THE DIRECTOR'S CIRCLE BOOK FOR 2005

The Johns Hopkins University Press gratefully
acknowledges members of the 2005 Director's Circle
for supporting the publication of works such as
The Secret History of Domesticity

Anonymous
Alfred and Muriel Berkeley
John J. Boland
Darlene Bookoff
Jack Goellner and Barbara Lamb
Charles and Elizabeth Hughes
Ralph S. O'Connor
Peter Onuf
Douglas R. Price
Anders Richter
David Ryer
R. Champlin and Debbie Sheridan
Daun Van Ee
Robert L. Warren and Family

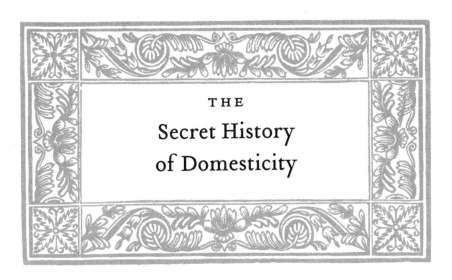

THE

Secret History
of Domesticity

Public, Private, and the Division of Knowledge

M ICHAEL M C K EON

The Johns Hopkins
University Press
Baltimore

© 2005 The Johns Hopkins University Press
All rights reserved. Published 2005
Printed in the United States of America on acid-free paper

2 4 6 8 9 7 5 3 1

The Johns Hopkins University Press
2715 North Charles Street
Baltimore, Maryland 21218-4363
www.press.jhu.edu

Library of Congress Cataloging-in-Publication Data
McKeon, Michael, 1943–
    The secret history of domesticity : public, private, and the division
of knowledge / Michael McKeon.
        p. cm.
    Includes bibliographical references and index.
    ISBN 0-8018-8220-6 (hardcover : alk. paper)
    1. Knowledge, Sociology of. 2. Material culture. 3. Privacy. 4. Con-
duct of life. 5. Social history. 6. Civilization, Modern. 7. England—
Social life and customs. 8. Privacy—England—History. 9. Privacy in
literature. I. Title.
    HM651.M38 2005
    306.4′2—dc22   2005000738

A catalog record for this book is available from the British Library.

For Rose, Carolyn, and Lucy

Contents

Illustrations

Acknowledgments

My greatest debt of gratitude is to Rutgers, the State University of New Jersey, which has supported my work on this project with a generosity that has exceeded all expectation. I am particularly fortunate to have taught at Rutgers under the leadership of Barry Qualls, Cheryl Wall, and Richard Miller. I hope this book will be seen to justify that support to some degree.

Many friends and colleagues gave me helpful advice on earlier drafts and versions of this book. In particular, Jonathan Kramnick commented on the lengthy and demanding first draft of part 1, and at a later stage Paula McDowell gave chapter 2 a close and painstaking reading. Their interest in and thoughts about this project have been important in sustaining my sense of working in a community of accomplished eighteenth-century scholar-critics. For valuable readings and commentary I also would like to thank the late Doug Canfield, Joseph Chaves, Anne Cotterill, Bill Dowling, Marcie Frank, Billy Galperin, Timo Gilmore, Annie Janowitz, Myra Jehlen, Kevin Pask, Mark Phillips, Gordon Schochet, and Carolyn Williams. I have received bibliographical help from Jason Gieger, Kristin Girten, Kimberly Latta, Erin Murphy, John Shanahan, and Sandra Young. I have benefited from discussions with Rutgers graduate students in courses I have taught that engaged some of the problems that are central to this book. And I have thrived in the vigorous atmosphere of period-field community created not only by my faculty colleagues but also by the Rutgers Graduate Student Transatlantic Eighteenth-Century Group.

James Winn kindly put at my disposal his expertise in Restoration and eighteenth-century music. Isabelle Bour, in Paris, and Brian Lockey, in Madrid, helped me secure images that were difficult to obtain through less direct means of communication. Most of the work of locating and ordering images, and of obtaining permission to use them, was done with care by Kristin Girten and Madhvi Zutshi. Madhvi, along with Deborah Allen, also attentively proofread the entire book after it was meticulously copyedited, and improved, by Joanne Allen. Margie Towery prepared the index with a professional eye to both accuracy and utility. Staff members of the Johns Hopkins University Press with whom I worked were unfailingly gracious and helpful, most of all Jackie Wehmueller, whose support and friendship I have learned to rely on with gratitude and pleasure.

Despite (and in some cases because of) the ongoing revolution in information technology, I have benefited from the knowledge and patience of the staff at the Warburg Institute Library, the Alexander Library at Rutgers University, and the Princeton University Libraries, of the latter especially Firestone Library, Marquand Library, and the Department of Rare Books and Special Collections.

My greatest intellectual debt is to Carolyn Williams, from whom I have the benefit of an intelligence whose acuteness and domestic proximity continue to be a very rare gift.

Introduction

This book began as an effort to address a set of questions central to our understanding of the past. On the one hand, the modern Western view of the public and the private, both the categories and the constitutive difference between them, has seemed to students of many disciplines a fundamentally new historical phenomenon. On the other hand, both the categories and their difference are a fundamental feature of traditional societies as well, whether we mean by "tradition" what precedes the modern period or what coexists with modernity in time independent of its singular character and influence. How new can this new sense of difference be? The same question is posed when we ask what we mean by "the modern period," or when we question the capacity of diachronic periodization to pinpoint a change in "Western" understanding, a change whose rate and quality clearly are subject to wide synchronic variation.

The Division of Knowledge

The title of this book states its central concerns in ascending order of generality. Most broadly, my interest lies in the comprehensive division of knowledge that takes place in the sixteenth, seventeenth, and eighteenth centuries and that separates modernity from tradition. What we mean by the modern division of knowledge can be clarified by comparing it to the comprehensive and correlative division of labor. As it happens, Karl Marx's ruminations on historical method use the category "labor" as their primary example:

> Labour seems a quite simple category. The conception of labour in this form—as labour as such—is also immeasurably old. Nevertheless, when it is economically conceived in this simplicity, "labour" is as modern a category as are the relations which create this simple abstraction. The Monetary System, for example, still locates wealth altogether objectively, as an external thing, in money. Compared with this standpoint, the commercial, or manufacture, system took a great step forward by locating the source of wealth not in the object but in a subjective activity—in commercial and manufacturing activity—even though it still always conceives this activity within narrow boundaries, as money-making. . . . It was an immense step

forward for Adam Smith to throw out every limiting specification of wealth-creating activity—not only manufacturing, or commercial or agricultural labour, but one as well as the others, labour in general. With the abstract universality of wealth-creating activity we now have the universality of the object defined as wealth, the product as such or again labour as such, but labour as past, objectified labour. . . . Indifference towards any specific kind of labour presupposes a very developed totality of real kinds of labour, of which no single one is any longer predominant. As a rule, the most general abstractions arise only in the midst of the richest possible concrete development, where one thing appears as common to many, to all. . . . Indifference towards specific labours corresponds to a form of society in which individuals can with ease transfer from one labour to another, and where the specific kind . . . has ceased to be organically linked with specific individuals in any specific form. . . . The simplest abstraction, then, which modern economics places at the head of its discussions, and which expresses an immeasurably ancient relation valid in all forms of society, nevertheless achieves practical truth as an abstraction only as a category of the most modern society.[1]

There are two points in this rich passage that I want to emphasize. First, Marx argues that what is required for the formulation of general and inclusive categories of knowledge—e.g., the conceptualization of labor "as such"—is a material experience of different concrete and particular kinds of labor. Second, he suggests that the division of knowledge—e.g., into different concrete kinds of labor—is coextensive with the abstraction of knowledge: to be aware of labor as such is also to be aware of several sorts of labor that this general category comprises. (The division of knowledge also occurs, we might extrapolate, at a slightly higher level of abstraction, where labor, along with other concrete and particular categories like "need," "money," and "value," is conceived as one part of a greater abstract whole, "the economic system.")[2] On the one hand, generality, totality, abstract universality, objectification; on the other hand, particularity, individuation, concrete multiplicity, mobility.

The specific division of knowledge on which this study focuses—the second concern of my title—is of course not that of labor and its several kinds but that which gives modernity its distinctive division between the public and the private. Here a clarification is in order. Marx uses the category "labor" to exemplify the historical dialectic of all material and conceptual development, whereas I have been using it as a general term for material activity itself, the generic counterpart of "knowledge" or conceptual activity. In other words, the categories "privacy" and "publicity" may be historicized in the same way that Marx historicizes "labor." To pursue his line of thought, we might hypothesize that however active and consequential those categories and their distinction may have been before the modern period, it is only then that they are conceivable "as such." That is, it is only then that a multiplicity of different kinds of public and private experience permits contemporaries to become "indifferent" to the more limited form of the distinction that, in part because the recognition of privacy and publicity has been limited "organically" to "specific individuals" and to "specific forms," has thus far been "predominant." At a certain moment, the multiplication of different conditions and behaviors that are also similar enough to be conceived as parts of a greater whole induces an abstraction, an awareness of that whole that may seem retrospectively to have pre-existed the constitutive multiplication of its parts. The example of the public and the private complicates that of labor, however, in that their modern abstraction is simultaneously a reflexive process, an objectification of categories over against each other.

The Public and the Private

The present study may be framed as an abstract and therefore deceptively simple hypothesis. In "traditional" cultures, the differential relationship between public and private modes of experience is conceived as a *distinction* that does not admit of *separation*. In "modernity" the public and the private are separated out from each other, a condition that both sustains the sense of traditional distinction and, axiomatically, reconstitutes the public and the private as categories that are susceptible to separation. What are the sociopsychological conditions that attend this change in how the relationship between two distinct categories is construed? One way I engage this question is through the notion that "traditional" knowledge is *tacit* in the sense of being deeply embedded in a political, social, and cultural matrix of practice whose guidance suffuses daily experience and discourages the separation out of knowledge for self-conscious examination. "Modern" knowledge is, on the contrary, an *explicit* and self-conscious awareness, characterized not by the way it saturates social practice but by the way it satisfies the canons of epistemology, which impose on knowledge the test of self-justifying self-sufficiency. Disembedded from the matrix of experience it seeks to explain, modern knowledge is defined precisely by its explanatory ambition to separate itself from its object of knowledge sufficiently to fulfill the epistemological demand that what is known must be divided from the process by which it is known.[3] Like labor, the private and the public are thrown into distinctive relief against what had been a relatively homogeneous plane of existence and has become a heterogeneous landscape of semiautonomous structures.

The modern separation out of the public and the private is therefore, like the abstraction of labor, a disembedding of figure from ground, an "explicitation" of what tacitly had always been there but now, in becoming explicit, also takes on a new life. More precisely, however, the modern disembedding of the public-private dyad entails their separation out not only from the common ground of tradition and social practice but also from each other: the division of public *from* private. The historical movement from distinction to separation is most strikingly expressed when the modern separation is evidently the result of a process of splitting that acknowledges the separability of what formerly had been most intelligible not "as such" but as parts of a greater whole. In the case of the public and the private (although less so than in the case of, say, the body and the spirit, nature and nurture, or tragedy and comedy), a potential for categorial separation is acknowledged in most traditional cultures by the parallel coexistence of two terms, with the result that the transition from tradition to modernity may take on, in this respect, the dominant appearance of continuity. One of the means by which I underscore the force of historical discontinuity as well, the long-term change from relations of distinction to relations of separation, is by recourse to a different sort of terminological or categorial development—the division of one term into two—that has played an important role in substantiating the notion that the modern relation of the public and the private has entailed a splitting of a former tacit whole into oppositional and self-sufficient parts. Some instances of this sort of development may be useful: *estate,* the public state/the private estate; *status,* sociopolitical rank/economic wealth; *gender,* natural sex/acculturated gender; *honor,* family lineage/personal virtue; *propriety,* social appropriateness/private property; *religion,* institutional and cultural/individual and personal; *subjecthood,* subjection to another/autonomous subjectivity; *knowledge,* external sense impressions/internal creative imagination; *romance,* historical veracity/falsehood or fiction; *individual,* indivisible and collective/independent and singular. Each of these divisions of knowledge has its own peculiar complexity. My claim is not a strict homology between them but a common and explicit use of the language of the public and the private that testifies to both a conceptual and a material separation out of the public from the private in the modern period.

Domesticity

The third and most specific concern named in the title of this book is domesticity. If the modern separation of the public from the private is the division of knowledge on which this study is centrally focused, the coalescence of the category of domesticity is perhaps its most visible and resonant expression. One reason for speaking of "the secret history" of domesticity is to convey my interest in the "prehistory" of that category before it emerges, as either a term or an idea, in the modern usage with which we are familiar (I explain another important meaning of the phrase below). Domesticity is both a species of modern privacy and unintelligible apart from our modern experience of publicity; its story can only make sense within the more general story of modern privacy and its separation out from the realm of the public. As much as any other categorial abstractions, the public and the private have been fruitfully susceptible to representation through spatial metaphor and its cardinal differentials outside/inside and high/low. And although its centrality to the modern idea of privacy is obvious in any case, the historical emergence of domesticity is peculiarly accessible to the awareness of both contemporaries and modern scholars because of its spatial and structural representability. The aim of chapters 4 and 5 is to exploit this capacity in the most direct manner available by discussing the spatial gendering of labor in the domestic economy and the articulation of "domestic space" in the architectural history of the home. But the spatial and structural representation of privacy and publicity themselves has also been an important index to their shifting meaning throughout the period of my concern, which helps explain my liberal use of graphic images and figures in other chapters as well. Still, the advantages of attending closely to the category of domesticity would be negated if either domesticity were collapsed into privacy or privacy into domesticity. Indeed, in lived experience the norms and values of domesticity and privacy were found to be capable of obstructing one another. While the understanding of domesticity as a subcategory of privacy seems to me sound in the broad sweep of social and intellectual history, throughout this study I have guarded against the assumption of their compatibility in all more local instances.

Form and Spatial Representability

Spatial figuration is most richly expressive in artistic and literary works, where the self-conscious representation of form is one of the most powerful aims of, and aids to, the articulation of meaning. For this reason I pay attention to issues of artistic composition—in paintings, engravings, and drawings—throughout this study. In literary works, form lacks the graphic concretion unique to the visual media and their technical armory. But formal structure achieved through language has a special and subtle kind of sensitivity that tells its own story, a truth recorded by the fact that the modern world witnesses the coalescence of not only "domestic space" but also "the domestic novel."

But the status of the domestic novel in the present work requires clarification. This is not in any basic sense a book about the history of the novel. In part 1 my purpose is to trace the several contexts of British experience that are most relevant to the transformation of traditional into modern attitudes toward the public and the private, beginning with the most general and "public" of these contexts and moving incrementally into the more "deeply interiorized" realm (to use a familiar modern metaphor) of private experience. Broadly speaking, this is a movement "inward," through the realms of the state and civil society, religion, printing and the public sphere, the state and the family, domestic labor, domestic architecture, gender differentiation, subjectivity, intimacy, and sexuality. As we pass from the most public to the most private realms as these are reconceived in the early centuries of modernity, our trajectory also describes the separation process as a devolutionary movement "downward," a progressive detachment of the normatively absolute from its presumed locale in royal absolutism and its experimental relocation in "the people," the family, women, the individual, personal identity, and the absolute subject. Yet even as this principle of the irreducibly absolute is translated inward and downward, the increasingly private spheres of experience in which it takes root recapitulate, in their own terms, the structural opposition between the public and the private that in a more abstracted view consigns them to the realm of the private.

Part 2 makes a more sustained effort to engage the discursive and formal features of privacy and domesticity by considering the transition from the traditional to the modern as a shift in attitudes toward the rhetoric of accommodation—of hermeneutics and pedagogy—that I identify as "formal domestication," a rhetoric that traditionally uses the easy familiarity of the private (and the profane) to accommodate the arcane obscurity of the public (and the sacred). Chapter 8 in particular studies a number of poetic, dramatic, narrative, and pictorial genres so as to illustrate how formal domestication both invites and pursues strategies of spatial representation.

In part 3 I concentrate on one branch of narrative in particular—not an identifiable genre but an association of forms to which I give the name "secret history" and which facilitates the study of peculiarly narrative techniques of formality that contemporaries explicitly distinguish through the language of privacy and publicity: literal and allegorical plot structure, first- and third-person voice, individual and typical characterization, the ethics of author and character and author and reader, actualizing and fictionalizing claims to authority. "Secret history" is a contemporary term that signifies the private revelation of high public secrets, a substantive ambition that bears a close relation to the rhetoric of formal domestication, with which it sometimes is combined. The contradictory nature of the secret history in both of these senses can be felt in its formal instability, its all-but-tangible contingency. Over the century and a half in which it flourishes, the secrets revealed by the secret history tend to become increasingly private, not public, and its formality tends to undermine the structure of domestication in its very operation, a tendency that may be summarized as the movement from domestication to domesticity. This sort of development—the assumption by the private realm of tendencies toward thematic and teleological significance that formerly had characterized only the public realm—plays an important role in the modern disembedding and apotheosis of privacy; but it is by no means the whole story of this study, in which publicity, in both its formal and its sociopolitical senses, will be seen to undergo its own positive revaluation. The emergence of the domestic novel at the end of the eighteenth century, in which both the movement from domestication to domesticity and this study itself find closure, is therefore not the payoff of my argument but a peculiarly persuasive, because structurally eloquent, example of the historical trajectory it argues, the movement from relations of distinction to relations of separation. Among the functions of part 3 is what it adds, through the detailed elaboration of contemporary thought about narrative, to the already rich vocabulary of public-private usage documented in parts 1 and 2. This accumulation and deep sedimentation of usage creates the conditions for what Marx calls the "indifference" of contemporaries to the specific and limited applications of the public-private dyad that heretofore have supported its tacit significance. Indifference to the specificity of these applications signals on the contrary the explicit awareness with which the abstracted terms now may be applied to an expanded range of phenomena, as well as the self-conscious separability of which they are increasingly capable.

Questions of Method

The vast scholarship on the relationship between the realms of the public and the private may be divided heuristically into two sorts. The first, exemplified by the many-authored and multivolume study *Histoire de la vie privée,* is a historical account of incremental and epochal change.[4] The second, exemplified by Jeff Weintraub's introduction to *Public and Private in Thought and Practice,* is an analytic account that uncovers the range of often incompatible models and meanings that have come down to us.[5] The heuristic nature of this division is illustrated by the fact that each collection also practices the method of the other: the writings of Philippe Ariès, Georges Duby, and Roger Chartier (to go no further) are deeply informed by the understanding that the history these volumes relate has historiographical implications, and Weintraub is keenly aware that his analytic categories have a complex history. But the contrast is useful because it helps me conceive and describe this book as an effort to extend this hybrid method in both directions. On the one hand, my historical narration is mindful of the way diachronic change creates the synchronic terms of analysis by which modern historical understanding, including my own, proceeds. By sustaining in some detail distinct treatments of socioeconomic, political, intellectual, and literary history I hope to lay the grounds for attending to the way these histories intersect with and reinforce one another. On the other hand, my analysis of the incompatibility between reigning models and meanings of the public-private relation that have come down to us aims to construe conceptual as historical contradiction, not only a static result susceptible to synchronic categorization but also a dynamic process susceptible to diachronic periodization. Indeed, my interest lies less in the retrospective and atemporal fact of separation than in the active experience of separation out from a ground whose power to make intelligible may, in the process of historicization, still be felt.

This brief discussion of method raises two questions. First, there is an evident relationship between the subject of this book—the division of knowledge in which the modern abstractions of the public and the private came into their characteristic relationship—and its method, itself a division of knowledge, which entails dividing the abstract, synchronic, and diachronic wholes of history into subsidiary categories and periods so as to subject these wholes, in turn, to division. A description of my historical method, although not the same, therefore has some bearing on my historical thesis about the division of knowledge. That is, I posit general hypotheses on the strength of particular evidence, generating further evidence as well as the impulse to refine the original hypothesis on this evidentiary basis; and I continue to oscillate between abstraction and concretion until I am content that the general hypothesis and its particular evidence are sufficiently and reciprocally supportive to offer a plausible interpretation of the phenomenon at hand. In fact, my aim here is to tell a general story about how the tendency toward conceptual division came to shape modern thought regarding the public and the private by relying to some degree on the fruits of that tendency to make my story not only persuasive but also accurate.

However, any effort to come to terms with the modern impulse toward division will soon encounter a major structural complication. In the modern, and most explicitly the postmodern, experience the momentum by which categories are separated out from one another very quickly produces a reciprocal and antithetical ambition to qualify and complicate separation by disclosing the sorts of *conflation* to which a too-easy separation may be subversively subjected and, by that conflation, better understood. One premise of this study is that by "the Enlightenment" we name that period in the emergence of modernity in which we can discern most clearly this close reciprocity of separation and conflation—the demystification not only of traditional distinctions but also of modern separations—whose ongoing dialectic comprehends modernity as such. The interplay of separation and conflation is a fundamental tool of modern thought. A central aim of this book is to document this interplay in the particular case of the relation of the public and the private, an aim that cannot be fulfilled without also documenting the early modern interplay between distinction and separation. To do justice to my relatively particularized subject, the modern division between the public and the private, therefore also requires having recourse to the most abstract categories available for the analytically historical study of the division of knowledge, the sequence of distinction, separation, and conflation. My claim is not that the completion of this sequence with respect to any particular conceptual node is always achieved in seventeenth- and eighteenth-century culture—the good news of the gospels was powerfully articulated as a conflation of the former separations between body and spirit, nature and nurture, tragedy and comedy—but that it is in this period that such an achievement becomes so common as to be systematic and definitive of the modern age.

A second question of method, related to the first, grows out of my ambition to combine extended historical narration with analytic self-consciousness, and it raises an objection that is common in some circles of academic study. The nature of the objection may be evoked by citing its most frequent negative signposts: *abstraction, reduction, teleology, evolution, master narrative.* From the perspective of this critique, abstraction is the bane of fruitful inquiry because it reduces the rich multiplicity of experience to an arid schematism. As my foregoing comments will suggest, however, the equation of abstraction with reduction is itself a reduction, a freezing of one stage of a process into the static product of inquiry. Abstraction is not a dogmatic shutting down but an experimental opening up of discovery, a way of generating concrete particularity by tentatively constituting a whole susceptible to analysis into parts. Abstraction entails not the occlusion but the explicitation of concretion, just as system may work not to exclude, but to ensure the acknowledgment of, contradiction. To characterize traditional knowledge as tacit and modern knowledge as explicit is therefore not to claim foundational truths but to make visible those concrete particularities that will both confirm and complicate these initial abstractions. To my understanding, the objection to teleology in argument is that it implicitly posits at the outset a result that is purported to emerge only as the result of inquiry. But this error in conceptualization seems to me very different from the historian's basic motivating premise, in which teleology is often supposed to inhere, namely, the premise that diachronically different phenomena—a before and an after—stand in some comparative and meaningful relationship to each other and that historical study invites speculation on what that relationship might be. *Post hoc non est propter hoc.* The blind circularity of this crude teleology should not be confused with the hermeneutic circularity of the sort that characterizes all interpretation and that, when openly acknowledged, enables rather than disarms historical method. Method is at risk of becoming crudely teleological only when—a crucial caveat—we lose our awareness that generalizing abstraction controls particularizing concretion (only) as concretion also controls abstraction.

The difference between historical method and what I have called crude teleology may be seen with unusual clarity when historical study focuses its attention on synchronic differences within a single diachronic cross section. To discern difference—e.g., between infrastructure and superstructure—manifestly need not posit causal or determinant relation. By the same token, to study the past in relation to the present does not logically condemn that study to an evolutionary bias—the bias that consists in treating the past as though it is fueled by the motor of a present toward which it more or less "inevitably" moves. On the contrary, only by comparing diachronically or synchronically different historical phenomena are we able to conceive and formulate how the abstract separation by which they are constituted as objects of study may be complicated and sophisticated beyond the capacity of evolutionary argument to explain. The insight that diachronic categories may be seen as "residual" or "emergent," for example, is unavailable to us unless we posit a determinate historical entity of which a later one is a residue, or one from which an earlier one may emerge.[6]

Properly conceived, master narratives are vitally important to historical study not because they seek a specious and unavailable "mastery" of the phenomena but because they provide a conceptual framework broad enough to set the engine of historical inquiry in motion. It is from this position that I would defend not only the conceptual breadth of this study but also its length, the amount of empirical data it undertakes to analyze. Although there are obvious limits, the breadth of study undertaken and the range of data examined are better seen as marking a seriousness of commitment rather than the illusion of mastery. In fact, to repudiate master narratives on principle is to court the illusion that the potential of a conceptual framework to "master"—to reduce and distort—the field of study might be avoided by a quantitative reduction in the size of the field itself. All other things being equal, the inclusiveness of the field of study militates against bias. The common tendency to interpret the modern division of knowledge (like the modern division of labor) as either "evolutionary" or "devolutionary"—that is, either progressive or regressive in its socioethical implications—is thwarted, not encouraged, by a field of study inclusive enough to provide alternative modes of contextualization.

I will end with two caveats. First, my concentration on British texts and contexts in this study has no better justification than the limits of my scholarly competence; however, I draw on French, Italian, and American material where needed. No presumption about the relative importance of British culture should be read into this limitation.

Second, in the ongoing debate over how to assess the ultimate value of modernity—over how to balance on all fronts what has been gained against what has been lost—I have aimed, without seeking to address it directly, to do justice to both sides of the question. If readers find that my efforts to understand and to rationalize the modernizing process sometimes sound like a justification of it, I urge them to view this study in its historical context. Living as we must on the crest of modernity's wave, we are to some extent obliged to judge it by the most recent and disastrous failures of the past two centuries. In this book I have tried to do what is perhaps more challenging and certainly as obligatory: to view the past not only as a prelude to our present but also as a response to its own past. The English people who are my subject fill a broad spectrum of experiential and ideological diversity, and yet at a certain level of schematic abstraction they may be understood and judged as a singular and integral instance mediating between the traditional or "premodern" on the one hand and modernity on the other. From the perspective of futurity it is the causal implications of this historical instance—what it turns out, beyond all agency, to have entailed—that make it most vulnerable to our condemnation. While I acknowledge and exploit the explanatory force of this perspective, I have also tried to discover an interpretive perspective from which the period of my concern can be seen to have had a motivated agency in changing what the past had given it.

The Secret History of Domesticity

Part One ✳ The Age of Separations

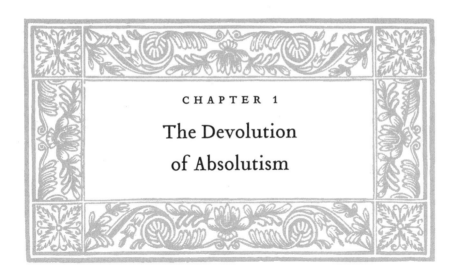

CHAPTER 1

The Devolution
of Absolutism

State and Civil Society

In 1767 Adam Ferguson, the Scottish Enlightenment man of letters, wrote that "[t]he practitioners of every art and profession may afford matter of general speculation to the man of science; and thinking itself, in this age of separations, may become a peculiar craft."[1] Ferguson's insight has a compound truth. The division of labor entails a division of knowledge not only in that specialized kinds of physical labor require specialized knowledges nor only in that thinking is itself a kind of labor but also in that in an "age of separations" the craft of thinking involves the division and subdivision of single into multiple categories of knowledge. The relationship between conceptual categories and the material categories they designate, hence between the division of knowledge and the division of labor, is a subtly dialectical one that cannot be reduced to any simple mechanism. Still, it is clear enough that both the idea and the experience—indeed, the very terminology—of the "public-private" distinction antedate Ferguson's age by many centuries. What sense can there be in looking to early modern English culture for evidence of this division's emergence out of a more singular and undivided whole?

Ferguson's concern in *An Essay on the History of Civil Society* is to characterize a category and a term—"civil society"—that are truly emergent in his own era, in no small part through the conceptual labors of Ferguson himself and his compatriots. "Civil society" takes form through tracing its history, its emergence out of what it is not. In Ferguson's analysis, civil society seems to become discernible and enunciable at the uncertain boundaries that coalesce within integral categories, boundaries between subject and monarch, between warrior and citizen, between family and country, between territorial inhabitants and state.[2] But his discussions are ambiguous. Civil society appears sometimes to be the precedent and coherent unit that encompasses divergent parts, at others rather the product of that divergence. Moreover, it is not clear how firmly Ferguson would distinguish between "civil society" and society as such. Does "civil society" refer to a society of "citizens," one already brought under and associated with state rule? Yet others—Bernard Mandeville, for example—will sometimes speak of "society" as such in just these terms, as what is constituted by "lawgivers" and the rule of "government."[3]

The ambiguity of "civil society" in its eighteenth-century usage, rather than vitiating the coherence of the category, underscores the dialectical nature of its emergence and utility.[4] The separation of "state" and "civil society" will serve in what follows as a procedural rather than ontological starting point, a conceptual nexus that provides access to the early modern division of knowledge in which the separation of the public and the private is intricately involved. It may be helpful to see "civil society" as the Enlightenment consolidation of the late-Renaissance category "society." As idea and as institution, "society" both pre-exists the Renaissance and comes into being over against the Renaissance "state," which in its own (reciprocally dialectical) emergence is both the antithesis of "society" and the very condition of its being. This is at once a conceptual and an objective process, customarily associated with the epoch of absolutism and its centralization of political power in royal hands.[5] Despite the obvious problems with the notion, historians have often been willing to associate the absolutist state with the emergence of state power as such because absolutism entails an unprecedented essay in separation, in easing the traditional dependence of political power on metaphysical and moral sanctions. This is a well-known story, especially in its paradigmatic Italian development. The absolute prince or monarch is he who practices the "art of the state," who exercises his dominion according not to overarching principles of justice, reason, and grace but to an autonomous "reason of state," the "mysteries" of rule, or *arcana imperii,* whose autotelic end is the maintenance of state power itself.[6] In the figures of speech that organize more traditional political theory (the body politic, the linked chain of micro- and macrocorrespondences) the state is distinguishable but not separable from the other estates of the realm; "reason of state" defines precisely the grounds of its separability.

The autonomization of state power gave to the Renaissance state a compelling coherence over against several disparate institutions: the pope, the emperor, the baronage, and most crucially, "society" itself, which is reciprocally defined by its "civility," by its relationship to and difference from the state. This early modern discrimination between "state" and "society" is no doubt the most important foundation for the modern discrimination between the realms of the "public" and the "private." Once postulated, however, the conception of absolute, self-justified authority could be detached from the "body natural" of the absolute monarch and embodied elsewhere: in the courtier, in Parliament, even in the common people. This was in part the consequence of opening up sovereignty to debate, of making tacit knowledge explicit. In 1616 James I declared that "[t]hat which concerns the mystery of the King's power is not lawful to be disputed; for that is to wade into the weakness of Princes, and to take away the mystical reverence that belongs unto them that sit in the throne of God. . . . [S]o it is presumption and high contempt in a subject to dispute what a King can do, or say that a King cannot do this or that, but rest with that which is the King's revealed will in his law."[7] To theorize absolutism, however, is also to render it vulnerable—or to acknowledge its vulnerability. The *arcana imperii* that are central to the theory of absolutism have already entered into the historical process of explicitation simply by virtue of having been acknowledged as such.[8]

From Tacit to Explicit

In 1628 Parliament petitioned Charles I to affirm his support of what it argued were the English people's accustomed freedoms from arbitrary governmental demands. In the debate that followed, it was suggested that the Petition of Right also affirm the customary locus of "sovereign power" in the monarchy. Sir Henry Marten argued strenuously against such an affirmation, however, saying that it would invite controversy too explicitly. "[T]his petition will run through many hands," he pointed out, and people would "presently fall to arguing and reasoning and descanting what sovereign power is—what is the latitude? whence the original? where the bounds? etc.—with many such curious and captious questions. . . . My Lords, I wish that the sovereign power of the King might ever be kept in a tacit veneration, and not had in public examination." Dissenting, in Commons debate, from the Grand Remonstrance of 1641, Sir Edward Dering expressed in subtly grammatical terms how making the tacit explicit disturbed the proper relation between king and people: "When I first heard of a Remonstrance, I presently imagined that like faithful Counsellors, we should hold up a Glass unto His Majesty: I thought to represent unto the King the wicked Counsels of pernicious Counsellors: the restless turbulency of practical Papists. The treachery of false Judges . . . I did not dream that we should remonstrate downward, tell stories to the People, and talk of the King as of a third Person. . . . [W]e pass His Majesty, and do remonstrate to the People . . . ."[9] Dering's point is only partly the inversion of hierarchy. He captures the enormity of unfolding events in the insolent detachment of third-person narration, which demotes the king from sovereign audience to mere character in a story that is fashioned by his subjects for his subjects.

The absolutist momentum would eventually outstrip its intended object: this was the prescient apprehension of Charles I (or of his speechwriters) seven months later. If the House of Commons were ceded the power it sought, he declared, "so new a power will undoubtedly intoxicate persons who were not born to it, and beget not only divisions among them as equals, but in them contempt of us, as become an equal to them . . . till . . . at last the common people . . . discover this *arcanum imperii,* that all this was done by them, but not for them, and grow weary of journey-work, and set up for themselves, [and] call parity and independence liberty . . . ." As a contemporary observed of the regicides seven years later, "They who fight to free themselves from an absolute power, are by that obliged for the time to take upon them the absolutest."[10] Over the long term, the indefinite transferability of royal absolutism fed the notion that even, perhaps only, the individual was endowed with an absolute authority.[11] At the same time, it encouraged the depersonalization of state authority, which manifestly persisted even when the head was forcibly detached from the rest of the body politic. Long before the regicide—a month before Charles's "Answer to the Nineteen Propositions"—Parliament was already content to distinguish between "the king" and "his kingdoms" in a way that prepared for this ultimate depersonalization: "We hope that his Majesty will not make his own understanding or reason the rule of his government, but will suffer himself to be assisted with a wise and prudent counsel, that may deal faithfully between him and his people: and that he will remember that his resolutions do concern kingdoms, and therefore ought not to be moulded by his own." Half a century after the regicide and in the midst of a related crisis, Algernon Sidney explicitly demystified the personality of royal sovereignty through an analysis of the language of the king's two bodies: "Truth can never conduce to mischief, and is best discovered by plain words; but nothing is more usual with ill men than to cover their mischievous designs with figurative phrases. . . . The people makes or creates the figurative head, the natural is from itself, or connate with the body. The natural body cannot change or subsist without the natural head; but a people may change and subsist very well without the artificial." As we shall see, the mobility of absolutism gave to the modern distinction between the public and the private both its foundation and its dynamic plasticity.[12]

Polis and *Oikos*

Of course, the association between the political state and the "public" is already present in classical antiquity: in the Greek distinction of the *polis* from the *oikos*, in the Roman republic and its concern with *res publica*. Half a century ago scholarly consensus conceived the distinction between the public and the private in the classical world as, in the terms of this study, a fundamental separation. The broad argument may be summarized from the influential writings of Hannah Arendt. "Private things" pertain to the material necessities of the household: to the physical labor of sustaining the human body and of reproducing the human species, hence to women, children, and slaves. Especially in Greek thought, private things were characterized by privation, not only because matters of bodily sustenance were thought to be properly hidden from public view but also because the household was deprived of the freedom that is built upon, and that lies beyond, the realm of necessity. Citizens of the *polis*, by contrast, were free not only because they owned land, by which the community was tied to the authority of the past, but also because they were released by the labor of their households' noncitizens from the necessity of devoting their time and attention to its maintenance. What citizens were freed to do was to guide the *polis*, a "political" activity that entailed the full actualization of the self, who exercised his free agency in his creative community with other citizens. Although the *polis* and the *oikos*, the public and the private, the realm of politics and the realm of the household and the family, were in experiential terms inevitably related, Greek political philosophy conceived their relationship in terms of the absolute difference between freedom and necessity.[13]

In recent years this paradigm has been questioned on a number of grounds. The putative antithesis between *polis* and *oikos* draws strength, it has been argued, from a confusion of two distinct "family" categories: the *oikos*, the household of persons and property; and the *genos*, the cult-oriented blood kin or clan. When the tension between ancestral *genos* and emergent *polis* in preclassical Greece is taken to bespeak also a historical estrangement of *polis* from *oikos*, the ongoing correlation of the latter two entities becomes obscured. The crucial figure here is, of course, Aristotle. Before Aristotle the relation between *polis* and *oikos* was understood both metaphorically and metonymically: the *polis* was conceived and arranged on the model of the family, that is, the *oikos*, whose economic management was also seen to be functionally inseparable from the financial relations of the *polis*, or state.[14] By theorizing the antithesis between the political activities of the citizen and the economic activities of household management in terms of the philosophical antithesis of freedom and necessity, Aristotle's *Politics* laid the ground for a more definitive separation between the family and the state in the tradition of political philosophy that flowed from his writings. But even Aristotle's authority is ambiguous on these matters. His use of the term *polis* can be both narrow and comprehensive, implying both the immediate community of citizens and the larger, geographical and sociological community of the city-state. Indeed, the question how the former is encompassed by the latter may be seen as the great problem that the *Politics* undertakes to explain.[15] Although Aristotle argues that "the state is by nature clearly prior to the family . . . since the whole is of necessity prior to the part," he also observes that "the state is made up of households . . . ." That is, his analysis acknowledges, even assumes, the functional embeddedness of the state within a historically prior social matrix.[16] Aristotle also affirms an analogical relationship between the family and the state: "The rule of a household is a monarchy, for every house is under one head: whereas constitutional rule is a government of freemen and equals. . . . A husband and father . . . rules over wife and children, . . . the rule over his children being a royal, over his wife a constitutional rule . . ." (1255b, 1259a–b). In short, the public-private relation, if conceived as one of absolute separation, is also conceived as one of relative distinction within a greater congruence.

This is not to deny the radical innovation of the Aristotelian analysis but to limit its scope. Moreover, intellectual history at the combined levels of high theory, legal superstructure, and common social practice is unlikely to return a simple picture.[17] For one thing, the theory of a separation between politics and the family in classical Greece is not borne out by its social practice. For another, Aristotle's unprecedented emphasis on the "public" affairs of the *polis* over against the "private" affairs of the *oikos* is not representative of the contemporary Greek, or even of the Athenian, perspective on these matters. According to one analysis, Aristotle foresaw "the divorce of the social from the overtly political, . . . a radical rupture between political and socioeconomic roles" that would characterize the developed Hellenistic cities of Asia and Africa of the future. If we accept this judgment, Aristotle's "prescience" in the *Politics* regarding the long-term separation out of the public from the private might be compared to his even more remarkable anticipation, in the *Poetics,* of the separation between history and poetry that would require another two millennia to be embraced by Western culture.[18] As for Roman antiquity, the interrelatedness of family and state was ensured by the interrelatedness of both private and public Roman law and domestic and political institutions.[19] Classical Rome gives us the very language of "public" and "private," but there is a wide divergence between their application in the republican era, when the centrality of the term "citizen" argues the continuing influence of Aristotelian theory, and in the imperial era, when the political authority of "citizenship" is overshadowed by that of "sovereignty" and the Roman law.[20]

The utility of the heuristic abstraction "public versus private in classical antiquity" lies in the way it obliges self-conscious enquiry to take a closer look at the inconsistency of the categorial parts of which it is composed. The revelation of inconsistency is a structural attribute of methodological abstraction; at what point does it tell against, not the method, but the epistemological value of the abstraction? There is no quantitative answer to this question. In the present case it may be useful to draw upon Marx's insight, discussed in the introduction, regarding the conditions necessary for the formulation of a conceptual abstraction that is "indifferent" to any concrete instance because it grows out of a multiplicity of instances whose number and variety preclude the dominance of the concrete and provide the basis for generalization. "Public" and "private" are of course already abstract terms in ancient usage. Indeed, we owe our English terms to classical Latin: *publicus* is related to *pubes* and specifies "the people" as "adult men" or "the male population," hence *privatus* takes in those who are deprived of such status.[21] Needless to say, these socially specific meanings are as familiar in early modern English usage as they are in ancient Roman. The difference is that extensions in the Roman usage—extensions of "public" to "the state," "universal," "general," "common," "shared"; extensions of "private" to "stripped of," "freed from," "special," "propertied"—are still closely linked to the concreteness of this etymological foundation, whereas the English usage has extrapolated broadly from it.[22] In classical Latin the public/private dyad expresses the quality of a particular social relationship; in modern English it is an expansive abstraction that, disembedded from the ground of that relationship, encompasses a universe of related but concretely distinct meanings.

Until the Renaissance, Christianity and the modes of social organization we have come to call feudalism variously encouraged an analogical way of thinking about the relation of the public and the private according to which politics and the household were understood to be distinct and unequal versions of each other rather than separable entities. The Renaissance revival of the broadly Aristotelian emphasis on the public to the exclusion of the private, associated most famously with the name Machiavelli, like other Renaissance revivals took a complex and unpredictable course. On the one hand, Machiavelli's separation of political from religious and moral considerations, centrally a reaction against the view that Christian morality should suffuse all branches of thought and action, made an initially controversial but lasting contribution to the modern division of knowledge.[23] For us this separation may be to some degree intelligible as a public/private issue because in modern experience religion has undergone an epochal "privatization" (a subject to which I will return); but for Machiavelli's contemporary readers the suspension of religious standards in politics would have had no such meaning. In *The Prince* (1532), the public/private issue would instead cohere around the question to which Machiavelli returns again and again with dogged fascination: How—on what principles and by what actions—might a private citizen rise to become a prince? But the umbrella answer to this question is "by reason of state," one hardly compatible with the Aristotelian ideal of a free community of free citizens. In *The Discourses* (1531), on the other hand, the citizen assumes the more recognizably authoritative status that he possesses in what has come to be called "classical republicanism." And this tradition of thought (to which I also will return) makes a real but limited contribution to early modern English ideas of publicity and privacy.

Because of these and other developments, the modern separation between the public and the private draws upon the classical tradition only in a complex and highly contradictory fashion. On the one hand, the classical management of the *oikos,* of the household economy, was transformed into a model for the management of the greater household—that is, for "political economy"—whose implications were yet very different from those of the medieval analogy between the family and the state. On the other hand, the residue of this transformation—the household divested even of its economic function—became the model for the "domestic sphere." Both of these emergent categories retain in the modern world their classical associations with privacy, even as each stands in oppositional relation to the other. A number of factors are involved in this process. In the agrarian "domestic economy" characteristic of premodern England economic production was organized around the household. With the early modern capitalist revolution, however, productive labor—defined as such by the fact of its remuneration—became an activity increasingly undertaken only by men and only outside the household. That is, the private work of economic production was separated out from the private household and undertaken for the market. At the same time, the function of the household was greatly altered and augmented as it gradually became the seat of primary socialization, of Puritan discipline and gentle cultivation, through which it took on those nonprivative private values that we associate with the ethos of the domestic sphere.[24] The etymological development of "political economy" therefore reminds us that the categories by which we commonly exemplify the difference between public and private are themselves resistant to that separation. Indeed, the market activity that undergirds political economy remains ambiguous even in its modern usage. Customarily we associate it with the "public" as it is distinguished from the "private" affairs of the household, but we also associate it with the "private" as it is distinguished from the "public sector" of the state and its political apparatus.

The State and the Family

Of the several medieval traditions of political thought that militated against the autonomization of reason of state, none is more central to present purposes than patriarchalist theory. Patriarchalism entailed an analogy between the state and the family that legitimated each institution by associating it with the "naturalness" of the other. As a theory of political obligation, patriarchalism enjoined upon subjects a subordination to the magistrate analogous to that of family members to the male head of the household. As Francis Bacon put it, if you would know the propriety of government in the greater sphere, look to its operation in the lesser: "So it cometh often to pass that mean and small things discover great better than great can discover the small; and therefore Aristotle noteth well, *that the nature of every thing is best seen in his smallest portions,* and for that cause he inquireth the nature of a commonwealth, first in a family, and the simple conjugations of man and wife, parent and child, master and servant, which are in every cottage . . . ."25 But we need to be careful with the language of analogy in characterizing the nature of what I am calling relations of distinction. Sir Robert Filmer's patriarchalist analogy is not simply a metaphor linking two separate entities; it defines the continuity between, the interpenetration of, things that are distinct but inseparable from each other.26

In a dynastic monarchy, moreover, the analogy between the state and the family is reinforced by their metonymic relationship: political sovereignty is a function of familial inheritance. Rendered explicit, this aspect of the doctrine was peculiarly vulnerable to skepticism. Answering Charles I's posthumous martyrology, John Milton wrote in 1649: "Indeed if the race of Kings were eminently the best of men, as the breed at *Tutburie* is of Horses, it would in some reson then be their part onely to command, ours only to obey." But since this proves not to be the case, it is a mistake to "nullifie and tread to durt the rest of mankind, by exalting one person and his Linage without other merit lookt after, but the meer contingence of a begetting, into an absolute and unaccountable dominion over them and their posterity." Ethical capacity is not genealogically embodied. Two years later Milton refuted the analogy itself: "[B]y calling kings fathers of their country, you think this metaphor has forced me to apply right off to kings whatever I might admit of fathers. Fathers and kings are very different things . . . ."27 And before the century was out John Locke published his definitive refutation: "[T]he Power of a *Magistrate* over a Subject, may be distinguished from that of a *Father* over his Children, a *Master* over his Servant, a *Husband* over his Wife, and a *Lord* over his Slave."28 Locke's "distinction" has the more definitive force of what I have been calling a "separation." Indeed, the several sorts of rule he treats come into being at different times and through different mechanisms.

Political government or the state originates, in Locke's famous analysis, through a "compact" by which individuals agree to relinquish some of the liberties enjoyed in the state of nature in order to secure and preserve their properties. Accordingly, those rights that are inseparable in the state of nature are to the end of security parceled out to a legislative, a judicial, and an executive branch of government. Contract theory rationalized the state's impersonality—so crucial to its conceptual constitution—as the effect not of the magistrate's but of the protocitizens' depersonalization. The institutions that make up the state, never embodied in the magistrate, are instead created by an act of collective disembodiment or detachment, a model of political authority diametrically opposed to the principles of personal embodiment that in different ways characterize both the royal doctrine of the king's two bodies and the unmediated reciprocity of lordship and service in feudal sociopolitical relations. Oliver Cromwell's New Model Army replaced the old hierarchy based on concrete feudal relations of personal loyalty by a depersonalized chain of command based on the abstract principle of merit.[29] Like Cromwell's army, Locke's compact overcomes what is becoming recognizable and nameable as a "conflict of interests," in this case the conflict that is inescapable in the state of nature, "where Men may be Judges in their own Cases . . . ."[30] It also defines the difference between the state of nature and the institutions of culture—paradigmatically, civil society and the state—as one between tacit and explicit knowledge. And yet with a logic that must at first seem counterintuitive, contract theory demystifies the analogical thinking of tacit knowledge only to replace it with the manifest fiction of the state of nature and the virtuality of its replacement, the contract by which state and civil society are reciprocally constituted.

The crucial importance of this contractual detachment—we might call it that of the subject from the object of justice—recalls the separation that grounds Locke's empirical epistemology, the separation of the object of knowledge from the subjective means by which it is known.[31] In the present context the parallel is instructive for two reasons. First, it reminds us that political theory and epistemology share the category "subject." The separation of subject from sovereign is like the separation of the knowing subject from the object of knowledge because it involves an experience of detachment, an awareness of oneself as a singular entity over against the context of one's customary and taken-for-granted embeddedness. In the argument that follows I will invoke this parallel from time to time in order to speak schematically of a shift in status from, on the one hand, that of a "political subject" who undergoes "subjection" to royal authority to, on the other hand, the status of an "ethical subject" who reflects upon his or her condition of "subjecthood" and thereby lays the ground for the growth of a reflexive and autonomous "subjectivity." (This shift has nothing to do with a putative removal from actual political relationships, which may or may not occur; it describes a change in the way people experience themselves in relation to external authority.)

This leads to the second reason for the instructiveness of the parallel between the political and the epistemological subject, namely, that it emphasizes how fully the modern theory of the state depends upon the cardinal principle of explicitness.[32] This is, of course, the essence of contract theory—that it entails the explicit consent of its participants. In this it contrasts with patriarchalist political theory, which in two respects occupies rather the realm of tacit knowledge: first, because analogous to being born into a pre-existent family, it presumes involuntary subjection; second, because its plausibility requires that the basic analogy of family and state not be examined too closely.[33] Filmer began his treatise on patriarchalism by assuring the reader that "I have nothing to meddle with mysteries of the present state. Such *arcana imperii,* or cabinet councils, the vulgar may not pry into. An implicit faith is given to the meanest artificer in his own craft; how much more is it, then, due to a Prince in the profound secrets of government . . . [?]" Algernon Sidney's reply was acerbic:

> Whilst Filmer's business is to overthrow liberty and truth, he, in his passage, modestly professeth *not to meddle with mysteries of state,* or *arcana imperii.* He renounces these inquiries through an implicit faith, which never enter'd into the head of any but fools . . . . Such as have reason, understanding, or common sense, will and ought to . . . suspect the words of such as are interested in deceiving or persuading them not to see with their own eyes, that they may be more easily deceived. . . . [T]he question is not whether that which is Caesar's should be rendered to him, for that is to be done to all men; but who is Caesar, and what doth of right belong to him . . . .[34]

But for this reason it is a misnomer to speak of the "theory" of patriarchalism. The point at which Filmer theorized the patriarchalist analogy marks the point at which it lost its tacit force and, by being asserted with a positivity foreign to tacit conviction, became vulnerable to refutation. The very substance of patriarchalism, we might argue, like that of absolutism, was countermanded by the manner of its articulation.

This said, however, let me pause briefly to register a caveat. Much of the following analysis turns on the distinction between tacit and explicit knowledge, specifically on the notion that the modern division of knowledge is broadly coextensive with the transformation of the first into the second. I would not stress as much as I do this particular way of articulating how historical change occurs if I did not believe in its utility. At the same time, the abstracted use of this formulation regarding a specific moment can suggest a once-and-for-all watershed between the traditional and the modern—an epochal point at which all that was once tacit became henceforth explicit—that is no part of my argument. The ongoing process by which the tacit becomes explicit is a local, multiple, reversible, overlapping, and uneven development that differs according to a wide range of variables. My argument is nonetheless based on the conviction that the figure of the tacit-rendered-explicit is justly concentrated on this historical moment in particular, a conviction whose abstract plausibility will depend entirely on the persuasiveness of the concrete examples and instances that follow.

On the face of it, the critique of patriarchalism, by emphasizing the incommensurability of "great" and "small," made a signal contribution to the separation of "public" from "private." To some, however, it seemed clear that Locke had not carried his empiricism far enough. The separation between the state and the family, based as it is on the notion of a voluntary compact between sovereign and subjects, encouraged many contemporaries to distinguish between, on the one hand, sovereigns who are just and rightly evoke the assent of their subjects and, on the other hand, sovereigns who are unjust and therefore resistible—the latter being those who wield the absolute authority of the patriarch. But does not this separation of state and family both logically and ethically enjoin an analogous distinction between the just and the unjust patriarch—the latter being he who wields the absolute authority of the tyrant over his unassenting wife and children? In the end, the separation between the publicity of the state and the privacy of the family reclaims, by detoxifying, their analogous relation. That is, social justice requires not a separation out of family from state that reinforces customary patriarchy in the family but a benign patriarchalism in the family analogous to that in the state.

Although she was a royalist who opposed political resistance on any grounds, the most cogent proponent of this view was Mary Astell. As it was then constituted, Astell wrote, marriage was a condition of "Private Tyranny" in which women assumed the status of "*Female Slaves.*"

> [I]f Absolute Sovereignty be not necessary in a State, how comes it to be so in a Family? . . . The Domestic Sovereign is without Dispute Elected, and the Stipulations and Contract are mutual, is it not then partial in Men to the last degree, to contend for, and practise that Arbitrary Dominion in their Families, which they abhor and exclaim against in the State? For if Arbitrary Power is evil in itself, and an improper Method of Governing Rational and Free Agents, it ought not to be Practis'd any where; Nor is it less, but rather more mischievous in Families than in Kingdoms, by how much 100000 Tyrants are worse than one.

Astell's argument capitalizes on the downward mobility of absolutism, which she hypothetically extends not only (as Locke does) to male but even to female subjects—to the "rational and free" agency of married women. Just as Locke's compact separates the state from those who choose, by alienating their rights, to constitute it, so the state of matrimony is made by the mutual consent—the "stipulations and contract"—of its respective participants. Yet the separation of the "public" institution of marriage from its "private" founders is fatally incomplete so long as marriage allows husbands to be absolute "judges in their own cases" and therefore requires wives to be "female slaves."[35]

Once rationalized as not simply a distinction but also a separation, the relationship between the public and the private tends to reproduce the force of a separation within the latter category. Indeed, the very disengagement of the state and the family permitted the theories of political and matrimonial obligation the illumination that comes with explicit and reciprocal reflection. This can be seen in the way Enlightenment discourse on marriage obsessively recurs to the competition between two kinds of marriage: the "arranged" marriage of "alliance" or "convenience" and marriage for love.

Daniel Defoe's treatment of this commonplace is as clear as any. Recalling Locke's discrimination between distinct kinds of authority, Defoe says, "I don't take the State of Matrimony to be designed as that of Apprentices who are bound to the Family, and that the Wife is to be us'd only as the upper Servant in the House." Family service is properly undertaken for material reasons; what Defoe calls "matrimonial whoredom" is a marriage similarly motivated—by financial or sexual desire, by "Money and the Maidenhead." Defoe's greatest interest is in the former, and his antagonist is a patriarchalist absolutism that turns fathers into tyrants and their marriageable children into "slaves": "As Matrimony should be the Effect of a free and previous Choice in the Persons marrying, so the breaking in by Violence upon the Choice and Affection of the Parties, I take to be the worst kind of *Rape;* whether the Violence be the Violence of Perswasion or of Authority; I mean, such as that of Paternal Authority . . . ." Like the establishment of the state, marriage is for Defoe a matter of contractual choice by ethical subjects, and he emphasizes the explicitness of the marriage choice as crucial to its success: "[T]hose Matches succeed best which are entered into with the most serious and thorough Deliberation . . . ."[36] It is as though the state, quarantined off from civil society, returns from within to control the terms by which society's most private institutions are organized. Many of the plots of eighteenth-century novels amount to a complex narrativization of the conflict between these "public" and "private" circumstances for marriage; I will return to this later to consider why it should be so.

Absolute Private Property

The process I have referred to as the devolution or downward mobility of absolutism can be seen in the complex historical relationship between royal absolutism and the institution of absolute private property. By explicitly articulating
tacit conceptions of monarchal authority, I have suggested, royal absolutism
also destabilized those conceptions by separating out the authority of the state
from what it governs, and the authority of the king from its personal embodiment. This movement can be seen as well in the development of attitudes toward property.[37] Although English common law conceived all property to be
held in fee from one's lord—which early on meant, ultimately, from the king—
the property of commoners was seen customarily as a use-right that might under different circumstances be both inclusive and exclusive, both shared with
others and conditionally "privatized" to some or one. The quintessential (and
momentarily paradoxical) mark of private property is unconditional alienability: to own something is to be able to disown it. It has been argued that this
right had been available to English people since the later Middle Ages.[38] Yet the
view of property as a matter of delimited use-rights rather than of disposable or
alienable things was the accustomed view in early modern England, and it was
compatible (at least in this respect) with contemporary elaborations of natural-
law theory, according to which God had originally granted dominion over the
earth and its resources inclusively, to all humanity; special contractual arrangements made it conditionally available for exclusive use as well. English common law and natural-law theory stand in sharp contrast to the view of Roman
law that property, or *dominium,* "is the power over resources which a *dominus,*
that is, a head of household, exercises over his *domus.*"[39] Filmer's version of absolutism was in this respect compatible with Roman law: God's original donation was an exclusive dominion over private things, unconditionally given to
Adam and thence to all monarchs.

In refuting Filmer's absolutism, Locke argued within the tradition of natural-law theory in order to counter this notion that property was an unconditionally exclusive, or absolute, possession of the monarch. Did he also depart
from natural-law theory to argue that land became the absolute private property of those who used it productively? That is, did Locke translate "absolutism"
from the monarch to the improving landowner? By suggesting something like
this more than forty years ago, C. B. Macpherson initiated a rigorous rereading
of the *Second Treatise* in the context of the natural-law tradition.[40] How "natural" is property in Locke? How restricted are the possibilities of its appro-
priation? How self-limiting are exclusive, individual use-rights? How protected
are inclusive, common use-rights? Macpherson's critics have successfully chal-

lenged the image of Locke as a straightforward proponent of "possessive individualism" without dismissing Locke's innovations in theorizing the separability of common from individual use-rights and of property as delimited use-rights from property as alienable things.

Our present concern is not with what Locke (or, indeed, Filmer) meant but with the way developments in property relations helped condition contemporaries' views on the separability of the realms of the public and the private. And from this perspective, the attention Locke gave to the legitimating force of land improvement in a money economy—where not only individual but even common use is arguably enhanced—is consistent with a growing presumption that estates were the absolute private property of their owners. This presumption gained strength in 1646 from the abolition of feudal tenures and the Court of Wards, which legally freed major landholders of their feudal ties to the king and enabled an unprecedented degree of long-term estate planning, experimentation, and investment.[41] Thanks to the abolition of feudal tenures, Defoe wrote, the English gentry held and inherited "their lands *in capite,* absolutely and by entail . . . . All the knight's service and vassalage is abolish'd, they are as absolutely possess'd of their mannours and freehold as a prince is of his crown." Defoe's contemporary John Lilly believed that "an absolute proprietor hath an absolute Power to dispose of his Estate as he pleases, subject only to the Laws of the Land."[42]

The separation out of absolute "private" possession from delimited and common use suggests a sense in which in eighteenth-century England common-law custom came to constitute a historically residual yet politically "rebellious" realm of the "public."[43] More dominantly, the "privacy" of propertied possession was attained over against the emergent publicness of state property, now depersonalized of royal identification. What has been said of Locke might be said as well of the abolition of feudal tenures: "In detaching the title to property from allegiance to a sovereign, he depoliticized property and turned it into an economic rather than a political category."[44] In this way the ground was laid for the modern association of the public sector with state "politics" and of the private sector with "economics"—with the market behavior of private individuals.

At the beginning of the seventeenth century Francis Bacon was able to use the terms "state" and "estate" interchangeably because the political state was inseparable from the king's economic estate.[45] By the end of the century this usage was no longer viable. The point can easily be overstressed. The well-known weakness of English absolutism during the seventeenth century, in comparison with that of France, already bespeaks a comparatively advanced separation of state from civil society, which in turn bespeaks a relatively advanced differentiation of political from economic functions. From the French viewpoint, an

English coextension of political and property-law issues in about 1600 seems dubious at best. This viewpoint sheds valuable light on the relative absence of feudal parcelization in England and on the early development there of both capitalism and class consciousness, in which political terms of conflict became overshadowed by economic ones.[46] At the same time, the comparative perspective should not obscure the signs that political and economic power nonetheless underwent a crucial stage of separation in seventeenth-century England.

In his celebrated visit to the citadel of the emergent private sector, the Royal Exchange, Mr. Spectator was struck "to see so many private Men, who in [past] Time would have been the Vassals of some powerful Baron, Negotiating like Princes for greater Sums of Mony than were formerly to be met with in the Royal Treasury!" The fortunes of these private merchants outstrip those of the feudal lords (and monarch) in whose vassalage their imagined predecessors labored; yet Addison assumes a mutuality between them and the modern-day "public," for they are "thriving in their own private Fortunes, and at the same time promoting the Publick Stock . . . ."[47] That this should appear noteworthy to Addison presupposes a more traditional expectation that private "economic" interests must give way to public "political" ones—that the public good must serve as the prior and procrustean measure of all private interests. By the end of the eighteenth century Adam Smith had formulated the most enduring version of the modern orthodoxy, which nicely reverses this traditional wisdom by arguing that the public interest consists of nothing but the sum and interaction of all private interests.[48] Smith's formulation has a long and rich precedence. A century earlier Richard Cumberland had argued that God and nature "occasion that we in some respect necessarily, whether we will or no, actually promote this general good. Nay, even at the very time we are gratifying our brutal appetites, and acting, even as much as we can against such a good. . . . [The] common good or public good [is] . . . the whole aggregate or sum total of all those various and several kinds of good, from which all individual, rational beings, collectively considered, can be benefited." Smith's famous words therefore must be understood to mark not the beginning but the culmination of a conceptual revolution through which the "public interest" became visible as a general category through its abstraction from a plethora of concrete individual cases.[49]

Interest and the Public Interest

The greatest obstacle to this momentous reversal was the tacit identification of the public interest with the national interest, and of the national interest with that of the absolute sovereign. "And where absolute Power is," wrote the third Earl of Shaftesbury after that obstacle had been removed by decades of conflict, "there is no PUBLICK."⁵⁰ This can be seen in the antiprotectionist corollary of Smith's postulation of the invisible hand: "To hinder . . . the farmer from sending his goods at all times to the best market, is evidently to sacrifice the ordinary laws of justice to an idea of publick utility, to a sort of reasons of state . . . ."⁵¹ This attitude could not long withstand the radical solvent of civil war. Commenting on a republican description of the costs of fighting him as "the publict burthens," Charles I wrote with melancholy understatement, "I thinke that the Kings ar part of the publicke."⁵² As we have seen, absolutist belief was undermined by many factors. On the eve of the Restoration, George Monck, its crucial efficient cause, focused attention on the role played by the civil wars themselves: "Before these unhappy Wars the Government of these Nations was Monarchical in Church and State: these wars have given birth and growth to several Interests both in Church and State heretofore not known; though now upon many accounts very considerable . . . I think upon rational grounds it may be taken for granted; *That no Government can be either good, peaceful or lasting to these Nations, that doth not rationally include and comprehend the security and preservrtion of all the foresaid Interests both Civil and Spiritual . . . .*"⁵³ "Civil" wars make the unknown known and the tacit explicit, dividing presumptive wholes into laboriously separated parts, including "civil" society on the one hand and "state" rule on the other. In fact, the language itself of "interest" came into play in order to acknowledge this irresistible separation, the impossibility of persisting in a unitary and unreflective identification of king with country.

The language of interest after the Restoration was remarkable, not for pertaining to economic rather than political issues—it addressed both—but for the extraordinary specificity and precision with which it seemed to account for an entire, heretofore unacknowledged spectrum of needs and wants. This is also true of the more celebrated development of this period, the rise, proliferation, factionalization, and reconstitution of political parties, a carnival of explicitation that is evident as well in the remarkable increase in the rate of parliamentary elections.⁵⁴ The flowering of political parties and of hotly contested elections made tangible the notion that a broad spectrum of interests not only existed but was relevant to the identification of the national interest. In the first decade of the Restoration period royalists and republicans, Anglicans and dissenters, not to mention other nascent "interests," participated in a discursive conflict over how "England's interest" was to be computed.⁵⁵ One outcome of this debate was the denial, central to the contract theory of government, that the state was coextensive with the monarchy. Thus Algernon Sidney maintained that government had been established, not for the king's interest, "but for the preservation of the whole people, and the defence of the liberty, life and estate of every private man."[56] According to Robert Ferguson, "God having in the institution of magistracy, confined such as shall be chosen rulers, within no other limits in reference to our civil concerns, save that they are to govern for the good of those over whom they come to be established, it remains free and entire to the people . . . to prescribe and define what shall be the measure and boundaries of the public good."[57] Again, the parallel with empiricism is instructive. On the one hand, once the epistemological subject is fully separated out from the object of knowledge—once royal "reason of state" is fully separated out from the state itself—the plausibility of their identification depends not on tacit assumption but on persuasive argument. To resist their separation, on the other hand—to conceive the authenticity of the former as grounds for positing the nature of the latter—can only appear tautological.

A more radical and far-reaching outcome of the debate on interest was the insistence not only that the public "good" is the sum of all private "interests" but also that when we think we are doing good, we are really fulfilling our self-interest. Bernard Mandeville's version of the contract theory of government reads more like a modern theory of socialization:

> [I]n the wild State of Nature . . . no Species of Animal is, without the Curb of Government, less capable of agreeing long together in Multitudes than that of Man; . . . But . . . it is impossible by force alone to make him tractable, and receive the Improvements he is capable of. The Chief Thing therefore, which Lawgivers and other wise Men, that have laboured for the Establishment of Society, have endeavour'd, has been to make the People they were to govern, believe, that it was more beneficial for every Body to conquer than indulge his Appetites, and much better to mind the Publick than what seem'd his private Interest. . . . It being the Interest then of [even the self-indulgent] to preach up Publick-spiritedness, that they might reap the Fruits of the Labour and Self-denial of others, and at the same time indulge their own Appetites with less disturbance, they agreed with the rest, to call every thing, which, without Regard to the Publick, Man should commit to gratify any of his Appetites, VICE; . . . And to give the name of VIRTUE to every Performance, by which Man, contrary to the impulse of Nature, should endeavour the Benefit of others, or the Conquest of his own Passions out of a Rational Ambition of being good.[58]

Locke gives us the agency of universal consent, the rational and qualitative trade-off of liberty for security, and the consequent separation out of state from civil society. For Mandeville, by contrast, the contract fiction is only barely serviceable to his intuition of a systematic and impersonal social mechanism in which original cause and choice are almost beside the point. The division of state from society, of "Lawgivers" from "People," paradoxically seems to preexist the contract itself; the governors possess a theatrically conspiratorial agency, the governed a nugatory agency consisting only in the bad faith of willing dupes; and the contractual trade-off is the quantitative one of self-interest for greater self-interest. Mandeville's nominalism supports the realism of his notorious maxim: "Private Vices, Public Benefits." What purports to be virtuous because "public" is really vicious because "private" but thereby also "public" because beneficial. But in this most famous version of his polemic, the depersonalization of the social system is incompletely accomplished, since Mandeville represents society as the intentional conspiracy of "Lawgivers and other wise Men." Later in his career he was to recognize that "all Inventions of this Sort [are] the joint Labour of Many. Human Wisdom is the Child of Time. It was not the Contrivance of one Man, nor could it have been the Business of a few Years . . . ."[59]

So in Mandeville's proto–social science the "privacy" of civil society, although distilled to the quintessence of self-regard, is nonetheless vitiated by what also seems to be a suprapersonal, quasi-public "social" agency. More commonly, however, the intentional pursuit and fulfillment of one's own economic interest is an unambiguous source for the modern notion of internal "privacy" that emerged in early modern England. This was conceived, crucially, as a negative liberty, a freedom from state control whose corollary was the autonomous agency of the individual subject.[60] In figure 1.1 the painful conflict between private wealth and public—that is, national—health ("publica salus") is represented as a sacrifice of the merchant's profit to supply his king with troops. Such conflict is perhaps inevitable in time of civil war. But the coalescence and estrangement of private from official public interest was potently represented also in the first years after the restoration of Charles II by the widely publicized plight of the "loyal cavaliers" who had fought for the king in adversity but went unrewarded by the "ungrateful" monarch after 1660. Here was the explicit spectacle of a national interest once assumed to be single now breaking up into parts. According to the Earl of Ailesbury, "'Whigism' really sprung by degrees from the discontent of noble families" and gentry whose ancestors had suffered for their "steadfast loyalties."[61]

The separation out of specifically mercantile from royal interests seen in this image and its legends was complicated by the aura of trade wars of the sort that engaged England with the United Provinces of the Netherlands during the middle years of the century, which, as contemporaries were increasingly aware, were a contradictory exercise in winning commercial advantage by severely disrupting commerce.[62] Of course, the collective management of individual economic activity is a tacit and universal assumption in premodern culture, evident not only in trade legislation but also in the organization of merchants into trading companies or guilds that celebrated the arts and "mysteries" of their craft and enjoyed royal protection against unaffiliated interlopers. Indeed, only

PUBLICA SALUS NUNC MEÆ MERCES.

PRO FŒDERE, REGE, ET GREGE.

1640.

Rob. Vaughan sculp.

See here a Merchant, who for's Countries good,
Leaves off his Trade, to spend both Wealth and Blood;
Tramples on Profit, to redeem the Fate,
Of his decaying Church, and Prince, and State.

Such Traffick, sure none can too highly prize,
When Gain is self is made a Sacrifice.
But Oh! how ill will such examples move,
If Lose be made the recompence to Love.

when it can be said to have an alternative, and when it therefore gains the coherence of self-conscious policy ("protectionism," "mercantilism"), does state control of the economy simultaneously come into its own and become vulnerable to challenge. The resulting conflict is one between positive and negative standards of freedom, to be free *of* a trade and to be free *from* interference with it. On the one hand: "It is not to be imagined by the desiring of a free Trade, that all sorts of people should be permitted to exercise the mistery of a Merchant . . . ." On the other hand: "It is repugnant to the very Law of Nature, to give the chief and general Commodity of a Country to a few; in which every free born Inhabitant may claim a material interest."[63]

Once again, the liberties of the civil-war years played a crucial role in enabling this conflict to coalesce. In 1646 an opponent of regulated merchant companies lodged a Leveller-inspired complaint against the "Machivilian empoysoned principles of king's cozening citizens of rights of liberty to which all civil government is subservient."[64] This notion of the tyrannical state as defrauder of individual rights bespeaks a model of negative liberty that could be derived both in repudiation of the absolutist teachings of *The Prince* and in ambivalent concert with the republicanism of the *Discourses*. Machiavelli's are central texts in the self-conscious revival of that strain of classical political theory that has come to be known variously as the discourse of "classical republicanism," "civic humanism," and "country ideology." But like other Renaissance revivals, the derivation of Florentine from classical political theory is a complicated affair.

The most powerful and lasting legacy of Machiavelli's indebtedness to one strain of that theory is, as we have seen, his radical autonomization of the state, and its perpetuation, over against all other concerns. Florentine civic humanism, responding not only to classical models but also to the very different features of the late-medieval culture within and against which it evolved, placed less emphasis on the opposition between the political and the domestic but a great deal more on the separation between the political and the religious.[65] The separability of reason of state from moral reason was the hallmark of Florentine civic humanism. The meaning of political freedom and virtue in the classical theory on which it drew depended on the separability of political action from household business, of freedom from necessity. However, this survived in Renaissance thought largely through implication and association, carried on the

FIG. I.I. (*opposite*) *The Lamentable Estate and distressed Case Of the Deceased Sr William Dick in Scotland, And his Numerous Family and Creditors for the Commonwealth . . .* (1657), A2r. By permission of the British Library, shelf mark 669 f.20 (53).

coattails of the ethos of the free citizen and his civic virtue. This can be seen in the fact that in Florentine civic humanism the meaning of political freedom and virtue cohered as a function of the citizen's independence not of the household but of the state itself and of the state's vulnerability to the necessities of time and fortune.

In their vision of free citizens collaborating in political activity, the ancient sources of civic humanism articulated an ideal of positive freedom by which citizens sustained the republic by their relations with it through their relations with one another. However, positive freedom must be a far more notional ideal in English civic humanism since the collectivity of citizens must maintain a watchful distance—a negative freedom—from the contingencies and corruptions of the state, which its members, if they aim to exercise their civic virtue, are nonetheless bound to serve. In other words, the contradictory character of civic humanist discourse derives from its defective adaptation to the basic tenet of emergent political culture in the early modern period, the separation of society from the state. The category "civil society," which coalesces in opposition to the early modern state, incorporates a crucial component of the classical *polis,* the citizenry itself. In civic humanist doctrine, the citizenry both is and is not of the state.

Civic Humanism or Capitalist Ideology?

The fact that England was for most of the century a monarchy rather than a republic was only the most obvious difficulty in accommodating the Florentine model of civic humanism to seventeenth-century English people. True, much of the century was spent engaged in a struggle against Stuart absolutism, to which republican theory was a real if radical solution; but the central civic humanist tenet of the free citizen and his civic virtue was already anachronistic with regard to that struggle. Civic humanists argued that only those citizens who already, in their private circumstances, were independent could, by principled state service, ensure the liberty of civil society as a whole. By virtue of their freedom from material necessity—translated from ancient sources as the financial and occupational independence enjoyed by English freehold landowners—such citizens, possessed of civic virtue, were able to undertake a career in public life (so runs the doctrine) unthreatened by the corruptions endemic to political patronage. They brought to the state the incorruptibility available only to those who are beholden to no one, and the result was a comprehensiveness and objectivity of judgment that was coextensive with the public good.[66]

But the possession of land could no longer have the pristine meaning in early modern England that it had held in classical antiquity. The centrality of real estate to the civic humanist view of authority—the conception of per-durable property as the indispensable criterion of political status because the necessary qualification for state service—bespeaks a view of politics and economics as inseparable from each other.[67] In civic humanism, this coimplication of political freedom within economic freedom from necessity through the dependence of the first on the second must pertain to the free citizen; but for contemporaries it was already quite practically associated with the residual claims of monarchy—residual precisely because the abolition of feudal tenures had recently legislated the separation out of politics from economics. Again, the republicanism that was rooted in the events of 1642-60 located the freedom of civil society in a broad principle of natural rights—however curtailed this was by the Levellers and later by Locke—according to which the satisfaction of the public interest required that of all private interests. We might suppose that the republicanism of civic humanism would have upheld its own, stricter curtailment of this principle, discovering in a minority of private interests—freehold landowners—the conditions necessary to sustain the public interest. But from the classical perspective on which civic humanism was based, the language of "interest" itself was by definition inappropriate. Indeed, for civic humanists, civic virtue was to be understood not even as a unique and normative private interest; on the contrary, it was to be understood as the capacity of "disinterestedness," the logical corollary of financial and occupational independence.[68]

In short, the calculus of public freedom versus private necessity that civic humanism derived from its reading of Aristotle yielded very different results in seventeenth-century England. The positive freedom of relation thought to define the identification between the classical citizen and the *polis* was actually being conceived as the negative freedom of the private citizen from the state, for which public service was done increasingly by professional salaried bureaucrats and soldiers. The negative freedom ascribed to the classical citizen from the necessities of the *oikos* was being conceived as the positive freedom of private citizens to join one another in relations of political economy and domestic intimacy. As the interestedness of the king himself became explicit, the identity of that social fraction, if any, that might claim the condition of disinterestedness was up for grabs.[69] This is perhaps only to say that civic humanism, like most political doctrines, had a complex relation to the historical context in which it was promulgated. But civic humanism is a special case not because of its contemporary character but because of what has been made of it by modern scholars.[70]

Civic humanism has been credited with an extraordinary role in the formation of modern political and economic discourse, hence in the modern reconception of the relation between the public and the private. Before the eighteenth century, it has been said, civic humanist discourse and its notion of a disinterested virtue was the only source for English people's conception of a public and politically relevant "virtue," indeed for a conception of public "personality." With the financial revolution of the 1690s, in this view, and with the consequent discovery of a mobile species of value and property not grounded in the politically charged soil of real estate, the civic humanist model of public virtue began to be challenged by alternative models, more compatible with an emergent commercial culture, that could valorize more successfully the public efficacy of private interests. In this respect, then, civic humanism has been ascribed a crucial agency in stimulating the emergence of capitalist (or "commercial") ideology, a development this line of thought has located in the early eighteenth century. By contrast, the contribution of seventeenth-century economic and religious debate to this emergence has been seen as negligible.[71]

Yet despite the claim that early-eighteenth-century England was indebted to civic humanism for its only conception of public virtue, the foregoing discussion suggests that by the seventeenth century, economic discourse already was learning both to separate and to reconcile private and public virtue, the pursuit of private interest and the fulfillment of the public interest. Moreover, this kind of reconciliation first began to be accomplished in conjunction not with the financial revolution of the 1690s but with the capitalist revolution itself, that is, with the commodification of land and labor that had begun to be visible to observers decades earlier. The English commercial system of the eighteenth century was not the cause but the consequence of capitalist development and ideology. The capitalist revolution of the countryside preceded and informed the commercial revolution, grounding it in a strong domestic market that was rooted in agrarian class relations.[72] Already by 1660 the civic humanist ambience—the political view of property—was not simply traditional but anachronistic. Detached from its presumptive royal owner, land was coming to be understood as contingent and mobile. By the end of the seventeenth century, when innovative instruments of investment and public credit were both raising the specter of mobile property and evoking its civic humanist repudiation, English people were already familiar with the idea that all property had the potential separability and autonomy that come with the circulation and exchange of substantive things as insubstantial commodities.

From the Marketplace to the Market

As we might expect, the phenomenon of exchange value was subject to sharp criticism on the communitarian principle of positive liberty. In 1622 Thomas Scott attacked all "Improuers of our Land" who "study to doe such acts, and invent such projects, as may vndo the publique for their priuate and inordinate desires," who "liue in this world as *in a market,* [and] *imagine there is nothing else for them to doe, but to buy and sell, and that the only end of their creation and being was to gather riches, by all meanes possible.*" Scott's prescient language captures "*the* market" in its infancy, before the explicit argument of simile has been transmuted into the virtual reality that the market has come to possess in the modern world.[73] In the same negative vein, John Bunyan's Vanity Fair allegorizes the sinfulness of the world as a universal market, limited neither in time ("[t]his *Fair* therefore is an Ancient thing") nor place ("he that will go to the [Celestial] City and yet not go thorow this Town, must needs *go out of the World*") nor commodity ("at *this Fair* are all such Merchandize sold, as Houses, Lands, Trades, Places, Honours, Preferments, Titles, Countreys, Kingdoms, Lusts, Pleasures, and Delights of all sorts, as Whores, Bauds, Wives, Husbands, Children, Masters, Servants, Lives, Blood, Bodies, Souls, Silver, Gold, Pearls, Precious Stones, and what not"). Bunyan's catalog of "what not" expresses both the richness and plenty of a tangible market of consumables and an intuition of "*the* market" of exchangeables, where a bewildering diversity of incommensurable use-values can be lined up and reconciled at the abstract level of exchange. The abstraction of the market went hand in hand with the abstraction of the economy, the self-willed activity of private citizens, from the political and public authority of the state. But as these passages suggest, the market was also an abstraction from the actual particularity of people, places, and things, a public place where the "private and inordinate desires" of individuals might find their iniquitous satisfaction.[74]

But exchange value was also being theorized at midcentury in the dispassionate and positive terms of a proto–political economy. Anthony Ascham did not need the institution of the stock market in the 1690s to observe, in 1649, that "money is an invention onely for the more expedite permutation of things." Such "things" are items of private property, whether land or labor. Locke was soon to make explicit the connection between "own" and "owner," propriety and property: "[E]very Man has a *Property* in his own *Person*. . . . The *Labour* of his Body, and the *Work* of his Hands, we may say, are properly his." "A mans Labour also," Hobbes wrote, "is a commodity exchangeable for benefit, as well as any other thing . . . ." William Petty thought the most important consideration in political economy was "how to make a Par and Equation between Lands and Labour, so as to express the Value of any thing by either alone." By such equations land undergoes an "expedite permutation" into something else: first into a monetary medium of exchange and then, for example, into labor. But as Locke continues, land may also be transformed by labor as it were from within. "Whatsoever then [man] removes out of the State that Nature hath provided, and left it in, he hath mixed his *Labour* with, and joyned to it something that is his own, and thereby makes it his *Property.* It being by him removed from the common state Nature placed it in, it hath by this *labour* something annexed to it, that excludes the right of other Men. . . . His labour hath taken it out of the hands of Nature . . . and *hath* thereby *appropriated* it to himself." When land is thus disembedded from common use, it is appropriated by the propriety of personality and made into personal property. The impersonality of land is thus both exchangeable for and miscible with the personality of a person's labor. Indeed, by the time Locke wrote these famous words, Richard Allestree had already used his metaphor of mixed land as itself a metaphor for the qualitative differentiation of personality: "Men have their parts cultivated and improved by Education, refined and subtiliz'd by Learning and Arts, are like an inclosed piece of a Common, which by industry and husbandry, becomes a different thing from the rest, tho the natural Turf own'd no such inequality. And truly had women the same advantage, I dare not say but they would make as good returns of it . . . ." Allestree's figure is extended and deepened by Mary Astell: "The Ladies, I'm sure, have no reason to dislike this Proposal, but I know not how the Men will resent it to have their enclosure broke down, and Women invited to tast of that Tree of Knowledge they have so long unjustly *Monopoliz'd.*"[75]

Metaphorical usages like these are important in part because they exemplify the mobile exchangeability of land in the realm of discourse as well as economics, a point to which I will return in a moment. But to conceive labor as an act by which land is disembedded from nature is not only a metaphor: it also figures the way in which metaphor itself disembeds discrete textual meaning from its context, transforming concrete literality into an abstract virtuality that both discards and preserves semantic features of the literal. The metaphor of the market—Scott's "living in this world as in a market"—has a similar reflexivity. But the conceptual movement from the literal marketplace to the virtuality of market exchange was also punctuated by way stations in which the process of virtual abstraction was ingeniously if incompletely accomplished through models of activity that were still tangibly actual, that is, institutional. In 1650 Henry Robinson proposed the establishment of an "Office of Addresses and Encounters" (also called a "Register of Addresses") to help put the poor to work. In Robinson's plan, virtualization would be achieved through centralization: "[A]t present, poore people, and others, spend much time, in running up and down, from one place to another to seeke employment, and sell their worke . . . ." Currently our arts, trades, and callings "are scituate some distance from one another, oftentimes unknown & In number Infinite . . . . [A]s yet there never was any publique place appointed which might have served as a Treasury, or Abridgment of all Accommodations desireable." The "Register of Addresses" would be a "common Center of Intelligence" where people "can but *leave* their names, with the place of their abode . . . ," and until something turns up "they may keepe at home . . . ." Notably, the abstraction of a single "public place" distills the "infinite" range of places of concern to a single reciprocity between that public place and "home," whose antithetical privacy is thrown into relief by this generalizing process.[76]

A century later, John and Henry Fielding established a Universal Register Office, whose importance the novelist rationalized in terms of civilization's progress from actual locality to (virtually) virtual universality:

> Man is said to be by Nature a Social Animal, . . . the members of the Body Corporate, like those of the Natural Body, having their several Uses and Qualifications, all jointly contributing to the Good of the Whole. . . . Now Society itself alone creates all these Wants [of its members], and at the same Time alone gives us the Methods of supplying them by the Invention of what is called Trade or Traffick. And yet as Societies of Men encreased into great and populous Cities and large extended Countries, the Politician found something still wanting; and this was a Method of communicating the various Wants and Talents of the Members to each other; by which Means they might be mutually supplied. Hence the Invention of Fairs, Markets, Exchanges, and all other Publick Meetings for carrying on Traffick and Commerce between Men . . . . All these Methods, however, are so far defective, as they fail to be universal . . . . This, as it seems, can only be attained, by providing some Place of universal Resort, where all the Members of the Society may communicate all their mutual Wants and Talents to each other. . . . Upon these Principles an Office was erected on *February* 19, 1749 [1750] . . . The Design of which Office is to bring the World, as it were, together into one Place. . . . [B]e the Wants of Persons ever so singular or extraordinary, 'tis highly probably they may have them supplied by enquiring at this Office . . . . [I]ts Use consists chiefly in its Universality, and this is entirely in the Power of the Public.[77]

Fielding adds that although patrons at first will want to "come to the Office themselves, . . . when the Public are once acquainted with the Method of transacting Business here, it may be done with as much Ease by Letter as by their Presence" (18). As society is metaphorically "corporate," like an actual body it requires methods of "communicating" the demand and supply of its many members that will make it "universal" on its own macroscale, that is, methods that will make it "the world as it were." Many places are therefore distilled into one, whose actuality, although unavoidable, will be minimized by the fact that doing business there will not require the physical "presence" of clients. The movement from the actual to the virtual proceeds by and large as one from the particular to the general, and the success with which this movement is accomplished is projected as a "high probability." As we will see, the principle of probability that underwrites the success of Fielding's Universal Register Office—the accommodation of "private" particulars to a "public" standard of the general—is closely related to the principle of probability that he and others elaborate in developing a theory of literary realism and the aesthetic.[78] There is nothing new, of course, about the susceptibility of things, land in particular, to figuration. But the richness of such usage among contemporaries may suggest a new level of inventiveness that is related to the new abstractability of land from its immemorial embeddedness. In years to come, writers would exploit the understanding of land's physical alienability to set off interior realms of human personality—thought, aesthetic experience—that possessed a more absolute propriety. Arguably, the separation out of an economic from a political view of landed property played a major role in the proliferation and transformation of pastoral and pastoralism during this period. In short, the mobility of land in later-seventeenth-century England facilitated a notion of personality very different from that available through civic humanist discourse; and the commercial mobility of all property accommodated personality to the norms of public virtue.

True, many contemporaries feared, as did Scott, that commercial exchange threatened to sacrifice the public good to private interests. But Ascham, for one, toyed with the notion that commerce was, on the contrary, no more than a new (admittedly more privatized) method of attaining the old end of the common good: "Instead of Community therefore we now have commerce, which *Commercium* is nothing else but *Communio mercium*," the public sharing of merchandise. Commerce is from this perspective like the political contract, an alienation of personal right or property predicated on the expectation of an advantageous return that is both private and public. Well before the outbreak of civil war, in fact, similar notions were being expressed by the more progressive mercantilist authors: "Is it not lawful for Merchants to seek their *Privatum Comodium* in the exercise of their calling? Is not gaine the end of trade? Is not the publique involved in the private and the private in the publique? What else makes a Common-wealth, but the private wealth, if I may so say, of the members thereof in the exercise of Commerce amongst themselves, and with forraine nations?"[79]

A creature of seventeenth-century experience and discourse, capitalist ideology and its reconciliation of private with public interest partakes of the familiar logic of absolutist devolution, whereby the absolute authority of the sovereign is internalized, over time, as a sovereign attribute of the individual citizen. Hobbes had used the voluntarist language of contract to insist on the necessity of a contract enforcer, Leviathan's absolute sovereign: "[T]he bonds of words are too weak to bridle mens ambition, avarice, anger, and other Passions, without the feare of some coercive Power . . . . Therefore before the names of Just, and Unjust can have place, there must be some coercive Power, to compel men equally to the performance of their Covenants, by the terrour of some punishment, greater than the benefit they expect by the breach of their Covenant . . . ."[80] Yet by the end of the century commentators had located within the self-interested desires of private citizens a prudential sensitivity to reputational "credit" and "trust" sufficient to enforce private covenants without recourse to the fear of a "coercive" public power.[81] In fact, it was on this model of the voluntaristic yet systematic interaction of private desires and interests that contemporaries imagined mysterious new public institutions as impersonal personalities, local and private motives somehow writ large and public. "[A]s the Publick Credit is *National,* not *Personal,* so it depends upon *No thing* or *Person,* No *Man* or *Body of Men,* but upon the Government, *that is,* The Queen and Parliament . . . . Neither does our Credit depend upon the Person of the Queen, *as Queen,* on the individual House of Commons, *Identically* . . . ."[82]

External legal authority might be replaced by internal sanctions because those sanctions, the prudence of economic self-interest, were deemed natural: "The Wants of the Mind are infinite, Man naturally Aspires, and as his Mind is elevated, his Senses grow more refined, and more capable of Delight; . . . it is the wants of the Mind, Fashion, and Desire of Novelties, and Things scarce, that causeth Trade." These are "wants" in the sense not of privative need but of lack, that is, of appetite or desire. "The main spur to Trade, or rather to Industry and Ingenuity, is the exorbitant Appetites of Men, which they will take pains to gratifie, and so be disposed to work, when nothing else will incline them to it . . . ."[83] Locke tried to limit the rule of want-as-lack by a utilitarian standard of want-as-need: "As much as any one can make use of to any advantage of life before it spoils; so much he may by his labour fix a Property in." But consumables like the produce of land—what is susceptible to spoilage—have a built-in limit on their usability that does not exist for other sorts of commodities. Indeed, the whole point of market exchange is that it frees objects from the tyranny of use by which natural objects are constrained. What counts for Fielding is not the naturalness but the sheer existence—the "reality"—of want-as-lack:

> [I]n Proportion to the Opulence of any Society, the Wants of its Members will be multiplied . . . . [T]he Wants of a Man worth a single Thousand Pounds bear no Proportion to those of him who is possessed of a hundred times that Sum. The Ethic Writer, indeed, will tell me, that none of these Wants arise from Nature. But let them arise from what they will, they are real, and to supply them is as essential to the Happiness of him who hath, or thinks he hath them, as it is to a Savage to supply any of those few Necessities with which a State of Nature, as some call it, abounds.[84]

In this way private desire could be understood as an invariable, unquenchable, hence absolute engine of individual economy. But its absoluteness could also be generalized as a collective "law" of the private realm that obviated the positive law of the state: a law of human nature, even the objective and natural "law of the market."[85] The "privacy" of economy, far from the connotation of "privation" and necessity that colored the Aristotelian view of household economy, was taking on the aura of negative liberty that would characterize modern political economy and that Charles I found oxymoronic in the revolutionary equation of "liberty" with "independence."[86] This is not to say, of course, that liberal economic thought and policy now swept the field. Rather, the seventeenth-century theorization of "the market" as a separate realm of choice and activity over against state policy and law ensured that modern economic discourse would be defined by the oppositional relationship of society and the state, "free enterprise" and "planning," the private and the public sectors.

My point is also, however, that by the end of the seventeenth century it was precisely this separation out of state from civil society that was facilitating the innovative terms in which ideas of public virtue and public personality might have bearing in the modern context. In this process the experience of international trade taught lessons that could be applied at the domestic level. The mercantilist theory that justified the trade wars of the seventeenth century was based on the view that wealth was a material entity and that there was a limited amount of it in the world. Trade wars were therefore a zero-sum game overseen by the all-important criterion of the balance of trade: the more wealth the Dutch possessed the less there was for the English. The discovery that private desire not only consumed but also created wealth was consonant with the reconception of the market as elastic and virtual, not a public emporium for the distribution of actual use values but the imagination of a space where an unlimited amount of private use values became available to the indeterminate needs and lacks of "the public." This reconception did not occur overnight. As Mandeville expressed it, private vices ensure public benefits. However, those who believed the pursuit of private self-interest was the key to the public welfare did not necessarily insist on the paradoxical nature of that process. On the contrary, many saw the logic whereby self-improving industriousness served the public good; after all, "industry" was itself a private good. One commentator advised: "Let the People of England . . . get their Livings by Industry, and never exceed the limits of their private Fortunes, and all complaints of venality and Corruption will fall to the Ground. . . . There is no sure Method, therefore, of preventing Corruption, but by preventing Necessity . . . . Let them secure private Virtue and they will see all public Virtue rise out of it."[87] This language of the 1730s bears the indelible marks of the Protestant doctrine that had come to maturity during the previous century. In the remainder of this chapter I will ask how religious discourse contributed to the economic elaboration of a public virtue separable from the state and grounded not in disinterestedness but in the satisfaction of private interests.

To traditionalists who thought "the wants of the mind" should be superintended by religious motive, the absoluteness of the profit motive seemed no more than a stand-in for that of absolutist prerogative and reason of state—at best a cynical parody of divine-right ordinance. According to Richard Allestree in 1667, interest "is the great *Idol* to which the world bows . . . . We sacrilegiously entitle our profit to all the Prerogatives of a Creator, give it an absolute unlimited dominion over us, allow it to prescribe us all our measures of good and evil; . . . Divinity has long since been made the handmaid of Policy, and Religion's modelled by conveniencies of State."[88] And yet religion, conceived as the realm of spiritual faith or "conscience," is justly seen (as is economic interest) as one of the great sources of the modern notion of internal "privacy." Traditional Christian culture tended to polarize religion and interest as antithetical forces—as the pursuit of the spiritual and the profane life, respectively. How did they become allies in the privacy of civil society? Here, as earlier, the distinction between explicit and tacit cultural knowledge will be of use.

The Protestant Separation

To posit a "traditional culture" is to conceive one in which religious experience is tacit in the sense that it suffuses all of life through the media of sacred time and spaces, habitual and ritual behavior, common practices, and unrationalized convictions—a state of mind that does not, incidentally, preclude impiety and sacrilege. In the fundamentally alternative model, "religion" has been separated out from the rest of experience as the specialized realm of worship, doctrine, and conscious belief in an immaterial and absent deity.[89] These are ideal types. If Roman Catholicism was a "traditional" culture for Protestants, it was a "modern" culture for pagan natural religions. Moreover, in seventeenth-century Protestant England religion still exercised its "traditional" function to, in Cicero's etymology, *re-ligare*—to bind a people together again in the precepts of public duty, or back to their superhuman foundations. My schematic abstraction aims not to obscure these truths but to help sensitize us to the historical singularity of what in the most general terms may "always" be said of human cultures.

In its very ambition to bind the people together English Protestantism fatally impaired the tacit efficacy of religion by making it an explicit program. One reason scholars have been willing to see civic humanism as the only source of a concept of public virtue in seventeenth-century England may be that they have misconstrued the process of secularization. In early modern England, it has been argued, secularization was not the mechanical separation of religion from politics and science but the religion of Protestantism itself.⁹⁰ The grand motive underlying all movements of Christian reform (the Protestant Reformation being only the most significant of these) has been not to "secularize" but to resanctify. What made the Reformation different was not its motive but its powerful techniques of explicitation, which purified religion by separating it out from the cultural matrix in which it customarily had exercised its relatively tacit sway. Paradoxically, the modern disembedding of religion, which altered it from the universal precondition of human existence to the personal and private experience of the individual, also defined it as the last refuge of "embedded" belief precisely because its metaphysics could not withstand the cold but normative scrutiny of empirical epistemology. The long-term result was the modern emergence not only of secularity but also of religion itself in the modern sense of the term.

To speak in this way is, of course, to anticipate two centuries of change. A more concrete and particularized perspective on this process must account for the way Protestants hopefully engaged in experiments that would vindicate true religion by disclosing the corrupt entanglement of Roman Catholicism in profane institutions and motives. The first such experiment was the Reformation itself, which threw Protestantism into deep relief by its explicitating periodization of past Christian practice as a fatal fall from pristine beginnings.

As a political act, Henry VIII's rebellion against Rome was an absolutist assumption of authority well symbolized by the English sovereign's embrace of the role of *defensor fidei,* "defender of the faith." By ostentatiously fusing church and state, Henry's reform both fulfilled the tacit promise of traditional culture—religion cannot be separated from secular life—and, in the very explicitness of that fulfillment, laid the ground for its modern undoing. This is the logic of absolutism and its devolution. By repudiating the patriarchal authoritarianism of pope and priest, reform reinforced the authority of the household patriarch to such a degree that it also undermined the role of the state in authorizing family worship, thereby weakening the appeal of patriarchalism and ultimately eroding intrafamilial hierarchy as well.⁹¹ Moreover, the theological substance of Protestant doctrine individualized the great question of salvation in a way that hastened this devolution of religious absolutism from pope to king to father and thence to the people. This is an old story that need be recalled only in its outlines.⁹²

In the eyes of its adversaries, the Roman Catholic Church interposed between God and the believer a hierarchy of ecclesiastical rituals and powers whose officious mediations encouraged irresponsibility, indifference, and hypocrisy while siphoning off power to the secular institution of the church. Reformation doctrine made the question of salvation explicit and self-conscious by placing it in the hands of Luther's "priesthood of all believers"—by making it a matter not of external authority but of internal conscience. One of John Foxe's Puritan martyrs told his Catholic inquisitors that thanks to "your rules of religion," before his conversion "I made no conscience of sin, but trusted in the priest's absolution, he for money doing some penance also for me, which after I had given, I cared no further what offences I did . . . so that lechery, swearing, and all other vices I accounted no offence of danger, so long as I could for money have them absolved." This continued until God "opened the light of his word, and called me by his grace . . . ."[93] Here the private light of conscience is opposed to "public" corruption in the double guise of economic interest and state authority.

For justification by external works the reformers substituted justification by internal faith or "grace," which the Calvinist doctrine of predestination ensured was utterly beyond the will or actions of the believer. "Good works" were fundamentally reconceived: industrious discipline was crucial to Puritans as a means not of instrumentally gaining grace but of gratuitously serving God and sanctifying his order. Through discipline in their private callings, the elect became "public" saints. "Thus may a private man become a magistrate," said William Perkins of the specifically political vocation. Another wrote: "Private persons are self-centered like clods of the earth, but public persons are turned into other men, and have a public spirit . . . ."[94] Language like this drew upon covenant theology and its conception of an explicit "covenant of grace" between Christ and his saints. The idea of the Protestant covenant was grounded in the "privacy" of unmediated interchange and agreement. But the covenant of grace was also conceived as a relationship of "public" representation, in which Christ and the believer stood in for "other men"—for all humanity or sometimes (recalling the slippery criterion of representation in the political theory of the contract) for the elect alone.[95] In the experience of the Puritan elect, then, there was an unbroken continuum linking private to public virtue.

But how do you tell that you are one of the elect? In the Roman Church, the reformers believed, grace was complacently ensured by ecclesiastical mediators. For Puritans, however, the only available sign of election was the subjective conviction of the believer. Puritanism made conscientious self-scrutiny central to salvation, providing modernity a model of how authority might be identified, through interiority, as authenticity. Theological developments like these may be related to the way in which the word "conscience," until the seventeenth century an inclusive term ill-distinguished from "consciousness," by the beginning of the eighteenth century was acquiring its modern, distinctively internal reference.[96] And in the vital struggle to attain the certainty of salvation, Puritan practice (if not doctrine) discovered in industrious discipline and the idea of the inward vocation, or "calling," an unsought instrumentality. This is, of course, the heart of Max Weber's celebrated thesis: not that discipline could, like popish works, "earn" grace but that it might signify, as a mark of divine approval, the fact that grace was already predestinate. For many correligionists, the Puritan replacement of a causal by a signifying relationship between public and outward labor discipline and private and inward grace triumphantly overcame the hypocrisy of the Roman Catholic theology of works. But for many others (and surely for their enemies), it only sophisticated popish hypocrisy, correlating the antinomies of spiritual and material success at the impregnable level of individual self-assurance.

In these distinct but related ways the doctrine of Puritan discipline contributed to the notion not simply that self-interested behavior was consistent with religious ends but even that their consistency was unparadoxical. By attending to the affinities between two different intellectual structures, Weber's thesis provides one answer to the question how religious faith and economic interest, the Protestant ethic and the spirit of capitalism, came to be allied in the early modern period.[97]

Why Protestantism in particular? After all, from Augustine on, Christianity had known that the interior realm of personal faith was where the battle for salvation must be waged, and the Protestant churches exercised no monopoly on conscience and its close examination.[98] Casuistry, the adjudication of moral precepts by applying them to specific dilemmas (or "cases") of conscientious choice, was first of all a Roman Catholic method of inquiry. In the Church of Rome, however, casuistry was the official and exclusive work of divines because salvation depended on priestly mediation. In Protestant cultures, by contrast, casuistry played an unofficial and advisory role in the counsel of individual believers, and it was undertaken there as much by the laity as by the clergy. Only when it was separated out in this way from the systematic soteriological procedures of the Roman Church did casuistry become a despised and "jesuitical" procedure, reminding Protestants not only of popish hierarchy but also of popish hypocrisy—the ratiocinative equivalent, as it were, of ritual absolution. "He is excused from sin," said one critic of Roman Catholic casuistry, "who ventures on it upon some probable reason."[99]

Yet casuistical modes of reasoning proved indispensable to English Protestants as well, for example, on political issues such as the right of resistance to established authority. In such cases the demands of "private" conscience characteristically were ranged against those of "public" policy. On the one hand, the absolutist Hobbes thought the doctrine *"that every private man is Judge of Good and Evill actions,"* as well as that *"whatsoever a man does against his Conscience, is Sinne,"* was "repugnant to Civill Society." For "with him that lives in a Common-wealth . . . the Law is the publique Conscience, by which he hath already undertaken to be guided. . . . [B]y Publique, is alwaies meant, either the Person of the Common-wealth it self, or something that is so the Common-wealths, as no private person can claim any propriety therein." In the wake of the Exclusion Crisis the archbishop of York made a similar if less absolute point: "There is nothing more in our mouths than *Conscience;* and yet there are few Things we have generally taken less Pains to understand. We sit down too often with this, That it is something *within us,* and we trouble ourselves no further about it. . . . *Conscience* . . . among other Ends, was given to Mankind for a Preservative and Security of the publick Peace . . . ." On the other hand, the absolutist Charles I, looking back on his acquiescence in the attainder of the Earl of Strafford in 1641, ruefully resolved against such absolutism: "[N]ever suffer me for any reason of State, to goe against my Reason of Conscience."[100]

Of course, in his endorsement of individual conscience and its absolute claims Charles was principally motivated by the fact that in the space of a single year absolute state power had already become well advanced in its momentous devolution from king to Parliament. Shortly after the Restoration of Charles's son a series of parliamentary statutes used the power of the state to constrain all religious activity that did not conform to Anglican doctrine.[101] This legislation brought "nonconformity" and "dissent" into existence, and "fanaticism" into common parlance. Pressured by this legal polarization of state and civil society, Nonconformists soon discovered how to conjoin conscience and interest as categories of the private that were opposed by the public state but representative of a higher public good, the interest of England. In this way the suspension of a public/private conflict (between interest and conscience) within the larger realm of the private depended upon the disclosure of such a conflict (between national and state interest) within the larger realm of the public.

The debates in which these arguments were made were informed by the sociological insight that persecution is one of the most efficient means of rendering tacit knowledge explicit—and politically dangerous. John Locke offered Anglicans the following advice in 1667:

> [T]he opprobrious name of fanatics . . . I think might with more prudence be laid aside and forgotten; for, what understanding man, in a disordered state, would . . . , by giving one common name to different parties, teach those to unite whom he is concerned to divide and keep at a distance one among another? . . . For the fanatics, taken all together, being numerous, and possibly more than the hearty friends to the

state-religion, are yet crumbled into different parties amongst themselves, and are at as much distance from one another as from you, if you drive them not farther off by the treatment they receive from you. . . . But, if you persecute them, you make them all of one party and interest against you, tempt them to shake off your yoke, and venture for a new government . . . .[102]

The heart of the tolerationist argument was that however "private" their interest might be, the "fanatics" were far too vital to the national interest to warrant discouragement. One writer observed that "the Sea-fareing Men, and the Trading Part of the Nation, dos in a great measure consist of Non-conformists; and that much of the Wealth and Stock of the Kingdom, is lodged in their Hands, who have no great Devotion for the present Liturgy, & Hierarchy of the Church of *England*. Wherefore we need go no farther to find out the cause of that general Damp upon Traffique and Commerce, then the Strictness of our Laws upon that Sort of People . . . . [I]t is certainly the great interest of the *English State,* and particularly of his *Majesty,* to take off all *discouragements* from his *Subjects,* (especially the *Trading part* of them) and to *unite the Nation.*"[103] Like trade, tender consciences were one of England's great interests; indeed, they were the same interest, conjoined in the sphere of civil society by a common vulnerability to state prohibition.

Antitolerationists responded to this radical reconceptualization—religion and economic interest ranged over against state interference—by explicitly reaffirming the more traditional attitude. Religion was not the equal ally but the subsuming sovereign of interest:

Men may amuse themselves, with the instance of the *United Provinces;* which, they say, flourish in trade and riches, by maintaining all Religions. But the question is of Religion, not of Trade, nor Riches. If it could be said, that their Religion is improved, with their Trade, the example were considerable. But, they that would restore and improve the Religion, that flourished in *England* thirty years ago, must not take up with the *base Alloy* of that which is seen in the *United Provinces.* Nor is this a reproach to them, but a truth of God's Word; that Religion and Trade cannot be both at once at the height.[104]

In this dispute we can see the modern view of public-private relations emerging from a medieval paradigm. On the one hand, religion and trade cannot be both at once at the height. The conflict between the two is intelligible according to the theological and moral distinction between things of the spirit and things of the flesh, virtue and vice, truth and interest, and it is sustained and administered by the superintending authority of religion itself, which adjudicates the limited degree of commercial enterprise that is tolerable in a Christian commonwealth. On the other hand, religion and trade are seen to cohere, through the public threat of state prohibition, as a private unit of individualistic under-taking that promotes the public good. State power articulates what is ultimately not a moral but a political distinction: between liberty and constraint, self-interest and the public interest. As capitalist ideology reconciles private self-interest, so the argument of religious interest reconciles private conscience with the public welfare. Public virtue and public personality are to be found not in the putative disinterest of men who serve the state but in the enlightened self-interest of those who keep their distance from it.

Conscientious Privacy and the Closet of Devotion

But this is not, of course, the end of the story; for despite the legislative vindication of religious dissent, the predominant face of religion in the modern world is not a public one. When governmental constraint was finally curtailed —when English state policy became officially one of religious toleration (with significant limitations, in 1689)—it may have been because English people agreed that heterodoxy served the public interest, but it was more profoundly because they had begun to isolate, from its more externalized manifestations, what increasingly seemed the quintessential interiority of religion. Once again, the argument is one of separation. By 1720 Benjamin Ibbot was able to argue that

> vices fall under [the magistrate's] Cognizance, as they are injurious to Mens *Civil Interests,* and destructive of the good *Order and Government of the World;* and not as they have an inherent *Turpitude* in them. . . . If the ill influence which these Vices have upon the *Peace and Welfare of Human Society,* could be separated from their *Immorality,* and their being *Transgressions of the Laws of God,* the *Magistrate* could have nothing to do with them; his Business being nothing else but to preserve the *Publick Peace and Quiet* . . . . But though we cannot actually separate the *ill Influence* any Vice has upon the *Society* we live in, from its being a Transgression of some *Divine Law;* yet in our Minds we may make this Separation, and consider every Vice as a mix'd Action . . . . [S]ecret Intentions and Designs of Wickedness, if they never break out into Act . . . can never be liable to Civil Punishments. But with Regard to the *Laws of God,* the Case is far otherwise. . . . For there is this remarkable and essential Difference between Mens *Civil* or *Temporal,* and their *Religious* or *Spiritual* Rights, that the *former* are *alienable* . . . . But the latter, their *Religious* or *Spiritual* Rights, are their unalienable Property . . . .[105]

That is, we have absolute ownership of our "secret intentions and designs"—of our private thoughts—in the eyes of the law, although not in those of the Law.

Absolutist Erastianism was challenged, the English church and state became at least in this sense separable, through the devolutionary "privatization" of religion as crucially a matter of "conscience": of thoughts not speech, of speech not action, of individuals not collectives. Thomas Sprat believed that "all wise Men should have two Religions; the one, a *publick,* for their Conformity with the People, the other, a *private,* to be kept to their own Breasts . . . ." Dryden thought that "Conscience is the Royalty and Prerogative of every Private man. He is absolute in his own Breast, and accountable to no Earthly Power, for that which passes only betwixt God and Him." Milton used the language of typological fulfillment—of the Law by the Spirit—to characterize the deep and internalized locality of conscience: "We must realize that only the written surface has been changed, and that the law is now inscribed on believers' hearts by the spirit."[106]

Seventeenth-century Protestants literalized this location through the institution of the devotional closet. Edward Wettenhall wrote that the closet of devotion was "by its end and designment, after a sort separate or sacred, a certain secret Chappel for my self . . . ." We are not to be misled by the richly figurative quality of his language. The biblical text on which the concept of the closet of devotion is based is Matthew 6:6: "But thou, when thou prayest, enter into thy Closet, and when thou hast shut thy door, pray to thy Father which is in secret, and thy Father, which seeth in secret, shall reward thee openly." "Some understand and interpret it," wrote Oliver Heywood, "not literally but mystically, making an Allegory of it as though it did import . . . the inner recesses or motions of the heart, but though that be a truth and duty, . . . yet, I humbly conceive, that is not the proper meaning of this place: for we need not interpret the plain word in such a borrowed sense . . . ." Heywood construed the closet Matthew speaks of expansively, as "a Safe place, or Cupboard, . . . or a locked Chest, . . . or . . . a close or secret chamber, a withdrawing-room, retiring-place, . . . a secret conclave or locked Parlour, where no company is to come," "the most retired room," even a "barn, or wood . . . ." "[M]y Closet would I have no unpleasant place," wrote Wettenhall, "as sweetly situated as any place in my house, that I might delight to be therein; and by no means a low or darksome room, but as high as I well could . . . . And if it might be my passage thereunto should be through two outer rooms, at least through one, the door or doors of which I might even have shut when I thither retired . . . ." Figure 1.2 reproduces the title page of Wettenhall's devotional guide. Apart from the ministering angel, the most noteworthy "furniture of my closet" are a bookshelf, a chair, and a desk with "two *paper books* (which when fill'd must be supply'd by two others), and a *Pen* and *Ink.*"[107]

These and other writers set the secrecy, solitude, and privacy of the devotional closet over against more public spaces for prayer, although not necessarily to the latter's disadvantage. In the words of Elnathan Parr, "Private is that

ENTER INTO THY
CLOSET.

Sold by Io: Martyn at y.̃ Bell in S.ͭ Paul's C. Yard

FIG. 1.2. Title page, Edward Wettenhall, *Enter into thy Closet: or, A Method for private Devotion . . .* ([1663] repr. 1684). By permission of the Folger Shakespeare Library.

which is used by private persons in private places . . . . But remember that never any man prayed wel privately, who contemned or neglected the publicke prayers in the Church." According to Francis Osbourne, "[P]rivate Christians [i.e., lay people] though neither ordained, nor learned in Arts and tongues, having the words of Christ dwelling in them richly, zealous of good works, may meet weekly if they please, in some of their owne private houses, upon some working day, to interpret and give the sense of some more usefull and more easie places in the booke of God . . . ." For the pious Mary Gunter (notably a Catholic convert), solitary prayer complemented family devotions: "[S]he resolved . . . that besides Family duties, which were performed twice every day, by the Chaplain jn the Religious house in which she lived . . . [a]nd besides the private Prayers which she daily read in her Ladies Bed-Chamber, she was thrice on her knees every day before God in secret . . . ." Thomas Lye suggested that if "thou canst not be so much in the *Pulpit* as thou would'st, oh! be more in thy *Closet:* it may be thou shalt not have so many opportunities to hear so many *Lectures,* be more conscientious in thy *meditations* in secret: it may be thou shalt not have that freedome with God in *publick,* be more earnest with God in *private* . . . ." And Heywood observed that "[m]any Sermons are lost for want of souls taking them home to their Closets, and turning them to Prayer . . . ."[108]

However universally acceptable devotion may have been, however, the language of closet prayer endorses as normative the movement from the outside to the inside. Heywood makes this point through the most extreme of ethical contrasts: the scribes and pharisees "were wont to perform their private devotions in publick places, meerly for vain-glory, to be seen of men, as in the *Synagogues,* or in the *Streets* . . ."; but Christ taught his disciples "to withdraw themselves out of the view of men, into some solitary place, and there perform that Duty . . . ." The differential between public and private devotion was also conceived normatively as one between remaining on the surface and descending to the very depths of sincerity, humility, and authenticity: "Publike is more solemne, but priuate ought to bee more frequent: publike makes more noyse, but priuate (for the most part) hath a deeper channell." "[P]rivacie is to bee chosen that beeing sequestred from company, wee may more fully descend into our owne hearts, and be freer from Ostentation and Hypocrisie . . . ."[109] George Herbert imagined this sometimes desperate descent as a sequence of nesting enclosures, each more private than the last but none so private as to bar access to "God's afflictions":

> O what a cunning guest
> Is this same grief! within my heart I made
> Closets; and in them many a chest;
> And like a master in my trade,

In those chests, boxes; in each box, a till:
Yet grief knows all, and enters when he will.

.   .   .   .

No smith can make such locks, but they have keys:
Closets are halls to them; and hearts, high-ways. . . .[110]

So the interiority of conscientious experience and experiment was correlated with the interiority of the domestic spaces in which these activities occurred, a correlation between micro- and macro-, bodily and architectural privacy, to which we will return in subsequent chapters.

The Puritan divine William Perkins thought "all courts of men are inferior to conscience, the tribunal which God has erected in every man's heart." Over the course of the seventeenth century the jurisdiction of the ecclesiastical or "spiritual" courts was steadily whittled away; the ordinance abolishing episcopacy in 1646 also abolished church courts.[111] After 1660 the old offenses of heresy and blasphemy ceased to be punishable in the extreme old ways. "England did not like making the exercise of conscience a felony." Rather, "conscience pushed to external disobedience of the law raised the specter of seditious conspiracy." To be actionable, blasphemy had to be intelligible as sedition, internal as external, religious as political offense.[112] In 1676 Lord Chief Justice Matthew Hale ruled that "wicked blasphemous words were not only an offence to God and religion, but a crime against the laws, State and Government, and therefore punishable in this Court. For to say, religion is a cheat, is to dissolve all those obligations whereby the civil societies are preserved . . . ."[113] "Liberty of Conscience," said a commentator in 1712, "is the free enjoyment of ones own private Opinion, and every Man because his Opinion is Orthodox to himself, hath a just title to it, so long as he doth not thereby disturb the Peace of the Church and State."[114] Like absolute private property, absolute private conscience is a possession to which the individual has "a just title," "subject only to the Laws of the Land." And like economic and political laws, religious legislation increasingly aimed not to constrain private liberties but to protect them from the constraints of other private parties.

What Is the Public Sphere?

The growth of the societies for the reformation of manners in London during the 1690s may be understood as a self-consciously private effort to continue the public work that the church courts were increasingly less willing or able to do.[115] However, the societies were obliged by the historical logic of their emergence to define their mission in terms more tangible—action not speech, speech not thoughts—than the spiritual courts had once envisioned. Their concern was strictly with "public vice": "Vice when it is private and retired is not attended with those provoking circumstances as when it revels in your streets and in your markets and bids defiance to God and Religion in the face of open day."[116] The members of the first such society were "most of them private men" who "thought something of a more universal nature, and such as private persons by their pains and purses might promote, more proper for them."[117] These private men were soon joined by some mayors, aldermen, and justices of the peace, and their work was expanded to include efforts to enhance the penal and judicial activities of the state.

The title page of a 1700 tract announced its very practical purpose to be *A Help to a National Reformation. An Abstract of the Penal Laws against Prophaneness and Vice. A Form of the Warrants Issued out upon Offenders against the Said Laws. A Blank Register of Such Warrants. Prudential Rules for the Giving of Informations to the Magistrates in these Cases . . . Printed for the Ease of Magistrates and Ministers and the Direction and Encouragement of Private Persons. . . .* Language like this suggests the integrative aim of *religare,* of binding together private morality and public policy. But the balance was exceedingly delicate, and criticisms of the movement were suggestively varied in their construal of its implications for the public-private relationship. Some critics thought the private was being dangerously subsumed by the public, that the societies were "[r]eally, the Societies of Informers, not reformers." The famous Dr. Sacheverell believed that religion "does not oblige us to charge men at random upon bare surmise and suspicion, or . . . to invade their private rights by usurping a jurisdiction which we have no title to justify . . . ." Other critics feared not subsumption but separation: "Separate societies and councils of reformation have always been reckoned necessary implements towards the subverting of an Establishment . . . ." "They are only seedlings of the good old cause and sprouts of the Rebellion of '41." Defoe anticipated a different sort of separation:

> How Publick Lewdness is expell'd the Nation,
> That *Private* Whoring may be more in fashion.

Defoe's point is not simply that the campaign against prostitution leaves adultery in a flourishing state. Reformation operates by a double standard: the prosecution of vice among the poor not only masks, but even fosters, the vicious manners of the gentle.[118] The very diversity of responses to the reforming societies bespeaks an uncertainty about how to place them. Were they a private supplement, a stimulus, or a challenge to state authority?

How do private individuals influence public policy? The questions raised by the reforming societies evoke Jürgen Habermas's characterization of the emergent public sphere of early-eighteenth-century England as "the sphere of private people come together as a public."[119] There are, of course, more traditional examples of this convergence. Figure 1.3 depicts in three stages a model country contest in the election of 1733: the welcoming of the candidates, the alfresco feast of the electors, and the chairing of the candidates after the polling is over. The Habermasian phrase enjoys a crude and highly tangible realization. The private people comprise men and women of all ages, and they come together as a public not only in the sense of actively engaging matters of public policy but also in the sense of literally bringing the indoors out into the open air of public discourse and celebration. The mobilization of crowds around election issues was not new, but the election itself, and its explicitly public-private interaction, took on a new public importance in this period.[120] The societies for the reformation of manners provide an unusually activist example of a different sort of private interest, one that entered the public sphere by generating its own institutional structure. Our sense of the potential scope of Habermas's phrase will be deepened by considering a comparable but longer-lived institution, the freemasons.

The masons began their corporate existence as a medieval craft guild, like most guilds formulaically endowed by a prince, commune, or great landowner with "liberties and privileges" to practice their trade according to the ancient and secret "mysteries" of the craft. This was a positive liberty—to be sure, a freedom from unprivileged interlopers, but more fundamentally a corporate freedom to protect trade and to regulate wages and labor according to prescribed rules of association, "whether the corporation was more or less autonomous, or was closely tied to the government of the commune."[121] The breakdown of protectionist policies under the impact of the developing market was a long-term process that subjected the principles of positive liberty of the old guild system to the principles of negative liberty entailed in the separation out of the state and its hitherto tacit authority from the multiple interests of civil society. England experienced this process earlier than other European countries, and freemasonry emerged from its guild status first of all in England. The freemasons were singular in the success with which they made this transition by recreating themselves as a professional organization self-consciously continuous with the old mysteries and practices but composed as much of gentlemen as of stonecutters and dedicated to the antiabsolutist ideals of equality, meritocracy, and fraternity. But these were also the ideals of the constitutional state as it was being redefined through the crises of Stuart rule. The masonic lodges of the early eighteenth century came together as a public in the most literal sense of the phrase. That is, they modeled their own organizations on those of the state and became "microscopic, and contractually founded and constitu-

tionally governed, civil societies. . . . Within this sociable meritocracy lies the first self-conscious attempt to create societies governed by the abstract principles of British constitutionalism."[122]

But imitation of the state in its emergent, constitutional identity was only half of the equation. The other half, more familiar in the Habermasian model of the public-sphere institution, was a critique of the state in its still powerfully residual authoritarian and absolutist identity, a critique that was also rooted in imitative motives. "The cult of secrecy was, from one angle, a kind of emulation, borrowing on the awe attached to the arcanum of absolutist statecraft . . . ."[123] Hence masonic lodges "were spaces in a new zone of civil society wherein aspects of the larger political and social order were mirrored and mimicked, yet also and simultaneously opened to scrutiny and criticism." From this perspective we can detect a parodic doubleness in the way the freemasons sustained the ancient rites of mysteriousness. "The ability to keep the secrets of masonry—rather than a practice of those mysteries—became the only means of identifying a true brother." These secrets were "words and signs used in the bonding of men who were different from one another in nearly every aspect of their lives, save their membership in a constitutionally governed private society."[124]

The example of the freemasons allows us to expand our understanding of the relationship between the state and the public sphere as Habermas and others have postulated it. Institutions of the emergent public sphere were far too various to be reduced to a single paradigm, but they all partake of a basic distance or detachment from the state that manifests itself in distinct ways. In the societies for the reformation of manners we see a fundamentally supplementary purpose that can approach the substitutional. The freemasons evince a more clearly parodic relationship in which imitation is balanced by criticism. Although to different degrees, evident in both is an oppositional impulse in which the motive to oppose is mixed with the motive to affect and to change.

Is the Habermasian thesis relevant also to those private models of "public virtue" and "public personality" whose innovative capacity to focus private experience on public affairs is premised on the equally innovative separation out of the public from the private? In Habermas's analysis, the modern relationship between the public and the private that begins to emerge in the early eighteenth century exhibits this fundamentally dialectical logic. The division of the state from civil society constitutes the realms of the public and the private with an antithetical coherence unavailable under the conditions of medieval culture.

FIG. 1.3. (*opposite*) Frontispiece, *The Humours of a Country Election*, 1733, in John Brewer, *The Common People and Politics, 1750–1790s: The English Satirical Print, 1600–1832* (Cambridge: Chadwyck-Healey, 1986). Princeton University Library.

But this definitive antithesis is the essential precondition for what is equally characteristic of modernity, the interpenetrative conflation of the public and the private realms. The Aristotelian opposition of the public and the private lacks this dialectical dimension, whereas the medieval relation lacks the antithetical separation on which a dialectical conflation depends. Habermas schematically represents the modern relationship of the public and the private as an opposition that is also an interpenetration. The public realm of state authority is opposed to a private realm that is composed of a market-driven civil society, an intimate sphere, and a public sphere that mediates between the private and the public realms.[125]

The present chapter suggests how this model of a participatory mediation generated from a context of separation may illuminate the peculiarly dynamic structure of later-seventeenth- and early-eighteenth-century thought. I have tried to capture this dynamic through the idea of the devolution of absolutism, which we now can see is structured by the fundamental principle of parody, of repetition with a difference. On the one hand, contemporaries are increasingly inclined to view behavior and institutions as possessing an unambiguously public or private character. On the other hand, they labor to acknowledge how behavior and institutions may take on, under specific circumstances, the private or public efficacy that their characters appear to preclude. Thus the pursuit of private religious conscience and private economic interest influences public policy and promotes the public good; thus the public House of Commons (or Parliament itself) represents and enforces the private needs and rights of the people over against the public authority of the monarchal state; thus the idea of a "Republic of Letters," like the freemasons, uses a model of the state to characterize the peculiar status of what Habermas calls the "literary public sphere." These are not all categories that Habermas offers as paradigmatic of public-sphere activity, to which I will return in subsequent chapters. There may be some use, however, in applying the term in this way so as to emphasize both its scope and its experiential lability. Habermas's category of the public sphere names the historically unprecedented space opened up between political authority and political subjects whereby the latter may participate in the former without being of it. The public sphere is a suppositional conflux of real places, like public elections or the meetings of the freemasons. But it is also, and most famously, a virtual "space" like the Republic of Letters or the contractual relationship of state and civil society, brought into being in equal parts by the participants' experience of their subjection to the state and by their consciousness of their own subjecthood.

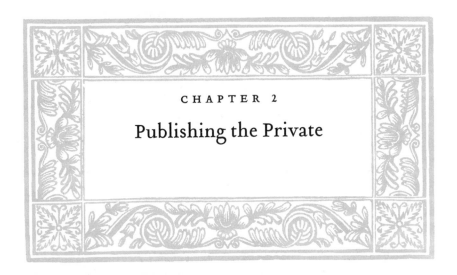

CHAPTER 2

Publishing the Private

The Restoration opposition to state interference that found its best argument in the intertwined freedoms of trade and conscience may be taken as a kind of symbolic register of the emergence into explicit discourse of the modern realm of the private. Yet in the medium through which this emergence largely occurred is to be found a third great source of modern privacy. This is, paradoxically, the medium of print, of publication. Print is the very mechanism by which the tacit is made explicit. Moreover, the history of print culture in the Enlightenment conjoins those distinct themes of negative liberty we have already encountered in the respective fortunes of trade and conscience: on the one hand, the material freedom of unrestrained industry and absolute ownership; on the other hand, the "spiritual" freedom of unrestrained belief, opinion, and expression. "And experience manifests," said a writer of the 1690s, "that wheresoever [liberty] of the Press is denied, there no Other is preserved."[1]

The Plasticity of Print

But for contemporaries the experience of print was as various as the uses to which it might be put. And although "publication" still meant scribal as much as typographical modes in the seventeenth century, most often it was the experience of print that focused people's imagination of the alternative to oral "privacy." John Milton thought the printing of *Eikon Basilike* (1649) shortly after Charles I's execution an act of public self-display both shameful and shameless: "He should have shut the dore, and pray'd in secret not heer in the High Street. Private praiers in publick, ask something of whom they ask not, and that shall be their reward." In a different context, the efficacy of print could seem pointedly private. John Dryden was "as much ashamed to put a loose undigested play upon the public as I should be to offer brass money in a payment. For though it should be taken (as it is too often on the stage), yet it will be found in the second telling; and a judicious reader will discover in his closet that trashy stuff whose glittering deceived him in the action." (The converse of this, perhaps, is Colley Cibber's remark that "[c]haracters, that would make the Reader yawn, in the Closet, have by the strength of . . . Action, been lifted into the lowdest Laughter, on the Stage.") Compared especially to print, speech was private in the root sense of being defectively privative, deprived of stability and permanence. One of Margaret Cavendish's characters knew that "those subjects that are only discourst off, in speech, flyes away in words; which vanisheth as smoak, or shadows, and the memory or remembrance of the Author, or Oratour, melts away as oyle, leaving no sign in present life, or else moulders as dust, leaving no Monument to after-posterity, to be known or remembred by; when writeing, or printing, fixes it to everlasting time, to the publick view of the World." Yet the evanescence of oral culture was also colored by the longing for an irrecoverable childhood, esteemed for the foundational values of female sociability that print seemed to set aside. Thus John Aubrey:

> The fashion when I was a boy (before the Civil warres) for the maydes to sitt-up late by the fire tell old Romantique stories of the old time, handed downe to them with a great deal of alteration. [My Nurse, Kath. Bushell of Ford, was excellent at these old stories.] . . . In the old ignorant times, before woomen were Readers, the history was handed downe from Mother to daughter, &c: . . . So my Nurse had the History from the Conquest down to Carl. I. in Ballad. . . . Before Printing, Old-wives Tales were ingeniose: and since Printing came into fashion, till a little before the Civil-warres, the ordinary sort of People were not taught to reade: now-a-dayes Bookes are common, and most of the poor people understand letters: and the many good Bookes, and variety of Turnes of Affaires, have put all the old Fables out of dores: and the divine art of Printing and Gunpowder have frighted away Robin-good-fellow and the Fayries.[2]

The experience of print was equivocal because its cultural meaning was determined by a complex range of factors. Among the industries of early modern England, the book trade was one of the first to experience the full rationalization of commodity production, and the peculiar logic of typographical reproduction was singularly compatible with that of production for the capitalist marketplace. Like other crafts, however, the book trade began as a medieval guild organization to which royal protection granted a positive freedom marked by its own peculiar mysteries and privileges. By the Restoration the division of labor had ramified the labor-extensive printing trade into a wide diversity of functions. "At the first beginning of Printing," wrote the printer Elinor James, "the whole Trade center'd in the Printer; but since it has been divided into three Branches [i.e., those of printer, bookseller, and stationer], Printing is the peculiar Priviledge of the Printer . . . ." This division was detailed by Sir Roger L'Estrange in 1663, on his appointment to the post of royal surveyor of the press. L'Estrange divides the labor of printing under two main headings, the "Promoters" and the "Publishers": "The Instruments for setting the work [of promotion] afoot are These. The *Adviser, Author, Compiler, Writer, Correcter,* and the Persons *for* whom, and *by* whom; that is [to] say, the Stationer (commonly), and the *Printer.* To which may be Added, the *Letter-Founders,* and the *Smiths,* and *Joyners,* that work upon *Presses.* The usual *Agents* for **Publishing,** are the Printers themselves, *Stitchers, Binders, Stationers, Hawkers, Mercury-women, Pedlers, Ballad-singers, Posts, Carryers, Hackney-Coachmen, Boat-men,* and *Mariners.*" Defoe's account of the printing trade sixty years later is in some crucial respects not very different: "Writing . . . is become a very considerable Branch of the English Commerce. The Booksellers are the Master Manufacturers or Employers. The several Writers, Authors, Copyers, Sub-writers, and all other Operators with Pen and Ink are the workmen employed by the said Master Manufacturers."[3]

Much recent scholarship has remarked what is evident here, namely, that during the Restoration period the authorial function had not yet been separated out and elevated to the central role it plays in modern views of book production, let alone aesthetic creation.[4] It is not just that authorship competes for importance here with a wide range of other labors. Even "in itself" authorship has the dispersed multiplicity of several overlapping categories. Joseph Moxon stressed that "the *Compositers* Judgment should know where the Author has been deficient," and he should be prepared to "discern and amend" and "get himself into the meaning of the *Author* . . . ."[5] Correlated as it is with the modern division of labor, the emergence of the author in the eighteenth century is a division of knowledge to which the devolution of absolutism also makes a crucial contribution.

When its guild status was solidified by the incorporation of the Stationers' Company in 1557, the book trade, like commercial "trade" in general, was already being associated with the negative freedom of Protestantism—more specifically, with the Reformation itself. A century later this had become a commonplace. Pretending to concur with his absolutist antagonist Samuel Parker in 1672, the year of Charles's abortive Declaration of Indulgence, Andrew Marvell made this ironic apostrophe to the printing press:

> The Press (that villanous Engine) invented much about the same time with the Reformation, that hath done more mischief to the Discipline of our Church, than all the Doctrine can make amends for. 'Twas an happy time when all Learning was in

Manuscript, and some little Officer, like our Author, did keep the Keys of the Library. . . . There have been wayes found out to banish Ministers, to fine not only the People, but even the Grounds and Fields where they assembled in Conventicles: but no Art yet could prevent these seditious meetings of Letters. Two or three brawny Fellows in a Corner, with meer Ink and Elbow-grease, do more harm than an *hundred Systematical Divines* with their *sweaty Preaching.*

Affirming that "the Reformation is wholly owing to the Press . . . ," Matthew Tindal argued the absurdity of a Protestant restraint on printing, since "as they owe their Religion to its Liberty, so they cannot hinder it without destroying that Religion which has no other Foundation than that of every ones having a Right to examine those Reasons that are for or against any Opinion, in order to make a true and impartial Judgment . . . ." An unrestrained press was therefore the very mechanism of Protestant explicitness and crucial to reason, "except an implicit Belief be a Duty, which must necessarily bring Men back again to Popery."[6] Freedom of the press was tantamount to freedom from papist absolutism.

Many Protestants associated the "implicit belief" enjoined by popery with orality. In *Religio Laici* (1682) Dryden argued that under Roman Catholicism "none but *Priests* were *Authoriz'd* to *know*."[7] As for laymen, "*God's* Word they had not, but the *Priests* they had" (line 383). The problem was one of "corruption," not only the political corruption of "*Interest, Church,* and *Gain*" (line 275) but also the epistemological corruption of unreliable transmission:

> If *written words* from time are not secur'd,
> How can we think have *oral Sounds* endur'd?
> Which *thus* transmitted, if *one* Mouth has fail'd,
> *Immortal Lyes* on *Ages* are intail'd . . .
> (lines 270–73)

Dryden calls the Reformation "a knowing Age" (line 388) in a sense not unrelated to Adam Ferguson's "age of separations."[8] Indeed, the layman poet's discrimination of God's word from that of the priests, his discernment of a specifically popish "interest," discloses a gap between church and laity analogous to that between state and civil society. Figuring scripture as the divine "*Will*" that adjudicates the inheritance of a landed "*Estate*" (lines 391-92), Dryden imagines the reformers making a "narrower search" of its terms (line 390) only to find that, contrary to priestly pretense, salvation is the private property of us all:

> Then, every man who saw the Title fair
> Claim'd a Child's part, and put in for a Share:
> Consulted Soberly his private good;
> And sav'd himself as cheap as e'er he cou'd.
> (lines 394–97)

Direct and universal access to the Book makes explicit the immediacy of that "private good" which the tacit knowledge of the church had subjected to public—that is, ecclesiastical—authorization. But the layman poet is also an Anglican, and he therefore is obliged to inquire into the limits of private liberty. In his depiction of Puritan sectarians Dryden exploits the familiar association of private trade with private conscience in the pejorative language of guild privileges:

> The *Spirit* gave the *Doctoral Degree,*
> And every member of a *Company*
> Was of his *Trade,* and of the *Bible free.*
> . . . .
> This was the Fruit the *private Spirit* brought;
> Occasion'd by *great Zeal,* and *little Thought.*
> (lines 406–8, 415–16)

Taken to an extreme, the devolution of absolute authority transforms positive into negative freedom, the normative "private good" into the fallible "private spirit" of enthusiastic license. So, having denied the public authority of the Roman Church over private conscience, Dryden invokes that of the Church of England:

> And, after hearing what our Church can say,
> If still our Reason runs another way,
> That private Reason 'tis more Just to curb,
> Than by Disputes the publick Peace disturb.
> (lines 445–48)

Publishing in the midst of the Exclusion Crisis, Dryden thus voices as well the emergent view that the privacy of private conscience—thought not speech, speech not action—consists in its not endangering "the public peace."

Understood as the publication of the private, the institution of printing seems to hold in suspension the separation it historically helped enforce. Is printing a public or a private activity? This conundrum is relatively inactive in the case of the Protestant publication of God's Word, which is only incongruously seen as private (although it could well be said to have enabled the "privatization" of God's Word within the hearts of believers). In the institution of preaching, however, Protestants had their own "oral tradition," which set the comparison with printing in a different light. Anglicans who supported penal laws against dissenters' preaching were likely also to support laws against publishing their writings—in other words, were likely to see a continuity between the two activities—but they might disagree on which activity was more "public." Here are two opinions. On the one hand, "there is no more occasion to believe it was meant that the Dissenters should preach to the People of the Church of *England* from the Press, than from the Pulpit, for otherwise the same Reasons would hold, for their coming into Churches to Preach against the Establishment, as for the more publick way of Printing against it . . . ." On the other hand, "[w]hen the *Parson* has done his Argument in the *Pulpit,* down it is handed to the *Coffee-House,* from thence into *private Families,* and so on, 'till the whole Nation is inflam'd."9 The latter tract, although it agrees that printing reaches more people, seems to envision it nonetheless as a process of increasingly private devolution, from church to coffeehouse to family. The unprecedentedly public activity of producing and distributing printed material is only completed by the unprecedentedly private activity of consuming it. It is in this spirit that the Methodist Anne Dutton maintains that what is printed and thereby "published to the *World*" is nonetheless "*Private* with respect to the *Church. Books* are not Read, and the Instruction by them given in the *public Assemblies* of the Saints: But visit every one, and converse with them in their own *private Houses.*" Printing "is one *Way* of private Converse with the Saints: Only it is a more *extensive one,* of talking with Thousands, which otherwise could not have been spoke with, nor can ever be seen *Face to Face in the Flesh.*"10

Daniel Defoe gives a classic account of the continuity of print with preaching as a universalizing and progressive process:

> Preaching of Sermons is Speaking to a few of Mankind: Printing of Books is Talking to the whole World. The Parson Prescribes himself, and addresses to the particular Auditory with the Appellation of *My Brethren;* but he that Prints a Book, ought to Preface it with a *Noverint Universi,* Know all Men by these Presents. . . . Tho' he that Preaches from the Pulpit ought to be careful of his Words, that nothing pass from him but with an especial Sanction of Truth; yet he that Prints and Publishes to all the World, has a tenfold Obligation. The Sermon . . . extends no farther than the strength of Memory can convey it; a Book Printed is a Record, remaining in every Man's Possession, always ready to renew its Acquaintance with his Memory, and always ready to be produc'd as an Authority or Voucher to any Reports he makes out of it, and conveys its Contents for Ages to come, to the Eternity of mortal Time, when the Author is forgotten in his Grave.11

Yet there are contradictions in Defoe's account as well. Here publication is represented as an act of depersonalization that abstracts both author and reader from the concrete presence of face-to-face exchange; and yet the very impersonality of the exchange imposes upon the author an unprecedented burden of personal and ethical obligation. Publication is here felt to be an act of supreme mastery, a "talking to the whole world"; and yet by virtue of this mastery it is also felt to entail an alienation, a loss of control over what has been said, a disowning of what henceforth remains in the possession of others. Publication has the commanding authority of objective truth; and yet the perdurability of the objects it produces is measured by the impermanence of their subjective producer—by the death of the author. These issues have an evident relevance to the tangled relation of the public and the private, and they haunt the imaginations of contemporaries.

Scribal Publication

Of course, publication was by no means synonymous with printing. In private letter-writing contemporaries found the figurative virtuality that Habermas would associate with the public sphere of print. Is not writing, asked Martin Billingsley, "the very mouth whereby a man familiarly conferreth with his friend, though the distance of thousands of miles be betwixt them?" William Fulwood called an epistle "nothing else but a declaration, by Writing of the mindes of such as bee absent, one of them to another, even as though they were present." The establishment of the Post Office in 1657 both facilitated this already widespread publication of words and sought to exert public—that is, state—control over it. According to Henry Coventry, the secretaries of state "may demand an Account of any letters that come to the Posthouse from anybody." Nor need they "ask anybodys leave but the King's . . ."; although "the opening of letters is what no man can justify, . . . reasons of state, or the King's particular demand" provided the usual authorization. According to a French observer, the English "have tricks to open letters more skillfully than anywhere in the world." Indeed they thought "it is not possible to be a great statesman without tampering with packets." In 1675 L'Estrange remarked that "not one of forty [libels] ever comes to the Presse, and yet by the help of Transcripts, they are well nigh as Publique."[12]

Although it was printed in 1710, the third Earl of Shaftesbury wrote that his "Advice to an Author" was composed for his own "private Entertainment" or for "such of my Acquaintance as are thus desperately embark'd" and "shou'd read [it] in better Characters than those of my own Hand-writing. . . . What I write is not worth being made a Mystery. And if it be worth any one's purchasing; much good may do the Purchaser. 'Tis a *Traffick* I have no share in; tho I accidentally furnish the Subject-matter. And thus am I no-wise more an AUTHOR, for being in *Print*. . . . I can hardly think that *the Quality* of what is written can be alter'd by *the Manner* of Writing . . . . Why a Man may not be permitted to write with *Iron* as well as *Quill*, I can't conceive . . . ."[13] In the seventeenth and early eighteenth centuries, typography complemented scribal publication and circulation, whose methods of making texts public already had been developed and exploited in directions that print replicated, extended, and transformed. Because it allowed authors to control the circulation of their writings more fully than did print, scribal publication also freed authors from the threat that published *arcana* would be consumed by the vulgar or censored by the state.

The inappropriateness of printed disclosure was most obvious in the case of the private, or "familiar," letter. "The truth is," wrote Thomas Sprat, "the Letters that pass between particular Friends, if they are written as they ought to be, can scarce ever be fit to see the light. . . . [T]hey should have a Native clearness and shortness, a Domestical plaines, and a peculiar kind of Familiarity, which can only affect the humour of those to whom they were intended. . . . In such Letters the Souls of men should appear undress'd: and in that negligent habit they may be fit to be seen by one or two in a Chamber, but not to go abroad into the Streets." The vicissitudes of civil war persuaded Dudley, Lord North, to have his poems printed, but they "were designed, as they tell you, to a domestique confinement, impatient of public view."[14] In other words, scribal publication provided texts a more nuanced spectrum of degrees of publicity, or of relative privacy, than was possible with print technology.[15] But for this very reason print's capacity to make the tacit explicit played a far greater role in fueling imaginative and legal responses to the phenomenon of publication during this period. And although scribal publication was commonly enhanced by the economics of patronage or theatrical presentation, "printing put commerce squarely at the center of textual production." According to Jonathan Swift, "A Copy of Verses kept in a Cabinet, and only shewn to a few Friends, is like a Virgin much sought after and admired; but when printed and published, is like a common Whore, whom any body may purchase for half a Crown."[16] But the hand copying of texts often served a ceremonial function that can only incongruously be called "private." This was a culture still dominated by patron-client relationships, and many manuscript publications "were first and foremost presentation pieces, not closet productions. They were 'private' only in the sense that the author, not the bookseller, had control of the manuscript."[17]

Print, Property, and the Public Interest

Jürgen Habermas has influentially associated the early modern formation of the public sphere with the opening years of the eighteenth century. If our concern is with its most fundamental institution, typographical reproduction and circulation, there is reason to prefer to this dating the outbreak of the English Civil War in the early 1640s.[18] True, the Glorious Revolution of 1688 and the lapsing of the restrictive Printing Act seven years later combined to ignite a published controversy so conspicuous as to suggest that matters of state sovereignty had become as openly debated as those of scientific truth: "We are intirely unsettled, as to the Government," said one author in 1697. "The King's Title and Legality of it, are as publickly disputed, as any Point of Natural Philosophy in the Schools at Oxford."[19] Contemporaries knew, however, that this crisis had a signal precedent in the momentous events of a half-century earlier. In fact, the record for the greatest annual number of publications, set in 1642, was surpassed only in the 1690s.[20] Two years after the Printing Act had been passed in 1662, a royalist, Richard Atkyns, counseled the newly restored Charles II that "the *Liberty* of the Press, was the principal furthering Cause of the Confinement of Your most Royal Fathers Person: for, after this *Act* [17 Car. 1, c. 10, abolishing Star Chamber in 1641], every *Male-content* vented his Passion in Print . . . the Common People that before this Liberty believed even a *Ballad,* because it was in Print, greedily suckt in these Scandals . . . the *Parliament* finding the Faith of the *Deceived People* to be implicitly in them, . . . so totally possest the Press that the King could not be heard: By this means the *Common People* became not only *Statists,* but *Parties* in the *Parliaments* Cause, hearing but one side . . . ."[21]

From this royalist perspective the explicitness ensured by the liberty of the press, because that liberty had been exploited especially by the parliamentary cause, somehow also ensured a tacit faith in Parliament. Of course, republican contemporaries gave the abolition of Star Chamber an interpretation more consistent with the principles of negative liberty that we associate with the idea of the public sphere. Because of the abolition, "the art of Printing will so spread knowledge that the common people, knowing their own rights and liberties will not be governed by way of oppression."[22] Yet one of the first acts of Parliament once it had taken on the king's absolute authority as regulator of the press in 1642 was to increase the positive freedom of the Stationers' Company so as to limit the negative freedom of the majority of the common people—for "very many, as well stationers and printers as others of sundry other professions not free of the Stationers' Company, have taken upon them to set up sundry private printing presses in corners, and to print, vent, publishe and disperse books, pamphlets and papers in such multitudes that no industry could be sufficient to discover or bring to punishment all the several abounding delinquents."[23] Indeed, any view of Parliament as a kind of protopress—as a sphere of open discussion over against the prerogative of the crown—is complicated by Parliament's refusal, for a century more, to permit its proceedings to be reported *by* the press.[24] Royalists like Atkyns were not the only ones to see the devolution of absolute authority from monarch to Parliament as an unauthorized continuation of absolutism by other means.

However, the ultimate problem for Atkyns was not that Parliament, but that the Stationers' Company, had come to speak for the state, whose only true voice was that of the monarch. This voice had been challenged most crucially, he argued, not in 1641 but in 1557, when the printing trade was incorporated by royal charter as the Stationers' Company. Although the trading company ostensibly operated according to royal privilege, its authority to register books for publication nonetheless seemed to Atkyns to usurp the right of the crown to authorize patentees directly. In condemning this usurpation, Atkyns uses language that mediates between the model of positive liberty that he defends and the model of negative liberty that, writing in 1664, he is obliged to employ in the very service of its repudiation.

On the one hand, writes Atkyns, the royal sovereign is coextensive with the national interest: "I could not but think a Publique Person and a Publique Purse must needs be concerned in so publique a Good." "*Printing* belongs to Your Majesty, in Your publique and private Capacity, as Supream Magistrate, and as Proprietor . . . ." Atkyns insists that a "Corporation being in it self a Petit-*State,* is inconsistent with *Monarchy,*" and he asks "[t]hat the King's Just Power and Prerogative, in the impowring and restraining *Printing,* . . . as a Matter of State, be Declared and Confirmed, as an Antient and Hereditary Right of the CROWN . . . ."25 Atkyns's model here is one of positive liberty in which the state cannot be separated from civil society; the only terms available for representing such a monstrosity are the contradictory ones of involuted hierarchy, a sovereign state within a sovereign state. The private interest of the booksellers has wrongly assumed the authority to represent the public interest that is the monarch's alone.

But on the other hand, Atkyns's language acknowledges, however disapprovingly, a model of negative liberty: the incorporation of the Stationers' Company marks the point at which the printing trade's economic interest was separated out from its political duty to the king. "And whereas before [1557] they Printed nothing but by the Kings especiall Leave and Command, they now (being free) set up for themselves to print what they could get most Money by . . . whereas they were before the King's Printers and Servants, they now grew so poor, so numerous, and contemptible, by being Concorporated, that they turn'd this famous ART into a Mechanick Trade for a Livelyhood." Thus the book trade is like landed property. Although the king maintains some royal lands "in Common," he also "[i]ncloseth several Parks, and gives the keeping of them to several Persons by *Patent* . . . these are still the Kings Parks, though kept by the *Patentees* . . . . Is not the Interest of the King and His *Patentees* so involv'd, that they cannot be divided? Just so is it by Inclosing *Printing* . . . ."26 Writing in the wake of the abolition of feudal tenures, Atkyns admits by implication what he expressly denies, the divisibility of interest from interest, state from civil society, political serviceability from economic alienability. Many scholars have remarked on the suggestive synonymy of "propriety" and "property" in early modern usage and on their separation out from one another over the course of the eighteenth century. In the present context this linguistic process encapsulates the conceptual shift from the guild mentality of positive freedom, in which economic interest is embedded within a customary ground of sociopolitical association, to the modern view that matters of propriety and property are best kept separate from each other lest the demands of the former impinge on the negative freedom of the latter.

Atkyns's assault on the privileges of the Stationers' Company fell on listening ears in Charles II's new government, and the resulting pressure forced the booksellers to make more explicit the nature of the interest whose rights they purportedly defended, and to do this (like Atkyns) on analogy with the ownership of real estate: "The Author of every *Manuscript* or *Copy*" has "(in all reason) as good right thereunto, as any Man hath to the Estate wherein he has the most absolute property."[27] Although the Stationers' Company was far from vindicated in this view, over the long term the devolution of absolute property in print from the state to distinct spheres of civil society prevailed, often enough in tandem with the real-estate analogy. John How, for example, thought the national interest regarding print was to be found not in the royal prerogative and its monopoly printing patents but in the interests of unprivileged printers, whose "*Right* and *Property*" in books goes unprotected against the greater power of "the most Considerable Dealers": "But when private Interest is oppos'd to publick Good, the Considerations of Honour and Justice are commonly laid aside." Unlike Atkyns, How sees the analogy between printing and landed property not in absolutist but in contractual terms. The first duty of the state is the negative one of securing its citizens in their absolute possession of private property. Property in books, he wrote, was nothing but "the Right of Purchase, to which no Man can lay a better Claim to Lands of Inheritance, or any Thing he possesses . . . . For considering that all other Trades are secur'd in their Property, 'tis a hard Case that the *Printing* Trade alone should not be protected equally with others . . . ."[28]

In compatible if not identical terms, Defoe finds the national interest neither in king nor in Parliament but in "the people," and he regards the stationers, whom Atkyns takes to be the very embodiment of private license, as, on the contrary, the public instrument of an absolutist Parliament: "The People of *England* do not believe the Parliament will make a Law to abridge them of that Liberty they should protect . . . . I cannot see how the supervising, and passing all the Works of the Learned part of the World by one or a few Men, and giving them an absolute Negative in the Press, can possibly be reconcil'd to the liberty of the *English Nation.*" By the latter decades of the eighteenth century Sir William Blackstone could radically reconceive the parallel between absolute printed and landed property such that the authority and interest of king, Parliament, and even bookseller were simply beside the point. According to Blackstone, publishing a book was "like making a way through a man's own private grounds, which he may stop at pleasure; he may give out a number of keys, by publishing a number of copies; but no man, who receives a key, has thereby a right to forge others, and sell them to other people."[29]

Print Legislation and Copyright

The downward mobility of absolutism in printing—from royal absolutism to the absolute private property of the author—is reflected in the broad history of print legislation. Henry VIII inaugurated the practice of granting royal patents of monopoly to printers and booksellers for publishing certain categories of books. Even before the end of the sixteenth century, however, the rights in copies of publishers not privileged in this way were also being recognized by the Stationers' Company, whose licensing register became the accepted sign of property in copies or copyright. In the first decades of the following century, exclusive property rights in individual works were being granted not only to booksellers but also to authors.[30] The Printing Act of 1662 extended these procedures, but the experience of the next few decades made clear their ineffectiveness in regulating printing, and for this reason the act was allowed to lapse after 1694. The complaints of How and Defoe were published, along with those of many others, during the brief and traumatic period of deregulation that succeeded that of inadequate regulation. For her part, Elinor James was vocal in arguing that "[p]rinting ought not to be a Free Trade; for it is an Art and Mystery . . . ." And in 1710 the so-called Copyright Act (8 Anne, c. 21) met at least some of the complaints by specifying, for a set period of years, absolute private ownership and exclusive right to publish for those who were registered by the Stationers' Company as copyright owners.[31]

Some scholars have been tempted to read in the 1710 Copyright Act the unambiguous establishment of the absolute property of authors in their publications. The language of the act makes no such specification: the exclusive right it establishes, so far from being exclusive to authors, is vested in whoever owns right in copies. In a series of important copyright cases during the later decades of the eighteenth century, the ownership dispute set original against later bookseller-publishers. The former claimed "authorial right"; the ownership rights of the "author" in the modern sense of the term never entered into the dispute.[32] However, the role of copyright litigation in defining the broad cultural view of where lay primary, "authorial" responsibility for books can be overstated. Charles II's attempt to control printing through the ferocious censorship efforts of Roger L'Estrange did much to focus attention on the author—i.e., the writer—as the primary agent of book production. Early on in his service as surveyor of the press, L'Estrange sought to specify the author as "the *first Mover*" of publication by assuming that anyone found with an unlawful book was "the Author of the said Book, unless he *Produce* the Person or Persons, from whom he receiv'd it." John Twyn was executed in 1664 for intending to print *Treatise of the Execution of Justice,* at least in part because he refused to identify its author. During the 1680 trial of another printer, Henry Care, Chief Justice Scroggs remarked that "[i]t is hard to find the author, it is not hard to find the printer."[33]

For some, the case for the author's ownership of books was made most persuasively with reference not to financial but to mental "possession." In 1720 John Dennis admitted to a belief that "nothing was more a Man's own than his Thoughts and Inventions. Nay, I have been often inclin'd to think, that a Man had absolute Property in his Thoughts and Inventions alone." Dennis boldly repudiates the analogy of absolute printed with landed property, not because he conceives landed property "politically" rather than "economically," but because he conceives an authorial ownership more real even than that of real estate: "The Money that is mine, was somebody's else before, and will be hereafter another's. Houses and Lands too are certain to change their Landlords; sometimes by Gift, sometimes by Purchase, and sometimes by Might; but always, to be sure, by Death. But my Thoughts are unalterably and unalienably mine, and never can be another's."[34] Dennis's remarks are not simply an exercise in abstract idealism. Condemning the plagiarism that consists in printing old plays with new title pages and author attributions, he posits a mental possession so absolutely private that even its alienation through objectification, publication, and sale only confirms its more fundamental inalienability.

Dennis is unconcerned here to account for the mechanism by which mental is transformed into financial possession, but others voiced their awareness that this transformation was utterly dependent on the emergence of a new entity capable of providing writers economic support. This was "the public," increasingly identified as the supplement, and ultimately as the replacement, of the financial institution of literary patronage. "The public" was of course an ambiguous term since it defined a phenomenon in no way coextensive with the normative publicness that contemporaries were learning to associate with the state and its functions. In the Popish Plot year of 1679 Chief Justice Scroggs feared that the public authority of the courts might be subjugated to the opinions of the public: "[I]f once causes come to be tried with complacency to popular opinions, and shall be insolently censured if they go otherwise, all public causes shall receive the doom as the multitude happen to be possessed; and at length every cause shall become public, if they will but espouse it."[35] By the same token, aristocrats were conventionally understood to serve the national and "public" interest by their patronage of writers.[36]

Yet there was also some logic to this usage, since what in the long term "the public" replaced—aristocratic and state patronage—was manifestly implicated in what Norbert Elias has called the "absolutist-courtly society" from which the modern state emerged. In 1760 Oliver Goldsmith in his Chinese persona declared that "at present the few poets of England no longer depend on the Great for subsistence, they have now no other patrons but the public, and the public collectively considered, is a good and a generous master." A contemporary situated this replacement in the context of the evolution of literary property:

> The public, therefore, properly speaking, are now become the patrons of learning; authors are grown so numerous, that all cannot be taken under the especial patronage of the great. From this deduction, we may clearly discover the reason why the author's exclusive right was never worth claiming before, nor indeed for some time after, the invention of printing. . . . [T]he right was always inherent, and might always have been executed: but we find that learning was, in its infant state, confined within a very narrow sphere. The author could have no dependance on the *number*, but on the *quality*, of his readers. . . . But since authors and readers are multiplied, the case is extremely different. The profits of a copy are now collected by slow returns from a number of purchasers; and if the author has not a right in all the copies which are multiplied from his original manuscript, he has, truly speaking, scarce any property at all.[37]

By this view, authorial right, always tacit, became explicit through the growth of the reading public. Nonetheless, the notion that public sales replaced literary patronage during the eighteenth century exaggerates what was a more protracted process.[38]

The coexistence of patronage and the literary marketplace preoccupied the most celebrated eighteenth-century authors as much as did the replacement of the one by the other. In the increasingly parodic apparatus introductory to *A Tale of a Tub* (1704)—the author's apology (added in 1710), the bookseller's dedication to a noble lord, the bookseller to the reader, the author's epistle dedicatory to Prince Posterity, the preface, the introduction—Swift amply documented the entanglement of patronage and public, the struggle to satisfy simultaneously the demands of a traditional and an emergent literary economy, the slow but implacable domination of "quality" by "number"—in effect, the laborious and contradictory birth of the author.[39] Shaftesbury wrote that "modern Authors . . . regulate themselves by the irregular Fancy of the World; and

frankly own they are preposterous and absurd, in order to accommodate themselves to the Genius of the Age. In our Days *the Audience* makes *the Poet;* and *the
Bookseller the Author* . . . ."[40] Pope's famously ambivalent suspension between
patronage and the public frames his entire career, from the preface to the *Works*
of 1717 to *The Dunciad* of 1742–43. His apocalyptic vision in the latter work and
in *Peri Bathous* (1727) imagines modern authorship under the control of capitalist entrepreneurs: quantity triumphant over quality, booksellers advising writers
on how to apply their metaphors,[41] publishers stealing, slandering, and corrupting writers with impunity. But the second book of *The Dunciad* has equally
harsh words for patrons; and because he was in fact deeply invested in the publication process, Pope's self-characterizations vacillate between the pose of the
private amateur, the *vir bonus* whose authorial status is evident in his diffident
integrity and disinterestedness, and the pose of the public professional, the man
of letters whose authorial status is evident in his success with "the public."[42]

One of the great artifacts of the coexistence of patronage and the public is
Samuel Johnson's grandly authorial disdain for Lord Chesterfield's belated willingness to make good his offer of patronage: "I hope it is no very cynical asper-
ity not to confess obligations where no benefit has been received, or to be unwilling that the Publick should consider me as owing that to a Patron, which
Providence has enabled me to do for myself."[43] For several decades after the
1710 Copyright Act, and despite its term limits, judicial practice tended to treat
copyright not only as authorial but also as perpetual, something like a natural-
law right. This tendency was supported by the landmark case of *Millar v. Taylor* (1769), then reversed by the celebrated ruling of *Donaldson v. Becket* (1774),
which reaffirmed the temporal limitations on copyright—hence also the implied existence of a "public domain," which begins where term limits expire.
Echoing Dennis, Boswell's Johnson memorably summarized the significance of
this compromise:

> There seems, (said he,) to be in authours a stronger right of property than that by
> occupancy; a metaphysical right, a right, as it were, of creation, which should from
> its nature be perpetual; but the consent of nations is against it, and indeed reason
> and the interests of learning are against it; for were it to be perpetual, no book, how-
> ever useful, could be universally diffused amongst mankind, should the proprietor
> take it into his head to restrain its circulation. . . . For the general good of the world,
> therefore, whatever valuable work has once been created by an authour, and issued
> out by him, should be understood as no longer in his power, but as belonging to the
> publick . . . .[44]

Speaking of *Donaldson v. Becket,* another observer remarked that literary works
"are, by this Reversal, declared to be the Property of any Person." Yet another

thought that ideas were indeed private possessions, but "the very matter and contents of . . . books are by the author's publication of them, irrevocably given to the public; they become common; all the sentiments contained therein, rendered universally common: and when the sentiments are made common by the author's own act, every use of those sentiments must be equally common."[45]

This view of the public domain has been associated with a distinctively modern valorization of literary circulation.[46] However, it evidently hearkens back as well to the precapitalist view of property as a matter of limited and inclusive use-rights rather than absolutely owned and unconditionally alienable things.[47] In the virtual space opened up by publication the public domain recreates the actual territory of the feudal commons, where the tacit distinction between private and public does not (yet) admit of their separation. The idea of the "public domain" helps make the paradox of the publication of the private explicit, even tangible. Elsewhere I have argued that "[b]efore the existence of patents and copyrights, the value of ideas was preserved by the maintenance of secrecy and by strictly private and elitist consumption. But once ideas can be owned, their value lies in disowning them by making them public—not only in the economic sense of the creation of surplus value, but also in the sense that the very meaning of conceptual ownership depends upon the knowledge of others of your ownership, upon their capacity to know your ideas without also being able to extract material profit from them."[48] The institution of the public domain completes this process by deprivatizing the capacity to profit from private ideas—by opening them up again, after the expiration of term limits, to the possibility of public exploitation.

Knowledge and Secrecy

The paradox of private property bears a profound relation to the paradox of the publication of the private; but it is not an essential ingredient. An unusually reflexive exemplar of this truth can be found in the commendatory verse preceding John Wilkins's *Mercury, or the Secret and Swift Messenger . . .* (1641), a study of techniques of coded and "secret" writing:

> Secrecie's now Publish'd; you reveal
> By demonstration how wee may Conceal.[49]

In the previous chapter I briefly considered freemasonry as representative of the public-sphere aptitude for turning the secrecy of traditional elites to its own ends. More fundamentally, of course, the public-sphere impulse toward secrets is the unambiguous one of disclosure. If the publication of what previously had been *arcana* was the dystopian nightmare of absolutist politics, it was also the utopian dream of experimental "science."[50] Historians of science have been increasingly careful to avoid imposing on early modern attitudes toward the relationship between what we would call natural "magic" and natural "science" the polarizing standards of modernity. Still, an authentic discriminant may lie in the fact that both the esoteric and the exoteric approaches to knowledge can be found in the discourse of magic, whereas only the latter survives as a scientific norm.[51] There is an evident connection between the esoteric secrets of medieval experiment, the *arcana imperii* of statecraft, and the "mysteries" of technical craft guild and trade practices—also between the respective and interrelated histories of their early modern dissipation. Medieval experiments in natural magic were recorded in "receipts," or recipes, which reduced the techniques of trial to formula, and their esoteric secrecy reflected that of the *arcana naturae* they investigated. The shift in thinking that permitted the widespread printing of these recipes in "books of secrets" in the late-medieval and early modern period, it has been suggested, may be seen as a subtle reconception of the parallel between experimental technique and the natural phenomena it sought to know. When the shared secrecy of the recipes and nature itself was seen to lie in the way the former's experimental procedure reflected the very structure of the latter, "nature could be understood in mechanical terms as a set of invisible 'techniques' nature employs for producing its various sensible effects. Hence nature's 'inner workings' might be replicated as one might replicate a technique by following a recipe." "Recipe books translated craft 'secrets' into simple rules and procedures, and replaced the artificer's cunning with the technologist's know-how."[52]

From this perspective, Machiavelli's book *The Prince,* if the Bible of absolutist politics, was also a "book of secrets" concerned to expose the *arcana imperii* to public view.[53] Although few would have justified the publication of *The Prince* on ethical grounds, Machiavelli's contemporary Alessio Piemontese offered an ethical rationale for the disclosure of his *Secreti* (1555), perhaps the most famous and influential of the books of secrets. "If the secretes were knowen of every man," he wrote disapprovingly, "thei should no more be called secretes, but publike and common"; but his convictions changed when his delay in divulging a secret remedy for bladder stones led to the death of the patient. "But yet not havyng the power to put it out of my fantasie, but that I was a verie homicide and murtherer, for refusing to give the Phisician the receipt and remedie, for the healyng of this poore manne, I have determined to publishe and communicate to the worlde, all that I have, beyng assured that fewe other menne have so many as I."[54]

Like other books of secrets, Alessio's was by modern scientific standards remarkably eclectic, fully one-third of it containing information on household economy (how to make soaps, preserves, cosmetics, tonics, cleansers, etc.).[55] Colored by a certain anti-elitism, both this eclecticism and Alessio's ethical concern recur in the Royal Society's *Transactions* (satirically immortalized in Swift's account of the Grand Academy of Lagado in part 3 of *Gulliver's Travels*), as well as in early debates on the society's research program. In 1674 an anonymous speaker argued that "[n]o Observation or Experiment, if truly made, is therefore to be sleighted, because it may seem to be but mean. For so far as we have any matter of fact before us, we have really advanced further than we were before. And many things which seeme trivial in them selves, may be a foundation for that which is of greater moment; . . . the meanest observation of what is really existent in nature, is more valuable than the most illustrious, if ungrounded, phancy."[56] Seeking to forestall anxiety about the sheer multitude of experimenters to be associated with the new society, Thomas Sprat asked his readers "[w]hether their Number being so large, will not affright private Men from imparting many profitable Secrets to them; lest they should thereby become common, and so they be depriv'd of the Gain, which else they might be sure of, if they kept them to themselves." Sprat answered his own question with the serviceable real-estate analogy:

> [A]ll, or the greatest part of such *domestick Receipts* and Curiosities, will soon flow into this *publick Treasurie.* How few Secrets have there been, though ever so gainful, that have been long conceal'd from the whole World by their *Authors?* Were not all the least Arts of Life at first private? . . . But if all this should fail, . . . the *Royal Society* will be able by Degrees to purchase such extraordinary Inventions, which are now close lock'd up in *Cabinets;* and then to bring them into one common Stock, which shall be upon all Occasions expos'd to all Men's Use. . . . The *Artificers* should reap the common Crop of [t]heir Arts: but the *Publick* should still have *Title* to the miraculous Productions.[57]

Robert Boyle was outspoken in his opposition to the "ethics of exclusiveness" entailed in esotericism; however, the maintenance of secrecy seemed to him important in some contexts, and he required his technical assistants to sign an oath of secrecy while in his service.[58] And on occasion the ethic of scientific openness conflicted with apparent reason of state: William Brouncker, the president of the Royal Society, concealed William Petty's manuscript treatise on shipbuilding because it was "too great an Arcanum of State to be commonly perused."[59] The exoteric approach to knowledge was nonetheless fundamental to the procedures of the Royal Society. At the center of these procedures was the notion of the "experiment," whose capacity to establish the probability of matters of fact was being recognized during the Restoration period as both an empirical and a rhetorico-theatrical phenomenon. To be known scientifically, facts had to be known and confirmed by witnesses—the more the better. This required that the physical scene of experiment be made to some degree open and "public." "In *Assemblies*," writes Sprat,

> the *Wits* of most Men are *sharper*, their *Apprehensions readier*, their *Thoughts fuller*, than in their *Closets*. . . . [L]et the wittiest and most eloquent Men think as largely as they can, on any Subject in private; yet, when they come into the publick . . . their *Argument* appears quite another thing to them . . . . Those, to whom the Conduct of the *Experiment* is committed . . . do, as it were, carry the Eyes and the Imaginations of the whole Company into the *Laboratory* with them. And after they have perform'd the *Trial*, they bring all the *History* of its *Process* back again to the *Test*. Then comes in the second great Work of the *Assembly*; which is to *judge* and *resolve* upon the Matter of *Fact*.[60]

But the actual witnessing of an experiment could also be multiplied by two additional methods of publication: through its replication under other circumstances and before other witnesses, and through its printing for consumption by "virtual witnesses." "The technology of virtual witnessing involves the production in a *reader's* mind of such an image of an experimental scene as obviates the necessity for either direct witness or replication."[61] The dependence of scientific experiment on a technology of public witnessing that includes that of print bears a striking relationship to the epistemology of witnessing evident in experiments with (printed) novelistic narrative that were contemporary with the Royal Society's first decades.[62] In the present context the exoteric technology of virtual witnessing is fruitfully understood as a subset of public-sphere technology, and the establishment of matters of fact through the quantitative multiplication of witnesses is fruitfully compared to the contemporaneous emergence of the category of public opinion.

Public Opinion

As we can see in Thomas Sprat, the ethical grounds for the publication of knowledge might easily coexist with the ambition to secure its ownership and profit. But the sine qua non of the public sphere, in Habermas's formulation, is the rendering of the tacit explicit. The rationality that sustains and animates the public sphere defines the very condition under which tacit knowledge becomes explicit: "Discussion within such a public presupposed the problematization of areas that until then had not been questioned," a process entailing the establishment, at least for a time, of a new realm of the tacit and the unproblematic. "The laws of the market, of course, prevailed because they were intrinsic; . . . The laws of the state, in contrast, needed to be explicitly enacted." Produced for and distributed through the market, cultural productions became commodities, hence "in principle generally accessible. They no longer remained components of the Church's and court's publicity of representation . . . . The private people for whom the cultural product became available as a commodity profaned it inasmuch as they had to determine its meaning on their own (by way of rational communication with one another), verbalize it, and thus state explicitly what precisely in its implicitness for so long could assert its authority." Thus rationalized, mere opinion acquired the ostensive self-consciousness of "public opinion": "The opinion of the public that put its reason to use was no longer just opinion; it did not arise from mere inclination but from private reflection upon public affairs and from their public discussion . . . ."[63]

In the seventeenth and eighteenth centuries the term "opinion," although it continued to mean belief that falls short of knowledge, in association with "public" came to signify as well a kind of collectivizable "knowledge in formation."[64] By 1777 Edmund Burke could write that "[i]n a free country every man thinks he has a concern in all public matters; that he has a right to form and a right to deliver an opinion upon them. They sift, examine, and discuss them. They are curious, eager, attentive, and jealous; and by making such matters the daily subjects of our thoughts and discoveries, vast numbers contract a very tolerable knowledge of them, and some a very considerable one. And this it is that fills free countries with men of ability in all stations."[65] The liminal quality of "public opinion"—the way it mediates between individual and group, fixity and dynamism, direct and indeterminate address—is captured by a distinction Sir William Coventry made one hundred years earlier: "As a privy councillor, I have taken my oath, but as a parliament man I have my opinion."[66] The emergence of the category of public opinion in England can arguably be dated to the midcentury years of the revolution, when it becomes intelligible in the context of Parliament's challenge to traditional "norms of secrecy and privilege," however unintended that challenge may have been.[67] The coalescence of public opinion can be seen most broadly as a function of the sheer density and self-consciousness of printed debate after the abolition of Star Chamber. As print proliferated, texts responded to other texts, compared and cross-referenced still other texts, addressed texts as though they represented communities of textual utterance or were themselves embodied speakers, creating a virtual but intricately realized network of speech acts, "an immanent style of criticism" whose increasingly confident negotiation of the discursive terrain fostered the spatial sense of a terrain, a determinate place one might enter and depart from at will.[68]

More particularly, the coalescence of public opinion was aided by changes in customary techniques of petitioning political authority that go to the very heart of the matter. By tradition, clients addressed petitions to their patrons; paradigmatically, political subjects petitioned the monarch. A witness to the debate surrounding Parliament's Grand Remonstrance of 1641, however, remarked that "the contestation now is whether to publish it in print to the public view or by petition to his Majesty." The implication of print was to constitute Charles I's subjects as susceptible to the propriety of direct address, to put them into, as it were, a competition with the king himself for the honor of primary deference.[69] A similar violation of decorum emerged in petitions to Parliament from the people. Customarily, popular petitions were to be channeled through lesser governmental bodies. When the Root and Branch Petition of 1640 was presented directly to Parliament by the London citizens it represented, George Digby "looked upon it then with terror, as upon a comet, a blazing star raised and kindled out of the stench, out of the poisonous exhalation of a corrupted hierarchy." The petition came not from the City Corporation "but from I know not what 15,000 Londoners" who themselves undertook to "prescribe to a Parliament."[70] In 1648 the plan to print three thousand copies of a Leveller petition evoked this objection: "[I]f it be a petition to the House, why is it printed and published to the people, before the presenting of it to the House? Is it to get the approbation of multitudes?"[71]

Customarily seen as private acts of communication, petitions to the king became public through publication. The effect of this innovation was to "corrupt hierarchy" and its customary spatial relations by opening up a very different sort of space between ruler and ruled, affording the tacit subjection of political subjects an unwontedly self-conscious subjecthood. What is new here is not the notion of a virtual collectivity: corporate entities like the official government bodies through which petitions traditionally issued—indeed, corporate entities like kingship—had already been imagined and legitimated. What is new is the unmediated constitution of "the people" and "the public" in this fashion, which amounted to an unauthorized extension of the corporate principle and encouraged royalists to fall back on literalistic protests against its quite conventional claim to adequate the actual quantitative parts ("multitudes") with the qualitative fiction of a corporate whole. Thus one royal declaration denied the legitimacy of any petition that "carried not the style [i.e., the signature] of all." A petition "implied no other consent than such as went visibly along with it."[72] Here was a mystery of representation that the sacred mystery of kingship himself was not prepared to credit. But public petitioning was here to stay, and during the Exclusion Crisis of 1678-81 the techniques of the civil-war years were taken to new heights of sophistication.[73]

Figure 2.1, whose date is that of the outbreak of hostilities between Charles I and Parliament, uses traditional techniques of emblematic representation to make the untraditional association between opinion and print. Opinion is a blindfolded "Ladie" or woman of quality, crowned by a "Coronet" and seated in a tree whose fruit is "idle bookes and libells" and whose roots are watered by a fool. Although clearly devalued, she has the power of a quasi-allegorical divine monarch who sits "[i]n state Maiestique," elevated above the world that rests upon her knee and that is absolutely "rvled & governed" by her. And yet Opinion's transcendent if arbitrary majesty is belied by her vulnerability to "th' giddie Vulgar" and by the fact that she can be "found in everie house and streete." An iconographic hybrid, Opinion entails a species of both public, political sovereignty and private, popular rule by the *vulgum mobile*. (The third figure in the image, although cavalier in dress, represents not courtly authority but the mediating function of the stranger wayfarer ["Viator"], a surrogate viewer who elicits for us the meaning of this mysterious emblem.)

A century and a half later, the representation of opinion has become not allegory but personification, not classical mock sovereignty but national embodiment, not an elevated goddess but a bluff, down-to-earth citizen and man among men (fig. 2.2). In 1795 John Bull is well on his way to becoming the standard figure for Britain or British public opinion.[74] Here (and in contrast to fig. 2.1) national opinion is fully separated out from the effete and courtly figure of the state, who speaks down to "Johnny" as though to a child or a simpleton who needs for his own good to be confined by lock and key, potent symbols of *arcana* and their disclosure in the tradition of the secret history, with which we will be concerned in later chapters. Making very clear what may be more silently understood in other representations of John Bull, this one depicts the virtual collectivity of nationhood—the "imagined community" of Britain—as the well-fleshed body of civil society's public opinion defined explicitly against the emaciated but dangerous publicness of the state. The state apparatus, the image of the enormous lock affixed to Johnny's mouth to prevent speech, bespeaks in part what now is felt to be the outrageous absurdity of efforts to constrain Englishmen's common birthright and in part the fact that the cartoon was occasioned by unprecedented measures to do just that—passage of the Seditious Meetings and Treasonable Practices Bills—in the wake of the French Terror.[75]

What Was the Public Sphere?

These crucial developments of the 1640s shed a powerful light on the origins of public opinion in English civil life. But they also clarify the very meaning of the category of the public sphere in its early modern emergence. Much of the debate surrounding Habermas's thesis has revolved around the question of inclu-

THE WORLD IS RVLED & GOVERNED by OPINION.

Viator　Who art thou Ladie that aloft art set
　　　　In state Maiestique this faire spredding
　　　　Vpon thine head a Towre-like Coronet,
　　　　The Worldes whole Compasse, resting on thy knee,

Opinio　I am OPINION who the world do swaie
　　　　Wherefore, I beare it, on my head that Tower
　　　　Is BABELS; meaning my confused waie
　　　　The Tree so shaken, my unsetled Bowre.

Viator　What meaneth that Chameleon on thy fist
　　　　That can assume all Cullors saving white.

Opinio　OPINION thus can everie waie shee list.
　　　　Transforme her self save into TRVTH, the right

Viator　And Ladie what's the Fruite, which from thy Tree
　　　　Is shaken of with everie little wind
　　　　Like Bookes and papers this amuseth mee
　　　　Beside thou seemest (veiled) to bee blind

Opinio　Tis true I cannot as cleare IVDGMENTS see
　　　　Through self CONCEIT and haughtie PRIDE
　　　　The fruite those idle bookes and libells bee
　　　　In everie streete, on everie stall you find

Viator　Cannot OPINION remedie the same.

Opinio　Ah no then should I perish in the throng
　　　　Oth giddie Vulgar; without feare or shame
　　　　Who censure all thinges, bee they right or wrong

Viator　But Ladie deare, whence came at first this fruite
　　　　Or why doth WISEDOME suffer it to grow
　　　　And what's the reason its farre reaching roote
　　　　Is water'd by a sillie Foole below

Opinio　Because that FOLLIE giveth life to these
　　　　I but retaile the fruites of idle Aire
　　　　Sith now all Humors utter what they please
　　　　Toth loathing loading of each Mart and Faire.

Viator　And why those saplings from the roote that rise
　　　　In such abundance of OPINIONS tree

Opinio　Cause one Opinion many doth devise
　　　　And propagate, till infinite they bee

Viator　Adieu sweete Ladie till againe wee meete

Opinio　But when shall that againe bee, Viator Ladie saie

Opinio　Opinion's found in everie house and streete
　　　　And going ever, never in her waie.

VIRO CLA.^{mo} D: FRANCISCO PRVIEANO D: MEDICO, OMNIVM BONARVM AR:
tium. et Elegantiarum. Fautori et Admiratori summo. D. D. D.　　*Henricus Peachamus.*

FIG. 2.1. *The World is rvled & Governed by Opinion,* 1642, etching by Wenceslaus Holler, verses by Henry Peacham. © Copyright The Trustees of the British Museum.

FIG. 2.2. *A Lock'd Jaw for John Bull*, 1795. © Copyright The Trustees of the British Museum.

siveness. In principle, the public sphere admits universal access. In practice, Habermas says, access to it is constrained by the same factors—education and the ownership of property—that define the actual reading public. The public sphere figures a discursive intervention into public matters of rule by all citizens, a universality grounded in an emergent capitalist ideology of negative liberty enacted through equal access to the fruits of commodity exchange. So, like the emergent scenario of the political contract, the public-sphere concept conflates the partiality of a nascent class interest with the universality of the human. But although Habermas thus emphasizes the ideological nature of the public-sphere concept, he also attributes to it a kind of utopianism, the capacity of an exclusiveness perpetually expanded by new inclusions (see 37, 85–88, 160). I will address first the practice, and then the principle, of public-sphere inclusiveness.

The most visible case in point regarding the inclusiveness of the emergent public sphere is that of women. Habermas has been chided both for ignoring women's exclusion from the public sphere and for ignoring their access to it— or to alternative publics, counterpublics, or "subaltern counterpublics."[76] In fact his position lies somewhere between these two claims. Habermas distinguishes between the "political" and the "literary" public sphere: on the one hand, the legal system and the franchise, both of which were grounded in the ownership of property; on the other hand, print. On the one hand, "[w]omen and dependents were factually and legally excluded from the political public sphere . . . ." On the other hand, women "often took a more active part in the literary public sphere than the owners of private property and family heads themselves" (56).[77]

According to Habermas, the relatively heterogeneous and inclusive character of the literary public sphere was crucial to the "full development" of the bourgeois public sphere for two reasons. First, the literary public sphere seemed to document, indeed to constitute, the public reality of humanity itself, to give voice to private individuals in their universal capacity as human beings.[78] Second, property owners, whose more narrow and exclusive interests were represented within the political sphere, embraced the ideological "fiction" that these two public voices were one: that the public sphere was indivisible, that the interests of property owners were identical with, and stood for, those of all humanity (56).[79] The distinction is meaningful but heuristic, since it leaves unsorted out a broad range of entrepreneurial and property-related activities and capacities in which scholars have recently shown early modern women to have been involved.[80] Still, the hypostatizing of counterpublics to accommodate female publicness is obviated by these broad but explicit guidelines concerning women's participation in the public sphere.

Another realm of public activity that critics have argued Habermas ignores in his concept of the public sphere is that of commoners and "plebeians"; and this criticism is at least theoretically justified by Habermas's self-limitation not only to the "bourgeois" public sphere but also to a "*liberal* model" of it that explicitly excludes "the *plebeian* public sphere" (xviii). Here the breadth of Habermas's chronology becomes a factor. The need for some such caveat becomes increasingly plausible as the analysis moves beyond the eighteenth century into a modernity dominated by the terms of class conflict and by, not the emergence, but the "transformation" of the public sphere that preoccupies Habermas's title.[81] But the period of our concern not only precedes this one; it also precedes class consciousness. Habermas's translator, Thomas Burger, notes that a key term in his subtitle and throughout the book—*bürgerlich*—may be translated as either "bourgeois" or "civil" (xv). In opting for the former (despite the currency of the term "civil society" in eighteenth-century discourse) Burger inadvertently muddies the already murky but deeply consequential waters of historical transition.[82] For the nonbourgeois character of the public sphere's first participants is central to its historical meaning. At this point, empirical questions concerning the practice of public-sphere inclusiveness bleed into questions about the fundamental principle it articulates.

Class terminology, however relevant it may be to the historical analysis of early modern England, is not relevant to the way early modern English people understood themselves. And yet the period of our sharpest focus—1640 to 1760—is also the one in which class consciousness is demonstrably emergent. Moreover, the history of the public sphere (unlike that, say, of agricultural technology) is coextensive with matters of consciousness: to ask how people came to inhabit the public sphere is the same thing as asking how people came to think of themselves as inhabiting the public sphere. It seems to me that the public sphere is historically intelligible in its emergence, not as a category of "bourgeois" society, but as a means by which English people made the transition from a status-based to a class-based system of social relations.[83] To declare that the petitioners of Parliament in the 1640s or the periodical essayists of the early eighteenth century were bourgeois, or to declare (because they were not) that Habermas's model of the public sphere is too exclusive, is to misconstrue the meaning and importance of that model. What the idea of the emergent public sphere names is a historically unprecedented episode in making the tacit explicit—a separation out of status from class, of (aristocratic) honor from (human) merit, of subjection from subjecthood, of state from civil society, of public from private—without which the question of inclusiveness is not even askable.

The significance of the early modern public sphere comes into focus when we approach it not from the present but from the past, not as social scientists testing its adequacy to modern liberal democratic standards of social justice but as historians aware of its context—aware, that is, of what it replaces. When Habermas says that participation in the public sphere bracketed differences in social status, he does not mean that participants either did not know or pretended not to know one another's status. And when he says that the public sphere involved private "people's public use of their reason" (27), he means neither that discursive conflict nor that "merely private interests were to be inadmissible . . . ."[84] Habermas's point is that social status was no longer (as it had been) the very precondition for participating in debate and that the validity of an argument, like the assumption of merit, was not seen (as it had been) to be predicated on status. The public-sphere ideal of inclusiveness is not the ideological formation of a self-conscious class strategically concerned to universalize its own interest. It is the discovery, in a society stratified by status, that the idea of the public interest (or the national interest, or the commonwealth) has meaning only if it is premised on the conviction that interests are multiple and that no single interest—not even that of the monarch—is universal or "absolute." The public sphere's impulse toward universality bespeaks, not a (bad-faith) claim to equality of access and representation (which most contemporaries would have dismissed frankly as neither possible nor desirable), but the will to act upon the notion of a discursive and virtual calculus capable of adjudicating between an indefinite number of inherently legitimate interests. This was to be by definition an explicit exercise in conflict.

The emergent public sphere was understood by contemporaries as a virtual collectivity, a metaphorical place of assembly constituted principally by publication and its readership. But it also was associated (unlike "the public domain") with actual spaces. This in itself was a development on an earlier social formation (as the market was on actual marketplaces). Before the 1666 Great Fire of London the nave of St. Paul's Cathedral served as the great emporium of oral news, a collectivity preternaturally and restlessly aural in expression. According to a contemporary frequenter of "Paul's walking," "The Noyse in it, is like that of Bees, a strange hum[m]ing or Buzz; mixt of walking Tonges and feet; it, is a kind of still roare, or Loud whisper." And from this perspective, the London coffeehouses, with the Paris *salons* the paradigmatic places of the public sphere, entail, in the words of a modern scholar, "a radical fracturing of the vast information exchange of Paul's into a multitude of separate, more specialized exchanges through which orally transmitted information would have passed more slowly and with less efficiency."[85] In hostile responses to the coffeehouses during the Restoration period we can sense the way this exchange network both evoked and challenged the antithetical relation of the public and the private, state and civil society. In 1672 Charles II complained that "there have been of late more bold and Licentious Discourses then formerly; and men have assumed to themselves a liberty, not onely in *Coffee-houses,* but in other Places and Meetings, both publick and private, to censure and defame the Proceedings of State, by speaking evil of things they understand not . . . ." This royal proclamation not only prohibited such "Writing and Speaking," but also required the "Hearers" of such discourse to reveal it to the authorities within the space of twenty-four hours. In 1675 the problem was seen as serious enough to require that coffeehouses be "put down and Suppressed," and proprietors forbidden "to keep any Publick Coffee-house," on grounds both public ("the Defamation of his Majesties Government") and private (tradesmen "mis-spend much of their time, which might and probably would otherwise be imployed in and about their Lawfull Callings and Affairs . . ."). Three weeks later a proclamation rescinded this wholesale ban on the condition that coffeehouse proprietors report defamatory discourse within forty-eight hours.[86]

In 1673 one of the secretaries of state was told by a correspondent that he dared "not write half what is spoken in public in every coffee-house." A tract published in the same year recounts: "By this time, the Politick Cabal-men were most of 'um set, and all the Rooms rung with nothing but a continued Noise of *Arcana Imperii,* and *Ragioni di stato* (in these places some think, most of our late Forms of Government were model'd, and there are, that say, *Machiavel* the *Florentine* was born in a Coffee-house)."[87] Coffeehouses could be found throughout the provinces as well as in London, and although they were patronized overwhelmingly by men, women not only attended coffeehouses but in some cases owned and managed them. Introduced in 1680, the Penny Post exploited the vast infrastructure of London coffeehouses for mail collection points.[88] Figure 2.3 depicts the interior of a coffeehouse with two "politicians" so intent on their discourse over the *London Gazette* that they discompose the serving boy and a fellow customer whose nightcap indicates that he has just risen from bed and come to the coffeehouse without changing his clothes. Figure 2.4 shows a larger interior with customers in a range of activities and postures, along with a number of domestic touches, including the dogs at play in the foreground. Everywhere people are reading newsletters and newspapers. The coffeehouse was "the Great Pond or Puddle of News."[89]

Publicness through Virtuality

One of the "other places" in which state proceedings were being dangerously publicized during these decades was poems on affairs of state.[90] This is clear even in royalist poems sympathetic to the official indignation at coffeehouses, through their unspoken metonymy of discursive medium and subject matter.

The Coffee-house Politicians.

Fig. 2.3. *The Coffee-house Politicians*, c. 1733. © Copyright The Trustees of the British Museum.

/ Paris Cher Monsi.ͬ Trolaria. /

FIG. 2.4. *A Coffee House,* eighteenth-century French (?) adaptation of Restoration drawing, in A. S. Turberville, *English Men and Manners in the Eighteenth Century* (New York: Galaxy, 1957).

Referring to the coffeehouses, Nahum Tate wrote:

> Look, look, the sovereign people here dispense
> The laws of empire to an absolute prince.

Another poet situated the coffeehouse absorption with public, state affairs within the more general tendency, consequent on our fall from a golden age of due degree, for commoners to ignore their own, private trade mysteries in favor of the *arcana imperii* of their betters (cf. Charles I on tradesmen's neglect of their "callings"):

> In former days, when men had sense,
> And reason rul'd both peer and prince;
> When honesty no crime was thought,
> And churchmen no sedition taught;
> When soldiers for their pay would fight,

> Without disputing wrong or right;
> When each mechanic kept his trade,
> Ere tailor's yards were scepters made;
> Before each coffee club durst prate,
> Or pry into affairs of State.

According to a third disapproving observer, this is a time "when every private and ordinary person turns statesman, and with a judicious gravity canvasses, and determines the particular interests and designs of Kings and princes."[91] By these accounts, the public preoccupation with state affairs is something like an occupational deformation, an engrossment of the political "profession" by amateurs. However, there is also the suggestion that when private "amateurs"—poets and coffeehouse patrons—become public politicians, it is in response to the fact that politics has already become, in Fielding's term, "pollitrics":[92] not "reasonable" and "honest" public service to the Commonwealth, but a private trade in self-service and self-interest. By this way of thinking, poems on affairs of state address not politics in the traditional sense of the term—rightly left to king, peer, and prince—but its absolutist degeneration, state politics. This is in fact the great rationale that justifies state poetry in its artful reproach to the art of the state. The very self-consciousness whereby one trade turns its attention to the work of another—whereby private poets turn to public state affairs—stands as a rebuke to the irresponsible self-absorption of the absolutist state.

The genre of state poetry was by definition private discourse about the public. Habermas finds concrete evidence of a public-sphere discourse most famously in the nascent genre of the periodical essay. In the person of Isaac Bickerstaff, Richard Steele opened the *Tatler* by soliciting a readership of "*all Persons, without Distinction*," especially "*the Fair Sex*," and he promised to categorize future material under the names of the several London coffeehouses.[93] Joseph Addison impersonated Mr. Spectator as quintessentially a private man in the public sphere: "I have passed my latter Years in this City, where I am frequently seen in most publick Places, 'tho there are not above half a dozen of my select Friends that know me . . . ." He makes the rounds of the coffeehouses, surreptitiously "over-hear[ing] the Conversation of every Table in the Room. . . . Thus I live in the World, rather as a Spectator of Mankind, than as one of the Species . . . and since I have neither Time nor Inclination to communicate the Fulness of my Heart in Speech, I am resolved to do it in Writing; and to Print my self out, if possible, before I Die."[94] Maintaining his privacy in public, Mr. Spectator promises to publicize the private: "It was said of *Socrates,* that he brought Philosophy down from Heaven, to inhabit among Men; and I shall be ambitious to have it said of me, that I have brought Philosophy out of Closets and Libraries, Schools and Colleges, to dwell in Clubs and Assemblies, at Tea-

Tables, and in Coffee-Houses. . . . Is it not much better to be let into the Knowledge of ones-self, than to hear what passes in *Muscovy* or *Poland* . . . ?" (*Spectator,* no. 10, 12 Mar. 1711).

In terms of journalistic policy, Mr. Spectator's privatizing self-detachment from the world goes hand in hand with his well-known ambition to "domesticate" the news of the day. The first step in this process had already occurred with the explosion of print that took place on the eve of civil war, when news books began to publish not only foreign but also "domestic" (i.e., English) news.[95] In this way, the realm of ("private") national news was separated out from the greater, international realm of "public" news. In the quoted passage Mr. Spectator takes this domestication deep into the privacy of the public sphere and beyond.[96]

Samuel Johnson mused at midcentury on the consequences of periodical publication for the status of the author. On the one hand, "those who labour in periodical sheets" are more vulnerable to criticism than those who publish free-standing writings because "their works are not sent into the world at once, but by small parts in gradual succession" and therefore seem to readers still in process of production and available to improvement. On the other hand, a similar attitude seems to distinguish manuscript from printed material: "When a book is once in the hands of the public, it is considered as permanent and unalterable; and the reader . . . takes it up with no other intention than of pleasing or instructing himself . . . . But if the same man be called upon to consider the merit of a production yet unpublished, he brings an imagination heated with objections to passages, which he has yet never heard . . . ." So serial publication is to single publication as manuscript production is to printing for "the public" as ongoing process is to finished product. But what about printed periodical papers, which by this logic would seem to combine process and product? Johnson does not address this question. He is preoccupied instead with the expectations of seriality ("an idea of unconnected essays"), among other conventions of the periodical-essay genre, that his readers bring to the *Rambler* from their familiarity with and love for the *Spectator.* But the expectations of readers—"that which they had before conceived"—should not be the final standard. Johnson's choice of words is for our purposes striking: "[T]here always lies an appeal from domestick criticism to a higher judicature, and the publick, which is never corrupted nor often deceived, is to pass the last sentence upon literary claims."[97]

One of the most ostentatious ways the private gets publicized in the periodical essay is through the publication of private letters. Even in itself, correspondence—personal sentiments exchanged with another person—evokes the mediating doubleness of the private made public. Steele and Addison raised this effect to another level by publishing the letters they received, making their private correspondents their public coauthors and their reading public private writers. The effect is only heightened when we realize that the private letters the essays printed were hopelessly mixed: some, although genuine, imitated the distinctive public style of Isaac Bickerstaff and Mr. Spectator; others, authentic in provenance, were yet rewritten by the essayists to their own ends; while still others were totally fabricated—public fictions of the private mode. Shaftesbury thought it had become a common "practice among Authors, to feign a Correspondency, and give the Title of *a private Letter* to a Piece address'd solely to the *Publick* . . . ." The relish of reading celebrated letter writers would be decreased if one did not know the identities of their correspondents. "But how much less cou'd we find pleasure in this reading, shou'd we take it into our heads, that both the Personages and Correspondency it-self were merely fictitious." Do Shaftesbury's remarks afford the basis for correlating the difference between the private and the public with that between the actual and the fictional? I will return to this question at the end of the chapter.[98]

The dialectical coimplication of the private and the public that can be felt at the moment of the public sphere's emergence sometimes was expressed through discourse in which the coexistence of orality, script, and print was artfully accomplished. Manuscript newsletters continued to circulate throughout the seventeenth century, to be joined toward the end of the century by the highly self-conscious oddity of printed newsletters that used script type fonts. In *Tatler*, no. 178 (27–30 May 1710), Bickerstaff, listening to newspapers being read aloud (as was the custom) in a coffeehouse, is bemused to hear a passage from one such hybrid: "His Style is a Dialect between the Familiarity of Talking and Writing," Steele says, "and his Letter such as you cannot distinguish whether Print or Manuscript." In a letter to the *Spectator* some think is by Pope, the publication of the private is made drolly ludicrous by the proposal to publish a "*News-Letter of Whispers*" in this hybrid style: "By Whispers I mean those Pieces of News which are communicated as Secrets, and which bring a double Pleasure to the Hearer; first, as they are a private History, and in the next place, as they have always in them a Dash of Scandal." One of the writer's sources will "communicate to me the private Transactions of the Crimp Table, with all the *Arcana* of the fair Sex."[99] *Tatler*, no. 67 (15 Sept. 1709), proposed using the Penny Post to establish a charitable society from which "there shall go every Day Circular Letters to all Parts within the Bills of Mortality, to tell People of their Faults in a friendly and private Manner . . . they who will not be reform'd by it, must be contented to see the several Letters printed, which were not regarded by 'em, that when they will not take private Reprehension, they may be try'd further by a publick one."

Through publication the category of privacy emerges from privation and coheres in the fulness of its freedom—its difference—from the very publicity by which it comes to be known. This "publicity" of the public sphere, so far from subserving the public policy of the state, was sometimes conceived as its alternative, wielding the innovative power not of physical force but of knowledge and prestige. "Absolute Princes," Bickerstaff remarks, "make People pay what they please in Deference to their Power: I do not know why I should not do the same, out of Fear or Respect to my Knowledge" (*Tatler,* no. 26, 9 June 1709). A virtual power, knowledge is no less powerful for that. Monarchs dispense honors; but so does the press. When he first saw one of his publications, writes the bookseller-translator Francis Kirkman, he was transfixed, for "the Name of the Translator being plac'd on the Title-page in large Characters, there was also added the honoured Word *Gent.* to import that the Translator was a Gentleman, that he was every Inch of him in his own imagination, and did believe that the so printing that word on the Title of the Book, did as much entitle him to Gentility, as if he had Letters Patents for it from the *Heralds-Office:* Nay, did suppose this to be more authentick because more publick."[100]

Kirkman's self-actualizing fantasy reminds us of the parodic doubleness of which the public sphere was capable,[101] a capacity Steele's Bickerstaff exploited fully. In *Tatler,* no. 144 (11 Mar. 1710), he proposed that he undertake the role of modern public "Censor": "It is allowed, that I have no Authority for assuming this important Appellation . . . . But if in the Execution of this fantastical Dignity, I observe upon Things which do not fall within the Cognizance of real Authority, I hope it will be granted, that an idle Man could not be more usefully employed . . . ." Bickerstaff's modest acknowledgment that he lacks "real" authority is belied by his conviction, only partly tongue in cheek, that the power of the public press to laugh pretension out of countenance exceeds the restraining capacities of the state apparatus, whether police or judiciary: "The Overseers of the Highway and Constables have so little Skill or Power to rectify this Matter, that you may often see the Equipage of a Fellow whom all the Town knows to deserve hanging, make a Stop that shall interrupt the Lord High Chancellor and all the Judges in their Way to *Westminster.*" In other numbers (e.g., *Tatler,* no. 110, 22 Dec. 1709) Bickerstaff presided over a figurative but highly elaborated "court of judicature" whose function was to consider cases of social impropriety whose "criminality" the state judiciary was unwilling or unable to try. Underlying all of these papers is the intuition that the role of the public sphere in modern culture is not so much to replace traditional state sanctions that have now been abandoned as it is to supply an explicit mediation between state law and social practice now that their traditional and tacit partnership has been dissolved.[102]

As these passages suggest, the virtuality of the public sphere was self-consciously exploited as a droll fantasy of imaginary power that also held more than a grain of truth. The parodic judicial function of the public sphere—its supplementary or even substitutive role as "court of public opinion"—was often specified by contemporaries as the peculiar and public task of satire. "Satyr can scourge," wrote Defoe, "where the Lash of the Law cannot." Despairing of "the Defectiveness of our Laws," Swift thought it

> very false Reasoning, especially in the Management of Public Affairs, to argue that Men are Innocent, because the Law hath not pronounced them Guilty. I am apt to think, it was to supply such Defects as these, that Satyr was first introduced into the World; whereby those whom neither Religion, nor natural Virtue, nor fear of Punishment, were able to keep within the Bounds of their Duty, might be with-held by the Shame of having their Crimes exposed to open View in the strongest of Colours, and themselves rendered odious to Mankind.

Defending the satirical ferocity of *The Dunciad,* Pope remarked that "Law can pronounce judgment only on open Facts, Morality alone can pass censure on Intentions of mischief; so that for secret calumny or the arrow flying in the dark, there is no publick punishment left, but what a good writer inflicts." And when he revived Steele's literary "court of judicature" years later, Henry Fielding saw it as a necessary supplement to the state judicial system, since "our lawes are not sufficient to restrain or correct half the enormities that spring up in this fruitful soil."[103] Like the societies for the reformation of manners, Augustan satire is a "private" experiment in "public" action motivated by the insight that the traditional and tacit coextension of politics, morality, and society was coming undone. Unlike in their case, however, the explicit virtuality of its "actions" has something to do with its actual efficacy.

Publication and Personality

Thus far in my discussion the notion of a virtualizing "depersonalization" has been so recurrent as to suggest that the modern category of the public is what remains once the element of personal embodiment has been abstracted away. Thus the modern state emerged through a depersonalization of political authority encouraged by the downward mobility of royal absolutism; contract theory rationalized the state's impersonality as the effect not of the magistrate's but of the citizens' disembodiment; absolute private property, closely associated with the personhood of its owner, was nonetheless defined by its alienability through commodity exchange, which seemed to feed the reservoir of the public interest even as it satisfied the private desires from which the commodity had been dissociated; the idea that everyone had access to the public sphere depended on the perception that, because of the depersonalizing mechanism of publication, no one had such access in her or his actual particularity. At the most general level, the power of published knowledge is allied to that of empirical knowledge as such: the impersonal authority of objectivity derives from the fact that it has been drained of that personal subjectivity on which it depends for its very constitution.[104] This is most true in the case of those publications that conspicuously lack any other sort of authority. L'Estrange defended the energetic suppression of tracts dating from the years of the regicide: "If it be objected that This Looks too farr Back; It may be Answer'd that *Persons* are Pardon'd, but not *Books*."[105] And Steele is, oddly, most compelling on the judicial force of the periodical paper when he most belittles it.

However, to speak of publication as a process of depersonalization alone risks losing sight of the powerful premise of personal identity—the sense of authorship as an inalienable possession, authentication, and responsibility—that is the precondition for its alienability through print. In Milton's words, "Books are not absolutely dead things, but doe contain a potencie of life in them to be as active as that soule was whose progeny they are; nay they do preserve as in a violl the purest efficacie and extraction of that living intellect that bred them." Swift's personified battle of the books was so striking that it seemed to demand a rematerializing caveat: "I must warn the Reader, to beware of applying to Persons what is here meant, only of Books in the most literal Sense. So, when *Virgil* is mentioned, we are not to understand the Person of a famous Poet, call'd by that Name, but only certain Sheets of Paper, bound up in Leather, containing in Print, the Works of the said Poet, and so of the rest." The dialectic of personal identity and its alienability organizes contemporaries' responses to the experience of publication. When the Faulkner edition of *Gulliver's Travels* (1726) appeared in 1735, it printed "A Letter from Capt. Gulliver, to his Cousin Sympson," a document that brilliantly caps Gulliver's fictional and virtual rage at the world even as it vents Swift's personal and actual irritation at finding himself publicly misrepresented in the first edition: "I hope you will be ready to own publickly, whenever you shall be called to it, that by your great and frequent Urgency you prevailed on me to publish a very loose and uncorrect Account of my Travels . . . . [Y]ou have either omitted some material Circumstances, or minced and changed them in such a Manner, that I do hardly know mine own Work."[106]

Pope exulted in satire's implacable and remorseless power to capture the inner truth of its subjects—and its author—and to publish it for all the world to see:

> I love to pour out all myself, as plain
> As downright *Shippen,* or as old *Montagne.*

In them, as certain to be lov'd as seen,
The Soul stood forth, nor kept a Thought within;
In me what Spots (for Spots I have) appear,
Will prove at least the Medium must be clear.
In this impartial Glass, my Muse intends
Fair to expose myself, my Foes, my Friends;
Publish the present Age . . . .[107]

To be sure, we know to qualify this exultation as the sentiments not of Pope but of his "persona." In the idea of the persona, literary critics allude to the ancient practice of literally masked speech in theatrical orality so as to acknowledge the figurative impersonality of ironic discourse—or perhaps of all literate and printed discourse. The unaccustomed pressure exerted by the experience of print on a rhetorical culture's consciousness that the public discourse of self-representation cannot be taken as the self (thus the notion of the rhetor's "ethical argument") owed to the fact that it seemed to encourage just such a confusion.

But print could also foster the illusion that books were one thing and persons quite another. A hundred years before Pope published, John Robinson anxiously reminded his readers that "[w]riting is the speech of the absent . . . . Great care is to be taken, and circumspection used in writing of Books; not onely (though specially for conscience of God); but also because the Author therein exposeth himself to the censure of all men." Lord Auchinleck, writing to his son, James Boswell, agreed that publication exposed the private self even when its authorship was spurious: "The News[paper] were brought to me, and therein was contained an account of the publishing some letters of yours; and one of them was insert as a specimen. . . . [I]t was extremely odd to send such a piece to the press to be perused by all and sundry. The gentlemen at Jedburgh . . . could not suspect the letter to be genuine. At the same time they said it was a cruel jest, as it was exposing you." By contrast, the patronizing men in Frances Burney's life—her father, even her king—aggravate her dread of public exposure by turning her self-sufficient and anonymous publication of her first novel into a private story that itself must be "published" abroad (thus patronage, usurped by publication, reasserts its authority). George III recounts that Mr. Burney "told me the whole history of her *Evelina*," and he asks Frances for her version:

"I—I only wrote, sir, for my own amusement,—only in some odd, idle hours."
"But your publishing—your printing—how was that?" . . .
"I thought—sir—it would look very well in print!" . . .
"But your father—how came you not to show him what you wrote?"
"I was too much ashamed of it, sir, seriously." . . .

"But how did you get it printed?"

"I sent it, sir, to a bookseller my father never employed, . . . in full hope by that means he never would hear of it." . . .

"But how was it," he continued, "you thought most likely for your father to discover you?"[108]

The experience of entering the public sphere of print confronted these and other writers with the specter of an abstract and impersonally knowing "public" that both dissipated and concentrated authorial personality and volition. Earlier I quoted Andrew Marvell's parodic apostrophe to the Protestant press. In the polemical assault on the savagery of Anglican intolerance that follows this apostrophe, Marvell, finding that the ethics of publication are more equivocal than they had seemed at first, registers his own brilliant version of this ambivalence. His method is to subject Samuel Parker's venomous writings to a close reading, in effect personalizing the role of the "public" by reenacting Parker's public self-exposure within the space of his own publication. I will briefly extract this thread of argument from Marvell's tightly knit fabric.

"Some Man that had less right to be fastidious and confident," writes Marvell, "would, before he exposed himself in publick, both have cool'd his Thoughts, and corrected his Indecencies: or would have considered whether it were necessary or wholsom that he should write at all" (7). Reviewing Parker's early history, Marvell finds that his talent always lay "in exposing and personating the Nonconformists"; and having for a time exercised his skill privately and orally, by "drolling upon the *Puritans* . . . at Chappel and Table . . . ," "nothing now would serve him but he must be a madman in print . . ." (10, 30, 31). Parker is an archpractitioner of intemperate railing, which by "*Projection*" he attributes to the very Puritans against whom he rails (116–17). But in the second part of *The Rehearsal Transpros'd* Marvell's polemical zeal is moderated by the misgiving, based on the response to the first part (including that of his adversary), that his own treatment of Parker may only have impersonated Parker's treatment of the Nonconformists. The title page of part 2 tells us that it was occasioned in part by a "*Letter left for me at a Friends House, Dated* Nov. 3. 1673. *Subscribed* J.G. *and concluding with these words;* If thou darest to Print or Publish any Lie or Libel against Doctor *Parker,* By the Eternal God I will cut thy Throat" (147). "I am sorry if that should occasion a distemper, which I ordered as Physick": Marvell's contrition is not immediately apparent in his elaboration of this medical conceit, whose reference to both pharmaceutical and clerical certification also puns upon the licensing of the press. "I cannot determine whether I being but a new unlicensed Practitioner, and the *Rehearsal Transpros'd* my first experiment, there might be some errour in the preparation . . . . But it has brought up such ulcerous stuff as never was seen; and whereas I intended it only for a *Diaphoretick* to cast him into a breathing sweat, it hath had upon him all the effects of a Vomit" (156–58). However, the filth of Parker's vomit is not entirely his own responsibility, and the reflections that follow have reference as much to Marvell's own procedure as they do to Parker's.

Because of the distance between writer and readers, Marvell writes, publication is

> an envious and dangerous imployment. For, how well soever it be intended, the World will have some pretence to suspect, that the Author hath . . . too good a conceit of his own sufficiency . . . . But among all the differences of writing, he that does publish an Invective, does it at his utmost peril, and 'tis but just that it should be so. For a mans Credit is of so natural and high concernment to him, that the preserving of it better, was perhaps none of the least inducements at first to enter into the bonds of Society, and Civil Government; as that Government too must at one time or other be dissolved where mens Reputation cannot be under Security. . . . [T]his Invective way . . . is a praedatory course of life, and indeed but a privateering upon reputation; wherein all that stock of Credit, which an honest Man perhaps hath all his age been toyling for, is in an hour or two's reading plunder'd from him by a Freebooter. . . . But he that hath once Printed an ill book has thereby condens'd his words on purpose lest they should be carried away by the wind; he has diffused his poyson so publickly in design that it might be beyond his own recollection: and put himself past the reach of any private admonition. . . . I am too conscious of mine own imperfections to rake into and dilate upon the failings of other men . . . . Yet the errours of [part 1 are] not . . . now revocable but by asking pardon of whosoever may have innocently mistaken my book . . . . (159–70)[109]

As for Parker, his "person I was so far ignorant of, that I could only take aim at his errours, and much less could intend any other of that function, but those few who might assume to themselves his Character . . ." (170).

In its intricately promiscuous figuration, Marvell's argument takes in much of the territory we have traversed thus far. One of the reasons for leaving the state of nature to form civil society is to empower the state to secure the private possessions of credit and reputation. Just as trade sanctions against piracy protect the commercial credit of traders, so the office of press licenser safeguards the discursive reputation of authors against unethical attacks. The parallel is fairly precise. Like the public sphere of print, commodity exchange is a sphere of private people come together as a public—a virtual realm of private freedom from public interference that may nonetheless require state authority to protect it from the depredations of competing private interests.[110]

When do medicines become poisons? When does private freedom become private license? The parallel between reputational and commercial credit lies only partly in their joint reliance on the traditional maxim that a man is no better than his word.[111] Printed words are commodities; but they are also like commodities. Both words and commodities, their power multiplied by the reproductive process, enter into a fetishizing public circulation that "condenses" them into materiality and "diffuses" them beyond the "recollection" of their makers.[112] Quickly separated there from the personal sanctions of their sources, they are liberated to damage not only others but even their putative possessors. Public circulation inevitably evades private responsibility, whether by its very structure—which disembeds communication from personal interaction—or by encouraging personal malice through a presumption of impunity. Print's depersonalization of the texts it puts into circulation only invites the licentious personalization of their objects—hence the importance of Marvell's personal disclaimer of reference to Parker's "person," a studied "depersonalization" of his invective predicated not on his conviction of the impersonality of print but, on the contrary, on his sensitivity to the power of its personalizations. Neither the absolutism of the reader nor that of the magistrate can substitute for the ethics of private conscience.

Anonymity and Responsibility

On the testimony of Marvell and others, to publish was to enter a territory highly sensitized to issues of ethical choice. Like the idea of the social contract, publication hypostatized the political subject as an ethical subject. How can public circulation be made to assume private responsibility? Marvell criticizes Parker for having published his works anonymously, which only aggravates the impunity of malice: "For every one that will treat of so nice and tender argument ought to affix his name, thereby to make himself responsible to the publick for any dammage that may arise by his undertaking. Otherwise though he has a License in his pocket, or he perhaps himself the Licenser, it is but a more authoriz'd way of libelling; . . . Whereas if men were obliged to leave that anonymous and sculking method both of Writing and Licensing, they would certainly grow more careful what opinions they vented . . ." (166). It is noteworthy that part 1 of *The Rehearsal Transpros'd* was itself published anonymously. The title page of part 2 forswears what Marvell now (166) calls "the license of Mascarade" and bears his name. Yet when he died five years later, Marvell was being sought for questioning about the authorship of an inflammatory work that he had just published in unabashed anonymity.[113]

Had Marvell been apprehended, he probably would have been charged with seditious libel for the written defamation of state personages and institutions. (Criminal libel was a broader charge not limited to matters of state; "slander" referred to spoken defamation, "scandal" to the defamation of peers; in common usage these technical terms were often interchangeable.)[114] The law against seditious libel was understood to protect "public" figures, who would be "render'd contemptible to their subjects . . . if they are suffer'd to be traduc'd by every private person, and expos'd all over the nation."[115] The exposure of real persons was central to the general charge of libel. "In truth," wrote Thomas Gordon, "most libels are purely personal; they fly at men rather than things; which proceeding is as injudicious as it is unmanly. It is mean to be quarrelling with faces, names, and private pleasures . . . ." However, there was some uncertainty about whether only public persons or also public institutions like the state could be libeled. Gordon's unquenchable populism persuaded him that besides libel against "magistrates" and "private men," "there seems to be a third sort of libels, full as destructive as any of the former can possibly be; I mean, Libels against the People."[116]

A decision of 1670 argued that libel was in general more actionable than slander because publication implied a higher degree of malice than (especially a single instance of) speech.[117] Since oral discourse is face-to-face communication, the availability of pertinent witnesses made the charge of slander relatively difficult to defend against. The documentary testimony of printed books made the charge of libel even easier to prove; but the possibility of anonymous publication could frustrate the assignment of responsibility for it. Under the 1662 Printing Act, prior state censorship prevented libelous publication, whether anonymous or signed—at least in theory. In fact, the 1662 act was allowed to expire because of its ineffectiveness on a number of fronts, and the pressure exerted thereby on the sanction of postpublication prosecution threw the problem of anonymity into relief after 1694.

The appeal of anonymous publication was not only its political prudence. As we saw in the case of freemasonry, the maintenance of a secretive privacy at the heart of the public sphere may have been one way in which authors, by evoking the aura of absolutist reason of state, internalized and turned against the state its own powers of mysteriousness. The publicity of print both dispelled and nurtured privacy. For example, Mary Astell's appendix to the second edition of her *Reflections Upon Marriage* (1703) dispels the mystery of its original anonymity in terms consistent with her basic assertion that if the (contractual) state is not like a family, the family should not be run like an (absolutist) state. Since curious readers of the first edition rightly doubted that a man would thus "have betray'd the *Arcana Imperii* of his Sex," the author now acknowledges that she is a woman, who designs nothing "but the Publick Good, and to retrieve, if possible, the Native Liberty, the Rights and Privileges of the

Subject."[118] Astell abandons the secrecy of anonymity at the moment that its stealthy analogy with the secrecy of the absolutist state, disclosed to public view, liberates for her an alternative analogy with the open publicity of the self-owned, absolute subject.

In her occasional Horatian ode to her husband, Anne Finch takes a different route to a similar destination.[119] Winchilsea has asked her to write on any subject during his day-long absence. Using her poetic pseudonym "Ardelia," Finch obliges by writing reflexively about the difficulty of fulfilling this request. The poem's central conceit is that poetic inspiration is hard to come by these days. Parnassus, the location of "the *Muses'* Court," has become an adjunct of the state. The Muses themselves, serviceable operatives likened to "Country-*doctors,*" are happy to turn their "Industry" Ardelia's way until they hear that she aims to write in praise of her husband. Erato, struck by the sheer unfashion-ableness of the topic, thinks it must be kept quiet:

> And 'twas their *Bus'ness* to take care,
> It reach'd not to the publick Ear,
> Or got about the Town:
>
> Nor came where Evening *Beaux* were met
> O'er *Billet-doux* and *Chocolate,*
> Lest it destroy'd the House . . . .
> (lines 46–51)

Others make their hasty "Excuses": Melpomene and Thalia are financially com-mitted ("Bond," "Fees," "Stipends") to the official patent theaters licensed by the government, while Pegasus is exhausted by requests for royal panegyrics on William and Mary. Inspiration, in short, is a public affair, whether patronage or public sphere, and the implication is that Ardelia's purpose is embarrassingly private. Urania alone approves it; but her aid is the paradoxical advice that no aid is needed—beyond what the poet already possesses in her own person:

> *Urania* only lik'd the choice;
> Yet not to thwart the publick Voice,
> She whisp'ring did impart:
> They need no Foreign Aid invoke,
> No help to draw a moving Stroke,
> Who dictate from the Heart.
>
> Enough! the pleas'd ARDELIA cry'd;
> And slighting ev'ry Muse beside,
> Consulting now her Breast,
> Perceiv'd that ev'ry tender Thought,

Which from abroad she'd vainly sought,
Did there in Silence rest . . . .
(lines 74–84)

Keeping quiet is positively revalued. And if the Muses are part of the state apparatus, the authority of the state is paradoxically a "foreign aid" extraneous to the domestic poetry of "the heart" and its private agency of autonomous self-inspiration.

For since the World do's so despise
Hymen's Endearments and its Ties,
They shou'd mysterious be;
Till We that Pleasure too possess
(Which makes their fancy'd Happiness)
Of stollen Secrecy.
(lines 91–97)

Finch's ode is unusual for its time, a poem in praise of "companionate marriage," which is antiquated (as Erato knows) but also unfashionable in the sense of being (as we with hindsight know) not yet fashionable. Like marriage, Ardelia's self-consultation has a "mysterious" interiority, a "stolen secrecy" akin to that of Protestant conscience, which bypasses the official mediators—of state, of church—so as to experience the authenticity of immediate and absolute devotion. The sense that this is a value devolved from and forfeited by public authority is enhanced by the circumstance adumbrated in the chronological detail of Finch's headnote. She and her husband both had been in service at the royal court, he to the Duke of York, later James II, and she to his wife, Mary of Modena. When James was deposed in 1688, they both assumed the status of nonjurors, unable to swear allegiance to the new king and queen, and soon after went into conscientious exile from court. Read with this knowledge, Finch's ode becomes intelligible as a poem in praise not just of privacy but of a secrecy inspired by the example of royal conjugality yet stolen away and domestically secreted once the world ceased knowing how to value it.[120]

A final example of the way anonymous privacy might capitalize on state secrecy is that of Jonathan Swift. Writing to Stella (Esther Johnson) in 1710–11, Swift, not yet surfeited with the ingratitude of state ministers, took a delicious pleasure in narrating the impact of his anonymous publications on people in high places, a pleasure heightened by his private expectations of public advancement. The intimacy of Swift's correspondence with Stella and Rebecca Dingley, its scribal form continually underscored by ostentatious effects of immediate address, provides a private and "feminine" alternative to the public and printed appeals to elevated men these letters narrate. The complicating overlap of public and private is considerable: Swift aspires at times to the role of the "secret historian" whose private discourse predicts public events; his recourse to what he calls "our language" evokes the secret codes both of lovers' discourse and of state politics, each being subject to its own peculiar mode of self-censorship; yet there are secrets of his published identity that Swift hides even from the women:

> I have finished my poem on the *Shower,* all but the beginning, and am going on with my *Tatler.* They have fixt about fifty things on me since I came [to London]: I have printed but three. . . . These letters of mine are a sort of journal, where matters open by degrees; and, as I tell true or false, you will find by the event whether my intelligence be good . . . . I fancy you'll smoak me [i.e., smoke me out] in the *Tatler* I am going to write; for I believe I have told you the hint. . . . My lampoon is cried up to the skies; but nobody suspects me for it, except sir Andrew Fountain . . . . The bishop of Clogher has smoaked my *Tatler* about shortening of words, &c. . . . After dinner came in lord Peterborow: . . . They began to talk of a paper of verses called *Sid Hamet.* . . . Mr. Harley bobbed [i.e., nudged] me at every line to take notice of the beauties. . . . I am not guessed at all in town to be the author; yet so it is: but that is a secret only to you. . . . Some bookseller has raked up every thing I writ, and published it t'other day in one volume; but I know nothing of it, 'twas without my knowledge or consent . . . . Yes, I do read the *Examiners,* and they are written very finely, as you judge. . . . You may count upon all things in them to be true. The author has said, it is not Prior; but perhaps it may be Atterbury . . . .[121]

Painfully aware of his political and social distance from the men whose favor he solicits, Swift identifies so fully with his female correspondents that he impersonates them, chides them for impersonating him, and can freely associate, through the theme of anonymity and false attribution, from the story of an adulterous pregnancy to that of his own publications.[122]

Among the fine truths Swift praised in the *Examiner* was his insight into the illicit pleasures bestowed by anonymity. The rewards of writing for a ruined cause, he writes, are many: "Not to mention the wonderful Delight of libelling Men in Power, and hugging yourself in a Corner with mighty Satisfaction for what you have done."[123] The Copyright Act of 1710 attempted to resolve the epistemo-economic problem of ownership that was aggravated by the lapsing of the 1694 act. In a parallel fashion, the Stamp Act of 1712 (10 Anne, c. 18) sought, in the wake of the 1694 expiration, a resolution to the politico-ethical problem of libel. Rather than return to the failed mechanisms of state censorship, the act of 1712 tried to shift responsibility from the state to the producing individuals by prohibiting anonymous publication. The logic of the legislation was that if the names of author or printer were required to appear on published works (with the penalty of a sizeable tax and the forfeit of copyright for noncompliance), their human bearers would be obliged to exercise prior self-censorship, that is, to internalize the negative authority of the state.[124]

The joint logic of the acts of 1710 and 1712 was that to be financially owned a printed work must be personally "owned"; nor was this the only condition that made the latter legislation controversial. Joseph Addison, noting the pseudonymity of the *Spectator* papers themselves, feared "that such an Expedient would not only destroy Scandal, but Learning. . . . There are few Works of Genius that come out at first with the Author's Name." There were few, he said, who would write "if they knew, before Hand, that they must not publish their Productions but on such Conditions" (*Spectator*, no. 451, 7 Aug. 1712). A group of London printers argued that the disclosure requirement would "very much discourage the publication of many excellent treatises, through the excess of modesty in some, who will rather stifle their performances than suffer their names to appear in print, though to a work deserving of the greatest applause . . . ." A self-identified Tory observed that "there may be a Thousand Things both Lawful, and indeed Useful to be Printed, which the Writer may not be willing to own," and he worried that if the Whigs "shou'd ever have the Mastery of the Press too; if we shou'd ever be debarred from Publishing our Fictions and Invectives, which will be the sure Consequence of compelling Authors to own what they do, we shall be routed for ever."[125] Another writer agreed only to disagree ("[T]here is a natural Bashfulness in the most flagitious Sinners, . . . [w]hereas a Printed Book never blushes, nor the Author, if his Name be not to it") and thought anonymous libelers were "as Highway-men in Masks." Conceiving the press as the replacement of an absolutist judicial system, yet another applauded the act, since "[a]s the Press is now used, it is a Paper-Inquisition; by which any Man may be arraign'd, judg'd, and condemn'd . . . without even knowing his Accusers."[126]

Some of these remarks suggest that the 1712 act forced contemporaries to meditate on the difference between the "political" motive of secrecy and the "personal" motive of privacy. The ideal of the negative freedom of the subject from state control opens up a space of subjecthood whose political character may become relatively vestigial. In any case, the 1712 act, after an apparent initial success, failed to achieve its ends, and eight years after its passage John Dennis was moved to insist that under current conditions, "if the writer of a Libel puts but a sham Name to it, he has a Dispensation by that *alias* to injure, slander, and threaten all that is Powerful and Noble in *Great Britain*. But that if anyone pretends to write ev'n a just Satire . . . without putting any Name at all to it; why the Action is abominable . . . ." In 1729 Pope complained not only of anonymous libels but also that "the immediate publishers thereof lay sculking under the wings of an Act of Parliament, assuredly intended for better purposes."[127]

A central problem with the Stamp Act of 1712 was that even if it succeeded in forcing those responsible for publication to name themselves, it still left them free to obscure—just enough to frustrate prosecution, but not also identification—the names of those their publications libeled. The personal reference of libels might be obscured by many means: contemporaries spoke of nicknames, initials, stars, "syncopated or fictitious Names," innuendo, circumlocution, insinuations, indirection, "putting Cases," irony, historical parallel, allegory, and the like.[128] Mr. Spectator published a parody of a libel that employed many of these obscuring devices (fig. 2.5), observing that "[i]t gives a secret Satisfaction to a Peruser of these mysterious Works, that he is able to decipher them without help, and, by the Strength of his own natural Parts, to fill up a Blank-Space, or make out a Word that has only the first or last Letter to it" (*Spectator,* no. 567, 14 July 1714).[129]

Strong protests were lodged against the reckless discovery of historical allegories. One tract complained that in the case of "Matters of Fact extracted from the best Historians, of Things transacted some Ages ago, how invidous is it in any Man to wrest an Author's meaning, and draw Parallels where none were design'd . . . . If this Method of Construction be allowed, what Writer can be safe?" The Duke of Wharton wrote that the charge of innuendo or "forc'd Construction"

> can change Countries, and make *Ancient Greece* and *Old Rome, Spain, Poland,* &c. appear to be only different Names for one and the same Nation; and shew that they all signify the same as the Word ENGLAND, in their Turns. It can make *Evil Ministers,* that liv'd never so many Ages ago, revive again, and prove them to be actually opening the present New Year with their Sinister Operations. . . . In fine, this *new-invented* Piece of *Law-Artifice,* that will not allow Writers to have their own Meanings, but will be ever devising new Meanings for them, can make as many Transformations out of a *plain* and *literal* Narrative, as are to be found in the *Metamorphoses* of *Ovid;* and in such Cases the *Lawyer* may render them as *plausible* as the *Poet,* and they must be own'd at the same Time to be as *beautifully* Fictitious.[130]

Complaints like these suggest that libel law may have helped make explicit the notion that there did in fact exist such a determinate thing as "an author's own meaning" and to put a premium on establishing what it was. Responsibility for the proper construction of obscure passages in works charged with libel—for determining whether, and to whom, personal reference had been made—lay ultimately with the jury. Interpretive criteria for this all-important task tended to rely on the notion how "the generality of readers" might construe words used "in their true and proper sense."[131] Thus political and legal policy undertook to establish something like the general "public" norms of reading and interpretation, which in cases of conflict would have priority over the semantic particularity and "privacy" of the authors themselves. So the public law of the land fostered the coalescence of a virtual "reading public"—"the generality of readers"—that averaged out the actual particularity of individual reader responses. Like the legal prohibition of anonymity, however, the legal attempt to define discursive meaning in this way also made a negative contribution to the coalescence of a private authorial meaning whose authenticity was most apparent when "misread" and overruled by the public courts.[132]

Libel versus Satire

Certainly the influence of libel law on literary theory is evident in the way contemporaries debated the role of personal reference in satire. In 1682 Thomas Shadwell chastised Dryden's procedure in the following terms:

> For libel and true satire different be;
> This must have truth, and salt, with modesty.
> Sparing the persons, this does tax the crimes,
> Galls not great men, but vices of the times.

But Dryden, although he claimed that "[m]ore libels have been written against me than almost any man now living," nonetheless believed that there were reasons "which may justify a poet when he writes against a particular person," for example, "when he becomes a public nuisance." This view is consistent with the notion that the public is the sum of all actual particularities rather than an abstract generalization of them. Others agreed that personal attack was politically and morally necessary. A contemporary collector of poems on affairs of state acknowledged that "the Original design of *Satyr* in its Primitive Institution, was only to expose the Deformity of Vice, without levelling any thing directly against the *Person;* but Corruption continually increasing, . . . it was found necessary for *Poets* to become more blunt . . . ." The tide of opinion on this issue, however, was turning in the opposite direction. Steele thought that "the Satyrist and Libeller differ as much as the Magistrate and the Murderer." Although he was opposed to the 1712 act, Addison thought libels had become "a kind of National Crime . . ." and considered "the finest Strokes of Satyr which are aimed at particular Persons, and which are supported even with the Appearances of Truth, to be the Marks of an evil Mind, and highly Criminal in themselves." Defoe justified impersonality not only on ethical but also on pedagogic grounds: "But the Design of this Book [*The Family Instructor*] is of a Nature above a personal Satyr; the Errors in Family Conduct are the Business here, not

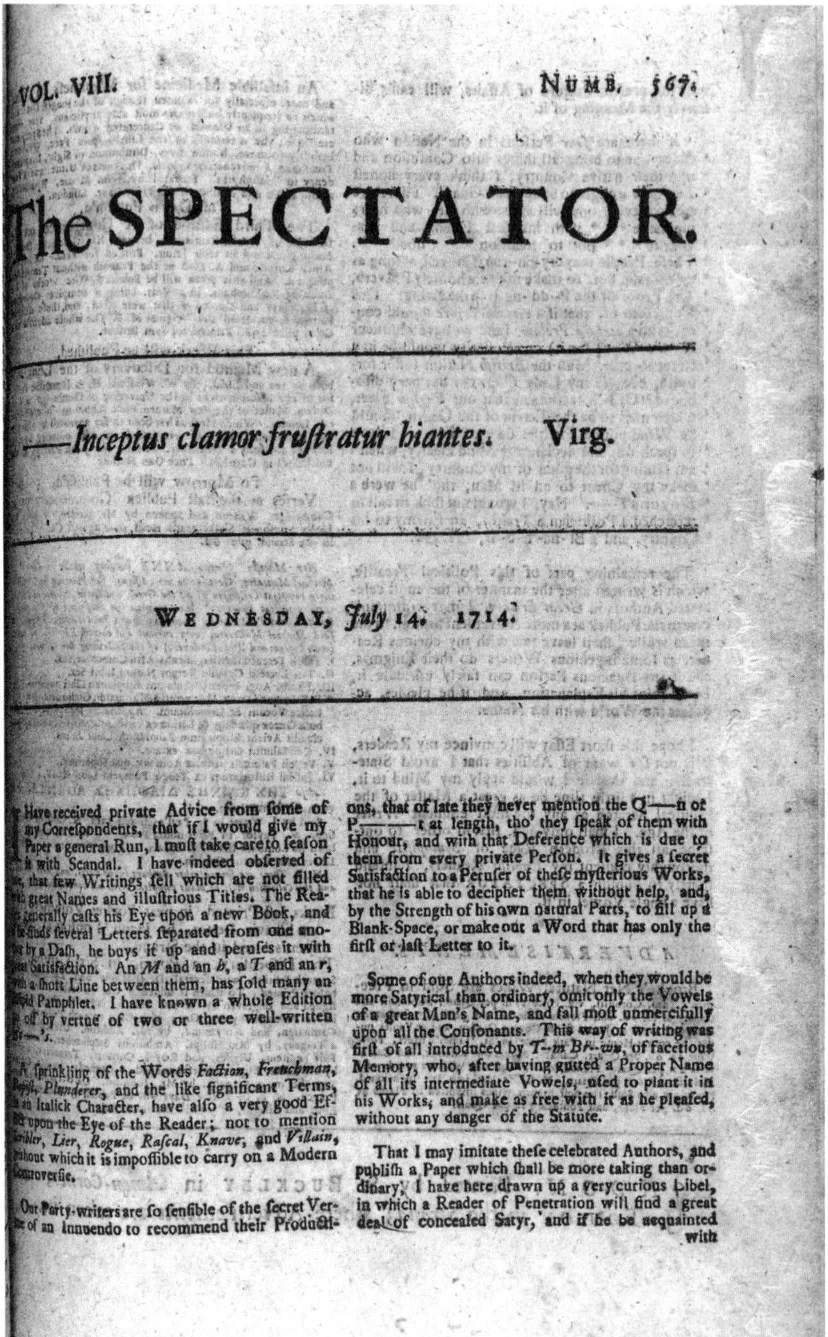

VOL. VIII.   NUMB. 567.

The SPECTATOR.

——*Inceptus clamor fruſtratur hiantes.*   Virg.

WEDNESDAY, *July* 14. 1714.

I Have received private Advice from ſome of my Correſpondents, that if I would give my Paper a general Run, I muſt take care to ſeaſon it with Scandal. I have indeed obſerved of late, that few Writings ſell which are not filled with great Names and illuſtrious Titles. The Reader generally caſts his Eye upon a new Book, and if he finds ſeveral Letters ſeparated from one another by a Daſh, he buys it up and peruſes it with great Satisfaction. An *M* and an *h*, a *T* and an *r*, with a ſhort Line between them, has ſold many an idle Pamphlet. I have known a whole Edition go off by vertue of two or three well-written *Et cæters*.

A ſprinkling of the Words *Faction*, *Frenchman*, *Papiſt*, *Plunderer*, and the like ſignificant Terms, in an Italick Character, have alſo a very good Effect upon the Eye of the Reader; not to mention *Scribler*, *Lier*, *Rogue*, *Raſcal*, *Knave*, and *Villain*, without which it is impoſſible to carry on a Modern Controverſie.

Our Party-writers are ſo ſenſible of the ſecret Vertue of an Innuendo to recommend their Produti-

ons, that of late they never mention the Q——n or P——t at length, tho' they ſpeak of them with Honour, and with that Deference which is due to them from every private Perſon. It gives a ſecret Satisfaction to a Peruſer of theſe myſterious Works, that he is able to decipher them without help, and, by the Strength of his own natural Parts, to fill up a Blank-Space, or make out a Word that has only the firſt or laſt Letter to it.

Some of our Authors indeed, when they would be more Satyrical than ordinary, omit only the Vowels of a great Man's Name, and fall moſt unmercifully upon all the Conſonants. This way of writing was firſt of all introduced by T——m Br——wn, of facetious Memory, who, after having gutted a Proper Name of all its intermediate Vowels, uſed to plant it in his Works, and make as free with it as he pleaſed, without any danger of the Statute.

That I may imitate theſe celebrated Authors, and publiſh a Paper which ſhall be more taking than ordinary, I have here drawn up a very curious Libel, in which a Reader of Penetration will find a great deal of concealed Satyr, and if he be acquainted with

FIG. 2.5. [Joseph Addison], *The Spectator*, no. 567 (14 July 1714). By permission of the British Library, shelf mark C71g1, no. 567 (14/7/1714).

with the present Posture of Affairs, will eaſily diſcover the Meaning of it.

' If there are *four* Perſons in the Nation who endeavour to bring all things into Confuſion and ruin their native Country, I think every honeſt *Engl-ſhm-n* ought to be upon his Guard. That there are ſuch every one will agree with me, who hears me name * * * with his firſt Friend and Favourite * * * not to mention * * * nor * * *. Theſe People may cry Ch--rch, Ch--rch, as long as they pleaſe, but, to make uſe of a homely Proverb, The Proof of the P--dd--ng is in the eating. This I am ſure of, that if a *certain Prince* ſhould concur with a *certain Prelate*, (and we have Monſieur *Z---n's* Word for it) our Poſterity would be in a ſweet P--ckle. Muſt the *Britiſh* Nation ſuffer forſooth, becauſe my Lady *Q--p--s--s* has been diſoſobliged? Or is it reaſonable that our *Engliſh* Fleet, which uſed to be the Terror of the Ocean, ſhould lie Wind-bound for the ſake of a ——. I love to ſpeak out and declare my Mind clearly, when I am talking for the good of my Country. I will not make my Court to an ill Man, tho' he were a *B---y* or a *T----t*. Nay, I would not ſtick to call ſo wretched a Politician a Traitor, an Enemy to his Country, and a Bl--nd--r--b--ſs, &c. &c.'

The remaining part of this Political Treatiſe, which is written after the manner of the moſt celebrated Authors in *Great Britain*, I may communicate to the Publick at a more convenient Seaſon. In the mean while I ſhall leave this with my curious Reader, as ſome ingenious Writers do their Enigmas, and if any ſagacious Perſon can fairly unriddle it, I will print his Explanation, and, if he pleaſes, acquaint the World with his Name.

I hope this ſhort Eſſay will convince my Readers, it is not for want of Abilities that I avoid State-tracts, and that if I would apply my Mind to it, I might in a little time be as great a Maſter of the Political Scratch as any the moſt eminent Writer of the Age. I ſhall only add, that in order to out-ſhine all this Modern Race of *Syncopiſts*, and thoroughly content my *Engliſh* Readers, I intend ſhortly to publiſh a SPECTATOR that ſhall not have a ſingle Vowel in it.

ADVERTISEMENTS.

This Day is Publiſh'd,

The Third Edition of A Conference on the Doctrine of Tranſubſtantiation, between His Grace the Duke of Buckingham and an Iriſh Jeſuit. Printed for Ferd. Burleigh in Amen-Corner, and A. Dod at the Peacock without Temple-Bar, price 4 d. And this Week will be Publiſh'd, The Works of the Duke of Buckingham, in 2 Vols. being a compleat Collection of his Plays and Comedies that were acted, and thoſe deſigned for the Stage, from the Original M. S. The whole adorn'd with Cuts, price 10 s. Printed for Sam. Briſcoe.

This Week will be Publiſhed,

A new Method for Diſcovery of the Longitude both by ſea and Land. By W. Whiſton. M. A. ſometime Profeſſor of the Mathematicks in the Univerſity of Cambridge, and H. Ditton, Maſter of the New Mathematick School in Chriſt's Hoſpital, London. Which Method has been ſo far approved by this preſent Parliament, that they have paſſed an Act, ordering 20000 l. Reward for ſuch a Diſcovery. Printed for John Phillips at the Black Bull in Cornhill. Price One Shilling.

To Morrow will be Publiſh'd,

Verſes at the laſt Publick Commencement at Cambridge. Written and Spoken by Mr. Euſden. Printed for Jacob Tonſon at Shakeſpear's Head over-againſt Catherine-ſtreet in the Strand; price 6 d.

Her Majeſty Queen ANNE having made a Grant to Michael Maittaire, Gent. or to his Aſſigns, for Printing and Publiſhing a compleat Collection of all the Greek and Latin Authors in Twelves, with compleat Indexes: There is, now (in purſuance of that Grant) Printed, and Publiſhed by Jacob Tonſon and John Watts, Aſſigns of the ſaid Michael Maittaire, very curious and correct Editions, in 12mo. (with Copious and Uſeful Indexes,) of the following Books, viz.
I. Publii Terentii Carthaginienſis Afri Comœdiæ Sex.
II. Titi Lucretii Cari de Rerum Natura Libri Sex.
III. Phædri Aug. Liberti Fabularum Æſopiarum Libri quinque; item, Fabulæ quædam ex MS. veteri à Marquerdo Gudio deſcriptæ, cum Indice Vocum & Locutionum. Appendicis loco adjiciuntur Fabulæ Græcæ quædam & Latinæ ex variis Authoribus collectæ; quas claudit Avieni Æſopicarum Fabularum Liber Unicus.
IV. Caii Salluſtii Criſpi quæ extant.
V. Vellcii Paterculi Hiſtoriæ Romanæ quæ Superſunt.
VI. Juſtini Hiſtoriarum ex Trogo Pompeio Libri XLIV.
Alſo ΤΗΣ ΚΑΙΝΗΣ ΔΙΑΘΗΚΗΣ ΑΠΑΝΤΑ. Novum Teſtamentum.
Sold by J. Wyatt in St. Paul's Church-yard, N. Cliff in Cheapſide, W. Taylor in Pater-noſter-Row, T. Vernun and J. Osborn in Lombard-ſtreet, J. Brown without Temple-Bar, and W. Lewis near Covent-Garden.
N. B. There are ſeveral other Authors in the Preſs, and near finiſhed; and this Collection will be made compleat with all convenient ſpeed.

Books juſt Printed, in neat Pocket Volumes, with an Elzevir Letter, by Jacob Tonſon at Shakeſpear's Head in the Strand.
The Diſpenſary, a Poem, in Six Cantos; the Seventh Edition, with ſeveral Deſcriptions and Epiſodes never before Printed; To which is added a Cut to each Canto, Deſigned and Engraven by the beſt Hands. The Shepherd's Week, in Six Paſtorals, by Mr. Gay, with Cuts to each Paſtoral. Care, Campaign, and Rolamond, by Mr. Addiſon. Diſtreſt Mother, a Tragedy, by Mr. Philips. Ambitious Stepmother, Tamerlane, Fair Penitent, Ulyſſes, and Royal Convert, Tragedies, written by N. Rowe, Eſq; Careleſs Husband, a Comedy, by Mr. Cibber. The Victim, a Tragedy, by Mr. Johnſon. Cato tranſlated into French. N. B. In a few Days will be Publiſh'd, Abramule; or, Love and Empire, Printed in the ſame Vol.

the Families themselves; and the Names and Persons so intirely conceal'd, and the real History so couch'd that it is impossible for any body, but the Persons themselves, to read the People by the Characters." Swift's remark to Pope—that "I hate and detest that animal called man, although I hartily love John, Peter, Thomas and so forth"—famous for the generality it seems to illuminate in Swift's satire, nonetheless must be set beside the same letter's observation that *Gulliver's Travels* will be published as soon as "a Printer shall be found brave enough to venture his Eares . . . ."[133]

Pope's ambivalence was a good deal more open. On the one hand, he claimed an ethical motive for his own use of "real rather than feign'd names" in *The Dunciad Variorum,* his "care to preserve the Innocent from any false Applications; whereas in the former editions which had no more than the Initial letters, he [Pope] was made, by Keys printed here, to hurt the inoffensive . . . ." By this rationale, the achievement of publicity is not impersonality but immortality, Defoe's "eternity of mortal time" endured not by the book but by its subjects: "Of the *Persons* [satirized] it was judg'd proper to give some account . . . since it is only in this monument that they must expect to survive . . ." (In *Tatler,* no. 92, Steele, "the public censor," had similarly promised to punish libelers themselves by "preserv[ing] them to immortal Infamy.") Four years later, on the other hand, Pope ridiculed "the mistaking a *Satyrist* [of institutions] for a *Libeller* [of persons]; whereas to a *true Satyrist* nothing is so odious as a *Libeller* . . ."—a disingenuous remark given the function of these words to advertise Pope's imitations of Horace, which contain some of his most personal satire. And he attributed to John Arbuthnot's influence the fact that in the prologue to the satires "I have, for the most part spar'd [his antagonists'] *Names* . . . ," a claim belied, once again, by the savage specificity of the *Epistle to Dr. Arbuthnot* (1735).[134] In *Joseph Andrews* (1742) Henry Fielding more credibly called himself a satirist rather than a libeler because "I describe not Men, but Manners; not an Individual, but a Species," and aim "not to expose one pitiful Wretch, to the small and contemptible Circle of his Acquaintance; but to hold the Glass to thousands in their Closets, that they may contemplate their Deformity, and endeavour to reduce it, and thus by suffering private Mortification may avoid public Shame. This places the Boundary between, and distinguishes the Satirist from the Libeller; for the former privately corrects the Fault for the Benefit of the Person, like a Parent; the latter publickly exposes the Person himself, as an Example to others, like an Executioner."[135] Of course, Fielding's discrimination of libel from satire also depends crucially on the difference between oral or coterie scribal publication and print.

Evidence like this would seem to confirm the contribution of libel legislation to defining not only the propriety of satiric reference but also the attractiveness of what a later age would call "realism"—avowedly fictional narrative that resembles, and borrows the authority of, factuality. In the present context it also contributed to the conception of a mode of published writing that resisted the ethically questionable effects of publicizing the private by confining its reference to "the public," that is, to generalizations of the personal. However, a determined state apparatus was quite capable of ignoring the logic of its own laws when it was expedient to do so. When the unfinished manuscript of his *Discourses concerning Government* (1696) was seized at his apartment and made the basis for a charge of high treason in 1683, Algernon Sidney protested, plausibly enough, that the manuscript was a general exercise in political theory rather than (as was alleged) a personal libel on Charles II. He also denied any intent to publish, observing that men "write in their own closets what they please for their own memory, and no man can be answerable for it, unless they publish it." Chief Justice George "Bloody Assizes" Jeffreys would have none of it. Collapsing the distinction not only between theoretical and practical "reflection" but also between thought, speech, and active dissemination, he ruled that "the imagination of a man's heart is not to be discerned; but if I declare such my imagination by an overt-act . . . it will be sufficient evidence of treason within that act." For Sidney, the physical space of the closet was an extension of one's own private person; for Jeffreys it was an extension of the coffeehouse and part of the public sphere. Sidney was executed on 7 December 1683, about the time when the following mordant lines were being circulated:

> Algernon Sidney,
> Of Commonwealth kidney,
> Compos'd a damn'd libel (ay, marry, was it!)
>   Writ to occasion
>   Ill blood in the nation,
> And therefore dispers'd it all over his closet.[136]

Characters, Authors, Readers

The public exposure of the personal met ethical opposition not only on the grounds that it injured the individuals so exposed but also because even if the exposure had no actual referent, it nonetheless publicized and disseminated vicious example. Jeremy Collier thought "libel" the operative term to reprove even this sort of discourse, in which characterization makes no pretense to personal representation: for a poet "to descend to Particulars, and fall to *Characterizing,* is no better than Libel, and Personal Abuse." Therefore, "[a]ll Characters of Immodesty (if there must be any such) should only be hinted in remote Lan-

guage, and thrown off in Generals."[137] The ethical liability of vicious representations was, of course, a point of intense debate regarding prose narrative
during this period.[138] That the controversy inaugurated by Collier in 1698 concentrated so exclusively on dramatic productions may owe in part to the fact
that in the voice of the narrator, narrative offers at least the opportunity for a
normative and framing moral commentary, which the unmixed dialogue of
drama does not.[139] (It also owed, no doubt, to the fact that the target of much
moral reform was nonliterate commoners.) In this respect, narrative is most
vulnerable when it sacrifices the distance of a distinct narrative voice by assuming a first-person address, even more by parodically impersonating the voice of
one whom the author aims to condemn.

In the "Apology" he attached to *A Tale of a Tub* (1704) six years after its first
printing, Swift was compelled to make this method of exposing vice explicit:
"There is one Thing which the judicious Reader cannot but have observed, that
some of those Passages in this Discourse, which appear most liable to Objection
are what they call Parodies, where the author personates the Style and Manner
of other Writers, whom he has a mind to expose. . . . Another Thing to be observed is, that there generally runs an Irony through the Thread of the whole
Book, which the Men of Tast will observe and distinguish, and which will render some Objections that have been made, very weak and insignificant."[140] Did
Swift feel obliged to teach his readers this lesson in textual interpretation because the techniques of irony and parody were as yet imperfectly understood by
English readers? What does the mysterious impersonality of impersonation—
both personalization and depersonalization, Swift's indignation and Gulliver's
rage—have to do with the paradoxical mechanism by which publication makes
the private public? We may make some progress in answering these questions
by sampling the richness of the Collier controversy.

Collier's insistence that the characterization of an evil person is necessarily
an evil characterization reminds us of Chief Justice Jeffreys's insistence that theoretical reflection is also personal reflection. And like libel law, it forced Collier's antagonists to make explicit the protocols of interpretation that tacitly obtained under customary conditions of performance and publication. One of
these was the distinction between the sentiments of a character and those of its
author, a distinction that seemed to contemporaries to invite the differential
terminology of "public" and "private." Implicitly rejecting the logic of persona
theory, Collier flatly asserted that "'tis the Poet that speaks in the *Persons* of the
Stage," and when they are vicious, his or her "*private Sentiments* fall under Censure." According to William Congreve, however, nothing should be "imputed
to the Persuasions or private Sentiments of the Author, if at any time one of
these vicious Characters in any of his Plays shall behave himself foolishly, or im-

morally in Word or Deed." Similarly, James Drake warned against confusing the poets' "private or real sense" with the "Sentiments, which they are obliged sometimes to furnish Villains and Extravagants with in conformity to their Characters," for in such characterizations the poet was "frequently necessitated to make use of Thoughts and Expressions very contrary to his own proper person."[141] Collier's antagonists correlate the private with the real or actual and the public with the rhetorical or fictional. The capacity to make a tacit distinction between character and author had long guided viewing and reading habits. What is new here is the explicit separation out of character from author, a move necessitated by their explicit coimplication in Collier's discourse.

Both arguments are aided by the understanding that the sentiments of the character exist in something like a public sphere, whereas those of the author have a private existence. But for Collier both the public sphere and literary characters are simple empirical extensions of actual particularity, of actual readers and actual authors, whereas Collier's antagonists hypostatize for them a separate realm of virtuality. That is, Collier's antagonists conceive the publicizing of the private through literary characterization as a process that alienates the "private or real sense" of the author's "own proper person," whereas Collier himself believes that when the private author creates a character and projects it into the public sphere, author and character constitute a continuous and homogeneous personality. The language of the debate reminds us, strikingly enough, of the difference between absolutist theories of political obligation and (Lockean) contract theory. In the former, private subjects are subordinated to and comprehended by the public authority of the magistrate. In the latter, the constitution of the public state by private subjects, undertaken with the express purpose of securing the property of the subject in his (but not her) "own proper person," requires a reciprocal alienation of the subject's nonproperty rights that necessarily reconceives what is proper to the private person. In the terms of this analogy (and on the commonsense face of it), the "contractarian" private author so familiar to modernity pre-exists the character he or she creates. But there is also a sense in which the author comes into existence only as he or she is separated out from character, as though the very being of authorship—the authenticity, the "private or real sense" of a deep interiority—results from the creative alienation of the superficial and worldly entity of literary character.

To modern eyes, both Collier and his antagonists work within a distinctly "didactic" framework—literature as engaged in an explicitly moral pedagogy—although the category of private and autonomous authorship toward which Collier's antagonists tend would seem to augur the emergence of a more "aesthetic" framework in which literature is one thing and morality quite another. But the explicitness that is the hallmark of the didactic—Collier's insistence on the moral accountability of the private author for the opinions of the public character—should caution us against seeing didacticism as the traditionality that the modernity of the aesthetic replaces. More persuasively, we might understand the didactic and the aesthetic as a dialectical unit, antithetical but interdependent instruments of explicit knowledge that sprout from the decay of true traditionality, which tacitly conceived all knowledge according to moral standards. In this respect as in others Dryden marks a crucial watershed. In his famous comparison of Horace's judicious raillery and Juvenal's ferocious, railing style of satire Dryden assumes that both poets excel in the twin (Horatian) categories of *dulce et utile,* "delight and instruction." But he is also willing to separate those two headings, and his correlation of Horace and Juvenal respectively with instruction and delight is suggestive: "[G]ranting Horace to be the more general philosopher, we cannot deny that Juvenal was the greater poet, I mean in satire. . . . [I]f we make Horace our minister of state in satire, and Juvenal of our private pleasures, I think the latter has no ill bargain of it. Let profit have the pre-eminence of honour, in the end of poetry. Pleasure, though but the second in degree, is the first in favour."[142]

In his notorious attack on the modern "English stage," Collier distinguishes between, but refuses to separate, the ethical status of private author and that of public character. Shaftesbury, his contemporary, carries this debate into the realm of written publication, and although he agrees with Collier on the correlation of author with privacy and character with publicity, he disagrees strenuously that they are ethically continuous. Rather, the ethical problem consists in the fact that publication separates character from author. Especially "indecent" are those authors who publish works—"*Meditations, Occasional Reflections, Solitary Thoughts*"—that claim to be personal and "self-discoursing," since "they never afford themselves the least time to think in private, for their own particular benefit and use" (1:164; 1:103). But these cases exemplify with unusual clarity what is generally wrong with modern authorship: to write for publication is to mischaracterize, to sacrifice authorial personality. "An Author who writes in his own Person, has the advantage of being *who* or *what* he pleases. He is no certain Man, nor has any certain or genuine Character: but sutes himself, on every occasion, to the Fancy of his Reader . . ." (1:199; 1:124). Such an author is like a "passionate Lover," "talking eternally of himself . . . whilst he is making diligent court," fabricating his character in the very act of being "personal" (1:175, 200; 1:110, 125). "Their *Page* can carry none of the advantages of their *Person.* They can no-way bring into Paper those Airs they give themselves in Discourse" (1:167; 1:105). "Our modern Authors . . . are turn'd and model'd (as themselves confess) by the Publick Relish . . . . In our Days *the Audience* makes the *Poet;* and *the Bookseller the Author:* with what Profit to the

Publick . . . let any one who has Judgment imagine." The system is one of supply and demand: "Read we must; let Writers be ever so indifferent. . . . [And so] our Authors[,] . . . making an exact Calculation in the way of Trade, to know justly the Quality and Quantity of the publick Demand, feed us thus from hand to mouth; resolving not to over-stock the Market . . ." (1:270, 264, 265; 1:168, 164, 165). Here Shaftesbury seems to have in mind a print economy. But the fundamental difference of the "modern" author is no more technological (i.e., typographical rather than scribal publication)[143] than it is generic or modal (written rather than performed publication).[144] The difference is rather between "modern" and "ancient" practices of authorship. Modern publication depersonalizes the author.

Shaftesbury's exemplary ancient is Socrates, whose dialogues, both spoken and written, vouchsafe us a public character faithful to his private one because they record the process by which, in accord with "that celebrated *Delphick* Inscription," he struggled to know himself. The Socratic method is for Shaftesbury something like what free association would be for Freud: a utopian technique for making the tacit explicit without sacrificing the self-knowledge that owes to the fact of its being tacit and in that sense unknown: "[O]ne wou'd think, there was nothing easier for us, than to know our own Minds . . . But our Thoughts have generally such an obscure implicit Language, that 'tis the hardest thing in the world to make'em speak out distinctly. For this reason, the right Method is to give 'em Voice and Accent." In the character of Socrates himself we feel this in the "exquisite and refin'd Raillery" by which he frames or distances himself from what he says and thereby "seem'd often to be very different from what he really was." We see this also in the "*second Characters*" of the dialogues, who in discourse with Socrates learn "to carry about with 'em a sort of *Pocket-Mirrour*" in which might be seen "*Two* Faces," one of Socrates and "the *other* like that rude, undisciplin'd and headstrong Creature, whom we ourselves in our natural Capacity most exactly resembled." By reading the Socratic dialogues we learn, "by virtue of the double Reflection, [to] distinguish ourselves into two different Partys." So philosophy would "hold us out a kind of *vocal* Looking-Glass, draw sound out of our Breast, and instruct us to personate our-selves . . ." (1:170-71, 194-96; 1:107-8, 121-22). Perhaps ancient wisdom can be modernized: if publication depersonalizes, it thereby also incites us to a deeper personal knowledge that resides in a figurative domesticity. The first step in publication, Shaftesbury advises, is for authors to pursue a "home *Regimen*," speak a "Home-*Dialect*," cultivate a "Home-Acquaintance and Familiarity," engage in "*Home*-Practice," and "enumerate . . . Home-affections" (1:167, 170, 172, 189, 2:139; 1:105, 107, 108, 118, 2:80).

Shaftesbury's reading of the Platonic Socrates reminds us that the present study's basic correlation of "ancient versus modern" with "distinction versus separation" and "tacit versus explicit" is a heuristic abstraction whose truth lies, at least in part, in the encouragement it gives to concrete complication.[145] Reading Plato, Shaftesbury finds in this ancient a model of explicitation, his publicizing of which will play a central role in the great modern coalescence of explicitation. The language of "double reflection" would seem to bolster the modern impulse toward "separation," not only between the public and the private but also within the latter domain. The private author must "multiply himself into *two Persons,* and be *his own Subject* . . . ." We must "discover a certain *Duplicity* of Soul, and divide our-selves into *two Partys*" (1:157, 169; 1:97, 106). The ancient philosopher was not, of course, Shaftesbury's only source for such formulations. Locke, the supervisor of Shaftesbury's early education, recently had characterized "reflection" as "that notice which the Mind takes of its own Operations . . . ," a kind of "internal Sense" whereby "the Understanding turns inward upon it self, *reflects* on its own *Operations,* and makes them the Object of its own Contemplation."[146] The reflexivity of Shaftesbury's Lockean epistemology, its conflation of mental subject and object, is enabled by the preconditional division or "duplicity of soul," the separation out of private subject and public object by which conflation becomes thinkable. Moreover, this mental operation recapitulates the separation and conflation that occur, as it were one level up, in the social operation of authorship. As the author learns the mental reflexivity of private and public microdomains, so the private author, his character separated from the public world in the process of publication, is equipped to overcome that separation through the very same mental reflexivity.

Again, it is important to stress that this achieved compatibility of the author's private character with that available to public readers bears a real but only superficial resemblance to the continuity of private author and public character we saw in Collier, since even to propose a similarity provides grounds for its refutation. For Collier and Shaftesbury, although nearly exact contemporaries, also exemplify, at least in this respect, the epochal difference between a culture of distinction and one of separation and conflation. In Collier, publication does not depersonalize: the morality of the private author can be distinguished, but it cannot be separated, from that of the public characters he depicts. In Shaftesbury, it is only the experience of the separation between the public and the private—the insight that publication depersonalizes—that enables their dialectical conflation, their reconciliation with each other. Shaftesbury sees this reconciliation as a profoundly moral achievement, but its morality, unlike Collier's, betrays the marks of the separation it has overcome by bringing the wisdom of intrapersonal study to the aid of personal authorship.

The third and final volume of *Characteristicks* contains what Shaftesbury calls "Miscellaneous Reflections on the preceding Treatises, and other Critical Subjects" (vol. 3, title page). These are "reflections" in several analogous senses of the term. They arise most profoundly from Shaftesbury's self-division, and from the internal self-study—as it were the reflection of public microreader on private microauthor—self-division allows him to do. But these reflections are also the product of that self-study, in which Shaftesbury the author seeks a truthful accommodation of his public, authorial character to his private person. He does so by simultaneously reading himself—reviewing his arguments and reminding us, through footnotes, where they were made—and directly addressing his reader: "My Reader doubtless, by this time, must begin to wonder thro' what Labyrinth of Speculation, and odd Texture of capricious Reflections, I am offering to conduct him." With an oblique and self-conscious air of authorial "Courtship" detoxified (if it is) by his earlier critique of such depersonalizations, Shaftesbury informs us that the time has come for him, "in my Capacity of *Author,* . . . to congratulate our *English* READER on the Establishment of what is so advantageous to himself; I mean, that mutual *Relation* between him and our-selves, which naturally turns so much to his Advantage, and makes *us* to be in reality the subservient Party. And in this respect 'tis to be hop'd he will long enjoy his just Superiority and Privilege over his humble Servants, who compose and labour for his sake." But the ironized vanity of authorial groveling—Shaftesbury imitating the raillery of his master Socrates—also carries the sobering charge of the reader's responsibility "to *read;* that is to say, to *examine, construe,* and *remark with Understanding*" (3:242–44; 3:148–49).[147]

As the author has strived to publicize a just representation of his own "inward Character" (1:339; 1:208), it is now time for the reader, with the aid of this "pocket-mirror," to read himself. From the outset, Shaftesbury's "Advice to an Author"—the subtitle and organizing topic of the essay that brings the first volume of *Characteristicks* to a close—has taken as granted the fact, not just of the relationship, but also of the analogy, between authors and readers. Momentarily casting a shadow over the comfortable Horatian maxim *dulce et utile,* he writes that authors, "whilst they profess only *to please,* . . . secretly *advise,* and give Instruction . . ." (1:155; 1:98). In his own practice Shaftesbury would disclose this secret, first, by openly acknowledging his own ambition to advise authors, and second, by acting on this ambition by advising himself through the strategy of dividing himself into author and reader and by offering this strategy as a model whereby other authors may keep themselves and their readers honest.

Particulars and Generals

The printing and circulation of books involves a movement from the personal to the impersonal, from the particular to the general, that calls to mind a number of other contemporary phenomena. Unlike traditional models of sovereignty, contract theory and the derivation of the public interest from a multitude of private ones begin at the level not of the whole but of the parts, which constitute the generality of the collective through the reciprocal accommodation of their particularity. Unlike traditional models of commerce, the idea of the market conceives value to be a general and homogeneous category available through the equalization of particular and distinct commodities.[148] In a related fashion, the publication of the private is a process by which a general readership coheres through the multiplication and dissemination of particular discourses. All three of these movements attain the level of the general by accounting for particulars in quantifying terms, and for this reason they invite and encourage the figure of the general as a concrete but virtual space composed of many actual particulars. Moreover, all three understand the particulars that constitute the general as having in that process of constitution left something behind, even if only temporarily—certain rights; value in use; privacy. Indeed, the common recourse to legal and ethical argument we have encountered may be understood as a response to this experience of objectification or alienation whereby the integrity of the actual particular as a constituent of the general is affirmed as the precondition for a process of virtual constitution in which that integrity is compromised.

My thinking on these issues has been aided by Charles Taylor's fruitful hypothesis of the modern "social imaginary," as well as by the work of others who have pursued this hypothesis in a number of different directions.[149] Inspired most clearly by Benedict Anderson's influential idea of the modern nation-state as an "imagined community," Taylor's hypothesis adds to the nation-state two other modern "social imaginaries," the market and the public sphere, and by this addition refines, through comparison, our understanding of the qualities they share.[150] Although the dyadic categories I have used in this study—distinction/separation, tacit/explicit, embedded/abstracted, actual/virtual—for the most part are not those deployed by Taylor, they are in the spirit of his hypothesis, and my use of them has benefited from the example of his terminology and analysis.

Broadly speaking, the modern social imaginary is one that comes into being through its own agency rather than through any external force. It is social because it is a general or collective entity, a relationship of individuals, and it is an "imaginary" because it has a virtual rather than an actual existence, one that consists in nothing but the activity of its self-constitution and self-perpetuation. Modern social imaginaries are therefore reflexive entities in the radical sense that they not only refer to themselves explicitly and self-consciously; they also constitute themselves through that explicitating act of self-reference. For this reason their deployment of a collective agency bears an illuminating relationship to the self-actualizing capacities of the linguistic performative.[151] These basic features of the modern social imaginary—virtuality, self-constitution, reflexivity—are germane to a fundamental quality of modern socioeconomic and cultural relations, the fact that they are relatively disembodied, mediated rather than face to face, disembedded from the substratum of physical presence and practices. Although in differing ways, modern social relations—the social contract, market exchange, public opinion—are normatively impersonal relations between "strangers" who have no actual experience of one another.[152] Finally, modern social imaginaries are "secular" in the double sense of that term, temporal and "of the age" rather than implicated in an eternal order, hence profane and worldly rather than sacred or religious.[153] The relevance of this hypothesis to the modern relationship between the public and the private that I have been documenting will be clear enough to readers.[154]

To speak of "modern social imaginaries" implies that one also may speak of traditional social imaginaries. And when Taylor employs related categories like "theory," "background," and "repertory" (we might wish to add "hegemony") to clarify what is distinctive about this one, he defends the notion that "social imaginary" usefully names a reciprocity of the individual and the community, as well as a reciprocity of understanding and behaving in the social world, that should be applicable to all societies.[155] There is indeed a real sense in which all social communities are self-constituted, sustained by the collective will of their individual members, just as there is a real sense in which communities are ontologically greater than the epistemological sum of the wills of their constituents. But modern social imaginaries—the social contract, market exchange, public opinion—also explicitly posit themselves as self-constituted even if common usage willingly suspends disbelief in this proposition by speaking of them as though they were actual, objective, and embodied entities that owe their continuing existence to something beyond the will of their constituents.[156]

My point might be clearer if we recall the generative idea of the modern nation-state as an "imagined community," in which there is something about the act of imagining that is not simply generic to all social formations but also peculiar to modern ones alone. Anderson is careful to argue the continuity, as well as the discontinuity, of the modern nation-state with the traditional religious community and dynastic realm. One of the most telling signs of discontinuity, however, is the difference between, on the one hand, the modern self-consciousness that I have been associating with the motive of explicitation and, on the other hand, the "*unselfconscious coherence*," the "axiomatic grip," the "automatic legitimacy" of tradition.[157] What Taylor's generalizing usage might invite us to call "traditional social imaginaries" are actual, embedded, and embodied collectives not only because this is their empirical and sociological status but also because their members understand themselves—through myth, story, theology, and theory—to be first of all not creative individuals but created parts of a totality that pre-exists individuality: creatures created by a collectivizing force beyond their own agency. *Creatura non potest creare:* this fundamental of Christianity underlies not simply what we recognize as "religious" belief but traditional ontology as such. But this is precisely what is absent in the modern social imaginary, in which "creation" is felt to be (at however deep a level of awareness) and justified as being (at the articulated level of political, economic, and cultural theory) a human rather than a superhuman capacity, a fiat of human imagination rather than of divinity. All social communities are, however tacitly, "imaginary"; modern social communities are also explicitly performative works of the imagination. And if this is so, it makes sense to ponder a fourth category whose emergence during the two centuries of our concern bears a crucial, even an explanatory, relevance to the formulation of the three "social imaginaries": the category of the aesthetic imagination itself.[158]

Actual and Concrete Particularity

To return to my argument, the abstract framework in which contemporaries reconceived the relation between the public and the private toward the beginning of the modern period was that of a relation between concrete but virtual realms of collectivity and actual individuals. If the character of modern privacy is bound up with the structure of dialectical recapitulation, whereby separation between private and public realms recurs, one level down, within the realm of the private, the modern public has the character and structure of a virtual collectivity constituted by the cognitive agency of all those actual, disembedded individuals who are, simply by virtue of that reflexive act of cognition, imaginatively reembedded as its component parts. But how can actual individuals be implicated in a virtual community? A case in point is the dispute between the particularity of libel and the generality of satire. The legal and ethical arguments against libelous discourse helped persuade writers to prefer satire as a method of public-sphere critique. But what can be the force of such critique if in criticizing public figures and institutions it avoids the dimension of the particular, the level of actual people? Fielding's rationale in *Joseph Andrews,* quoted above, offers one answer to this question. In confining itself to the realm of the general, satire does not necessarily lose touch with the particularity of private individuals. Rather, it engages that particularity by offering readers a concrete individual, a fictional character, from whom they can learn through an equalizing process of identification—holding the glass to thousands of private readers in their closets—which depends on and is enabled by generalizing from the realm of the actual to a realm that is virtual but also concrete. Only within this general realm, Fielding implies, can the private transaction of ethical improvement be achieved. To remain in the realm of actual particularity is, on the contrary, to resign oneself to the public exposure (or, in Shaftesbury's critique, the public deformation) of the private, to sacrificing the private to the public instead of bringing the private into public discourse.

The effect of Fielding's rationale is to separate out two aspects of particularity, actual and concrete particularity, whose difference had lain dormant in traditional ways of thinking about that category in the absence of the unprecedentedly normative force of empirical actuality in early modern experience. I will return to the importance of this separation in subsequent chapters. For the moment it is enough to remark its relevance to the idea of concrete virtuality that is central to the modern doctrines of realism and the aesthetic. The emergence of these doctrines amounts to the emergence, not of fiction, but of our kind of fiction, which openly proclaims its fictionality against the backdrop of its apparent factuality.[159] Only through the modern valorization of the actual—of the factual, the empirical, the historical—does the ancient and equivocal whole of "fiction" become resolvable into separate and unequivocal parts: falsehood and fiction, deceit and the aesthetic mode of truth, what is made up and what is made.

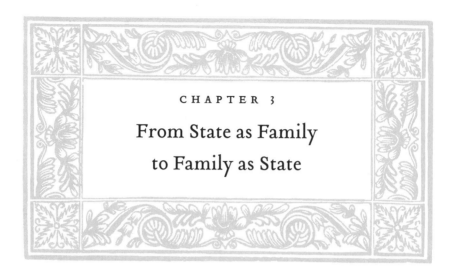

CHAPTER 3

From State as Family
to Family as State

Thus far our inquiry into the early modern separation out of the publicness of the state from the privacy of civil society has concentrated on three interrelated factors: the coalescence of a notion of individual economic rights and interests; the elaboration of a notion of interior religious conscience; and the typographical publication of the private. All three of these factors involve the dialectical constitution of the categories "public" and "private" over against each other; all three display the dialectical tendency to replicate, within the realm of the private, the oppositional relationship that is figured by the opposition between the two realms. The fourth and final factor in this process is the establishment of what Habermas calls the "intimate domain" or "sphere" of the modern conjugal family. It will be worth our while to consult Habermas briefly for an overview of this category.

In Habermas, the early modern separation out of the public and private realms raises as many questions as it answers. The private realm against which public state authority is ranged is itself a complex amalgam: not only is the public sphere to be understood as a part of that private realm; the privacy of civil society is composed of market exchange on the one hand and the "intimate sphere" (*Intimsphäre*) of the modern conjugal family on the other.[1] How can the intimate sphere of the family be concomitant with commodity exchange on the market given their evident antithesis as, respectively, private and public entities? Habermas finds the answer to this question in the dialectical logic of a broadly schematic historical understanding. With the early modern capitalist revolution, the private work of economic reproduction was increasingly separated out from the private household and undertaken for the market. "Modern economics was no longer oriented to the *oikos*," says Habermas; "the market had replaced the household . . ." (20). Yet economic activity, defined over against public state control, retained its ancient association with privacy, conceived not as privation but as negative freedom from constraint. The household, deprived of its (private) economic function, increasingly assumed the (private) status of the modern family, also valued for its negative freedom from public control. "To the autonomy of property owners in the market," Habermas writes, "corresponded a self-presentation of human beings in the family. The latter's intimacy, apparently set free from the constraint of society, was the seal on the truth of a private autonomy exercised in competition" (46). "The status of private man combined the role of owner of commodities with that of head of the family, that of property owner with that of 'human being' *per se*" (28–29). As we see in the centrifugal tension between property and propriety, however, the seal was defective. Although the intimate role materially depended on the market role, family intimacy was experienced in diametrical opposition to its economic ground. The logic, the powerful momentum, of a "privacy" conceived as a freedom from public dependence enforced a sense of the family as founded in the principles of "voluntariness, community of love, and cultivation [, which] were conjoined in a concept of the humanity that was supposed to inhere in humankind as such and truly to constitute its absoluteness: the emancipation . . . of an inner realm, following its own laws, from extrinsic purposes of any sort" (47). So, the separation of public and private was replicated one level down: "the process of the polarization of state and society was repeated once more within society itself" (28).

Nor does the mechanism of replication end there. The modern "home," the thoroughly privatized replacement of the traditional household, nonetheless reproduced a divided domain within its own walls. "The line between private and public sphere extended right through the home. The privatized individuals stepped out of the intimacy of their living rooms into the public sphere of the *salon*, but the one was strictly complementary to the other" (45). Gradually internalized within the home, the *salon* came to simulate, within one fragment of the private realm, the authentic public sphere whose role was to channel the discourse of the private realm to the greater realm of the public. In a related fashion, the negative freedom of the private family was consecrated by a contractual model of marriage that, promising individual autonomy, also recreated the subordination of private to public authority in the unequal relationship of husband and father to wife and children. The dialectical ambivalence of early modern marriage—its equilibrium between absolutist authority and contractual choice (or between a patriarchal and a downwardly mobile absolutism)—was expressed in the oft-reiterated "conflict between marriage for love and marriage for reason, that is, for economic and social considerations" (47), a kind of parental reason of state set over against the amatory freedom of the children. The terminus of this dialectical movement ever inward Habermas finds in the category of subjectivity, "the innermost core of the private" (49), "the source of privateness in the modern sense of a saturated and free interiority" (28), whose experimental laboratory was the epistolary and autobiographical literature of the public sphere. According to Habermas, the private work of this "literary public sphere" was critically instrumental in formulating the terms of rational debate as it transpired within a distinguishable "political public sphere" (see 51–56).

Habermas's hypostatizing of a public sphere within the early modern realm of the private has exerted a powerful influence over recent scholarship in the area. One liability of this focused attention, however, has been a relative neglect of the larger historical argument within which the thesis of an emergent public sphere acquires its dialectical meaning. Habermas gives us a model for understanding how the dichotomizing logic of the "public/private" opposition may be coextensive with the assimilative logic of a "public-private" continuum. Within a synchronic cross section of historical experience the realms of the public and the private may be lived as exclusive and oppositional. Pursuing a diachronic perspective on historical experience, on the other hand, relativizes the exclusivity of the realms and establishes their metonymic interpenetration. Yet as we have just seen, the continuity of the public and the private is fully accessible even within a synchronic framework, since the constitutive opposition between public and private tends to be replicated, one level down, within the private realm (indeed, this is a central implication of positing a public sphere "within" the private realm). In the everyday experience of contemporaries, the antithetical terms of politics and economics, of market and family, of sociofinancial alliance and love, were lived as simultaneous dimensions of personal existence. The model has an extraordinary descriptive power and explanatory potential. Yet although Habermas devotes some illuminating space to showing how the model may be derived from the particularities of the British experience (see 56–67), the application is cursory by the standards of the foregoing analysis. In this and the next several chapters I will concentrate on what Habermas calls the "intimate sphere" in the context, and in the terms, that have organized my account thus far.

State as Family

At the beginning of this study I discussed briefly the role of patriarchalist theory in explicitly formulating, and thereby destabilizing, the tacit traditionality of the analogy between the family and the state. Richard Greenham's curt sum-mation of the analogy in 1612 exemplifies how the distinction between its component parts need not imply their separability: "Care in superiors, and fear in inferiors, cause a godly government both private and public, in family, church and commonwealth." John Hayward provides a more expansive version: "The whole worlde is noethinge but a greate state; a state is no other than a great familie; and a familie is no other than a greate bodye. As one God ruleth the worlde, one maister the familie, as all the members of one bodye receiveth both sence and motion from one heade, which is the seate and tower both of the understanding and of the will: so it seemeth no less naturall, that one state should be governed by one commaunder." Yet even at this time, well before Filmer's theorization of the patriarchalist analogy, commentators were finding it less than transparent in its details on both sides of the analogy—and from both sides of the Protestant church. The vastly influential Puritan writers John Dod and Robert Cleaver believed that "[i]t is impossible for a man to understand how to govern the common-wealth, that doth not know to rule his own house, or order his own person; so that he that knoweth not to govern, deserveth not to reign." But they also believed that "[a]ll in the family are not to be governed alike. There is one rule to govern the wife by, another for children, another for servants." And in 1593 the eminent Anglican Richard Hooker raised the problem that the metaphor entails a metonymy—that if the state is like the family, it is also composed of families: "To fathers within their private families nature hath given a supreme power . . . . Howbeit over a whole grand multitude having no such dependencie upon any one, and consisting of so many families, as every politique societie in the world doth, impossible it is that any should have complet lawfull power but by consent of men, or immediat appointment of God; because [no one has here] the natural superioritie of fathers . . . ."[2] Indeed, even Filmer's views on family relations, expounded apart from *Patriarcha*, are a good deal less absolutist than the bald patriarchalist analogy would lead us to suppose. And we might conclude from this that despite *Patriarcha*, Filmer's notion of private order was more nuanced than his notion of public order, were it not for the fact that *Patriarcha*'s theory of kingship itself, when read closely, is also less straightforward than it has been taken to be.[3]

The persuasiveness of the metaphor of family and state derived in part from its metonymic underpinnings, that is, from the fact that royal sovereignty was determined by dynastic or familial inheritance. Viewed from this perspective, however, the history of the royal house of Stuart must have appeared to many a century-long allegory of family crisis: the desertion and murder of the husband-father, Charles I; the widowhood of the wife-mother, England; the belated return of the eldest son, Charles II; the rivalry of fatally defective heirs (the imperious younger son, the Duke of York; his bastard nephew, the Duke of

Monmouth); the futile effort to extend the line through James II; the anomalous rule of the mother, Anne; and the conveyance of the estate to Hanoverian interlopers. Along the way, royalists hopefully accommodated the unfolding events of the public realm to the reassuring private model. At the beginning of the century James I had declared with confidence, "I am the Husband, and all the whole Isle is my lawfull Wife . . . ." In 1643 the royal chaplain reminded his readers that "the King is also *sponsus* Regni, and wedded to the kingdom by a ring at his Coronation . . . ." In accounting for the outbreak of civil war, public-sphere debate recurred constantly to the mutual "jealousies" of king and people and to the "love" those jealousies presupposed:

> Jealousie in State, like that of Love,
> hath a double passion, of feare and hate.4

But by the late 1640s the dire condition of the royal party called for harsher analogies between family and state. In four "dialogues" printed in 1648, the decade-long effort to establish a reformed national church to replace the Anglican is figured as a grotesque scene of childbirth: Mistress Parliament is a whore who, surrounded and supported by "gossips" variously representing the evils of rebellion, is delivered of a terrible monster without a head (i.e., a king).5 And in the same year a royalist tract imagined the impending marriage of "Mr. King and Mrs. Parliament" to be blocked by "Captain Army," who forbids publishing the banns so that the king's "Estate may goe in the line of the Righteous, the men of Israel, the godly, and well-affected party . . . ." Mistress Parliament, he says, is "a woman of a light carriage, inconstant, and likely to be fruitlesse . . . ."6

The regicide was irresistibly a patricide, but what was the role of the father's wife in this scenario? In the schematic allegorical framework of *Hudibras* (1663, 1664, 1678) Samuel Butler makes Interregnum England an innocent widow courted by Puritan suitors.7 But England the father's wife could also be figured as the regicide. The fourteenth-century law of petit treason (25 Edw. 3, st. 5, c. 2) provided that "if any servant kill his Master, any woman kill her husband, or any secular or religious person kill his Prelate to whom he owes Obedience, this is treason." In 1663, a year after the last execution for regicide, the chief justice of the King's Bench, ruling on the case of a runaway wife, observed that "[w]hen the wife departs from her husband against his will, she forsakes and deserts his Government; erects and sets up a new jurisdiction; and assumes to govern herself, *besides* at least, if not *against,* the law of God and the law of the land. Therefore it is but just, that the law for this offence should put her in the same plight in the petit commonwealth of the household, that it puts the subjects for the like offense in the great commonwealth of the realm."8

Celebrated as another sacred wedding of prince and people, the Restoration unraveled so quickly that by 1667 John Dryden was reassuring the City of London that "[n]ever had Prince or People more mutual reason to love each other, if suffering for each other can indear affection. You have come together a pair of matchless Lovers, through many difficulties; He, through a long Exile, various traverses of Fortune, and the interposition of many Rivals, who violently ravish'd and with-held You from Him: And certainly you have had your share in sufferings." Less than ten years later, John Ayloffe's Britannia complained that

> A colony of French possess the court;
> .   .   .   .
> Thus fairy-like the King they steal away,
> And in his place a Louis changeling lay.

Taking the Sun King as her model, Louis's personified regime urges Charles to

> Taste the delicious sweets of sov'reign power;
> 'Tis royal game whole kingdoms to deflower.
> Three spotless virgins to your bed I bring,
> A sacrifice to you, their god and King . . . .

On the eve of the Glorious Revolution, Elinor James tried to persuade Parliament not to depose James II: "[C]onsider that *he* has been *misled* by *strangers,* as many *Men* has been *misled* by *strange Women,* yet they are not willing their *Wives* should turn *them* out of *doors* and take other *Husbands* . . . ."9

The difficulty of holding the customary analogy together under the strain of its close analysis is yet more evident in the willingness of parliamentarians to regender its terms. Henry Parker argued that comparisons between prince and father, prince and husband, "do illustrate some excellency in Princes by way of similitude, but must not in all things be applyed . . . , for the wife is inferiour in nature, and was created for the assistance of man, . . . but it is otherwise in the State betwixt man and man . . . ." To justify the gender reversal Parker had recourse to another traditional figure (like this one, deceptively self-evident in its tacit application): "[T]he Head Politicall . . . receives more subsistence from the body than it gives, and being subservient to that, it has no being when it is dissolved . . . . [T]he verie order of Princes binds them not to be insolent, but lowly; and not to aime at their owne good but secondarily, contrarie to the Florentines wretched Politiques." The new analogy was succinctly applied by another writer in support of the regicide: "When my *Wife* turneth *adultresse,* my *Covenant* with her is broken, And when my *King* turneth *Tyrant,* and continueth so, my *Covenant* with him is also broken." In a single stroke, king becomes a perfidious adulteress, Parliament and people the dishonored husband.10

These developments provide a compelling context for John Locke's famous use of contract theory, a year after the English people "deserted" the government of James II, to refute the patriarchalist identification of magistrate with father and husband. But the pressure of explicitation can be seen even more subtly in the temptation to slide from the metaphorical to the metonymic dimension of the relation between state and family so as to facilitate understanding it not only in analogical but also in causal terms. In John Milton's analysis, "No effect of tyranny can sit more heavy on the Common-wealth, then this household unhappiness of the family. And farewell all hope of true Reformation in the state, while such an evill as this lies undiscern'd or unregarded in the house." In 1654 Milton warned "the English People" that "[i]f, having done with war, you neglect the arts of peace . . . Unless you expel avarice, ambition, and luxury from your minds, yes, and extravagance from your families as well, you will find at home and within that tyrant who, you believed, was to be sought abroad and in the field—now even more stubborn." Among the weapons with which Milton countered the hagiography of Charles I after his death was a deep disdain for his monarch's bearing with the queen, Henrietta Maria: "Examples are not farr to seek, how great mischeif and dishonour hath befall'n to Nations under the Government of effeminate and Uxorious Magistrates. Who being themselves govern'd and overswaid at home under a Feminine usurpation, cannot be but farr short of spirit and autority without dores, to govern a whole Nation." Writing in 1650, the year after the faithful husband (or the faithless wife) of the nation had been decapitated, Henry Neville drew upon the domestic experiments proposed by radical sectarians during the previous decade to satirize the political ambitions of aristocratic women on both sides of the conflict, reversing Milton's cause and effect:

> There was a time in *England,* when men *wore the Breeches,* and debar'd women of their *Liberty;* which brought many grievances and oppressions upon the *weaker vessels;* for, they were constrained to converse only with their *homes and closets* . . . . In consideration whereof, and divers other inconveniences, by the tyranny of men, the *Ladies Rampant* of the times, in their last *Parliament,* knowing themselves to be a part of the *free people* of this Nation, unanimously resolved to assert their own *freedoms;* and casting off the intolerable yoak of their *Lords* and *Husbands,* have voted themselves the *Supreme Authority* both at home and abroad, and setled themselves in the posture of a *Free-State,* as may appear by their *Practises.*[11]

In a similar vein, a tract of 1647 closely parodied the republican language of commoner petitions for redress of grievances by making the petitioners "Shee-Citizens" whose radicalism turns out to be not political but sexual. The demand of these voracious women is that they be allowed to pursue their natural rights to sexual intercourse with whomever they desire. Alluding to the Leveller leader John Lilburne, the author asserts that "to us . . . [,] according as that stiffe stander for the subjects Liberties Col. *Lilburne* hath noted, belongeth every immunitie of *Magna Charta* . . . ."[12] The reduction of political to sexual libertinism aims to demonstrate the corrupting effect of state on familial affairs, but it also defends against Leveller-inspired women's petitions that vainly sought to extend the concept of the freeborn citizen to women.[13] A similar motivation lies behind the diverse material that invokes the notion of a "parliament of women," whose volatility lies in the fact that sexual reduction is often hard to tell from the genuine radicalism of utopian politics.[14] Figure 3.1, the frontispiece of a royalist tract, offers an image of women making the law in Parliament that inadvertently may undercut the derision with which the tract aims to meet the idea of a parliament of women.[15]

Although it worked with the same components, the causal analysis of the relation between the family and the state inevitably detached those terms from the automatic reciprocity of signification entailed in the customary analogy. Writing in 1685, after the Exclusion Crisis but before the deposal of James II, Robert South thought it "but too frequent a complaint, that neither are men so good husbands, nor women so good wives, as they were before that accursed rebellion [i.e., the civil war] had made that fatal leading breach in the conjugal tie between the best of kings and the happiest of people." Figure 3.2 extends South's apprehension to fathers and children. Playing on the popular maxim "Cobbler, stick to thy last," the image illustrates the thesis that book learning can be a dangerous thing. The cobbler has so immersed himself in radical political ideas (note the many books on his shelf) like Bishop Benjamin Hoadley's justification of subjects who resist their rulers that his own proper trade has suffered. Moreover, the lesson has traveled from state to family: the cobbler's son attacks his father for failing to maintain the family. However, the prognosis might be made more favorable by locating determinacy not in the public but in private experience:

> *Marriage* will reform the Mischiefs of the Debauch'd, and bring these Nations to a regular and quiet *Temper:* For a *Family* is the *Epitome* of a Kingdom, and it naturally resolves into a Government, which cannot subsist without *Rules* and Order . . . . And as *Marriage* does all this, so it goes farther, by leading a Man to consider, that there can be no Assurance, no nor pretence of Obedience from a *Wife, Children,* or *Servants,* but under the protection of the Government we live under; so that, perhaps, he that was before an *Enemy* to *Authority,* is now, by becoming a *Party* (as *that* he will have in his *Family* will make him to be) a *Convert* to *that* in the *State,* which he expects to be *Master* of in his *House.*

The efficacy of private experience is here thrown into sharp relief against the comparatively passive ground of the public—a reversal in emphasis that has

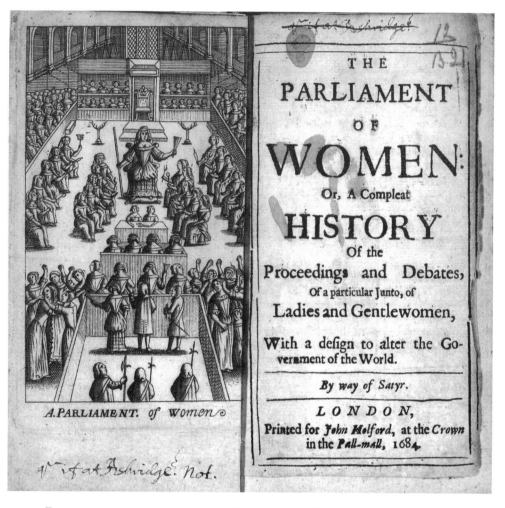

FIG. 3.1. Frontispiece and title page, *The Parliament of Women . . .* (1684). By permission of The Huntington Library, San Marino, California.

great importance for the largest themes of this study. And the effect is still, as when the public realm is treated as determinant, to break the spell of the similitude through the very act of rationalizing it. On occasion the spell is broken not through the relatively outspoken metonymy of causal argument but by bringing to the fore the familial metonymy that fuels all dynastic monarchy. When Mary agreed to reign with her husband William, lending the throne the luster of genealogical sovereignty while forswearing her own sovereign author-

FIG. 3.2. Frontispiece, *Crispin the Cobler's Confutation of Ben H[oadley]* . . .
(1709). By permission of the British Library, shelf mark 94.e.21.

ity, it seemed to some that she had been stripped of her majesty and reduced to the status of one more sad token in the private traffic in women—

> [P]oor Moll who stole her father's crown
> For terror of her husband's frown.[16]

Family as State

Testimony like this suggests that the family crisis of the seventeenth-century English state increasingly evoked reflections on the state of the English family itself. However, it was not only that political upheavals had sensitized English people to their familial "equivalents"; the family itself was in the process of transformation. To appreciate the volatility of the family-state analogy in the later seventeenth century, that is, we must attend to historical developments not only in the political realm but also in the realm of the family: not only in the theory and practice of state sovereignty but also in the law and practice of marriage. But first, a word on the inclusiveness of the term "family" in the early modern period.[17]

When people speak of the family at this time they are likely to have in mind one (or more) of three senses of the term that we tend to distinguish from one another. First and perhaps most important, "family" was a term of primarily spatial designation, referring to all those who lived under the same roof—in the same household—under the acknowledged authority of its (usually male) head. Second, "family" had a temporal inflection that evoked one's lineage, genealogy, and ancestry, specifically the diachronic dimension of "blood" relations but by extension those aspects of wealth, prestige, and power whose synchronic coalescence might be assumed by virtue of one's lineage. The sense of lineage might easily coexist with that of household. A major development of this period, however, is the growing tension between the two, which we see expressed in the conflict between marriages of alliance and marriage for love, as well as in the separation out of birth and worth that I elsewhere have associated with the critique of aristocratic ideology.[18] Third, the language of "family" was used to refer to the circle of kin both within and outside the household. The standard kinship terms in this period are similar to those in our own; but this is a deceptive correspondence in that early modern usage was far looser in its application, incorporating a broader but variable range of reference depending on specific contexts of use. However, the inclusiveness of these kin terms also diminished in the seventeenth and eighteenth centuries, becoming more restricted and definitive over the course of this period. In addition, collective kin terms like "relations," "friends," and "connexions" shuttled back and forth between what we would call familial and nonfamilial reference, often serving to designate a basic kin relation without specifying its particular nature. Our own usage makes clear that these collective categories too have become separated out from familial reference during the modern period.

In the following discussion of how the public terms of state rule were used to investigate and signify the nature of the family, my focus is on the act of marriage and the nuclear unit, which are central both to the constitution of households and to the issue of lineage that fuels the power struggles between parents and children, husbands and wives, through which the analogy with princes and people is pursued. It is important to recognize, however, that contemporaries did not identify household-families by their conjugal core.[19] Indeed, the self-conscious application of public, political categories to the understanding of private, familial ones had the effect not only of separating out the state from the family but also of separating out those meanings of "the family" which we take for granted from the vast network of social relations within which they had been embedded.

True, the English custom whereby married couples moved out of the old households in order to establish new ones gave the nuclear unit an integral if temporary coherence. But domestic service was so common that "between a quarter and a third of all households contained servants," hence the majority of those who established new household-families "also lived at some stage in their lives in households to whose members they were not related."[20] The household was of course hierarchically divisible: family proper and servants might be distinguished as the "great" and the "little" family, and servants as "upper" and "lower" servants.[21] So, within the private realm of the family there were distinctions reminiscent of that between the family itself and the state. Indeed, as Milton could blame political problems, so Richard Allestree could blame the servant problem, on family disorder: "And sure we need not wonder at the universal complaint that is now made of ill servants, when we reflect upon this ill government of families."[22] Embodying traditional assumptions of social inequality, the master-servant relationship was nonetheless now given "a new lease of life" as a model of social relations by its adaptation to, and support of, the inequality of the emergent wage-labor contract.[23] If the household hierarchy was constituted by principles of both unity and division, the general effect of social development at this time was to emphasize—as in the conjugal unit itself—division over unity. On the one hand, the master and mistress of the household exercised something like an "absolute" "public" authority of employment and discipline over their servants, an authority both reflected and resisted in the contemporaneous growth of protounion "confederacies" among domestic laborers. On the other hand, servants were notoriously privy to, and open about, the secrets of their employers. As legal proceedings for the separation of married couples became common during the eighteenth century, domestic servants proved invaluable in providing testimony about the intimate behavior of their betters. This testimony was "public" not only in that it was given in court but also because salacious evidence pertaining to adultery received an enormous amount of publicity through the publication of court proceedings and scandal periodicals.[24]

Coming Together

Medieval canon law had treated marriage as a sacrament and therefore indissoluble. It countenanced two different forms of marriage. In noble and gentle families, where marriage played the crucial role of legitimating the genealogical transmission of property, the full formality of a public and clerically supervised church ceremonial was expected. Among common people, canon law accepted "contract" marriages—private verbal contracts, or "spousals," accompanied by popular ritual—as binding. The degree to which the Protestant Reformation altered these marriage practices varied according to national culture. From one easily available perspective, the English Reformation was nothing less than a revolt against the "patriarchal"—i.e., papal—control of divorce, remarriage, and the production of a legitimate heir, and in these terms it presented a highly visible challenge to canon law on marriage. Yet perhaps in part because it was undertaken so clearly as a matter of state policy and to further state ends, the English Reformation left medieval marriage laws basically intact, unlike in the other Protestant countries of Europe. True, marriage ceased to be a sacrament (although it remained a spiritual act, hence indissoluble), and the authority of the Roman Catholic Church was replaced by that of the Church of England. Nevertheless, English marriage remained subject (except during the brief Interregnum hiatus) to canon law and its church courts until the Marriage Act of 1753.[25]

At the Council of Trent in 1563 the Catholic Church reasserted its spiritual and financial control over marriage in Catholic countries by requiring that private contracts be validated by public church ceremonies. In post-Reformation England the church courts pursued a similar aim by trying to enforce public weddings in church so as to reconcile the canon law of contract marriage with the common law controlling the ownership of property. The policy had a real success; but it entailed such corruption that the church courts sustained bitter attack as "the bawdy courts."[26] The civil war brought with it the abolition of the church courts (1646) and of weddings according to the rites of the Church of England (1653). And although these were restored along with monarchy and episcopacy in 1660, the Interregnum abolition's encouragement of experimentation with informal and private modes of marriage and separation only heightened their popularity during the following century. By the 1753 Marriage Act, any marriage not accompanied by official public procedures was deemed null and void.[27] Although common wisdom has understood the 1650 act against sexual misconduct as the manifestation of a specifically Puritan prudery, its most recent historian places it in a long tradition of comparable efforts (what distinguishes it is the judicial role taken by the state rather than the church) and associates it with a general and "growing idealization of married love and domestic life." The centerpiece of the act, the strict punishment of (female) adultery, was conceived as a remedy for a public crime, not a private injury—a crime, that is, against the continuity and stability of the Commonwealth.[28]

In debates about marriage in post-Reformation England the "public/private" opposition has several distinct if overlapping meanings. With respect to "contract" marriage, it suggests the difference between the spiritual and patrimonial sanctions of official ceremony and the informality of popular custom, a distinction in which the interests of church and state are conjoined over against those of the free English subject. This can be heard in the report of a visitor to South Wales in the 1760s, who found that "the late [1753] Act of Parlamt is lookd upon only as a Cruel and wicked restraint upon the liberties of the Mine Country. . . . Some Couples (especially among the miners) either having no friends, or seeing this kind of public marriage too troublesome and Impracticable, procure a man to wed them privately which will not cost above two or 3 mugs of ale."[29] The conflict between marriage licensed by church and state and contract marriage was thus felt to figure the familiar symbolic conflict between the absolute will of the sovereign and the liberty of the subject.

A different sense of the "public/private" opposition may be seen in responses to the growth of an alternative to contract spousals, "clandestine" marriage. Because clandestine marriages were (unlike mere contracts) performed by a clergyman according to the Book of Common Prayer, they were legally binding with respect to common-law property rights. On the other hand, clandestine marriages dispensed (as did contracts) with the official banns and license and might be performed anywhere but in the parish church of one of the spouses. These conditions underscore the centrality of the motive of secrecy announced in the very name of the procedure. If the "privacy" of contract marriage connotes folk custom unregulated by church or state forms and interests, the "privacy" of the clandestine marriage assents to that regulation so long as it does not compromise the crucial secrecy of the union. Touring England at the end of the seventeenth century, Henri Misson was struck by the importance of the secrecy motive in English marriages. Clandestine marriage, he found, appealed to most people with "the slightest claims to gentility," who were unwilling "to have their affairs declar'd to all the world in a public place, when for a guinea they may do it snug and without noise. . . . One of the reasons that they have for marrying secretly, as they generally do in England, is, that thereby they avoid a great deal of expense and trouble."[30]

As Misson implied, reasons for desiring secrecy varied. Most couples anticipated opposition to the marriage from some level of "authority," whether parish, employment, or family. In the cultural imagination, however, and perhaps also in reality, the most common reason for clandestine marriage was to frustrate the opposition of parents and "friends" who deemed it unsuitable. In locating the threat to free contract in the authority of church and state, contract marriage conceived the public/private opposition as a matter of conflict *between* the public realm and the private realm.[31] In shifting the locus of the threat from the church and state to the family, clandestine marriage conceived the public/ private opposition instead as a matter of conflict *within* the private realm. Before 1754, clandestine marriages were quick, cheap, and relatively easy to be had, most of all in the vicinity of the Fleet in London. Figure 3.3, published in 1747, depicts the interior of a public room in a tavern where a "Fleet wedding" is being celebrated. The artist has borrowed liberally from Hogarth, including the representation of a skimmington ride (see fig. 4.7), which in Hogarthian fashion (see fig. 3.5) casts a premonitory pall over the festivities below. The 1753 Marriage Act, which invalidated all clandestine marriages, contained a clause authorizing a parental veto on marriages of children under twenty-one years of age. Henceforth the only recourse for children whose parents' sense of interest frustrated the official acknowledgment of love was travel to Scotland, particularly Gretna Green, which was just across the border and became known for its marriage trade.[32] In figure 3.4 Thomas Rowlandson emphasizes the violence of the conflict between parental authority and the liberty of the child-subject by the liberal brandishing of pistols and whips, not to mention the very high dudgeon evident in the face of the father.

Unlike political sovereignty, marriage had always demonstrably been based on some form of consent; hence it was always plausible to conceive it in contractual terms. Moreover, the express consent of both parties was deemed requisite by most early modern writers on marriage.[33] Indeed, the consensual basis of marriage was a potent weapon in the hands of those who, like Henry Parker, were opposed to the patriarchalist theory of political obligation but not necessarily to the broader logic of the patriarchalist analogy:

> In Matrimony there is something divine . . . but is this any ground to infer that there is no humane consent or concurrance in it? does the divine institution of marriage

FIG. 3.3. *The Sailors Fleet Wedding Entertainment*, 1747. © Copyright The Trustees of The British Museum. For complete rendering of figure text, see Plate 12.

take away from freedome of choice before, or conclude either party under an absolute formalization? . . . And if men, for whose sake women were created, shall not lay hold upon the divine right of wedlock, to the disadvantage of women; much less shal Princes who were created for the peoples sake, chalenge any thing from the sanctity of their offices, that may derogate from the people.

In 1644 Parker made contractualism in the family a pointed model for contractualism in the state. In 1680 William Lawrence left the latter application unstated, not because he rejected the logic of the analogy but because he had faith in the logic of metonymy. That is, he thought that if the radical conjugal contractualism for which he argued were to prevail in the royal family, its metonymic fulfillment would ensure political rule compatible with the will of the

FILLIAL AFFECTION, or A TRIP TO GRETNA GREEN.

FIG. 3.4. Thomas Rowlandson, *Fillial Affection, or a Trip to Gretna Green*, 1785. BM Sat 6861. © Copyright The Trustees of the British Museum.

people: "Private Marriage, or carnal knowledge, is of two sorts, the one without publick Witness, the other without any Witness at all . . . . The Law of *England* makes all private Marriage, and carnal knowledge, without publick Witness, Fornication. . . . [A]ll persons ought to be left liberty of Conscience, to marry publickly or privately, with or without Witnesses, as it suits best with their conveniences and occasions, as is the use and practice in all other civil Contracts . . . ."[34]

When Locke famously argued that princes rule not by absolute sovereignty but by contractual agreement, he might be said to have refuted the analogy between family and state with one hand while affirming it with the other. For his contractarian argument models princes not on fathers but, implicitly, on husbands: elsewhere in the *Second Treatise* Locke expresses the conventional view that "*Conjugal Society* is made by a voluntary Compact between Man and Woman . . ."; and he adds that "the *Power of the Husband* being so far from that of an absolute Monarch, . . . the *Wife* has, in many cases, a Liberty to *separate* from him . . . ."[35] The severity of seventeenth-century constitutional crisis ensured that explicitation of the patriarchalist analogy most often involved asking the question, (How) is the state like the family? Locke's reply to this most pressing of questions was skeptical. But the demands of the analysis also led him to ask the corollary question, (How) is the family like the state? Locke's negative (if incomplete) answer to this corollary—the family is not like the absolute state—clearly served the contractarian ends of his argument about the nature of public government. But by momentarily reversing the direction of the inquiry he did what many contemporaries were also beginning to do: he made the private government of the family the primary question. If the traditional idea of the conjugal contract provided a model and stimulus for the emergence of political contract theory, political contract theory in turn provided a stimulus for explicitating and demystifying the plausibility that tacitly had been accorded the "contractualism" of traditional marriage.

Not that the patriarchalist analogy had tacitly operated as a one-way street; the late-medieval law of petit treason makes this clear enough. And in the early decades of the seventeenth century the discursive use of state rule to illuminate the nature of the family was by no means unheard of.[36] Still, there may be some basis for seeing the period between the Restoration of the house of the Stuarts and its replacement by a new family lineage in 1714 as crucial in the history of the patriarchalist analogy. By this I refer not to the demise of the analogy (which is no doubt still with us) nor to its public-sphere explicitation, which rendered it a problematic object of study, but to a shift in the weighting of its component parts. If we conceive the analogy as an exercise in interpretive signification, the realm of the family had tended until this historical moment to be placed in the position of the "signifier" and thereby to be used experimentally to interpret or construe the nature of the state. Henceforth this relationship is rebalanced in the opposite direction: the family assumes the place of the "signified," and the state becomes one important means for signifying it, for making sense of the nature of the family. We can see evidence of this rebalancing in a range of public-sphere discourse—poems, plays, essays, conduct books, letters —in which the private family is of central interest and the public state is brought to bear on its understanding. I will return to this issue of a fundamental shift in the balance of signification in order to investigate it within the formal development of a single discourse, the secret history.[37] There my claim will be that a transformation in the discursive status of the family, from a signifier of meaning that lies elsewhere to the very embodiment of signification, can be seen on the level of literary form.

I suggested above that clandestine marriage encouraged people to internalize the public/private opposition that obtained between the church and state on the one hand and the contracting couple on the other, to conceive it as a matter of conflict within the private realm of the family. In this internalization the tyranny of church and state most often reappears as parental tyranny. In Thomas Shadwell's *Lancashire Witches* (1682) the country gentleman Sir Edward Hartfort despairs of marrying off his clownish son to Theodosia, the daughter of a local justice; but he hopefully enumerates to his own daughter, Isabella, the material attractions of young Sir Timothy Shacklehead. "Thou knowest, my Child, how this cross match will strengthen and advance my Family." Both women have only contempt for their respective intendeds. "Well," says Isabella to Theodosia, "we are resolved never to marry where we are designed, that's certain. For my part I am a free English woman, and will stand up for my Liberty, and property of Choice." Theodosia agrees: "And Faith, Girl, I'le be a mutineer on thy side; I hate the imposition of a Husband, 'tis as bad as Popery." In Thomas Otway's *Atheist* (1683) Portia makes the application as explicit as it could be. Declaring liberty "an English Woman's natural Right," she asks: "Do not our Fathers, Brothers and Kinsmen often, upon pretence of it, bid fair for Rebellion against their Sovereign: And why ought not we, by their Example, to rebel as plausibly against them?" A few years earlier Richard Leigh had written that

> In *arbitrary Families,*
> Which seem *Domestique Tyrannies,*
> *Parents,* with *Turkish Rigors* sway . . . .

Using the more allusive language of "bondage" and "liberty," Mary, Lady Chudleigh's Melissa enlarges on those tyrannies from the viewpoint of the daughters:

> Unhappy they, who by their Duty led,
> Are made the Partners of a hated Bed;
> And by their Fathers Avarice or Pride,
> To Empty Fops, or Nauseous Clowns are ty'd;
> · · · · · · · · · · · · · · · · · ·
> But such as may be from this Bondage free,
> Who've no Abridgers of their Liberty;
> No cruel Parents, no imposing Friends,
> To make em wretched for their private Ends,
> From me shall no Commiseration have,
> If they themselves to barbarous Men inslave.[38]

In these passages we see a certain range in the extent to which public are accommodated to private matters. Some of the passages openly display the act of internalization through a full articulation of the analogy, while in others the public realm remains more allusively visible in the way its language of power and authority colors the representation of what is ostensibly a private concern.[39] This could be said also of several periodical essays. In one number of the *Tatler* Richard Steele's Mr. Bickerstaff has "often admired at the Barbarity of Parents, who so frequently interpose their Authority in this grand Article of Life." Soon after he describes a branch of his own family that endlessly replays this same generational scenario: "the Father" squanders one-third of the estate, forces "his eldest Son" to marry for money, and presides "as a Tyrant" over the household until his death releases the son to begin the cycle again (*Tatler,* nos. 185 and 189, 15 and 24 June 1709). Mr. Spectator will soon extend the theme: "A Parent who forces a Child of a liberal and ingenious Spirit into the Arms of a Clown or a Blockhead, obliges her to a Crime too odious for a Name" (*Spectator,* no. 437, 22 July 1712). Here the confrontation between the couple's choice and the parents' constraints is described in a characteristically urbane idiom that still evokes that other confrontation—between the subject's liberty and the sovereign's absolute will.

In her letters to Sir William Temple during the Interregnum, Dorothy Osborne finds the public state of affairs an apt figure for her private dilemma in the marriage choice. Her wealthy father had been impoverished by the fines Parliament levied on his estate in punishment for his support of Charles I, and Dorothy's family hoped for a larger fortune than a match with William Temple might provide. Having entered into a clandestine engagement to William, Dorothy has lately asked him if she may be released from it. Now she writes him with sad ambivalence about her cousin's decision to repudiate love in favor of fortune, and she responds to William's question "how," if he releases her from her marriage pledge, "I intend to dispose of my self":

> Alasse were I in my owne disposall you should come to my Grave to bee resolved, but Greif alone will not kill. All that I can say then is, that I resolve on nothing but to Arme my self with patience, to resist nothing that is layd upon mee, not struggle for what I have noe hope to gett. I have noe End's nor noe designes nor will my heart ever bee capable of any, but like a Country wasted by a Civill warr, where two opposeing Party's have disputed theire right soe long till they have made it worth neither of theire conquest's, tis Ruin'd and desolated by the long striffe within it to that degree as twill bee usefull to none . . . .[40]

Dorothy's comparison of her heart to England wasted by the internecine conflict of "two opposing parties" calls to mind Shaftesbury's injunction that "[we] divide ourselves into two parties."[41] But for him self-division is a dynamic strategy of self-knowledge, whereas hers is a psychomachy between agents that are beyond her own disposal. The public ruin of civil war is both metonymy and metaphor, both instrumental in the unlooked-for devastation of private English families and emblematic of the diurnal devastation of the marriage choice, that is, of being subject to the choice of others.

Several of the *Tatler*'s scathing accounts of elite courtship draw heavily upon notes, based on personal experience, that were provided by Steele's friend Edward Wortley (see *Tatler,* nos. 199 and 223, 18 July and 12 Sept. 1710). In her letters to Edward from this period, two generations after that of Dorothy Osborne and Sir William Temple, Mary Pierrepont records her response to Edward's highly secret—and indecisive—courtship of her at a time when her noble father has already begun arrangements for her marriage to a wealthy but unloved aristocrat. The correspondence is suffused with the aura and apprehensions of absolutist politics:

> I have no hand in the makeing of Settlements. My present Duty is to obey my Father. . . . [M]y Father may do some things disagreable to my Inclinations, but passive Obedience is a doctrine should allwaies be receivd among wives and daughters.⁴² . . . I should think your Correspondance a pleasure if it was Among the number of the permitted. But you know it is forbidden, and I am in pain when I do any thing that must be a Secret. . . . [I] do not think I have any hand in makeing Settlements. People in my way are sold like slaves, and I cannot tell what price my Master will put on me. . . . My Family is resolv'd to dispose of me where I hate. I have made all the Opposition in my power; perhaps I have carry'd that opposition too far. However it is, things were carry'd to that height, I have been assur'd of never haveing a shilling, except I comply. . . . That Threat would not have oblig'd me to consent, if it had not been joyn'd with an Assurance of makeing my Maiden Life as miserable as lay in their power, that is so much in their power I am compell'd to submit.

Despite these words, Mary and Edward slowly come to terms with the idea of a secret elopement and marriage, and Mary begins to essay the language of private love:

> I wanted courrage to resist at first the Will of my Relations, but as every day added to my fears, Those at last grew strong enough to make me venture the disobliging them. . . . A Man that marrys a Woman without any advantages of Fortune or Alliance (as it will be the case) has a very good title to her future Obedience. . . . With you, I quit all things but your selfe, as much as if we were to be plac'd alone together in an inaccesible Island, and I hazard a possibility of being reduc'd to suffer all the Evils of poverty. . . . If we retire into the country, both your fortune and Inclination require a degree of privacy. . . . [Y]ou must not be far off if you intend to do it, for I own I cannot, nor dare not, resist my Father, and I know he has power over me to make me do whatever he pleases. . . . I read over some of your first Letters, and I form romantic Scenes to my selfe of Love and Solitude. . . . I tremble for what we are doing. Are you sure you will love me for ever? . . . [A] Woman that disobliges her Family and engages the world against her, risques a great deal . . . .⁴³

Mary and Edward eloped four days after this last letter. Many years later she wrote to her daughter: "This Richardson is a strange fellow. I heartily despise him, and eagerly read him, nay, sob over his works in a most scandalous manner. The two first tomes of Clarissa touched me, as being very resembling to my maiden days."44

When it was published almost thirty years ago, Lawrence Stone's innovative and widely influential study *The Family, Sex, and Marriage in England* touched off a protracted and fruitful debate about, among other things, the marriage motives of English people in past times. Did affection, companionship, and love become central to courtship considerations only in the eighteenth century? Did the motives of family and financial interest tend to exclude the more personal concerns of the couple itself before the great watershed of modernity? Scholars have been right to question this too-simple reading of the history of English marriage, especially in the case of the lower orders but even among gentility, and Stone himself affirmed more recently the inextricable intermixture of marriage motives in traditional English culture.45 But if the eighteenth century was not singular in experiencing, or in distinguishing between, the marital motives of love and interest, it may nonetheless have been unprecedented in separating them out so decisively into oppositional conflict. As we have already seen, the emergent language of "interest" necessarily entailed not only the notion of competing interests but also that of alternative kinds of interest. What seems truly innovative about this period is its extraordinary concentration upon the question of the marriage choice, and upon the paradigm of a basic opposition—embodied in typical familial (or simply human) personages—between love and money.

Of course, the terminology and emphases vary, and there is some value in attending to some of the variations recorded by a culturally significant source like the *Spectator* papers. In one essay, a man of comfortable if modest means writes that "[i]t is the Fashion with Parents (how justly I leave you to judge) to make all Regards give way to the Article of Wealth. From this one consideration it is that I have concealed the ardent Love I have for" his beloved (no. 304, 18 Feb. 1712). In another, the "intended Son-in-law . . . had all along regarded this Alliance rather as a Marriage of Convenience than of Love" (no. 164, 7 Sept. 1711). Elsewhere the difference is between "estate" and "person," and it is not really a conflict at all: "Where the Choice is left to Friends, the chief Point under Consideration is an Estate: Where the Parties chuse for themselves, their Thoughts turn most upon the Person" (no. 261, 29 Dec. 1711). On the other hand, an elder son complains that his parents think he "must be settled, it seems, not according to my own, but their Liking" (no. 533, 11 Nov. 1712). Likewise, a daughter wonders "whether I shall be govern'd by the vain World, and the frequent

Examples I meet with, or hearken to the Voice of my Lover, and the Motions I find in my Heart in favour of him" (no. 278, 18 Jan. 1712). Steele distinguishes more evenly between the "insipid" and the "happy" married life. In the first, "the young Lady's person is no more regarded, than the House and Improvements in Purchase of an Estate . . ."; "[t]he happy Marriage, is where two Persons meet and voluntarily make Choice of each other, without principally regarding or neglecting the Circumstance of Fortune or Beauty" (no. 149, 21 Aug. 1711). And to an "impatient Gentleman" torn between "a beautiful young Creature" of "no Fortune" and the fear that it "would utterly ruine my Reputation for Discretion to marry such a one," Steele curtly replies: "Would you marry to please other People, or your self?" (no. 254, 21 Dec. 1711).

The first plate of William Hogarth's celebrated series *Marriage à-la-Mode, The Marriage Contract* (fig. 3.5) is a deeply nuanced graphic representation of the marriage of convenience or alliance between the son of a gout-stricken aristocrat and the daughter of a wealthy City alderman and banker or merchant. The earl's coronet, designating his property, can be seen everywhere, even on the flanks of the two dogs who, chained together, reflect the enforced attachment of the young couple. The two families are both mixed and segregated: the fathers on the left balance the children on the right, but only the fathers show any signs of close engagement, over the documents of this financial exchange, the earl's redeemed mortgage and the marriage contract itself; the children turn away from each other in postures emblematic of their mutual and future antipathy. Most pertinent to our present concerns are the paintings that cover the walls of the earl's chamber and elegantly proliferate (in the words of Hogarth's interpreter) "images of violence, torture, and martyrdom" that cast their dark significance onto the scene below.[46]

Readers will be familiar with other variations on this general theme, which becomes ubiquitous especially in novelistic narrative, and I will return to its significance at a later moment. For the present a few observations will suffice to suggest how the devolution of public and political to private and familial levels of conflict opens up the potential for subdivisions of conflict on the latter terain. First, the conflict between love and money entails a separation out, against one another, of motives that hitherto had seemed sufficiently similar— as two kinds of inordinate passion—to obviate their explicit disengagement. I have remarked elsewhere that the two major strands of novelistic narrative in the early eighteenth century direct their animus respectively against lust and the lust for money. Recently it has been argued, moreover, that the development of the novel depends upon, and articulates, a gradual separation out of sexual from economic desire.[47] Second, the logic of my current argument suggests that in the conflict between love and money we see, as it were, a private version of

FIG. 3.5. William Hogarth, *The Marriage Contract.* Plate 1 of *Marriage-à-la-Mode,*
1745, in William Hogarth, *Hogarth: The Complete Engravings,* ed. Joseph Burke and
Colin Caldwell (New York: Abrams, 1968). Princeton University Library. For complete
rendering of figure text, see Plate 13.

the public confrontation between the liberty of the subject and the tyranny of
the absolute sovereign. However, in the internalization of this public contest two
important adjustments have been made. The language of political power remains important in the private paradigm, personated most often by the figure of
the parents, the father, the family, or "friends." Yet there is also a tendency to
reconceive power, once it has been "privatized," in economic rather than in
strictly political terms. The personal danger of physical "enslavement" comes to
include that of reification and commodification. Third, with the movement
from public to private conflict there comes an opportunity to particularize the
way conflict gets embodied in both its superordinate and its subordinate categories.

At the public level, tyranny is tyranny no matter what political body enacts it. At the private level, however, to embody tyranny in the parents (or the father) is to choose against an alternative possibility. Over the course of the century there is a growing awareness that the category "family" is susceptible to an ideologically significant subdivision between consanguineal and conjugal kinship relations, between the "old" family into which one was born and the "new" family one makes through marriage. And depending on the degree of emphasis, the association of tyranny with parental, i.e., consanguineal, or "public," relations may imply a corresponding valorization of conjugal, or "private," ties.[48] Again, in the public conflict over affairs of state, the subject whose liberty is at stake tends to be neutrally gendered, hence perhaps generically "male." In the private conflict over the marriage choice, men are often the victims of parental tyranny, but there is a tendency for women to predominate in this role. With the marriageable woman in particular, then, will become associated a set of values redolent of interiority—personhood, one's own liking, the heart, the self, love—which nonetheless bear the residual marks of a "political" (i.e., public) signification.

Being Together

In the sources I have cited thus far, the analogy between the family and the state concentrates our attention on the moment of origin: by what authority, contractual choice or absolute decree, is the institution first established? One *Spectator* number focuses upon this moment only to modulate to something rather different. Two young people, deeply in love, would marry, but they are frustrated by the knowledge that "[h]is Father was a very hard worldly Man, and proud; so that there was no Reason to believe he would easily be brought to think there was any thing in any Woman's Person or Character that could ballance the Disadvantage of an unequal Fortune." The son "offer'd to marry me privately, and keep it so till he should be so happy as to gain his Father's Approbation, or become possessed of his Estate." A clandestine ceremony is held, a certificate is signed by participants and witnesses, and "Octavia" rusticates herself "in a resigned Expectation of better Days." But when the certificate is accidentally destroyed and Octavia applies to her husband for another, "I find both the Witnesses of my Marriage dead, and that my Husband, after three Months Cohabitation, has buried a young Lady whom he married in Obedience to his Father. In a Word, he shuns and disowns me," and Octavia discovers that the secrecy she once had embraced is now her downfall: "Should I talk it to the World, what Reparation can I expect for an Injury I cannot make out?" So, the

opening conflict between "hard" father and loving children turns into one between hard men and loving woman (*Spectator,* no. 322, 10 Mar. 1712).

Thomas Shadwell provides an earlier, comic version of this complication: A
young gentleman, having long endured financial "Slavery" to his father, finally
comes into his estate wishing to marry another's wife, who is herself displeased
with her miserly and antiquated husband. "[M]y Mother betray'd me in my
Youth to the slavery of thy Age," she tells her husband. "Thou didst promise to
be a Father to me; thou canst not be a Husband, and wilt not be a Father—but
a cruel Tyrant." "Will this Tyrannie never be at an end? must I be always thus
abridg'd of Liberty? . . . I will have the liberty of a She-Subject of *England.*" Her
husband replies, "Nay then I will use my Conjugal authority," and locks her in
her chamber. She cross-dresses as a captain, demands that he "return her Portion, or settle her Jointure," and tricks him into signing a separate maintenance
agreement. The new marriage that is intimated at the end of the play signifies a
joint liberation: the son is free of his father, the wife is free of her husband.[49]

These two texts are "transitional" in the sense that they mediate between the
first and the second phases of meaningful analogy between public and private,
political and familial, society. The first phase concerns the origins of society. It
consists, as we have seen, in the analogy between two levels of conflict: on the
one hand, the negative freedom of contractual consent versus the tyranny of
absolute will; on the other, the negative freedom of amatory choice versus the
tyranny of marriages of "alliance" or "convenience." The second phase of the
analogy concerns the nature of society once it has come into being and centers
on the issue of property ownership. In the public and political realm we encountered a distinction between absolute sovereign ownership and absolute private ownership by the civil subject, but also a slippage whereby the former devolves into the latter. To what extent is this phenomenon discoverable in the
private realm of marriage? What becomes of a woman's property rights once she
becomes a wife?

As we might suppose, once the focus is on the married state itself rather than
on how it comes about, the likelihood that the conjugal ties between wife and
husband will be valued over against the consanguineal ties of children and parents dwindles considerably, and the husband becomes a prime candidate for the
epithet "tyrant." In 1773 the well-known bluestocking Hester Chapone used the
patriarchalist analogy to inform private married gentlewomen of their "public"
duties with a sententiousness that seems to bespeak a certain cultural sanction:
"It is with a family as with a common wealth, the more numerous and luxurious it becomes, the more difficult it is to govern it properly."[50] The sanction did
not come easily. By English legal tradition, a woman who married changed her

status from that of *feme sole* to that of *feme covert*. Husband and wife became one person under law, distinguishable but not legally separable. The wife, having no separate legal existence or personality, was powerless to transact legal business, including the ownership of property. To the considerable extent that domesticity emerged when this traditional view of marriage was still common, its inconsistency with the emergence of privacy and the principle of negative liberty was, at least in the case of wives, undeniable. As William Lawrence observed, a "Law would be thought very absurd and unjust, which should Enact, That no Man or Woman should sue one another in the Common-wealth; what horrible wickednesses and villanies would be committed by the two Sexes, one against another; but it is more unjust to make such a Law in Families, and more unjust to make such a Law between Men and their Wives, then in Families: For in the Common-wealth, such as are persecuted in one City, can fly to another. In Families such as like not one anothers company, and are unmarried, can be received and have protection in other Families. But Men and their Wives are chained together, and cannot avoid the injuries of one another, and have no remedy . . . ." In the words of Richard Allestree, "there is so strict union between a man and his wife that the law counts them one person and consequently they can have no divided interest." Allestree's language recalls the absolutist subsumption of all private interests under that of public monarchy. Under these conditions, the relation of husband and wife might well be compared to that of absolute sovereign and slave. As we have seen, these were Mary Astell's terms. "He who has Sovereign Power," she continued,

> does not value the Provocations of a Rebellious Subject, but knows how to subdue him with ease, and will make himself obey'd; but Patience and Submission are the only Comforts that are left to a poor People, who groan under Tyranny, unless they are Strong enough to break the Yoke, to Depose and Abdicate, which I doubt wou'd not be allow'd of here. For whatever may be said against Passive-Obedience in another case, I suppose there's no Man but likes it very well in this; how much soever Arbitrary Power may be dislik'd on a Throne, not *Milton* himself wou'd cry up Liberty to poor *Female Slaves,* or plead for the Lawfulness of Resisting a Private Tyranny.[51]

Writing in the signal year 1689 Shadwell appears to prove Astell's point. In his dedicatory epistle to *Bury Fair* Shadwell ridicules "the Doctrine of *Passive Obedience* and *Non-resistance*" and defends the deposal of kings "when the compact on which Government is founded is broken . . . ." But the play ends with Gertrude, until now an independent-minded woman, accepting the proposal of the reformable libertine Wildish by saying that she has "ever held *Non resistance* a Doctrine fit for all Wives, tho' for nobody else." According to Richard Leigh,

> Each *House*, a *Kingdom* is in short,
> And govern'd, like the *Turkish Court.*
> The *Wife*, no *Office* seems to have,
> But of the *Husband*'s prime she-*Slave.*
> For she apart no *Rights* can claim,
> Nor has no Title to her *Name.*

In a poem by Ned Ward, a similar sentiment is one of the means by which the crafty bawd persuades a young virgin into prostitution:

> *Husbands* maintain an *Arbitrary* Sway,
> Whilst the Poor *Wife* must *Suffer,* and *Obey;*
> And like a Kingdom into Slav'ry drawn;
> Thro' *Fear,* not *Love,* upon her Tyrant Fawn.

Chudleigh, like Astell and Shadwell writing after the Glorious Revolution, made the disparity between public and private relations explicit. Her persona Melissa asks:

> Must Men command, and we alone obey,
> As if design'd for Arbitrary Sway:
> Born petty Monarchs, and, like *Homer's* Gods,
> See all subjected to their haughty Nods?
> . . . .
> Passive Obedience you've to us transferr'd,
> And we must drudge in Paths where you have err'd:
> That antiquated Doctrine you disown;
> 'Tis now your Scorn, and fit for us alone.

Sarah Fyge Egerton thought "[p]oor womankind's in every state a slave," but most of all in marriage:

> Then comes the last, the fatal slavery:
> The husband with insulting tyranny
> Can have ill manners justified by law,
> For men all join to keep the wife in awe.
> . . . .
> We yield like vanquished kings whom fetters bind,
> When chance of war is to usurpers kind;
> Submit in form; but they'd our thoughts control,
> And lay restraints on the impassive soul.

Amid sentiments like these, John Crowne's application of revolution principles to the case of rebellious wives is a decidedly minority (albeit opportunistically libertine) stance. In *City Politiques* (1683) Florio defends Rosaura's infidelity to her husband by saying that "she is a true Whig and has revolted from you because you did not pay her nightly pension well. . . . Our principles are: he is not to be regarded who has a right to govern, but he who can best serve the ends of government. I can better serve the ends of your lady than you can, so I lay claim to your lady." And when Rosaura says that "you have my consent," Florio adds: "So, I have the voice of the subject too . . . ."[52]

Precisely because wives were in theory so totally subjected to their husbands, seventeenth-century writers on marriage tended to distinguish their status from that of slavery. As John Wemyss wrote, a wife's conjugal subjection "differeth far from servile subjection, for he that is servilely subject worketh for another: but the wife worketh not for another but for herself, for she and her husband are one."[53] But despite this common reading of marriage as an absolute unity of interests, the formal abolition of feudal tenures in the public realm found some measure of corollary in the alterations made, within the private realm, in the law of marriage settlement during the later seventeenth and early eighteenth centuries.[54] The development of the prenuptial "strict settlement" among elite families during the Restoration encouraged contemporaries to separate out from "the family" those components—the heir, his wife, the eldest son, youngest sons, and daughters, as well as the depersonalized estate itself—to which varying amounts of explicit financial attention now seemed warranted.[55] This development might be seen as a precondition for one central phenomenon with which we are currently engaged, the separation out of financial from amatory motives in the marriage choice. Of more immediate relevance in the present context are those financial arrangements that, despite legal tradition, provided for married women's separate property: principally, jointure (for use in the event of widowhood) and pin money (for use during the marriage itself). Both jointure and pin money could also be contracted for postnuptially. Although the long-term practical significance of these innovations has been hotly debated by historians, to contemporaries they seemed to set in motion, within the intimate sphere not just of the family but of marriage itself, the downward mobility of absolute private property from "public" husbands to "private" wives. Thus the character of a modern "city lady": "She opposes the *Monarchy* of a Husband, with the *Undeterminable* Privileges of a *Wife*. . . . Doing *what she Lists*, is her *Liberty*; a separate *Maintenance* is her *Property*, and claims that by her *Original Contract*."[56]

Once again we may have recourse to the periodical essay. Steele was a staunch defender of "companionate" marriage rightly conceived, and he could use the language of absolutist politics to ridicule husbands whose fear that marriage betrays their "Softness" and "Effeminacy" leads them to assume the ab soluteness of a tyrant. Desiring "to appear to their Friends free and at Liberty," they "grow Tyrants that they may seem Masters. Because an uncontroulable Command of their own Actions is a certain Sign of entire Dominion, they wont so much as recede from the Government even in one Muscle of their Faces" (*Spectator,* no. 236, 30 Nov. 1711). But it seemed to Steele excessive that a wife might possess her own property—as well as the absolute liberty to alienate it as she would. Like the parental marriage of convenience, this threatened to transform an affective into a crassly monetary association. Indeed, in Steele's eyes the most evident culprit here was precisely "the covetous Tempers of the Parents." The problem with pin money and jointures, which Steele understood to be quite recent inventions, was that they rendered the state of matrimony "terrible," making young people distrustful and intimating "that they are very soon to be in a State of War with each other . . . . Thus is Tenderness thrown out of the Question; and the great care is, What the young Couple shall do when they come to hate each other?" To Steele it seemed expressive enough to figure this venality as an "Auction," or as "the Sale of our Women" (*Tatler,* nos. 199 and 223, 18 July and 12 Sept. 1710).57 But in briefly imagining the state of matrimony as a state of war, Steele adumbrated a singular public metaphor for this private aberration that Addison would illuminate more fully.

Addison's vehicle is Josiah Fribble, who writes to complain that in order to marry "a young Woman of a good Family," he was obliged to enter "into a Treaty with her longer than that of the Grand Alliance. Among other Articles it was therein stipulated, that she should have 400 *l.* a Year for *Pin-money* . . . ."58 Taxed by this obligation, Mr. Fribble inquires of his wife whether he might be freed of his quarterly payments, whereupon she threatens to have him arrested. So Mr. Fribble asks Mr. Spectator to "inform us if there are any Precedents for this Usage among our Ancestors; or whether you find any mention of *Pin-money* in *Grotius, Puffendorf,* or any other of the Civilians." In Addison's witty fiction the wife's desire for a modicum of financial autonomy transforms the matrimonial state of nature into a state of war. Addison shortly alludes to a widow whose mercenary demand for pin money led her outraged suitor to conceive that "she thought him her Slave" (*Spectator,* no. 295, 7 Feb. 1712). According to Locke, "[H]e who attempts to get another Man into his Absolute Power, does thereby *put himself into a State of War* with him . . . . [H]e who makes an *attempt to enslave* me, thereby puts himself into a State of War with me. He that in the State of Nature, *would take away the Freedom,* that belongs to any one in that State, must necessarily be supposed to have a design to take away every thing else . . . ."59 Mr. Fribble looks to Grotius and Puffendorf to discover whether natural law may override the mortal aggression entailed in the demand for pin money, an aggression comparable to that of one nation against another on the high seas, located by Locke in the state of nature because not subject to the positive law of particular nations.[60]

Mr. Spectator agrees with Mr. Fribble that "the supplying a Man's Wife with *Pin-money,* is furnishing her with Arms against himself," because it contravenes the two fundamental principles of the state of nature, freedom and equality. In Locke's words, "The *State of Nature* has a Law of Nature to govern it, which . . . teaches all Mankind, who will but consult it, that being all equal and independent, no one ought to harm another in his Life, Health, Liberty, or Possessions."[61] Mr. Spectator allows that pin money may be warranted to offset glaring matrimonial imbalances, "[b]ut where the Age and Circumstances of both Parties are pretty much upon a level, I cannot but think the insisting upon *Pin-money* is very extraordinary . . . . I cou'd . . . wish . . . that they had rather call'd it *Needle-money,* which might have implied something of Good-housewifry . . . ." Addison's bantering tone is typically self-protective. Behind the patently absurd claim of equality in marriage lies the stern implication that it is only the provision for wifely equalization that unbalances the integrity of the marriage unit. In effect, Addison's complaint is that pin money transforms a tacit distinction into an explicit separation. "Separate Purses, between Man and Wife, are, in my Opinion, as unnatural as separate Beds. A Marriage cannot be happy, where the Pleasures, Inclinations and Interests of both Parties are not the same" (*Spectator,* no. 295, 7 Feb. 1712).

In the wake of 1641 and 1688, an acknowledgment of the reality and authenticity of separate interests had become the necessary ground for any effort to satisfy the public interest. Even one level down, where the public realm was reconceived as the family, the logic of that argument seemed powerful, if problematic in its consequences. At the microlevel of the married couple, however, the downward mobility of absolutism—whose dynamic purport was, paradoxically, to withhold from any person absolute authority over any other person— came to a halt, at least for men like Addison. If the husband could not be absolute master in his own house, then he must be a slave, and the wife absolute mistress. Alternatively, if the wife insisted upon that unconditional possession of property that elsewhere signified autonomous privacy, it must be negatively revalued as an evasion of authentic privacy, of "good housewifery." But the analogy between family and state did not, for all this, become unworkable at the microlevel of marriage. Rather, its terms must be shifted from civil society to the state of nature among nation-states, where all parties might be supposed free and equal in the absence of pin money and its singular bellicosity.

Less than a week after this number of the *Spectator* appeared, Addison, perhaps not fully satisfied with his attempted solution of the problem of married women's separate property, published another letter from a dejected husband. John Anvil, an upwardly mobile commoner grown wealthy in scrap iron and knighted for his pains, decided to establish a family with "a Dash of good Blood in their Veins" and accordingly "made Love to the Lady *Mary Oddly*, an Indigent young Woman of Quality. To cut short the Marriage Treaty, I threw her a *Charte Blanche,* as our News Papers call it, desiring her to write upon it her own Terms. She was very concise in her Demands, insisting only that the Disposal of my Fortune, and the Regulation of my Family, should be entirely in her Hands." A previous number has amusingly informed us that *carte blanche* is one of those terms of "Modern Military Eloquence" publicized through journalistic accounts of the present war with the French (*Spectator,* no. 165, 8 Sept. 1711); hence this marriage too is figuratively located in an international state of nature fallen into war. Lady Mary quickly makes the absoluteness of pin money look like peanuts. She tells Sir John how to run his business, redecorates his entire house, replaces his servants by her own, raises their children as though they were exclusively hers, changes her husband's very surname, and announces that "I was no longer to consider my self as Sir *John Anvil,* but as her Husband . . ." (no. 299, 12 Feb. 1712). In short, the wife assumes the place of the husband— the world turned upside down—and takes absolute control of the family.[62]

Steele made a related effort to grapple with the challenge of married women's separate property. A correspondent whose wife is now pregnant with their fifth child begs Mr. Spectator to persuade him that she will not "be delivered of something as monstrous as any thing that has yet appeared to the World; for they say the Child is to bear a Resemblance of what is desired by the Mother."[63] This is not the first time the letter writer has had such concerns. During each of her previous pregnancies, his wife's "Fancy" has been so "exorbitant" as to take in not just "Eatables and Drinkables" but "Equipage and Furniture, and the like Extravagancies." Fearful that her irrational wishes will transform his children into monsters, her husband has undertaken to fulfill all these desires by purchasing their objects, on the unstated theory that if the wish is answered, its force will be spent. However, he begins now to lose patience and wonders "if there be any way to come at these wild unaccountable Rovings of Imagination by Reason and Argument . . ." (*Spectator,* no. 326, 14 Mar. 1712).

How is this related to the problem of separate property? Like Lady Mary Anvil, this wife threatens to take over the family. Her power lies in, not external, but (as it were) the "internal property" of her imagination, rendered fungible by her husband's understanding that its sway will be neutralized if he buys her anything she wants. It is as though a marriage settlement stipulating the provision of separate property has been internalized within her mind—which is what her husband implies when he complains that "[t]his exceeds the Grievance of Pin-Money; and I think in every Settlement there ought to be a Clause inserted, that the Father should be answerable for the Longings of his Daughter" (*Spectator*, no. 326, 14 Mar. 1712). The old folk superstition is refurbished to explain a modern system of demand and supply. The figure of the wife allegorizes the emergent type of the woman of leisure and her double "property": imaginative desire born of unwonted passivity, and its fulfillment through material expenditure and consumption. And the relation of private to public, family to state, wife to husband, finds its most radical internalization in the intrapsychic contest between imagination and reason.

In this number, Steele associates married women's separate property with imaginative production and material consumption. In my final example, pin money is tied to writing and publication. Isaac Bickerstaff, called away on business, gives his half-sister, Jenny Distaff, the authority to write and publish that day's number of the *Tatler*. The result ambiguously enacts the consequences of women's access to the public sphere. Jenny hopes to exploit Isaac's privilege as a private man come together with other men in public—to borrow, in effect, her brother's liberty, secrecy, and property. Having been authorized to dispatch the news "with Liberty to speak it my own Way," Jenny has at her disposal "all the Papers in [her brother's] Closet, which he has left open for my Use on this Occasion." The discourse that follows pointedly assumes a female audience and pursues the special interests of women. At one point Jenny transcribes a letter from a gentleman of her acquaintance whose triviality and indolence outdo what is usually ascribed to women. She adds:

> Sure, if our Sex had the Liberty of frequenting publick Houses, and Conversations, we should put these Rivals of our Faults and Follies out of Countenance. However, we shall soon have the Pleasure of being acquainted with 'em one Way or other, for my Brother *Isaac* designs, for the Use of our Sex, to give the exact Characters of all the Chief Politicians who frequent any of the Coffee-houses from St. *James's* to the *Change* . . . . This will be of great Service for us, and I have Authority to promise an exact Journal of their Deliberations; the Publication of which I am to be allow'd for Pin-Money.

That is, women do not need access to coffeehouses if they have access to the public sphere of print, which is not only like separate property but also exchangable for it. True, shortly thereafter Jenny bungles a Latin tag rummaged from her brother's papers, and we wonder whether her promise of an exact transcription from the coffeehouses may clash with her determination to "speak it her own way." However, she turns quickly to her assignment of printing a packet of news on affairs of state "in the very Stile and Words" of her brother's coffeehouse contact, and the number ends successfully in the familiar, anonymous "male" voice of the foreign correspondent (*Tatler*, no. 10, 3 May 1709). Does this vindicate Jenny's liberty or advertise its absence? In either case, her absorption in the public sphere adumbrates (especially in contrast with her effeminized male friend) a gender reversal that Daniel Defoe makes explicit: "All Manner of Discourse among the Women, runs now upon State Affairs, War, and Government; Tattling Nonsense and Slander is Transposed to the Males, and adjourned from the *Toilet*, to the *Coffee-Houses*."[64]

Putting Asunder

The first two phases of both political and familial society concern their original establishment and their ongoing existence. The third and final phase pertains to their termination. Because marriage was held to be indissoluble, divorce was unavailable through the church courts. For those without property, desertion or elopement was the common means for achieving a de facto separation. When property was an issue, wife sale gave some among the lower orders a public and highly ritualized method of legitimating its transfer within the community (if not also in the courts).[65] The ostentatiously mercenary motive linked plebeian wife sale and patrician arranged marriage in the minds of many; both might be called "Smithfield bargains" (in which the wife is thrown in on what is an essentially financial deal). But although the elaborate symbolism of the wife sale was fully compatible with the ethic of authoritarian absolutism that pervaded parental arrangements, in fact the ritual presumed the consent of all three of the principal parties involved.[66] Traditionally the church courts granted separation "from bed and hearth" (*a mensa et thoro*) in the case of adultery or extreme cruelty, and without permission to remarry. The general decline of the church courts toward the end of the seventeenth century brought with it a decline in the prosecution of adultery. By extending the action of trespass to include civil suits involving the seduction of—"criminal conversation" with—other men's wives, the common-law courts in some sense took over this moral function, but with no clear effect on the incidence of legal separations. However, successful "crim. con." prosecutions played a role in facilitating the first legal divorces in England, those by private act of Parliament, which carried permission to remarry.[67]

Although the first such act dates from 1552, the pattern was really established after the Restoration. The socioeconomic profile of those who obtained parliamentary divorce was quite sharply defined, since apart from some suits in the 1690s, its exclusive object was "the preservation of the patrilineal descent of property in the legitimate male blood line." For this reason, its early development is closely tied to the public politics of the later seventeenth century, the familial crisis of the royal house of Stuart. In 1670 Parliament granted Lord Roos permission to remarry (and hence de facto to divorce) in order to produce a legitimate male heir. Charles II supported the bill—he was said to have attended sessions in the House of Lords incognito, judging the proceedings "better than a play"—because he was without an heir by Catherine of Braganza. His brother James, heir to the throne, was understandably opposed to the bill. From 1692 to 1700 the Duke of Norfolk brought three bills for divorce before Parliament on similar grounds, strengthening his comparatively weak case sufficiently over time for it to be finally granted in the latter year.[68] An anonymous satire written in the wake of the first attempt made clear the analogy between private and public "divorce," between the Norfolk suit and the epochal deposal of King James II four years earlier. In this poetic fiction the Whig John Tillotson, archbishop of Canterbury, addresses the Whig Gilbert Burnet, bishop of Salisbury, on the subject of Norfolk's designs:

> A virtuous wise lord, that is troubled in mind
> How to get rid on's wife and a new portion find,
> By my pious advice a divorce has designed,
>   which nobody can deny.
> · · · · · · · · · · · · · ·
> Our master and dame[69] we shall please in the thing,
> And ourselves justify, for spouse, bishop, and king
> All used to be made with the help of a ring,
>   which nobody can deny.
> Parting kings and their crowns, abdication we call;
> For supplying full sees, we new bishops install;
> Yet both's but divorcing, when all comes to all,
>   which nobody can deny.[70]

It seems plausible that the short-term upsurge of divorce cases accepted by Parliament during the 1690s owed not only to the Norfolk case but also to the public, constitutional "divorce" of James II by his "wife" the people of England. However, many of these other cases diverged from the patrilineal purposes of Roos and Norfolk, and some were brought by commoners and women. Thereafter the number of parliamentary divorces fell again, and their socioeconomic character returned to the narrow aristocratic model.[71]

It is striking that both kinds of "divorce" were parliamentary accomplishments, privately overruling the indissolubility of public rule and publicly overruling the indissolubility of private relationships. The analogy worked in both directions. If developments in marriage law helped construe the constitutional crisis of James's deposal, the revolution of 1688 suggested how private separations might be, if not "glorious," then at least "bloodless." In fact, although marriage had always been in some quasi-literal fashion "contractual," "contractarianism" became an active force in marriage law only when the political fiction of contract theory was successfully acted out, "better than a play," in public. But supporters of the revolution were careful not to advocate current cases of parliamentary divorce in such a way as to fuel Jacobite accusations that Whiggism entailed disorder in the family. One such author argued that the proper private analogy for the public deposal of James II was not the wife's right of separation from a dangerous husband but the right of anyone to self-defense against rape or murder. The author continued: "I have heard you compare a king to a father and to a husband, and subjects to children and to a wife. These comparisons may be used in a moral sense, to press the moral duties between them. But in a strict sense, such as we are upon now, they are false." In other words, the analogy instructed how to be ethical but not political subjects. The very provocativeness of the conjunction of the Norfolk divorce case and the Glorious Revolution may have persuaded commentators to sidestep the private-public analogy it seemed to invite and to focus their attention on the merits of each case in studious separation from the others.[72]

Parliamentary divorce was deemed "private" because it was not achieved through any of the competing legal systems—canon law, common law, chancery—extant during this period. A final recourse for the termination of marriage, the private separation agreement, was "private" for much the same reason. Included in such agreements were separate maintenance contracts that by various means ensured wives financial support (and relieved husbands of their responsibility for their wives' debts) upon separation. Once again, Restoration comedy bears witness to the way state contract theory might signify and illuminate familial behavior. Thomas Southerne's Mrs. Friendall reflects upon her husband's violation of his contractual obligations: "[I]n a marry'd State, as in the Publick we tie our selves up, indeed; but to be protected in our Persons, Fortunes and Honours, by those very Laws that restrain us in other things; for few will obey, but for the Benefit they receive from the Government." John Vanbrugh's Lady Brute declares: "Why, what did I vow? I think I promised to be true to my husband. Well; and he promised to be kind to me, But he hasn't kept his word. Why then I'm absolved from mine. Aye, that seems clear to me. The argument's good between the king and the people, why not between the husband and the wife?"[73]

In these self-conscious analogies the law is conceived as a "public" instrument that transfers from the "public" realm and its coordination of "public" king and "private" subject a parallel principle for the "private" coordination of "public" husband and "private" wife. Separation agreements flourished increasingly during the Restoration and the early eighteenth century. By the end of the century, however, their success had generated a judicial backlash that protested the implications of their logic for the marriage institution itself.74 How can husband and wife contract to separate from each other if the wife is not a legally separate person and if marriage is indissoluble? Contractual separation contradicts the unique contractualism of marriage. When Lord Chancellor Eldon enunciated these principles in 1805, he also alluded to the analogous public stakes—the stakes for "the great family of the public"—of this seemingly private innovation:

> Independent of the effect of the contract of marriage itself, the rule upon the policy of the law is, that the contract shall be indissoluble, even by the sentence of the law . . . . [P]eople should understand that they should not enter into these fluctuating contracts: and, after that sacred contract they should feel it to be their mutual interest to improve their tempers. . . . It is admitted every where, that by the known law, founded upon policy, for the sake of keeping together individual families, constituting the great family of the public, there shall be no separation *a mensa & thoro*, except *propter saevitiam aut adulterium* [except for cruelty or adultery].75

However, the dialectical dynamic of the analogy between the family and the state can be felt in the fact that by the end of the eighteenth century, yet before the French Revolution had resensitized the minds of English people to the fragility of "the great family of the public," the very "privacy" of the marriage contract seemed to argue against the intrusions of public law. "Adultery ceased to be a part of the history of cuckoldry and became a domestic tragedy, less a matter for public scorn (though that was still there) and more a part of private pain." Preparatory to refusing action on a separate maintenance contract, Justice Francis Buller remarked in 1788 that "[d]issensions existing between man and wife are in all events very unfortunate: when they become the subject of consideration to third persons, they are very unpleasant, and if the case requires that the conduct of each party should be commented upon in public, it is a most painful task to those whose lot it falls to judge on them." By this emergent way of thinking, the radical "privacy" of marriage contradicts its analogous relation to "public" state sovereignty even though one mediatory aim of the "public" law had been precisely the protection of "private" conjugal interests.76 Moreover, public disclosure, whether of arcane secrets or of private intimacies, is again suggestively expressed by recourse to the detachment of the "third person."77

There remains one other, drastic means by which the separation of husband and wife might come about: the death of the husband. If accomplished by his wife, this amounted not simply to murder but to the crime of "petit treason" in the "petit commonwealth" of the family. If not (and in any case), the death of the husband transformed the wife into a widow, restoring to her the legal personality of the *feme sole,* which had been sacrificed through marriage. Widowed gentlewomen gained control over their jointures. Widows of the middling sort, whose husbands had been merchants or businessmen, often carried on their husbands' trades and became, collectively, a significant factor in business activity, especially in London.[78] A crucial difference between the ways Dryden and Butler figure the courtship of England during the Interregnum is that by imagining the nation as a widow Butler allows her the absolute possession of her own property, giving her a power of active resistance to all suits that seem to threaten her self-interest.[79] And if political crisis could be figured as widowhood, widowhood might be figured in turn as political crisis—or triumph. William Cavendish, Duke of Newcastle, concludes a play with its widowed protagonist, Lady Haughty, explaining why "I am resolved never to marry" by describing the sort of ideal she would find acceptable:

> *Till such a man I find I'le sit alone,*
> *And triumph in the liberty I owne:*
> *I ne're will wear a matrimonial Chain,*
> *But safe and quiet in this Throne remain,*
> *And absolute Monarch o're my self will raign.*[80]

Tory Feminism and the Devolution of Absolutism

William Cavendish uses the public figure of the absolute monarch to signify the negative liberty of the private widow, who has been freed from the chains of marriage. The image cannot fail to recall the trope that has recurred through much of this inquiry into the modern relation of the public and the private, the devolution of absolutism. To conceive royal absolutism as "downwardly mobile" is to imagine its detachability from royalty as such, the paradoxical separation out of a concept of integrity, autonomy, and autotelic self-sufficiency from its essential and inseparable public embodiment. Absolutist doctrines like patriarchalism and divine right were unstable compounds because they tried to promulgate explicitly what could be sustained only by tacit custom.[81] "Absolutist theory wrenched the idea of hierarchy from its context in the nature of things and made it a matter of the prince's will." Like public-sphere practice, the detachment and reapplication of absolutism has the doubleness of parody, composed as it is of both imitation and criticism. In the words of Anthony Ascham, "[T]hey who fight to free themselves from an absolute power, are by that obliged for the time to take upon them the absolutest."[82]

Ascham's maxim suggests the state of affairs in which absoluteness becomes relative, a property of each member in turn of the great hierarchy of super- and subordination. Cavendish's usage implies several such relative absolutes: that of the family freed from its serviceable signification of the state; that of the widow freed from legal coverture; but also that of the "self," its freedom paradoxically intimated by the subjecthood of self-subjection, by the liberation entailed in the reflexive separation out of private self from public self. At this lowly rung of the hierarchy the devolution of absolutism becomes instrumental in disclosing interior realms of autonomy and privacy, the secret precincts of the self. One powerful impetus for this excavation of interiority, we have seen, was the Protestant development of casuistry and the idea of the absolute liberty of conscience—of thoughts if not speech or actions. Mary Astell's use of the public figure of absolutism to signify a more private condition clearly depends on this Protestant development:

> The Men therefore may still enjoy their Prerogatives for us, we mean not to intrench on any of their Lawful Privileges;[83] our only contention shall be that they may not outdo us in promoting his glory who is lord both of them and us; and by all that appears the generality will not oppose us in this matter, we shall not provoke them by striving to be better Christians. They may busy their Heads with Affairs of State, and spend their Time and Strength in recommending themselves to an uncertain Master, or a more giddy Multitude, our only endeavour shall be to be absolute Monarchs in our own Bosoms. They shall still if they please dispute about Religion, let 'em give us leave to Understand and Practise it.

Astell's usage posits a species of autonomous privacy, not for widows enjoying a negative freedom from the rule of their husbands, but for women in general in a man's world, utterly deprived as they are of direct access to the public realm. Chudleigh's Melissa follows suit:

> Your's be the Fame, the Profit, and the Praise;
> We'll neither Rob you of your Vines, nor Bays:
> Nor will we to Dominion once aspire;
> You shall be Chief, and still your selves admire.
> The Tyrant Man may still possess the Throne;
> 'Tis in our Minds that we wou'd Rule alone:
> Those unseen Empires give us leave to sway,
> And to our Reason private Homage pay . . . .

For neither woman does the possession of an absolute privacy of mind or bosom result from the removal of a constraint (like marriage) that has hitherto deprived her of her freedom. It results from the insight that the state of privation can help identify for excavation that interior, "unseen" realm of privacy that lies beyond its jurisdiction.[84]

The devolution of absolutism was, as we have seen, an uneven development whose course, progress, and coloring varied according to a broad range of factors. Supremely sensitive to the relativizing instability of the contemporary political terrain, the royalist Dryden knew its hold on the political imagination. Addressing King Boabdelin, Dryden's Almanzor is content to let others render unto Caesar his due deference:

> Obey'd as Sovereign by thy Subjects be,
> But know, that I alone am King of me.[85]

Almanzor's implication, like Lady Haughty's, is that to be free of subjection to another is to be subject to oneself. Dryden articulated another, more fully privatized sense of the devolution of absolutism, we may recall, when he was deprived of public subjecthood after his conversion to Roman Catholicism: "Conscience is the royalty and prerogative of every private man. He is absolute in his own breast, and accountable to no earthly power, for that which passes only betwixt God and him." As a Catholic convert living in a Protestant nation, Dryden experienced the extreme degree of external deprivation that was for Englishwomen a congenital condition, and it evidently deepened his sense of privacy as a virtual space hollowed out from within. But the congenital experience of Englishwomen was by no means uniform. Astell and Chudleigh find in their public privation something like the cautious elation of integrity. But for Dorothy Osborne, the reflexivity of self is absorbed by the pall of civil war, and the potential of private agency is demoralized by a public privation that seems universal. Very different kinds of public privation might encourage the apprehension of a private inwardness. For Shaftesbury it is the way publication, by deforming personality, incites self-study. For John Dennis it is the expropriating powers of plagiarism and the immaterial endurance, beyond all theft, of cognition itself: "I have often been inclined to think that a man had absolute property in his thoughts and inventions alone. My thoughts are unalterably and unalienably mine, and never can be another's."[86]

William Cavendish's wife, Margaret, applied the figure of the absolute monarch to herself most directly in order to describe the adolescent experience of "making the World my Book . . . . I found the World too difficult to be understood by my tender yeers, and weak capacity, that till the time I was married, I could onely read the letters, and joyn the words, but understood nothing of the sense of the World, until my Lord, who was learned by experience, as my Master, instructed me. . . . Thus my minde is become an absolute Monark, ruling alone, my thoughts as a peaceable Common-wealth . . . ." The well-known obscurity of Cavendish's writing has something to do with her ambition to use language literally and figuratively in the same breath, an ambition that makes the movement of royal absolutism as it devolves to its "subject" unusually hard to follow. Here the privation that prefigures the private rule of mind over thoughts would seem to be the condition of youthful innocence and ignorance, not ostensibly gendered unless aggravated by Cavendish's sex and requiring special pedagogic intervention by "my Lord" and "Master." In another passage, Cavendish describes with exceptional force the civil deprivation of English-women at large, then strikingly shifts her ground:

> And as for the matter of Governments, we Women understand them not; yet if we did, we are excluded from intermeddling therewith, and almost from being subject thereto; we are not tied, nor bound to State or Crown; we are free, not Sworn to Allegiance, nor do we take the Oath of Supremacy; we are not made Citizens of the Commonwealth, we hold no Offices, nor bear we any Authority therein; we are accounted neither Useful in Peace, nor Serviceable in War; and if we be not Citizens in the Commonwealth, I know no reason we should be Subjects to the Commonwealth: and the truth is, we are no Subjects, unless it be to our Husbands, and not alwayes to them, for sometimes we usurp their Authority, or else by flattery get their good wills to govern; but if Nature had not befriended us with Beauty, and other good Graces, to help us to insinuate our selves into men's Affections, we should have been more inslaved than any other of Natur's Creatures she hath made; but Nature be thank'd, she hath been so bountiful to us, as we oftener inslave men, than men inslave us; they seem to govern the world, but we really govern the world, in that we govern men . . . . [W]e govern as it were by an insensible power, so as men perceive not how they are Led, Guided, and Rul'd by the Feminine Sex.[87]

Sounding less like her husband than like Astell and Chudleigh, Cavendish associates female deprivation, not with the institution of marriage, but with civil life as such. To be an Englishwoman is to be so thoroughly bereft of public personality as to be deprived of the status of the civil and ecclesiastical subject. More strikingly than those other women, however, Cavendish suggests how the wholesale deprivation of women in the polity makes it possible to imagine a different kind of subjecthood, one not of the political but of the ethical subject. In Cavendish's analysis, the utter "privacy" customarily experienced by women—the sheer privation of political community and its positive freedom—is the key to the modern ethos of privacy as negative freedom: "We are not tied nor bound to state or crown; we are free."

But at this crucial point, Cavendish abruptly redirects her attention from the state to the family. Rather than attempting to describe in direct terms the contents of the space enclosed by the negative freedom of women in the polity (as the autonomous realm of thought and invention, for example, or as the capacity for self-subjection), Cavendish qualifies her denial ("we are no Subjects") by acknowledging that wives are subjects to their husbands. Is this a positive or a negative freedom? a political or an ethical subjecthood? On the one hand, Cavendish says, the natural inequality of the sexes might have made their relationship one of absolute master and slave (the sort of relationship the absolute monarchy of William's widow, Lady Haughty, avoids). On the other hand, the natural difference between the sexes, which gives women access to the inner "Affections" of men, ameliorates the master-slave relationship by making it figurative and dialectical: the sexual attractions of women "inslave" men more than men enslave women. Nor can this be a merely metaphorical "power," grounded as it is in the physicality of sexual difference. Addressing the sexual relations between wife and husband, the Puritan divine William Gouge argued that the usual conditions of inferiority and subjection were here suspended: "There may not only be a fellowship, but also an equality in some things betwixt those that in other things are one of them inferiour and subject: as betwixt man and wife in the power of one another['s] bodies: *for the wife* (as well as the husband) is therein *both a seruant, and a mistress, a seruant to yeeld her body, a mistresse to haue the power of his.*"[88] Like ethics but in a different way, sex levels the playing field.

Cavendish's apparent recourse to the weary Petrarchan conceits of the male poets, or to what may seem to us the unsatisfying trope of the woman behind the man, should not blind us to the way the condition of conjugal subjecthood, rather than diverting us from the inquiry into the negative freedom of the ethical subject, instead offers something like an experimental theater of operations. Cavendish's move to the figurative level of subjection acknowledges the crucial element of difference that informs the patriarchalist analogy, the difference between the monarch and the husband, which turns on the (natural) difference between men and women. Deprivation in the polity affords a radical freedom from subjection that finds its nearest expression in the mutuality of marriage. Marriage provides a metaphorical figure for absolute rule that opens up the interior territory of the ethical, where power ceases to be merely physical and physicality ceases to be merely a matter of strength, where the literally disempowered acquire strategic volition and the ability, in Cavendish's self-consciously conjectural phrase, to "govern as it were by an insensible power." For a moment the little commonwealth of marriage looks, not like a microversion of the polity, but, for women at least, like its utopian form, a social arrangement that conduces to the sort of virtual privacy that Astell and Chudleigh conceive only in the privation of civil life. More broadly, the devolution of absolutism is shared by all three women as an experience of extreme virtualization and interiorization, a transit from the actual privations of public absolutism to the innermost privacy of mind, breast, affections, and sexuality, a transit from subject-hood to something like "subjectivity." Astell's remarks on the psychological re-wards of arbitrary subjection are relevant here:

> There is not a surer Sign of a noble Mind, a Mind very far advanc'd towards perfec-tion, than the being able to bear Contempt and an unjust Treatment from one's Su-periors evenly and patiently. For inward Worth and Real Excellency are the true Ground of Superiority . . . . And when a Superior does a Mean and unjust Thing, . . . and yet this does not provoke his Inferiors to refuse that Observance which their Sta-tions in the World require, they cannot but have an inward Sense of their own real Superiority, the other having no pretence to it, at the same time that they pay him an outward Respect and Deference . . . .[89]

In the space between outward injustice and inward self-justification flowers the interiorized absolute of the ethical subject.

The specificity of this experience as a gendered phenomenon is crucial. Chudleigh's "sway over unseen empires," Cavendish's "government by insensi-ble powers," Astell's "inward sense of superiority"—in its devolution to women absolutism manifests itself in a peculiarly immaterial, interior, metaphorical, virtual, and ethical form because in their sociocultural existence women are de-prived of the potential for that material and actual sufficiency on which the movement from necessity to freedom is predicated and through which the de-volution of absolutism might be registered. For men as a group, the experience of taking on some portion of the absolute sovereignty that had tacitly accrued to the monarch alone might assume the form of augmented political authority, economic ownership, or social entitlement. For women as a group (if also for particular men under special constraint or with special insight, like Dryden, Shaftesbury, and Dennis), the explicitation and dissemination of absolutism could only be experienced—and therefore was able to be experienced—in the subjective dimension. As crucial as this gendered specificity may be, however, it is equally crucial that we recognize its generality, that is, the way the "female" experience of the interior absolute participates in the broader and ungendered process of absolutist devolution before it is separated out as a distinctively "fem-inine" quality.[90]

As we know, feminine subjectivity becomes a fundamental outpost of the realm of privacy in modern thinking. The importance of attending to its "pre-history," before it can be said to be definitively gendered, is related to the im-portance of the phenomenon that has come to be called "Tory feminism."[91] Why did the first generation of women writers to define what looks to us like a protofeminist position on the political rights of women subscribe not to "Whig" contractualist tenets but to the "Tory" principles of divine right, patri-

archalism, and royal absolutism? Tory feminism seems counterintuitive because
the basic feminist premise that women possess political rights would seem to require a model of political relations, like the contractarian model, that acknowledges the volitional agency of civil subjects. Why would women who rejected
this way of thinking about the polity have been the ones who first began thinking in this way about the status of women?

Contemporaries understood, as we tend not to, that seventeenth-century
contractarian political theory had no particular implications for the political
status of women. There were two reasons for this. First, the contract by which
the state of nature is abolished and the political state is first separated out from
civil society was understood to have been preceded by the marriage contracts
that had obtained in the state of nature and that persist in civil society. Speaking of "the Natural State of Mankind" before the Fall, the contractarian James
Tyrrell wrote that "all the Authority that can be suppos'd could have been then
necessary for the Good and Happiness of Mankind, would have been no more
than that of the Husband over his Wife, or that of Parents over their Children,
the former of which would not have been an Absolute Coercive power neither . . . ." Tyrell was on firm ground. Samuel Pufendorf, with Grotius the natural-law theorist most frequently invoked by contemporaries, wrote that "*Fathers of Families,* who being the chief Rulers before the Institution of Publick
Governments, brought into such Governments the Power which they before
held over their Wives, their Children, and their Servants. So that this Inequality being more Ancient than the Erection of Civil Society, can by no means owe
its Original to them; nor do they [public governments] give this Power to the
Fathers of Families, but leave it in their Hands as they found it."[92]

Canny opponents of contractarian thinking parodied it by pursuing its logic
in a direction that looks feminist but really presupposes the tacit knowledge
that the marriage contract preempts all political contracts. In the words of the
Jacobite George Hickes,

> They cannot tell us upon this hypothesis, whether the supreme Power belongs to all
> the people promiscuously, that have the use of reason, without any regard to Sex or
> condition, or onely to qualified persons, to Men onely, and men of such a condition
> and sort. If men only have a share and interest in the supreme Power, by whose or-
> der and authority, or by what Salique law of Nature were Women excluded from it,
> who are as usefull members of the Commonwealth, and as necessary for humane so-
> cieties as the men are? Who gave the men authority to deprive them of their
> birthright, and set them aside as unfit to meddle with Government; when Histories
> teach us they have wielded Scepters, as well as Men, and Experience shews, that
> there is no natural difference between their understandings and ours, nor any defects
> in their knowledge of things, but what Education makes[?]

The plausibility of Hickes's argument is meant to show readers, not the difficult questions raised by contractarian thought, but the way its erroneous premises conduce to the absurdity involved in questioning the authority for women's deprivation. Similarly, the wit of John Arbuthnot's "Doctrine of the original Right of Cuckoldom" depends at bottom on the conviction that with respect to original rights, at least, the marriage contract and the civil contract have nothing in common. "[O]ne day looking over his Cabinet," John Bull finds a paper in which his wife has laid out her principles: "It is evident that Matrimony is founded upon an original Contract, whereby the Wife makes over the Right she has by the Law of Nature to the *Concubitus vagus* [inconstant copulation], in favour of the Husband, by which he acquires the Property of all her Posterity; but then the Obligation is mutual: And where the Contract is broken on one side, it ceases to bind on the other; where there is a Right, there must be a Power to maintain it, and to punish the offending Party. This Power I affirm to be that Original Right, or rather that indispensable Duty of Cuckoldom, lodg'd in all Wives . . . ."[93]

However, contractarianism was irrelevant to the rights of women not simply because marriage precedes polity but more fundamentally because women were deemed naturally inferior to men. The contractarian view of the state of nature as one of political equality did not suppose that people were physically and mentally equal. Women voluntarily entered into subjection to men through marriage contracts, it was thought, because they recognized that it was in their interests to receive the protection that marriage afforded. Like all women, most men were naturally inferior to the best of men, whose physical and mental superiority was naturally sustained by the laws of heredity and socially acknowledged by noble or gentle status. Early modern contract theory used the possession or non-possession of property as a standard by which to exclude the majority of men from full political rights. Like women who consented to the marriage contract, inferior men were understood by contractarians to enter the state of subjection entailed in the political contract on rational grounds, for their own protection. The dependence of women (in marriage) and men (in the polity) was both the sign of their inferiority and the justification for their subjection to superior men. This understanding sheds light on Steele's and Addison's means of expressing their extreme discomfort with jointures and pin money—by associating them with a natural-law state of war. Similarly (although without the public metaphor), John Trenchard thought that the present trend toward large marriage settlements "inverted the very ends of marriage, and made wives independent on their husbands, and sons on their fathers. . . ."[94]

The irrelevance of political contract theory to the status of women may help explain what is wrong with our assumption that "the first feminists" are likely to have been Whigs; but it leaves unanswered the question why they should have been Tories, or rather, why they should have been female Tories, for to pose the question in this way goes some distance toward answering it. What distinguishes Cavendish, Astell, Behn, and Manley from Hickes, who shows himself to be as capable as they at reflecting critically on the subjection of women?[95] None of these writers affirm the rights of women with the direct and unambiguous commitment to principle we expect of feminist advocacy. But whereas Hickes is pointedly parodic in his critique, the obliquity we sense in the others is a matter less of strategic rhetorical purpose than of deep-seated ambivalence, an unwillingness to pursue the issue to its end because of a conflict in principles so deep as to be inexpressible in its own terms and available to us only through a mixed tone of muffled bitterness, passionate regret, and open-ended irony. What distinguishes Hickes from the others is the fact that he is a man, hence lacking the chronic experiential basis for their division of mind between the outrage and the prudence of having to seek public protection from others. But since the necessity of public constraints may also mother the invention of unknown private freedoms, this division of mind was accompanied by one between the obvious losses and the secret gains entailed in being deprived of those (external) freedoms over which external authority has some control. As the denial of positive liberty can provide the ground on which negative liberty is nurtured, so the material inconsequence of thoughts compared to speech and action may be the precondition for the modern excavation of immateriality—of conscience, consciousness, and the unconscious.

What unites these women with Hickes is their dedication to a vision of social hierarchy at a time when the traditional stratification of society is beginning to sustain a rational and pragmatic inquiry from which it will not recover. As "Tories," the Tory feminists are comparatively sensitive to what is lost when the inequalities between people—the natural hierarchy of inferiority and superiority that is socially marked by the degrees of status and by the differential of subordination and superordination—cease to organize the kinds of relationship they possess in the social fabric. But as women, the Tory feminists are also sensitive to the way the sexual is being separated out from the social at this time, disembedded from the broad homogeneity of social status as that singular criterion of natural difference that needs to be not simply preserved but acknowledged as a fundamental determinant of personality. This is a gradual process whose full effects cannot begin to be felt in the half-century, from the Restoration to the ascendancy of the Hanoverians, that defines the long generation of Tory feminism. However, even toward the end of this period contemporaries were experimenting with the notion not only that the natural standard of blood was a defective social discriminant but also that the natural standard of sexual difference could not be ignored. Common men who bridled at their customary subjection could take comfort and courage from the ongoing demystification of the social maxim that birth equals worth. But even as the criterion of the natural was being explicitated and expelled from social doctrine, it was being insinuated into sexual doctrine. Both of these developments were consistent with a growing skepticism about the utility and propriety of conceiving the human order as a hierarchy of the better and the worse. The belief that birth equals worth, on the decline, justified inequality, but the belief that sex is biologically determined, on the rise, replaced inequality by the purportedly neutral judgment of natural difference. And yet the coming of the idea of natural sexual difference had fundamental and unforeseen consequences for the future.[96]

Privacy and Pastoral

The relationship between the public and the private has always been an aspect of pastoral poetry. Still, there may be some use in supposing, in early modern pastoral, a revaluation of the public-private distinction parallel to developments we already have seen in other kinds of early modern discourse. Especially for eighteenth-century writers, the *beatus ille* of Horace's second epode was the *locus classicus* for conceiving the distinction as a palpable process, a retreat from city to country undertakable by a single person.[97] Is it plausible to see the seventeenth and eighteenth centuries as a period in which writers consolidated the idea of pastoral retreat as an active agency, not the passive "privation" of merely private existence—the simplicity of a subsistence-level innocence—but the negative liberty of a chosen solitude? Certainly the active agency of pastoral retreat quickly becomes a commonplace in poetry of this period, sometimes in association with a woman's, perhaps even a wife's, innermost desires. Anne Finch provides an especially telling example because she also conceives her retreat as "absolute":

> Give me O indulgent Fate!
> Give me yet, before I Dye,
> A sweet, but absolute Retreat,
> 'Mongst Paths so lost, and Trees so high,
> That the World may ne'er invade,
> Through such Windings and such Shade,
> My unshaken Liberty.

There is, moreover, a public dimension to this private idyll. Although Finch's speaker would enjoy her retreat with a "*Partner,*" she imagines as filling this role not her husband but the female friend to whom she dedicates her poem. The love of the friend Finch links not only to her speaker's absolute private retreat but also to her deliverance from the "Dark Oblivion" caused by the public fall and exile of the absolutist James II, whose loyal followers included Finch and her husband.[98]

On the verge of elopement, the young Mary Pierrepont had figured her secret marriage as a private pastoral retreat from "the world"—more specifically, from the absolutism of her father's mercenary marriage plans. Toward the end of her life, and long since separated from Edward, Mary was pleased to revalue this figure so that not marriage but singleness became the precondition for the "Solitude" of Horatian "retreat." Living like a *feme sole* at her Italian villa, Mary evinces the "improvement" both of herself and of her country estate. Her pastoralism now entails the highly georgic virtues of industry and productivity that flourish in the absence of external interference: "I have been this six weeks, and still am, at my Dairy house, which joins to my Garden, . . . I have fitted up in this farm house a room for my selfe . . . . My Garden was a plain Vineyard when it came into my hands not two years ago, and it is with a small expence turn'd into a Garden that . . . I like better than that of Kensington. . . . All things have hitherto prosper'd under my Care. My Bees and silk worms are double'd, and I am told that, without accidents, my Capital will be so in two years time." Under such conditions, the privacy of domestic retirement merges with that of absolute private property. In the terms of Habermas, the intimacy of the human being per se, "apparently set free from the constraint of society, [is] the seal on the truth of a private autonomy exercized in competition."[99]

Natural-law theories of the origins of culture were influenced inevitably by ancient pastoral traditions of the golden age and the Garden of Eden, which in their own way also addressed the question how—and by what authority—the state came to be separated out from civil society. In Aphra Behn's primarily classical version, natural liberty is sexual love, at first unfettered but then subjected to the harsh laws of "Tyrant Honour," which teach women to replace the immediacy of desire by the fatal indirection of "coy disdain":

> Those Fopperies of the Gown were then not known,
> Those vain those Politick Curbs to keep man in,
> Who by a fond mistake Created that a Sin;
> Which freeborn we, by right of Nature claim our own.
>
> . . . .
>
> Oh cursed Honour! thou who first didst damn,
> A Woman to the Sin of shame;
> Honour! that rob'st us of our Gust,
> Honour! that hindred mankind first,
> At Loves Eternal Spring to squench his amorous thirst.

The earnestness of Behn's implicit address to a female audience gives her pastoral libertinism a powerful candor—until we find at the end of the poem that the speaker is gendered male and that the sincerity of his words is complicated by the witty deviousness of his *carpe diem* motive ("Then let us *Sylvia* yet be wise, / And the Gay hasty minutes prize"). What we took to be natural discourse turns out always to have been mere convention.[100]

Mary Leapor's revision of Christian pastoralism, "Man the Monarch," is also a revision of patriarchalist theory:

> Amazed we read of Nature's early throes,
> How the fair heavens and ponderous earth arose;
> How blooming trees unplanted first began;
> And beasts submissive to their tyrant, man:
> To man, invested with despotic sway,
> While his mute brethren tremble and obey;
> Till heaven beheld him insolently vain,
> And checked the limits of his haughty reign.

Evidently "Tyrant man" is generic, his "check" the Eve-induced Fall; but neither assumption proves to be correct. Heaven limits man's sway by giving the animals the power to evade "his fruitless rage": "But where! ah, where shall helpless woman fly?" Nature's "favourite," woman is created beautiful but vulnerable. Nature

> Beholds a wretch, whom she designed a queen,
> And weeps that e'er she formed the weak machine.

And at this point the speaker reveals that she is passing on to us one of those anonymous and dubious old wives' tales:

> A tattling dame, no matter where or who—
> Me it concerns not, and it need not you—
> Once told this story . . . .

This is history from below, a countermyth to set against the official and male version of what happened in Eden: the Fall is not general but female, occasioned not by female curiosity but by Adam's jealousy.

> He viewed his consort with an envious eye;
> Greedy of power, he hugged the tottering throne,
> Pleased with the homage, and would reign alone;
> And, better to secure his doubtful rule,
> Rolled his wise eyeballs, and pronounced her *fool.*
> The regal blood to distant ages runs:
> Sires, brothers, husbands, and commanding sons,

> The sceptre claim; and every cottage brings
> A long succession of domestic kings.

Leapor unfolds the implications of Tyrrell's contractarian view of marriage as a prelapsarian institution. Patriarchal right is a natural aberration of nature, the artifice of tyranny; domestic privacy is grounded in a pristine political usurpation.[101]

This radical sort of revision attacks not so much the analogy between the family and the state, between private and public life, as its specifically patriarchalist application, whereby the role of wives is understood to be a kind of political subjection. Natural-law theory authorized an alternative to domestic absolutism, not to domestic politics as such. But because the terms of the patriarchalist model were those in which the analogy itself first became openly available for reflection, they often provided the basis for alternative experiments. Joseph Addison attempted several such experiments; one takes the form of genial mock heroic. The indulgent "Philogamus" writes in to praise Mr. Spectator for having "drawn so many agreeable Pictures of Marriage," and he goes on to claim that "I look upon my Family as a Patriarchal Sovereignty, in which I am my self both King and Priest." For Philogamus, the simile is a droll hyperbole, emphasizing affective distance as much as structural similarity. When he tells Mr. Spectator that he "take[s] great pleasure in the Administration of my Government in particular," he means that he goes so far as to "Review" "my little Troop" of children from time to time (*Spectator*, no. 500, 3 Oct. 1712).

In another paper, Addison uses the resonant archaism of the "little commonwealth" to describe the solitude of a conjugal pastoral retreat:

> *Aurelia*, tho' a Woman of Great Quality, delights in the Privacy of a Country Life, and passes away a great part of her Time in her own Walks and Gardens. Her Husband, who is her Bosom Friend, and Companion in her Solitudes, has been in Love with her ever since he knew her. . . . Their Family is under so regular an Oeconomy, in its Hours of Devotion and Repast, Employment and Diversion, that it looks like a little Common-Wealth within it self. They often go into Company, that they may return with the greater Delight to one another; and sometimes live in Town not to enjoy it so properly as to grow weary of it, that they may renew in themselves the Relish of a Country Life.

Addison's coordination of pastoral with patriarchalist associations has a complex effect. By emphasizing the public-private register of pastoral opposition—country life as the negative liberty of a chosen solitude—he encourages us to consider the little commonwealth in a similar light. To choose the country over the town is like choosing the little over the great commonwealth. Yet the happiness of both choices depends on a sense of having preserved in each—of having internalized—the positive essence of what has been left behind. Pastoral *otium* incorporates a pleasing georgic *negotium*. The private family, structured by mutuality rather than sovereignty, yet runs on the highly regulated rhythms of a thriving public polity. Modeled on the great world, an emergent domesticity combines the best of both worlds. Fulvia, Aurelia's urbane antithesis, sees domesticity as sheer privation, "looks upon Discretion, and good House-Wifery, as little domestick Virtues, . . . [and] thinks Life lost in her own Family, and fancies her self out of the World . . . ." For Aurelia, domesticity has the dignity and consequence of a little world made cunningly (*Spectator,* no. 15, 17 Mar. 1711).

Addison's portrait of country life and its industrious employment finds an idealized public realm encapsulated within the private. In the eighteenth century, the new science of political economy projected a positively revalued domesticity outward, from the rural country to the country of Britain. This movement might also be described as a kind of "macropastoralism," in which the realm of the domestic defines, now on an international scale, the normative center of things.[102] According to Adam Smith, "[E]very individual endeavours to employ his capital as near home as he can, and consequently as much as he can in the support of domestick industry . . . . In the home-trade his capital is never so long out of his sight as it frequently is in the foreign trade of consumption. He can know better the character and situation of the persons whom he trusts, and if he should happen to be deceived, he knows better the laws of the country from which he must seek redress. . . . Home is in this manner the center, if I may say so, round which the capitals of the inhabitants of every country are continually circulating, and towards which they are always tending . . . ."[103] Smith's remarks remind us that our double meaning of the word "domestic" is the unobjectionable relic of the once-powerful patriarchalist analogy, reduced now to the common-sense logic of proportionality: the single "home" is to what lies beyond its bounds as the single nation is to foreign nations. Although this is no part of his own thesis, Smith might have added that in the colonialist practice of an emergent political economy the home front is also distinguished by being the only domain within which free-trade doctrine has a real application. With respect to its colonies, the domestic and metropolitan center maintains a frankly mercantilist or protectionist policy according to which the norm of natural liberty in trade is superseded by the higher law of economic control and exploitation. We may sense here a parallel with what feminist thought must see as the inconsistencies of contractarian political theory, whose norm of natural rights is superseded by the natural inferiority of women and preceded by the inequalities of the marriage contract.

The principal aim of this chapter has been to document how changes in the way the patriarchalist analogy was employed between 1650 and 1750 suggest the self-consciousness with which English people were rethinking not only the state but also marriage and the family, as well as the growing centrality, even normativity, of the "intimate sphere" that is implied by these changes. I have argued that these experiments in decoupling the patriarchalist analogy exemplify the explicitation of formerly tacit knowledge that is broadly characteristic of this period. Another great example of this historical process is what happens to the traditional and tacit relationship between, not the family and the state, but the household and the world of work. The "secret history" of domesticity is the history of that category as its separation out from the realms of political rule and economic labor constitutes it as something that is both fully precedented and, by virtue of its unprecedented separation out, something new in the history of English culture. The following two chapters aim to document how the household became the private realm of domesticity.

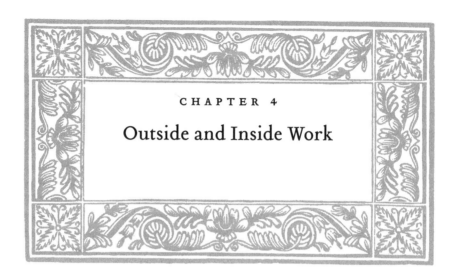

CHAPTER 4

Outside and Inside Work

The Habermasian language of the "public sphere" has a spatial resonance that is crucially metaphorical. If we inquire into the spatial distinction between the public and the private as it is construed in literal terms, however, we commonly encounter a vocabulary of outside and inside. We think of the coffeehouse as the archetypal site of public-sphere intercourse, but by the mid-eighteenth century contemporaries were mindful of the degree to which political expression and agitation that cut across differences in social status and gender could be experienced out of doors, in the open air. To some degree there is nothing new in this. Graphic depictions of collective activities often evoke and elaborate the aura of traditional social ritual, like the public execution. In figure 4.1 William Hogarth represents the confrontation between public justice and popular sentiment—between the state and the "people"—as a vast amphitheater or coliseum teeming with closely particularized plebeian responses to the entertaining and edifying spectacle of crime and punishment. Uniting these variegated spectators is the common element of distraction, whether by or from the spectacle, that places this collective scene less in the modern setting of a public sphere (despite the front-and-center mercury woman) than in the ancient tradition of bread and circuses. Figure 4.2 depicts not traditional subjection but an emergent subjecthood, not the passive consumption of public spectacle but the activism of a literalized public sphere, where a broad assortment of people, united by the common will to criticize state policies, debate the peace and a tax on consumables according to interests and idioms peculiar to their several trades. As the legend reads, "BRITANIA'S *Sons of all Conditions/Amazing! now are Politicions/. . ./Thus boldly cavil and debate/On matters that concern the ST——* . . . ." All private trades merge to form the public "trade" of politicians; the very streets have become an oppositional House of Commons. The virtuality of the public sphere—private people "come together" on public issues—is here given an actual outdoors spatialization, and the tone of voice mixes mild exasperation with genuine admiration.

These images help point a question that follows from the hypothesis that modernity is marked by a reversal in the priority, the determinant status, of the normative collective on the one hand and the individual on the other.[1] If social formation henceforth begins with the individual rather than being, as traditionally, the foundation that precedes and justifies individual activity, what does collectivity look like when, under the modern regime, it seeks to claim its own authority? It may be useful to speak of a three-part typology of mob, crowd, and public. The mob, or *vulgum mobile,* is closest to the traditional negative instance of collectivity, the merely many (cf. *hoi polloi*) undistinguished by any qualifier—except for the fact of undirected movement. The mob has the

FIG. 4.1. William Hogarth, *The Idle 'Prentice Executed at Tyburn.* Plate 11 of *Industry and Idleness,* 1747, in William Hogarth, *Hogarth: The Complete Engravings,* ed. Joseph Burke and Colin Caldwell (New York: Abrams, 1968). Princeton University Library. For complete rendering of figure text, see Plate 14.

FIG. 4.2. *The Politicians*, 1763, in John Brewer, *The Common People and Politics, 1750–1790s: The English Satirical Print, 1600–1832* (Cambridge: Chadwyck-Healey, 1986). Princeton University Library. For complete rendering of figure text, see Plate 15.

pure collectivity of actual embodied people without individual shape or agency other than the supramotivated capacity of random liquidity or flow. According to the reigning idiom, those few individuals who possess honor are "quality"; all the rest are sheer quantity deprived of all quality, whether in movement or at rest. In 1687 Aphra Behn dedicated a farce to a "Man of Quality," who would, "thro' all the humble Actions and trivialness of Business, find Nature there, and that Diversion which was not meant for the Numbers, who comprehend nothing beyond the Show and Buffoonry."[2] Especially as theorized in recent decades, notably by George Rudé and E. P. Thompson, the eighteenth-century plebeian, or popular, crowd is a more complex social formation, an agglomeration of the many qualified by a kind of active anonymity and by the sort of political instrumentality that may be called upon to address a variety of needs and occasions. Actual and embodied like the mob, the popular crowd nonetheless entails a subsistent strategic potential that exceeds any punctual purpose or empirical composition. The public (public opinion, the public interest, the public sphere, the public domain, the reading public) extends this potentiality and excess into disembodied virtuality. Unlike the mob and the crowd, the public explicitly derives its authority from the actual individuals it comprehends and supersedes. The public might be figured not as a flow or an agglomerated totality but as a quotient, a totality of qualitative subjects quantified by averaged typicality. This is the positive and normative instance of collectivity in modern life across (as we have already seen) a broad range of experience.

The typology of mob, crowd, and public names the central modes of "political" collectivity in the eighteenth century in a sequence of escalating modernity. However, to acknowledge another important mode of coming together that emerges at this time, one seemingly devoid of political meaning or purpose, we need to abandon the strict schematism of this typology. The access of eighteenth-century English people to variously inclusive places of public sociability, especially in London but also in the provinces, is familiar to scholars of the period. Streets, walks, squares, parks, assemblies, pleasure gardens—the broad development is one of increasingly heterogeneous public spaces.3 What unites these spaces is the premise of a public occasion that is indeterminate, ongoing, and officially unmotivated: the occasion of taking the air, walking the streets, bringing into and out of focus a stranger in a crowd of similarly familiarizable strangers, a crowd that momentarily embodies a public that is otherwise, and in any case, subliminally but perpetually present. In his second trip to London, at the age of twenty-three, James Boswell experienced the gestalt oscillation between figure and crowd so characteristic of the modern city, whereby antithetical values—solitude and society, anonymity and celebrity, privacy and publicity—can exchange places so quickly as to assume each other's qualities for a moment. "London," Boswell writes, "is undoubtedly a place where men and manners may be seen to the greatest advantage. . . . [T]he immense crowd and hurry and bustle of business and diversion, the great number of public places of entertainment . . . agitate, amuse, and elevate the mind. Besides, the satisfaction of pursuing whatever plan is most agreeable, without being known or looked at, is very great." Coming home at the end of a day on the town, Boswell slips contentedly into his old clothes and writes to himself in his journal. "While I can thus entertain myself, I must be happy in solitude. Indeed there is a great difference between solitude in the country, where you cannot help it, and in London, where you can in a moment be in the hurry and splendour of life." However, when he attends a magnificent rout at Northumberland

House, Boswell "felt a little awkward this night, as I scarcely knew anybody in the room. . . . I was curious to find of how little consequence each individual was in such a crowd."⁴ The bittersweet privacy of solitude is experienced nowhere so pungently as in a public crowd.

The delightful choreography of "holyday gambols" on Greenwich Hill in figure 4.3 celebrates one of those modes of public sociability that lack a political motivation, and yet the legend, which advertises an alternative to the court, the Mall, to assemblies and balls, implies a more pointedly demotic rebuke to "[y]e sweetscented Sirs." Ostensibly urged to exchange the "stale languid follies" of indoor London formality for the innocent hedonism and frankly chaotic hilarity of the suburban outdoors, these sirs, we sense, are actually confirmed in the appropriateness of spaces that are "as dull as Yourselves." The rebuke is greatly intensified in figure 4.4, where beefy butchers turn their outdoor meat stall in the Strand into a makeshift penal stocks to punish a "Pigmy . . . Fop" for presuming to assert his authority on their turf. As the legend suggests, social justice for this territorial infraction is achieved by realizing an implicit gender inversion: the status-coded effeminacy of the fop, despised by all "Women of Sense," is derided by displaying it before them in the public meat market. Figure 4.5 depicts a similar reversal. Street people transform into their own public thoroughfare the private space of a haughty lady's coach that is blocking "Free Passage" at Charing Cross. "The Lady much ruffled, soon alterd her Tone . . . ."⁵ Over a century earlier than this print, Henry Peacham claimed that sedan chairs "are places fit for privacie, or meditation, where a man may reade or studie, even in the midst of the throng, and open street . . . . By [coaches] is made a publique difference, betweene *Nobilitie,* and the *Multitude* . . . . [T]hey are . . . the moving closets of brave Ladies, and beautiful virgins, who in common sence, are unfit to walke the streets, to be justled to the kennell, by a sturdie Porter . . . ."⁶

These disparate materials suggest two generalizations about the cultural significance of spatial distinctions in eighteenth-century Britain. First, if the several social ranks experienced an unprecedented degree of public intermixing at this time, the out-of-doors was understood to be the realm of commoners—the

Fig. 4.3. (*opposite, top*) *Greenwich Hill or Holyday Gambols,* 1750, in John Brewer, *The Common People and Politics, 1750–1790s: The English Satirical Print, 1600–1832* (Cambridge: Chadwyck-Healey, 1986). Princeton University Library. For complete rendering of figure text, see Plate 16.

Fig. 4.4. (*opposite, bottom*) *The Beaux Disaster,* 1747, in John Brewer, *The Common People and Politics, 1750–1790s: The English Satirical Print, 1600–1832* (Cambridge: Chadwyck-Healey, 1986). Princeton University Library. For complete rendering of figure text, see Plate 17.

Ye ex enervated Sons who are sick of the Sport,
And the stale languid Follies of Ballroom or Court,
For a Change leave the Mall to Greenwich resort.

GREENWICH HILL
or *Holyday Gambols.*

There heighten'd with Raptures, which never can pall,
Youl own, the Delights of Assembly and Ball,
Are as dull as Yourselves, & just nothing at all.

The BEAUX DISASTER.

Ye Smarts whose Merit lies in Dress,
Take warning by a Beaux Distress,
Whose Pigmy Size & ill-turn'd Rage
Ventured with Butchers to engage.

But they unus'd Affronts to brook,
Have hung poor Fribble on a Hook,
While foul Disgrace, expos'd in Air,
The Butchers Shout, & Ladies stare.

Satyr so strong, ye Fops, must strike you
Flow can you think y Fair will like you,
Women of Sense, in Men despise
The Anticks, they in Monkeys prize.

FIG. 4.5. *Stand Coachman, or the Haughty Lady Well Fitted*, 1750, in John Brewer, *The Common People and Politics, 1750–1790s: The English Satirical Print, 1600–1832* (Cambridge: Chadwyck-Healey, 1986). Princeton University Library. For complete rendering of figure text, see Plate 18.

people, the many, the mob—and gentry who sought to impose their sense of indoor privacy, privilege, and enclosure on the openness of the outdoors were trespassers deserving of punishment by shaming.7 But second, the difference between the outdoors and the indoors was also understood to be broadly gendered. So on the matter of schematic spatial categorization, status and gender criteria cut across one another: although it would obviously go too far to say that "common sense" prohibited women from appearing outdoors, the coding of outside and inside as male and female territories had deep roots in British culture.

There are obvious complications. For one thing, if (as I have just suggested) status and gender criteria cut across one another, male commoners and female quality may seem to have experienced a consistent spatial identification with, respectively, the outdoors and the indoors, while male quality and female commoners experienced a more contradictory one. Such consistency was more notional than real. Had Margaret Cavendish, Duchess of Newcastle, ever addressed them, the rewards of aristocratic enclosure presumably would have sounded very different from her complaint that women "are kept like birds in cages to hop up and down in our houses, not suffered to fly abroad . . . ."[8] For another, since women entered into a metaphorical but deeply consequential legal "coverture" when they married, marital status divided women's spatial identification quite as fully as did social status: the term "spinster" evolved to designate nubile but unmarried women by the fact of their labor for a market that lay beyond the confines of the home.[9] Recent scholarly controversy over the domestic ideology of "separate spheres" has been fueled by these among other complications. Is the emergence of separate spheres in eighteenth-century England an optical illusion caused by the reductive abstraction of subtle and scattered tendencies—or, on the contrary, is it caused by a refusal to see that English culture has always been one of separate spheres? Even granted the eighteenth-century emergence of separate-spheres ideology as a prescriptive and hortatory discourse, what, if anything, does this tell us about social practice? And how can a tangled history of this sort be compatible with our powerful sense of a normative bond in modern culture between the female and the private?

It seems to me that a qualitative change in both ideology and practice is undeniable over the long term, but a change composed of incremental and uneven shifts that plausibly bespeak continuity as much as they do discontinuity.[10] For this reason, the domestic ideology of separate spheres may be peculiarly responsive to an analysis based on the model of an early modern shift from relations of distinction to relations of separation or division, a model of change in which the ideological explicitation of a cultural knowledge that had been tacitly embedded within social experience is both cause and consequence of a correlative division of labor. Not that material history is unequipped to tell this story; rather, the abstract narrative of the transition from feudalism to capitalism needs to be understood at each of its concrete and interlocking junctures, which include but also exceed the network of factors we allude to in the umbrella notion of an "advent of industrialization."[11] One function of domestic ideology is to reconcile the increasingly common argument for the ethical superiority of women with the persistence, perhaps even aggravation, of their socioeconomic subordination.[12]

In early-eighteenth-century periodical papers we find an increasingly common insistence on the fact of sexual difference (a subject to which I will return in chapter 6) and on its correlation with the separation of the public from the

private. Waggishly ridiculing the way fashionable women dabble in party politics, Joseph Addison finally resorts to a stern, plain style: ""Female Virtues are
of a Domestick turn. The Family is the proper Province for Private Women to
Shine in."¹³ Yet it is only now that the family, as it becomes fully separated out
from the state, can be seen not only to possess a normatively private character
but also to enclose a subtly distinctive and authentically public character, which
the conceptual entanglement of family and state inevitably had rendered incon-
ceivable.¹⁴ In order to understand how the modern revaluation of the domestic
came about, we need to recall that the ancient *oikos* had a double destiny in the
modern world: that of the household and that of the economy. Conceived in
relation to the state, the household and the economy are partners in privacy.
Conceived in relation to each other, however, the household and the economy
provide a paradigm case of the opposition between the private and the public.
We may begin to understand the deceptively simple ideology of separate
spheres, evidently emergent in Addison's words, as a function of this dialectic.¹⁵

The Domestic Economy and Cottage Industry

The domestic ideology of separate spheres spatializes an incremental and long-
term sexual division of labor—a separation out of men's and women's work—as
the mutual exclusion of "outside" and "inside" labor in terms of the dichotomy
between waged and unwaged labor. The distinction, if not the separation, was
traditional. At the beginning of the sixteenth century, economic production
was dominated by what historians have variously called the "domestic system,"
the "domestic economy," and the "family economy," a system in which the
household was the major unit of production. Attempts to generalize about how
this domestic economy was undermined in early modern England are frustrated by crucial variations in households based on differences in region and social status. Still, it can be said that in 1500 all women were also housewives, involved in production both for the subsistence of the household and for the
market. The domestic economy operated according to a schematic sexual division of labor—between female inside and male outside work—that was in
practice rather flexible and scarcely operative on smaller holdings. In such an
economy, husbands exercised the authority of the head of a household that was
organized as an integrated working relationship.¹⁶

The breakdown of the domestic economy, and the concomitant withdrawal
of women from work deemed economically productive, was most immediately
the result of agrarian capitalist innovation. The flexibility of traditional work
relations depended on customary arrangements and property use-rights that
capitalist improvement rendered unprofitable. The flourishing of absolute pri-

vate property, enclosure, and the consolidation of large estates increasingly denied to lesser farmers the subsistence conditions on which their households had depended. The loss of commons rights—not only grazing but also gathering fuel and gleaning harvest leavings—deprived women in particular of customary labor. When farmers lost access to land, their wives lost the means to keep a cow and practice dairying, a common form of women's work. As a result, outside work traditionally available to women simply disappeared at the lower social strata. At the higher social strata, increased sensitivity to price levels and market demand marginalized dairying in favor of more profitable production or transformed it into a commercial activity under the control of hired managers.[17]

The flexibility and equilibrium that were entailed in the sexual division of labor characteristic of the domestic economy can be sensed in traditional representations—and rebukes—of the breakdown of domestic gender hierarchy. This is because the instruments of women's inside and outside work played an important role in the ritualized enactment of domestic disorder. In the ritual of the skimmington ride a noisy and rowdy procession of villagers would punish a local instance of the unbalanced household by the shameful spectacle of the husband and wife, usually impersonated by neighbors, paraded on horseback, the submissive and likely cuckolded husband seated back to front, berated and beaten by the domineering scold his wife.[18] Figure 4.6 depicts "Lady Skimmington" dismounted and beating her husband with a skimming ladle. Samuel Butler's character of "The Henpect Man," taking its imagery from the skimmington, draws on the patriarchalist analogy to give weight to the enormity of this inversion: he "[r]ides behind his Wife and lets her wear the Spurs and govern the Reins. . . . When he was married he . . . changed Sexes with his Wife, . . . [who] has the Tuition of him during his or her Life; and he has no Power to do any Thing of himself, but by his Guardian. His Wife manages him and his Estate with equal Authority, and he lives under her arbitrary Government and Command as his superior Officer."[19] As Butler puts it, domestic absolutism has devolved to the wife.

Butler's account of a skimmington in *Hudibras* (1663), pt. 2, canto 2, lines 591–664, was a *locus classicus* of its graphic representation, twice illustrated by Hogarth, as well as by other artists. Figure 4.7 shows Hogarth's large illustration, in which the wife brandishes the dairy ladle while the husband meekly untwists the distaff.[20] For our immediate purposes what is interesting in these images of the woman on top is the fact that they depict, not a simple exchange of tools, but the transformation into a weapon of discord of what ordinarily signifies the normative outside authority of the housewife. One historian has suggested that the popularity of the skimmington ride in seventeenth-century

England bespeaks not a straightforward intensification of the sexual division of labor but, on the contrary, a relative increase in female outside authority through the growth of the market economy—and male misgivings about that increase. Early in the century Gervase Markham advised of the housewife's diet: "Let it proceed more from the provision of her owne yard, then the furniture of the Markets; and let it be rather esteemed for the familiar acquaintance she has with it, then for the strangenesse and varity it bringeth from other Countries." Markham's (unjustified) dovetailing of market and foreign produce reinforces the association of the housewife with the domestic on the levels of both household and nation.[21]

FIG. 4.6. *Skimmington beats her husband,* mid-seventeenth-century etching in David Underdown, *Revel, Riot, and Rebellion* (Oxford: Oxford University Press, 1985). Princeton University Library.

FIG. 4.7. William Hogarth, *Hudibras and the Skimmington*, 1726. No. 7 of twelve large illustrations for Samuel Butler's *Hudibras* (1663, 1664, 1678), in William Hogarth, *Hogarth: The Complete Engravings,* ed. Joseph Burke and Colin Caldwell (New York: Abrams, 1968). Princeton University Library.

What happened to that portion of the agrarian economy not organized through the household? Over the course of the eighteenth century there was a general decrease in the agricultural employment of women, and work patterns for men and women outside the household diverged in a number of ways. Increasingly, female employment was concentrated in spring activities like dairying and calving, while male labor was specialized in the fall harvesting of cereal crops, which required heavier technology. Especially in the latter half of the century, moreover, male real wages rose as female real wages declined. By limiting quasi-independent domestic production, capitalist improvement exerted pressure on what was increasingly understood as "the labor market" so as to throw women into competition with men. This was especially true in the fall, when the vulnerability of laborers in cereal production to structural unemployment put a premium on the availability of nonharvesting jobs. That men tended to prevail in this competition was both a cause and a consequence of developing conceptions of familial income as primarily male income.[22]

In recent years economic historians have had recourse to the category "protoindustrialization" to acknowledge the way eighteenth-century cottage industry both extended and transformed household production in the domestic economy.²³ "The obvious way of industrial expansion in the eighteenth century was not to construct factories, but to extend the so-called domestic system."²⁴ In some respects domestic manufacture seems to have favored women's work by employing higher proportions of women and children than did factories and by exploiting what were seen as female skills through a division of labor that might go so far as maintaining separate manufacturing households composed exclusively of women and children. Figure 4.8 pictures such a household of women spinning, reeling, and boiling flax, laborers for whom "productive" inside work and the reproduction of the family (thus the boy at the fire) are coextensive activities. A charge against wool spinners in 1687 complained that "many young women, healthful and strong, combine and agree to cot and live together without government, and refuse to work in time of harvest and give great occasion for lewdness." Crowds of machine wreckers that included women destroyed the larger spinning jennies that were used in factories but spared smaller ones in use at home.²⁵

SPINNING—REELING WITH THE CLOCK-REEL—BOILING YARN.

FIG. 4.8. *Spinning—Reeling with the Clock-Reel—Boiling Yarn,* early-eighteenth-century drawing. Mary Evans Picture Library.

CARDING, DRAWING, AND ROVING.

FIG. 4.9. *Carding, Drawing, and Roving,* late-eighteenth-century engraving in Edward Baines, *History of the Cotton Manufacture in Great Britain* (1835; reprint, London: Cass, 1966). Princeton University Library.

However, as the subdivision of manufacturing processes ramified labor into separate and relatively unskilled stages, women's waged labor was both augmented and "sweated": reduced skill levels led to an oversupply of labor, a lowering of wages, and a lengthening of work hours needed for subsistence. In 1775 Richard Arkwright took out a patent for a series of carding, drawing, and roving machines for preparing silk, cotton, flax, and wool for spinning. Figure 4.9 shows a room occupied by these machines in a large mill near Preston. Like the flax workers in figure 4.8, these female laborers are industriously dispersed throughout the indoor space. But the productive processes of the labor require a room too vast and heavily reinforced to be adapted from the "inside" space of the household, and the tasks performed by the women are far more partialized than those of the cottage flax workers. The derivation of factory industry from household industry also ensured that female wage scales in the factories, modeled on the hierarchical inequality of the family, would be lower than those for male laborers. In the market as in civil society, gender-based subordination was predetermined by subordination in the family.[26]

The subcontracting of labor to families that was a central feature of cottage industry went hand in hand with the decay of the guild system, which had closely regulated craft production by (among other means) effectively excluding women from many trades. Here as in other areas of civil society, the decline of state protectionism and the shift to a model of negative liberty promised a more inclusive and extensive participation, and although the guild system's gender exclusions enjoyed a vestigial persistence into the modern labor market, eighteenth-century women did gain access to the trades and to apprenticeships, although in smaller numbers and for shorter periods than did men.[27] In the seventeenth and early eighteenth centuries, changes in the demography of women —increased age at marriage, decreased incidence of marriage—created a large pool of cheap female labor that was apprenticed and employed in a wide range of trades and occupations.[28] The decrease in female employment in the latter half of the eighteenth century is closely connected to a rise in fertility, whose principal causes are, correlatively, a fall in the age of women at first marriage and a rise in the number of women who married. It seems plausible to connect these developments: "As female employment became more precarious and lowly paid, there were obvious reasons to marry younger as defense against the unemployment which was increasingly the lot of women."[29]

Unlike in other areas of civil society, the negative liberty of the expanding market met powerful resistance in the standards of positive liberty embodied (despite the "marriage market") in the family and its ongoing ethic of what might be called gender "protectionism." The systems of gender and social status, accommodated to each other under the traditional and tacit structure of hierarchy, were discomposed once the model of hierarchical subordination began to be seriously challenged in the early modern period. One case in point among many is the way the more-or-less coherent trajectory of the rise of the professions is shadowed by gender considerations. In the early seventeenth century, people were already learning to value the skills of an occupation as John Dennis later did his own mental capacity—as a portable sort of property that was more absolutely "owned" than real estate. William Perkins explained that the popular adage that "an occupation is as good as land" had substance "because land may be lost, but skill and labour in a good occupation is profitable to the end because it will help at need when land and all things fail."[30] But as the emergent category of profession became detachable from status as a quasi-autonomous possession, it also became less available to women. In the late seventeenth century, "trade tokens used by local shopkeepers and small masters carried the initials of the man and woman's first name and the couple's surname, but by the late eighteenth century only the initials of the man were retained."[31] The replacement of status by class attitudes (hence of positive by negative norms of freedom) in contemporary essays at social description is broadly correlated with the growing preference for occupational and professional categories.[32] But although working men are increasingly identified by occupational designations, working women tend to be categorized by marital status.[33] (In figure 4.2, whose aim is to represent a broad spectrum of occupations, the mercury woman provides an exception to this rule.)

An early-seventeenth-century commentator advised men to avoid "housewives trades (as brewer, baker, cook, and the like) because they be the skill of women as well as of men and common to both," a warning that both acknowledges and (with hindsight) casts in doubt the occupational status of women's work. (This notion of "housewives trades" may explain the otherwise puzzling evidence that for a time women might be apprenticed in "the art of the housewife" or "in the occupation of housewifeship.")[34] The professionalization of trades and occupations transformed the old guild system according to the model of the career open to talents, one mark of which was the ability to fulfill the demands of a body of specialized practice that had been separated out from the mystique both of arbitrary status privilege and of unrationalized "folk" knowledge. Figure 4.10 and its explication illustrate the cultural work needed to legitimate the emergent profession of the physician as one of "art," not quackery. At the bedside of the sick, an intervening angel "gently" promotes the expertise of the physician over the well-meant but erroneous remedies of the folk healer. But the healer is also a woman, whose clothing connects her far more firmly to the authority of the physician than to the outmoded "trickes" of the traditional cunning woman. In thus conflating "the errours of the people" with the errors of women, the image both acknowledges and denies (once again) the possibility of female professionalism.[35]

The Economic Basis of Separate Spheres

At the higher social levels the differential process of class formation led women and men who aspired to a proto-"bourgeois" gentility to value female idleness, in the strict sense of eschewing all modes of production for the market. In such households women's work was increasingly oriented toward "female" accomplishments, while cheap wage labor did much of what had once been the inside work of wives.[36] In plate 1 the separation of outside labor from inside domesticity is expressed through the vertical division of the canvas. On the left is the world of men, money, and industry; on the right, the wife and mother attended by children and servants (the placement of the boy, presumably heir to the family fortune, bridges the divide). The open window framing the outside world of work is echoed by the interior window provided by the painting, which frames

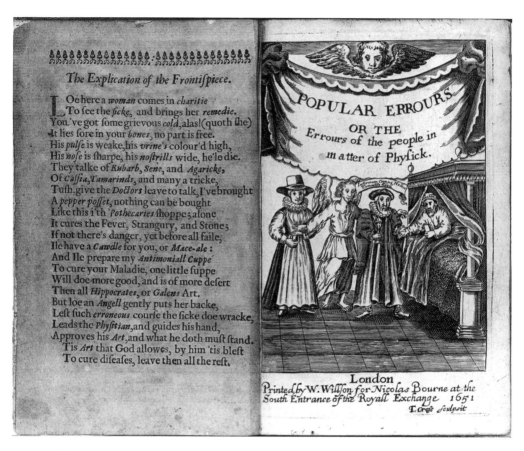

The Explication of the Frontispiece.

LOe here a *woman* comes in *charitie*
To fee the *ficke*, and brings her *remedie*.
You've got fome grievous *cold*, alas!(quoth fhe)
It lies fore in your *bones*, no part is free.
His *pulfe* is weake, his *vrine's* colour'd high,
His *nofe* is fharpe, his *nostrills* wide, he'le die.
They talke of *Rubarb*, *Sene*, and *Agaricke*,
Of *Caffia*, *Tamarinds*, and many a tricke,
Tufh, give the *Doctors* leave to talk, I've brought
A *pepper poffet*, nothing can be bought
Like this i'th *'Pothecaries* fhoppe; alone
It cures the Fever, Strangury, and Stone;
If not there's danger, yet before all faile;
Ile have a *Cawdle* for you, or *Mace-ale*:
And Ile prepare my *Antimoniall Cuppe*
To cure your Maladie, one little fuppe
Will doe more good, and is of more defert
Then all *Hippocrates*, or *Galens* Art.
But loe an *Angell* gently puts her backe,
Left fuch *erroneous* courfe the ficke doe wracke,
Leads the *Phyfitian*, and guides his hand,
Approves his *Art*, and what he doth muft ftand.
Tis *Art* that God allowes, by him 'tis bleft
To cure difeafes, leave then all the reft.

POPULAR ERROURS

OR THE
Errours of the people in
matter of Phyfick.

London
Printed by W. Willfon for Nicolas Bourne at the
South Entrance of the Royall Exchange 1651
T. Crose fculpfit

FIG. 4.10. Frontispiece and title page, [James Primrose], *Popular Errours or the Errours of the people in matter of Physick,* translated from Latin by Robert Witty (1651). By permission of the Folger Shakespeare Library.

a suburban villa. George Morland's title, *The Fruits of Early Industry and Economy,* draws our attention to both the figurative and the literal fruits of labor. It also gives the divided image an implicit temporality: if the right side has flourished through the labors of the left, its current coherence and integrity belie, we might suppose, a more mixed and "protoindustrial" past. In more modest families than Morland has depicted here, husbands and wives turned increasingly to wage labor, seeking work outside the home. Both lost thereby the traditional liberty to define the tasks entailed in their work; but laboring women were also losing even the opportunity for wage labor.[37] Historians have documented the "hidden investment" made by families and especially by women in the flourishing of what has aptly been called "the family enterprise."[38] But as that enterprise became more thoroughly intertwined with production for the market, wives were losing the flexibility once enjoyed in household labor, which was in the process of becoming "housework," the exclusive domain of women and increasingly denigrated not only for its unproductivity but also by its nonremuneration.

In the developing terms of eighteenth-century political economy, the unproductivity of housework made it no different from the public services and the professions.[39] What distinguished housework was the fact that it was unwaged. But the difficulty of establishing agreed-upon criteria for an analytic distinction between productive and unproductive labor led classical economy over time to translate the implications of that distinction into the terms of one between market and nonmarket labor, a process that can be seen in the development of the British census. In the census of 1851 the categories of female occupation included nonmarket household work along with paid occupations. Twenty years later the categories were similar but more ambivalently annotated: the "occupation" of wife and mother was deemed "a noble and essential" one, but female factory workers were seen as engaged in "specifically productive work." In the 1881 census wives and other women engaged in domestic duties were relegated to the "Unoccupied Class," and in 1891 the "Domestic Class" was restricted to those employed in paid domestic service, while the "Unoccupied Class" had disappeared altogether from the occupational assessment, even though the accompanying commentary acknowledged the enormous impact that would be made on the market if those responsible for housework ceased doing it.[40]

Historians have expended some energy trying to explain the economic devaluation of housework in the modern era, which may have been encouraged by the "protoindustrialization" of cottage industry.[41] When household production was undertaken primarily for subsistence but also for the market, we might speculate, it was relatively easy to credit the value of things both qualitatively and quantitatively, both in "private" use and in "public" exchange. But when the household temporarily became a primary site for the production of commodities, the comparatively low exchange value of women's work for the market degraded the value of women's work as such. If monetary quantification was increasingly the requisite mechanism for assessing productivity, housework was unproductive—a conclusion that was reinforced when cottage industry subsided and labor for the market was definitively concentrated outside the household. A predictably complicated relationship in other respects, the separation out of the private economy from public royal politics is like the separation out of the public, productive economy of the market from the private, unproductive economy of the household in that it "makes sense" as a division between quantitative and qualitative criteria of value; that monarchs and women thus become bedfellows is both strange and intelligible.

The flexible gendered distinction between inside and outside work was well on the way to becoming the ossified gendered separation between use and exchange, consumption and production, private necessity and public freedom. This was least so at the lower levels of social status. Still, we may hear the expectations of futurity—marriage as the only safe apprenticeship for a woman—in these midcentury words of warning about the "art and mystery" of the mantua maker, a female-associated occupation that (like millinery) had acquired at the sales end a rather shady reputation:

> It is a Misfortune to the Fair Sex, when they are left young to their own Management, that they can scarce avoid falling into the many Snares laid for them by designing Men . . . . [T]heir natural Innocence and Good-nature make them credulous, and too soon yields them a Prey to the affected Sighs and perjured Oaths of those who have no other View but their Ruin. . . . Parents, who bind their Daughters to this Business, must not think they have done their Duty, when, according to the Phrase, they have put a Trade into their Hands; . . . They ought to watch their Motions, and assist their unexperienced Years with good Advice; and never think themselves discharged of their Parental Duty, till they have settled them in the World under the Protection of some Man of Sagacity, Industry, and Good-nature: a Woman is always under Age till she comes (in the Law Phrase) to be under Cover. A Youth may be set a-float in the World as soon as he has got a Trade in his Head, without much danger of spoiling, but a Girl is such a tender, ticklish Plant to rear, that there is no permitting her out of Leading-strings till she is bound to a Husband.[42]

So by this analysis, the separation of work from housework, of "public" productive labor from "private" domestic marriage, was a function of the process by which the logic of the market slowly but implacably saturated the values of civil society at large. Indeed, housework might be seen as something like the limit case of capitalist exploitation in the technical sense of the term. The disparity between the labor expended in housework and its money equivalent, so great as to be absolute, is expressed by the extraction of a "surplus value" whose computation exceeds the powers of the market system itself. True, women's work was comparatively devalued in the precapitalist regime of the domestic economy as well, and the gender protectionism of this passage is wholly traditional. But the starkness of the modern dichotomy as it is expressed through the absolute difference between payment and nonpayment provides a telling example of how relations of distinction are both continuous and discontinuous with relations of separation.[43]

This is not to say that the household ceased to be a site of remunerated la-

bor. By the end of the eighteenth century domestic service was probably the
most important occupation for women after agriculture; indeed, during much
of the preceding period the distinction between female domestic service and female service in husbandry had been hard to make, at least in rural contexts. By
the same token, the private-public continuum of women's service in private
homes, lodging houses, public houses, and inns is suggested by the inconsistency in attitudes about where vails (tipping) were appropriate and where they
were not. There is a consensus among historians that domestic service became
"feminized" over the course of the century. A 1776 tax on male servants effectively prevented those in husbandry or apprenticeship from doing housework,
whereas the heavy employment of girls in domestic service tended to exclude
them from apprenticeships and other occupational training.[44] In two wealthy
City of London parishes around 1700, female servants "represent four out of
every five domestics and were the only domestics in over three-quarters of the
households."[45] As we have seen, domestic servants were regarded as part of the
family, and a large proportion of wives setting up new households already had
served in others as domestics. The fact that domestic money wages supplemented the use-based barter of service for room and board must only have enhanced, at least in the lower social orders, the comparability of girls, female servants, and wives as distinguishable but inseparable versions of a single domestic
category. Among gentility the divisions were sharper, but the fundamental
complementarity was similar.[46] Hence the gradual ossification of the gendered
division between inside and outside work was paralleled and complicated on an
intragender basis within the inside space of the home. At the same time, the
most privatized of gentle families experienced a recapitulation of the public-private relation within the realm of the private, a phenomenon that has become a
familiar feature of this study: "Those children in homes totally separated from
[domestic economy] now found a microcosm of the outside world within their
own households through domestic servants."[47]

Housewife as Governor

A central question for historians of separate spheres is the relationship—and
the putative disparity—between the austere prescriptions of didactic discourse
and the relative liberality of social practice. In 1737 a male author assured his
readers that "women are not form'd for great Cares themselves, but to soothe
and soften ours; their Tenderness is the proper Reward for the Toils we under
go for their Preservation; and the Ease and Chearfulness of their Conversation,
our desireable Retreat from the Labours of Study and Business. They are confined within the narrow Limits of Domestick Offices, and when they stray be-

yond them, they move excentrically, and consequently without Grace."⁴⁸ One of the most notorious public places into which women might stray was open political advocacy. Early in the century Addison famously ridiculed women for "patching" (wearing face and body patches) and other methods of publicizing their party affiliations (e.g., *Spectator,* nos. 57 and 81, 5 May and 2 June 1711). Figure 4.11 conveys one of many, largely hostile responses to the spectacle of Georgiana, Duchess of Devonshire, canvassing for Charles James Fox in the Westminster election of 1784. Drawing on some of the imagery of the skimmington ride, *The Devonshire Amusement* depicts Georgiana and her husband improperly sphered: she flamboyantly campaigns out-of-doors in windswept dishabille; he, unmanned, sits at home changing diapers. Vestiges of an older, antipatriarchalist formulation persist in the fact of Fox's opposition to the public authority of the monarch and its implications for domestic authority, but these are subsumed by the more dominant imagery of separate spheres within the realm of the private. The case of women in politics might be taken to exemplify the gap between prescription and practice; and yet even the prescriptive discourse was more complicated than this would suggest. One tract, firm on the gendered significance of outdoors and indoors, is also clear that inside work is a form of responsible "government": "It is the Husband's Duty to manage all things without-doors, and the Wives to take care of all within. In fine, I say, it is the Husband's Duty to furnish Money, and the Wives to govern the Family."⁴⁹ True, conventional language of domestic government can be found in Renaissance conduct books.⁵⁰ But if the "public" status of the housewife's domestic labor was nugatory by the emergent standards of political economy, its cultural status, registered by figurative borrowings from the public realms of politics and business, was on the rise. As Margaret Cavendish had affirmed in the previous century, wives "govern as it were by an insensible power."⁵¹

The first stage in the household's apotheosis was, in Christopher Hill's phrase, "the spiritualization of the household," the post-Reformation transfer of regulatory authority from the church and priesthood to Puritan male heads of households. The second stage is comparable to the way the public (the ecclesiastical and state) apparatus of moral reform was taken over in the early eighteenth century by private institutions like satire, periodical pedagogy, and the societies for the reformation of manners—what Habermas would call public-sphere instruments of the private realm. In this second stage the public regulation of both morals and finances was internalized in the domestic and private role of wife and mother. And whether or not it was openly acknowledged, this internalization was often accompanied by the conviction that the state fundamentally depended on the family. Thus Milton described "the houshold estate" as that "out of which must flourish forth the vigor and spirit of all publick en-

FIG. 4.11. *The Devonshire Amusement*, 1784. Courtesy of the Lewis Walpole Library, Yale University.

terprizes . . . ." Attributing to Aristotle the observation "that the Estate of Republics entirely hang on private Families, the little Monarchies both composing and giving Law to the great," Richard Allestree thought it "evident that the disposal of Families and all Domestic concerns therein lies chiefly on the Wife . . . ." Although its long-term force is clear enough, the fundamental difference between the "traditional" patriarchalist analogy and the "modernizing" response to it can be hard to discern in local usages like these. This is because the critique of the analogy—the analytic separation out of state and family—often enough prepares for the metaphorical conflation of public with private functions within the realm of the domestic. One important factor in the transition from the first to the second stage was Protestant doctrines of conscience, marriage, and the calling. In 1622 William Gouge reassured certaine weake consciences, who thinke that if they haue no publike calling, they haue no calling at all . . . . Which consequence if it were good and sound, what comfort in spending their time should most women haue, who are not admitted to any publike function in Church or commonwealth? or seruants, children, and others who are wholly imployed in priuate affaires of the familie? But . . . a consciomable performance of houshold duties, in regard of the end and fruit thereof, may be accounted a publike worke. . . . Wherefore if they who haue no publike calling, be so much the more diligent in the function of their priuate callings, they shall be as well accepted of the Lord, as if they had publike offices.[52]

Given the attentiveness with which the patriarchalist analogy was being anatomized at this time, it is not surprising that increasingly explicit efforts to model the family on the state (rather than the tacitly assumed reverse model) should have been mindful of the analogy's limitations. John Locke found the figure of the absolute monarch relevant only to childrearing, and even then only with reference to younger children: "I imagine every one will judge it reasonable, that their Children, *when little,* should look upon their Parents as their Lords, their Absolute Governors, and as such, stand in awe of them: And that, when they come to riper Years, they should look on them as their best, as their only sure Friends; and as such, love and reverence them." Only "whilst he is a Child" is it "fit" that one's son be one's "obedient Subject." Adolescent girls may be another matter, if Samuel Johnson's correspondent "Bellaria" is any indication. Fatigued by warnings about the attentions of men, the beautiful Bellaria complains that while grownups like her mother and two aunts "keep poor girls close in the nursery, they tyrannize over us in a very shameful manner, and fill our imaginations with tales of terror, only to make us live in quiet subjection, and fancy that we can never be safe but by their protection. . . . These ladies, Mr. Rambler, have had me under their government fifteen years and a half, and have all that time been endeavouring to deceive me by such representations of life as I now find not to be true." We are to understand, however, that Bellaria's absolutist language expresses not the reality of her upbringing but the same naïveté that persuades her that she has been the victim of deception. Skepticism about the absolutist extreme only refined the inquiry into how the activities of the mother and housewife might be represented in terms of the juridical, the executive, and the financial functions of the state. Secreted within the status of the *feme covert,* contemporaries found, was the office of the benevolent magistrate and the authority of ethical precept.[53]

"It is with a family as with a common wealth," Hester Chapone wrote, "the more numerous and luxurious it becomes, the more difficult it is to govern properly." The most important locus of the housewife's governance was, by consensus, her responsibility for the early education of children. "The Care and

Education of Children, both with respect to their Bodies and Minds, is by Nature given all along to the Mother, in a much greater Proportion than to the Father."⁵⁴ But if there was agreement on the fact of this arrangement, attitudes toward it varied considerably, often in the coded language of inside versus outside. The alarmist author of *Satan's Harvest Home* maintained that "[o]ur Fore-Fathers were train'd up to Arts and Arms; . . . [T]he Boy . . . was taken early from the Nursery and sent to the Grammar-School . . . . The School Hours over, . . . then sought he the Resort of other Boys, either in the Fields, or publick Squares of the City; where he hard'ned himself against the Inclemency of the Weather . . . ." Nowadays, however, "Little Master is kept in the Nursery 'till he is five or six Years old, at least, after which he is sent to a Girl's School . . . . [H]is whole Animal Fabrick is enervated for want of due Exercise; . . . for, till he went to the *Girls School,* he seldom or never was out of the Nursery . . . ." Writing seventy-five years earlier, John Aubrey told a very different story. The boy should be "bred carefully at home" until twelve and then sent to school. "It is now that he is entered to be of the world, to come from his innocent life, tender care, and indulgence of his parents, to be beaten by his school fellows, to be falsely accused, to be whipped by the master, to understand his tyranny. . . . 'Tis here he begins to understand the world, the misery, falseness and deceitfulness of it . . . ."⁵⁵

Perhaps the two most influential treatises on domestic conduct in the early eighteenth century were those by Richard Allestree and the Marquis of Halifax, both of whom appreciate the profound importance of the mother's pedagogic power. Allestree's formulation emphasizes an empiricist epistemology: "[A]ll mankind is the Pupil and Disciple of Female Institution: . . . the time when the mind is most ductile, and prepar'd to receive impression, being wholly in the Care and Conduct of the Mother." Halifax, addressing his daughter and sounding at times like a Machiavelli of the nursery, stresses political opportunism: "You must begin early to make them *love* you, that they may *obey* you. This Mixture is nowhere more necessary than in Children. . . . You are to have as strict a Guard upon your self amongst your *Children,* as if you were amongst your *Enemies.*" Since they too had once been children, this approach applies to husbands as well: Although "there is *Inequality* in the *Sexes,* . . . you have it in your power not only to free your selves, but to subdue your Masters, and without violence throw both their *Natural* and *Legal Authority* at your Feet. . . . The first part of our Life is a good deal of it subjected to you in the *Nursery,* where you Reign without Competition, and by that means have the advantage of giving the first *Impressions;* after wards you have stronger Influences, which, well manag'd, have more force in your behalf, than all our *Priviledges* and *Jurisdictions* can pretend to have against you. You have more strength in your *Looks,* then we have in our *Laws* . . . ." Halifax's extension of the wife's power over her children to her power over her husband may seem to smack of Petrarchan bad faith, but Mary Astell makes the same point more persuasively. How great, she says,

> is the influence we have over [men] in their Childhood, in which time if a Mother be discreet and knowing as well as devout, she has many opportunities of giving such a *Form* and *Season* to the tender Mind of the Child, as will shew its good effects thro' all the stages of his Life. . . . But besides this, a good and prudent Wife wou'd wonderfully work on an ill man . . . . Doubtless her Husband is a much happier Man and more likely to abandon all his ill Courses, than he who has none to come home to, but an ignorant, forward and fantastick Creature. . . . The only danger is that the Wife be more knowing than the Husband . . . .[56]

The danger Astell apprehends in the domestic realm is the same one that Renaissance writers had warned of at court: the devolutionary problem of the omnicompetent courtier whose service to his prince is so expert that it goes beyond the accomplishments of the prince himself. And the implicit parallel between husband and prince should not obscure for us another implication of Astell's remarks. Although Locke invokes the drastic developmental difference between children and adults so as to limit the applicability of the absolutist figure to the practice of familial education, Astell's words, like those of Halifax, suggest that the pedagogic influence of mother over child is continuous with that exercised by wife over husband. The domestic reformation of the rake, no less than the socialization of the child into adulthood (or the macrosocial reformation of manners), is aptly expressed in a civic register. Thus "Chastity Loveworth" indignantly wonders of Steele why the "looser Part of our Sex . . . indulge the Males in Licenciousness whilst single, and we have the dismal Hazard and Plague of reforming them when married?" Several of her suitors have gone so far as to claim "that all Women of good Sense ever were, and ever will be, Latitudinarians in Wedlock; and always did, and will, give and take what they profanely term Conjugal Liberty of Conscience" (*Spectator,* no. 298, 11 Feb. 1712). Against such libertinism was directed an emergent discourse that reversed and privatized the patriarchalist analogy so as to conflate the reformative powers of a female-dominated interior space with the authority of public government:

> *Marriage* will reform the Mischiefs of the Debauch'd, and bring these Nations to a regular and quiet *Temper:* For a *Family* is the *Epitome* of a Kingdom, and it naturally resolves into a Government, which cannot subsist without *Rules* and Order; so that even the extravagant, who, like the *Beast* of Prey, ruffles and delights in Disorder Abroad, will take Pleasure to be quiet in his *Denn;* he makes a Tumult in a *Tavern,*

but will not endure it in his *House*; . . . [T]he Converse of a *vertuous Wife* may, and oftentimes does take off the unwarrantable Delights of a *single* and debauch'd Conversation.

In Butler's traditionalist character of the henpecked husband the fact that the wife "has the tuition of him" is one important barb of the satire. The developing scenario of the reformed rake will make this normative.[57]

The radical force of Mary Wollstonecraft's writings depends greatly on her recognition that in the balance of power between the sexes education is the central issue. This insight depends, in turn, on the explicitation of the category of gender that was a byproduct of the emergent biologization of sex. "Gender"—the social construction of "sex"—only became theorizable by hypostatizing sex over against it as a natural and invariable constant.[58] "I have," Wollstonecraft remarks dryly,

> probably, had an opportunity of observing more girls in their infancy than J. J. Rousseau. I can recollect my own feelings, and I have looked steadily around me; yet, so far from coinciding with him in opinion respecting the first dawn of the female character, I will venture to affirm, that a girl whose spirits have not been damped by inactivity, or innocence tainted by false shame, will always be a romp, and the doll will never excite attention unless confinement allows her no alternative. Girls and boys, in short, would play harmlessly together, if the distinction of sex was not inculcated long before nature makes any difference.[59]

Modern feminists sometimes are disappointed by the apparent endorsement of domesticity entailed in Wollstonecraft's criticism of conduct books that are "more anxious to make [women] alluring mistresses than affectionate wives and rational mothers . . ." (79). But for Wollstonecraft as for many of her contemporaries, the emergent concept of domesticity—the practice of being a wife and mother—can promise a utopian determinacy very far from its later connotations. She has read the books on education, and she has arrived at the "profound conviction that the neglected education of my fellow-creatures is the grand source of the misery I deplore" (79). But the locus of the problem is also that of its solution. "[H]ave women who have early imbibed notions of passive obedience, sufficient character to manage a family or educate children?" (119). Rightly educated, the female child becomes the domestic wife and mother whose crucial role is to reproduce her experience for the succeeding generation. In her highest optimism Wollstonecraft envisions the present moment as the time "to effect a revolution in female manners . . . and make them, as a part of the human species, labour by reforming themselves to reform the world" (132). "By individual education, I mean . . . such an attention to a child as will slowly

sharpen the senses, form the temper, regulate the passions as they begin to ferment, and set the understanding to work before the body arrives at maturity . . ." (102).

Thus does domestic labor beget the most public of achievements. Yet the
very force of Wollstonecraft's sociological imagination can outstrip her utopian
optimism, making her despair of piecemeal, "private education" as a mechanism of social change: "Men and women must be educated, in a great degree,
by the opinions and manners of the society they live in. In every age there has
been a stream of popular opinion that has carried all before it, and given a family character, as it were, to the century. It may then fairly be inferred, that, till
society be differently constituted, much cannot be expected from education"
(102). The inference is perhaps to be seen in William Godwin's blistering attack
on the institution of marriage, and more broadly in his critique of "the irregular transfer of property" as providing the "interior and domestic history" of "the
evils of political society."[60] In any case, the momentous change in education for
which the individual wife and mother might be responsible therefore may require for Wollstonecraft a change in socialization—a collective social revolution. Nor is it clear anyway that the public effects of the housewife's private labor are possible without a truly public existence: "It is plain from the history of
all nations, that women cannot be confined to merely domestic pursuits, for
they will not fulfil family duties, unless their minds take a wider range . . ."
(294). "But in order to render their private virtue a public benefit, they must
have a civil existence in the State, married or single . . ." (262). In other words,
women must be afforded the public status of men.

Skeptical as Wollstonecraft may have been regarding the status of women
and its immediate prospects, she treats the emergent institution of domesticity
not as the problem but as a realm of pedagogic possibility. For the generality
of her contemporaries, the wife was also understood to exercise a species of sovereign power regarding the economy and management of the household. Allestree played an important role in disseminating the revolutionary doctrine that
was to replace the traditional view of women as simply an inferior version of
men. This was a doctrine of sexual difference, of separate but equal: the emergent separation of the sexes was grounded in the explicit assertion of their ultimate—which is to say their spiritual—equality: "That spiritual Essence, that
ray of Divinity owns no distinction of Sexes . . . . [A]ll Ages and Nations have
made some distinction between masculine and feminine Vertues . . . ."[61] If
sexual difference is manifested in the division between the public and the private, Steele suggests, it simultaneously grounds the discovery of a "public" administrative authority within the province of the private: "[T]he Soul of a Man
and that of a Woman are made very unlike, according to the employments for

which they are designed. The Ladies will please to observe, I say, our Minds have different, not superior Qualities to theirs. . . . To manage well a great Family, is as worthy an Instance of Capacity, as to execute a great Employment . . ." (*Tatler*, no. 172, 16 May 1710). And a correspondent wonders at the rarity of the man wise enough to seek a wife "who will manage that Share of his Estate he intrusts to her Conduct with Prudence and Frugality, govern his House with Oeconomy and Discretion, and be an Ornament to himself and Family . . ." (*Spectator*, no. 268, 7 Jan. 1712).

According to Hannah Woolley, "To govern an House is an excellent and profitable employment; there is nothing more beautiful than an Houshold well and peacably governed . . . ." Handbooks on housewifery stressed that the management of money was an integral part of domestic "employment." The preface to one of these lists the skills in which it offers instruction, "[q]ualifications extremely useful in every Station of Life, especially to those who have the Management of Families, and the Regulation of domestic Expenses." The author of what is essentially a cookbook addresses ladies for whom "the prudent Management of Family Affairs is your particular Province," assuring them that "I have had a great deal of Experience in Business of this Kind and endeavoured to fix a Standard, so that good Housewifry and Oeconomy, may go Hand in Hand." And according to Lady Sarah Pennington, "The Management of all Domestic Affairs is certainly the proper Business of Woman; and unfashionably rustic as such an Assertion may be thought, 'tis certainly not beneath the Dignity of any Lady, however high her rank, to know how to educate her children, to govern her servants, to order an elegant Table with Oeconomy, and to manage her whole family with Prudence, Regularity and method." Indeed, Halifax had warned his daughter that "the old *House-keeper* shall make a better Figure in the Family, than the *Lady* with all her fine Cloths, if she wilfully relinquish her Title to the *Government* . . . ." Eliza Haywood both concurs and apotheosizes the wifely role of governor to a fully ethical status:

> Even Persons of the highest Rank in Life will suffer greatly both in their Circumstances and Peace of Mind, when she, who ought to be the Mistress of the Family, lives in it like a Stranger, and perhaps knows no more of what those about her do than an Alien. But supposing her an excellent Œconomist, in every Respect what the World calls a notable Woman, methinks the Husband would be yet infinitely happier were she endued with other good Qualities as well as a perfect Understanding in Houshold Affairs:—The Governess of a Family, or what is commonly call'd Houskeeper, provided she be honest and careful, might discharge this Trust as well as a Wife; but there is, doubtless, somewhat more to be expected by a Man from that Woman whom the Ceremony of Marriage has made Part of himself:—She is, or ought to be, if qualified for it, the Repository of his dearest Secrets, the Moderator of

his fiercer Passions, the Softner of his most anxious Cares, and the constantly chearful and entertaining Companion of his more unbended Moments.[62]

Such was the persuasiveness of this developing vision of the housewife as governor that it also might be turned around to create a vision of the governor as housewife. This was William Wordsworth's reflection on the failure of Napoleon Bonaparte:

> 'Tis not in battles that from youth we train
> The Governor who must be wise and good,
> And temper with the sternness of the brain
> Thoughts motherly, and meek as womanhood.
> Wisdom doth live with children round her knees . . . .[63]

In the language of "management," "employment," "business," and "government" may be heard not only an alacrity to acknowledge the regulatory function of household governance but also a recognition that under the emergent regime of sexual difference and its innovative division of labor wives are becoming principally responsible for the kind of duties that had occupied both wives and husbands under the older, domestic economy. This way of thinking about the relationship between men's and women's work entails both metaphor and metonymy: women's inside duties are not only like men's outside duties; they also make them possible. We have already encountered this idea in the claim that "marriage will reform the mischiefs of the debauched, and bring these nations to a regular and quiet temper."[64] John Trenchard emphasized how his relentless concern for liberty and property found pertinent the politics of domestic as well as public life. With the cause of women, he writes,

> the cause of liberty is blended; and scarce any man will be much concerned for publick happiness, unless he enjoys domestick: Publick happiness being nothing else but the magistrate's protecting of private men in their property, and their enjoyments. It is certain, that a man's interest, in point of happiness and pleasures, is in no instance so much concerned as in that of marriage . . . . Our wealth does also depend in a great measure upon domestick sympathy and concord; and it is a true proverb, that *A man must ask leave of his wife to be rich:* so great a share of his substance and prosperity must remain in her power, and at her discretion, and under her management, that if he would thrive and be happy himself, he must make her so.

Trenchard adds the familiar, paradoxical corollary: if domesticity is continuous with public affairs, it is also separate from them: "It is miserable folly, to put yourself in a circumstance of being uneasy in your own house, which ought to be a retreat from all the ruffles and disappointments that you meet with elsewhere . . . ." The paradox exemplifies the way the modern principle of privacy connects seemingly separate institutions. Recalling Habermas, "To the autonomy of property owners in the market corresponded a self-presentation of human beings in the family. The latter's intimacy, apparently set free from the constraints of society, was the seal on the truth of a private autonomy exercised in competition." On the basis of Trenchard's remarks we might add that the protection of private men's property is a comprehensively public and private labor, one of wise magistrates and devoted wives. The cultural role of the wife is to officiate over the private retreat where the husband enjoys his negative liberty from the public struggle for autonomy—even as her office orchestrates in little a benign, even utopian version of that struggle.[65]

The metonymic relationship between private domestic accomplishment and public stature was composed of several strands. For one thing, in the later eighteenth century it became common to measure the achievements of a culture by those of its women: "[W]hat age or country, distinguished in the annals of fame, has not received a part of that distinction from the numbers of women, whom it produced, conspicuous for their virtues and their talents? Look at this, in which you live: does it not derive a very considerable share of its reputation from the female pens, that eminently adorn it?" Female learning, but also, more broadly, feminine sociability and welfare, came to be seen as a yardstick of national development: "[T]he rank . . . and condition, in which we find women in any country, mark out to us with the greatest precision, the exact point in the scale of civil society, to which the people of such country have arrived; and were their history entirely silent on every other subject, and only mentioned the manner in which they treated their women, we would, from thence, be enabled to form a tolerable judgment of the barbarity, or culture of their manners."[66] The converse also holds: "In proportion as real politeness and elegance of manners advance, the interest and advantages of the fair sex not only advance also, but become more firmly and permanently established."[67]

But the domestic virtues, although significant as an abstract measure of national civility, were most important as an active determinant of that condition. The most tangible connection between the domestic woman and the national welfare can be seen in the relationship between a developing (and unwarranted) concern about national underpopulation and the cult of motherhood. In the seventeenth and early eighteenth centuries, wet-nursing was a flourishing mode of paid domestic labor among the middling sort and the elite. Figure 4.12 is a mid-seventeenth-century image of a wet nurse feeding an infant with other children in her charge. The scene is framed by others—a bedside lying-in and a visit to the apothecary shop—in such a way as to represent their common concern with pediatric health as a spatial coextension. About midcentury there began a campaign to promote breast-feeding that was so successful that by the

De Morbis Puerorum

Gul Vaughan fecit

1770s and 1780s nursing had largely been transformed from paid to unpaid labor, from a class-stratified to a strictly gendered activity.[68] This was a domestication in both senses of the term. One of the reasons why mothers' milk came to be preferred to that of wet nurses was the old apprehension that the latter method of breast-feeding might introduce into the infant milk (and therefore blood) that was contaminated by a foreign and/or racial otherness. Like the early acquisition of the "mother tongue," breast-feeding was an individual and national experience in acculturation best undertaken by the mother.[69] Jonas Hanway, governor of the Foundling Hospital in 1756, was only one of the better-known proponents of the notion that Britain's national and imperial greatness depended on an augmented population growth, in which maternal breast-feeding was thought to be highly instrumental: "[T]he more subjects, the more labor, the more labor the greater the national income; & the private opulence." "Increase alone can make our *natural* Strength in *Men* correspond with our *artificial* Power in *Riches,* and both with the Grandeur and Extent of the *British Empire.*" This was to become a connection of enormous importance in the succeeding century.[70]

So the removal of married women from the productive workplace they had enjoyed in the domestic economy complicated rather than precluded their participation in public life. A final example of this can be seen in the emergent understanding that middling and elite married women had important roles even as individual players in the market economy—the roles of philanthropist and consumer. According to the enormously influential Hannah More, "[C]harity is the calling of a lady; the care of the poor is her profession."[71] By tradition, hospitality had been administered through the great household. Toward the end of the seventeenth century, personal giving was moving from inside to outside, from the household to public agencies, a movement that "completed the separation of hospitality to the prosperous and alms to the poor that had always been latent in household culture."[72] By the end of the following century, charitable associations established and run by women had become fairly common.[73] At the same time, individual acts of stewardship continued to be esteemed as a means by which domestic women might exercise their skills at financial management outside the home.

In the past few years, the growth of consumer culture in eighteenth-century England and women's major contribution to that growth have become the ob-

FIG. 4.12. (*opposite*) Frontispiece, J. S., *Childrens Diseases Both Outward and Inward* (1664), in Wendy Wall, *Staging Domesticity: Household Work and English Identity in Early Modern Drama* (Cambridge: Cambridge University Press, 2002). Princeton University Library.

ject of much scholarly research. If the work of housewives played a questionable role in the productivity of the market economy, their signal importance as consumers was becoming visible to contemporaries at the same moment that political economy was discovering the dialectical truth that consumption is an indispensable factor in the generation of national productivity. On the one hand, the posture of the consumer tied married women to the ancient and dead-end tether of subsistence and necessity—or worse, to the all-purpose evil of "luxury." On the other hand, consuming women were crucial to the economy. As Adam Smith wrote, "Consumption is the sole end and purpose of all production; and the interest of the producer ought to be attended to, only so far as it may be necessary for promoting that of the consumer." According to Karl Marx, "Consumption creates the need for *new* production, that is it creates the ideal, internally impelling cause for production, which is its presupposition. . . . Production is consumption, consumption is production. . . . The political economists call both productive consumption."[74] From the standpoint of a prudent domesticity, female consumption was consumerism, shopping, fashion; from that of political economy it was a vital wheel in the machinery of public life. At the beginning of the nineteenth century a contemporary used this image of the machine to figure, not public society, but private domesticity itself—specifically (and with an ironic justice) the machine that now did the job that had once been the prototypical inside work of wives: "A large family is a complex machine, composed of a great number of individual and subordinate parts. . . . It should ever be so constituted, that, like the silk-wheels at Derby, when any one part goes wrong, that part may be stopped and repaired, without arresting the motion of the rest."[75]

The Whore's Labor

The wife's cultural role depends entirely on where we find her. If stably married, she may well be intelligible as the magistrate of the little commonwealth. If unhappily married or in the process of marriage—either becoming or ceasing to be a wife—she is on the contrary subject to magistratic power, which is to say both to political and mercenary "enslavement," and to the profoundly ambivalent contingencies of freedom. Indeed, the household family itself, figuratively modeled as it was on the outside world, was less a sanctuary from than a breeding ground for its public dangers. One key to this intercourse was domestic service. Over the course of the eighteenth century most of the seductions and illegitimate childbirths in one Chelsea parish involved servants in domestic settings.[76] According to a midcentury tract, female domestic service and prostitution were scarcely distinguishable stops on the same circuit: "The Town being over-stock'd with *Harlots,* is entirely owing to those Numbers of *Women-Servants,* incessantly pouring into it from all Corners of the Universe, and those Debaucheries practis'd upon 'em in almost all the Families that entertain them: *Masters, Footmen, Journeymen, Lodgers, Apprentices,* &c. are for ever attempting to corrupt . . . . Many of them are as restless as a *new Equipage,* running from Place to Place, from Bawdy-House to Service, and from Service to Bawdy-House again; . . . So that in Effect, they neither make good Whores, good Wives, or good Servants, and this is one of the chief Reasons why our Streets swarm with Strumpets."

Whores, wives, and servants: another tract, alluding to the great thoroughfare of continuous streetwalking that connected the East End to the West End of London, added the notoriously vulnerable millinery-shop girls to this gamut of domestic labor and debauchery. Speaking of milliners' apprentices, this author claims that "nine out of ten of the young Creatures that are obliged to serve in these Shops, are ruined and undone: Take a Survey of all the common Women of the Town, who take their Walks between *Charing-Cross* and *Fleet-Ditch,* and, I am persuaded, more than one Half of them have been bred Milliners, have been debauched in their *Houses* [i.e., shops], and are obliged to throw themselves upon the Town for Want of Bread, after they have left them." Bernard Mandeville saw a related pattern of circulation and exchange in the urban life cycle of syphilis: "[T]his Disease has its Spring and Source entirely from publick Whoring, and from thence creeps into private Families; so it likewise receives continual Supplies and Recruits thro' the same Channel . . . ."[77]

It was the public nature of prostitution that most disturbed contemporaries. In 1650 Jeremy Taylor wrote that one of the most beneficial "*[w]orks of spiritual Almes and mercy*" is "[t]o redeem maydens from prostitution and publication of their bodies." A century later, Saunders Welch complained that prostitutes

> swarm in the streets of this metropolis to such a degree, and bawdy-houses are kept in such an open and public manner, to the great scandal of our civil polity, that a stranger would think that such practices, instead of being prohibited, had the sanction of the legislature, and that the whole town was one general stew. . . . [C]ertainly there is a wide difference between vice hiding its head and skulking in corners, and vice exposing its face at noon-day. What idea must foreigners have of our policy, when in almost every street they see women publickly exposing themselves at the windows and doors of bawdy-houses, like beasts in a market for publick sale, with language, dress, and gesture too offensive to mention; and find themselves tempted (it may be said assaulted) in the streets by a hundred women between Temple-Bar and Charing-Cross, in terms shocking to the ear of modesty[?][78]

The public nature of prostitution was offensive in part because it appeared to betray the indeterminate but strongly sensed boundaries between the public and the private. The extremity of this offence was a relatively recent development that was a result of its separation out from other, related offences.

As late as the early eighteenth century, "whoring" was still a general term for almost all extramarital heterosexual activity. "To denounce a woman as a whore was to accuse her of sexual immorality and carried no necessary implication of payment." Streetwalkers, fornicators, and adulterers were seen as fundamentally alike. Bernard Mandeville has been credited with playing an important role in separating sexual desire from financial interest in assessing the motives for prostitution, a process that was fed both by contemporary efforts in moral philosophy to discriminate between more and less vicious kinds of passion and by the growing tendency to see women as naturally modest rather than (as by tradition) naturally lubricious. By midcentury the moralizing attitudes of the societies for the reformation of manners were being challenged and supplemented by the humanitarian concerns of the Magdalen Hospital for the Reception of Penitent Prostitutes, which took its charges to be victims of economic deprivation, not predators fueled by an inborn lust.[79] This complemented the notion that prostitutes were public persons, engaged in a particular form of outside work that set them apart from merely lustful adulterers. By this way of thinking, reform was a peculiarly Protestant sort of industrious work discipline, and penitence entailed the willingness to undertake an acceptable form of productive labor. Thus John Fielding proposed "a public Laundry . . . to reform those Prostitutes whom necessity has drove into the Streets, and who are willing to return to Virtue and obtain an honest Livelihood by severe Industry."[80]

But this thinking also encouraged speculation on the commonalty of private women (like maidens and wives) and public women (like prostitutes): if they possessed a common sense of shame, what distinguished them was little more than the financial motive. Indeed, Steele and Defoe urge us to see the private publicness of the wife, who could be bought and sold, as a complex counterpart of the public privateness of the prostitute, who would be bought and sold.[81] The wife's "employment," anomalous in its nonremuneration, is essential to the nation's economy. The whore's employment, shocking for its remuneration, is anathema to the nation's self-ideal. The market devaluation of the wife's inside work is by a certain logic the other side of the coin of the market's valorization of the whore's outside work. The wife's economic unproductivity is balanced by her conjugal reproductivity, the whore's shameful productivity by her profligate unreproductivity. The whore—the woman whose business is sex, the *feme sole* as *feme covert*—seems to mark the extremity of both female publicity and female privacy. Contemporaries recognized this suggestive indeterminacy, which is reflected in their overlapping and inconsistent application of the public/private formula.

During the Restoration period, prostitution was broadly if drolly recognized as a "trade" best left to enjoy its own squalid negative freedom (or, with the rise of the societies for the reformation of manners, best treated as a sinful activity to be punished to the full extent of the law).[82] Lists of whores at work in London were published at regular intervals in the early years of the Restoration. One such publication testified to the fact that by virtue of sheer unfettered enterprise, the trade had elaborated, within its own public practice, a distinction between those who practiced in "public" (i.e., in brothels) and those who practiced in "private" (i.e., on the streets): "Now the privat Whores have got the Knack on't to knock in corners, so that all our Cattel . . . cannot . . . persuade a Gallant to enter their Forts, . . . Ergo, Publick trading is destroy'd by private correspondencies and actings, which was not formerly [i.e., in 1660–61] when our lists of whores were printed."[83]

Figures 4.13 and 4.14 show two plates from Marcellus Laroon the Elder's engravings of the criers and hawkers of London, a collection that illustrates the broad diversity of street vendors who vocally advertised their wares during the Restoration. These include the *London Curtezan,* a fashionably dressed streetwalker, and *Madame Creswell,* a famous bawd (one of the interlocutors in *The Whores Rhetorick,* discussed below). The courtesan exemplifies the high end of the "private" trade. Her mask and fan associate her with the dissolute theater but also with the stylish ladies who might be seen there and at the masquerade. The mask remained an eloquent sign of the labile high-class courtesan. In figure 4.15 another such streetwalker in the notorious Covent Garden area of the 1740s is arrested by members of that other body of nocturnal outside laborers, the night watch. Looking like a lady of quality returning home from a masquerade, she is held in an immobile posture, as though she were a display-window mannequin. The elegant courtesan played herself in the very act of disguising herself as her betters. In 1785 the *Times* pointed out that efforts to bar prostitutes from public places were bound to fail owing to the fact that fashionable women liked to appear racy by copying the makeup and clothing of streetwalkers. Two years later the *Times* reported that "a young harlot" had mistaken "a young lady" for a fellow streetwalker; "the virgin was conveyed home in a fit, and the prostitute dragged to the watchhouse in a frenzy."[84] The appeal of the streetwalker—of the "private" whore—was thus bound up with her proximity to her putative, more categorically private antithesis. This goes some distance, perhaps, toward rationalizing the oddity that solicitation that occurred in public—that is, on the streets—was called "private," whereas solicitation that occurred in private domiciles was called "public"; another explanation might be that "public/private" here means "corporate/individual."

Mandeville's 1724 defense of public brothels was also based on the under-

London Curtezan
La Putain de Londres
Cortegiana di Londra

M. Lauron delin.

P. Tempest exc.
Cum Privilegio

FIG. 4.13. Marcellus Laroon the Elder, *London Curtezan,* c. 1688, in *The Criers and Hawkers of London,* ed. Sean Shesgreen (Stanford, CA: Stanford University Press, 1990). Graphic Arts Collection, Department of Rare Books and Special Collections, Princeton University Library.

Madam Creſwell
Vne Maquerelle
Vecchia ruſiana

M. aaroon delin.   P.Tempeſta.
                                                    Cum priv.lege

Fɪɢ. 4.14. Marcellus Laroon the Elder, *Madam Creswell*, c. 1688, in *The Criers and Hawkers of London,* ed. Sean Shesgreen (Stanford, CA: Stanford University Press, 1990). Graphic Arts Collection, Department of Rare Books and Special Collections, Princeton University Library.

FIG. 4.15. *The arrest of a prostitute in Covent Garden*, c. 1740, in Tony Henderson, *Disorderly Women in Eighteenth-Century London: Prostitution and Control in the Metropolis, 1730–1830* (London: Longman, 1999). Princeton University Library.

standing that by current policy, "public" were being sacrificed to "private" interests. The tract provides a classic instance of the Mandevillian logic of "private vices, public benefits." His point is that prostitution should be publicly supported and regulated by the state, but not for the usual (and increasingly archaic) protectionist reasons. Despite its obvious libertine excess, the problem with prostitution was not that it enjoyed too absolute a negative liberty but that it was not free enough: that it was criminalized as a private vice. Like other private vices, prostitution served a social need, and the public policy of turning a blind eye with occasional gestures at punishment had antisocial consequences: in fact, "publick Whoring is neither so criminal in itself, nor so detrimental to the *Society,* as private Whoring . . . ." Mandeville's public-private distinction is that between prostitution and adultery, and he speaks of prostitutes as "profess'd Courtezans" and of prostitution as a "Profession," proposing that it be accorded something like guild status by "not only the erecting Publick Stews, . . . but also the endowing them with such Privileges and Immunities . . . as may be most effectual to turn the general Stream of Lewdness into this common Channel."85 Needless to say, Mandeville's proposal was not taken up. And years later, the effort of the Disorderly Houses Act of 1751 to crack down on bawdyhouses seemed misguided to some, and for related reasons: "If all the private Wh——s and Adul——es that are in the Land were to be mustred upon Salisbury Plain, the Common Ladies [i.e., "public" brothel prostitutes] would appear no bigger than the Army of the Israelites, when they went to engage a great Host of their Enemies . . . ." Here the problem of "private whores" explicitly takes in the problem of adultery, reinforcing Mandeville's point that the failure to provide vice an official public sanction and outlet only aggravates its private noxiousness. But others thought the 1751 act had fallen short of its estimable purpose. Although Welch saw the logic of Mandeville's safety-valve argument —and of the notion that one passion might be pitted against another—his guarded language seems to apprehend not adultery but masturbation: he does not "suppose it practicable totally to suppress whoreing; the consequence of which, were it possible to effect it, might be the encrease of a horrid vice too rife already, though the bare thought of it strikes the mind with horror . . . ."86

Prostitutes operating out of brothels or bawdyhouses (whether or not controlled by bawds) in fact were greatly outnumbered not only by "private" adulterers but also by "private" streetwalkers.87 That the brothel nonetheless loomed so large in the popular imagination may owe to its provocative aura of the domestic, its parodic evocation of "housework." Bawds were commonly known as the "mothers" of their "families."88 Henry Fielding described the bawdyhouse as though it were the mirror reflection of the tutelary family household at mid-century, "an age when brothels are become in a manner the seminaries of edu-

cation, and that especially of those youths whose birth makes their right institution of the utmost consequence to the future well being of the public: for
whatever may be the education of these youths, however vitiated and enervated
their minds and bodies may be with vices and diseases, they are born to be the
governors of our posterity." In 1749 Fielding endured public criticism for calling out the military to suppress a bawdyhouse riot in the Strand that was entering into its third night of activity. The riot was caused by seamen who had been
demobilized after the War of Jenkins' Ear and ransacked a house where some of
them had been refused reparation for theft. Figure 4.16 depicts this scene:
sailors build a bonfire out of the furniture and belongings of the bawdyhouse,
whose detail, except perhaps for its specialized reading matter—a sermon, a Tyburn confession, but also *Onania* and Mandeville's *Modest Defence of Publick
Stews*—emphasizes its close resemblance to the average domestic household.[89]

Indeed, brothels are not only like family households; they may spring up
within them. And although in all other things the *feme covert* was a legal nonen-
tity, in such cases the wisdom of the law acknowledged her domestic "governor-
ship" sufficiently to punish her along with her husband for brothel-keeping. Or
as Fielding put it, "[N]otwithstanding the Favour which the Law in many
Cases extends to married Women, yet in this case the Wife is equally indictable,
and may be found guilty with her Husband." Fielding based this judgment on
legal authority, which ruled that brothel-keeping was "an offense as to the government of the house in which the wife has a principal share."[90] Like the authorities whose job it was to recognize and prosecute libel, those whose penal
province was prostitution nurtured an expertise in identifying clues that both
concealed and revealed the public nature of an ostensibly private domestic
dwelling: "[T]hough there is no particular sign upon them, yet, from the door
being kept upon the jar, the particular manner in which they are painted, the
blinds and curtains, it is very well known what sort of houses they are."[91] As political allegory of the Restoration and early eighteenth century sometimes
claimed the innocence of mere "romance," what has been called the "sentimentalization" of the public brothel (including its self-presentation as a private
household) in the later part of the century may also harbor a political motive.[92]
By the same token, perhaps, the Magdalen penitentiary was modeled, according to contemporaries, on the "well-regulated private family": its male founders
called themselves "Fathers," and its matron was seen as "a good mother to all
her little family."[93] Figure 4.17 depicts a Magdalen penitent whose posture recalls that seen in the closet of devotion (see fig. 1.2). The divine light of grace
before which the female subject kneels is now explicitly represented as light
taken in from the outside. The angel is replaced by textual aids to interior ref-

ormation—the Book of Common Prayer, the institutional Table of Diet—and by the instrument of women's inside work, the spinning wheel.

Especially during the Restoration period, the difference between the private and the public whore also might mean the difference between the common prostitute (whether housed or pedestrian) and the true courtesan, the *cortegiana honesta,* the whore at court.[94] In Easter week of 1668 large crowds of apprentices attacked and pulled down a number of brothels, accompanied by slogans and symbolism that tied the rioting to grievances over recent legislation prohibiting liberty of conscience. The motives for the Bawdy House Riots, as they came to be called, are difficult to sort out. A recent study suggests that their logic was to connect standing laws against Nonconformists with those against prostitution: if the government was intent on enforcing the former, the rioters would enforce the latter as well. One strand of this logic, adumbrated in

FIG. 4.16. *The Tar's Triumph or Bawdy-House Battery,* 1749, in Derek Jarrett, *England in the Age of Hogarth* (New Haven, CT: Yale University Press, 1986). Princeton University Library.

FIG. 4.17. Frontispiece, Jonas Hanway, *Thoughts on the Plan for a Magdalen House* (1758), in Miles Ogborn, *Spaces of Modernity: London Geographies, 1680–1780* (New York: Guilford, 1998). Princeton University Library.

pamphlets, was the hypocrisy and corruption of persecuting the "poor Inferior Whores" of the brothels and celebrating the "most exquisite Whoores" who were "the bosome freinds of Kings and Archbishops." Addressed as the representative of these public, state whores was Charles II's mistress Barbara Villiers, Countess of Castlemaine, a recent convert to Roman Catholicism whom Charles had given rooms in Whitehall. "But here it was said," wrote Samuel Pepys, "how these idle fellows have had the confidence to say that they did ill in contenting themselfs in pulling down the little bawdy-houses and did not go and pull down the great bawdy-house at White hall." So the bawdyhouse held a powerful imaginative sway, mediating as it did between the private family and the public state, the common household and the royal household.⁹⁵

Throughout the prostitution discourse of this period there runs not only the thread of public-private ambiguity but also the impulse, even when the inside is thought to be no different from the outside, to strip away the public facade so as to disclose the private interior of truth. The impulse is clear enough in the titles of two of the wandering-whore tracts: *Strange Newes from Bartholomew-Fair, or, the Wandring-Whore Discovered, Her Cabinet unlockt, her Secrets laid open, vnvailed, and spread abroad . . . By Peter Aretine* (1661) and *The Wandring-Whores Complaint for W'ant of Trading Wherein the Cabinet of her Iniquity is Unlockt and All Her Secrets Laid Open* (1663).⁹⁶ In Jonathan Swift's poem "A Beautiful Young Nymph Going to Bed. Written for the Honour of the Fair-Sex . . ." (1734) the private cabinet the speaker unlocks and systematically rifles is the streetwalker's own squalid bedroom and its bodily leavings. The single-minded relentlessness of the disclosure is mitigated in part by the pathos of Corinna's dreams and in part by our realization that Swift's target is not so much the public hypocrisy of the fair sex as that of male love poetry supposedly written in its honor.⁹⁷

The Whores Rhetorick

Nowhere was the complex ambivalence of contemporary attitudes toward prostitution registered more acutely than in the English adaptation (a great deal more free than a translation) of Ferrante Pallavicino's *La retorica delle puttane* (1642). I will devote extended attention to this tract.⁹⁸ Self-consciously shaped by a number of literary models, *The Whores Rhetorick* (1683) preserves from its Italian progenitor a fundamental link to the books of secrets, and especially to "all the subtilties in *Machiavel* with *Guicciardin's*, and *Boccalin's* sage Advertisements . . . ." Like *The Prince*, *The Whores Rhetorick* takes the radically skeptical position that human behavior may be reduced to pragmatic rules of art (reason of state, reason of prostitution), that the only metaphysical authority to which the whore is subject is that of an amoral Machiavellian *fortuna*. Dorothea is "a young and most beautiful Virgin" whose father "had much more Nobility in his Veins than Money in his Purse . . . ." This was because he was one of those Cavaliers who supported Charles II in "the last intestine broils," watched their family estates sink with their monarch's fortunes, and were shocked to see their loyalty go unrewarded after the Restoration. Now destitute, Dorothea sees the ironic appropriateness that the "Goddess of Fortune" should be her antagonist: "Is it then from this insensible Divinity that our whole Sex remains accursed, condemned to subjection, and called by the other part of mankind, light, giddy, capricious and unconstant?" But Mrs. Cresswell, a notorious London bawd whom the English version identifies as one of the two speakers of the tract, reassures her young disciple of her potential *virtu,* telling her there are "blessings for thee in store; if with an industrious and vigilant hand, thou wilt turn Fortunes wheel to thy own humour." The aged Cresswell is able to make this claim because she has undertaken to leave to Dorothea "all the choice se-crets of my Soul, all those Soveriegn Receipts" of esoteric knowledge at her dis-posal, that is, to teach her the mysteries of prostitution.[99]

Machiavelli's prince succeeds through force and fraud. Lacking access to the former, the whore must depend upon the latter; hence her crucial reliance on "rhetoric," defined as "that which makes an absolute Orator" and associated by the author with the ancient art of sophistry (22, 20–21).[100] As we might expect, a Machiavellian perspective on prostitution has frequent recourse to the com-parison between the private whore and the public magistrate. Like the other bawds of London, Mrs. Cresswell pursues the "State-Policy" of a "Supervisor of Love" (74, 41); she has "serve[d] the publick . . . to the joy, comfort and support of the whole amorous Republick" (38). Dorothea learns quickly: "Why Moth-er," she says, "I think you design to make me a States-woman, as well as know-ing in the Rules of Rhetorick. I shall endeavour to imitate the wise Prince, to shew neither partiality, nor cowardize in the administration of my Republick" (58). Elsewhere the prostitute's dominion takes on a more absolutist coloring. Even the most abject of whores "govern the World," says Cresswell. "If privy Councellours, Judges, Aldermen, Doctors, Dukes, Lords, Colonels, Knights and Squires maybe made beasts on by these stupid Jades; how thinkest thou might the Cullies be handled by Women of sense and understanding?" (45). Other maxims are no less calculating and absolutist. "With young Men, that have lately dropt from under a Mothers or a Tutors Wing; a Whores great work is at first, rather to captivate their Heart, than win their Purse; because enjoying the first, entitles her to an absolute Soveraignty over the last" (79).

The public-private figure is also construed along a religious axis, emphasiz-ing not just the broad analogy between prostitution and spiritual practices ("A

Whore must not forget that her Bed is the Altar" [95]) but more specifically the themes of liberty and submission that suffuse contemporary religious controversy. The whore covers the ecclesiastical spectrum: she mortifies her flesh like a primitive Christian; she is like a young girl entered into monastic life; Dorothea is a "young Probationer" to the bawd's "Lady Abbess," or to "the *Jesuites* . . . Seminary"; but the whore is also "a latitudinarian in Love," like the Calvinist "Elect" or the familists who meet in "dark Conventicles," and possessed of a "Fanatick Parson's" eloquence (13, 59, 160, 101, 94, 71, 113, 68, 136–41). As for the whore's clients, although "all Men are of a Romish perswasion" in their devotion to "obscene images" (like Aretino's erotic postures), those "who have dyed Martyrs in the cause of *Venus*" should be avoided so as not to offend "Votaries . . . of a *Geneva* stamp," who abhor "*Passive Obedience*" (127–28).[101]

The whore is referred to throughout as a "Trading Lady," and mercantile terms of art pervade the tract, sometimes evoking the problematic conditions of overseas intercourse that natural-law theory evolved to adjudicate. Thus a whore who allows a "pert man of War" to enter her "streights" "without first disbursing the usual tax . . . would discredit her Government, bring her Policy in question, and encourage every pitiful Privateer to steer the same course, in hopes of the like success." Here the whores come close to exercising directly a public, state authority. Elsewhere they are figured as private merchants who, free of their trade, constitute a trading company with whom the author himself wittily hopes to have informal affiliation: "If you become free of your amorous caresses, [the author] promises to regulate himself . . . it is hoped you will grant me liberty to trade, though I cannot properly as one of your body politick, yet very well as an interloping Merchant." The author's affiliation apparently is justified by his authorship of this very tract, a craft handbook that provides "the Rules of a Profession" and "the Mysteries of this Trade." Guild mysteries resonate not only (as we have seen) with the *arcana* of absolutist politics but also with the *ars amandi*, whose secrecy is redoubled in the scandalous intimacy of prostitution (66–67, 97–98, 14–15, 19).

The Whores Rhetorick seems less inclined to associate prostitution with one particular economic, religious, or political practice than to entertain a range of professional analogues simultaneously. Clearly, the author aims to accommodate the debased activity of prostitution to the norms of professional life—even as those norms are glancingly thrown into question. Yet beneath the explicit level of simile is adumbrated another comparison that sheds a different light on this apology for prostitution. The author seeks a "liberty to trade" from the London whores not simply because he writes about their profession but also because their profession is like his (11, 15). Like theirs, the author's job is to "gratifie all Mankind" (17). As Cresswell says at one point to Dorothea, "You must look on it as the great business of your life, to please others, and enrich your self" (53). To this extent *The Whores Rhetorick* is a discontinuous allegory of the emergent profession of authorship. Perhaps it may even be said to allegorize female authorship in particular and thereby to articulate the relationship between authorship and prostitution as analogous (and exceptional) means by which women may exercise a public profession.[102] When Cresswell says she "could shew thee a noble precedent" for a whore having sex with both father and son, Dorothea replies: "I guess your meaning. It is an intrigue might afford matter for a Novel, which would in part take off the scandal of translating daily such numbers of *French* ones, that are in my mind, fitter for the necessary House [i.e., privy] than the Closet" (135). Less than a year after the publication of *The Whores Rhetorick* there appeared in print the first part of Aphra Behn's *Love-Letters Between a Noble-Man and his Sister,* a "novel" purporting to be a *roman à clef* translated from the French and replete with scandalous noble intrigues of this sort. In this way, the author appears to allude to the imminent publication of a narrative written about whores and by a woman commonly accused of literary prostitution.[103]

Certainly the author is concerned to distinguish the public profession of the whore from the private status of the wife. To this end the whore is seen as a kind of antiwife, and the basic terms of opposition are the same as those operative in contemporary efforts to separate out the basic antithetical motives for marriage: love versus interest/money. Whores "relinquish all those frailties that render the Sex weak and contemptible." The frailty of love is not clearly distinguished here from that of sexual desire: the "chief happiness" of wives lies "in gratifying their carnal and obscene desires; whereas a Whores interest and worldly lucre ought to be considered as her first, last, and her greatest wish." Playing upon the status of the married woman as a *feme covert* who is legally dead, Cresswell advises Dorothea to behave like "a person dead in Law," to "devest your self of all Womanish . . . weakness and pusillanimity . . . ," to "be sure to believe your person dead as to all Laws, except those prescribed by your own interest." So the prostitute is the *feme sole* whose disguise as the legally dead *feme covert* provides the cover for a singularly libertine life (111–12, 155, 160).

How singular is such a life? Although the legal status of *feme sole* is available to others besides prostitutes, this tract pointedly concentrates on the whore alone, "without regarding the married Women, Widow, or superficial Maid; who do not obey the dictates of interest, but prostitute themselves meerly to gratifie their libidinous appetites" (47). The ironic imputation of prostitution to those who are not officially prostitutes is acute; but why not exempt also widows? This is especially surprising given the resemblance between the author's portrait of the self-interested whore and Butler's extended characterization of the widow in the recently published *Hudibras*.[104] One similarity in particular deserves comment. Cresswell advises Dorothea to receive all love sonnets with the utmost enthusiasm, in accord with the general principle that the whore's discourse must be replete with "sophistry," "a medley of lyes and fictions" (121). Cresswell's advice follows directly upon her instruction that "[y]ou must study a particular way of commending every thing he wears" that momentarily reads like a parodic reversal of the poetic *blazon:* praise "the briskness of his raillery, the fringe of his Gloves, his Lace, the smoothness of his Face, the redness of his Lip, his jantee way of picking his Teeth, the foretop of his Peruque . . ." (120). The impression of mock love poetry is furthered later on in the tract, when Cresswell instructs Dorothea on the technique of lascivious kissing:

> You must not forget to use the natural accents of dying persons, as my Heart, my Life, my Soul, I Dye, let us Dye together, and the like, which imply a counterfeit, if not a real sense. You must add to these, ejaculations, aspirations, sighs, intercision of words, and such like gallantries, whereby you may give your Mate to belive, that you are melted, dissolved, and wholly consumed in pleasure, though Ladies of large business are generally no more moved by an imbrace, than if they were made of Wood or Stone. (148)

These passages are striking not only because they acknowledge the hypocrisy of male love poetry but also because they invite the woman (reinforcing the conjunction of author and whore) to fashion her own knowing version of it. When Butler's Hudibras undertakes to court the wealthy widow, his best Petrarchan flights meet with only a cold and penetrating skepticism. "I cannot *Love* where I'm *belov'd*," complains the widow:

> *Love-passions* are like *Parables,*
> By which men still mean something else:
> Though *Love* be all the worlds pretence,
> Mony's the *Mythologique* sence,
> The real substance of the shadow,
> Which all Address and Courtship's made to.
> . . . .
> For you will find it a hard *Chapter,*
> To catch me with *Poetique Rapture,*
> In which your *Mastery* of *Art*
> Doth shew it self, and not your *Heart:*
> Nor will you raise in mine *combustion,*
> By dint of high *Heroique* fustian:
> Shee that with *Poetry* is won,
> Is but a *Desk* to write upon;

And what men say of her, they mean,
No more, then that on which they *lean*.
Some . . .

. . . . .

Use her so barbarously ill,
To grind her Lips upon a *Mill,*
Until the *Facet Doublet* [105] doth
Fit their *Rhimes* rather then her mouth;
Her mouth compar'd t'an *Oyster's,* with
A Row of *Pearl* in't, stead of *Teeth;*
Others, make *Posies* of her *Cheeks,*
Where *red,* and *whitest* colours mix . . . .[106]

Like the whore, the widow is in a position to expose the conceits of love poetry for what they are: the crass materialism of a putative idealism; the narcissistic self-display of a seeming servility; the reification of the poetic subject as mere poetic apparatus; the studied brutality of the *blazon.*[107] The position that enables this exposure, that of material interestedness, is also what enables prostitution to function as the professional (but crucially regendered) equivalent of Petrarchan hypocrisy. If the whore's devotion to money over love superficially reminds us of the patriarchalist absolutism of the father, it pertains more accurately to the devolutionary absolutism of absolute private property, of the widowed *feme sole.*

However, our doubts about the singularity of the whore are fed, in *The Whores Rhetorick,* by more than just her comparability to the widow. Arguing the importance of having a multitude of clients, Cresswell calls it "the height of folly to depend on the supplies of one Purse . . ." (56). Yet it might develop, she admits, that "'one of your favorites,' jealous of his rivals," offers Dorothea an "easy and pleasant station" too good to be refused, one that includes "a convenient maintenance setled during your own life, in case of any contingency, as a rupture between you, his death, or the alteration of his humour" (59). And soon enough Cresswell enjoins Dorothea to

> raise your aspiring thoughts and consider how you may best make your self capable of enjoying a third part of your future Husband's estate, if you should chance to survive him. The Lawyers call this Dower in their Jargon, and tell us it is one of their Ladies prime favorites, and seems in her eyes the most pretious Jewel, next to Life and Liberty, that she wears about her rusty and wrinkled Neck. If these Gentlemen of the Robe would pardon the misprision (for so I am sure they miscall it) I should think this careful provision for married Women might be well termed the courtesie of *England* . . . . (59–60)

The turn in the argument is unsettling, for it encourages us to see the relationship between public whore and domestic wife not antithetically but instrumentally. Marriage is the futurity of prostitution; to be a successful whore is to pursue one's interested liberty so profitably as to verge on the status of a wife. The adulterous "courtesy" of the courtesan dovetails with the common-law "courtesy" of the marriage settlement.[108]

Soon after, the bawd returns to the antithetical formulation we have learned to expect from her. But the surprising dovetailing of wife and whore is not entirely suppressed, and it recurs strikingly toward the end of the tract as Cresswell's skepticism reaches its culmination. The world is run by deception, she says. Indeed, "[m]arryed Women do daily discover new fine methods to abuse their Husbands . . . ." Dorothea replies: "I see married Ladies have likewise their State-policy." After her long discourse Cresswell regrets her failing voice, "else I could make a longer harangue on the marryed Dames State-Policy than I have done on the Whores Rhetorick." True, wives and whores may be distinguished by their respective susceptibilities to lust and the lust for money. But the difference between sexual and financial desire seems insignificant in the face of common interest: "Honour in Women advances them only to act the Whore in a higher sphere . . ." (62, 105, 150, 155).

This reversal colors our experience of the entire tract. The professional promiscuity of the public whore bleeds into the "professional" adultery of the private wife. Marriage for love is one crucial tactic in the more general strategy of marriage for interest. The liberty of the *feme sole* emulates the arguably greater liberty of the *feme covert*. The whore's rhetoric is in the end indistinguishable from the wife's rhetoric: as *The Prince* addresses the new man, so *The Whores Rhetorick* addresses nothing less than the new woman. From one perspective, this is recognizable as the misogyny of a peculiarly Italianate libertinism, whose corrosive cynicism prognosticates the failure of the legal innovations in married women's separate property in England with which it is contemporary and of which it is acutely aware. From another perspective, however, this only extends and fulfills the utopian politics of the freedom of the private subject, which is logically predicated on the status of the married woman as the last and most concentrated instance of absolute private authority achieved through the internalization of patriarchalist absolutism. The wife's privation, the prison of her coverture, is the precondition for her secret productivity.

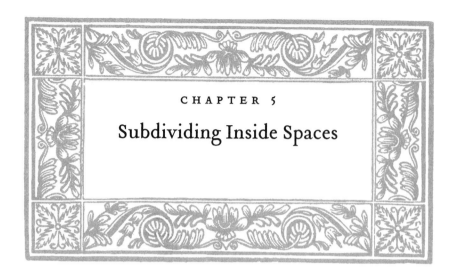

CHAPTER 5

Subdividing Inside Spaces

The transition from cottage industry to the factory system has a well-known significance in the emergence of modern culture. In Max Weber's words, "The modern rational organization of the capitalistic enterprise would not have been possible without . . . the separation of business from the household, which completely dominates modern economic life . . . ."[1] Industrial production is only the most obvious instance of this transition. The rise of the professions entailed the separation out not only of specialized technical practices but also of specialized workplaces. As with the cottage industry and protoindustrialization, a brief glimpse of "protoprofessional" space at this transitional moment affords some insight into one aspect of the modern public-private relationship.

Separating Out "Science"

Perhaps the most consequential of all divisions of knowledge in the early modern period is the separation out of "the sciences" in the modern sense of the term: from *scientia* in the traditional meaning of knowledge as such; from the arts and the humanities; and from all practices indifferent to the strictest principles of empirical epistemology. The development of modern science is coextensive with the development of what we have learned to call "laboratories," whose family resemblances distinguish them from the disparate range of spaces —monasteries, theaters, altars, domestic kitchens and closets—in which "natural philosophers" of all sorts were accustomed to practice their arts.[2] These practitioners—alchemists, astrologers, apothecaries, unnatural natural historians, collectors, quacks, antiquarians, virtuosi—helped mediate the emergence of the modern figure of the "scientist." In contemporary depictions of their

practices the particularity of a distinctive and specialized kind of space is precisely what is absent. What these images share looks retrospectively like a parasitic dependence on the more "traditional" sorts of inside space, as well as some
representational commonplaces that seem for that reason alone to bespeak a
common enterprise.

A number of seventeenth-century, primarily Dutch genre painters were fond
of the subject of the alchemist at work. Figures 5.1 and 5.2, paintings of the mid-
to later seventeenth century by Thomas Wijck and his younger contemporary
Richard Brakenburgh, illustrate the coextension of "public" laboratory and
private household space within a single shared interior through the depiction of
male alchemical activity alongside female housework and maternal care. In
Wijck's painting, the alchemist is set back from his family by the doubly vaulted
structure of the deep but open interior space. He sits at his desk reading, surrounded by books and a globe, a studious and contemplative figure whose beret
and fur-trimmed cloak are those of a scholar. Suspended from the ceiling are
specimens, a reptile and a turtle, whose presence and placement are, as we will
see, a representational convention that helps define the common ground between the disparate practitioners of protoscience (cf. fig. 4.12, the entrance to
the apothecary's shop). In the left foreground an alchemical distillation occupies
part of the stove. To its right are the alchemist's wife and two children, the son
helping his mother prepare food and the daughter, perhaps too young for real
work, nonetheless imitating her mother's diligence. On the table are bread and
a pitcher, on the floor a jumble of alchemical and culinary utensils. Light enters
the foreground space from windows that look out onto a village scene. This is a
household in which work and housework enjoy a harmonious coexistence.

In Brakenburgh's painting, similar elements are arranged to very different effect. The space is dark but not deep, the limits of the background defined by
the dim outlines of furniture and the seated group, a typical and familiar image
from other Netherlandish genre painters. The foreground—indeed, the painting—is dominated by the standing figure of the alchemist's wife, whose grace-
ful frustration organizes the sense of ironic disjunction that permeates the scene
she surveys. A small child clinging to her skirts, she expostulates with her husband, her right hand gesturing toward four more children in the left foreground: one plays alchemist on the floor, two sit forlorn at a small empty table,
and another points to an empty cupboard. On the other side of the room, his
eyes wide with excitement, is the alchemist, monopolizing the fire and surrounded by the clutter of his instruments, his eldest son behind him gaily aping
his father by pumping the lever of the hearth bellows. The conventionality of
the alchemist paintings militates against reading them, as some have done, as
efforts at the "realistic" representation of early laboratory space.[3] Still, the inter-

FIG. 5.1. Thomas Wijck, *The Alchemist,* seventeenth century. Oil on panel. Eddleman Collection 00.03.06, Chemical Heritage Foundation Collections, Philadelphia, PA. Photo: Will Brown.

FIG. 5.2. Richard Brakenburgh, *An Alchemist's Workshop with Children Playing,* late seventeenth century. Oil on canvas. Eddleman Collection 00.03.11, Chemical Heritage Foundation Collections, Philadelphia, PA. Photo: Will Brown.

penetration of public and private spaces, of scientific experiment and the domestic household, is consistent with what we know from other sources about the early practice of natural philosophy.[4] What Brakenburgh registers, however, is a growing skepticism about the figure of the alchemist that itself becomes conventional in genre paintings and other cultural commentary in the eighteenth century and that has some bearing on this spatial coextension.[5] The central irony concerns what is gradually being exposed as the grandiose impracticality of the alchemical ambition, and it is pointed by the failure of the dreamy head of household to support his family with his labor. But the resulting disjunction between the alchemist's work and his wife's vain efforts at housework depends for much of its effect on the way Brakenburgh makes us feel their incompatibility within the same domestic space.

One of William Hogarth's large engraved illustrations (1725) for Samuel Butler's *Hudibras* (1663), set in the astrologer Sidrophel's chambers (fig. 5.3), depicts the knight holding off Sidrophel and his assistant Whachum as Ralpho runs to fetch the constable (pt. 2, canto 3, lines 1013–70). As in the alchemist paintings, the astrologer's sanctum is cluttered with arcane paraphernalia, including books, a globe, and suspended specimens of fish and reptiles. Moreover, the presence of a cat places the scene of *arcana naturae* in a larger if largely suggested domestic setting (cf., in figs. 2.4 and 4.8 and plate 1, the domesticating conventionality of the household pets in the home-work spaces of coffeehouse, flax spinners, and business office). Figure 5.4, *Dr. Silvester Partridge's Predictions* (1719), is more obviously part of a household space. The astrologer, casting nativities for his customers, is surrounded by books, equipment (some of it alchemical), and suspended specimens.

FIG. 5.3. William Hogarth, *Hudibras beats Sidrophel and Whacum*, 1726. No. 8 of twelve illustrations for Samuel Butler's *Hudibras* (1663, 1664, 1678), in William Hogarth, *Hogarth: The Complete Engravings*, ed. Joseph Burke and Colin Caldwell (New York: Abrams, 1968). Princeton University Library.

FIG. 5.4. Elisha Kirkall, *Dr. Silvester Partridge's Predictions*, 1719, in Charles Saumarez Smith, *Eighteenth-Century Decoration: Design and the Domestic Interior in England* (New York: Abrams, 1993). Princeton University Library.

The motif of the suspended specimen links these representations of alchemists and astrologers, both partly embedded in the household, to a third
practice of early modern natural philosophy, the cabinet of curiosities. The
term "cabinet" first referred to a cupboard with shelves and drawers that held
assorted small natural and cultural rarities. Although it continued to have this
meaning, by the seventeenth century the word might also designate the larger
space—a closet or a chamber—that contained such cabinets.6 The wall structure we see behind Dr. Partridge fits the original description well enough, but
its contents are more serviceable than collectible; the cabinet of curiosities was,
not surprisingly, a luxury of the nobility and/or the wealthy. A private space
within a private space, the cabinet encapsulated the great world within its odd
and wondrous confines, and it announced its owner to be a gentleman of polite
and cosmopolitan understanding. Public museums owe their origins to these
private collections, which graced the estates and palaces of the Renaissance patriciate. Figure 5.5 is the first known illustration of such a museum, every inch
of wall and ceiling filled with the recondite secrets of the universe. The son of
the owner, the apothecary Ferrante Imperato, points out some choice specimens to elegantly attired visitors, while at their feet two domesticated lap dogs
counterbalance the wild beasts overhead and remind us that this seemingly
public museum is part of the apothecary's private family palace.7

When the Royal Society announced the existence of its museum "repository"
in 1666 it was described as a place where the gifts of benefactors would be preserved for posterity "probably much better and safer, than in their own private
Cabinets."8 Something of the early modern transformation of "science" from a
collection of *arcana naturae* to the vast domain of material knowledge can be felt
in the relationship between these cabinets and John Locke's domestication of
epistemology as a process of furnishing and familiarizing the cabinet of the
mind: "The Senses at first let in particular *Ideas,* and furnish the yet empty Cabinet: And the Mind by degrees growing familiar with some of them, they are
lodged in the Memory, and Names got to them."9 It may be unwarranted to
read in Locke's metaphorical account of "lodging," then "naming," a systematic
organizing motive. Nonetheless, we may speculate that what distinguishes the
traditional cabinet of curiosities from the modern museum is not only its publicness but also its explicit aim to rationalize. One central ambition of the cabinet
of curiosities is to amass objects that amaze not only in their odd singularity but
also in the way this singularity is reinforced by the arbitrariness of their arrangement. In rationalizing its objects according to geographical, temporal, and cultural criteria, the modern museum on the contrary emphasizes collectivity over
singularity, even—in allowing for empty spaces that will be filled by future specimens that are known to exist but not yet possessed—virtual collectivity.

FIG. 5.5. *Ferrante Imperato's Museum in Naples,* 1599, in *The Origins of Museums: The Cabinet of Curiosities in Sixteenth- and Seventeenth-Century Europe,* ed. Oliver Impey and Arthur MacGregor (Oxford: Clarendon, 1985). Princeton University Press.

The Royal Household

The separation of workplace from household is an almost universal feature of capitalist development, although it proceeded at different rates in different locales. Like the inn and the alehouse before it, the coffeehouse brought the private activity of food consumption into the public realm of market exchange. Images of eighteenth-century coffeehouses show traces of domestic living space, not only likely culinary articles (hearths, dish cupboards, and buffets) but also less predictable details like paintings, mirrors, and a customer still dressed for bed (see figs. 2.3 and 2.4). "They say," wrote Joseph Moxon in 1684, "Such a One has set up a *Printing-House,* when thereby they only mean he has remov'd the Tools us'd in his former House." Indeed the state's apprehension of

"Printing-houses, and Presses erected in byplaces and corners, out of the Eye of Government" led to the Interregnum parliamentary requirement that printers work *only* in "their respective Dwelling-Houses, and not elsewhere." In this exceptional way, then, domestic space was to have the visibility of public space: according to Moxon, illicit printers had "to get a Hole Private," where they might do their work "With More Secrecy Privaty and Securaty."[10] On the other hand, in the centers of large provincial towns, lockup shops, where the family lived off the premises, did not become common until after the middle of the nineteenth century.[11] In figure 3.2 we have an image of what the coextension of household and workplace looked like at the lower levels of common life.

However, the separation of workplace from household is only the most obvious manifestation of the way the division of the private from the public was spatialized in early modern interiors. In the development of elite dwelling structures from the fifteenth through the eighteenth centuries we have a graphic account both of the long-term transition from relations of distinction to those of separation between the public and the private and of the way this change proceeds through the successive rediscovery, within the private realm, of a capacity for further subdivision. The risk of this kind of survey lies in the methodological necessity of a starting point, which, however heuristic its originating status, by the nature of the operation never undergoes the complicating analysis to which later stages are programmatically subjected. I trust the reader will understand this as a formal consequence of method rather than as a substantive claim as to the immutability of medieval interiors, which I have neither the motive nor the knowledge to make.

In the mid-seventeenth century, John Selden looked back to a time when the hall was "the place where the great lord used to eat (wherefore else were the Halls made so big?), where he saw all his servants and tenants about him. He ate not in private, except in time of sickness: when once he became a thing cooped up, all his greatness was spilled." In the late-medieval household, the maintenance of greatness required public spectacle and display, nowhere more so than in the ceremony of eating. But the openness of the great household went hand in hand with the ritualized expression of hierarchy, deference, and social place, which required a system of distinctions between spaces that marked differences in status that were also permeable to the basic principle of social totality. Francis Bacon acknowledged the most important of these architectural distinctions when he wrote that "you cannot have a perfect palace, except you have two several sides; a side for the banquet, . . . and a side for the household; the one for feasts and triumphs, and the other for dwelling."[12]

But Bacon's distinction cannot be correlated with our notions of the divide between the public and the private in any decisive way. This can be seen in figure 5.6, a schematic diagram of the great house, whose basic distinction between the household of magnificence and the household of service cuts across Bacon's categorization. On the one hand, "public" feasts are set apart from "private" dwellings. On the other hand, feasts in the great hall are coextensive with the service rooms that produce them and distinct from the sequestered magnificence of the lord and his nuclear family in the great chamber. The dais step marks the barrier between these two households; but the screen marks another barrier, between those visitors who were admitted to the great hall to dine with the lord and those who might be offered no more than a drink at the buttery bar—as well as the servants engaged in food preparation. At the end of the screens passage is the door to the house, a third barrier between house and courtyard, which supplements the more fundamental act of social filtering that occurs at the gatehouse, "the immediate limit of the lord's territory." Viewed in this way, the great household exemplifies the model of the "linear house," the central aim of whose layout was to map, as a "visual expression of hierarchy," the successive degrees of access to the lord. All distinctions subserve this purpose of social subordination, which subsumes the several divisions between chamber and hall, hall and service rooms, house and courtyard, gatehouse and outside territory.[13] Indeed, the inapplicability of a consistent "public versus private" distinction even to these several divisions is clear from basic ambiguities in usage (thus life in the great chamber entails both the ultimate publicity of "magnificence" and the ultimate privacy of absence from public display). "Private" and "public" have a real but locally variable utility in this system, whose organizing coordinates are determined rather by a status hierarchy for which the difference between the public and the private in our sense of those terms is of ancillary importance.

Broadly speaking, innovation in interior design and usage began at the highest level of the social hierarchy and filtered downwards. Between the fifteenth and the early sixteenth centuries it became increasingly customary for the lord, his family, and his most immediate guests to dine in the chamber rather than in the hall. In the royal household this development—a withdrawal of public state into semiprivacy, which might equally be seen as an adaptation of private space to semipublic uses—occurred as early as the beginning of the fourteenth century. Thus began the slow process by which the great hall was transformed, by the seventeenth century, from the place of collective dining to the place where one first enters the house itself, the entrance hall. As if in confirmation, a century later Henry VII initiated a subdivision of the great chamber into its ceremonial and its personal aspects, the latter of which included the privy chamber (also called the secret chamber) or bedchamber, whose servants alone were likely to come into anything more than the most formal contact with the king.

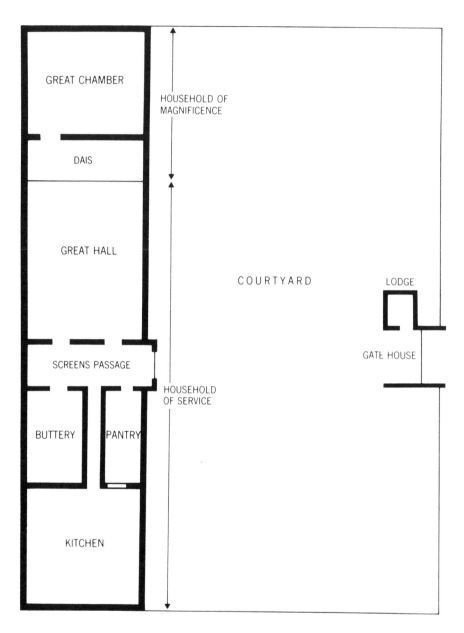

FIG. 5.6. Schematic diagram of the great house, in Felicity Heal, *Hospitality in Early Modern England* (Oxford: Clarendon, 1990), fig. 21 (p. 28). By permission of Oxford University Press.

Now the structure of the royal household was triadic: privy chamber, chamber, household. According to one historian, "the process of withdrawal and subdivision entered a new phase" in the following reign, when Henry VIII created a new room, the presence chamber, to assume the functions of the old chamber, which now was to house the newly founded yeomen of the guard. Meanwhile the privy chamber became a private dining and reception chamber, subdivided from the royal bedchamber by a withdrawing room. Figure 5.7 is a schematic diagram of the king's apartments in the palace at Whitehall as they reflected these changes in the century between 1540 and 1640.[14]

A Restoration alchemical writer used the linearity of the royal interior to domesticate his vision of mystical theology as an exacting rite of sequential passages: "As in a *Royal Palace* we must pass through many rooms and *apartments,* before we come to the *Presence-chamber* of the Prince, so in *Eternal Nature* the *forms of darkness* must be pass'd through and after these the *Fire* and *Water,* before we can come to the *Love-fire,* which the Holy Trinity hath chosen for his *Presence-chamber*."[15] At the same time, however, it is not hard to see signs of the future in this plan. One general feature that will have important consequences in the later design of interiors is the way in which the subdivision and multiplication of rooms challenges the structure of the linear house and its incremental expression of hierarchy. Indeed, the ramification of architectural space with which the following pages will be concerned had its corollaries in other sorts of interiority. John Locke, a contemporary of the alchemical writer just cited, also used the figure of the royal presence chamber to express how exacting must be the access of our senses to our understanding: "There are *some* Ideas, *which have admittance only through one Sense* . . . . And if these Organs, or the Nerves which are the Conduits, to convey them from without to their Audience in the Brain, the mind's Presence-room (as I may so call it) are any of them so disordered, as not to perform their Functions, they have no Postern to be admitted by . . . ." To do justice to the actual complexity of cognition, however, Locke is obliged to undercut the model of uniform linearity—there are five senses, not one—that the analogy otherwise might have conveyed, and we are left instead with the image of multiple passages radiating out from a singular center.[16] Another foretaste of futurity in this plan is the privy gallery (G), a mediating passageway that promotes privacy in principle by obviating the need to pass through other rooms in order to gain access to one's chosen destination. A third notable feature of this plan is the use of the closet as a sort of extended withdrawing room (H, I), a development that at this point requires a brief elaboration.

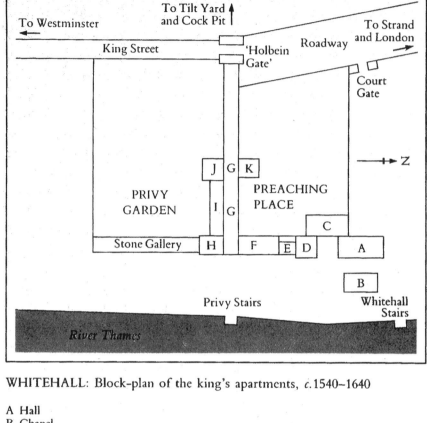

WHITEHALL: Block-plan of the king's apartments, *c*.1540–1640

A Hall
B Chapel
C Guard Chamber   Yeomen of the Guard
D Presence Chamber   Gentlemen Pensioners, Knights and
                                   Esquires of the Body, Carvers,
                                   Cupbearers, Sewers, Gentlemen
                                   Ushers, Grooms
E Closet (i.e. private chapel)
F Privy Chamber   Gentlemen, Gentlemen Ushers, Grooms
G Privy Gallery
H Withdrawing Room
I Lesser Withdrawing Room, closets
J Bedchamber
K Council Chamber   Privy Councillors

FIG. 5.7. Block plan of the king's apartments, Whitehall, c. 1540–1640, in *The English Court: From the Wars of the Roses to the Civil War* (London: Longman, 1987), ed. David Starkey et al. Copyright © Jutland Ltd. Reproduced by permission of Curtis Brown Ltd., London, on behalf of the copyright owner. Princeton University Library.

Cabinet and Closet

The cabinet of curiosities is only one of several architectural streams that fed the emergence of the domestic closet—the closet of devotion might be described as accessible only through a linear "withdrawal"[17]—but it plays an important role in this process. Indeed, "closet" tends to be the preferred term for what the French called a *cabinet,* although the latter word is also common enough in English domestic discourse.[18] Like the cabinet of curiosities, the closet was a comparatively small space that enclosed yet smaller ones, and its contents could be quite diverse. In Elizabethan England, aristocratic closets were intimate spaces in which the intricate interiors of sonnets and miniatures might be read and viewed. John Donne evoked this association of the privacy of small rooms with that of small poems over against the discursive publicity of obsequies and chronicles:

> And if unfit for tombes and hearse
> Our legend bee, it will be fit for verse;
> And if no peece of Chronicle wee prove,
> We'll build in sonnets pretty roomes . . . .

One of the great practitioners of the miniature, Nicholas Hilliard, wrote that limning "is for the service of noble persons very meet, in small volumes, in private manner." "[I]t is a kind of gentle painting. . . . [I]t is secret."[19]

Figure 5.8 shows designs for a closet by Hilliard's contemporary Robert Smythson. The minutely honeycombed space is apparently to be used as a business room, since it features sites for desks, writings, loose papers, and ink, as well as for a map. In 1669 Samuel Pepys records: "Then down with Lord Brouncker [navy commissioner and president of the Royal Society] to Sir R. Murray [i.e., Moray] into the King's little elaboratory under his closet, a pretty place, and there saw a great many Chymicall glasses and things, but understood none of them."[20] "Nine feet upon three and a half deep . . . is the least you can allow to the Closet," wrote the architect Sir Roger Pratt in 1660.[21] As Smythson's plan would suggest, the closet (like the cabinet of curiosities) was also a place for keeping books, themselves often rare curiosities, and it provided the model for the domestic room that in the seventeenth century began to be separated out as the "study" or "library."[22] Among the mercantile patriciate of Renaissance Italy, all parts of the household were the wife's province except for the study, where the paterfamilias kept, paradoxically, the family "books and records." (The seeming paradox is explained by the fact that these "private affairs" were "things outside the house," familial in the sense of being crucial to the patrilineal succession, of which the wife was an essential but insubstantial facilitator.) So in the ideal plan of Leon Battista Alberti the separate bedrooms of husband and wife gave off onto, respectively, a library (*libraria cella*) and a dressing room.[23] In England two centuries later, the closet is not so much un-gendered as serviceably double-gendered, a condition aptly expressed by one of the scholastic conundrums we are told Butler's Hudibras has mastered:

> What *Adam* dreamt of when his Bride
> Came from her Closet in his side . . . .[24]

And by the following century the functions of the closet, the study, and the cabinet had been sufficiently separated out to be conflatable under the general and broadly ungendered aegis of private space. In 1700 the marriage articles of William Congreve's Millamant require that she be able to "[c]ome to Dinner when I please, dine in my dressing room when I'm out of humour without giving a reason. To have my Closet Inviolate; to be sole Empress of my Tea-Table, which you must never presume to approach without first asking leave." Toward

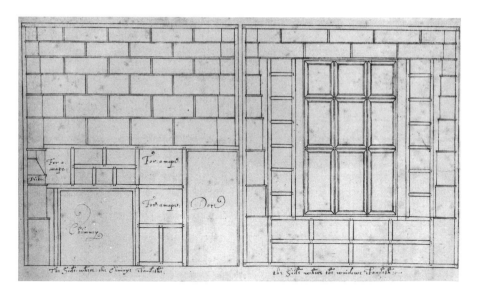

FIG. 5.8. Robert Smythson, design for a closet or business room, c. 1600. *Above*, elevation of two walls, showing a "Deske," three places "For a mape," and "Chimney"; legends: "The Side: where: the Chimnye standethe:" and "The Side where the windowe standethe:—" *Facing page, top*, elevation of one wall, with scale, showing two desks and places "For writings," "For loose Papers," and "For: Incke." *Facing page, bottom*, elevation of one wall showing two desks, three places "for writings:" and two places "For Incke"; legend: "The ende of the Clossette." RIBA Library Drawings Collection, London.

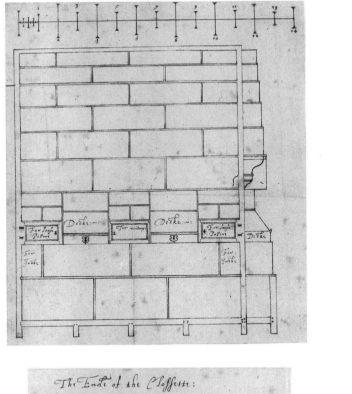

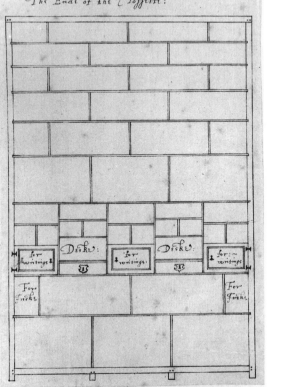

The Endß of the Cloßßett:

the end of the eighteenth century, Samuel Johnson observed that "Mankind was not then [in Shakespeare's England] to be studied in the closet; . . . He that will understand Shakespeare, must not be content to study him in the closet, he must look for his meaning sometimes among the sports of the field, and sometimes among the manufactures of the shop." "The call for books was not in Milton's age what it is in the present, To read was not then a general amusement . . . . The women had not then aspired to literature, nor was every house supplied with a closet of knowledge."[25]

Returning now to my summary account of innovative features in the early modern royal household, we need to be cautious about finding evolutionary implications here for the emergence of "modern" attitudes toward the public and the private, since their meaning in this respect depends entirely on the variant ways in which the Tudor and early Stuart monarchs actually used these spaces.[26] Still, the early terminology of "withdrawal" in royal and noble domestic arrangements warrants speculative generalization. The common element of "privacy" in these early plans is a function of withdrawing from the ceremonial display of magnificence in the dining ritual, a privation of the public "presence" (which by the sixteenth century had itself been hived off into a separate space) from which it negatively derives its meaning. The development of domestic architecture in the following two centuries may be imaginatively encapsulated in the transformation of the withdrawing room from a negative into a positive space, from a public absence to a private sort of presence, a process that was marked by idiomatic usage in the positivizing shift from "withdrawing room" to "drawing room."

Secrets and the Secretary

Before we leave the royal household, it will be instructive to consider how this speculative generalization might be substantiated by attending more closely to the nature of the relationship between the monarch and his or her most intimate counselors. To speak of the royal household is not, of course, to speak of the government, whose central executive consisted, by the seventeenth century, of the monarch, the two secretaries of state, and the privy council. The dynastic nature of English sovereignty is manifested in the critical importance of the royal household in English political life, and in the seventeenth century government and household were significantly intertwined: the chief officers in the household were also members of the privy council, while the two secretaries of state frequently dined at court.[27] In 1677 Andrew Marvell drew attention to the conflict of interests experienced by members of the House of Commons who were also members of "his Majestie's houshold, or who attend upon his royal person, to forget by any chance vote, or in being absent from the House, that they are his domestick servants . . . ." Under Louis XIV the *grand cabinet* evolved as a larger and more public version of the *cabinet,* and the king's came to serve as his *cabinet de conseil,* where Louis's privy council met to discuss state affairs.[28]

In his capacity as secretary to Cromwell's Council of State, John Milton is said to have had printed in 1658 a manuscript by Sir Walter Raleigh whose title asserts both the importance of such a body in English politics and its status as one repository of the absolutist state's *arcana imperii: The Cabinet-Council: Containing the Cheif Arts of Empire, and Mysteries of State; Discabineted In Political and Polemical Aphorisms . . . Published by John Milton, Esq.* Raleigh's tract exemplifies a polemical strategy that became very familiar during the seventeenth century, a disclosure, or "discabineting," of hitherto tightly held state secrets, a publication of the private that alludes, in its own discursive form, to the knot of political esoterica that it exists to untie.[29] "[I]n every state of what quality soever," writes Raleigh, "a secret or Cabinet-Council is mainly necessary. . . . [W]ithout Counsel, no Kingdom, no State, no private house can stand . . . ."[30] Charles II favored public gatherings. By the time Marvell was warning the public about the ties between Charles's government and his household, the king's withdrawing room had become quite open, and even his bedchamber, where the king's daily levee was commonly held, was accessible to principal officers of state and privy councilors. Hence his more truly exclusive closet (or cabinet) was the meeting place for his cabinet council. (The midcentury poet Thomas Randolph, fantastically imagining his own body as a country house, made this invitation to the reader: "Within the inner closet of my brain / Attend the nobler members of my train.")[31] This was also where the king kept clandestine appointments with all sorts of people, who gained secret admittance by means of the back stairs and by arrangement with William Chiffinch, whose office was Senior Page of the Back Stairs and Keeper of the King's Cabinet-Closet.[32] By the early eighteenth century the utmost privacy of the private realm—the intimacy of the household's most interior space—had passed on its name to the privacy of the public realm's most exclusive circle of power, the cabinet.

The relationship between the king and his principal secretaries partook both of the courtier ethos that suffused Renaissance court culture and of a glorified species of domestic labor service. The secretary was a special sort of courtier whose responsibilities received close attention from contemporaries. The most influential authority on the subject, Angel Day, insisted on the etymological significance of the title "secretary":

> [I]n respect of such *Secrecie, trust,* and *assurance* required at the handes of him who serveth in such place, the name was first giuen to be called a *Secretorie,* and that by

the *etymologie* of the verie word it selfe, sounding in true coniecture, *quasi custos,* or *conseruator secreti sibi commissi, a keeper or conseruer of the secret vnto him committed.*

By this reason, we do call the most secrete place in the house, appropriate unto our owne priuate studies, and wherein wee repose and deliberate by deepe consideration of all our waightiest affaires, a *Closet,* in true intendment and meaning, a place where our dealings of importance are shut up, a roome proper and peculiar to our selues. And whereas into each other place of the house, it is ordinarie for euery neere attendant about us to have accesse: in this place we doe solitarie and alone shut up our selues, of this we keep the key our selues, and the use thereof alone doe onelie appropriate unto our selues.[33]

Such an understanding clearly was, in a secular register, consistent with the devotional function of the closet. John Bunyan's allegory fused the two: just before Christiana sets out on pilgrimage she is visited by God's "messenger," whom we recognize to be his secretary: "[M]y name is *Secret,* I dwell with those that are high. . . . *Christiana,* the merciful one has sent me to tell thee that he is a God ready to forgive . . . . He also would have thee know that he inviteth thee to come into his presence, to his Table, and that he will feed thee with the Fat of his House . . . ."[34] Robert Beale, secretary of the Privy Council and sometime principal secretary under Elizabeth, thought a "Secretarie must have a speciall Cabinett, whereof he is himselfe to keepe the Keys, for his signetts, Ciphers and secrett Intelligences, distinguishing the boxes or tills rather by letters than by the names of the Countryes or places, keepinge that only unto himselfe, for the names may inflame a desire to come by such things."[35]

So the secretary's cabinet, like the collector's, contains items that are curious in part for their geographical localism. Unlike the collector, however, the secretary labored for another and was obliged always to keep in mind the difference between his own possessions and those of his master or mistress:

In the Collecc[i]on of thinges I would wish a distincc[i]on used betweene that w[hi]ch is publicke and that w[hi]ch is private,—that is, a separac[i]on betweene those thinges w[hi]ch are her Ma[jes]tie's Recordes and appertaines unto her and those w[hi]ch a Secretarie getteth by his private industrie and charge. Heretofore there was a chamber in Westm[inster] where such thinges, towards the latter end of K[ing] Hen[ry] 8, were kept and were not in the Secretarie's private Custodie . . . . I would wish a Secretarie kept such thinges aparte in a chest or place and n[o]t to confound them w[i]th his owne.[36]

On the one hand, the inner sanctum defines the private apotheosis of public royalty. On the other hand, the privacy of the secretary is even more private than that of his monarch. We may sense a tension here that recalls the omnicompetence both of the courtier and of the housewife. Day expressed the total subservience of the secretary to the "absolute direction" of his "*Lorde or Mais-*

ter" by drawing an "*analogie* or proportion" between secretary and closet: "The *Secretorie*, as hee is a *keeper and conseruer of secrets,* so is hee by his Lorde or Maister, and by none other to bee directed. To a *Closet,* there belongeth properlie, a *doore,* a *locke,* and a *key;* to a *Secretorie,* there appertaineth incidentlie, *Honestie, Care,* and *Fidelitie.*" But the subservience of the secretary cannot be truly absolute in an age of explicitation, as Day implies in his careful acknowledgment that the secretary "carieth a maner of subiection to that partie [his master], who for the time of such service, is at his hands to bee reuerenced and obeyed."[37] And in the remainder of this section of his book Day expands on the capacity of the secretary to be a friend as well to his master, a relationship that decidedly blurs the boundaries of status hierarchy.

To Day's contemporaries it seemed accurate to describe the authority of the secretary as something like an autonomized and internalized possession of the master's authority. Secretaries were called "inward men." Nicholas Faunt saw the secretary as his master's "owne penne, his mouth, his eye, his ease and keeper of his most secret Cabinet." Robert Cecil, principal secretary during the latter years of Elizabeth's reign, thought the secretary was "created by himself, and of his own raising."[38] Language like this recalls the schematic scenario of a devolving absolutism—the movement from subjection to subjecthood to subjectivity—that we have already associated with the civil subject, the wife, and the widow. The present context provides a spatial analogue for this scenario, the movement from the privation of presence entailed in the withdrawal of the monarch from public display to the replete privacy of the secretary, who in serving his master serves, even constitutes, himself.

In the dialectic of master and secretary we may be reminded of a number of relationships that already have arisen in this study, such as that between reader and author as described by the Earl of Shaftesbury: the author "secretly advise[s]" his reader with a hyperhumility characteristic of one confident in his own superiority but also, by virtue of his own industrious self-reading, fully justified in that confidence.[39] Like Shaftesbury's author, the figure of the secretary is a nascent ethical subject because he has internalized the dialectic of sovereignty and subjection within his own being. The secretary has the self-denying serviceability of Addison's Mr. Spectator, especially as darkly reembodied in Tobias Smollett's Misanthrope: "I now appear in the world, not as a member of any community, or what is called a social creature; but meerly as a spectator . . . . I feign myself deaf; an expedient by which I . . . become master of a thousand little secrets, which are every day whispered in my presence, without any suspicion of their being overheard. . . . In consequence of my rank and character I obtain free admission to the ladies, among whom I have obtained the appellation of the Scandalous Chronicle; . . . they divest their conversation of all

restraint before me, and gratify my sense of hearing with strange things, which
. . . would compose a curious piece of secret history . . . ." But the secretary also
shares ground with the figure of the wife in relation to her husband, who is empowered by being, in Eliza Haywood's words, "the Repository of his dearest
Secrets" and by, in Mary Astell's, "an inward Sense of [her] own real Superiority."[40] As a category of labor, however, the secretary undergoes a gendered bi-
furcation in the modern period. At the higher levels of public (i.e., state) professionalism the secretary remains primarily a male figure; at the lower levels of
private (i.e., corporate) wage labor the office of the secretary becomes relatively
menial and therefore relatively female. Indeed, the lability of the secretary has a
sexual as well as a social dimension. In the homosocial intimacy of seventeenth-
century male friendship at this level of social interaction there is an erotic component that parallels the amatory energy with which the emergent model of
marriage for love challenges the traditional model of the dynastic marriage of
alliance, a parallel that contemporary discourse is increasingly inclined to test as
a competition.[41]

Noble and Gentle Households

In royal and noble households the woman's levee was less officially designed for
politics or business than the man's and was held in her bedroom or dressing
room. The latter space seems to have been an English refinement—the term enters the language in the middle of the seventeenth century—perhaps because
unlike in France, in England couples tended to share the same bedchamber.
Still, figure 5.9, rare in its representation of a seventeenth-century English interior as early as 1640, depicts an English lady's fashionable bedchamber that incorporates a dressing table covered by a table carpet and a *toilette* made of linen
and lace, on which rests a dressing box with a built-in mirror. This is the period
in which the ancient female arts of cosmetics are being separated out from culinary contexts and given an increasingly specialized status. In 1675 the lady's accomplishments in "Preserving, Physick, Beautifying and Cookery" could be
pictured as transpiring in distinct spaces that nonetheless were part of a single
domain of domestic expertise (fig. 5.10). A Restoration critique of women for
the luxurious excess of their dressing rooms met with the retort that "it is a general Desire in Men, that their Ladies should keep Home, and therefore it is but
reasonable they should make their Homes as delightfull as it is possible . . . ." In
the eighteenth century the dressing room often functioned as a private sitting
room that (like the closet) contained a writing desk and table and might be
larger than the bedroom itself. When the French word *garde-robe* was used to

refer to a dressing room it designated a smaller closet off the bedchamber. Otherwise it named a wardrobe or (also) the place where the close-stool was kept.

Separate *appartements des bains* were unusual in the seventeenth century, although Ham House and Chatsworth (see below) had them, the former in a "Withdrawing-Roome." Most often people bathed piecemeal in basins or tubs placed for that purpose in their dressing rooms. Figure 5.11, entitled *Femme de qualité déshabillée pour le bain,* shows a woman sitting with her lap dog on a daybed, fashionable in 1685, washing her feet in a vessel that is set next to a perfume burner (*cassolette*), while her visitor's stagy pose of *politesse* just fails to shield his eyes from the intimate sight. Chamber pots sat in the bedchamber, under or next to the bed, or in an adjoining pantry when not in use. The more substantial close-stool might be elaborately worked, like "the Chest" in Swift's poem "The Lady's Dressing Room" (1732), whose "counterfeit . . . Disguise" makes euphemism palpable. Close-stools too might be left, as was Swift's, in full view, but they often were privately placed in separate small rooms or cubicles, or "water closets" (before the eighteenth century close-stools tended to share a room with a servant). Swift's ekphrastic close-stool, alluding as it does to the larger poetic enclosure of which it forms one part, aptly captures the synecdochic profusion characteristic of these female rooms, where multitudinous containers seem to be larger and smaller variations on one another.[42]

When the birth of a child approached, the bedroom was temporarily (for as long as a month) transformed into another sort of female room, the lying-in chamber, where the ceremony of childbirth was performed. Both the ceremony and its spatialization had deep roots in traditional English culture, and they continued to dominate social life across the social ranks until the end of the eighteenth century and the consolidation of the man-midwife's expertise. This was a "private," but also an emphatically collective, activity. The bedroom was insulated from the outside, its air excluded by blocked keyholes, daylight shut out by the use of heavy curtains. The housewife withdrew from her customary physical labor and sexual services, taking to her bed in the company of the midwife—a distinct category of waged female household labor—and her several gossips (from "god-sib" or "god-sibling," a woman invited to witness the birth for the purpose of the later baptism). In figure 5.12, the frontispiece of a popular eighteenth-century midwifery manual, the mother lies in a canopied four-poster in a comfortable bedroom that is illuminated by firelight and furnished with a dressing table, a framed painting, and the customary domestic pet and chamber pot, closely attended by six women who feed her the traditional caudle and swaddle the newborn baby. (In a humbler household the lying-in space might be confined to the bed itself; see fig. 4.12.) The lying-in ceremony could

FIG. 5.9. *An English lady's bedchamber,* c. 1640, in Peter Thornton, *Authentic Decor: The Domestic Interior, 1620–1920* (New York: Viking, 1984). Marquand Library, Princeton University Library.

FIG. 5.10. (*opposite*) Frontispiece, Hannah Wooley, *The Accomplisht Ladys Delight* (1675). Department of Rare Books and Special Collections, Princeton University Library.

be seen as a ritual of woman on top, positive where the skimmington ride is negative because gender reversal is expressed here not through physical and verbal domination but in the aura of a self-sufficiently female household that simply excludes men. This may go too far, however: in a tract of 1683 a husband is made to remark that "for gossips to meet . . . at a lying-in, and not to talk, you may as well dam up the arches of London Bridge, as stop their mouths at such a time. 'Tis a time of freedom, when women, like parliament men have a privilege to talk petty treason."[43]

The well-known replacement of the midwife's authority by the man-midwife's has recently been complicated by scholars in a number of ways. Before this development of the later eighteenth century, the man-midwife was already

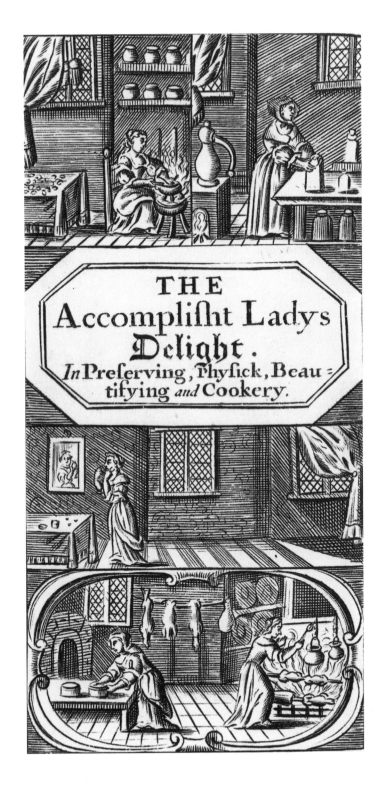

THE
Accomplisht Ladys
Delight.
In Preserving, Physick, Beautifying *and* Cookery.

Femme de qualité déshabillée pour le bain.

FIG. 5.11. *Femme de qualité déshabillée pour le bain,* 1685, in Peter Thornton, *Seventeenth-Century Interior Decoration in England, France, and Holland* (New Haven, CT: Yale University Press, 1979). Marquand Library, Princeton University Library.

a known and accepted figure, customarily called in to supplement the supervisory role of the midwife when a dead birth necessitated the medical expertise of obstetric surgery. His ascent to the supervisory role, a professionalizing male takeover of women's traditional inside work, was made possible by the class aspirations of upwardly mobile wives to the social cachet his services provided. One of the most sought after man-midwives, William Hunter, was the first to

FIG. 5.12. Frontispiece, *Aristotle's Compleat and Experienc'd Midwife . . .* (1733). Wellcome Library, London.

resolve the anatomy of the placenta, was resistant (as most midwives were) to intervention by the use of forceps, and was highly empathetic with the expectant mothers he served as a kind of private secretary:

> The world will give me credit, surely, for having had sufficient opportunities of knowing a good deal of female characters. I have seen the private as well as the public virtues, the private as well as the more public frailties of women in all ranks of life. I have been in their secrets, their counsellor and adviser in the moments of their greatest distress in body and mind. I have been a witness to their private conduct, when they were preparing themselves to meet danger, and have heard their last and most serious reflections, when they were certain they had but few hours to live.

Providing for "female characters" something like the medical equivalent of free indirect narration, Hunter was a remarkable pioneer in the benign but implacable exploration of the female interior: the lying-in chamber, the womb, the secret privacy of mind and body.[44]

The search for domestic privacy "took a variety of forms, depending upon who was excluding whom in order to achieve it."[45] The family sought privacy from domestic servants; males and females increasingly were thought to require segregation from each other; children had to be separable, if not entirely separated, from adults; personal privacy was required for reading, writing, contemplation, and bodily evacuation; and all members of the household sought privacy from the outside world of uninvited visitors. Below the apogee of the royal household, the linear model in English domestic design was successfully challenged in the seventeenth century by a symmetrical model that gained strength at least in part through the great popularity of Andrea Palladio. In the linear model, as we have seen, two elongated suites of rooms, *en enfilade* (in English usage, "rooms of parade"), extend in opposite directions from a central hall. Roger North thought such a ground plan "fit for a colledge or hospitall, to be devided into cells, and chambers independent of each other; but not for a dwelling house, that ought to have a connexion, and unity, without crossing to and fro from one part to the other . . . ." Thomas Fuller put it succinctly: "[L]et not the common rooms be several nor the several rooms common." Symmetry replaced linearity primarily through the use of a double-pile ground plan, which compacted space into a deeper rectangle and thus enabled one to choose one's route through the house, facilitating both circulation and privacy.[46] The basic difference between the two models can be seen in figure 5.13, which presents simplified plans for several English country houses. Doddington, in Lincolnshire (A), built about 1595, illustrates the older, linear model. Charlton House, in Kent (B), built in 1607–12, modifies the linear model; while the other diagrams show variations on the double-pile plan, some of which, by expanding space through the

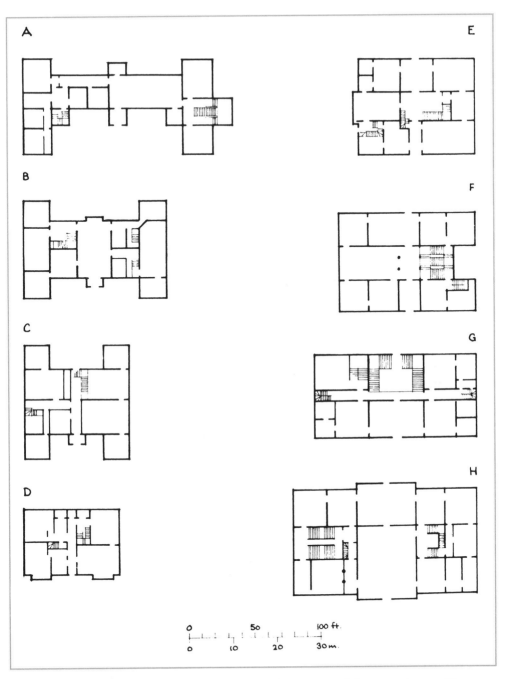

FIG. 5.13. Simplified ground plans of seventeenth-century English country houses: (A) Doddington; (B) Charlton House; (C) Swakeleys; (D) The Dutch House, Kew; (E) Melton Constable; (F) Tring (Wren); (G) Coleshill (Pratt); (H) Horseheath (Pratt). Drawing by John Morrey. In John Bold, "Privacy and the Plan," in *English Architecture Public and Private: Essays for Kerry Downes,* ed. John Bold and Edward Chaney (London: Hambledon, 1993). By permission of Hambledon and London. Marquand Library, Princeton University Library.

use of a triple pile in order to solve problems created by the extreme compaction of the double pile, also created new difficulties in circulation.

Coleshill, in Oxfordshire (formerly Berkshire) (G), designed by Sir Roger Pratt and built in 1657–62, is "the supreme, yet atypical, example of the double pile form," using service stairs, closets, and especially the passageway or corridor to maximum effect.[47] Figure 5.14 provides a more detailed view of Coleshill. The great hall, two stories high, accommodates the main staircase and functions not (as of old) as a dining area where the lord's magnificence is publicly displayed in the ceremony of service but as an elegant room of entry to the house. The corridor and two sets of back stairs ensure the separation of the family and guests from the servants, who dine separately in the basement, to which the kitchen and its food preparation have also been relegated. The arrangement of bedchambers, withdrawing chambers, and closets into several sets of rooms composed of a larger and two smaller, inner spaces aims at flexibility of use.[48]

Pratt thought the bedchambers "must each of them have a closet, and a servant's lodging with chimney both of which will easily be made by dividing the breadth of one end of the room into two such parts as shall be convenient and to the servant's room a pair of backstairs ought to be adjoining . . . [and] so contrived . . . that the ordinary servants may never publicly appear in passing to and from for their occasions there." North believed that in such country houses the main entry "must not be the common passage for all things, in regard your freinds and persons of esteem should pass without being annoyed with the sight of foull persons, and things, which must and will be moving in some part of a large and well inhabited dwelling. . . . The like is to be sayd of stayres. For the cheif must not be annoyed with disagreeable objects, but be releived of them by a back-inferior staircase," for although "it is no unseemly object to an English gentleman . . . to see his servants and buissness passing at ordinary times, . . . if we consult convenience, we must have severall avenews and bolting holes . . . ."[49] Yet North was disdainful of urban architects who built for quality even though their use of small spaces was justified not only by the profit motive but also by the aim to achieve that privacy which he applauded in the great country houses. Indeed, North's words against the professionalized architecture of the townhouses of quality might also apply to Coleshill. He sneered at the many ways "aggreable to litleness, whereby all the grandure proper to quality is layd aside; large rooms, great tables and glasses, capacious chimneys, spacious hangings, are not be found, as when the nobility built their owne houses. Nay, the evil spreads, so that country gentlemen of value and fortune, in their new erected seats, creep after the meanness of these town builders and order their houses in squares [i.e., double-pile] like suburb dwellings . . . ."[50]

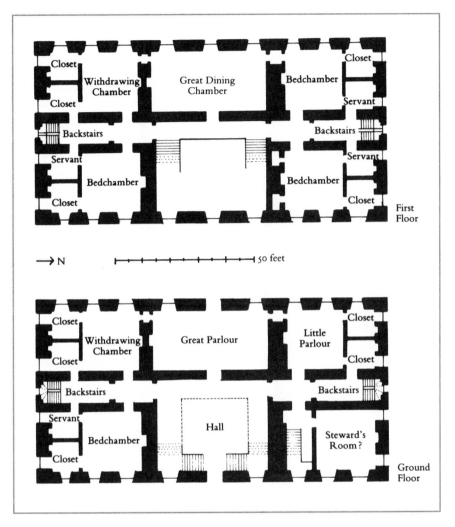

FIG. 5.14. Ground- and first-floor plans, Coleshill, Oxfordshire, built 1657–62, in Mark Girouard, *Life in the English Country House: A Social and Architectural History* (New Haven, CT: Yale University Press, 1978). Copyright Yale University Press. Princeton University Library.

What distinguishes a house like Coleshill is not just service stairs and corridors (which pre-existed it) but the explicitness of their deployment, "the articulation of the need for them and the overall form of their accommodation" to the aim of separating the labor of maintaining the house from the leisure of inhabiting it.[51] In a related fashion, the tendency to dissociate the hall from ceremonial dining (which also had precedents) and to remove the kitchen from the dwelling quarters (which did not) expresses a growing consensus that eating together was no longer the paradigmatic ritual of a communal status hierarchy and that the production of food should be segregated from its consumption.[52] In the linear plan of tradition, the household of service encompasses the entire spectrum of status hierarchy, a finely calibrated continuum of social degrees in which the display of eating in the great hall is only the most important ritual of distinction. In such a system, the only crucial difference is between the absolute magnificence of nobility and the service done by those who are variously dependent upon it. In the emergent plan, a continuous and graded hierarchy of social distinctions has been replaced by a complex network of social spaces in which the incremental ladder of status difference has been reduced to a dyadic separation between the public and the private, production and consumption, labor and capital at domestic leisure: between those who labor at the house and those, whether family or their guests, who inhabit it. Labor comprises both the inside work of domestic servants and the outside work of "business" that is brought into the house.[53] The separation between the public and the private, available repeatedly but discontinuously throughout the house, suggests the emergent terms of class conflict, in which the abstract category "labor"[54] both produces domestic space and is secreted within its interstices. Privacy is the recourse of absolute property, of the owners of the means of production in their capacity as consumers. At the same time, however, the relative ease of mobility between social categories that characterizes a class system of social relations—prefigured in the lability of the early modern secretary—ensures that the social identity of the actual people who fill the antithetical categories of production and consumption, labor and capital, will be highly variable.

The Curtain Lecture

This class system of separation, so different from the status system of distinction, also differs from the increasingly ossified sexual division of labor, in which an equally dyadic separation between the public and the private has a basically gendered structure. The separate-but-equal ideology of sexual difference that infiltrated English culture in these years had some familiar effects on behavior in domestic interiors—like the postprandial English custom, which seems to have begun during the Restoration and which was regarded on the Continent as a barbarism, whereby the women withdrew to the drawing room, leaving the men to drink and smoke in the dining room.[55] But as we have already seen in the case of the housewife, the modern separation of the sexes was consistent with a devolutionary movement whereby women internalized authority that previously had been gendered male. A complex case of such movement can be seen in a seventeenth-century convention of domestic representation. The skimmington ride, we recall, was a ritual enactment of the disordered household that invited vivid graphic depiction (see figs. 4.6 and 4.7). Under the emergent regime of sexual difference, the skimmington view of the wife as, by Butler's implication, tutor, manager, and governor modulated from a negative to a normative weighting.[56] This modulation was mediated by an image, which exists in several versions, that might be seen as a literal domestication of the skimmington ride. The most common name for what the image depicts is a "curtain lecture," which Johnson's *Dictionary* (1755) defines as "a reproof given by a wife to her husband in bed."[57]

One version of this image, shown in figure 5.15, appears as the frontispiece to Thomas Heywood's *A Curtaine Lecture . . .* (1637). Husband and wife are side by side in an elaborate fourposter bed, canopy and curtain further enclosing what is already a scene of intimate enclosure. An hourglass, a candle, and a table carpet rest on the bedside table, a pillow and chamber pot on the sideboard of the bed. A crescent moon signals the lateness of the hour. The wife, propped up, bends over her prostrate husband, lecturing: "Vera praedico" (I proclaim the truth). On her nightgown is inscribed, "Her night rayle," a term for a dressing gown that puns on her railing lecture. The husband says, "Milieri ne credas" (Do not believe women). The couple's posture closely replicates that of the skimmington couples, but here the scene of woman on top is private and indoors, made meaningful by being set in what is, broadly speaking, the wife's territory (in a related fashion, Heywood's frontispiece publishes typographically what the skimmington ride published abroad by ritual enactment). The legend reads: "When *Wiues* preach, 'tis not in the *Husbands* power / To haue their *Lectures* end within an hower / If *Hee* with patience stay till shee haue donne / *Shee'l* not conclude till twyce the Glasse bee runne."

A second version (fig. 5.16), printed as the frontispiece to Richard Brathwaite's *Ar't asleepe Husband? A Bovlster Lectvre . . .* (1640), is very similar to this one. The bed is curtained and canopied, on the floor beside it are a chamber pot and slippers, and the wife, half-sitting, is almost identically poised over her husband, who has turned away from her as if in sleep. Indignantly the wife demands, "Dum loquor ista, taces" (You over there, are you silent while I speak?), while the husband blocks her out: "Surdo canis" (You preach to deaf ears). The

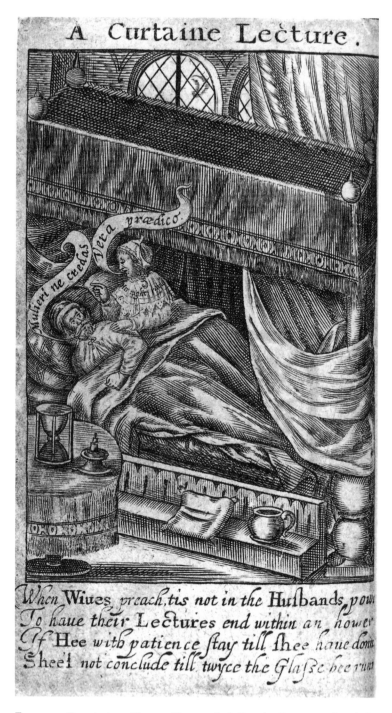

FIG. 5.15. Frontispiece, Thomas Heywood, *A Curtaine Lecture* . . . (1637). By permission of the British Library, shelf mark C.117.a.1.

legend reads: "The *wife* a wondrous racket meanes to keepe, / Whilest *Husband* seemes to sleepe but does not sleepe: / But she might full so well her *Lecture* smother, / For ent'ring one Eare it goes out at t'other." If the curtain lecture may justly be seen as a literal domestication of the skimmington ride, it also softens and moralizes ("preach") the violence of that encounter to accord with its setting: the wife has no weapon but her tongue, which internalizes the "racket" of rough music, and the husband's subordination is figured by no more than his forbearing posture and passive resistance.

A third version of the curtain lecture, although unaccompanied by graphic illustration, is worth noting for the way it complicates the tone of the encounter, largely through its political specificity. The premise of *A Curtain-Conference,* a royalist broadside published in 1659 in the last days of the Protectorate, is that John Lambert, major general of the army and an influential figure under Cromwell, lies in bed with his wife bitterly lamenting his fall from public prominence. Form reflects content in the publication of private discourse that documents how a public hero becomes a private buffoon.[58] Perhaps for no better reason than that this is a mock-heroic deflation of a hated enemy, the wife and her domesticating desires come off sympathetically. Beginning with Lady Lambert, the conversations goes as follows:

O My Dear Heart, my love and Joy, my own sweet *Jonny,* why so sad?
LAMBERT. *Jonny!* I thou mayest well call me so, for I have made it appear to all the world (For all I was accounted a Grand Polititian) that I am but a *Jonny.*
LA. Prithee be of good cheer, (dear Chuck) and receive a little comfort from the embraces of thine own dear Wife, who hath a long time, as a desolate widow, mourned for want of thee.
LAM. Sweet *Jonny,* dear Chuck, and what not? am I not full enough of grief already, but thou . . . must (like the wife of *Job*) add unto mine afflictions, by flouting me with such ridiculous Titles, as *Jonny* and Chuck, which in plain English is no more then Fool or Chicken[?]

If the woman is on top here, it is by championing a mode of society—domestic affection and companionship—more durable than that desired by the major general. The husband's shame in the skimmington is that of an ineffectual cuckold and/or drunkard; Lambert is parodied for being, not a public hero, but a mere private lover.[59] In a final version of the curtain lecture (fig. 5.17), printed about 1685 with words written by Thomas Durfey and set to music, the affective tone and terms of the skimmington have been reversed. The husband, an aggressively self-righteous libertine whose sword and whip lie ominously on the table, drunkenly rants fully dressed in the middle of the bedroom. His wife lies patiently, mildly attempting to persuade him to return to his conjugal bed and to her. His "Rambling . . . blades" stand opposed to her "stiching . . . maids" and "gossips"; he would stay "a month from home," she would have him "repos'd" there. Under these circumstances the title seems ironic; this is a rake sorely in need of reformation.[60]

The schematic abstraction of the account of historical transition in the architecture of domestic interiors as I have given it thus far inevitably obscures its unevenness. For one thing, the historic separation of production from consumption in the country house was hardly inexorable. At Wilton House, in Wiltshire, in 1786, the Earl of Pembroke thought that "a steward's office *in the house* would be the very devil. One should never be free an instant from meeting people full of words and wants." Within a few months, however, he had become "convinced of the absolute indispensable necessity of a land-steward, doing nobody's business but mine, living and boarding in the house, and transacting everything in my office."[61] Evidently the pleasures of ownership might be enjoyed both through the privatizing removal of labor and through its public display. More broadly, if the fashion for Palladio and for Italian classicism reinforced native tendencies toward the separation of the public from the private in English architecture during the early part of the seventeenth century, it is also true that the growing popularity of the French formal *appartement* in the middle years of the century revived the linear model—but with differences from the more traditional English layout. On the one hand, the formal plan reflected French—and a modified English—absolutism in its commitment to a sequence of rooms of increasing exclusivity. On the other hand, the French plan favored a symmetrical effect that might be achieved not through the double-pile plan but by balancing two great apartments against each other off a central structure. The major attraction of the French plan was the elegant sequencing of rooms *en enfilade,* which was especially admired as a model for the layout of those state apartments in English country houses that were adapted to accommodate visiting royalty in the splendor of an independent suite occupying most or all of one floor of the house.[62]

Ham House, in Surrey (fig. 5.18), built in the 1630s, was given a form comparable to that of the double pile in the 1670s by doubling the central range of the original structure. This created matching apartments for the Duke and Duchess of Lauderdale on the ground floor of the house. On the first floor, the new range of rooms completed a single state apartment whose sequence comprised the original staircase (a), great dining room (b), withdrawing room (c), and gallery (d), as well as the added suite of antechamber (e), state bedchamber (f), and closet with alcove (g). At Chatsworth, in Derbyshire (fig. 5.19), the state apartment was located on the second floor of the south front. The Elizabethan design of the house facilitated a 1680s remodeling that highlighted the

FIG. 5.16. Frontispiece, [Richard Brathwaite], *Ar't asleepe Husband? A Bovlster Lectvre*
... (1640). By permission of the Folger Shakespeare Library.

THE CURTAIN LECTURE. The Words by Mr. Durfey.

I

he. *Of all Comforts I'm miscarried,*
When I Play'd the Sot and married.
'Tis a trap ther's none need doubt on't.
Those that are in't would fain get out on't.
she. *Fy my dear pray come to bed.*
That napkin take and bind your head,
Too much Drink your brain has dos'd,
You'l be quite alter'd when repos'd.

he. *Oons tis all one if I'm up or Lye down,*
For as soon as the cock Crows Ile be gon.
she. *Tis to grieve me, thus you leave me,*
Was I, was I made a wife to lye alone.

II

he. *From your Arms my self divorcing,*
I this morn must ride a Coursing.
Sport that far excells a Madam,
Or all wives have been since Adam.
she. *I when thus I've lost my Due.*
Must hug my Pillow wanting you,
And whilst you tope all the day
Regale in Cups of harmless Tea.

he. *Pox what care I drink your slops till you dye,*
Yonder's brandy will keep me a month from home.
she. *If thus parted I'm broken hearted.*
When I, when I send for ye my dear pray come

III

he. *Ere Ile be from Rambling hindred,*
Ile renounce my spouse and kindred.
To be sober I have no leasure,
Whats a man without his pleasure.
she. *To my grief then I must see,*
Strong Ale and Nants my rivalls be,
Whilst you tope it with your blades,
Poor I sitt stiching with my maids.

he. *Oons you may go to your gossips you know,*
And there if you can meet a friend pray do.
she. *Go you Joker go provoker.*
Never, never shall I meet a man like you.

processional formality of a grand sequence from great dining chamber to antechamber, withdrawing chamber, bedchamber, and closet. But the original design prohibited the achievement of the desired symmetry through reconstruction, so the effect was created instead by the *trompe l'oeil* device of a large mirror that was set into the wall of the dining chamber, reflecting back the sequence of doors in the existing apartment as though it were a perfectly balancing apartment of "rooms of parade."[63] Seventy-five years later the device—or perhaps the linear plan itself—had lost its charm. In 1763 Philip Yorke thought the rooms of the state apartment at Chatsworth "of little use but to be walked through."[64] The linearity of the formal plan was modified in many eighteenth-century houses to create a circuit of reception rooms that preserved but relativized the sense of a stately procession into the interior. At the opening assembly of the newly built Norfolk House, in London, in 1756 (fig. 5.20) guests circled around the first floor of the deep, triple-pile space through rooms of varied hues and decor, from the antechamber to a closet "filled," according to one guest, "with an infinite number of curiosities," and back again to the antechamber. Here if not elsewhere in Norfolk House the ceremonial function of the quasi-public assembly outweighed all considerations of privacy, and the dressing room, bedchamber, and closet were probably seldom used by an individual. The Norfolk House plan became standard for London houses in the next couple of decades.[65]

The capacity to provide efficient public assembly is not, of course, the broadest lesson to be learned from this brief tour of royal and stately homes before the nineteenth century. That lesson can be summarized succinctly by comparing the ground plans of Longleat House (Wiltshire) when it was built about 1570 and when it was remodeled in the early nineteenth century (figs. 5.21 and 5.22).[66] In the plan of c. 1570 there is little evidence of a distinction between public and private spaces: there are no corridors off which private rooms might be hived, and the left and right wings of the house are sequenced as rooms of parade; servants and family share the same living spaces; no water closets or dark closets provide excretory privacy; and the hall functions as a general dining place for all members and guests of the household.

The modernization of c. 1809 provides the entire ground floor with a rectangular system of corridors and galleries that both allows private entry to the outer rooms that feed off it and divides the family rooms, on the outside left

Fig. 5.17. (*opposite*) *The Curtain Lecture*, c. 1685, words by Thomas D'Urfey, in Charles Saumarez Smith, *Eighteenth-Century Decoration: Design and the Domestic Interior in England* (New York: Abrams, 1993). Marquand Library, Princeton University Library.

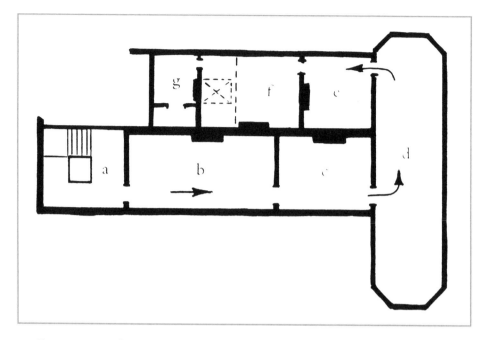

Fig. 5.18. First-floor plan, Ham House, Surrey, built 1630s, in Peter Thornton, *Seventeenth-Century Interior Decoration in England, France, and Holland* (New Haven, CT: Yale University Press, 1979). Copyright Yale University Press. Marquand Library, Princeton University Library.

Fig. 5.19. (*opposite, middle*) Remodeling of the state apartment on the second floor of the south front of Chatsworth, Derbyshire, 1680s, with *trompe l'oeil* mirror; and (*opposite, top*) floor plan of same apartment; in Mark Girouard, *Life in the English Country House: A Social and Architectural History* (New Haven, CT: Yale University Press, 1978). Copyright Yale University Press. Princeton University Library.

Fig. 5.20. (*opposite, bottom*) Ground plan of Norfolk House, London, built 1756, in Mark Girouard, *Life in the English Country House: A Social and Architectural History* (New Haven, CT: Yale University Press, 1978). Copyright Yale University Press. Princeton University Library.

and front of the house, from the inner and back areas where the servants are given their own living spaces. (The exception to this division is the lady's maid's room, which offers service at a slight but discreet remove from the family suite.) Family members and servants alike are provided with their own sets of water closets and staircases, and the hall has ceased to function as a communal dining place for either family or servants. In 1871 Robert Kerr, comparing the old and

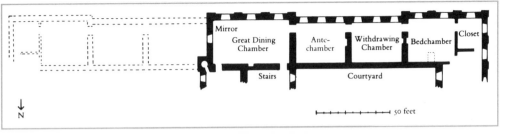

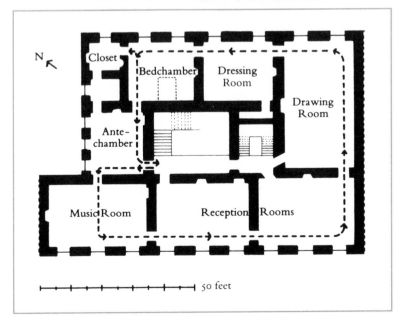

the new plans of Longleat, remarked on "the confusion which prevail[s] in this old plan . . . the want of special purpose in the rooms, the want of intelligent relationship between them, and the particular defectiveness of the means of communication; but in the new plan all these evils vanish as if by magic . . . . [N]othing of the kind is to be found . . . in even the best of the eighteenth-century Mansions." The futurity of the stately home lay, however, in publicity as well as privacy. By the mid-eighteenth century the well-known conversion of England's stately homes into show houses for tourist consumption was already under way. This involved less a physical than a cultural reconstruction, and public curiosity about how "the other half" lived was transfixed no more by aristocratic magnificence than it was by the wonderful intricacy of interiority through which the aristocratic itch for privacy by this time had been relieved.[67]

Households of the Middling Sort

"The historians taught us long ago that the King was never left alone," wrote Philippe Ariès. "But in fact, until the end of the seventeenth century, nobody was ever left alone."[68] I have already remarked that innovation in interior design observed a trickle-down pattern; but this leaves open the question whether the quest for privacy among the middling social orders was fueled primarily by motivations of status or of class aspiration. There is little doubt that below the status level of the nobility and gentry, wealthy yeomen and merchants replicated many of the changes in domestic architecture already discussed in the assimilationist spirit of emulating their betters.[69] But differences in building within those groups confirm that it was not the qualitative codes of status hierarchy but the quantitative, class-based criterion of income that determined how innovation trickled down. That is, the impulse toward physical privacy was experienced as a universal human value rather than as proper to the socially elevated alone. What had begun as an elite withdrawal from collective presence had become the architectural expression of an emergent individualist norm.

In 1724 an unidentified Bristol architect prepared plans and elevations for several townhouses to be occupied by merchants. The largest plan (fig. 5.23), for a house in which the merchant's clerks also will live and work, is accompanied by extensive notes that testify to the importance of already familiar privacy considerations. Each floor of the house contains a central hall that permits private access to each of its main rooms. "At the Entrance you find a Vestibule [A] for the Conveniency of Common people attending till they can be spoken to, or Strangers Servants to wait in and is therefore separated from the [great] Stairs that they may not be at liberty to walk about and that the Family may pass privately about their affairs." The semihexagonal shape of the vestibule distances

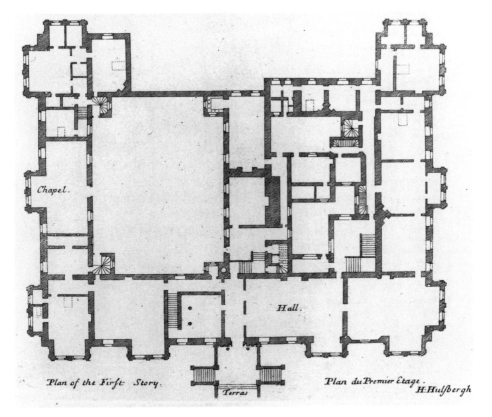

FIG. 5.21. Ground plan of Longleat House, Wiltshire, 1570, in Colen Campbell, *Vitruvius Britannicus, or The British Architect . . .* (1717), 2:69. Marquand Library, Princeton University Library.

the front door from the adjacent compter (or business room) and withdrawing room so as to spare their inhabitants "any inconveniency" caused by entry. Intended "for the Mistress of the House to entertain Company in," the withdrawing room [B] has "a Private door to the Staircase for her Servants to bring any thing (without exposing it to people who may be waiting in the Vestibule,) . . . ." The separate parlor behind [C], primarily an "Eating Room," can also be used to accommodate more company or "to make a Shew . . . ." As the right half of the ground floor is dedicated to the nuclear family and the entertainment of their guests, so the left side is given over to work.[70] The compter [D] "has a private door by the Back stairs to retreat without being seen by people that are visiting, and the conveying away anything that should not be exposed to view: and by it is the Back Stairs, to the Chambers that the young Men may

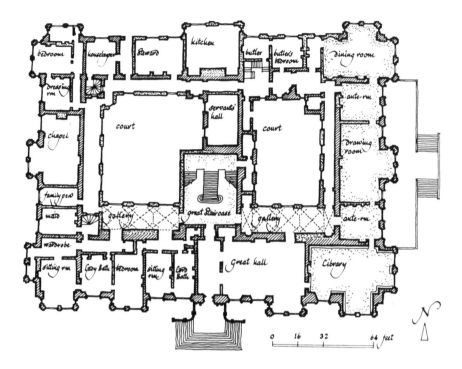

FIG. 5.22. Ground plan of Longleat House, Wiltshire, c. 1809, in Derek Linstrum, *Sir Jeffry Wyatville, Architect to the King,* Oxford Studies in the History of Art and Architecture (Oxford: Clarendon, 1972), fig. 1 (p. 57). By permission of Oxford University Press. Marquand Library, Princeton University Library.

at night go to their Beds and in the morning come to their business without disturbing or dirtying the best part of the House. Beyond the Back:stairs is a Private Parlour where the Master may treat with any Dealer . . . ."[71] So the labor of the clerks is comparable to that of the servants. Still, the author recommends, perhaps to protect the family from the spread of scandal, that in dining arrangements the clerks "have as little occasion as may be to mix and converse with Common Servants from whom they seldom learn any good." Other features of the plan are familiar from our survey of country houses. Three of the four best bedchambers (H, J), all on the first floor, have a "Light Closet" (K), the two front ones built so as to "be perfectly Private." The front chambers also contain "large dark Closets" (c), "of great conveniency for the holding Close: Stools and many other Family necessarys." The detached kitchen and associated offices are in the rear court, below separate sleeping accommodations for servants.[72]

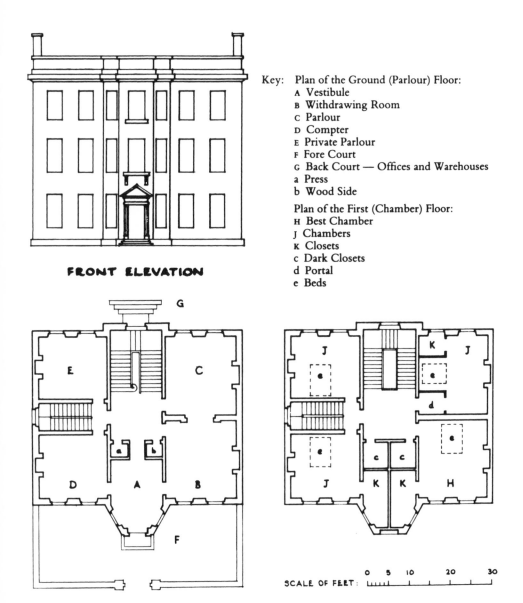

FRONT ELEVATION

Key: Plan of the Ground (Parlour) Floor:
       A Vestibule
       B Withdrawing Room
       C Parlour
       D Compter
       E Private Parlour
       F Fore Court
       G Back Court — Offices and Warehouses
       a Press
       b Wood Side

       Plan of the First (Chamber) Floor:
       H Best Chamber
       J Chambers
       K Closets
       c Dark Closets
       d Portal
       e Beds

SCALE OF FEET: 0   5   10   20   30

GROUND (PARLOUR) FLOOR   FIRST (CHAMBER) FLOOR

DESIGN OF A HOUSE FOR A MERCHANT. 1724.

FIG. 5.23. Front elevation and ground- and first-floor plans of a house for a merchant in Bristol, 1724, in John Bold, "The Design of a House for a Merchant, 1724," *Architectural History* 33 (1990). Redrawing by John Morrey of original in Bristol Record Office. By permission of John Bold and John Morrey. Marquand Library, Princeton University Library.

The same architect who was responsible for this plan also designed three more modest townhouses for merchants, two small units on either side of a larger one.[73] A comparison of these three plans (fig. 5.24) with that of the largest townhouse we have just explored provides a graduated scale of privacy, all within a single status group, whose differences are dictated not by degrees of status emulation but by the quantitative standard of available space and money. The ground floor of the central plan in figure 5.24, like that of figure 5.23, has four rooms, a main stairs, and a back stairs.[74] Here the much smaller hall space in the area of the main stairs still separates the family from the "common people" and "strangers' servants" they would otherwise encounter at the front of the house. But the diminished hall space provides separate entry for only the two back rooms; the front rooms must be entered through what is here called the "Hall," which assumes the function of both hall and vestibule in figure 5.24. The separation of business from family affairs is maintained, although less adequately, by placing the hall entries to the compter and the best parlor diagonally across (hence at the greatest distance) from each other, which, however, deprives the compter of a "private door by the back stairs." As a result, clerks have easy access to the compter from the front door, but they also mix with guests and visitors heading for the best parlor. The mistress of the house is also deprived of the "private door to the staircase" for her servants to avoid people waiting in the hall. In the two smallest plans, privacy continues to be served, and to be compromised, by space limitations. These mirror reflections of each other reduce the number of rooms by one and pursue a linear model from the family rooms in the front to the compter in the back. An entry hall provides separate access to the best parlor and to the staircase, but from the latter one has only walk-through access to the two back rooms. Traffic from the outside mixes with family and servant affairs, although the clerks are successfully segregated adjacent to the back stairs.[75] Kitchen and servants' quarters remain detached from the main house.

The differential achievement of privacy that is evident in this comparison of households of variant income levels below the gentry level can also be seen chronologically, in the way the Yorkshire farmhouse of a successful yeoman-clothier was refashioned in the sixteenth and early seventeenth centuries. When it was built about 1500, High Bentley, in Shelf (Yorkshire), had a linear structure whose aisled hall was characteristic of the Halifax region of the West Riding (fig. 5.25). The passage, echoing the screens passage in the late-medieval great house (see fig. 5.6), separates the hall and chambers from the workshop. A century later the workshop space was more than doubled, creating a wing that balanced that of the private chambers. And in 1661 the separation of consumption from production space was completed by several strategies. Both food

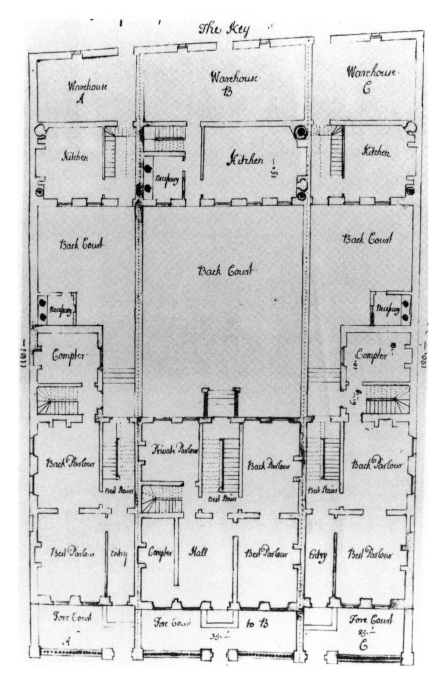

FIG. 5.24. Ground plans for three merchants' houses in Prince Street, Bristol, c. 1725, in Mark Girouard, *The English Town* (New Haven, CT: Yale University Press, 1990). Copyright Yale University Press. Marquand Library, Princeton University Library.

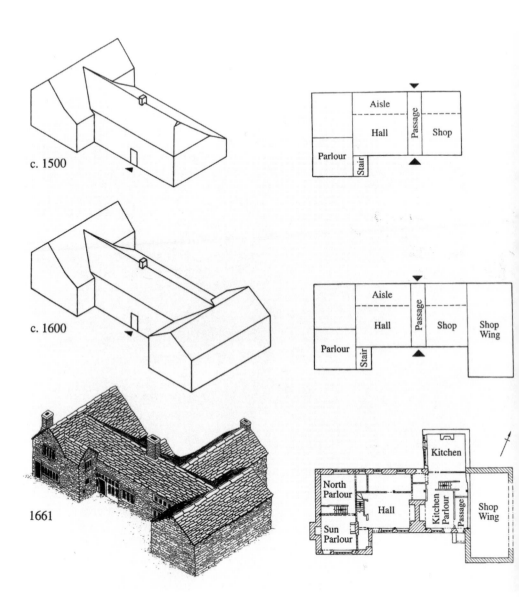

Fig. 5.25. Elevations and ground plans for High Bentley, Shelf, Yorkshire, c. 1500, c. 1600, and 1661, in Colin Platt, *The Great Rebuildings of Tudor and Stuart England: Revolutions in Architectural Taste* (London: University College of London Press, 1994), fig. 67 (p. 156). Marquand Library, Princeton University Library.

preparation and servants were removed to a new kitchen wing with its own hearth; the original passage was moved to the wall of the added shop wing, while the original shop was converted to domestic purposes; the hall was modernized for family use and entertainment; and the front door, which had opened into the passage, was moved to the side to create a separate lobby entrance.[76]

Where the Poor Should Live

When Daniel Defoe toured this Yorkshire countryside in the 1720s he was struck by the prosperity and industry not only of the "Manufacturers Houses" but also of the "Number of Cottages or small Dwellings, in which dwell the Workmen which are employed, the Women and Children of whom, are always busy Carding, Spinning, &c. so that no Hands being unemploy'd, all can gain their Bread . . . . This is the Reason also why we saw so few People without Doors . . . ."[77] The condition of existing manufacturers' cottages looked considerably bleaker to the architect John Wood fifty years later. The humanitarian Wood believed there was a "regular gradation between the plan of the most simple hut and that of the most superb palace; that a palace is nothing more than a cottage IMPROVED; and that the plan of the latter is the basis as it were of plans for the former . . . ." Yet when he surveyed the cottages of laborers not only in husbandry but also in the "manufacturing counties," he found them "to be shattered, dirty, inconvenient, miserable hovels, scarcely affording a shelter for beasts of the forest . . . ." Affected by contemporary currents of sentiment and sensibility and determined to make a difference, Wood, unwilling to be only "the melancholy spectator" of such scenes, thought it "necessary for me to feel as the cottager himself; for . . . no architect can form a convenient plan, unless he ideally places himself in the situation of the person for whom he designs . . . ." So he surveyed the opinions of the cottagers, as well as their habitations, and found, among other complaints, that their domiciles "were *inconvenient* for their want of room . . . ." Interpreting this as a problem not just of space but of separate space, Wood decided that as a basic principle "there should be one lodging room for the parents, another for the female, and a third for the male children . . . ," at least those children over the age of nine. Wood designed plans and elevations for four types of cottages, their differences depending strictly on the number of people that would inhabit them. The cottages, proposed for an area east of Bath (Wiltshire), adhere to a close economy in their construction and would most likely be built "at parochial expense."[78]

By contemporary housing standards, Wood's modest plans are utopian. "Humanity shudders," wrote the Marquis of Bath's steward, "at the idea of the industrious labourer, with a wife and five or six children, being obliged to live or rather to exist, in a wretched, damp, gloomy room, of 10 or 12 ft square, and that room without a floor; but common decency must revolt at considering, that over this wretched apartment, there is only *one* chamber, to hold all the miserable beds of the miserable family."[79]

Although horizontal subdivisions of space provide some of the best evidence of the quest for privacy among the middle and upper status groups, country houses and townhouses also shared a broad commitment to a model of vertical stratification in which servants' quarters and household production were relegated to the top and the bottom of the house. The urban tenements of the poor evince a comparable model: the poorest lived in garrets and cellars, where the crowding and the squalor were even worse than in the middle stories. "It will scarcely appear credible," observed a medical doctor at the end of the eighteenth century, "though it is precisely true, that persons of the lowest class do not put clean sheets on their beds three times a year; . . . that from three to eight individuals of different ages often sleep in the same bed; there being but one room and one bed for each family. . . . The room occupied is either a deep cellar, almost inaccessible to the light, and admitting of no change of air; or a garret with a low roof and small windows, the passage to which is close, kept dark, and filled not only with bad air, but with putrid excremental effluvia from a vault at the bottom of the staircase." Another doctor confirmed that "[i]n a large proportion of the dwellings of the poor a house contains as many families as rooms . . . ." Common lodging-houses were similar. According to the Middlesex justices, "It is now become a common practice, in the extreme parts of the town, to receive into their houses persons unknown, without distinction of sex or age on their paying one penny or more per night for lying in such houses without beds or covering, and . . . it is frequent in such houses for fifteen or twenty or more to lie in a small room." In 1826 the working-class reformer Francis Place looked back: "In a few years from this time it will hardly be believed that an immense number of houses were built in narrow courts and close lanes, each house being at least three stories and many of them four stories above the ground floor. That in these courts and lanes the dirt and filth used to accumulate in heaps and was but seldom removed, that many of these tall houses had two, three and sometimes four rooms on a floor, and that from the garrets to the cellars a family lived or starved in each room."[80]

The living conditions of the poor force on our attention a criterion of spatial privacy that is less compellingly obvious among their betters. At the higher social levels the boon of spatial privacy is sought in the physical separation of quality from commoners, of family from servants, and of one person from another. What is thrown into relief by these accounts of the poor, a good deal more brutally than the incidence of close-stools and water closets among the nobility, gentry, and middling sort, is the criterion that consists in separating persons from their own and others' bodily waste. True, standards of health, cleanliness, and delicacy have their own history and cannot simply be equated with standards of privacy. But there is some justice in seeing the growing intolerance of the proximity of bodies and their excrement as one measure of the growing norm of individualism and autonomy—and in this sense, of privacy—in the modern period (although the term "privy" had been in use since the fourteenth century). This was of course an outside as well as an inside issue. In the middle decades of the eighteenth century a series of public acts drained stagnant pools, replaced kennels in the middle of roads by gutters at their sides, and covered over filthy open drains of refuse.[81] For the poor, who effectively dwelled outside as much as they did inside houses, these reforms represent something like the equivalent of replacing the chamber pot by the segregated close-stool in more respectable houses. Still, Wood's plans are sensitive, as we will see, to these inside needs as well.

The quest for privacy at the most indigent level, especially if it is a matter of public (i.e., parochial) policy, severely tests what Wood hopefully calls the "regular gradation" between palace and hut. In the latter, at least, there is a strict equivalence in the relation between cost and privacy that is far less flexible than in the country houses we have been examining: the more money, the more space; the more space, the more rooms. Nonetheless, Wood shows considerable ingenuity in his designs. Figure 5.26 depicts one of his plans for one-room cottages; here two such cottages are joined together, their back-to-back chimneys offering "the great conveniency of having cupboards or shelves on each side of them, as the saving of materials." (Needless to say, cupboards and cabinets of curiosities, although physically similar, imply very different modes of existence.) Pantries are marked by the letter C. The privy is attached to the shed, divorced from the living space but of relatively easy access to its inhabitant. "These cottages, with a piece of ground for a garden, would serve . . . two women, or a man and his wife, either without a family, or with one or two children."[82]

In providing four variations on a basic two-room plan, figure 5.27 evinces a sensitivity to bed placement as a cardinal criterion of privacy. In No. 1 the single bed is in the bedroom (C). In No. 2 the "porch" (A) is made into an "inside porch" (i.e., a foyer) whose construction "makes a very convenient recess E for a bed, which in this sample is thrown open to [and effectively enlarges] bed room C, the most proper situation for a bed for small children . . . ." No. 3 achieves the same recess effect in the other room (B) "for the sleeping place of an adult," whose propriety and convenience differ from those of a child. This difference is further pursued in No. 4, where the recess is enlarged and more fully enclosed by partition, a design that says to Wood that "it must have a window," which in turn requires the division of the shed into pantry (E) and fuel storage/privy (F).[83] In No. 1 of figure 5.28, very little more space is deployed to design three-room cottages in which the bed recess acquires the status of a (windowed) bedroom (F) largely by moving its entrance from one of the other rooms (B) (as in fig. 5.27, No. 4) to the "passage" (C) that is created by one wall of the recess and that enables private access to each of the three rooms. No. 2 uses its additional 4.5 feet of length to move the front door from the porch— where in No. 1 it shares the space of storage (B) and privy—to its own separate entry on the east. The passage (A) into which the front door opens, however, sacrifices private access to one of the rooms (G).[84]

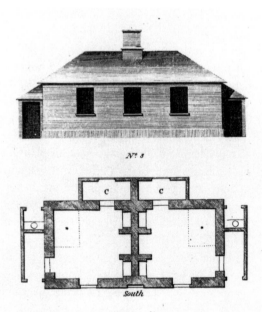

FIG. 5.26. Elevation and ground plan for two one-room attached cottages, Bath, Wiltshire, in John Wood, *A Series of Plans, for Cottages or Habitations of the Labourer, Either in Husbandry, or the Mechanic Arts* . . . (1792). Department of Rare Books and Special Collections, Princeton University Library.

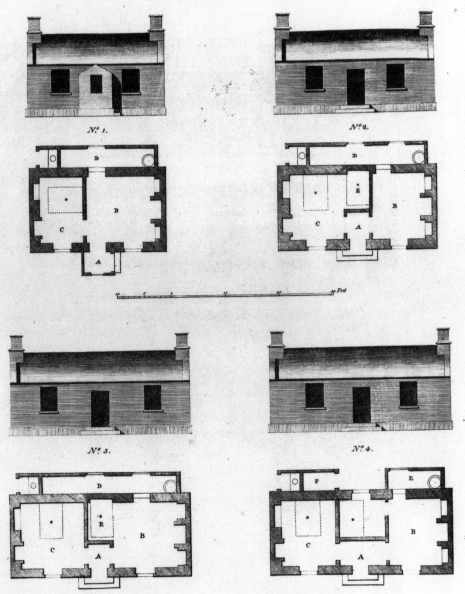

Engraved at the expence of John Wood, Architect, after his own original designs and published by him Jany 1.^{st}1781

P.Begbie Sculp.^r

FIG. 5.27. Elevations and ground plans for two-room cottage (four variations), Bath, Wiltshire, in John Wood, *A Series of Plans, for Cottages or Habitations of the Labourer, Either in Husbandry, or the Mechanic Arts . . .* (1792). Department of Rare Books and Special Collections, Princeton University Library.

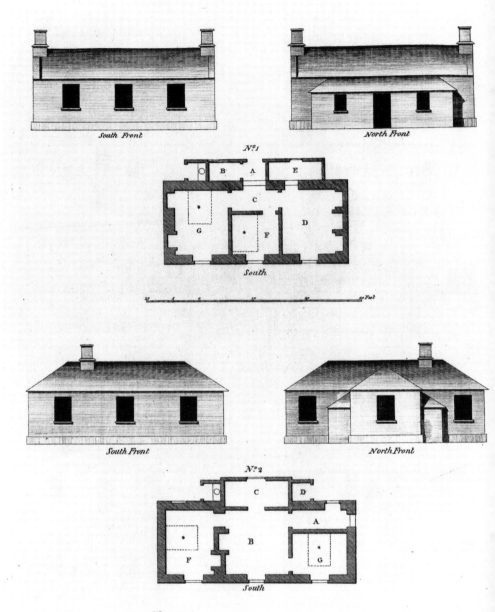

FIG. 5.28. Elevations and ground plans for three-room cottage (two variations), Bath, Wiltshire, in John Wood, *A Series of Plans, for Cottages or Habitations of the Labourer, Either in Husbandry, or the Mechanic Arts . . .* (1792). Department of Rare Books and Special Collections, Princeton University Library.

"Farms presented the greatest challenge to the separation of domestic life from production."[85] In 1785 Thomas Stone thought that "[w]ith regard to a house to be built upon any farm, a parlour, kitchen, hen-house, dairy, and cellar are absolutely necessary; with chambers and garrets upon large farms, and chambers in the roof upon small ones."[86] In the 1750s William Halfpenny designed a number of farmhouses, like Wood with a close eye to cost. Figure 5.29 shows plans for two small houses. No. 1 largely ignores the challenge to separate domestic living space from productive workspace in order to situate the kitchen (C) at the center of the house, having access both to the pantry or cupboard (D) and to the passage (B) to the front entrance (A) (note that Halfpenny's plan reverses the order of Nos. 1 and 2). For convenience the kitchen also communicates directly to the "Milk-Room" (E) and the cellar (F), which abut on it, al-

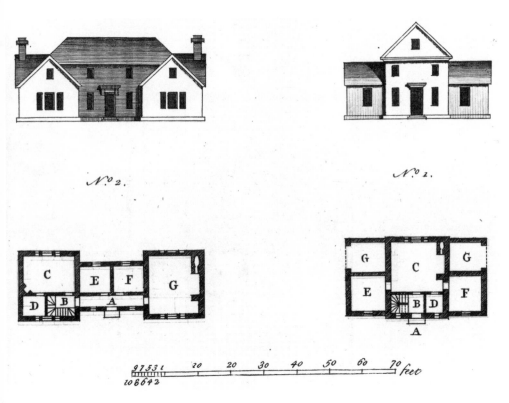

FIG. 5.29. Elevations and ground plans for two small farmhouses, in William Halfpenny, *Useful Architecture in Twenty-one New Designs for erecting Parsonage-Houses, Farm-Houses, and Inns . . .* (1752). By permission of the British Library, shelf mark 1264.c.16.

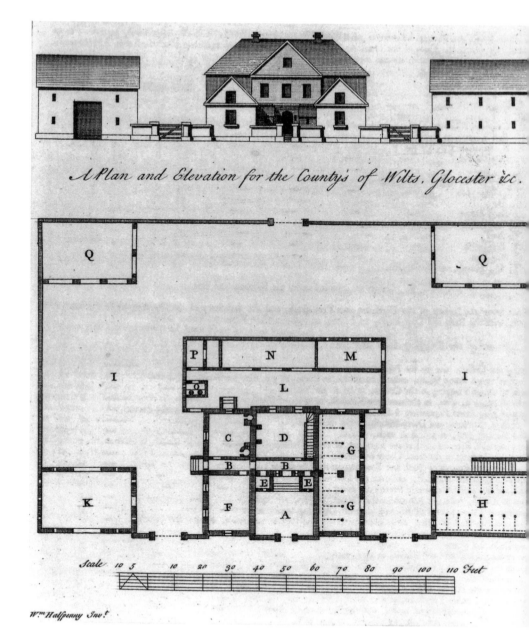

FIG. 5.30. Elevation and ground plan for farmhouse and yard, in William Halfpenny, *Twelve Beautiful Designs for Farm-Houses . . .* (1750). By permission of the British Library, shelf mark 1482.ee3.

though not to the similarly situated husbandry sheds (G), which are by that detail alone defined apart from the contiguous kitchen. In No. 2 the challenge to separate living space from workspace is once again largely avoided in that the house, which also might serve as a parsonage, has only a "Milk-House" (E) and cellar (F) to link it to productive farm labor. Instead these two rooms are used to make a separation, within the domestic space of the house, between the productive labor of the kitchen (G) and the leisured consumption of the parlor (C), closet (D), and first-story bedchambers, which are approached by the stairs. None of the four principal rooms can be entered from any of the others; all have private access to the connecting passage (A, B).[87]

In another publication Halfpenny offered designs for farmhouses that situate them within the full context of the farm and its productive facilities. In these plans he uses the placement of rooms, and especially entryways, to make subtle but significant distinctions between several kinds of animal husbandry as they stand in spatial relation to the domestic core of the house. In figure 5.30, the central parlor (D), which contains stairs up to the first-floor bedchambers, communicates to the passage (B), which also gives private access to the kitchen (C) (with which the parlor shares a chimney but not a doorway), pantries (E), front court (A), and "Dairy-Room" (F). Although the stables (G) abut on both the passage and the parlor stairs, they can be entered only from the outside, through the barnyard (I) or the back court (L). The latter space, which contains (outdoor) privies (O), can be reached through the kitchen, parlor, or stables and in turn communicates to the more detached area of the "Hog-stye" (P), the shed (N), and the "Calf-house" (M). Entirely detached from the domestic quarters and located at the four corners of the barnyard are the barn (K), the "Cow-house" and grainery (H), and two shelters for livestock and carts (Q). The effect suggests the concentric ripples of a pool, their comparative distance from the parlor dictated no doubt by issues of labor efficiency but also by propriety-inflected considerations of privacy.[88]

The logic of division and subdivision we have observed in the design of interior spaces entails a basic structural principle rather than a predictable and consistent body of results. We can generalize about the broad movement from a model of linear hierarchy to one of separation and difference, for example, so long as we remain responsive to the specific variations that this simple abstraction subtends. At the same time, it is important to see that the specificity of these variations, even their intelligibility as such, depends on the capacity of abstraction to enclose a field that both includes and exceeds them. One factor in the density of this field is the complex counterpoint of status and gender criteria in the proliferation of outside and especially inside spaces. But these criteria are themselves in flux, and in ways that can be clarified by bringing to bear on them the same modes of particularizing analysis and generalizing abstraction that are useful in understanding the history of spatial arrangements. In the case of gender, this was evident in chapter 4 in my effort to engage the well-known hypothesis of "separate spheres" in association with the idea that "sexual difference," if from the broadest perspective a given of human culture, is from a more focused point of view a crucial development of modern culture. The following chapter will consider more closely the evidence for the modernity of sexual difference over against the more traditional and hierarchical notion of gender, as well as the hypothesis of a long-term shift in the norms of social categorization from a system of status to one of class.

As the emergence of modern attitudes toward the public and the private is an incremental rather than a rapid historical process, so its contributing elements (e.g., systems of social and gender categorization) evince a comparable pattern of change. The most comprehensive abstraction of such patterns that I have used in this study is that of the movement from relations of distinction to relations of separation, and I have stressed the likelihood that in a period of change such as this one, evidence of what can be abstracted as "before" and "after" will be overlapping and coextensive. The title of Alexander Ross's tract of 1651—*Arcana Microcosmi: or, the hid Secrets of Man's Body disclosed*—points in two directions: backward, to the view of the universe as a vast continuum of correspondences between greater and lesser, outside and inside versions of each other; and forward, through the disclosing force of a devolutionary absolutism that, by rendering tacit correspondence explicit, discovers secreted difference where similarity formerly had been assumed. In 1639 William Austin used the language of correspondence to a related end. In a book about "the excellency of the creation of woman," Austin observed that "the *female body* hath in it not only *all the rooms* and divisions in the *male* body, but diverse others besides that he hath not . . . . She is therefore so *largely* made, with so many *more rooms* then the *masculine* building, because she must contain *another house* within her, with an *unruly guest,* and all *provision* necessary for him."[89] The brunt of Austin's argument has the traditionalist force of distinction, not separation: male and female are, like house and body, greater and lesser spaces. Yet the distinction he makes between the bodies of men and women, although it draws on a knowledge of anatomical difference familiar to traditional thought and easily reconciled therein with a belief in the morphological continuity of things, also plays with the figure of proliferating domestic interiors to suggest in the female body a capacity for incorporation and interiority that in coming years will seem more and more to bespeak not simply a distinct but a separate sort of being.

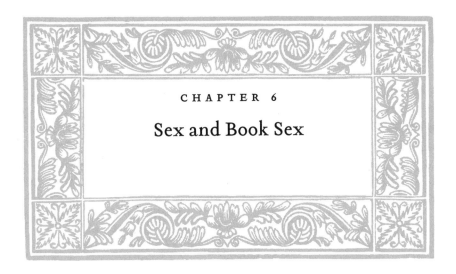

CHAPTER 6

Sex and Book Sex

As we move inward in our study of how the realms of the public and the private were explicitly separated out in the early modern period, we continue to encounter the opposition between the collective and the individual first intimated in the separation of the state from civil society. And as our vision adapts to this increasingly internalized structure of opposition, we find that the terms of the opposition are recapitulated within the latter pole. Indeed, the "privacy" of the individual can be conceived to consist not only of interrelations with other private individuals and institutions (like the normative experience of the property owner or the housewife) but also of the intrarelations that exist within any single individual. We already have seen how the third Earl of Shaftesbury conceives this internal recapitulation of opposition as a microdialogue between the individual's interiorized "author" and "reader."[1] Bernard Mandeville sees this internal dynamic as one of two different but complementary perspectives on the individual. On the one hand, the individual may be conceived as serving the ends of the greater whole of which it is one constituent part. On the other hand, the individual may be conceived as an integral and self-sufficient whole composed in turn of constituent parts. Moreover, like Shaftesbury, Mandeville finds the language of the public and the private fruitful in formulating this dialectical relationship:

> [T]o judge impartially, we ought to view things on all sides, and . . . all men ought to be consider'd two different ways.
>
> FIRST, as to their occupation, the station of life, which either choice or necessity has put them in. And here we chiefly mind the usefulness and dignity of their callings, their capacities with all qualifications requir'd for the exercise or performance of their functions. In this view we have no regard for the persons themselves, but

only the benefit they may be of to the publick, if they please and their service be wanted; and so they are only look'd upon as parts and members of the whole society.

SECONDLY, every person is to be consider'd as an entire individual, a wonderful machine, endued with thought and a will independent of any thing visible from without. In this view we look upon him as a necessitous being, subject to hunger and thirst, and having many passions to gratify, and at the same time a vast compound, or lesser world, with a sovereignty, and court of judicature within, having a private welfare and preservation of his own to mind, altogether abstract from the good of the publick.[2]

Mandeville's formulation bears a momentary and deceptive resemblance to the relation of distinction that organizes the traditional epistemology of hierarchical correspondence. In that sort of relationship the nature of the "lesser world" is understood to follow implicitly and by extension from that of the greater. However, the specificity with which Mandeville is able to divide the individual into his or her component, "public" and "private" parts depends on a prior separation out of the individual and the collective sufficiently explicit to permit their rearticulation. Only because the "lesser world" is felt to diverge fundamentally from the greater one can the terms of the latter be used metaphorically to suggest the structure of the former. The category of "the persons themselves," constituted by its division from the collective, can then be set in relation to "the whole society" in a way that cannot be read back into traditional analogies like the body politic, the ship of state, and the state as a family, which coordinate individuals strictly as parts of structured wholes rather than as structured "persons themselves." I use the generalizing language of "traditional" and "modern" epistemology to suggest determinant historical and cultural tendencies, not categorical capabilities. Shaftesbury's ancient mentor Socrates was a master of the explicitating mode of inquiry (thus the painstaking analogy between the soul and the state on which *The Republic* is built) that his modern follower employs when, in his notebook meditations, he exhorts himself to render his mental images explicit, to put them into words, "making them speak out & explaine themselves as it were viva voce, and not tacitely & murmeringly . . . ."[3]

What is the relationship between the coalescence of the idea that "private" personality has a systematic structure and the coalescence of the category of sex "as such"? For the past two decades or so, evidence has accumulated on several scholarly fronts suggesting that the later seventeenth and eighteenth centuries experienced a fundamental reorientation in attitudes toward sexuality. Like much of the material I have discussed thus far, this was a long-term and uneven process. That such a change occurred is most apparent at the macrolevel, when we compare the everyday assumptions that sixteenth- and twentieth-century

English people bring to sexual matters. That it was a multifarious change is clear from the impossibility of specifying those factors, and those moments, that were most crucial to it, as well as from the fact that until the past few decades historical study of a highly sophisticated sort found it plausible to comprehend this period in the absence of such a hypothesis—as many scholars continue to find today. Only additional scholarship in the history of sexuality can bring evidence that will make this hypothesis persuasive to the consensus of early modern scholars, and in the following pages I will adduce my own contribution to this effort. But it may also be at least suggestive to consider this hypothesis in the context of the schematic understanding of historical change that I have been pursuing in this book. For within that context the sexuality hypothesis takes its place alongside a disparate range of others—concerning politics, social relations, religious experience, epistemology, literature—all of which share the fundamental structure entailed in the movement from relations of distinction to relations of separation.

English people have, of course, always been aware of sex. But the tacit category "sex" became unprecedentedly explicit in this period because it was disembedded from the sociocultural, economic, and religious ground that heretofore had made "it" functional and purposive in (what modern thinking has come to see as separable, hence) "other" terms. English people have always understood the disparity between men and women as essential to their experience of the world. But the customary distinction between the genders along a shared and common spectrum was replaced over the course of this period by the tendency to view men and women as basically different from each other, as separate ways of being whose difference is crucially marked by a preference for the other sex and crucially mediated by the existence of a category of people who, on the contrary, prefer the same sex. Historical change is by definition diachronic. But the complexity of this shift from "tradition" to "modernity" has been underscored by scholars' recognition that the period in question is striated by synchronic differences in sexual attitudes and practices, along the lines of social and regional difference, of a sort that broadly corresponds to its overarching diachronic difference. (It may be useful to compare the richness and depth of this overlay of the diachronic and the synchronic to that which must obtain in accounting for the "transition" from an oral to a literate or print culture.) Indeed, this factor of synchronic diversity—the habits of commoners versus those of gentility, of English practices versus those said to obtain in the Americas—played an important role in the way contemporaries themselves learned to abstract sex and gender from their tacit givenness. The following discussion offers an extremely cursory overview of findings in fields of study that are currently in productive ferment, and it emphasizes evidence that seems to have a particular bearing on the relation between the public and the private that is the central concern of this study.

Sex

At the beginning of our period, and especially at the plebeian level, sexual activity that focused on the couple and involved vaginal penetration tended to be closely associated with marriage and procreation. Otherwise, and more commonly, sex was likely to be a more collective, semi-"public" affair—even masturbation, let alone the broad range of nonpenetrative acts of petting, fondling, bundling, and the like that modern discourse tends to consign to the category "foreplay" but that was traditionally experienced as fully constitutive of sexual activity (no doubt birth control played a part in this). For men as well as women, sex involved different parts of the body, among which the conjunction of the genital organs was central only to the specifically purposive end of reproduction. The modern tendency to associate sexual activity with the specific act of penetration and with the demonstrable fact of penile ejaculation makes sex more ostensibly "natural" not in the sense of its procreativity (which was always manifest) but in the sense that it concentrates attention on the natural differences between male and female anatomy.[4]

Dominant premodern strands of medical thinking took an alternative view of these matters. According to Galenic and humoral theory, genital anatomy was differentiated along a hierarchical continuum. Because women have less body heat than men, their sex organs are morphologically an underdeveloped —an inverted and internalized—version of men's, and the comparative lubricity of women is explained by the fact that they seek to raise their bodily temperature through copulation. The chronology of cultural change as significant as that of our present topic is inevitably difficult to pin down. Nonetheless, there seems to be some basis for saying that over the course of the seventeenth century the traditional, "one-sex" model of anatomy was incompletely challenged and replaced by the modern, "two-sex" model according to which the difference between men and women is not a matter of distinction along a common gradient but a radical separation based on fundamental physiological differences. Women are not an undeveloped and subordinate version of men; they are biologically and naturally different from them—the "opposite" sex.[5] Needless to say, there is an arresting congruence in the spatial language by which the tacit distinction between kinds of work and kinds of bodies is figured. But whereas the modern ideology of separate spheres intensifies to the point of dichotomy the outside-inside distinction, the separation that is entailed in the modern two-sex model is achieved at the expense of the spatial figure.

This overview of the transition from a traditional to a modern attitude toward sexuality in Western culture is consistent with the long-term change I have invoked from time to time in the preceding pages, the change from a positive to a negative model of liberty in conceiving the normative relationship between individuals and communities. According to traditional views, bodily and mental health is achieved through temperance, a state of balanced equilibrium that depends upon the individual's capacity and willingness to control his or her passions. By this understanding, individuality is to a considerable extent a function of self-control.[6] What begins to counter this norm in the early modern period is the growing conviction that liberty requires the liberation of the passions from control, whether that of the self or that of external institutions like the state—in other words, that individuality entails individualism. That these are vast generalizations synoptic of local multiplicity and variation is best seen, I think, not as a conceptual weakness or danger but as the groundwork of their conceptual utility and strength.

The early modern valorization of empirical knowledge, which gave "nature" an unprecedentedly material grounding and sensible access, encouraged the view that sex was "natural" and hence a thing in itself. The word "sex" itself was generalized from particular reference to "the two divisions of organic beings distinguished as male and female respectively" and also made to signify, more abstractly, "the class of phenomena with which these [distinctions] are concerned." As a result of this linguistic abstraction, it became possible to write not only about "the male sex" or "the female sex" but also about "sex" as such.[7] Already entailed within this grand abstraction, however, is the analogous abstraction that consists in conceiving the male and the female sex as "organic divisions" by virtue of their biological determinacy, the disembedding of "man" and "woman" from a complex experiential network of social and legal status so as to isolate each as a fundamental and differential physiological identity. The scientific "discovery" of definitive anatomical difference was not so much the cause of this change in thinking (which affected people who were quite unaware of it) as one cause among many in a cultural transformation characterized (as we have seen) by an overdetermined tendency toward separation out and explicitation. Still, the deep connection between an emergent scientific method and the emergent disclosure of the discrete and private realm of the sexual is suggested by the language of a sixteenth-century anatomical guide that "endeavoured to set wyde the closet doore of natures secretes . . ." and by that of the seventeenth-century enthusiast who "happened upon the ever-vernant and private walkes of *Naturall Philosophie,* (which are not accessible to all, nor every one admitted, but onely Students, by their prerogative and Priviledge) where (having an eye not incurious) it being lawfull to enter the very bowels (as I may say) of her secresies, not without infinite pleasure I penetrated her *Arcana,* and opening her *Cabinet,* finding her full of *Curiosities,* and [had] free licence to take what I thought fit . . . ."8

The long-term dichotomization of gender difference was also reinforced by a contemporaneous abstraction of sodomitical behavior as defining a kind of proto-"homosexual" identity. Although the correlative terms "homosexual" and "heterosexual" were of much later coinage, recent research suggests that the "molly" subculture of early-eighteenth-century London coalesced alongside the biologization of the male and female genders as their functional correlate, a sort of "third gender" composed of exclusive male sodomites. Under the one-sex regime sodomy was condemned as a sinful behavior that might be indulged by a variety of men. In fact, a normative aristocratic masculinity, defined by the crucial fact of superior power, could entail sexual relations both with women and with young male commoners (the latter according to a differential that would seem to be based on age and social status rather than gender, although when gender difference is conceived on a hierarchical continuum the biological underdevelopment of plebeian boys also assimilates them to the female gender). Under this traditional regime, finally, the defining condition of masculinity was not sexual prowess but the capacity for violent behavior, whether toward other men or toward women.9 Under the emergent two-sex regime, by contrast, masculinity came to be consistent only with an anatomically gender-based differential and definable by sexual behavior. Indeed, we might speculate that it was "only through the emergence of this new gender role that the two 'orthodox' genders simultaneously came into being as the normative choice of difference made intelligible by the alternative and negative choice of sameness. . . . The proto-homosexuality of sodomy . . . functioned within the system of sexuality as a structural anomaly, bestowing on the difference between masculinity and femininity a normative coherence achieved through a mediating term that was at once both and neither."10

Although it is not strictly relevant to my current concern with the early modern disembedding of sex, it makes sense at this point to pose briefly a question that is important to my organizing interest in the public-private relationship. If biologized sexual difference became the single most definitive determinant of personal identity for modern Western culture, what did it replace? The obvious answer to this question is that it has no traditional equivalent because the notion of personal identity presumes a condition of abstracted and individualized autonomy that is foreign to premodern culture. However, the idea of a naturally determined marker of social status does play a central role in the system of lineage that dominates most traditional cultures. In England the most important signifier of social difference before class consciousness developed in the late eighteenth and nineteenth centuries was the possession or nonpossession of honor, which was understood to be a heritable entity that was entailed in the blood and passed on to succeeding generations as a biological aspect of genealogical inheritance. Of course, premodern English people knew as well as we to distinguish between nature and nurture as well as to presume their interaction. As Delarivier Manley observed, "It is easie to judge why Persons of Quality have generally more Penetration, Vivacity and Spirit, than those of a meaner Rank: For . . . good Nourishment, and the Juice of Nice Meats, which mixes with the Blood, and other Humours of the Body, subtilizes them, and renders them more proper for the Functions of Nature."[11] But because people saw the relationship between nature and nurture as one of distinction more than of separation, they had no difficulty in reconciling the evidence of social determination with the belief in a natural "social essence." The intense and intimate preoccupation with the royal succession with which this study is so often concerned is only the most ostensible sign of the belief in the preeminence of the bloodline—as well as of that belief's increasing vulnerability.

Under the aegis of the early modern empiricist revolution, the demystification of this view—the broad if not universal repudiation of the belief that nobility has a natural grounding—roughly coincided with the discovery that gender difference is in fact so grounded. From a bird's-eye view we can see that in seventeenth- and eighteenth-century England the baton of natural determinacy was passed from birth to sex, from the system of social status to the system of gender identity. The modern insistence on a differentiation between nature and nurture more rigorous than that evinced by Delarivier Manley ensures that our conviction that sex is natural depends on our ability to draw the line between this and its appearance, what looks natural about sex but is really cultural. This is the ambition of Manley's French contemporary François Poullain de la Barre, one of the most influential propounders of the emergent argument of gender difference. He observes of "some *Physitians*" that "[w]hen they perceive the *Two Sexes* more distinguished, by that which regards the civil, than particular, Functions; they fancy to themselves, that so they ought to be; And, not discerning exactly enough, betwixt that which proceeds from Custom and Education, and that which comes from Nature; they have attributed to one and the same Cause, all which they see in Society; imagining, that when *God* Created *Man* and *Woman,* he disposed then in such a manner, as ought to produce all the Distinction which we observe betwixt them."[12]

This dialectic is acknowledged in the tendency, a product of the late-twentieth-century feminist movement, to speak of the sex/gender system and to use "gender" to designate "sexual difference" that is really socially constructed. By this way of thinking, premodern culture evinced not a sex/gender but a gender system because biological sexuality was traditionally embedded in its sociocultural ground to such a degree as to preclude the dichotomization of sex and gender.[13] By hypostatizing biological sex—and thereby making explicit a division between natural sex and cultural gender—the modern system both augmented the reification of gender as sex and sophisticated the demystification of sex as gender. In George Lillo's domestic tragedy the seductress Millwood's response to the charge that "[t]o call thee woman were to wrong the sex" shows a distinctly modern intelligence about an age-old phenomenon: "That imaginary being is an emblem of thy cursed sex collected, a mirror wherein each particular man can see his own likeness and that of all mankind."[14]

To speak of the traditional "embedding" of biological sexuality in its sociocultural ground, it should be clear, does not imply that the "bed" was singular and unchanging. A case in point is the Renaissance institution of court pederasty.[15] Pederasty names the kind of same-sex behavior that required a decisive difference in generation, power, and status between its participants and that worked, like the patron-client relationship, to cement hierarchical super- and subordination through the performance of one man's dependence on another's power. From a modern perspective this is definitively a "sexual" behavior. Within early modern culture, however, pederasty was experienced as a political relationship of dependence and empowerment, a "sexual" instance of subjection comparable, at least in this respect, to the subjection of the wife to the husband's power. In the schematic view of political change that I have invoked from time to time the ideology of negative liberty became thinkable when distinction became separation, when the absolute and tacit condition of subjection to another became explicitly intelligible as a relationship between absolute subjectivities. As the devolution of absolutism made political subjects into ethical subjects, we might infer, so it relocated the increasingly antiquated political practice of pederasty within the general category of sodomy, a "sexual" practice that remains ethically abhorrent but is politically neutral. Indeed, this line of thought might suggest a way to concretize the hypothesis that it is in this period that same-sex and different-sex behavior are separated out over against each other. If to contemporaries pederasty bespoke not "sodomy" in general but the absolutist order of hierarchical subjection, the subjective reciprocity of gender difference, bonded to a repudiation of sodomy that is more precisely a repudiation of pederasty, become intelligible as a rebellion against royal and aristocratic absolutism. In these terms marriage might be seen as an affirmation of the private liberties of the subject even if it also might enclose, as we have seen, a struggle between "public" male tyranny and the "private" female subject.

One consequence of these changes concerns women and generation. By the old way of thinking, reproduction depended heavily on female mentality and consciousness: women were sexually voracious, hence inclined to copulate; conception required that women experience the pleasure of orgasm; images in the mind of the conceiving woman were liable to be imprinted on the body of her child. The shift to a more strictly biological view of generation obviated these beliefs in the importance to conception of the woman's state of mind and contributed to, on the one hand, the modern view of women as comparatively modest, passive, and passionless and, on the other, the modern identification of female difference with the generative organs and of female identity with motherhood.[16] Physical generalizations about "women's nature" are on the face of it no more abstractive than are mental generalizations, and yet we might be justified in supposing that the emergent conviction of a physical grounding encouraged a more confident and overarching abstraction of the nature of women. Hannah Woolley's ambition in her compendious handbook of 1675 was to cut across and to "control for" all the concrete contingencies of social, regional, and generational diversity, to write "such a Book as might be a *Universal Companion* and *Guide* to the Female Sex, in all *Relations, Companies, Conditions,* and *states* of *Life* even from *Child-hood* down to *Old-age;* and from the Lady at the *Court,* to the Cook-maid in the *Country* . . . ."[17]

Aristotle's Master-piece

And yet the problem with adducing this sort of evidence—Woolley alongside Manley and Poullain—is clear enough. The chronology and unevenness of the transformation with which we are concerned are such that for any given moment evidence both for the old and for the new dispensation is likely to be available. Persuasive documentation of diachronic difference may be found at either terminus of this long-term transition, but what is found in the middle range is overlap and mixture. To some degree this reflects not simply the nature of long-term change but also the medium on which we depend for our knowledge of it. "Cultural lag" was built into the origins of print culture. "The advent of printing transformed the conditions under which texts were produced, distributed and consumed. But this was accomplished in a most deceptive way— not by discarding the products of scribal culture but by reproducing them in greater quantities than ever before. The *ars artificialiter scribendi* was first and foremost a duplicating process."[18] For this reason the coalescence of "sex as such" in early modern culture may be a matter not only of contents but also of form: a matter not only of new attitudes toward sex but also of a quantitative explicitation of sex, an explosion in the publication, dissemination, and consumption of texts about "it."[19]

A case in point is the most popular English manual about sexual anatomy and activity of the eighteenth century (and beyond). With variations in title and contents, *Aristotle's Master-piece* was reprinted frequently over the course of the century that scholars have increasingly depicted as a watershed in attitudes toward sex and gender, and yet it tends to endorse traditional far more than innovative ways of thinking about these matters.[20] Indeed, if vaginal penetration was less central to premodern sexual culture and practice than it has since become, *Aristotle's Master-piece*—and this is evident also by modern standards—is focused on conception, not sex. Constant through all its editorial variations is an organizing interest not in the process but in the product, not in generating pleasure but in generating offspring—or in avoiding it, since the knowledge the book imparts might also be used to contraceptive ends.[21] Yet a comparison of some of the frontispieces that accompany the several editions of the book provides food for thought about how its central interest in reproduction might variously be construed.

Much of what *Aristotle's Master-piece* contains justifies locating it in the genre of birthing and midwifery manuals, as does the tract with which it sometimes was printed (see fig. 5.12).[22] Some editions of the book feature frontispieces that express the anxiety of imaginatively induced monstrous births. In figure 6.1 a naked woman in an outdoor setting stands beside a black child over the legend: "The Effigies of a Maid all Hairy, and an Infant that was black by the Imagination of their Parents."[23] Other editions picture close facsimiles of this woman and child, without the explanatory legend, in postures that are identical to those of figure 6.1 but that now, in an altered setting, convey the sense that they have stepped from a still-visible outdoors into the relative privacy of the room in which they are standing, the book-lined study of a learned doctor who sits at his desk writing; the woman's genitalia are now covered by a floral design (fig. 6.2).[24] This (quite artificial) juxtaposition of images may call to mind the story told by figure 4.10, of the male physician angelically preferred to the woman; and the costumes of the two doctors are very alike (as is that of Wijck's scholarly alchemist in fig. 5.1). If that frontispiece does indeed depict a scene of "modernization" in which the customary, plebeian household lore of the female is displaced by the special knowledge of the male professional, the appearance of the doctor in figure 6.2 may give to this edition of *Aristotle's Master-piece* a similar aura.

That impression is strengthened by yet another version of the frontispiece, figure 6.3, in which a naked woman, modestly if partially draped and devoid of monstrous body hair, stands in a book-lined study before a doctor who writes at his desk but, unlike in figure 6.2, is also attentive to the woman, to whom he seems to be speaking.[25] More suggestive still is the room itself. Books and an astrolabe sit on the doctor's desk, while on the walls and from the ceiling are sus-

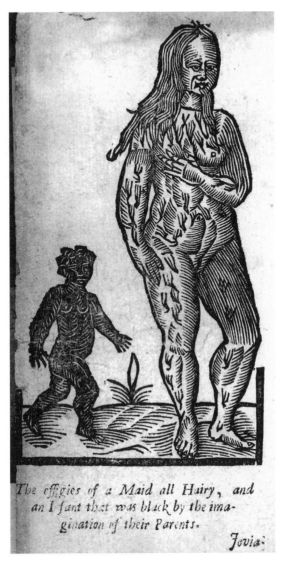

The effigies of a Maid all Hairy, and
an I fant that was black by the imagination of their Parents.

Jovia:

FIG. 6.1. Frontispiece, *Aristoteles Master-piece, Or The
Secrets of Generation displayed in all the parts thereof.* . . .
(1684). Yale University, Harvey Cushing/John Hay
Whitney Medical Library.

FIG. 6.2. Frontispiece, *Aristotle's compleat master-piece . . .*, 12th ed. (1722?). Wellcome Library, London.

pended exotic reptilian specimens. These furnishings associate the room with a number of "protoscientific" spaces we have already encountered: the apothecary shop, the cabinet of curiosities, the museum, the alchemist's house, the astrologer's house (see figs. 4.12, 5.1, 5.3, 5.4, 5.5). There is a family resemblance between both the dress and the seated posture of these adepts of the *arcana naturae,* but the natural artifacts of celestial, terrestrial, and subaqueous wonder that surround the astrologer (for example) are demoted, in the doctor's study, to the status of decoration by the dominating presence of the female body, her private parts sedately poised for private disclosure and examination. The surrounding space is presumably domestic; and if we recall the gendered exclusivity that lay behind Alberti's ideal study, it is as though we see here the terms by which that principle might permissibly be breached: if the female subject is rendered a natural object of investigation. By the same token, we might suppose, figure 6.3 answers the question raised by the angelic exclusion of women and their folk remedies in figure 4.10: they are permitted back into the domestic interiors provided they shed their authority along with their clothing.[26]

The point of these tendentious appositions of images is not to argue a developmental narrative in the successive editions of *Aristotle's Master-piece* (the mixed chronology of the frontispieces alone militates against such a reading) but to release or enhance some of the semantic potential that lies within each image in isolation from the others. In figure 6.3, we might wish to conclude, the privacy of both "woman" and "sex" have been separated out through the abstractive force of protoscientific explication. A final frontispiece both does and does not support this reading. Figure 6.4 depicts a relationship of outdoors and indoors similar to that shown in figure 6.2, but here the view through the doorway reveals a garden being tended, while in the (also) more fully domesticated indoor scene the doctor sits at a table with a cup in his hand, attended by a fully clothed housewife or servant; a curtain of clouds embossed with astrological, hermetic, and Hebraic characters overarches the entire scene. The verses under the frontispiece read:

> I've Read this Useful Tract, and therein find
> The lively Strokes of *Aristotle's* Mind:
> And they that do with Understanding Read,
> Will find it is a *Master-piece* indeed:
> For in this Subject there is none can Write,
> (At least so well) as that Great *Stagyrite.*
> He Nature's Cabinet has open laid,
> And her *Abstrusest Secrets* here display'd:
> Here modest Maids and Women, being Ill,
> Have got a *Doctor* to advise with still:

FIG. 6.3. Frontispiece, *The works of Aristotle in four parts . . .*
(1777). Wellcome Library, London.

Where they mayn't only their Distempers see;
But find a Sure, and Proper Remedy
For each Disease, and every Condition;
And have no other need of a Physician:
For which Good End I'm sure it was design'd,
And may the Reader the Advantage find.[27]

These verses situate *Aristotle's Master-piece* within the broad terrain of the book of secrets: as in his other treatises, "Aristotle" here lays open nature's cabinet to reveal her abstruse secrets, which are the secrets not of statecraft nor of trade-craft but of women's bodies. But the title page describes the book's "second part" in terms—"A Private Looking-Glass for the Female-Sex"—that encourage us to read the verses more attentively. Their implication is that what is private about *Aristotle's Master-piece* is not only its female contents but also its availabil-ity to the female reader. And the verses attest not so much to the mastery of "Aristotle's" learning as to its legibility by "they that do with Understanding Read."[28] That is, the process the verses envision is one not of subjection but of internalization: not the subjection of the female object to the objective author-ity of the male subject but the internalization of male authority in a book that, typographically abstracted from any actual and gendered scene of pedagogy, may be internalized by the female subject in the privacy and virtuality of the scene of reading. The female reader, having "no other need of a Physitian" than this book, may proceed to self-examination and self-remedy.

The autonomization of sex as such in the early modern period was condi-tioned by a number of factors that themselves may have been inconsistent with one another. In this discussion of *Aristotle's Master-piece* the emphasis has been on the disembedding of procreation from the *curiositas* of natural wonders, but also from the expertise of extrinsic practitioners. Along with the cult of moth-erhood and the concentration of a more diffused premodern sexual activity into vaginal penetration and the telos of orgasm, this might seem to confirm that the explicitation of "sex" went hand in hand with a modern tendency to focal-ize on reproduction as such.[29] However, reproduction itself also might be un-derstood as the ground within which traditional thinking about sex was cus-tomarily and tacitly embedded. The factor that then united (and to some degree still unites) a broad spectrum of proscribed sexual activities—prostitu-tion, sodomy, masturbation, fornication, adultery—was the absence of a pro-creative purpose. The figure of the whore plays a pivotal role in this spectrum: overdetermined though it was, the early modern fascination with the whore grew in part from her seeming embodiment of copulatory sex stripped of its ra-tionale. Of course, other rationales were available. On the one hand, prostitutes were condemned for having sex for the *wrong* reason—for money, not procre-ation—and even married women were vulnerable (as we have seen) to the charge of "matrimonial whoredom" if their marriage (hence their sexual activ-ity) seemed to have either a monetary or a too strictly lascivious motivation. On the other hand, prostitutes were condemned for copulating in the *absence* of the only *good* reason. Here the correlative category is not the matrimonial whore but the "he-whore," the exclusive male sodomite whose sexual activity despica-

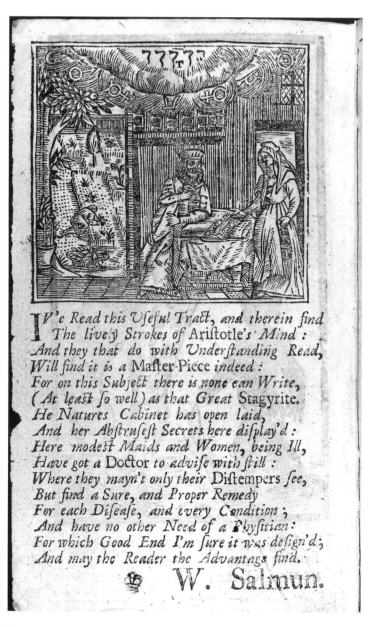

I'Ve Read this Useful Tract, and therein find
The lively Strokes of Aristotle's Mind :
And they that do with Understanding Read,
Will find it is a Master-Piece indeed :
For on this Subject there is none can Write,
(At least so well) as that Great Stagyrite.
He Natures Cabinet has open laid,
And her Abstrusest Secrets here display'd :
Here modest Maids and Women, being Ill,
Have got a Doctor to advise with still :
Where they mayn't only their Distempers see,
But find a Sure, and Proper Remedy
For each Disease, and every Condition ;
And have no other Need of a Physitian :
For which Good End I'm sure it was design'd ;
And may the Reader the Advantage find.

W. Salmun.

FIG. 6.4. Frontispiece, *Aristotle's Master-piece Compleated* . . . (1702). By permission of the British Library, shelf mark 1485.aaa.31. Verses attributed to William Salmun.

bly defied the social virtues of procreation and the perpetuation of the lineage.³⁰ We might speculate that the emergence of sex as such required that the blanket prohibition of nonprocreative sex as sin be replaced by a closer inquiry moti- vated not so much (at least at first) by a higher tolerance for nongenerative cop- ulation as by an explicitating impulse to sort out these variously reviled activi- ties in their particularity.

Onania

Like *Aristotle's Master-piece,* the eighteenth century's most popular book on mas- turbation perpetuates aspects of the traditional, one-sex model even as it offers an unprecedentedly medicalized assault on the ancient sin of Onan. Pur- portedly first printed in 1710, *Onania* tripled in length through successive print- ings before taking on a supplement almost as long as itself. This phenomenal growth obviously testifies to the popularity of the tract, especially since it was achieved by incorporating and responding to letters sent in by readers of previ- ous editions, a policy that gave *Onania* something like the status of a periodical paper for medical self-help and that established the public-sphere status of mas- turbation as the secret that everybody not only knows but also knows that everyone knows. The virtual collectivity of masturbation confirms its multi- farious actuality. As *Onania*'s author remarks at one point, "[M]y Lord *Roches- ter* has reckoned it among the Things that are not only universal, but never to

c   e   a   s   e

. . . .".³¹

Onania begins with a sentence that succinctly summarizes its main con- cerns: "SELF-POLLUTION is that unnatural Practice, by which Persons of either Sex, may defile their own Bodies, without the Assistance of others, whilst yield- ing to filthy Imaginations, they endeavour to imitate and procure to themselves that Sensation, which God has order'd to attend the carnal Commerce of the two Sexes, for the Continuance of our Species" (1). Most immediately striking, perhaps, is the fact that although masturbation had by no means been a solitary practice, *Onania* consistently treats it as such—as though the burden of sin- gling it out for attention were borne in part by understanding it as a singular activity. In conjunction with the emphasis on "self-pollution," in fact, the antithesis between "their own" and "others," between "either Sex" and "two Sexes," in this opening sentence goes some distance toward identifying what is unnatural about the act as not just its nonreproductivity but especially its au- tonomy. One correspondent similarly speaks of his "hurtful Secret" as "sinful Self-Conversation" (108, 109). The title page of the *Supplement* condemns "that filthy Commerce with ones self . . ."; a correspondent confesses to "this Criminal Knowledge of my self," and its author separates out masturbation as "that Branch of Uncleanness, that without Witness, may be committed with one's self . . ." (96, 48).

The autonomy and the secrecy of onanism are mutually reinforcing. Proposing "to speak of those peculiar Causes, which belong to this Sin, and hardly any other," the author comes to the second cause, which "is the Secrecy, with which SELF-POLLUTION may be committed: All other Actions of Uncleanness must have a Witness, this needs none. . . . the Secrecy of this Sin has betray'd many into it, whom hardly any thing else would have tempted" (11).[32] The secrecy of the act entails a corresponding anonymity of publication: "I request that you wou'd in this Matter be as private as you can," writes one correspondent; and regarding both their sin and its physical consequences two masturbating twins confide that "we have till now kept it secret, and not made any Body acquainted with it . . . . Our Names must be conceal'd . . ." (*Onania,* 46, font reversed [on secrecy and privacy, see also 101, 104, 151]; *Supplement,* 90, 91). Initials, syncopated names, and pseudonyms are the most commonly used means to this end. Sensitized to the issue of secrecy, the author devotes some space to refuting the complaint that he has "betray'd the Secrets of my Patients": "As to the revealing of Secrets, the exposing of Patients publickly, and the breaking of one's Trust, . . . the charge is ridiculous . . . from such Letters there is no more to be discover'd or gather'd, to any one's prejudice, than there is from every Case and History, related in any practical Book of Physick or Surgery . . ." (*Supplement,* v, 52–53).

So the author of *Onania* wrote in the tradition of the book of secrets made public. Resorting to some of the same literary devices used by libelous discourse, moreover, writing about onanism thus betrayed a similar sensitivity to the publication of the private.[33] To put this another way, *Onania* is committed, as is realism, to the casuistical "case history," which separates out the concrete particularity of what is "history-like" from the actual particularity of what is historically accurate.[34] At a certain point, however, a correspondent raises a question that is analogous to this one about the invasion of privacy but that proves a good deal less tractable. It also exemplifies how the discourse of masturbation helps bring the category of sex to the verge of explicitness. The correspondent C.T. wonders whether the "filthy imaginations" that enable masturbation may be more opprobrious than masturbation itself: "I look upon the impure Imaginations which often go along with, and always facilitate the operation [of masturbation], to contain the greatest Part of its Sinfulness, and have thought I might allow my self in it, could I but separate the Action from those its usual attendants, which I have experienc'd to be very possible." The question is analogous to the problem of how to guard against the invasion of privacy that occurs through the publication of real names because it too concerns the separability of actual particularity (in this case, the act of masturbation) from the concrete particularity of the virtual (the imagination of that act). The author applauds the impulse behind this experiment, but he doubts its feasibility. The thought is indeed worse than the act, he agrees, "but that you can separate the Action from those usual attendants, as you affirm, I cannot easily believe" (108–9, 120).

Of course, the differences between this question and the problem of how to detoxify libel are as apparent as are their similarities. Most important, the analogy involves a radical internalization: what concerns the correspondent is not a public-sphere event—not a making public to many people the secrets of some or one—but an action that occurs, at least by the terms of the libel problem, strictly within the private realm of the individual subject. Once translated to the internal realm, moreover, the status of concrete virtuality changes. In the macroinstance the virtual improves on the actual: what is imagined there is an ethically positive product of the transformation of libel into satire or realism. In the microinstance, however, what is imagined is original and ethically negative. Finally, the author believes that the public-sphere possibility of separating actual from concrete particularity is frustrated within the private realm of the individual subject, perhaps because of its too-intimate confines. And this belief only reinforces onanism's autonomy, solitude, secrecy, and privacy with the aura of its irreducibly virtual interiority.

How does the silent and imperfect analogy between the workings of the imagination and the publication of the private clarify how masturbation helps explicitate sex as such? The analogy comes close to being broached when the author warns his reader early on of the extreme delicacy of the task before him. Indeed, the warning goes beyond analogy, suggesting that the macro- and the microinstances—the problem of publication and the problem of imagination—are related not only metaphorically but also metonymically:

I Would have the Reader reflect on the Matter I treat of, which differs much from other Points of Morality; for in handling other Topicks, a Man may safely say whatever he thinks any way advantageous to his Design . . . . But in arguing against Uncleanness, especially this sort of it, which of all, as it is the most loathsome, the same Liberty is not to be taken, but a Man is extremely confin'd, and is oblig'd to express himself with the utmost Circumspection and Caution, for fear of intrenching upon Modesty; which as I promis'd I would not be Guilty of doing, I shall all along with the greatest strictness observe, as knowing that I shou'd be oblig'd to name some Things that might betray my Readers into the remembrance of what it is much better that they should for ever forget, as they would not then be able to set such a watchful Guard upon their Thoughts and Fancies, but that some foul or filthy Desires would in Spight creep in; the least imagination only of which, would render them Odious in God's sight, who seeth the Heart, and Delights in none but those who are pure and upright there; with which Apology, hoping it will be sufficient for what Omissions and Obscurity I have been guilty of, I conclude this Chapter. (14–15)

The metonymic relationship between the author's publication and the reader's imagination turns on the fact that the authorial danger of "naming" here concerns not proper names (hence the risk of libel) but "things"—ideas and images—whose risk lies in their filthiness: if the author is too particular in the language he publishes, the reader's imagination will become dangerously corrupted. And in describing the mechanics of such corruption the author of *Onania* finds that the language of Protestant conscience will carry him only so far. True, it carries him some distance: in the microinstance of the reader's imagination the equivalent of the readership of the author's publication is (an internalization of) God, the passively receptive counterpart of the divine vocation, for which the act of masturbation is already sinful in its most original and immaterial conception.[35] What God reads is the reader's conscience, which is to say his most private representations: not his actions or speech but his very thoughts. The author's care "to express himself" in public is balanced by the reader's private "guard upon his thoughts and fancies": thoughts are more private than words, but even thoughts and fancies are none too private for "God's sight." Moreover, it is the author's care in expression that determines, at least to some degree, the reader's ability to guard his thoughts from becoming susceptible to God's judgment.[36]

And yet the language of Protestant conscience, expressly designed to excavate the interior space of consciousness, stops short at this juncture because it is unequipped to plumb the realm that lies beyond it, that of the unconscious. As we have seen by now in a range of instances, the process of separation out is dialectical. On the one hand, to separate categories from each other is to disengage what previously had been connected. On the other hand, separation out enables an engagement between what previously had been too coextensive to admit of relationship. In the absence of the category of the unconscious the author relies instead on the faculty of memory and its uncanny ability to bring into mind what once was there but now is not.[37] In this analysis, the position of the reader is assumed not by (even an internalization of) God but by the secular subject him- or herself—or rather, by the "public," imagining aspect of that subject, to which its "private" productions become known through the failure of what is in effect a censoring process. And the danger of corruption here is not simply one of the mind's infiltration from without. Instead, it is the author's uncircumspect naming of certain things that, from without, causes the remembrance of what has been there deep within and should forever have been forgotten. This remembrance in turn impairs the operation of the mind's "watchful guard," which allows filthy desires to creep into the imagination, not from without but from the memory, the "within" that is internal even to the "within" of the mind itself.

So the entire system involves two levels of censorship. First, in the macroinstance of publication, the author aims to impose a prepublication censorship on his writings through his intentional "omissions and obscurity," by which certain things go unnamed; the purpose of the 1712 Stamp Act was to force authors to practice just this sort of self-censorship. Second, in the microinstance, the reader normally imposes a censorship or watchful guard on his or her own thoughts and fancies to ensure that foul or filthy desires do not attain "the least imagination"—that is, do not creep into the "public" imagination from the "private" precincts of memory. (In the macroinstance of publication there is also the potential for a third level, a kind of postpublication censorship that is interposed between these two, a censorship that normatively prohibits the circulation of offensive things that have escaped the author's prepublication censorship; this had been the purpose of the 1662 Printing Act, which lapsed in 1694.)[38]

The secularity of the language the author uses to describe the reader's own internal guard is dictated not only by the unavailability of such terminology in the depth psychology of Protestantism but also by the fact that it otherwise would intimate that we know things deeper than the imagination, things that God Himself does not see. For the most part, however, these protopsychoanalytic formulations of an internal censorship mechanism are compatible enough with the language of religious conscience. Having printed a letter from N. Pedagogus, the author of *Onania* warns that "[t]o Answer it as you desire, I must have leave with freedom to examine and dive into the Sentiments of your Heart; [and] discover the struggles that seem to be there between Virtue and Passion . . . . [B]y continuing in the Sinful Practice you live in, you act against the Dictates of your own Reason, and raise Arguments to Skreen your self from your own Fears" (154). Protestant compunction dictates a continuous and conscientious vigilance over one's own mental productions as the sign both of sin and of salvation. No doubt in part because it insists on seeing masturbation as a solitary activity, *Onania* is saturated with the Protestant impulse toward self-examination and self-experiment, which helps mobilize the explicitating motive that is evident in the book's restless ambition to tease apart this from that sort of secrecy or privacy, actual from concrete particularity, candor from rationalization, sinful from innocent passions and pleasures.

This explicitating motive is as evident in the author's correspondents as it is in the author himself. At one point in his long letter Pedagogus refers to a masturbating priest of his acquaintance, "an Example of Piety" who nonetheless "is no more concern'd for the gratifying of his Senses *per se ipsum,* than he is when he enjoys the Company and Society of his Wife; . . . which I am pretty sure he would not do, if he thought it was a Sin" (142–43). Agreeing with the author that masturbation is "an Abuse of the Creative Power," a female correspondent remarks that "what is in it self Evil, Marriage can't make Good, therefore I conclude the Marriage-Bed defil'd, the Man and Wife committing Sin, when the End can't be had for which that Sensation was given; for tho' the Man be at all Times capable of Generation, the Woman is not . . . ." Conjugal copulation at such times is "the same in my Opinion with SELF-POLLUTION and SODOMY" (86). Another correspondent is concerned "lest your seeming to prefer Uncleanness with the different Sex, before that with ones self, should tempt some young Persons who have never yet known any other kind of Uncleanness but the latter, to exchange it for that greater Sin of *Fornication*" (106). Like the Protestant casuistry of salvation, in other words, the casuistry of masturbation subdivides not only the inquiring subject into a psychomachia of interiorized faculties and interests but also the seemingly straightforward rule of chastity itself into an assemblage of variables and qualifications. And in peeling away the ethical differences between fornication, adultery, contraceptive conjugal copulation, sodomy, and masturbation, the experimental investigation circles in toward the as yet unformulated category for which its language controls, sex itself—the "constant" that affords these differences their status as variables. Masturbation makes a crucial contribution to this experiment, it would seem, because its construal as a solitary activity appears to clear away those ultimately extraneous factors that are introduced by the presence and participation of other people.

Recent scholarship has recognized the importance of the relationship between ethical introspection and the emergence of sex as such. Michel Foucault suggested that the modern "discourse on sex" was indebted to techniques of religious confession. "By integrating it into the beginnings of a scientific discourse, the nineteenth century altered the scope of the confession; it tended no longer to be concerned solely with what the subject wished to hide, but with what was hidden from himself, being incapable of coming to light except gradually and through the labor of a confession in which the questioner and the questioned each had a part to play." Foucault's followers have extended this insight to account for the emergence of pornographic discourse and to articulate this emergence with that of sex as such—not just its disclosure but its very existence: "To teach individuals that the truth of their sex was hidden was a means of getting them to look for it and, in looking for it, expose more of their self to correction. . . . The technique of confession is not an apparatus revealing the existence of sexuality to knowledge; it is a means of bringing western sexuality into existence by attaching it to an apparatus of knowledges in which it must be revealed."[39]

The preceding discussion of *Onania* suggests that Foucault's thesis needs to be both backdated and Reformed: that the specifically Protestant development of conscience and casuistry is vital to the process by which sex comes into being in the early modern period by virtue of its always being there as a "constant," a temporarily forgotten memory.[40] To speak of the emergence of sex as such is to mark the difference between a traditional view of lust as oscillating and transitory and the modern view of sexual desire as a steady and constant condition of personality. The Protestant injunction of conscientious self-scrutiny, self-discipline, and self-control—of the self by the self—presupposed and reinforced the integrity and perdurability both of the activity of discipline and of that which was disciplined. Foucault's critique of "the repressive hypothesis"—of the notion that modern culture has been concerned to prohibit, deny, and silence sex—is most fruitful when seen to insist not on the opposite (modern sex as "discursively" promoted) but on the dialectical truth of both repression and promotion. (The reciprocal repression and promotion of sex thus exemplifies the dialectical principle entailed more broadly in the publication of the private.) Sex becomes a "hidden," "secret" entity not under medieval confession but through the introspective powers of Protestant conscience and its impulse toward control. Only if sex is transitory can it be at times absent. The constancy of an entity, its persistence over time, predicates its integrity, its existence as such. "From the modern point of view, . . . sexuality can only appear to be absent, since it must always (really) be at work. Modern men and women thus suppose that sex is hidden (rather than absent) when it is not present. This makes sex fundamentally mysterious. . . . It is because of the new conscience that a new sense of sex's mysterious place in the human psyche comes about. Far from simply repressing sex, conscience also creates it."[41]

This dialectic, and the close proximity of conscientious and sexual privacy, is aptly conveyed by a conversion narrative of the mid-seventeenth century. While a prisoner in the Fleet, the speaker observes a woman in a building across from him and, submitting both her and her domestic space to his moralized surveillance, discovers she is a prostitute. He writes to her in verse:

> For know (*Amanda*) to thy griefe, even I
> Have pri'd into thy secret passages,
> And have observed with a watchfull eye

> Such as to thee come with Embassages,
> And understood their private messages.
> I know their suits, and whereunto they tend.
> And see destruction wait upon the end.

After much discourse, Amanda confirms her conversion from the profession of one who solicits sexual invasion in conscientious language that, if we knew no better, might seem instead to sustain the solicitation:

> Rifle my Chests, my Boxes, and my Trunkes,
> Seize all the goods within them, thou shalt finde,
> Such things as those are farre unmeete for Punkes,
> They suite not any longer with my minde.[42]

If we return now to the question raised by the correspondent C.T., we may gain a better idea of why the imagination might seem to him, and to the author, more heinous than the act of masturbation itself. The imaginative virtuality of satire and realism, whose concrete particularity is an extrapolation from the actual particularity of real people, elevates it ethically above libel. The imagination that is appropriate to masturbation, however, precedes and facilitates the act, its filth marking its intimacy with (in religious terms) the secret sinfulness of the heart, or with (in secular terms) the mysterious repository of sex itself. That is, the virtuality of the satiric and the realist imagination is the product of a sublimating process, and what it in turn produces is the concrete particularity—the immateriality—of satire and realism. However, the virtuality of the masturbatory imagination, perhaps produced by images and ideas from without, in turn produces the filthy materiality of masturbation itself.[43]

One of the most striking features of *Onania,* and of the innovative line of thought it represents, is its unprecedented medicalization of masturbation, its preoccupation with the thesis that self-abuse is "bad" for you not only in moral terms, as a sin, but also in physical terms, as a disease. The modern emergence of sex as such depends greatly (as I have suggested) on its biologization. How is the relationship between the physical and the psychoethical aspects of sex negotiated in this discourse? Is sex a physical or a mental phenomenon? That the coalescence of sex at this time seems to occasion a version of the mind/body problem is related to the fact that it notably partakes of the ambiguity of "sense" that to some degree infiltrates all empirical knowledge. Sex is what remains "when the End can't be had for which that Sensation was given" (86), a material sensation deprived of its ideal reproductive telos but through that very deprivation something we have a sense of: an object of reflective knowledge, an immaterial desire.

The theory of sublimation provides one sort of answer to the mind/body problem. The ancient discourse of "Longinus" entered the eighteenth century through the filter of empirical epistemology. According to John Locke, "The *Impressions* that are made on our *Senses* by outward Objects, that are extrinsical to the Mind; and *its own Operations,* proceeding from Powers intrinsical and proper to it self, which when reflected on by it self, become also Objects of its contemplation, are . . . *the Original of all Knowledge.* . . . This is the first step a Man makes towards the Discovery of any thing, and the Groundwork, whereon to build all those Notions, which ever he shall have naturally in this World. All those sublime Thoughts, which towre above the Clouds, and reach as high as Heaven it self, take their Rise and Footing here . . . ."[44] In Jonathan Swift's notorious formulation, the mechanical operation of the spirit, the *"lifting up of the Soul or its Faculties above Matter,"* is a universal accompaniment to all great human achievement. "[T]he Seed or Principle, which has ever put Men upon *Visions* in Things *Invisible,* is of a Corporeal Nature . . . ." "Human Understanding, seated in the Brain, must be troubled and overspread by Vapours, ascending from the lower Faculties, to water the Invention, and render it fruitful." We see this in religious inspiration, which owes to "certain subterraneous *Effluviums* of *Wind"* that cause, especially in female priests, "a Pruriency by the Way, such as with due Management, hath been refined from a Carnal, into a Spiritual Extasie." Moreover, "the very same Principle that influences a *Bully* to break the Windows of a Whore, who has jilted him, naturally stirs up a Great Prince to raise mighty Armies . . . ." "What secret Wheel, what hidden Spring could put into Motion so wonderful an Engine" as occasioned the vast ambitions of Henry IV of France before they were brutally frustrated by assassination? "It was afterwards discovered, that the Movement of this whole Machine had been directed by an absent *Female,* whose Eyes had raised a Protuberancy" in that eminent monarch. "Now, I would gladly be informed, how it is possible to account for such Imaginations as these in particular Men, without Recourse to my *Phaenomenon* of *Vapours,* ascending from the lower Faculties to overshadow the Brain, and thence distilling into Conceptions . . . ."[45]

These assertions, themselves parodic of a species of literary wind or enthusiasm, serve a number of satiric ends. But they also offer the era's most brilliant account of human culture as a libidinal economy in which the most varied sorts of achievement may be traced to, and explained by reference to, a sexual substance that resides deep in our bodies and that, consisting of vapors, effluvium, wind, gas, exhalation, is neither matter nor spirit but both at once. Like the repressive hypothesis, the sublimation hypothesis simultaneously points in two directions, both denying and affirming the reality and force of sexuality. Its very absence suggests a deeper presence; its "public" control implies a "private" liberty. The imagination that facilitates onanism is filthy because it is a mental manifestation of sex itself, a species of sexual wind or vapor that, did it not issue in the material activity of masturbation, might instead issue from the mind in the form of an imagination cleansed of the bodily. Biology proves the naturalness of sexual difference; conscience confirms the constancy of sex; sublimation cultivates the sexual soil that grounds all human achievement. In the introduction to *A Tale of a Tub* Swift anticipates this digression on the sublimation process by describing the "three Methods" by which to satisfy "an Ambition to be heard in a Crowd . . . ." The first of these three "Engines of Orators"—the Nonconformist pulpit, the criminal's ladder at Tyburn, and the mountebank's stage—is represented in an original sketch for the *Tale* that depicts auditors seated in a conventicle and addressed by a Puritan saint who is elevated above them in his tub but is himself overseen by the four winds, which bow the trees outside and infiltrate the room through a large window (fig. 6.5). The ostentatious emission of wind at all three levels does the work here of transforming hierarchically different activities to a sameness that is the essence of sublimation theory. Our author, the Grubæan Sage, performs a hermeneutic version of this when he importantly informs us that "this Physico-logical Scheme of Oratorial Receptacles or Machines, contains a great Mystery, being a Type, a Sign, an Emblem, a Shadow, a Symbol, bearing Analogy to the spacious Commonwealth of Writers, and to those Methods by which they must exalt themselves to a certain Eminency above the inferiour World" (55, 59, 61).

Book Sex

Whatever the actual circumstances in which it is practiced, masturbation has the distinctive quality of being, whether or not a solitary, in any case an autoerotic, activity. The opening sentence of *Onania* suggests the importance of this distinction. By "yielding to filthy imaginations," onanists "endeavor to imitate and to procure to themselves" the sensation of "carnal commerce" with another (1). This language suggests that if the masturbatory imagination is singularly tarred with the brush of materiality, the implications of mind/body complementarity in masturbation may also be turned around. Not only the imagination that facilitates masturbation, that is, but even the act itself is "imaginative" and virtual because substitutive for actuality, like Aristotelian tragedy an "imitation of an action" rather than the action itself.[46] Thus Mandeville distinguishes the "lewd Trick" of masturbation from having "actual Commerce with Women," wondering that any man would "prefer this boyish solitary Amusement before the actual Embraces of a fine Woman . . . ."[47] This is the spirit in which Samuel Pepys remarks that "I have used of late, since my wife went, to make bad use of my fancy with whatever woman I have a mind to—which I am

FIG. 6.5. Original design for plate illustrating the introduction to [Jonathan Swift], *A Tale of a Tub*, in *A Tale of a Tub, To which is added The Battle of the Books and the Mechanical Operation of the Spirit* (1704, 1710), ed. A. C. Guthkelch and D. Nichol Smith, 2nd ed. (Oxford: Clarendon, 1958). Princeton University Library.

ashamed of and shall endeavour to do so no more."[48] In these terms, masturbation is antisocial not only for being unproductive of offspring but also for being a solitary substitute for sociability. Indeed, the promise of masturbation is, as Pepys's words hint ("whatever woman I have a mind to"), to deliver (some of) the rewards of sociability without its inconvenience and negative consequences. This formulation permits us to sense a relationship between masturbation and not only the Aristotelian pleasures of the imagination but also the virtuality that unites the political contract, the commercial market, and the public sphere.[49]

On the face of it this might seem odd since the contract, the market, and the public sphere are nothing if not sociable. But the self-evidence of their sociability is a hard-won achievement of modern experience, since all three are solutions to the problem posed by the early modern separation out of the private from the public and the individual from the social and by the discovery that traditional standards of sociability ignore the interests of most individuals. Consequently, all three sustained criticism (as did masturbation) for being antisocial, that is, for attending too closely to—indeed, for countenancing the existence of—the individual disembedded from traditional collectivity. This is perhaps most obvious in the case of the market, whose seventeenth-century virtualization laid the foundation for eighteenth-century political economy and its paradox that not only sociability but also material productivity is best served when individuals act self-interestedly. By elaborating theories of circulation and exchange value, modern economic orthodoxy has validated this paradox. Modern attitudes toward masturbation, devoid of this possibility, are torn between minority approval and majority condemnation of its narcissistic and solipsistic evils.[50]

The multiple publications of *Onania* coincided with the theorizing of the pleasures of the imagination as what would come to be called an "aesthetic" effect, and its author's awareness of the causal connection between masturbation and the silent reading of "literary" texts was acute. This is clear not only in explicit references to that connection (see, e.g., 10, 163; *Supplement*, 153) but also in what we have already seen of the author's defensiveness about his own "circumspection and caution" in this very book (15). To warn of evil risks inciting to it: "I shall be forc'd to make use of some expressions in this Chapter," he admits, "which tho' spoke with a Design the most remote from Obscenity, may, working by the reverse, perhaps furnish the Fancies of silly People with Matter for Impurity . . ." (16–17). Such a reversal is especially to be feared in works of casuistry, whose pedagogy involves teaching by concrete example. Indeed, as the learned prelate Jeremy Taylor wrote, "[T]here are some spirits so Atheistical, and some so wholly possessed with a spirit of uncleannesse, that they turn the most prudent and chaste discourses into dirt and filthy apprehensions: like cholerick stomacks changing their very Cordials and medicines into bitternesse; and in a literal sense *turning the grace of God into wantonnesse:* They study cases of conscience in the matter of carnal sins, not to avoid, but to learn wayes how to offend God and pollute their own spirits: and search their houses with a Sun-beam that they may be instructed in all the corners of nastinesse."[51] So the early novel was only one of the genres criticized for publicizing images that raised rather than quelled the lubricity of sexual desire.[52] Several things would have to happen before this could emerge as not an unintended reversal but a frankly calculated purpose of writing, an emergence that we might expect to be corre-lated with that of the category of sex as such. The name we give to this sort of writing is of course "pornography"—literally, "engraving or writing about pros-titutes"—a term that enters English discourse in the later nineteenth century.[53] By this etymological logic, the sexual activity of prostitutes provides a synec-doche for sexual activity as such. Why should this be so?

In the seventeenth century, women still possessed their traditional associa-tion with excessive sexual appetite. Their normative modern association with the modesty and purity of "romantic" love was already well established before the end of the eighteenth century. By modern standards, *The Whores Rhetorick,* a late-seventeenth-century text, is perplexing in its willingness to characterize (at least the stereotype of) the wife indiscriminately by her devotion to "love" and to "libidinous appetites." According to this way of thinking, love and sex-ual desire are conjoined over against the alternative passion of prostitutional "interest." One hundred years later, the "love" of the wife will be sharply distin-guished from the "interested sexuality" of the prostitute. This transformation is fundamental to modern gender ideology. But the radical discontinuity it marks should not obscure an equally fundamental thread of continuity. Both the lu-bricity of traditional woman and the purity of modern woman are consistent with the belief that their sexual activity is justified when undertaken conjugally, to the end of procreation. By the same token, whores, whether "traditional" or "modern," are reviled because their sexual activity lacks this justifying end. Of course, the emergence of "pornography" as the accepted term for writing about sex cannot be explained by any single factor. Still, prostitution and sex writing were linked by, among other things, the apparent concentration of each upon "sex" as such as a category of experience that could be separated out from its customary involvement in greater purposes.

Certainly the association of sex with the more general category of woman is intensified during this period. True, women were traditionally known to be both the seat of generation and, for reasons that to moderns must seem equally extraneous to sex as such, inordinately lustful. But the mutual implication of sexual being and conscientious vigilance in the Protestant habits of introspection deepens the association of sex and women in the modern period. I have already suggested how introspection predicates the constancy of sex, hence the need for its constant control. I have also discussed how, at a less ultimate stage of interiority—that of the modern family—the "public" agency of moral control (government, management, employment) comes to be associated with the wife and mother, the magistrate of the little commonwealth. Her business is not precisely control, however, but the pedagogy of self-control. Customarily associated with the vicissitudes of *fortuna,* women have for that reason customarily been enjoined to follow the rule of constancy. But the constancy required by traditional culture, although "sexual," is rather different from that which continues and replaces it in the modern period. The patrilineal rule of female constancy as chastity, embedding sexuality in sociality, superintended the purity of the family lineage along a diachronic axis. Modern female constancy provides a model rather for the purity of each of the individual ethical subjects that compose the synchronic unit of the modern family.[54] The modern "culture of constancy" holds out the promise "that people can successfully control their behavior and feelings in a much more thorough way than was previously believed."[55] The new sexual purity of the modern married woman is justified and sustained by her new responsibility for inculcating the techniques of self-control within her husband and children, who signify in their very embodiment her own controlled sexuality. Although her purity is therefore consistent with a "love" dissociated from "libidinous appetites," it marks her as, not asexual or antisexual, but the moral regulator of sexuality—in her own way engaged, like the prostitute (once again), in "sex work." This understanding may render more intelligible the startling usage whereby "woman" was known generically, throughout the eighteenth century, as "the sex."[56]

Reading (and writing) pornography was widely recognized as a valuable stimulus to the filthy imaginations on which masturbation depended, and the nonprocreative expenditure that resulted from this sort of reading experience only underscored the vulnerability of all imaginative literature to the charge of occasioning a catharsis that substituted for reality. Later in the century, novels of sensibility would be faulted for the antisocial vicariousness entailed in evoking and expending charitable emotions within a wholly imaginative and imaginary setting.[57] It is in this regard that a recent study has described pornography as "the auto-erotic techniques of book-sex."[58] Of course, masturbation and pornography did not require each other, but their combination reinforced the extreme privacy associated with both solitary sex and silent reading. This is clear from one reader's apprehensions for the "Modest young Lady" who finds herself reading the warm passages in Samuel Richardson's *Pamela* (1740): "[I]f

Nature should be too powerful, . . . tho' Shame and the Censure of the World may restrain her from openly gratifying the criminal Thought, yet she privately may seek Remedies which may drive her to the most unnatural Excesses."[59]

One of the most celebrated scenes of masturbation occurs in Pepys's *Diary* soon after he purchases the notorious *L'escolle des filles* (Paris, 1655) "in plain binding," "a mighty lewd book, but yet not amiss for a sober man once to read over to inform himself in the villainy of the world." Having bought the book at his Strand bookseller, Pepys puts it aside until the next morning, then recounts his movements with his usual precision, allowing us to search his house with Jeremy Taylor's sunbeam so as to discover its secret corner of nastiness. Since 1660 Pepys had been living in the City in a rambling building that accommodated both work and domesticity, the Navy Office as well as lodgings for its principal officers. On the morning in question he divided his time between his private chamber in his domestic lodgings and his office in the public domains of the building, "doing business and also reading" a bit of his new purchase. At noon he returned from his office to his lodgings to dine with acquaintances, after which the men moved "into our dining-room," where they spent the afternoon singing and drinking wine. After his guests departed, Pepys retired once more to his chamber sanctum, where he read the entire book, ejaculated, then burned it; "and so at night to supper and then to bed." To narrate the crucial event Pepys reverts to the Anglo-French pidgin he reserves for intimate matters, which, like the techniques of other diarists and of libelers who would escape prosecution, is a method by which to conceal and reveal simultaneously (*Diary*, 8–9 Feb. 1668, vol. 9, *1668–9*, 57–59).[60]

Plate 2 confines its attention to the private chamber itself. A century after Pepys recorded his encounter with French pornography, the French watercolorist Pierre-Antoine Baudouin captured a modest young lady at a moment of suspended reading, perhaps of *Pamela* or the infamous *Fanny Hill*. The scene is one of multiple enclosures and receding interiors. The apertures of the lady's *cabinet* are doubly sealed off from the outside, its door and window covered by a decorated screen and drapery that echo the dishabille of its occupant, whose right hand ventures beneath her disheveled dress.[61] Farther to her right, the writing desk is piled with assorted texts—weighty volumes, maps, a globe —that promise their reader a mediated access to the world; one of the books announces itself to be a history of voyages. To her left, a diminutive duodecimo slips from the lady's fingers onto the top of a tiny house that encloses a miniature dog asleep, its legs absently extended, like those of its mistress, in sensible reverie.

From our intimately invasive vantage point we may be tempted to allegorize the human figure as reclining between intellect and animality, the spirit and the senses (the guitar, the dog sated with its food), the mind and the body. But it is more that she is poised between two kinds of reading, two virtual spaces of outer and inner pleasure, voyages of outward discovery and of self-exploration. This is an account of masturbation very different from the ones conjured up by the fevered anxiety of *Onania*—not the loss, but the delicate calibration, of control. Indeed, a suggestive comparison might be made with figure 6.3, which depicts another cabinet devoted to knowledge of the natural world. But here the Aristotelian doctor has been replaced by the woman herself, a picture of contemplative self-study, the object of examination turned subject. On the one hand, pornography subjectifies scientific experiment; on the other, it material-izes conscientious introspection. On the threshold of the senses, masturbation here escapes the twin fates of medicalization and moralization by using the imagination to move first upward, then downward into self-knowledge.

The evidence of book sex argues that so far from being primordially the most "intimate" of concerns, sex was aided in its modern privatization by, among other things, the technology of print and its solitary consumption. Be-fore the modern period, we might say, sex was either "public" in the sense of serving the great collective ends of perpetuating the family and the species or (more precisely) "nonprivate" in the sense of being coextensive with—not sep-arated out from—these great ends. Under such conditions, the discourse of sex as it appeared in jest books, chap books, broadsides, and the like had the status of a shared joke rather than a private gratification. It was more obscene than pornographic, more concerned with social commentary and punishment than with sensual arousal.[62] Certainly the experience and spectacle of sex were far more public during the Restoration and the early eighteenth century than later on in the very real sense that sexual activity, both "foreplay" and penetration, was much more commonly seen and done in public places.[63]

When we turn our attention to the characteristics of seventeenth-century writing on sex in England, we find that its single-minded concentration on sex as such is quite elusive.[64] If we take the aim to arouse sexual desire and to gen-erate sexual pleasure as definitive of a form concerned with sex as such, the sta-bilizing of such a form in Europe is consigned by some scholars to the later decades of the following century.[65] What about the Renaissance foundations laid by Pietro Aretino, his peers, and his followers? The answer to this question may be anticipated by a brief and speculative glance at the historical semantics of "libertinism" in England, which bears some relevance to the emergence of pornography. From the sixteenth century through the English Civil War, "lib-ertinism" referred principally to religious antinomianism, aggravated by in-creasingly radical critiques of Calvinist predestination.[66] Its politico-philosoph-ical and sexual reference was a significant but secondary formation. By the end of the Restoration and during the first decades of the eighteenth century both the politico-philosophical and the sexual meaning of the term competed equally with the religious sense that centered in the deist movement, so that "libertine" possessed at this time a broadly allusive and polysemous range of reference. The history of the term thereafter, and into the nineteenth century, is a steady process of specialization whereby the sexual meaning of the word becomes increasingly dominant and its religious and politico-philosophical significance correspondingly vestigial.[67]

Protopornography: Sex and Religion

The religious significance of what came to be called "pornography" is profound and complicated. The fully sexualized spirituality or "sacred eroticism" evident in some seventeenth-century English devotional modes is rooted in earlier Christian practice.[68] The dialogue form pursued by *The Whores Rhetorick* and much early pornography is an inheritance from Aretino's *Ragionamenti* (1534–36), where the pedagogic interaction between experienced bawd and innocent novice draws deeply on the confessional and casuistical technologies of the Christian church.[69] The indebtedness of emergent pornography to religious forms and knowledge is evident in the range of ways its autonomy as such—the aim to arouse sexual desire and to generate sexual pleasure—was compromised by overarching religious purposes. These purposes, all arguably products of religious libertinism, nonetheless covered a considerable spectrum. At one end of the spectrum were efforts, like those of the Dilettanti Society, to elevate sexuality by showing its importance in pagan and Christian worship and to elaborate for it a religious ethos and superstructure.[70] At the other end of this spectrum was the negative purpose of anticlerical and antireligious satire, which so fully saturates seventeenth- and eighteenth-century pornography as sometimes to seem inseparable from it.[71] Such libertine satire attacks religious hypocrisy—the lie of a moral authority inhering in the transcendence of the flesh—by depicting the ecclesiastical agents and ceremonies of the spirit engaged in grossly carnal pursuits.

This might take the direct form of coarse obscenity—the randy monk with a huge erection—or the witty approach of equivocating indirection. At an earlier stage in this argument I reviewed Andrew Marvell's complex response to the Anglican divine Samuel Parker's published polemics against Nonconformity. Early on in this response Marvell provides an example of the indirect approach as he narrates Parker's entry into religious life, soon after his ordainment, as chaplain in the household of Gilbert Sheldon, archbishop of Canterbury:

[H]aving soon wrought himself dexterously into his Patrons favour, by short Graces and Sermons, and a mimical way of drolling upon the *Puritans,* which he knew would take both at Chappel and Table; [Parker] gained a great Authority likewise among all the domesticks. . . . [B]eing of an amorous Complexion, and finding himself (as I told you) the *Cock-Divine* and *Cock Wit* of the Family, he took the priviledge to walk among the Hens . . . . And they that perceived he was a Rising-Man, and of pleasant Conversation, dividing his Day among them into Canonical hours, of reading now the Common-prayer, and now the Romances; were very much taken with him. The Sympathy of Silk began to stir and attract the Tippet [an ecclesiastical band] to the Pettycoat and the Petticoat toward the Tippet. The innocent Ladies found a strange unquietness in their minds, and could not distinguish whether it were Love or Devotion. . . . Till, having before had enough of the Libertine, and undertaken his Calling only for Preferment; he was transported now with the Sanctity of his Office, even to extasy . . . .[72]

Marvell practices a mode of translation familiar to us from the analogy of state and family—except now the place of the state is occupied by the professional offices of religion, and the analogy of public and private is deliberately disabled by its adequation to the antithesis of sacred and profane. Parker vainly tries to accommodate episcopacy to domesticity, the chapel to the table, common prayer to romance, the tippet to the petticoat, *caritas* to *amor.* Inspired by Marvell's satiric practice, Swift famously adapted it to the critique of the competitive religiosity of the Puritan saint: "Upon a certain Day, while he was far engaged among the Tabernacles of the *Wicked,* he felt the Outward Man put into odd Commotions, and strangely prick'd forward by the inward: An Effect very usual among the Modern Inspired. . . . the *Saint* felt his *Vessel* full *extended* in every Part (a very natural Effect of strong *Inspiration;*) and the Place and Time falling out so unluckily, that he could not have the Convenience of Evacuating upwards, by Repetition, Prayer, or Lecture; he was forced to open an inferior Vent. In short, he wrestled with the Flesh so long, that he at length subdued it . . . ."[73] As we have seen, Swift's religious satire adumbrated a theory of sublimation that isolates sexuality as such both as the "private" expression of religious inspiration and as its irreducible ground. The author of *The Whores Rhetorick* had already deployed a still clearly alchemical version of this theory in seeking inspiration from the London prostitutes: "A little of that sharpness you inspire into your Lovers Urine, would give my periods a grateful relish: and . . . sublimate my fancy beyond the feculent dregs of matter, which at present doe strangely retard its motion."[74] Sex is the as yet unspecified substance that underlies religiosity and that is more or less stealthily signified by the ostensibly antithetical movements of faith.

Seen in this way, the pornography that inheres in libertine religious satire might be understood as a method of making the analogy between "public" and "private" in a deliberately undermining way, so that the resemblance of the second to the first is crucially charged by their dissimilarity. Indeed, this instability, the deliberate disablement of analogy, may be central to the pornographic mechanism as such: excitation through flagrant impropriety. Sex is the uncanny double of our public professions, the shared joke or hidden secret that is revealed once public motives and purposes have been skeptically stripped away. Thus the negative, (anti)religious ends of religious satire tend to modulate into positive, self-sufficiently erotic ends. This fundamental, constitutive ambivalence of pornography is well evoked by a passage in *The Whores Rhetorick* that describes an Aretinian posture: "I have seen a certain draught of Pictures that would serve sufficiently on this occasion, hanging one way it might be set up in a Cathedral, but the reverse was able to seduce a Hermit [i.e., a religious recluse] into obscene thoughts. Such a Model as this may be had, and at an easy rate, it may appear barefaced in your Lodgings, and on occasion, with an easy motion, turning the upside down, the obscenity appears, of power to raise a luxuriant heat, and a beastly appetite. . . . This pleasing spectacle will ever sensibly affect the seeing organ, so turning the leaf according to what diversity the eye discovers, as most pleasant, a harmonious discord will thence arise . . . ."[75]

Protopornography: Sex and Politics

If pornography began in service to religious libertinism, it quickly showed its affinity with the libertine critique of political absolutism as well. As we saw in chapter 3, the *arcana imperii* were easily and parodically reconceived not only as familial but also as sexual mysteries, the secret truth of libidinous imperatives that motivated and explained public policy. Sexual knowledge, like secrecy, lies deep within. In the late Renaissance, leadership in the production of pornography passed from Italy to the paradigmatically absolutist regime of the French state, and English pornography is utterly dependent on French models and translations, at least until John Cleland's *Memoirs of a Woman of Pleasure* (1749). Nevertheless, the literature of the Restoration period provides as good examples as can be found anywhere of protopornography's embeddedness in political argument.[76]

This is of course something of a truism. Anglicans and Nonconformists, Tories and Whigs, ascetics and libertines, all thought that the return of Stuart monarchy and of Charles II's "body natural" inaugurated a reign of moral debauchery. Royal politics, being ultimately dynastic, were structurally inseparable from issues of "sexuality"—that is, from a close attentiveness to matters of conception, childbirth, adultery, and bastardy in public places. Still, the tenor of court life during the first three decades of the Restoration played a special role in encouraging attacks on Charles's reign for permitting the reduction of the public to the private, of politics to sex: for collapsing the patriarchalist analogy into a dissolute identity.

The writings of John Wilmot, Earl of Rochester, alone are sufficient to document this development. What follows is two-thirds of the notorious poem for which he was said to have been banished temporarily from court in 1674:

> In the Isle of Brittain long since famous growne
> For breeding the best C—ts in Christendome,
> Not long since Reign'd (oh may he long survive)
> The easiest King and best bred Man alive.
> Him no Ambition mov'd to get Renowne
> Like a French Foole still wandring up and downe,
> Starving his People, hazarding his Crowne.
> Peace was his Aime, his gentleness was such
> And Love, he lov'd, For he lov'd Fucking much,
> Nor was his high desire above his Strength:
> His Scepter and his Prick were of a length,
> And she may sway the one who plays with t'other
> Which makes him litle wiser then his Brother.
> For Princes Pricks like to Buffoones at Court
> Doe governe Us, because they make Us Sport.
> His was the sauciest that did ever swive,
> The prowdest peremptory Prick alive:
> Thô Safety, Law, Religion, Life lay on't
> Twou'd breake thrô all to make it's way to C—t.
> Restlesse he Rowles about from Whore to Whore
> With Dogg and Bastard, always goeing before,
> A merry Monarch, scandalous and poore. . . .⁷⁷

The poem is distinctive in its use of roughened iambics that move into and out of an accentual or "ballad" meter (it concludes: "I hate all Monarchs and the Thrones that they sitt on / From the Hector of France to th'Cully of greate Brittaine"). And Rochester thereby sustains the impression of an elite vulgarity, the hybrid voice of a social coalition united in radical response to the shameful royal spectacle. In a related way, Charles is both deficient (contrast the "French Foole" Louis XIV) in absolutist intensity and excessive in his own, scarcely voluntary species of absolutism. Utterly innocent of political "Ambition," Charles would yet trample "Law" and "Religion" to have his sexual way. So the difference between Charles and Louis is not as great as at first it appears to be. John Evelyn told Pepys that "the king of France hath his maistresses, but laughs at the foolery of our King, that makes his bastards princes, . . . and makes his mistresses his maisters" (*Diary,* 26 Apr. 1667, vol. 8, *1667,* 183). Of course, this is not really Charles at all, but his emblem of office. The synecdochic scepter stands for the "political body" of kingship as distinguished from the "natural body" of the king. Charles's substitutive synecdoche, his prick, is rather a "private part"[78] that stands for itself, the body natural masquerading as the body political. In a poem contemporary with Rochester's, Charles's "prick foams and swears he will be absolute."[79] More precisely, Charles's prick stands for one part of the natural man against another. Absolute power has devolved from the world of the scepter to that of the prick, from the public to the private realm, where it psychomachically "governs" the king's reason. As a result of this substitution, however, it is not only Charles but also his people who are governed by the royal libido.

"Peace was his Aime": according to one of Pepys's contacts in 1667, shortly after the end of the Second Anglo-Dutch War, "I do not find the Change at all glad of it, but rather the worse, they looking upon it as a peace made only to preserve the King for a time in his lusts and ease, and to sacrifice trade and his kingdoms only to his own pleasures . . . . [Parliament fears] the nation in certain condition of ruin, while the King, they see, is only governed by his lust and women and rogues about him" (*Diary,* 27–28 July 1667, 8:354–56). Moreover, as both Pepys and Rochester suggest, the royal prick may finally be, not an absolute and autotelic power, but a tool in the hands of evil counselors and whores. John Lacy, using the commonplace term of absolutist abjection, asks: "Was ever prince's soul so meanly poor, / To be enslav'd to ev'ry little whore?" This is perhaps overly inclusive. Nell Gwynne had lately been singled out as one royal whore who could tell the difference between a prick and a scepter:

> Hard by Pall Mall lives a wench call'd Nell.
> King Charles the Second he kept her.
> She hath got a trick to handle his p——,
> But never lays hands on his sceptre.
> All matters of state from her soul she does hate,
> And leave to the politic bitches.
> The whore's in the right, for 'tis her delight
> To be scratching just where it itches.[80]

What seems like the collapsing of analogy into identity, of public policy into sexual intimacy, crucially depends on the dynastic nature of Stuart monarchy. Charles's office requires that we attend not only to the ways he is like a father-husband but also to the ways he is one. His domestic ways do not recommend him: Charles is a promiscuous begetter of bastards, shamefully "effeminate" in the still active sense of being in thrall to female sexuality.[81] In other words,

Charles is at least in this respect an antidomestic "libertine." Although sexual and political libertinism are in principle complementary—both eschew the constraints of authority and rule—in the practice of Stuart kingship they seem to bear a more contradictory relation to each other. On the one hand, sexual and political libertinism are opposed because Charles's prick *replaces* his scepter: it is his debauchery that makes Charles cede the absolutist ambition to enslave his people. On the other hand, they are allied because Charles's prick *is* his scepter: his debauchery has politically absolutist consequences.[82]

These dialectical implications of the king's sexual absolutism were pursued most relentlessly, perhaps, in the fragmentary closet drama *Sodom and Gomorah,* a thick burlesque of heroic drama that was composed sometime in the 1670s and bears an obvious relation to Rochester's "Satyr" on Charles II.[83] Thus King Bolloxinian:

> Let other Monarchs who their Scepters beare
> To keepe their subjects lesse in loue yᵉⁿ feare
> Bee slaues to Crownes, my nation shall be free:
> My Pintle onely shall my scepter bee.
> My laws shall Act more pleasures then Comand
> And with my Prick I'le gouerne all the land. (303)

But unlike Rochester's "Satyr," *Sodom and Gomorah* satirizes Charles not as the devotee of courtesans but as the royal sodomite. Earlier I observed that the emergence of different-sex behavior as a normative standard over against the negative standard of same-sex behavior might sustain a sociopolitical reading if we were to see in the growing hostility toward "sodomy" at this time a more focalized animus against pederasty, the "sexualized" enactment of absolutist subjection. Does *Sodom and Gomorah* invite such a reading?

The main action of this fragmentary play is summarized in the "Prologue":

> Almighty Cunts, whom Bolloxinian here
> Tyr'd with their tedious toyle does quit Casheire;
> From thence to Arse hee hath his Pricke conueyed
> And think itt Treason to behold a maid. (302)

Although it is never fully specified, the politics of different-sex behavior seems to be not that Bolloxinian-Charles has declared it treasonous but that until now it has been enforced by the absolute prohibition of its same-sex alternative. This is the implication, at least, of the fact that the king now asserts his royal prerogative in language that cannot fail to recall Charles's 1672 Declaration of Indulgence, which dispensed with penal laws against Roman Catholics and Nonconformists that had been put in place by the Cavalier Parliament a decade earlier. Bolloxinian-Charles gives the order to one of his courtiers (identified in the dramatis personae as a "Catamite of hono^r"):

> Those who my pleasure serue I must requite
> Henceforth Borastus sett the Nation free:
> Let Conscience haue itts force of liberty.
> I do proclaim that Buggery may be vsd
> O're all the land so C—t be no abus'd. (305)

What are we to make of the implicit analogy between the royal indulgence of popery and of pederasty? For one thing, the present question of historical interpretation—to what degree was increasingly outspoken opposition to sodomy a way of speaking out against pederasty?—makes uncertain how we are to construe the cultural meaning of the same-sex behavior that Bolloxinian-Charles would indulge. On the one hand, a royal declaration of this sort has the national scope of "all the land" and therefore would seem to refer to male sodomy in general. On the other hand, the spirit of the declaration ("Those who my pleasure serue I must requite") is more specifically pederastic, which is also true of the sort of sodomy that is plentifully represented throughout this court-set drama. The 1672 Indulgence was widely seen as a hypocritical strategy that used the pretense of a liberalized religious policy toward Protestant dissent to encourage both English popery and a secret rapprochement with French absolutism.[84] By analogy, perhaps, Bolloxinian-Charles represents his pederastic patronage of his courtiers as a blow for private liberty of conscience and against public (i.e., parliamentary) absolutism, a libertine, natural-law resistance to conjugal tedium and tyranny.[85] "C—ts no longer I admire," complains the king, "The Drudgery has worn out my desire" (304). This is partly a matter of habituation, partly a function of childbirth ("Products spoile C—ts . . ." [325]), and partly the grinding subjection of a microabsolutism:

> Faces may Change but C—t is but C—t still,
> And hee that ffucks is slave to womans will. (323)

As another "Catamite & fauorite to the King" puts it:

> How simply was the Letchery of old,
> How full of shame, how feeble & how cold,
> Confin'd to a formality of law
> When women nere her husbands P——tle saw
> But when tame lust or duty made him draw,
> Then fuckt with such indifferent delight
> As if Pr. stood agst the will in spight;
> ffirst rubd, then spent, then groaned & soe good night.
> Wee the kind Dictates of our sense pursue:

> Wee study pleasures still and find out new. (323)

So a robust Protestantism is to Roman Catholicism as different-sex is to same-sex behavior. Antipopery was the most popular platform in English politics in the years before the Popish Plot, and the widespread association of the Roman Church with tyranny and absolutism makes clear how unpersuasive the Bolloxinian view of this analogy would be to the generality of readers. Certainly Queen Cuntigratia sees the royal declaration differently. The mother of her maids of honor warns:

> That day of marriage you may justly rue
> Since he will neither Swiue nor suffer you.
>   *Cunt.* That tyranny does much augment my Greife:
> I can command all but my Cunts reliefe. (307)

And she admonishes her husband:

> Yoᵣ Pr: hath long diuorct it selfe from me
> And rob'd C—t of itts pleasing misery.
> Woud you att home f—ke as kind husbands shou'd.
> I would not by base meanes defile yʳ bloud. (312)

One of her maids urges the Cuntigratia to see herself, and not her royal husband, as the one who is subjected to unjust tyranny—and to rebel against it.

> Tho' hee a Tyrant to yoᵣ honoᵣ bee,
> Yoᵣ C—t may Clayme a subjects liberty. (315)

Cuntigratia determinedly goes in search of the "stallion" General Buggeranthes and thereby of her autonomous subjecthood (315). But the nation is soon infected by "epidemicall" sexual complaints, and Bolloxinian-Charles finally asks the royal physician, a "Man of Philosophy" (329) how to redress these evils:

> To love & nature all their rights restore:
> ffuck women & lett Bugg'ry be no more.
> Itt does that Propogable end destroy
> Which nature gave wᵗʰ pleasure t'enjoy. (330)

And the "Epilogue," spoken by a courtesan, extends this natural-rights moral:

> Can Arse holes fire, tho' it be feirce & great,
> Infuse more than a C—t immortall heat?
> ·   ·   ·   ·   ·   ·   ·   ·   ·   ·   ·   ·   ·
> Veiw the intreagues of swelling C—t & arse
> And tell me wᶜʰ of 'em best help yoᵣ Tarse!
> The haires of Pr & C t about do roul,
> Curle in pure love & ticles down each soul.
> Thus wee are made pregnant . . .

. . . .

> Naked weele lye to entertayne yor Tarses,
> Soe you will but forsake mens beastly arses. (332)

Sodom and Gomorah uses the language of anal and vaginal penetration with such promiscuous and anarchic relish that it cannot be read definitively as a satire against court pederasty. Indeed, readers may find that discursive means have become ends: that the very heat of its descriptive details places it in an advanced position on the scale running from obscene political satire to pornography. But the parallel between popery and same-sex activity is so telling that it encourages us, through shared themes of hierarchical super- and subordination, to see not a broad attack on sodomy but a pointed attack on pederasty as the "sexual" expression of absolutist subjection in the state. In fact, by applying the explicitated and fully intelligible categories "Protestant" and "Catholic" to the less cultivated field of sexual behavior, the parallel may ensure that readers will conceive sexual difference as susceptible to a comparably explicit understanding. We are used to thinking of seventeenth-century "religion" itself as incompletely separated out from "politics." The parallel between popery and pederasty in *Sodom and Gomorah* brings to contemporary awareness not only how deeply "sexuality" is embedded in "politics" at this time but also the terms of their separability. Again, the libertine nihilism of the drama (nobody comes off well here) and the aura of hasty opportunism that hangs about its moral make it very hard to read *Sodom and Gomorah* as a brief for emergent, private norms of gender difference and sexuality. Yet we might do worse than look to *The Rape of the Lock* (1714) and its own tacked-on ending for a comparable if more coherent abstraction from its more public ground of what modernity will regard as the privacy of domesticity.[86] Perhaps this is what "companionate marriage" looks like early on in the process of its disembedding from the ground of patriarchal patrilineage: "Woud you att home f—ke as kind husbands shou'd, / I would not by base meanes defile y^r bloud. / . . . / The haires of Pr & C t about do roul, / Curle in pure love & ticles down each soul. / Thus wee are made pregnant . . . ."

The absolutist art of the state came into being in Renaissance Italy through the separation out of reason from reason of state, ethics and the study of virtue from politics and the study of *virtù*.[87] From the political perspective, reason of state is a superior form of reason, divested of its irrational ethical idealism. From the ethical perspective, reason of state is not reason at all but passion or interest. In the dynastic politics of Restoration England the rationality of absolutist reason of state became questionable when its separation from ethical idealism became questionable: not only because of absolutism's irrational dependence on doctrines like the divine right of kings, nor only because it irrationally supported the interest of the king against the patently greater interest of the nation state, but also because Stuart absolutism seemed to sacrifice reason of state to sexual libertinism, politics as such to sex as such. So the Renaissance separation of ethics from politics was recapitulated at another level by the Restoration separation of political rationality from the irrationality of sexual desire.

For the sexual libertine, of course, these were simply two different kinds of passion. The problem with Charles II was not only that he tried to combine them but also that, under the necessity of choice, he seemed uncertain about which was more nobly and profitably indulged. Rochester was inclined to reverse even the terminology—the "great" versus the "little"—by which the comparative valuation of public and private affairs was customarily made. To Henry Savile he wrote: "Livy and sickness has a little inclined me to policy. When I come to town I make no question but to change that folly for some less, whether wine or women I know not . . . . They who would be great in our little government seem as ridiculous to me as schoolboys who with much endeavour and some danger climb a crab-tree, venturing their necks for fruit which solid pigs would disdain if they were not starving." Scant months before the English state expelled the English king for his absolutist passions, Sir George Etherege remarked: "How pleasanter it is to jolt about in poor hackney Coaches to find out the harmless lust of the Town than to spend the time in a Roome of State in whispers to discover the ambitious designs of Princes."[88]

What are the implications of these sentiments for the question of pornography in Restoration England? In his effort to defend Rochester's poetry against the (anonymous) criticisms of the Earl of Mulgrave, Charles Wolseley was pushed to make a number of distinctions that led to the effective separation out of what moderns tend to mean when they refer to texts as "pornographic." Alluding to Rochester's rumored deathbed conversion in 1681, Mulgrave had judged his songs to be quite inferior:

> Here, as in all things else, is most unfit
> Bawdry barefac'd that poor pretence to Wit,—
> Such nauseous Songs as the late Convert made,
> Which justly call this censure on his Shade;
> Not that warm thoughts of the transporting joy
> Can shock the Chastest or the Nicest cloy,
> But obscene words, too gross to move desire,
> Like heaps of Fuel do but choak the Fire.
> That Author's Name has undeserved praise,
> Who pall'd the appetite he meant to raise.[89]

Wolseley first challenges Mulgrave's confusion of poetic form and content—that is, the belief "that the Wit of a Poet was to be measur'd by the worth of his

Subject . . . . [I]n all true Poetry, let the Subject or Matter of the Poem be in it self never so great or so good, 'tis still the Fashion that makes the Value . . . ."⁹⁰ Second, Wolseley is moved to separate questions of wit from those of morality: "Wit it self, as it may sometimes be unseasonable and impertinent, so at other times it may be also libertine, unjust, ungrateful, and every way immoral, yet still 'tis Wit . . ." (24). Third, he argues that such distinctions require that we know the intended audience of a poem: Rochester did not "design those Songs [Mulgrave] is so offended with to be sung for Anthems in the King's-Chappel, any more than he did his other obscene Writings (however they may have been since abus'd) for the Cabinets of Ladies, or the Closets of Divines, or for any publick or common Entertainment whatever, but for the private Diversion of those happy Few whom he us'd to charm with his Company and honour with his Friendship" (25). In other words, posthumous publication has depersonalized Rochester's authorship, circulating his private writings indiscriminately throughout the public sphere—which includes private sites other than his own coterie, ones that he did not intend his songs to address and to which they are obviously inappropriate.

Wolseley's first two points may well remind us of the way dramatists, under attack by Jeremy Collier, would soon be moved to defend themselves by making explicit the tacit and consensual protocols of reading: authors are not ethically coextensive with their characters.⁹¹ Wolseley's third point, although it also tends toward the disembedding of the author as an autonomous ethical subject and agent, may have required, more than these two, the special conditions of a mature print culture to cohere as a critical canon. In any case, it is only now that Wolseley draws the distinction that is crucial to the explicitation of pornography as such. Mulgrave faults Rochester not, Wolseley observes, for obscenity but for "bawdry barefac'd": obscenity "too gross" to achieve the end its author "meant," namely, the "rais[ing]" of "appetite." "Does he think," Wolseley asks, "that all kind of obscene Poetry is design'd to *raise Appetite*? Does he not know that obscene Satyre (of which nature are most of my *Lord Rochester's* obscene Writings, and particularly several of his Songs) has a quite different end, and is so far from being intended to raise, that the whole force of it is generally turn'd to restrain *Appetite,* and keep it within due Bounds, to reprove the unjust Designs and check the Excesses of that lawlesse Tyrant?" (27–28). If Mulgrave wishes to experience the kind of obscenity he imagines Rochester to have intended, "let him read *l'Escole des Filles* [i.e., the book over which Pepys masturbated]; and if the obscene Words and Descriptions he will meet with there do not raise his Appetite, the World will be apt to conclude it not only very dull but absolutely dead . . ." (29). Wolseley divides the category of obscene poetry into two subcategories. The first, obscene satire, aims to criticize vices that arise ultimately from appetitive license. The second, which we have learned to call (obscene) pornography, aims to arouse sexual desire and to generate sexual pleasure.

In the century that separates the Glorious from the French Revolution, pornography came into its own as a genre by learning to concentrate its attention on the raising of sexual rather than the restraining of religious and political passions. This was not a simple process. Scholars of the later period see political libertinism both as the empowering engine of sexual libertinism and as a major force in its narrowing specialization. Pornographers accommodated the belief in the universality of rights and of access to goods by pursuing in narrative the principle that bodies should be available and interchangeable regardless of political, social, and sexual difference. By subsuming all more particular oppositions under the abstract antithesis of master and slave—abstract in the sense of having universalized heretofore particular matters of absolutist politics—the Marquis de Sade both took this principle to its logical extreme and participated in pornography's depoliticization. By the early decades of the nineteenth century London radicals were turning from political—and politically charged pornographic—publications to the recognizably modern brand of pornography, in which the arousal of sexual desire and the generation of sexual pleasure are pursued as ends in themselves.[92]

The Law of Obscene Libel

Pornography came into focus as a distinct entity in eighteenth-century Britain not only through the acuity of readers like Wolseley but also through "public" efforts to channel and contain its singular "privacy." In the instance of pornography, however, the terms of state regulation were not immediately available under existing English law, so they were derived from two distinct areas of common and church law. The case through which the law of obscene libel was constituted was that of the notorious pornographer Edmund Curll (1725–28).[93]

In the early-eighteenth-century rationalization of a law prohibiting obscene and pornographic publications we can see the effort to conceive the privacy of sexuality as related to, yet different from, the privacy of personal particularity. Wolseley's claim that the "end" or "design" of Rochester's songs might be judged by identifying the particular private audience for whom he originally wrote them has proved an important method in literary criticism. For the law, however, a different standard of judgment was required. Libel law defined the privacy of personal reputation on the pattern of the law protecting private property,[94] but the offence committed in publishing the privacy of sexual discourse has nothing to do with the personal reputation of a particular victim.

Therefore the syncretic law of obscene libel both drew upon the model of libel law and looked to the domain of ecclesiastical law for a model by which the real victim, the public itself, might be protected from the knowledge of sexual privacy.

As with marriage law, the evolution of obscenity law entailed jurisdictional disputes between the church courts and the common law. Ambiguous overlaps between the two, a traditional and even defining feature of English law, were becoming more difficult to tolerate as the distinction between religious and secular concerns was gradually aggravated by the developing notion of their separability. In 1676 Lord Chief Justice Matthew Hale had argued "that Christianity is a parcel of the Laws of England and therefore to reproach the Christian religion is to speak in subversion of the law." And four years after prepublication licensing had been abolished, the Blasphemy Act (1698) had explicitly sought to specify the range of "religious" offences that could be prosecuted at common law.[95]

Curll's case was argued over the course of three years, from 1725 to 1728.[96] Curll was brought before the King's Bench in 1725 principally for having published, the year before, a new English edition of *Venus in the Cloyster, or the Nun in her Smock* (1683), a translation that had first appeared in the same year as Jean Barrin's French original, *Vénus dans le cloître, ou la religieuse en chemise* . . . . Although Curll was quickly found guilty, the judgment was arrested on jurisdictional grounds. There was no disagreement on whether Curll's publication should be prosecuted. In the words of dissenting Justice Fortescue, "I own this is a great offence; but I know of no law by which we can punish it" (col. 159). There were several problems. True, the format of the offence dictated a temporal indictment, for the crime of libel: "The Spiritual Courts punish only personal spiritual defamation by words; if it is reduced to writing, it is a temporal offence . . . there is no instance of the spiritual court's intermeddling, where it is reduced to writing, or in print" (cols. 156, 158–59). However, "libel" is a "technical word": "This is for printing bawdy stuff, that reflects on no person: and a libel must be against some particular person or persons, or against the government. It is stuff not fit to be mentioned publicly" (cols. 159, 157). Like *Onania*, that is, *Venus in the Cloyster* "named" not actual persons but filthy ideas and images. So far from fitting the classic description of libel, *Venus in the Cloyster* seemed to Justice Fortescue "rather to be published, on purpose to expose the Romish priests, the father confessors, and Popish religion" (col. 158). (Thus Fortescue's reading also suggests that *Venus in the Cloyster* was intelligible in modern terminology more as "obscenity" than as "pornography," that its sexual libertinism was felt, at least by this reader, to be embedded within its religious libertinism.) The defenders of the judgment challenged this notion that libel necessarily had a particular—and probably personal—reference. On the contrary, it "is to be governed by the epithet, which is added to it. . . . [I]n this case it may stand as an obscene little book" (cols. 159, 157).

To justify this broad construction, the defenders of the judgment against Curll had to refute a second, closely related objection to the propriety of trying him before the King's Bench. According to their skeptical colleagues, *Venus in the Cloyster* was an act not of temporal illegality but of spiritual immorality. It was "an offence 'contra bonos mores,'" and "[w]hatever tends to corrupt the morals of the people, ought to be censured in the Spiritual Court . . ." (col. 153). To this it was replied that the King's Bench also superintends offences *contra bonos mores*. According to the attorney general, Curll's publication "is an offence at common law, as it tends to corrupt the morals of the king's subjects"— by undermining "government," "religion," or "morality"—"and is against the peace of the king" (cols. 158, 154). But then how do we distinguish temporal from spiritual offences? "I do not insist that every immoral act is indictable," continued the attorney general, "such as telling a lie, or the like: But if it is destructive of morality in general; if it does, or may, affect all the king's subjects, it then is an offence of a public nature. And upon this distinction it is, that particular acts of fornication are not punishable in the Temporal Courts, and bawdy houses are" (col. 155). Justice Reynolds clarified this "reasonable distinction": "Acts of immorality" like fornication, and other such "offences of the incontinent kind," are admittedly "of spiritual cognizance only; but then those are particular acts, where the prosecution is *pro salute animae* of the offender, and not where they are of a general immoral tendency . . ." (cols. 158, 155, 159). By implication, the common law, in moving against bawdy houses, prosecutes not particular but general acts, and it does so for the health not of the particular offender but of the general public.

In order to buttress this view that the temporal courts were charged with the duty of protecting the moral health of the public, the attorney general cited the precedent of Sir Charles Sedley's case. In 1663 the libertine Sedley had been convicted not for libel but for misdemeanors against the king's peace. Sir Charles had "shewed his naked body in a balcony in Covent Garden to a great multitude of people," on whom he also had rained down bottles filled with urine (col. 155). How does this serve as a precedent for the judgment against Curll? Dissenting Justice Fortescue argued that Sedley's conviction for breach of the peace depended on the physical force used in "throwing out bottles upon the people's heads," a use of force lacking in Curll's case. Against this, however, it was maintained that the use of "actual force" was not required for a conviction for breach of the peace; moreover, "it was plain the force used in Sedley's case was but a small ingredient in the judgment of the Court . . . ." Instead it was claimed that in prosecuting Sedley the King's Bench had acted principally as "the *custos morum* of the king's subjects," as the guardian not of their physical but of their moral well-being. It was not the physically dangerous bottles but the immoral display of nakedness that was at issue here. Indeed, according to Justice Reynolds, by this standard Curll's case "is surely worse than sir Charles Sedley's case, who only exposed himself to the people then present, [naked,] who might chuse whether they would look upon him or not; whereas this book goes all over the kingdom" (cols. 159–60, 154, 155–56). When the judgment came up again in 1728, Fortescue had been replaced by another judge, and the original verdict was unanimously upheld. In this way, the criminal offence of "obscene libel" entered English law.

The arguments accompanying Curll's case suggest that "obscene libel" is an amalgam of spiritual and temporal considerations, fashioned as a temporal offence but bearing important spiritual concerns. With respect to both jurisdictional domains, it borrows some features, while rejecting others; but in all these operations the common, overriding aim is evidently to emphasize the generality and to minimize the particularity of the offence. From the temporal domain, "obscene libel" retains the fundamental fact of written or printed format, which underscores (by constituting) the broad generality of the victim of this crime, the reading public, as an important factor in its severity. By the same token, however, it rejects the temporal domain's focus on the particularity of the (likely personal) victim of the crime of libel. From the spiritual domain, "obscene libel" retains the generality of the issue of morality with which it is concerned. That is, its interest lies in public morality, in an immorality perpetrated on the public rather than (as in the common notion of libel) in something perpetrated on a particular person or institution. And by the same token, obscene libel rejects the particularity of the person to be remedied by spiritual censure, the individual "incontinent" or sinner.

From a modern perspective, "stuff not fit to be mentioned publicly" seems an apt description of what most people mean by obscenity or pornography. For Fortescue, however, it expressly excludes "bawdy stuff," implying instead a view of libel as presupposing the privacy of a particular victim: only private particulars are unfit—like reputational "property"—to be made public and general. Curll's case enabled the criminal publication of the private to be dissociated from the particularity of its victim and contents: henceforth it might be criminal to make something publicly known that, although private, was yet not of a particular nature. In the model of libel that had been evolving over the past few decades, what is publicized is, typically, the private-as-particular. If privacy—stuff that should not be mentioned publicly—is dissociated from particularity, knowledge of the private is not necessarily knowledge *about* a particular person but knowledge *of* matters that are themselves deemed private by nature. Moreover, the damage connected with this knowledge of the private is inflicted not on the object but on the subject of knowledge—not on a particular person who is thereby known but on the public that knows, and by that knowledge. Hence the damage is not defamation but corruption.

So the law of obscene libel made several important contributions to the modern articulation of the public and the private. First, it added weight to the idea, evident in other areas we have already investigated, that privacy was separable from actual particularity. Second, it reinforced the virtual existence of a reading public, and with an impact arguably greater than that of libel law. For although both laws required that the norm of "the generality of readers" be constituted by the courts so as to provide the basis for a semantic judgment of the texts in question, the law of obscene libel also hypostatized "the public" as the all but palpable victim of the crime.[97] Beyond this, the emergence of obscene libel as a distinct legal category helped mediate the emergence of sex as such —specifically, as a special sort of private knowledge. Coalescing as a kind of discourse that aims at arousing sexual desire and generating sexual pleasure, pornography isolates the privacy of sex as such from its public—from its religious, political, and reproductive—embeddedness. The law of obscene libel acknowledges and reflects this development by dissociating the damage done to the public by publishing the privacy of sexual knowledge from the damage done to particular people by a range of private knowledges that might be had of them through publication. The outcome of sexual knowledge is corruption: not a unit of knowledge but an internal disposition to know immorally. In this respect Satan was the first obscene libeler. Against his forces, however, the law of obscene libel managed to enlist the power of the state in the great battle that contemporary satire and moral reformation movements sometimes saw as strictly an extralegal struggle.

Curll himself suffered minimally for his role in the precedent-setting case that bears his name.[98] Several years later he was caricatured at the height of his powers in an engraved triptych representing scenes of labor in a printing house, which will repay our attention (fig. 6.6). Published in 1732 in the *Grub-Street Journal,* "The Art and Mystery of *Printing* Emblematically Displayed" is accompanied by an "explication," reminiscent of Swift's Grubæan Sage in *A Tale of a Tub,* that provides a fully fivefold interpretation of the picture's esoteric sense, evoking the hermeneutic excess and bad faith characteristic of contemporary libel and its prosecution.[99] The "most obvious" or "natural" reading, says the explicator, is that the picture depicts the trade "mystery" of printing itself and that the creatures engaged in its several stages reflect the craft nicknames given to their tasks (thus, for example, the visual pun on the "printer's devil").

"From this natural explication it is evident," the author insists, "that all the figures are intended to represent characters, and not any particular persons . . . ," most of all the two-faced master printer: "the application of that figure to any particular person, who either is at present, or has been formerly a printer, must be the effect of ignorance, or of malice, or of both." But a "political interpretation" of the picture is also to be had: the ass is an informer, the three beasts in the central panel are "persons of quality" signifying various aristocratic vices, the Janus figure is a "great states-man," and "the press represents the squeezing of the people . . . ." By this reading the design is clearly *treasonable*," but the reading is also vulnerable since it is the work of John ("Orator") Henley, who formulated it in revenge for a third interpretation that reads Henley himself as the two-faced figure. The fourth interpretation, produced by "some coffee-house wits," applies the scene to "the charitable corporation," candidly represented here as a pawnshop: the ass is hocking something of value, the "double-

FIG. 6.6. Title page, *Grub-Street Journal*, no. 147 (26 Oct. 1732). Bodleian Library, University of Oxford, shelf mark N.22863.

faced gentleman" signifies the hypocritical director, the press is the charitable "engine of extortion and cruelty," and what appear to be newspapers and books are actually pawned goods from the East Indies, which becomes apparent when we decipher their titles by inverting them, disclosing "words not at all stranger than . . . names of East-India goods, which we now and then read in the newspapers."[100]

But it is the fifth reading of the picture, by the explicator himself, that implicates Curll in the design, in effect converting the general, "satirical" exegesis of the master printer in the first construction into a particular, libelous reference to a real "bookseller." The scene is still a printing house, but now the beasts are explained as representing either types of printers or types of authors, to whom the bookseller gives directions. At this point in the reading the Janus-faced bookseller is also no more than a type, the sort who "has frequently, printed, at his own charge, religious and impious, godly and lewd books . . . ." But in turning to the third panel of the triptych, the explicator suggests that "the devil seems to denote a particular bookseller, stripped of all his false ornaments of puffs, advertisements, and title pages, and *in propria persona,* putting up his own and other peoples copies, books, some of pious devotions, others of lewd diversion, in his literatory" (*Grub-Street Journal,* no. 148, 30 Oct. 1732). Three contiguous titles confirm this multifaceted duplicity of piracy and moral equivocation: *Onania, Rochester's Poems,* and *Manual of Devotion.* Both as graphic design and as verbal explication, "The Art and Mystery of *Printing* Emblematically Displayed" engages many of the issues that are central to the emergence of the category of obscene libel as the publication of the depersonalized privacy of sexuality that offends the depersonalized virtuality of the public.

———

This chapter concludes part 1, whose work has been to account for the early modern separation out of the public from the private over a range of discourses and practices. The broad logic of this account has been to move from the macro- to the microconditions of separation, from the realm of the public into the realm of the private, acknowledging along the way the tendency of each phase of this movement to recapitulate within its more internalized dimensions the oppositional terms of the more external public/private structure of which it also constitutes one part. The separation out of pornography makes a useful transition to the discussion that follows in part 2. What we have come to call the domestic novel had an emergence in eighteenth-century Britain roughly parallel to that of pornography, and both generic categories are germane to the more inclusive category "domesticity," with which this study is centrally concerned. Pornography and the domestic novel plainly share a number of features at the level of content. In part 2 I will turn my attention to matters of form, building on some of the ideas of part 1 to conceive an idea of domestication, the formal counterpart of the domestic. "Domestication" names a process, a pedagogic and hermeneutic technique of understanding that transpires in a diverse range of traditional and early modern texts. As I intend to use it, domestication stands in relation to the domestic as form does to content, but also as process does to product: domestication is to the domestic as means is to end. As we will see, however, there is a more precise and fundamental sense in which the process of domestication begins rather than ends with the domestic—a sense in which domestication achieves its purpose when its domestic content, its pedagogic and hermeneutic function having been attained, gives way to something else. And in this sense of the term, "domesticity" comes into being as a cultural norm when domestication itself—the process of employing the domestic to other ends—becomes culturally superfluous.

Part Two ✳ Domestication as Form

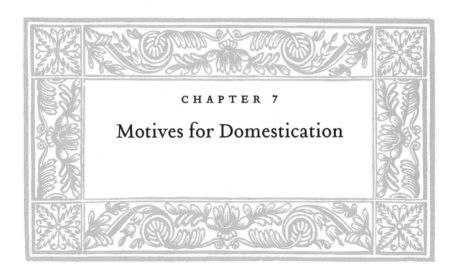

CHAPTER 7

Motives for Domestication

The Productivity of the Division of Knowledge

In the modern division of knowledge that has been my broadest subject in the foregoing pages we can observe three principles in operation that have bearing on the relation between the domains of the public and the private. The first principle, that of explicit separation, consists in the way the traditional and tacit habit of distinguishing between the public and the private gradually becomes concentrated into an explicit motive to separate them. And although it is fully predicated in a prior distinction, the separation out of public from private necessarily constitutes them as categories that are not only newly separate but also therefore new: unprecedented, in their self-standing integrity, by any traditional dispensation. Absolute as it may appear to be, however, this first principle is systematically complicated by a second principle, that of dialectical recapitulation. This second principle names the way the momentum of categorial separation is carried over to its products, relativizing the division between public and private by successively discovering within each newly constituted domain of privacy the components of the old distinction—and incipient separation. This recapitulation has been most evident in what I have called the devolution or downward mobility of absolutism, which begins (speaking schematically, not chronologically) with the separation out of state from civil society and which transports "public" authority from greater to lesser spheres: paradigmatically, from the political to the economic, from the economic to the domestic, from the domestic to the female, the subjective, and the sexual. Evidently a process of "privatization," this is also one of "internalization" insofar as the clarification of, or solution to, problems in the greater sphere is programmatically sought within the lesser sphere.

The third principle at work in the modern division of knowledge bears a reciprocal relation to these first two. If modernity involves the systematic multiplication and authorization of private entities—rights, opinions, interests, desires, ethical subjectivities, genders—it also is obliged to reconceive the nature of the realm of the public, which can, precisely by virtue of its impersonality, acknowledge and comprehend this indefinite potential of private entities. I speak now not of "the state"—the institutionalized and bureaucratized public realm of government and its apparatus—but of a category of publicness that is as unprecedented as the system of proliferating privacies it comes into being to embrace. What is required of such a public is the dynamic flexibility of a whole that will accommodate an unlimited and perpetually changing number of parts. The modern public is able to do this because it derives its own, virtual entity from the parts that compose it. Its primary boundaries are defined neither by space nor time nor suprahuman authority but by the reflexive self-affiliation of its individual parts. These parts are persons, actual individuals that comprise a virtual population whose makeup shifts constantly according to the patterns of participation, mobility, and circulation that move its component parts through the system of dialectical recapitulation—the public-private differential—of modern life.

In premodern cultures knowledge begins with the positing of a macrowhole, an a priori sociopolitical and ethico-epistemological totality. Names for this whole include God, the Fathers, the public; its primordial totality is conceived in many ways, as *in illo tempore,* Creation, the Garden of Eden, and in general by obscurely evoking its fullness through metaphorical comparisons with one or another of its privative and partial components. By one monotheistic version of such a paradigm, only the Creator can create, and what he creates is called interchangeably human beings and human community. By the alternative paradigm of modernity, the creature is so far creative that individual and society are defined by their difference, and individual is prior to society as nature is to culture. In the modern view, knowledge begins with an indeterminate number of private microwholes whose autonomy is expressed through figures of an original state of nature or the blank screen of cognition. Knowledge of the public follows upon knowledge of these preexisting private entities, whose plenitude provides the basis on which the indefinite inclusiveness of the virtual realm of the public is constituted. This is also to describe the difference between a positive and a negative model of liberty.

To speak in these terms suggests that the modern division between the public and the private is best understood not as a mutual exclusion but as a tool to think with. The instrumental metaphor is warranted, perhaps, by the proximity between the division of knowledge and the division of labor. Adam Smith begins *The Wealth of Nations* (1776) with the observation that the latter division has been responsible for "the greatest improvement in the productive powers of labour." By this means, indeed, the lesser may be seen to possess its own greatness, the "trifling" its own "importance"; this is in fact one lesson of Smith's famous account of "the trade of the pin-maker," which, like the remoter recesses of privacy, depends for its very existence on a succession of divisions and separations. Evidently "a very trifling manufacture," once it is known to be "divided into eighteen distinct operations" this trade becomes intelligible, in Smith's amused inflation, as "the important business of making a pin . . . ."[1]

Part 1 of this study gives ample testimony to contemporaries' awareness that the improvement in the productive powers of material labor is a mixed good, and "productivity" in the realm of knowledge is hard to fathom as a concept, let alone to evaluate as a consequence of division.[2] And yet the comparison between labor and knowledge is compelling, in part because it suggests that the public/private division of knowledge, broadly conceived as a historical movement beyond individual agency, nonetheless has something like a strategically motivated dimension, an ambition to make knowledge more efficiently "productive." The case can be made most directly where a demonstrable division of knowledge is causally related to a manifest division of labor—like the separation between home and workplace. Whatever else may be said of it, the modern concentration of what is deemed productive labor outside the home is, like Smith's pin-making trade, a materially productive development. In what sense is the conceptual gender division that accompanies this division of labor a culturally productive development?

The difficulty we have in answering this question has to do with the incommensurability of terms: in what language do we translate between the quantitative measure of material and the qualitative measure of cultural improvement? In other words, the obstacle to the accommodation of labor and knowledge in this fashion lies in the irreconcilability of the very principles—of quantity and quality—by which their separation is historically defined.[3] Indeed, the adequation of labor and knowledge silently and necessarily subsumes the particularizing, qualitative norm of the latter under the generalizing—the quantifying and adequating—norm of the former. This is the implication, at least, of contemporaries' ironic visions of novel-writing as a mode of commodity production that adequates difference as similarity. One late-eighteenth-century reviewer begins by observing that "[w]hen a manufacture has been carried on long enough for the workmen to attain a general proficiency, the uniformity of the stuffs will render it difficult to decide on the preference of one piece beyond another; and this must be our apology for not entering into a discussion of the merits of the novel now before us, which, at the same time that it exhibits nothing to shock our feelings, affords nothing to attract particular attention, either as to materials or workmanship."4

A more promising approach to exploring the productivity of the division of knowledge therefore may require that we shift the inquiry from cases like this one, where divisions of labor and knowledge sustain a close relationship, to ones where developments in knowledge, more intelligible as a distinct activity, may be seen to generate the notion of "productivity" in their own terms. Here we might have recourse to conventional usages like the early modern patriarchalist analogy between the state and the family, where the relation between greater and lesser, although poised on the brink of separation, is still conceived as a distinction informed with possibility. In the words of Francis Bacon that I have already quoted, "mean and small things" like the family can be used productively to "discover great" things, like the nature of a commonwealth.5 The relationship between small and great has the practical utility of a hermeneutic and pedagogic method.6 And although according to the principles I have been pursuing in this study the language of "division" is unsuitable to the relation of distinction that governs the utility of the patriarchalist analogy, we nonetheless gain an insight here into how the division of knowledge may be felt to be productive in a qualitative rather than a quantitative sense of the term.

Again, according to John Cheke, "dissension we see in small houses, and thereby may take example to great commonwealths. . . . and thereby learn to judge of great things unknown, by small things perceived." Thomas Gataker thought that "evils are the more grievous, the nearer and more inward they are," and that "domestical evils vex a man most." While "precepts show us what we should do, examples go further," and "domestical examples are of all others the most powerful."7 We may feel, however, that in these formulations of the patriarchalist analogy something more also is going on. Cheke and Gataker make clear that method may be detached from domestic experience and applied in a way similar to other contemporary approaches to the production of knowledge. One of these is the maxim that concrete examples conduce to abstract precepts. True, the implication of Gataker's remarks is not simply that the most proximate examples are the best guides but that the realm of the domestic itself possesses a distinctive exemplarity that improves upon the obscurity of abstract precept. However, this is a useful observation precisely because it enables us to see that in techniques like the apprehension of precept by example there operates a formal activity of "domestication" that in the patriarchalist analogy is redoubled on the level of content. One common figurative meaning of the verb "to domesticate" is, after all, "to naturalize" or "to familiarize" the great, the distant, the worldly, the strange, or the foreign by "bringing it home"—through the medium of the little, the proximate, the local, the familiar, or the native.

Using example to instantiate precept is a mode of "domestication" in this formal sense of the term, but the patriarchalist analogy combines this method with an example that is domestic in substance as well. To turn this around, the domestic is evidently not only a social but simultaneously an epistemological practice. The sociopolitical utility of the familial, we might say, is confirmed by the epistemological utility of the familiar. But to recognize this double feature of the patriarchalist analogy—to see that it involves a notion of the "domestic" on the epistemological level of form as well as on the sociopolitical level of content—involves the explicit acknowledgment of separability that also underlies the modern disenchantment with that analogy. The long-term, modern separation out of the family from the state, of the private from the public, clearly signals the end of this partnership. The separation out of domesticity transvalues it from a means to an end, from an instrumental signifier to a self-sufficient signified within which formal domestication may proceed (or such is the promise) with augmented efficiency. And this suggests a simple answer to the question of the productivity of the division of knowledge. The separation out of the family from the state is "productive" precisely because it enables their comparison, concentrating our view on the qualitative differences between the family and the state with the result that the modern understanding of each "in its own terms" becomes possible.

The aim of this chapter is to investigate a range of modes—some "discursive," some "literary"—that employ formal domestication, often but not always in partnership with a substantive domesticity, at the historical moment when the traditional distinction between the public and the private is in the process of issuing in their modern separation, hence when the productivity of tacit distinction is being replaced by that of explicit separation. In subsequent chapters I will pursue this process in a range of genres, and then as a peculiarly narrative phenomenon; one of the questions will concern the kind of productivity that is peculiar to the generic division of knowledge that gives British culture the domestic novel.

Domestication as Hermeneutics

Formal domestication bears an evident relationship to biblical hermeneutics, particularly the Christian doctrine of accommodation. John Milton gives the doctrine a concise and lucid formulation: "[O]ur understanding cannot in this body found it selfe but on sensible things, nor arrive so cleerly to the knowledge of God and things invisible, as by orderly conning over the visible and inferior creature . . . ."[8] As Henry Vaughan inquired, "Do we not see divers birds . . . such as are commonly known to us, with other meaner Creatures as *silk-worms* and the *humble-bee,* which yet are not so contemptible, but they may serve us for noble instances . . . seeing there is in them a *living spirit* . . . [?]"⁹ Protestant iconoclasm renewed both the promise and the danger of hermeneutic accommodation and its strategic reliance on "sensible things" to get beyond the realm of the senses.¹⁰ In the following few pages I aim to give no more than a suggestion of how the idea of formal domestication may be thrown into relief by conceiving it as a hermeneutic technique.

The relationship between hermeneutic accommodation and the sort of domestication we see in the patriarchalist analogy between the family and the state is a formal one: as the low may help us know the high, the little the great, and the private the public, so the profane, "visible and inferior creature" may lead us to the sacred and "invisible" Creator. Associating his allegorical method in *The Pilgrim's Progress* (1678, 1684) with that of Christ's parabolic teachings, John Bunyan knows that "a dark Similitude / Will on the Fancie more it self intrude, / And will stick faster in the Heart and Head, / Then things from Similies not borrowed."¹¹ Domestication lies at the very heart of the Christian drama of the Incarnation and Passion—in which the Creator accommodates himself to the status and suffering of a common creature—and is expressed in the development of a literary style, the *sermo humilis,* answerable to its lowly yet elevated substance.¹²

But the peculiar nature and development of English Protestant teaching made the intercourse between a formal domestication and a domestic content more insistent, in Protestant hermeneutics, than it had been before the Reformation. The formal accommodation of divine spirit (or precept) through human materiality (or example) that was central to Christian thought was given optimistic reinforcement, at the level of content, by the Protestant will toward internalization and privatization. The Protestant theology of grace individualized salvation as a matter of private conviction (whether or not in alliance with the privacy of economic individualism and interest). And the long-term legacy of Reformation history entailed the devolution of absolute authority from pope to king to spiritualized household and individual conscience. Given that trajectory, it is not surprising that Protestants tended to put a special premium on the humblest—the "meanest," "basest," "homeliest"—signifiers of grace. Under Roman Catholicism, a select minority found the blessing of humility in a life of ascetic renunciation; under Protestantism, all Christians might find the blessing of humility in the lowly callings of their daily lives. "[W]hatsoever our callings be," wrote John Dod and Robert Cleaver, "we serve the Lord Christ in them. . . . Though your worke be base, yet it is not a base thing to serve such a master in it." William Perkins believed that "the works of every calling . . . are done in faith and obedience, and serve notably for Gods glory, be the calling never so base. . . . The meaneness of the calling, doth not abase the goodnesse of the worke . . . ." According to Joseph Hall, "The homeliest service that we doe in an honest calling, though it be but to plow, or digge, if done in obedience, and conscience of God's Commandement, is crowned with an ample reward . . . ."[13]

Precisely because it is not rigorously allegorical in form, John Foxe's *Book of Martyrs* (1563, 1570) allows us to see how the hopeful logic of formal domestication can evoke and suffuse its substantive counterpart. In Foxe's lives of the Protestant saints homely detail is saturated with the paradigmatic aura of Reformation history at large, and the domestication of salvation stories makes speaking of low, sensible things to low, common people the key to transcendent truth. This narrative strategy was not without its complications. By wresting authority from Rome, Henry VIII had subjected religious affairs to the public authority of the English state in the very process of their "domestication" and privatization. This contradiction for the most part remained latent during the Marian persecutions, permitting Foxe to overlay the publicity of Roman Catholic absolutism with that of state absolutism so as to throw the private authority of the English saint into unambiguous relief. This moral antithesis was clearest when reinforced by social criteria, as in the case of Alice Driver, a common woman who "was an honest poor man's daughter, never brought up in the university, . . . but I have driven the plough before my father many a time . . . ." Driver's lack of traditional book learning gives her the cultural independence of the empirical subject, who, untutored, reads and interprets "God's book" according to scrupulous standards of literal sense that confound the self-serving hermeneutics of her inquisitors. Resisting a sacramental reading of scripture, she refutes the identity of "sign" and "signified," of Christ's "bread" and his "body," championing a semantics of plain sense and leaving her Catholic examiners speechless.[14]

Similarly free of traditional authority, Roger Holland admits that "I am unlearned. I have no sophistry to shift my reasons withal; but the truth I trust I have, which needeth no painted colours to set her forth. . . . Wherein shall a young man direct his ways, but by the word of God? and yet you will hide it from us in a tongue unknown." Before his conversion Holland was an apprentice given to a "licentious liberty" paralleled by "that liberty under your auricular confession, that I made no conscience of sin, but trusted in the priest's absolution . . . ." Reformed by "a servant in the house" whom he soon marries, Holland trades license for self-discipline, "wanton company" for domesticity, and institutional absolution for the private absolutism of individual conscience (8:473–76). But the devolutionary momentum of domestication does not require the lowness of the commoner. "Mistress Joyce Lewes, a gentlewoman born," is "brought up . . . infected" by the worldly follies of gentility until she begins "to wax weary of the world" and is reborn, through her conviction "that she was chosen to eternal life," into the conscientious aristocracy of grace. Confronted by the institutional mediation of two priests who have "come to hear her confession," Lewes replies with self-sufficiency that she already "had made her confession to Christ her Saviour." Betrayed by her husband, who, "like a murderer of his own wife . . . carried her to the bloody bishop," Lewes is executed for her comprehensive defiance of patriarchal absolutism—but not before she is joined in her parodic negation of "the idolatrous mass" ("I drink to all them that unfeignedly love the gospel of Jesus Christ, and wish for the abolishment of papistry") by friends and neighbors, and "specially the women of that town, [who] did drink with her . . ." (8:401–5).

In Roman Catholic lives of the saints individual resistance to temporal powers ultimately may be folded back into the overarching plan of ecclesiastical and divine hierarchy. In Protestant soteriology the exemplary life of the individual saint is concretized and separated out so emphatically that it may acquire at least the semblance of self-standing autonomy. *The Pilgrim's Progress* is perhaps our most striking instance of this phenomenon, an allegory whose "literal sense" so adequately domesticates its figural meaning as to risk becoming, itself, the self-sufficient signified. Bunyan's salvation story is figured as a narrative of physical and social mobility—not only the flight of a solitary common man from home, family, and neighbors but also his rise from the disparate tyrannies of feudal custom to the centralized bureaucracy of the modern nation-state.[15] As we have seen, one achievement of early modern culture was to posit male enterprise as not only the public antithesis but also the private counterpart of the female sphere of domesticity. If the rebuke to royal absolutism is given by the radically devolutionary conviction that only the individual has absolute authority, domesticity both sustains and socializes that rebuke by suggesting that the ultimate site of absolute authority in the modern world may be the family, which anchors the mobile individual within the ethical collective that is overseen by the authority of the individual who stays at home. Bunyan writes at a time when the Reformation spiritualization of the household, not yet having reached this ultimate stage, has nonetheless already infused the private family with primary responsibility for religious instruction. Consequently *The Pilgrim's Progress* involves a domestication on the levels of both form and content.

Through much of his pilgrimage, Bunyan keeps before us and Christian the poignant memory of the family he has left behind (17–18, 21–22, 42–43), and he punctuates the pilgrimage with ambivalent episodes of domestic and familial potential that adumbrate a domestication in the most literal sense of that term. These episodes include the Village of Morality, where Christian is encouraged to hear that "thou mayest send for thy wife and Children to thee to the Village, where there are houses now stand empty, one of which thou mayest have at reasonable rates . . ." but where the entire family to which he has been referred, it turns out, lies in deadly bondage. Christian's pilgrimage also takes in the highly articulated house of the Interpreter, who leads Christian from one room to another (a "private Room," a "very large *Parlour*," another "little Room, where sat two little Children . . ."), each of which presents Christian with a hermeneutic conundrum (in the parlor, the working of the Gospel on the Law is domesticated by the way sprinkled water helps sweep up dust). At Doubting-Castle Christian and his "brother" in Christ Hopeful are punished for trespass by Despair and his wife, "Mrs. *Diffidence*," whose nightly curtain lecture concerns the fate of the prisoners they have confined in their dungeon below.[16] By contrast, the House Beautiful is populated by young virgins who discourse with Christian and have "him into the Family; and many of them meeting him at the threshold of the house, . . . [s]o when he was come in, and set down, they gave him something to drink . . ." (16–19, 23–25, 93–95, 38–39).

To some degree, the serial ambivalence of these episodes bespeaks the contradictory status of the domesticated family within traditional Christian thought. "For whosoever shall do the will of my Father which is in heaven," said Jesus, "the same is my brother, and sister, and mother. . . . And everyone that hath forsaken houses, or brethren, or sisters, or father, or mother, or wife, or children, or lands, for my name's sake, shall receive an hundredfold, and shall inherit everlasting life."[17] Familial kinship ties are one of those low, sensible things that both define what the Christian must leave behind and model the Christian's alternative destination. Six years after the appearance of part 1 of *The Pilgrim's Progress*, Bunyan published a second part, in which domesticity enters the content of the allegory far more thoroughly than it had in the first because it tells the story of how Christian's solitary pilgrimage is recapitulated by that of his wife Christiana and their four sons. Christiana learns that her husband "has a House now given him to dwell in . . ." and that "[t]he Prince of the Place has also sent for me . . . ," that "he inviteth thee to come into his presence, to his Table, and that he will feed thee with the Fat of his House . . . ," and that all will be "glad when they shall hear the sound of thy feet step over thy Fathers Threshold" (150, 147).

Christiana and her circle leave home to get home, the collective personification of domesticity in transit between distinct versions of itself. A flight from "the world," this is also a flight into the world, a "set[ting] foot out of Doors," an act of going public that Bunyan strikingly marks as such by figuring the publication of the second part of *The Pilgrim's Progress*— Christiana's part—as her pilgrimage: "Go, now my little Book, to every place, / Where my first *Pilgrim* has but shewn his Face, / Call at their door: If any say, *who's there?* / Then answer thou, *Christiana is here. / . . . /* Tell them that they have left their House and Home, / Are turned Pilgrims, seek a World to come . . . ." In part 1 (she tells her sons) Christiana failed both their "fathers" by staying at home: "I have sinned away your Father, and he is gone; he would have had us with him; but I would not go my self; I also have hindred you of Life." Through her own publication, however, Christiana's book completes what her husband's only began as the New Testament fulfills the Old: "Besides," says Bunyan, "what my first *Pilgrim* left conceal'd, / Thou my brave *Second Pilgrim* hast reveal'd; / What *Christian* left lock't up and went his way, / Sweet *Christiana* opens with her Key" (152, 135, 146, 139, font reversed).

When it was first published in 1678, Bunyan's book implicitly—in the very name of its protagonist—purported to provide an allegorization universal in its exemplarity. The appearance of a second part retrospectively qualifies that achievement: the privacy of a feminine and collectivized domesticity carries on the public work initiated by (what we now may see as) Christian's individual male adventure. If he stands as our exemplary representative, Christiana and her children concretize his comparatively abstract and preceptual example by making salvation a genealogical and family affair. As Gaius asks, "[I]s this *Christian*'s wife, and are these *Christian*'s Children? I knew your Husband's Father, yea, also, his Father's Father. Many have been good of this stock . . . I have heard of many of your Husband's Relations that have stood all Tryals for the sake of the Truth[,] . . . men antiently of the Family from whence your Husband came." As for Christian's sons (says Greatheart), they "take all after their Father, and covet to tread in his Steps." "Wherefore let *Christiana* look out some Damsels for her Sons," continues Gaius, "to whom they may be Betroathed, *&c.* that the Name of their Father, and the House of his Progenitors may never be forgotten in the World. . . . [M]ay I advise, take *Mercie* into a nearer Relation to thee. If she will, let her be given to *Mathew* thy eldest Son. 'Tis the way to preserve you a posterity in the Earth. So this match was concluded, and in process of time they were married" (216–17). Thus the materfamilias, now *feme sole,* arranges a marriage that is also a love match, and her posterity populates not only the world to come but first of all the world at large.[18]

In the image of Christiana's key Bunyan expresses the way a substantive "domestication" may operate as a lowly means to an end that lies beyond it—even, more radically, as a typological fulfillment, an end in itself. Critics have hypothesized a seventeenth-century "Protestant poetics" whose distinction is (among other things) to "domesticate" Christian typology and soteriology in several dimensions. The increasingly commonplace identification of the Old Testament Jewish Nation with the modern English Nation of "Israelites"—the "naturalization" of the foreign as "native"—is one obvious example. By means of this sort of "historical" allegorization the ongoingness of English history, even the life history of the individual saint, becomes a screen upon which is projected the abstract and cosmic drama of salvation.[19] "I did toward Canaan draw; but now I am / Brought back to the Red sea, the sea of shame. / For as the Jews of old by God's command / Travelled, and saw no town: / So now each Christian hath his journeys spanned: / Their story pens and sets us down."[20] The apparent humility of George Herbert's speaker conceals two errors: the naive reduction of New Testament Promise to Old Testament Law (which is part of the poet's lesson) and the vain nationalization and individualization with which biblical typology is fulfilled in the English saint (which is not). In John Dryden's *Absalom and Achitophel* (1681) Old Testament history seems to stand, in relation to English history, as signifier does to signified.[21]

Herbert is perhaps our greatest master at expressing the ambivalence of Protestant domestication, its hermeneutic powers and the risks attendant on those powers. In his poem "Redemption" he exploits the doubleness of Christian "lordship," as Bunyan does that of the Christian "family," to accommodate Christ's Passion as a hopeful opportunity for socioeconomic betterment:

> Having been tenant long to a rich Lord,
>   Not thriving, I resolved to be bold,
>   And make a suit unto him, to afford
> A new small-rented lease, and cancell th' old.
> In heaven at his manor I him sought:
>   They told me there, that he was lately gone
>   About some land, which he had dearly bought
> Long since on earth, to take possession.
> I straight returned, and knowing his great birth,
>   Sought him accordingly in great resorts;
>   In cities, theatres, gardens, parks, and courts:
> At length I heard a ragged noise and mirth
>   Of theeves and murderers: there I him espied,
>   Who straight, *Your suit is granted*, said, and died.[22]

Like the houses in Bunyan's Village of Morality that now stand empty, the speaker's tenancy is no better than bondage to the Law, and in seeking a new lease of Grace he concentrates into his own, local salvation story the central event of Christian history. Christ himself, figured as an improving (land)lord of the "manor," both vindicates and repudiates this accommodation. His epochal descent to humble and sensible human form echoes the speaker's domestication of his own sin as the dependence of an agrarian copyhold lease. Seduced by the materializing force of his allegory, the speaker looks for his "rich Lord" in rich surrounds, and we are shocked by his double error. In seeking the "great" he has aimed both too high—the lord hangs out with the mean and common—and too low—his lordship is insensible and eternal.

Herbert's poem is a domesticated token that may be redeemed in exchange for the understanding of Christ's Passion its domesticity both figures and obscures. Carefully teasing apart the layers of his redemption metaphor, Herbert elaborates the terse, preceptual figure into an exemplary story of estate settlement that does not so much conclude as evaporate into thin air. Jonathan Swift's allegory of estate settlement in *A Tale of a Tub* (1704, 1710) offers no likelihood of auto-evaporation because at least part of its point is to exhibit the hermeneutic vice of indefinite construability that is also its subject. Swift's allegory of the public history of the Christian Church is figured by the domestic story of three brothers at large in Restoration London and bent upon turning their dead father's will to their own private interests. "Once upon a Time," it begins, "there was a Man who had Three Sons by one Wife, and all at a Birth, neither could the Mid-Wife tell certainly which was the Eldest." William Wotton thought this a blasphemous "*Farce*" that smacked of the gossip's or "Common Old Wives Introduction . . . ." Swift briefly and impatiently continues in a Bunyanesque, generically romance vein—"they travelled thro' several Countries, encountred a reasonable Quantity of Gyants, and slew certain Dragons"—then drastically domesticates his tale to the present time and place: the three brothers "Writ, and Raillyed, and Rhymed, and Sung, and Said, and said Nothing; they Drank, and Fought, and Whor'd, and Slept, and Swore, and took Snuff: They went to new Plays in the first Night, haunted the *Chocolate*-Houses, beat the Watch, lay on Bulks, and got Claps . . . ." Wotton might have complained of Swift what Clarendon had said of Hobbes, that "under the notion of translating proper and significant words and terms . . . into vulgar and common Language, . . . [he] hath in truth traduced the whole Scheme of Christianity into Burlesque . . . ."[23]

And yet it was in the nature of scriptural accommodation that the line between translation and desecration was difficult to draw, and the propriety of Christian domestication could not be judged ahead of time. In book 5 of *Paradise Lost* (1667) Milton provides an instance of accommodation that is remarkable in the way it thematizes its epistemological concerns within, and through, an explicitly domestic setting. Anticipating a visit from the seraph Raphael, Eve gathers from the Garden a wealth of "savoury fruits" and "nectarous draughts" with which to prepare "Dinner" in their "Silvan Lodge" for "our Angel guest, as hee / Beholding shall confess that here on Earth / God hath dispenst his bounties as in Heav'n."[24] Eve's eager comparison becomes the topic of dinner-table conversation. This is "unsavory food perhaps / To spiritual Natures," Adam remarks doubtfully. Raphael replies that "Intelligential" creatures can happily eat the food of "Rational" creatures because they are able to "transubstantiate" it, "[a]nd corporeal to incorporeal turn" (bk. 5, lines 401–2, 408, 409, 438, 413). Having eaten his fill, Adam now seeks to satisfy his hunger "to know / Of things above his World . . . ," and the angel proceeds to describe how creation is a vast scale of steps "[d]iffering but in degree, of kind the same." Food and understanding, matter and spirit, cohere in a gradual but integral process of transubstantiation:

> time may come when men
> With Angels may participate, and find
> No inconvenient Diet, nor too light Fare:
> And from these corporal nutriments perhaps
> Your bodies may at last turn all to spirit, . . .
> (bk. 5, lines 454–55, 490, 493–97)

This is an act simultaneously of ontological modulation and hermeneutic accommodation, and it echoes other ways in which the great may be domesticated by the little—spirit by matter, knowing by eating, ontology by domesticity, theology by poetry. Forty years later Richard Steele undertook to accommodate the already arduous language of Milton's instant classic to the urbane idiom of emergent middle-class culture. Adam and Eve's quarrel after the Fall, Steele writes, "to a Modern will appear but a very faint Piece of Conjugal Enmity . . . ." Translated "out of Heroicks, and put into Domestick Stile," Milton's verse undergoes in turn its own parodic domestication, into the comic-journalistic-novelistic prose that will both replace and extend epic poetry in the modern world. Thus Adam: "Madam, if my Advice had been of any Authority with you when that strange Desire of Gadding possessed you this Morning, we had still been happy . . . ." And as Steele remarks, Eve's spirited self-defense against the charge that her vulnerability to Satan precipitated their fatal transgression, "allowing for the Improvements of Time, . . . gave him the same Provocation as if she had called him Cuckold." In this way the Fall of humanity is accommodated to bedroom farce and the expulsion from Eden to a skimmington ride.[25]

Steele's translation reminds us that with the Renaissance rediscovery of the ancient learning, textual hermeneutics had an impact on modern historiography. That is, the age-old effort of Christian hermeneutics to accommodate spirit through matter provided a model for contemporary efforts, "allowing for the improvements of time," to accommodate ancient achievements through modern practice—even to accommodate pagan through modern Christian poetic machinery. Here the perplexing line is that between translation and more or less self-conscious anachronism. And these efforts too may be illuminated as acts of domestication in both the formal and the substantive senses of the term, if within the latter we include the "naturalization" of the strange, the foreign, and the remote to the familiar, the native, and the present. In *Peri Bathous* (1727) Alexander Pope includes this sort of domestication under the heading of "the *Pert Stile*"; needless to say, perhaps, he has only ironic praise for it: "But the Beauty and Energy of it is never so conspicuous, as when it is employ'd in *Modernizing* and *Adapting* to the *Taste of the Times* the Works of the Antients. This we rightly phrase *Doing* them *into English*, and *making* them *English*; two Expressions of great Propriety, the one denoting our *Neglect* of the *Manner how*, the other the *Force* and *Compulsion* with which, it is brought about. It is by Virtue of this Stile that *Tacitus* talks like a *Coffee-House Politician, Josephus* like the *British Gazeteer, Tully* is as short and smart as *Seneca* or Mr. *Asgill* [an MP and pamphleteer], *Marcus Aurelius* is excellent at *Snipsnap* [smart repartee], and honest *Thomas a Kempis* as *Prim* and *Polite* as any Preacher at Court."[26]

In his best-known antiromance Charles Sorel has his characters debate the historicizing notion "that we must permit the ancients to be mad after their mode; and if we should talk idly in our way, and accommodate our selves to our own times, as they did to theirs, we must make the Gods ride in Coaches or Sedans instead of Chariots, and we should feign that *Cupid* shoots at us with a Pistol, instead of an arrow, and the fiction were much more natural . . . ."[27] Taking a page from Sorel's book (and from Ariosto's before him), Milton has Raphael pose the problem of accommodation, asking, ". . . how shall I relate / To human sense th' invisible exploits / Of warring Spirits . . . ?" a rhetorical question to which he replies, ". . . what surmounts the reach / Of human sense, I shall delineate so, / By lik'ning spiritual to corporal forms . . . ." Raphael then confidently attributes to Satan the invention of artillery (bk. 5, lines 564–66, 571–73, bk. 6, lines 470–93; on Ariosto, see 335n). (Milton's programmatic response to this sort of problem in *Paradise Lost* is, of course, to deny the analogy between the problem of biblical accommodation and the problem of modern historiography. The putative superiority of ancient to modern learning is not to be confused with the manifest inferiority of pagan to Christian faith, and throughout the poem the poet insists that his argument is "Not less but more Heroic than the wrath / Of stern *Achilles* . . ." [bk. 9, lines 14–15].)

Pursuant to his political-satirical agenda in *Absalom and Achitophel*, Dryden in turn attributes the invention of artillery to Old Testament personages: "Some thought they God's Anointed meant to Slay / By Guns, invented since full many a day: / Our Authour swears it not; but who can know / How far the Devil and *Jebusites* may go?" Elsewhere freed of this strategic purpose, Dryden too was able to anticipate the Christian accommodation of pagan machinery with some confidence: "The perusing of one chapter in the prophecy of Daniel, and accommodating what there they find with the principles of Platonic philosophy as it is now Christianised, would have made the ministry of angels as strong an engine for the working up heroic poetry, in our religion, as that of the Ancients has been to raise theirs by all the fables of their gods . . . ." A year later, however, Dryden was more pessimistic about the efficacy of this sort of domestication: "If I undertake the translation of Virgil, the little which I can perform will shew at least that no man is fit to write after him in a barbarous modern tongue. Neither will his machines be of any service to a Christian poet. . . . 'Tis using them too dully if we only make devils of his gods: as if, for example, I would raise a storm, and make use of Aeolus, with this only difference of calling him Prince of the Air. What invention of mine would there be in this; or who would not see Virgil through me; only the same trick played over again by a bungling juggler?"²⁸ In 1712 Addison published an "Edict" prohibiting Christian poets from using "Heathen Mythology" and "the Pagan Creed"—in particular, "I shall not allow the Destinies to have had an Hand in the Deaths of the several Thousands who have been slain in the late War [of the Spanish Succession], being of Opinion that all such Deaths may be very well accounted for by the Christian System of Powder and Ball."²⁹

In the previous pages I have introduced the notion of formal domestication by comparing it to methods of biblical hermeneutics and then, by extension, to historiographical efforts to close the gap between antiquity and modernity, the classical and the vernacular languages, once Renaissance thought had made their separation inescapable. In some of the foregoing examples formal domestication is accompanied by a substantive domesticity; in others it is not. The ambivalence of Christian accommodation, the uncertainty that it can achieve its end, is a constitutive feature of the form. Yet especially in those Protestant versions where form is reinforced by content we may begin to see how the common and the lowly can be associated with the authority not only of the means but also of the end itself. In the following section I will enlarge the implications of formal domestication by discussing its use as a pedagogic method.

Domestication as Pedagogy

At the beginning of this chapter I cited several proponents of the patriarchalist analogy in whom the pedagogic motive is evident enough. Others make clear that the utility of the method is supported by the fact that in this case, at least, pedagogic method is enhanced by pedagogic experience: living in a family teaches people how to live in a commonwealth. According to William Perkins, the family is "the Seminarie of all other Societies . . . . For this first Societie, is

as it were the Schoole, wherein are taught and learned the principles of author-
itie and subjection." Perkins's followers concurred: "Besides," writes William
Gouge, "a family is a little Church, and a little commonwealth, at least a lively
representation thereof . . . . Or rather, it is a schoole wherein the first principles
and grounds of gouernment and subiection are learned: whereby men are fitted
to greater matters in Church or commonwealth." And John Downame invites
his readers to "consider that the family is the Seminary of the Church and
Common-wealth; and as a private schoole, wherein children and servants are
fitted for the public assemblies, as it were the Universities, to performe, when
they meete together, all religious duties of Gods worship and service."[30]

A familiar instance of the pedagogy of domestication that consists in teaching precept by example is the rhetoric of exemplarity as it was widely practiced
by early modern historians. This is a formal domestication that has nothing to
do with the substantive realm of the domestic. That is, exemplarity moves from
the local instance to the general application, but its examples are effective because they are taken not from the realms of the mean and the small but from
the public precincts of greatness: only the lives of illustrious men and women
can teach a pattern of virtue. By the same token, the distinction between historical and biographical writing, although traditionally understood as one between
a focus on the public and a focus on the private life, took for granted that the
exemplars of "private" life would be great men, figures of public importance. In
the eighteenth century, biographical exemplarity underwent a revolution that
replaced the illustrious by the domestic example. This encouraged methods of
formal domestication that also exploited the signifying, even the explanatory,
powers of a substantive domesticity, as Macaulay suggests: "As the history of
states is generally written, the greatest and most momentous revolutions seem
to come upon them like supernatural inflictions, without warning or cause. But
the fact is, that such revolutions are almost always the consequences of moral
changes, which have gradually passed on the mass of the community, and
which ordinarily proceed far before their progress is indicated by any public
measure. An intimate knowledge of the domestic history of nations is therefore
absolutely necessary to the prognosis of political events."[31]

More radically, the revolution in biographical exemplarity resulted in the
discovery that the domestic realm was the self-sufficient signified, the key not
to public history but to history as such. According to Samuel Johnson, "[T]he
business of the biographer is often to pass slightly over those performances and
incidents, which produce vulgar greatness, to lead the thoughts into domestick
privacies, and display the minute details of daily life, where exterior appendages
are cast aside, and men excel each other only by prudence and virtue." This
bears some relation to the business of the fiction writer. "In the romances for-

merly written, every transaction and sentiment was so remote from all that passes among men, that the reader was in very little danger of making any applications to himself." The "familiar histories" of today "may perhaps be made of greater use than the solemnities of professed morality, and convey the knowledge of vice and virtue with more efficacy than axioms and definitions." Not that Johnson lacks respect for the solemnities either of morality or of public life; rather, he believes that moral precepts are most reliably learned from the ethical examples of private life: "The good or ill success of battles and embassies extends itself to a very small part of domestick life: we all have good and evil, which we feel more sensibly than our petty part of publick miscarriage or prosperity."[32] In speaking of the familiar histories of the day Johnson might have been describing the practice of Tobias Smollett. In the preface to *Roderick Random* (1748) Smollett suggests that the "remoteness" of the old romances amounted to a kind of cultural "disguise." And although he foresees "that some people will be offended at the mean scenes in which [his hero] is involved, I persuade myself the judicious will . . . find entertainment in viewing those parts of life, where the humours and passions are undisguised by affectation, ceremony, or education; and the whimsical peculiarities of disposition appear as nature has implanted them."[33] And as the Puritan divines remind us, "household stuffe" is the very epitome of "mean things."[34]

Others seconded Johnson's assessment of the business of the biographer. According to Oliver Goldsmith, "The relations of great events may surprize indeed; they may be calculated to instruct those very few, who govern the million beneath, but the generality of mankind find the most real improvement from relations which are levelled to the general surface of life; which tell, not how men learned to conquer, but how they endeavoured to live . . . ." Toward the end of the century John Bennett addresses "a young lady" on the topic of biography in similar terms: "Instead of wars, sieges, and victories or great atchievements, which are not so much within the province of a female, it presents those domestick anecdotes and events, which come more forcibly home to her bosom and curiosity." The familiar language of interiority ("home to her bosom") discloses the generality of human nature, strikingly enough, in the ultimate particularity of private sentiment. Another biographer writes that whatever people's outward differences, "yet follow them close, enter with them into their cabinets, or, which is still more, into their private thoughts, and the dark recesses of their minds, and they will be found pretty much on a level."[35]

In these observations we see formal domestication so intently focused on the substantive realm of the private and domestic that the sort of signifying role it plays in patriarchalism—the evocation of a public signified through a private signifier—has disappeared entirely. Or perhaps we should say that the aim of signification has been internalized within the realm of the private, where "mean," domestic content increasingly is found able to do the sort of epistemological work that formerly had seemed to require a pedagogic fulfillment in the realm of the public. For what becomes explicit in these observations is that the signifying purpose of domestication is served when we gain access to a "public" dimension in the sense not of sociopolitical greatness but of ethico-epistemological generality. In one of the *Rambler* passages quoted above, Johnson commends biography for preferring "domestick privacies" to "vulgar greatness" because the differences that owe to "exterior appendages" are there "cast aside" and we confront more directly the realm of the ethical—of "prudence" and "virtue"—that we all inhabit in common. A few lines earlier Johnson makes clear that the end of biographical particularization is the capacity to generalize: "[T]here is such an uniformity in the state of man, considered apart from adventitious and separable decorations and disguises, that there is scarce any possibility of good or ill, but is common to human kind." Indeed, "the common" is a fruitful term in contemporaries' meditation on the movement from the "private" to the "public" because its semantic richness mediates between the sociopolitical sense of the private realm and the epistemological payoff of generality that traditionally had seemed available only through the sociopolitical sense of the realm of the public. On the one hand, the common refers (as here) to that which is uniform in human nature, what is general and common to us all, much as the public domain renders information "universally common." On the other hand, the common inheres in "domestick privacies" and "the minute details of daily life," through which we can learn more about a man, "by a short conversation with one of his servants," "than might be collected from publick papers . . . ."[36]

Johnson's point here is that neither the lives of commoners nor the testimony of common servants is a privileged means for sifting the general from the particular. And yet both implications seem to hover above his sense—and to inform his judgment about the difference between the heroic romances of the past and the comic romances that are popular with "the present generation": "The task of our present writers is very different; it requires . . . that experience which . . . must arise from general converse, and accurate observation of the living world. . . . Other writings are safe, except from the malice of learning, but these are in danger from every common reader; as the slipper ill executed was censured by a shoemaker who happened to stop in his way at the Venus of Apelles." Like the common shoemaker, the "common reader" has an epistemological advantage that bears some relation to his sociopolitical status. As the protagonist of contemporary fiction "is levelled with the rest of the world," so the advantaged reader of such fiction is a lowest common denominator, one to whose place the rest of the world has been leveled.37 Like the idea of the common, the language of leveling Johnson shares with Goldsmith ("relations which are levelled to the general surface of life") and the anonymous biographer ("they will all be found pretty much on a level") points in two directions. On the one hand, the leveled is common in the sense of being general; on the other hand, the leveled has a sociopolitical commonness or "meanness" that gains access to the general by virtue of its lack of distinction.

And, as Edmund Burke suggests, by virtue of its openness to debate: "In free countries [like England], there is often found more real public wisdom and sagacity in shops and manufactories than in the cabinets of princes in countries where none dares to have an opinion until he comes into them."38 The sagacity or reason of the public sphere is a function of its free debate, its open contention of interests, for what issues from this debate is public opinion, a collective species of disinterestedness. This is a relatively unfamiliar Burke, who writes three years after being elected to Parliament as member from Bristol and one year after the American colonies have, in a cause with which Burke sympathized, declared their independence from British rule. With Johnson's analogy between the common reader and the common shoemaker, Burke's praise of "the public wisdom and sagacity in shops and manufactories" suggests not simply (as we have heard) that public matters must be domesticated in order to be understood by common people but that common people may be an instrumental key to the formulation of public policy. By 1777 the idea of a virtual and self-authorizing public sphere had become for most people, as for Burke, a mandatory means of acknowledging the reality of a public realm constituted by the collective will of the people and posited over against the institutionalized publicness of the state apparatus. One hundred years earlier the idea was still in its formative stages. When did the collective, common sagacity of the common people first become thinkable?

In speaking of parables as a species of "Poetry in an home and countrey dresse," William Davenant describes domestication as form in terms of domesticity as content: parables "make reason familiar with Sense, and inforce the gravest and most considerable Truths from the smallest and most domestique hints . . . ." Implicit here is a certain level of audience. Domestication characteristically addresses the rude, rustic, and untutored: "the generality of mankinde are solely instructed in their senses, and by immediate impressions of particular objects, never vexing their heads with reviews and subtle examinations . . . ." And yet the appeal to the senses is one Davenant finds effective regarding both "the common people" and the inquisitive and learned "*Virtuosi.*"39 Similarly, Bacon observes that the parabolic appeal to the sensible example, prevalent "in the old times, . . . the understanding of men being then rude and impatient of all subtleties that did not address themselves to the sense . . . ," is still needed today "if any one wish to let new light on any subject into men's minds . . . ."[40] This is recognizably the language not only of an old exemplarity but also of the new philosophy. That is, as the old argument for teaching by example becomes colored by the positive, protoscientific revaluation of sense impressions, its repudiation of abstract rationalism bespeaks both a traditionalistic, rhetorically oriented deference to unsophisticated minds and an emergent, epistemologically oriented advocacy of empiricist cognition. The "rudeness" and "meanness" of domestication—paradigmatically, speaking of low, sensible things to low, common people—is transformed by a growing belief in the epistemological value of lowness.

Over the course of the eighteenth century the category of disinterestedness came to designate, in several domains of knowledge, a mode of judgment that contemporaries conceived to be "public" because of its powers of generalization, its capacity to rise above the local and "private" conditions in which knowledge germinates to establish what might justly be called a realm of dependably common knowledge. The hermeneutic and the pedagogic are ancient motives for domestication that in this period were found to contain, in their own movements toward discovery, that end to which they formerly had been thought to be no more than a means. The modern coalescence of the category "disinterestedness" coincides with, and is intimately related to, this historical crisis in which formal domestication finds its fulfillment in domesticity. I hope to make the case that the idea of disinterested judgment, the capacity to generalize from the singular to the common, is found early on to reside as much in "mean" and "base" commoners as in other social groups.

Disembedding Epistemology from Social Status

This hope appears to run counter to prevailing scholarly consensus. Recent historians of political and social thought, science, and the aesthetic have argued that in seventeenth- and eighteenth-century British culture the capacity for knowledge was generally thought to be correlated with a disinterestedness available only to independent male landowners of gentle social status.[41] To assess this claim we need to understand how the question of disinterestedness first became one that English people were moved to ask.

The discursive emergence of "disinterestedness" in the seventeenth century is bound up with the explicitation of the idea of "interest" and "the public interest" that came with the midcentury experience of civil war.[42] To generalize: before the civil wars there was a tacit identification of the public interest with the national interest, of the national interest with that of the sovereign, and of the sovereign with transcendental founts of authority. The civil wars created a crisis of domestication; that is, they forced English people to look critically and skeptically at the customary assumption that in human sovereignty we experience an accommodation of divinity. This assumption was not an explicit doctrine of the divine right of kings but a more powerfully implicit aura of the numinous with which royal sovereignty was imbued by the rituals and mysteries of sacred and pre-Christian kingship and which made the question of monarchal "disinterestedness" not impertinent but unintelligible. The separation of the king's natural from his political body in 1649 was the most important demystification of the king's aura on the level of symbolic action. At a lower level, however, the civil wars also complicated the idea of the public interest by contributing to the separation of the state from civil society, making explicit the existence of multiple private interests that had to be taken into account in the assessment of the public interest.

The idea of civic disinterestedness comes into being, we may speculate, as an effort to replace the presumed neutrality and comprehensiveness of sovereign authority—its coextension with the public interest—by its closest available equivalent once the tacit "disinterestedness" (or omni-interest) of the sovereign had been challenged through explicitation. Was the argument of domestication—the understanding of human authority as a profane signifier of the sacred, as a concrete example of abstract Law—still viable? The efforts to justify both Cromwell and Charles II are well known, as is the correlation between the stridency of those efforts and their inadequacy to the hopeless task of renovating a tacit knowledge. What transpired instead was a replacement of the traditional coordination of the public and the private, as in the doctrine of the king's two bodies, by an oppositional separation between the public good and those private interests—including that of the king—that might threaten it.[43] And over the long term what was found to be needed was the explanation of authority as a derivation not from on high but from below: not the argument of a domestication downward, from a realm yet more "public" than that of royalty, but the argument of a refinement upward, from the low and private precincts of the common. Domestication was a traditional mode of accommodation that remained active throughout this period. What I am calling refinement, the authorization of empirical interest itself as the foundation of disinterestedness, was broadly consonant with a body of attitudes (pride, self-sufficiency, creativity, worldliness) that also were traditional, but only by virtue of being thought destructive of human community. What was new in this period was therefore not refinement but its indulgence. So the search for a plausible principle of disinterestedness ultimately took a form similar to what I have described in the development of hermeneutic and pedagogic motives, the movement from domestication to domesticity.[44]

During the decades following the Restoration the question was, on whom might fall the sovereign's once-tacit mantle of "disinterestedness"? How strong is the claim that the accepted wisdom on this was that of civic humanism, namely, gentle male landowners? It must be said in passing that even to pose the question in these modestly historical terms creates difficulties, since scholarly advocates of civic humanism do not come fully to terms with the fact that England, being a monarchy, already possessed a political model of incorruptible authority more compelling than that offered by Roman republicanism and that when the monarchal model became unviable, civic humanism was only one of several contenders for the honor of disinterestedness.[45] Nonetheless, it was an important contender for a while, and the authoritative disinterestedness of male landowning gentility was not restricted to matters of impartiality in civic judgment; it also was extended to the realms of natural philosophy and aesthetic taste.

Although distinguishable, the civic, scientific, and aesthetic species of disinterestedness are closely entwined in their early development. Early on, the ethico-epistemological meaning we attribute (although with significant variations) to disinterestedness in these three capacities often has a politico-social coloring. This appeal to gentility needs to be understood in its rhetorical dimension. In the decades after the Restoration the language of gentility is still useful as a means to make what are primarily epistemological and ethical attributions because the latter are still, by modern standards, relatively unseparated out from social standing. True, the division of knowledge had already proceeded some distance. By the beginning of the eighteenth century the category "gentleman" had lost its denotative socioeconomic specificity. As Deane Bartlett remarked in 1713, "It is a clear settled Point, that the Gentleman should be preferred to the Mechanic. But who is the Gentleman, and who the Mechanic, wants to be explained."[46] It may be plausible to see contemporaries using the traditional vocabulary of social status experimentally in an effort to render an emergent value system intelligible and familiar. This can be sensed, for example, in the way the bookseller-translator Francis Kirkman played upon the attributive powers of print in 1673.[47] Kirkman does not suppose the reader will mistake him as possessed of gentility and aristocratic honor. He uses these terms to accommodate a novel, seemingly analogous but really very different mechanism of public authentication—not the Heralds Office but the printing press. By the same token, contemporaries looked to absolute property ownership, hence to gentility, as a means of conveying a conception of disinterestedness as independence of mind that seemed available through other means as well.[48]

It did not take long for the separation out of ethico-epistemological from material independence to be accomplished. But we also need to note in passing that contemporaries were aware of preconditions other than gentility for material independence. Much has been made of Mr. Spectator's landed independence, for example, as a requirement for the disinterested spectatorship crucial to his urban existence: "Thus I live in the World, rather as a Spectator of Mankind, than as one of the Species; by which means I have made my self a Speculative Statesman, Soldier, Merchant and Artizan, without ever medling with any Practical Part in Life. I am very well versed in the Theory of an Husband, or a Father, and can discern the Errors in the Oeconomy, Business, and Diversion of others, better than those who are engaged in them . . . ."[49] The detached posture of the spectator is not peculiar, however, to those whose financial independence owes to their gentle landed status. The following week Addison describes his preferred and like-minded readership, whose common idleness has a number of causes. Among these are "the Fraternity of Spectators," notably including "contemplative Tradesmen," "who live in the World without having any thing to do in it; and either by the Affluence of their Fortunes, or Laziness of their Dispositions, have no other Business with the rest of Mankind but to look upon them." Another category of the comfortably idle whom Mr. Spectator solicits as his readers comprehends the inhabitants of "the female World," "who have so much Time on their Hands" and whose qualifications he underscores by facetiously characterizing their trivial leisured pursuits as "Employments," "Business," "Work," and "Occupations" (*Spectator*, no. 10, 12 Mar. 1711).

Delicately balanced as the passage is between solidarity and satire, does it invite us to consider not only contemplative tradesmen but also leisured women as enjoying a species of disinterestedness?[50] When Addison celebrated traders on the Royal Exchange as "private Men" liberated from baronial vassalage to serve the "common Interest," he effectively affirmed that the material independence arrogated by civic humanism to landed gentility alone had become, by the last years of the seventeenth century, a common possibility (*Spectator*, no. 69, 19 May 1711). Steele had already proposed a female readership for the *Tatler*, "in Honour of whom I have invented the Title of this Paper." He thus eagerly makes his own the female leisure activity of "tattling," which in most contexts has an exclusively dismissive connotation. Is not this, too, a freedom of mind that is facilitated by a freedom from "business" (*Tatler*, no. 1, 12 Apr. 1709)?[51]

Of course, there is an obvious difference between the financially based disinterestedness of the tradesman or landed gentleman and that of the leisured domestic *feme covert*. The first results from a condition of financial independence, the second from one of financial dependence (whatever putative disinterested-ness that leisure may enable). And yet both would seem to entail an easy de-tachment from what pass for the affairs and interests of the great world. Samuel Johnson suggestively complicates this comparison. Pursuing in a more psychol-ogizing direction Mandeville's sociological skepticism about the possibility of disinterested behavior, Johnson creates in Rasselas an exemplar who gives the lie to the civic humanist association of material independence in private with dis-interested judgment in public life. Precisely because he has been relieved of all (private) material needs, the Prince of Abyssinia is beset by (private) imagina-tive desires. Johnson's paradoxical topic in *Rasselas* is "[t]he wants of him that wants nothing," and his protagonist discovers what Johnson reduces, in the *Rambler,* to a general truth: "It is impossible to supply wants as fast as an idle imagination may be able to form them . . . ." Johnson's point in this essay is that unhappiness stemming from a sense of unsatisfied need is general to the human condition—to landlords and merchants, wealthy misers and polite wits, young lovers and their insensible elders—because whatever our conditions, the satis-faction of actual wants is only the precondition for the creation of imaginary and insatiable wants. And the real test of this truth comes not from the gentle-man landowner (to whom Johnson assumes it to apply) but from the extreme case of the leisured lady, "born with an exemption from care and sorrow, . . . upon whom one age has laboured after another to confer honours, and accu-mulate immunities . . . ," and yet beset by "numerous and restless anxieties . . . ." In arguing the inescapable preoccupation of the leisured lady Johnson also implies that of the propertied gentleman, whose material independence is no guarantee of his independence of mind.[52]

A corollary of this, perhaps, was the recognition that the material depend-ence of the commoner might be compatible, if he was a truly ethical subject, with a capacity for disinterestedness. By forsaking luxury and returning "to the more easy and natural Means of national Industry," William Arnall wrote, the populace might become "honest, just and disinterested" and avoid the "various Misfortunes attending Slavery and Debauchery." The civic humanist restriction of disinterestedness to independent gentle landowners represents the most tra-ditional and tacit version of the doctrine, in which the essential coextension of that mental capaciousness with that status group needed no rationalization. Landed male gentility axiomatically and exclusively entailed "public virtue." Once the question of interestedness began to be posed explicitly, however, some commentators learned to explain the disinterestedness of independent land-owners in the more rational terms of access to education: elite landowners owed their capacity for disinterestedness not to the fact of their private ownership but to the knowledge that comes with independence from subsistence labor. Once this door is opened, of course—once disinterestedness is seen to be a function of not birth or its privileges but experience—the separation out of epistemology from social status is well under way. Authority that had seemed by custom an automatic condition of rank could be loosened, detached, and applied elsewhere. Thus John Locke argued that the sociopolitical condition of "subjection," when figuratively extended in an epistemological direction, takes on a more authentic meaning: "[T]his, at least, is worth the consideration of those who call themselves Gentlemen, That however they may think Credit, Respect, Power, and Authority the Concomitants of their Birth and Fortune, yet they will find all these still carried away from them, by Men of lower Condition who surpass them in Knowledge. . . . [H]e is certainly the most subjected, the most enslaved, who is so in his Understanding."[53]

Scientific Disinterestedness

Perhaps the most persuasive testimony to the correlation of disinterestedness in natural philosophy with the independence of male gentility comes from Robert Boyle. "Being a bachelor," he recalled, "and through God's bounty furnished with a competent estate for a younger brother, and freed from any ambition to leave my heirs rich, I had no need to pursue lucriferous experiments, to which I so much preferred luciferous ones, that I had a kind of ambition . . . of being able to say, that I cultivated chemistry with a disinterested mind."[54] But this testimony to the correlation of gentility with disinterestedness does not necessarily represent the general views of contemporary natural philosophers. According to one historian of science, "The defense of the mechanical arts against the charge of baseness . . . implied . . . the rejection of a . . . conception of science . . . as a disinterested contemplation of truth, as an investigation that comes into being and is pursued only *after* the things necessary to life have been attended to." To put this in more positive terms, the epistemological condition of scientific disinterestedness was quickly separated out from questions of social status.[55]

Robert Hooke, Boyle's commoner assistant, agreed with his boss that the natural philosopher should devote him- or herself to "luciferous" experiments, but he also insisted on defending the potential "baseness" of such work in terms that carry a socially leveling implication: "Those things which others count Childish and Foolish, he may find Reasons to think them worthy his most attentive, grave and serious Thoughts . . . . Other things which the Generality would account an Employment about Niceties and Trifles, he finds to be the shortest and easiest way to his Journey's end, and . . . from the turning of a Straw, is able to foresee a Change in the great Ocean of the Air. He ought therefore . . . not to neglect or pass by any [circumstances] as trivial, or childish, or base and mean, and the like . . . ." Laboring to formulate the protocols of scientific method, Hooke's implication is "leveling" not in any doctrinal sense of social equalization but in the methodological sense of pronouncing inimical to objective standards of observation all customary, socially coded preconceptions about what is proper or worthy of attention. This seems clear enough, at least, when we read his striking suggestion that scientific observers adopt a technique of radical self-estrangement aimed at counteracting whatever might be their usual assumptions, whether social, professional, national, or broadly experiential:

> And an Observer should endeavour to look upon such Experiments and Observations that are more common, and to which he has been more accustom'd, as if they were the greatest Rarity, and to imagine himself a Person of some other Country or Calling, that he had never heard of, or seen any thing of the like before: And to this end, to consider over those Phenomena and Effects, which being accustom'd to, he would be very apt to run over and slight, to see whether a more serious considering of them will not discover a Significancy in those things which because usual were neglected: For I am very apt to believe, that if this Course were taken we should have much greater Discoveries of Nature made than have been hitherto. For I find it very common for Tradesmen, or such as have been much versed about any thing, to give the worst kind of Description of it for this purpose; and one that is altogether ignorant and a Stranger to it, if he be curious and inquisitive, to make the most perfect and full Description of it. And the like may be observed also in such as travel into other Countries, that they will give a better Description of the Place than such as are Natives of it; for those usually take notice of all the things which because of their Newness seem strange, whereas a Native passes over those because accustom'd to them. I grant that a Native, or one that has been more accustom'd and vers'd in a thing or place, shall be able to answer Questions propounded much better: But a Stranger shall be best able to make the Queries . . . .[56]

Hooke's and others' efforts to define the grounds of scientific disinterestedness are richly suggestive for our understanding of how the categories of the public and the private enter into the contemporary discourse on epistemology. Hooke here calls not for education but for diseducation, a state of mind divested of customary assumptions, a process of defamiliarization theoretically available, he believes, to all observers, whatever the particular "family" of assumptions in which they are customarily embedded. Elsewhere he remarks that the "*reformation* in Philosophy" he promotes requires not "any strength of *Imagination,* or exactness of *Method,* or depth of *Contemplation* . . . as a *sincere Hand,* and a faithful *Eye,* to examine, and to record, the things themselves as they appear. . . . No *Intelligence* [i.e., information] from Men of all Professions, and quarters of the World, is to be *slighted* . . . ."[57] What is sought is a disembedding of a common empirical measure of "things themselves" from the distracting diversity of customary prejudice. Thomas Sprat, the first historian of the Royal Society, gives this advocacy of the "common" a formulation that goes somewhat further than Hooke does in the direction of social leveling: "If we cannot have a sufficient Choice of those that are skill'd in all *Divine* and *Humam* Things (which was the ancient Definition of a Philosopher) it suffices, if many of them be plain, diligent, and laborious Observers: such, who though they bring not much Knowledge, yet bring their Hand, and their Eyes uncorrupted: such as have not their Brains infected by false Images . . . ."[58]

Not that Sprat disagrees with Boyle that the "free and unconfin'd" condition of gentlemen is important in ensuring the dominance of luciferous over lucriferous experiments. On the contrary, he too would "commit the Work to the Care of such Men, who, by the Freedom of their Education, the Plenty of their Estates, and the usual Generosity of noble Blood, may be well suppos'd to be most averse from such sordid Considerations." Like many others, however, Sprat was also sensitive to "the universal Complaints of those who direct the *Education* of great Men's Children . . . ," whose heads are filled "with difficult and *unintelligible Notions,* which neither afford them Pleasure in Learning, nor Profit in remembring them . . . . [T]heir present *Honour* cannot be maintain'd by intemperate *Pleasures,* or the gawdy Shews of Pomp, but by true *Labours* and *industrious Virtue.*" On the one hand, and in accord with the traditional habit of subsuming the question of epistemological capacity under the aegis of social hierarchy, gentility may plausibly be accorded the intellectual freedom of material independence. On the other hand, as the socializing influence of custom and education becomes increasingly evident during these decades, intellectual freedom comes to be understood as a function not just of a public and material but, more subtly and profoundly, of a private and cultural independence.[59]

Sprat's language recalls the celebrated Baconian "doctrine of Idols," which confronts the problem of interestedness by conceiving the experiential obstacles to secular understanding on analogy with the sinful obstacles to grace. Necessary for both conditions, Bacon argues, is as much the negative, and prior, identification and eradication of error as any positive acquisition of truth: "The Idols and false notions which are now in possession of the human understanding, and have taken deep root therein, not only so beset men's minds that truth can hardly find entrance, but even after entrance obtained, they will again in the very instauration of the sciences meet and trouble us, unless men being forewarned of the danger fortify themselves as far as may be against their assaults." By this way of thinking, the pedagogy of domestication may be a counterpedagogy that reverses the damage done by traditional education. Understanding requires that we forsake what we have learned: "the several classes of

Idols, and their equipage . . . , must be renounced and put away with a fixed and solid determination, and the understanding thoroughly freed and cleansed; the entrance into the kingdom of man, founded on the sciences, being not much other than the entrance into the kingdom of heaven, whereinto none may enter except as a little child." Bacon's nascent critique of acculturation encourages the radical notion, reflected in Sprat and then in Smollett, that "elite" social status may corrupt and infect, rather than solicit and improve, the understanding, an idea that invites a language of epistemological leveling whose social implications are obscure but suggestive: "But the course I propose for the discovery of sciences is such as leaves but little to the acuteness and strength of wits, but places all wits and understandings nearly on a level."[60]

Like that of the common reader, the commonness of the common observer implies both generality and sociopolitical lowness. Not that disinterestedness necessarily demands, for Bacon, the tabula rasa of the uneducated commoner; but a "freed" understanding is a matter of strictly epistemological, not material or traditionally cultural, independence. This is also the implication of the deist John Toland, who contrasts the tortuous exegesis of the Old Testament to the parabolic teachings of Jesus: "The Poor, who are not suppos'd to understand Philosophical Systems, soon apprehended the Difference between the plain convincing Instructions of Christ, and the intricate ineffectual Declamations of the Scribes. . . . No wonder then if the disinterested common sort, and the more ingenuous among the Rulers, did reject these nonsensical Superstitions . . . . [W]hy may not the Vulgar likewise be Judges of the true Sense of Things . . . ?"[61] In this way, disinterested methods of reading nature may be felt to converge with those of reading scripture at the level of the common.

So the goal of disinterested observation was approached through the ideal of an individual observer of leveled understanding, an ideal that promised access to a species of the common whose generality might also be felt to imply a certain "vulgarity." But the inquiry into how to attain scientific disinterestedness also pursued a different strategy, taking the interestedness of the individual and the group as a given but aiming to countervail such bias through a method of collective generalization. Given the power of socialization, disinterestedness— freedom from the corruptions of private interest—may best be achieved by consulting not a single man cleansed of obfuscating interest, nor one select body of men, but a socially and occupationally diversified spectrum of people. "The whole Care" of the Royal Society, writes Sprat, "is not to be trusted to *single* Men; not to a *Company* all of *one Mind* . . . ." By an

> equal Balance of all Professions, there will be no one Particular of them overweigh the other, or make the *Oracle* only speak of their *private* Sense . . . . It is natural to all Ranks of Men, to have some one Darling, upon which their Care is chiefly fix'd. . . .

So much is to be found in Men of all Conditions, of that which is call'd *Pedantry* in Scholars; which is nothing else but an obstinate Addiction to the Forms of some private Life, and not regarding general Things enough. This Freedom therefore, which [the Royal Society] use, in embracing all Assistance, is most advantageous to them; which is the more remarkable, in that they diligently search out, and join to them, all extraordinary Men, though but of ordinary Trades. . . . All Places and Corners are now busie and warm about this Work: and we find many noble Rarities to be every Day given in not only by the Hands of learned and profess'd Philosophers: but from the Shops of *Mechanicks;* from the Voyages of *Merchants;* from the Ploughs of *Husbandmen;* from the Sports, the Fish-ponds, the Parks, the Gardens of *Gentlemen* . . . .[62]

This line of thought bears some relation to another of Sprat's suggestions, which is to attain disinterestedness not by an estrangement of the individual from what is customary to himself or herself but by familiarizing that individual with a broad range of what is customary in the experience of other people: "I know it may be here suggested; that they, who busie themselves much abroad about learning the Judgments of others, cannot be unprejudic'd in what they think. But it is not the *knowing,* but the peremptory *Addiction* to other *Tenets,* that sowers and perverts the *Understanding.* Nay, to go farther; that Man, who is thoroughly acquainted with all Sorts of *Opinions,* is very much more unlikely, to adhere obstinately to any one particular, then he whose Head is only fill'd with Thoughts, that are all of one Colour." Even as he offers this insight, in fact, Sprat seems to modulate from a psychological to a sociological register, reconceiving disinterestedness as a matter not of rendering the individual capacious but of achieving capaciousness by collecting individuals together. "It being now so requisite," he continues, "to premise this general Collection, it could not be better made, than by the *joint Labours* of the whole [Royal] *Society.* . . . [T]he Task being shar'd amongst so great a Number, will become not much more than a Business of *Delight.*"[63]

In these pages Sprat formulates a fundamental principle of scientific method —the idea of experimental repeatability—that improves upon the haphazard and uncontrolled process by which the varied interests of many people's experiences are collected together so as to cancel each other out. Experiment formalizes this generalization of experience by methodically limiting—"controlling for"—the capacity of varied interests ("variables") to color what thereby may be understood as a constant of nature. But the experiment is not complete unless it is repeatable under circumstances that indefinitely generalize this process of methodical control. As Hooke puts it, "In the making of all kind of Observations or Experiments there ought to be a huge deal of Circumspection, to take notice of every the least perceivable Circumstance that seems to be significant either in the promoting or hindering, or any ways influencing the Effect. And to this end, . . . it were very desirable that both Observations and Experiments should be divers times repeated, and that at several Seasons and with several Circumstances, both of the Mind and of Persons, Time, Place, Instruments and Materials . . . ." At this level of generality the qualitative assessment of disinterestedness, whether by social status or by other signs, has been demoted to the condition of a variable that must be controlled for if the invariable constant of the natural is to be separated out with success.

Experiment begins in the local, particular, and "private" realm of common sense impressions, and it ends in the quantitative abstraction of the general and the common that is embodied in the "public" laws of nature. These are the "ways by which Nature may be trac'd, by which we may be able to find out the material Efficient and Instrumental Causes of divers Effects, not too far removed beyond the reach of our Senses, and which do not very much differ from such Effects as are more material and obvious to our Senses." The removal Hooke describes is one from the actual particularity of sense impressions to the virtuality of generalization about causes and effects, a removal that leaves behind the variable "interests" that militate against generalization.[64] In two ways this amounts to a methodological formalization of the process by which the ethico-epistemological core of disinterestedness is separated out from its peripheral involvement in the social. First, Hooke's essay in scientific method is analogous to that separation out: the removal of causation beyond the reach of the senses is like the removal of disinterestedness beyond the reach of social status. Second and more fundamentally, Hooke's method exemplifies the results of that removal: namely, the process of generalization that is entailed in working within the virtual realm of the ethico-epistemological.

Hooke's views on scientific generalizations about causation soon would be sophisticated by David Hume's "maxim, that no objects have any discoverable connexion together, and that all the inferences, which we can draw from one to another, are founded merely on our experience of their constant and regular conjunction . . . ." Our raw material can be nothing but experience: not external objects but our internal sense impressions of them. The more constant and regular our experience of their conjunction, the more probably can we generalize to a connection between the objects themselves. Hume's method distills the control for variables into the quintessence of quantitative aggregation. "Interest" is coextensive with irreducible singleness. The disinterestedness of knowledge is a mathematical proposition that depends in equal parts on the indefinite multiplication of instances and the generalizing abstraction from their singular particularity.[65]

As we have seen, the early writers on scientific method experimented with several ways of achieving disinterestedness: at the level of the individual, by consulting persons who were independent of material need or of occlusive education; at the level of the collective, by abstracting from the actual sense impressions of individuals through collaboration, repetition, and publication so as to establish a realm of probability from which actual variables have been extracted.[66] We begin where all empirically grounded method must begin, with the actual particularity of the senses, which is transmuted into a generalization of actual experience that is probable (not despite the fact that but) because the virtual has replaced the realm of the actual. The virtual realm of scientific probability, constituted through a movement from particulars to generals, therefore may be compared to the virtual product of another method by which contemporaries reconceived the relation between "private" particulars and "public" generals, the nation-state. In concert with the public sphere, contract theory is itself a strategy to institutionalize disinterestedness.

Civic Disinterestedness

Boyle's belief that the obviation of luciferous labors ensured the disinterestedness of his luciferous activities is the rough equivalent of the civic humanist conviction that the disinterestedness required for political authority is a function of material independence. By the same token, the idea that scientific disinterestedness is, on the contrary, a quantitative achievement whereby multiple private interests are reciprocally cancelled out or controlled for bears an evident relation to seventeenth- and eighteenth-century efforts to theorize a political system of government of, by, and for "the people." Sprat's appreciation of the man "who is thoroughly acquainted with all sorts of opinions" recalls the category "public opinion," whose long gestation covers the period of my major concern in this study. So on the one hand, the modern discourse of civic disinterestedness looks back to debates in the 1640s over whether it is quality or quantity, the social status or the number of their signers, that authenticates public petitions to the king and Parliament.[67] On the other hand, it looks ahead to American postrevolutionary debates in the 1780s over how best to guard against the destructive forces of faction in a democratic system of government.

Faction pits "a common impulse of passion, or of interest," against a greater common value, "the rights of other citizens" or "the permanent and aggregate interests of the community." James Madison famously prefers "republican representation" to "pure democracy" as a method of "controling the effects of faction" for reasons that bear some analogy to the way scientific method controls for the constants of natural law. First, by delegating government "to a small number of citizens elected by the rest," republican representation is able "to refine and enlarge the public views, by passing them through the medium of a chosen body of citizens" who, partly for patriotic and partly for structural reasons, are able to generalize those views beyond "temporary or partial considerations" better than the people themselves are likely able to do. Second, "the greater number" of citizens presupposed by a representative system takes in "a greater variety of parties and interests," which makes it "less probable" that a faction will be empowered by "a common motive" sufficiently to harm the whole and more likely that the representative body will be able to resist such empowerment.[68]

The manifest differences between scientific and political method nonetheless admit an analogy at the abstract level of their common effort to adjudicate between particulars and generals. Madison figures this process, "the delegation of the government," as a kind of sieve that winnows out the "temporary or partial" so that public opinion is both "refined" and "enlarged," more fully purified of strictly private interest and hence abstracted to a more fully public generality. The refining sieve of republican representation may be compared to the experimental process by which the "temporary or partial considerations" that obtain in any single and local experience—the variables that Hooke calls the "several Circumstances, both of the Mind and of Persons, Time, Place, Instruments and Materials"—are "not too far removed" or, in Madison's metaphor, winnowed away both by the control mechanism that structures the formal experiment itself and by the winnowing effect of experimental repetition. Like scientific method, republican method is premised on a strict separation out of the principle of representativeness from that of social hierarchy. Both the particular elements with which the processes begin (individual voting citizens and individual experiences) and their respective filtering mechanisms (the elected citizens and the experiment) play their roles irrespective of status considerations—a fact that reminds us of how far this republican model of disinterested government is from the "republicanism" of the civic humanist tradition, for which epistemological disinterestedness, instead of being mediated by this filtering process, is an immediate function of social status, that is, land ownership.

This gesture at evoking the modern meaning of civic disinterestedness requires, however, that we also acknowledge the force of a different strand of political thought contemporary with the *Federalist* papers. This is the modern theory of conservatism, articulated most fervently by Edmund Burke in his *Reflections on the Revolution in France* (1790). It would be hard to imagine two texts more antithetical in their civic principles than these, and I do not intend to claim an affinity between Madison and Burke on how the authority of political judgment may be ensured by a method of quantifying abstraction. Indeed,

PLATE 1. George Morland, *The Fruits of Early Industry and Economy,* 1789. Philadelphia Museum of Art/Art Resource, NY.

PLATE 2. Pierre-Antoine Baudouin, *La Lecture,* c. 1760. Gouache on paper. Musée des Arts décoratifs, Paris.

PLATE 3. Pieter Aertsen, *Christ in the House of Martha and Mary,* 1553. Museum Boymans van Beuningen, Rotterdam, The Netherlands. Kavaler/Art Resource, NY.

PLATE 4. Joachim Bueckelaer, *Kitchen Piece with Christ in the House of Martha and Mary,* 1565. Photo: The National Museum of Fine Arts, Stockholm, Sweden.

PLATE 5. Vincenzo Campi, *Christ in the House of Martha and Mary Magdalen,* late sixteenth century. Galleria Estense, Modena, Italy. Alinari / Art Resource, NY.

PLATE 6. (*Facing page*) Jacopo Robusti Tintoretto, *Christ with Mary and Martha,* c. 1567. Alte Pinakothek, Munich, Germany. Scala / Art Resource, NY.

PLATE 7. Diego Rodriguez Velázquez, *Christ in the House of Martha and Mary,* 1618. National Gallery, London, Great Britain. Erich Lessing/Art Resource, NY.

PLATE 9. Joseph Highmore, *Pamela Fainting,* 1743–1744. Oil on canvas. No. 3 of twelve scenes from Samuel Richardson's *Pamela* (1740). National Gallery of Victoria, Melbourne, Australia. Felton Bequest, 1921.

PLATE 8. Johannes Vermeer, *Christ in the House of Mary and Martha,* c. 1655. National Galleries of Scotland, Edinburgh.

PLATE 10. Joseph Highmore, *Pamela Preparing to Go Home,* 1743–1744. Oil on canvas. No. 4 of twelve scenes from Samuel Richardson's *Pamela* (1740). National Gallery of Victoria, Melbourne, Australia. Felton Bequest, 1921.

PLATE 11. Joseph Highmore, *Pamela in the Bedroom with Mrs. Jewkes and Mr. B.*, 1743–1744. No. 7 of twelve scenes from Samuel Richardson's *Pamela* (1740). Tate Gallery, London, Great Britain / Art Resource, NY.

THE SAILORS FLEET WEDDING ENTERTAINMENT.

Jack, rich in Prizes, now the Knot is ty'd, |The Bawd, now from her Daughter's charge | The Lawyer grins, and Peg with wanton Glance|The Skimmington Observe. Mirth to provoke
Sits pleas'd by her he thinks his maiden Bride, |relie'd|With pleasure smiles to think how he's deceiv'd;|Seems much delighted by Tom's antic Dance.|Sam points the Horns, with many a bawdy Joke.
But tho' a modest Look by Molly's shown, |Experienc'd in the Trade, and void of Shame,|Kit kisses Kate, vows she shall be his Wife;|For Spouse's Cloaths the Baily's Crew are seen
She only longs for what she oft has known.|To her the Man in Crape imparts his Flame.|While Cat & Dog resemble nuptial Strife.|And change, oh sad Mishap! the jovial Scene."

Publish'd according to ... Act of Parliament, November y 10.17.47. Price 6d. by M. Cooper   *Nov. 1747*

PLATE 12. *The Sailors Fleet Wedding Entertainment*, 1747. © Copyright The Trustees of The British Museum.

Text at bottom reads:

"Jack, rich in Prizes, now the Knot is ty'd,
Sits pleas'd by her he thinks his maiden Bride,
But tho' a modest Look by Molly's shown,
She only longs for what she oft has known.

The Bawd, now from her Daughter's charge relie'd
With pleasure smiles to think how he's deceiv'd;
Experienc'd in the Trade, and void of Shame,
To her the Man in Crape imparts his Flame.

The Lawyer grins, and Peg with wanton Glance
Seems much delighted by Tom's antic Dance.
[K]it kisses Kate, vows she shall be his Wife;
While Cat & Dog resemble nuptial Strife.

The Skimmington Observe. Mirth to provoke
Sam points the Horns, with many a bawdy Joke.
For Spouse's Cloaths the Baily's Crew are seen
And change, oh sad Mishap! the jovial Scene."

PLATE 13. William Hogarth, *The Marriage Contract*. Plate 1 of *Marriage-à-la-Mode*, 1745, in William Hogarth, *Hogarth: The Complete Engravings*, ed. Joseph Burke and Colin Caldwell (New York: Abrams, 1968). Princeton University Library.

Text on pages reads, left to right: family tree scroll, "William Duke of Normandy"; page under window, "Plan of the New Building of the Right Honble . . . ."; page in hand of standing man, "Mortgage"; page to right of table, "Marriage Settelm^t of The R^t Honble, Lord Viscount Squanderfield."

The IDLE 'PRENTICE Executed at Tyburn.

PLATE 14. William Hogarth, *The Idle 'Prentice Executed at Tyburn*. Plate 11 of *Industry and Idleness*, 1747, in William Hogarth, *Hogarth: The Complete Engravings*, ed. Joseph Burke and Colin Caldwell (New York: Abrams, 1968). Princeton University Library.

Text reads: center, "The last Dying Speech and Confession of Tho. Idle"; bottom, "Proverbs Chap: I. Verss. 27, 28. When fear cometh as desolation, and their destruction cometh as a Whirlwind; when distress cometh upon them; Then they shall call upon God, but he will not answer."

Speech bubbles, *top, left to right:*

"With all my Heart, Liberty & Property and no Excise."

"Come, Neighbour, here's wishing the King better Counsellors."

"The Devil it is! then all is over with us. What new Tax will they find out next?"

"Dam me, Will the Citizens are finely humour'd. this Paper says the Excise Bill is signed[.] Here has been foul Play I doubt.

"by my Soul, Sir, I cannot do it for fear of offending his Lairdship, for ye ken he's a Man [?] a' muckle Authority."

"Mr. Macdonald, will you undertake to write me a smart Remonstrance against Arbitrary Power?

"Ah Farmer Russet, is this the boasted Liberty of Englishmen?"

"Wounds! could n't he suffer our Apples & Pears to go Scot-free?"

"Surely this Peace was a Master-piece."

"How long d'ye think it will last?"

"Why till our Enemies are in a Condition to declare War again."

"The French only want to recover Breath"

"We all know who's at the Bottom of it."

"I was told it had no Bottom at all."

Speech bubbles, *bottom, left to right:*

"Sing Tantararara [?]. Tax all." [paper in ballad-singer's hand:] "Tax all. A New Ballad"

"All will have an End at last."

"Nothing like striking while the Iron's hot."

"Then e'en let the Block have [?] it's Chip again."

"this Stu——t is a Chip o' the old Block."

"I should like it well enough if I [?] and well paid for it as some Folks."

"Don't you think you & I might be offered [a place?] at C——, Jack [.] We are us'd to do dirty Work."

"So the Scotchman is resolv'd to go through Stitch with it ."

"I am going to shave the Deputy of our Ward and there I shall hear all about it."

"My Lord has given us Authority to search for the Losses [?]."

[paper in squatting man's hand:] "Magna Charta"

Text at bottom reads:

"Britania's Sons of all Conditions . . . .
Amazing! now are Politicions
Bards, Parsons, Lawyers and Physicians
E'en low Mechanicks too pretend . . . .
To rail at what they cannot mend ————

The Taylors from their Stitching cease
To damn my Lord Excise & P————
"Bute"
The Cobler too will quit his Stall . . . .
And o'er his Pint the Scotchmen mawl

The fellow too that trims your Lamps,
Will freely talk of Fleets and Camps,
Stand up for Pitt & England's Right
And hope their Tricks will come to Light

Thus boldly cavil and Debate . . . . . .
On matters that concern the St————
And for their Plea this Proverb bring . . .
A Cat may look upon a King. ————"

March 1763

Plate 15. *The Politicians,* 1763, in John Brewer, *The Common People and Politics, 1750–1790s: The English Satirical Print, 1600–1832* (Cambridge: Chadwyck-Healey, 1986). Princeton University Library.

PLATE 16. *Greenwich Hill or Holyday Gambols*, 1750, in John Brewer, *The Common People and Politics, 1750–1790s: The English Satirical Print, 1600–1832* (Cambridge: Chadwyck-Healey, 1986). Princeton University Library.

Text at bottom reads:
"Ye sweetscented Sirs who are sick of the Sport
And the stale languid follies of Ballroom or Court;
For a Change leave the Mall & to Greenwich resort,

There heighten'd with Rapture, which never can pall,
You'l own the Delights of Assembly and Ball,
Are as dull as Yourselves—& just nothing at all."

The Beaux Disaster.

PLATE 17. *The Beaux Disaster, 1747*, in John Brewer, *The Common People and Politics, 1750–1790s: The English Satirical Print, 1600–1832* (Cambridge: Chadwyck-Healey, 1986). Princeton University Library.

Text at bottom reads:

"Ye Smarts whose Merit lies in Dress,
Take warning by a Beaux Distress.
Whose Pigmy Size, & ill-turn'd Rage
Ventur'd with Butchers to engage.

But they unus'd Affronts to brook
Have hung poor Fribble on a Hook.
While foul Disgrace, expos'd in Air,
The Butchers shout, & Ladies stare,

Satyr so strong, ye Fops, must strike you
How can you think ye Fair will like you,
Women of Sense, in Men despise
The Anticks they in Monkeys prize."

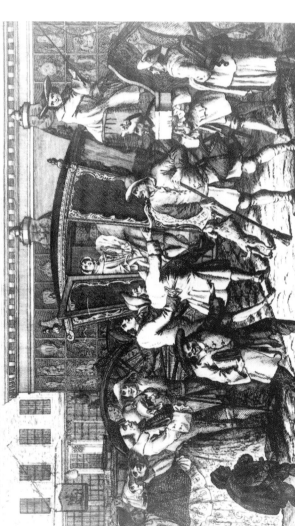

STAND COACHMAN, OR THE HAUGHTY LADY WELL FITTED.

PLATE 18. *Stand Coachman, or the Haughty Lady Well Fitted,* 1750, in John Brewer, *The Common People and Politics, 1750–1790s: The English Satirical Print, 1600–1832* (Cambridge: Chadwyck-Healey, 1986). Princeton University Library.

Text at bottom reads:

"At a Toy Shop hard by Charing Cross t'other Day,
A Lady's Coach stood quite across the Foot Way:
A Person did civily th' Coachman intreat
To pull up, and let him pass over the Street;

But being that Favour most rudely denied,
By John on the Box, and his Lady beside;
The Gentleman finding that Words would not do,
He op'd the Coach Doors, and genteely went thro':

The Mobb seeing this, they all laugh'd at the Whim,
And swore 'twas as free for the rest, as for him.
So hoisting each other; just like a Ship's Crew
Bespatter'd and dirty, began to march thro':

The Lady much ruffled, soon alter'd her Tone,
And call'd to her Coachman in haste to move on:
'Tis hop'd the fair Ladies from hence will beware
How they stop a Free Passage with such haughty Air.

for Burke the quantifications of "sophisters, economists, and calculators" are not the solution but the problem.[69] The relevance of Burke's conservatism to the modern idea of disinterestedness lies not in its analytic account of whence the authority of political judgment derives but in its affective account of what makes political judgment authoritative, hence effective, in the minds and hearts of its subjects. Despite himself a man of Enlightenment, Burke argues that the legitimacy of the French monarchy lies in its existence, not its essence. The sanctity of traditional authority is not an intrinsic virtue but a historical product, and its political efficacy depends on our having sufficient distance from it to value it with the disinterestedness of self-conscious detachment. We believe in aristocracy despite our epistemological detachment from it precisely because of our historical detachment from it. "You see, Sir, that in this enlightened age I am bold enough to confess that we are generally men of untaught feelings, that, instead of casting away our old prejudices, we cherish them to a very considerable degree, and, to take more shame to ourselves, we cherish them because they are prejudices; and the longer they have lasted and the more generally they have prevailed, the more we cherish them" (98–99). Quantification, bankrupt as a representative method of transforming particulars into generals, comes into its own as the principle of historical duration.

Between the aristocratic reverence for tradition as such and the conservative reverence for tradition's affective and social utility lies the yawning gulf of explicitation. Burke's task, to praise the tacit from a position of explicitness, is also to praise the principles of positive liberty with the belated knowledge that what had seemed only distinct are really separable and separate powers. To accomplish this task he has recourse to the notional category of feudalism and its outmoded oxymora: "Never, never more shall we behold that generous loyalty to rank and sex, that proud submission, that dignified obedience, that subordination of the heart which kept alive, even in servitude itself, the spirit of an exalted freedom. . . . It was this which, without confounding ranks, had produced a noble equality and handed it down through all the gradations of social life. It was this . . . which mitigated kings into companions and raised private men to be fellows with kings." If the penetrability of public by private life is by the cold light of modernity an illusion, it is a pleasing illusion: "But now all is to be changed. All the pleasing illusions which had made power gentle and obedience liberal, which harmonized the different shades of life, and which, by a bland assimilation, incorporated into politics the sentiments which beautify and soften private society, are to be dissolved by this new conquering empire of light and reason. All the decent drapery of life is to be rudely torn off" (86–87).

Burke's elegiac tone is belied, however, by the sense that there is a middle way between the unavailable disinterestedness of nobility and royalty and the

spurious disinterestedness of the political quantifiers. By this middle way, pragmatic social efficacy becomes available to belief at the moment it loses its tacit
social efficacy. In fact, our historical distance from the antiquated politics of the
ancien régime gives them an imaginative power over us that fuels their pragmatic efficacy. We cherish tradition disinterestedly, not because of its essential
value but because it gives us pleasure to do so, and in our affective response to
its pleasing illusions lies the ground of its social utility: not the immediate coherence of cultural embeddedness but the mediated pleasure of self-conscious
reenactment. Modern conservative thought is grounded in this skeptical posture, which involves a commitment to the disinterestedness proclaimed and
perpetuated in the perdurability of civic institutions. It is opposed to the liberal
commitment to disinterestedness achieved through the sieving of actual particulars by political representation (or, as in the case of Burke the American sym-
pathizer, through the generalization of public opinion).[70]

Contemptuous of the notion that traditional social hierarchy bears any but
an "accidental" relation to virtue, Johnson told Boswell that "I would no more
deprive a nobleman of his respect, than of his money. I consider myself as acting a part in the great system of society. . . . I would behave to a nobleman as I
should expect he would behave to me, were I a nobleman and he Sam. Johnson. . . . Sir, there would be a perpetual struggle for precedence, were there no
fixed invariable rules for the distinction of rank, which creates no jealousy, as it
is allowed to be accidental."[71] Johnson's notion of "acting a part in the great system of society" is echoed by Burke's claim that "[t]here ought to be a system of
manners in every nation which a well-informed mind would be disposed to relish. To make us love our country, our country ought to be lovely" (88). That we
live in a virtual "society" and "nation" that can be abstracted from our daily
lives sufficiently to be experienced as "systematic" is part and parcel of the language both men use to signify the detached disinterestedness with which our
social participation is intelligible to us.

As we will see, Burke's and Johnson's ideas of civic disinterestedness gained
coherence through their writings on aesthetic disinterestedness. But the coextension of the two concepts can also be seen in the language of those who wrote
against conservatism. William Godwin, as skeptical as Burke about the justice
of the representative sieve, nonetheless has a few good words to say about it in
refuting Burke's plea for "salutary prejudices." "The system of political imposture divides men into two classes," one of which understands of the other that
"[w]e ought to gain over their judgments through the medium of their
senses . . . ." Godwin is indignant that the latter should be deprived of "that
chance for additional wisdom, which would result, from a greater number of
minds being employed in the enquiry, and from the disinterested and impartial

spirit that might be expected to accompany it." But he draws comfort from the insight that explicitation is a sign of weakness, not strength, using the (pre-)Coleridgean language of aesthetic belief to characterize and dismiss the strategy of Burkean conservatism: "But, at the same time that he tells us, we should cherish the mistake as mistake, and the prejudice as prejudice, he is himself lifting the veil, and destroying his own system. . . . [T]he moment they begin to write books, to persuade us that we ought to be willing to be deceived, it may well be suspected that their system is upon the decline."[72]

Aesthetic Disinterestedness

Received wisdom on the emergence of the aesthetic in eighteenth-century Britain would have us begin our investigation with the third Earl of Shaftesbury. According to this line of thought, aesthetic disinterestedness first comes into view inseparable from the hypothesis of sociopolitical disinterestedness through absolute land ownership and that the uncoupling of this association begins only at the end of the eighteenth century. It seems to me that this claim is vulnerable on several counts. The argument that a civic humanist version of aesthetic theory dominated eighteenth-century discourse is belied by the single, commanding example of William Hogarth.[73] And we can hear something of Hogarth's perspective in Johnson's grudging praise of Thomas Gray's *Elegy Written in a Country Church-Yard* (1751), in which the criterion of the common-as-general may be felt to suggest also that of the common-as-commoner: "In the character of his *Elegy* I rejoice to concur with the common reader; for by the common sense of readers uncorrupted with literary prejudices, after all the refinements of subtilty and the dogmatism of learning, must be finally decided all claim to poetical honours."[74] Johnson's praise finds thematic confirmation in Gray's imagination of

> Some village-Hampden that with dauntless breast
> The little tyrant of his fields withstood . . . .[75]

What in another context might be a pointedly inadequate domestication of public politics into the littleness of rural life is here self-sufficiently significant. The pathos of the unfulfilled commoner, set off by the antithetical signifiers Hampden and Charles I, is the fully meaningful signified that evokes our common sympathy. The young Edmund Burke provides a sentiment similar to Johnson's and reminiscent, in its populist empiricism, of his views on public opinion around the time of the American Revolution: "The true standard of the arts is in every man's power; and an easy observation of the most common, sometimes of the meanest things in nature, will give the truest lights, where the greatest sagacity and industry that slights such observation, must leave us in the dark . . . ."[76] But if we seek an alternative to the civic humanist belief that disinterestedness presupposes social rank and financial independence, we need not wait for the middle decades of the century. Indeed, the writings of Shaftesbury himself provide that alternative.

There is no doubt that the diffuse but pervasive social ambience of the *Characteristicks* is that of a polite gentility. For Shaftesbury, however, the paradigm case of disinterestedness is not social but religious. "I cou'd be almost tempted to think," he writes, "that the true Reason why some of the most heroick Virtues have so little notice taken of 'em in our holy Religion, is, because there wou'd have been no room left for *Disinterestedness,* had they been entitled to a share of that infinite Reward, which Providence has by Revelation assign'd to other Dutys."[77] "*Disinterestedness*" consists in "the *Love of God or Virtue* for GOD or VIRTUE's sake" (2:272; 2:153). Interested virtue, motivated by the anticipation of reward, is in these terms no virtue at all. However, the paradigm case of religion does admit a social application. The "Vulgar," Shaftesbury knows, thus apply "the Notion of a future Reward or Punishment to their immediate Behaviour in Society," but "the liberal, polish'd, and refin'd part of Mankind" have a more disinterested standard of behavior (3:177; 3:108). Again, "the mere Vulgar of Mankind often stand in need of such a rectifying Object as *the Gallows* before their Eyes. Yet I have no belief, that any Man of a liberal Education, or common Honesty, ever needed to have recourse to this Idea . . . ." What is the sociopolitical significance of Shaftesbury's distinction between the "vulgar" and the "refined" and "liberal"? The distinction is ostensibly epistemological and ethical. It is the difference between (on the one hand) a spurious "philosophy," for which the criterion of value is "the Number and Exquisiteness of *the pleasing Sensations,*" whose sacrifice is resisted "except on the condition of being repaid in the same Coin, and with good Interest into the bargain"; and (on the other) that authentic philosophy in which "WORTH and MERIT are substantial, and no way variable by *Fancy* or *Will;* and . . . HONOUR is as much it-self, when acting *by it-self,* and *unseen,* as when *seen,* and applauded by all the World." And although "the vulgar" may sound to us instinct with sociopolitical aspersion, that implication is frustrated by the fact that Shaftesbury comfortably refers to the self-interested vulgar here as "gentlemen" (1:123–26; 1:77–79).

Elsewhere a sociopolitical resonance might appear more readily available. "A Man of thorow *Good-Breeding,*" Shaftesbury writes, "whatever else he be, is incapable of doing a rude or brutal Action. He never *deliberates* in this case, or considers of the matter by prudential Rules of Self-Interest and Advantage." As we have seen, for Shaftesbury true philosophy is disinterested contemplation and action. "To *philosophize,*" he continues, "in a just Signification, is but to carry *Good-breeding* a step higher. For the Accomplishment of Breeding is, To learn whatever is *decent* in Company, or *beautiful* in Arts . . ." (1:129, 3:161; 1:81, 3:99). Here the crucial term is "good breeding." But Shaftesbury is notably silent when it comes to claiming either social rank or financial independence as the hallmark of good breeding, and the term itself is ambiguous in contemporary usage. Although allusive to the intrinsic, natural advantage of "good birth," good breeding suggests something closer to good nurture or upbringing, which is implied in Shaftesbury's description of it as what might be "learned." Indeed, the susceptibility of the term to entail whatever current fashion requires is the topic of one of Addison's humorous efforts to distinguish between town and country life (see *Spectator*, no. 119, 17 July 1711).

At the very least we need to recognize that "good breeding," like "sensibility" and the metaphorical category "taste," is one of those quasi-somatic terms that were fashioned by eighteenth-century writers to replace, within a culture increasingly skeptical about the literal and bodily innateness of nobility but increasingly taken with arguments from the natural, the honor that traditionally distinguished those of noble birth.[78] For Shaftesbury, disinterestedness consists in the ethical conviction that not only virtue but also truth and beauty are their own reward. And for this reason they may be less available in association with material ownership than they are in its absence. "[T]aken with the Beauty of the Ocean" and seeking "how to command it," the Doge of Venice goes "in Nuptial Ceremony . . . to wed the *Gulf*" so as to call it "properly *my own.*" Yet in that action he "has less *Possession* than the poor *Shepherd,* who from a hanging Rock, or Point of some high Promontory, stretch'd at his ease, forgets his feeding flock, while he admires *her Beauty.*" Shaftesbury points the moral by remarking how "absurd" would be he who, viewing a beautiful landscape, "shou'd for the *Enjoyment* of the Prospect, require the *Property* or *Possession* of the Land" (2:396–97; 2:221–22). As in the developing discourse of scientific disinterestedness, Shaftesbury's effort to detach the abstract integrity of disinterested virtue from expectations of sensible reward or punishment is closely related to his effort to disembed the virtual criterion of the ethico-epistemological from what might appear to be its actual sociopolitical ground.

In this (artificially constructed) development of Shaftesbury's idea of disinterestedness we have moved from a negative to a positive view of its implicit psychology. That is, we have moved from an understanding of disinterestedness as lacking any expectation of tangible reward to a view of it as entailing an intangible sort of "reward" whose value is predicated on the fact of its intangibility. The "in-itself-ness" of virtue, truth, and beauty is tied up with their insensibility, their virtuality. We may recall Shaftesbury's portrait of the spurious "philosopher" as one who "rates life by the number and exquisiteness of the pleasing sensations." Of course, it would be easy enough to construe the enjoyment of a beautiful prospect as involving a "pleasing sensation." But Shaftesbury's language suggests that he aims to distinguish more finely between pleasures that are sensible and those that are not. Elsewhere in *Characteristicks* he remarks that one who engages in mathematical discovery, although "merely of speculative Truths," nonetheless "receives a Pleasure and Delight superior to that of Sense." Where the "scientific" writers in natural philosophy stress the language of quantitative generalization, Shaftesbury tends to prefer the language of a purifying abstraction. These are related ways of articulating how disinterestedness is broadly understood to require a movement "upward," a "removal" (in Hooke's words) from the actual particularity of the realm of the senses and of the sociopolitical. I have argued that in the traditional, hermeneutic and pedagogic, motives for formal domestication we can see at this time a complex but fundamental adaptation to the idea that the domesticating strategy "downward" may be not only a means to an "upward" end but also an end in itself. These ostensibly opposed movements were in fact complementary. The aim of achieving disinterestedness encouraged contemporaries to discover in the realm of the private an unprecedented source of authority. What traditionally had been restricted to the public province of hierarchical sociopolitical status coalesced into view, within the private realm, as an ethico-epistemological transformation of itself. The movement of formal domestication downward to "the common" was increasingly understood to facilitate thereby an upward movement of generalization or abstraction to "the common" that suffused the realm of the private with a distinctively if metaphorically "public" species of importance.

Shaftesbury's discrimination between sensible and speculative pleasures may well remind us of Addison's argument in the first of his *Spectator* papers on the pleasures of the imagination. Indeed, Shaftesbury and Addison and Steele, whose publications on aesthetic disinterestedness are exactly contemporary, are in broad agreement on these matters. One major difference, however, is that Shaftesbury's appreciation for the epistemological upward movement from the sensible to the speculative entirely bypasses the middle ground of the imagination, which in his view is too sullied by the senses to engineer a dependable refinement of them. Consequently the negotiation of disinterestedness in Shaftesbury has no mediator, and we are left with the sense that despite his empiricism, the middle ground that is his destination is a suburb of the speculative, and that a Neoplatonic domestication of what lies beyond us is a far more effective way to reach it than is a refinement of what lies below. However, by focusing his attention on the faculty of the imagination, Addison developed the inquiry in a way that would be crucial to the clarification of aesthetic disinterestedness. Sensible pleasures are nothing if not interested, and Addison, like Shaftesbury in his Lockean empiricism, also treats all knowledge as rooted in sense experience. But more in the manner of the empiricist Hooke, Addison is concerned to define the nature of a kind of knowledge that is removed but "not too far removed beyond the reach of our Senses"—detached from but also rooted in the irreducible ground of sense experience and its constitutive interestedness.

And yet it is not Hooke's "scientific" (nor, as in Shaftesbury's example, mathematical) knowledge but imaginative knowledge that concerns Addison. He opens his discussion with a three-part division—traditional enough in itself except perhaps in distinguishing the faculties according to their distinct sorts of "pleasure"—that establishes the imagination as a mediatory faculty: "[t]he Pleasures of the Imagination, taken in their full Extent, are not so gross as those of Sense, nor so refined as those of the Understanding."79 Addison's faculty of the understanding, we might infer, roughly corresponds to the realm of knowledge that Hooke seeks to attain, hence Addison's goal, the imagination, is even less "far removed beyond" the reach of the senses than Hooke's. Addison's project does, however, require a discrimination between those senses that are less and those that are more conducive to the pleasures of the imagination. And on this score Addison prefers sight to feeling (in part) because of its mediatory qualities, because it "converses with its Objects at the greatest Distance . . . ." Hence he begins his discourse by affirming that it is most of all the sense of vision that "furnishes the Imagination with its Ideas . . . ." But feeling is to sight as the unmediated senses themselves are to the imagination. The unrelieved rudeness of sensible things is conceived as an extreme condition whose "gross" and potentially "Criminal" pleasures require the moderating distance of the imagination. Addison's language here has a suggestively moral inflection that recalls, once more, Shaftesbury's principled correlation of the good and the beautiful and that requires us to see the emergent alternative to a sociopolitically embedded notion of disinterestedness not simply in epistemological but also in ethical terms: "A Man should endeavour . . . to make the Sphere of his innocent Pleasures as wide as possible, that he may retire into them with Safety, and find in them such a Satisfaction as a wise Man would not blush to take. Of this Nature are those of the Imagination . . ." (*Spectator*, no. 411, 21 June 1712).80

But a detachment from the interested grossness of sense impressions is only one half of the process in which the imagination participates. At the other extreme of the senses is the utterly "refined" pleasure of the understanding, refined in the sense of being the result of a process that comprehensively filters out the gross and interested pleasures of sense impressions. The pleasures of the understanding, Addison acknowledges, are finally "more preferable," but "those of the Imagination are as great and as transporting as the other. . . . Besides, the Pleasures of the Imagination have this Advantage, above those of the Understanding, that they are more obvious, and more easie to be acquired." They do not "require such a Bent of Thought," such an extremity of "Labour" and "Difficulty," as is needed to experience the pleasures of the understanding (*Spectator,* no. 411, 21 June 1712). Addison's language here cannot help remind us of the hermeneutic and pedagogic motives that drive the engine of formal domestication. And if his account of how the imagination refines the senses is finally more innovative, Addison pays due attention to the way the images produced by the imagination also are derived through domesticating the understanding. This is a process of using figuration to undo, to some degree, the hyperrefinement by which the understanding has transformed some of its sensible raw materials into pure ideation. Thus in the last paper on the pleasures of the imagination Addison allies the pleasures of the imagination with the use of "Similitudes, Metaphors, and Allegories": "By these Allusions a Truth in the Understanding is as it were reflected by the Imagination; we are able to see something like Colour and Shape in a Notion, and to discover a Scheme of Thoughts traced out upon Matter. And here the Mind receives a great deal of Satisfaction, and has two of its Faculties gratified at the same time, while the Fancy is busy in copying after the Understanding, and transcribing Ideas out of the Intellectual World into the Material" (*Spectator,* no. 421, 3 July 1712). As works of the imagination refine the senses, making them also cognitively accessible, so they domesticate the understanding, making it figuratively available to our materiality. Indeed, these are not two analogous processes but two aspects of the same process.

The "aesthetic" quality of Mr. Spectator's spectatorship, hence its relevance to the aesthetic pleasures of the imagination, seems clear enough.[81] As one among several examples Addison provides, the "contemplative Tradesman" would seem to qualify as a member of "the Fraternity of Spectators who live in the World without having any thing to do in it," not because he is without social interestedness, but for his capacity to assume an epistemological distance from it. The genial oxymoron of the contemplative tradesman emphasizes a disinterestedness that is not the product of material independence but rather stands out in relief against a background of interestedness, and in a later number Steele recurs to the topic while characterizing spectatorship, in a Shaftesburyan fashion, as "a Delight known only to those who are turned for Speculation: Nay they who enjoy it, must value things only as they are the Objects of Speculation, without drawing any worldly Advantage to themselves from them . . . ." Having made this preface, Mr. Spectator proceeds to narrate the consequences of a recent "Resolution to rove by Boat and Coach for the next

Four and twenty Hours, till the many different Objects I must needs meet with should tire my Imagination . . . ." Near the end of this ramble he finds himself at the Royal Exchange, playing the role of the contemplative, virtual tradesman amid a bustle of actual ones: "As other Men in the Crowds about me were pleased with their Hopes and Bargains, I found my Account in observing them, in Attention to their several Interests. I, indeed, look'd upon my self as the richest Man that walk'd the *Exchange* that Day; for my Benevolence made me share the Gains of every Bargain that was made" (*Spectator*, no. 10, 12 Mar. 1711; no. 454, 11 Aug. 1712).[82]

Steele's apparent play on the visual, the meditative, and the financial senses of the word "speculation" both recalls and expands Shaftesbury's discrimination between sensible and speculative pleasures.[83] The paper reinforces our general impression that at issue in the idea of aesthetic disinterestedness is the delicate differential between the immediacy of material interest and the capacity to be liberated from it, one personified most acutely not by the freehold gentleman but by the contemplative tradesman. At the same time, Mr. Spectator's recourse to the metaphorical language of "accounts" and "riches" specifies this differential between the active and the contemplative as a movement between the literal and the figurative, the actual and the virtual. Worldly activity—whether landed, trading, or monied—plays a complicated role here, negatively defining disinterested activity by being what it is not in the very special sense of providing the literal model for a negation achieved through figuration. The relative disinterestedness of the aesthetic is detached from sensible experience as the metaphorical is detached from the literal, both escaping and sustaining its connection to the interestedness of sense impressions. But we have just heard how figuration—"Similitudes, Metaphors, and Allegories"—is also the technique by which "a Truth in the Understanding is as it were reflected by the Imagination," which "transcrib[es] Ideas out of the Intellectual World into the Material." Avoiding the overabstraction of the refined, preceptual understanding, the imagination also avoids the underabstraction of the literal and the real by fashioning an exemplary metaphor that figures both but is reducible to neither. Refining the senses in the direction of the virtual, the imagination also domesticates the understanding in the direction of the actual, and they meet on the "common" ground of what is both mean and general.

It should be clear by now that in its frequent association with aesthetic categories like "taste," the eighteenth-century language of "refinement" refers not to sociopolitical status—the gentility that is a precondition for having refined taste—but to the ethico-epistemological process whereby judgment is purified of its sensible grossness through virtualization (thus for Madison "refinement," although a sociopolitical process, is a means by which sociopolitical partiality may be neutralized).[84] This is not a simple task; indeed, it requires a kind of practice—extensive reading and conversation, the comparison of, and capacity to sympathize with, disparate productions—that is circumstantially more accessible to gentle than to common people.[85] But the difference between a categorical prerequisite and a facilitating factor is in this context crucial, and the meaning of refinement here may be substantiated by a famous passage in Addison that recalls one we have already considered in Shaftesbury. True, the passage might seem at first to confirm the special relationship between disinterestedness and gentility, since it explains how "[a] Man of a Polite Imagination, is let into a great many Pleasures that the Vulgar are not capable of receiving." However, Addison's differentiation between the "polite" and the "vulgar" seeks less to establish a social opposition between the "literally" gentle and the common than to accommodate an emergent, ethico-epistemological distinction between those select men of taste who command a polite imagination and the majority—not commoners but people of common capacity—who do not.

Addison's notion of the "polite imagination" recalls his treatment of "good breeding," and the discrimination is best seen in cultural, not social, terms. This quickly becomes clear when the difference between the "polite" and the "vulgar" is clarified as one between those who contemplate a landscape and those who own it (cf. Shaftesbury's description of the "vulgar" as "gentlemen"): "A Man of a Polite Imagination . . . meets with a secret Refreshment in a Description, and often feels a greater Satisfaction in the Prospect of Fields and Meadows, than another does in the Possession. It gives him, indeed, a kind of Property in every thing he sees, and makes the most rude uncultivated Parts of Nature administer to his Pleasures: So that he looks upon the World, as it were, in another Light, and discovers in it a Multitude of Charms, that conceal themselves from the generality of Mankind" (*Spectator*, no. 411, 21 June 1712). Again, the parallel with Shaftesbury's sentiments is close. The capacity for disinterestedness is signaled by the metaphorical nature of absolute "property," a kind of "possession" that improves upon the merely sensible grossness associated with the rude, uncultivated literality and interestedness of actually owning "real" estate. To put this another way, the polite exercise of the imagination marks the separation out of the "propriety" of appropriate behavior from the "propriety" entailed in appropriating things, which henceforth will have its own denomination, "property."[86]

Like elite education, material possession is cast in the light of an interested obstacle to disinterested "taste," whose metaphorical distance from the realm of sense impressions is quite as important as its metaphorical proximity to that realm. If anything, the "commonness" of being without freehold estate liberates one from the "generality of Mankind" to assume the uncommon status of the

"Man of a Polite Imagination." Addison's emphasis on secrecy and concealment in *Spectator*, no. 411, reminds us that this distinction between the general incapacity of mankind and the singular capacity of the few is also one between public and private pleasures. And if the capacity of disinterestedness is developed to stand in for the sovereign's coextension with the public interest (for his now-discredited freedom from private bias), there is some logic to its figuration as a "private" independence from "public" materiality and materialism. First explicit separation, then dialectical recapitulation. Once it has been separated out from the realm of the public, the realm of the private subdivides into two realms of private activity, absolute property ownership and the absolute imagination, which then are reconceived as, respectively, public and private preserves.[87]

Behind Shaftesbury's and Addison's peculiarly topographical figurations of aesthetic disinterestedness there lies a rich tradition of usage. In his remarkable virtualization of the country house poem, Thomas Randolph methodically internalizes the material elaborations and possessions of rural gentility. As his title proclaims, Randolph's poem is a defense of poetry whose defiance of a substantive domesticity draws its strength from the poetic resources of formal domestication. And the poem draws to a close in a witty condemnation of the marriage market that gives new meaning to the *beatus ille* trope of solitary rural retirement.[88]

Although this is not Randolph's emphasis, the resonant image of the garden has played an important role in the argument of aesthetic disinterestedness, its densely significant virtuality overdetermined by centuries of classical and Christian usage. Set beside Randolph's, Andrew Marvell's famous poem in praise of pastoral *otium* coalesces as an early contribution to the discourse on the pleasures of the imagination and their disinterestedness:

> Meanwhile the mind, from pleasures less,
> Withdraws into its happiness:
> . . . .
> Annihilating all that's made
> To a green thought in a green shade.[89]

In his observations on dramatic technique John Dryden both coincides with Marvell and anticipates Addison: "The words of a good writer, which describe it lively, will make a deeper impression of belief in us than all the actor can persuade us to, when he seems to fall dead before us; as a poet in the description of a beautiful garden, or a meadow, will please our imagination more than the place itself can please our sight."[90]

Charles Cotton's erotic parody of the topographical survey genre ("the present state of . . .") imagines the female body as a beautiful rural countryside of which fine "Landskips" can be painted—although here the virtual picture is inferior to the reality and scarcely innocent since its value lies in serving as a kind of Aretinian stimulus to masturbation: "[T]he whole Country of Betty-land shews you a very fair prospect, which is yet the more delightful the more naked it lies; it makes the finest Landskips in the world, if they be taken at the full Extent; and many of your rich husbandmen will never be without them hanging at their bed sides, especially they that have no Farms of their own, meerly that they may seem to enjoy what they have not: some there are that so really believe they possess the substance by the sight of the shadow, that they fall to till and manure the very Picture with that strength of Imagination, that it is a hundred pounds to a penny they do not spoil it with their Instruments of Agriculture . . . ."[91] Viewing the landscape from the summit of Grongar Hill, John Dyer moralizes the prospect that lies before him:

> O may I with myself agree,
> And never covet what I see . . . .[92]

And by the mid-eighteenth century Edward Young can use the trope of the imaginary garden to domesticate pastoral domesticity with programmatic confidence. So long as it is subordinated to "the sacred interests of Virtue, and the real Service of mankind," writing offers "a sweet Refuge" that "opens a back-door out of the Bustle of this busy, and idle world, into a delicious Garden of Moral and Intellectual fruits and flowers . . . . With what a Gust do we retire to our disinterested, and immortal Friends in our Closet . . . ? How independent of the world is he, who can daily find new Acquaintance, that at once entertain, and improve him, in the little World, the minute but fruitful Creation, of his own mind?"[93] Young's sweet mental refuge is a metaphorical space whose concreteness bespeaks both the exemplary accommodation of abstracted and overly disinterested writing and the refining sublimation of actual and overly interested sensations.

As we have seen, the conditions under which the imagination produces its greatest pleasure, according to Addison, are established (at least in part) by a refining process that distances aesthetic response from the empirical ground of sense perception. In describing this process he moves methodically through three increasingly extreme stages of detachment. First, Addison designates the sense of sight as the most "delightful" of our senses because it "converses with its Objects at the greatest Distance . . . ." Second, he distinguishes between the "Primary" and the "Secondary" pleasures of the visual imagination: respectively, those "which proceed entirely from such Objects as are before our Eyes" and those "which flow from the Idea of Visible Objects, when the Objects are not actually before the Eye, but are called up into our Memories . . . ." Addison finds the latter, virtual pleasures to be "of a wider and more universal Nature than those it has, when joined with Sight" because of that "Action of the Mind, which *compares* the Ideas that arise from Words, with the Ideas that arise from the Objects themselves . . . ." Finally, of these virtual pleasures Addison favors those that "proceed from Ideas raised by *Words*" or "Description," which "runs yet further from the thing it represents than Painting" or the spectacular aspect of dramatic presentation (*Spectator*, no. 411, 21 June 1712; no. 418, 20 June 1712; no. 416, 28 June 1712). In fact, Addison's preference for verbal description over visual presentation is in this respect so strong that when he speaks of the pleasure of tragedy, he seems to have in mind not a viewing but a reading experience: "[I]t does not arise so properly from the Description of what is Terrible, as from the Reflection we make on our selves at the time of reading it" (*Spectator*, no. 418, 30 June 1712).

This striking progression toward the most detached—which is to say the most disinterested—conditions of imaginative experience implies that imaginative pleasure is so deeply embedded in sensible pleasure that several stages of separation out are required to permit its flowering "as such." What is achieved by these successive stages is a virtualization of the actual that is powerful enough to allow the reflexivity entailed both in comparing and in appreciating the difference between what we now experience through representation and what we usually experience in the actual presence of the object—a virtualization that most succeeds when we possess the extreme detachment provided by verbal description. This last point cannot fail to remind us of Shaftesbury's explicitation of the virtual and reflexive relationship between the public and the private through the relationship between the author and the reader.94 The detachment from the sensible object that is afforded by the experience of both reading and writing a "description" is one principal means by which the detachment of the reader from the author and, within the author, of one authorial "party" from another, becomes possible. In both respects, detachment entails the explicit separation out of categories that normally are tacitly conjoined, with the result that the subjects and formal procedure of knowing the object itself becomes available, along with those actual objects that thereby are known, as a concrete and virtual object of knowledge. This detachment is the mechanism by which disinterested judgment is achieved. But it is an immanent process, not a transcendent product, and it is achieved through the ongoing, dialectical interplay between actual, or private, and virtual, or public, experience. It is therefore not surprising that the practical working out of what we mean by imaginative or aesthetic response took place most thoroughly with respect to printed narrative and what came to be called its "realism." However, aesthetic response received its first theorization with respect to drama, as, it should be noted, an ethico-epistemological inquiry independent of questions of sociopolitical status. The following discussion can do no more than highlight the most significant features of this crucial episode in dramatic theory.

Aesthetic Response

Hooke, we recall, formulated his view of scientific disinterestedness by recourse to the principle of experimental repeatability, which enabled him to guard against interested bias by controlling for variations in "Persons, Time, Place, Instruments and Materials." In a related fashion, the debate over the pseudo-Aristotelian unities of time and place was the earliest context in which the aesthetic frame of mind was discovered to involve the sort of detachment from the actual particularity of the conditions of performance that is achieved experimentally through repetition and virtual witnessing. The standard rationale for the necessity of preserving the two unities of time and place was credibility. In the most extreme version of this argument, the audience would not credit the action on stage either if there was a disparity between the amount of time taken to represent the play and the amount of time represented within it or if the scope of the space represented in the play departed from the physical dimensions of the stage itself. Skepticism about the two unities in England is at least as old as Philip Sidney: "[T]he poet, he nothing affirms, and therefore never lieth." For "[w]hat child is there, that, coming to a play, and seeing *Thebes* written in great letters upon an old door, doth believe that it is Thebes?"[95]

Sidney's skepticism entails the tacit insight that the particularity we desire and expect of dramatic representation is concrete, not actual, and that the empirical ground of our pleasure lies somewhere between the literal reality available through our sense impressions and the conceptual abstraction accessible to our understandings. But if the insight is tacit, the Renaissance debate over the two unities helped precipitate a separation out of those elements, actual and concrete particularity, on whose separability depended the explicit recognition of the difference between empirical and aesthetic judgment. Our most enduring image of the consequences of being unable to separate empirical from aesthetic judgment, the creation of Sidney's contemporary Miguel de Cervantes, is that of Don Quixote passionately wading into Master Pedro's puppet theater with sword unsheathed (fig. 7.1). The madness of the Don, his confounding of the real and the unreal, is exemplary of an age for which the authority of empirical factuality has gained such stature that the authority of the virtual will have to be theorized into explicitness as the experience neither of madness nor of actuality but of the aesthetic.

When Dryden entered the debate seventy years after Sidney wrote, his approach to these questions was colored by concurrent debates over the episte-

FIG. 7.1. *Don Quixote and Master Pedro's Puppet Theater,* copperplate designed by F. Hayman, in *The History and Adventures of the Renowned Don Quixote. Translated from the Spanish of Miguel Cervantes Saavedra. . . . by T[obias] Smollett* (1755). Department of Rare Books and Special Collections, Princeton University Library.

mology of scientific experiment.[96] To some contemporaries, the only authoritative "experiment" was experience; and for them the artificiality of the experimental setting and its specialized instruments rendered experimentation vulnerable to the charge of being unnatural and therefore inconclusive. Dryden's Crites lodged a related complaint about the "experimental" nature of Shakespeare's history plays: "[I]f you consider the historical plays of Shakespeare, they are rather so many chronicles of kings, or the business many times of thirty or forty years, cramped into a representation of two hours and an half, which is not to imitate or paint nature, but rather to draw her in miniature, to take her in little; to look upon her through the wrong end of a perspective [i.e., a telescope], and receive her images not only much less, but infinitely more imperfect than the life: this, instead of making a play delightful, renders it ridiculous." Crites indicts the representational compression of place and time of a formal domestication whose pedagogic aim is frustrated by the reductive distortion it entails. However, the resulting problem of "unnaturalness" in the dramatic presentation is one not, as in the scientific experiment, of inconclusiveness but of ridiculousness, of the incredibility of what is presented. "For what is more ridiculous," adds Lisideius, "than to represent an army with a drum and five men behind it . . . [?]" In this way, the problem expands from that of time and place to that of dramatic representation as such, and Neander soon replies on this broader plane: "[W]hy may not our imagination as well suffer itself to be deluded with the probability of it, as with any other thing in the play? For my part, I can with as great ease persuade myself that the blows which are struck are given in earnest, as I can that they who strike them are kings or princes, or those persons which they represent."[97]

Addison takes up the Aristotelian line of thought where Dryden's Neander leaves off:

> The two leading Passions which the more serious Parts of Poetry endeavour to stir up in us, are Terror and Pity. . . . But how comes it to pass, that we should take delight in being terrified or dejected by a Description, when we find so much Uneasiness in the Fear or Grief which we receive from any other Occasion? . . . When we look on such hideous Objects, we are not a little pleased to think we are in no Danger of them. We consider them at the same time, as Dreadful and Harmless; so that the more frightful Appearance they make, the greater is the Pleasure we receive from the Sense of our own Safety. . . .
>
> This is, however, such a kind of Pleasure as we are not capable of receiving, when we see a Person actually lying under the Tortures that we meet with in a Description; because, in this Case, the Object presses too close upon our Senses, and bears so hard upon us, that it does not give us time or leisure to reflect on our selves. (*Spectator*, no. 418, 30 June 1712)

If Dryden expands the discussion from time and place to dramatic representation, Addison employs his earlier distinction between the three kinds of pleasure to expand the argument yet further so as to encompass all products of the imagination.

When Samuel Johnson took up the problem of the two unities in the preface to his edition of Shakespeare's works, he remarked that "[t]he necessity of observing the unities of time and place arises from the supposed necessity of making the drama credible." But it "is false, that any representation is mistaken for reality; that any dramatick fable in its materiality was ever credible, or, for a single moment, was ever credited. . . . Delusion, if delusion be admitted, has no certain limitation . . . . The delight of tragedy proceeds from our consciousness of fiction; if we thought murders and treasons real, they would please no more. Imitations produce pain or pleasure, not because they are mistaken for realities, but because they bring realities to mind."⁹⁸ "A play read," Johnson observes, "affects the mind like a play acted. It is therefore evident, that the action is not supposed to be real, and it follows that between the acts a longer or shorter time may be allowed to pass, and that no more account of space or duration is to be taken by the auditor of a drama, than by the reader of a narrative, before whom may pass in an hour the life of a hero, or the revolutions of an empire."⁹⁹ Although twentieth-century criticism has commonly seen the early modern doctrine of the two unities to express a (misguided) devotion to ancient precept, its devotion is more evidently to the distinctly modern precepts of naive empiricism and to the literalism that is also clear in the narrative claim to historicity. What unites these positions, both of which are fleetingly but vigorously asserted during this period, is their common subsumption of Addison's pleasures of the imagination under the pleasures of the senses. The demands we make of aesthetic belief, they claim, are the same as those we make of empirical belief.

In an earlier chapter I remarked on Henry Fielding's role in separating out libel from satire, and thereby actual from concrete particularity, in his articulation of a doctrine of narrative realism.¹⁰⁰ Although these are not the dominant terms in which the doctrine of realism gets formulated, Fielding (also a dramatist) makes his case in terms of the empirical protocols of time and place. In *Joseph Andrews,* we recall, Fielding aims to describe "not Men, but Manners; not an Individual, but a Species." He is therefore a "Biographer" rather than either a "Topographer" or a "Chorographer," historians of place or time who are scrupulous as to the spatial or temporal factuality of their narratives, "[b]ut as to the Actions and Characters of Men, their Writings are not quite so authentic . . . . Now with us Biographers the Case is different, the Facts we deliver may be relied on, tho' we often mistake the Age and Country wherein they happened . . . ." As his use of the term "fact" suggests, Fielding insists that his narrative is as much a "history" as are topography and chorography: "for whereas the latter [are] confined to a particular Period of Time, and to a particular Nation; the former is a History of the World in general . . . ." Fielding's "general" factuality, not limited to the "particular" details of time and place, is an instance of concrete particularity. And this distinguishes it not only from the actual particularity of the other sorts of historians but also from "Romances," which "without any Assistance from Nature or History, record Persons who never were, or will be, and Facts which never did nor possibly can happen . . . ." The particularity of Fielding's narrative is virtual; that is, it mediates between the ground of the actual and the idealisms of romance (a negative counterpart of Addison's "understanding") and occupies its own realm of "factuality."[101] As in the works of other contemporary writers on biography, Fielding's "biography" has the particularity and privacy of the individual life divorced from the temporal and spatial registers by which we measure the actuality of public life. But in his usage biography also has the capacity to generalize about human character beyond the temporal and spatial confines of actual particularity, and it thereby lays claim to being a species of public knowledge.

Aesthetic Judgment

In separating out the pleasures of the understanding from those of the imagination the debates on dramatic theory are engaged in an experimental division of knowledge whose most fundamental form is that of the early modern division between the sciences and the arts.[102] The ostensible effect of the quarrel of the ancients and moderns was to rationalize and reinforce the chronological division between antiquity and modernity that the quarrel takes as its hypothesis. This effect was achieved, however, by means of another, unlooked-for division of knowledge whose "productivity" would be difficult to question. Certain kinds of ancient knowledge, it was found, were vulnerable to criticism based on modern evidence that had been unavailable to the ancients and that was demonstrably superior to theirs, whereas other kinds of ancient knowledge, although subject to criticism, were invulnerable to the sorts of evidence by which a definitive judgment of truth or value might be made. "Is it not evident in these last hundred years," says Dryden's Crites, "(when the study of philosophy has been the business of all the virtuosi in Christendom), that almost a new nature has been revealed to us? that more errors of the school have been detected, more useful experiments in philosophy have been made, more noble secrets in optics, medicine, anatomy, astronomy discovered, than in all those credulous and doting ages from Aristotle to us? so true it is, that nothing spreads more fast than science, when rightly and generally cultivated."[103] This could not be said of "the arts" because the standards of achievement in the sciences are quantitative, whereas those operative in the arts are qualitative. Although these are not his terms, Johnson begins his preface by acknowledging this fundamental difference and the difficulty it poses for those who would assess value in the arts and by proposing a solution to this difficulty. In the present context Johnson's discourse in the preface helps us see that the emergence of the modern category of the aesthetic is a hopeful solution to the problem that had been raised by the quarrel of the ancients and moderns, a response to the apparent lack of a standard of judgment in the arts. That a merely "qualitative" standard of judgment should now be seen as deficient testifies both to the extraordinary authority that had accrued to empirical epistemology during the past century and to the resulting sophistication of thought about what quantitative measure allowed one to do.

"To works," Johnson writes, "of which the excellence is not absolute and definite, but gradual and comparative; to works not raised upon principles demonstrative and scientifick, but appealing wholly to observation and experience, no other test can be applied than length of duration and continuance of esteem. What mankind have long possessed they have often examined and compared, and if they persist to value the possession, it is because frequent comparisons have confirmed opinion in its favour." Johnson seeks what might be called the closest equivalent, for works of "art," to the standard of judgment available for works of "science," and he discovers it in the quantifiability of which both empirical and aesthetic experience is susceptible. "As among the works of nature no man can properly call a river deep or a mountain high, without the knowledge of many mountains and many rivers; so in the productions of genius, nothing can be stiled excellent till it has been compared with other works of the same kind."[104] But the comparison of qualitatively different objects cannot in itself yield a standard of aesthetic value because differences in quality are by definition incomparable. What is needed is a mechanism of quantification, a standard by which qualitatively different works can be rendered comparable, and Johnson finds this standard in the test of time, which he borrows from Horace (see *Epistles* 2.1.39) but applies in a strikingly modern way. Shakespeare

> has long outlived his century, the term commonly fixed as the test of literary merit. Whatever advantages he might once derive from personal allusions, local customs, or temporary opinions, have for many years been lost . . . . The effects of favour and competition are at an end; the tradition of his friendships and his enmities has perished; his works support no opinion with arguments, nor supply any faction with invectives; they can neither indulge vanity nor gratify malignity, but are read without any other reason than the desire of pleasure, and are therefore praised only as pleasure is obtained; yet, thus unassisted by interest or passion, they have past through

variations of taste and changes of manners, and, as they devolved from one generation to another, have received new honours at every transmission.[105]

In Johnson's analysis, the test of time enables judgments of aesthetic value because it entails a generalizing abstraction similar to that by which standards of
disinterestedness in both the arts and the sciences are met. In Hooke's scientific
method, the repetition of experiments disembeds the constants of positive
knowledge from the "several Circumstances, both of the Mind and of Persons,
Time, Place, Instruments and Materials." In Madison's civic method, "controlling the effects of faction"—the people's "variety of parties and interests," their
"temporary or partial" concerns—requires that the republic "refine and enlarge
the public views, by passing them through the medium of a chosen body of citizens . . . ."[106] In Fielding's "biography" the actual particularity of qualitatively
different things is generalized and transformed into the concrete particularity of
a representative type by winnowing out the "facts" of time and place from the
"facts" of action and character. Johnson extends this principle from its use in
defining the aesthetic nature of the belief we invest in fictional representations
to its use in judging the aesthetic value of such representations. We judge
Shakespeare to be good because the winnowing effect of sheer temporality—by
which the winds of time gradually scatter to oblivion the particular "advantages" of the "personal," the "local," and the "temporary," the effects of "opinion," "faction," "interest," and "passion"—leaves behind no other motive for
viewing or reading his plays than the general "desire of pleasure" and no outcome of that motive but the general experience of "pleasure" as such: Addison's
"pleasures of the imagination." Johnson hereby anticipates Burke's quantification of time. Historicity, in its sheer contingency the very criterion of particularity and difference, is in its duration also the means by which particularity
may be generalized and difference rendered similar. As in his own treatment of
"biography," Johnson here argues that it is through the common-as-particular
that we arrive at the common-as-general, "considered apart from adventitious
and separable decorations and disguises" and therefore "common to human
kind."[107]

Johnson also anticipates William Wordsworth's defining act of romantic poetic theory. *Lyrical Ballads* (1800, 1802) was published, he writes, "as an experiment, which, I hoped, might be of some use to ascertain, how far, by fitting to
metrical arrangement a selection of the real language of men in a state of vivid
sensation, that sort of pleasure and that quantity of pleasure may be imparted,
which a Poet may rationally endeavour to impart." For "all men feel an habitual
gratitude . . . for the objects which have long continued to please them: we not
only wish to be pleased, but to be pleased in that particular way in which we

have been accustomed to be pleased." Like Johnson, if not so explicitly, Wordsworth writes with the division of knowledge in mind. The *Lyrical Ballads* is an "experiment" whose aim is to produce "pleasure" as a determinate entity, known not only as to quality but also as to "quantity," known by the criterion of duration for the kind of object and the kind of process that produces it. Indeed, the "knowledge both of the Poet and the Man of science is pleasure . . . ," and Wordsworth begins his poetic experiment at the empirical level of sense impressions: "I have wished to keep the Reader in the company of flesh and blood . . . [and] I have at all times endeavoured to look steadily at my subject . . . ." He has chosen as his subject "incidents and situations from common life" represented "in a selection of language really used by men" in "[h]umble [the 1800 edition reads 'Low'] and rustic life . . . ." This is to speak of low, sensible things, "because, in that condition, the essential passions of the heart find a better soil," and "the manners of rural life germinate from those elementary feelings . . . ." Moreover, the life of rural commoners is likely to afford a common language "because, from their rank in society and the sameness and narrow circle of their intercourse, being less under the influence of social vanity, they convey their feelings and notions in simple and unelaborated expressions." Wordsworth describes the emergent capacity of aesthetic disinterestedness in terms that are familiar to us from his predecessors; and if he risks being accused of a "triviality and meanness, both of thought and language," he also believes in the abstract universality of this language, which, "arising out of repeated experience and regular feelings, is a more permanent, and a far more philosophical language, than that which is frequently substituted for it by Poets . . . ."[108]

In order to achieve these ends, however, the poet must be a master at achieving the effect of aesthetic distance and virtuality that he seeks to produce, as affect, in his readers. If he describes common incidents in "a selection of language really used by men," he also must "throw over them a certain colouring of imagination . . . ." The poet must have the "ability of conjuring up in himself passions which are indeed far from being the same as those produced by real events, yet . . . do more nearly resemble the passions produced by real events, than anything which, from the motions of their own minds merely, other men are accustomed to feel in themselves . . . ." Indeed, "it will be the wish of the Poet to bring his feelings near to those of the persons whose feelings he describes, nay, for short spaces of time, perhaps, to let himself slip into an entire delusion, and even confound and identify his own feelings with theirs . . . ." Like Hooke, however, who would assume toward his objects a generalizing perspective that is "not too far removed beyond the reach of our Senses," Wordsworth would have the poet select language that is effective in "removing what would otherwise be painful or disgusting in the passion . . . ," language that "will entirely separate the composition from the vulgarity and meanness of ordinary life . . . ." And he extends his temporal discourse ("for short spaces of time") to make clear the poet's need to maintain a detachment from the poetic object of study. For poetry "takes its origin from emotion recollected in tranquillity: the emotion is contemplated till, by a species of re-action, the tranquillity gradually disappears, and an emotion, kindred to that which was before the subject of contemplation, is gradually produced, and does itself actually exist in the mind." In fact, Wordsworth's famous defense of verse and meter is similarly couched in terms of the distance it allows readers from too immediate an experience of the real (in Addison's words, when "the Object presses too close upon our Senses"), and it reminds us of earlier arguments that theatrical artifice like the violation of the two unities, so far from impairing aesthetic response, is essential to its pleasure. For "from the tendency of metre to divest language, in a certain degree, of its reality, . . . there can be little doubt but that more pathetic situations and sentiments, that is, those which have a greater proportion of pain connected with them, may be endured in metrical composition, especially in rhyme, than in prose."[109]

Social Psychology and Political Economy

Wordsworth locates the special capacity for sympathetic identification in the figure of the poet, who is therefore the avatar of both aesthetic effect and aesthetic affect. But as we have already seen in the cases of scientific and civic disinterestedness, the epistemological dialectic between individual and general, sense and understanding, private and public that is the hallmark of the aesthetic is also the ambition of other systems of knowledge. Indeed, the idea of the "social imaginary" articulates the upward movement of winnowing refinement if not also, at least as currently formulated, the downward movement of formal domestication.[110] The most successful effort to elaborate, for social theory, a dialectic of "upward" and "downward" movements comparable to that put forward in the idea of the aesthetic is Adam Smith's *Theory of Moral Sentiments* (1759), which Smith called moral philosophy but we, capitalizing on the more highly ramified division of knowledge that divides us from the Enlightenment, might call social psychology. Smith's basic working part, like that of aesthetic theory, is the imagination. "As we have no immediate experience of what other men feel," he writes, "we can form no idea of the manner in which they are affected, but by conceiving what we ourselves should feel in the like situation. Though our brother is upon the rack, as long as we ourselves are at our ease, our senses will never inform us of what he suffers. They never did, and never can, carry us beyond our own person, and it is by the imagination only that we can form any conception of what are his sensations." Reflecting the influence of theatrical experience, Smith gives the name of "spectator" to he who thus identifies with another, and he calls that other whose feelings are imagined by the spectator the "person principally concerned." Smith's spectator is thus a generalization of Wordsworth's poet.[111]

In the theory of the aesthetic, imagination is, like understanding, a means by which we refine or distance ourselves from our own sense impressions. In Smith's theory of moral sentiments imagination is the means by which we overcome the distance between our own and others' sense impressions. All (empirical) knowledge presupposes a detachment of the knowing subject from the object of knowledge. The aim of imaginative sympathy is, by acknowledging and exploiting it, to defeat this detachment. The virtual reality of "society" is produced by imaginative acts of sympathy, which transform the actual particularity of others into the concrete particularity of others-as-ourselves, who thereby become susceptible to collective generalization. But in Smith's thinking the actual particularity of others also takes the place occupied, in the aesthetic, by the understanding, that alien land to which we have only difficult access. Accordingly Smith often figures this mental process as one of domestication, an imaginative act of the spectator's "bringing the case home to himself" that receives its most striking application in reference to our sympathy with the dead: "[W]hen we bring home in this manner his case to our own bosoms, we feel upon this, as upon many other occasions, an emotion which the person principally concerned is incapable of feeling, and which yet we feel by an illusive sympathy with him." In this way, Smith says, the dead "haunt" the minds of the living (10, 71). But if we understand the extreme example of sympathy with the dead as he intends us to, we must see that it is, as such, an uncanny experience of being haunted by another, an imaginative exercise in bringing home to our "private" selves a specter from a "public" realm beyond our own dimension of existence.

At this fundamental level sympathy is therefore an inescapable faculty of "man" the social animal. But sympathy can also be achieved well or badly. The ethical dimension of Smith's theory turns on the reciprocal efforts of the spectator and the person principally concerned to modulate their emotions—respectively, to raise and to "lower" the "violence" of their pitch—so as to approach each other, "for the harmony of society," halfway. Smith treats the ability to modulate the emotions in this fashion as constituting "two different sets of virtues": the sociable, feminine, "amiable virtues" of "humanity" and the self-governing, masculine "virtues of self-denial." These gendered virtues, Smith insists, stand in dialectical rather than antithetical relation to each other.[112] For "as nature teaches the spectators to assume the circumstances of the person principally concerned, so she teaches this last in some measure to assume those of the spectators." The reciprocity of sympathetic identification makes us all by turns both spectators and persons principally concerned (22, 23; see also 190–91). A theory of social harmony, Smith's treatise is therefore also a theory of individual or psychological harmony: the relationship between the spectator and the person principally concerned is, writ large, already familiar to us as the relationship between the upwardly refining "private" senses and the downwardly domesticating "public" understanding.

In fact, Smith's philosophy is fulfilled as moral only when the ethical spectator is required to internalize this social dialectic—to "humble the arrogance of his self-love" by looking upon himself as the person principally concerned. This is the route to both social harmony and self-knowledge: we know ourselves only as we sympathetically internalize the social other. Recalling the mode of self-estrangement that Hooke advocated for the disinterested study of the external world "not too far removed beyond the reach of our Senses," Smith writes that "[w]e can never survey our own sentiments and motives, we can never form any judgment concerning them; unless we remove ourselves, as it were, from our own natural station, and endeavour to view them as at a certain distance from us." Bring the natural man "into society, and he is immediately provided with the mirror which he wanted before. It is placed in the countenance and behaviour of those he lives with . . ." (83, 110). The conditions requisite for ethical privacy are established once "natural man" and his innate privation is situated in the publicness of social existence, for it then becomes possible sympathetically to internalize others as a kind of public version of one's private self. "This is the only looking-glass by which we can, in some measure, with the eyes of other people, scrutinize the propriety of our own conduct. . . . I divide myself, as it were, into two persons; and . . . I, the examiner and judge, represent a different character from that other I, the person whose conduct is examined into and judged of" (112, 113). Here Smith names these respectively public and private "characters" of the self by the terms "I" or the "spectator," and the "agent" or "person whom I properly call myself" (113). Elsewhere he associates this internalized spectator with the detachment of "a third person, who has no particular connexion with" either myself or my neighbor but "who judges with impartiality between us" (135; see also 191). Both usages, it is worth remarking, describe a dialectical and extraliterary process of internalizing the public view in terms that evoke the literary.[113]

In Smith's customary usage, the spectator who achieves sympathetic identification with the person principally concerned is variously "impartial" and "indifferent"—but not "disinterested," since Smith's premise is that we judge well of others not by escaping but by exploiting our ineluctable self-interestedness. Society coheres not from "generous and disinterested motives" (86) but because we project onto others an image of ourselves and introject within ourselves an image of the other. For Smith, the Golden Rule, "the great law of Christianity" (25), expresses the fundamental dialectic of self and society that his own theory seeks to sophisticate, and he describes "conscience" as a kind of "consciousness" that, internalizing the public function of the "social mirror" as a private version of public regard, seems to entail intention and yet achieves ends that bespeak a higher sort of agency (86–87, 134). "It is reason, principle, conscience, the inhabitant of the breast, the man within, the great judge and arbiter of our conduct[,] . . . [i]t is from him only that we learn the real littleness of ourselves . . ." (137). The most general "harmony of society" therefore is achieved by abstracting from the irreducible particularity of the self. Through the specularity of self-regard we discover "the man within" and, thereby, the virtual multiplicity of others, and by this measure we learn "the real littleness of ourselves."

Now if the microdialectic is an internalization of the macrodialectic, another name for the impartial spectator must be the imagination, that mental faculty that regulates, and in which are met, the respectively upward and downward movements of the spectator and the person principally concerned. But although the imagination is a—perhaps the—central player in Smith's moral philosophy, he does not deploy it, as Addison does, as a mediator between the senses[114] and the understanding, terms that have a minimal role to play in Smith's analysis. As an analytic category, Smith's imagination has been detached from its strict function in faculty psychology and become a free-floating principle of sympathy that names, both in society and in psychology, that image-making power that accommodates to each other high and low, outside and inside, public and private in all dimensions of human life. In other words, although Smith's dominant concern in the *Theory* is with social interaction, methodologically speaking he begins with individual psychology and its powers of imagination, which provides a model for developing a theory of social sympathy. Consequently Smith feels free to leave the categories of sense and understanding relatively undifferentiated from each other. Even when the model of social sympathy is reinternalized as a tripartite system of psychological relations, the difference we find in Addison between the imaginative, upward "refinement" of the crude senses and the imaginative, downward "domestication" of the rarefied understanding is of no importance to Smith. These are not substantively separate faculties but structurally separate selves. We can see this in the fact that Smith is content to describe not only the downward but also the upward activity as one of domestication (see 21), a process of "bringing home" that applies equally to spectator and person principally concerned because the only significant difference between them is also their sameness, the fact that each is an other to the other. Smith can write a treatise on social relations that borrows freely but loosely from faculty psychology because the separation out of psychology (from the bodily) and of its component faculties (from each other) is sufficiently advanced to permit the abstraction of the imaginative faculty as a psychological microfunction that can be applied to the macroanalysis of many psychologies—that is, to understanding social sympathy.

In this way, the study of more "public," social formations grows out of the study of a more "private" faculty psychology, categories which first can be divided from each other and then conflated as the discipline of social psychology. Something similar may be said of Smith's role in establishing the discipline of political economy.[115] The idea of conscience as the impartial spectator within helps mediate the gap between religious and secular apprehensions of a supraindividual, "public" systematicity in which the private will both does and does not participate. In *The Wealth of Nations* Smith uses the famous figure of the "invisible hand" to perform a comparable mediation between a traditional, providential notion of system that passes human understanding and its secular adumbration: "It is not from the benevolence of the butcher, the brewer, or the baker, that we expect our dinner, but from their regard to their own interest. We address ourselves, not to their humanity but to their self-love, and never talk to them of our own necessities but of their advantages" (bk. 1, chap. 2; 1:26–27). This microeconomic insight into the priority of self-love can be expressed, at the macroeconomic level, as a natural preference for domestic industry:

> [E]very individual endeavours to employ his capital as near home as he can, and consequently as much as he can in the support of domestick industry. . . . Every individual is continually exerting himself to find out that most advantageous employment for whatever capital he can command. It is his own advantage, indeed, and not that of the society, which he has in view. But the study of his own advantage naturally, or rather necessarily leads him to prefer that employment which is most advantageous to the society. . . . He generally, indeed, neither intends to promote the publick interest, nor knows how much he is promoting it. By preferring the support of domestick to that of foreign industry, he intends only his own security; and by directing that industry in such a manner as its produce may be of the greatest value, he intends only his own gain, and he is in this, as in many other cases, led by an invisible hand to promote an end which was no part of his intention. (Bk. 4, chap. 2; 1:454, 456)[116]

In Smith's analysis, social psychology and political economy are complementary methods of reconciling individual and society, particular and general, methods that demystify common sense from opposite directions. What appears to be sociable is grounded in self-limitation; what appears to be self-interested serves the social. The separation out of the particularity of the self from the generality of society is the precondition for discovering methods for their confla-

tion, methods that permit passage from the actual realm of qualitative difference, in which individuals participate as individuals, to the virtual realm of
quantitative comparability that defines their social existence. "Every faculty in
one man," Smith writes in *The Theory of Moral Sentiments,* "is the measure by
which he judges of the like faculty in another." As the spectators "are constantly
considering what they themselves would feel, if they actually were the sufferers,
so [the person principally concerned] is constantly led to imagine in what manner he would be affected if he was only one of the spectators of his own situation. As their sympathy makes them look at it, in some measure, with his eyes,
so his sympathy makes him look at it, in some measure, with theirs . . ." (19, 22).

The equivalent of sympathy in the economic system—that is, the mechanism of "measure" that translates qualitative difference into quantitative comparability—is the capacity of the market to turn objects of consumption and
use into objects of circulation and exchange, or commodities. The "real measure" of exchange value, "the real price of all commodities," is the "quantity of
labour which we exchange for what is supposed at the time to contain the value
of an equal quantity. . . . But though labour be the real measure of the exchangeable value of all commodities, it is not that by which their value is commonly estimated," a result that is achieved, "not by any accurate measure, but
by the higgling and bargaining of the market, according to that sort of rough
equality which, though not exact, is sufficient for carrying on the business of
common life" (bk. 1, chaps. 4–5; 1:46, 47–48, 49). Once translated into the generalizing measure of exchange, qualitatively incomparable use values become
quantitatively comparable and exchangeable. So the market adaptation of private consumables to public sharables (or commodities), of real to virtual value,
is the economic mechanism by which the adaptation of particular self-interests
to the general social interest is accomplished. It is in this sense that the market,
like sympathy, is the measure of disinterestedness. A century before Smith
wrote, a popular author put it in the following terms: "The market-price is generally the surest rule, for it is presumed to be more indifferent then the appetites of men."[117] In the system of political economy the market corresponds
to the sympathetic mechanism of social psychology by which private feelings
become susceptible to a process of imaginative identification.[118]

Aesthetic Value and Exchange Value

As it emerged in early modern debates in dramatic theory, what we have
learned to call the idea of the aesthetic might be seen as a prototype or working
model for adjusting qualitative difference to quantitative comparability that
was highly relevant to (what we have learned to call) scientific method, political
theory, social psychology, and political economy. Certainly the analysis of aes-

thetic experience offered contemporaries a compelling technique for negotiating the developing rift between individual and society, between the private and the public. On the one hand, the aesthetic became intelligible as a mode of belief grounded in the actual particularity of sense impressions but imaginatively freed of their empirical liabilities (in Addison's terms, their literal, material, and criminal grossness); on the other hand, the aesthetic offered a standard for judging the value of human products based on a multitude of individual responses but purified of all obfuscating admixtures (in Johnson's terms, their personal, local, and temporary advantages). That contemporaries knowingly connected the aesthetic to some of these other emergent practices is clear from the testimony of Alexander Pope.

Along with its more specific ambitions, *Peri Bathous,* Pope's parody of "Longinus's" ancient text, aims to shed light on the sublimation process by which immediate material experience is distilled in the alembic of the imagination. What is the nature of the relationship sublimation posits between the imagination and materiality?[119] We have already considered Swift's efforts to answer this question. According to his speaker, we recall, the multiplicity of human achievements may be reduced to the powerful influence of a single bodily mechanism.[120] Pope's speaker, a Scriblerian cousin of Swift's, acknowledges the force of this biologically grounded argument in his third chapter. But perhaps because his topic is more specific than Swift's—not all human achievements but poetry in particular—his search for material causes is correspondingly more focused, and it takes him in the direction of not bodily materialism but the politico-economic materialism of contemporary theatrical and literary production. Quantifying Horace's requirement that poetry be both *dulce et utile,* Pope's speaker suggests that "[i]f the Intent of all Poetry be to divert and instruct, certainly that Kind which diverts and instructs the greatest Number, is to be preferr'd" (391). An obvious example is the success of the popular theatrical entertainments of the day, evident in "the universal Applause daily given to the admirable Entertainments of *Harlequins* and *Magicians* on our Stage" (395).

Pope's emphasis on quantity bespeaks his well-known if ambivalent impatience with the growing authority of the public taste in cultural life—and so his speaker affirms that "[t]he Publick are better Judges of what is honourable, than private Men" (431).[121] In the present context, however, his emphasis also clarifies the adaptation of quality to quantity, of particular difference to general comparability, that is the hallmark of much early thinking about the aesthetic. If Swift points us toward the bodily theory of sublimation so familiar to us in the modern materialism of psychology, Pope turns that theory in a socioeconomic direction that grounds not only historical materialism but the social sciences in general. In both theories the determinant force in cultural development is mean, base, and homely, the lowest common denominator of human need and desire. Aesthetic refinement is the individual counterpart of this social sublimation process, whose ostensible exaltation of ideal achievement deeply affirms the foundational priority of matter.

Johnson's test of time, for example, whereby we judge poetic achievement according to how far pure "pleasure is obtained" from generations of consumers, is parodically illuminated by Pope's remark about "our wiser Authors," that "[t]heir true Design is *Profit* or *Gain;* in order to acquire which, 'tis necessary to procure Applause, by administring *Pleasure* to the Reader . . ." (391). Johnson's mechanism of quantification is the winnowing effect of temporality, "length of duration and continuance of esteem." Pope's is a more opportunistic project in spatial amplification: "1. IT is propos'd that the two *Theatres* [Drury Lane and Lincoln's Inn Fields] be incorporated into one Company; that the *Royal Academy of Musick* be added to them as an *Orchestra;* and that Mr. *Figg* with his Prize-fighters, and *Violante* with the Rope-dancers, be admitted in Partnership. 2. THAT a spacious Building be erected at the Publick Expence, capable of containing at least ten thousand Spectators, which is become absolutely necessary by the great addition of Children and Nurses to the Audience, since the new Entertainments." Five times the capacity of the current Drury Lane Theatre, Pope's project might be constructed on the site of Somerset House, or (obviating the need for new building) accommodated by Westminster Hall. The influence of political institutions on Pope's conception of how both actual and virtual generality might be derived from particularity is evident in part in the plan to provide seating in the theater for both houses of Parliament, the legal courts, and the aldermen of the City of London and in part in the plan for a "*Council of Six* to sit and deliberate on the Merits of *Plays.* The *Majority* shall determine the Dispute; and if it should happen that *three* and *three* should be of each Side, the President shall have a *casting Voice . . . .*" Seated "in some conspicuous Situation in the Theatre," the Council of Six "may give *Signs* (before settled and agreed upon) of Dislike or Approbation. In consequence of these Signs the whole Audience shall be requir'd to *clap* or *hiss,* that the Town may learn certainly when and how far they ought to be pleas'd" (437).

In these respects, Pope's account of poetic quantification through the collectivization of theatrical response would seem to draw upon, and to satirize, the corruptions of representative government. Perhaps the same may be said of chapter 15 of *Peri Bathous,* "*A Receipt to make an* Epic Poem," where Pope has recourse to the tradition of the secret recipe book to satirize the modern mechanization of poetic composition (84–87).[122] Elsewhere in the treatise, however, the quantifying methods of economic production are clearly his model:

It is therefore humbly offer'd, that all and every Individual of the *Bathos* do enter into a firm *Association,* and incorporate into *one Regular Body,* whereof every Member, even the meanest, will some way contribute to the Support of the whole; in like manner as the weakest Reeds when join'd in one Bundle, become infrangible. To which end our Art ought to be put upon the same foot with other Arts of this Age. The vast Improvement of modern Manufactures ariseth from their being divided into several Branches, and parcel'd out to several *Trades:* For instance, in *Clock-making,* one Artist makes the Balance, another the Spring, another the Crown-Wheels, a fourth the Case, and the principal Workman puts all together; To this Œconomy we owe the Perfection of our modern Watches; and doubtless we also might that of our modern Poetry and Rhetoric, were the several Parts branched out in the like manner.[123]

NOTHING is more evident than that divers Persons, no other way remarkable, have each a strong Disposition to the Formation of some particular Trope or Figure. . . . Now each man applying his whole Time and Genius upon his particular Figure, would doubtless attain to Perfection; and when each became incorporated and sworn into the Society, . . . a Poet or Orator would have no more to do, but to send to the particular Traders in each Kind . . . . I THEREFORE propose that there be contrived with all convenient Dispatch, at the publick Expence, a *Rhetorical Chest of Drawers,* consisting of three Stories, . . . and every Drawer shall again be sub-divided into Cells, resembling those of Cabinets for Rarities. . . . Every Composer shall soon be taught the Use of this Cabinet . . . . (428–29)

And so the productivity of the division of labor is directly yoked to the productivity of the division of knowledge with an ingenuity that only emphasizes the incommensurability whereby quantity is adequated to quality, scientific and technological achievement to literary and artistic achievement.[124] True, the separation out of aesthetic value from exchange value is qualitatively productive in that it allows us to see these two entities as qualitatively different (i.e., not simply greater and lesser versions of each other), hence more precisely conceivable "as such" rather than constituted by qualities that are coextensive aspects of the same entity. Moreover, the force of the division is to attribute to aesthetic value qualities that characterize it as (precisely) a criterion of qualitative value, over against the quantitative standards adjudicated by exchange value. But Pope's trenchancy addresses both his present and ours. On the one hand, his satire of the modern tendency to separate and then conflate draws on a number of early modern developments—the liberalization of trade guilds, the evolution of the book of secrets, the public utility of private cabinets of curiosities—that have commanded our attention in previous pages. On the other hand, Pope anticipates, with a prescience that now seems remarkable, not only political economy but its critique fifty years before the conflation of the political and the economic has even been accomplished. As critique, *Peri Bathous* adumbrates the affinity of the modern work of art and the commodity, between aesthetic value and exchange value, at a historical moment when the language of the aesthetic and of exchange, joint products of the ongoing effort to theorize the adjustment of actual particularity to concrete virtuality, have a great deal more in common than in contradiction.[125]

Posterity will be persuaded to see art and the commodity as antithetical, a separation out that, however productive, leaves something important behind on both sides of the division. What appears to get lost, already for Pope but definitively in the evolved form of the aesthetic so familiar in our own time, is precisely the sense of an adjustment, a continuous and dynamic oscillation between the actual and the virtual, the particular and the general, that defines the emergent relation between the private and the public during this period. What dominates the modern idea of the aesthetic is instead one pole of this dialectic, a (therefore) frozen sense of concrete virtuality as monolithic and self-subsistent, virtual yet somehow posited with an idealized objectivity that needs no subjective stimulus. Pope's satire freshens the minority but by now stale insight into the commodity fetishism of the literary work by reminding us that a generalizing depersonalization—of the author, of the reader/spectator, of the uniform quantity of pleasure "administered" to the consumer—is at the heart of the new publicness. What has disappeared is the reciprocal privatization of author and reader, the reflexive self-consciousness of self-creation, the unpredictability of a system whose actual and virtual components are in constant flux. I have suggested that the formulation of the modern aesthetic be seen as a reaction to and a compensation for the early modern division of the arts from the sciences, which determined one of these newly constituted bodies of knowledge to be defective by the very standards of empirical rationality that generated the division itself. The homology between the putatively antithetical values of literary aesthetics and economic exchange is undeniable and deeply suggestive for the genealogy of both categories. But the relation seems to me most powerfully explanatory when understood not even as a causal reciprocity but as one component of the yet larger historical phenomenon that is the subject of this study.[126]

Looking back on the early decades of the seventeenth century, we see a set of social practices whose outspoken dominance seems to express that culture's dedication to the principle of positive liberty: the absolute state, a mercantilist policy of economic protectionism, aristocratic ideology. The very visibility of these practices, however, the fact that they are explicitly theorized and widely publicized only at this time, suggests the alternative view that the principle of positive liberty is in crisis—a view that is buttressed by evidence of a growing fascination with doctrines of the social contract, the public sphere, commodity exchange, and (somewhat later) the aesthetics of sympathetic identification.

In the previous pages of this chapter we have reviewed some aspects of the development of the idea of disinterestedness in the seventeenth and eighteenth centuries. By this analysis, the contemporary understanding of the conditions required for disinterestedness might broadly be said to have shifted from a socioeconomic to an epistemological emphasis in a way that reflects the broad shift from a paradigm of positive to one of negative liberty. Of course, disinterestedness is nothing if not an epistemological phenomenon. But the insistence on the separation of the subject from the object of knowledge that is the cornerstone of empirical epistemology disembedded epistemology itself from its age-old lodgings in the philosophical substratum of tradition. As the tacit presumption that "disinterestedness" was the singular capacity of royal ontology was challenged on several fronts, its status *as* a strictly epistemological capacity became more evident. The challenge to aristocratic disinterestedness posed by the example of commoners (and to a lesser degree by women) was primarily motivated not by social animus but by the increasing recognition that "interestedness" is a function not simply of material dependence but more broadly of education, acculturation, experience.

The hermeneutic and pedagogic motives for domestication, so far from losing their traditional utility, were gradually weaned of their association with speaking to low, common people of low, sensible things and became available as techniques for producing a common knowledge—that is, knowledge independent of particular status, class, or gender association. The vulnerability of seeking disinterested judgment in the (inevitable) interestedness of particular social groups might be overcome, it was found, by methodically consulting and coordinating qualitatively distinct social groups. By extension, the achievement of disinterested knowledge might best be won through the quantitative method of collective generalization. But the hallmark of disinterestedness is the abstraction from interest, which is not a product—not the absence of interest, as in the model of positive liberty and its independent landholder—but a process: the generalization of a virtual collectivity of knowledge from the actual knowledge of interested individuals. Aesthetic experience offered contemporaries a compelling model of this process. However, by the time society, the nation-state, the market, and the realm of aesthetic experience had become established as virtual collective entities in the nineteenth century, only the latter realm fully retained its aura of the imaginary. Indeed, we might suppose that the apotheosis of literature and the arts as the repository of a now-codified aesthetic experience was a necessary complement to the institutionalization of those other realms as operationally empirical actualities. Modern culture paid a heavy price for this disciplinary polarization. On the one hand, over the course of the nineteenth century the coalescence of social, political, and economic inquiry under the aegis of the "social sciences" bespoke the ambition of attaining "positive" knowledge through a mediation between the senses and the understanding that would bypass altogether the mediatory powers of the imagination. On the other hand, the development of the aesthetic realm over this same period so favored one pole of the imagination over the other—virtual generality over actual particularity, textual reflexivity over contextual reflection—that it obscured the dependence of aesthetic response, judgment, and value on an active and continuous oscillation between these two poles. The "alienation effect" that Bertolt Brecht was obliged to theorize and practice in the twentieth century was understood, in the eighteenth century, to be built into the aesthetic itself.

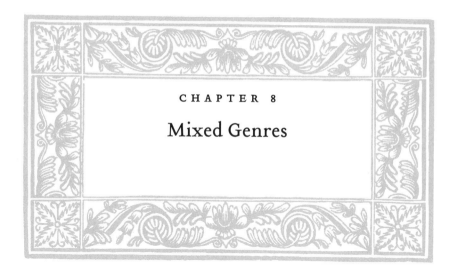

CHAPTER 8

Mixed Genres

As we have come to understand it, formal domestication is motivated by the ambition to interpret and to teach at the generalized level of the "common." Its historical dynamism in our period, the momentum with which a signifying recourse to the mean and the low learns to find its fulfillment in its own significance, may also be conceived broadly as a thematization of form, a long-term transition from domestication to domesticity. In the previous chapter my aim was to illuminate this process in epistemological terms: as a development in attitudes toward problems of knowledge that required for its realization the separation out of the category of epistemology itself from its traditional sociopolitical substratum. Evidence for this epistemological transition may also be found in the local history of genres. Elsewhere I have argued that the origins of the novel as a separate genre are theorized persuasively, on this broad model, in terms of the thematization of form.[1] In the third part of this study I will turn to narrative form and, at a certain point, to the novel genre in order to address the emergence of the domestic novel out of the more disparate, and frequently domesticating, terrain of the secret history. My aim in this chapter is to provide a brief and highly selective account of how the development of some other, traditional literary genres exemplifies the dialectical interplay between domestication and domesticity. My attention here will be directed especially at the structural delicacy and acuity with which authors negotiate the movement of traditional forms from relations of distinction to relations of separation, a movement that characteristically evokes a reflexive awareness of generic mixture but that in some cases also precipitates what categorial separation makes possible: reflexive experiments in formal conflation. Like pictorial composition, the formal structures of linguistic discourse offer a seemingly tangible register of the conceptual world. Indeed, self-conscious experimentation with (what modernity learned to call) "literary" form stands in relation to the conceptualization of reality rather as example does to precept. So far from being irrelevant to a historicity that lies beyond, formal reflexivity provides a serviceable skeleton key to it.

Tragicomedy

The cheerful spirit in which Steele domesticates the quarrel in the Garden in *Paradise Lost*[2] seems closer to that of a secular experiment in genre formation than to the customary sobriety of Christian accommodation. As such, it invites comparison with another of Steele's experiments: "When unhappy Catastrophe's make up Part of the History of Princes, and Persons who act in high Spheres, or are represented in the moving Language, and well wrought Scenes of Tragedians, they do not fail of striking us with Terror; but then they affect us only in a transient Manner, and pass through our Imaginations, as Incidents in which our Fortunes are too humble to be concerned . . . ." This is the now-familiar language of the emergent aesthetic, which Steele uses to broach the possibility of a more leveled approach to the common experience of humanity. "Instead of such high Passages," he continues, "I was thinking it would be of great Use, (if any Body could hit it) to lay before the World such Adventures as befall Persons not exalted above the common Level. This, methought, would better prevail upon the ordinary Race of Men, who . . . believe nothing can relate to them that does not happen to such as live and look like themselves." Steele proceeds to narrate a "wonderful Tragedy" that befell a married couple living "very distant from the rest of their Family, in a lonely Country House." His editor remarks that "Steele here looks forward to 'bourgeois tragedy.'"[3] Steele also looks back to the hybrid genre of "tragicomedy," which is rooted in classical antiquity but flowers, in association with the mixed form of the satyr play, during the Renaissance.[4]

Presupposing as it does an explicit antithesis between tragedy and comedy, the early modern flourishing of "tragicomedy" reminds us that in some important instances the division of knowledge by which relations of distinction become ones of separation was itself an ancient phenomenon. Nor did the experimental conflation of tragedy and comedy have to wait for the Renaissance: Steele's startlingly comic accommodation of the quarrel in the Garden is itself accommodated and redeemed by the *felix culpa* of Christian historiography. Realism, it has famously been argued, results in antiquity from the reconception of the low and comic as susceptible to high and serious treatment.[5] In the hands of both Steele's contemporaries and modern critics, "tragicomedy" is a loose category comprising several ways in which the generic mixture to which it refers can be registered. Most obviously, tragicomedy may blend serious and comic emotions. In "bourgeois" or "domestic" tragedy of the sort Steele imagines, common people suffer elevated passions.[6] In double-plotted plays a low and comic plot usually stands in foil relationship to a high and tragic one (although not in the sort of explicitly signifying relationship that is entailed in formal domestication).[7]

Modern critics tend to juxtapose the affective and the formal aspects of tragicomedy, although they do not always accord the latter—the divided plot structure—tragicomic status.[8] Notoriously prone to accommodate Shakespeare's plays to the tastes of the present age, Restoration adapters found both the affective and the formal elements to be active in his drama, and they often revised so as to throw the tragicomic Shakespeare into relief.[9] Thomas Betterton titled his 1700 revision of the Henry IV plays *K. Henry IV. with the Humours of Sir John Falstaff. A Tragi-Comedy. . . .*[10] But the range of opinion was broad. Although he acknowledged that many of Shakespeare's greatest tragedies might be described as tragicomic, Addison nonetheless believed that as an exclusive model for tragic drama, tragicomedy, "the Product of the English Theatre, is one of the most monstrous Inventions that ever enter'd into a Poet's Thoughts. . . . The same Objections which are made to Tragi-Comedy, may in some Measure be apply'd to all Tragedies that have a double Plot in them. . . ."[11] George Lillo, author of the most original and successful "domestic tragedy" of the eighteenth century, eschewed the divided plot but embraced the Shakespearean precedent in justifying his experiment in accommodation: "Tragedy is so far from losing its Dignity, by being accommodated to the Circumstances of the Generality of Mankind, that it is more truly august in Proportion to the Extent of its Influence, and the Number that are properly affected by it." The result, two centuries before Arthur Miller, is a tragedy of "the common man" that engages both the quantifying and the social aspects of "the common" by combining formal domestication with a substantive domesticity:

> Forgive us then, if we attempt to show,
> In artless Strains, a Tale of private Woe.
> A *London* Prentice ruin'd is our Theme . . . .[12]

Contemporary critics debated the merits of tragicomedy according to standards of unity, propriety, and decorum: Is it useful to inquire into the significance of Restoration tragicomedy as a "mixed genre," an experiment in formal domestication? What is achieved by self-consciously conflating elements that have been defined in opposition to each other? Of course, the topic requires extended treatment; I will confine myself here to some thoughts about two quite different examples of the kind.

Dryden's Neander thought that in comedy "the persons are only of common rank, and their business private, not elevated by passions or high concernments as in serious plays." But Dryden also celebrated his own "tragi-comedies," by which he meant the double-plotted play, "so moving in the serious part of it, and so pleasant in the comic, as might deserve a more than ordinary care in both."[13] His *Marriage à la Mode* (1672)[14] is suggestive for our purposes because the rigorous formal division between its high and low plots, sustained by the microformality of a strict "separation of styles"—the elevated "public" pentameters of the high-plot nobility versus the low "private" prose of Restoration courtiers—only sets the stage for their energetically persistent conflation. Not that Dryden's high and low characters are involved in any sustained interaction. In fact, on the two occasions when this does occur the effect is to reinforce a basic sense of the extreme social distance between "high" and "low."[15] Nor is the dovetailing of the plots just a matter of discovering that both are preoccupied with the problem of how marriage is to be sanctioned. Nor (again) is it even simply that both plots conceive the marriage problem in terms (alliance versus love, absolute authority versus contractual choice) that resonate with the patriarchalist analogy between the public state and the private family. What is most striking in *Marriage à la Mode* is the fact that with some consistency the ideological emphases we might expect to find within each of its plots are if anything reversed.

It is the heroic Leonidas, for example, who insists to his presumptive father, "I would not marry, Sir; and, when I do, / I hope you'll give me freedom in my choice. . . . Duty's a Name; and Love's a Real thing." And it is the libertine Palamede who admits that "I have given my consent [to an arranged marriage], for fear of being disinherited; and yet know not what kind of woman I am to marry." Or again, although Dryden's heroic high plot is based on the venerable aristocratic family-romance convention of revealed parentage, its correlation of inner worth with outer birth is managed with such skeptical inconsistency that it is less the integrity than the conventionality of the trope that impresses us. True, in its libertine play with the mutual exclusion of "wife" and "mistress" the comic low plot assumes this sort of skepticism from the outset. And yet by ingeniously exploiting the imaginative mechanism of mimetic desire, Palamede and Rhodophil learn to love their wives, with aesthetic disinterestedness, as though they were whores, thereby knitting up into a whole the old courtly split between love and marriage (2.1.286–87, 4.4.46, 1.1.107–9).

In other words, the ostentatious separation between public and private that formally frames *Marriage à la Mode* is the prelude for discovering within each realm a reprise of that separation whereby the framework of values each might be expected to enforce is obscured, if not opposed. This is not a case of formal domestication: Dryden's double-plotted dramatic structure nowhere purports to provide an explicit signifying system in which the low serves to illuminate the high, the little the great. And yet the effect of their contradictory conjunction is the recognizable one of dialectical recapitulation, where the understanding generated by the separation of categories includes that of their inseparability.

If we ask how the distinction between the public and the private spheres was formally dramatized before their separation had laid the ground for the sort of experimental conflation we see in *Marriage à la Mode,* one answer might be the court masque. Of course, this "before" is less chronological than cultural (although as we have seen, in the English experience the civil wars truly constituted an epochal watershed).[16] In the masques of the Jacobean and Caroline periods we see the product of an extraordinarily cohesive, artfully maintained subculture where some of the most familiar markers of the public/private divide—state versus civil society, gentility versus commoners, audience versus players, the political versus the domestic—are at most implicit within a fluid continuum of appearance and reality. Increasingly a celebration of absolute monarchy, the court masque took as its subject the indivisibility of royal magnificence. As monarchy simultaneously possessed a "natural" and a "political" body, so the royal or aristocratic masquer was simultaneously reality and representation: in Ben Jonson's words, "objected to sense" and "subjected to understanding," "outward show" and "inward parts," "present occasion" and "lasting mystery," "personater" and "person," actor and actor.[17] "[T]he 1630s saw the last practical application at an English court of mental habits that made little separation between different areas of knowledge."[18] Of course royal absolutism, so far from being "indivisible" in the first half of the seventeenth century, had already begun that long devolutionary process through which the authority of the public realm came to seem transferable to private entities, and in recent years the court masque has been reconceived as in its own way a means of representing political conflict.[19] Nevertheless, the tension between the public and the private, dramatic personater and person, was greatly aggravated by the wholesale crisis of the civil wars and would be paralleled and extended by the separation between public and private, dramatic character and author, that was enforced by the moral crisis of the 1690s.[20]

Only a year before *Marriage à la Mode* was first performed Milton gave the world a very different sort of tragicomedy. To be sure, *Samson Agonistes* (1671) was prefaced by an explicit condemnation of "the Poet's error of intermixing Comic stuff with Tragic sadness and gravity; or introducing trivial and vulgar persons, which by all judicious hath been counted absurd . . . ."[21] Nor does Milton share Dryden's penchant for double plotting. But *Samson Agonistes,* like *Paradise Lost,* is profoundly informed by the Christian principle of the *felix culpa,* which grafts onto the scrupulous classicism of Milton's conception of tragedy the comic, because redemptive, resolution of Christian history. And if the subject of Milton's private closet drama is Samson's typological role in the cosmic Christian plot, the poem accommodates this high matter through several sorts of domestication. As most readers are fitfully aware, *Samson Agonistes* practices a "Protestant poetics" by being allusively concerned with the individualized, even autobiographical, soteriology of its author, as well as the historical and national fate of the English, God's chosen people. These formal domestications are thematized, moreover, through a plot that concerns the problematic relationship between the household, the state, and the cosmic plan: not only the putative analogy but also the complicating metonymy between the little and the great. In effect Milton asks Locke's question: what is the relationship between "the Power of a *Magistrate* over a Subject," "that of . . . a *Husband* over his Wife," and that of the Creator over his creatures?[22]

Milton's Samson, like Dryden's Leonidas, has rejected his parents' matrimonial authority; as his father Manoa says, "I cannot praise thy marriage choices, Son, / Rather approv'd them not . . ." (lines 420–21). But the son's rebellion against the "public" authority of the father, motivated by the privacy of love, is simultaneously figured as an act of private conscience motivated by deference to a higher Father. Of his first marriage Samson says, ". . . she pleas'd / Mee, not my Parents, that I sought to wed, / The daughter of an Infidel: they knew not / That what I motion'd was of God; I knew / From intimate impulse, and therefore urg'd / The Marriage on . . . ." By this Samson means that he, although "a private person," yet "was no private but a person rais'd / With strength sufficient and command from Heav'n / To free my Country . . ." (lines 219–24, 1208, 1211–13).[23] By the same token, however, Samson's humiliation threatens a "house" and a "home" that are simultaneously domestic, civil, and divine (see lines 447, 515–17, 633–34, 1733).

Samson's "intimate impulse" names both an amatory and a vocational interiority, both a negative and a positive liberty with respect to paternal authority. And when Samson accuses Dalila of "Matrimonial treason" (line 959) he both relies on patriarchalist analogy (the family is like the state) and refers to her literal, Philistine betrayal of the Jewish cause. That is, Dalila spurns the private subjection of the *feme covert* in favor of political and public subjecthood: "Why then / Didst thou at first receive me for thy husband, / Then, as since then, thy country's foe profest? / Being once a wife, for me thou wast to leave / Parents and country; nor was I their subject, / Nor under their protection but my own, / Thou mine, not theirs . . ." (lines 882–88). Samson subscribes to the Chorus's vision of "domestic good": ". . . God's universal Law / Gave to the man despotic power / Over his female in due awe, / . . . not sway'd / By female usurpation . . . ."

Usurping this power in the domestic sphere, Dalila not only condemns her husband to the most privative privacy within that sphere—to "live uxorious to thy will / In perfect thraldom . . . ," "to sit idle on the household hearth / A burdenous drone . . ."—but also (and thereby) assumes an unwonted public authority (lines 1048, 1053–55, 1059–60, 945–46, 566–67).[24] Laying military siege to Samson (lines 402–5), the public-minded Dalila wins from him the *arcana imperii* of the Jews, "the secret gift of God," "his holy secret," which she ensures is "publish'd" to the enemy (lines 201, 497, 498).[25]

Dalila has a more sympathetic view of her decision to go public. For one thing, hers was an untenable choice between two species of male despotism: Philistine "Magistrates," "Princes," and "Priest[s]" all had pressured her to betray her husband on the grounds "that to the public good / Private respects must yield . . ." (lines 850, 851, 857, 868–69). But in any case, to be the *feme covert* of a public hero looked to her very much like the lonely liberty of the *feme sole:* "I knew that liberty / Would draw thee forth to perilous enterprises, / While I at home sat full of cares and fears / Wailing thy absence in my widow'd bed . . . ." Blind and subjected, Samson now may experience the internalized magistracy of the wifely helpmeet, residing "[a]t home in leisure and domestic ease . . . , / . . . where my redoubl'd love and care / With nursing diligence, to me glad office, / May ever tend about thee to old age . . . ." Not public alliance or convenience but conjugal and domestic love has been her real motive (lines 803–6, 917, 923–25). Samson's reply is scathingly sarcastic: "But Love constrain'd thee; call it furious rage / To satisfy thy lust" for *Philistian* gold . . . ." In her private as much as in her public capacity Dalila is corrupted, preferring money to love and the interested status of widow to that of wife: "Cherish thy hast'n'd widowhood with the gold / Of Matrimonial treason . . ."—which for Samson is tantamount to Defoe's "matrimonial whoredom" (lines 836–37, 831, 958–59).[26]

Romance

Dryden's and Milton's "tragicomedies" may help suggest the range of ways contemporaries used mixed dramatic forms to investigate the relationship between—through the self-conscious "mixing" of—the several overlapping realms of publicity and privacy. In the romance mode, the most ostentatious example of such mixture in formal terms is the seventeenth-century "political / allegorical romance,"[27] which programmatically domesticated high affairs of state through fictional and more or less transparent "romance" narratives. A treatment of such narratives, and of their implications for the emergence of the domestic novel, will be reserved for later chapters. For the moment I want to reflect on the mixed nature of "romance" itself as exemplary of the way the early modern mixture of forms may sometimes emerge not from self-conscious experimentation but in the discovery that traditional and singular modes have always enclosed a tacit heterogeneity that under modern conditions of increasing explicitation now begins to look contradictory.

I have argued elsewhere that "print helps transform romance into a self-conscious canon. But it also helps 'periodize' romance as a 'medieval' production, as that which the present age—the framing counterpart of the classical past—defines itself against. Medieval romance, in which the antecedents of our 'history' and 'romance' coexist in fluid suspension, becomes 'medieval romance,' the product of an earlier period and increasingly the locus of strictly 'romance' elements that have been separated out from the documentary objectivity of 'history' and of print, the technology to which it therefore owes (at least in part) both its birth and its instantaneous obsolescence."[28] Premodern "romance" was thus distinguishable but inseparable from "history." The relationship between "romance" and "epic" at the beginning of the modern period is more complicated than this, but there are some elements of similarity. The ease with which modernity attributes to romance and epic, respectively, the fundamentally antithetical concerns of love and war was alien to medieval thinking. When Renaissance scholars began to apply the formal standards of (Aristotelian) epic to romance and to find the latter wanting, the result was not a definitive separation out but rather the elaboration of a category of "heroic poetry" in which the best of epic and romance might stand together.[29] In the seventeenth century, however, readers became increasingly preoccupied with a content-based tension between romance and epic, love and war, which also affected the viability of Petrarchan love conceit.

Very early in the century Shakespeare's *Troilus and Cressida* articulated the emergent problem with unparalleled force, taking as its occasion the primordial war for love, the Trojan War. If the state is like a family, says Ulysses, when "[t]he unity and married calm of states" is shattered, "[e]ach thing meets / In mere oppugnancy . . . / . . . [and all] lose their names . . . ." Love and war, pushed to parodic identification, absorb, corrupt, and repudiate each other. On one side, Pandarus sings for Helen and Paris:

> Love, love, nothing but love, still love still more!
> For, O, love's bow shoots buck and doe.
> The shaft confounds not that it wounds,
> But tickles still the sore.
> These lovers cry, O ho! they die!
> Yet that which seems the wound to kill
> Doth turn O ho! to Ha, ha, he!
> So dying love lives still.

On the other side, Thersites tersely summarizes the Greek cause: "All the argument is a whore and a cuckold, a good quarrel to draw emulous factions and bleed to death upon."[30] Writing at midcentury, after intestine war has divided a seemingly integral nation and at the moment when the king's political is separated from his natural body, Richard Lovelace can yet hold love and war together in a delicate dialectic of heroism:

> I.
> Tell me not (Sweet) I am unkinde,
>   That from the Nunnerie
> Of thy chaste breast, and quiet minde,
>   To Warre and Arms I flie.
> II.
> True; a new Mistresse now I chase,
>   The first Foe in the Field;
> And with a stronger Faith imbrace
>   A Sword, a Horse, a Shield.
> III.
> Yet this Inconstancy is such,
>   As you too shall adore;
> I could not love thee (Deare) so much,
>   Lov'd I not Honour more.[31]

War, domesticable as love but a "stronger" version of it, both supplants love and preserves it at a higher level. Love, sublimated to the higher level of chastity, becomes a nonlove that joins war in its nonwar sublimation as the love of honor. Male honor, sustained in marriage by female chastity, in war sustains love through its own form of asexual devotion.

After the Restoration, the heroic nexus of romance and epic, love and war, was chronically suspect. In this respect the period's great monument to heroic poetry is arguably not *Paradise Lost* (1667) but *Hudibras* (1663–64, 1678) because Butler's concern is more evidently than Milton's the problematic coextension of love and war.[32] Indebted as he is to Spenser and Cervantes, Butler calls his poem a romance; but although he finds in that form the same mixture that marks "heroic poetry," distinction has become a formal separation of styles. In the first part of *Hudibras* Butler observes that just as Empedocles claimed that the world "[w]as made of *Fighting* and of *Love:* / Just so *Romances* are, for what else / Is in them all, but *Love* and *Battels*? / O'th' first of these w' have no great matter / To treat of, but a world o'th' lat[t]er . . . ." Yet he begins the second part: "But now t'observe *Romantique* Method, / Let rusty Steel a while be sheathed; / And all those harsh and rugged sounds / Of Bastinado's, Cuts and Wounds / Exchang'd to Love's more gentle stile, / To let our Reader breathe a while . . . ."[33]

Having ostentatiously modulated from war to love, however, Butler demonstrates not only their stealthy conflation but also its utter monstrosity. Playing Dulcinea to Hudibras's Don Quixote, the Widow visits him in the stocks only to find herself subjected to a Petrarchan lecture on the cruelty of the beloved: "*Loves* power's too great to be withstood, / By feeble humane *flesh* and *blood.*" "Why are you *fair,* but to entice us / To *love* you, that you may despise us?" (pt. 2, canto 1, lines 349–50, 329–30, pp. 111, 109). The Widow replies: "*Love-passions* are like *Parables,* / By which men still mean something else . . ." (pt. 2, canto 1, lines 441–42, p. 113). The irony of these parables is that their low, sensible address does not reveal abstract truth; it conceals "something else" yet lower. What the Widow refers to is, in part, the passion for money: she is a wealthy *feme sole,* and much of the rest of this canto concerns Hudibras's unsuccessful efforts to engineer the settlement of her estate to his advantage. But the Widow also refers to another kind of sensible passion, one that lies behind the metaphysical sufferings of the Petrarchan love poet. This becomes clear when Hudibras launches into a *blazon* whose figurative barbarity, masquerading as amatory devotion, the Widow interrupts to denounce.[34] The hypocrisy of male love poetry hides the brutal truth of male passion as verse does the "plainness" of prose: "This has been done by some, who those / Th' ador'd in *Rhime* would kick in *Prose;* / And in those *Ribbins* would have hung, / Of which melodiously they sung. . . . But I do wonder you should chuse / This way t'attack me with your Muse . . ." (pt. 2, canto 1, lines 481, 639–40, pp. 114, 118). Behind the figurative masochism of the Petrarchan poet lies the literal sadism of the patriarchal despot.

Butler's disclosure of "war" at the heart of "love" enacts the separation out of the one from the other as (with only apparent paradox) a conflationary desublimation. For if love and war are inextricably bound up with each other, they are so not in the manner of tacit distinction but as physical violence—low, sensible things—is the antithetical yet authentic ground and meaning of amatory idealism. If we now recall that *Hudibras* is an allegory of the Interregnum period that domesticates the nation as a wife widowed by regicide,[35] the appropriateness of this domestication becomes clear. The critique of Petrarchan hypocrisy figures forth, at the private level of courtship, the public hypocrisy of religious warfare. *Hudibras* is a comprehensive indictment of the civil wars as a grotesque amplification of the Protestant confidence in the powers of accommodation. Justifying physical violence as a low and sensible means of achieving elevated spiritual ends, the English civil wars are desublimated—in a related sense of the term "domesticated"—by Butler as a degradation of *caritas* into a whoring lust for power:

When *civil* Fury first grew high,
And men fell out they knew not why;
When hard words, *Jealousies* and *Fears,*
Set Folks together by the ears,
And made them fight, like mad or drunk,
For Dame *Religion* as for Punk,
Whose honesty they all durst swear for,
Though not a man of them knew wherefore:
When *Gospel-trumpeter,* surrounded
With long-ear'd rout, to Battel sounded,
And Pulpit, Drum Ecclesiastick,
Was beat with fist, instead of a stick:
Then did Sir *Knight* abandon dwelling,
And out he rode a Colonelling.
    (pt. 1, canto 1, lines 1–14)

Butler's desublimation of English culture is a coolly and corrosively skeptical diagnosis that conflates religion and the politics of warfare so as to show their shocking incongruity, the ineluctability of their separation.[36] And yet this substantive theme is established through a formal technique of domestication that presumes the persuasive congruity of private and public estate settlement, the family and the state, courtly "love" and civil "war." This contradiction places *Hudibras* at the center of the Restoration effort to investigate the boundaries between the private and the public. And the contradiction is evident at another level of literary form as well: in the doggerel plainness of Butler's "Hudibrastics," which in the same gesture lay claim to and refute poetic smoothness and decorum. "Plainness" is coded here as private candor. As the Widow tells the knight, "I like this plainness better, / Then false *mock-passion, speech,* or *letter* . . ." (pt. 2, canto 1, lines 481–82, p. 114). As our speaker tells us, romance idealizes; "But as for our part, we shall tell / The naked Truth . . ." (pt. 1, canto 2, lines 35–36, p. 30). The prosaic lowness of Butler's diction and the roughness of his tetrameters simultaneously evoke and evade both the canting obliquity of prevailing "political" discourse ("hard words") and the seductive lubricity of romance and Petrarchan discourse.[37]

Of the many poets who continued Butler's investigation, it is with Rochester that I will conclude this discussion of romance as a mixed form, not because he writes romances but because his poetic treatment of the relation between love and war is as compelling as any. Rochester extends the idealizing conventions of Petrarchan love poetry—love as war—far enough for us to watch the first autodesublimate, with stunning speed and ferocity, into the second. In "A Ramble in St. James's Park" the suffering lover, confronted by the inconstancy of his imperious beloved, is torn between a theatrically self-pitying narcissism and the thuggish abusiveness of a brute:

> Gods! that a thing admir'd by me,
> Shou'd taste so much of Infamy.
> . . . .
> Ungrateful! Why this Treachery
> To humble fond, believing me?
> . . . .
> May stinking *Vapours* choak your *Womb,*
> Such as the *Men* you doat upon;
> . . . .
> *And may no* Woman *better thrive*
> *That dares prophane the* Cunt *I Swive.*[38]

We have already seen how Rochester uses Charles II to figure the incestuous mutual exclusion of sexual politics: sex corrupts politics, politics corrupt sex.[39] A Latin apostrophe to Charles II, attributed to Rochester, appears at the end of the anonymous *Fifth Advice to a Painter* (1667): "The following lines, written by some unknown idle rascal, were found on the threshold of the royal bedchamber: 'You shun battles and chase beauties, hate what is warlike and make your wars in bed. Being fond of peace you love the weak. You seem like bold Mars only in the works of Venus, but like Venus in the arms of Mars.'"[40] In this form, the contradictory exchange between love and war recalls the apprehension that public men of war are "effeminated" by private love, which is also one of the directions taken by the trope of the curtain lecture.[41] "The Disabled Debauchee" is a lighter treatment of the exchange, a poem in heroic stanzas organized by an epic simile that compares the speaker's bittersweet retirement from a life of debauchery to that of "some brave Admiral, in former War / Depriv'd of force . . ." (lines 1–2, p. 44). The subtle apposition through which the simile is first established, then enclosed within the dominant narrative of sexual renunciation and nostalgia, brilliantly underscores the negation at the heart of the poem: that love and war are most alike when both have ceased to be. Addressing Chloris, his former partner in sexual battle, the male speaker concludes magnanimously by offering contemplative counsel to her ongoing activity:

> Thus, Statesman-like, I'll sawcily Impose,
>   And, safe from Action, valiantly Advise;
> Shelter'd in Impotence, urge you to blows:
>   And being good for nothing else, be Wise.
> (lines 45–48, p. 45)

An alternative strategy to a similar end is the cheerful palinode "Nestor," where Nestor's cup from the *Iliad* is made the model for an anticup—"Engrave no Battail on its Cheek / (With warr I've nought to doe"—in whose curious design war is definitively replaced by its interiorizing "domestications":

> Cupid and Bacchus my saints are:
> May drink and love still reign.
> With wine I wash away my cares,
> And then to cunt again.
> (lines 9–10, 21–24, pp. 41–42)

By 1670 an influential treatise was able to assert that epic "Poems make some Military Act, or Politic Conduct, their Theme, and only descant upon Love at Pleasure; whereas *Romances,* on the contrary, have Love for their Principal Subject, and don't concern themselves in War or Politicks, but by Accident."[42] The separation out of love and war marks the effective demise of Petrarchan conceits and "heroic poetry." In one number of the *Tatler* Isaac Bickerstaff investigates a young woman's complaint "[t]hat the Expressions mentioned in the Papers [i.e., love letters] written to her, were become meer Words, and that she had always been ready to marry any of those who said they died for her; but that they made their Escape as soon as they found themselves pitied or believed" (*Tatler,* no. 110, 22 Dec. 1709).[43] But it may also be plausible to connect the death of the old forms with the birth of a new one—pornography. Only when sex is detached from its subservient dependence on dynastic, political, and religious ends—only when sex becomes separated out as "sex as such"—does it become possible self-consciously to conflate sex and (politico-bellico-rhetorical) violence in such a way as to serve the ends of sexual desire and pleasure through the complex network of responses we have come to call "masochism" and "sadism."

Mock Epic

To address the formal instability of romance and "heroic poetry" in this period is inevitably to raise the subject of antiromance and the mock heroic. Literary history rightly regards the decades from 1660 to 1740 as the great age of sundry mixed forms—mock epic, burlesque, travesty, lampoon—that share a basic parodic or ironic motive. Contemporaries were preoccupied with the phenomenon of parodic reversal. Some, like Sprat, observed that it was potential in rhetorical usage itself: "[A]ll things are capable of abuse from the same *Topicks* by which they may be commended . . . ." Others, like Butler, ascribed the problem to generic convention: "Heroicall Poetry handle's the slightest, and most Impertinent Follys in the world in a formall Serious and unnaturall way: And Comedy and Burlesque the most Serious in a Frolique and Gay humor . . . ." Swift found it necessary to remind readers how to read irony and parody correctly.[44]

Moreover, there was some agreement that the unstable relation between praise and blame, between the serious and the comical, had become aggravated in modern times. This is implicit in Swift's impersonation of an archmodern hack who, with ingenious idiocy, explains why it is that people tend to be insulted by panegyric and affirmed by satire. And it is explicit in the third Earl of Shaftesbury's remark that "[v]ile *Encomiums,* and wretched *Panegyricks* are the worst of *Satirs:* . . . For in reality the Nerve and Sinew of modern *Panegyrick* lies in a dull kind of *Satir;* . . . Such is the Sterility of these *Encomiasts*! They know not how to praise, but by Detraction. If a Fair-One is to be celebrated, HELEN must in comparison be deform'd; VENUS her-self degraded. That a *Modern* may be honour'd, some *Antient* must be sacrific'd." When Pope borrows Shaftesbury's phrase to anchor the gruff candor of his address to George II—"But Verse alas! your Majesty disdains; / And I'm not us'd to Panegyric strains: / . . . / Besides, a fate attends on all I write, / That when I aim at praise, they say I bite. / A vile Encomium doubly ridicules . . ."—he also borrows Swift's implicit approach insofar as the poem he writes is a purposely vile encomium on the modern George Augustus based on Horace's praise of his normative ancient prototype Octavius Augustus.[45]

If the long shadow cast by ancient virtue helped blur the line between praise and blame for contemporaries, so did the experience of status inconsistency.[46] Once the coextensive components of an integral virtue—status, wealth, place, power—had begun systematically to be separated out by social change, the correlation of inner "goodness" and outer "greatness" became subject to increasing query and critique. As a consequence, the presumptive ethical basis for elevating the "high" over the "low," the "public" over the "private" man, became questionable. Thomas Gordon wrote that "[t]he common people generally think that great men have great minds, and scorn base actions; which judgment is so false, that the basest and worst of all actions have been done by great men: Perhaps they have not picked private pockets, but they have done worse; they have often disturbed, deceived, and pillaged the world: and he who is capable of the highest mischief, is capable of the meanest: He who plunders a country of a million of money, would in suitable circumstances steal a silver spoon; and a conqueror, who steals and pillages a kingdom, would, in an humbler fortune, rifle a portmanteau, or rob an orchard." This is the formula that underlies some of the sharpest political satires of the period, like John Gay's *The Beggar's Opera* (1728) and Henry Fielding's *Jonathan Wild* (1743).[47]

In the preface to his narrative Fielding makes the conflation of high and low, public "statesman" and private "thief," in suggestively residential terms: "[W]ithout considering Newgate as no other than human nature with its mask off, . . . I think we may be excused for suspecting, that the splendid palaces of the great are often no other than Newgate with the mask on. . . . [T]he same morals [are] in one place attended with all imaginable misery and infamy, and in the other, with the highest luxury and honour." In short, "[t]here is a nearer connexion between high and low life than is generally imagined . . . ." As we might expect, however—and by the very logic of his argument—Fielding's moral conflation of the public and the private is predicated on their moral separation. Or rather, the ethical conflation of public and private "greatness" depends on the ethical separation of public "greatness" from private "goodness": "The truth, I apprehend, is, we often confound the ideas of goodness and greatness together, or rather include the former in our idea of the latter." And to exemplify the former Fielding has recourse to an alternative residential norm, the virtuous domesticity of Thomas Heartfree, whom Fielding condemns ironically for having "married a very agreeable woman for love, . . . a mean-spirited, poor, domestic, low-bred animal, who confined herself mostly to the care of her family, placed her happiness in her husband and her children, followed no expensive fashion or diversions, and indeed rarely went abroad . . . ."[48]

Like many contemporary works, *Jonathan Wild* is radically mock-heroic in that it goes beyond the use of ancient heroism as a norm for the critique of modern knavery to criticize, by the standard of goodness, the ancient standard of greatness as well.[49] Embedded in this sort of ethical critique, however, is a more neutral ambition to get to the heart of things that takes much of its force from the new-philosophical impatience with acculturated and circumstantial knowledge at all levels. Thomas Gordon's emphasis on the arbitrariness of "fortune" recalls the deep ambivalence of Swift's digression on madness in *A Tale of a Tub* (1704, 1710). Like Pope in *Peri Bathous* (1727) but to different ends, Swift engages here in an act of desublimation: cultural achievement is grounded in the lowest common denominator, the body, and lucky circumstance is all that separates the hero from the madman.[50]

Crucial to this sort of disclosure, Swift's speaker fears, is a scientific method willing to go beyond the superficiality of the senses, a rational faculty that comes "officiously, with Tools for cutting, and opening, and mangling, and piercing, offering to demonstrate, that [physical bodies] are not of the same consistence quite thro'. . . . Yesterday I ordered the Carcass of a *Beau* to be stript in my Presence; when we were all amazed to find so many unsuspected Faults under one suit of Cloaths . . . ." Of course, Swift is satirizing the modern's lack of stomach for this sort of rational-material "Anatomy." But he is also satirizing the equally modern ambition—which the allegory of the three brothers forces us too to display—to "inspect beyond the Surface and the Rind of Things . . . ," to anatomize "the prime Productions of our Society, which . . . have darkly and deeply couched under them, the most finished and refined Systems of all Sciences and Arts; as I do not doubt to lay open by Untwisting or Unwinding, and either to draw up by Exantlation, or display by Incision" (173, 66–67). Gulliver tells a professor at the Grand Academy of Lagado that "in the Kingdom of *Tribnia*" it has become a ridiculous national obsession of "the Natives called *Langden*" to discover "the mysterious Meanings of Words, Syllables and Letters" by anagrammatic and other means. This leaves readers with the untenable choice of either respecting the critique and living with their own shallowness or confirming its accuracy by domesticating "Tribnia" and "Langden" as Britain and England.⁵¹ Marked by the separation out of "surface" from "depth," the period could hardly fail to be guilty of both by turns.

The relationship between the superficial and the deep acquires a more stably normative character in modern thought than that expressed by Swift, one that stands in complex homology with the relationship between the great and the little. Both are central to the ironic mechanism of mock heroic as well as to the method of the new philosophy. Indeed, the familiar valorization of depth over surface that emerges at this time may help us understand how the relation of little to great is subtly altered under conditions of modernity. In the traditional scheme of universal correspondence the little stood in relation to the great (e.g., the family to the state) in a hierarchical continuum of tacit distinction, each level illuminating, in its inferiority, the superiority of the next. We have already seen evidence of Bacon's interest in this sort of correspondence of microcosm to macrocosm, but the relationship is susceptible to other formulations as well: "[T]hings that are mean or even filthy, . . . no less than the most splendid and costly, must be admitted into natural history. For whatever deserves to exist deserves also to be known . . . . Moreover . . . from mean and sordid instances there sometimes emanates excellent light and information." In this argument for knowledge of the little, the promise of illumination is comparatively open ended: the "information" to be gathered is not governed by its presumed relevance to the great. In his panegyric "To the Royal Society" Abraham Cowley writes from a similar perspective:

> Nature's great Works no Distance can obscure,
> No Smallness her near Objects can secure.
>> You've taught the curious Sight to press
>> Into the privatest Recess
> Of her imperceptible Littleness.
> . . . .

> You've learn'd to read her smallest Hand,
> And well begun her deepest Sense to understand.[52]

In Cowley's panegyric the implicit valorization of depth ("her deepest Sense") over surface does not control our view of the relation of smallness to greatness, but it supports the separation out of the little as potentially consequential in its own right. Broadly speaking, this is the modern view. The technique of formal domestication accords with the traditional scheme of correspondence. When formal domestication combines with domesticity on the level of content, microinteriority begins to be accessible in its own right as a space for innovative "objective" discovery. Yet the separable autonomy of the private recess also bespeaks a "scientific" detachment sufficient to disclose, wholly within the freestanding sphere of the little, a dialectical recapitulation of its relationship with the sphere of the great. Here the new philosophy and Puritan meditation met on common ground. John Flavell, one of the most popular of the Protestant spiritualizers, assumed that his homely topics "some of my Readers will call the slightest and most Trifling subjects of Meditation . . . ." "It hath been long since observ'd," however, "[t]hat the World below is a Glass to discover the World above; *Seculum est speculum.*" Flavell hoped "to make such holy improvements of all these earthly Objects which daily occur to your senses, and cause them to proclaim and preach to you Divine and Heavenly Mysteries . . . ."[53] The new philosopher Robert Boyle was the author of one of the most influential treatises of Protestant meditation, *Occasional Reflections upon Several Subjects* (1665). Even as their experiments were motivated by the assumption that the little may be consequential in its own right, new philosophers continued to find evidence of universal correspondence that might seem to validate the hierarchical relation of little to great: "[A] Drop of Water, the Diameter of which exceeds not a Line, may be a Sea, not only as daily Experience shows, in the Capacity which it has of containing, and affording Sustenance to Millions of Animals, but also in the Similitude which these very Animals may bear to several known Species in that part of the Creation, which is the Object of our naked Eyes. . . . [T]he peculiar Inhabitants of several Portions of Matter often bear a near Resemblance to each other, tho' they differ extreamly in Magnitude."[54]

Observations like these sustained the efforts of physico-theologians to incorporate scientific data into Christian ideas about the unity of Creation. However, the strategy of exploiting the secular revelations of experimental method to theological ends had its costs. In concentrating on what was empirically verifiable in the structural design of Creation's microparts, William Paley's version of the argument from design abandoned the demonstration that design was also evident in the macrostructure of universal correspondence: "The proof is not a conclusion which lies at the end of a chain of reasoning, of which chain each instance of contrivance is only a link, and of which, if one link fail, the whole falls; but it is an argument separately supplied by every separate example. . . . The proof in each example is complete; for when the design of the part, and the conduciveness of its structure to that design is shown, the mind may set itself at rest . . . ."55 Oliver Goldsmith's Chinese visitor already had dismissed even the secular version of this sort of separation out of the small: "I have frequently compared the understandings of [the learned] to their own glasses [i.e., microscopes]. Their field of vision is too contracted to take in the whole of any but minute objects, they view all nature bit by bit, now the proboscis, now the antennæ, now the pinnæ of—a flea. . . . Thus they proceed laborious in trifles, constant in experiment, without one single abstraction by which alone knowledge may be properly said to encrease . . . ."56 Increasingly an expression not of the tacit distinction characteristic of traditional categorization but of the self-conscious conflation enabled by explicit separation, the argument from design ultimately foundered on the reef of secular and anti-Creationist notions of natural unity like evolutionary theory.57

Addison's attitude toward discoveries made through the microscope oscillates between enthusiasm for their proof of correspondence and the belief that the little only distracts us from the great. In one number of the *Tatler* he remarks that "[p]hilosophy had ranged over all the visible Creation, and began to want Objects for her Enquiries, when the present Age, by the Invention of Glasses, opened a new and inexhaustible Magazine of Rarities . . . ." Addison then imagines Galen extolling the microscope and assuring him "that we see in these little Animals different Natures, Instincts and Modes of Life, which correspond to what you observe in Creatures of bigger Dimensions." In another number, however, although he "would not discourage any Searches that are made into the most minute and trivial Parts of the Creation," Addison derides the interest scientific virtuosos display in "the Refuse of Nature": "Observations of this Kind are apt to alienate us too much from the Knowledge of the World, and to make us serious upon Trifles . . . . [W]hatever appears trivial or obscene in the common Notions of the World, looks grave and philosophical in the Eye of a Virtuoso" (*Tatler*, no 119, 12 Jan. 1710; no. 216, 26 Aug. 1710). Addison's remarks bring us close to the mock-epic attitude. One of the most celebrated new-philosophical stimuli to this attitude—surely among Bacon's "mean or filthy" things—was Robert Hooke's illustration of an enlarged louse in his *Micrographia* (1665), whose mock-heroic possibilities Andrew Marvell immediately exploited and others, contemporary and modern, have been quick to observe.58

The invention of the microscope captured the English imagination. Hooke

was as eloquent as anyone on the theological utility of its revelations. "To conclude," he wrote of a magnified gnat, "take this creature altogether, and for
beauty and curious contrivances, it may be compared with the largest Animal
upon the Earth. Nor doth the Alwise Creator seem to have shewn less care and
providence in the fabrick of it, then in those which seem most considerable."
Mock-heroic possibility, real but muted in this passage, is less clearly available
when Hooke focuses more directly on the microcosm itself: "[B]y the help of
Microscopes, there is nothing so small, as to escape our inquiry; hence there is a
new visible World discovered to the understanding. . . . [I]n every *little particle*
of its matter, we now behold almost as great variety of Creatures, as we were
able before to reckon up in the whole *Universe* it self. . . . [W]e may perhaps be
inabled to discern all the secret workings of Nature . . . ."[59]

And yet as the microworld increasingly is justified in its own terms, the old
model of correspondence returns, transformed, as the phenomenon of interiorization. This return is suggestively adumbrated by Hooke's observations on the
reflective powers of the many "hemispheres" of which the eye of a fly is composed (see fig. 8.1, top): "In so much that in each of these *Hemispheres,* I have
been able to discover a Land-scape of those things which lay before my window,
one thing of which was a large Tree, whose trunk and top I could plainly discover, as I could also the parts of my window, and my hand and fingers, if I held
it between the Window and the Object; a small draught of nineteen of which
[hemispheres], as they appear'd in the bigger Magnifying-glass to reflect the Image of the two windows of my Chamber, are delineated in the third *Figure* of
the 23. *Scheme*" (see fig. 8.1 bottom, further enlarged).[60] What looks, at the first
level of magnification, like a multipartite but uniform surface of opacity is
found, at higher levels of magnification, to be an extreme interior replete with
images of reflected exteriority—a "landscape." Within the diminutive eye of
the fly is enclosed the chamber's windows, the domestic eyes that, internalized
within the yet-lesser eyes of the insect, invert the relationship between outer
and inner, container and contained. One is reminded of the phantom domestic
interior at Chatsworth in Derbyshire, where an artfully placed mirror transforms opacity into the illusion of transparency, except that here the effect is not
to deepen a single dimension of interiority but to render it multidimensional.[61]
The dynamic of mock-heroic incongruity, always potential within microscopic
magnification, is transformed by the interiorizing process into a positive reciprocity. We can see this in Edmund Burke's acknowledgment that there is a
sublime of the small as well as of the great:

> [A]s the great extreme of dimension is sublime, so the last extreme of littleness is in
> some measure sublime likewise; when we attend to the infinite divisibility of matter,

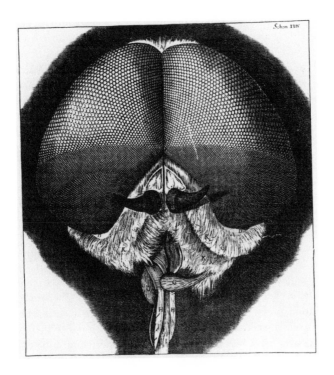

FIG. 8.1. The eye of a fly at two levels of magnification, in Robert Hooke, *Micrographia* . . . (1665; facs. reprint, New York: Dover, 1961). Princeton University Library.

when we pursue animal life into these excessively small, and yet organized beings, that escape the nicest inquisition of the sense, when we push our discoveries yet downward, and consider those creatures so many degrees yet smaller, and the still diminishing scale of existence, in tracing which the imagination is lost as well as the sense, we become amazed and confounded at the wonders of minuteness; nor can we distinguish in its effect this extreme of littleness from the vast design itself.[62]

In another sense, the (surely unintended) spirit of mock-heroic plays about the edges of a long, sympathetic letter to Eliza Haywood's *Female Spectator* whose aim is to persuade female readers to take up nature walks,

> extremely proper for such of the Fair, who are too volatile to have Patience to go through those tedious Volumes, which are requisite for the understanding all other Sciences. . . . But all those Curiosities, which are discoverable by the naked Eye, are infinitely short of those beyond it . . . . The Glasses which afford us so much Satisfaction are as portable as a Snuff-Box, and I am surprized the Ladies do not make more Use of them in the little Excursions they make in the Fields, Meadows, and Gardens. . . . [Nature] furnishes Matter for agreeable Conversation, especially for the Ladies, who cannot always be furnished with Discourse on the article of Dress, or the Repetition of what fine Things have been said to them by their Admirers . . . . As Ladies frequently walk out in the Country in little Troops, if every one of them would take with her a Magnifying Glass, what a pretty Emulation there would be among them, to make fresh Discoveries?——the *Royal Society* might be indebted to every fair *Columbus* for a new World of Beings to employ their Speculations.

Here the mock-heroic effect is one of "domestication" in the fully substantive sense of the term, depending as it does not on the microscopical enlargement of the little but on the patronizing elevation of women and their "little" preoccupations to the comparatively great role of "fair Philosophers." And yet the domestication, being moral, is not only diminishing. For the author's premise is that women are made for more serious pursuits than "The Play,——the Opera, ——the Masquerade and Ball . . . ." "To have their Names set down . . . in the Memoirs and Transactions of [the Royal Society] would be gratifying a laudable Ambition, and a far greater Addition to their Charms than the Reputation of having been the first in the Mode . . . ."[63]

The metonymy of microscope and snuffbox suggests we are in the territory of *The Rape of the Lock*. Before turning to Pope's consummation of the mock-epic form, however, I will look briefly at Dryden's paradigmatic exercise in, as Sprat put it, turning the topics of commendation to abuse. *Mac Flecknoe's* mock-heroic method is to deploy the topics of classical and Christian heroism in praise of figures who cannot bear their foundational and typological weight.[64] This is an epic of *translatio* and succession—"To settle the succession of the State" (line 10, p. 54)—of Virgilian *auctoritas* and Christian fulfillment, whose topics are used to accommodate the domestic history of English poetastry. But to say this is to acknowledge that Dryden's mock epic is also, explicitly and significantly, a "mock-political allegory" in which the customary signifying relationship between the private and the public is reversed: *Mac Flecknoe* uses the public story of especially Roman state succession—of sacred absolute sovereignty—to accommodate the private story of literary "succession." To put this another way, Dryden's poem is a *translatio imperii* that achieves its own translation into a *translatio studii,* a cultural endeavor that uses the familiar public material of state affairs to disclose, in the obscure privation of pre-"literary" affairs, an emergent domestic (i.e., national) dramatic canon.

Dryden's most ambitious work in this deceptively inconsequential poem is the constitution of "literature" as a historical entity. And although the basis for this is already given in the normative institution of the "poet laureate," the difficulty of the enterprise is signaled by the fact that the history of literature can only emerge negatively (hence the utility of mock epic). Literary succession is figured first of all as a parodic privation, in the lineage of Dekker-Heywood-Shirley-Flecknoe-Shadwell (lines 87, 29, pp. 56, 54), then—only by negative definition—in the normative line of Fletcher-Jonson-Sedley-Etherege (lines 79–80, 151, 163, pp. 56, 58). A coherent conception of literary high culture waits (at least in this poem) upon the coalescence of the low culture of Grub Street, which is quite precisely localized in the City and its agglomeration of authors, stationers, booksellers, most of all the mass of books that "almost choakt the way" (line 103, p. 57)—all components of a vast and burgeoning print culture. So even as the aesthetic privacy of literature is separated out from the publicity of more worldly activities, the literary sphere is subdivided into its high "private" and its low "public" subspheres, the latter being distinguished by their enthrallment to publicity and publication (lines 94–105). And the accommodating distinction between literary and state affairs on which Dryden's poem is constructed looks very much like the parodic conflation of literary and state affairs that is enabled by their ongoing separation.[65]

Is *Mac Flecknoe* not only a "mock-political allegory" but also a political allegory? That is, does the figurative framework of ancient Roman state affairs also accommodate modern English state affairs? Although published in 1682, *Mac Flecknoe* is known to have been composed in 1676, as momentum for the outbreak of the Popish Plot was building. John Dennis later thought that the anonymous *Mac Flecknoe* was among the "Libels which have pass'd for Satires";[66] did some read it as a libel on figures of state? Writing (and circulating) his poem at a time when Whiggish fortunes were in the ascendant, Dryden may well have seen fit to hide the ultimate referent of his mock epic under the allegorical cover of "literary" satire.[67] By this reading, *Mac Flecknoe* becomes a comic anticipation of *Absalom and Achitophel,* one whose doubled mask—typology layered over by "literature"—permits it to be a good deal more frankly critical of Charles's self-indulgent passions (his passion for the bastard Duke of Monmouth, his passion for court whores) than Dryden allows himself to be in that poem.[68]

Pope's greatest mock epic is no doubt *The Dunciad* (1728, 1729, 1742–43), in several ways an exercise in formal domestication. Following Dryden, Pope domesticates the public *translatio imperii* of ancient Rome to the private *translatio studii* of modern England: "[T]he Action of the Dunciad is the Removal of the Imperial seat of Dulness from the City to the polite World; as that of the Aeneid is the Removal of the empire of *Troy* to *Latium.*"[69] And like Dryden, Pope conceives this modern action as a phenomenon of print and the commodification of culture, a focus perfected by the substitution of the notorious theatrical entrepreneur Colley Cibber for Lewis Theobald as King of the Dunces in the 1742 *Dunciad* and deepened by Pope's claim that the poem was occasioned by the invention of printing and the liberty of the press ("Martinus Scriblerus, of the Poem," 49). To this occasion Pope domesticates Homer's purpose in writing his lost comic epic, the *Margites,* "the first Dunciad" and "the first Epic poem" (48). And in 1743 Pope adapts this mock-epic genealogy to the domesticating relation of the little and the great. The *Odyssey,* the *Iliad,* and the *Aeneid* are examples of the "*greater Epic,*" the *Margites* and the *Dunciad* of the "*little Epic.*" "There must still exist some analogy, if not Resemblance of Qualities, between the Heroes of the two Poems; and this in order to admit what Neoteric critics call the *Parody,* one of the liveliest graces of the little Epic" ("Ricardus Aristarchus of the Hero of the Poem," 254–56).

But if the *Dunciad* exemplifies the technique of formal domestication, the poem's content, although private because "literary," is not domestic. *The Rape of the Lock* (1714) shows not only what such a doubly domestic mock epic might look like but also how the *Dunciad* might have attained this shape had it exploited more fully the precedent of the *Iliad.* Like *Hudibras, The Rape of the Lock* exploits this precedent quite fully; the poem begins:

> What dire Offence from am'rous Causes springs,
> What mighty Contests rise from trivial Things,
> I sing—— . . .[70]

In calling his poem "heroi-comical" (139) Pope makes a preliminary generic classification whose clarifying refinement will come only through close reading. Is the poem a "mixed genre" in the conventional sense of the mock epic, in which mixture is the result of conjoining the mighty epic mode of the ancients with the trivial matter of modernity, or in the radical sense that, finding mixture tacit in the ancient epic itself, teases apart its elements into the tension of explicit separation? By thus alluding to the *Iliad* in his opening lines, Pope invites us to see his poem in the latter terms, as a modern imitation of an ancient action that is in itself a mixture of the mighty and the trivial, of war and love. In what I am calling its conventional sense, mock-heroic parody domesticates the great through the little—the ancient through the modern, the public through the private—as a privation, a lack: you cannot get there from here. But by disclosing privation in the public realm of the ancient as well, radical mock heroic gives access to ancient epic as a source for modeling an emergent reconception of negative privation as positive privacy. This radical extrusion of a positive "neo-epic" from the conventional negativity of mock epic is one important literary means by which modernity experimentally carves out a positive space of interiority—that is, a space in which liberty is valued as a negative liberty from relation, in this case subordinate relation to ancient authority.

The Rape of the Lock represents one moment in modernity's long-term conceptualization of negative liberty. Still bound to ancient epic through a complex relation of formal domestication, Pope's mock epic also experiments with substantive images of domesticity that posit for privacy a positive value that is (negatively) free of the disvalue of sheer privation.[71] In fact, substantive domesticity is potential within, and generated out of, formal domestication: as Pope says in his dedicatory epistle to Arabella Fermor, "[T]he ancient Poets are in one respect like many modern Ladies; Let an Action be never so trivial in it self, they always make it appear of the utmost Importance" (142). Pope is speaking here of epic machinery, whose metaphorical relationship to modern ladies is revealed, in the poem itself, to be a fully metonymic sublimation. For Pope's mock-epic machinery, the sylphs are nothing but the spirits of dead coquettes, whose duty it is to guard the honor of those still living (canto 1, lines 51–78, pp. 149–51). To accommodate ancient form entails positing modern "femininity."[72]

This is the image of domesticity that dominates *The Rape of the Lock*: the leisured pursuit of a "feminized" modern gentility, whose ceaseless activity is sexual warfare conducted through the elegant, elaborate, and minutely detailed rituals of the London *beau monde:* the "sacred Rites of Pride" by which Belinda arms herself with "*Cosmetic* Pow'rs" (canto 1, lines 128, 124, p. 154); the Baron's altar pyre built and consumed to propitiate the god of love (canto 2, lines 35–46, pp. 159–60); the game of omber (canto 3, lines 19–100, pp. 168–72); the rape of the lock itself (canto 3, lines 147–54, p. 176); the descent to the Cave of Spleen (canto 4, lines 15–88, pp. 181–87); and the climactic Petrarchan battle ("*O cruel Nymph! a living Death I bear,/* Cry'd *Dapperwit,* and sunk beside his Chair./ A mournful Glance Sir *Fopling* upwards cast,/ *Those Eyes are made so killing*—was his last . . . ," canto 5, lines 61–64, p. 200). The domestic interiors within which these rituals transpire have the ambivalence of a trivial privacy that yet purports to enclose the public world—especially evident in the feminine intimacy of Belinda's toilet, in which "[t]he various Off'rings of the World appear . . ." (canto 1, line 130, p. 155). Yet as Pope's threadbare Petrarchisms make clear, this is a domesticity that, however modern, still clings to the heroic fiction that love is war in other terms, and vice versa.

From this perspective, Pope's 1717 addition of Clarissa's speech to canto 5— pedagogically intended, he later said, *to open more clearly the* MORAL *of the poem*"—has the purpose of proposing a second, more fully modernized version of domesticity by which to domesticate the rape of Helen and the Trojan War to modern English culture (p. 123; canto 5, line 7n, p. 195). In other words, once divided from the public, the private realm of domesticity undergoes its own refining subdivision into the comparatively public *beau monde* on the one hand and the intimate interiority of the domestic family on the other. The seeds of the second lie dormant in the first. The "*Love*" propitiated by the Baron is the conventionally adulterous love of the "*French* Romances" (canto 2, lines 37, 38, p. 160), and Clarissa's donation of the fateful scissors concludes as an epic simile for amatory combat: "So Ladies in Romance assist their Knight, / Present the Spear, and arm him for the Fight" (canto 3, lines 129–30, p. 175). However, the love that Ariel discovers in Belinda, a secretive and interior emotion, seems of a different sort:

> As on the Nosegay in her Breast reclin'd,
> He watch'd th' Ideas rising in her Mind,
> Sudden he view'd, in spite of all her Art,
> An Earthly Lover lurking at her Heart
> Amaz'd, confus'd, he found his Pow'r expir'd,
> Resign'd to Fate, and with a Sigh retir'd.
> (canto 3, lines 141–46, p. 176)

The desublimation of the Baron's love, were it needed, would reveal the rooting of courtly idealism in the secrecy of sexual desire, a rooting broadly consistent, in its bedrock materialism, with the market-grounded desublimation that Pope exposes in *Peri Bathous* and that (albeit with a far greater indulgence) is everywhere to be found in the glittering commodities of *The Rape of the Lock*. But Ariel's intimate insight seems to descry a secret that, if material ("earthly"), has a more affective authenticity. Dependent until now on her supernatural sylph for her "Ideas" of love (thus the erotic "Morning-Dream" with which the poem begins, canto 1, line 22, p. 146), Belinda here evinces a disparity between the superficial "Art" of coquetry taught by Ariel and the deep authenticity of what modernity has learned to call "romantic" love.

Throughout the course of the poem Pope's ostentatious and implacable chain of signifiers for the lock whose rape is his subject matter has the effect of separating out those elements of outer and inner, matter and spirit, that the signifying continuum purports only to distinguish: hair-lock-prison-guard-chastity-honor-virtue (cantos 2, lines 19–24, 1, lines 67–78, 3, line 103, 4, lines 105–12, pp. 159, 150–51, 172, 188–89). The emergent modern solution to this division will be an unprecedented conflation of inner and outer: love and marriage. Pope claimed that he had written *The Rape of the Lock* to overcome the estrangement, caused by the actual rape of the lock, between two noble families already interfiliated through several marriages of alliance. Pope hoped to "laugh them together again," an act of matchmaking at the familial level that might seem to turn on patching things up between "Belinda" and "the Baron" through yet another ("public") dynastic marriage of alliance—or would it be a ("private") marriage of free choice and love?73

Clarissa's speech is silent on love. But it does seek to portray the type of a "modern lady" who is *not* like the "ancient poets"—who knows the difference between the "trivial" and the "important." Clarissa, suspicious of Petrarchan idealism ("Why Angels call'd, and Angel-like ador'd?," canto 5, line 12, p. 196), points her moral by aligning the normative opposition between surface and depth (between "Beauty" and "good Sense," "Face" and "Virtue," canto 5, lines 16, 18, p. 196) with the opposition between the dominant, and her own, version of domesticity. That is, Clarissa's clear choice is between the Petrarchan "power" of the coquette and the utilitarian power of the housewife's unpaid productivity:74

> Oh! if to dance all Night and dress all Day,
> Charm'd the Small-pox, or chas'd old Age away;
> Who would not scorn what Huswife's Cares produce,
> Or who would learn one earthly Thing of Use?
> . . . .
> But since, alas! frail Beauty must decay,
> Curl'd or uncurl'd, since Locks will turn to grey,
> Since painted, or not painted, all shall fade,
> And she who scorns a Man, must die a Maid;
> What then remains, but well our Pow'r to use,
> And keep good Humour still whate'er we lose?
> (canto 5, lines 19–22, 25–30, pp. 196–97)

That Clarissa's moral is quickly drowned out by the mock-heroic clamor of figurative militarism only underscores its anticipation of a time when domesticity will be freed of its dependence on formal domestication.

Pastoral

In an earlier chapter I observed that eighteenth-century pastoral undergoes a development related to this anticipation. The privacy of retreat is revalued, I suggested, from the status of a normative but merely passive privation to that of an active agency, the negative liberty of a chosen solitude that might even take the form of a chosen marriage. Pastoral is the final poetic "mixed genre" I will examine in this chapter—although the appropriateness of that category may seem questionable. After all, the instability of pastoral's mixture is a congenital condition of the genre, a function of its constituting aim to describe nature art-fully, a conflationary aim that responds to the antithetical separation of art and nature, which the pastoral tradition also takes as its premise. The implications of this aim for the relation between the public and the private, the city and the country, the high and the low,[75] have a special relevance to our concerns with both the form of domestication and the content of domesticity.

If much formal domestication presumes the posture of speaking of low, sensible things to low, common people, pastoral manifestly fulfills the first but not the second of these conditions. The broad tendency of Renaissance pastoral was to make this apparent imbalance the key to pastoral's formal domestication by treating the genre as a sociopolitical and cultural allegory, an accommodation of the great through the little, the courtly through the rustic, the worldly through the "homely," actual through concrete particularity. The purpose of this fundamental pastoral figuration was seen to be fully pedagogic and hermeneutic. George Puttenham thought Virgil's *Eclogues* were composed "not of purpose to counterfait or represent the rusticall manner of loues and communication: but vnder the vaile of homely persons, and in rude speeches to insinuate and glaunce at greater matters, and such as perchance had not bene safe to haue beene disclosed in any other sort, which may be perceiued by the Eglogues of *Virgill,* in which are treated by figure matters of greater importance then the loues of *Titirus* and *Corydon.* These Eglogues came after to containe and enforme morall discipline, for the amendment of mans behauiour . . . ."[76]

By the end of the seventeenth century a revolution in this domesticating project was under way. Spurred by daring projects like Jacopo Sannazaro's piscatory eclogues, pastoralists were increasingly preoccupied with a different problem in domestication. Thomas Tickell, for example, was moved to inquire how far might one "lawfully deviate from the Ancients" by naturalizing and nationalizing the eclogue in a modern and English direction; and in a famous series of essays in the *Guardian* he undertook, among other things, to "recommend this our Island as a proper Scene for Pastoral under certain Regulations, as will satisfie the courteous Reader that I am in the Landed Interest."[77] Because this inquiry concerned the representation not of real courtiers but of realistic rural settings and people, it encouraged pastoral to treat rural life less as the signifier of a courtly signified than as its own signified, a sensible and material reality susceptible to objective, even microscopic, examination. Tickell argued that although we are not obliged to represent them as "dull and stupid," the minds of shepherds "must be supposed so rude and uncultivated, that nothing but what is plain and unaffected can come from them," a point that reminds us of new-philosophical assertions that disinterested description could be expected from common people (*Guardian*, no. 23, 7 Apr. 1713). Over the long term, pastoral abandoned the Renaissance investment in the allegorical structures of formal domestication[78] and embraced the thematic description of country life and domesticity as an end in itself. Tickell's call for a domestication of pastoral in the nationalizing sense of the term is not very far from Joseph Warton's paradigmatically "pre-romantic" answer to the question where fancy can be found in the modern age: "Turn your Thoughts inward. Look but at Home and you'll soon find you need not go so far as Afric or Asia to seek her."[79]

Signs of this turn may be found already in the several *Guardian* periodical papers, one of whose subtexts is a debate on the comparative pastoralist virtues of Alexander Pope and Ambrose Philips. "The Reason why such Changes from the Ancients should be introduced," wrote Tickell, "is very obvious; namely, that Poetry being Imitation, . . . we must take up the Customs which are most familiar, or universally known [i.e., to current readers], since no Man can be deceived or delighted with the Imitation of what he is ignorant of" (*Guardian*, no. 30, 15 Apr. 1713). Addison praised Philips for just such a domestication: "One would have thought it impossible for this Kind of Poetry to have subsisted without Fawns and Satyrs, Wood-Nymphs and Water-Nymphs, with all the Tribe of Rural Deities. But we see he has given a new Life, and a more natural Beauty to this way of Writing, by substituting in the Place of these antiquated Fables, the superstitious Mythology which prevails among the Shepherds of our own Country" (*Spectator*, no. 523, 30 Oct. 1712). When Pope, parodically impersonating Tickell, recalled having deemed it "a principal Fault to introduce Fruits and Flowers of a Foreign Growth, in Descriptions where the Scene lies in our Country . . . ," his purpose was to belittle Philips for having "described *Wolves* in *England* in his first Pastoral" (*Guardian*, no. 40, 27 Apr. 1713).[80] However, Pope was by no means a strong advocate of modern or English domestications in pastoral: "So that we are not to describe our shepherds as shepherds at this day really are, but as they may be conceiv'd then to have been . . . ." Even Spenser takes the naturalization of Theocritus's "simplicity" too far toward "rusticity," his "plain" style too far toward the "clownish." The Greek's Doric dialect had its own propriety, "whereas the old *English* and country phrases of *Spenser* were either entirely obsolete, or spoken only by people of the lowest condition." Pope nonetheless was careful to domesticate the ancient laurels to English "Willows" in his own winter eclogue.[81]

According to Tickell, Sannazaro went beyond the limits of "lawful deviation" in pastoral domestication when he "changed the Scene in this kind of Poetry from Woods and Lawns, to the barren Beach and boundless Ocean . . ." (*Guardian,* no. 28, 13 Apr. 1713; on Sannazaro see also no. 32, 17 Apr. 1713). Yet surely Swift had already exceeded Sannazaro in the microscopic precision with which his famous pastoral lines localized, in Steele's words, "[t]hings exactly as they happen . . . . They are a Description of the Morning, but of the Morning in Town; nay, of the Morning at this End of the Town . . . ." Swift's "Description," first published by Steele in the *Tatler,* domesticates ancient pastoral through its intense localization and specification to the City of London: country becomes city, shepherd becomes jailor, the natural signs of dawn's approach become a cultural frenzy of license and labor. Steele calls this poem, like its companion piece, the "Description of a City Shower," an example of "Local Poetry." The later poem, in particular, describes a scene as mixed as its form: "various Kinds" of people are driven together by the rainstorm; ancients and moderns are conflated by epic simile; and in a climactic "epic" translation, a vast flood "of all Hues and Odours" washes westward, down from Smithfield to Holborn-Bridge, a natural force that submerges all cultural difference within the uniformity of the flood (and of the concluding triplet). "Mock pastoral" has all the complexity here of mock epic; and as *The Rape of the Lock* lays claim to the status of a miniaturized and revitalized epic, so one seeks among alternative categories to identify the nature of Swift's achievement in his "Descriptions": mock pastoral, antipastoral, urban pastoral, counterpastoral, neopastoral (Tatler, no 9, 30 Apr. 1709; no. 238, 17 Oct. 1709).

This achievement, suggestive in Swift, becomes fully programmatic in John Gay's *Shepherd's Week* (1714).[82] The domesticating impulse is evident as early as Gay's title, which concentrates and miniaturizes Spenser's twelve-month calendar into a six-day week. In "The Proeme" Gay parodies the "Dedicatory Epistle" by Spenser's E.K., as well as Philips's preface to his own pastorals, with an economy that permits the satire of "rustic" antiquarianism to coexist alongside Gay's palpable appreciation for the "simple" specificity of (what we would call) English popular culture, which his poem effectively celebrates.[83] Gay promises us an Anglicizing and "naturalizing" domestication, "a true homebred Tast" of "the Manners of our own honest and laborious Plough-men, in no wise sure more unworthy a *British* Poet's imitation, than those of *Sicily* or *Arcadie* . . . . Furthermore, it is my Purpose, gentle Reader, to set before thee, as it were, a Picture, or rather lively Landscape of thy own Country, just as thou mightest see it, didest thou take a Walk in the Fields at the proper Season . . . ." Domestication leads easily to domesticity: "Thou wilt not find my Shepherdesses idly piping on oaten Reeds, but milking the Kine, tying up the Sheaves, or if the Hogs are astray driving them to their Styes" ("Proeme," 1:90–91, font reversed).

True, this sounds in some ways closer to the old domestic economy than it does to an emergent domesticity. Gay's preoccupation with the low, sensible things of "popular culture" does not sharply distinguish between the socioeconomic vulgarity and the chronological traditionality that still dovetail, at this time, in the rural. Although this is only one dimension of his complex persona, at times Gay approaches his material in the spirit of a cultural and historical preservationist. Hence the work of the housewife has here the breadth of a comprehensive, inside-and-outside "huswifry."[84] In the elegiac "Friday" Bumkinet recalls his beloved Blouzelinda:

> Sometimes, like Wax, she rolls the Butter round,
> Or with the wooden Lilly prints the Pound.
> Whilome I've seen her skim the clouted Cream,
> And press from spongy Curds the milky Stream.
> (lines 59–62, 1:115)

Grubbinol relates Blouzelinda's death:

> Mother, quoth she, let not the Poultry need,
> And give the Goose wherewith to raise her Breed,
> Be these my Sister's Care—and ev'ry Morn
> Amid the Ducklings let her scatter Corn;
> The sickly Calf that's hous'd, be sure to tend,
> Feed him with Milk, and from bleak Colds defend.
> (lines 113–18, 1:117)

Elsewhere, Gay's pastoral complaints feature not lovelorn swains but lovelorn maids, whose domestic skills only underscore the injustice of their plight. In "Tuesday" Marian complains:

> Ah Colin! canst thou leave thy Sweetheart true!
> What I have done for thee will *Cic'ly* do?
> Will she thy Linnen wash or Hosen darn,
> And knit thee Gloves made of her own-spun Yarn?
> Will she with Huswife's Hand provide thy Meat,
> And ev'ry *Sunday* Morn thy Neckcloth plait?
> (lines 31–36, 1:102)

In "Wednesday" Sparabella depreciates her rival:

> The cleanly Cheese-press she could never turn,
> Her awkward Fist did ne'er employ the Churn;
> If e'er she brew'd, the Drink wou'd strait grow sour,
> Before it ever felt the Thunder's Pow'r:
> No Huswifry the dowdy Creature knew;
> To sum up all, her Tongue confess'd the Shrew.
> (lines 41–46, 1:106)

Of course, it is the traditional work of pastoral to celebrate the humble innocence of country life, and Gay's eclogues, although a discontinuous imitation of Virgil's, are closely indebted to them. What nonetheless sets Gay apart from the tradition is the sense of a purpose as much archaeological as ethical. The nostalgic retrospection on the Golden Age that colors pastoral in its temporal dimension[85] becomes in Gay an active project of retrieval—of minutely detailed customs, habits, beliefs, oral traditions—that is formalized by his conclusion of the poem with "*An* ALPHABETICAL CATALOGUE. OF Names, Plants, Flowers, Fruits, Birds, Beasts, Insects, and other material things mentioned in these Pastorals" (1:123–26).[86] The use of this catalog, Gay says (with a glance at Spenser's E.K. that is only partly ironic), may come "when these Words in the course of transitory Things shall decay," and someone else may "render these mine Eclogues into such modern Dialect as shall then be understood . . ." ("Proeme," 1:92, font reversed). As Gay has domesticated Virgil, so some future poet will domesticate Gay (much as Steele recently has domesticated *Paradise Lost*). And although his interest is quite broadly cultural, Gay seems to find in women and their work—in the realm, that is, of protodomesticity—the crucial register of pastoral concern.

Given the importance of Spenser in his parodic project, Gay could hardly be ignorant of the allegorical premises that informed the pastorals of the preceding age. What is his attitude toward this kind of formal domestication? In the "Proeme" Gay briefly disparages the "*Court Clowns, or Clown Courtiers*" that populate such pastoral (1:91). But his "Prologue" dedicates *The Shepherd's Week* to Henry St. John, Viscount Bolingbroke, at the moment of his greatest political power, and it proceeds to celebrate Bolingbroke and the ladies of Queen Anne's court through an explicit parallel with the fictional personages of his eclogues. Lest we take this as a key to the poem's higher, "public" meaning, however, Gay concludes to Bolingbroke:

> Lo here, thou hast mine Eclogues fair,
> But let not these detain thine Ear.
> Let not Affairs of States and Kings
> Wait, while our *Bowzybeus* sings.
> ("Prologue," lines 87–90, 1:95)

The "material things" of common and domestic experience are not to be confused with the public realm from which they are in the process of being definitively separated out. Even in his imitation of Virgil's Fourth Eclogue, the prototype for pastoral allegory, Gay stops short of what the form at first promises:

> Sublimer Strains, O rustick Muse, prepare;
> Forget a-while the Barn and Dairy's Care;
> Thy homely Voice to loftier Numbers raise . . . .
> ("Saturday," lines 1–3, 1:119)

Where Virgil proceeds to prophesy the millennial triumphs of a great Roman consul, Gay treats us, and his bucolic auditors, to the proverbs, folklore, and ballads of the singer Bowzybeus, an encyclopedic rule book and guide to rustic and commoner wisdom.[87] Prepared for a sublimating ascent to the elevated realm whose meaning and glory justify this vulgar world, the poet discovers that the domesticity of country life may be its own justification.

In the decades that follow the experiments of Philips and Pope, Swift and Gay, pastoral continues to undergo a transformation that will bring it, by the end of the century, very close to the project in aligning the empirical account of a "public," external nature with the constitutive power of a "private," internal subjectivity that posterity calls "romanticism." In another context I have suggested how this process may be broadly conceived as an inquiry into the construability of pastoral "retreat." In eighteenth-century English pastoral the venerable topos of the landed gentleman's retirement from the cares of city and court life devolves to a new range of experience: female; proto–laboring class; "macropastoral" colonialism; urban interiority; and, of course, the internalized, "micropastoral" landscape of the mind. One innovation in pastoral poetry, however, crucial to my present concerns, by the end of the previous century already had reached what many take to be the apex of its development. I will close this treatment of pastoral as a "mixed genre" with a brief consideration of the country house poem.

Until quite recently critics have seen the genre of the country house poem as a qualitatively exalted but quantitatively limited form, chronologically bounded by Ben Jonson's prototypical "To Penshurst" toward the beginning of the seventeenth century and Andrew Marvell's richly syncretic "Upon Appleton House" in the middle. A recent reconception of the form, however, has collected seventy-seven poems or poetic excerpts that span the entire century and intimate relevant texts both before and after, not to mention in other national cultures.[88] Based on the evidence of this collection, the proposed development of the form sheds a suggestive light on the topics of domestication and domesticity. Three phases have been distinguished. The first, extending from the beginnings to about 1640, most fully justifies the contention that the form should be called not the country house poem but the estate poem because it concerns itself less with the great house itself than with its surrounding estate, and especially its gardens (1). In this phase of the form's development the estate is seen as an emblem of its owner, and one central preoccupation of the form is the decline of housekeeping and hospitality. From 1640 to 1660 this preoccupation is replaced by themes of retirement and privacy expressive, if not fully a function, of the enforced seclusion experienced by Interregnum royalists. In the third and final stage, from the Restoration onward, the estate becomes "an indispensable moral correlate." Its role as a microcosm of themes pertinent to the nation-state, heretofore "implicit," becomes increasingly "explicit" as georgic topics are used to extend the concerns of a small social elite to national and international dimensions. At the same time, the focus of the estate poem is increasingly architectural and house-centered. Although the collection concludes with Pope, it is the Augustan period in which "estate poems came into their own; and eighteenth-century exemplars were far more numerous than seventeenth" (18–24).

This brief survey of the country house poem suggests a pattern broadly consonant with the dialectic—the movement from the distinction to the separation and thence to the conflation of categories—that has organized much of my analysis in this study. "Estate poem" characterizes a discourse for which owner, house, estate, and state stand in implicit relation to one another and for which the hierarchical and reciprocal social relations of the "late-feudal" polity are still a predominant concern. "Country house poem" may become a more appropriate term for later examples of the form, which articulate a separation out of estate from state sufficient to encourage their explicit and experimental conflation and of house from estate adequate to emphasize domestic exterior and interiors as possessing a degree of semantic autonomy.[89]

The development is highly schematic and cannot bear the weight of close application.[90] Moreover, the change it traces should not obscure the continuity on which that change is dependent. Already in Virgil's First Eclogue we hear the fundamental comparison that is by turns implicit distinction, explicit separation, and experimental conflation. *Sic parvis componere magna solebam:* "And so the great I measured by the less," says the shepherd Tityrus of his naive expectation that great Rome would be like his native Mantua (Eclogue 1, line 23, Dryden's trans., p. 4). In its broadest implications Tityrus's hopeful domestication haunts the history of pastoral poetry's inquiry into the relationship between the greater and the less, the city and the country. Indeed, the passage immediately follows Tityrus's obscure allusion to one who ensured his rural *otium* and therefore cannot be deemed "less than god" (Eclogue 1, line 8, Dryden's trans., p. 3), an allusion that points Virgil's concern here with the politics of land redistribution after the civil wars and that parallels the pastoral domestication of greater by less with the public-private aura of political allegory.[91]

Virgil's resonant line echoes through the much briefer history of the country house poem. Speaking of both the house and the poem, Nun Appleton and "Upon Appleton House," Marvell declares:

> Humility alone designs
> Those short but admirable lines,
> By which, ungirt and unconstrained,
> Things greater are in less contained.
> (lines 41–44)

In accord with this optimistic view of domestication and its powers, the opening of Marvell's country house poem reflects contentedly on the grandiosity of seventeenth-century domestic (and poetic) innovation: "Within this sober frame expect / Work of no foreign architect" (lines 1–2).[92] But the proud superfluity of a "hollow palace" (line 19) is tempered by the speaker's reciprocal concern that the modesty of the house (and the poem) may be strained to contain its owner, Lord Fairfax:

> Yet thus the laden house does sweat,
> And scarce endures the Master great:
> But where he comes the swelling hall
> Stirs, and the square grows spherical . . .
> (lines 49–52)

Marvell's apprehension that his poetic enclosure may be inadequate to its ends is a conceit that helps rationalize the persistence of his poem's "mock-heroic" effects, the sense of parody that plays about its self-conscious formal innovations. But the ambiguity of domestication is also central to Marvell's sensitivity regarding what the house is called upon to do. Is the Protestant dwelling a fully positive secularization of the former Catholic nunnery? Is Fairfax's public greatness adequately accommodated by the privacy of a domestic retirement? On the one hand, if the master's elected rustication figures England's prelapsarian grace before the civil war, retirement to his garden can be imagined as a righteously motivated case of conscience:

> For he did, with his utmost skill,
> Ambition weed, but conscience till—
> Conscience, that heaven-nursèd plant,
> Which most our earthy gardens want.
> (lines 353–56)

On the other hand, the speaker will not totally suppress his deep misgiving that the domestication of Fairfax has simply replaced the greater by the less, public action by private "imagination":

> And yet there walks one on the sod
> Who, had it pleasèd him and God,
> Might once have made our gardens spring
> Fresh as his own and flourishing.
> But he preferred to the Cinque Ports
> These five imaginary forts . . . .
> (lines 345–50)

Much later, however, when the speaker's "slow . . . survey" (line 81) has led us out from the house to the garden, meadow, flood, and on into the deepest recess of the wood where he has "encamped my mind" (line 602), we meet Maria, Fairfax's daughter and heir, who embodies a more exemplary model of domestication. Her future confirms the positivity of a Protestant secularization, for Maria has

> been from the first
> In a domestic heaven nursed,
> Under the discipline severe
> Of Fairfax, and the starry Vere;
>
> .   .   .   .
>
> Hence she with graces more divine
> Supplies beyond her sex the line . . . .
> (lines 721–24, 737–38)

The domestication of Fairfax's greatness, his translation from Lord-General of the public state of England to proprietor of the private estate at Nun Appleton, is a lengthier but no less successful route to the same end. With the help of the poetic line, Maria will extend her genealogical line through the virtues and habits of domesticity, and Fairfax's house, now apostrophized by the speaker, will vindicate his initial promise that "things greater are in less contained"—the best one can hope for, perhaps, in a fallen world:

> 'Tis, not what once it was, the world,
> But a rude heap together hurled,
> All negligently overthrown,
> Gulfs, deserts, precipices, stone.
> Your lesser world contains the same,
> But in more decent order tame;
> You, heaven's centre, Nature's lap,
> And paradise's only map.
> (lines 761–68)

Christ in the House of Martha and Mary

I will conclude this selective survey of mixed genres with an instance from the formal history of not poetry but painting. According to the gospels, after Jesus raised Lazarus from the dead he visited Lazarus's sisters, Martha and Mary, in the town of Bethany.

> Now it came to pass, as they went, that he entered into a certain village: and a certain woman named Martha received him into her house. And she had a sister called Mary, which also sat at Jesus' feet, and heard his word. But Martha was cumbered about much serving, and came to him, and said, Lord, dost thou not care that my sister hath left me to serve alone? bid her therefore that she help me. And Jesus answered and said unto her, Martha, Martha, thou art careful and troubled about many things: but one thing is needful; and Mary hath chosen that good part, which shall not be taken away from her.[93]

In the long tradition of biblical commentary this gospel scene has been variously interpreted in reference to the dyadic values with which it suggests Martha and Mary may be associated: the active and the contemplative life, works and faith, the present and the future, the temporal and the eternal. Generalization about the development of this hermeneutic history is of course difficult. Still, it is possible to discern a broad movement from an earlier view of Mary's virtue—the "one thing needful"—as more highly valued within a "traditional symbiosis" in which the imitation of both women is normative for the exemplary Christian life to a later disposition whereby the "mixed life of action and contemplation" was "replaced by a tendency to separate the two lives" and to value them independently of each other.[94] This sort of development accords with our schematic understanding of the division of knowledge as a movement from relations of distinction to relations of separation. When we turn to visual interpretations of the gospel scene, however, we find that the altered medium affords the representation of value relations a new, and subtly expressive, dimension. In the following discussion my aim is not to test the hypothesis of a parallel development from distinction to separation in pictorial representations of the scene—indeed, I focus only on sixteenth- and seventeenth-century depictions—but to explore in a more synchronic fashion the complex range of images to which artists had recourse in this period as evidence of a mixed genre comparable to those we have already encountered in literary media. The Martha and Mary paintings constitute a "genre" not only in the general, broadly formal sense of the term but also in the specifically art-historical sense that they fall into the category of "genre painting," which designates images of common and everyday life as distinguished from subjects drawn from the realm of biblical, mythological, and heroic tradition. Or rather, the Martha and Mary scenes exemplify religious painting that uses the conventions of genre painting in innovative ways to thematize its concern with the crucial relationship between the spirit and the flesh, the sacred and the secular, the great and the lesser. Their "mixture" therefore may be understood as symptomatic, like that of some of the literary works I have already discussed, of an early modern tendency toward secularization in the full sense of the term: as a sacralizing accommodation of elevated religious motives both through and to the profane experience of daily life.

In the paintings of Martha and Mary this crucial relationship is interpreted most fundamentally by the placement and postures of the two sisters themselves with respect both to each other and to the figure of Christ. Luke says that Mary "sat at Jesus' feet, and heard his word," and some of the many paintings in this pictorial tradition follow the gospel account literally, situating her on the floor beside Jesus in postures ranging from rapt attention to prayerful adoration. More picture Mary seated next to Jesus on a low chair, stool, or pile of cushions that maintains her position, virtually universal in these paintings, as the humblest of the three points that define the triangular composition of sacred figures (see plates 3, 5,[95] 6, and 8[96] and figs. 8.2, 8.4, 8.5, and 8.6). Martha, by contrast, sometimes is placed in height between Jesus and Mary (plates 3 and 7 and fig. 8.3) but more often, standing, defines the highest point of the triangle.

These relative placements are subject, of course, to moral interpretation. In traditional secular contexts domestic activity broadly connotes a mode of privacy as privation that is more familiar but less powerful than the public realm. In religious and particularly Protestant contexts, however, the domestic may assume the aspect of a "public" worldliness whose power pales beside that of the privatized spirit. In Vermeer's painting (plate 8) Martha faces the viewer and, tending to her domestic duties, places a basket of bread on the table, while her sister, head propped on her hand, gazes pensively into Jesus's eyes. Christ seems to gesture toward Mary as he speaks to Martha, instructing her in the one thing needful. Yet the eucharistic nature of Martha's service and her central positioning in the scene suggest a balanced assessment of the relationship between the devotional and the worldly, faith and works. In the painting by Seghers (fig.

Fig. 8.2. (*opposite, top*) Pieter Aertsen, *Vanitas. Still-life with Jesus, Mary, and Martha, Sisters of Lazarus*, 1552. Kunsthistorisches Museum, Gemaeldegalerie, Vienna, Austria. Erich Lessing/Art Resource, NY.

Fig. 8.3. (*opposite, bottom*) Jacopo and Francesco Bassano, *Christ in the House of Mary, Martha, and Lazarus*, c. 1577. Sarah Campbell Blaffer Foundation, Houston, Texas.

FIG. 8.4. Joachim Bueckelaer, *Kitchen Maid*, 1574. Kunsthistorisches Museum, Vienna, Austria.

8.5) hand gestures seem to capture both Christ's gentle reproach and the gentle complaint from Martha that motivates it, while Mary, by contrast, looks bemused, even bashful. The majority of the paintings are concerned in this way to represent the act of discourse between Jesus and Martha, with Mary's silence bespeaking a contemplative mode expressive of the one thing needful. But Mary is not entirely still. Jacopo and Francesco Bassano (fig. 8.3) represent her spiritual devotion through the act of kissing Christ's hand, and in both of Aertsen's paintings (plate 3 and fig. 8.2) Mary folds her hands in a prayerlike gesture, while in the latter Jesus blesses her by placing his right hand on her head. Over the mantle is inscribed, "Mary has chosen the best part."[97] Only in Tintoretto's

FIG. 8.5. Gerard Seghers, *Jesus in the House of Martha and Mary*, c. 1620. Museo Nacional del Prado, Spain.

painting (plate 6) does Martha seem forcefully to address her sister, whose right hand silently but subtly responds to the dynamic intensity of Christ's gestures in a way that suggests the deepest of engagements.

Yet Martha's authority is not ostensibly diminished thereby. Rather, the tendency of these several depictions is to underscore, through Martha's spatially mediatory posture, the iconographic doubleness of her role as servant to the demands of the body. On the one hand, she stands in opposition to the one thing needful that shall not be taken away by death. On the other hand, the needs of the flesh are (as we have seen) an ancient, and highly conventional, accommodation of the needs of the spirit. This hermeneutic relationship between Martha and Mary is well represented by the Bassano brothers (fig. 8.3), whose Martha intimately leans into the sacred triangle on her right even as she gestures eloquently with her outstretched left arm toward the enabling sustenance being prepared at the table and fireplace. With consummate economy Vermeer (plate 8) achieves a similar effect through the vertical axis of his painting, whose upward movement is defined by one hand of each of his subjects and culminates in the mediatory figure of Martha, a triangle within a triangle, and the eucharistic mystery of her offering.

To speak in these terms is only to begin to address the expressiveness with which the artists interpret Luke's moral meaning through the variable triangulation of Martha, Mary, and Jesus.[98] Scholars have shown, moreover, how other details in the depiction of the religious triangle—architectural decorations, other biblical figures—are used to underscore the didactic message that the conjunction of the two sisters themselves is meant to convey.[99] Yet the iconography of the Martha and Mary scenes is powerfully accentuated also by the situation of that triangle within the larger space of the canvas. From this perspective, the semantic significance of its internal variations is reinforced—or complicated—by variations in the way the triangle itself is placed within the painting's external frame. One compositional extreme is exemplified by plates 5 and 7 and figure 8.4. Here the triangle is set deep into the background of the painting, rendering its figures diminutive in comparison with those in the foreground and closeting them with such closure as to suggest that they exist in an entirely different dimension. This is most striking in the spare simplicity of Velázquez's painting (plate 7), whose tightly framed triangle has been read by some as though viewed through a wall opening (for which no hatch is, however, visible) and by others as a mirror's reflection of what lies, off-canvas, in the space of the viewer.[100] The choice between window and mirror defines the ambiguity of this, if not every, domestic servant in the Martha and Mary paintings: is Velázquez's central figure observant, or oblivious, of the sacred scene that transpires in some numinous way "behind" her?

FIG. 8.6. Joachim Wtewael, *Kitchen Scene with Christ, Martha, and Mary*, c. 1620–1625, location unknown. In Anne W. Lowenthal, *Joachim Wtewael and Dutch Mannerism* (Doornspijk, The Netherlands: Davaco, 1986). Princeton University Library.

Dominating the foreground in these three paintings is a genre scene, a still life of food and its preparation by domestic servants. And by this basic juxtaposition the relationship between flesh and spirit, foreground and background, large and small, encompassing genre scene and framed sacred subject, recapitulates in other terms the relationship between the figures who are enclosed within the latter frame.[101] Is it plausible to conceive of this composition, on analogy with formal domestication, as a "genericization" of the biblical, an accommodation of the elevated by means of the lowly? In other Martha and Mary paintings the compositional structure is similar but the contrast somewhat less stark owing to the implication of an architectural continuity between the foreground and the background spaces. Thus in plates 3 and 4 and figures 8.2 and 8.6 the sacred scene is recessed rather than definitively cut off from the foregrounded scenes of work and still life. Here the apparitional sense of discontinuity evident especially in Velázquez is modified to one of contrast between entities that nonetheless share a phenomenal space, a contrast in some cases heightened by the monumental presence of the female servants and/or the cornucopian foodstuffs. The perspectival contrast calls to mind, in the literary medium, the grotesque but intimate disparity between Gulliver and the Brobdingnagian maids who carelessly display their flesh to him (*Gulliver's Travels*, pt. 2, chap. 5), but here the tiny Gulliver is in some fashion replaced by the tiny devotional scene, and the naked candor of the maids is replaced by the brazen display of the servants and their naked skewered poultry. Plate 5 and figure 8.4 extend this kind of visual perspectivism to the level of outright concealment. In figure 8.4 the extreme miniaturization of the sacred triangle in the right background is parodically balanced by the trussed fowl in the left foreground. In plate 5 a spitted fowl partially obscures the sacred inset and, perhaps, the figure of Martha herself. In plate 4 one of the cooks, apparently unaware of the scene, all but blocks our view of it. We may well be reminded (a Swiftian parallel once again seems apposite) of Wotton's complaint that the allegory in *A Tale of a Tub* makes Christian history into a "farce," or of Clarendon's charge that Hobbes's *Leviathan* "hath traduced the whole scheme of Christianity into Burlesque."[102]

As in Milton's accommodation of knowledge to eating,[103] the Martha and Mary paintings turn on the issue of the adequacy of outward, material consumption as a figure for inward, spiritual sustenance. And like the prelapsarian scene in the Garden, these images might be understood provisionally as domestications that use domestic means to achieve their formal ends. But does the visual experience of traversing the distance between the material foreground and the spiritual background in these images elicit the sense of a successful accommodation or the conviction that you cannot get there from here? As John Bunyan warned the readers of his Christian allegory:

Take, heed also, that thou be not extream,
In playing with the out-side of my Dream:
Nor let my figure, or similitude,
Put thee into a laughter or a feud;
Leave this for Boys and Fools; but as for thee,
Do thou the substance of my matter see.[104]

The analogy between literary allegory and what has been called "mannerist inversion"[105] is compelling in part because it obliges us to remark not only the similarities but also the differences between the verbal and the visual techniques. The Martha and Mary paintings allow easy access to the similarities. Unlike in the celebrated inversion in Breughel's *Icarus,* for example, where one is struck by the displacement of attention from the more to the less significant detail, in these paintings on sacred themes (as in Bunyan's allegory of the humble pilgrim) the displacement also carries the hermeneutic weight of the Christian doctrine whereby the humble is revalued as the great and the elevated as the lowly. But the visual medium is much more powerfully—one might say "literally"—figurative than the verbal, and the cognitive process of visual interpretation depends far more heavily on the interplay of images that are in the first instance nonconceptual. Of course, Christian art deploys a vast storehouse of visual symbols whose meaning habitual usage has made to inhere in the images themselves. But although both symbols and allegories signify, the essence of allegory and its interpretation is that it also moves in time.[106] In the apprehension of language, as Lessing famously argued, temporality—and therefore the potential for allegorical interpretation—is a condition of the medium; in the apprehension of visual images it is not.[107] In the Martha and Mary paintings that exploit spatial depth, as we have been observing, the reflexive relationship between biblical and generic subjects and the movement of the eye by which this reflexivity is grasped approximate to the temporal movement whereby abstract meaning allegorically accrues to concrete things. But the immediacy and simultaneity of those things in the visual medium, some of which bespeak concrete materiality and others abstract spirituality, give to the process of signification a greater volatility than it has in language. As a result, allegorical discovery in these paintings often balances (as we have seen) on the edge of parody or irony. Indeed, the irony of these paintings is deeply grounded in, and doctrinally authorized by, the way the physical size and proximity of the generic and sacred subjects seem to stand in inverse relation to their moral value. But unlike in literary allegory, the apprehension of similarity on which "genericization" depends is impeded by the fact that difference is represented with an inescapably palpable simultaneity and immediacy.

From this fundamental perspective, the domesticating promise of these generic domestic scenes would seem to be minimal. In fact, the close attention paid to material detail may even persuade us that, as in some early novelistic narratives, the announced end of spiritualization is belied by the allure of the materiality that (according to this hypothesis) purports to be no more than an instrument toward our edification.[108] But the hermeneutic powers of the domestic are at play in these paintings at several levels. In Wtewael's (fig. 8.6), for example, the way the cook's posture mirrors that of Martha, herself demonstratively busy (unlike many of her representations) at active kitchen work, complicates our reading of the sacred triangle. Is Martha to be seen as recapitulating the materialistic and mock-heroic inflation of the servant, or does her place in the closely concentrated scenario of the sacred establish, on the macromodel of the servant, a symbiotic relationship between the active flesh and the contemplative spirit? More striking still is the visual parallelism in plate 5. Here the body of the cook (is she in fact a macro-Martha, not obscured by the fowl but translated from the religious to the genre scene?) echoes that of the contemplative Mary, whose right arm and downcast eyes draw our eyes to the open book in her lap. But what are we to make of the spatial correspondence between this emblem of spiritual nourishment and the succulent slice of salmon fingered by the buxom cook—itself a suggestive symbol, scholars tell us, of the female genitals?[109] In the accommodating movement of our vision from front to back, from large to small, and from one sort of interiority to another, similarity and difference engage each other in close battle to preserve in this scenario if not an innocent then at least a positive hermeneutic.

The Martha and Mary paintings mark a contradictory moment in the emergence of modern privacy. The sexuality of their kitchen scenes vies with the spirituality of the religious enclosures they front for the position of subjectively, if not ethically, privileged mediator of interiority. Like the architectural inside spaces that were increasingly hived off from public living areas over the course of the seventeenth century,[110] the sacred spaces in these paintings seem to define the privacy of an interiorized retreat. And yet the vertiginously hermeneutic relationship between inside and outside encourages us to see in the kitchen spaces, as well, an interiority that is not only domestic and sexual but also spiritual—indeed, to see there a negotiation of the shifting boundaries between these several private domains.

In the painting by Wtewael (fig. 8.6), how are we to understand the relationship between the cook herself and the table that, standing just behind her and hence slightly nearer to the sacred background scene, is set with a eucharistic still life of pure white cloth, bread, and wine?[111] The plate also holds some fish, the universal symbol of Christ and a genre detail that recurs insistently and ambiguously throughout the Martha and Mary still lifes. Within such settings the sliced salmon and the array of whole fish, the latter as phallic[112] as the former is vulval, the trussed and spitted birds and wildlife, bespeak a preoccupation not only with *voluptas carnis* but also with the sacred mysteries of sacrifice and transubstantiation.[113] Meanwhile, in the background, Wtewael's contemplative Mary, and even more Seghers's (fig. 8.5), betrays in the languid droop of her arm a literal inclination toward the animal.[114] Aertsen's foreground (fig. 8.2) is unusual in being devoid of human figures. Instead it contains, besides the enormous haunch of meat, a massive cabinet or strongbox whose door is ajar so as to reveal precious objects and documents inside; on the door itself hangs a fat money bag, and in it a set of keys hangs from the lock. These are the keys of Martha, authorized and "careful" mistress of the house. In consort with major compositional lines in the painting, the mouth of the strongbox directs us back to the mouth of the fireplace that frames the authority of Christ at the painting's vanishing point. If the strongbox and its glittering contents complement the foodstuffs with symbols of not bodily but financial materialism, they also complement the light of the fireplace in the background, conjoining Martha with Jesus as caretakers of, and keybearers to, their respective kingdoms.[115]

The oppositional clarity of the relationship between foreground and background is complicated in a different way in Aertsen's other painting (plate 3). Here the foreground genre scene itself, although architecturally unified as a single elegant kitchen, is perspectivally subdivided into three planes. Closest to the viewer are tables topped with alimentary and botanical still lifes. Behind these, on the left, is a generic grouping, perhaps of kitchen servants,[116] dressed in contemporary clothing. A group on the right mirrors this one but recedes farther into the background of their common space. Here the four disciples, biblically attired, include the youthful John, on the floor, and the seated Peter, who (following folk tradition) is tipsy and lecherous, a figure of fleshly license attended by a voluptuous and complaisant cook whose modern dress identifies her with those on the extreme left. Engraved above the fireplace are Hebrew characters of no particular meaning. Members of each group glance across the centuries toward the domain of the other, ignoring the sacred scene that unfolds behind them in an open courtyard whose light and architectural detail sharply divide it from the dark wainscoting of the foreground space with which it is nonetheless continuous.[117] The depth of the composition creates a scale of sizes suggestive of a moral differential that is complicated both by the mirroring effect in the foreground groups and by their sartorial anachronism, which carries the mixture of the biblical and the generic a step further. Of course, the idea of conscious anachronism may itself be still, if barely, anachronistic for this period.[118] But the modern habit of periodization is emergent in a way that is broadly analogous to that of both secularity and privacy, and Aertsen's mixed costumes augment, whatever his motive, the effect of his mixed genre. Bueckelaer (plate 4) follows Aertsen in many of these details and effects but with variations, especially the relative compaction of the foreground space and its more emphatic distance from the background scene. The contemporary and biblical figures, more inter-mixed and concentrated in the middle and at the right of the canvas, do not convey the relatively symmetrical opposition between historically distinct groups that we sense in plate 3. They attend either to their work or to the view-er, composing a more integral group that, rather than framing, all but blocks out the sacred scene that is set off-center in the deep background.

Although they have made no appearance in this discussion of "allegorical" inversion and the ostentatious interplay of foreground and background, those paintings of Martha and Mary that abstain from such formal effects would seem already to have been accounted for in my brief, opening remarks on the range of ways in which the sacred triangle itself has been treated. And yet to re-turn to them after this discussion is also to see them in a new light. In some of these images sartorial anachronism is sustained (in a highly traditional fash-ion) simply by the representation of Jesus in biblical robes and the sisters in modern dress. In Tintoretto's painting (plate 6) the contrast is emphasized and spatialized by the glimpse we have of the biblically attired disciples outside the background window and of the contemporary kitchen maid, a bit closer, tend-ing the fire on the right. In the Bassano brothers' painting (fig. 8.3) Jesus seems to emerge from outside through an ancient stone arch on the left and into the space of a modern kitchen bustling with domestic activity and culinary still lifes.

For the most part, however, the contrast between the biblical and the generic is understated because the biblical seems to have been "internalized" within the generic.[119] That is, the accommodation of the profane and familiar domestic setting to the representation of the sacred event and its spiritual meaning is so successful that the evidence of it as a highly ostensible hermeneutic activity is all but absent. This is not to say that internalization obviates interpretation. On the contrary, the range of spiritualization—the semantic variety entailed in the way the artists triangulate their central figures—is as subtle and various as it might be. In Tintoretto's painting (plate 6) we see Martha the authoritative house mistress; in the works of the Bassano brothers (fig. 8.3) and Vermeer (plate 8) we see her worldly care spiritualized into a sublime devotion. Seghers (fig. 8.5) gives us a Mary whose contemplative mood borders on the mundane and prosaic (in this instance perhaps a sign of the failure of accommodation); in Vermeer (plate 8) we see reflected in her deep absorption the hypnotic spell cast by the charismatic man of wisdom; Tintoretto (plate 6) captures in Mary a medley of reserve and fascination generated by the vocal dynamism both of her sister and of her remarkable guest. In short, what these paintings sacrifice in planar complexity and explicit hermeneutic reflexivity they make up in the depth of emotion that inhabits the faces and bodies of Martha and Mary, who, by coalescing before us in the foreground, become more-than-human emblems that are also fully human. In Velázquez (plate 7) the ineffable compound of thought and feeling is found in the face of the maid-servant, and the sisters themselves reside in the biblical background, obscure and rudimentary types waiting to be animated by the intermingled emotions illuminated in the generic foreground. In Tintoretto (plate 6) and Vermeer (plate 8) Martha and Mary have been fully subsumed by the world of the everyday. The mixed genre has become uniform; domestication has been absorbed by domesticity.

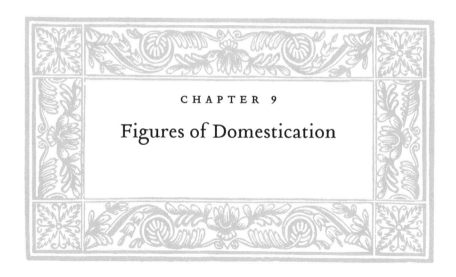

CHAPTER 9

Figures of Domestication

The history of the mixed forms reviewed in the preceding chapter varies considerably: some of them contemporaries found to be tacit within traditional forms; others took shape through self-conscious experimentation. Yet over and above these differences there is a shared impulse to bring together distinct levels of discourse, variously conceived as the great and the little, the high and the low, the important and the trivial, the noble and the common, the male and the female, the sublime and the bathetic, the abstract and the concrete, the universal and the local—discursive dyads that express in different ways the problematic relationship between the public and the private. Crucial to these mixtures is their instability. In some cases the very sense of mixture may be minimized by a still-effectual tendency to treat its terms as distinct but interdependent and inseparable, even where (as often) one term is given a normative weighting. In all such cases, however, the very impulse toward mixture may be felt to be energized by a will to test the inseparability of the terms, even the normative nature of their relation. In many of these mixed forms, moreover, the normative relation of terms is expressed through the "domesticating"—the pedagogic-hermeneutic—serviceability of one to the other as means to end or signifier to signified. And in these cases the instability of the mixture is registered, at least in part, through the intimation that the lesser term in the pair may be capable of internalizing the end or signification toward which it is conventionally held to be no more than serviceable.

The present chapter will extend this formal inquiry beyond the mixed forms already surveyed into the realm of prose narrative. Techniques of narrative domestication show all the variety already evident in those mixed forms, and I will not try to recapitulate that variety here. My aim is rather to cast into relief two rhetorical figures that have been implicit within much of the foregoing material but that coalesce as distinctive strategies of domestication, possessing their own traditions of discourse, in specifically narrative practice. The first of these figures, closely associated with the traditions of patriarchalist analogy and political allegory, involves the strategy by which domestic narrative is elaborated in order to distill or concentrate broad-based issues of policy and political principle. The second figure, associated with exemplary pedagogy and the casuistical case study, involves the strategy by which domestic narrative is elaborated in order to particularize or concretize abstract ethical principle.

Although contemporaries make local use of these figures in distinct contexts and to distinct ends, they would separate them out from each other no more decisively than they would politics and ethics. Both make an essential contribution to the emergent discourse of civil society, to what Habermas calls the public sphere. And both evince the instability characteristic of all mixed forms during this period, in this case the potential of a substantive domesticity to replace and recapitulate the work of formal domestication by which it has been generated. At the same time, one part of the interest in attending to concentration and concretization as distinct rhetorical figures possessing their own discursive traditions lies in the fact that their distinction enunciates an emergent division of knowledge—between the political subject and the ethical subject—that takes on fundamental significance in modern attitudes toward the public and the private.

Narrative Concentration

Narrative concentration is a technique for reducing broadly conceived and widely ramified narratives to stories of simpler scope and more circumscribed dimensions. A method of formal domestication, narrative concentration has a widespread application that is of course by no means limited to the generation of specifically domestic story that is now my central focus.[1] The best-known of such stories, owing less to its narrative interest than to its central character's later career as a political symbol, is no doubt that of John Bull. Formulated by John Arbuthnot as an allegory of European affairs around the War of the Spanish Succession, the story turns on the fate of the empire after the death of Charles II of Spain, figured as the "very great Landed Estate" of the deceased Lord *Strutt*. The war is concentrated as a lawsuit aimed at forestalling Louis XIV's (Lewis Baboon's) engrossment of the estate; however, England is figured not as a landowner but as a bluff tradesman, "John Bull the clothier."[2]

Politics

Jonathan Swift's political writings provide several shorter, and finally more interesting, examples of concentration where (as also in *A Tale of a Tub*'s ecclesiastical allegory) the domestication of public affairs issues in the domesticity of a landed estate. In the following passage Swift "concentrates" the fall of the Whigs and the public credit in 1710: "For my own part, when I saw this false Credit sink, upon the Change of the Ministry, I was singular enough to conceive it a good Omen. It seemed, as if the young extravagant Heir had got a new Steward, and was resolved to look into his Estate before things grew desperate, which made the Usurers forbear feeding him with Mony, as they used to do." Matters of public, state policy are distilled here to the essence of private estate management. Two decades later Swift has similar recourse to domestic concentration regarding the expedients required to combat Irish economic crisis: "Suppose a gentleman's estate of 200*l.* a year should sink to one hundred, . . . and suppose the said gentleman utterly hopeless and unqualified ever to retrieve the loss; how is he otherwise to proceed in his future oeconomy, than by reducing it on every article to one half less, unless he will be content to fly his country, or rot in jail? This is a representation of Ireland's condition . . . ." Several paragraphs later Swift returns to the representation: "If my steward comes and tells me, that my rents are sunk so low that they are very little more than sufficient to pay my servants their wages, have I any other course left, than to cashier four in six of my rascally footmen, and a number of other varlets in my family, of whose insolence the whole neighbourhood complains[?]"[3]

These narrative concentrations are momentary and opportunistic interventions within larger discursive arguments. At one point in his journalistic career Swift reflected, with characteristic obliquity, on their rhetorical uses. "When I first undertook this Paper," he writes, "I was resolved to concern my self only with *Things,* and not with *Persons.* . . . [But] the *Things* I have Occasion to mention, are so closely linked to *Persons,* that nothing but *Time* (the Father of *Oblivion*) can separate them. Let me put a parallel Case . . . ." Swift proceeds to imagine himself an estate holder who suddenly finds himself "over Head-and-Ears in Debt, although I were sure my Tenants paid their Rents very well, and that I never spent all my *Income* . . . ." In such a situation, he continues, his friends, knowing which of his employees bore responsibility for these matters, could be counted on to link thing to person and to advise him to fire "Mr. *Old-fox* my Receiver, and take another." Elaborating the fiction, Swift imagines his tenants to be involved in squabbles and (since he is also justice of the peace) his clerks to have mismanaged his legal cases. The good advice of his friend is to punish the persons responsible—"*Will Bigamy,* the *Seneschal* of my *Mannor*" and "*Charles* and *Harry*, my two *Clerks*." Swift then makes the lesson of the parallel between estate and state explicit: "It is the same Thing in the Conduct of publick Affairs . . . barely to Relate the Facts, at least, while they are fresh in Memory, will as much reflect upon the Persons concerned, as if we had told their Names at length." The analogy between private and public affairs is instructive enough. But the rhetorical strategy Swift really teaches is not that of explicit simile but that of surreptitious allegory, since the attentive reader may take the process one step further and correlate the private offices of receiver, seneschal, and clerks in Swift's fiction with their closest actual public equivalents so as to infer the identities of guilty parties at the state level even though the discursive domain of the political and the public has not been broached. This, at least, may be the implication of the footnotes that were added to the text when Swift's collected works were published almost thirty years later and "the facts" were no longer "fresh in memory." For the footnotes frankly serve as a key by supplying the names of the public ministers who correspond to the names of Swift's fictional servants. The other possibility, of course, is that however suggestive it may have been, Swift's fiction became truly functional as a political allegory only when the names could be supplied with impunity.[4]

Swift preceded these uses of narrative concentration with one of similar import—comparing state policy to estate management—whose formality is, however, a good deal more elaborate and freestanding. "The Story of the Injured Lady," composed in 1707, is a letter written by one who, "[b]eing ruined by the Inconstancy and Unkindness of a Lover," hopes that "a true and plain Relation of my Misfortunes may be of Use and Warning to credulous Maids, never to put too much Trust in deceitful Men."[5] Despite appearances (and as its subtitle suggests), Swift's epistolary fiction is a state allegory directed against England's 1707 Act of Union with Scotland. The eponymous injured lady is Ireland, mistress of a good estate, who, having been seduced by England with a promise of marriage, is now distressed to see her suitor engross her estate and propose marriage instead to her rival, Scotland.

This will be a "publick Wedding" (7), a cynical marriage of alliance, not love: as the injured lady complains, "in Marriage there ought to be an Union of Minds as well as of Persons" (4). She herself is the victim of conjugal deception: her suitor, once having gained "Possession," quickly reneged on his "solemn Vows and Protestations of Marriage" (5). As in *A Tale of a Tub*, Swift's exploitation of the allegory is subtle and ingenious, shaping the domestic scenario to disclose the most singular and salient features of the political situation. Significantly, sexual "possession" is made to stand for the colonial expropriation that in gender relations is legitimated only by marriage: the lady is reduced to the state of a *feme covert* even though she actually remains a *feme sole*. Hence the gentleman quickly finds "Fault with the Government of my Family," acts the "Conqueror," and "expected his Word should be a Law to me in all Things . . ." "[O]ne Third Part of my whole Income is spent on his Estate, and above another Third by his Tolls and Markets . . . ." "[A]ll I now desire is, only to enjoy a little Quiet, to be free from the Persecutions of this unreasonable Man . . ." (5, 6, 7, 8).

The rhetorical premise of Swift's impersonation is that the enormities of English rule will be rendered more legible and odious if domesticated as a private and gendered perfidy. Most strikingly, what had seemed a flaw in an otherwise seamless allegory—the absence of conjugal ties—turns out to be a crucial opening in the argument. This becomes clear in "The Answer to the Injured Lady," which immediately follows her "Story," a brief reply written in the voice of the lady's male addressee. His responses plainly derive their considerable political force from the domestic setting. First, the speaker reproaches the lady for letting her personal hatred of her rival interfere with a more politic female solidarity against the oppressor, who might then have "lessened his Severity to you out of perfect Fear." Second, the speaker points out that the lady's abjection is within her own power to undo. "Having yielded up your Person, you thought nothing else worth defending, and therefore you will not now insist upon those very Conditions for which you yielded at first." The consequences of "possession"—of the loss of chastity, of colonial occupation—are not fixed but negotiable. To behave like a *feme covert* is to forfeit the opportunity of behaving like the boldest of *femes sole* and play "the Trick, very well known among Women of the Town, to grant a Man the Favour over Night, and the next Day have the impudence to deny it to his Face" (10–11). In short, the speaker advises that she, her family, and her tenants draw up articles repudiating the gentleman's financial control (11–12).

As an early document in his long and celebrated campaign against English rule in Ireland, Swift's "Story of the Injured Lady" is predictably brilliant in its polemics. As a concentration narrative it raises some interesting questions. Swift's "subject" here is plainly not the status of women in a patriarchal culture, yet this is just as plainly one of the topics the "Story" is inescapably "about." Reading for the political signified, at what points and in what ways do we—did Swift's intended audience—read "for" the domestic signifier? Taking its shape from the recent public history of Anglo-Irish relations, to what degree does Swift's private figure in turn reshape that history according to a home-grown domestic politics that is as fully in flux, during the early eighteenth century, as the macropolitical realm?[26] These questions are not susceptible to definitive answers; nonetheless, some observations may be in order. Viewed through the microscope of gender relations, English colonialism becomes visible as an act of seductive ingratiation that relies as much on the psychosocial suggestibility of the colony as it does on metropolitan military incursion. By the same token, the guerilla theater of the wife-as-whore illuminates the possibilities for an Irish policy of political resistance in a way that is perhaps unavailable elsewhere on the contemporary political scene.[7] On the other hand, the derivation of private story from issues of public policy may give domestic narrative a special coloring. What if we compare Swift's story with one of "literal" derivation—one derived, that is, not from political affairs but from an older tale on the same theme of domestic seduction and betrayal?[8]

Delarivier Manley's novella "The Wife's Resentment" is a formal "domestication" in the sense of her dedicatory statement that "I have attempted, in modern English, to draw [old stories] out of obscurity . . . ." That is, it modernizes and Anglicizes an Italian tale with a Spanish setting that had already been retold in an English Renaissance version.[9] Circumstantially Manley's story differs from Swift's in two ways: where the injured lady is "born to a good Estate" (4) and never actually marries her oppressor, Manley's Violenta is a virtuous commoner whose marriage is deprived of its authority by her noble husband's denial of it and by his later bigamy.[10] Hence Violenta's "possession" is strictly a matter of sex, not real estate.

Painfully aware that she lacks "redress" both as a woman and as a commoner, Violenta is nonetheless remarkable in being a common woman whose sense of honor is that of a male aristocrat (146, 148, 161). Hence her "honorable resentment" (157) more than amply supplies the power of redress denied by her social circumstance, and she takes bloody revenge on her husband, whose mutilated and dismembered body she triumphantly hurls from her bedroom window into the street below. Violenta's redress, fueled by the antiquated and self-consciously alien social ethics of a traditional novella, takes the histrionically idealized and utopian form proper to a heroic prodigy. The redress Swift urges upon the injured lady, tempered by the pragmatics of contemporary state politics, would entail a strategically restrained agency more closely attuned to the status of the contemporary *feme sole.* In this instance, at any rate, the productivity of the division of knowledge that furnishes the working parts of concentration narrative can be seen in the way it appears to coordinate the public and the private in a dialectical reciprocity whereby each refines the adaptability of the other to emergent and analogous sociopolitical imperatives.

Economics

One of the best-known concentration narratives of the period is Daniel Defoe's extended and radically discontinuous allegory of Lady Credit, which he returned to again and again over the course of five years in his periodical *Review.*[11]

Defoe begins this series with an apology: "[N]or did I design to have pursu'd the meer Allegory of CREDIT to the National Affairs; but I see such room for Publick Service in it, that I thought it my Duty to make this mention of it . . ." (*Review* 3, no. 5, 10 Jan. 1706, p. 20). "Merely" private, the domestic story of credit nonetheless undertakes a great public service. How does the concentration operate?

The only things constant about Defoe's figure of Credit are her sex and the fact that her character is fundamentally (but not entirely) gendered—that is, constituted along a broad spectrum of stereotypically female behavior toward male figures.[12] The spectrum is indeed broad. Credit is a "coy Mistress," a "coy Lass," a "Coy Dame" who, if disobliged, will "slip from you without any Warning" and go away "in a Huff . . ." (3, no. 5, 10 Jan. 1706, pp. 17, 19; 6, no. 31, 14 June 1709, p. 123). But if sometimes a "jade," she is also a "Friend." And her value is "inestimable": Credit is a "Vertuous" and "Beautiful Virgin Lady" who is not simply a "nice Gentlewoman" but a lady of "Quality" and a "Beautiful Countess" (3, no. 5, 10 Jan. 1706, p. 18; 6, no. 32, 16 June 1709, p. 125; 7, no. 117, 23 Dec. 1710, p. 466; no. 102, 18 Nov. 1710, p. 405; no. 116, 21 Dec. 1710, p. 461).

Defoe concentrates his central action—the universal desire for public credit and the effort to pursue a national fiscal policy to maximize it—into a marriage-market courtship narrative in which the prize is an heiress and an estate settlement of unimaginable allure. Lady Credit's suitors fall into two categories. First and most important, she is courted by the crown heads of Europe—foreign monarchs in competition with England, but also (in a series of chronological retrospections) a line of English monarchs, variously successful in their courtship, stretching back to Henry V and forward to the currently reigning Queen Anne. "Courtship" is therefore gendered but not sexed: to court Lady Credit means, on the level of the signified, to persuade her to "dwell" in the country of the royal suitor. Lady Credit has both "Jilted" and "been jilted"; and if she "indeed was never constant to any of her Lovers," this is testimony to the magnitude of the stakes involved and not simply to her female fickleness (8, no. 38, 21 June 1711, p. 156; 3, no. 5, 10 Jan. 1706, p. 18).

True, there is something of the imperious Petrarchan lady in Lady Credit, for she "tyrannizes over Youth, Beauty, Vertue, Estate . . ." to such a degree that Defoe can only advise us to "Pay Homage to this Idol . . ." (6, no. 31, 14 June 1709, p. 123).[13] Certainly she is difficult to read, and she has a basically contrary bent that makes her most available when least courted and needed (3, no. 5, 10 Jan. 1706, p. 19; 6, no. 32, 16 June 1709, p. 126). Yet there is something quite constant in her own desire—a desire for peace and quiet redolent of domestic retirement—which her suitors nonetheless have found very difficult to satisfy. When Charles II ordered the Stop of the Exchequer in 1672 to help finance the

Third Anglo-Dutch War, Credit's mother, Commerce, "big with Child of her" at the time, was so "frighted by the Shoutings of the Rabble" that she nearly miscarried. "Ever since this, the Lady has had an Aversion to Rabbles and Tumults . . ." (7, no. 116, 21 Dec. 1710, p. 462). And although for the past seven years she has lived happily in England, the recent disorders caused by Dr. Sacheverell's polemics on behalf of high-flying Tories and Jacobites have so disturbed her that she now considers leaving for France (see 7, no. 58, 8 Aug. 1710; no. 59, 10 Aug. 1710; no. 102, 18 Nov. 1710; no. 116, 21 Dec. 1710; no. 117, 23 Dec. 1710; no. 134, 1 Feb. 1711; no. 135, 3 Feb. 1711; no. 136, 6 Feb. 1711).

The second category of Lady Credit's suitors follows from Defoe's distinction "between Publick and private, or Personal Credit," that of the nation and that of the individual tradesman: "[A]ll Publick Credit is deriv'd, tho' at some distance, from private Credit, and yet it reciprocally Contributes to the Support of its said remote Parent—And thus they become dependant upon one another" (7, no. 118, 26 Dec. 1710, p. 470). Although the distinction is in itself unexceptionable, we may wonder whether, coming as it does within the realm of the private as defined by Defoe's act of concentration, it exemplifies the familiar tendency toward dialectical recapitulation whereby the separation between the public and the private becomes internalized within the latter realm. In another number Defoe offers a pertinent allegorical genealogy. The sisters Prudence and Vertue were married to, respectively, Probity and Wisdom, and each union issued in daughters—Credit and Reputation—very "like one another" but given "Tuition . . . adapted to two very different kind of appearances in the World . . . ," namely, "publick Affairs" on the one hand and "personal Character" on the other (7, no. 55, 1 Aug. 1710, p. 215). But then what is the relation between "personal Credit" and "personal Character"? Are there two kinds of credit, or is the private sort really "reputation"?

These are, of course, fruitful ambiguities because they exemplify the way the separation out of the public and the private, so far from being definitive, is rather an instrument for thinking more productively about the boundaries between publicity and privacy. In another number Defoe indulges the notion that personal or private credit has a meaning distinct from that of private reputation, and the result is that Lady Credit's other, nonnational, species of suitor comes into view. Despite her elevated quality, Lady Credit not only is willing to "Sociate with the meanest Shop-Keeper, Country Wooll-Comber, or petty Chapmen" but "will keep Company with none but the Industrious, the Honest, the Laborious, and such . . . ." True, if commoners lack these virtues, she will abandon them as quickly as she will monarchs; "they must expect no more Assistance from her, till they take up, turn over a new Leaf, and reform the Crime." But if the meanest tradesman applies himself diligently, "[s]he'll set him up without a Stock, [and] marry him without a Portion . . . ." The tale is poignant enough, reminding us as it may of Foxe's story of the bad apprentice Roger Holland reformed by the love of a good Protestant. Yet the allegory seems for a moment to have turned back upon itself like a Möbius strip. Narrative concentration, undertaken to express the public realm of the financial signified by means of a signifying figure of private courtship and marriage, enters so enthusiastically into its work that it comes to signify itself: not the national competition for public credit but the domestic experience of conjugal upward mobility. And as if to mark this reversal, Defoe breaks off at this point to say: "Let us leave this part of her Conduct, and View her in Publick Business . . ." (7, no. 57, 5 Aug. 1710, pp. 221–22).[14]

What I have called a reversal in the allegory of Lady Credit clearly underscores the problem in understanding that Defoe's narrative exists to investigate. The phenomenon of "public credit" was perhaps the most remarkable of all the instruments that coalesced, during the 1690s, in what we have learned to call the Financial Revolution; and public finance was in turn the most remarkable branch of private economic enterprise that was separated out during the seventeenth century as a distinct category over against the heretofore monolithic power of the centralized political apparatus. Like freedom of conscience, freedom of trade spearheaded the establishment of negative liberty—liberty from state legislation—that first defined the existence, and simultaneously the autonomy and integrity, of civil society. Credit was to financial investment as financial investment was to trade, the extreme instance and great cynosure of individual choice and agency, of freedom from external control. Indeed, what made credit so mysterious was that its objective possession depended on its subjective perception: the public is to the private as objective capital is to subjective credit. The problem of credit—the fact that its highly consequential actuality is grounded in an insubstantial virtuality—therefore makes it ideally suited to narrative virtualization.

Moreover, credit exemplified with unparalleled lucidity the devolution of absolutism. In one number of the *Review* Defoe has Lady Credit declare to him that she "could never consist with Arbitrary Power, because Property had there no Fence . . . . [T]hose absurd Doctrines of Absolute Submission, &c. were so many Declarations of War against her . . ." (7, no. 135, 3 Feb. 1711, p. 538). Yet "'[t]is a strange thing to think, how absolute this Lady is; how despotickly she governs all her Actions . . . ." Credit is a "perfect free Agent acting by Wheels and Springs absolutely undiscover'd . . . . No Law can reach it, Acts of Parliament cannot influence it . . . ." "[N]ot *the Queen,* not *the Parliament,* not all the Arts and Powers of Government in the World can force Credit . . ." (3, no. 5, 10 Jan. 1706, p. 18; 6, no. 31, 14 June 1709, p. 122; 7, no. 102, 18 Nov. 1710, p. 407).

Thus, credit internalizes the absolutism of the monarch as an engine of its own self-government. A self-moved mover, credit has an autotelic integrity whose representation paradoxically requires that it be divided against itself. As the essential expression of free agency, credit is beyond the control of its possessor, an infinite regress of negative liberty. Defoe articulates this paradox in a number of ways. If credit cannot be forced by law, it is also nothing but the force of others' attitudes. A subjective construction, it grounds objective value. Credit is "the great Mystery of this Age," "neither a Soul or Body[,] . . . neither visible [n]or invisible[,] . . . a Being without Matter, a Substance without Form" (6, no. 32, 16 June 1709, p. 125; no. 31, 14 June 1709, p. 122).

In his restless quest to distill credit into intelligibility Defoe has recourse to several other tactics. One of the most striking of these is the allegorical genealogy, one example of which has already been cited (for others, see 3, no. 5, 10 Jan. 1706; 5, no. 107, 2 Dec. 1708; 7, no. 116, 21 Dec. 1710; and 8, nos. 38, 21 June 1711, and 39, 23 June 1711). Successively revising and contradicting one another, Defoe's genealogies well express both the power and the limits of the customary, familial means at his disposal for defining the nature of an unfamiliar entity.[15] How is credit related to "honor" (see 3, no. 5, 10 Jan. 1706, p. 17; and 6, no. 33, 18 June 1709, p. 131)? How is it related to "reputation" (7, no. 55, 1 Aug. 1710, p. 215)? Within this context we can see the ingenuity of Defoe's dominant, and most effective, accommodation of credit, the figure of the marriageable woman. Female nubility had traditionally been defined paradoxically by an objective "chastity" (later, "honor")[16] accessible through subjective "reputation." And of course women had traditionally been subject to an objectifying commodity exchange. However, the autonomization of market enterprise in the latter half of the seventeenth century affected the marriage market as it did all others, and developments in marriage settlement laws, as well as in attitudes toward the social status of women, gave to the figure of the propertied *feme sole* an unprecedented aura of public agency even as "woman" was being shaped to become a vessel of ultimate private interiority. Marriage was a primary means not only of exchange but also of investment, and the *feme sole,* increasingly separated out from the patriarchal family by the prospective "marriage of love" even if also still susceptible to the "marriage of alliance," was increasingly intelligible as both the object and the agent of financial investment.

To speak in these terms is to acknowledge what has been evident for some time in our reading of the *Review* essays. If Defoe's concentration narrative is motivated by the aim to understand public credit by means of the figure of the marriageable woman, its semantic vector also—inevitably—points in the opposite direction, as surely as does that of a tract (like Defoe's *Conjugal Lewdness*) that is explicitly concerned to define the proper grounds of marriage. The "pri-

vate" figure of woman illuminates the "public" institution of credit, but the figure of credit also illuminates woman.

An enthusiastic advocate of credit, Defoe nonetheless shares with his more
conservative contemporaries a traditionalist apprehension of usury, the generation of money from money. How can credit be distinguished from usury? Defoe's fundamental principle in this regard is that "nothing encreases the Stock of
the Nation, but a real and intrinsick Value encreasing." One purpose of his allegorical genealogies is to elaborate categories that set the limit case of credit by
instancing financial instruments that increase not "intrinsic" but "imaginary
Value." These are various: Projecting, Ensuring, Wager; most of all, Stock-job-
bing. And Defoe concentrates these financial instruments in ways that have important implications for his parallel experiment in defining the normative
boundaries of the marriageable woman. Projecting and Ensuring are the bastard twin daughters of Trade and Avarice, who are incestuously impregnated by
their father to produce more bastards, including Wager and Stock-jobber, both
of whom become prostitutes (5, no. 107, 2 Dec. 1708, pp. 427–28; 6, no. 31, 14
June 1709, p. 121). Elsewhere Defoe dismisses "the abortive Births of gaping
Projectors, . . . with their empty Unperforming Proposals," and he characterizes
Stock-jobbers as "*Sodomites*" who seek to defile Credit's "Honour and Chastity"
(3, no. 5, 10 Jan. 1706, p. 18; 6, no. 32, 16 June 1709, p. 127). By figuring the unproductivity of these extreme financial instruments as bastardy, incest, abor-
tion, prostitution, and sodomy Defoe simultaneously tries to set the outer limits of public agency for the nubile woman, whose financially productive status
on the marriage market, dangerously comparable to that of the prostitute, he
definitively distinguishes from prostitution (and from the other procreative
anomalies with which he associates it) by the fact of her legitimate procreative
productivity.[17]

In Defoe's hands, the concentration narrative is an exploratory device of surprising flexibility, permitting a reciprocal illumination of signified and signifier
that frustrates the separation of the public from the private even as it formally
sustains that separation. I will conclude this reading by addressing one aspect of
the process that so far has gone unremarked. If the central fiction of Defoe's
narrative is one of conjugal courtship, the specific nature of Lady Credit's character frequently turns that fiction in an unanticipated direction. Lady Credit's
suitors seek from her the confidence needed to increase their financial assets;
she seeks from them the peace and quiet necessary for that confidence to flourish. As a result, the role of the suitor is often colored by that of the medical spe-
cialist capable of alleviating the effects of public tumult. And behind this coloration lies—at least in the realm of the signified—the venerable figure of the
body politic. At times of peace "Credit is the Health of every Party . . . ." "[A]s

by Veins and Arteries, it conveys its quickening Spirits to all the remotest Parts of that Politick Engine the Constitution . . . ." By the apparent logic of this figure, at times of tumult Lady Credit's state "*Physicians*" must administer "*Cordials*" and return her to her "Native Diet . . . [to] preserve Her Health, and strengthen her Constitution . . ." (7, no. 118, 26 Dec. 1710, p. 471; 6, no. 32, 16 June 1709, p. 125).

But Defoe's concentration involves a significant slippage. For his application of the figure on the level of the signifier transforms credit from one element in the bodily constitution of the commonwealth to the body itself. In becoming Lady Credit, credit becomes a woman of extreme bodily susceptibility whom discord is liable to "thr[o]w . . . INTO FITS." On the most disturbing occasion of this sort, Defoe reports, "she is fallen into a Relapse," and "her Distemper is turn'd into the *Falling-Sickness* [epilepsy]," which is "peculiar to sundry Constitutions, more than to others, and particularly has been a Family-Distemper, among this Ladys Ancestors" (7, nos. 58, 8 Aug. 8 1710, p. 227, and 59, 10 Aug. 1710, p. 229). In the next few decades English people will learn to medicalize female "sensibility" as the neurasthenic condition of hysteria. In the vulnerability of credit Defoe anticipates this somatizing internalization by domesticating the disordered polity as the disordered woman. Genealogical inheritance intimates biological anatomy: the disease of the polity becomes a "family distemper" and then a female disease.[18]

Narrative concentration comes into being when a problematic aspect of public (political, social, economic) actuality is thought to be potentially more tractable to understanding when distilled into the virtual dimensions of a private story. In the second figure of domestication with which I am concerned in this chapter the problem that motivates recourse to narrative strategy is public not in the sense of actuality but in the sense of generality or abstraction. My first exemplar will be, once again, Defoe, because he uses the concretizing procedure as precisely and as self-consciously as anyone.[19] After Defoe, I will turn to Eliza Haywood, whose periodical, the *Female Spectator* (1744–46), is in its own way as inventive as Defoe's conduct manuals in deploying narrative concretization, especially as it prompts us to ask how issues of gender may vary and particularize its deployment.

Narrative Concretization

In an earlier discussion of the technique of teaching precept by example I considered concretizing abstract ethical principle as a mode of formal domestication. This technique received special application in the long history of casuistry. Casuistry specializes exemplary teaching by its premise that to concretize abstract principle is pedagogically useful not only because example is easier to grasp than precept but also because it is in the nature of ethical questions to reveal their complexity only when posed in their circumstantial specificity, as particularized cases of conscientious behavior. Casuistry renders ethics fully problematic by articulating a circumstantial context whose "real-life" density, often a product of conflicting ethical demands, complicates the relative simplicity of abstract principle when viewed in isolation.

Making Ethical Subjects

The relevance of Defoe's casuistical conduct manuals to the themes, and even the form, of his novels was acutely remarked and demonstrated years ago.[20] In this argument, formal interest lay primarily in the way plots generated by casuistical intent have an episodic, paratactic structure that is still evident in Defoe's novelistic plots, although moderated there by the continuity characteristically established through first-person narration. But Defoe's conduct books also use first-person narration—along with third-person narration and dialogue. In the following several pages I aim to focus on the phenomenon of concretization in Defoe's conduct books as a method of teaching the "publicity" of abstract principle through the "privacy" of concrete example; along the way I will also inquire into the relevance to this pedagogic process of his shifts in narrative point of view.

To say that Defoe's conduct manuals attend primarily to the ethical rather than to the political subject is to acknowledge that in this very division of labor we can see evidence of a fuller conceptual separation than that visible in the great Renaissance conduct books like Castiglione's *The Courtier*. For the subject to be treated as an ethical rather than as a political entity presupposes a "private" social status: only in its "privation" of the political does ethical subjectivity come into view as that which is independent not only of (tacit) political subjection but also of (explicit) political subjecthood. Within the family, however, Defoe rediscovers the public-private differential in a variety of forms that can bear a suggestive relation to the abstract-concrete differential of his pedagogic method. Indeed, one benefit of reading early modern conduct manuals, in which formal domestication is a variable but substantive domesticity is a constant, is the light it sheds on what we mean when we speak of the "instability" of discourses like that of patriarchalism. If the logic of such discourse is that the familial gives us easier and plainer access to the political, this logic falters with the discovery that under conditions of social change the realm of the family is no plainer in its rules and structure than is that of the state.

Concretization speaks of low, sensible, and humble things. By the same token, Defoe can appear to imply that it is in those who are relatively low in the familial hierarchy, like younger siblings, that we see the highest possibility of truly ethical conduct. The innocently knowing inquiries of the child are often enough the chief avenue for moral improvement in Defoe's conduct books. And in a work like *The Compleat English Gentleman* the formal reduction achieved by concretization seems to stand in symbiotic relation to the ideological reduction of aristocratic primogeniture.[21] Like others before him, Defoe attempts here to retain the category "gentleman" by emptying it out from the inside, replacing the tacit presumption of a correspondence between external birth and internal worth by the explicit insistence on the latter's priority.

This is also a demystifying exercise in desublimation. "[H]aving made an Idol of our own, . . . we would have all the meaner World fall down and worship him." Instead Defoe undertakes a scientific demonstration that the "Idol" of gentility has its sources in the same humoral "Mixture" from which we all have sprung: "Nay, I will grant an invisible Influence of the Blood," he says with mock indulgence, which "fir'd the Creature with a superior Heat differing from those which mov'd in the Vessels of a meaner and lower Kind of Creature . . . , as if he were . . . not made of the same Materials as the rest of the Species of Men" but was rather possessed of "some sublime Particles in the Animal Secretion, which will not mix with the hated Stream of a mechanick Race . . ." (16–17). Ironically using "the Language of the Times, which I must comply with . . . ," Defoe would in fact insist on the very opposite truth, a secret that remains hidden only so long as traditional knowledge remains tacit: "[A]ll Great things begin in Small, the highest Families begun low, and therefore to examine it too nicely, is to overthrow it all" (13). Instead of birth, blood, and descent as definitive of gentle status Defoe proposes "Learning, Education, Virtue and good Manners . . ." (18), thereby aligning himself with the position that the "privacy" of inner value, fully separable from the "publicity" of outer social status, is a complex function of education and socialization.

But the truth of this secret is conveyed to us most strikingly in the formal register, when Defoe characteristically breaks off his preceptual argument and moves instead to exemplary story, which is framed by the detachment of a first-person narration but quickly modulates to the unmediated first-person of dialogue. "I once met casually with one of those sons of ignorance [a traditional nobleman] in a country coffee-house. He had in his company two clergy-men and his younger brother" (43). The ensuing dialogue between the younger and the elder brother offers a concrete familial model, in a primogenitary culture, for the socio-ethical precepts Defoe has until now been enunciating. In doing so, it provides a body of circumstantial detail about the two brothers that transforms the discourse from relatively straightforward advocacy to a more nuanced casuistry. "I wouldn't giv[e] you my fox-hounds," says the elder brother with some poignancy, "for all your vast coleccion of books, tho' my father was to give you his library to joyn with 'em" (57). Embedding abstract argument in the experiential ground of the familial and the familiar, Defoe discloses a cultural divide whose force is not to obscure his advocacy but to make it more significant because more densely available to us. This quality depends on the first-person narration but especially on the immediacy of dialogue, which captures the protagonists in intimately detailed self-characterization.

In an earlier chapter I looked briefly at the way another of Defoe's conduct books, *Conjugal Lewdness; or, Matrimonial Whoredom* (1727), uses the "public" language of the state to accentuate what is wrong with many "private" marriages.[22] In the present context it is instructive to see how this lesson, first pointed by the vestigial signs of narrative concentration—that is, by the metaphorical internalization of politics within the realm of domesticity (parental "despots" versus amatory "subjects")—thereafter continues to be taught within that realm by successive acts of narrative concretization. Evident throughout this manual, the several stages of concretization can also be seen in the space of a single page. At one point in *Conjugal Lewdness* Defoe begins with a precept about the deplorable priority "public" marriages of alliance and interest seem to have over "private" marriages of love: "Matrimony is now looked upon only as a politick Opportunity to gratify a vitious Appetite: . . . the Money and the Maidenhead is the Subject of our Meditations . . . ." From here it is a short step to exemplary, if still generalized, formulation: "[T]he best of Women are betrayed by [appetite] into the hands of the vilest of Men, and in the grossest manner abus'd; . . . the modest and most virtuous Lady is impudently defloured, and the Night's Enjoyment boasted of the next Day in the Arms of a Strumpet . . . ." And with the following paragraph, the fledgling story is poised for flight: "A —— B—— was a Gentleman of Figure and Fortune . . ." (33).

Yet Defoe's concretized narration, persisting for the space of another page, ends rather abruptly: "If this unhappy Story were a Romance, a Fiction, contrived to illustrate the Subject, I should give it you with all its abhorred Particulars, as far as decency of Language would permit; that the abuse of Matrimony, which is the Subject I am now to enter upon, may be exposed as it deserves. But when Facts, however flagrant, are too near home, and the miserable Sufferers already too much oppressed with the Injury, we must not add to their Afflictions by too publick a use of the Calamity to embellish our Story . . ." (34–35). Defoe's diction only emphasizes the seeming obscurity of the problem. The domesticating momentum that has been established thus far by successive concretizations is now joined by the force of the claim to historicity, a claim whose empirical reference to the facts of actual people (itself implicit in the syncopated names), by bringing things "home" in a distinct but apparently compatible sense of the term, would seem only to redouble the effectiveness of the formal domestication. But instead the claim to historicity has the effect of curtailing concrete narration. And this is because if these are real people, to make their private story "publick" will only "add to their Afflictions" by extending the sort of unethically interested exploitation—"gratify[ing] a vitious Appetite"—that the example is elaborated to reprove. Narrative concretion brings things home in a way that both invites and militates against the impulse to bring things home through empirical actualization.

In earlier chapters we observed that the early modern excavation of the domain of privacy, having increasingly self-conscious recourse to the category of "particularity," over time explicitly separates out those facets of the category that until then had required nothing more definitive than implicit distinction. The modern separation of the public from the private required the disengagement of the particularity of concreteness from the particularity of historico-personal actuality. Only thus could satire be separated from libel, obscene libel from (personal) libel, literary character from authorial ethics, aesthetic experience from strictly sensible experience.[23] The separation out of concrete from actual particularity aided in the emergent division between the "literary" and the "historical" by substituting for the actual particularity of the claim to historicity the concrete particularity of probabilistic "realism," permitting literature to be "personal" in the sense of privacy and intimacy without also being "personal" in the sense of actual reference.[24] In the pertinent passage from *Conjugal Lewdness* Defoe uses the claim to historicity to extend the particularizing force of concretion, only to find that the ethical implications of publishing (of making public) the private-as-actual are very different from those of publishing the private-as-concrete. We can pursue this problem in another of Defoe's conduct books.

Defoe's *The Family Instructor* (1715) begins with a discourse on method motivated by a sense of crisis: "[W]e live in an Age that does not want so much to know their Duty *as to practise it* . . . , in which Men will frankly own a thing to be their Duty, which *at the same Time* they dare omit the Practice of . . . . One Part of this Work is pointed *at such* . . . . The Way I have taken for this, is *intirely new,* and at first *perhaps* it may appear something *odd,* and the Method may be contemned . . . . If then, . . . this mean and familiar Method, should, by its Novelty, prevail, this will be a happy Undertaking . . . ."[25] Were this a more traditional work, Defoe might begin with "a List of Authorities in Scripture for catechising and instructing of Children . . ." (8). Instead he undertakes a method that is "mean and familiar" in that it begins at the other end, not with abstract "duty" but with the concrete "practice" of a recognizable family. And once again, the particularity of this method entails an exemplary concreteness that Defoe inconsistently allies with the particularity of actual personality. Defoe prefaces "The First Dialogue" of *The Family Instructor* by introducing his cast of characters: the father, who "appears knowing enough, but seems to be one of those professing Christians . . ."; the mother, "likewise a formal loose-living Christian . . ."; and the child, "who is here made the Inquirer, [and] has no *Questions* put into his Mouth but what are natural and rational . . . ." In a similar vein of "naturalized" concretion, "[t]he Scene of this little Action is not laid very remote, or the Circumstance obscure . . ." (9–11). Defoe's language here suggests, not historicity, but a concerted effort at a concrete exemplarity based in a casuistical verisimilitude or probability;[26] yet he leaves the door open to actuality: for "the Author, resolving not to give the least Hint that should lead to Persons, has been obliged to leave it uncertain to the Reader, whether it be a History or a Parable . . ." (10–11).

Later on in the manual, Defoe turns his attention to a different category of cases, in whose treatment we can observe the conjunction of several distinct means of marking the public-private differential. The first part has "treated of a Father's Conduct with his Houshold . . . . The ensuing Part will go the same Length in the following Cases, *viz.* (1.) Masters to Servants, (2.) Servants to Masters, and to Fellow-servants, (3.) Companions and 'Sociates one to another . . . . The Scene lies now," he adds, "among the meaner Sort of People . . ." (164–65). Subdividing the private family into its relatively "mean" and its more elevated components, Defoe proceeds to apply to the mean part of the family—in the first instance, the relationship of two apprentices—the "mean and familiar" method he has already used to treat the more elevated. "There lived in a Country Town, an industrious Trading Man, in middling Circumstances, . . . a serious, useful Christian in every Respect . . . . There was in the same Town, a wealthy Shop-keeper, a Man in great Business, . . . so that he had really no Time to think of, or to spare, about religious Affairs. . . . It appears by the Story in hand, that two young Lads, much about the same Age, and pretty near the same Time, came Apprentices to these two Men . . . ." But the boys are very different in their spiritual values; and it so happens that "[t]he sober religious Lad was unhappily put Apprentice to the rich Shop keeper, who regarded no Religion but his Trade; and the wild prophane Boy was put Apprentice to the religious Tradesman . . ." (165–67). Confirming here the proximity of casuistical and scientific method, Defoe sets up an experiment in which variables and controls are established with empirical precision.[27] That is, apprentices are paired with masters so as to ensure that the proclivities in which they have been educated will be explicitly tested rather than tacitly reinforced by their work experience. Moreover, this recourse to the evidence of the senses is repeated, we might say, at the level of narrative point of view. For Defoe now modulates from a formally elevated third-person narration to the concreteness of first-person "dialogue," as though to permit the case to generate, as unmediated "practice," its own highly particularized sense data.

Defoe concludes this dialogue by extracting the dutiful precepts its concretizing practice has thrown into relief. To this end, however, he is first obliged to meditate on the particularity of his characters: "[A]s even this History, will be the same thing as a Parable to the Ages to come, in which it may I hope be as useful as now; and, *above all,* as this Work is design'd for a general, not a particular Reproof, I am willing to let it lie hid entirely, as to *Persons,* that it may perhaps, look less by that means like a History, than really it is." Defoe insists on the actual particularity of his characters, hence on "the Civility shewn them in concealing their Names . . . . But the Design of this Book is of a Nature above a Personal Satyr; the Errors in Family Conduct are the Business here, not the Families themselves; and the Names and Persons so intirely conceal'd and the real History so couch'd that it is impossible for any body, but the Persons themselves, to read the People by the Characters" (190–91). In *Conjugal Lewdness* Defoe rationalized obscuring the actual particularity of his characters as necessary to avoid the exploitation of those to whom they refer. Here the rationale concerns as much what is needed to maximize the effects of his pedagogy on his readers. As exemplary concretion serves the end of preceptual abstraction ("Errors in Family Conduct"), so concrete particularity must facilitate a reproof that is "general" (and not of "the Families themselves"). Actual particularity persists as a powerful rhetorical commonplace, but its pedagogic utility is rendered uncertain by its apparent detachability from concrete particularity, which enables the passage from example to precept that actual particularity may compromise. Concrete particularity can negotiate the public-private differential because its "private" particularity is in this way continuous with a "public" generality. Actual particularity is not, because its "private" particularity frustrates "public" generalization.

In this respect the diachronic confirms the synchronic view. "History" is to "Parable" as the actual particularity of the present is to the concrete particularity of the future. If exemplary story remains pedagogically effective (as Defoe believes it does), it must do so because of its concrete, not its actual, particularity. The generality of the emergent notion of a "reading public" militates against the idea of a public grounded in external reference to actual persons. Over the long term, the reading public will be separated from the empirically existent public as the aesthetic imagination is separated from sensible cognition of the external world and as the self-contained and perdurable pleasures of reading are separated from those attributable, in Samuel Johnson's words, to "personal allusions, local customs, or temporary opinions . . . ."[28]

To summarize: both concentration and concretization use the "privacy" of concrete narrative as a means to what are conceived as greater ends, and in their traditional usage those ends are sufficiently intertwined to militate against their separation out as fundamentally different strategies of domestication. A crucial factor in the shift from distinction to separation is the ascendancy of empiricist thought and its insistence on the epistemological norm of sensible actuality, a factor whose role in that separation can be seen in the way each of these two strategies of domestication reflects the importance of actual particularity. In the strategy of concentration, actual particularity has the central importance of the telos, the end toward which signification operates. That is, concentration uses the concrete particularity of narrative to disclose actual particularity at the level of the public—that is, the political—signified. The strategy of concretization also uses the signifying appeal of the concrete particularity of narrative, but to the distinct end of disclosing a signified that is public by virtue not of its actual particularity but of its ethical abstraction. Consequently, actual particularity enters the concretization process not as an end on which the entire process is predicated but as an invasion from without, an ambivalent acknowledgment of empiricist authority. The traditional commitment of concentration to the representation of elevated public personages, although reinforced at this historical moment by the empiricist standard of actual particularity, over time will come to seem less interesting and important to its practitioners than the stories in which that representation traditionally has been accomplished. In a different but related development, concretization over time will learn to forgo its ambivalent invocation of actual particularity at the level of the signified.

Female Ethical Subjectivity

In moving now to Eliza Haywood I will pursue evidence of this development in the techniques and purposes of concretization narrative. Although Defoe's conduct manuals and Haywood's monthly periodical, the *Female Spectator* (1744–46),[29] are generically disparate, Haywood's understanding of her aim in this work brings her pedagogy into close proximity with Defoe's. In her first number she tells us that in order to "secure an eternal Fund of Intelligence," she has established a network of well-placed "Spies," domestic and foreign, who will aid her in "penetrating into the Mysteries of the Alcove, the Cabinet, or Field" so as to disclose "all the Secrets of *Europe* . . ." (1.1.8).[30] Midway through the run, however, a correspondent takes issue with this claim. Haughtily addressing Haywood as "*Vain Pretender to Things above thy Reach!*" he complains that

> Tho' I never had any very great Opinion of your Sex as Authors, yet I thought, whenever you set up for such, you had Cunning enough to confine yourselves with-

in your own Sphere, or at least not to raise the Expectations of the Public by such *mountainous* Promises as you have done, when you could not be insensible they must in a short time discover themselves to be but of the *Mole-hill* kind. . . . Every body imagin'd you had a Key to unlock the Cabinet of Princes,—a Clue to guide you through the most intricate Labyrinths of State . . . . Are you not under most terrible Apprehensions that . . . you should be taken for an idle, prating, gossiping old Woman, fit only to tell long Stories by the Fire-side for the Entertainment of little Children or Matrons, more antiquated than yourself? . . . To deal plainly with you, the Lucubrations you have hitherto published [might be] recommended as Maxims for the well regulating private Life; but are no way fit for the polite Coffee-Houses, or to satisfy Persons of an inquisitive Taste. (2.8.117–20)

Both Haywood and her antagonist use here a trope central to the discourse of the "secret history" that had flourished around the turn of the century—the trope of the royal cabinet of clandestine letters, crammed with absolutist *arcana imperii* made scandalously but justifiably public through publication. In its simplest form a secret history might consist of a published correspondence purporting to be by real public figures. More elaborately but very commonly, it was a scandalous memoir or *roman à clef* whose "key" opened the "cabinet" either as narrative concentration successfully evoked the identity of the public figures to whom the secret history silently referred or (if necessary) as an appended index that explicitly identified the intended political referent.[31] But whereas Haywood's language associates her periodical essays with the weighty privacy of a secret history that contains public scandal, her correspondent derides them as no better than old wives' tales, whose privacy is the traditional, privative sort characteristic of oral culture, gossips, and women.

Undaunted by this assault on the low, "mole-hill" triviality of her publications, Haywood suggests that her correspondent may have taken her too literally. "I never proposed, nor, I believe, did any body but this Letter-Writer expect that these Lucubrations should be devoted merely to the Use of News-Mongers:—A Change-Broker might, I think, have as much Cause to resent my taking no Notice of the Rise or Fall of Stocks" (2.8.123). Perhaps he missed the playful melodrama of Haywood's promise to penetrate the mysteries of the cabinet and the secrets of all Europe. Granted, the "Turns and Counter-Turns in Politics" may sometimes require "that Intelligence he wants me to receive from the Cabinets where they were hatch'd;—and yet perhaps, if once revealed, there would appear so little in them, that one might justly enough compare them to the Knots Children tye at School in Packthread, only to puzzle one another to undo again" (2.8.124).

Against her correspondent's infantile notion of political intelligence Haywood argues "that *The Female Spectator* is not altogether so indolent and insensible to public Transactions as he imagines . . . ," an argument that goes in two directions. First, Haywood makes clear her own, more sophisticated understanding of public-sphere access and the privileges of critical reason. "The Power of making War and Peace, is indeed lodg'd in the Hands of whoever sits upon the Throne." But the power of the "People of *England*" lies in "enquiring by [their] Representative[s] in Parliament the Motives by which the Sovereign is induced to declare a War, or conclude a Peace"; in "enquiring how, and for what Ends their Money is laid out." "The meanest Person has also an equal Right with the greatest, to expect a satisfactory Account in every thing relating to the Common-Wealth . . ." (2.8.127–29). But second, the road to public affairs runs, for Haywood, through the realm of the private. Both her "cabinet" and her "key" have a decidedly internal reference, one that justifies her "long Stories" because it evokes a rhetoric not of concentration but of concretization, not of actual but of concrete particularity.

"Many little Histories, it is true, are interspers'd" throughout the *Female Spectator,* Haywood acknowledges, "but then they are only such as serve to enforce *Precept* by *Example*" so that the reader will see "the Resemblance of himself in the Character of another" (2.8.125–26). Because "my Ambition was to be as universally read as possible," Haywood thought that "being made acquainted with other People's Affairs should at the same Time teach every one to regulate their own" (1.1.6). She aimed "to engage the Attention of those I endeavoured to reform, by giving them such Things as I knew would please them: Tales, and little Stories to which every one might flatter themselves with being able to find a Key, seemed to me the most effectual Method . . . . For this End it was I chose to assume the Name of the *Female Spectator* rather than that of *Monitor,* as thinking the latter by discovering too plainly my Design, might in a great Measure have frustrated it with the Gay and Unreflecting, who are indeed those for whom this Work was chiefly intended, as standing most in need of it" (4.24.362–63).

Haywood's apologia strikes a number of familiar chords—like speaking of low, sensible things to low, common people, including the women and men addressed by Bunyan's Christiana and her typological "key."[32] The women addressed by the *Female Spectator* are anything but common; but we have already observed the proximity of commoners and women in the pedagogy of domestication. Explicitly female in its associations, Haywood's exemplary teaching addresses the lowness of female readers through the lowness of trivial and private stories. But as her critic demands, what does this sort of ethical self-regulation have to do with public ends? Although Haywood moderately distances herself here from the spectatorial title, her trenchant disavowal of crudely public, "news-mongering" purposes cannot help remind us of the Addison who wondered whether it was "not much better to be let into the knowledge of ones-self, than to hear what passes in *Muscovy* or *Poland* . . . ."[33] Yet Haywood also disavows a sharp segregation between public and private "news." In fact, her self-defense depends on the argument that self-regulation is central to public affairs: "[T]he better we regulate our Actions in *private Life,* the more we may hope of *public Blessings* . . . . [A]n Endeavour to rectify the Morals of *Individuals,* is the first Step ought to be taken for rousing up a *general* Ardor for" preserving our English freedoms (2.8.125, 129).

Early on in her unusually long and eclectic career Haywood wrote a number of what she called "secret histories" that bear some relation to concentration narratives about actual personages.[34] Although she never abandoned this practice, her later writings are generally concerned less with overtly "political" allusion than with overtly moral teaching, and critics have devoted some energy to interpreting the significance of this development. Haywood's hostile correspondent and her own apologia offer some aid in this interpretation. Early and late, making the private public remains the common end in Haywood's writings, and print—"the Guardian Angel entitled the *Liberty of the Press*" (2.8.125)—remains the common means to that end; but the *roman à clef* and teaching by example differ significantly in the way their methods of "publication" anticipate and supplement print. Where early on the figure of the key stood for apprehending the direct resemblance of the concentrated story to public affairs that were both secret and of public importance, later it refers to apprehending the resemblance of the concretized story to the reader's own private experience.

This is a pedagogy of affective identification that involves the "publication" of the private in two distinct phases. First, in the payoff of narrative concretization, concrete story is generalized to abstract, "universal" ethical precept; second, ethical self-regulation "in private life" provides the basis for "public blessings." "It may be judged that on the Business of Love I am too serious," Haywood remarks at one point, "but I know nothing more concerns the Happiness of Mankind than that by which their Species is to be propagated, and which by being ill conducted, makes all the Miseries of civil Life." Like Defoe's, Haywood's method is manifestly casuistical, but with the significant corollary that the ethical subject provides grounding for the political subject, whom Haywood conceives less in the agon of sovereign subjecthood than in the formation of civic subjectivity. "A Man who is discontented in himself, and uneasy with those at Home, is an unfit Member of Society elsewhere" (4.24.360–61). The early modern separation out of the self from the home, and of both from "society elsewhere," helped contemporaries conceive the contiguity of those realms with a specificity and self-consciousness unavailable to the traditional view of their tacit relation.

As we therefore might expect, Haywood emphasizes not the actual but the concrete particularity of her exemplary personages. In the process she substantiates, through another use of the "key" figure, our sense that for her the concretization so common in the *Female Spectator* is a mode of formal domestication comparable but clearly alternative to the concentration characteristic of the *romans à clef* she used to write. Haywood says that "tho' I shall bring real Facts on the Stage, I shall conceal the Actors Names under such as will be conformable to their Characters; my Intention being only to expose the Vice, not the Person. . . . [T]he sole Aim of the following Pages is to reform the Faulty, and give an innocent Amusement to those who are not so . . . ." And she directs a solemn warning to those who "shall pretend to fix on any particular Person the Blame of Actions they may happen to find recorded here, or make what they call a Key [i.e., a guide to personal references] to these Lucubrations . . ." (1.1.8–9). And yet the claim to historicity, however gratuitous it may seem, is nonetheless still made. How does Haywood's technique of concretization diverge from Defoe's? What does it mean to say that her method of teaching by example is peculiarly "female"? What might this have to do with her notion that public blessings are dependent on private self-regulation, that the political subject is a function of the ethical subject?

Narrator as Mother

Haywood's commitment to ethical reform in the *Female Spectator* is so plain that well into the periodical one correspondent employs, with some fondness, the salutation "*Dear Female Moralizer*" (2.9.179). And as we have seen, in the final number she reveals that she had thought at first to call her periodical the *Female Monitor* (4.24.363). Whereas her hostile correspondent had found her exemplary teaching too heavy on the example (and thereby too female), Haywood tells us here that other readers have complained that on the contrary "I moralize too much, and that I give them too few tales"—in other words, that her exemplary teaching was too heavy on the teaching. Haywood's reply to this complaint tells us something about how she herself would gender her procedure: "I was willing to treat [my readers] with the Tenderness of a Mother, but not, like some Mothers, to continue my Indulgence to their Ruin" (4.24.362–63). To be a good mother in narrative terms is not simply to accommodate "male" precept through "female" example but rather to balance example with precept, identificatory absorption with regulation. Haywood is willing to embrace the notion that storytelling is female because she means by that a normative, "maternal" sort of storytelling that serves a simultaneously ethical and public purpose.[35]

How does this work in practice? What do Haywood's concretizations sound like, and how do they compare with Defoe's? In the first number of the *Female Spectator* Haywood makes a preceptual distinction between a mature love based on a rational apprehension of the other and the more common immaturity of flighty infatuation. Briefly concretized by the vignette of Tenderilla at a concert (1.1.11–12), this precept is then clarified as the necessity of knowing the sincerity of the other (1.1.12–14), then re-concretized by the more extended story of Martesia's clandestine marriage and its aftermath (1.1.14–23). Now the problem of "indiscreet Marriages" is acknowledged to reflect as much on the parents as on the "young Ladies themselves:—Parents are sometimes, by an over Caution, guilty of forcing them into Things which otherwise would be far distant from their Thoughts" (1.1.23). "Nature in all Ages is abhorrent of Restraint, but in Youth especially . . . ," and a "Woman is in far less Danger of losing her Heart, when every Day surrounded with a Variety of gay Objects, than when by some Accident she falls into the Conversation of a single one" (1.1.24). The sexual vulnerability paradoxically bred by the overprotection of girls can be seen in the contrast of English and Continental, of rural and urban, attitudes toward upbringing. Momentary character formation—Eagaretta, Arminia (1.1.25)—now prepares for Haywood's dilation into the relatively full-scale story of Seomanthe: her enforced seclusion by a jealous aunt; her seduction, elopement, and clandestine marriage; her financial spoliation and abandonment by her villainous husband (1.1.26–32).

What does this sort of story have to do with ensuring "public blessings"? Book 2 begins with an account of a private meeting of the *Female Spectator's* editorial staff that is interrupted by a woman whose gossiping stereotype seems calculated to appeal to readers like Haywood's hostile correspondent—one of "a Race of Mortals, who will tell you all their own Secrets in two Hours Acquaintance . . ." and expect you "to listen to the vociferous Trifle they are big with . . . ." The woman "forced her Passage through my Servants, and flew directly to the Room where we were sitting . . . , tenacious of a Welcome for the News she brought, which she told me was of so much Consequence, that she could not have slept all Night without making me Partaker of it." The trifling news is about an absurdly "unequal Match" between the young Bloometta and the ancient Pompilius, yet it happily occasions an editorial conversation on a topic of the greatest importance, marriage, "on which the Happiness of Mankind so much depends; . . . that which prevents those numberless Irregularities and Confusions, that would else overthrow all Order, and destroy Society . . ." (2.1.72–75). In this way, parodically "trifling news" unexpectedly provides the key to unlock the cabinet of secrets crucial to public sociability.

Having thus asserted the public consequences of bad marriages, Haywood summarizes at somewhat greater length the unhappy case of Bloometta and

Pompilius, ending with a preceptual caveat against such marriages, especially unequal matches like this one (2.1.75–77). What follows is a series of cases variously exemplary of this comprehensive precept. Unbeknownst to him, Celinda engineers with their two fathers a marriage of alliance with Aristobolus, only to find that he has been permanently alienated by this presumption (2.1.77–84). Several brief examples ensue, then the sad story of how Dalinda and Macro fell into the respective habits of "Slavery" and "Tyranny" (2.1.88); more brief examples; and then the story of Bellair and Miseria (2.1.89–92). Haywood follows these with a precept: "A Sympathy of *Humours* is therefore no less to be consulted, than a Sympathy of *Inclination* . . ." (2.1.92). Now we hear the case of Vulpone and Lindamira (whose multiple inequality includes his being "older than her Father"), who secretly correspond and marry, then are pained to hear her parents issue "an immediate Order to her to quit the House that Instant, and never presume to see them more" (2.1.95, 102). The sequence ends with two more examples, one of which concerns a sensible daughter who is compelled "by the arbitrary Will of her Father" to marry a foolish fop, a story that soon diverges into a discussion of the number of "Coxcombs and Finikins" at large these days (2.1.104).[36]

Three points are worth making. First, the public importance of these private stories is asserted, at the outset, in causal terms: civic order requires conjugal order. But second, this metonymic claim is buttressed by a metaphorical claim—conjugal order is like the greater social order—that seems a significant but vestigial remnant of the old patriarchalist analogy filtered now through a progressive critique. And this can be felt in the degree to which Haywood's cases use the figurative language of political absolutism: "force," "tyranny," "arbitrary will."[37] Third, the relationship between the "publicity" of abstract precept and the "privacy" of concrete example in Haywood's usage has not only balance but even a sense of dialectical reciprocity: if examples originate as concretizations of precept, they develop according to their own narrative demands so as to elicit an ongoing refinement and reformulation of precept. On the level of both form and content, Haywood's pedagogic method encourages us to see private activity within the context of, rather than as an alternative to, public concerns. And yet if the formal evocation of public concerns sometimes seems to require a passing claim to historicity—to actual particularity—this does not threaten to obstruct storytelling as it can in Defoe.

Author as Example

In the preceding chapter I quoted from a long letter by a naturalist who urged Haywood's female readers to rusticate themselves armed with magnifying glasses whereby to learn from Nature itself "all that Books can teach us of this

Part of Natural Philosophy . . . ."[38] At the end of this letter Haywood extols the aims of its "ingenious Author," then enters into her own long discourse on her correspondent's subtext, the education of women (3.15.155, 157). At the center of this discourse is the precept that reading—not only the Book of Nature but also the books of humankind—is the chief method by which women "may attain that amiable Quality, in which are comprehended all other good Qualities and Accomplishments . . ." (3.15.174). However, the precept is concretized not in the usual way, through narrative, but in a detailed, twenty-page account of the sort of learning most valuable for women to obtain, as well as of the principal books in which that learning may be found. As we complete this discourse we realize that Haywood herself, the amiable teacher teaching, here provides the example by which her own precept has been concretized. The reflexivity of this process, the way in which the formal activity of authorship not only enables but also exemplifies the author's substantive argument, is a subtle but persistent feature of the *Female Spectator,* whose overarching argument—whose casuistry—concerns nothing but the proper place of women in the world at large, that is, "in public."[39]

Concretely exemplifying the general precept that women should occupy a place in the world, the figure of the publishing author is present from the first number of the *Female Spectator,* in which Haywood carefully constitutes the collective authorship of her periodical. Invoking the "precious Memory" of her "learned Brother" Mr. Spectator, the speaker nonetheless diverges from Addison's example in a number of ways. Neither beautiful nor young, she is a reformed "Coquet" of whose early self-publication the best that can be said is that "the Public may reap some Benefit from it . . . . I flatter'd myself that it might be in my Power to be in some measure both useful and entertaining to the Public . . ." (1.1.4–5). As soon as "I commenc'd Author," however, she found that her singularity was not sufficient to engage the public, and so she invited three acquaintances to fabricate with her a collective or corporate authorship whose components "are to be consider'd only as several Members of one Body, of which I am the Mouth" (1.1.7–8).

On the face of it a reinforcement of the depersonalization basic to publication (and evident in the anonymity of the *Female Spectator*), authorial collectivity counters the powerful premise of personal identity that is, in effect, the other side of alienation through print. But here the act of depersonalization that produces publication is itself a "public" process of consensus, which precedes and confirms its printed enactment. Consensus establishes positive liberty through association. In the *Female Spectator's* editorial collective, "every one has the Liberty of excepting against, or censuring whatever she disapproves; nothing being to be exhibited to the Public, without the joint Concurrence of all" (1.2.71–72). Public consumption is prefigured by an authorial public of productive ethical subjects. Elsewhere Haywood speaks of "the Mystery of our little Cabal," parodically inflating this corporate authorship as though its composition were an *arcanum imperii,* an absolutist secret of state whose public force lies in the fact that it alone remains private (2.24.383). In these several ways, Haywood thematizes her authorial status and procedure as a model of how women might go public without sacrificing—indeed, while enhancing—their privacy: their autonomy, agency, and safety.

What are the alternatives to which authorship provides a preferable mode of being in public? To answer this question I will return to one of Haywood's sequences of exemplary teaching. The sequence begins with a letter from Sarah Oldfashion, who is both indignant and distraught at her daughter's attraction to the pleasures of "public places." When she was a girl her time was consumed chiefly by instruction in the "necessary Accomplishments of my Sex . . . . I trained up my only Daughter in the same Manner I had been bred up myself . . ."; and all went well until she turned fourteen and Ranelagh Gardens "gave Notice there would be public Breakfasting every Morning.—This gave a Turn very vexatious to me, and prejudicial to the Education I intended to bestow on her . . . ." Oldfashion doubts the propriety of permitting this girl, "over whom Heaven and Nature has given me the sole Authority, to conduct herself in this Fashion . . . ," and she implores the Female Spectator to "set forth, in the most moving and pathetick Terms you can, the Folly of gadding eternally to these publick Places . . . . A public Reproof from you may, perhaps, be more effectual than all the private Admonitions" of friends. She resolves that if the Female Spectator fails her, she will seclude Biddy in a very private place, remotest Cornwall (1.5.261–67).

Haywood's response to this plea is fully sympathetic and deeply eloquent on the vanities of public gadding. But with what we may now recognize as a characteristic sensitivity, she strenuously warns Oldfashion against forcible rustication lest Biddy "throw herself into much greater Misfortunes than she was sent thither to avoid, merely to prevent the too great Caution of those who have the Power over her . . . . I am wholly against running such a Hazard by exerting Authority in this Manner" (1.5.267–71). The case is no less problematic for being familiar: how can we reconcile the pedagogic authority and the protective impulses of the parent with the child's resentment of prohibitions and her longing for the excitement of public places? In Haywood and elsewhere, civil authority has served for some time as a largely negative and monitory parallel to family authority. What begins to emerge here is the notion that authorship—perhaps especially female authorship—provides a more positive model for (even alternative to) the normative exercise of authority in the family. Oldfashion, unsure whether to assert her maternal pedagogic authority over frequenting "public places," calls upon the pedagogic authority of the author to issue a "public reproof" from the alternative public place of the periodical press, a virtual place Oldfashion's request implicitly assures Haywood her daughter will visit. The mother's identification with her daughter entails regulating Biddy's upbringing by imposing upon it the model of her own; Haywood balances regulation by an empathetic absorption in the daughter's point of view, thereby exemplifying the characteristics of the good mother (see 4.24.363).

The relationship between actual public places like Ranelagh and virtual public places like the periodical press is one of both difference and similarity. In a later issue Haywood gives an "Eye-witness" account of the near-allegorical chaos that ensues when a "fine Lady"'s enormous hoop petticoat becomes entangled in the horns of "an old Ram" who is leading "a large Flock of Sheep" through the narrow streets of London. "The rude Populace, instead of pitying, insulted her Misfortune, and continued their Shouts till she got into a Chair, and was quite out of Sight" (3.25.185–86). Figure 9.1, printed at the same time as this issue of the *Female Spectator,* depicts a similar "lady's disaster" involving not an old ram but a young chimney sweep. The preoccupation of the mock-pastoral legendary verse with what is "to be seen below," along with the sweep's "black distorted features" and those of the "leering Jew," emphasizes the social and racial defilement in store for elevated ladies who expose their privacy to "publick Jest."[40] Toward the end of the long sequence initiated by Oldcastle's letter Haywood berates the immodesty with which "some Ladies come into public Assemblies:—They do not walk but straddle; and sometimes run with a Kind of a Frisk and Jump;—[and] throw their enormous Hoops almost in the Faces of those who pass by them . . . ." "Far be it from me," she adds characteristically, "to debar my Sex from going to those public Diversions which, at present, make so much Noise in Town . . . . It is the immoderate Use, or rather the Abuse of any Thing, which renders the partaking it a Fault . . . ." And yet "the Men are so censorious, that they look on all those of our Sex, who appear too much at these public Places, as setting themselves up for Sale, and, therefore, taking the Privilege of Buyers, measure us with their Eyes from Head to Foot . . ." (1.5.297–99). But how far is this experience from the painful scrutiny Haywood, in this published journal that is literally "up for Sale," endured from her hostile male correspondent?

Haywood continues: The pleasure of public entertainments not only "takes us much out of our own Houses:—The Idea of it is apt to render us Indolent in our Affairs, even the little Time we are at Home . . ." (1.5.301). Indeed, "[i]t's a great Pity, methinks, that People of Fashion have not frequent Entertainments of this Nature at their own Houses; where only select Companies being admit-

FIG. 9.1. *The Lady's Disaster*, 1746, in Amanda Vickery, *The Gentleman's Daughter: Women's Lives in Georgian England* (New Haven, CT: Yale University Press, 1998). Princeton University Library.

ted, all the Dangers, the Indecencies, the Mischiefs which attend rambling to public Assemblies would be avoided . . ." (1.5.318). This solution to the problem—the literal internalization of public life within the home—is attractive but utopian, at least in this form, since domestic experience cannot be counted upon to admit such internalization. A case in point is Sarah Oldfashion, who in a later issue complains to the Female Spectator for having advised her to send her daughter into the country, an experiment that has ended in a clandestine and highly unequal marriage to a gentleman's groom. Reflexively invoking her journal as an objective place of public access, Haywood replies: "Whoever will give themselves the Trouble to turn back to the Fifth Book of the *Female Spectator*, will find I was totally averse to her sending the young Lady into a Place, where she could meet with no Diversions to compensate for the Want of those she left behind." In fact, it turns out that Oldfashion ignored the Female Spectator's advice so far that she restricted Biddy to exclusively "female" domestic arts "instead of ordering she should be indulg'd in all those innocent Sports a rural Life affords . . ." (3.15.176). Oldfashion thus shows herself to be one of those partial mothers who allows preceptual strictness to overbalance exemplary "indulgence."

This error in maternal pedagogy leads Haywood to a suggestive expansion on the topic of the female arts: "Nor can I by any means approve of compelling young Ladies of Fortune to make so much Use of the Needle, as they did in former Days, and some few continue to do:—There are enough whose Necessities oblige them to live wholly by it; and it is a Kind of Robbery to those unhappy Persons to do that ourselves which is their whole Support:—In my Opinion, a Lady of Condition should learn just as much of Cookery and of Work, as to know when she is imposed upon by those she employs in both those necessary Occasions, but no more:—To pass too much of her Time in them may acquire her the Reputation of a notable *House-wife,* but not of a Woman of *fine Taste,* or any way qualify her for polite Conversation, or of entertaining herself agreeably when alone" (3.15.176–77). Implicit in Haywood's opinion is the recognition that the sexual division of labor has rendered the female arts not only anachronistic and unproductive but also counterproductive to the interests of those lower-class women whose day labor depends on them.[41] But what does she mean by her ideal of the woman of fine taste, apparently an alternative both to excessive housewifery and to excessive public gadding? Haywood suggests an answer when she rhetorically inquires of "any young Lady, under the abovementioned Confinement, if she had not rather apply to Reading and Philosophy than to Threading of Needles" (3.15.178).

Sarah Oldfashion's second letter comes just after the long passage, already described, in which Haywood responds to a naturalist's advice that leisured ladies venture forth to read the Book of Nature by dilating on the books of culture. Her extended exemplification here of the learned woman is part of her effort to show the "Way toward acquiring that *fine Taste* which is so much talked of, and so little understood . . . . [F]or when we have a perfect *good Taste in Essentials,* we cannot be without it in Things of a more trifling Nature" (3.15.160, 174). Haywood's hostile correspondent, we may recall, invoked "Persons of inquisitive Taste" and "the polite Coffee-Houses" in describing those who must remain dissatisfied by the pedagogy of the *Female Spectator* (see 1.8.121). But "taste" and "politeness" are synthetic categories elaborated to crystallize a notion of empirically evident cultural distinction that might replace the outmoded reliance on attributed and presumptive distinction—that is, on embodied aristocracy and the absolutist polity.[42] The logic of Haywood's advice is that the reign of taste and politeness liberates us from the tyranny not only of political and social status but also of gender hierarchy.

Leisured ladies may best assume a public stature neither by frequenting public places that maximize their vulnerability nor by persisting in behavior that the decline of the domestic economy has rendered unproductive and vacuously symbolic, but by partaking in the public sphere of reading and writing published texts. Women, denied political subjecthood with the denial of the franchise and the holding of public office, are the quintessential ethical subjects, participating (in Habermas's terms) not in the "political" but in the "literary" public sphere.[43] In this very segregation, however, women become crucially instrumental in overcoming, through a self-consciously internalizing conflation, the modern separation between the political and the ethical domains to which men, because of their privilege, remain more subservient. It is noteworthy not only that with the *Female Spectator* Haywood achieves a productive employment, but also that the public-sphere labor of her editorial collective is internalized in the actual privacy of her own domestic space: "The Rendezvous is kept at my Lodgings, and I give strict Orders, that no Person whatever shall be admitted to interrupt our Consultations . . ." (1.2.72). This is productive labor by women that takes place within the domestic arena yet is not housework, and it thereby renews in very different terms the distinction, insusceptible of separation, between house and work characteristic of the older domestic economy (cf. fig. 4.8).

However, it is equally noteworthy (to return to the question with which this chapter began) that this participation in the division of labor—materially and quantitatively productive for both Haywood's and the public interest—is entwined with a division of knowledge whose qualitative productivity is unquestionable and whose achievement owes significantly to the efforts of women like Haywood. By this I mean the modern discrimination between the political and the ethical subject, between subjecthood and subjectivity.

Part Three ✳ Secret Histories

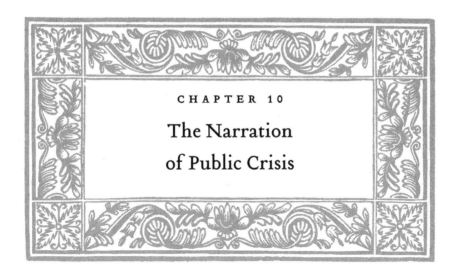

CHAPTER 10

The Narration
of Public Crisis

What Is a Secret History?

It is a point of common understanding that "privacy" is not the same as "secrecy." Secrecy involves an act of "intentional concealment," whereas privacy, a central principle of negative liberty, names "the condition of being protected from unwanted access by others."[1] From one perspective, the category of secrecy might be thought to heighten the early modern separation out of the public from the private by imputing to the private a volitional agency in avoiding or evading public disclosure. But secrecy is first of all a category of traditional knowledge, not a privative privacy but that which distinguishes an elite from the deprived majority and which paradoxically comes to be fully known as secret only under the apprehension of its discovery. This is the abstruse and esoteric knowledge that marks the exclusivity of "secret societies," the "mysteries" of guild practices known only to initiates, and the "receipts" of natural magic that eventually were published in "books of secrets"—also the arcane motives and purposes of ruling sovereign elites, whose authority is bound up with their essential unknowability.

In the early modern period the secrecy of secret knowledge was threatened not only by revolutionary technologies of disclosure, like print, but also by explicit doctrines of disclosure: Protestant conscientiousness and its imperatives of self-examination and enlightenment; the new philosophy, whose language of surface and depth was only the most powerful figure for the scientific excavation, demystification, and desublimation of secrets. "We are to overcome the Mysteries of all the Works of Nature . . . ," said Thomas Sprat of the Royal Society. The ambition applied also to the mysteries of human nature; and in the conjunction of these doctrines of disclosure there coalesced a conviction of the existence of "sex" as such, secreted at the obscure center of human motivation. Different though they might be, moreover, the secrets of sovereign rule, scientific inquiry, and sexuality all shared the terminology of a concretely spatial interiority: to discover them required inspecting out-of-the-way places like "cabinets," "closets," and "corners." Thus were the "mysteries" of the royal "Cabinet-Council" "discabineted" by publication. But thus too was the publication of "[t]he Wandring-Whores Complaint" described as a process "[w]herein the Cabinet of her Iniquity is Unlockt and All Her Secrets Laid Open."[2] Usage like this suggests that in the period of our concern the languages of secrecy and privacy overlapped to a degree that may seem to us imprecise—even that the establishment of privacy as an authorized realm in the modern world depended on a general deauthorization of secrecy. The key that protected privacy was wrought from the key that concealed secrets.

If this begins, at least, to evoke the semantic range of "secrecy" in our period, what were "secret histories"? The idea of a secret history presupposes the idea of a manifest and official but necessarily partial version of things. In the midst of civil war the Leveller Richard Overton posed the rhetorical question, "If the King conquer, the Parliament will be Traytours to posterity by Cronicle; for who writ the Histories of the Anabaptists but their Enemies?"[3] The secret history is both a logical entailment and a solution to the problem of the fact that history gets written by the winners. Although they may flourish elsewhere, secret histories are a mandatory mode in cultures that have discovered the fundamental interestedness of knowledge but have not yet developed ideologies and mechanisms designed to ensure the access of all interests to the means of knowledge production and dissemination.

The phrase "secret history" itself became familiar to Anglophone culture through the English translation of the *Anecdota* of Procopius (c. AD 550) in 1674, whose title means "unpublished things."[4] The Procopian precedent quickly provided a popular model for the disclosure of state secrets. The material prefatory to a Restoration translation from the French praises the author for having written "a sort of Cabinet, Historical Inquisition" that "has refin'd upon *Procopius* his Pattern . . . ." But the "Author's Preface" to this translation also makes clear the broader relevance of the secret history to the development of biography in the following century and even to the separation out of concrete from actual particularity:

> [T]he Historian considers almost ever Men in Publick, whereas the Anecdoto-grapher only examines 'em in private. Th' one thinks he has perform'd his duty, when he draws them such as they were in the Army, or in the tumult of Cities, and th' other endeavours by all means to get open their Closet-door; th' one sees them in Ceremony, and th' other in conversation; th' one fixes principally upon their Ac-

tions, and th' other wou'd be a Witness of their inward Life, and assist at the most private hours of their leisure: In a word, the one has barely Command and Authority for Object, and the other makes his Main of what occurs in Secret and in Solitude. . . .

Not but that the Writer of Ἀϛεκδοτα draws a Picture of Persons, as exact, and as faithful, at the least, as can be done by the Historian; but he does it after his own Mode: He represents only as much of the Man's Out-side, as is necessary to know his Inside; and as the good and bad dispositions of the Mind, are only to be disclos'd in the Manners, 'tis also for the Manners that he reserves his liveliest Colours, and finest Materials.

By the same token, the form of the secret history joins the diversity of contemporary writings that insist upon the utility of seeming "trifles" in disclosing the "greatest" of things: "I pretend likewise . . . to relate with a serious Air, the smallest trifles, when they have been th' Origine or occasion of the greatest Matters." The translator concurs: "For Irresolution and Passion prevail equally in the Great, as in the Vulgar. And often a little Cabinet-pique, or Bed-Chamber Quarrel, occasions a rumbling World, and is the source of the greatest Transactions."[5]

As these words suggest, the significance of the trivial and the private in secret histories is first of all that they bear a causal relation to great and public happenings. But the allure of the secret history was also that it might entail a stealthy formal domestication: read aright, what appears to be an exotic tale or history turns out to have present and public application. This may be the implication of the decision to reissue the 1674 translation of Procopius in 1682, although too late to fan the flames of the Exclusion Crisis, as *The Debauch'd Court. Or, the Lives of the Emperor Justinian, and his Empress Theodora the Comedian.* In other words, the mode of secret history that is inspired by the translation of Procopius draws strength from, and dovetails with, the mode of political allegory that had flourished since the beginning of the seventeenth century. In this chapter and those that follow I will use the term "secret history" in this relatively broad sense, to include not only the narratives of the Restoration and early eighteenth century that explicitly call themselves "secret histories" but also those (like the *romans à clef*) that signal their secrecy through allegorical, amatory "romance" plots that sanction techniques of close reading to uncover their deepest public meaning. In this inclusive sense of the term, secret histories might take the form of third-person exposé, first-person memoir, epistolary collection, or romance fable, with or without explanatory key; often anonymous, they might claim the authenticity either of detachment from or of intimate involvement with the events at issue; they even might be written in verse, not prose: poems on affairs of state were said to give "the best *Secret History* of our late Reigns, as being writ by such great Persons as were near the Helm, knew the Transactions, and were above being brib'd to flatter, or afraid to speak the truth."[6]

Secret histories are secret in two ways. In disclosing traditional or elite secrets they make public a history of secrets; but in this act of illicit disclosure they constitute themselves as (potentially) libelous histories that need to sustain their own secrecy by obscuring the identity either of their authors or of those figures they aim to expose. As *chroniques scandaleuses,* secret histories both reveal the scandals of people in high places and by that revelation partake in scandal themselves—*scandalum magnatum* (the defamation of peers) or, less technically, the flagrant violation of propriety entailed in bringing the high low. Secret histories both dispel and promulgate secrets, turning the secrecy of their targets to their own advantage; hence they might be seen as parodic or mock histories that stand in a similarly ambiguous relation to official histories as mock epics do to the heroic tradition.[7]

Secret histories are mixed forms not only in this sense, however, but more generally as they tend to deploy the varied methods of formal domestication. Like the letters they contain, the cabinets from which secret histories are sometimes supposed to emanate have a double charge of objectivity and subjectivity, publicity and privacy, state affairs and amatory affairs. The contents of cabinets, once disclosed, have the potential for scandal that is either high or low, either political or sexual—or both by turns, as the *roman à clef* domesticates state politics through the "sexual politics" of amatory intrigue and erotic romance. Indeed, in a nation-state like England, where royal sovereignty depends on familial-dynastic inheritance, the metonymic contiguity of the political and the sexual guarantees that political secrets will be understood in terms of sexual secrets.

However, as patriarchalist discourse becomes increasingly explicit, hence strained, over the course of the seventeenth century, the separation out of the family and the state from their customary and tacit analogy exerts pressure on their traditional metonymic relation as well. Under this pressure, the sexuality of political dynasty, the intimate privacy of the body natural that grounds the body politic, acquires the potential to undermine it, to desublimate the secret and scandalous truth of sovereignty so as to reveal that the "deepest meaning" of the story is in fact not public but private. This is only to substantiate the basic ambiguity of the secret history's publication of the private—and perhaps to suggest that the form is ultimately dedicated neither to the realm of the public nor to that of the private but to an experimental inquiry into the limits of their emergent separability. Indeed, the restless insistence of this inquiry can be felt in the way the domestication entailed in the secret history's concern with the "private" intrigues of a romance plot involves, from another point of view, the estrangement from the familiar that is implicit in the exoticizing detachment of Italianate romance names, an effect frequently reinforced by the geographical alienation of a tale that takes place far from home.

This is, of course, a fundamental feature of those secret histories that employ the allegorizing technique of the *roman à clef*, and it distinguishes their more complicated hermeneutics of domestication from the basic mechanisms of concentration and concretization as we have examined them so far. The overriding purpose of formal domestication is to accommodate what is difficult of access by figuring it in more familiar and available terms. The purpose of political allegory, however, is simultaneously to reveal and to conceal reference: to tell a story that allusively signifies affairs of state (hence the need for a key) while at the same time purporting to contain its own key, to signify nothing beyond itself. This ambiguity is a feature of the broader category of the fable or the parable. As Francis Bacon observed, "Parables have been used in two ways, and (which is strange) for contrary purposes. For they serve to disguise and veil the meaning, and they serve also to clear and throw light on it."[8] The allegorical ideal of an equilibrium between revelation and concealment was not easy to put into practice. As the deist John Toland optimistically put it, "The knowledge of the nature of things, is much better convey'd by allegories than fables: for allegories do onely cover the Truth, while fables confound and quite overwhelm it."[9] My aim in the final part of this study, very far from being exhaustive, is to focus on selected moments in the history of the secret history so as to obtain a sense of its form and its development during this period. In concluding the study with a consideration of the emergent domestic novel I will suggest that the history of the secret history offers us an illuminating model of how the modern understanding of the relationship between the realms of the public and the private becomes established at this time.

Sidney and Barclay

To speak of a founding text in the tradition of the English secret history is to invite dispute. Nonetheless, there may be general agreement that Philip Sidney's *Arcadia* deserves this title.[10] Several versions of Sidney's prose romance exist; I will confine my discussion to the *Old Arcadia,* which was written sometime between 1579 and 1581. Sidney tells the story of Duke Basilius of Arcadia and his beautiful daughters, Pamela and Philoclea, who are courted by the wandering princes and cousins Musidorus and Pyrocles. The justification for reading the *Old Arcadia* as a political allegory lies in the fact that it is a pastoral romance and therefore invites the kind of allegorizing that Renaissance readers generally thought proper to the pastoral mode. In *A Defence of Poetry* (1595), which was written about the same time as the *Old Arcadia,* Sidney agrees that pastoral "sometime out of Meliboeus' mouth can show the misery of people under hard lords or ravening soldiers" or "under the pretty tales of wolves and sheep, can include the whole considerations of wrong-doing and patience . . . ."[11] His narrative is punctuated by collections of eclogues attributed to the shepherds of Arcadia, and in "The First Eclogues" we are told of these shepherds that "of all other things, they did especially delight in eclogues; wherein sometimes they would contend for a prize of well singing, sometimes lament the unhappy pursuit of their affections, sometimes, again, under hidden forms utter such matters as otherwise were not fit for their delivery." In his dedicatory epistle to his sister, Sidney referred to the *Old Arcadia* as an "idle work" and a "trifle," a description that might seem to encourage her to find "matter" under its "hidden form."[12] Moreover, the penalties against seditious publication (hence the motive to disguise one's meaning), although different from those in place a hundred years later, were a sobering reality of this period.[13]

The episodes in which the wandering princes first confront their beloveds in disguise support our sense of a reflexive relationship between Sidney's content and form, the sense that disguise on one level implies disguise on the other. Having consulted the Delphic oracle, Duke Basilius hopes he will evade its obscure prophecy by taking his family into pastoral retirement. As we might expect, the vain attempt to hide from the world only brings the world into his hiding place. When Musidorus sees the rusticated Pamela, he disguises himself as the shepherd Dorus, whose "meanness" Pamela acknowledges even after he saves her from a marauding bear and she begins to suspect "that he came of some very noble blood—so noble a countenance he bare, and so worthy an act he had performed" (55, 53). Pyrocles, already having fallen in love with Philoclea's picture, disguises himself as "an Amazon lady going about the world to practise feats of chivalry and to seek myself a worthy husband" (18). Musidorus is neither deceived nor amused. Anticipating the Earl of Shaftesbury's advice to an author, "O sweet Pyrocles," he says, "separate yourself a little, if it be possible from yourself, and let your own mind look upon your own proceedings . . . . [T]his effeminate love of a woman doth so womanize a man that, if you yield to it, it will not only make you a famous Amazon, but a launder, a distaff-spinner, or whatsoever other vile occupation their idle heads can imagine and their weak hands perform" (18, 20).[14] But Pyrocles' disguise is nonetheless effective: not only Philoclea but also her parents, Basilius and Gynecia, fall in love with him-her. Although in different ways, then, both men renounce the public for the private, "soldiery" for love (53), their adventures culminating in "this captiving of us within ourselves which hath transformed the one in sex, and the other in state . . ." (43).

Sidney encourages us to connect clothing and stories as related methods of using debased and outward appearance to hide—but only partially—elevated inner truth. Seeing through Pyrocles' disguise, the lovesick Gynecia confronts him by saying, "Take pity of me, O Cleophila, but not as Cleophila, and disguise not with me in words, as I know thou dost in apparel" (95). We readers might be taken in by Cleophila's appearance were not our narrator careful to reveal what he has concealed by speaking to us of "her (for still, fair ladies, you remember that I use the she-title to Pyrocles, since so he would have it) . . ." (38). Similarly, Musidorus-as-Dorus tells Pamela the provocatively transparent tale of Musidorus, who falls in love with "the Arcadian duke's eldest daughter" and "clothed himself in a shepherd's weed, that under the baseness of that form he might at least have free access to feed his eyes with that which should at length eat up his heart. In which doing, thus much without doubt he hath manifested: that this estate is not always to be rejected, since under that veil there may be hidden things to be esteemed" (105–6). No fool, Pamela "well found he meant the tale by himself, and that he did under that covert manner make her know the great nobleness of his birth. . . . She did immediately catch hold of his signifying himself to be a prince, and did glad her heart with having a reasonable ground to build her love upon" (106). But Pamela is cautious: "[N]ow what could induce a princess to go away with a shepherd?," she asks. "'Principally,' said he, 'the virtuous gratefulness for his affection; then, knowing him to be a prince; and lastly, seeing herself in unworthy bondage.' Pamela found in her conscience such an accusing of secret consent thereto that she thought it safest way to divert the speech, lest in parley the castle be given up" (107).

So readers of the *Old Arcadia* appear on solid ground in suspecting that through the romance veil of these exotic adventures will be visible, if only fitfully, the public matter and actual particularity of English politics in high places. Moreover, the notion of Pamela's "unworthy bondage" to her parents and the "secret consent" she detects in her own "conscience" suggest that the patriarchalist analogy may be at work here through a concentration of royal absolutism as parental tyranny and of political liberty as amatory freedom of choice. Certainly the issue is alive at the private level of romance. "[T]here was a general opinion grown the duke would grant his daughters in marriage to nobody" (11). Until Pyrocles appears before her in the disguise of Cleophila, the younger sister, Philoclea, "had obediently lived under her parents' behests without the framing (out of her own will) the forechoosing of anything . . ." (108–9). But Philoclea's parents, maddened by love for Cleophila, are now their daughter's rivals. Pyrocles-Cleophila tricks Basilius and Gynecia into thinking each will rendezvous with him-her, then presents himself to Philoclea divested of the now-unnecessary disguise. Philoclea is devastated: "[D]o you think to deceive me in Pyrocles' form, as you have done in Cleophila's? Or rather, now you have betrayed me in both those, is there some third sex left you into which you can transform yourself, to inveigle my simplicity?" But desire wins out, and "with her consent" their love is consummated (234–35, 299).

Has Sidney deceived us with the outward form of pastoral romance as Pyrocles has deceived Philoclea and her father with the outward form of Cleophila? Pamela, the elder and more conscientious sister, asks Musidorus to "govern your love towards me as I may still remain worthy to be loved. . . . Let me be your own (as I am), but by no unjust conquest. Let not our joys, which ought ever to last, be stained in our own consciences. . . . I have yielded [i.e., consented] to be your wife; stay then till the time that I may rightly be so" (197). Later on Pyrocles affirms of his friend that "with Pamela's consent, he was to convey her out of the thraldom she lived in . . . until her father's consent might be obtained" (392–93). The four lovers may suffer cruelly for their actions, since it turns out that "the wickedness of lust is by our [Arcadian] decrees punished by death, though both consent . . ." (406). (How) does this language of "consent," especially in the context of its political antithesis "unjust conquest," enjoin us to read at the level of the public signified?

In 1580 "unjust conquest" has an unquestionably political resonance. Our expectations of a vital political correlate for amatory "consent," however, may be whetted by later usage that reflects the revolutionary explicitation of political thinking that occurred during the middle years of the following century. Indeed, the correlation between parental tyranny and political absolutism does not have the confidently formulaic quality at this time that it obtained after the Restoration. This is to suggest not that patriarchalist thought lacks the force it would later acquire but rather the opposite: that because patriarchalism (still) has the force of something like tacit knowledge, it is articulated in matter-of-fact ways that militate against the explicit and particularized unfolding of a public-private differential that only begins to become commonplace a century hence.[15] True, the *Old Arcadia* is replete with cases of the correspondence between public and private experience, a correspondence that Sidney makes available to his readers with an easy understatement that borders on the taken for granted.[16] But the formal domestication entailed in political allegory, although well rationalized by pastoral theory, in practice is harder to document.

No attentive reader can doubt the broad relevance of the political crisis represented in Sidney's romance to the crisis through which he actually lived. During the years in which the *Old Arcadia* was being composed, the central policy issue at court was Queen Elizabeth's highly controversial proposed marriage to the Roman Catholic Duke of Anjou, an alliance to which Sidney was strongly opposed and which by the nature of the case lent itself to trenchant public/private formulation. Anjou was seen by most observers as a shifty, ambitious, and dangerous figure. To Sidney the royal match was symptomatic of Elizabeth's indecisiveness and passivity on matters of foreign policy just at the moment when strong English leadership was imperative in the struggle to pursue the international Protestant Cause.[17] At the height of this state emergency, with Basilius disabled and the state rudderless, Sidney describes "the whole multitude fallen into confused and dangerous divisions" (320) in language that resonates with the discourse of political typology that the Renaissance had inherited from classical antiquity and naturalized as its own.

Moreover, the irresolution and ineffectuality Sidney feared in Queen Elizabeth are broadly represented by the romance figure Duke Basilius in several striking ways. His retreat from the world is prompted by an oracle to whose counsel he has had superstitious recourse, and there Basilius suffers the ludicrously inappropriate infatuation with the duplicitous Pyrocles-Cleophila that ends only with the deep and deathlike sleep he falls into when accidentally administered a poison. Within this broad framework, however, the correspondence of romance and politics, of the family and the state, is achieved less through the active hermeneutic of political allegory and its signification of actual particularity than through the consistency of an overarching philosophical perspective. To argue the case for the *Old Arcadia* as a *roman à clef* requires a sensitivity to the status of politics and ethics as adjacent and compatible systems of value, for Sidney and for his contemporaries, rather than a close interpretation of discursive reference of the sort that contemporary views of pastoral meaning might appear to sanction and demand.[18] In the end this may be no more than to confirm the status of the *Old Arcadia* as the founding text of the golden age of English political allegory precisely by virtue of the inertial force it exerts against its own moving parts, which are distinguishable but not easily separated out. The severity of Elizabeth's sedition laws cannot be ignored, of course, as a real contributing factor.

The most influential secret history of the seventeenth century was arguably the Scotsman John Barclay's *Argenis,* published in Latin in 1621 and translated into English three times before the decade was out. *Argenis* is an allegorical *roman à clef* whose subject, the religio-civil wars of the Huguenots that had ended two decades earlier, is domesticated as a romance narrative about the pursuit and eventual marriage of Argenis, daughter of King Meleander of Sicily.[19] *Argenis* partakes of both narrative concentration and concretization. One of Barclay's translators, Kingesmill Long, "compared it to a greater Globe, wherein not onely the World, but even the businesse of it is represented; it being (indeed) . . . a perfect Glasse of State . . . , an institution or ordering both of King and Kingdome; and that not more effectuall in Precepts, than in examples."[20] Another translator, Sir Robert Le Grys, observes that in the figure of Argenis is concentrated "the Crowne of France, and the right of succession to it . . . ." Le Grys also remarks that "thorow the whole worke he [Barclay] doth personate himselfe" under the name of Nicopompus, a strategy that at one point in the narrative enables Barclay to explain his rhetorical procedure with unusual clarity.[21]

Fired with the ambition to provide the elevated personages of his age with frank counsel, Nicopompus is also mindful that the reward of those who "rayle" with "rash and unseasonable censure" and "contumelious Libel" is likely to be "the Gallowes" (Long, 192). He therefore proposes a strategy of indirection, which he compares to the device of the sugar-coated pill and believes will sustain, despite the fact of publication, an aura of detached privacy. "I . . . will not, as guilty men call them which trouble the Common-wealth, to a publique triall" (Le Grys, 131). "But I will circumvent them unawares, with such delightful circumstances, as even themselves shall be pleased, in being taxed under strange names" (Long, 192).

> I will compile some stately Fable, in manner of a Historie; . . . The Readers will be delighted with the vanities there shewne incident to mortall men: and I shall haue them more willing to reade mee, when they shall not find mee seuere, or giuing precepts. I will feed their minds with diuers contemplations, and as it were, with a Map of places. . . . I know the disposition of our Countrie-men: because I seem to tell them Tales, I shall haue them all: they will loue my Booke aboue any Stage-play, or spectacle on the Theater . . . . While they reade, while they are affected with anger or fauour, as it were against strangers, they shall meete with themselues; and finde in the glasse held before them, the shew and merit of their owne fame. It will perchance make them ashamed longer to play those parts upon the Stage of this life, for which they must confesse themselves justly taxed in a fable. (Long, 192–93)

Barclay's paradoxical strategy involves a narrative estrangement that will induce in his readers a false sense of security sufficient to force a stealthy familiarization—the shock of self-recognition—when it is least expected. Le Grys' translation suggests that this is the (in this case false) security provided by imaginative or aesthetic distance: "I will feede their mindes with diuers contemplations, as it were with a Landskip. Then, with the imaginations of danger, I will stirre vp in them pittie, feare, and horror" (Le Grys, 131). Like Shaftesbury and Addison,[22] Le Grys uses the image of a landscape to suggest the mediatory pleasures of the imagination, which domesticates abstract precept as exemplary metaphor even as it refines literal as figurative experience. However, here the refinement subserves a domesticating purpose; and this may owe in part to the quality of Barclay's intended audience.

Domestication has become most broadly intelligible to us as a method of accommodating elevated matters by speaking of low, sensible things to low, common people—and to women. But Barclay anticipates a more elite audience that would consist principally of the very personages about whom he writes—"the greatest men," including the king himself (Le Grys, 130). His generically romance plot, from one plausible perspective a "domestication" of high public activities to amatory intimacy, from the perspective of the public actors themselves quite plausibly works rather to defamiliarize their own actions by projecting them onto an alien and fanciful terrain, a "Globe" or "Map" of places other than their own. Reading *Argenis* as though looking through a "glass" or window, Barclay's readers (at least in this ideal scenario) safely identify with his protagonists until they are brought up short by the realization that the "glass of state" is really a looking glass, or mirror, that the state is really their own and that identification is really a mask for identity. Within this scenario, Barclay's translators took it upon themselves to enhance the likelihood of readerly self-recognition through the "naturalizing" redomestication entailed in an English translation. In his epistle dedicatory Le Grys advised Charles I that "though it [*Argenis*] had a forraine birth, it was first conceived in this your Kingdome . . . . I may with reason hope, that the raising another Title to it for your Maiesty, by naturalizing of it vpon your Maiesties command, will not diminish your fauour . . ."(Le Grys, "To His Most Sacred Maiestie," A2v). And Long included in his version of the narrative a poetic address to the translator that contained this promise: "Ile court thy ARGENIS: who by thy paine/Is naturaliz'd, and doth in ENGLISH reigne . . ." (Long, A4r).[23]

In an earlier discussion I juxtaposed the concretizing methods of the contemporaries Daniel Defoe and Eliza Haywood in order to suggest how gender difference might enter into the eighteenth-century development of formal domestication. Here it will be useful to juxtapose Haywood's method with that of Barclay, compounding gender comparison through a more extended, diachronic comparison that will provide a different perspective on a similar phenomenon. Like Haywood, Barclay would use narrative concretization to establish the concrete particularity required for aesthetic identification and ethical reform; like her, he would "expose the Vice, not the Person": "So shall vices, not men be galled . . ." (Le Grys, 131). Unlike Haywood, however, Barclay would use concrete as a cover for actual particularity.[24] The contrasting methods of Barclay and Haywood offer an occasion for tentative generalizations about the long-term development in techniques of formal domestication. In Barclay's work of the 1620s we may experience the emergent separation out of political subjecthood from ethical subjectivity as an ongoing process of formal adjustment in which the explicit separation of actual from concrete particularity has not yet overmastered their tacit distinction. In Haywood's work of the 1740s these separations have proceeded so far that she conflates the contrastive terms by internalizing the former within the latter, reflexively establishing the author as the exemplary woman of taste, the ethical subject who labors productively within the virtual public space of print.

The diachronic and the synchronic perspectives on the development of formal domestication are of course complementary. In chastising her for claiming a public relevance she fails to demonstrate, Haywood's hostile correspondent makes clear his view that this is a peculiarly female and childbearing failing, that of "an idle, prating, gossiping old Woman, fit only to tell long Stories by the Fire-side for the Entertainment of little Children or Matrons . . . ." In his "Clavis" Le Grys uses very similar language to characterize the sort of work careless readers might take *Argenis* to be: "an idle Romance, in which there were no other fruit conteined, but fantasticall tales, fit onely to put away the tediousnes of a Winter euening . . ." (Le Grys, 485).[25] The principal difference between these two statements is that the earlier one is gender neutral, while the later one is gendered female. A more complex but comparable difference will be found if we compare the way Barclay and Haywood develop the secret history's stock figure of the key to the cabinet.

I have suggested that over the course of her career Haywood refigures the "key" as a device for opening, not the "public" reference of character to actual personage, but the "private" correspondence between character and reader—a correspondence overseen by the maternal narrator and the exemplary author through the careful and self-conscious equilibration of absorption and regulation, example and precept. The dominance of the former sense of the "key" in *Argenis* needs no fuller proof than the appended "clavis," which confirms its status as a *roman à clef.* Yet the figure is briefly but suggestively elaborated within the text as well.

In book 2 of *Argenis,* Poliarchus (Henry IV of France) retrieves from pirates a "treasure" stolen from Queen Hyanisbe (Elizabeth I of England), who is most overjoyed at the return of "one little Cabinet . . . . This Cabinet shee held dearer than her life; wherein, shee knew, was the fate of her sonne" (Long, 170–71, 179–81).[26] Toward the end of *Argenis,* in book 5, Poliarchus and Hyanisbe's son, rivals for the hand of Argenis, together present themselves to her father, King Meleander (Henry III of France). Fulfilling a solemn promise made to Hyanisbe, her son delivers some letters to Meleander, along with the cabinet Poliarchus had seized from the pirates. One of the letters discloses to the astonished monarch that Hyanisbe's son is also his own. "There was a small key inclosed in the Letter," Barclay adds, "wherewith the Cabbinet was to be unlocked . . . ." Within the cabinet Meleander finds more letters and a ring, "with some private tokens of secret businesse, which made the old man give beliefe to what *Hyanisbe* had written." Eager "to have so great and publique businesse generally knowne," he announces the discovery and embraces his new-found heir, whose change of fortune clears the way for marriage between Argenis and Poliarchus (Long, 699–704).

By integrating the figure of the key to the cabinet with the venerable family-romance trope of discovered parentage, Barclay illuminates some of the broader cultural implications of the kind of secret history he has undertaken. The author of a secret history that takes the form of the *roman à clef* is like Queen Hyanisbe: both provide keys to their cabinets of secret knowledge, within which can be found tokens that affirm the identity of elevated personages sufficiently to justify that their readers—us, King Meleander—"give beliefe." "Identity" here is of the sort that only one in a maternal role can affirm, the identity of dynastic lineage. It is therefore a "private" and "secret businesse"—amatory romance, sexual reproduction—that, once "generally knowne" or published, becomes a "great and publique businesse." Alluding to Hyanisbe's treasure, Barclay's translator sees himself as extending the labor of author and mother: "[W]hile it spake not *English,*" Argenis "was close lockt from all those, to whom Education had not given more Languages, than Nature Tongues: I have adventured to become the Key to this Peece of hidden Treasure . . ." (Long, "Epistle Dedicatorie," A2v). The role of the author-translator as mother is to confirm the lineal succession from son to king, ethical to political subject, private romance to public politics, secrecy to history.

In the quite different form of secret history that Haywood practices,[27] the narrator-author as exemplary mother provides the key not to political identity but to ethical identification. That is, she sustains the relation of private to public, not by affirming the authenticity of lineal succession after the fact, but by actively promulgating the correspondence between example and precept, child and citizen, narrative characterization and reading public. Her aim is to ensure not a "horizontal," diachronic relatedness (the dynastic continuity of father to son, the semantic continuity of reference to referent) but the "vertical," synchronic relatedness of ethical modeling and regulation (among private readers, between private readers and narrators, between private readers and private citizens). Unlike in *Argenis,* however, where the analogy between mother and author-translator analogizes narrative content to form through the ancient authority of the family romance, in the *Female Spectator* the figure of the narrator-author has internalized that of the mother.

This is not to deny the existence of exemplary (or counterexemplary) mothers on the level of Haywood's narrative content, Sarah Oldfashion being a case in point. It is rather to suggest what Haywood's hostile correspondent has already made obvious, the gendering of narrative method in the *Female Spectator.* As we will see in succeeding readings, the sex of the author, no doubt relevant to this particular difference between Barclay's and Haywood's narratives, nonetheless cannot explain it. The temptation to claim transhistorical links between "gender and genre" is a powerful one especially in the case of romance (although an essential tie between women and the novel has also had its advocates), which I will address shortly. To discover the significance of such associations, however, requires that we understand them in their historical contingency, thereby augmenting the powerful but totalizing truism of "patriarchy" with the knowledge of how and why male domination and female opposition take different forms at different times and places.

Opening the King's Cabinet

Whatever contribution was made by these translations of Barclay's *Argenis* to justifying Charles I's absolutist policies was insufficient to stave off civil war. In 1642 the king expressed concern lest "the common people . . . discover this *arcanum imperii,* that all this was done by them, but not for them . . . ."[28] Three years later Charles's forces were decisively defeated at the battle of Naseby. Copies of his private letters were captured and quickly published under a title that insisted on their status as an authentic secret history that in its own way disclosed the true identity of the king: *The Kings Cabinet Opened: or Certain Packets of Secret Letters & Papers, Written with the Kings own Hand, and taken in his Cabinet at Naseby-Field, June 14. 1645. By Victorious Sr. Thomas Fairfax; Wherein many mysteries of State . . . are clearly laid open . . . . Published by speciall Order of the Parliament.*[29] The letters revealed the profound gap between Charles's "two bodies"—between his public and private professions. As their contemporary editors put it, "Hee calls us a Parliament publikely, yet acknowledges us not a Parliament secretly . . . ." A case in point is the royal response to the Irish Rebellion. In a letter of late 1644 Charles instructs his Lord Lieutenant in Ireland to prosecute a speedy peace with the rebels—"all this in Cypher you must impart to none, but those three already named, and that with injunction of strictest secresie . . ." (19). His editors remark that Charles thereby "prostitutes his pardon and grace to the Irish Rebels . . . . To bargaine away our Acts of Parliament by such clandestine ingagements, as passe onely by papers, and dare not looke upon the light, supposes us to be slaves of the basest aloye . . ." (45).

The Kings Cabinet Opened is like a *roman à clef* divested of its romance signifier. What is published is the bare truth of history; yet the allegorical differential between signifier and signified remains in the felt disparity between the king's private motives and the recent, public professions we are now encouraged to recall. As the editors of the volume urge Parliament, "[H]aving now taken the dimention of the King's minde by his secret Letters, turne about a while and looke upon the same in his publike Declarations. See if you can reconcile his former promises to his present designes . . ." (49). The authentic truth of private conscience lies in speech more than in action, but in thought yet more than in speech. The striking implication of this injunction is a fundamental reversal in values. The "bare truth of history" is felt to lie, not in a public realm of behavior to which a private plot gives us obscure access, but in that private plot itself. Charles's "former promises" in his "public declarations" turn out to provide a (deceptive) signification of the "present designs" within "the king's mind." The realm of the private takes on the semiotic authority of the public realm, and what it entails is the "identity" of the king in the sense, not of name and lineage (we know these already), but, more intimately, of mind and motive. The *arcana imperii,* once disclosed, are transformed from public reason of state to the private reasons of Charles I.

This privatizing line of thought could be given a positive royalist inflection. Reflecting "*Upon His Majesties Letters taken and divulged,*" John Gauden took the king's own voice to remark that his enemies speak

> as if I were wholly confined to the Dictates and Directions of others; whom they please to brand with the names of Evill Counsellours.
>
> Its probable some men will now look upon me as my own Counsellour, and having none else to quarrell with under that notion, they will hereafter confine their anger to my self: Although I know they are very unwilling I should enjoy the liberty of my own Thoughts, or follow the light of my own Conscience, which they labour to bring into an absolute captivity to themselves . . . .[30]

Looking back after the Restoration at the conditions of his own imprisonment in the 1640s, James Howell wrote: "Among many other Barbarismes which like an impetuous Torrent have lately rush'd in upon us, the interception and opening of Letters is none of the least. . . . 'tis a plundering of the very brain, as is spoken in another place. We are reduced here to that servile condition, or rather to such a height of slavery, that we have nothing left which may entitle us free Rationall creatures; the *thought* it self cannot say 'tis free, much less the *tongue* or *pen.*" From this perspective, Charles is not antagonist but victim, the publicizing of his letters not a blow for freedom from absolutist tyranny but an absolutist invasion of the royal "brain"'s freedom. The public cabinet of state secrets devolves into the private absolutism of the epistolary self: this is the implication not only of Gauden's language of liberty and absolute captivity but also of Howell's metaphor that to "make this scrutiny within myself" is to "enter into the closest Cabinet of my Soul . . . ."[31]

A royalist verse satire made explicit the application of this conscientious critique to the case of *The Kings Cabinet Opened:*

> The *Basiliskes* are turn'd to *Closet-Spies,*
> And to their *Poys'nous* adde *Enquiring* eyes:
>
> · · · · · · · · · · · · · ·
>
> Who now have waded through all *Publick* aw,
> Will break through *Secrets* and prophane their Law.
>
> · · · · · · · · · · · · · ·
>
> Nature gave Reason power to find a way,
> Which none but these could venture to betray.
> 'Two close safe Pathes she did bequeath to men,
> 'In *Presence, Whisper;* and at *Distance, Penne.*
> Publick *Decrees* and *Thoughts* were else the same,
> Nor went it to *Converse,* but to *Proclaim.*

Like later participants in the debate on how to assign property in printing, the poet uses the analogy of absolute landownership to extend the critique of the rebels' disclosure:

> Conceipts were else but *Records,* but by this care
> Our *Thoughts* no *Commons,* but *Inclosures* are:
> What bold *Intruders* then are, who assail
> To cut their Prince's *Hedge,* and break his *Pale*?[32]

The regicide of 1649 was accompanied by the royalist publication of Charles's hagiography, *Eikon Basilike, The Portraiture of His Sacred Majesty in His Solitudes and Sufferings.* "To counteract the damage done by the contents of the king's cabinet, it was essential to believe that the piety and forgiveness expressed in the posthumous book came from the still more secret cabinet of the king's heart."[33]

However, *The Kings Cabinet Opened* specifies Charles's intimate realm more precisely than this. If the parliamentary view is of a radical disparity between the king's public and private selves—between his bodies "politic" and "natural"—the royalist view is that his enemies treacherously assault the traditional, dynastic solidarity of the king's two bodies as expressed in the coextension of monarchy and family. In one of his secret letters Charles asserts that "in pursuance of their great design of extirpating the Royall Bloud, and Monarchie of England they [the English rebels] have endeavoured likewise to lay a great blemish upon his Royall Family, endeavouring to illegitimate all derived from his Sister, at once to cut off the interest and pretensions of the whole Race, which their most detestable and scandalous designe they have pursued . . ." (42). For Charles, the metonymic relation between the royal family and the (royal) state exercises a tacit authority. For Parliament, that relation, rendered explicit and volatile by events of the past decade, has become suspect, an intimation of a world turned upside down. From the parliamentary perspective, the private royal family, no longer the serviceable engine of a sovereign state succession, on the contrary is now being accorded priority over, and elevated above, the public state.

Indeed, it is the realization that this reversal is under way that dictates the logic of turning to Charles's private papers to learn the truth of state affairs. The evidence for the reversal lies in the tenor of the letters themselves. Many of them are addressed to the Roman Catholic Henrietta Maria ("Deare heart"), intermixing ejaculations of love and affection with matters of policy and affairs of state. "It is plaine here," say the editors, "that the Kings Counsels are wholly managed by the Queene, though she be of the weaker Sex, borne an Alien, bred up in a contrarie Religion, yet nothing great or small is transacted without her privitie & consent. . . . The King professes to prefer her health before the exigence, and importance of his owne publikes affaires" (43). The royalist poet is acerbic (and opportunistically feminist) on this complaint:

> they reasons vex,
> And tell the world Shee's of the Weaker Sex.
> In what wilde Braines this Madnesse first began!
> They're wondrous angry, 'cause the Queen's no Man.
> . . . .
> Fond Sirs forbear, do not the world perplex:
> *Reason* and *Judgement* are not things of *Sex.*
> . . . .
> But as all Publick Knowledge barr'd must be,
> So *Houshold-Acts* must have their *Mysterie:*
> No Circumstance can passe, no Servant made,
> But must be wrapt in *silence* and close *shade.*
> (172–73)

In the eyes of the royalist, the rebels are absurdly mock-heroic, treating domestic trifles as though they had the mystery and weight of state affairs. The rebels give the same mock-heroic incongruity a more radical valence. Amatory intimacies have usurped the place of public judgment, a perversion intimated by the (conventionally) amatory language the editors use to announce that usurpation: we "may see here in his private Letters what affection the King beares to his people, . . . [and] consider with sorrow that it comes from a Prince seduced out of his proper spheare . . ." (A3r). Similarly, Lucy Hutchinson had little hope for a kingdom "where the hands that are made only for distaffs affect the management of sceptres." And in response to *Eikon Basilike* Milton wondered "what concerns it us to hear a Husband divulge his Household privacies, extolling to others the virtues of his Wife; an infirmity not seldom incident to those who have least cause. . . . How fitt to govern men, undervaluing and as-persing the great Counsel of his Kingdom, in comparison of one Woman."[34] The evidence of *The Kings Cabinet Opened* suggests that the reduction of the public to the private, of politics to sex, of mastery to "effeminacy," for which contemporaries took Charles's son to task forty years later[35] was not simply an effect of "the merry monarch's" character but also the culmination of a dynamic at the heart of Stuart absolutism.

Opening the Queen's Closet

Ten years after the publication of *The Kings Cabinet Opened*, the king dead and the queen in exile, the "mystery" of "household acts" was publicly affirmed in the printing of *The Queens Closet Opened. Incomparable Secrets in Physick, Chyrurgery, Preserving, Candying, and Cookery. As they were presented unto the Queen by the most Experienced Persons of our times, many whereof were honoured with her own Practise, when she pleased to descend to these more private Recre-ations. . . .*[36] The strategic posture of this volume is hard to pin down. Suffused with an allusive knowledge of the tradition in which it would seem to play an obliquely ironic role, *The Queens Closet Opened* also adopts an authentically ele-giac tone of royalist regret, while making a creditable contribution to an exis-tent genre of domestic lore. The publication is a labor of love, "the Original pa-pers being most of them preserved in my own hands, which I kept as so many Reliques, and should sooner have parted with my dearest blood, then to have suffered them to be publick. But since my Soveraign Mistress her banish-ment, . . . I found no less then two other Copies abroad . . . my friends . . . ad-vised me to dispatch my original copy to the Press to prevent those false ones; for otherwise I should not have thought it less then Sacriledge, had not the lock been first pickt, to have opened the Closet of my distressed Soveraign Mistress without her Royal Assent. . . . thank the times, not me, for otherwise these pre-cious leaves, had never been in common . . ." ("Epistle to the Reader," A3v, A4v, font reversed). For a moment two worlds dovetail: the expertise of the battle-field and that of the kitchen; the military strongbox and the domestic recipe book; Charles and Henrietta Maria—the woman behind the man.[37]

The history of cookbooks provides a case study in the productivity of the gendered division of both labor and knowledge. The category of housewifery was first conceived and published as a subcategory of husbandry and thereby seen as part of the province of estate management. With social mobility and ur-banization, cookbooks began to be separated out from this general province to-ward the end of the sixteenth century and directed at a female audience. Indeed, a useful record of the gendered division of labor can be found in the ongoing specialization of estate management as registered in the history of "domestic" guidebooks (first the separation of husbandry from housewifery, then the alienation from the latter of increasingly professionalized trades like distillation and medicinal practice).[38] The first cookbook in English written specifically for women is John Partridge's *The Treasure of Hidden Secrets. Commonlie called, The Good-huswives Closet of prouision, for the health of her Houshold* . . . (1573). This and subsequent publications in the following century make clear the riskiness of reading *The Queens Closet Opened* only as a parodic, "private" allusion to *The Kings Cabinet Opened*—or even as exemplifying a strictly female genre: *The Ladies Cabinet Opened: Wherein is found hidden severall Experiments in Preserving and Conserving, Physicke, and Surgery, Cookery and Huswifery* (1639);[39] *The Closet of the Eminently Learned Sir Kenelme Digby Kt Opened: Whereby is Discovered Several ways for making of Methgelin, Syder, Cherry-Wine, &c. Together with Excellent Directions for Cookery* . . . *Published by his Son's Consent* (1669); *The Gentlewomans Cabinet Unlocked. Wherein is contained many excellent Receipts for neat Dressing of divers sorts of Meats* . . . (1688). That Hannah Woolley relied on *The Queens Closet Opened* for the compilation of her own popular cookbooks is clear not only from her explicit acknowledgment of it[40] but also from the title of one of her publications: *The Queen-like Closet; or, Rich Cabinet: Stored with all manner of Rare Receipts for Preserving, Candying & Cookery* . . . (1670). But if the title of Henrietta Maria's book is thus quite adequately explained by the publication history of the cookbook genre, we are nonetheless justified in seeing it, I think, as a watershed in the early modern gendering of labor. For by self-consciously parodying *The Kings Cabinet Opened* it also distances its own securely private purposes from the less determinate ones of its counterpart. Like the profession of the secretary, the practice of domestic cookery is one of those activities whose primary modern associations mark its devolution to the domain of the private and the female even as its most exalted practitioners are usually male and "public" (i.e., remunerated on the market).[41]

Scudéry

One of the innovative forms that exemplify the tendency of seventeenth-century love and war, romance and heroics toward "mixture"[42] is what modern English readers call the French heroic romance, which exerted a profound influence on certain strains of the English secret history. The classics of the genre date from the early decades of the century and bear a formal relation to Barclay's *Argenis* close enough to justify contiguous classification.[43] However, the works of Madeleine de Scudéry, published under her brother's name between 1641 and 1661, are ultimately more pervasive in their impact on English literary culture, and I will confine my brief remarks to her three heroic romances. Scudéry's work is a product of the midcentury Parisian salon subculture, a complex network of overlapping and intersecting coteries led by women and dedicated to the exploration and practice of delicacy, civility, and affective interiority in all realms of social life.

Scudéry's voluminous narratives, extreme in the alien exoticism of their locales and chronologies, are disparately allusive to contemporary French personages ranging from the most elevated court figures to Scudéry and her own circles. The French heroic romance characteristically, if variously and inconsistently, took the form of a *roman à clef.* A key was actually published for Scudéry's longest work, *Artamenes, or the Grand Cyrus* ([Fr., 1649–53], trans. 1653-55), in which Cyrus himself represents the Prince of Condé, a leader of the aristocratic Fronde. Scudéry's vast tapestry is also populated by frequenters of the salons, notably that of Catherine de Rambouillet and Scudéry's own salon, the *Samedi.* The translator of the English version remarked that "the Intrigues and Miscarriages of War and Peace are better, many times, laid open and Satyriz'd in a *Romance,* than in a downright History, which being oblig'd to name the Persons, is often forc'd for several Reasons and Motives to be too partial and sparing; while such disguis'd Discourses as these, promiscuously personating every Man, and no Man, take their full liberty to speak the Truth."44

Scudéry's narratives therefore operate as secret histories in this most immediate, political sense of the term. But as the mixture of great and not-so-great personages in *Cyrus* might suggest, Scudéry works the public-private differential in a number of familiar ways. Like her predecessors in the heroic romance, she constructs her narratives from a central action punctuated by interpolated, interconnecting stories, or *recits,* that are told by her characters and that sustain an elaborate structure of variety in unity whose public-private resonances are momentary and shifting but highly suggestive. "Third-person impersonal narration is constantly superseded by the first-person *recit.* The *recit* turns the past into speech, and speech overwhelms action. A combat in the narrative present will immediately lead to speech, to history, to the past—as if action must be erased by words."45 One of the *recits* in *Clelia. An Excellent new Romance* ([Fr., 1654–60], trans. 1656–61) is itself a *roman à clef,* the history of Artaxander as told by the character Amilcar, who is both the signified of Artaxander and the signifier of the contemporary poet Jean-François Sarasin.46 Like Barclay's translators, Scudéry's play upon the personifying and domesticating potential of English translation: John Davies tells "the Ladies" of *Clelia's* "paines willingly taken for your *beautifull Sex* in passing the Seas, and changing not only her *Language* but her *Country* . . . ."47

In her most famous innovation, Scudéry's Clelia, asked by her friends to provide a definition of "tenderness," promises "to give you the Map of that Country," a promise that produces, not the expected explanatory "Letter," but a design "that so resembled a true Map, that there was Seas, Rivers, Mountains, a Lake, Cities and Villages . . ." (see fig. 10.1). The *Carte de tendre* is a cartographic concretization of abstract affective states (not only tenderness but indifference, indiscretion, sensibility, generosity, etc.) whose primary function is to guide readers toward a state of tender friendship or platonic love that negotiates a spectrum of dangers, including that of marriage. Clelia begs Herminius, soon to be her tender friend, "not to shew it but to five or six persons whom she desired should see it . . . ." But in a development that has the allegorical aura of the transition from coterie manuscript exchange to typographical mass circulation the map quickly becomes known to many more than this, and Herminius is sharply reproved: "[D]o you think I imagined, this spective fancy had anything pleasant, but for our *Cabala* in particular to become publick, and that I made to be seen by five or six persons which have noble spirits, should be seen by two thousand who scarce have any, and who hardly understand the best things?"[48] Scudéry's *Cabala* is perhaps one of Haywood's sources for her own authorial "Cabal" in the *Female Spectator,* and its publication expresses the basic ambivalence of a politico-amatory secret whose ultimate value may require its disclosure.

On the level of content, Scudéry's heroic romances are shot through with the sensibility of an author highly conscious of the power dynamic at work in gender relations—also of the ameliorative, even utopian, possibilities of a manifestly "feminine" sensibility. To what extent are the variously domesticating features of Scudéry's narrative form gendered female? (The question might be asked, more unexpectedly, of Bunyan's Protestant allegory: Christiana replaces Christian as our representative pilgrim, but Scudéry's town, "A Great hart," becomes Bunyan's personified "Mr. Great-heart," Christiana's indispensable guard and guide.) That is, how far do she and her contemporaries conceive the heroic romance, especially in her hands, to be a female form? The preface to Scudéry's last heroic romance, *Ibrahim* ([Fr., 1641] trans. 1652), famously affirms the propriety of interior assessment in the characterization of the hero: "It is not by things without him, it is not by the caprichioes of destiny, that I will judge him; it is by the motions of his soul, and by that which he speaketh." Like the other addresses to the reader in her works, this preface is generally attributed to her brother Georges, who instances Scudéry's predecessor Honoré d'Urfé as the great master of this technique: "[H]e goes searching out in the bottom of hearts the most secret thoughts . . . ."[49] The evidence of gender neutrality in this valorization of the interior approach is supported by that of an equally famous section in Scudéry's last heroic romance.

Debating with her friends the relative merits of "history" and "fable," Clelia elicits from Herminius an account of what each requires. The historian, says Herminius, "must have a universal knowledge of the World, of the interests of Princes and the humours of Nations; policy must not be unknown to him, nor the art of War; he must understand to describe battles; and, which is most of all necessary, he must be able perfectly to represent those Wars of the Closet which are met with in all Courts, which consist in intrigues, delusions, and negotiations true or feign'd, and which notwithstanding are of such importance, that 'tis in them the seeds are sow'd of the most considerable Wars, and on which the ruin or felicity of Nations as well as the verity of History depends."⁵⁰ The claim that private "Wars of the Closet" are prior to, and the seedlings for, public warfare may well remind us of Haywood's insistence that example teaches precept and that the ill propagation of the species ensures the miseries of civil life. The difference is that unlike in Haywood, there is no explicit sign here that narra-

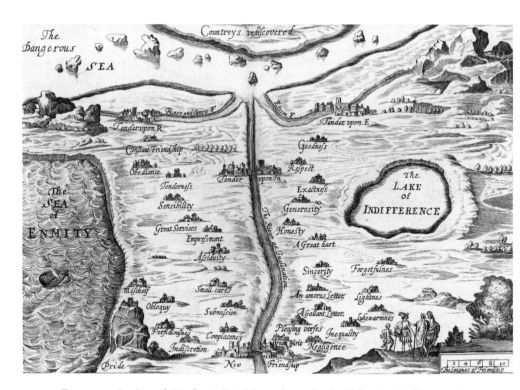

FIG. 10.1. *La Carte de Tendre,* in [Madeleine de Scudéry], *Clelia. An Excellent new Romance . . .* (1654–60), trans. J. Davies, 1655. Bodleian Library, University of Oxford, shelf mark fol. BS. 143, between A5 and A6.

tive technique that takes seriously the wars of the closet is to be associated with women writers or readers in particular. And when Herminius turns to the normative method of "fable," his account seems only to deepen and extend the exemplary pedagogy of the historian rather than to set forth a (potentially gendered) antithesis to it.

It is easy to hear in Scudéry's Herminius an echo of Barclay's spokesman Nicopompus. Beyond the qualifications of the historian, he says, the fabulist "must also know . . . the secrets of all hearts . . . . But above all things, he must know how to take away plainnesse and drinesse from morality, and set it off in a dresse so natural and so agreeable, that it may divert all those to whom it gives instruction; and as Ladies break not their Looking-glasses which show them the defects which they amend when they know; so they may not hate a work wherein they oftentimes see things which none durst speak to them of . . . ." Readers of such a fable will be spared "the pains of Travelling, to become persons of worth and accomplisht; since there may be made so handsom a Map of the World, that it might be seen in Epitome without going forth of their Closet."[51] At least in theory, the glass of state metamorphoses from window to mirror; the world at large is epitomized and concentrated into a fabulous map, and the map is secreted within the domestic privacy of the closet.

Women and Romance

Scholars tend to assume the widespread association of women and romance in early modern England on a number of grounds, but perhaps most often on the evidence of the male authorial anticipation of a female readership. The evidence is real (as we have just seen in the preface to the English *Clelia*) but difficult to interpret. How is the association of gender and genre based on anticipated (female) readership of romances complicated by the association of gender and genre based on actual (male) authorship of romances—including authors like Sidney, Spenser, Shakespeare, and Milton? Do the claims of Addison, Steele, Dunton, and others to be writing for women argue an analogous association between women and the periodical essay? How do we distinguish negative expectations of women reading romances from negative expectations of women reading narratives, or of women reading as such? Does the fact that women and romance often are criticized for the same things (triviality, loquacity) warrant the inference that the critique of romance and the critique of women implicate each other? How can we balance stated expectations of women reading romances against the quantity of articulated anticipations of male readership of romances, or of a readership (e.g., commoners, youths) whose sex is not specified? What do we—what did contemporaries—mean by "romance"?

Can we extrapolate from expectations of, for example, French heroic romance—or of one of Scudéry's heroic romances—to attitudes toward romance as such?[52]

The association of women and romance seems to have become so axiomatic in the modern world as to enjoin caution lest we project present attitudes onto the past. And yet the very familiarity of the association also may enjoin us to pinpoint the historical moment when the association became axiomatic. It seems to me that in the case of women and romance, however, the gendering of genre is a variable and discontinuous phenomenon. Romance is an ancient, singularly complex mode whose ideological and cultural import at any moment depends on which of its multiple historical accretions may be thrown into relief by a given context of elaboration. Even the self-evidence of romance's femininity in the modern world is challenged by the actual vicissitudes of modern literary history.[53] The feminization of romance has a decidedly uneven development that consists of opportunistic and locally conditioned movements that do not seem susceptible to monolithic generalization. Part of my argument in succeeding chapters will be that the comparatively clear association of women with romance that scholars of early modern literature would disclose in the sixteenth and seventeenth centuries is a product of the later eighteenth century and of its institutionalization and stabilization of domesticity.

The King Out of Power

With the Interregnum and the eclipse of monarchy, secrecy and its secret history temporarily assumed a particularly royalist coloring.[54] The *arcana imperii* were now doubly so as actual empire passed to a republican commonwealth and protectorate whose state powers encouraged the production of "royal romances" that used the obliquity of romance *arcana* to orchestrate royalist opposition to state *arcana*. In such a context, the aspect of the patriarchalist analogy that focused on issues of obligation was especially useful in adumbrating, through the private institution of the marriage contract, the public problem created for English people by Cromwell's act of 1650 requiring all English citizens to subscribe to the Commonwealth Engagement, that is, to "*declare and promise, that I will be true and faithful to the Commonwealth of England as it is now established, without a king or House of Lords.*"[55] In these terms, the marriage plots of royal romances both concentrated and concretized the problem of engagement, on the one hand condensing the political contract to the lineaments of a nuptial contract, on the other reconceiving the abstract paradox of consent to be bound as the pragmatic experience of a habituation in self-regulation.[56]

When it was published in 1653, *Cloria and Narcissus* was prefaced by an account of its origins that assumed the tone of the average common reader, despite his simplicity suspecting that there might be more there than meets the eye: "It was my chance being beyond-sea, to have the perusing of some of this story, which according to my sense and understanding then, appeared not onely delightfull in the reading, but seemed to my capacity to containe in many places mysteries, belonging to the transactions of forraine parts either at present, or not very long before put in execution . . . ." The only suggestion of a domestic (i.e., English) reference comes in a remark about the unusual accessibility of this text to English readers: "[F]or many yeers past, not any one Romance, hath been written in the English tongue; when as daily from other Nations, so many of all sorts fly into the World to be seen . . . ."⁵⁷ Eight years later, a retitled and considerably expanded version of this text appeared, even though, as its straightforward preface made clear, vastly altered political circumstance now seemed to obviate the obliquity of romance: "You have now the whole Work of *the Princess Cloria,* otherwise called, *The Royal Romance;* some of it being printed formerly in the worst of times; that is to say, under the Tyrannical Government of *Cromwel;* when but to name or mention any of the Kings concernments, was held the greatest crime, almost could be committed against that Usurpation . . . ."⁵⁸

Now the romance could be openly acknowledged to signify and domesticate "the Kings concernments." And yet the return of Stuart monarchy did not render the romance plot expendable. On the contrary, *The Princess Cloria* is now candidly declared one of those "mixed" forms, its "Style and manner of Contrivance, being mixt between Modern and Antick . . ." (A1v).⁵⁹ The reader is instructed not to "look for an exact History, in every particular circumstance; though perchance upon due consideration you will finde, a certain methodical coherency between the main Story, and the numerous Transactions that passed, both at home and abroad . . ." (A1r). Freed from acute political necessity, the mixed form of the secret history learns how to justify itself on epistemological and ethical grounds. "[I]t is impossible otherwise [than in such romance] to express inward passions and hidden thoughts, that of necessity accompany all Transactions of consequence, when as States-men now and then in Treaties judge of effects, by the very looks and countenances of such, they have occasion to deal withal in Businesses of any importance . . ." (A3r). Made safe by a change in political regime, the attractions of actual particularity are now challenged by those of concrete particularity: "[T]he common Occurrences of the World, do not arrive alwayes at a pitch high enough for example, or to stir up the appetite of the Reader, which things feigned may do under the notion of a Romance . . ." (A3r). Exemplary narrative teaches best the precepts that actual history, their living source, is nonetheless pedagogically less powerful to convey.

Indeed, histories of "former Ages are no other, then certain kinde of *Romances* to succeeding posterity; since they have no testimony for them but mens probable opinions; seeing the Historical part almost of all Countreys is subject to be questioned . . ." (A3r–A4v).

Inward as the clue to outward, example as the clue to precept: these signifying relationships, familiar to us from other essays in exemplary and domesticating pedagogy, sustain the aim to speak to an inclusive, even common, readership that was evident in the earlier, protectorate version *Cloria and Narcissus.* But the Restoration had fractured the tenuous integrity of royalist "secrecy," obviating the new, expansive, opposition-building hermeneutics of the king in exile while reinvigorating the old, absolutist hermeneutics of the king in state. Hence the comprehension of commoners was no longer so attractive. According to the preface to *The Princess Cloria,* the public meaning of "the Story is no way difficult to be understood by any, who have been but indifferently versed in the Affairs of *Europe;* and for others of the more vulgar sort, a bare *Romance* of Love and Chivalry, such as this may be esteemed to be at the worst, will prove entertainment enough for their leasure . . ." (A1v–A2r). As the absolutist Cardinal Mazarin remarks within *The Princess Cloria* itself, "[S]ecrets of State to the common people, resemble Speculative Divinity, onely known to the learned studiant, and not to be debated without an interpreter, lest outward sense, turn all rather to Atheisme then sollid Doctrine . . ." (568).[60] According to another "royal romance," "[s]o keen and eager were the Talens of our Statizing Censors, as this Royal Romance would not upon its first production or presentation be admitted to the Presse." It was published in 1659, soon after Richard Cromwell's abdication, when Stuart monarchy was about to become once again not the object but the agent of "statizing censorship."[61]

The King In Power

The failure of the restored king to restore the conditions of tacit authority that his grandfather had tried (paradoxically) to enunciate was overdetermined by, among other things, the robustness of a literary public sphere that had been flourishing for two decades. Once set in motion, the explicitating capacities of literary circulation in general and of typographical reproduction in particular were beyond the powers of the state to suppress. In Sir Roger L'Estrange Charles II had an indefatigable royal surveyor of the press whose efforts to police the public disclosure of *arcana imperii* were unprecedented but largely ineffective. Undeterred by the king's 1660 Declaration of Indemnity and Oblivion, poems on affairs of state, replete with potentially libelous innuendo, proliferated early on in the decade, many of them purporting to disclose governmental scandal of one sort or another.[62] In 1667 John Dryden published *Annus Mirabilis: The Year of Wonders, 1666. An Historical Poem* in part to rebut these secret histories with a narration of current events that, he implied, was "ti'd too severly to the Laws of History" to be vulnerable to challenge. Premised on the patriarchalist maxim "Realms are housholds which the Great must guide," Dryden's poem used a texture of metaphor (if not a full-blown allegory) both to concentrate the national disasters of plague, war, and fire into a parable of familial crisis and to concretize them as the terrestrial workings-out of a typological providence.[63]

Later the same year Andrew Marvell circulated a poem that epitomized what Dryden was worried about. Climaxing a series of poems based on the Horatian topos *ut pictura poesis, The Last Instructions to a Painter* beat Dryden at his own concentrating game.[64] Marvell's fiction is of England as "our Lady State" sitting for a portrait whose imaginary execution is preceded by the poet's real one by way of advice on what the painter should emphasize. This organizing representation of the public as the private, the great as the little, authorizes an extraordinary array of satiric (but also libelous) techniques by which Marvell reduces England's leaders to contempt. The brilliance of the strategy lies, at least in part, in the fact that the poet's and the painter's arts of reduction are the positive and productive version of what those leaders do without knowing it:

> Here, Painter, rest a little, and survey
> With what small arts the public game they play.
> (lines 117–18, p. 160)

Replaying the unconscious mock heroics of the great with the crucial difference of knowingness, the poet instructs the painter to "through the microscope take aim" (line 16, p. 157); and no episode better reflects Marvell's virtuosic microscopy than his domestication of the British navy's humiliation by representing it as a skimmington ride:

> The court as once of war, now fond of peace,
> All to new sports their wanton fears release.
> From Greenwich (where intelligence they hold)
> Comes news of pastime martial and old,
> A punishment invented first to awe
> Masculine wives transgressing Nature's law,
> Where, when the brawny female disobeys
> And beats the husband till for peace he prays,
> No concerned jury for him damage finds,
> Nor partial justice her behaviour binds,
> But the just street does the next house invade,

> Mounting the neighbour couple on lean jade,
> The distaff knocks, the grains from kettle fly,
> And boys and girls in troops run hooting by:
> Prudent antiquity, that knew by shame,
> Better than law, domestic crimes to tame,
> And taught youth by spectácle innocent!
> So thou and I, dear Painter, represent
> In quick effígy others' faults, and feign
> By making them ridiculous, to restrain.
> (lines 373–92, p. 167)

The court's decision to sue for peace is a characteristically corrupt *arcanum*, a cynical and stealthy diminishment of heroic pretence—"So therefore secretly for peace decrees, / Yet as for war the Parliament should squeeze" (lines 123–24, p. 160)—which the poet punishes in kind by comparing this public perfidy to a domestic shaming ritual. The husband is England, the wife is the Dutch, and the skimmington ride encompasses both the way the brawny Dutch "beat" the English and the way the cowardly English beg for "peace." But since the punishment ritual is performative, not direct, the actual ride is not undertaken by the transgressing "couple": "So Holland with us had the mastery tried, / And our next neighbours, France and Flanders, ride" (lines 395–96, p. 167). The ride tames "domestic crimes" not only in the obvious sense but also because the major onus of blame must fall, not on the foreign enemy, but on those at home who have betrayed their people. But because it is the state itself that is to blame, justice is to be found not in the public "law" but in the "just street," the will of common English people as "taught" by the diminishing power of satiric art.[65]

Although this episode is a relatively faint illustration, *The Last Instructions* is suffused with the strategic reduction of public politics to private sex, an extreme act of concentration that was justified, as we have seen, by the increasingly common perception that under Charles II, state affairs had become enthralled to libertine self-indulgence. Near the end of the poem Marvell pictures, with amusing reflexivity, the careworn Charles suddenly awakened by a vision of England, "our Lady State," who has been the allegorical subject of the poem's portraiture from the beginning. The problem is that unlike us readers, Charles does not recognize her at first; and the reason for this is her external appearance:

> Naked as born, and her round arms behind
> With her own tresses, interwove and twined;
> Her mouth locked up, a blind before her eyes,
> Yet from beneath the veil her blushes rise,
> And silent tears her secret anguish speak;

> Her heart throbs and with very shame would break.
> The object strange in him no terror moved:
> He wondered first, then pitied, then he loved,
> And with kind hand does the coy vision press
> (Whose beauty greater seemed by her distress), . . .
> (lines 893–902, p. 180)

A superficial and salacious reader, Charles takes the signifier for the signified and overlooks the "secret anguish" for the "coy vision." Marvell's secret history ensures that we do not.

We have already considered the contribution Marvell's country house poem of the 1650s made to the pastoral discourse of the lesser and the great. In 1677 John Lacy travestied the already suggestive language of "Upon Appleton House," concentrating house into cunt and shrinking Fairfax's magnificence into Charles's tumescence:

> C--t is the mansion house where thou dost swell.
> There thou art fix'd as tortoise is to shell,
> Whose head peeps out a little now and then
> To take the air and then creeps in again.[66]

The king's secret rendezvous, sexual and other, were facilitated by William Chiffinch, who in 1666 was appointed Senior Page of the Back Stairs and Keeper of the King's Cabinet-Closet, a private room off Charles's bedchamber. Chiffinch was known as a procurer both sexual and political, and his influential domain was the interior recesses of the royal palace. The Earl of Rochester tells of Chiffinch's role in brokering potential new mistresses for Charles. Roger North thought "[t]he back-stairs might properly be called the spy office where the King spoke with particular persons about intrigues of all sorts" and Chiffinch "discovered men's characters which the King could never have obtained by any other means."[67] Broadly speaking, of course, the sexualization of politics was built into the English system of dynastic succession. The most important complication in the reign of the later Stuarts was the uncertainty of the succession, which brought intimate issues of marriage, divorce, and childbirth to the forefront of the political agenda. Political secrets were therefore never far from sexual secrets.[68]

L'Estrange's greatest success in at least temporary concealment was the secret treaty of Dover of 1670, which reversed current pro-Dutch and anti-French policy by stealthily establishing an alliance with Louis XIV whereby England and France would prosecute war against the United Provinces and Charles, on his own timetable, would openly embrace Roman Catholicism. As the first clause of the secret treaty put it, "articles so secret and advantageous to both monarchs have been agreed upon that a treaty of similar importance can hardly be found in any period of history." The treaty was so secret that not only most of Charles's Privy Council but even most of his inner "Cabal" were deprived of its terms—elaborately "disinformed," in fact, by the careful fiction of a bogus treaty identical to the real one but omitting the popish conversion clause.[69] Since the English Reformation had fused church and state by making the English monarch *defensor fidei,* the conversion of Charles meant the conversion of the English state. Charles professed "such confidence in the fidelity and affection of his subjects that none of them, not even those who (as yet) have been denied a full outpouring of divine grace, will fail in their due obedience to their sovereign." Recognizing the need for a backup plan, however, the secret treaty also provided for French financial and military support in enforcing the transformation of England into a Catholic state.[70]

The secret treaty of 1670 thus subordinated the apprehensions of "divine grace" to "due obedience," private conscience to (the king's view of) state interest. To Marvell this perverse subjection of religion to politics had been generally characteristic of Roman Catholic legislators, who "instead of squaring their governments by the rule of Christianity, have shaped Christianity by the measures of their government, have reduced that straight line by the crooked, and bungling divine and humane things together, have been always hacking and hewing one another, to frame an irregular figure of political incongruity." The opening of Marvell's notoriously incendiary polemic, anonymously published seven years after the secret treaty of Dover, aligns the secret, and not so secret, history of England in recent times with this venerable practice: "There has now for divers years a design been carried on to change the lawful Government of England into an absolute Tyranny, and to convert the established Protestant Religion into downright Popery . . . ."[71]

For English Protestants, the *arcana ecclesiae* of popish patriarchy dovetailed seamlessly with the *arcana imperii* of absolute monarchy. Marvell's tract helped distill the fear of popery into the disclosure of the most celebrated, and polymorphously political, secret of the period, the Popish Plot: the putative Catholic conspiracy to assassinate Charles II and place his papist brother, James, Duke of York, on the throne. As evidenced by the secret treaty of Dover, the plot was not quite the figment of conspiracy theory that modern historiography has tended to suggest it was. The outrage Marvell and others felt was fueled, moreover, by the discovery and publication of secret letters, some written in cipher, that had been carelessly circulated by Edward Coleman, the Roman Catholic secretary to the Duke and Duchess of York, in an effort to drum up for James the sort of papist financial support that the secret treaty of Dover already had won for Charles.[72] The publication of Coleman's letters in 1681 by order of the House of Commons recalls, in a lower key, the dismay with which the publication of *The Kings Cabinet Opened* was met after the battle of Naseby.

That the Popish Plot cast Charles in the role of passive victim may owe to the still operative (if threadbare) fiction that the king himself "can do no wrong"[73]—and to the consequences of ignoring that fiction, still very live in people's memories. Yet the portrayal of Charles as a relatively innocent pawn of evil counselors and secretaries fits with the oddly privatized image of the king that emerged from current views of him not only as a libertine sex addict but also (as we will see) as a loving husband betrayed by his brother's political ambition. For the next eight years the English press was filled with discoveries of popish and Tory—and then, as the political tide turned, of fanatic and Whiggish—perfidy. For L'Estrange, this was truly an "Age of *Narratives*."[74] In the last years of the decade the intractable problem of Stuart absolutism would be permanently settled by, not regicide, but James's exclusion and replacement.

The secret pledge of French arms and money testifies that Louis XIV was a tireless booster of English Catholicism—"anxious," as the treaty of Dover put it, "to contribute to a design glorious not only for the King of England, but for the whole of Catholic Christendom." And when the Duke of York's wife died in 1671, Louis found it easy to show his support also in the "private" register, exerting his influence to ensure that the heir to the English throne remarry a Frenchwoman. Two years later the marriage contract between James and Mary of Modena was sealed, and the wedding completed by proxy. James told the French ambassador that he sentimentally regarded his bride as Louis's daughter; the marriage was kept secret, at least for a while, from the English Parliament and people. The queen was by now acknowledged to be barren, and some were urging Charles himself, clearly against his brother's interests, to seek a divorce and marry again.[75] Although diverted in 1670 by the rare spectacle of a nobleman granted parliamentary permission to divorce and remarry,[76] the king kept his own counsel on the inflammatory issue of a royal remarriage.

The Secret of the Black Box

Charles's nuptial contract with Catherine of Braganza in 1661 had been in the time-honored dynastic tradition of the public marriage of alliance. In 1680 he was obliged to issue a declaration denying an earlier, secret love match—specifically, "a most false and scandalous Report of a Marriage or Contract of Marriage supposed to be had and made between Us and one Mrs *Walters*, alias *Barlow*, now deceased, Mother of the present Duke of *Monmouth* . . . ." Lucy Walter had been Charles's mistress while he was in exile in The Hague, and she had given birth to a son in 1649. What the king called "this idle Story" of his son's legitimacy was said to be documented by proofs of marriage contained in a mysterious black box.[77] Responding to Charles's declaration with a skepticism bred of the civil-war years, Robert Feguson laid down the principle "[t]hat the denials of Kings are not to be subscribed unto with an implicite Faith, but that we ought to use the same discretion in believing or not believing what they say, that we esteem our selves priviledged to use towards others in the credit which they require we should give unto them." Ferguson claimed that Charles had said "not long ago, *He vvas harrassed out of his Life, by the importunity of his Brother* . . . ," recalling as well that the Duke of York had also tried to renounce his first wife, Anne Hyde. "And it may be, he thinks it will be some extenuation of what he did himself, if people can be brought to believe that it is a Disease natural to the Family, and which runs in a Blood." As for Charles, "some of us can remember, how through immoderate love to her being reduced to a condition that his Life was dispaired of, and the late *Queen* his *Mother* receiving intelligence both of his Disease and the Cause of it, she consented to his espousing of her, rather than that he should consume and perish in his otherwise unquenchable flames."[78]

Ferguson's purported memory sits oddly with his skepticism, given the romance conventionality of the story of the black box, audible here in the language of Petrarchan lovesickness. In fact a scant month earlier Ferguson had made just this objection:

> But in truth the whole referring to the Black Box is a meer Romance, purposely invented to sham and ridicule the business of the Marriage, which indeed hath no relation to it. For they who judg'd it conducible to their present Interest to have the *D.* of *M's.* Title to the Crown not only discredited but exposed, thought it necessary, instead of nakedly enquiring whether he be the *Kings Legitimate* or only *Natural* Son; to bring upon the Stage a circumstance no way annexed with it, supposing that this being found a Fable, the *Marriage* it self of the *K.* with the said *Ds. Mother,* would have undergone the same Censure.

From this perspective, the token of the black box is a kind of secret cabinet whose potential authenticity is deliberately undermined by the otiose fictionality of its romance roots. And in any case, Ferguson's advocacy of Monmouth's cause here goes beyond the claim of his legitimacy altogether: for "what is all this to the reality of the Marriage, seeing it might be transacted, as most other Marriages are, *In verbis de presenti,* and of which no other Proof can be expected besides the Testimony of such as were personally present [?]" Indeed, "'[t]is of no great concernment, who is the immediate apparent Heir in the *Regal Line,* if we do but consider that the *Parliament* of *England* hath often provided a Successor to the Government, when the Interest of the Publick hath required it, without the least regard to such Punctilio's."[79]

Ferguson's argument for "private" contract marriage over "public" licensing by church and state was made more cogently by William Lawrence, who maintained that "the Marriage now under consideration, was a Lawful, Holy, and Indissoluble Marriage by the Moral Law of God, as declared both in Nature and Scripture." For Lawrence the criterion of God's moral law was the natural fact of coitus. One of the many purposes served by Dryden's use of Old Testament typology to defend Charles in *Absalom and Achitophel* was that it allowed him to seem, at least, to address this argument by setting his story

> In pious times, e'r Priest-craft did begin,
> Before Polygamy was made a sin;
>
> .   .   .   .
>
> When Nature prompted, and no law deny'd
> Promiscuous use of Concubine and Bride; . . .[80]

To call a story "mere romance" at this time, as Ferguson does that of the black box, was to indict it of improbability at best, more likely of manifest falsehood.[81] And indeed, the story of the black box fits the familiar pattern of the family romance, in which the hero's father is discovered to be royalty. By contrast, political allegory that employed a patent romance signifier was in a sense exempt from this charge precisely because it ostentatiously embraced its fictionality. By formally assigning to the reader the responsibility for its reference to real people, the *roman à clef* was able, at least in theory, to avoid the incredulity appropriate to claims about actual particularity—an epistemological freedom analogous to its supposed impunity from prosecution for libel.[82]

As if in recognition of its liability, the incredible romance of the black box was reformulated in 1682 as a political allegory. Its author, describing it as a "Novell," prefaced the narrative with praise of "Novels, *Romances,* and *allegorical Writings.*" The story begins after the defeat of Charles I, when Conradus, King of Otenia (Charles), falls in love with Lucilious (Lucy Walter).[83] But since "it was not the custom of the Kings of *Otenia* to marry a Subject," the Prince of Pardina (James) advises his brother to marry Lucilious "with all the privacie imaginable" and with only himself and a priest as witness. Lucilious, still troubled by the inequality (and therefore convinced of the legitimacy) of such a marriage, demurs. Conradus undertakes to persuade her "with all the Rhetorick that Love and Passion could invent," and following the joint intimacies of subterfuge and candid love talk "they were privately married according to the Prince of *Purdino*'s Advice; and about Ten Months after she was brought to Bed

of a Son . . . ." When Conradus is restored to the throne and Pardina, "disavowing all Contracts of Marriage between" himself and his own wife, urges his
brother to follow suit, the king at first refuses, instead *"openly and publickly ac-
knowledg*[ing] *and own*[ing] [Lucilious] *for his Wife.*" However, Conradus is
soon persuaded to reverse himself, remarries with public ceremony, and publicly denies his former marriage. Now the duplicitous sway of the younger over
the older brother is extended from these private matters to public issues of politics and religion. Having believed in a popish plot, Conradus is now convinced
by Pardina rather of the reality of a Protestant plot. And after further adventures the narrative breaks off at the point when Conradus hears talk that "there
are some few persons yet living, who were present both at the Kings Marriage
with his Mother, and at the Birth of the Prince."[84]

Despite its slapdash composition, *The Perplex'd Prince* negotiates the several
dimensions of the porous public-private divide with considerable interest. Its
mechanism of formal domestication entails, in accord with the *roman à clef*
form, a one-to-one correspondence between public politics and romance story
(Conradus is king as Charles is king), but not the concentration of public politics into private domesticity. And yet the formal nuance of concentration is
communicated by a number of substantive factors. Most notably, the choice
between the two wives is formulated in terms of a choice between private and
public modes of marriage that correlates with other details so as to divide the
narrative into two subtly different modes of being. The privacy of the first marriage, accompanied as it is by the intimate dalliance of courtship, confirms our
impression that it is a love match occasioned by the private choice of husband
and wife. The official ceremony of the second marriage accords with its pragmatic status as a matter of policy that exceeds the now-distracted will of the
perplexed prince. In this way, the gathering momentum of marriage for love as
an emergent ideological force in the intimate sphere supports the political argument for Monmouth by challenging ideas of legitimacy based on *arcana imperii* with the putatively more evident authenticity of the heart.

This is also the authenticity of empirical fact. For given the depth of controversy at this time over what constitutes conjugal legitimacy, the marriage of
Conradus and Lucilious has a quite arguable legitimacy that is based in the
common sense of popular custom, for which its flat denial shows only an expedient and elitist contempt. The younger brother Pardina is the architect of this
policy and the fount of contempt for the people. The persistence of something
like public opinion over against this outworn version of the public interest can
be discerned in the voice of "some few persons yet living" who quietly maintain
the truth of this secret history in the face of official lies. The romance token of
the secret black box has been refashioned, in short, as the private integrity of

the people. The king himself, although the official and supreme representative of the public realm, is a basically sympathetic man manipulated by his own state apparatus. He is sincere and constant in his love for a wife who, in her deep association with the authenticity of the private realm, is also thereby associated with the "private" people, who are similarly beloved by their monarch even as they are obliged by his betrayal of them to come together (in the Habermasian phrase) as a "public" over against him. So the politics of exclusion are sustained by an ideal of negative liberty that coalesces as a reaction, in the macroworld of national politics, of civil society against the state, but that is "secretly" grounded in the microworld of affective conjugal experience. In this way *The Perplex'd Prince* can be felt to domesticate the actual particularity of its political figures not just as the concrete particularity of romance figures but also as the concentrated love plot—a "novell"—of a weak but good man forced by familial tyranny to forswear his one true love.

The formal complexity of Dryden's great poem on the Exclusion Crisis grows out of its use, not of romance as allegorical signifier, but of scripture as typological signifier. Even so, the instability of *Absalom and Achitophel* as a signifying system bears some relation to that of *romans à clef* like *The Perplex'd Prince*—even to their more ostensible efforts to adjudicate the public-private divide.[85] A year after that tract was published, a refutation of it appeared that adopted the strategy of turning Dryden's poem into a *roman à clef*. The author made sure to resurrect the self-parodic token of the black box: Achitophel "gave out that there was a Certain Instrument preserved in a Black Box, being the Contract of Marriage between *David* and *Absalom*'s Mother, and a settlement of the Crown upon the Issue he might have by that Lady." Moreover, the tract evinces a canny awareness of how the Whig politics of exclusion aimed to exploit the patriarchalist analogy between state and family. By this understanding, Achitophel would make Absalom "depend upon him and his Faction, until that having thus divided and destroyed the Royal Family, by its Domestical Divisions, he might by that means reduce the Monarchy into a Common-wealth, or Democracy."[86] As in hermeneutics, so in politics: the family is the key by which to unlock the state.

The Secret of *The Holy War*

In Christian allegory, politics, if it figures at all, is the signifying agent rather than the signified end of domestication. This is the case in John Bunyan's *The Holy War* (1682), which uses the concrete language of absolutist statecraft to domesticate the abstractions of the spirit. Bunyan's plot is that of Christian history and individual soteriology, a history that is revealed to the reader as a secret history on the level of both form and content. Mansoul, a town in the domain of Universe ruled by King Shaddai, is under siege by Diabolus. King Shaddai decides to let Mansoul fall to the invader, telling his son Emanuel that it will be his future duty to recover the lost territory. The concretion of the Trinity is completed by the Lord Chief Secretary, who, as Emanuel says, "always has been the chief dictator of all my Fathers Laws, a person altogether well skill'd in all mysteries, and knowledge of mysteries as is my Father, or as my self is. Indeed he is one with us in nature . . . ." Once King Shaddai has made his decision, he orders his keeper of secrets to draw up a "fair Record of what was determined, and to cause that it should be published in all the Corners of the Kingdom of *Universe.*" This record, "[t]he secret of Shaddai's purpose," is the holy scriptures, in effect God's reason of state. The Lord Chief Secretary also teaches the people of Mansoul how to "make and draw up Petitions to my Father"—that is, prayers.[87] When Emanuel entertains the people "with some curious riddles of secrets drawn up by his Fathers Secretary," the margin identifies these riddles also as the scriptures. But this is, of course, what Bunyan does for his readers as well in telling us one of "those *Histories* / That *Mansoul,* and her Wars *Anatomize.*"

> Nor do thou go to work without my Key,
> (In mysteries men soon do lose their way)
> And also turn it right if thou wouldst know
> My riddle, and wouldst with my heifer plow.[88]
> It lies there in the *window,* . . .[89]

Bunyan's "window" is the margin of his text, identified as such with economical reflexivity by a note in the margin adjacent to this line that reads, "The margent." A parallel reflexivity governs the relationship between the two secret histories, Bunyan's text and the scriptures onto which he, like the king's secretary, opens a window. Bunyan's syncretism reconciles the *arcana imperii* and the *arcana ecclesiae* with such credibility that it comes as something of a surprise when his modern editors offer a reading supportive of the notion that *The Holy War,* a political allegorization of spiritual life, may also be read as a political allegorization of politics—specifically, those of the Exclusion Crisis. When the tide turned against the exclusionists toward the end of 1681, royalists inaugurated a policy of replacing existing corporation charters and councillors with new ones more sympathetic to James's eventual accession. Bunyan's editors read an early episode in the narrative, when Diabolus takes possession of Mansoul and "is entertained" (the margin tells us) "for their King," as referring to this campaign.[90] Thus Bunyan briefly opens a window onto the secret, actual particularity of Diabolus, the ultimate absolutist, who can be no other than Charles himself.

If Bunyan's *The Holy War* is the most unlikely *roman à clef* of the Exclusion Crisis, Aphra Behn's *Love-Letters Between a Nobleman and his Sister* (1684, 1685, 1687) is its most remarkable one—indeed, the most important *roman à clef* of the Restoration period. The following chapter is devoted to it.

The three parts of Aphra Behn's *Love-Letters Between a Nobleman and his Sister* (1684, 1685, 1687) span—and well exceed—the period of royalist reprisal against those who had fomented the idea of the Popish Plot. And although it was preceded by John Dryden's ideologically compatible exercise in key narrative poetry, parts 1 and 2 of *Absalom and Achitophel* (1681, 1682), the volatile political atmosphere in England in the latter part of the decade still justified the circumspection of political allegory.[1] At the same time, the formal development in Behn's narrative method may reflect, among other things, changing political conditions. Although all three volumes capitalized on the secrecy of anonymous publication, the epistles dedicatory to the latter two volumes, unlike the first, are signed "A.B." The dedicatory epistle and "The Argument" preceding the first volume inform readers that the work to follow is a translation of a French narrative about (like Barclay's *Argenis*) the wars of the Huguenots. But Behn is as ready to reveal as to conceal, to accommodate as to defamiliarize. Of one of her personages she says: "I have added a word or two to his Character that might render it a little more parallel to that of a modern Prince in our Age . . . ." Two other characters she refers to as "a French Whigg" and a "true Tory." Perhaps most pointedly, Behn dismisses "publick" rumors of her dedicatee's clandestine "Amour" by comparing them to "the imposition of the late Popish Plot upon the Town," another "nonsensical History past for authentick with unthinking man . . . ."[2]

This comparison economically conjoins not only past with present, French politics with English politics, but also public politics with the publication of private amours; and in doing so it provides a "key" to the way Behn's story of illicit love, complete with romance names and rhetoric, signifies illicit politics and warfare. This signification is intimated by the information that the lovers' letters, of which much of this epistolary romance consists, "were found in their Cabinets, at their house at St. *Denice* . . . ," a doubly domestic enclosure of private *arcana amoris* that echoes that of the public *arcana imperii* whose disclosure is the common purpose of secret histories ("The Argument," 10, font reversed). But the formal domestication undertaken by *Love-Letters* goes beyond this fundamentally patriarchalist analogy (the family is like the state), since in England's dynastic monarchy the sovereignty of the state is itself a family affair; hence a contiguity of the private and the public, of love and politics, exists on both levels of the analogy. A fundamentally important consequence of this complication is the phenomenon of dialectical recapitulation, evident in the presence of both "private" and "public" elements on both the "private" (signifying) and the "public" (signified) levels of allegorical semantics. Behn's allegory thus obscures on the level of content, even as it posits on the level of form, the difference between the private and public realms. The experimental slippages between these two realms that Behn engineers throughout *Love-Letters,* although broadly and deeply motivated, owe at least some of their importance to this peculiarly (if not uniquely) English understanding of state sovereignty. More generally, her secret history offered a searching inquiry into the grounds for the relationship between state and family, political and personal life, public and private realms of experience, at a historical moment when they seemed poised between the tacit connectedness bequeathed by tradition and the explicit separation enjoined by modernity. To aid her in this project, Behn's experimental deployment of the *roman à clef* form allows her to oscillate between reference to the actual particularity of historical personages and the concrete particularity of "characters" whose broad exemplarity defines the virtual collectivity of a public readership.

Love versus War?

Behn's story concerns the "private," scandalous love affair of Forde, Lord Grey of Wark (Philander), and his sister-in-law Lady Henrietta Berkeley (Silvia). But Lady Henrietta's sister and Lord Grey's wife, Lady Mary Berkeley (Mertilla), had already succumbed to the seductive charms of the Duke of Monmouth (Cesario), the illegitimate son of Charles II.[3] More important, Lord Grey was deeply involved in state affairs, most notably as a loyal supporter of Monmouth throughout this entire period. In 1680, with the Popish Plot raging, Monmouth was the overwhelmingly popular Whig choice to replace the cryptopapist Duke of York in the royal succession. In 1683 the royalist reaction generated several executions growing out of the Rye House Plot, a "Protestant Plot" no less dubious than the Popish. And in 1685 Monmouth himself was executed for leading a failed military rebellion against the new king James II; Lord Grey, still a prominent supporter, managed to obtain the king's pardon.[4] Monmouth, a great public figure, was prohibited from becoming the greatest by the "private," familial fact of his bastardy, which, although hotly disputed,[5] gave the king's younger brother precedence over the king's eldest son in the royal succession. The Exclusion Crisis was therefore a political and public event of the highest consequence that turned on the most intimate secrets of sexual and conjugal behavior.

By the same token, Behn's *Love-Letters* is a secret history of this crisis that takes the form of a private romance whose political overtones are not nearly secret enough to escape our notice. Indeed, Behn may teach us to discern a public purpose in her very disavowals of it. When she denies in "The Argument" of part 1 that hers is a "mixed" form—"'tis not my business here to mix the rough relation of a War with the soft affairs of Love"—we have scant basis for questioning her claim (10; see also 426).[6] But if, as I propose, one central ambition of *Love-Letters* is to inquire into the fluid relationship between the public and the private at the moment of its fundamental transformation, we may need to take Behn's denial of formal mixture with a grain of salt. An inquiry such as this, moreover, is likely to encounter the fluidity of gender difference as well: are the capacities of women suited to the treatment of love but not of war?

The inquiry is most immediately available to us in the way Philander's seduction of his sister-in-law Silvia leads both of them to ponder the relationship between the familial authority of the father and the political authority of the king. Saturated as it is with political implication, Philander's amatory discourse assumes an analogy between the tyrannical absolutism of private and public institutions, between marriage and the state. By this way of thinking, matrimonial law has no more lasting hold over us than do the slavish oaths of allegiance made by our ancestors. Adultery, even affinal incest, are inviolable liberties of the subject. "No tyes of blood forbid my Passion," writes Philander in his first letter to Silvia; "and what's a Ceremony impos'd on man by custome? what is it to my divine *Silvia,* that the Priest took my hand and gave it to your Sister? What Alliance can that create? why shou'd a trick devis'd by the wary old, only to make provision for posterity, tye me to an eternal slavery[?]" (11–12).

Impatiently awaiting Silvia in a rustic retreat, Philander remarks, "[H]ere's no troublesome Honour, amongst the pretty inhabitants of the Woods and Streams, fondly to give Laws to nature, but uncontroul'd they play and sing, and Love; no Parents checking their dear delights, no slavish Matrimonial tyes to restrain their Nobler flame" (35). Even this early in the narrative, Philander's Whiggish and libertine antinomianism may remind us of the treacherous pas-

toralism of Behn's poem "The Golden Age" (1684). The speaker of that poem—
to all appearances a disinterestedly philosophical and sympathetic panegyric to
our prelapsarian liberty from the customary tyrannies of the sexual honor
code—in its very last lines is gendered as a self-interested male seducer whose
carpe diem to his coy mistress "*Sylvia*" suggests that his high-mindedness may
be only one more patriarchal ploy for exploiting women. If sexual politics mirror state politics, Philander's Silvia (or at least her "Tory feminist" author)
might well suspect that a candid system of gender inequality mitigated by the
female entitlement to paternalist protection is far preferable to a careless and irresponsible utopianism that promises all but provides for nothing.7

And the analogy between libertine love and libertine politics, once made explicit, is questioned by Silvia on both principled and prudential grounds. True,
the politics are themselves familial: Philander supports the ambition of Cesario-
Monmouth to exclude and replace his uncle against the authority of his father,
the king. But Silvia stoutly denies that their royal father has "play'd the Tyrant,"
and she demands of Philander, "[W]ou'd you . . . establish a King without Law,
without right, without consent, without Title . . . ?" Moreover, the lessons of
his public ambition have chilling implications for Philander's private desires:
"[I]f *Silvia* cou'd command, *Philander* shou'd be Loyal as he's Noble; and what
generous Maid wou'd not suspect his Vows to a Mistress who breaks 'em with
his Prince and Master . . . [?]" (40, 42, 23). In this single respect the analogy
holds for Silvia, although not as Philander would have it. Dreading the implications of the metaphorical relationship between Philander's private love and
his public politics, Silvia, transforming metaphor into metonymy, refigures that
relationship as a competition within the realm of the private, between two
"mistresses":8 "[D]oes not *Silvia* ly neglected and unregarded in your thoughts?
hudled up confusedly with your graver business of State, and almost lost in the
ambitious crowd? Say, say my lovely Charmer, is she not, does not this fatal Interest you espouse, Rival your *Silvia,* is she not too often remov'd thence to let
in that haughty Tyrant Mistress? . . . [F]or two such mighty contradictions and
enemies as Love and ambition, or revenge can never sure abide in one Soul together . . ." (38-39). But Philander is hypocritical enough to renounce his political principles if they seem, as now, to interfere with his amatory ambition; and
in response to Silvia's critique of his public support for Cesario he disingenu-
ously repudiates its private and familial implications as well: "[I]t really shocks
ones nature to find a Son engag'd against a Father . . ." (46).

Philander also patronizes the incongruity of Silvia's political sophistication,
finding its source in his own love for her, which levels political as amatory "secrets": "How comes my charming *Silvia* so skill'd in the Mysteries of State?
where learnt her tender heart the Notions of rigid business? where her soft

Tongue, form'd only for the dear Language of Love, to talk of the concerns of Nations and Kingdoms? 'tis true, when I gave my Soul away to my dear Councellor, I reserv'd nothing to my self, not even that secret that so concern'd my Life . . . . 'tis not enough that we tell those we Love all they love to hear, but one ought to tell 'em too, every secret that we know . . . ." Indeed, capitalizing on Silvia's metonymy of the "rivals" love and politics, Philander refutes the implication of the metaphor (political forewarns of amatory betrayal) by willingly subjugating politics to love: "I design no more by this great enterprize, then to make thee some glorious thing, elevated above what we have seen yet on Earth . . . . Love gave me Ambition . . ." (43–47).

In this most consummately artful of his letters, Philander exemplifies in his own rhetoric the "language of love" he has just ascribed to women. One of Philander's preferred love languages is, of course, Petrarchan metaphor, by which private love is figured (as here) as the public "command and Dominion" of women over men, who are but "slaves and Vassals to the Almighty Sex" (44). Soon after he disarms his literal "Rival" Foscario in a duel over Silvia—a little war for love—Philander evinces the opportunism of his language use by disarming his rival of his Petrarchisms: "[B]y the style he writes, I dread his Sense less than his Person . . ." (87). Later on Silvia confirms this opportunism:

> Yes, *Philander,* I have received your Letter, and but I found my name there, shou'd have hop'd it was not meant for *Silvia:* Oh! 'tis all cold—Short—Short and cold as a dead Winters day. . . . What is become of all the tender things, which, as I us'd to read, made little nimble pantings in my heart, my blushes rise, and tremblings in my bloud, adding new fire to the poor burning Victim! Oh where are all thy pretty flatteries of Love, that made me fond, and vain, and set a value on this trifling Beauty? Hast thou forgot thy wondrous Art of loving? Thy pretty cunings, and thy soft deceivings? Hast thou forgot 'em all? Or hast forgot indeed to love at all? (144)

Lest we experience Silvia's own language as naive "female" transparency, however, she here turns Petrarchan masochism ("poor burning Victim") to self-description, just as elsewhere she practices the surgical brutality of the "male" *blazon* (see 26, 29–30, 89). And after all, it is Silvia who first names the technique: "The Rhetorick of Love is half-breath'd, interrupted words, languishing Eyes, flattering Speeches, broken Sighs, pressing the hand, and falling Tears: Ah how do they not perswade; how do they not charm and conquer; 'twas thus with these soft easie Arts, that *Silvia* first was won!" (33).

The subtlety with which Behn manages the formal structure of her secret history enables us to see that the question "What's the relation between war/politics and love?" can be translated into the question "How are Silvia and Philander's politics related to their ethics—and (discontinuously but insistently) to their gender?" Behn ensures that the first question remains unanswerable in its own terms. The public resonance of cabinets, keys, and spies echoes throughout the minutely articulated private spaces of her narrative. In a pair of writing tablets Philander reminds Silvia that she has "the other Key of these Tablets, if not they are easily broke open . . ." (48). Silvia's maid Melinda fears that her mother the Countess "will possibly set Spies in every corner . . . ," and Silvia, anticipating a secret rendezvous, writes Philander: "'Tis almost dark, and my Mother is retir'd to her Chamber, my Father to his Cabinet, and has left all that Apartment next the Garden wholly without Spies. I have by trusty *Silvia* sent you a Key *Melinda* got made to the Door, which leads from the Garden to the back-Stairs to my Apartment, so carefully lock'd, and the original Key so closely guarded by my jealous Father . . ." (53, 55). As if to prove the substance of this warning, soon the Count somberly delivers to Silvia's "Cabinet" a letter from Philander editorially superscribed "*To* Silvia. *That which was left in her hands by* Monsieur, *her Father, in her Cabinet*" (90).

In different ways, both lovers are haunted by the incongruous but confusing proximity their affair has engendered. What is the household, what is the state? Which is personal, which political? "[B]etray'd" by "houshould spies," Silvia complains that she is now "arraign'd and convicted, three Judges . . . sate in condemnation on me, a Father, a Mother, and a Sister . . . ." Her household has become the very seat of the law, and Silvia vows to "turn . . . from these domestick, melancholy objects, and look abroad . . ." (90–93). Philander, en route from Silvia's amatory arms to Cesario's rebellious cabal, fears he will confuse these two secret histories, so that "when he comes into the grave Cabal he must betray the story of his heart, and in lieu of the mighty business there in hand be raving still on *Silvia,* telling his joy to all the amazed listeners, and answering questions that concern our great affair, with something of my love . . ." (71). Which is the "great affair" and which the trivial, which the "mighty business" and which the inconsiderable? The confusion is reinforced by public judicial action. Soon after this letter, Philander writes "*From the* Bastill" (i.e., the Tower of London) that he has been "arrested at the suit of *Monsieur* the Count, your Father, for a Rape on my lovely Maid . . ." (106–7). Yet no sooner is he cleared of the father's rape charge than he is "stopt and seiz'd for high Treason, by the King's messengers, . . ." and again "found guilty enough to be committed to the *Bastile*" in connection with the Rye House Plot (114–15). Family and state, materializing into separability, for that very reason become subject to relentless conflations that border on radical parody or mock heroics, in which the identity of the "great" and the "trivial" is up for grabs.

One of Silvia's arguments against her lover's participation in the rebel cabal is that Cesario, no friend to Philander, is known to have seduced Mertilla, Silvia's sister and Philander's wife: why help crown the head of someone who has crowned you with the cuckold's horns? (43). But Philander feels only gratitude and empathy for "my disorder'd Rival": as he puts it with studied ambiguity, "I lov'd him for't, pleas'd at the resemblance of our Souls, for we were secret Lovers both . . ." (17). Cesario repays Philander the compliment: "I'll allow you, my Dear, to be very fond of so much Beauty as the world must own adorns the Lovely *Silvia;* I'll permit Love too to Rival me in your heart, but not out-rival Glory; hast then my Dear to the advance of that, make no delay, but with the Mornings dawne, let me find you in my Arms . . ." (63). Cesario's homosocial aubade ties war to love, partaking equally of martial intimacy (from arms to arms) and of the male bond forged by loving the same woman.⁹ As love and war abet each other, so the homoerotics of gendered speech inform the homosociality of the martial cabal.

Philander's response to his two arrests, for private and public crimes, is double. To foil the charge of rape he enjoins his man Brilljard (William Turner) to marry Silvia and testify to this in court; to foil the charge of high treason he disguises Silvia in "your Boys cloaths" and escapes with her and Brilljard to Holland (113, 115). So ends part 1 of *Love-Letters,* with Silvia doubly disguised: privately, in the coverture of a clandestine marriage later acknowledged a "*mock-Marriage*"; publicly, in the covering of "a youth of quality . . ." (123, 277). Only the secrecy of the private disguise limits its constraints on her liberty; but the public disguise makes her "pleas'd with the Cavalier in her self" and "gave her a thousand little Priviledges, which otherwise wou'd have been deny'd to Women" (126).

The three travelers quickly meet the well-placed young Dutch nobleman Octavio. "[A]t first sight he inclin'd *Phillanders* heart to a friendship with him, and on the other side the lovely person of *Phillander,* the quality that appear'd in his face and mein oblig'd *Octavio* to become no less his admirer" (122–23). The attraction is not very different from that between Octavio and Silvia. Briefly renamed Fillmond, Silvia, who "captivated the Men no less than the Women . . . ," made of Octavio "as absolute a Conquest as 'twas possible for her suppos'd Sex to do over a man, who was a great admirer of the other . . . ." Silvia both conceals and reveals the "secret" of her sex: Octavio "had a secret hope she was not what she seem'd, but of that Sex whereof she discovered so many softnesses and beauties . . . ." That is, he hopes she is a woman; but her female sex is less important to him than her feminine gender—and her status ("quality," like Philander) (123, 127). Well aware of the "thousand little privileges denied to women," Behn associates these privileges, not with unalterable sexual, but with manipulable gender, difference, whose masquerade permits Silvia not just to play the cavalier but to discover "the cavalier in her self." At the same time, *Love-Letters*—like all of Behn's writings—is subliminally aware of, and inquisitive about, her culture's emergent temptation to think of sex as an essential and definitive condition of existence, separable from the social embeddedness of gender, as the family now begins to seem from the state.

Thus Behn has her characters behave as though they were personages in a *roman à clef,* adopting disguises and "feign'd names" in this foreign country and having adventures "worthy . . . to be related intirely by themselves in a Novel" (123, 127). A temporary illness forces Silvia to abandon her male disguise, and Philander tells Octavio both his secret histories: "all the story of his Love with the charming *Silvia;* and with it all the story of his Fate . . . ." Octavio replies that "his affairs were already but too well known . . . ," by which he means the second of Philander's secret histories, his state affairs: the United Provinces have ordered his deportation as a "declar'd Enemy to the French [i.e., English] King . . ." (128). Philander proposes to sway the Dutch with the secret history of his love affair, but Octavio assures him that it will be of "little force with these arbitrary Tyrants of State . . . ," and Philander reluctantly departs, leaving Silvia with Octavio and Brilljard (133).

Love versus Friendship

The movement of action at the end of part 1 from "France" to Holland, from domestic to foreign territory, involves (with incidental paradox) an increased emphasis on private over public "affairs." This is also the moment at which Octavio enters the story, the only central character in *Love-Letters* whose historical reference—whose actual particularity—cannot be positively assigned.[10] It is as though Behn, having established the signifying relationship between her private and her public plots in part 1, now temporarily consigns the latter to the shadows of her narrative in order to pursue the way the romance plot engenders politics in other terms. Schematically speaking, Cesario's homosocial relation with Philander is now replaced by Octavio's, implicitly extending the public implications of male friendship without explicitly insisting on them.[11] As the love affair of Silvia and Philander is triangulated through Octavio, so the friendship of Octavio and Philander is triangulated through Silvia—and around the control of epistolary information. Two weeks after his departure from Holland, Philander renews his correspondence with Silvia and Octavio, adopting the expedient of enclosing letters to her within those addressed to him. These two agree that the cool tone of Philander's first letters bespeaks some "mystery" in his motives, and Silvia, uneasy, recalls to her beloved the loss of "my Virgin innocence" as though it were a deep mystery of state: "I sate inthron'd in awful vertue, crown'd with shining honour, and adorn'd with unsullied reputation, till thou, O Tyrant *Love*! with a charming usurpation, invaded all my glories . . ." (140, 147, 145–46).

For different reasons they also agree that Philander must now be told of Octavio's love for Silvia. Octavio makes a "frank Confession," posing the difficult case of a conflict between his "*Constant*" and "Eternal" friendship for Philander and his love for Silvia, which (some would say) must "reign . . . absolutely" in the heart. Octavio insists to Silvia that his two passions can coexist peacefully there, but privately he wonders whether the absolute tyrant may be not (heterosexual) love but (homosocial) friendship—if "he shou'd not chuse to dye and quit *Silvia* rather then be false to friendship . . ." (167, 168, 169). As though reading his mind, Silvia derides the casuistry of making a "*publique confession*" of love to one's rival, which she rather takes to be "a piece of Gallantry and diversion to *Philander* . . ." (168, font reversed). Octavio evades her efforts to confirm her suspicion that Philander has betrayed her with another woman, and Silvia tells him that "you have given a much greater testimony of your friendship for *Philander,* than your passion for *Silvia* . . . . I find Honour in you men, is only what you please to make it . . ." (194). And in part 3, after much more water has passed beneath the bridge, Octavio tersely corroborates her skepticism to Philander: "[A] Friend's above a Sister, or a Mistress" (377).

How is the rivalry between male homosocial friendship and heterosexual love related to Behn's central preoccupation with the relationship between the public and the private? The structural complexity of *Love-Letters* ensures that our answer to this question will depend on which level of that relationship we are addressing. Within the private realm of the family, Silvia's faith in Philander has been motivated by her conviction that he opposes the parental tyranny of arranged marriages in favor of the freedom of lovers. But the gender-neutral competition between the interest of parents and the love of their children is insidiously underwritten, Silvia finds, by the stealthy and gendered competition between men's friendship with each other and men's love of women. The apparently libertine opposition to parental authority is ultimately grounded in a deeper commitment to male solidarity, and the antinomian love of women is found in the end to be a subset of the aristocratic exchange of women. So when Silvia's family closes ranks against her love affair, Philander quickly arranges her marriage to his servant Brilljard "so that no Authority of a Father," as Silvia later explains it, "could take me from the Husband" (276). Can one oppose the authority of the father by imitating it; or is this an instance of the supposed libertine reverting to patriarchal type?

Or again, when Octavio confesses his love for Silvia to his friend, Philander's love for her has already cooled, and he cheerfully gives Octavio "my leave to Love the Charming *Silvia,*" thereby passing on the former lover to the friend

(170). Indeed, in what he calls a "pay-back" for this secret about Octavio's new love affair, Philander exchanges the secret of *his* new love affair; and Octavio is astonished to learn that it involves none other than his own sister Calista, who had been "bred in a Nunnery . . . [and] married to an Old ill favour'd jealous Husband, no Parents but himself to right her wrongs . . ." (177–78). So Octavio too has carelessly played the role of the patriarch by abetting his sister's forced marriage. Moreover, now he decides to redouble that perfidy through an act of homosocial friendship that parallels but supersedes the recent exchange of secrets—namely, an adulterous exchange of sisters. For rather than frustrating Philander's fulfillment with Calista, Octavio conceals his sibling relation to her so as to justify (at least by his tortured logic) his own fulfillment with Silvia. Addressing Calista in his thoughts, Octavio exclaims: "[S]ince thy Brother cannot be happy: but by the Sisters being undone, . . . yield to *Philander* and make me blest in *Silvia!*" (178). So far from protecting Calista from a brutal husband, Octavio later apologizes to that husband for "letting the Revenge of *Calista's* Honour alone so long," by which he means the very cuckolding in which he now colludes (350, font reversed).

Behn's achievement here goes beyond the exposure of heterosexual marriage customs as systematically concealing their real motive force, namely, aristocratic "friendship" and the homosocial exchange of women, property, and political interest. For her target is not so much aristocratic matrimonial ideology as the hypocrisy of the libertine who purports to combat tyranny with the freedom of love so as to better serve his own ends. Within the private realm of the family the lesson is powerful enough: the freethinker who promises liberation from traditional matrimonial constraints is likely to prove the most opportunistic of patriarchs when the chips are down. But the lesson also applies in the public realm of state politics: libertine rebels against the absolute authority of the king are the least likely to honor the liberties of others than themselves. As Silvia later writes, "What cou'd I expect . . . [from] thou that betray'd thy Prince, abandon'd thy Wife, . . . ravisht thy Sister, and art in open Rebellion against thy Native country . . . [?]" (218). In both the private and the public realm the lesson is most pertinent to the status of women, who have most to gain but also most to lose in these egalitarian projects of reform. "Tory feminism" is the name we have given to the seemingly paradoxical phenomenon whereby the first English feminists tend also to be royalists.[12] The paradox is perhaps mitigated by Behn's perspective on what protoliberalism looked like to many of her contemporaries: an unprincipled and irresponsible utopianism that would supplant a system of gender inequality whose very candor carries with it the assumption that women are entitled, if not to equality, then at least to the paternalistic protection of men.

How can we generalize thus far about the kind of relationship Behn's deployment of the *roman à clef* would posit between the private and the pubic levels of her political allegory? The complex pattern of amatory "affairs" Behn has established does not so much signify as allude to the actual particularity of elevated personages currently involved in public "affairs," building a structure of concrete examples whose several facets reflect alternative models from which precepts may be abstracted that are central to both private and public affairs. Crucial to Behn's hermeneutics is not the direct "political" correlation of character and personage (e.g., Philander and Lord Grey), which is soon known and accepted, but the construction of a broad "ethical" grid of private possibility— or probability—for reading "public" events. Under what circumstances (if any) is breaking a vow of amatory constancy (or an oath of political allegiance) not a betrayal but a legitimate choice? How can we adjudicate the contest between exchange as marriage (or succession) and exchange as adultery and divorce (or exclusion and substitution)? How is the exchange of brothers (like York and Monmouth) like the exchange of sisters (like Silvia and Calista)? Is tyranny (whether forced marriage or absolute monarchy) mitigated, or sophisticated, by libertinism (whether sexual or political)?

The figures by which this amatory case of conscience is represented give it a deep coloration of absolutist politics without cracking the private code in any definitive way. Philander ends his letter to Octavio confessing his new love with a postscript noting his enclosure of a letter to Silvia, which "I need not oblige you to deliver: You see I give you opportunity" (177). In addressing Octavio Philander addresses Silvia's most intimate concerns, while in writing to Silvia he really writes to Octavio. Homosocial friendship has not so much defeated heterosexual love as enclosed it within its own, more ample purview. This exchange of secrets initiates a complex interaction carried out through the exchange (and withholding) of letters and women. Philander, by allowing Octavio to conceal or reveal both his secret and his letters to Silvia, invites him to engage in the ambivalent censorship that does both by turns. Torn between friendship and love, Octavio, resolving "now rather to die than to confess *Philanders* Secret . . . ," at another moment is "ready to unravel all the Secrets of *Philanders* letter . . ." (179, 196). Silvia, obsessed with Philander's "secret" (187, 198, 201, 205), both knows and evades her knowledge of it, taking Octavio's casuistical evasions as evidence that he is less the lover of Silvia than the friend of Philander. As if acknowledging the power of friendship, she tells Philander to "preserve him next your Soul, for he's a Jewel, fit for such a Cabinet . . ." (192). Octavio, "absolutely" "subdued" and "conquered" by Silvia (197, 202, 203), in fact possesses the key to absolute power over her, the knowledge of Philander's *arcana amoris.*

Fathers versus Children

When Philander is deported by the Dutch authorities as an enemy of their allies, he leaves behind the unstable triangle of Silvia, Brilljard, and Octavio. The
triangle soon begins to dissolve. Brilljard, inflamed both by Silvia's beauty and
by the promise of their matrimonial tie, becomes jealous of her favors to Octavio and "seeks presidents of usurp'd dominion, and thinks she is his Wife, and
has forgot that he's her creature, and *Phillanders* Vassal" (125–26). That is, Brilljard's belief in his private superordination over Silvia is contradicted by his public subordination to her. In the allegorical dimension of publicity, however,
Brilljard, the reader may reflect, has precedents for dominion over Silvia in
York's (another younger son) or Monmouth's (another adulterer) aspirations to
rule England.[13] And when he learns that Octavio and Silvia are about to be
joined in clandestine marriage, Brilljard tells the Dutch that Octavio, like Philander, aims to "betray the State" (262). The lie works: Silvia, dressed "in mans
Cloaths, that she might not be known," is taken for Octavio's accomplice and
seized along with him (263).

There now ensues a bewildering flurry of public-private reversals. The
Dutch quickly discover that they have mistaken a woman for a man and a private for a public scandal—"that this Caballing with the *French* [i.e., English]
Spies, was only an innocent Design to give himself [i.e., Octavio] away to a fine
young Lady . . ." (266). Brilljard, his back to the wall, ingeniously shifts his
ground: the private *is* a public scandal, he maintains, a treason not against the
state but against exemplary "public" ethics itself. "[Y]ou had a Plot to betray the
State," he tells Octavio, because "if all the Youth should follow your Example,
you would betray Posterity it self; and only mad Confusion would abound: in
short, my Lord, that Lady who was taken with you by the Messenger, was my
Wife . . ." (268–69). At first the notion that private bigamy is public treason
meets only with derision. Sebastian, Octavio's uncle and a powerful senator in
the States General, replies to Brilljard, "Why, what Sir, then it seems all this
Noise of Betraying the State was but a Cuckold's Dream. Hah! and this wonderful and dangerous Plot, was but one upon your Wife Sir . . ." (269).[14]

But soon enough his nephew's infatuation with Silvia and the charges of "Effeminacy" it inspires persuade Sebastian to reconsider the public significance of
the charge (280). For one thing, the uncle has learned that Silvia "was not only
a Wife, but a scandalous Mistress too . . . ." For another, Octavio, like Sebastian, is also a senator, and in "neglecting to give his Attendance on the Publick . . . he is become a Scandal to the Common-Wealth . . ." (281). "Why, this
is flat Adultery," says Sebastian; "a little Fornication in a civil way, might have
been allow'd . . . . A little Pleasure—a little Recreation, I can allow: A Layer of

Love, and a Layer of Business—but to neglect the Nation for a Wench, is flat Treason against the State . . ." (281). Now the enraged Octavio, like Philander before him, radically revalues things. Compared with his elevated and *"Nobler Love,"* state politics are no more than a *"sordid Business"* taken up with "useless Trifles" (281, 282). Adamant, the patriarchal uncle insists that he will cut Octavio out of his inheritance unless he abandons Silvia and agrees to an arranged marriage (284). Sebastian's tyranny *in loco parentis*[15] is buttressed by a profound misogyny: he "bore an unaccountable Hate to the whole Sex, and therefore was pityless to all [Octavio] could say on the Score of Love . . . . He said, if he were to make Laws, he would confine all young Women to Monasteries, where they should never see Man till Forty, and then come out and marry for Generation sake, no more . . ." (283, 285).

Sebastian's is a strictly "public" approach to marriage, its purpose being the perpetuation of the male lineage. Once he sees Silvia, however, "his old Heart burnt in the Socket": from being a patriarchal father Sebastian becomes (with an ease and logic Behn has taught us to understand) a libertine lover like Octavio, his public-private value system turned on its head. Ordering that Silvia be moved "to his own House," Sebastian laments to his nephew that "If I go to the State House I mind nothing there, my Heart's at home with the Young Gentlewoman . . ." (287, 290). Overtones of patriarchal exchange between uncle and nephew thus complicate their rivalry as libertine lovers. In the event, however, Sebastian surprises the young lovers in Silvia's chamber and in the confusion is accidentally shot to death.

No sooner has this disaster occurred to Octavio and Philander's sister Silvia than they hear of a parallel disaster involving Philander and Octavio's sister Calista. Realizing that the patriarchal cuckold Clarinau is in pursuit, Philander prepares for flight by dressing Calista up in "a Suit of Mans Cloths," including "one of my Pistols . . ." (308–9). But Clarinau encounters them before they make good their escape, and taking his cross-dressed wife for her presumed lover, he attacks her. Wounded, Calista wounds her husband in turn, then flees to a nunnery in Brussels to recover. Clarinau, seeking what Behn calls "the Revenge of a Man of Honour"—not a duel, that is, but "the private Stab, for private Injuries"—follows his wife to Brussels (348). There he spies Philander leaving Silvia's lodgings, waits until evening, then returns for vengeance. But as it happens, Clarinau mistakes Octavio for Philander, wounds him, and is himself wounded once more, now by Octavio, who helps Clarinau to his lodgings only to return the next morning to find Philander asleep in the arms of the faithless Silvia. Octavio challenges his friend to a duel in which both are wounded. But even after the duel Philander is still so enraged at Octavio for "betraying" his "Friendship" that Silvia fears "he look'd on himself as a Person injured by close private ways, and would take . . . Revenge, and have hurt [Octavio] when he . . . little dream'd of it . . ." (356, 362). Silvia's fears recall the "private stab" that Clarinau has already unsuccessfully attempted. Put to the test, in other words, the libertine's code of friendship dovetails with the patriarch's code of honor. When the work of the homosocial bond is not to render women serviceable, it is to wreak cowardly vengeance on male rivals.

Effeminacy and the Public Wife

These are some of the principal private intrigues through which Behn entangles the categories of the public and the private even as she employs them. What about the public realm of Exclusion politics? Sandwiched between the stories of the two tyrannical fathers, Sebastian and Clarinau, Tomaso (Shaftesbury / Sir Thomas Armstrong) narrates to Philander news of the rebel Cesario in the aftermath of the Rye House Plot. And as we might expect by now, it does not take long for the story of state politics to become entangled, with unexceptionable logic, in a story of familial and amatory politics. For Cesario, in hiding from the king's forces, "happen'd in this his Retreat to fall most desperately in Love" (320). While yet in his minority, Cesario had been joined to his wife through a "forced Marriage," the conjugal equivalent of civil despotism "wherein he was not capacitated to chose Good or Evil . . . ." Now he has fallen in love with Hermione (Lady Henrietta Wentworth), whom he assures is "both his Mistress and his Wife . . ." (324, 399). Cesario's claim regarding his private status cannot be supported by law, even in futurity, for "'twas impossible to find any Cause of a Separation between" him and his wife, the Princess. That is, not only divorce but even a private separation agreement is out of the question. What Cesario means by this is that because his marriage to the Princess was motivated not by (private) love but by (public) interest, it has no moral legitimacy. Satisfied for the moment with his "thousand solemn Vows," Hermione later prevails on Cesario's accomplice, Fergusano (Robert Ferguson), to help "bring him absolutely under her power" through a mock marriage ceremony— "tho they do not make publick Declaration of this . . ." (323, 411, 412).

Ferguson "the Plotter" was an important player in Exclusion politics, a former Presbyterian preacher who helped foment radical Whig causes from the Popish Plot to Monmouth's Rebellion. In figure 11.1, Ferguson, assigned the "Knave" card, preaches to Monmouth's rebels before battle. The "Queen" cards juxtapose the love of the people with martial disaster as the tribute of local schoolgirls is flanked by military rout. In Behn's narrative, Ferguson becomes the ill-concealed Fergusano, the "*High-land Wizard*," master of "the black Art." Astrologically convinced that Cesario was "born to be a King," he leagues with

Hermione to conjure up a dumb show for Cesario, who thinks he sees "his proper Figure in a Glass" torn between embracing the martial arts of kingship and, "disarm[ed] . . . of those Ornaments of War," subsiding "with all Effeminacy" into "the soft Arms of Love" (402, 399, 398, 405, 406, 407). Enthralled by love, the effeminated Cesario reminds us of comparable cases, like Basilio and Cleophila or Charles I and Henrietta Maria. Indeed, the trope of the masculine woman as the power behind the effeminate public man seems like a courtly version of the skimmington ride.[16] Moreover, Cesario's ambivalence regarding the apparently absolute choice between love and war, private and public, evokes Behn's insistence that she herself treats of love, not war, recalling both Philander on the supposed limits of female expertise and the conventional rhetorical posture of the political allegorist. So Fergusano's magic glass is a rival of Behn's own glass of state, this very narrative. Of course, Ferguson earned his role in *Love-Letters* as mystifier of past and future at least in part through having asserted that Monmouth was "born to be a king" by virtue of the legal and moral legitimacy of Charles's marriage to Monmouth's mother, Lucy Walter.[17]

So if politics quickly leads to love, love as quickly shows its political coloring. Cesario himself sees that the question of his private status is connected to that of his public status by ties that are both metaphorical and metonymic. To Hermione he renounces his wife the Princess as he does "all Pretenders to him except herself . . . . [I]f ever Fortune favoured him with a Crown, he would fix it on her Head, and make her in spight of all former Ties and Obligations Queen of *France* [i.e., England]" (324, 323, 399). The family is like the state: Cesario declares Hermione a legitimate pretender to marriage, as he himself is to monarchy; the spirit, if not the letter, of the law—love if not interest—proclaims Monmouth England's true "husband."

And when Cesario's conviction flags, Fergusano is prepared to play the same role in public affairs as he has in private. He insists on the need for a "Declaration"—perforce public, unlike the "declaration" of marriage—"to draw out a Scene of fair Pretences for *Cesario* to the Crown of *France,* and the lawfulness of his Claim: for let the Conquest be never so sure, the People require it, and the Conqueror is oblig'd to give some better reason, than that of the strength of his Sword, for his Dominion over them" (409, font reversed). The appearance of legality, as important in monarchy as in marriage, binds the two institutions together. But the crucial criterion in both is not the external and public authority of the law but the internal and "private" sanction supplied by love—Cesario's love for Hermione, "the people's" love for Cesario. This is Behn's parodic version of contract theory: as Cesario has "contracted" (323) with Hermione, so the mutual affection of prince and people provides the basis for Cesario's claim to sovereignty. It is in this spirit that Fergusano exclaims to Cesario "how much

FIG. 11.1. Playing cards illustrating Monmouth's Rebellion, 1685, in *Poems on Affairs of State: Augustan Satirical Verse, 1660–1714*, vol. 4, *1685–1688*, ed. Galbraith M. Crump (New Haven, CT: Yale University Press, 1968). Princeton University Library.

a greater interest he had in the Hearts of the People, than their proper Monarch" (408); Cesario is to Charles II as Hermione is to the Princess. Reversing Brilljard's charge against Silvia and Octavio, private bigamy, if sanctified by love, provides a legitimating model for the public alteration of the royal lineage. Its analogy to bigamy, that is, provides one key to adjudicating the legitimacy of rebellion against the king.[18]

Our confidence in Behn's royalism may dull us to the intricacy and precision with which the public case against Monmouth's qualifications is made through the private. At the same time, we must recognize that Behn's version of the *roman à clef,* although clearly grounded in reference to actual particularity, just as clearly does not turn on a one-to-one coding. The point of the sequence I have just reviewed has only begun to be made when we see that the character Cesario stands for the actual Monmouth—since he also stands for Lady Henrietta, Robert Ferguson, Charles II, and the English people, in that he partakes piecemeal of these disparate characters in the set of shifting foil relationships by which his own ethical status comes to be defined. Behn does not simply condemn Cesario and thereby indirectly condemn Monmouth. She depicts the Exclusion Crisis as a case of conscience in which abstract issues of state are concretized as private character types (the lover, the beloved, the pretender, the ruler, the effeminate, the ambitious, the moralist, the legalist, the libertine, the bigamist, the politician, the magician) whose multiple overlappings constitute the complex status of a man like the king's bastard.

This is the fruit of Behn's analogical entanglement of love and politics. At the same time, however, she works on the level of metonymy, where she deftly achieves a comparable entanglement. On the one hand, the relationship of love and politics is ominously disjunctive: Cesario would be content to sacrifice all for love—"to live and die in the Glory of being hers alone, without wishing for Liberty or Empire . . . ." Tomaso fears that Cesario has been "perfectly effeminated into soft Woman" by his devotion to Hermione, and warns him "not to suffer his Passion to surmount his Ambition . . ." (324, 325). On the other hand (and equally ominously), love and politics are closely conjoined thanks to Hermione's peculiar powers. She not only believes that Cesario is the "finest Man in the World" but also relishes the idea that he will "prove the greatest . . . ." For his part, Cesario loves Hermione for her "*Masculine*" grace: "*Hermione* was a Friend as well as a Mistress, and one with whom . . . he could Discourse with of useful things of State, as well as Love; and improve in both the Noble Mysteries, by her Charming Conversation." The *arcana imperii* and *amoris,* however clearly gendered they may be, are not so clearly sexed. Hence later on, as Monmouth's rebels plan their invasion of England from Brussels, "all the world made their Court to *Hermione* . . . . [I]f any Body had any Petitions, or Addresses to make to the Prince, 'twas by her sole Interest; she sate in their closest Councils, and heard their gravest debates; and she was the Oracle of the Board . . ." (322, 325, 335, 396–97). The point here is not "sexual transgression" but political irresponsibility manifested in the inversion of gender roles. Monmouth recalls the royal effeminacy of both Charles I and, through the figure of Sidney's Basilius, Elizabeth I.[19]

Not content to complicate the dichotomy between public politics and private love, however, Behn analyzes one product of this complication—what might be called the type of the public wife—wherein she finds in turn a private and a public exemplar. Under cover of night Cesario has been paying prudent visits to "Madam his Wife, who was very well at Court, maugre her Husbands ill Conduct . . . ." On one such evening they are surprised by the king, who also "often made her Visits"; and Cesario, a state traitor playing a domestic traitor, "had no time to retire but into Madam the Princess's *Cabaret* . . . ." The lawful husband who is also an illicit rival hides in his wife's inner chamber; the illicit intruder who is also the lawful monarch "asked her who she had conceal'd in her Closet," then "urged her to give him the Key of her *Cabaret* . . . ." Like other domestic interiors Behn has set before us, this one promises both revelation and concealment. The Princess pleads Cesario's case so well "that at last she had the Joy to perceive the happy Effects of her Wit and Goodness, which had mov'd Tears of Pity and Compassion from his Majesty's Eyes . . . ." The wife's candid depiction of her husband as a deserving object of mercy is the key that opens the closet—but only to the husband's duplicitous stagecraft. Or as Tomaso puts it, the king's pity "was *Cesario*'s Cue to come forth . . . ," whereupon he "call'd up all the Force of necessary Dissimulation, Tenderness to his Voice, Tears to his Eyes, and Trembling to his Hands, . . . till the Pardon was pronounced" (328–30). Cesario's pose as his majesty's most "faithful Subject" is short lived, however, since he balks at signing his confession in deference to the "Friends" it might implicate. "*Sir, if you have any better Friends than my self,*" says the king, "*I leave you to 'em,*" and Cesario is banished from court (331, 334).

The Princess's intimate intervention with the king on her husband's behalf contrasts with Hermione's public incitement of conflict between king and husband. The final pages of *Love-Letters* (425–39) narrate the largely military circumstances of Cesario's defeat by the royal army. Commoners and women ("the dirty Croud" and "the Ladies") are his main supporters; men of quality are put off, in part by his claim, however reluctant, of "the title of King" (426). Showing himself to be "much more of a Souldier than the Politician . . ." (428), Cesario is nonetheless torn between despair at his leave-taking of Hermione and frustration at Fergusano's insistence that battle be delayed, on astrological grounds, until the new moon. Once in combat he fights valiantly, but God favors the royal forces, and "Love, that coward of the Mind, . . . had unman'd his great Soul" to such a degree that he forgoes the noble Roman expedient of falling on his sword (432, 434). In prison "[h]e spoke, he thought, he dreamt of nothing but *Hermione*; . . . even on the Scaffold, where he was urged to excuse, as a good Christian ought, his Invasion, his Bloodshed and his unnatural War; he set himself to justifie his Passion to *Hermione* . . ." (438).

Gender without Sex

The "public" "Adventures of *Cesario*" that Tomaso narrates are framed by, and replay, the more thoroughly "private" episodes of Sebastian and Clarinau (319): the effeminization and contested authority of the patriarch; the duplicity of the unfaithful child-lover; the unyielding conflict between "love" and "friendship." The major differences between these otherwise comparable cases of conscience concern the ethical status of the patriarch. In effect, Behn uses the concrete particularity of the private figures Sebastian and Clarinau—their efforts to sustain the absolute subjection of their daughters and sons—to throw into contrastive relief the actual particularity of the public figure Charles II, whose mercy and mildness (Behn would have us see) evince a very different, and more authentic, authority. Precisely because the family is like the state, the spectacle of bad fathers can illuminate that of good monarchs. The bastard Octavio may be justified in his successful (but accidental) murder of his uncle Sebastian; but the bastard Cesario, who soon will fail to murder and supplant his uncle James, the newly crowned king, would not be so justified. At the same time, however, the increasingly complex articulation of private cases of conscience may begin to suggest in them a priority over the realm of high politics, for which they are supposed to provide a "glass." Perhaps public affairs serve private ends, rather than vice versa; or (to put it differently), perhaps private affairs are coming to internalize public ends. Thus Philander, "being now fully bent upon some Adventure to see *Calista* if possible, . . . feign'd that he was sent to by Cesario . . . ." And in what earlier on would have seemed a non sequitur, "being upon Love Adventures" Philander makes sure to bring his "pocket Pistols" (348, 350).

This ambiguity in the hermeneutic function of the private in relation to the public is also replayed, throughout *Love-Letters,* in the social register. The conundrum faced early on by Philander and Silvia—which is the great affair and which the trivial?—Behn poses in the ongoing, parodic relationship of her aristocrats and their servants. Here the central "private" triangle of Philander, Silvia, and Octavio itself assumes the "public" stature of a "high" plot when set against its "low" reenactment by the servants Brilljard and Antonett.[20] On this lowest of levels, amatory activity can appear crude enough to valorize, by its negativity, both the public and the more elevated private levels of action. Indeed, there may be a connection between the movement of action down the social hierarchy (from masters to servants) and the desublimation of grandly political to vulgarian sexual motives. However, the debasement of the low plot can also, more radically, exert a reductively mocking influence on both its higher counterparts.

Silvia writes Octavio imploring him to reveal to her "your Secret" of Philander's inconstancy (201). But in relying on their servants to mediate their epistolary affairs, the masters overlook the danger that their servants may also emulate their masters and seek to take their places. This is especially evident in the case of Brilljard, the parvenu younger son who has tasted the upward mobility of the servant who becomes his mistress's husband. Brilljard, the gentleman's gentleman, is in effect a secretary gone bad, capitalizing on his access to the secrets of his betters to better himself. The sexualization of epistolary secrecy, always latent within its predominantly political denotation, now becomes explicit. Brilljard asks Antonett "to get one of *Octavio*'s Letters out of her Ladies Cabinet" and substitutes for it a forgery that crudely equates Silvia's "secret" with her sexuality: "Since I have a secret which none but I can unfold . . . Give me leave to say that you fair Creature have another secret, a joy to dispence, which none but you can give the languishing *Octavio* . . ." (204).[21]

This exchange of counterfeit letters may be seen as a bold internalization of the *roman à clef* form—fictional names standing for real people—within the boundaries of Behn's fictional and private realm. Duped by the forgery and incensed at Octavio, Silvia plots against him a yet bolder internalization of the *roman à clef* than the exchange of counterfeit letters, namely, the exchange of counterfeit clothing and bodies. Having carefully "drest up" Antonett in "fine point Linnen," Silvia "imbrac'd her, and fancy'd she was much of her own shape and bigness . . ." (211). Silvia aims to punish Octavio for (what she thinks is) his presumption by substituting her maid for herself (in Behn's words, "by the exchange of the Maid for the Mistress" [221]). Meanwhile, however, Brilljard prepares himself to counterfeit Octavio: "[H]e washt and perfum'd his Body and after drest himself in the finest Linnen perfum'd, that he had, . . . nor was his shape which was very good, or his stature unlike to that of *Octavio* . . ." (211). As a result, the downstairs couple unwittingly substitutes for the upstairs couple, satisfying no one but reinforcing in our minds the question of how far, and with what implications, the private is able to stand in for and signify the public.

Of course, scenes like these depend not only on a social but also on a sexual differential. This is emphasized when, after the counterfeit assignation ends uncertainly, Silvia assesses Antonett to reassure herself that Octavio (in fact, Brilljard) has not suspected the dupe: "[S]he imbrac'd her, she kiss'd her bosom, and found her touches soft, her breath and Bosom sweet as any thing in Nature cou'd be . . ." (224). Here homoerotics subserve a more basic dynamic of social leveling, suggesting the degree to which Behn and her culture understand sexual difference to be embedded within—not yet separated out from—status difference. The significant differential between the public and the private, the high and the low, is not in this case that between man and woman but that between mistress and maid. By the same token, Brilljard's sexual desire is inseparable from his social desire, which was ignited by the status inconsistency of his unequal marriage to Silvia and which is now evident in his anxiety over "the Treachery he shew'd in this Action to his Lord" Philander (211). Later on Brilljard succeeds in having sex with Silvia, who "found too late she had discovered too much to him, to keep him at the Distance of a Servant . . ." (272). Now the secretary has access to his mistress's secrets in the epistemological, carnal, and social senses of the term, and the consequence of her "discovery" to him is a fall into domesticity: "*Silvia* longs for Liberty, and those necessary Gallantries, which every day diminish'd; she lov'd rich Cloths, gay Coaches, and to be lavish; and now she was stinted to good Housewifery, a Penury she hated" (374). Only when she has entered into a new intrigue with a new Petrarchan lover intent on performing metaphorical "*Services*" will Silvia be able to reestablish a suitable distance from Brilljard, "not suffering even her Domesticks [i.e., domestic servants] to approach her . . ." (422).

These remarks build upon a broader analysis made earlier in this study.[22] When sexual difference is still embedded within social, legal, and cultural custom, women are conceived, not as fundamentally different, but as inferior versions of men. But as "natural," biological distinctions between the sexes emerge from this social embeddedness in the early modern period, they gradually become the definitive criterion by which normative sexual desire is separated into dyadic categories defined by the absolute difference of anatomy and object choice. But this is the wave of the future—which is to say that Behn's notion of gendered behavior comfortably crosses sexual borders even as it anticipates a much stricter correlation of gendered behavior with biologically given sexual characteristics. By the same token, in its current volatility patriarchalism "means" both the tacit implication of the family within the state and its emergent autonomy as a separate realm of domesticity possessed of its own rule-governed behavior.

These issues are also engaged by the comedy of errors that follows upon Philander's temporary inability to consummate his love for Silvia. Writing to her afterward, he sets the scene of his impotence as an epistolary mock heroic, a Bunyanesque vanquishment of "the Giant Honour" followed by the amatory "Siege" of Silvia's "sacred Fort."[23] On his failure, however, and in "fear of being discover'd," Philander retreats in the unmanly cover of the maid "*Melinda's* Night Gown and Head dress," only to be accosted by Silvia's father "*Monsieur* the Count, who taking me for *Melinda* who it seems he expected, caught hold of my Gown as I would have pass'd him . . . ." The son, unexpectedly identifying with the father-in-law ("to go had disappointed him worse than I was [disappointed] with thee before"), acquits himself without being discovered (56–61).[24] And we may recognize in the encounter between Count Beralti and the cross-dressed Philander an identification based not only in their comparable roles as seducers nor only in the homoerotic overtones of their comic misalliance (this is the scene in which the Count confidently places his penis in Philander's hand) but also, and most tellingly, in the homosocial alliance of father and son engaged in the exchange of the daughter. The encounter is subversive—not of sexual difference (for the modern system of sexual difference is not yet sufficiently established to be susceptible to subversion), but of the supposed politico-social difference between the old patriarchy and the new libertinism.

Behn precedes this scene by another intimate masquerade, this time epistolary in nature. Silvia, surprised by her mother and her friend the Duchess of —— in her "Apartment" while "writing in her Dressing-Room, giving her only time to slip the Paper into her Comb-box," watches in horror as the Duchess seizes "the Box and opening it, found the Letter" meant for Philander, and boldly prepares to read it aloud. Improvising quickly, Silvia pretends she has written a counterfeit letter in code for her maid Melinda to send her beloved Alexis "under the name of *Silvia* to *Philander:*" "all being resolv'd it should be read, she her self did it, and turn'd it so prettily into Burlesque Love by her manner of reading it, that made Madam the Dutchess laugh extreamly . . ." (52–53). The thinnest of lines (a mere "manner of reading") divides love from burlesque love—which is to say, at least in part, love among the aristocracy from love below stairs. Silvia and Philander thus are first joined in their love, not physically, but by their joint impersonation of their maid Melinda, for whom they are misread through the counterfeit codes of clothing and writing. Melinda later supplies her lover's father with the key to this epistolary romance: "*Alexis* at this time meant no other than my Lord, which pleas'd the good man extreamly, who thought it a good omen for his Son . . ." (53). Affinal incest, comically figured by the spectacle of a common social leveling, becomes intelligible as sexual scandal expressive of social scandal.

Love-Letters is replete with instances of women being taken for men. The implication of such scenes is not, I think, sexual transgression but social mobility; and the crucial figure is of course Silvia. This seems clear enough in the early scene, already described, when Silvia-as-Fillmond meets Octavio and discovers "the cavalier in herself." Toward the end of *Love-Letters* Silvia, now estranged from both Philander and Octavio, replays this masquerade in a different key. Because her "Head ran on new Adventures," she decides to dress "in Man's Cloths," and in disguise as the "Young Cavalier" Bellumere she encounters "a very handsom young Gentleman" named Alonzo (385, 386, 418). Like Octavio before him, Alonzo knows Silvia first as a man; unlike him, Alonzo is "absolutely deceiv'd in her," so that her "Demonstrations of Love . . . he mistoke for Friendship, having mistaken her Sex" (387, 388). Their first interaction proceeds on this homosocial, and potentially homoerotic, basis. But more than Octavio before him, Alonzo has misgivings about the lack of accord between Bellumere's gendered attractions and "his" apparent sex: "I am too passionate an Adorer of the Female Sex, to incommode any of my own with Addresses[,] . . . which yet the Course of all my Fiery Youth, through all the wild Debauches I had wandered, had never yet betray'd me to . . . least . . . Beauty had o'er-come my Vertue" (394, 422). If Octavio (and Philander) evinces the type of the "traditional" aristocrat whose sexual desire is determined by gender, not sex, Alonzo seems rather to evoke the emergent modern type, for whom gender must be sexually grounded.

But if Alonzo's experience is limited by this stipulation, Silvia's is enlarged by it. This is because the "eternal Friendship" to which they apparently must be reconciled admits Silvia once more to the "privileges" of homosocial fraternity. And through this male intimacy she learns that she has already attracted Alonzo's attention in her female guise—or guises: for Alonzo has seen and admired Silvia not only as a great "*Beauty*" whose evident familiarity with gentlemen persuades him she is a "*Whore*" but also as a "lovely unknown" he views one day walking "Mask'd" in the park (393, 417). On the basis of this knowledge Silvia "verily believed her Conquest was certain: He having seen her three times, and all those times for a several Person, and yet was still in Love with her: And she doubted not when all three were joyn'd in one, he would be much more in Love than yet he had been . . ." (420). This soon comes to pass, and Silvia's composite identity as the handsome Bellumere, the beautiful whore, and the lovely unknown—a kind of *roman à clef* she performs for Alonzo-as-audience—is rendered singular by the climactic revelation that she is a woman. For Alonzo this is a real loss that nonetheless entails a greater gain: "[S]ince you have made me lose a Charming Friend; it is but just I find a Mistriss; give me but your permission to Love . . ." (422). And yet the secret of Silvia's identity is by no means exhausted by this revelation, for we sense in her an enlargement of capacity that, facilitated by the masquerade of male friendship, persists beyond it.

How does Silvia's masterful management of Alonzo compare with the respective performances of Hermione and the Princess as exemplary "public wives"? In fact Behn narrates Silvia's intrigue with Alonzo in alternating conjunction with that of Hermione and Cesario. Like Silvia, Hermione undergoes a mock wedding ceremony of which "they do not make publick Declaration . . ."; like Silvia, Hermione pleases by her "*Masculine*" grace; hence like Silvia she is "a Friend as well as a Mistress" (412, 335). And in the space of a page the force of Hermione's "sole Interest" in affairs of politics and war echoes Silvia's pursuit of her own "Interest" in affairs of love (396–97). How does Behn's juxtaposition of Silvia with these other exemplary female cases refine our sense of her own ethical exemplarity?

The competition between arranged marriages of alliance and chosen marriages for love, which becomes such a potent expression of the public-private split in the eighteenth-century novel,[25] plays a relatively unimportant role in this narrative. This is in part because Behn here conceives herself to be performing in a different genre and in part because the institution of marriage among the gentle is not yet sufficiently intelligible as anything but a public alliance to have internalized within itself the competition between interested and amatory, public and private, motives. For all Behn's characters, marriage exists to serve an end that lies beyond itself, the end of perpetuating the male line: "to produce a race of Glorious Hero's" (Silvia); to extend "the race of old nobility" (Mertilla); "for Generation sake, no more" (Sebastian); "to make provision for posterity" (Philander) (25, 75, 285, 11). And yet the competition between interest and love —indeed, the ascendancy of interest over love—is increasingly prominent in Behn's efforts to account for Silvia's state of mind (cf. 346, 347, 384, 414). How does her more extended masquerade as a man now illuminate the ethical meaning of her apparent development as a character?

It may be useful to see the gendered conflict between friendship and love, which has been prominently thematized throughout *Love-Letters*, as a means, precedent and alternative to the conflict between interested and amatory motives for marriage, by which Behn figures the public-private differential within the realm of private experience. Within marriage, "interest" can have only the negative valence of that which impedes or constrains the personalized integrity of love. But as we have seen,[26] the emergence of the category of individual self-interest plays a vital role in constituting that realm of modern privacy to which personal love also makes its crucial contribution. As the idealizing glue that traditionally binds gentlemen together in honorable relationships of homosociality, friendship is antithetical to self-interest. But as the homosociality of market-driven behavior becomes more normative, the model of male friendship could increasingly acknowledge, as a positive good, the economic interest that had always provided it a tacit basis. Especially in contrast with the still suspiciously "effeminate" male love of women, male friendship comes to mediate the value of autonomous choice and agency even as within marriage "love" is learning a comparable function.

From Epistolary to Third Person

Earlier in *Love-Letters* the narrator contrasts the duplicity of Philander and Silvia in a way that illuminates Silvia's enlargement when disguised as a man. Lying, says the narrator, is "infinitely more excusable in her Sex, there being a thousand little Actions of their Lives liable to Censure and Reproach, which they would willingly excuse and colour over with little Falsities; but in a Man, whose most inconstant Actions pass oftentimes for innocent Gallantries, and to whom 'tis no Infamy to own a thousand Amours, but rather a Glory to his Fame and Merit: I say, in him (whom Custom has favoured with an Allowance to commit any Vice and boast it) 'tis not so brave" (312). This, Behn's version of the double standard, justifies Silvia in clearing an expansive middle ground—that of the man—between the antithetical poles of lovely but masked unknown and beautiful but brazen whore, which customarily define the sphere of female identity.

These antithetical poles also define, of course, the untenable choice between public and private capacities customarily available to women: either the self-effacing virtue of the maiden or wife in private coverture or the self-interested vice of the prostitute in the public marketplace. As we have seen, Eliza Haywood's practice would later propose the literary public sphere as a solution to this untenable choice.[27] For Behn's protagonist, however, the ambivalent relationship between the public and the private that I have been arguing is the central concern of *Love-Letters* can be felt in the apparently implacable progression from her early status as "private" maiden to her final status as "public" whore. Most readers, at least, feel a marked shift in Silvia's character over the course of the entire narrative. In part 1 she seems an innocent inflamed and seduced by her libertine brother-in-law. By part 2 Silvia's innocence already seems a memory, replaced by a calculation, dissimulation, and duplicity that Behn asks us to see also as universal female traits: "[S]he therefore dissembled her thoughts, as women in those cases ever do, who when most angry seem the most Galliard, especially when they have need of the friendship of those they flatter" (142; see also 157–58, 160). And by part 3 the alteration is yet more striking: "[T]o render her Character impartially, she had also abundance of disagreeing Qualities mixt with her Perfections. . . . Nevertheless she was now so discreet, or rather Cunning, to dissemble her Resentment . . ." (257–58; see also 278, 345, 354, 359, 363, 384).

Now, it is notable that all such characterizations of Silvia—and there are many—come in the voice of the third-person narrator, who also, like the vicious side of Silvia's character, emerges only after part 1 of *Love-Letters*. And we are therefore justified in asking, What has changed: Silvia's character, or our access to it? Is *Love-Letters* the story of a woman's fall into ethical depravity, or is it the story of a woman's discovery of how to narrate the ethical fullness of her characters? The public-private question of Silvia's ethical development, in other words, seems entangled with the public-private question of Behn's development as a narrator.

The transition from the first to the second part of Behn's narrative, which involves a shift of scene from "France" to Holland, also entails a shift in narrative method. Part 1 is purely epistolary, a cabinet of letters unadorned save by its opening "Argument." Part 2 is (as its title page proclaims, facing 116) a "Mixt" narrative, combining first-person "Letters" with an intermittent third-person "History of their Adventures."[28] Reading Defoe has encouraged us to ask how a modulation between first- and third-person narration might articulate the private-public differential.[29] Is the narration of part 2 "mixt" in a sense related to the way *Love-Letters* purportedly refuses to "mix" love and war? How far was this formal change conditioned by swiftly moving developments in the volatile political context of 1684–85?

Behn inaugurates this shift in narrative method with no fanfare at all. Like part 1, part 2 opens with an "Argument." Unlike its predecessor, however, the second "Argument" is not set off by italics from the letters that follow it, and it persists for eight pages, then merges with (or incorporates) the epistolary discourse that will constitute the major portion of this part, providing continuity between its letters with some consistency. As a result, our awareness of the difference between epistolary and narratorial voice is discreetly minimized, an effect that is furthered by the fact that Behn's narration, far from being "omniscient," is punctuated by first- and second-person references that evoke, however fleetingly, the epistolary, direct, and self-conscious address of one person by another (cf. 160, 165, 191, 202, 209, 246).[30] Given the relative unobtrusiveness of Behn's narrative mixture, what difference does it make in the way we read her secret history? What does Behn gain by her modulation from a purely epistolary first-person narration in part 1 of *Love-Letters* to an increasingly active, at one point even embodied, third-person narrator in parts 2 and 3?

Common sense would assign third-person narration the role of supplementing the immediate "privacy" of first-person letters with a more "public" mediation. But third-person narration can also convey to us inner motives that are unavailable through epistolary form. That is, the intrusion of third-person narration "from the outside" can reveal "internal" motives that the first-person letter writers themselves have neglected. This increase in knowledge is especially evident when the object of narrative illumination is itself a letter; for example, Silvia "then read over the Letter she had writ, which she lik'd very well for her purpose . . ." (168). Third-person narration can also clarify what letters have obscured. When Silvia writes Octavio after the upstairs-downstairs bedroom farce in which the maid has masqueraded as the mistress but the servant has, unbeknownst to Silvia, also substituted for the master, Octavio reads her letter in total confusion. Then "he read the Letter again, and . . . tho all was riddle to him; he found 'twas writ to some happier man than himself, . . . And now he believ'd he had found out the real Mystery, that it was not meant to him . . ." (223). Indeed, third-person narration can reveal what letters intentionally conceal—an unsurprising claim given Behn's display of the subterfuge and duplicity of which disingenuous, even counterfeit, letters are capable. Truth, like conscience, lies inside: in words, not actions, but even more, in thoughts, not words. Much of what happens in *Love-Letters* entails the disclosure of inner truths that the supposed candor of letters has covered over. And this suggests that Behn's addition of the third-person point of view in the latter parts of *Love-Letters* gives her a more efficient means of achieving what she already has attempted, more rudimentarily, in the epistolary mode, namely, an inquiry into the relation between the "private" and the "public" on the level of narrative form. What is notable, of course, is that the success of the "public" mode of third-person narration lies in its ability to capture the privacy of her characters *better* than the "private" mode of the letter form. Like the technology of typographical publication, the technique of third-person narration of the sort Behn improvises in parts 2 and 3 of *Love-Letters* is paradoxically both a public and a private enterprise, unearthing a hitherto unsuspected depth of interiority through external acts of inquiry and disclosure.

The language of the third person has made several appearances in this study. In the mid-eighteenth century Adam Smith gave a schematic account of sympathy as the synthetic product of a reciprocal adjustment, as it were upward and downward, of two persons' passions so that they meet in the middle ground. A social order in which this sort of adjustment between persons is normative is likely to be composed of persons each of whom has internalized it as a psychological adjustment between two "persons" or "characters" who lie within, the public-turned-private "spectator" and the private "agent," "I" and "myself." And at this more thoroughly privatized level the synthetic product of adjustment is given its own name: the "impartial spectator," who sees with the eyes of "a third person."[31] One hundred years earlier, Sir Edward Dering was shocked to find that the Grand Remonstrance of the House of Commons was addressed not to Charles I but to the English people: "I did not dream that we should remonstrate downward, tell stories to the People, and talk of the King as of a third Person." By addressing the people rather than the king, Parliament (more pointedly, Commons) appeared to detach itself from the sovereign partnership of the "mixed constitution," to speak as a third-person narrator who mediates between prince and people as between one "character" in the story it tells and another—indeed, to align itself, by its mode of address, with that character whose interests it "represents."[32] These usages bear a suggestive relationship to Behn's experiment in third-person narration. Based on their example, the language of the third person would appear to name not precisely a "public" or even necessarily a collective process but one by which both the public and the private (I and myself, king and people) as they subsist within the realm of actuality are consolidated by a concrete virtuality—the "we" of Parliament, the impartiality of the spectator—whose detachment, structurally more comprehensive than that of the actual public, is also more faithful to the actual particularity of the private agents or "characters" it encloses.[33]

But it is easy to simplify the nature of the gendered identification between Behn and Silvia—for example, to anticipate in their relationship as writers a kind of narrative surrogacy. True, Silvia does more than her share of writing, and Behn encourages us to connect her writing with her increasing female "artifice." Relatively early on in the narrative, Silvia fears that she has been raped by Brilljard while in a swoon: "she lookt on him as a Ravisher, but how to find that Truth . . . she call'd up all the Arts of Women to instruct her in, by threats she knew 'twas vain, therefore she assumed an Artifice . . . ." She tricks him into acknowledging that his "rape upon her Bosom" fell short of fruition, then frustrates his hopes of finishing the work by "[s]natching a Penknife that lay on her Toylite, where she had been writing, which she offered . . . to his bosome . . ." (149, 157–58). Silvia's instrument mediates suggestively between two distinct methods of addressing treachery, weaponry and writing (in courtly humanist discourse, "arms and letters"), both of them male-identified. In the protracted transition from epistolary form to third-person narration, as the narrator's voice increasingly fills in for the voices of her characters, it also allows some of them to reverse the process by more or less self-consciously serving as surrogate "artists," that is, narrators. Silvia's principal performance as surrogate narrator occurs when, in a gesture of full disclosure soon after the inception of part 3, she "begg'd a thousand Pardons of [Octavio] for having conceal'd any part of her Story from him, but she could no longer be guilty of that Crime, to a Man for whom she had so perfect a Passion . . . ." Octavio, initially overcome with emotion, soon cries, "*Now I attend thy Story:* She then began anew the Repetition of the Loves between herself and *Philander;* which she slightly ran over, because he had already heard every Circumstance of it, both from herself and Philander; till she arriv'd to that part of it where she left Belfont, her Father's House . . ." (275). Of course, Silvia's ellipsis is also the narrator's, who here "runs over" Silvia's "repetition" because like Octavio, we readers have heard it already in part 1 of *Love-Letters,* where both Silvia and Philander write in their own voices. Indeed, the opening of Silvia's story may remind us of the opening—the title page—of Behn's recapitulatory part 3: *The Amours of Philander and Silvia: Being the Third and Last Part of the Love-Letters Between a Noble-Man and his Sister* (facing 252).

In this way, Behn seems to secrete herself within Silvia's voice, which now shifts to the first person as repetition gives way to the disclosure of new information:

> I was no sooner miss'd by my Parent, but you may imagine the diligent Search that would be made, both by *Foscario,* whom I was to have married the next day, and my tender Parents; but all Search, all *Hu-an-Crys* were vain; at last they put me into the weekly *Gazette,* describing me to the very Features of my Face, my Hair, my Breast, my Stature, Youth and Beauty, omitting nothing that might render me apparent to all that should see me, offering vast Sums to any that should give Intelligence of such a lost Maid of Quality. *Philander,* who understood too well the Nature of the common People, and that they would betray their very Fathers for such a proferr'd Sum, durst trust me no longer to their Mercy . . . . [T]hey every Moment expected the People should rise against their King, and these Glorious Chiefs of the Faction were obliged to wait and watch the Motions of the dirty Croud. (275–76, font reversed)

Silvia's narration is evocative on a number of fronts. By telling us the story of someone else telling her "official" history, she reminds us that we are in the process of reading another such account, putatively her alternative, "secret history" but evidently also another serial publication that for a price renders her "apparent to all that should see me." The public organ of the state, the London *Gazette* does the "public" work of parents and prospective husband, seeking to ensure the smooth transition from one to the other by publishing her (private) bodily parts to "the dirty crowd," the (reading) public, whose hypothetical, mercenary betrayal of their actual fathers evokes their anticipated betrayal of their betters, not only their king but even their rebel leaders. This is the devolution of absolutism: money, the universal solvent, persuades the people to uphold and betray by turns the patrilineal succession of states and families. As the *Gazette* strips Silvia of her cover so as to hasten her coverture, so *Love-Letters* reveals the private Frenchwoman Silvia to signify the public body of England, torn between the patriarchal authority of the royal succession and that of royal exclusion (Silvia also tells us now about the plan to have her married to Brilljard "so that no Authority of a Father could take me from the Husband" [276]). The *Gazette*'s relatively modest *blazon* may even remind us that Behn begins *Love-Letters* with a much fuller one, elaborated to the point of parody and descriptive of Mertilla, Silvia's sister and, as the first of Philander's amorous abductees, her foil (9).

Something like the inversion of this narrative surrogacy can be attributed to the later account of the ceremony whereby Octavio is invested as a monk in the Order of St. Bernard. Despite the presiding authority of "all the Fathers that officiated at the High-Altar," the ceremony is presented as a crowning artifice of Behn's narrator, who imaginatively presides over it and whose concrete particularity is actualized at least to the point of personalization and feminization: "I my self went among the rest to this Ceremony," she begins, "having in all the time I lived in *Flanders,* never been so curious to see any such thing . . . . [W]holly ravished with what I saw and heard, I fancied myself no longer on Earth, but absolutely ascended up to the Regions of the Sky. . . . *Silvia* swounded several times during the Ceremony . . . . For my part, I swear I was never so affected in my Life, . . . and was myself ready to sink where I sate, when he came near me . . . . But as I have said, she was not of a Nature to dy for Love; and charming and brave as *Octavio* was, it was perhaps her Interest, and the loss of his considerable Fortune, that gave her the greatest Cause of Grief" (379–84). If third-person narration is like publication, the intrusive presence of Behn's "I" also privatizes the narrator, separating her out as a character whose affective powers rival those of Silvia herself. Behn's narrator fully stands in for Silvia here, artfully identifying with her, exposing her, momentarily substituting for her.[34]

Passages like these, where Silvia and her narrator formally exchange places, might well be taken as definitive of their relationship as practitioners of the "Arts of Women" (157). And yet it is not female but male characters who perform the service of surrogate narration most fully—notably Tomaso and Philander, the latter of whom at one point even converges momentarily with the narrative "I" (319–41, 230–42).[35] Indeed, a moment's reflection might lead us to expect this of an author whose basic anonymity, effectively a male disguise like those Silvia assumes, gives her "a thousand little Priviledges, which otherwise wou'd have been deny'd to Women" (126). *Love-Letters* is the story neither of a ("private") character's nor of a ("public") narrator's ethical development but of their interdependence. The gendered identification between the narrator and the heroine in this narrative is found less at the metonymic level of surrogacy or substitution than at the metaphorical level, where Silvia learns from the example of Behn's narrator how to practice the gendered "Arts of Women" with the ethical latitude normally accorded men, "whom Custom has favoured with an Allowance to commit any Vice and boast it . . ." (312). What Silvia learns from her narrator is how to deploy a more comprehensive sort of "self-authorship" so as to accrue to herself the integrity and depth of ethical subjectivity. Often enough she does this through male disguise—by taking upon herself the public, political subjecthood of a man. As Fillmond, Silvia is "pleased with the Cavalier in her self," as though to cross-dress is to gain access to a latent, and otherwise unavailable, dimension of interiority. Employed by women, the notorious and immemorial female arts are contrivances of duplicity. Employed by women passing as men, the female arts can be transformed from scandalous into intimate secrecy, from duplicity into interiority.

From Female Duplicity to Female Interiority

Male impersonation is perhaps the most explicit way in which the morally flat duplicity of Behn's female characters is transformed into an ethically deep interiority. More subtly and thoroughly, however, Behn authorizes this transformation through the formal mechanism of third-person narration itself. What I have called the shift in Silvia's character evident to most readers tends to cast a negative light on her ethical status because it often entails the disclosure, within her deepest mental recesses, of motives that her narrator argues are in justice "more excusable in her Sex" precisely because they are by custom less excusable, more "liable to Censure and Reproach," than they are "in a Man" (312). And the cumulative effect of Behn's narrative excavations is to normalize these motives by accommodating them to the excusable, even commendable, mentality customarily gendered masculine. Over time Silvia's feminine "jealousy" is masculinized as the active ambition for "revenge"; the "female arts" become difficult to distinguish from simple "artifice" and "art"; most important, the programmatically mercenary inconstancy of being a "whore" yields to the emergent civic virtue of pursuing one's own "self-interest."

This is most powerfully expressed in a passage that directly follows the narrator's speculation on the venality of Silvia's grief at Octavio's monastic investiture: "[S]he had this wretched Prudence, even in the highest Flights and Passions of her Love, to have a wise Regard to Interest; insomuch that it is most certain, she refused to give herself up intirely even to *Philander* . . . . How much more then ought we to believe that Interest was the greatest Motive of all her after Passions?" (384). The first thing to observe here is that the narrator's retrospective disclosure of a prudential self-interest in what had seemed, under the strictly epistolary conditions of part 1, the innocent passion of Silvia's love underscores the interdependence of her character development and the development of Behn's narrative technique. But second, Behn's anatomy of Silvia's passions here separates out self-interest as, however volatile a force, sufficiently attuned to the virtue of prudence to warrant being called the greatest and most powerful of the "after passions." This is not to explain away the undeniable negativity of Silvia's motives as her narrator sometimes discloses them to us but to suggest a historical context of ambivalence regarding the category of self-interest by which to understand the meaning of that negativity.

The pursuit of one's own self-interest, traditionally proscribed for men as well as women, is gradually being reconceived at this time as, properly understood, not negative at all but a natural norm of human behavior. This is, of course, first of all a male norm. But Behn's experimental accommodation of self-interest to women as well as men is one part of her comprehensive inquiry into the relation between the private world of ethical signification and the public world of political significance. *Love-Letters* begins in the imitative stealth of political allegory, which entails this manifestly unequal relationship of private signifier to public signified. Like cross-dressed women, the *roman à clef* both reveals and conceals, mimetically signifying and domesticating a higher, greater, and more powerful model. But as the masquerade becomes sophisticated and habituated, its powers of signification are increasingly internalized within the mechanism of the private signifier itself. The public-private differential remains constant, but the hermeneutic "key" to characterization shifts from the macrolevel of the allegorical mode, in which character is disclosed as a correspondence to public exteriority and actual particularity, to the microlevel on which third-person narration, establishing its own public realm of exteriority, digs out the private space of character in all its concrete particularity.

This is not, of course, "what happens" in *Love-Letters*. To speak in these terms is to abstract a complex and untidy process into a paradigm whose deceptively clear outlines are suggestive of an order of which Behn's narrative does not partake but in which it unevenly participates as historical process. Over the long term of the following century or so, the parodic imitation of male political subjecthood will be transmuted into the autonomy of female ethical subjectivity, and political allegory like Behn's will be replaced by what we have come to call the domestic novel. *Love-Letters* itself never loses its formal status as a *roman à clef*—another way of saying that it never loses its profound commitment to public political commentary on the Exclusion Crisis and its aftermath. By the same token, marriage never loses its status here as a public institution for the perpetuation of the patriline—which is to say that it never hints at a capacity to mediate the emergent norm of the "female arts" of self-interest through the practice of domesticity. When Silvia sets parental "interest" against personal "love," only the former is intelligible as an impetus toward marriage; the latter appears possible only in the absence of a "formal ceremony" (112). Unlawful in *Love-Letters*, pregnancy is experienced as a "dangerous" health risk or as a negative privation rather than as a positive and prospective privacy: Silvia's "being big with Child had kept her from appearing in all publick places . . ." (311, 415).

Childbirth marks for Silvia, only less explicitly than for the novitiate Calista, the end rather than the beginning of a relationship: "This great Affair being well over, [Silvia] considers herself a new Woman . . . ." Calista "commanded the Child should be removed where she might never see it . . ." (365, 315). And yet the emergence of self-interest as a notionally normative motive for women as well as men, although uncertainly distributed along a spectrum running from prostitution to self-determination, itself has a crucial meaning within the abstract paradigm. Interest, not (yet) conceivable as a positive factor in the sort of marriages for love on which domesticity will be based, may nonetheless be given an experimental positivity in exploring the personal motives of women at large in the world.

The change in Behn's narrative technique over the course of *Love-Letters* is paradigmatic of a shift in the emergence and development of the domestic novel. Epistolary form gives way to third-person narration as the sheer existential secrecy of letters is found to be less meaningful than the secrecy of the motives that lie behind and beneath them. The key to the cabinet of character modulates from one to the other dimension of the letter form: from the objective and documentary to the subjective and affective. The secrets of political history become less compelling, less revelatory than the secrets of the private—the casuistical and psychological—case history. Letters, always explicitly informational about events and personages, become more internally and reflexively symptomatic of character. The literal reading of letters does not subside as a running index of the capacity to "read" or "write" character through another's or one's own characteristic style, but it tends to be subsumed more and more within the pedagogic self-consciousness of the narrative voice, on which we learn to rely with some hermeneutic confidence (cf. 144, 210–11, 243, 378, 414, 436). And here too the key that opens the cabinet of secrets is, if conspicuously pedagogic, also deeply affective. Once she is able to compare for herself the letters Philander has been filtering through the mediating censorship of his "friend" Octavio, Silvia becomes a very knowing reader: "This Letter raised in her a different Sentiment from that of the Story of his Misfortune; and that taught her to know that this he had writ to her was all false and dissembl'd . . ." (312).

We might even say that the kind of "friendship" that early on makes Philander and Octavio privileged correspondents becomes in time a property of the narrator, who distributes knowledge evenly both to her characters and to her readers. But if she does not play favorites, Behn's narrator also does not promote a simple model of how knowledge, once distributed, gets known. If she has the authoritative privilege of a "friend," her characters have the intuitive susceptibility of "lovers." "Lovers," the narrator tells us at one point, "the greatest Cullies in Nature, and the aptest to be deceived, tho' the most quick-sighted . . . do the soonest believe . . ." (317); and all Behn's characters are lovers. What she refers to here is not simple credulity, however, but a kind of protoaesthetic willingness to suspend disbelief and to enjoy the virtual pleasures of the imagination: "[S]he suffered herself to be convinc'd of all he had a mind to have her believe"; "Thus he flatters, and she believes, because she has a mind to believe; . . . and yet so well he dissembled, that he scarce knew himself that he did so . . ."; "[H]e fear'd himself put upon, which the Advantage he was likely to reap by the Deceit, made him less consider than he would perhaps otherwise have done"; "[H]e wishes, and has a secret hope that either she is not in fault, or that she will so cozen him into a belief she is not, that it may serve as well to sooth his willing heart . . ." (260, 344, 345, 244). The normalization of self-interested behavior in the real world, experimentally extended in *Love-Letters* even to women, is accompanied by the opening up of a virtual realm in which the pleasures of disinterested belief are potentially available to everyone.[36]

If Behn thus treats her characters as lovers and her lovers as imaginative subjects, over the course of the narrative she also learns to treat her readers as lovers. Most often the narrator of parts 2 and 3 will relate to us directly the sort of secrets that in part 1 could be vouchsafed only through letters. But occasionally she summarizes letters, at some length, through indirect speech (see, e.g., 414); and at times she ostentatiously omits to tell us secrets we sense formerly would have seemed worthy of epistolary exchange: thus Philander and Cesario "exchang'd their Souls to each other, and all the Secrets of 'em. After they had discours'd of all that they had a mind to hear and know on both sides, *Cesario* inquir'd of him of *Silvia*'s Health . . ." (378). The effect of this sort of omission might be to undermine our confidence in the narrator were we not also aware of her aim to internalize, within us, the hermeneutic capacity to assess relevance, significance, and character—to make us, like credulous lovers, also "quick-sighted." On this level of reading, Behn would teach us, not the identity of actual persons, but how to identify with concrete characters.

When Silvia and Octavio finally find sexual consummation, Behn's narrator confides that "'[t]would be too Amorous to tell you more; to tell you all that Night, that happy Night produc'd . . ." (279). Is this because the account would be too intimate? Too tedious ("*all* that night produced")? Or too doggedly literal-minded for our quick-sighted imaginations? Soon afterward Silvia and Octavio again find themselves in bed together: "Oh, who can guess their satisfaction?" wonders the narrator. "Who can guess their Sighs and Love? their tender Words half stifled in Kisses; Lovers! fond Lovers! only can imagine; to all besides this Tale will be Insipid" (302). Learning to read character in *Love-Letters* involves learning to supplement the public reference of the *roman à clef* with the private exemplarity of what is "characteristic." When Octavio, "being Master of the Key, flies to *Silvia's* Door like Lightening, . . . [h]e opens the Chamber-door, and goes softly to the Bed-side, . . . and . . . opened the Curtains, and found Silvia sleeping with Philander in her Arms. I need make no Discription of his Confusion and Surprize; the Character I have given of that gallant, honest and generous Lover, is sufficient to make you imagine his Heart . . ." (351). Knowing Octavio's character as Behn has presented it to us thus far, we should be in a position to assess his likely emotions according to what might be called a principle of "internal" probability. And in doing so we will only be following the example of Silvia when she infers the unlikelihood that Octavio wrote the letter counterfeited by Brilljard: "[E]very Action of your life has been too generous to make me think you writ what I have receiv'd . . ." (243). In the end, Behn vindicates *Love-Letters* as a "probable Story," not by avoiding "Pretences of State," but by internalizing probability within her method of characterization.37

Love-Letters and Pornography

To say that Behn would teach us to read like lovers is to say that she would "seduce"38 us into the intuitive sensibility possessed by those who attend to the evidence of the real with a preternatural interestedness that is perpetually poised for flight into the "disinterested"—the immaterial and virtual—realm of imaginative pleasure. Quite early in *Love-Letters* Behn gives us a striking example of this sort of closely attentive reading in a letter from Silvia to Philander. Philander's go-between has hinted to Silvia that a letter from Philander lies secreted in a basket of strawberries he has just delivered to her and her mother as they strolled in the garden at Bellfont, the family seat. Luckily the letter remains in the basket after the strawberries have been carelessly evacuated, its incriminating leaves concealed by counterfeit "Leaves of Fern put at the bottom between the Basket and Letter . . . ." Silvia secures the basket until she can "return to my apartment, where opening the Letter, and finding you so near and waiting to see me[,] I had certainly sunk down on the floor had not Melinda supported me, who was only by, something so new, and till now so strange, seiz'd me at the thought of so secret an interview, that I lost all my senses . . . and 'twas a pretty while before I recover'd strength to get to my Cabinet, where a second time I open'd your Letter, and read it again with a Thousand changes of Countenance, my whole mass of Blood was in that moment so discompos'd, that I chang'd from Ague to Feaver, several times in a Minute; oh what will all this bring me to? and where will the raging fit end? I dy with that thought, my guilty pen slackens in my trembling hand, and I Languish and fall over the unimploy'd Paper . . ." (32).

This scene of silent reading—the extreme solitude of its enclosed privacy brought home by the progressive interiorization from country seat to garden to basket to apartment to cabinet to the twice-opened letter itself—dramatizes the autoerotic virtuality of pornography.[39] The vicariousness of "so secret an interview" depends as much on the intimate presence of the desiring subject's own body as it does on the absence of the desired other. The letter Silvia reads is itself saturated with Philander's anticipatory imagination ("I wait . . . the tedious approaching Night that must shelter me in its kind shades, and conduct me to a pleasure I faint but with imagining . . . as soon as 'tis duskish, imagine me in the Meadow behind the Grove . . ." [31]), which is yet deprived of the literate aid available to Silvia herself. Her pen, which (as we have seen) she will learn to wield as one of several instruments of "male" self-direction, here operates as a "guilty" stimulus to self-pleasure, its public function, like the writing paper's, "unimploy'd" while Silvia, in touch only with herself, "dy[s] with that thought . . . ."

Pornography is an aesthetic experience in that its pleasures depend on its virtuality, its imaginative detachment from the materiality it evokes. Silvia's reading of Philander's letter would seem in theory to exemplify the effects of what Addison calls the "Polite Imagination," which provides "a secret Refreshment in a Description" and "makes the most rude uncultivated Parts of Nature administer to" one's "innocent Pleasures."[40] Of course, this does not work in the present case. Silvia's pleasures, although imaginative, do not thereby avoid the "gross" pleasures of "sense," but privatize them as the effect of self-administration.[41] Nor is she comfortable with the solitude of her experience—with the substitution of virtuality for reality, of absence for presence: "But oh where art thou? I see thee not, I touch thee not; but when I hast with transport to imbrace thee, 'tis shadow all, and my poor Arms return empty to my Bosome; why, oh why com'st thou not? . . . Impatient Love betrays me to a Thousand folly's, a Thousand rashnesses: I dy with shame, but I must be undone and 'tis no matter how, whether by my own weakness *Philander*'s Charms, or both . . ." (38).

Like prostitution and sodomy, masturbation was reviled (among other reasons) for its unproductivity. In traditional cultures the productive propagation of the species is the teleological origin and end of marriage.[42] In late-seventeenth-century England this grand conjugal motive is in the process of being complicated and altered by expectations of familial experience that eventually will coalesce under the aegis of domesticity. The coalescence of pornography if not masturbation—of book-sex if not solitary sex as such—is roughly contemporary with that of domesticity. A formal domestication that stops well short of domesticity, is *Love-Letters* plausibly seen as pornography? A century after their publication, Behn's allegory seemed intelligible as pornography just as Bunyan's allegory, *The Pilgrim's Progress,* was being read as a novel.43 Not that Behn's amorous scenes are ostensibly motivated by the exclusive and freestanding aim to arouse sexual desire and to generate sexual pleasure characteristic of (modern) pornography and its engagement of "sex as such." Suffusing them with its own pent-up power is the secrecy of state affairs and their tantalizingly imminent disclosure: most immediately, the figurative provocation of the secret cabinet and letter opened to voyeuristic public scrutiny; ultimately, the promise of allegorical signification that is built into the very form of the *roman à clef.* And yet the amatory romance narrative, everywhere offering us the key to its political reference, in the very plenitude of its domesticating semiotics conceals as much as it reveals, much as the allegorical technique of *The Pilgrim's Progress* reveals by concealing its religious reference.

We can put the question with a crude clarity: does the sex in *Love-Letters* have an ulterior motive? It is not hard to find cases that support an affirmative answer to this question. In the scene of Octavio's investiture ceremony we have an example of eroticized religious observance reminiscent of a familiar technique of anticlerical satire.44 Is Behn's purpose here to reflect on, by desublimating, the religious hypocrisy of Octavio? Of the monastic order? Of the ceremony's spectators? Certainly the reduction of an elevated "publicity" to a base privacy—of which this dovetailing of the sacred and the profane provides an extreme example—has satiric precedents in *Love-Letters.* But the relevance of such a blatant instance to Octavio seems unjustified by the context,45 which supports a milder and more general irony regarding the industrious futility of his courtship of Silvia, whereby likely success with "the world" comes only with the decision to renounce it ("he won that day more Hearts, without Design, than ever he had gain'd with all his Toils of Love and Youth before . . ." [382]). Still, the eroticizing of Octavio's investiture can hardly be said to exist, as it were, "for its own sake." And anyway, the test case is surely those scenes, common enough, where the broadly hermeneutic process of formal domestication seems to be suspended by the sheer multiplicity, detail, and length of the signifying activity—and yet domesticity is not the result.

Philander's narration of his initial, "unnatural impotence" with Silvia (57–60) adumbrates what becomes a broadly recognizable pattern. What is the source of Philander's impotence? Raising and dismissing "all the little circumstances that might occasion this disaster," Philander recurs to the momentary fears that punctuated his passionate approach to Silvia with uncertainty and delay: the "apprehension" of being surprised by Count Beralti (lately seen in pursuit of Melinda); the "sudden fright" at Silvia's immobility. Silvia herself is suspended between movement and stasis, approach and withdrawal: her "sighs interrupting every syllable" of caution, her look that "contradicted all her little Vows . . ."; invoking Philander's former "Vows" of "resistance" even as she presses his hand in "silent soft incouragement"; his hands "unknown," yet "permitted" to "traverse" her prostrate body; her deep desire disclosed beneath a counterfeit restraint ("not all your Art and Modesty could hide it . . . [,] could keep the Sparks concealed"). Demurral and deferral become for both lovers the enabling condition of sexual desire. As "I waited," Philander complains, his "Fire . . . by your delay consum'd it self in burning." The alternating rhythm of Philander's account, subtly accentuated by the way his voice falls into and out of iambic pentameters,[46] suggests that his impotence—the falling sign of passion's power—is only the expressive occasion and model for a more general patterning that orchestrates the eroticism of the entire scene.

In Brilljard's later "rape upon her Bosom" Silvia is again in a position in which the frustration of fulfillment by the ambivalence of external circumstance is echoed by the liminality of her own agency and desire (148–49). From the narrator's perspective (which is also close to his), Brilljard plays the double agency of servant and self-service. "[I]nstructed by her self in the way how to deceive her," he goads Silvia into a desperation at Philander's inconstancy from which she sinks into a swoon. Torn between solicitude and appetite, Brilljard extends his arms "both to save her from harm and to give himself the pleasure of grasping" her body, then is so moved by "the pleasure of that dear burden, that he forgot to call for, or to use any aid to bring her back to life . . . ." Interrupted in "his cowardly Conquest" by two knocks at the chamber door, Brilljard "knew not what to do, whether to refuse answering or to re-establish the reviving sense of *Silvia* . . . ." He opens the door to admit Octavio.

Brilljard, "the daring Husband-Lover" and "very *Machiavel*" who knows that "to be the greater Enemy you ought to seem to be the greatest Friend," now cedes his place in Silvia's chamber to Octavio, whom Brilljard regards as something like his own Machiavellian double, "a Lover in the disguise of a Friend" (149, 152, 155–56). And Octavio, ignoring Silvia's disdain, from his own perspective retells to her the story, now one of his discovery of her, with a voyeuristic detachment that discloses, beneath the cover of her honorable "ignorance" ("not knowing any thing of the freedom" Brilljard had taken), Silvia's circumstantial complicity in, and ambiguous knowledge of, what has happened. "Pardon the effect of a Passion," says Octavio, "that cou'd not run into less extravagancy at a sight so new and strange, as that she shou'd in a morning with only her Night Gown thrown loosely about her lovely body, and which left a thousand Charms to view, alone receive a man into her Chamber, and make fast the door upon 'em, which when (from his importunity) was open'd he found her all ruffled, and almost fainting on her Bed, and a young blushing youth start from her Arms with trembling Limbs, and a heart that beat time to the Tune of active love, faultering in his speech, as if scarce yet he had recruited the sense he had so happily lost in the Amorous incounter . . ." (156, font reversed).

The "pornographic" quality of Octavio's narration is the complex effect of several convergent factors. Himself a shocked reader of Silvia's behavior, Octavio gives us a key to—"opens the door upon"—this story in a way that is all the more telling for being a retelling, possessing the paradoxical, keyhole detachment and impersonality ("she," "her," a "man," a "youth") of objective reality thrown into high relief against the now too-closely motivated realism of the first telling (this is what has been said / this is what I saw). Octavio both does and does not address his beloved with subjective directness; Brilljard both is and is not in possession of his "sense"; Silvia both is and is not a willing participant. Stung by Octavio's key to the secrets of her interview with Brilljard, Silvia deploys her own key: "[S]urveying of her self, as she stood, in a great Glass, . . . she found indeed her Night Linnen, her Gown, and the bosome of her Shift in . . . disorder . . . ." Reading herself as we read her in the "glass" of her *roman à clef,* Silvia momentarily breaks through the thick texture of her concrete particularity to remind us of the actual particularity she sometimes possesses, by virtue of Behn's formal domestication, as the concentrated embodiment of England, importunately subjected to the seductions of the various "suitors" in the Exclusion Crisis but slowly taking on the skills of self-determination.[47] "[A]djusting her Linnen and Gown with blushes that almost appear'd criminal," Silvia also reminds us that the hermeneutic activity in which Behn engages us, perpetually shifting between concealment and revelation, is a formal paradigm for the patterned oscillations of reading pornography.[48] In its most abstracted formulation, this pornographic oscillation can be seen as the fundamental disparity between sexual and epistemological knowledge—between the will toward sexual activity and the unwillingness or inability to acknowledge it.

If this is an emergent pornography, the modern development of sex "as such" is not simply the open-ended indulgence of what tradition employs to other ends but the "internalization" of that traditional pattern of behavior itself. If "traditional sex" is circumscribed and contained through its temporary instrumentality to something else (procreation, political and religious dogma), "modern sex" takes over and internalizes that oscillation between instrumental presence and normative absence as the hallmark and engine of its own self-serving pleasure. Of course, the patterning of sexual experience has a physiological, hence transhistorical, basis. But so long as sex is understood as lust, and as at least "officially" a means to other ends, its physiologically induced pattern of oscillation is no more than the distinguishing mark of a temporary presence, a flow that undergoes its own ebb in the absence of instrumental demand. Modern sex, understood as an indwelling and permanent state of "desire," is "a steady and constant condition of personality"[49] that is defined by the ongoingness not only of its secret and unquenchable plenitude but also of the rhythms by which this plenitude is insinuated, resisted, dilated, obscured, descried, deferred, then revealed in the momentary stasis of fulfillment before subsiding once more into the latent depths of the perdurable "self."

From the perspective of Behn's *Love-Letters,* it may make sense to see domesticity and pornography as a discursive doublet: broadly contemporaneous in their emergence; similarly occasioned by an epochal challenge to the credibility of the traditional, diachronic narrative of patrilineal succession; but striking out in new directions as different from each other as love and lust, wife and whore, private and public. Part of Behn's labor is, of course, to test the reality of the difference between these categories. Although *Love-Letters* never normalizes marriage or "good Housewifery" (374) as the proper end of love, it advances a strong account of love as a negative and private liberty from external constraint—in Philander's words, as that which "no force, no art, not interest, honour, wealth, convenience, duty, or what other necessary cause" may hinder (99). In his "rape upon her Bosom," Brilljard's lust for Silvia is also described as a powerful impulse of negative liberty, "without controul, forgetting all respect of persons or of place . . ." (148).

Behn writes in the midst of a transition in attitudes toward female sexuality. The traditional association of female "love" and "lust" over against "interest" is in the process of modulating to the modern view of female love as sharply opposed to lust, the two incorporating their own very different—respectively maternal and prostitutional—sorts of interestedness. As pornography ostentatiously transforms sexual desire and pleasure from a means to a public and procreative end into a private and self-satisfying end in itself, so the domestic novel will convert procreation from a mechanism of public and transgenerational perpetuity into the very principle of a deep and private self-sufficiency. Partaking incompletely in both these processes, *Love-Letters* tells the story of a public, political crisis through a domesticating technique that is poised on the verge of becoming, in the most imaginatively various of ways, its own signified. Twenty-odd years after its publication, Richard Steele provided a summary domestication of Behn's story suitable for consumption by the *Tatler*'s reading public. In Steele's version, "*Silvia*" and "*Philander*" are exclusively private persons, and their story bears no trace of allegorical signification. Wishing to marry for love, they are frustrated by her father's genial conviction that each can find a more "advantageous Offer." Gallantly siding with the lovers, Mr. Bickerstaff uses their story to exemplify the precept that "[t]here is no Calamity in Life that falls heavier upon human Nature than a Disappointment in Love, especially when it happens between Two Persons whose Hearts are mutually engaged to each other."[50]

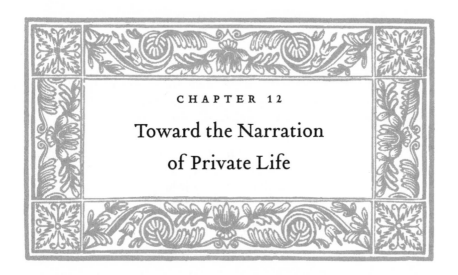

CHAPTER 12

Toward the Narration
of Private Life

A *roman à clef* that employs a recent episode of French history and an Italianate romance framework to domesticate the high politics and scandal of the Exclusion Crisis, Aphra Behn's *Love-Letters* orchestrates much that has occupied our attention in earlier chapters. Is the family like the state? Can the familiar matters of the family stand for the arcane matters of state affairs? The ambivalence of Behn's response to these questions is suggested by the instability of the genres—tragicomedy, romance, mock epic, pastoral—she exploits with such eclectic finesse. As a secret history *Love-Letters* both dispels and promulgates secrets, publicizing elite history under the mask of allegory and anonymity. Behn draws fully and inventively on the rhetoric of narrative concentration to figure forth the actual particularity of her characters. But she also indulges the allied rhetoric of narrative concretization in a way that substitutes concrete for actual particularity and satire for libel, obscuring the privacy effect entailed in references to historico-personal identity but enhancing the privacy effect entailed in the imaginative identification with exemplary characters.

Although this is a movement between one and another species of personal privacy, *Love-Letters* may also be felt to mediate, within that movement, between a history of public and of private secrets, of *arcana imperii* and *arcana amoris*. Indeed, for long stretches Behn's secret history feels less like an allegorical domestication than like a literal representation of "domesticity" as such—or at least of private as distinct from public experience. The aim to disclose secrets remains constant, but the pressure Behn puts on the distinction between two analogous realms of the secret challenges that distinction both by obscuring their boundaries and by intimating the internalizability of questions of state policy within the discourse of familial ethics.

Motivated by the explicitation of a once-tacit system of sovereignty that has been endemic since the outbreak of civil war in the 1640s, *Love-Letters* sets out to reveal and to vindicate the conditions of political subjection that obtain under Restoration monarchy, using the disparate exemplary models available in her private plot as multiple and alternative foils for the paradigmatic subordination of subject to king. But in pursuit of these ends she is obliged to inquire into the ethical subjectivities that refine and complicate the political subjecthood of her characters, a criterion that sophisticates, by internalizing, the quest for personal disclosure. In aid of this inquiry Behn experimentally modulates her narrative point of view from an epistolary first-person to a third-person technique that opens up, within the domain of ethical subjectivity, the difference between words and thoughts, interpersonal and intrapersonal discourse. The effect of this modulation in technique is not simply to mark as normatively revelatory the intrapersonal language of motivation made available to us by third-person narration but more broadly to mark the oscillation between distinct points of view—between narrative words, figural words, and figural thoughts—as itself the formal sign of interiorization. To put this another way, Behn teaches her readers to seek the key to personality not only in the actual identity of the public figures to whom her characters refer but also in the process by which they become available to ethical identification. This process is nowhere so palpable as in the relationship between Silvia and her narrator. Behn shares with her protagonist a technique of disguise peculiarly suited to a historical moment in transit between a traditional system of gender hierarchy and a modern system of gender difference. Like Silvia's cross-dressing, Behn's anonymity and its default maleness is a parodic imitation of a political subjecthood unavailable at the lower reaches of the gender hierarchy but serviceable as a model for the autonomy of ethical subjectivity that will become one criterion of female difference under the emergent sex-gender system. Behn's genre, the *roman à clef,* is also an analogue for cross-dressing, a strategy for domesticating, through parody, the authority of a higher realm. In time the disguise will become dispensable because a different kind of authority will have been lodged at the level of the signifier.

The subtle volatility of Behn's experiment with the metaphorical relationship between the family and the state is thoroughly conditioned, of course, by their metonymic relationship, the literal dependence of state order on family order. The unspoken but overriding question after the Restoration of Charles II in 1660 was, Can state sovereignty continue to be based on patrilineal principles of inheritance? The long view of historical hindsight tells us that after 1688–89 the answer to this question was no. For royalists like Behn in the 1680s, however, the more immediate question was how to construe the irregularities of the Stuart line as the consequence of rebellion rather than as endemic to the line itself. *Love-Letters* addresses a number of private, familial issues raised by the public, political events of the 1680s. In the matter of marriage, how do we adjudicate the competing legitimacy claims of civil and canon law, of clandestine and spousal contract ceremonies, of family interest and personal love? In the matter of estate settlement, how do we adjudicate the competing inheritance claims of natural sons and younger brothers, lineal and collateral heirs, priority in the succession and the legitimacy of the succession? Of the antithetical evils entailed in the limit cases of positive and negative liberty, which is worse—patriarchal tyranny and absolutism or patriarchal libertinism and "effeminacy"? What are the grounds for a legitimate matrimonial separation? By the time the third part of *Love-Letters* was published in 1687 Charles II, the patriarch, and Monmouth, the natural son, were dead, and the opposition effort to exclude York, the younger brother, from the line of inheritance had been replaced by the effort to depose him, as James II, from the estate and throne of England.

The Secret of the Warming Pan

Overdetermined by the weight of disparate circumstance, the Glorious Revolution was undoubtedly hastened by the announcement of the birth of James Frances Edward, Prince of Wales, in June 1688. Until that moment, dismay at the accession of the papist James II in 1685 had been mitigated by the knowledge that his legitimate heir nonetheless ensured a Protestant succession. Mary, James's eldest child by his first wife, was raised as a Protestant and married to the staunch Protestant William of Orange. Attempts to produce a Roman Catholic heir by James's second wife, Mary of Modena, had resulted in several miscarriages and infant deaths. Some attributed these failures to James's sexual libertinage and likely infection of his queen, although James had succeeded in fathering a number of "eminent ninnies" on celebrated courtesans. Aphra Behn's and John Dryden's panegyrics on the birth of the prince thickened the event with public historical allusion; for others, however, the appropriate discourse was the secret history and the disclosure of scandal in high places.[1] For the most part this amounted not to political allegories like Behn's *Love-Letters* but to empirically oriented reports of what had really happened in the queen's bedchamber on 10 June 1688. These reports recounted what quickly came to be known as the Warming-Pan Scandal.

Running as a thread through the several contiguous layers of this discourse is a single theme: the scandalous mixture of the public and the private. Shortly after the birth, James himself complained that "pamphlets flew about filled with all the ribaldry and calumny that malice and wit were capable of inventing, where under the notion of novels and private relations of what passed at court, the horridest crimes were laid to the Queen's charge." Here the mixture is itself discursive and generic, a function of public-sphere circulation. Another observer remarked that "concerning the Prince of Wales' birth . . . men are grown very learned. It is shameful to hear what discourse is common amongst them, even to footmen and lackeys." A crucial problem with the discursive mixture is that it entails, as here, a social mixture, the reflection of commoners on their betters. What people were saying was that the queen had not been pregnant and that the Prince of Wales was in fact a suppositious child: that under cover of secrecy a newborn baby had been smuggled into the queen's bedchamber in a warming pan (customarily used to heat the inner recesses of the bedclothes). A renovated Popish Plot, the Warming-Pan Scandal replaces the younger son's attempt to kill his brother by his attempt to counterfeit his own son. And at this intimately familial layer of the scandal, where the mixture of public and private is figured as the intrafamilial substitution of one generation for another, social mixture also reappears in alliance with religious mixture. A year later, a poem looked back to "the Golden Days"

> Ere it was heard a Queen did bear
> In Protestant land a Popish heir,
> And ere at eight months' end 'twas known
> A child was born without a groan; . . .

As in classic family romance, the revelation is one of true parentage. Now the deceptively diminutive container of the family secrets holds not (like the black box) the authentic documents but the authentic infant himself. However, in this version of the family romance—indeed, this is the whole point—even the identity of the mother is uncertain. Rumor has it that she is the wife of a bricklayer (or "tiler") named Cooper, a wet nurse who was sent for when the infant fell ill in the months after birth; hence the queen

> was made the lawful mother
> Of tiler's children's youngest brother,
> Who was begot, or born, or made,
> A Prince of Wales in masquerade, . . .

As for the father, another poem imputed paternity alternatively to Cooper or to Cardinal Ferdinando d'Adda, papal nuncio at the Court of St. James (fatherhood is amusingly confirmed by the baby-talk pun on the nuncio's name):

> (Bless'd d'Adda!), 'tis a venial crime
> That shall repair our breach of state;
> While all the world congratulate, . . .[2]

The whole shameful secret is evoked in the title of a broadside: *The Sham Prince Expos'd. In a Dialogue between the Popes Nuncio and bricklayers Wife* (1688). Edward Petre, James's Jesuit confessor and clerk of the Royal Closet, was also accused, like d'Adda, of fathering the prince, perhaps on the queen herself. Figure 12.1 gives some sense of the visceral, "racial" English response—and vulnerability—to Roman Catholicism. The unholy family triangle consists of Mary, the child, and Father Petre, the Jesuit's swarthy hand wrapped possessively around the queen's chest (the fraudulence of the birth was supposedly confirmed by the size and darkness of the child). The queen rocks the baby's cradle; on the table is an orange, and on the baby's coverlet is his toy, a tiny windmill, which alludes to another rumor that the real father was a miller. Based in the literality of royal succession, this depiction of the family romance also domesticates and concentrates the Counter Reformation in Father Petre's sinister embrace: and what rough beast . . . ?

Eight years after the event, a tract aiming to share "my Intelligence into this *Secret History*" claimed that the true mother was one Mary Grey, a pregnant "Gentlewom[a]n" who was brought from Ireland, lodged in "the *Narrow Gallery*, between the *Queen*'s Appartment and the great Chappel," and delivered of a child "but a little time before the late *Queen* pretended to be Delivered of a *Prince of Wales*."[3] The specificity of locale is common in discourse on the Warming-Pan Scandal, and it translates the scandalous mixture of the public and the private into the language of interior design. Yet another pamphlet was printed with a meticulously detailed fold-out floor plan of St. James's Palace (see fig. 12.2) annotated with a dotted line to show the "supposed" route of the suppositious child in its warming pan from the lying-in of the true mother to that of the false one. In this version of the plot the birth mother was lodged not in the narrow gallery on the near side of the chapel but in the chambers on the far side, adjacent to the cloisters. The line describes a zigzag path from the outermost precincts of the palace along lower passages underneath the chapel, then up again along galleries that snake their way past (but not through)[4] innumerable private recesses, to the queen's "ruel" and finally up to her very bedside. It is a journey less between the public and the private than between two different models of domestic privacy—from a room in which to recline that is scarcely separated from the other household functions whose space it shares (garden, cloisters, chapel, cemetery, stables) to a scene of indulgent intimacy, divided and subdivided into specialized quarters all devoted to the care of the private royal body. What ties together the two domains is the secret substitution of low for high, which is also intimated by the pamphlet's intense preoccupation with how the birth was witnessed, a preoccupation whose effect is to pressure the analogy of the king's two bodies to breaking point.

FIG. 12.1. *Father Petre, Queen Mary, and the Prince of Wales*, Amsterdam, 1688, mezzotint attributed to Pieter Schenck. © Copyright The Trustees of the British Museum.

If the queen's body is inseparably politic and natural—if state sovereignty is a function of family lineage—then private acts are also public. In accord with this understanding, royal sovereignty traditionally had been affirmed by spectacles in which the body of the monarch, publicly displayed, had stood in for monarchy as such. The succession crises of the seventeenth century made this tacit metonymy explicit, and therefore problematic. The private and the public bodies could no longer be presumed to be coordinate: private acts must be *made* public. And the crucial means of doing this reliably, absorbed from the increasingly normative epistemology of empiricism and already at work in contemporary legal, scientific, and narrative procedures, is the testimony of witnesses to the evidence of the senses, especially visual evidence. According to some, the queen's bedchamber had been filled with people on 10 June, and in October the court published the deposition of forty-three witnesses authenticating the birth of the Prince of Wales, an official history of the birth aimed at establishing the collective credit of its actual and virtual witnessing.[5] To some observers these seemingly scrupulous conditions rendered the notion of a successful conspiracy no more likely than the plot of a *roman à clef* like the old French heroic romances. Such observers "desire to be informed, Sir, in what Region or Age there ever was such a *Hocus-Pocus* Trick play'd. Nay, (omitting the Authors of *Cassandra, Grand Cyrus,* and Men in that Class of Fancy) They demand, whether *Bays* durst for shame venture on a *Plot* founded on this impossible Supposition: That a *Great Queen,* living publickly, and after her *usual manner,* in a *thronged, prying,* and *suspicious Court,* was, not only to carry a *fictitious Great Belly Nine Months* undiscover'd; but was also with the like Success to be *brought to Bed* in a *Chamber* crowded with *Persons* of both *Sexes,* and many of them utter *Enemies* to *Her* and *Hers.*"[6] But secret historians were not convinced; and this was only partly because those who testified to what they had seen were not the right sort of witness. The author of the pamphlet that reproduced the palace floor plan cited law (*De inspiciendo ventre,* "on the inspection of the belly") on how strictly royal childbirth was to be monitored:

> The Queen ought by the very obligations of her own Interest, that no objection might have been made against the birth, to have given notice of the House and Room she intended to lie in, that the Princess [Anne, James's youngest daughter and future monarch], or any for her, might have search'd such Room, and be satisfied there was no false doors, traps, or other conveniences for Juggling; or if there were, to nail them up; . . . not suffering any more than one door (whereas here there was three or four) to keep a guard at that door, for so many days before the delivery, *&c.* . . . but instead of this, the house was designedly concealed till within a few hours of her coming . . . . [A cheat] must needs have been descried by persons conveniently and privately placed about the Court, in or near the very Chamber she in-

tended to be in, . . . which might have been well performed by any belonging to the
Houshold or Bed-Chamber . . . .

That is, "it ought to have been publick to extremity, but on the contrary it was
private to a nicety. . . . [P]rivacy being the only thing desired, men of Riches,
Authority, and ill Consciences, are those of all others, that can the most easily
attain their desires . . . ."[7]

Although the plural subject of this sentence would seem to be generic, the
author may in fact intend a gendered specification, for an important objection
to the sort of witnesses that were present at the birth turns on their sex. And if
the queen's "interest" lay in the event's being public and open, the king's "interest" lay paradoxically in exploiting publicness to ensure privacy and secrecy.
Princess Anne's presence, it is argued, would have "saved the trouble of mens
being there, and by that means [i.e., her absence] they had had the liberty to
make the Birth more publick, because in the publicknesse consisted their Interest. The Kings introducing men was only to make a fair pretence of covering
her, and not letting the Women see what is usual in true births."[8] The presence
of men is thus a specious sort of publicness whose covert effect is privacy—a secret interest, that is, masquerading as disinterestedness. Another author invokes
gender difference to specify women as not the only, but surely the most material, agents in the chain of disinterested or "indifferent" witnessing by which
the private events of the bedroom ought to have been made public. According
to this author, the birth should have been attested to by

> the personal certain knowledg of proper *Witnesses* suitable to the case and concern,
> in so great a *number,* and of such unspotted fame, undoubted Authority, and perfect
> indifferency, that the Proofs of its *Birth* could never have been reasonably drawn into
> doubt or question . . . . [This required] Women to have testified their Personal sight
> and perception of that very individual Child coming naturally out of the *Queens*
> womb, and men to have witnessed their immediate free and full sight and inspection
> of that very Child by the womens assistance in his pure natural nakedness . . . .[9]

Female witnesses seem to ensure not only expertise in matters of pregnancy
and childbirth but more generally a standard of propriety and decorum. And
yet the virtual witnessing of the queen's body that the tract's own reportage substitutes for the actual witnessing the women might have done shows no signs
of either. After all, "the Protestants throughout *Europe* . . . wanted and desired
satisfaction about the *Queens great Belly* and her delivery . . . ," which "ought to

FIG. 12.2. (*opposite*) Folding plan prefixed to *A Full Answer to the Depositions* . . .
(1689). By permission of the British Library, shelf mark 522m5(23).

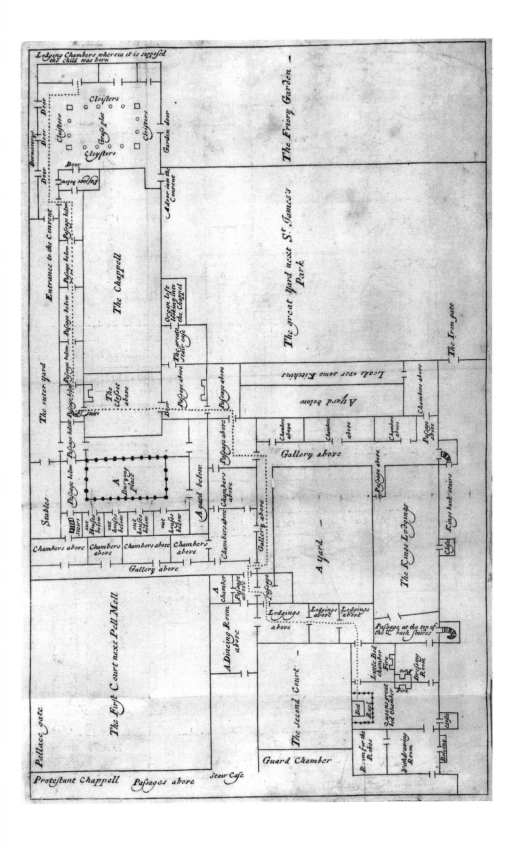

have been most freely exposed to the whole World . . . ."[10] As tacit belief, the doctrine of the king's two bodies customarily had authorized the concealment of the *arcana imperii* from public view. Now explicitated with an almost experimental deliberation, it authorizes instead the full publication of the private. One thinks of Swift's ingenuous virtuoso: "Last Week I saw a Woman *flay'd,* and you will hardly believe, how much it altered her Person for the worse."[11] The difference here is that the female body has the ritual privacy of royalty and that what is exposed goes to the most secret space of female sexuality. Hence the authors describe the size and shape of the queen's belly, breasts, and nipples, the regular flow of menses, and the paucity of breast milk with a public air of clinical disinterest that paradoxically bespeaks a deeply private and quasi-pornographic investment.[12]

Science, politics, and pornography converge in the discourse of public disclosure. Even the disclosers are sensitive to the practical problem of where to draw the line between publicity and privacy: "Now when I talk of a publick acting, I don't mean that they should have exposed her Majesty in the presence of dull doltish Teagues [i.e., Irishmen], villanous Jesuits, and bigotted flattering Courtiers . . . . Nor do I mean that all parties whatsoever that desired it might come in . . . ."[13] And at least one contemporary made a direct connection between the birth of the Prince of Wales and the death of Charles I as comparable events in the breakdown of the doctrine of the king's two bodies. In 1703 a Jacobite wrote: "I cannot imagine what you would have, unless you would either have had ye Q[uee]n delivered, as her father-in-law was beheaded, at her Palace gate on a scaffold, or else have had her discharge all her Ladys of honour and persons of Quality and send for ye Good women out of St. James market to come to her labour."[14] Here gender mixture is entangled with status mixture, the requirement of female witnesses with a demand for an epochal status inversion comparable to that of the regicide spectacle.

Figure 12.3 is a Dutch print depicting the queen's lying-in chamber crowded with people poised for medico-political intervention and unlikely to provide the sort of disinterested testimony required by those who criticized the handling of the royal birth. The setting is a hospital for *"Les Hypochondres."* Just to the right of center is the officiating Dutch doctor, who holds a urinal and cries in Dutch: "Away, . . . such a rabble must go to the mad-house. I have many cures to perform, before every thing can be set right." The figure to the right of the doctor may be William of Orange, who restrains the pugnacious figure in front of him, an enraged James II. To James's right is Louis XIV, who wears on his head the world in flames and is also enraged and restrained by two Algerines. In the left foreground a cardinal, squatting on a bed pan, has already drawn his sword; to his left a priest readies an injection. The focus of all this activity occupies the right side of the print. In the extreme right foreground sit a nurse and the putative mother, the miller's wife; the child, too large to be a newborn infant, plays with a windmill. Behind this group the queen lies in bed. Father Petre, twice represented, takes the queen's pulse on her right side and, standing behind her, holds up his fingers in token of secrecy like the two women with the child. The paintings framing the arch depict two famous wonderful births, of Bacchus from the thigh and Minerva from the head of Jupiter.

What is the relationship between authority and publicity? Once the doctrine of the king's two bodies is subjected, like the Queen's belly, to public-sphere inspection, the natural and private body of the monarch becomes, not a fence against interference with the political and public body of monarchy, but the easiest access to it. In a parallel fashion, commentators on both sides of the issue, confronted by the question of the child's legitimacy, have final recourse not to the *arcana imperii* of royal authority but to the commonsense experience of private citizens. Thus George Hickes deplored the demand for absolute certainty in the parentage of the Prince of Wales, arguing that "no suspicions or presumptions, how great soever, would defeat the title of a child owned by private parents." And his correspondent Robert Jenkin recalled a suppositious birth "but a few years ago in a private family, unknown to the supposed father." To make absolute certainty the criterion of legitimacy, wrote Thomas Wagstaffe, would "make suppositious not only all princes, but all men in the world." Moreover, it strained credulity to imagine that a father, whether or not royal, would willingly prefer a stranger over his own natural offspring: "Will any man adopt an heir when he does not know but he may have one of his own? Much less will he pick up one from a dunghill to inherit the glory of his ancestors, when his own loyns may afford him many branches to support it. Let all married men and women, who have any sense of children, consult your own bowels, and then let them believe this if they can."[15] Even by Jacobites, then, ultimate appeal is made not to the esoteric doctrines of public kingship but to the intimate impulses of private conscience. This is the domesticating discourse of disinterestedness—speaking of low, sensible things to low, common people.

The Private Lives of William, Mary, and Anne

The accession to the throne of William and Mary in 1689 and then of Anne in 1702 made patriarchalist principles explicit, and therefore problematic, in related ways. One of the state medals struck on the coronation of Mary (see fig. 12.4) pictures a bust of the queen on the obverse and on the reverse a parental eagle flying toward the meridian sun carrying one eaglet (the legitimate daughter Mary) in its talons but dropping another (the illegitimate son James) to

Arlequin Deodat, & Pamirge Hypochondriaques.

Weg riep den Doctor, sulk gespuys
Moet na het Dol en gecken huys:

Ick heb noch vry wat te geneesen
Eer alles op syn stel sal wesen.

Oseling f. d exc Giaeco

De Duytse Doctor, en de vreemde Patienten.

N.1. HOe Arlequin? Hoe Deodat?
Geharnast als een dol soldaet?

N.2. Ik ben Monarch die 't al kan dwingen,
'k Heb gantsch Europe syn defensingen,
Te land, ter zee, in 't Oost in 't West
Heb ik mijn leer en er gevest:
Wie derft mijn vrienden tegenblaffen?
Wie my bepalen, sonder straffen?

N.1. Hoe past dit harnas desen snaek?
De man is Hypochondriaecq;
Sijn water is vol turbulentie,
Maer sny hem af sijn appendentie,
En stuyt het mamelien in de Son.

N.3. De Meester-knecht riep, dat is Bon,
En sloot hem op. Doen was sijn tieren
Om ruymte en vryheyt van quartieren:

N.4. Om 't naer gesucht van een Prelaet
Die 't bloet en mergh gelijk afgaet.
Dit deed den Doctor ordineeren

N.5. Dat hem d'Apthecker moest klisteeren.
Strax muts en rok uit, en in 't hemt,
Van festien Meesters overstemt,
Tot Consistoriael purgeeren
Met een Incisie, om te weeren
't Besette Hypochondrium,
En voortgang van het Gallicum.

N.6. Ick (schreeut een derde) kan doen kloven
De aerde aen 't Centrum, en hier boven
Begruilt mijn bres het firmament
Soo dra mijn kunst werd aengewent.

N.7. Die wierd gepakt van Algernon,
En vlugh getrepaneert, machinen
Van rook en wint, ontvloogen t'brein:
Doen riep hy: 't is een pak desien
En een hoverdige verblintheit,

Dat broers sich slaen van een gesintheyt.
So biechtte hy voor een Canon.
Dat hem ruym overgapen kon.

N.8. Het Modens Vrouwje dat wou kramen,
Sy riep vast al de Doctors samen;
Maer dese Doctor seyd, dat werk
Is voor de Paters van de Kerk.
Hier op laet sy 'er binnen komen
Met wy- en suyver-quast van Romen.

N.9. Het heylyg kussen, seyd het wijf,
Brengt zegen op 't onvruchtbaer lijf.
Doch elk stont even zeer beteutert,
Om dat het geestslijk zaet zelfs leutert.

N.10. Des zocht men al de moeders op,
En levert die gewenste Pop.

N.11. Nu sit de Munnick in de boeken
Om 't geeftslijk goet net op te soeken,
Dat komt heur toe voor sulken vont.
Maer wie stopt nu de Quakers mont?

N.12. Wel Meester Tam en Schotse Jorden
Die sullen Patienten-luy worden.
John sal Sherif, boy meester sijn.
Doe riep de Meestres, sonder pijn
Van toestel, sonder smert, of hindree,
Haeft ik onsterffelijke kindren.
Dat is een kunst: de Monarchy,
Spijt Erraf-recht, staet vast door my.
Sus! riep de Mispaep, onder eeden,
Mach dit van niemant sijn beleeden;
Want al ons kluwen is verwart.
Hoe! Heeroom benje nu benart?
Ach, seyt hy, alles wort vermaegelt;
't Is of het volk en schapen hagelt;
Wy, onsen Baes en Deodaet,
Zijn door de Ketters buyten mat.

the earth; the legend reads, "NON PATITVR SVPPOSITITIOS" (a suppositious [child] is not permitted). The most immediately available Tory domestication of William's authority was as the usurping rapist of a feminized English state. One poet managed to combine this with the slur of sodomy by alluding to the king's relationship with Hans Willem Bentinck, Earl of Portland, a devoted friend of William's who had come over with him from Holland and whose intimately homosocial relations with his master were rumored to deviate with regularity into the homoerotic:

> If a wily Dutch boor for a rape on a girl
> Was hanged by the law's approbation,
> Then what does he merit that buggers an Earl
> And ravishes the whole nation?[16]

More subtly, the case of Mary extended in a gendered direction the dilemma of choosing between natural son and younger brother. Unlike both Monmouth and York, Mary was the former king's legitimate lineal heir; but she was also a *feme covert,* and so the question was whether priority lay with her subjection to her father or with her subjection to her husband.[17] The revolution settlement ensured that the latter interpretation prevailed, but not without benefiting from the lineal aura entailed in the paternal inheritance. As joint monarch, Mary was a public-private mixture in a special, gendered sense distinct from that dictated by the doctrine of the king's two bodies; for "because Mary's public and private identities were fused into one royal body, writers could identify wifely submission with an ideal of political virtue or political obedience, without acknowledging the difference between the public and the private contexts in which these qualities existed."[18] However, from the simpler perspective that soon would become known as Jacobitism, Mary was, in terms both public and private, a traitor.[19] Queen Mary's reign thus epitomized, in the most public mode imaginable, the way in which English law subordinated the patrilineal rules of status to the patriarchal rules of gender.

A poem of 1689 captures the paradoxical nature of the joint monarchy with brilliant concision and wit. During the first year of their reign, William and Mary spent more of their time at Hampton Court than at Whitehall, a rustication that encouraged Fleetwood Sheppard to conjure up a vision of the married couple in the privacy of their domestic retirement:

FIG. 12.3. (*opposite*) Romeyn de Hooghe, *Arlequin Deodat, et Pamirge Hypochondriaques,* Amsterdam, 1688, engraving. © Copyright The Trustees of the British Museum.

A DESCRIPTION OF A HAMPTON COURT LIFE

> Man and wife are all one
>> In flesh and in bone,
> From hence you may guess what they mean:
>> The Queen drinks chocolate
>> To make the King fat,
> The King hunts to make the Queen lean.
>> Mr. Dean says grace
>> With a reverend face,
> "Make room!" cries Sir Thomas Duppa,
>> Then Benting uplocks
>> His King in a box,
> And you see him no more till supper.[20]

Clearly some exegesis is needed. The serious project of this amusing poem, we might infer, is to reconcile the unfamiliar condition of a monarchy made dual by marriage with the familiar doctrine of the king's two bodies. How does the corporate nature of the public institution of kingship (which binds together the private, or "natural," embodiment of the monarchy of the moment with its public "political" ongoingness) incorporate the corporate nature of the private institution of marriage (which spiritually binds together two natural bodies as one)? The question is made yet more difficult (or perhaps constituted in its difficulty) by the fact that William's greater authority derives from his private role as husband, whereas Mary's lesser authority derives from her public role as lineal heir to the throne.

To pose, if not to answer, this question Sheppard transports us to the intimate sphere of the royal domestic arrangement at suburban Hampton Court to pursue the common round of daily life among royalty, where the public terms of state rule are eerily domesticated as the private terms of the conjugal household. Here the corporate nature of kingship persists not in the reciprocity of prince and people nor even in that of the public and the private "body" but in the symbiosis of a husband and wife who, pursuing their own quotidian, gendered desires in the normal course of things seem to exert a magical influence on each other's bodies. Sheppard evokes this strictly physical symbiosis by alluding both to the biblical account[21] of our first parents' marriage and to the nursery rhyme of Jack Sprat and his wife.[22] The sharing of sovereignty is then expressed by the oneness of a royal flesh that somehow manages to lick the platter clean.

But this sort of secret sharing may also imply that in a pinch the one can assume the role of and substitute for the other. Here the household servants play an important part. As the diurnal routine unfolds, Henry Compton, dean of

Fig. 12.4. Obverse and reverse of medal struck on the coronation of Queen Mary, 1689, in Edward Hawkins et al., *Medallic Illustrations of the History of Great Britain and Ireland to the Death of George II*, 2 vols. (London: Spink & Son, 1969). Princeton University Library.

the Royal Chapel, says grace, and when lunch is over, Hans William Bentinck, the First Gentleman of the Bedchamber, sequesters William until suppertime. For a nap? The uplocked "box" suggests a quasi-voluntary confinement within a yet more interior sanctum of the bedchamber, like a cabinet or a closet, and "Benting" is the concupiscent Earl of Portland. Like an element of dreamwork, the image of the king in a box has the supersaturated obscurity of overdetermination. As a figure of radical privatization, it carries the theme of somatic symbiosis to the ultimate point of substitution—masturbatory self-identity, transvestism, sodomitical reflexivity?—in any case "man" taking pleasure in his own flesh and bone to the exclusion of wife.[23] However, the third of William's subordinates to be named, Sir Thomas Duppa, is not really a servant of the royal household at all but Usher of the Black Rod, whose duty it was to escort the king into Parliament, those public "houses" whose imperious governance at Whitehall is now concentrated into the narrow confines of domestic enclosure at Hampton Court. For centuries "the King in Parliament" had served as shorthand for the correlative and indivisible authority of monarchy and Parliament. Over the course of the century of revolution, however, the phrase had come to acknowledge the depleted authority of the king by explicitating that condition under which his power was greatest: when he was in Parliament.[24] So the crucial transition from private, domestic house to public, parliamentary house is mysteriously domesticated as a postprandial privation, a royal withdrawal from royal presence; as William makes do without Mary, so Parliament makes do without William. And the muted echo of "jack-in-the-box" reinforces the more general insinuation that domestication is infantilization, with the king reduced to a knave mechanically popping up, and off, on schedule.[25]

Unlike Mary, her younger sister Anne, although married, ruled alone; but most of her pregnancies ended in miscarriage, and none of her children survived childhood. In one respect this was a blessing: any claim to the legitimacy of the succession based on the necessity of blood ties was vulnerable to Jacobite argument that this acknowledged the Glorious Revolution to have been unlawful.[26] Deprived, in any case, of the public authority of the mother entailed in the metonymic mediation of the royal patriline, Anne sought to exploit the metaphorical dimension of that authority by fostering her image as the figurative mother of her country.[27] But the weakening of patriarchalism under the force of its explicitation was transforming the tacit potency of that analogy into little more than a pleasing similitude for power. It has been argued that the spectacle of Anne's reign is a crucial stage in the long-term "domestication" of motherhood, that is, in its separation out from public life. By 1708 "queenly maternity had been defined as a symbolic category indicative of the distance *between* political agency and female experience."[28] But the reign of Queen Anne also marks, more broadly, an important stage in the decline of court culture, hence in the separation of government from the royal household as such; and the queen's bedchamber was more definitively a private, domestic space than such rooms had been in earlier reigns.[29]

The growing power of public-sphere explicitation was evident in other ways as well. In 1712 a pamphleteer who regretted the lapsing of state restraints on the press in 1694 took no comfort in the fact that "those Libellers who exercise . . . their venomous Talent, have no opportunity during so just and mild and wise a Reign [as Queen Anne's], than by making false and malicious guesses at Secrets of State." For this "way of guessing at political Mysteries, and then publishing as matter of fact, a bare surmise, is the most dangerous piece of Malice that can be exercised against Government . . . ." As in the past, it is no easy matter for people "to project or to penetrate into any of the sacred Mysteries of the State." The problem is that now the potential mischief of unpunished libel obliges government to demystify its own *arcana imperii:* "[I]f the Populace upon the first appearance of any State-Measures, cannot penetrate into the depths of them, the prime Minister must either take the Key out of his Pocket, and *coram nobis* [in our presence] decypher his meaning, or else be threatened with some impending fate."[30] On this evidence, the office of the prime minister, evolving to fill the power vacuum left by the demise of mystic kingship, assumes that the state is accountable to the public sphere. The modern ministerial bureaucracy is a lock that comes with its own key. The displacement of criticism from monarch to evil counselors that becomes so conventional in seventeenth-century political discourse is over the long term succeeded, not by the view that it is always the king who errs, but by the authorization of the "cabinet" minister as a political agent whose responsibility is independent of the largely symbolic *arcana imperii* vested in the monarchy itself.

So Anne's failure to produce an heir helped weaken, by making explicit, the tacit coordination of the public and the private, the state and the family. By the dialectical logic of historical crisis, however, the problematic separation out of categories is closely accompanied by their problematic conflation. Historical circumstance facilitated this logic through the rise to power of the upstart Sarah Churchill, Duchess of Marlborough, the royal favorite whose illegitimate authority over the queen of England was most notoriously castigated by Delarivier Manley. In *The Secret History of Queen Zarah, and the Zarazians . . .* (1705) Manley made Churchill the domestic and internal vanguard of William's foreign usurpation, the very type of the evil counselor and, more broadly, of social disorder.[31] Moreover, the feminocentric court facilitated by Churchill's rise to power added a sense of familial imbalance, even perversity, to the fact of Anne's childlessness, as though the legitimate (and ideally male) heir had been dis-

placed by parvenu female outsiders devoid of genealogical authority. As Groom
of the Stole, Churchill was the supreme bedchamber favorite whose hotly rumored say in policy matters challenged the supposed privatization of the royal
household.[32] But soon enough it was Sarah's ironic fate to be displaced, in turn,
by Abigail Masham, a more extreme instance of perversity both in her social
origins and in her sexual opportunism—including same-sex indulgences with
the queen herself, of which Churchill in particular was convinced. In a Whig
attack of 1708 Masham's salacious control of the more private architectural
precincts allows the despised Robert Harley (soon to be Earl of Oxford) access
to royal favor:

> Whenas Queen *Anne* of great Renown
>   *Great Britain*'s Scepter sway'd,
> Besides the Church, she dearly lov'd
>   A Dirty Chamber-Maid.
>
> . . . .
>
> Her Secretary she was not,
>   Because she could not write;
> But had the Conduct and the Care
>   Of some dark Deeds at night.
>
> The Important Pass of the Back-Stairs
>   Was put into her hand;
> And up she brought the greatest Rogue
>   Grew in this fruitful Land.
>
> And what am I to do, quoth he,
>   Oh! for this Favour great?
> You are to teach me how, quoth she,
>   To be a Slut of State.[33]

To Sarah's frustration, it now seemed necessary to insist on policing the queen's
private bedchamber so as to rid it of the public influence that she herself had
wielded there. Tories like Henry St. John (soon to be Viscount Bolingbroke)
were outraged: "Unhappy Nation, which expecting to be Govern'd by the Best,
fell under the Tyranny of the Worst of her Sex!" The Whigs' "First Attempt was
to take that Privilege from Her, which the Meanest of Her Subjects enjoy, and
Slavery was to pursue Her even into Her *Bed-Chamber*."[34] Sarah's efforts to prevail on the queen to cashier Abigail as a threat to the nation backfired. Not
Masham, but she and her husband, the Duke of Marlborough, were judged to
be the public problem and were dismissed from service.[35]

    After Anne died, John Dunton told the secret history of Masham's public influence in the form of a mock sermon on the text of Isaiah 3:12: "As for my People, Children are their Oppressors, and Women Rule over them. O my People, they which lead thee, cause thee to Err, and destroy the Way of thy Paths." Here the charge of usurpation is deflected from the Whiggish William to the Tory Masham. She "snatches the Scepter out of her Sovereign's Hands, and Rules like an Absolute Monarch. *Abigail the Favorite Reign'd like a King.*" Queen Anne, "thus shackled in her Cabinet, her Person as it were a captive, and *King Abigail* in Possession of Affairs, the Catastrophe was dismal, for the *poor Queen* very suddenly, and I know not how, makes her Exit into another World . . . ." Masham and her creatures are therefore "Traytors" who "made all Things ready for the Reception of the Pretender." Queen Anne and King Abigail: To modern ears, the most shocking scandal is likely to seem the sexual, but for Dunton, the order of gender and sexuality subserves a more fundamental sociopolitical and familial order, which Masham's ascendancy puts out of joint: "A general Confusion of all Degrees, without respect of Age or State . . . the whole State is all out of Order . . . ."36

The Privatization of the Secret History

But this is to pass too quickly over the last years of the Stuarts. What happened to the discursive form of the secret history in the immediate wake of the Glorious Revolution? For some writers, the task of raking over the remains of the Stuarts required the allegorical form of the *roman à clef.* According to its "Translator," *The Amours of Messalina, Late Queen of Albion* (1689) seemed "to carry the appearance of an *Historical Novel,* and contains most of the *Cabinet Contrivances* of the *Court* of *Albion* for these last four Years . . . ."37 More common were classically modeled exposés from below that dispensed with formal domesticating mechanisms, like *The Secret History of the Reigns of K. Charles, and K. James II.* (1690), which invoked Suetonius as precedent. Despite the absence of a "romance" signifier, however, the language of intimately amatory motivation explains public politics in both metaphorical and metonymic terms. "[N]o Prince in the World could ascend a Throne with more Love and Affection" than did Charles in 1660: the people, "inflam'd" by and "infatuated" with him, "ador'd" their restored monarch, while Parliament "doated" on him. But from the beginning Charles was ruled by baser passions: ingratitude toward his people's loyalty, revenge for his father's fate, and a lascivious debauchery fueled by cryptopopery, "a Devotion so conformable to his lustful Inclinations." Indeed, the keys to Charles's policies are the twin secrets of his effeminate and papist subjection.38 Another tract, purportedly discovered in Charles's strongbox after his death, is a three-hundred-page parody of his father's *Eikon Basi-*

like, in which Charles narrates the long "history" of his double ambition: to be an absolute Roman Catholic sovereign and an absolute debauchee.[39]

Secret historians who eschewed the allegorical form of the *roman à clef* were finding, as Aphra Behn had done, that the public-private differential was available to them in other registers as well. One author, working in "the Dark, and almost inscrutable Recesses of the French Cabinet-minutes" to reveal the perfidy of Louis XIV, felt obliged to apologize for rendering the actual particularity of his subjects in an epistolary mode:

> And 'tis hoped no body will quarrel, that this *Piece* which is Entituled by the Name of a *Secret History,* &c. should be written in an *Epistolary* way, when it be considered that such a *Form* was indispensibly necessary under the Circumstances of the *Author,* and his *Noble Correspondent,* and that there is a very engaging part naturally couched under such a method of bringing *State-Arcana's* to light, by way of *Letters,* which, in the very Notion of them carry something of secrecy; Though after all, the Reader cannot but observe an Air of History to run, in a manner, through the whole composition . . . .[40]

In other words, the epistolary mode is justified not only because of its literal authenticity but also because its air of authenticity has both a public and a private dimension, an actual and a concrete particularity. As secret histories are secret with respect to both their topics and their authorship, so the letter form testifies to both an objective and a subjective first-person veracity. To promise the revelation of public secrets reveals the existence of private ones, including the relationships of confidence and trust that subsist between authors and their noble correspondents. Another tract opens with a "Vindication of Secret History" that looks back to Cicero and insists that such works must be "written with Sincerity, and by a Person throughly acquainted with the Matters of Fact, which he commits to his Paper. I had the good Fortune to attend on the Noble Lord, who is the Subject of the following Narration . . . ."[41] However, in this secret history the narration itself is apparently devoid of public reference. Yet another work, pointedly about real public personages, nonetheless so weights its concern toward amatory intrigue that the "public" nature of its disclosures seems, as in considerable stretches of Behn's *Love-Letters,* quite nominal. The "cabinet" now "opened" is clearly a domestic, not a diplomatic, space. The "Author's Preface" tells us that "the better part of the Memoires, from whence this Little History is drawn, came out of the Cabinet of Madam Maintenon, and were partly written with her own Hand." The history itself begins:

> Amongst all those Effects that Love has produced, one sees nothing that surprizes him more, than when it joyns the Scepter to the Crook, and by its influences makes those Conditions of Life that stand at the greatest distance from one another, so

united and reconciled, that the two Parties forget not only what they have been, but also what they owe to themselves . . . .[42]

The reconciliation of crook and scepter recalls the social and sexual scandal of the trowel and prick figures we have already encountered.[43] And yet here the focus seems to have slipped from the actual particularity of the celebrated personages to the exemplary nature of their amatory relationship, whose force is precisely to dissolve public difference into the intimate homogeneity of which love is capable.

In this way, secret historians might find themselves scrutinizing the privacy of their own relations to publicity more than they do publicity itself. Such claims to notable liaison did not go unchallenged. Pierre Bayle was skeptical about the veracity of the much-translated Marie d'Aulnoy—who was if anything more popular in England than in France—although he carefully displaced his skepticism into the public sphere:

It is a pity the public cannot be persuaded that she deserves much credit. It has prevailed, as a general opinion, that her works are a mixture of fictions and truths, half romance, and half history . . . . It is an inconvenience which daily gets ground by the liberty that is taken to publish the secret amours, the secret history, &c. of such and such lords famous in History. Booksellers and authors do all they can to make it believed that these secret Histories have been taken from private manuscripts . . . .[44]

As Bayle's language suggests, however, to demystify history as fiction also has the potential to facilitate the private pleasures of the imagination, whose "secret Refreshment" (according to Joseph Addison) may afford us a "greater Satisfaction" than the more gross and public pleasures of the senses.[45] There is a similar potential in Richard Steele's observations on French memoirs, which echo Bayle's:

To read the Narrative of one of these Authors, you would fancy there was not an Action in a whole Campaign, which he did not contrive or execute; yet if you consult the History, or *Gazettes* of those Times, you do not find him so much at the Head of a Party from one end of the Summer to the other. . . . There are others of that gay People, who (as I am inform'd) will live half a Year together in a Garrat, and write an History of their Intrigues in the Court of *France*. . . . I do hereby give Notice to all Booksellers and Translators whatsoever, That the Word *Memoir* is *French* for a Novel . . . .[46]

In this reversal, official histories reveal the secret mendacities of secret histories. Steele's arch critique is a prelude to the careful, century-long elaboration of the difference between empirical and aesthetic truth, the actual particularity of public imposture and the concrete particularity of private self-representation.

One of the most spectacular secret histories of the seventeenth century, *The Kings Cabinet Opened* (1645), had published the captured letters of the most public Englishman of all, the king himself.[47] In 1692 Charles Gildon extended this remarkable invasion of public privacy by promulgating the fiction that he was publishing letters of private citizens sent through, and stolen from, the public post.[48] Gildon (or his Continental model) was of course aware of the tradition of which his work constituted a complex modernization: at one point he refers to "the fate of all those who have hitherto attempted these *Secret Histories,* who have made bold to sacrifice the Justice and Reputation of *Princes* to their own private Malice, . . . and therefore have not scrupl'd to broach the most Circumstantial Particulars of things that could never have possibly be[en] known, if true." He also understood the proximity of his discursive domestication to the (sexualized) excavations of the Royal Society:

> [W]hile your *Virtuosi* are poring over the Unaccountable Secrets of *Dame* NATURE, we are busie in searching into full as intricate a Subject; The Humours and Nature of Men, while they are conversing with Labour and Study, with the *Mineral, Vegetable,* and *Animal* Kingdoms, our Pleasure leads us in Chase of the Secrets of the *Rational World* . . . . They are like our Travellers who ramble abroad to see Foreign Countries, before they know any Thing of their own . . . .[49]

Gildon's tract is one of those efforts (like the Spectator Club or Haywood's band of female spectators) to literalize the virtuality of the public sphere as a small group of actual people—in this case a "Club" of friends who, encouraged by an initial misadventure, periodically steal packets of mail and convey them to the country in "a great Box or two" to read, debate, and moralize the epistolary contents, "there being LETTERS proportion'd to all Capacities and Tastes . . . ." The rusticated retreat imitates the activity of letter writing itself: one club member remarks that letters are "the pulling off the Mask in a Corner of the Room, to shew one another their Faces."[50] *Post=Boy* combines the documentary objectivity of a collection of familiar letters with the editorial moralizing of a conduct book. More than this, Gildon's project enacts the emergent agency of "civil society," not so much as a critique of but as a supplement to or replacement of state functions. Steele was soon to imagine his periodical as a "court of judicature"; Gildon compares his Club to the legislative body of a little "*Common-wealth.*"[51] In repossessing them from a government agency, *Post=Boy* valorizes the diurnal, domestic, and commonly amatory secrets of private citizens not (as with *The Kings Cabinet Opened*) to mitigate their political subjecthood but to refine their ethical subjectivity. The tract enforces the imperative that private subjects "speak to" each other in the collectivity of print, framing this public discourse with the Club's own metapublic discourse to ensure a proper moralization. The process is exemplified when the Club members read a letter from a young girl who has been affronted and defrauded by her guardian. They decide to publish the letter, accompanied by their own "wholsom Admonition" to reform the guardian's treatment of his dependant, "who he believes has neither the Power to do what she threatens, nor the will to discover it to a Third Person, that might assist her."[52] Gildon's language permits us to see the analogy between the elaboration of public opinion as a sphere of cultural reflection and its equivalent at the microlevel of narrative style, the development (as in Behn's *Love-Letters*) of a third-person mode of address. In both cases the relative "publicity" of reflexivity throws into relief a discourse that is otherwise too private to be accessible as such, paradoxically enhancing its privacy in the process.[53]

The Strange Case of Beau Wilson

It is instructive to consider Gildon's *Post=Boy* as an exercise in treating private *arcana amoris* as self-sufficient vehicles for conveying meaning that traditionally would need to be transported to the level of the public signified in order to attain the semantic force of *arcana imperii*. An event of the same period attracted a range of public notice that, although very different in form and import from Gildon's collection, nonetheless deserves to be pondered in a similar light. In a diary entry for 22 April 1694 John Evelyn recorded that "A [very young] Gentleman named Wilson, the [younger] son of one that had not above 200 pounds per Annum: lived in the Garb & Equipage of the richest Noble man in the nation for House, Furniture, Coaches & 6 horses, & other saddle horses; Table & all things accordingly: Redeemed his Fathers Estate, gave portion to his sister . . . ." Not long after, Evelyn tells us, Mr. Wilson was killed in a duel by John Law over an obscure entanglement involving Wilson's sister, Law's mistress, and a house of questionable repute.[54] The obscurity of the entanglement should not distract us, Evelyn believes, from the central issue. "But the Mysterie," he continues, "is, how this so young gentleman, a sober young person, & very inoffensive, & of good fame, did so live in so extraordinary Equipage; it not being discovered by any possible industry . . . . It did not appeare he either was kept by Women or Play [gambling], or Coyning [counterfeiting], Padding [foot-padding]; or that he had any dealing in Chymistry [alchemy] . . . . All which was subject of much discourse and admiration . . . ."[55]

Wilson and the She-Favorite

This skeletal narrative, in which the mystery of Wilson's upward mobility seems to be expressed through his lack of agency in the several scenarios Evelyn considers and discounts, was filled in thirteen years later in an epistolary adden-

dum to a translation of one of Marie d'Aulnoy's secret memoirs. The internal title page of *The Lady's Pacquet of Letters* goes some distance toward involving it
in the atmosphere of international secrecy for which d'Aulnoy was so celebrated: "The Unknown Lady's Pacquet of Letters, Taken from her By a *French*
Privateer in her Passage to *Holland.* Suppos'd to be written By *several Men of
Quality.* Brought over from St. *Malo's,* by an *English* Officer, at the last Exchange of Prisoners." The running heads are more succinctly suggestive: "The
Lady's Pacquet broke open."[56] Delarivier Manley, the anonymous author of the
Pacquet, thus broadly associates its diverse contents with the public events of
the Nine Years' War. But her account of Beau Wilson (his common nickname),
contained in the first of her forty-one letters, adumbrates a political context
more contemporary with the episode itself, which occurred several months before Mary II died. Not that the king and queen are centrally involved in the action. Rather, they maintain a shadow presence as the public origin or limit case
of a problem that is most fully explored within more private precincts. The
most remarkable feature of the Beau Wilson mystery in Manley's telling is that
"secrecy," detached from any secure and definitive grounding in the public or
the private, becomes something like a free-floating norm that has a life and purpose of its own.

Like Evelyn, Manley offers a set of hypotheses for Wilson's largely involuntary enrichment: he was supported by a wealthy lady; he had been vouchsafed
"*The Grand Secret*" of the philosopher's stone; he had robbed the Holland mail;
he was kept by "the *Jews*" (6). Unlike Evelyn, however, who does no more than
survey the field of public-sphere debate, Manley offers a solution to the mystery, although not in her own voice and framed by some misgivings. The sub-
heading for letter 1 reads, "Being a Discovery and Account of Beau Wilson's secret Support of his publick Manner of Living, and the Occasion of his Death,"
and it is narrated by a "man of quality" to a lady whom he addresses as "Madam." A "young Lady" of his acquaintance has brought to his attention the case
of "an elderly Gentlewoman" who shortly assumes the role of interpolated narrator (3).[57] The man of quality feels obliged to distance himself (as does Manley
herself) from this figure. "But before you imagine her the Speaker," he says, "allow me to say something by way of Introduction. . . . [Y]ou must do me the
favour to imagine you hear a malicious Person making [the following relation]
to me" (4, 7). The elderly gentlewoman's malice derives from the fact that she
"had been a Favorite (in a late Reign) of the then She-Favorite, but has since
been abandon'd by her . . . ." The great vice of the she-favorite, and the source
of her servant's bitter resentment, is the vice of ingratitude: "Once I was
belov'd, trusted and favour'd, or I had not been a manager of guilty Secrets. . . .
[I]f I had been base, 'twas more than once in my power to ruin her, this un-

grateful Lady! this Person accomplish'd in Ingratitude" (3; 7, font reversed). The narration of Manley's letter is therefore a formal enactment of the epistemo-ethical ambiguity of the sort of secret history that is told by one who was once secretary—"manager of guilty secrets"—to the great but now, galled by ingrati-tude, would make the private public. But as we will see, this is also what Man-ley's story is about.

One night, after her attendance "in the King's Closet," the she-favorite and her own favorite, the elderly gentlewoman, are strolling in Kensington Gardens when they come upon the melancholy and dejected figure of Beau Wilson, whose appearance irresistibly charms the she-favorite into "an Amour of Se-crecy." Taking coach for London, she charges her servant to "discover who he was." Acting as go-between, the gentlewoman facilitates an assignation that an-swers to all of her mistress's expectations. "She begg'd my Conduct and Secrecy in the management of an Affair upon which her Pleasure and her Interest (two considerable Points) depended. She said, she was resolv'd to shew what a For-tune it was to be her Favourite; . . . could he be but secret, (which she would not doubt) her Pride should be, to raise his Fortunes equal to his Merit" (7, 8, 11). Manley's heroine has something of the impetuous imperiousness of Defoe's Lady Credit.[58] Herself dependent (like most women) on a more powerful man, she nonetheless accrues to herself such power, such relative autonomy, that she can render men in turn her passive and effeminate favorites. In Wilson's case, however, one power remains in his possession, the power of sustaining a secret: "All you have to perform, on your part," says the gentlewoman, "is to reserve your self intirely for her, and never, by an indiscreet Curiosity, endeavour to dis-cover her"—that is, never, "like the *Psyche* in *Apuleius*," endeavor to discover who she is. So long as Wilson abides by this requirement—in effect, that he re-frain from becoming a living "key" to her identity—"you shall be the only Favourite" (12, 13, font reversed). If the gentlewoman feels compromised by the favoritism of this promise, she shows no sign of it. "Thus, for a long time, did our happy Lovers taste uninterruptedly the Sweets of Love" (13).

But Wilson's curiosity grows, and one night the she-favorite, frustrated at its persistence, asks the gentlewoman to meet Wilson "in my place" in order to re-inforce his agreement to secrecy. "I went accordingly, he took me for his Lady; tho' instead of being in Bed, I sat within the Curtains upon the Bed side . . ." (15). The gentlewoman's makeshift masquerade brings home to us the instabil-ity of not only (as in Behn's *Love-Letters*) the difference between political and amatory alliance but also that between the favorite and the favorer. Wilson ag-gravates this instability. Mistaking political imperative for Petrarchan love-play, he complains that the she-favorite must harbor a "vile distrust of my Hon-our . . . . Pray guess how obliging this must be to a Lover, who would die to serve, but never can deceive you." Beside herself with impatience, the gentle-woman drops her disguise and denounces Wilson as "Ungrateful!" and a "Fool and Traytor" both to his own fortune and to the contract he has made with her (16, font reversed). When the great lady hears of Wilson's response—and more, that by chance he has already discovered her identity—she agrees that the polit-ical language must be given a literal force: "[I]f this Discovery be made to oth-ers, I have Money, and Rage has industry, to find out needy Villains to dispatch the Traytor" (19).

Yet Wilson is not merely a love-besotted Petrarchan; he is a principled "lib-ertine" lover who believes his love lacks authenticity if not grounded in the free will, and hence the knowledge, of an ethical subjectivity that is incompatible with the passive archaism of a client's mere "gratitude" to his patron. And so he begs that he be permitted "to serve her out of Love, as before out of Grati-tude. . . . Can I be properly said to have a Passion for her whilst she was un-known? 'Tis only then since she was reveal'd to me, that mine can be call'd such . . . . I could not, with good Sense, pretend to love what I did not know; . . . Will she not have reason to be better satisfy'd with me, when my Heart, fil-l'd with her fair Image, has voluntary Fondness? When all my Transports are ex-cited by her Beauty, and that I consider nothing in the Possession of her, but her own Charms?" (17–18, font reversed). Through these last words Wilson also becomes intelligible to us as a "progressive" hero who rejects "public" in favor of "private" motives, external inducement in favor of internal merit, money and interest in favor of love.

On the evidence of this confrontation, we might find it plausible to see the mystery of Beau Wilson's status inconsistency as a consequence of the devolu-tion of absolutism, which relativizes the difference that separates each stage of the social and political hierarchy—or that divides the role of patron from that of client—to such a degree that gratitude, favoritism, and treachery cease to be definitive markers of status and place and become instead a sliding scale, a dif-ferential by which all in turn can be measured and held accountable. Everyone becomes a secretary, a keeper of secrets. The gentlewoman, a case in point, is a favorite of the great lady and also, with her, a favorer of Wilson (12), hence critical of the ingratitude and treachery both of her superordinate and of her subordinate rival, yet also capable of identifying with Wilson as favorite over against both their common favorer and their common rival favorite (soon to make his appearance). At this point in her narration, the scrupulous interpo-lated narrator admits that she is passing beyond her immediate knowledge of "matter of fact" and entering the realm of the "circumstantial" (20); the story it-self passes from the comic to the tragic.

The gentlewoman gathers that her mistress has "pick'd up a new Favorite," who receives a confidential charge—but "[t]his was a Secret which I was not to be let into" (20, 21). She and Wilson are now allied as former favorites. Soon after, the gentlewoman learns that Wilson has been killed in a duel, and she is astonished to find that his antagonist is the great lady's new favorite, a Mr. L——. Legally unpardonable, he is "miraculously" enabled to escape from prison lest on the gallows he "exclaim'd against the Ingratitude and Treachery of those who set him to work . . . ," and he is suddenly enriched (like Wilson before him) with "a Sum sufficient to arm him against Ingratitude" (23). "With me 'tis not so well," says the gentlewoman, who sees from Wilson's fate that "I must not let her [the great lady] know the discovery I had made; for such a dangerous Secret to one steep'd in Blood, would not have been long suffer'd to sleep in my Breast." On the other hand, "[a]ffairs have chang'd Faces; the King is dead, she no longer fears him; and concerning not her self for the discretional part, leaves me at liberty to say what I please . . . ." Now the gentlewoman's interpolated narrative ends, and the man of quality concludes his letter to the unknown lady by deferring to the judgment of his addressee on the story's credibility, in the process signaling his own place in the unmoored chain of patron and client, favorer and favorite: "I subscribe implicitly to your Opinion, as to the truth of it, and desire in the next that you will favour me with the knowledge of it" (23–24).

As for us—the last link in the chain—what have we learned from Manley's secret history? What secrets have been revealed? How is the she-favorite's morbid fear of disclosure, itself something of a mystery, clarified by our knowledge that it was the king alone whose knowledge of the Wilson alliance she dreaded? Most of all, is the affair of Beau Wilson and the she-favorite a private or a public matter? We know from Evelyn and other sources that the "late Reign" in which these events occurred is that of William and Mary, that the king who prohibited John Law's pardon because he "was always inexorable upon the account of Murder" is he whom many English people thought at the least "ungrateful" and perhaps a "traitor" for displacing James II (3, 23). Indeed, as we have seen, some thought the latter epithet particularly applicable to Mary, an Englishwoman who threw her lot in with her foreign husband rather than with her royal father. Is the great lady the she-favorite of Queen Mary? Why does Wilson rebuff the gentlewoman's demand that he cease his ingratitude and leave the country by declaring: "Never, Madam, . . . so long as our happy Monarch Reigns, and my Goddess possesses his Favour" (16). Is the great lady the she-favorite of the king himself? What is at stake in the secret of Wilson's history? What are we to make of the great lady's fantastic imagining, once convinced of the need to silence Wilson, that "I mean with my own Hands to taste the sweets of Murder and Revenge. Were I to meet with him in the King's

574 ❋ Secret Histories

Closet, on such an errand, it should be thus" (19)? What are we to make of her emphatic correlation of herself with the queen: "Is not the whole Nation upon Enquiry whence he derives his Fortune? Should they but think he knew me, 'twere all unravel'd; for who but the Queen and me could support a Favourite at such a shining height?" (19). What are we to make of the gentlewoman's starker assertion: "His expences were so vast, that, as the Town said, none but a Queen could support, without ruining her self; which . . . well deserves to be set down as a principal Article in the account of secret Service, &c." (13)? Is the she-favorite really Queen Mary?

These are questions of character motivation that the nature of Manley's narrative dictates must be answered by having recourse to the realm of actual particularity. And the most plausible solution to the mystery of the she-favorite/great lady's identity is that she is Elizabeth Villiers, in 1694 William's only courtesan in a sea of eager homosocial courtiers.[59] This solution is compatible with the highly suggestive innuendos cited in the previous paragraph (which also seem to imply other solutions than this one), and yet it feels almost beside the point. For the effect of those innuendos is not really to confirm any of our suspicions about the actual particularity—the identity—of the she-favorite but to suffuse with the spice of public (even royal) scandal our efforts to know her secret, enhancing our consumption of the story with the exotic yet familiar flavor of *scandalum magnatum*. Not only Beau Wilson but the elderly gentlewoman, the man of quality, even Manley herself, possess the key to this potential *roman à clef*; but the cabinet never quite gets opened. We may understand this as Manley's strategy to titillate her common readers with the affairs of quality; but it may also make sense to see her as engaged in an experimental effort to accommodate to the everyday life of common people a taste of what traditionally pertained only to their betters. In the emergent novel, the public rise and fall of princes is both superseded and extended by the closet drama of social mobility. Ingratitude toward one's subordinates, an early symptom in the centuries-long decay of "feudal" reciprocity, in Manley's story is already a status-neutral vice of which everyone is capable, a failing not of social rank but of subjective "character." And if the proliferation of favorites, ungratefuls, and traitors undermines our confidence that we can discover the objective identity of any of these "public" figures, we are thereby enabled to move more easily between them in an ongoing process of subjective identification.

But the argument can be overstated. In its broadest outlines, Manley's solution of the mystery of Beau Wilson's upward mobility manifestly accords with a "traditional" view both of how to read and of how things happen in the world. Sociopolitical agency lies with the status elite: whether benevolent or corrupt, "public" or "private," the secret cause of change at the lower levels of existence is to be found in the motives of the great, which hold the public key to the meaning of private events. Even the apparently anomalous can be reconciled with this view of things. What looks like a transgressive gender reversal—the aristocratic rake as woman, the subjected and seduced as beautiful male "beau"—is consistent with the traditional lability of gender categories, which at least appear to conform to social, political, and legal dispensation.[60] In fact, it is only against this stable ground of status hierarchy that the authenticity of Beau Wilson's voluntarism, his ethical subjectivity, can be thrown fitfully into relief. And if the gender reversal exposes Manley's hero to an emergent model of female virtue, it does not compromise his masculinity.

The Sodomitical Wilson

Seventeen years after the publication of the *Lady's Pacquet of Letters* and twenty-nine years after the events it seeks to explain, there appeared an extraordinary reinterpretation of the Beau Wilson affair that also took the form of an anonymous epistolary packet: *Love-Letters Between a certain late Nobleman And the famous Mr. Wilson: Discovering The true History of the Rise and surprising Grandeur of that celebrated Beau* (1723). What is immediately noticeable about the title of this tract in the present context is that it seems to allude to Behn's *Love-Letters* and thereby to invoke that by-now famous *roman à clef* (along with the *Lady's Pacquet*) as an intertextual foil.[61] Unlike that of its two predecessors, the anonymity of these *Love-Letters* has not been definitively deciphered.[62] Also unlike those tracts, this one concludes the twenty, highly circumstantial and elliptical letters that narrate the Wilson affair with "Observations on the Foregoing Letters" that clarify them to such a degree as to constitute something like their mandatory key.

The "Preface" to the letters, besides suggesting that a "Key" in the more usual sense of the term may be published in due course, briefly engages the reader's questions as to "Whether the Facts are true, and the Letters genuine." The "editor" alludes here to the familiar hearsay about the source of Wilson's riches (later summarized as "French Money, the Jew's Jewels, Mistresses; or else, a Contract with the Devil") before commending to us the "Probability" of this "true History," whose "Originals were found in the Cabinet of the Deceas'd, which had pass'd thro' some Hands, before the private Drawer, the Lodgment of this Scene of Guilt, was discover'd." And the scandalous fact at the center of this revelation and documented in detail by the letters is that Manley's narration gets it both right and wrong: Wilson was indeed raised and supported by an aristocratic rake, but that rake was a man, not a woman.[63] The hearsay "Conjectures" that have been "publish'd from Mouth to Mouth" thus far are now superseded by a definitive typographical "Publication" that (in well-chosen words) "sets the Matter quite upon another Bottom," and the editor, abhorring "the Scandal of the Vice here described thro the Course of these Papers," suggests we pursue an ingenious policy in reading them: "It is easy enough to take away all Offence of this Kind, by applying the Passion of these Letters to distinct Sexes, which we desire the Reader to do, and then he'll be a better Judge of the Spirit of the Writer. All the Weeds will then vanish, or be turn'd into Flowers, and in that View let them be seen" (13, 14). Such is the scandal of sodomy, in other words, that its *arcana* must be reencrypted even in the process of their disclosure. If the secret history of the Wilson affair is one of sodomitical behavior, for the sake of morality this intimate signified must be domesticated in turn as the signifier of an alternative and less scandalous signified, illicit love between the sexes. Same-sex sodomy must serve as an allegory for different-sex fornication—at the reader's discretion.[64]

The virtuosity with which the anonymous *Love-Letters* parodies Behn's *Love-Letters*—and to a lesser degree Manley's *Lady's Pacquet*—is remarkable. In Behn's text same-sex love is at least countenanced through Octavio's and Alonzo's misapprehensions of the cross-dressed Silvia, supplementing different-sex love in its representation of an intimately private realm whose ultimate difference from the public realm of war and politics Behn even so keeps in constant dispute. The later *Love-Letters* begins in the same vein. Although the correspondence opens obscurely *in medias res* (as the editor's "Observations" point out), there is enough here to suggest that Wilson has misconstrued the amatory Petrarchan conceits of the nobleman's missing first letter as a literal "Challenge" to "Combat" (35, 15). Indeed, in this respect Wilson resembles not only Silvia's suitors but even more Manley's Wilson in misreading, not the clothing, but the language of the other: thus he remarks that at first he could not tell if "Love or Rage had dictated those ambiguous Phrases, which lay liable to variety of Constructions . . . ." Now realizing that it is love, not war, that is on the mind of his noble correspondent, Wilson (inadvertently taking his editor's advice to read allegorically) nonetheless mistakes a man for a woman: "For tho' I'm not afraid to meet a brave Man's Sword, the Indearments of a fine Lady are infinitely preferable" (16).

Quickly disabused of this error as well, Wilson happily succumbs to the nobleman in the "Crime you . . . descended to encourage me in," then joins him in planning how to enjoy their aberrant love—not affinal incest but sodomy—while keeping it secret, not an easy task since others are plotting to disclose the source of Wilson's sudden wealth (26). So at the playhouse, Wilson writes, "sometime to disguise my secret Affection, I survey Beauty with as much seeming Delight as other Men . . ."; alternatively he is advised by the nobleman to cross-dress when attending their "private Meetings" (24, 20). But as this very letter informs us, the appearance of different-sex love can be unlocked by the key of same-sex love. In effect, Behn's private realm of amatory intimacy is definitively subdivided into its public and private components: different-sex love comes to stand in relation to same-sex love as public surface does to private substance. It is as though Alonzo's sexuality as we supposed it to be, expressive of an incipiently modernizing tendency to ground gender in biological sex, has now been generalized to English culture at large. The division of gender that results from this grounding—the modern separation out of masculinity from femininity—already legible in Behn as the separation of publicity from privacy, is now mirrored in an analogous division of "sexuality," the mutual exclusion of different-sex and same-sex love.

This becomes clear in the elaborately allusive "Counter-Plot[s]" that Wilson and the nobleman engineer to frustrate the plots of those who would discover the secret of Wilson's social elevation (40). The atmosphere of imperiled privacy and secrecy that pervades Behn's *Love-Letters* is sustained in great part by its dominating action: bodies moving furtively from one interior space to another, in flight from, or in disguise to evade recognition by, other bodies in hot pursuit. The brief section of the anonymous *Love-Letters* that pointedly recalls this action heightens the effect by slyly insinuating a bodily significance for the unaccustomed "back" openings of architectural spaces. Thus Wilson employs "a back Passage to the House": he "went in the Street Way, as usual," and soon after there appears "a Chair at the Back Door, which was immediately fill'd by one in the Habit of a Lady" who later is seen to "return to the Back Door, and shortly after, Wilson went out at the Street Door directly Home" (37). Knowing he is being observed, the cross-dressed Wilson arranges to be seen another evening entering the apartment, not of the nobleman, but of his French steward next door, and he encourages the suspicion that "it could not be my Lord that Wilson came to, he being at that Time out of Town; that perhaps the Steward might not be so great an Enemy to the French Interest as he pretended . . . ." The nobleman, pretending to participate in the plan to catch Wilson engaging in (not illicit sex but) treasonous politics ("I shall be the activest in this Farce," he warns his beloved, "and, perhaps, rudely press for the Secret: Be wary . . ."), surprises Wilson with the steward's daughter and exclaims: "I perceive this is only a Plot on the French Petticoat . . . ," then ridicules "the Pains they had all taken about such a Trifling Intrigue" (18, 39–40).

The episode closely parodies the contest between Octavio and Brilljard to impose their respective readings of Octavio's affair with the cross-dressed Silvia on his uncle Sebastian—but with significant differences. For in Behn's *Love-Letters* the farcical encounter asks a serious question about the political implications of private behavior (in this case, the familial "treason" of bigamous adultery), whereas in the anonymous *Love-Letters* the farce is itself an answer, a confident and carefully staged ploy to mislead Wilson's pursuers regarding the nature of his private activity. As the editor remarks, "this Management may convince the World that his Lordship was no less a Politician in his private Affairs, than he was in the Publick . . ." (36). The structure of the misunderstandings is the same, but in the later text the implication of state politics is no more than a temporary gambit to divert potential suspicion of sodomy toward suspicion of treason, then to dispel both by revealing treason to be only fornication. As in Behn's narrative, illicit sexual activity mediates here between the public and the private registers; but whereas in Behn the familial treason of fornication is dangerous as it participates in either realm, here it stands for the relatively safe and socially normative, hence "public," value of different-sex activity over against the dangerous public activity of treason. Sodomy, absorbing the intimate secrecy of both *arcana imperii* and *arcana amoris,* becomes the limit case of aberrant privacy. At the same time, however, in the allegorical structure of signification that the tract parodically takes over from the form of the secret history, sodomy also occupies the privileged place of the "public" signified, the semantic referent and "true meaning" of different-sex fornication.

As we have already seen, the anonymous *Love-Letters* is also aware of, and allusive to, the version of the Wilson affair contained in Manley's tract. As Wilson tells the nobleman, the main prosecutor of the plots aiming to make his private support public is "a certain GREAT LADY who knows all her Actions are back'd by a superiour Power . . . ." Our editor informs us that this is none other than "Mrs. V.——l——s" and that her plots are motivated partly by "that Curiosity, natural to her Sex," and partly by her desire to quash rumors that she "was the Person who had thus rais'd" Wilson, since "if such a Report spread, it might Occasion a Difference between her and the Power who supported her . . ."—that is, the king (20, 36; cf. the innuendo of 18). Elizabeth Villiers is aided in these intrigues by one whom the editor calls Johnasco and whom we may recognize as John Law, who in this version of the story is hired by Villiers to entrap Wilson but is persuaded by him to turn counterplotter against Villiers with him and the nobleman (37–39). Thus, what is in Manley the dark secret whose threatened revelation occasions Wilson's murder becomes here the erroneous rumor that facilitates Wilson's concealment of his darker secret. True, the last letter in the series is from Wilson "To Mr. L——," graciously negating Law's apparent belief (his letter is absent) that Wilson has expressed "Dishonour to your Family . . ." (34). But the duel itself is never directly mentioned, except insofar as Wilson's initial misreading of the nobleman's figurative conceits amounts to a parodic and proleptic anticipation of it.[65] The diatribe against ingratitude, the web of favoritism, and the problem of the decay of hierarchy that so preoccupy Manley are for the most part replaced here by the satisfactions of watching the two lovers prosecute their private "unruly Passion" (as the nobleman calls it) with public impunity (22). Indeed, crucial to the parody of Manley's version is this implicit correction of the counterintuitive notion that in the hotbed of homoerotic indulgence for which William's court was notorious, Wilson should have owed his social elevation to different-sex intrigue.[66]

It would be a mistake, however, to say that Manley's "social" concerns are here simply demystified as, replaced by, or domesticated into "sexual" ones. For one thing, Manley herself solves the mystery of Wilson's social rise by attributing it to an enabling sexual liaison. For another, the anonymous *Love-Letters* has its own social preoccupations. The sodomitical relationship is structured in traditional terms, along social and generational lines, as one between the aristocratic and courtly libertine seducer and the young commoner. As the editor observes, the nobleman's letters make their own stylistic claim to historicity, being "too polite and written with an Air too peculiar not to be distinguished from the Productions of a feigned Intrigue. The Thing Speaks itself, and any one, without Preface or Commentary, might easily see by the naked Letters, that they could not come from any Person, but one of Birth, and Figure, and many other Court like Accomplishments" (13–14). Indeed, the editor may seem here to protest too much the self-evidence of first-person style even in the absence of third-person commentary of the sort he provides. For in his later "Observations" he remarks on how, by the evidence of Wilson's letters, "especially by Letter IX, he seems to be perfectly skill'd in the Art of Insinuation; whether inspir'd by my Lord's excellent Genius, or his Gold, I will not pretend to determine . . ."; and the letter in question does sound prodigious (40, 23). Can Wilson put on the style of an aristocrat as he puts on female dress? The question raised, in other words, is not only, Does first-person voice speak itself? nor only, What is the relationship between writing and clothing style? but also, What is the relationship between altering one's social status and altering one's gender?

By tradition, the biological grounding of social status in family lineage made social mobility hard to conceive except as a species of fraud, whereas the ease of gender mobility was licensed by a cultural willingness to overlook the available evidence for a biological grounding of "sexual difference." How does the anonymous *Love-Letters* extend the modernizing experimentation with these categories already evident in Behn's *Love-Letters*—even by allusion to that precedent text? In one letter, Wilson tells the nobleman that walking in the Mall the day before, he had found a packet of "six and thirty Letters from a very great Man to a Lady, who must have dropt it just then . . . ," a packet that also contains "an Order for fifty Pounds, payable to the Bearer . . ." (28). Wilson seizes this opportunity to flatter his lover through the unequal comparison between the "low and wrangling" "Spirit" of these found epistles and the "infinitely more Force" apparent "to those who have the Honour to have a frequent Correspondence with your Lordship" (28). The insinuation is complicated even if we resist the temptation to read this as the author's raillery against Behn's efforts, in Philander's letters to Silvia, to imitate the libertine style. In that case, the author may be heard to reflect on Behn's stylistic failures not only as a commoner but also as a woman. And in any case, the issue of sex as well as status may appear to be raised by the suggestive language of "frequent Correspondence." Is the contrast one between not only epistolary but also sexual styles, between the mercenary lowness of different-sex affairs and the loftiness of same-sex love?

The pattern for such a contrast had already been established in the Earl of Rochester's song "Love to a Woman" which sustains the traditional paradigm of the aristocratic rake whose normative masculinity entails sex with both women and boys even as its misogyny hints at the separation out of a dutiful and incompetent different-sex pragmatism from the easy and careless raptures of same-sex sodomy.[67] The nobleman's misogyny in the anonymous *Love-Letters* depends heavily on the contrast between his own amatory idealism and the materialistic values of "those abject Wretches" for whom love is a "Trade," "the low Subtilties of the inferiour Sex, who, to enhance their Price, play at fast and loose . . ." (29, 22). Part of Behn's purpose in her *Love-Letters,* we surmised, was to discredit the supposed radical egalitarianism of a Petrarchan libertine like Philander as at bottom no better than the misogyny of a patriarchal tyrant like Sebastian, a purpose that was consistent not only with Behn's royalist politics but also with her protofeminist discrimination between male and female entitlements. The purpose of the anonymous *Love- Letters,* we might infer, is to exploit this emergent polarization of gender difference by extending its terms in the direction of sexual difference, simultaneously affirming and superseding the increasingly explicit dichotomization of man and woman through a historically unprecedented dichotomization of different-sex and same-sex activity—what modernity would learn to call "heterosexuality" and "homosexuality."

The importance of misogyny in facilitating this separation out of the two "sexualities" lies in its crude but effective ability to clear a space between a man's love for a woman and a man's love for another man. In reality, male sodomites were arguably no more likely than different-sex lovers to be misogynist; but extreme hatred of women helped distinguish the phenomenon of sodomy at a time when cultural construal was increasingly inclined to see it as constitutionally exclusive of sexual desire for women. The definitive separation out of the genders, once set in motion, could be rationalized persuasively by reference to empirical biological difference. No such "natural" basis was available for authorizing the separation out of the sexualities, and cultural discourse was obliged, at least for a time, to rely on the seeming psychologic whereby a passive lack of desire entailed an active motive of disgust. (This process was reinforced by the contemporary development of related cultural assumptions, like the narrowing of the term "effeminate" to refer not to both sodomitical transvestites and men who are sexually obsessed with women but to the former alone, as though a single term could not comprehend such mutual exclusion.)[68]

From the perspective of an emergent normative "heterosexual" culture, misogyny was a vice fully compatible with the "unreproductive" degeneracy of the sodomite, which led contemporaries to dovetail the critique of sodomy with the critique of aristocracy—the latter when viewed as a corrupted social group whose effete enervation and genealogical failures also bespoke a fatal unreproductivity.[69] In the correspondence between Wilson and his nobleman, by contrast, the commoner's social rise is implicitly and positively colored by a sense of his "sexual" rise to the clandestine but transcendent status of exclusive sodomite. "No, my Lord," writes Wilson, renouncing the love of women, "the Greatness of my Passion created and inspired by you, has disdained to share a Pleasure with that base, low, dull, insinuating Sex; let not one of them presume to hope the least Thought, in your exalted Mind, or noble Appetites, and condemn the ideal medling insipid World . . ." (26). The nobleman replies that sex with a woman is "a Trifle I despise" (27). Hitherto we have understood the strategic use of the language of the base, low, and trifling to underscore a powerful revaluation of private and diurnal experience: what traditionally has served only to signify something higher than itself begins now to assume the status of a self-subsistent signified. The misogyny of the anonymous *Love-Letters* revalues this revaluation: now the privacy of different-sex love is truly base in comparison with what it can do no more than signify, the "exalted" and more profoundly intimate love between men. Now different-sex love does the work of representing shallow worldliness, as in Philander's libertinism public norms and ends had done.

The vision is one of a pure and private love uncorrupted by the materialism of reproduction and its mundane monetary imperatives, hence linked in this valorized fashion to the epistemological "disinterestedness" that some were attributing to gentility and nobility.[70] In this way, the anonymous *Love-Letters* uses the languages of social and sexual categorization to illuminate each other, the social serving to figure forth a relatively autonomized sense of "sexual identity" not yet available in its own terms and the sexual providing for the solution of Wilson's status inconsistency a categorial lability not yet available (as it would be, through the modern language of class) for the description of mobility in social relations.

The sodomitical solution to the problem of status inconsistency—the radical privacy entailed in the sodomites' exemption from all reproductive and conjugal materialism—could lay forceful claim to being the purest negation of the discredited tyranny of forced marriage based on money and interest because it entailed a quintessentially negative liberty, private love liberated altogether from the marriage institution itself. In this respect, the nonreproductive purity of Wilson and the nobleman's sodomy is analogous to that of Silvia and Philander's incest. But this was not, of course, the solution that was in the process of being embraced by a normative heterosexual culture. From that viewpoint, the emergent paradigm of private life was instead rooted in a criterion of inner merit, the virtue of conscientious discipline that by its nature cut across the old status lines, justifying social mobility but also positing women as virtue's natural possessors, and that found its fulfillment in marriage for love and in the production and reproduction of the domestic family.⁷¹ And because it is not Wilson and the nobleman, but the editor, who has the last word in the anonymous *Love-Letters,* we end the tract with something more ambiguous than their utopian version of sodomitical society.

More abruptly than Behn's, the anonymous *Love-Letters* also moves from an epistolary first-person to a third-person narration. And like that earlier differential, this one has the effect of clarifying and "making public" what was obscure when the reader had only the characters' own voices as a source of knowledge about them. Indeed, the effect is a good deal more revelatory here than in Behn's narrative. This is not only because our editor provides one important *clef* to the *roman* in the classic sense of identifying the actual particularity of the great lady (if not also of the nobleman himself). As his preface emphasizes, the editor now makes typographically public what had been a singularly intimate scribal correspondence, and much of his work consists simply in rendering the text intelligible to us by providing the context needed to make sense of the sometimes paratactic, sometimes proleptic concision of the letters.

But the differential between first- and third-person narration also expresses the distance between an obscure and esoteric subculture and an explicitating effort to accommodate it to the knowledge of the dominant culture, to bring it into the light of day. Like other secretive subcultures I have touched on in this study—trade guilds, masons, conscientious Protestants, Newgate criminals, ladies' dressing rooms, Pepys's diary, Swift's journal to Stella—the sodomitical subculture of "mollies" that coalesced in London at the end of the seventeenth century and the beginning of the eighteenth had its own cant language that bespoke both its radical difference from and its obliquely parodic similarity to what its own existence helped constitute as normative culture.⁷² A sense of this is well conveyed by a tract of 1691:

Now wait on *Beau* to his *Alsatia,*
A Place that loves no *Dei Gratia;*
Where the Undoers live, and Undone,
In *London* separate from *London;*
Where go but Three Yards from the street,
And you with a new Language meet:
Prig, Prigster, Bubble, Caravan,
Pure Tackle, Buttock, Purest Pure. . . .[73]

The uncanny quality of the correspondence between Wilson and the nobleman owes less to their use of special diction like this, however, and more to the way recognizable attitudes of sexual intimacy are defamiliarized through their self-consciously perverse refinement and application to same-sex relationships. Sodomy's parodic reflection on different-sex culture, which generally evinces all the ambivalence of mock-heroic form, becomes darkly parasitic when, at the end of his "Observations," the editor tells the story, not of Wilson's murder at the hands of John Law, but of the nobleman's victimization of a country girl named Cloris.[74] The connection is not arbitrary: Cloris is first referred to when Wilson reproaches the nobleman for being seen in the company of "a new favourite Mistress," paralleling the entrance of Law as the great lady's "new Favorite" in Manley's *Lady's Pacquet* (20) and suggesting that Cloris has a comparable narrative function in the anonymous *Love-Letters*. In the correspondence itself the nobleman quickly dispels Wilson's fears of "that changeling Sex": "[I]t's true, I had her dirty Maidenhead," but only to shore up his reputation as a ladies' man (24–25). The details supplied by the third-person overview, a complete and self-contained four-page narrative, are more damning.

Cloris has come to town at the request of her parents "that she might have the Advantage of a genteeler Education than the Country could afford . . . ." At the same time, her guardian "took Care to instill into her the Principles of Modesty and Vertue, as the surest Guards against the too frequent Temptations of Men." Cloris and the nobleman, a frequent visitor at her guardian's, soon develop a mutual enmity, and he decides to seduce her on a bet that women are so naturally vicious that they can be corrupted even under the least promising of conditions (41). He quickly succeeds and resolves "to keep Cloris in so grand a Way, as might make the loss of her Reputation the more remarkable . . . ." But the nobleman soon tires of the charade and drops her: "All the delightful Idea's she had form'd of her future Grandeur, and the splendid Way of Living she was just arrived at, were now changed to the dreadful Apprehensions of future Shame and Wants . . ." (42). Not only Law, apparently, but also Wilson himself—both Manley's version of him and this one—is a foil for Cloris, who falls from her sudden height not through the external agency of a fatal challenge but because of the misogynist cruelty of her seducer. Now pregnant by him, Cloris gains access to the nobleman as Wilson does, by cross-dressing, and she confronts him with his perfidy in "basely deluding her from her Parents and Family, destroying her Virtue and Reputation"—and, when that confrontation fails, with a pistol. "[P]retending to take him for a Bully (tho' her Voice, Discourse, and effeminate Fears must needs discover her to him)," the nobleman beats the cross-dressed Cloris so savagely that after three or four days "she was deliver'd of a dead Child, two Months before its Time, and immediately expir'd." "This barbarous Usage to a Woman," says the editor, "and with Child by himself, plainly shews what a Hatred he had to the whole Sex; for no Man that was not given to the most abandon'd Vices could treat them whose tender Delicacy courts and invites our Protection, with such unheard of Cruelty" (43–44). By the tract's ethos, the nobleman's actions display the extreme misogyny of the sodomite, who hates not simply women but reproduction as such, even his own.

This shocking episode, which brings the anonymous *Love-Letters* to an abrupt close, must be read against both accounts of Wilson's rise, not only Manley's but also the first-person account that just precedes the Cloris episode here. And in the latter regard, it is as though the "key" function of the third-person "Observations" now modulates from providing circumstantial context for the story to offering an altogether new story in its place. Indeed, it is as though the editor were following his own advice to "take away all Offence of this Kind, by applying the Passion of these Letters to distinct Sexes . . ." (14). Does it make sense to see the third-person, different-sex Cloris plot as a domestication of the first-person, same-sex Wilson plot? In place of the utopian fable of same-sex love secretly enjoyed under the very noses of authority the editor propounds a fable, no less utopian for being tragic, of female virtue seduced and abandoned by aristocratic libertinism. In the process, the mystery of unexplained upward mobility, which is the primary motivation for the Wilson plot, becomes a secondary feature of the Cloris plot, still present as a fact but no longer mysterious because implicitly explained by the seduction plot of which it forms one episode in a greater telos. Yet in making this substitution of one story for another, the editor only extends the labor of formal domestication that is already at work in the first-person narration that his discourse frames. As Manley's tragic tale of corruption in high places is domesticated by the epistolary correspondence into a comic tale of private and illicit pleasures invisible even to the elite, so that correspondence itself is domesticated into a tragic tale of (failed) domesticity. By this reading, the expansion of the first- to a third-person perspective permits a far more fundamental remoralization than that achieved in Behn's *Love-Letters,* yet one that leaves the most abstract moral—the formal principle of seeking legibility in the local and the trifling—intact.

Now, if it is just to say that the tale of Cloris rewrites the tale of Wilson by domesticating its same-sex secrecy as different-sex domesticity, we cannot forget the lesson taught by much of the preceding argument in this study: that domesticity is itself the product of a traditional mode of domestication that uses the familiarity of private affairs to accommodate the elevated realm of public politics. In chapter 6 I suggested that at the turn of the eighteenth century the moral abomination of sodomy may have held for contemporaries the more specifically sociopolitical aura of pederasty, a practice of courtly absolutism whose taken-for-granted subjection of client to patron was increasingly susceptible to explicitation and critique as, like commercial protectionism and legally enforced religious conformity, a state infringement on the rights and liberties of ethical subjects. This hypothesis drew a guarded measure of support from a view of *Sodom and Gomorah* (c. 1673–78) that read its powerful analogy between the indulgence of popery and the indulgence of pederasty as conducive to the moral that different-sex behavior and its "Propogable end" are in tune with natural-rights theory and the liberty of the subject.[75] Can the domestication of Wilson's by Cloris's story be seen in a similar light?

Sodom and Gomorah is so centered in the royal court that we are obliged to read the general practice of male sodomy as the particular practice of pederasty. This is clearly not true fifty years later. The anonymous *Love-Letters* dates from the period that succeeds both 1688 and 1714, when royal absolutism was permanently ejected from the body politic and political patronage was learning to operate more on the basis of financial corruption than on the basis of bodily exploitation. It also dates from the period when the sodomitical subculture of the molly had become explicit enough to inaugurate the long process whereby sodomy was transformed from a traditional sociopolitical practice in which all men might engage into a modern state of being, personhood, and identity. Not that the aura of pederasty is entirely absent from the anonymous *Love-Letters.* His very writing style shows the nobleman to be a man of "Birth, and Figure, and many other Court like Accomplishments," and Wilson himself seems to have learned enough of that skill to make him a likely pederastic acolyte (14, 23, 40). That Wilson has been "raised" prodigiously is of course the very premise of the mystery that occasions these several tracts about him, although the revelation that he has been favored by the nobleman is colored more by the spectacle of Wilson's upward mobility in the world than by that of his preferment within the hierarchy of the royal court. Still, when he accuses Wilson of allowing another man to kiss him, the nobleman briefly indulges the language of the sub-

ordinate's "black Ingratitude," characteristic of the old regime and its deep regard for personal obligation (29). And Wilson reminds his aristocratic lover
that if his "Crime" of sodomy betrays his "Spirit of Ambition," "it is a Crime
you first descended to encourage me in" (26).

Beyond this, however, evidence for a specifically political and pederastic relationship between Wilson and the nobleman is hard to find. The admittedly
active theme of being preferred over others is not political and pederastic but
gendered and relentlessly misogynist: Wilson's same-sex affair is in competition,
not with the affairs of other male courtiers, but with the very model of different-sex love, and to this extent it is less exemplary than fully parodic of pederasty and its sociopolitically embedded, purely instrumental and opportunistic
vision of same-sex love. As in relation to pederasty, to say that the anonymous
Love-Letters parodies Behn's *Love-Letters* is to recall the truth that parody is both
imitative and critical. Like the emergent molly culture with which it is contemporary, the anonymous *Love-Letters* is generated by a creatively oblique mim-
icry of the emergent culture and socioliterary conventionality of gender difference. Moreover, as the anonymous story of Wilson intertextually parodies and
revises the different-sex stories of both Manley and Behn, so in intratextual
terms the story of Cloris parodies and revises the Wilson story in the process of
adumbrating emergent domestic narrative. "[P]oor Cloris," possessed of "a
lively Vivacity in her Looks" but also "some awkward Country Airs," is sent to
London "to instill into her the Principles of Modesty and Vertue, as the surest
Guards against the too frequent Temptations of Men" (41). In his seduction of
Cloris the nobleman is the very type of the patriarchal tyrant, a composite of
the father and the husband guilty of "deluding her from her Parents and Family, destroying her Virtue and Reputation . . ." (43).[76] What I have called the
"failed domesticity" of the Cloris story is better seen as that subspecies of domestic narrative in which tragic failure provides the most exquisite closure and
of which we need seek, for an example, no further than Richardson's *Clarissa*
(1747–48).

However, the fable of female virtue cannot easily stand as a corrective domestication of the same-sex fable in the way I have suggested. For one thing,
the heroine's modesty and virtue are questionable from the start: it is her "Tart-
ness" and inclination to "ill-natur'd Satire" that draw the nobleman's wrath in
the first place (41). More important, the two fables resist this kind of structural
analogy because they are inseparably connected by the figure of the nobleman,
whose brutality toward Cloris and his unborn child the editor insists is a function of his sodomy. To read the second story as a more legible version of the
first—to imagine Cloris's nobleman as a "heterosexual" analogue to Wilson's
"homosexual" nobleman, his private character thrown thereby into more illu-

minating public relief—accords with the editor's advice on how to read the "Scandal" of this "Publication" without "Offence," but only at the expense of his advice about how to read the hitherto hidden "Probability" of this "true History" (14, 13). In the end it may be useful to think of the "mystery" that the anonymous *Love-Letters* sets out to unravel as just this: Are same-sex love and different-sex love similar or different; distinct or separate; parts of the same "private" whole or respectively "private" and "public" wholes unto themselves? However we answer this question, there is no doubt that the anonymous *Love-Letters* plays a significant role in the complicated negotiation of public-private relations from which domesticity emerges as a cultural institution. Publicity is to domesticity as domesticity is to sodomy. Along with other species of illicit and unproductive sex—fornication, adultery, masturbation, prostitution— sodomy defines that realm of intimacy which is yet more private than domesticity itself, the realm of excess that makes domestic privacy normative.

A shrewdly sardonic parody, the anonymous *Love-Letters* equally balances a painstaking attention to imitative form and the cool detachment of critique. Its brilliance, like Behn's, is that of a late and highly reflexive stage of domestication. The aim of this chapter has been to attend to one important dimension of the passage from domestication to domesticity: the privatization of the secret history. The revelatory significance of private lives, writers find, may lie not so much in the public weight of the subject as in the rich domain of privacy itself, which under the microscope of the secret history is seen to enclose its own deeper and quite unsuspected secret, a swarming universe of public-private relations. The passage from domestication to domesticity, clearly a gravitation from the elevated to the everyday—from one sort of content to another—is also, in secret histories that are also *romans à clef,* a gravitation from form to content. That is, the intricate superstructure of allegorical signification, once mandated by hermeneutic and pedagogic imperatives, comes to feel superfluous, even counterproductive. In the two *Love-Letters* that superstructure is so relativized by multiple and inconsistent applications that it often seems a metaphorical strategy within the realm of the private rather than a means of getting from that realm to one of higher semantic status. In this respect the final stage of domestication, its replacement by domesticity, is the obviation of allegory through its internalization.

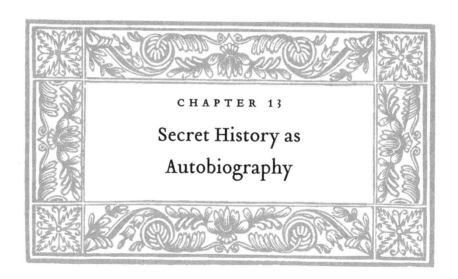

CHAPTER 13

Secret History as
Autobiography

Preface on Congreve

What is the relationship between a secret history and (as the anonymous *Love-Letters* calls itself) a "true history"? I have argued elsewhere that the latter term is a crucial category in the emergence of an empiricist approach to novelistic epistemology.[1] Although the epistemological burden of the secret history is also considerable given its ambition to disclose what hitherto has been hidden from view, it may make sense to see its truth-telling aim as less pure and unmediated than that of the true history, partly because it so often bears an admixture of so-ciopolitical retribution and partly because its avenue to the truth so often is the self-consciously elliptical path of allegorical signification. Especially early on, the novelistic "true history" entails a claim to historicity whose import is not only the actual particularity of its characters—their real existence—but also an unmediated narrative access to them. The political allegory of the *roman à clef* operates on very different assumptions. And of course its characters are under-stood to be not only actual but also of public import.

But it would be a mistake to impose an abstract principle of mutual exclu-sion on the complex practice of contemporary narrative. A case in point is William Congreve's *Incognita; or, Love and Duty Reconcil'd. A Novel* (1692). Like Behn's Incognito, Congreve's Incognita is a beautiful woman disguised, at one point, as a man. Like Behn's narrative, Congreve's is a highly reflexive story in which disguise on the level of content is mirrored by a self-conscious acknowl-edgment of formal masquerade. And like the plot of *Love-Letters*, *Incognita*'s plot is preoccupied with the conflict between parental "tyranny" and the "free-dom of choice" of young lovers, that is, between the "duty" and "love" of the subtitle. But Congreve gives no sign of writing a political allegory; the closest he comes to suggesting that his Italianate romance setting may have an English referent is to stress the implacability of the Italian revenge code by remarking that it "descend[s] lineally like an English estate, to all the heirs male of [the] family." The mystique of Congreve's formal masquerade is generated, not by the implication that he has written a *roman à clef*, but by his unflagging skepticism about the plausibility of his fiction and the credulity of those who take it too seriously, whether characters or readers. Where Behn encourages the idea that lovers and readers internalize a capacity for ethical identification, Congreve concludes an account of his hero's fantastic description of his beloved by saying of it that "none but lovers who have experience of such visions will believe." Taken in the context of Behn's *Love-Letters, Incognita* reads like a genial satire— in the tradition of the Continental antiromance and, later, of Fielding's narratives—both of the naive claim to "true history" and of the more esoteric sort of historicity that was characteristic of the *roman à clef* and that Behn was in her own way also superseding.²

One year after Congreve's death, however, *Incognita* was reprinted with the following domesticating caveat: "Tho' the Scene of the foregoing Novel be laid in *Italy*, every Incident was transacted in *England*. But as some of the Persons are dead, and others living, yet 'till they are all gather'd to their Fathers, I dare not presume to decypher any one Character especially since some Folks . . . threaten to prosecute us *to the Extent of their Fortunes, and the Hazard of our own Lives* . . . ."³ The status of this posthumous claim is hard to assess. Still, the epilogue to *The Way of the World* (1700) provides evidence of Congreve's position on a related issue, the relative merits of libel and satire, actual and concrete particularity:

> Others there are whose Malice we'd prevent;
> Such, who watch Plays, with scurrilous intent
> To mark out who by *Characters* are meant.
> And tho' no perfect likeness they can Trace;
> Yet each pretends to know the *Copy'd Face*.
> These with false Glosses, feed their own Ill-nature,
> And turn to *Libel*, what was meant a *Satire*.
> May such malicious *Fops* this Fortune find,
> To think themselves alone the *Fools* design'd . . . .⁴

Manley's *New Atalantis*

When she published her letter on the Beau Wilson affair, Delarivier Manley was in the process of establishing herself as the most notorious and scandalous English practitioner of the *roman à clef*. One of the ways Manley put her mark on that form was by accentuating more than others had done the fictionality of the "romance" level of the narrative, thereby insinuating its merely signifying status, even the logic that a sober truth therefore must lie beyond it. This can be seen even on the title page of her first great success, *The Secret History of Queen Zarah, and the Zarazians; being a Looking-glass for —— In the Kingdom of Albigion. Faithfully Translated from the Italian Copy now lodg'd in the Vatican at Rome, and never before Printed in any Language*, where the title is followed by "(Albigion, Printed in the Year 1705)." Both the figure of the looking glass and the claim to being a domestication from a foreign language look back to Barclay's *Argenis* and its classic play with the uncanny trope of the strange rendered familiar.[5] Here Manley is at pains to dissuade readers from the misconception that "this was a Modern History, and related to several Affairs Transacted near Home . . . . I wou'd have them rest satisfied the whole *Story* is a *Fiction* . . . ." Her most famous work, *Secret Memoirs and Manners Of several Persons of Quality, of Both Sexes. From the New Atalantis, an Island in the Mediterranean. Written Originally in Italian* (1709), claims a double linguistic domestication: "The following adventures first spoke their own mixed *Italian,* a Speech corrupted, and now much in use through all the islands of the Mediterranean; from whence some industrious Frenchman soon transported it into his own country; and, by giving it an air and habit, wherein the foreigner was almost lost, seemed to naturalize it: A friend of mine . . . put it into my hands, with a desire it might visit the court of Great Britain."[6] Manley's secret histories meet contemporary experiments in pastoral on the broad highway of linguistic domestication.[7]

Unlike that of Behn's, the publication of Manley's *romans à clef* was followed, after a variable period of time, by the publication of their keys.[8] As guides to the actual particularity of the personages whose public affairs have been concentrated into the privacy of their amatory intrigues, these keys can be equivocal—selective, eclectic, their signifying powers depleted by the appearance of identifying names that are variously inadequate for identification purposes. In such cases, what is unlocked by the key is not the real name of a public person but an amplification of private pseudonymy.[9] Far more than in Behn's *Love-Letters,* moreover, the scandalous public activities of the great—paradigmatically, at war and in politics—seem to be all but swallowed up by their scandalous private activities, by their lust and their lust for money. It is as though the allegorical valence of the relation between the state and the family has been overbalanced by a metonymic valence heavily weighted toward the semantic primacy of the family—sexual love, the generative motive, marriage and estate settlement, but also exploitative seduction, rape, adultery, bigamy, incest, and financial corruption. The implication of these factors is a reading experience that involves less identifying the real people who suffer these vices than, superficially but voraciously, identifying with exemplarily vicious characters.

Perhaps the most distinctive feature of Manley's version of the secret history is her impulse to focus attention on the nature and mechanics of the form itself, to thematize narrative form as content. This is most evident in the *New Atalantis,* where the office of narration is objectified through the creation of three allegorical characters who alternately tell the story we read. The procedure bears a general relation to Barclay's in *Argenis;* also to Behn's in *Love-Letters,* where a narrator first coalesces out of epistolary form, then extrudes surrogate narrators out of her characters, and finally, if fleetingly, becomes a character herself (in a related development, the epistolary form that controls the first part of *Love-Letters* becomes thematized in the latter two parts through the letters the characters write to one another). In the *New Atalantis,* the division of narrative labor is achieved, more immediately and ostentatiously, in the initial labor of narration itself. As Swift begins his ecclesiastical allegory in *A Tale of a Tub* (published five years before the *New Atalantis*), Manley begins her political allegory as a fairy-tale romance: "Once upon a time . . ." (4).[10] But although her narrative surrogates—Astrea, Virtue, and Intelligence—proceed to narrate the adventures of characters who are named in the usual mode of political allegory (as "romance" embodiments of purportedly real people) they are themselves of a different, more traditional and concretizing order of allegory since their names are personifications of abstract entities. Although they exist on the same level of represented action as the romance embodiments they discuss, these narrators are set off from those other characters by a cloak of invisibility that bespeaks their ontological difference on the level of content (see 9, 13) as, in the formal dimension, their narrative function is typographically set off by identifying dialogue tags in the manner of dramatis personae.

These explicitating effects may encourage us to attend more closely to the fact that Manley's three narrators provide distinct versions of her own procedure as a secret historian.[11] High-mindedly didactic, Astrea returns to earth to provide the young heir apparent to the throne a moral education attuned to the modern corruption of manners, guided in her turn by her mother, Virtue, a longtime expert in human depravity. Soon after commencing their travels, however, these divinities have recourse to a far more worldly informant, Intelligence, "groom of the stole" and "first lady of the bed-chamber to the Princess Fame," whose interest in corrupt manners is rather more quantitative than qualitative. An omnivorous gatherer of secret information, Lady Intelligence is dedicated not to moral improvement but to secrets as such—examples detached from their precepts—which she both conceals and reveals, both hoards and divulges, to her mistress (13). Of a decidedly lower social status than Astrea and

Virtue, Intelligence is not a moral but a social being, on the one hand a reincarnation of traditional misogynist embodiments like Fama, Rumor, and Gossip, on the other hand a demoralizing modernization of this tradition through its association with oral and printed "intelligence" or news and its public-sphere circulation.[12] Indeed, Manley is careful to disengage herself from the full force of the traditional misogyny by introducing at one point a temporary surrogate narrator, the gossip Mrs. Nightwork, a crude commoner whose ominous "night work," suggestive of both character assassination and infanticide, defines an extreme against that of the divinities, hence a polarity within which Lady Intelligence assumes the middle ground as Manley's intricate self-articulation.

By representing this middle ground with considerable self-irony, Manley enables it to constitute not her ideal but her normative representation of secret history. Lady Intelligence claims the power not of truth-telling but of domestication. She stands in relation to the elevated divinities for whom she acts as a kind of tour guide, as Manley's "translated" secret histories themselves do to their English readers, affording them an uncanny glass that is nominally a window but also stealthily a mirror: "You have hit, ladies, upon my very business; I entertain strangers with vast respect, they give me the greatest attention; for all I say is generally new to foreigners (when they appear in a strange court) . . ." (13). By the same token, Lady Intelligence claims, not the disinterestedness that only a sovereign can truly command, but the power to disclose, with an exhaustiveness bordering on impartiality, the interestedness of those by whom the sovereign is surrounded. Speaking of the "Empress" (i.e., Queen Anne), she tells Astrea and Virtue that

> [w]ere she but to judge of all things by her own eyes and ears, all things would be administered with the same impartiality and justice as if your self had held the balance, but alas! what defence is there against the corruption of favourites and the by-interests of ministers? 'Tis impossible a prince can come to the knowledge of things but by representation, and they are always represented according to the sense of the representator. Either avarice, revenge, or favour, are their motive, and yet how is it possible to prevent it? A prince knows not how to distinguish by the out, and are seldom let into the inside. . . . Therefore, till there can be found upright ministers and disinterested favourites, grievances there will be . . . . (110)[13]

In the absence of such ideal public servants, Lady Intelligence provides the next best service as official collector and disseminator of secrets, she who renders the private public. But Manley also gives us a portrait of "upright ministers and disinterested favorites" in the community of women called "the new Cabal" (154). Already current in seventeenth-century England as a term for private, esoteric, and secret interpretation derived from the reading of the Jewish cabbala, "cabal" acquired a specific political meaning in the 1660s, when it was used to refer to the group of five advisers, or "secretaries," from whom Charles II sought special counsel. "Cabal" also served conveniently as a kind of secret code or key to the actual particularity of the group's membership, since it was an acronym for their initials: Clifford, Arlington, Buckingham, Ashley (soon to be the first Earl of Shaftesbury), and Lauderdale. An informal council that helped explicitate the emergence of a state authority separable from the sovereign and one model for the modern ministerial cabinet of the eighteenth century, the Cabal was a known but self-consciously secretive state apparatus (two of its members signed the secret treaty of Dover).[14]

Manley's "new Cabal" and its "mysteries" therefore can be seen as a domesticating improvement on the old Cabal, a replacement of its public office by a private equivalent: not men but women, not state officials but private citizens, not the great commonwealth but a "little commonwealth," dedicated not to *arcana imperii* but to *arcana amoris* (161).[15] "Secrecy is . . . a material article" for the new even more than for the old Cabal in the sense of defining not simply a group practice but also what the group is materially committed to (155). Representing the institution of female friendship as opposed to that of marriage, the new Cabal is a secret group composed as much as possible of *femes soles* secreted from exposure to and by husbands. Marriage they view skeptically as motivated not by love but by convenience, it being "the custome of the world, that has made it convenient (nay, almost indispensable) for all ladies once to marry" (156). In the commonwealth of marriage women have no private property because their property is legally arrogated to their husbands. "In this little commonwealth is no property; whatever a lady possesses is, *sans ceremone,* at the service and for the use of her fair friend . . . mutual love bestows all things in common " (161). The abolition of absolute private property can be achieved, in other words, not only by a return to customary use-rights or even to the state of nature but also by the abolition of marriage.

The principles on which the Cabal excludes men are related to those on which it opposes marriage. The new bride is instructed by the Cabal "lest she let her husband into a mystery (however innocent) that may expose and ridicule the community . . ." (156). But society with men in general exposes female privacy to a similar vulnerability, and the Cabal has "wisely excluded that rapacious sex who, making a prey of the honour of ladies, find their greatest satisfaction (some few excepted) in boasting of their good fortune, the very chocolate-house being witnesses of their self-love where, promiscuously among the known and unknown, they expose the letters of the fair, explain the mysterious and refine upon the happy part, in their redundancy of vanity consulting nothing but what may feed the insatiable hydra [i.e., of scandal]." As one member of the Cabal protests, men "find their account in treachery and boasting, their pride is gratified, whilst our interest is in mutual secrecy, in natural justice and in mutual constancy." It follows that those members who are "released from the imposing matrimonial fetters are thought the ornament of the Cabal and by all most happy. They claim an ascendant, a right of governing . . ." (154, 155, 156).

If this description of the behavior of men in the public sphere reminds us of Intelligence (and Manley) herself, this is no accident, since the acquisition of autonomy requires the parodic imitation—preferably with a forgiving self-irony—of those who possess it. Hence the Cabal not only "exclude the men" but also "propagate their principles of exposing them without mercy . . ." (155). Hence, too, "[t]hey do not in reality love men, but"—recalling not only Lady Intelligence but also Behn's Silvia—"dote on the representation of men in women. Hence it is that those ladies are so fond of the dress en cavaliere . . ." (235).[16] Far more than Behn, however, Manley fully acknowledges, even elaborates, the scandal of same-sex love that clouds female friendship, and Lady Intelligence herself admits, not without distaste, that "some things may be strained a little too far" by some of the members (154). When considering a "novice" for admission to the Cabal, "they strictly examine her genius, whether it have fitted her for the mysteries of the Cabal, as if she may be rendered insensible on the side of Nature. Nature, who has the trick of making them dote on the opposite improving sex, for if her foible be found directed to what Nature inspires, she is unanimously excluded . . ." (156). As in the anonymous *Love-Letters,* we have the impression here that the empirical and biological grounding of gender difference that is under way in these decades is accompanied by an emergent sense of sexual difference, of the mutual exclusion of same-sex and different-sex love. It is never suggested (nor could it be) for these women, as it is for Beau Wilson and his nobleman, that exemption from reproductive and conjugal materialism constitutes a positive norm of privacy. But Manley's deep preoccupation throughout the *New Atalantis* with the tangled nexus of ideas that cohere in the image of the gossip—purveying tittle-tattle, publishing secrets, reproducing intelligence, midwifing childbirth—may justify our speculation that the Cabal (which is said to include some writers) adumbrates a vision of female publicity alternative to the standard one of, in Astrea's words, "the hymenial union" (161).[17]

So both Manley's account of Lady Intelligence and Lady Intelligence's account of the new Cabal sensitize us to the self-awareness of the secret history that the *New Atalantis* exemplifies. Manley's narrative reflexivity is carried to an extreme point when, in the second volume of that work, we are introduced to a surrogate narrator named Delia, who is none other than Manley herself, and for the space of several pages secret history dovetails explicitly with autobiography. In the process, state secrets are concentrated into family secrets, and the political subject is refashioned as the ethical subject. The rapprochement between secret history and autobiography may be Manley's most significant formal achievement, an important stage in the process whereby the tradition of formal domestication discovers in the exemplary lives of common people not simply the means to but the end of narrative pedagogy.[18]

The story Delia tells is one of seduction, perversity, and betrayal, and its status as a domesticating concentration is made explicit by its analogous relation to English history after the Restoration. Delia's father was a "loyal" royalist during "[t]he inhuman civil wars that rent asunder the kingdom," but "when afterwards that a calm succeeded and the royal line was restored, . . . the suffering loyalty of our family, like virtue, met little else but it self for a reward" (222–23). That is, Roger Manley was one of those loyal "cavaliers" whose unrelieved financial distress after 1660 became an ominous example for those who feared the consequences of Charles II's ingratitude (softened and broadened by Manley to "an ungrateful people" [223]).[19] Upon his death Delia's father leaves her and her younger sister in the care of their much older first cousin, Don Marcus (John Manley), whom he previously had taken into his own care, "a man and with my father in the next chamber when I was born" (224). According to Delia, although he could "talk of honour, of loyalty," her cousin was a turncoat who helped Henriquez (William of Orange) defeat "the reigning prince, . . . naming it the glorious cause," then "revolted back to the royal party . . ." (224–25; Manley's "glorious cause" economically conflates two Whiggish euphemisms for rebellion, the "Good Old Cause" and the "Glorious Revolution"). Thus in his public life Don Marcus displays the sort of ingratitude and treachery her father had suffered as an unrequited royalist; but he also does this in his private life, and directly against Delia's father. For Don Marcus proposes marriage to Delia when she is barely a teenager, and she agrees in "gratitude," if not love, only to discover, when pregnant with his child, that he is already married. To Delia this makes him a "conscious traitor," "the traitor that had seduced me to ruin by a specious pretence"; and the only relation who might "espouse my cause" was "the very traitor that had undone me . . ." (224, 226). So public yields to private "treason," and the defender of a specious "cause" is the villain at blame in a just one. Don Marcus's tortured confession of his "double villain[y]" has likely reference to his violation of both Delia's and her father's trust, but it may be felt to take in as well the doubly public and private dimension of his perfidy—"my father's form perpetually haunting his troubled dreams, reproaching him as a traitor to that trust which, in the pangs of death, he had reposed in him and, as a double villain, casting an impure, an indelible stain upon the honour of a family which was so nearly his own . . ." (225).

Thus in telling her own, private story Delia simultaneously tells the public story of her times. We are reminded of Behn's accommodation of rebellion against one's monarch to the terms of bigamous marriage: similarly, as Don Marcus embraced William while James was on the throne, so he married Delia without securing a divorce. Moreover, the disruption of family order wreaked by Don Marcus "in his guilty house" cannot fail to recall the aura, if not the facts, of disorder in the House of Stuart's efforts to coordinate the royal family's patrilineage with political prudence during the critical decade of the 1680s. Besides the exogamous bigamy, there is more than a whiff of endogamous incest in Don Marcus's status both as a guardian-father figure to Delia (he was "with my father in the next chamber when I was born") and as her sibling (to Don Marcus Delia's father acted "more like a father than an uncle"), not to mention Delia's bastard "wretched son" (224, 226). In this way her autobiographical distress articulates a historical distress.[20]

But we are not wrong to hear some of Intelligence's skeptical self-irony in Delia's narration. She begins it with a sober claim to historicity based on "the native love I have for truth"; but in her account of childhood trips "into the country to an old out-of-fashion aunt" she soon willingly gives us pause: "[F]ull of the heroic stiffness of her own times, [the aunt] would read books of chivalry and romances with her spectacles. This sort of conversation infected me and made me fancy every stranger that I saw, in what habit soever, some disguised prince or lover" (223–24). Delia thus informs us of her susceptibility to (a disastrously incestuous version of) family romance in words that make us ponder momentarily whether political allegory of the sort the *New Atalantis* entails is also to be seen as a kind of fanciful "infection," a projection of the "heroic" onto the everyday. Is John Manley no more Don Marcus than he is Delia's father or brother? The effect of this passage is not so much to destroy the semantic structure of allegorical signification as it is to increase the porosity of its internal borders, so that the objective and "public" status of characters like Don Marcus is felt to flow, at least to some degree, from the private subjectivity of the narrator Delia.

But if the seal between narrator and character becomes thereby less watertight, Delia's self-knowing narration opens up an analogous, interior space between her status as knowing narrator and her status as known character, her "private" and her "public" capacities. Or is it the other way around? Of her "cousin guardian's" declaration of love Delia continues: "I was no otherwise pleased with it than as he answered something to the character I had found in those books that had poisoned and deluded my dawning reason. However, I had the honour and cruelty of a true heroine and would not permit my adorer so much as a kiss from my hand without ten thousand times more entreaty . . ."

(224). Here we see both processes conjoined. On the one hand, Delia the narrator makes explicit the extent to which Don Marcus the character is her projection of "the character" found in romance. On the other hand, Delia the narrator "publicly" reflects on—assumes something like a third-person point of view regarding—Delia the Petrarchized "private" character. So when Don Marcus reveals his bigamy to Delia shortly after she remarks that "I had always loved reading to which I was now more than ever obliged or much of my time had hung upon my hands," we may wonder if this obligatory idealism may have colored her bombastic response to the bad news: "But, alas! my surprise and grief were beyond the ease of words, beyond the benefit of tears. Horror! amazement! sense of honour lost! the world's opinion!" (225, 226).[21]

Even Astrea is impatient with Delia's romance suggestibility—if not with her plight: "I am weary of being entertained with the fopperies of the fair. How is it possible to hinder the women from believing or the men from deceiving? The penalty must be there and something of a quicker sense (if possible) than that of honour lost!" And Astrea looks forward to a day when women will be truly served, not by the Petrarchan hypocrisy that Delia has imbibed—"not by false-deluding praise, heart-breaking sacrifice, or fond complaints of cruelty and charms, but in being their champion against all unlawful invaders" (228). The force of Astrea's critique is dulled, of course, by her own dependence on the sort of idealizing chivalric (if not Petrarchan) conceit from which Delia herself suffers. Lady Intelligence, for her part, speaks with characteristic pragmatism of the inadequate legal penalties currently in force against the corruption of female innocence, and she takes seriously the pressing problem of "honour lost," a refrain that recurs five times in four pages (226–29).

My point is not that Manley definitively ironizes political allegory in this passage but that, consistent with an effort to conflate secret history with autobiography, she accommodates it to the secrets of interiority in such a way that the difference between the public and the private retains not an absolute meaning but the force of a differential marker—a form with variable content—of interior space. And if Manley would have us reject the fustian language that deceitfully idealizes reality (maybe even—ultimately and proleptically—the allegorizing insistence that private affairs must be elevated to the heroics of public politics), this is precisely because the problem itself is so pressing. "Is there no retrieve for honour lost?" This is Manley's very serious articulation of the double standard:[22] "Unequal distribution! Why are your [i.e., the male] sex so partially distinguished? Why is it in your powers after accumulated crimes to regain opinion? When ours, though oftentimes guilty but in appearance, are irretrievably lost?" (227). Why need public opinion about women—their "reputation"—be so fragile and tenuous? What is the nature and scope of women's public "honour"? In 1714 Manley published an autobiography that fills in the spaces surrounding Delia's brief account of her life.[23] Cast, like her earlier and more famous work, as a *roman à clef,* it carries forward the project of shifting the allegorical weight of that form from the public signified to the private signifier, from the political to the ethical subject. It also carries forward the crucial question, Is there no retrieve for a woman's honor lost?

Manley's *Rivella*

Rivella was written very quickly after Manley learned from Edmund Curll that Charles Gildon was already at work on her biography. With the agreement of both men Manley took over Gildon's planned title and wrote her anonymous autobiography in the space of a few weeks, presenting it as a biography through the conceit that it was transcribed from a conversation between two men, who, it has been suggested, are "fictional counterparts" of Curll and Gildon.[24] According to this conceit, the biography passed rapidly from the utter privacy of oral discourse to script and then twice into print: Sir Charles Lovemore told the story (whether in English or in French is not said) to the Chevalier D'Aumont, who wrote it down overnight and gave it soon after to its French publisher, who printed the version that later was translated into English and published in London by Curll ("The Translator's Preface," 41). The suggestion that the two interlocutors at some level represent the actual particularity of Curll and Gildon is fruitful, since the latter pair's real involvement in the production of the text enriches the concrete particularity of the way in which the former pair "produce" Rivella, who never appears in *Rivella* in her own person.

But why, having wrested the narration of her story from one discrediting biographer, does Manley choose to tell it through another? *Rivella* is a secret autobiography in the sense both of telling secrets about the self and of sustaining the secrecy of that telling.[25] As the first-person Delia ironically estranges herself from herself in the *New Atalantis,* so the third-person ceding of her character's narrative agency in *Rivella* expands rather than contracts Manley's agency as autobiographer, augmenting the detachment obtained through anonymous authorship by that of pseudonymous narration. That is, Manley forgoes the public authority of both authorship and narration in order to exercise their secret power. Nor should we forget Behn's precedent in narrative surrogacy: the most likely voice in which to extend experimentally the range and authority of personal honor is not female but male. Moreover, if we compare the triad of Lovemore, D'Aumont, and Rivella to that of Astrea, Virtue, and Intelligence, the fact of gender difference in the former grouping can be felt to augment the formal public-private differential already available through status difference.[26]

The most significant innovation of *Rivella* is its paradoxical combination of the *roman à clef* with autobiography. Like all penetrating contradictions, this one results from the pursuit of similarity into opposition. The aim of political allegory is to use the private to adumbrate the public. In the autobiographical *Rivella*, the public signified is the actual particularity of the author herself, a private person whom the formal aura and apparatus of the *roman à clef* transform into a public figure, an objectification of subjectivity. The aim of autobiography is to split the subject into a private and a public component, the character and the narrator, so that the former is subjected to the analytic examination of the latter. In *Rivella*, autobiographical self-division becomes the engine of allegorical signification, a subjectification of objectivity. *Rivella* takes the logic of the *roman à clef* as far as it can go in one direction, doubling back on its own private signifier and collapsing the difference between private and public only to rediscover it within Rivella's persona. The secret history retains its ambition to conceal and reveal the secrets of high life even as it internalizes this ambition in a proleptically psychological exercise in the case history, where the interiority of low life becomes populated by versions of the self.[27] Manley's technique bears some comparison to Behn's shift from an epistolary first-person to a third-person narration. In fact, they might be seen as alternative methods of doing justice to that element of secrecy that lies in form as well as content— in the telling of the secret history rather than simply in what it tells.

Rivella fulfills a notable tendency of Manley's earlier secret histories by making the public reference of her fancifully named characters all but nugatory. True, they all have actual particularity (this is the promise of autobiography as much as of the *roman à clef*), but it is the actual particularity of private citizens, not public figures. Figure 13.1 reproduces the key that was printed with the second edition of *Rivella*.[28] Some of its identifications feature a conventionally obscure syncopation, for example, "Mr. C." is "Mr. *C——t*, Son to the Lord *B——re*"; others are obscure to the point of impenetrability: "Lord *Crafty*" is "——." However, Curll's key is most strikingly impenetrable not in its syncopations but in the fact that the actual particularity it discloses is often enough that of private people whose names signify no more, to the impersonal public-sphere reader (as distinguished from local denizens and/or Manley's personal acquaintances), than do the signifiers by which they are known in the text. Thus "*Petty-pan* Merchant" is identified as "Mr. *Hungerford*, a Pastry-Cook in *Limestreet*," and "*Flippanta*" is "Servant to *Rivella*." This descent into the realm of the private is well represented by the following sequence of entries: first "The Man *Hilaria* was in Love with" is identified as "Mr. *Goodman*, the Player"; then the key continues: "He kept a Mistress in the next Street," a textual signifier identified by "Mrs. *Wilson*, of the Pope's-Head Tavern in *Cornhill*." Even a pub-

A KEY to the Adventures of *RIVELLA*.

RIVELLA,	Author of the *Atalantis*.	*Mrs Manley.*
Sir *Charles Lovemore*,	Lieuten. Gen. *Tidcomb*.	

Pag.

5 Mr. C.	Mr. C——*t*, Son to the Lord B——*re*.
13 Mr. S——*le*,	Mr. *Steele*.
19 *Lysander*,	Mr. *Carlisle*.
30 *Hilaria*,	Late D——*fs* of *Cleveland*.
31 A Lady next Door to the poor Recluse,	Nominal Mrs. *Rider*, Sir *Richard Fanshaw*'s Daughter, Sister to Mrs. *Blount*, Housekeeper to the Lord *S.*—*rs*.
33 Count *Fortunatus*,	D—— of *M*——*gh*.
——Kitchin-Maid married to her Master,	Pretended Madam *Beauclair*.
34 Her Patroness's Eldest Son,	Duke of *C*——*nd* and *S*——*ton*.
——Young Lady of little or no Fortune,	Late Lady *Poultney*'s Daughter, D——*fs Ditto*.
35 The Man *Hilaria* was in Love with,	Mr. *Goodman*, the Player.
——He kept a Mistress in the next Street,	Mrs. *Wilson*, of the Pope's-Head Tavern in *Cornhill*.
37 The First Dutchess in England,	Late Dutchess of *Norfolk*.
45 Sir *Peter Vainlove*,	Sir *Thomas Skipwith*.
48 Mrs. *Settee*,	Mrs. *P*——*m*.

Lord

FIG. 13.1. [Delarivier Manley], key to *The Adventures of Rivella . . . The Second Edition. To which is added A Compleat Key* (1715). Department of Rare Books and Special Collections, Princeton University Library.

FINIS.

lic figure like "*Hilaria*" ("Late D——ss of *Cleveland*") means more to the narrative for her private relationship with Rivella as Hilaria than for what is added by the knowledge that she is "really" Cleveland. Or rather, our knowledge of Cleveland feeds our understanding of Hilaria, not the reverse. But the tendency of earlier narratives that is here fulfilled can also be seen not as an abandonment of the public but as an internalization of it within a private story, where the energy that subtends the basic signifying relationship of public and private in the *roman à clef* is rechanneled into plot and characterization. Indeed, the central theme of this private story is the conflict between two models by which private women may attain public status in the world.

Manley's autobiography begins in the voice not of one gentleman but of three: the Englishman Lovemore, the Frenchman D'Aumont, and D'Aumont's Gentleman of the Chamber, or secretary. It is the latter who narrates the introduction, in which the conversation of his superiors occasions the narration of Rivella's history, and who subsequently publishes that history in French (41). Not surprisingly, the conversation is a prelude to *Rivella*'s central inquiry into the public status of private women. As though in parody of Dryden's *Essay of Dramatic Poesy* (1668), Manley's work is a gentlemanly debate along national lines about how best to enjoy not drama but women. In both debates a crucial issue concerns whether immediacy or detachment is the key to experiencing pleasure.[29] D'Aumont, the Frenchman, insists that if women are appealing in "the theory"—in intellect, wit, conversation, and writing—they are likely to be so also in "the practic"—in love and sex. Lovemore, the Englishman, is less inclined to treat the theory as a dependable guide to the practice, and D'Aumont chides him for being "a novice . . . in what relates to women . . ." (44, 45). The relationship between theory and practice, explains the Frenchman, is especially close when the former takes the latter as its subject matter, when conversation and writing are actually about love and sex. In this respect no modern writer equals "your famous author of the *Atalantis*," he says, and he reminds Lovemore of three erotic scenes in that text that are "such representatives of nature, that must warm the coldest reader . . . . After perusing her inchanting descriptions, which of us have not gone in search of raptures which she every where tells us, as happy mortals, we are capable of tasting[?]" (44–45).

The scenes themselves mimic D'Aumont's account of them. In each a character is seduced by a virtual representation, raised to a pitch of desire by a detached contemplation that ends in actual fulfillment with the represented object. Two are scenes of voyeurism, the third an act of "dangerous reading" (the pornographic text is Ovid), which therefore precisely parallels D'Aumont's account of Rivella's ability as an author to link theory to practice, writing to sex.[30] But the linkage depicted within the scenes from the *New Atalantis* is absent in the scene of reading such scenes that D'Aumont describes, which raises desire through the autoerotic virtuality of pornography but leaves the reader—both D'Aumont and us—to go "in search of raptures," to find actual fulfillment, elsewhere. Appearing now to understand the Frenchman, Lovemore answers the question where those raptures are to be found by saying: "For my part, I believe they are to be met with no where else but in her own embraces." "That is what I would experience," agrees D'Aumont.

But are they really in agreement, or has the difference between the virtual and the actual only been reformulated? The Frenchman seems to seek a pornographic experience, a story of Rivella that is as seductive as the stories she herself tells, whereas the literalistic Englishman appears to think his friend's expectation is that Lovemore will link theory to practice, providing D'Aumont discursive preparation for "her own embraces." And he may be right: "I would have you paint her with as masterly an hand," adds the Frenchman, "as she has painted others, that I may know her perfectly before I see her" (45). Is Lovemore's role that of private pornographer or public pimp? By the end of the introduction, the issue of national difference in which the debate about women has been grounded has evaporated because the difference between the two male perspectives has become indecipherable. And as D'Aumont's voice (not to mention that of his secretary) is all but subsumed by Lovemore's, their nationalistic debate is subsumed by the larger question of the nature of female honor, which the debate had obscurely adumbrated. But the question of female honor also carries forward the formal question raised by the debate. Is the role of narrative to link the concrete particularity of its imaginative signifiers to an actual particularity by which they may be signified and fulfilled, or should it restrict its concerns to the virtual realm, leaving signification and fulfillment to the realm of the actual—or even internalizing them (as autobiography does secret history) within the virtual as imaginative versions of that realm?

Although it takes a number of forms, this basic ambiguity suffuses Rivella and the act of its narration. We encounter it most quickly in Lovemore's effort to "produce" Rivella in the time-honored trope of a *blazon*. Torn between the elevating idealism of the figure and his own impulse toward a more empirical and literal description, Lovemore denies all metaphor to Rivella's body parts, absurdly aggravating the trope's already considerable fetishism: "Her hands and arms have been publickly celebrated; . . . Her neck and breasts have an established reputation . . ." (48). More broadly, the problem is that Lovemore not only reads Rivella, he also loves her, a practical application of theory that nonetheless remains virtual because his love has never been requited. In Lovemore Manley creates an alter ego who is both outspoken in Rivella's praise and candid about her shortcomings. Manley-as-Lovemore provides Rivella an objective subjectivity: he is her male Petrarchan subject, her "slave"; but the authenticity of his abjection obliges him to narrate also her "male" Petrarchan lovesickness for another, her subjection to the beautiful young Lysander (57, 54–55). So Lovemore expansively fills the role in *Rivella* that, in a more limited way, Delia does in the *New Atalantis*. In fact, he refers us to Delia for an account of the "four miserable years of her life" when Rivella entered into a bigamous relationship (60). But there are points at which the two personae's stories overlap, and the differences are suggestive.

Delia had attributed her early introjection of "the honor and cruelty of a true heroine" to the course of romance reading set by her aunt. Lovemore both denies the former tendency and obscures the latter condition. "I loved her," he writes, "but she did not return my passion, yet without any affected coyness, or personating a heroine of the many romances she daily reads. Rivella would let me know in the very best language, with a bewitching air of sincerity and manners, that she was not really cruel, but insensible . . ." (53–54). As for the aunt, if she is the "severe *governante,* worse than any *duenna*" Lovemore mentions as being in charge of her "severe . . . education," she seems an unlikely source for a romance curriculum. More arresting in this regard is the way Lovemore describes his own childhood friendship with Rivella, "who had the misfortune to be born with an indifferent beauty, between two sisters perfectly handsom; and yet, as I have often thought my self, and as I have heard others say, they had less power over mankind than had Rivella. . . . My father's estate lay very near Rivella's father's government. I was then a youth, who took a great deal of delight in going to the castle, where three such fair persons were inclosed." The aura of fairy-tale romance is heady enough, but it is also clearly attributed: "I had used to please my self in talking romantick stories to her, and with furnishing her with books of that strain" (52). If Rivella is susceptible to romance fancy, evidently, it is through the influence of Lovemore (she even links her infatuation with Lysander to Lovemore's love letters [54]), whose apparent commitment to the body over the mind is belied by his imaginative enthrallment to Rivella. Despite his opening skepticism about the power of "theory" to dictate "practic," Lovemore's love for Rivella is a matter of his vulnerability to her "power," to which her "indifferent beauty" is quite irrelevant. But what does this say about Manley, who has in turn imagined Lovemore? Rivella may not "personate" a romance heroine, but Manley personates Lovemore, a devoted male admirer who is also her "official" (auto)biographer. On matters of fact the romancing Lovemore is demonstrably undependable;[31] yet he is deeply earnest in "[v]aluing my self . . . upon the reputation of an impartial historian . . ." (74). What does Manley intend—what does she accomplish—by this indulgent but judgmental, this patently partial, projection?

Lovemore's partiality, obvious enough in substantive terms, also has a strictly formal basis. His "public," third-person detachment is limited by the fact that he is also a "private" character whose viewpoint can be refined, even relativized, by his own narration of Rivella's viewpoint. But their relationship is a good deal more subtle than one of ironic inversion. As her narrator, Lovemore is Manley's "male projection," not as (for example) Behn's cross-dressed Silvia is a projection of male privilege, but as he embodies and enacts her feminine sensitivity to customary male advantage. Similarly, Rivella is Manley's "female projection" of how her customary female disentitlement might be lived from a masculine perspective. The sympathetic facility with which Manley manages this double projection bespeaks a gender reciprocity between "public" narrator and "private" character, a common ground that her virtual personae occupy. Echoing Delia on the double standard in the *New Atalantis,* Lovemore acknowledges that "the charter of that sex [i.e., women] being much more confined than ours, what is not a crime in men is scandalous and unpardonable in woman, as [Rivella] her self has very well observed in divers places . . ." (47). What Lovemore and Rivella principally share is an abiding interest in the question, Is there no retrieve for a woman's honor lost? And although their answers to this rhetorical question differ greatly, the autobiographical authenticity of *Rivella* is an outgrowth of their mutual engagement.

Lovemore's failure to establish the intimacy of the *arcana amoris* with Rivella is clear in the fact that she ignores his invitations to a private epistolary exchange: "[S]he answered none of my letters, nay forgot to read them; when I came to visit her, she shewed me a pocket full which she had never opened . . ." (56–57). Fearing that she will be called away to court to serve as "Maid of Honour" to James II's queen, Lovemore proposes a clandestine "marriage unknown to our parents," a potential marriage for love in which, however, Rivella refuses to take the role of rebel against paternal tyranny ("she feared to displease her father . . ."). In pained retrospection, the narrator regrets this lost opportunity by which "all those misfortunes that have since attended her, in point of honour and the world's opinion, had probably been prevented . . ." (59). These begin with "the misfortunes" of the king himself, whose deposal not only precludes Rivella's chance for honor at court but also saddens her father so much "that he died soon after, in mortal apprehension of what would befall his unhappy country." "Here begins Rivella's real misfortunes," says Lovemore; and he adds with callous moralism that "it would be well for her that I could say here she died with honour, as did her father" (60). Fastidiously avoiding it himself, Lovemore now refers us to Delia's account of the bigamous marriage, twice more alluding to it as "her misfortunes" (61).

As in Behn's *Love-Letters* and her own *New Atalantis,* Manley seems thus to compare rebellion with bigamy, England's public with her own private misfortunes. And yet the relationship is more attenuated here, suggesting less a domesticating allegory than a causal chain of circumstance whereby the (public) fate of the king leads to the death of the father, to the guardianship of the cousin, and finally to the (private) fate of the daughter. And the species of public honor with which Lovemore is principally concerned is not that of the court or of the Stuart line but that of the public sphere—that is, "the world's opinion." However, despite *Rivella*'s general flattening of political allegory, it is not devoid of the domesticating motive. To appreciate this we need to consider Rivella's relationship with Hilaria (the Duchess of Cleveland). "Rivella may well call it her second great misfortune to have been acquainted with that lady, who, to excuse her own inconstancy, always blasted the character of those whom she was grown weary of, as if by *slander* and *scandal,* she could take the odium from her self, and fix it upon others" (64). As these words suggest, however, Lovemore sees Hilaria in negative terms not only because she will soon do harm to Rivella's reputation but also because Hilaria is an extreme example of Rivella, a masculine woman who publishes scandal. Hence Hilaria is also a negative foil for Lovemore, Manley's public narrator. We can see this in Hilaria's cynical version of the double standard: "She read [Rivella] a learned lecture upon the ill-nature of the world, that would never restore a woman's reputation, how innocent soever she really were, if appearances proved to be against her; therefore she gave her advice . . . to make her self as happy as she could without valuing or regretting those, by whom it was impossible to be valued" (62). As Lovemore still "preache[s]" his moralizing "doctrine" to Rivella, so Hilaria delivers a "learned lecture" on the same topic, but as devoid of ethics as Lovemore's is oversupplied with them (69).

We also sense the opposition between Lovemore and Hilaria later on, when she temporarily becomes the subject of his narration and her libelous approach to scandal subtly infiltrates his own, more privatized procedure. Hilaria's taste for libelous allegory comes with her character. Like Behn's Hermione and her own she-favorite and queen, Zarah, Manley's Hilaria is one of those powerful gentlewomen whose *arcana amoris* are scarcely distinguishable from the *arcana imperii.*[32] When Lord Crafty (Ralph Montagu) discontinues an affair with her, she prevails on the king to remove him from his ambassadorship to Paris "upon secret advice that she pretended to have received of his corruption and treachery." But Crafy obtains and publicizes a cache of "fatal letters" sent to Hilaria by "a certain person," "full of amorous raptures for the favours she had bestowed." "What could be said against such clear evidences of her disloyalty?" The king orders Hilaria "to forgive the Ambassador; to whom he returned his thanks for the care he had taken of his glory . . ." (75–76).

But the story does not really hang together. Why Hilaria's "disloyalty"? Cleveland had not been Charles's mistress for years. And what about Montagu's purported "treachery"? Why does Charles instead go so far as to thank him for his "care"? These obscurities suggest a subtext of state affairs that has been inadequately concentrated into a love-affair plot. *Rivella*'s editor fruitfully suggests (76n1) that Manley alludes here to an episode of 1677–78 that fed into the Popish Plot by precipitating the fall of the government. Like Lovemore's plot, the episode began with Cleveland's efforts to tarnish Montagu in Charles II's eyes. As in the love plot, moreover, Montagu responded by threatening to publish a "fatal" correspondence. However, the letters in question had been addressed not to Cleveland but to himself, and the "certain person" with whom Montagu had corresponded was the Earl of Danby, whose letters documented the king's continuing receipt of secret subsidies from Louis XIV in exchange for a favorable foreign policy. The incriminating letters were read before the House of Commons with the king's approval deleted, and Danby was impeached. Montagu's disclosure was an effort to recoup his political losses at Cleveland's hands by gaining a pension from the French for his aid in undermining Danby.[33] As an overdetermined virtual signifier, Hilaria thus stands for two actual personages, the peripheral Cleveland and the central Danby.

We may even hear an allusion to this formal complication—this ambivalence between domesticating allegory and merely private narration—in Hilaria's attempt to explain away the "disloyalty" of her love letters as an illusion bred by differences in linguistic culture. The correspondence aimed only at "amusement," not "consequences," she says; but French and English are "widely different; that which in one language carried an air of extream gallantry, meant no more than meer civility in t'other" (76). Hilaria's excuse reminds us of the differences in national culture on which depends the hermeneutic uncertainty of *Rivella,* an English translation from a French publication that may in turn have originated in an English dialogue. The ultimate ambiguity of the introductory debate about women frustrates our effort to code the content of French (D'Aumont) versus English (Lovemore) approaches to them in any definitive way. However, the "widely different" categories of linguistic culture do define a formal differential by which to distinguish two opposed attitudes toward semantics: one, for which words signify beyond themselves—theory implies practice, "civility" connotes "gallantry," "amusement" entails "consequences," virtual posits actual particularity, the private bespeaks the public—and the other attitude, for which words, however plurisignificant they may be, mean no more than what they say. We may be tempted to read in Lovemore's lability as a narrator, his susceptibility to a partial ventriloquizing of Hilaria's allegorical mode, a lucid gendering of narrative modes. But the gender-heterogeneity of both these figures—Lovemore's male internalization of the feminine, Hilaria's female internalization of the masculine—suggests that Manley is deploying the categories of gender, like those of nationality, in a "traditional" rather than a "modern" fashion, resulting in a relativizing differential rather than a relation of definitive difference.

As it turns out, Rivella vindicates her personal honor against Hilaria's slanders, and despite his characterization of the Hilaria episode as Rivella's second great misfortune, Lovemore acknowledges that "[a]ll the world was fond of Rivella . . ." (67). Lovemore's oversensitivity to the vulnerability of Rivella's reputation to the world's calumnies now meets Rivella's more masculine sense of self-sufficiency head-on. With an affecting paternalism, Lovemore "begged she would retire to my seat in the country, where she might be sure to command with the same power as if it were her own, as in effect it must be, since my self was so devoted to her service. I made her this offer because it could no longer do her an injury in the opinion of the world which was sufficiently prejudiced against her already . . . ." Although with respect and in friendship, Rivella replies that she could never live with a man with whom she is not in love. "She told me her love of solitude was improved by her disgust of the world; and since it was impossible for her to be publick with reputation, she was resolved to remain in it concealed." On the one hand, a pastoral retirement from the world under the virtuality of male protection, "as if" commanding her own power; on the other, a solitary retirement within the world in the secrecy of a writer and *feme sole* ("'Twas in this solitude," Lovemore admits, "that she composed her first tragedy . . ." [67]). Adopting a posture that comports perfectly with her coming career as an anonymous author of political allegories, Rivella now defines the disparity that will control the remainder of this autobiography: the more its narrator rues the destruction of Rivella's public reputation, the more its protagonist vindicates her reputation through public activity. I will touch briefly on the major episodes in this plot before turning to its climax, the publication and prosecution of the *New Atalantis*.

The first episode Lovemore introduces with the following words: "Behold another wrong step toward ruining Rivella's character with the world; the incense that was daily offered her upon this occasion from the men of vogue and wit. Her appartment was daily crouded with them" (68). Rivella's entry into the literary public sphere is championed by Lovemore's nominal foil Sir Peter Vainlove (Thomas Skipwith), who specializes in virtual love affairs carried on through the public circulation of private *billets-doux*. Lovemore, scandalized by this behavior, nonetheless recirculates some of their epistolary exchange for D'Aumont's and our satisfaction. Vainlove's literary antics embody the ambiguous relationship between amatory theory and practice. Although "scandalous chronicle" represents him as sexually dangerous, he is also rumored to be "rather dangerous to a woman's reputation then her vertue . . . ." Still, Lovemore regrets "Rivella's folly; that could suffer the conversation of a wretch so insignificant to her pleasures, and yet so dangerous to her reputation" (73–74). We are reminded of Hilaria's opportunistic distinction between "mere civility" and "extreme gallantry" in epistolary affairs and, behind that, of the way Manley strategically uses an amatory correspondence to domesticate a political one. Is Rivella foolish because she truly forfeits her public reputation or because she does so without even gaining the benefits of real pleasures?

The second episode, which occupies the greater part of the remainder of this autobiography, consists in Lovemore's narration of what he twice calls the "secret history" of the complex and protracted Albemarle lawsuit (102, 89). A case in chancery trying the legitimacy of rival wills left by the second Duke of Albemarle, the celebrated lawsuit dramatizes both the authority of the public state apparatus to settle a private family estate and its vulnerability to private manipulation and intrigue. Lovemore's attention is divided between narrating Rivella's part in the Albemarle case to highlight "those occasions that have to her prejudice, made most noise in the world" and showing us how she might instead have achieved "the reparation of her own honour" by marrying a man she meets through the case (102, 105). At first Lovemore warns against the amiable Cleander (John Tilly): "One affair with a married man did a woman's reputation more harm than with six others." And by the conclusion of the lawsuit Rivella has become "the town talk by her scandalous intriegue with Cleander . . ." (86, 103). But when Cleander's wife dies and he is able to marry Rivella, both he and Lovemore are astonished that she instead urges Cleander, who is plagued with creditors, to make a match with "a rich young widow" lest she "see him poor and miserable, an object of perpetual reproach to her heart and eyes; for having preferred the reparation of her own honour, to the preservation of his." "One must be a woman of an exalted soul to take the part she did," writes Lovemore; but "I would have disswaded her from that romantick bravery of mind, by advising her to marry her lover . . . ." However, Rivella is adamant; and "she led her life mostly in the country, and never appeared in publick after Cleander's marriage . . . ." Once he dies, moreover, "I know nothing memorable of Rivella, but that she seemed to bury all thoughts of gallantry in Cleander's tomb; and unless she had her self published such melting scenes of love, I should by her regularity and good behaviour thought she had lost the memory of that passion" (105, 106, 107).

Lovemore's charge of romance idealism reminds us of his own penchant for it. How does that penchant affect his climactic narration? From Lovemore's partial perspective (which is also partly Manley's), Rivella now resigns herself to a life of writing about love rather than living it, of publishing "gallantry" rather than enacting it, of virtual theory rather than actual practice—choices that seem to be consistent with the heroic foolishness of preserving another's honor as a solitary *feme sole* rather than retrieving one's own through the public privacy of marriage. But is marriage the only avenue to a woman's honor? Indeed, is marriage honorable if it amounts, as in Lovemore's own earlier proposal, to the possession of a merely metaphorical power ("as if it were her own") in rustic coverture (see 67)? As though to compound this question Lovemore turns immediately to Rivella's publications. The publishers and printer of the *New Atalantis* have just been arrested, and Lovemore finds Rivella herself "in one of her heroick strains; . . . she told me that her self was the author of the *Atalantis,* for which three innocent persons were taken up and would be ruined with their families; that she was resolved to surrender her self . . . so to discharge those honest people from their imprisonment" (107). The "heroic strains" of this self-sacrifice are compatible with the "romantic bravery" of the one just made for Cleander. To avoid her "perish[ing] thro' want in a goal [i.e., a gaol]," Lovemore offers to help Rivella escape the law through flight. Stung by the potential "reproach" of her private "conscience," Rivella wonders again what "would become of the poor printer, and those two other persons concerned, the publishers, who with their families all would be undone by her flight? . . . [S]he could not bear to live and reproach her self with the misery that might happen to those unfortunate people." To follow Lovemore's casuistical advice,[34] in fact, would be to do "a dishonourable thing" (108, 109).

This is a signal moment in the narrative, where Manley's two autobiographical personae, her narrator and her protagonist, are split apart through direct confrontation, and it is heightened by the epochal conflict between Protestant standards of private conscience and aristocratic standards of public honor that suffuse it. Rivella's determination to protect these "families" underscores the counterintuitive promise of the solitary *feme sole* to serve the family better than the *feme covert* is able to do. Lovemore's insistence that a woman's honor requires the protections of conjugal coverture forces Rivella finally to articulate the counterprinciple that a woman's honor, like a man's, depends on honorable behavior, which in turn presupposes the autonomous agency of an ethical subject capable of truly conscientious choice. So far from being "romantic," this is a condition of actual responsibility as distinct from the ethically deprived state of both the political subject who is subjected to his sovereign and the *feme covert* who, with her family, is subjected to her husband. Embracing the dialectical liberty of self-subjection, Rivella "surrendered her self" to the law and is soon released (110). Her reproach to Lovemore is delicately devastating. A "friend" advises self-interestedly, "out of the greatness of his friendship"; a "man

of honour" advises honorably, "wherein his friend or himself must suffer . . . ."
"[M]y honour was found defective," Lovemore continues, "how perfect soever
my friendship might appear" (111). What Lovemore derides as heroic romance
is the authentic heroism of the private citizen behaving conscientiously in the
public sphere.

In this way *Rivella* tells us how to retrieve a woman's honor lost. Lovemore's
opposition of honor in marriage to dishonor outside it is refuted by the acknowledgment of the essential continuity of personal and "family" responsibility in both spheres of action. Does this include honor within publication,
where the virtuality of experience renders ethical responsibility tricky if not
moot? True, the act of publication itself has an actuality for which responsibility may be assigned or taken. And Rivella has shouldered the conscientious burden implicit in Marvell's warning that "he that hath once Printed an ill book
. . . has diffused his poyson so publickly in design that it might be beyond his
own recollection: and put himself past the reach of any private admonition."[35]
But the "act" that is published through publication has a virtuality for which
the very possibility of responsibility depends on a semantic interpretation of
reference. Indeed, Rivella is able to escape prosecution for the publication for
which she has admitted responsibility because she denies responsibility for its
actual reference, which she now disowns by invoking its "romantick names, and
a feigned scene of action . . . ." Like Hilaria, who denies that her letters are
"criminal" because they are "designed only for amusement, without presuming
to aim at consequences," Rivella denies "that she had a farther design than writing for her own amusement . . . without intending particular reflections or
characters" (111, 76, 110).

The ethical significance of Rivella's acknowledgment that she is the author
of the *New Atalantis* is bound up with the epistemological and proprietary significance of the emergence of the category of authorship as evidenced by the
legislation passed in the years between the publication of the *New Atalantis* in
1709 and that of *Rivella* in 1714.[36] Given the logic of this legislation, can Manley establish an ethical space that would permit her to own the actuality of her
actions without also owning the actuality of their reference? We may be reminded of the contemporary effort to separate libel from satire and of the way
the playwrights responded to Jeremy Collier's challenge by separating the actual
from the virtual ethics of characterization.[37] The central issue concerns the responsibility of private persons for public actions now that the latter category includes both the actuality of real-world behavior and the virtuality of public-
sphere behavior.

Manley confronts the new with the traditional tools she finds to hand.
When her denial of actual reference is met with official skepticism, Lovemore

writes, she has recourse to the traditional doctrine of "*inspiration*" in order to articulate the peculiar sort of responsible nonresponsibility she has for the characters of the *New Atalantis*. If her characters evoke actual personages, she suggests, this may owe not to her own, internal, bad motive but ("knowing her own innocence") to the external inspiration of "evil angels" (110). Of course, Rivella's suggestion cries out to be read either as cynical bad faith (from the perspective of the state) or as canny subterfuge (from the perspective of the political subject). But there is some value in reading it also as the struggle of the ethical subject to adapt the language of religio-poetic possession by a greater force to the protoaesthetic autonomy of authorship, a seemingly impregnable space of negative liberty from public interference that is, however, vulnerable to a new sort of "evil angel," the reader and the virtual construction of textual meaning. Indeed, it is the traditional public—the legal apparatus of the state— that claims the authority to codify the protocols of reading for "the generality of readers" that are normative in the new public sphere.[38]

In his own words Lovemore already has made the legal case against Rivella's act of publication, "the barbarous design of exposing people that never had done her any injury" (107). And although the case is soon dropped, Rivella is informally punished along the way by means peculiarly fitted to the crime. First she is "close shut up . . . from seeing or speaking to any person, without being allowed pen, ink, and paper . . ."; then she is made a public spectacle by the attorney general, "several times exposing her in person to walk across the court before the bench of judges . . ." (110, 111). That is, her virtual crimes become her actual punishments. Rivella's self-defense against the charge of libel is inconsistent but resourceful. Although in court she denies any design to expose actual people, to Lovemore she proudly admits providing an example of journalistic courage for the male sex by "throwing the first stone" at hypocrites who "advance themselves" "by the pretence of public good . . . ." Moreover, her "tattle of frailties" is relatively harmless, since she spares the "truly vertuous" and in any case "did but take up old stories that all the world had long since reported . . ." (108).

The inconsistency of Rivella's self-defense bespeaks not Manley's hypocrisy but the experimental nature of her inquiry into the mysteries of publishing ethics and aesthetic responsibility. Contemporaries like Defoe can be heard engaged in similar inquiries;[39] but we can also detect in Manley's language of "tattle" and "old stories," as in her exemplary stone-throwing, an acknowledgment of a gender dimension that is absent in Defoe's characteristic self-examinations. Like Lady Intelligence, Rivella would modernize the traditional gendered figure of the gossip. But if Intelligence refines gossip in the direction of news and its circulation through the virtual space of the public sphere, Rivella, in alliance here with Lovemore, pursues the old vocational duties of telling tales and mid-wifing childbirth so as to refine gossip in the direction of female creativity and the virtuality of aesthetic experience. The putative inconsequence of Rivella's "tattle," the way it dovetails with the image of her as a woman brought "to her trial for writing a few amorous trifles purely for her own amusement," is most resonant as it suggests not the secretly public reference of what purports to be merely private (as though the private needs the public for its fulfillment) but the ethical disinterestedness and fullness of female trifles and the end of amusement.

The debate between Lovemore and Rivella, between narrator and character, is Manley's autobiographical psychomachy, an interiorized inquiry into the nature of female honor that is also an inquiry into the honor of female privacy. In Rivella Manley has insisted on the heroic honor of single women at work in the public sphere of private life. In accord with this basic principle, Lovemore truly persuades Rivella, and at least partly speaks for Manley, in his ostensibly most partial opinions: "[W]hen I would argue with her the folly of a woman's disobliging any one party, by a pen equally qualified to divert all, she agreed my reflection was just, . . . and that hence-forward her business should be to write of pleasure and entertainment only, wherein party should no longer mingle . . . . She now agrees with me, that politicks is not the business of a woman, especially of one that can so well delight and entertain her readers with more gentle and pleasing theams . . ." (112). It is easy to read these lines as a repudiation of "politics" in the modern, comprehensive sense of the term rather than as a disengagement from party animosities by a major player at a moment when her own party is undergoing what will turn out to be a permanent divestment of power.[40] Although we are right to credit the evident polarization of Manley's two personae over the question of how a woman's honor might be retrieved, she gives us little basis here for such an oppositional reading on the issue of whether a "pen equally qualified to divert all"—whether a writer possessed of an aesthetically generalizing capacity for giving pleasure—should repudiate the divisively particularizing business of (party) politics. How does the larger context of *Rivella* itself clarify the meaning of this repudiation?

It seems to me that the embrace of writing "of pleasure and entertainment only, wherein *party* should no longer mingle" profits from being read as a tentative embrace of "theory" as disengaged from "practice," of aesthetic rather than empiricist ambition, hence of concrete rather than actual particularity in characterization. One justification for this reading can be found in the fact that it is at this point in the narrative that Manley reopens the introductory frame of her narrative, the debate between Lovemore and D'Aumont on how women are best enjoyed. That debate had ended ambiguously, we recall, in that the central question whether theory and practice are linked in women is never directly answered. Theory and practice are exemplified there by conversation or writing on the one hand and love or sex on the other. Manley's own pornography provides a case in point. Is the end of the *New Atalantis* both to arouse and to satisfy sexual desire or to arouse a desire that must be satisfied elsewhere? Does the pleasure of knowing Rivella entail reading her or also enjoying her sexually? Having declared the business of women to be, not politics, but to "delight and entertain her readers with more gentle and pleasing theams," Lovemore now adds that Rivella "has accordingly set her self again to write a tragedy for the stage. If you stay in England, dear Chevalier, till next winter, we may hope to entertain you from thence, with what ever Rivella is capable of performing in the dramatick art. But has she still a taste for love, interrupted young Monsieur D'Aumont? Doubtless, answered Sir Charles, or whence is it that she daily writes of him with such fire and force? But whether she does love, is a question" (112).

In this distinction between writing and doing Lovemore echoes his earlier inference that since Cleander's death Rivella's gallantry has been virtual rather than actual, more published than enacted (107). But as he proceeds, Lovemore begins to wonder whether he has fulfilled his companion's opening request that he "paint her with as masterly an hand . . . as she has painted others" (45). Echoing himself again on Rivella's powers to entertain her readers, Lovemore confesses doubt that he has followed her example: "I might have entertained you much more agreeably . . . [and] raised your passions in her favour; I should have brought you to her table well furnished and well served; . . . from thence carried you (in the heat of summer after dinner) within the nymphs alcove, to a bed nicely sheeted and strowed with roses, jessamins or orange-flowers, . . . and there have given you leave to fancy your self the happy man, with whom she chose to repose her self, during the heat of the day . . ." (113).

All at once we are back in the world of the *New Atalantis*—or rather, of the highly selective *New Atalantis* that D'Aumont cites in the introduction and that accords with Rivella's courtroom revision of that work as devoid of "particular reflections." The development of pornography played an important role in the transition from the dutiful signifying process of domestication to the confident thematization of domesticity because in learning to dispense with its dependence on religious, philosophical, and political ends by pursuing sexual desire and satisfaction as an end in itself, pornography provided a relatively conspicuous model for the establishment of aesthetic virtuality and self-sufficiency. *Rivella* concludes as it began, with ingenuous male enthusiasm for a release ambiguously caught between the virtual and the actual, the imagination and the senses, a release that is the hallmark of pornography: "*Allon's* let us go my dear

Lovemore, interrupted young D'Aumont, let us not lose a moment before we are acquainted with the only person of her sex that knows how to *live* . . ." (114). On the one hand, it is as though the closing of the narrative circle makes the intervening adventures of Rivella evaporate into thin air. On the other hand, the "pornographic" frame sets off a secret history no less compelling for being, in the end, its own key. In these terms, Manley's withdrawal from (party) politics amounts, not to a repudiation, but to an embrace of a more dependably principled public activity, the activity of publication.

Postscript on Pope

The striking turn toward autobiography in Manley's practice of the *roman à clef* can be observed in related literary forms. Alexander Pope advertised his Horatian verse *Epistle to Dr. Arbuthnot* (1735) as a "Bill of Complaint" against malicious critics who had attacked "not only my Writings (of which being publick the Public judge) but my *Person, Morals,* and *Family* . . . ."[41] In the opening of the poem itself Pope famously spatializes this invasion of privacy as an assault on his domestic retreat in suburban Twickenham:

> Shut, shut the door, good John! fatigu'd I said,
> Tye up the knocker, say I'm sick, I'm dead,
> . . . .
> What Walls can guard me, or what Shades can hide?
>
> They pierce my Thickets, thro' my Grot they glide, . . .
> (lines 1–2, 7–8, p. 96)

Pope's entreaty to his friend profanely echoes Christ's injunction to "shut thy door" to the devotional closet so as to "pray to thy Father which is in secret . . . ."[42] Not in devotion but rather in retribution for this invasion of his privacy Pope promises a satiric counterattack on his enemies that, although personal, will avoid libel by avoiding proper names: "Many will know their own Pictures in it, there being not a Circumstance but what is true; but I have, for the most part spar'd their *Names* . . ." (95, font reversed). Pope's verse epistle succeeds handsomely in its retributive aims (although not without naming some names). And yet the deeper we proceed into his argument, the more we find that the demotion of others serves the cause of self-promotion, that retribution requires a certain species of devotion, that satire mutates into autobiography. The attack on Sporus (Lord Hervey) shows the syntactic and pronominal subtlety of this process:

> His Wit all see-saw between *that* and *this*,
> Now high, now low, now Master up, now Miss,

And he himself one vile Antithesis.
Amphibious Thing! that acting either Part,
The trifling Head, or the corrupted Heart!
Fop at the Toilet, Flatt'rer at the Board,
Now trips a Lady, and now struts a Lord.
Eve's Tempter thus the Rabbins have exprest,
A Cherub's face, a Reptile all the rest;
Beauty that shocks you, Parts that none will trust,
Wit that can creep, and Pride that licks the dust.
Not Fortune's Worshipper, nor Fashion's Fool,
Not Lucre's Madman, nor Ambition's Tool,
Not proud, nor servile, be one Poet's praise
That, if he pleas'd, he pleas'd by manly ways; . . .
(lines 323–37, pp. 119–20)

Assuming a continuity between the pronouns of lines 325 and 337, the inattentive reader will fail to see the third-person speaker's shift at line 334 from the public to the private register, from objective to subjective reference. The true subject of the poem emerges negatively, dialectically defined by what he is not but also thereby entwined with his antithesis. As the amphibiousness of Sporus bleeds into that of the speaker himself, the delicate formal modulation replays the antithetical structure that the poem describes—the "mock-heroic" mixture of high and low, master and miss, lord and lady, Hervey and Pope, satire and self-devotion. Satiric depersonalization, in putative flight from libel, swerves into autobiography. Indeed, for much of the poem we see Pope, like Manley and Behn, experimenting with voice through partial projections of himself onto his "characters"—not only Hervey but Dennis, Dryden, Addison, and Arbuthnot himself. In the penultimate paragraph of the epistle this process comes to a climax when Pope projects his apologia onto his own father, memorializing and identifying with him in eighteen heartfelt lines ("The good Man walk'd innoxious thro' his Age"; "Oh grant me thus to live, and thus to die!" [lines 395, 404]) to such a degree that he fulfills his opening, obscurely allusive intimation that he would seize the opportunity of private retreat to "pray to thy father" (in a footnote Pope lovingly records the inscription he wrote for his parents' church monument).

Pope's greatest performance in political allegory, *Windsor-Forest* (1713), works in the tradition less of the secret history than of the loco-descriptive prospect poem, whose tangled roots go back to the country house poem, Renaissance pastoral allegory, and Virgilian georgic. His most important English precedents for this are John Denham's *Coopers Hill* (1642, 1655, 1668), Andrew Marvell's "Upon Appleton House" (wr. c. 1651), and John Dryden's "To My Honour'd

Kinsman, John Driden, of Chesterton" (1700). In ways that are both obvious and surprising, *The Rape of the Lock*, published a year after *Windsor-Forest* and in the same year as *Rivella*, lays claim to being Pope's most important contribution to the secret history. Besides exemplifying what I have called a "double domestication," *The Rape of the Lock* is also a *poème à clef* in that the romance names of its main characters refer to real people. In his key to the poem, Pope's modern editor makes clear that the actual particularity of Pope's characters is significant to him for private rather than public reasons—as they are members of a distinguished circle of "Roman Catholic families owning land in the home counties" rather than in any political capacity they may have had.[43] On the heels of the Jacobite Rising a year later, however, Pope himself published a pseudonymous and parodic key to his poem that reveals it to be a popish concentration narrative, "a Ridicule on the late Transactions . . . ." "What confirms me in this Opinion, is an accidental Discovery I made of a very artful Piece of Management among [the author's] Popish Friends and Abetters, to hide this whole Design upon the Government, by taking all the Characters upon themselves." In other words, the complaints of private individuals at having been made the butt of Pope's burlesque are a crafty papist conspiracy to distract attention from his public target, state affairs. By this reading, Belinda really signifies Great Britain or Queen Anne (or, more broadly, "the Popish Religion, or the Whore of *Babylon*"); the Baron signifies the Earl of Oxford; the poem's epic machinery "is a Satyr on the Ministers of State in particular"; and the lock itself represents the Barrier Treaty of 1715 (a byproduct of the Treaty of Utrecht by which Holland was ensured a military buffer for protection from French hostilities). The author finds precedent for "this mysterious way of Writing . . . in the Key to the curious romance of *Barclay's Argenis* . . . ."[44]

Pope went so far as to annotate his own copy of *The Rape of the Lock* according to his *Key*'s specifications.[45] Figure 13.3 reproduces these annotations. Here Pope has unlocked the private, domesticated signifiers of the first page of *The Rape of the Lock*: he identifies the lock as the Barrier Treaty, "*C——l*" as "Caryl" (John Caryll, who proposed the poem to Pope), and Belinda as Queen Anne. Moreover, the verso facing this page (fig. 13.2) bears the first of six engravings by French artists, illustrating in another medium the intimate scene of domestic privacy (see canto 1, lines 13–20) that Pope's annotations attest is no more than a crafty disguise for public secrets. The juxtaposition of image and annotated text reminds us that the conceit of an external political reference only replays, in another register, the conceit of domestication with which the poem itself is already concerned. For we see depicted in the engraving the disclosure of another sort of "public" secret, unknown to all those who bind their "narrow Views to Things below." What we see is Belinda's sylph prolonging her

FIG. 13.2. First engraving in Alexander Pope's copy of *The Rape of the Lock* (1714), verso facing first page of poem. Department of Rare Books and Special Collections, Princeton University Library, shelf mark Ex 3897.374.13c.2.

THE
RAPE *of the* LOCK.

The Barrier Treaty

CANTO I.

HAT dire Offence from am'rous
Caufes fprings,
What mighty Quarrels rife from
trivial Things,

I fing——This Verfe to C**ARYL** Mufe! is due ;

This, ev'n *Belinda* may vouchfafe to view :   *C. Arm.*

Slight is the Subject, but not fo the Praife,

If She infpire, and He approve my Lays.

B   Say

FIG. 13.3. First page of Alexander Pope's copy of *The Rape of the Lock* (1714), annotated by himself, recto facing first engraving. Department of Rare Books and Special Collections, Princeton University Library, shelf mark Ex 3897.374.13c.2.

sleep with a dream that reveals a "secret Truth" known only to "Maids" and "Children," namely, that when we say female "*Honour*" we signify the legion of supernatural sylphs by whom the likes of mortals such as Belinda are perpetually guarded (lines 35–37; see also lines 77–78). A modern critic has suggested that in *A Key to the Lock* Pope, like the popish conspirators he describes, is trying to distract attention from the *Rape*'s putative reference to state affairs by preemptively extending to absurdity the technique of political decoding.[46] If posterity has been more inclined to view the publication of the *Key* as Pope's playful jibe at the reigning impulse to discover public meaning in private events, this is at least in part because *The Rape of the Lock* memorably affirms the meaningfulness of private events in the very act of seeming to trivialize them.

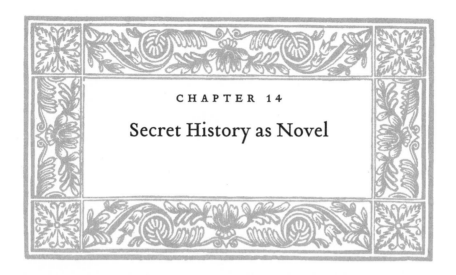

CHAPTER 14

Secret History as Novel

The publication of *Rivella* in 1714 roughly coincided with a watershed in English public affairs: the end of the War of the Spanish Succession; the fall from power of the Tory Party; the death of the last of the Stuarts; the accession of the first Hanoverian, a foreigner whose English was broken but whose Protestantism was secure; and the (first) resounding defeat of those who sought to restore the Stuart pretender to the throne of England. This historical concatenation would seem to have made mandatory the disclosures of secret history. Yet we note with some uncertainty that one highly relevant publishing phenomenon, collections of "poems on affairs of state," seems now to lose the popularity it had sustained for the past half-century or more. How does the watershed of 1714–15 punctuate the history of the secret history we have been tracing? Although there is no simple answer to this question, I hope to provide grounds for viewing the decades that follow as fundamental in the ongoing "privatization" of the secret history, that is, the gradual shift of normative weight from the public referent to private reference—more precisely, the gradual absorption of the public realm's traditional priority and privilege by the realm of private experience.

Autobiography turns biography inward. How is this understanding augmented by the looser notion that autobiography also turns the allegorical secret history inward? The techniques of Puritan introspection hold a privileged place in the generic development of autobiography. What can be said of the looser formal influence on autobiography of the secret history's technical armory? Manley's autobiographical *Rivella* applies the techniques of the *roman à clef* on several levels. Through much of the seventeenth century the *roman à clef* was figured as a "glass of state" endowed with the power to both conceal and reveal.[1]

Moved to extremes of passion by the strange spectacle of foreigners in love and at war, aristocratic readers were shocked (at least in theory) to discover that the glass was also a looking glass that reflected their own images back to them, transforming the pleasing detachment of identification into the rueful self-knowledge of identity. Over the course of the eighteenth century the figure of the (looking-)glass also proved useful in the epistemological account of the state of self-consciousness. Locke had named the two great sources of knowledge "sensation" and "reflection." Whereas the senses "from external Objects convey into the mind what produces there" sense perceptions or sensations, reflection is the "*Perception of the Operations of our own Minds* within us . . . ." Reflection is therefore a kind of "internal Sense" by which "the Understanding turns inwards upon it self, *reflects* on its own *Operations,* and makes them the Object of its own Contemplation."[2] We have seen how the third Earl of Shaftesbury soon after made the Socratic dialogue the model for "a sort of *Pocket-Mirrour*" or "*Looking-Glass*": "Whatever we were employ'd in, whatever we set about; if once we had acquir'd the habit of this *Mirrour;* we shou'd, by virtue of the double Reflection, distinguish our-selves into two different Partys."[3] And at mid-century Adam Smith used the image of the mirror to suggest the degree to which self-knowledge requires bringing "society" inward: "We suppose ourselves the spectators of our own behaviour, and endeavour to imagine what effect it would, in this light, produce upon us. This is the only looking-glass by which we can, in some measure, with the eyes of other people, scrutinize the propriety of our own conduct."[4]

The aim of allegorical secret history is both to conceal and to reveal the actual particularity of public personages. And in Manley's autobiography as in these epistemological figures of speech, attention remains focused on the actual particularity of the subject even if that subject is partialized and fragmentary, subdivided into its objective and subjective, "public" and "private" components (as Lovemore and Rivella, locked in conflict, both signify the actual Delarivier Manley). However, the looking-glass figure may also be used to evoke concrete particularity. This is the case, for example, with satire as it was carefully distinguished by contemporaries from libel. Swift's famous remark reminds us that the concrete particularity of satiric reference had its drawbacks: "Satyr is a sort of *Glass,* wherein Beholders do generally discover every body's Face but their Own; which is the chief Reason for that kind of Reception it meets in the World, and that so very few are offended with it."[5] Fielding's equally famous aim regarding what we have learned to call the novel is more confident—that is, the ambition "to hold the Glass to thousands in their Closets, that they may contemplate their Deformity, and endeavour to reduce it, and thus by suffering private Mortification may avoid public Shame."[6] My ambition in this chapter is to describe the relationship between ongoing experimentation with the secret history on the one hand and the emergence of the (domestic) novel on the other—not so much in the spirit of a genre study (whereby the former would be seen as a determinant formal influence on the latter) but rather as a model for the broad historical transformation that has been my subject throughout this book. The relationship between the secret history and the novel is useful as a model of how the realms of the public and the private are reconfigured in modern culture because narrative form is a richly expressive and suggestive guide to what otherwise may be too abstractly conceived only in terms of the devolution of absolutism, the shift from categorial distinction to separation and conflation, the modulation of formal domestication into domesticity, and the like. Like the graphic arts, literary form throws conceptual discourse into the high relief of shape and structure.

Defoe and Swift

Reading the early novel in the context of what the title of this book calls "the secret history of domesticity" suggests the liabilities of the critical division between the domestic novel and the adventure novel. *Robinson Crusoe* (1719) is commonly cited as an exemplar of the latter form[7] even though the domestication of the island—its familiarization, Anglicization, and domiciliation—lies at the heart of what most fascinates us in Defoe's novel. The ideological conflict between "masculine" economic and "feminine" domestic individualism is too quickly substituted for what we have seen is rather a dialectical relationship between two parts of a greater "private" whole.

But *Robinson Crusoe* is deeply preoccupied with the hermeneutic and pedagogic problems of formal domestication as well.[8] Defoe's claim to historicity may be seen as a privatization of the sort of actual particularity to which allegorical secret histories allude: "*If ever the Story of any private Man's Adventures in the World were worth making Publick, and were acceptable when Publish'd, the Editor of this Account thinks this will be so. . . . The Editor believes the thing to be a just History of Fact. . . .*"[9] But if Robinson is to be understood as a real person, his story is told "with a religious Application of Events" and aims at the reader's spiritual "*Improvement*" (1). And as *The Pilgrim's Progress* (1678, 1684) is a Christian allegory whose hermeneutic signifying system seems to assume a life of its own, *Robinson Crusoe* is its mirror reflection, a fully literalized narrative still marked by the vestiges of Christian allegory.

Shortly after its publication, and in the voice of Robinson Crusoe, Defoe meditated on the nature of the truth his novel aimed to tell, elaborating especially on the suggestiveness of its allegorical aura: "the story, though allegorical, is also historical . . . ."[10] The remark points in two directions. On the one hand, Defoe adds that "there is a man alive, and well known too, the actions of whose life are the just subject of these volumes, and to whom all or most part of the story most directly alludes . . ." (ix–x), and some readers accused Defoe of writing a veiled autobiography by concentrating his own life into that of his protagonist.[11] The charge draws strength from the fact that *Robinson Crusoe* is a conversion narrative whose basic structure is therefore that of the Puritan spiritual autobiography. As Manley divides herself into "two different parties," Rivella and Lovemore, so Defoe divides Robinson into the private, sinful character who is the subject of the story and the public, repentant narrator who tells the story from a postconversion perspective. Is *Robinson Crusoe* too an autobiography? Or is the allusion to "a man alive" to be read as the framing trope of a secret history that obliquely reveals the private life of a public minister of state?[12]

On the other hand, the "Robinson Crusoe" of *Serious Reflections* adds that "when in these reflections I speak of the times and circumstances of particular actions done, or incidents which happened, in my solitude and island-life, an impartial reader will be so just to take it as it is, viz., that it is spoken or intended of that part of the real story which the island-life is a just allusion to . . . . All these reflections are just history of a state of forced confinement, which in my real history is represented by a confined retreat in an island . . ." (xii). Defoe's words may be taken to imply a more comprehensive concentration of public into private "confinement," of a general "state" into a particular "retreat." And he invites us to ponder the rhetorical utility of such a concentration, which both domesticates the great and estranges the familiar: "Facts that are formed to touch the mind must be done a great way off, and by somebody never heard of. . . . [T]he scene, which is placed so far off, had its original so near home" (xiii). This sounds like an invitation to political allegorizing, and Defoe's advice that we attend to "the times of particular actions done" is worth following. Robinson's first shipping, it turns out, takes place in 1651, and the fatal voyage that shipwrecks him on the island in 1659; Robinson leaves the island in 1686 and arrives back in England in 1687 (7–8, 40, 70, 278). Within this chronology, Robinson's private confinement closely corresponds to the period of the Restoration, when dissenters like Defoe suffered the public confinement of Stuart absolutism. Is *Robinson Crusoe* a political allegory? "How like a King I look'd," he remarks shortly before he leaves the island. "First of all, the whole Country was my own meer Property; so that I had an undoubted Right of Dominion. *2dly*, My People were perfectly subjected: I was absolute Lord and Lawgiver; . . . However, I allow'd Liberty of Conscience throughout my Dominions" (241). Is the key that unlocks Robinson's actual particularity Defoe's imagination of a sort of king in exile, an anti-Stuart monarch who sustains on his island the sort of toleration that Charles II had banished from the British Isles until it can return with the Glorious Revolution?[13]

Defoe's obscurity on the temporality and epistemology of his novel exemplifies the problematic sort of discourse that ushered in the modern sense of the aesthetic as a kind of knowledge that combines "private" particularity with "public" generality. Related experimentation with the public-private differential can be seen on the substantive level of *Robinson Crusoe*. Defoe's novel is an ambivalent conversion narrative: that is, it tells the story of a man who strenuously spiritualizes his desire for "deliverance" only to find that the signifying letter of material life has the power to absorb and transfigure the spiritual signified it purports to subserve. Like children who defy their parents by eloping in a love match, Robinson is motivated by a standard of negative liberty that requires him to leave home in order to get home. Although he may possess the metaphorical status of anti-Stuart "absolute lord and law-giver," his character results more profoundly from the metonymic devolution of absolutism that transforms political subjection to the father into the ethical subjectivity of the private citizen. At one point Robinson drolly observes: "It would have made a Stoick smile to have seen, me and my little Family sit down to Dinner; there was my Majesty the Prince and Lord of the whole Island; I had the Lives of all my Subjects at my absolute Command" (148). But the "absolute command" he assumes on the island is first of all a self-command even if by the end of the novel it also takes on a political, commercial, and colonial literality. And the great *arcanum* Robinson internalizes as his own is his conviction of a divine calling, "those secret Hints, or pressings of my Mind" that early on we are asked to see as the signs of sin but gradually become consecrated as the voice of God (175, 14, 188, 198, 202, 232–34, 250).

The compound character that Robinson attains through this internalization of "public" decree within private conscience is the highly experimental identity of the Christian capitalist. In his father's house he bridles at the protectionist constraints put on his willful rambling. Having internalized his father as his will, Robinson undergoes an autoreformation and becomes an ethical and ostentatiously charitable subject (285–88). Mediating between these identities of the disobedient rebel and the Christian capitalist is the proving ground of the island, where solitary confinement paradoxically liberates Robinson to become an ethical subject not by altering his acquisitive, antisocial motives but by removing him from their register, society: "I had nothing to covet; for I had all that I was now capable of enjoying: I was Lord of the whole Mannor; or if I pleas'd, I might call my self King, or Emperor over the whole Country which I had Possession of. There were no Rivals. I had no Competitor, none to dispute Sovereignty or Command with me. I might have rais'd Ship Loadings of Corn;

but I had no use for it . . . . [A]ll I could make use of, was, All that was valuable" (128–29).

Oddly enough, Robinson's utopia of primitive accumulation resembles that of the domestic housewife, who, segregated from public intercourse with the decline of the domestic economy, reconstitutes the role of absolute governor within her own private "manor." Like the housewife's, Robinson's labor is unremunerated because untouched by the market and exchange value;[14] unlike her, he is self-sufficient because there exists no public alternative to his private home, which is in effect coextensive with the world. Economic and domestic individualism, rooted in the same soil of negative liberty, are nonetheless players in a zero-sum game and come into conflict where they touch—where the home and the (female) homemaker are programmatically protected from the solvent force of the market. In *Moll Flanders* (1722) and *Roxana* (1724) Defoe doggedly pursues this conflict. In *Robinson Crusoe* he avoids it with an alacrity that some readers mistakenly see as narrowly masculinist: in a single sentence we hear of Robinson's marriage, fatherhood, and widowing, a mere punctuation in the promise of "farther Adventures" (305). But the propinquity of home and adventure is evident everywhere in *Robinson Crusoe,* and nowhere more than in the proliferation of "my little Family" and of the "houshold Stuff and Habitation" (148, 69)—tent, cave, kitchen, cellar, storehouse, dining room, bower, country house—that populate the scene of Robinson's greatest adventure, the island itself.

If *Robinson Crusoe* is therefore only parabolically about the devolution of absolutism from public monarch to private citizen, *Gulliver's Travels* (1726) is explicitly focused on the myriad ways state authority fails those it subjects to its power.[15] Gulliver is astonished to hear the normative King of Brobdingnag decline his offer of the "Secret" of gunpowder—to hear him "let slip an Opportunity put into his Hands, that would have made him absolute Master of the Lives, the Liberties, and the Fortunes of his People. . . . He professed both to abominate and despise all *Mystery, Refinement,* and *Intrigue,* either in a Prince or a Minister. He could not tell what I meant by *Secrets of State,* where an Enemy or some Rival Nation were not in the Case."[16] But whereas Defoe's premise is the superiority of industrious privacy to the corruptions of absolutist secrecy, Swift imagines a public rule so tacitly authoritative as to prompt Gulliver to address it as "Master." With the Houyhnhnms there are no secrets because there is no separation between civil society and the state. Gulliver, torn between the modernity of separation and the futile wish to achieve mere distinction through laborious conflation, evinces the duplicity of the secret historian who deplores secrets of state even as he purveys them. In Glubbdubdrib his self-righteous indignation is contradictory: "Here I discovered the Roguery and Ignorance of those who pretend to write *Anecdotes,* or secret History; who send so many Kings to their Graves with a Cup of Poison; will repeat the Discourse between a Prince and chief Minister, where no Witness was by; unlock the Thoughts and Cabinets of Embassadors and Secretaries of State; and have the perpetual Misfortune to be mistaken. Here I discovered the true Causes of many great Events that have surprized the World . . ." (pt. 3, chap. 8, 183). Swift's own play with the possibility that his narrative is an allegorical secret history about actual particulars is far more pervasive than Defoe's, characteristically combining solid evidence of his allegorizing intent with irresistible enticements to overinterpret.

Jane Barker and Mary Hearne

Perhaps because of their extreme political jeopardy, recognizably Jacobite political allegories are not easy to find in the years following the '15. It has been argued that several of Jane Barker's narratives published between 1713 and 1726 should be read as "Jacobite novels" that bear "strong political resonances for contemporary readers attuned to Jacobite interpretive codes."[17] This may be a fair account so long as we keep in mind how far these "codes" are from the domesticating rhetoric of concentration and concretization at work in authors like Behn and Manley. Barker's narratives tell the stories of private people whose relation to public events is one of tenuous evocation rather than tangible signification.[18] True, reminders of historical events of Jacobite importance—especially James II's defeat, exile, and death—occasionally provide the stories with a background temporal setting, and some of Barker's characters, we are told, have played tangential roles in that history. Moreover, domestic events (thwarted love, familial conflicts, forced and chosen marriages, bigamy, spinsterhood) that in *romans à clef* might bear a determinate relationship to public events proliferate in these narratives. But rather than possessing a specifically public resonance, such events diffuse a broadly affective climate of regret, loss, and melancholy, a wistful nostalgia that is compatible with Jacobite ideology strictly at the level of feeling. Actual particularity is dissolved in the virtuality of emotional atmosphere.[19]

On the face of it, the companion narratives of Mary Hearne bear a closer formal relation to the tradition of the secret history. Each of them a single extended epistolary production, each also contains the confidential exchange of letters within its plots, which are peopled by personages whose names either are of romance provenance or are syncopated or truncated, in the self-censoring mode, after the initial letter ("Lady D——"). The first of the two volumes that comprise Hearne's three narratives is dedicated to Delarivier Manley and fea-

tures a hero named Philander who at one point is discovered reading "the famous Mrs. *Behn*'s Novels"; the second volume ends by claiming of its characters
that "tho' I have concealed their Names, when you read their Story, it will fully
explain to you who they are . . . ."[20] But the implication of political allegory is
not so easily made explicit as these words would suggest. Are Hearne's narratives infused (despite the politics of these mentors) "with Whiggish, pro-
Hanoverian intent"?[21] Even more strictly than in Barker, reference to the actual
particularity of public affairs is largely limited to background sketches of the
two fathers in *The Female Deserters:* one served the Tory ministry under Queen
Anne, the other (recalling Delia's Cavalier father a generation earlier)[22] "was ruined by his Loyalty among others, who had follow'd the Fortunes of King *James*
II" (9, 11). A single theme, generational conflict on the marriage choice, is
treated in Hearne's three narratives, whose structural similarities are underscored by the fact that they are first-person nested narratives. In *The Lover's
Week* Amaryllis writes her friend Emilia the story of her love affair with Philander. *The Female Deserters,* a second letter from Amaryllis to Emilia, brings that
story up to date in a frame that contains the amours of Calista and Torismond
as told to Amaryllis by Calista, who incorporates in her story the amours of Isabella and Polydor as told to her by Isabella. The effect of this nesting structure
is to involve the successively enclosed stories in something akin to the "privatizing" differential available through third-person narratives like the latter two
parts of Behn's *Love-Letters* while avoiding the explicit shift in person.

Does Hearne invoke Behn and Manley because she, like them, is writing *romans à clef?* We are told at the end of *The Female Deserters* that the stories have
been narrated to us in something close to reverse chronological order (109).
This detail, reinforcing our sense of Hearne's careful attention to structure and
in combination with the hints of public reference I have just cited, may invite
interpretive ingenuity. If the last is really the first, then we might read the three
nested narratives as a concentration of the royal history of England from 1685 to
1715. By this reading, the three women are successive embodiments of England
herself as she is passed along the succession of English royalty. Isabella, in love
with Polydor (the Duke of Monmouth), is "dying for Fear" that her father
(Charles II) will learn of this "Secret." In the event, it is Polydor's father (who in
this reading also must be Charles II) who discovers the secret, commands his
son "not to think any more of her," and finally ships him overseas. Meanwhile,
Isabella, affianced against her will to Lycippus (the Duke of York), leaves home,
only to find that "the Publick talk of the whole Country" is her "Desertion
from her Father . . ." (*Female Deserters,* 32, 52, 67). Calista, more fortunate than
Isabella, is urged by her father (James II) to follow him into retirement. And although Calista "could not think of leaving my Family" (*Female Deserters,* 92),

her devoted lover, Torismond (William of Orange), seduces her, then persuades her "to pass the rest of your life with me . . . ." She happily agrees, anticipating "a far greater Tranquility than I once thought could have been enjoyed in this Life" (*Female Deserters,* 105, 106). The third figure for England (now Britain), Amaryllis, is advised by her patriarchal guardian aunt (Queen Anne) to accede to an arranged marriage with the duke of A—— (the Tory ministry?). Instead Amaryllis resolves on "Desertion" with Philander (George I? more radically, Parliament?), who takes her to a brothel, which she is nonetheless assured is "as safe as if you were in the Royal Palace of *St. James*'s . . ." (*Lover's Week,* 35, 28). That night Philander seduces Amaryllis; she, disdaining female affectation, is concerned only that their "Secret" be kept. Soon Philander finds what he calls "a small Country-Seat" where "we shall pass the Remainder of our Lives in an agreeable Solitude," resolved "to quit all publick Places . . ." (34, 41–42, 45–46).

Justified by little more than these incidentals (and compromised even by some of them), the political allegorization of Hearne's narratives, bolstered by reader expectations that are decades old and by now second nature, has a real plausibility that vindicates the notion of a "Whiggish intent." And yet to take this as the semantic center of Hearne's intent requires that we dull our sensitivity to a broader and deeper preoccupation with the private lives of figures whose concrete particularity solicits our identificatory judgment on the way "we" live today. Hearne violates chronology, we may feel, in order to emphasize how traditional and still common ways of thinking about love and marriage, children and parents, subjectivity and subjection, fall short of ethical possibility. She constructs something like a typology of "female deserters," three women whose responses to the age-old injunction to leave one man for another are radically at variance with one another. As we hear their stories in this particular succession, we experience the progressively greater difficulty Calista and Isabella have in adopting the privatized posture of the ethical subject as unfortunate but unnecessary. True, their circumstances vary in tangible ways, but the evitability of Isabella's abjection—our sense that it might have been otherwise—owes to the fact that we already have the experiences of Calista and Amaryllis with which to compare her "fate."

What Amaryllis's story bespeaks is the possibility of a domestic female privacy, obscurely evocative of parliamentary democracy, that is consistent with autonomy and freedom. What her story shares with the other women's—and perhaps with Hearne herself—is the premise that this domestic ideal is inconsistent with the institution of marriage. Amaryllis's retirement is not privation but a chosen privacy, which she, unlike Manley's Rivella, is able to combine with love because the expendability of marriage to achieve this end is acceptable to both her and her lover. The daughter is able to desert the public scrutiny of the "father" without sacrificing herself to the husband. That is, Hearne experiments with the notion that the domestic house may be a setting for women's ethical responsibility so long as it is the (parliamentary?) house neither of the father nor of the husband. Calista and Isabella are bound by chains of deference, passivity, and dependence that, thrown into relief by the example of Amaryllis, seem almost fanciful and mind-made, a matter of bad faith. Raised to the macrolevel of historical experience, the psychological condition of bad faith finds its counterpart in the transitional moment when old convictions, threadbare enough to be seen through in places, continue to be worn in the absence of any comfortable replacement; Amaryllis, by contrast, seems to possess a whole new wardrobe. And yet even this considerable historical insight appears motivated less by the ambition to identify and characterize actual particularity than by the broad ethics of negative liberty that were in part generated by the public affairs of the past century and that remain intact in the shape of plot and character after the actual particularity of those affairs, along with its formal means of signification, have largely been weathered away. The private has internalized the concerns of the public (as Parliament has those of absolute monarchy?) just as Amaryllis, responsive to the moral threat of public scandal, reconceives that threat as a private matter responsive in turn to her own ethical volition. This is not to deny the semantic contiguity of Hearne's narratives and public politics but to conceive the latter as a residue or sediment that permeates the practice of the former with a powerfully determinant but fundamentally different meaning.

Hearne's formal procedure is, of course, an important means by which actual is converted to virtual and concrete particularity. In all three of her stories the lover first receives a truncated name denoting his actual particularity and then is renamed in the romance mode—twice (Philander and Polydor) by the lover himself signing a love letter and once (Torismond) by the internal narrator ("for so I shall now call him," says Calista) (*Lover's Week,* 5; *Female Deserters,* 11, 31).[23] Hearne thereby retains a formal connection to the *roman à clef,* but despite the final claim to historicity (*Female Deserters,* 108–9), we read the names not as a coded disguise for reality but as a virtual representation of it. The knowledge that Isabella's misfortunes transpire within a Jacobite family is important to us not because they illuminate—let alone refer to or signify—Jacobitism but because that knowledge subtly deepens our understanding of her misfortunes. Public passions give insight into private passions: the secret history of the Stuart family provides a gloss on the secret histories of private individuals. But psychology takes priority over chronology. Amaryllis is a fully ethical subject rather than a still partially political one not because she embodies the progressive principles of Whig history at the moment of their modern take-

off but because she fully internalizes from the examples of Calista and Isabella—from their concretization of abstract precept—what they can only live
out in partial subjection to tacit social rule. Amaryllis has pride of place in the
telling of the stories precisely because hers comes last, and the comparative fullness of her autonomy is reflected in her place in the chain of narrative dependence comprised of Hearne's companion texts. Calista and Isabella are both narrated by Amaryllis, alone among the three in having become an ethical subject
and therefore the only character who also can be her own narrator, her "privacy" coordinated with her "publicity."

Haywood's Secret Histories

By the 1740s Eliza Haywood had little respect (as we have seen) for the notion
that the only kind of "secret histories" worth disclosing were public ones of actual particularity.[24] Two decades earlier, however, the phrase was a frequent one
on her title pages, and it is worth asking what she meant by it. The question has
no simple answer. Two of these narratives follow the form of the allegorical secret history sufficiently to possess appended "Keys." *Memoirs of a Certain Island Adjacent to the Kingdom of Utopia* (1725) alludes to Manley's precedent
both in its title and in being principally told, like the *New Atalantis,* by a
frankly allegorical figure, a *"Celestial Intelligence,"* who narrates a series of "histories."

   The key to Haywood's *Memoirs* (see fig. 14.1) translates the several Italianate
romance names into syncopated ones. But the narrative also contains private
names that have not been romancified, and in several places its key tellingly
omits information that in a more traditional *roman à clef* would be self-evidently crucial. The key table, after all, correlates in the left column our only evidence (the fictional names we encounter in the narrative) with a column on
the right that specifies the actual people they stand for. In this key, however, the
lefthand column carelessly leaves several spaces blank, and we are obliged to return to the relevant page (whose number the key provides) to learn the identity
not, it should be stressed, of the signified but of the signifier: thus "the chevalier
d'Eshart" is the signifier of "Col. M——*y*" (17), "the Dutchess *de Cruizilla*" is
the signifier of "Dss. S——*y*" (19), "the Wife of the Chevalier *Brisoe*" is the
signifier of "Mrs. *Br*——*nt*" (33), and "That Woman" is the signifier of "Mrs.
H——*ll*" (34).[25] It is as though the most basic priorities of the *roman à clef*
have been not just muddled but inverted, so that the interpretive mystery we
are asked to solve pertains not to the actual but to the virtual identity of the
names, and the process of signification more often than not seems mysteriously
to correlate one "private" figure with another. In Haywood's other key narra-

tive, *The Secret History of the present Intrigues of the Court of Caramania* (1727), the key is more functionally conventional in its form insofar as the lefthand column fully supplies the romance signifiers used in the text (see fig. 14.2). This permits us to focus on the anomaly this key nonetheless shares with the key to the *Memoirs,* namely, that the signifieds of the righthand column are entirely syncopated and therefore only "solve" the problem of actual identity posed by the romance signifiers with another species of signifier. In figure 14.2 the reader of this copy of Haywood's *Secret History,* undaunted by the syncopations, has filled in their blank spaces, in effect (and necessarily) treating the putative solutions to the mystery as another mystery in need of solution.²⁶ Although this reader's industry appears to tell a different story, the evidence of Haywood's keys generally suggests that the key is becoming a vestigial convention of the *roman à clef* form, still in use but increasingly dysfunctional and unconcerned to unlock the mystery of actual particularity for which it is designed. The appeal of figure 14.2 would seem to bear more comparison with that of a crossword puzzle.

In other narratives of the 1720s the presence of the titular phrase in the absence of a key bespeaks varying degrees of privatization to which Haywood is subjecting the mode of the secret history. Little more ties one of these stories— *The City Jilt; or, the Alderman turn'd Beau: A Secret History* (1726)²⁷—to that mode than the title itself. Another "secret history" opens with a claim to historicity that broadly associates it with the rhetoric of actuality characteristic of the forthright "true history"; but the accompanying claim to exemplarity aligns it more specifically with the rhetoric of concretization than with the allegorical indirection and public reference of the "secret history" its title announces: "But, the following little History (which I can affirm for Truth, having it from the Mouths of those chiefly concerned in it) is a sad Example of what Miseries may attend a Woman, who has no other Foundation for Belief in what her Lover says to her than the good Opinion her Passion has made her conceive of him."²⁸ The "secrets" that the novella conceals and reveals with crucial epistolary interpolations are the private ones of "disobedience to Parents," "*ill requited Love,*" and illicit subsistence "with Child" (170, 155, 180). Yet the intrigues of its private plot are sustained by the politically resonant language of the "Traitor," the "Tyrant," the "Spy," "Ingratitude," "unexampled Perfidy," "free Consent" and "breach of Promise," "the Mystery of her concealing herself," and "Orders . . . to confine me to my Chamber" (183, 211, 187, 223, 204, 208, 155, 171). In other words, the conventional markers of public reference seem to haunt this private story, culminating in a remarkably sequenced disclosure of identity.

Cleomira (the British Recluse of the title) and Belinda have told each other their pathetic stories of seduction and abandonment, and the latter now nar-

(1)

A

K E Y.

Pag.			
7.	L	Ucitario,	C———gs.
9.		Conbree,	D. P————d.
11.		Marcus,	L. G——ge.
	Mirazaida,		Mrs. Le———n.
12.	Lady,		Cfs. C————y.
	Marthalia,		Mrs. Bl———t.
13.	Gratiana,		Mifs Ch———ld.
14.	Romanus,		Mr. Tr——rd.
17.			Col. M——y.
19.			Dfs. S———y.
21.			E. P——gh.
			Mrs. Th——n.
23.	Miranda,		Mrs. M——r———n.
33.			Mrs. Br———nt.
34.			Mrs. H————ll.
35.	Conftantius,		Mr. G. H————ll.
	Lauranus,		Mr. A. H————ll.
39.	Somerius,		Mr. So————rs.
	Philarchus,		Mr. Sy———s.
	Burtonius,		Mr. B———n.
	Arthario,		C———r H———tt.
	Merfus,		H———rl———y.
43.	Gloaticia,		Mrs. S——nf——m.

Ma-

FIG. 14.1. Key to [Eliza Haywood], *Memoirs Of a Certain Island Adjacent to the Kingdom of Utopia . . .* (1725). Department of Rare Books and Special Collections, Princeton University Library.

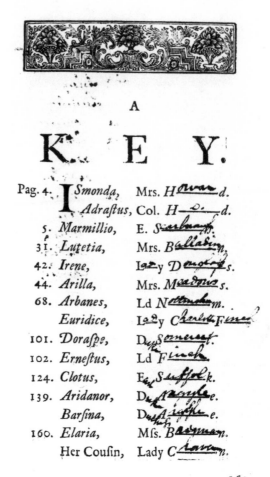

A

KEY.

Pag. 4. Smonda,   Mrs. H————d.

      Adraſtus,   Col. H————d.

  5. Marmillio,   E. S————.

 31. Lutetia,   Mrs. B————.

 42. Irene,   Laꞁy D————s.

 44. Arilla,   Mrs. M————s.

 68. Arbanes,   Ld N————m.

    Euridice,   Laꞁy C————.

101. Doraſpe,   D————.

102. Erneſtus,   Ld F————.

124. Clotus,   E——S————k.

139. Aridanor,   D————e.

    Barſina,   D————e.

160. Elaria,   Mſs. B————.

    Her Couſin,   Lady C————.

165.

FIG. 14.2. Key to [Eliza Haywood], *The Secret History of the present Intrigues of the Court of Caramania* (1727). Department of Rare Books and Special Collections, Princeton University Library, shelf mark Ex 3777.2.384.

rates the conversation with two ladies through which she discovered that the name her villain had given her—Sir Thomas Courtal—was a false one:

> Sir *Thomas Courtal* (cried they both out) for Heavens sake who are you talking of? . . . Bless me! (said one of them) I know him not; nor I (cried the other) I thought we had all this while been speaking of my *Lord*—— ——
>
> Here *Belinda* made a full Stop, as considering whether she should name him; and after about a Moment's Reflection—You will pardon me (said she to the RECLUSE) if I conceal the real Name of this ungrateful Man . . . . (217)

Belinda's full stop looks like the typographical syncopation of a secret history, and since this accords with her motive of concealment, it is easy to read the passage as an allusion to an actual particularity of whose knowledge both Cleomira and we are deprived. However, another discovery soon caps this one and brings the narrative to a close. A detail in Belinda's story has brought Cleomira to the crowning recognition that their two villains are one and the same man: "I might from the very beginning of your Story have imagined it—might have known that such prodigious *Charms* and such prodigious *Villainy* were no where blended but in my perfidious but still dear *Lysander!*—Your *Courtal!*— my *Lysander* are the same, and both are found only in the Person of the too lovely, faithless, *Bellamy*" (222–23). For readers whose anticipation has been piqued for scandal by Belinda's preceding full stop this last name must be fraught with anticlimax. For although "Lord Bellamy" might well name the actual particularity of a great man of Georgian England, in fact it has the concrete particularity of a fictional name that does not refer beyond the text, and it supplies, not the identity of the villain, but a placeholder by which our identification with the protagonists is augmented.

The accommodation of the secret to the true history in *The British Recluse* is apparent in other narratives by Haywood published during the 1720s. *The Mercenary Lover* (1726) justifies its subtitle by the prefatory promise of, not public disclosures but "*a Sad, but true Account of the Misfortunes of a Family . . . .*" "Secrets" are not lacking, but they are the "fatal," "guilty," "dreadful Secret[s]" of "Adultery and Incest" incurred by private people whose particularity we are never asked to suspect (as in the parallel case of Behn's Silvia and Philander) may be actual.[29] Behn's influence may also be felt in Haywood's *Fantomina* (1725), which takes Silvia's multiple impersonation a step further. Silvia, it will be recalled, persuades Alonzo that she is a different person in each of her guises as the handsome Bellumere, the beautiful whore, and the lovely unknown.[30] Haywood's protagonist hides the "Secret of her Name and Quality" from Beauplaisir by successively disguising herself as a playhouse courtesan and "Prostitute," "the Daughter of a Country Gentleman" named Fantomina, a "rude Country Girl" and domestic "Maid" named Celia, "the sorrowful *Widow*" "Mrs. *Bloomer*," and (with the aid of not just clothing but also letters) the mysterious Incognita.[31] In the course of this serial fornication she adds to the secrets of her name and quality the fact that she is "with Child" (246), and in the female sanctuary of her lying-in chamber she is forced to reveal to the astonished Beauplaisir that she is "really" the "Court beauty" he had admired around the public places of London but never suspected he knew, let alone had impregnated (247–48, 233).

Read as a truncated adaptation of Behn's *Love-Letters*, *Fantomina* is notable for the way the protagonist's disguises proliferate to cover the spectrum of female social identity. Perhaps this proliferation compensates for Haywood's aestheticizing withdrawal from public reference, hence also from the reflexive relationship between character and author, the parallel performances (available to a *roman à clef*) before the respectively micro- and macroaudiences of Silvia's Alonzo and Behn's readers. Is it fruitful to see this compensation as the work of internalization, whereby Haywood's more privatized secret history sustains the dialectical inquiry into the public-private relationship by transferring it from the "external" differential of actual-virtual particularity to that—located within the virtual realm—of female personality (city and court beauty, courtesan, widowed heiress, country gentility, domestic servant, single mother, cipher)? A related "adaptation" consists in the way Haywood's Beauplaisir echoes Behn's Bellumere. The latter figure is not a man but a male role taken by the female as one of her disguises, an incognito (or pseudocognito) who has no corresponding number in Haywood because her protagonist limits herself—and the performed range of female personality—to female impersonation. Does Haywood's Fantomina stand in relation to Behn's Silvia as Behn's Alonzo may to her Octavio, a harbinger of an emergent system of gender and sexual difference?

The most explicit adequation of the secret history to the epistemology of the true history comes in the preface to Haywood's *The Fair Hebrew:*

> There are so many Things, meerly the Effect of Invention, which have been published, of late, under the Title of SECRET HISTORIES, that to distinguish this, I am obliged to inform my Reader, that I have not inserted one Incident which was not related to me by a Person nearly concerned in the Family of that unfortunate Gentleman, who had no other Consideration in the Choice of a WIFE, than to gratify a present Passion for the Enjoyment of her Beauty.
>
> I found something so particular in the Story, and so much Room for the most useful and moral Reflections to be drawn from it, that I thought I should be guilty of an Injury to the Publick in concealing it.[32]

As in *The British Recluse,* the historicity of this secret history is underwritten by the testimony of an eye- or earwitness, a claim whose concern with actual particularity has to do not with public identity (this is undoubtedly a private "family") but with the element of the authentically "particular" that ensures the exemplary efficacy of the story. It is on this privately ethical score—and not for the political morality of exposing great men to public scandal—that the author decides against "concealing it" from "the Publick." Haywood ends her narrative with the brisk precept it concretizes: "This Example of a Wife so dearly purchased, is sufficent to warn Mankind from a too hasty Marriage" (53).

The principal work done by the Jewish milieu in *The Fair Hebrew* is to throw into the darkest relief the generational conflict between the absoluteness of patriarchal power and the childrens' liberty of choice. The beautiful Kesiah is no exception to the Jewish law that forbids all women "to appear with Faces uncovered" in synagogue. At "Home . . . she was never suffered to go abroad without her Father, one of her Brothers, or some other Relation . . ." (2, 4). Haywood's relentless theme is "*Jewish* Power" and "the Subjection of the *Jewish* Laws," represented both figuratively and literally by enclosure within the "Father's House" (47, 46, 13, 15, 21). As for Kesiah, "[t]he strict Restraint she was kept in by her Parents, had heightened her Desire of Liberty, and she looked on their Care, as a kind of Bondage" (8). When the Christian Dorante falls in love with her, she finds an opportunity to escape her domestic imprisonment and its perpetuation—for in the normal course of things "she should perhaps be forced to Marry a *Jew* . . ." (10). The lovers commence a "private" correspondence and manage to elope shortly before Kesiah's father finds a love letter in "a little Cabinet" (7, 16). The conflict now assumes explicitly public proportions: Kesiah "was not only married lawfully to DORANTE, but the better to secure herself from her Father's Power, she entirely renounc'd *Judaism*, embrac'd *Christianity,* and was baptized, and receiv'd into the Church of *England,* with all the Forms and Ceremonies necessary to render it dangerous, for even the Authority of a Parent to give her any Interruption" (19). As Kesiah represents it to her father, this is a classic case of alliance versus love, family tyranny versus the freedom of the subject: she chooses "to renounce her Father, Family, and Religion to embrace [Dorante's], because she loves him . . ." (22). But individual freedom of choice finds an unexpected ally in the state: marriage law pits the religious apparatus of the English state against Jewish law and the tyranny of the family.

In fact Haywood's Judaism only aggravates an already English problem. The fathers combine against the children: Dorante's father, Morosino, warns him that if he perseveres, he "must expect to be discarded by me, and made an alien to my Name and House . . . ." Morosino's vow "to disinherit him, and make his younger Son the sole Master of his Possessions after his decease" is soon enacted, and Dorante suffers literal imprisonment for debt (20, 25, 49, 48). Ensuring that her point has been made, Haywood reinforces it with the interpolated

"*History* of MIRIAM," a foil for Kesiah whose fate starkly exceeds hers. A Jewish woman seduced and impregnated by a gentile libertine, Miriam is made to suffer "the Letter of the Law." First "confin'd close Prisoner in my Chamber . . . ," she then is conducted to a lying-in chamber—customarily a female sanctuary and, like the room in figure 5.12, furnished with an open hearth—where her uncle, in an apotheosis of patriarchal absolutism, sacrifices her newborn child in the fire (30, 39, 42–43).

On the opening page of *The Fair Hebrew* Haywood invokes a convention of secret-history discourse—the cabinet of state effeminated and rifled by love—that momentarily gives a false lead into her ensuing narrative: "The insinuating Glances of two lovely Eyes have Power to melt the roughest Warrior to Effeminacy, make the Statesman forget his cunning, unlock the Cabinets of Princes, and from the Altar draw the suppliant Votary . . ." (1). Haywood's powerful fable intimates everywhere its availability to the allegorical strategies of the secret history, its potential for application to political struggles between the public state and private organs of civil society. Its most terrible representation of absolutist tyranny is provided by the pitiless engine of the Jewish law, rendered more chilling by the aura of arcane and preternatural mystery in which it is shrouded. And yet the very terror of the depiction may bespeak its aesthetic distance from the sort of actual public politics to which it might (but clearly does not) refer. Heretofore inseparable from politics, the absolutism of religion is becoming, especially in its exotic non-Christian guise, a numinous source of dread, the affect we feel in the presence of an atavism whose power is as much psychological as political.

Richardson's *Pamela*

If the category of the "domestic novel" warrants subgeneric status, Samuel Richardson's *Pamela* (1740) is both its first and its most fully realized exemplar. Richardson's action is set entirely in domestic spaces, his protagonist is a domestic servant who becomes a (domestic) wife, and his concerns revolve exclusively around the concentric spheres of intimate privacy. In what useful sense is *Pamela* also intelligible as a secret history, or an internalization of public concerns? How might it be seen not only as a paragon and innovative prototype of domesticity but also as a thickly sedimented record of the process of formal domestication by which it came to be what it is?

The most evident residue of the domestication process in *Pamela* bespeaks not the *roman à clef* but romance.[33] As Richard Steele self-consciously domesticated *Paradise Lost,* so (according to Anna Laetitia Barbauld) Richardson domesticated his generic plot of the chivalric romance: "That kind of fictitious writing of which he has set the example, disclaims all assistance from giants or genii. The moated castle is changed to a modern parlour; the princess and her pages to a lady and her domestics, or even to a simple maiden, without birth or fortune . . . ."[34] Pamela's own version of this domestication is only more Christian than Barbauld's: "For you see by my sad Story, and narrow Escapes, what Hardships poor Maidens go thro', whose Lot is to go out to Service; especially to Houses where there is not the Fear of God, and good Rule kept by the Heads of Families."[35] Richardson intimated the romance provenance of his novel on its title page, not only by referring to his protagonist by the slightly archaic term "damsel" but also by giving her a name unusual enough to call to readers' minds Philip Sidney's Pamela, who, like Richardson's, is nearly raped by her beloved (1).[36] Of course, the *Old Arcadia* is also a subtly understated *roman à clef* about the most elevated of public figures. Richardson is happy to hear Pamela described as an allegory, although the implication is not political but religious: "[W]ho could have dreamt, he should find, under the modest Disguise of a *Novel,* all the *Soul* of Religion . . . ?" (9).[37] Moreover, Richardson makes a powerful claim to historicity regarding Pamela's actual particularity ("the Story must have happened within these Thirty Years past"), although his prefatory role as "editor" is soon compromised by the term "author" (3, 4, 5, 6, 10). Most strikingly, perhaps, Pamela's master, tormentor, and eventual husband is first known to us only by the name of "Mr. *B——*" (see 17, 20, 57), a syncopation conventionally suggestive of real existence.[38] Enough of a public figure to sit in Parliament (71), he is also a local justice of the peace whom Pamela early on fears may send her to jail and put her on trial for theft (63). And if *Pamela* lacks an appended key to the political identities it conceals and reveals, "this little History" does end with its ethical equivalent, a key to, or "a few brief Observations" on, the exemplary status of each of its characters in turn, and a guide to the propriety of our identification with them (409–12).

Family Politics

The aura of not only actual but even public allusion adumbrated by these details is conveyed most subtly by the texture of metaphorical politics in which Richardson embeds the conflict between Pamela and Mr. B. As a result of this embedding, their conflict fitfully but forcefully assumes the proportions of a national engagement between collective opposing forces, and *Pamela,* read in this way, becomes available to us as a subtle evocation—even, a concentration narrative—of something like the civil wars of the past century. On the one hand, Mr. B., at one point explicitly supposed "a King," is more accurately seen as an absolute despot who inflicts his "sad" and "lawless Tyranny" on his servant. While still in the Bedfordshire house Pamela asks her parents: "Is there no

Constable . . . to take me out of his House? For I am sure I can safely swear the Peace against him . . . ." And from being "a free Person" she soon becomes "a sordid Slave," a "*Prisoner*" thrown into "Bondage" in the Lincolnshire house, where her jailer "locks me . . . in" with "two Keys" (72, 203, 147, 64, 126, 127, 109, 130, 104). Pamela, on the other hand, is an "*artful Creature* . . . enough to corrupt a Nation . . . ," a tirelessly plotting "Rebel" whose "downright Rebellion" and "Crime of *Læsæ Majestatis*" or "Treason against my Liege Lord and Husband" consists in circulating "treasonable Papers" and making of the domestic servants a "Party" of "Confederates" against their and her master (144, 66, 116, 334, 199, 68, 144, 202, 231). Pamela's chief weapon against authority is publication. Indeed, she libels her master: Mr. B. is "very much displeased with the Freedoms you have taken with my Name . . . ." Imprisonment in Lincolnshire was necessitated by Pamela's treacherous disclosure of the *arcana imperii,* her "Letter-writing of all the Secrets of my Family," by which she "has corrupted all my Servants at the other House" in Bedfordshire (41, 74, 163). Demanding now that she produce her "sawcy Journal," Mr. B. warns that "[i]f a Criminal won't plead with us here in *England,* we *press him* to Death, or till he does plead. And so now, *Pamela,* that is a Punishment shall certainly be yours, if you won't tell without" (203). And in response to the notion that husbands, however wrong, are not to be disputed, Pamela saucily invokes one of the most radically suggestive conceits of the revolutionary years: "This would bear a smart Debate, I fansy, in a Parliament of Women" (371).[39] The humor of these last two passages is consonant with a parodic motive as imitative of the public model as it is critical of its continued relevance. Richardson's very proximity to the *roman à clef* tradition complements our confidence that he is not writing such a narrative.

A recent strain of criticism has urged that we see Richardson and Fielding as constituting the second wave of the rise of the novel, writing in explicit opposition to and correction of a first wave of scandal novelists comprised of Behn, Manley, and Haywood. In this view, the central failings of the first wave in the eyes of the second are their sexual profligacy and the fact that they are popular and successful authors—and, for some critics, the fact that they are women. Posterity has conspired with Richardson and Fielding in burying the names and achievements of these first novelists; for a variety of reasons contemporary literary criticism is called upon to right this injustice.[40] Certainly both Richardson and Fielding made clear their distaste for what Behn, Manley, and Haywood had written, although with neither the decisiveness nor the like-mindedness that has been implied. In a letter of 1750 Richardson referred to three contemporary woman writers as "a Set of Wretches . . . to make the Behn's, the Manley's, and the Heywood's, look white," and in a 1739 preface that has been attributed to Richardson he praised Penelope Aubin against the negative example of contemporary female authors, who, "like the *fallen Angels,* having lost their own Innocence, seem, as one would think by their Writings, to make it their Study to corrupt the Minds of others, and render them as depraved, as miserable, and as lost as themselves."[41] It is harder to find Fielding criticizing his three predecessors, at least in the moral terms Richardson favored. Perhaps the best-known of his reflections is also the most cogent. In *Joseph Andrews* (1742) Fielding criticized "the Authors of immense Romances, or the modern Novel and *Atalantis* Writers; who without any Assistance from Nature or History, record Persons who never were, or will be, and Facts which never did nor possibly can happen . . . ."[42] Fielding's concern here is clearly with questions of truth telling, not sexual depravity, and the context of his reference to Manley's *New Atalantis* makes clear that the *roman à clef* was not what he meant by getting assistance from history.

Sex and gender conflict is perhaps too automatically the lens through which we are inclined to read the meaning of eighteenth-century literary critical judgments. Whatever the merits of the case that Behn, Manley, and Haywood are first-wave novelists, it seems to me worth considering that a crucial issue for both Richardson and Fielding concerns the allegorical method of the secret history and its dedication to disclosing (if also veiling) the actual particularity of its characters. The ethics of the secret history are tightly implicated within the morality of the political critique that is its motivating end. Richardson and Fielding were interested in making the ethics of private, domestic relations a distinct and central focus of their work rather than treating them as epiphenomenal to, because only instrumental toward, an attack on the state for its moral failure to govern responsibly. This is to some extent the difference between libel and satire as ethical projects. Of course, Fielding was willing enough to risk the charge of libel, as his career as a dramatist and his authorship of *Jonathan Wild* (1743) make clear. Much of the foregoing argument, moreover, has been that the secret histories of the Restoration and early eighteenth century evince an ethical interest similar to the one I am associating here with the novels of Richardson and Fielding. Indeed, the opposition of the latter authors to the narratives of the former might well express an impatience with what appeared the formal inadequacy of a moral commitment they shared.

Manifestly not a veiled allegory of public events, *Pamela* derives a great deal of its critical edge from the metaphorical concretion by which a signifying politics invests its amatory signified with socio-ethical weight. If Mr. B. and Pamela are not actually tyrant and rebel, their characters are subtly inflected by these political types. Where in a *roman à clef* the private character provides a key to the public personage, here the political type is a key to the ethical instance. Not that Mr. B. and Pamela are "type" or "stereotyped" characters: on the contrary, the delicacy and precision of novelistic characterization depend on the hypothesis of a differential between type and instance on which minute adjustments in ratio can be achieved. The differential between type and instance depends, in turn, on a separation out of general and particular, "public" and "private" aspects of character that takes its place beside a range of separations that have been our concern in this study.[43] Political type is the key to ethical instance in *Pamela* because the abstract and absolute opposition between tyrant and rebel in seventeenth- and early-eighteenth-century English culture helped generate what I have elsewhere called the conflict between "aristocratic" and "progressive" ideologies, whose opposition is respectively typified by antithetical commitments to "birth" and "worth" as the foundation of socio-ethical value.[44] On one occasion alone Pamela is willing to articulate her convictions in the broadly generalizing terms of ideological commitment and sociopolitical right, that is, when she refutes Lady Davers's letter to her brother Mr. B. (221–22). Otherwise the conflict is expressed and worked out in the socio-ethical terms of personal relations. No longer serviceable in the traditional manner, the distinction between the state and the family that had sustained patriarchalist analogy has devolved into a separation decisive enough to permit the enlistment of the detached realms of politics and religion in a metaphorizing illumination of the family. In *Pamela* the focus of this illumination is marriage.

Richardson's inquiry into the conditions by which marriage is authorized capitalizes on the dialectical interaction between ideas of family and state authority that had transpired during the previous century. Mr. B.'s efforts to seduce his servant are based in a traditional opposition between marriage as a public institution and love–sexual pleasure as private gratifications. And once his immediate advances fail, Mr. B. cunningly plots to gain power over Pamela by assuming a paternalistic role in her disposition, claiming that he would save her from a foolish marriage for love that she herself had plotted: "I have, *to oblige her Father,* order'd her to be carry'd to one of my Houses . . ." (100; see also 90–93). Alternatively Mr. B. plots to force Pamela into a marriage of his own convenience with Parson Williams (85–86, 131–32). But he leaves open the loophole of Pamela's consent, and to Williams's proposal she replies: "I'll see myself quite at Liberty before I shall think myself fit to make a Choice" (132). Mrs. Jewkes even tells her "as a Secret" that her master is plotting to force Pamela into a "Sham-marriage" with the Swiss M. Colbrand, who will then sell her to Mr. B.; but Mr. B.'s demonstrated respect for his servant's right of consent persuades us, with Pamela, that this must be "horrid romancing!" (157).[45] This respect is formalized in the "Articles" Mr. B. soon after solemnly presents to Pamela for her consent, attesting (as he writes) to the "Value I set upon the

Free-will of a Person already in my Power." The articles amount to a radical liberalization of Mr. B.'s approach thus far, since they commit him to all but the authorizing title of husband: "[Y]ou may appear with Reputation, as if you was my Wife. . . . You shall be Mistress, of my Person and Fortune, as much as if the foolish Ceremony had passed . . ." (166). This is a contract that would fully satisfy Mrs. Cresswell's requirements for her young disciple Dorothea in *The Whores Rhetorick;* but Pamela bluntly predicts her parents' noncompliance in a proposal that would entail "the Prostitution of their poor Daughter," and she refuses to consent (165).[46]

Once an anonymous note warns Pamela that Mr. B. plans to trick her with a false marriage officiated by "a sly artful Fellow . . . he has hir'd to personate a Minister," Pamela is beset by fears—not wholly unjustified, as Mr. B. later admits—that recur almost up to the wedding itself (196, 230). For the exact form of the wedding still remains to be decided.[47] Mr. B. says, "I think, my Dear, it shall be very private; I hope you are not afraid of a Sham-marriage . . . ." By "private" he means "at this House," for "it must be very publick if we go to Church." But Pamela demurs on conscientious grounds, and Mr. B. promises to have his "little Chapel," consecrated long ago but since then used as a lumber room, returned to its first purposes as "a little House of God" (236, 257). The diminutives seem to answer the need for a private authenticity to balance the public authority with which the two "will solemnize our Nuptials," but when the official marriage license arrives, Pamela tells us that "my Heart flutter'd at the Sight" (257, 274). A "publick Wedding" would have ensured the presence of a suitable female confidant for Pamela; but Lady Davers, the lingering representative of paternal tyranny, hopes "to hinder your Nuptials" should she learn of them in time. Mr. B. will publish the banns and "declare it when we go to *Bedfordshire,* which won't be long." So in the end the ceremony is performed in a flurry of "Secrecy" and as "privately as possible" without incurring on Pamela's part the suspicion of a sham (282, 283–84).

Yet Lady Davers continues to dismiss it as a "Sham-marriage" until she is finally reconciled to Pamela and her brother. "Dost thou think thou art really marry'd?" she demands of Pamela in a climactic scene of domestic combat around the dinner table. "[Y]ou see I am a kind of Prisoner," Pamela says to Mrs. Jewkes, who calmly serves courses while the two women trade verbal blows—and in the case of Lady Davers, physical ones too. She dares Pamela to utter "one bold Word, that I may fell thee at my Foot." But when Pamela tries to leave the room and Lord Jackey draws his sword on her, she throws herself on Lady Davers's mercy "and clasp'd my Arms about her, forgetting, just then, how much she was my Enemy . . . ." Although this is not her literal meaning, for Mr. B.'s sister his marriage to Pamela is a "sham" most of all if it really did have the legitimacy of public forms because it contravenes a much higher public good by accomplishing "the Disgrace of a Family, ancient and untainted beyond most in the Kingdom . . ." (321, 323, 325, 328, 329, 330). It turns out that Lady Davers had been seeking an aristocratic arranged marriage for her brother for years, whereas Mr. B., presumably as a result of his ethical reformation by Pamela, turns out to be a surprisingly staunch supporter of marriage for love (224, 341, 231, 366–67, 370, 385). This does not mean, however, that he also has rejected patrilineal principles—as he makes clear when, in a momentary fit of rage, he denounces his sister's interference in the following terms: "Leave my House this Instant!—I renounce you, and all Relation to you; and never more let me see your Face, or call me Brother" (347).[48]

If (as many readers think) the latter pages of *Pamela* are less interesting than the earlier ones, this may be because, as the Machiavellian Marvell put it, "The same arts that did gain / A power, must it maintain."[49] But Pamela and Mr. B.'s marriage, based on love rather than alliance, aims to be as much a republic as a principality. Like Pamela, it turns out, Mr. B. too was "brought up wrong" (77; cf. 366). He begins his familiar discourse on marriage by saying that "I hope I shan't be a very tyrannical Husband to you," and the positive picture he paints is explicitly defined against the negative example of absolutist aristocratic tradition: "I have been a close Observer of the Behaviour of wedded Folks, and hardly have ever seen it to be such as I could like in my own Case." "Convenience, or Birth and Fortune, are the first Motives, Affection the last . . ." (365, 367, 366). And although Pamela finds more than enough basis for irony in "this awful Lecture"—hence the parliament of women—Mr. B. is at pains to outline a contract by which "her Compliance with me [is] reasonable, and such as should not destroy her own free Agency . . ." (369, 367). A comparison with Aphra Behn's *Love-Letters* is instructive. As Pamela is "tried" by Mr. B. and Mrs. Jewkes, so Silvia is "betrayed by household spies" and "arraigned and convicted" by her family. As Pamela rightly fears a "sham marriage," so Behn gives us the "mock Marriage" between Silvia and Brilljard and the private ceremony between Cesario and Hermione of which "they do not make publick Declaration . . . ." But whereas in *Love-Letters* the public events of the Exclusion Crisis provide, however inconsistently, an allegorical backdrop for these private actions, in *Pamela* the political language deepens the depiction of what are definitively private engagements. This is to say not only that Behn has written an allegorical secret history whereas Richardson has not but also that in *Pamela* the "little" realm of the domestic is able to sustain the "great" themes of public discourse. When Pamela, still fearing the worst of her master, realizes that she loves him (" . . . and before I knew what was the Matter, it look'd like Love"), the language of political conflict, so far from disappearing, finds a yet deeper level of interiority: "O my treacherous, treacherous Heart! to serve me thus! . . . O perfidious Traitor, for giving up so weakly, thy *whole Self*. . .!" (214, 215).

Housework as House Work

The home has little to recommend it in *Love-Letters*. Marriage exists "for Generation sake, no more." Silvia, badgered by her parents, longs to "turn from these domestick, melancholy objects, and look abroad," and when she later lives very briefly with Brilljard she "longs for Liberty, and . . . was stinted to good Housewifery, a Penury she hated." For Pamela, however, domesticity is privation only so long as she is being persecuted by Mr. B. After his ethical conversion, "my Prison is become my Palace" (293). In Pamela's role as the "governor" of her domestic palace financial transactions are primary.[50] She looks forward to being "employ'd in the Family Accounts" and the "Family Oeconomy" (227, 226). Mr. B. gives her a substantial amount of money, which is nonetheless "very short of that Proportion of my Substance, which, as my dearest Wife, you have a Right to." He tells her to "give . . . what you think fit, out of these, as from yourself," but at first Pamela seeks his guidance on the appropriate size of each of her gifts to the servants, soon after developing the confidence to decide this for herself (306, 296, 383-85). "I am resolv'd to keep Accounts of all these Matters," she writes, "and Mr. *Longman* has already furnish'd me with a Vellum-book of all white Paper . . . . And I have written in it, *Humble* RETURNS FOR DIVINE MERCIES; and lock it up safe in my newly presented Cabinet." Mr. B. will see "(but nobody else) how I lay it out, from Quarter to Quarter; and I will, if any be left, carry it on, like an Accomptant, to the next Quarter, and strike a Ballance four times a Year . . ." (387–88). In all of these offices the housewife is, of course, governor by virtue of her husband's greater authority. But at the end of the novel Mr. B. informs Pamela that "my Line is almost extinct; and a great Part of my Estate, in case I die without Issue, will go to another Line; and other Parts of my personal Estate, will go into such Hands, as I should not care my Pamela should lie at their Mercy. I have therefore, as human Life is uncertain, made such a Disposition of my Affairs, as will make you absolutely independent and happy . . ." (404).

Pamela's description of her private account book must remind us that there is an analogous domain in which her "absolute independence" is established, that of her private journal. If *Pamela* forgoes dependence on external, political allegory, this is in part because it elaborates its own, internalized allegory, by which the seriousness of its domestic subject is justified. *The Whores Rhetorick* (1683) allegorizes (female) authorship as prostitution; *Pamela* allegorizes it as domesticity. Crucial to this development is Pamela's more secure confinement in the Lincolnshire estate, a "handsome, large, old, and lonely Mansion, that looks made for Solitude . . . ." Her fellow servant Mr. Longman had "set me up" (as though she was an apprentice in the trade of scrivener) with writing materials—"above forty Sheets of Paper, and a dozen Pens, and a little Phial of Ink; which last I wrapt in Paper, and put in my Pocket; and some Wax and Wafers"—and now she literalizes the mysteries of her craft by secreting her writing implements around her bedroom closet so as to foil the surveillance of Mrs. Jewkes (102, 96, 105).[51]

And now, too, although in a different sense, Pamela's prison becomes her palace. Liberated from housework, Pamela has "so much Time upon my Hands, that I must write on to employ myself." Her individual letters become a continuous journal, also "to amuse and employ her Time." This self-employ-ment, a labor that looks like leisure, is the house work that permanently frees Pamela from housework because it transforms her writing from political into aesthetic "plotting." Unlike her later accounts book, this private journal is read by Mr. B. without her knowledge, and over time he succumbs to its emotional power: "[T]here is such a pretty Air of Romance, as you relate them, in your Plots, and my Plots, that I shall be better directed in what manner to wind up the Catastrophe of the pretty Novel." Suspended between the real and the vir-tual, Mr. B. retraces her steps around the estate as he reads about them, and "when he came to my Reasonings, about throwing myself into the Water, he said, Walk gently before; and seem'd so mov'd, that he turn'd away his Face from me . . . . O my dear Girl! you have touch'd me sensibly with your mournful Re-lation, and your sweet Reflections upon it" (134, 94, 201, 208). Mr. B. is disin-terested, not deluded: he willingly suspends his disbelief so as to enjoy the pe-culiar pleasure of aesthetic knowledge.[52] When Pamela protests of her papers that "all that they contain you know, as well as I," he replies: "But I don't know . . . the Light you put Things in . . ." (207). Pamela's romancing has become an exercise not in lying but in emotional transport.

Pamela's shift from housework to house work has the utopian aura of pro-ductive labor. Delarivier Manley had narrated the actuality of Rivella's produc-tivity in the public sphere of publication even as her narrator Lovemore denied it the honor that only marriage can provide women. Like Pamela, Rivella exe-cuted "the barbarous design of exposing people that never had done her in-jury"; and like Pamela, she is locked up, deprived of her writing instruments, and made a public spectacle. Pamela's house work, by contrast, remains unpro-ductive and unremunerated, like that of the housewife.[53] Yet it circulates as script in a public sphere of rural gentry some of whom are "Stranger[s]" whom Pamela has never even met, who seem to agree that her exemplarity is produc-tive, if not of money, then of ethical subjects (334–35, 339–41, 374, 377). And long before it receives this public legitimation, Pamela's journal undergoes a

highly secret circulation under the tiles near the sunflower by the back door of
the garden (113). Once reconciled with Mr. B. but before their wedding, Pamela
herself is "circulated" among the gentry. She becomes a theatrical object for
them, dressed as a "pretty Rustick" and viewed at a "Distance" down "the
longest Gravel Walk in the Garden," and then in an affecting scene played in
the presence of her father (242–44, 249–50). The spectacle of Pamela is a kind
of "glass" in which the gentry see not her "public" meaning but themselves: the
authenticity of her upward mobility, the fact that she has become, despite her
rustic garb, like them. Soon after this scene Pamela confirms its results in solitude by dressing herself once more in her lady's castoff clothing; "and taking my
Fan in Hand, I, like a little proud Hussy, looked in the Glass, and thought myself a Gentlewoman once more . . ." (256).[54] In this sense *Pamela* is not a glass
of state but a glass of gentility, not an allegorical reflection of the great by the
little but a metonymic model of how the little may become the great.

The change in Pamela's mode of labor is coextensive with the change in her
mode of narration from multiple letters to singular "novel," and although
Pamela remains a first-person narrative, the effect of this change may be compared to that achieved by Behn when she shifts from first- to third-person narration in *Love-Letters* (89–94). Paradoxically the effect is enhanced by the temporary intrusion of the third-person editor to narrate Pamela's journey from
Bedfordshire to Lincolnshire, when she is unable to write, since something of
the authority of his narrative detachment ("We shall now leave the honest old
Pair, praying for their dear *Pamela*") contributes to the aesthetic detachment
we now begin, with Mr. B., to experience in the act of reading her (94). This is
due, at least in part, to the self-consciousness her imprisonment imposes on her
writing, the reflexivity with which her representation of things increasingly incorporates its own scribal secrecy as one of its objects. Indeed, her secrecy enforces a benign sort of duplicity that recalls the "female arts" of Behn's Silvia.
One great difference, of course, is that Pamela does not succumb to her libertine seducer, whereas Silvia does, hence she exercises her female arts in the cause
of virtue where Silvia does in the cause of vice. If *Love-Letters* is, among other
things, an experiment in transforming the morally flat duplicity of its protagonist into an ethically deep interiority, *Pamela* extends that process considerably.

Richardson turns the sartorial trope of the secret history to this end by having Pamela hide her writings on her own person.[55] In an example of writing to
the moment that comes early in the novel, Pamela tells her mother that "I
Broke off abruptly my last Letter; for I fear'd he was coming; and so it happen'd.
I thrust the Letter into my Bosom, and took up my Work, which lay by me; but
I had so little of the Artful, as he called it, that I look'd as confused, as if I had
been doing some great Harm." Pamela's letters have not yet become her "work."

There is more subterfuge than subjectivity in her impulsive act, and Mr. B., echoing Behn's narrator, is convinced that she "has all the Arts of her Sex," for "she is a mighty Letter-writer!" (40, 45). When Pamela learns to hide her letters on her person by design, to fashion a secret cabinet of her own body, she weaves a complex image of duplicity, creativity, pregnancy, exemplarity, and reflexivity whose strands are mutually reinforcing: "But I begin to be afraid my Writings may be discover'd; for they grow large! I stitch them hitherto in my Undercoat, next my Linen" (120). The "discovery" of Pamela's secret writings, their publication first to Mr. B. and then to others, makes her private interiority publicly available as an exemplary model of ethical subjectivity. Here Richardson evokes the two means of creativity and self-expression traditionally and normatively available to women, childbirth and dress, even as he goes beyond them to suggest an analogous but emergent alternative: the female arts as exemplary self-representation through writing. Richardson's fictional autobiography meets Manley's highly mediated "actual" autobiography and Haywood's monitorial spectator at the point where writing by women can begin to be experienced as in the broadest sense "productive."[56]

But at a cost. Behn encourages us to see Silvia's duplicity as a modest effort to rebalance the double standard, and her pleasure in impersonating men is consistent with this view. Pamela takes no pleasure in impersonating men because her unassailable virtue obviates it. The exemplarity of Pamela's interiority depends on the fact that plumbing its depths seems to expose no viciousness: she is not equal to men; she is different from them. By seeking and winning success in the public sphere Rivella employs her female arts in a way that successfully approximates the interested behavior of men. The only sign that Pamela is pursuing her own self-interest comes not in the motives that lead her to write but in the effect her writing has on other people. By this means Richardson empowers his female paragon in the public sphere without compromising her virtue with the will to public power through publication. *Pamela* thus helps contributes to the peculiar pattern by which women novelists of the later eighteenth century exercise unprecedented authority in the public sphere even as their novels depict female characters whose respectability requires that they be largely innocent of public activity.

Clothing: Ethics, Knowledge, Sex

And yet Richardson deploys with some daring the power of clothing to figure the proximity of interiority and duplicity, of secrecy and sexuality. "[J]ust now, as I was in my Closet, opening the Parcel I had hid under the Rose-bush, to see if it was damag'd by lying so long, Mrs. Jewkes came upon me by Surprize, and laid her Hands upon it; for she had been looking thro' the Key-hole, it seems. I know not what I shall do! For now he will see all my private Thoughts of him, and all my Secrets, as I may say." Pamela summarizes the contents of the parcel for her parents, then consoles herself that "how badly I came off, and what follow'd, I still have safe, as I hope, sew'd in my Undercoat, about my Hips." But Mr. B. demands to see this second parcel as well: "Now, said he, it is my opinion they are about you; and I never undrest a Girl in my Life; but I will now begin to strip my pretty *Pamela;* and hope I shall not go far, before I find them." He "began to unpin my Handkerchief . . ."; then "may-be, said he, they are ty'd about your Knees with your Garters, and stoop'd. . . ." Pamela admits defeat. "I went to my Closet, and there I sat me down, and could not bear the Thoughts of giving up my Papers. Besides, I must all undress me in a manner to untack them" (197, 198, 204). To divulge "all my private thoughts" sounds perilously close to sexual surrender. Indeed, in this novel sexual violation sounds very close to forced knowledge. In the rape scene, Mr. B. desires most of all Pamela's explicit acknowledgment "that you are in my Power!": "Swear then to me . . . that you will accept my Proposals!" (176). In modern culture sex will acquire the autotelic status of a primary mode of knowledge. But Mr. B.'s desire here seems less emergent than residual: for him sex serves an epistemological end that lies beyond itself.

Is Richardson's depiction of sex pornographic? It is obviously implausible to see him as intending to arouse sexual desire and generate sexual pleasure in his readers, although some of his critics thought this might be the effect of his novel.[57] In its prefatory material Aaron Hill had puffed Pamela in terms that brought the analogy between language and clothing to the verge of suggestiveness. The parody of this passage by Fielding's Parson Tickletext pushed it over the edge: "The thought is every where exactly cloathed by the Expression; and becomes its Dress as *roundly* and as close as *Pamela* her Country Habit; or *as she doth her no Habit,* when modest Beauty seeks to hide itself, by casting off the Pride of Ornament, and displays itself without any Covering . . . . Oh! I feel an Emotion even while I am relating this: Methinks I see *Pamela* at this Instant, with all the Pride of Ornament cast off."[58] Richardson's title page boasts that Pamela "is intirely divested of all those Images, which, in too many Pieces calculated for Amusement only, tend to *inflame* the Minds they should *instruct.*" The dialectic between vice and virtue, pleasure and instruction, is a familiar one, but Richardson's formulation of the pedagogy may be too simple: all that is required, apparently, is a conscious "calculation" for both, and in the correct order. Even the language of a prudent "divestment," meant to preclude pleasures unjustified by a higher instruction, seems to imply a prior presence still available in the very reassurance of its removal. The Protestant injunction of conscientious self-scrutiny and self-control bespeaks the constancy not only of the self—the subject—but also of its (e.g.) sexual object, whose symptoms must periodically be acknowledged and stripped away.[59]

The eroticism of Richardson's first novel tends toward pornography not because he aims to arouse sexual desire and generate sexual pleasure but because the relentlessness with which he makes sexual desire and pleasure stand for other things—knowledge, power, social status—over time tends to invest the signifier with the authority of a self-sufficient signified, an end in itself. This is especially true where Richardson relies on the sartorial figure to achieve his pedagogic aims. The passage from *Pamela*'s preface that Fielding's Tickletext makes his own alludes to the early scene in the novel where Pamela, believing she is on her way home to her parents' house, cheerfully embraces this social descent by dressing down: "I trick'd myself up as well as I could in my new Garb, and put on my round-ear'd ordinary Cap . . . and when I was quite 'quip'd, I took my Straw Hat in my Hand, with its two blue Strings, and look'd about me in the Glass, as proud as any thing.—To say Truth, I never lik'd myself so well in my Life. O the Pleasure of descending with Ease, Innocence and Resignation!" But no one recognizes her in her country habit, and Mr. B., inflamed by this seemingly innocent display, accuses Pamela of wanting to "disguise yourself, to attract me . . ." (60, 62).

Pamela had meant to use her clothing to signify her social humility, just as Richardson would use "the modest Disguise of a *Novel*" to signify "all the *Soul* of Religion" (9). The notion that clothing and language may function as "disguises" in a negative sense of the term is a common one in *Pamela*. It is in this sense that William Webster, in one of the two letters that preface the first edition, urges its "*Editor*" toward unrevised publication by alluding to this same compelling scene of Pamela's dressing down: "[L]et us have *Pamela* as *Pamela* wrote it; in her own Words . . . . Produce her to us in her neat Country Apparel . . . . Such a Dress will best edify and entertain. The flowing Robes of Oratory may indeed amuse and amaze, but will never strike the Mind with solid Attention" (7–8). But Webster's critique of excess language and clothing borders on a critique of formal domestication, the positive sense of "disguise" that Richardson applies to himself and to his heroine, both of whom would use low and mean forms (the novel, country apparel) to accommodate religious and moral behavior. In response to Mr. B's accusation that in changing her dress Pamela is only trying to "attract" him, she accuses him in turn of "pretending not to know me, on purpose to be free with me . . . . I have been in Disguise indeed ever since my good Lady, your Mother, took me from my poor Parents" (62, 65). Richardson thus parodically invokes the family romance trope of discovered parentage, thinly disguising through imitation his intent to criticize its implication that worth derives from birth. The ideological import of this critique comes through clearly enough, but like Mr. B., we are sometimes in danger of becoming preoccupied with the disguise, amused and amazed by it—in danger, that is, of taking the signifier for the signified. On the most general level, of course, this is Richardson's great achievement: that in our reading of *Pamela* formal domestication obtrudes on our attention like the colossal remains of a prehistoric species that now serves as the skeleton of some strange new creature, neither a casuistical tract nor a *roman à clef* but a domestic novel. However, the transmutation of form inevitably leaves the relation between signifiers and signifieds in some dispute. The sartorial imagery of dressing up and dressing down, in particular, takes on a life of its own in *Pamela,* intimating a literally underlying secret that both those actions subserve.

Soon after Pamela puts on her country apparel, she goes "to Mrs. *Jervis*'s Chamber; and Oh! my dear Father and Mother, my wicked Master had hid himself, base Gentleman as he is! in her Closet, where she has a few Books, and Chest of Drawers, and such-like." "I pulled off my Stays, and my Stockens, and my Gown, all to an Under-petticoat; and then hearing a rustling again in the Closet, I said, God protect us! but before I say my Prayers, I must look into this Closet. And so was going to it slip shod, when, O dreadful! out rush'd my Master, in a rich silk and silver Morning Gown" (64, 66). That this last detail strikes us as distracted irrelevance is testimony to Richardson's usual skill in giving his moral instruction the domesticated accessibility of a pleasurable plot. Its relevance is pedagogic—Mr. B.'s viciousness is confirmed by the luxurious excess of his clothing, which contrasts with the virtuous sparseness of Pamela's "under-petticoat"[60]—but Richardson's language is so sensible that its moral charge as a figure of speech is thickened to opacity, and we find ourselves reading for the clothing (or the lack of it) alone. The aesthetic mechanism—the refinement of gross sense impressions, the virtualization of sensible into imaginative pleasures—for a moment sputters to a halt. In his painting of this scene (plate 9) Joseph Highmore uses graphic arts more successfully, perhaps, than Richardson does linguistic ones to emphasize the moral burden of the seemingly irrelevant detail. Mr. B. leans acutely over Pamela in a posture of heightened, almost balletic grace. Light pours from the left side, just off canvas, onto the two reclining figures, illuminating them in different ways. Pamela's cotton pillow, cap, face, and petticoat absorb the light into themselves, whereas Mr. B.'s silk cap, morning gown, and right stocking reflect the light with a rich, luxuriant sheen of their own that complements the theatrical elegance of his attitude. His slippers are a brilliant red, and the outer layer of his gown is turned up to reveal the corner of an even more opulent red-and-gold-bordered jacket underneath. In suggesting nothing at all underneath her under-petticoat Pamela's simple costume bespeaks not salaciousness but sincerity, the absence of duplicity. Mrs. Jervis, almost imperceptible in the background, clasps her hands at the ethically fraught tableau.

The visual display of Pamela—to Mr. B., to her fellow servants, to the rural gentry—is a vital means by which Richardson tests and confirms the propriety of her social elevation. Confirmation comes in the form of the generalized aesthetic pleasure experienced by all those who see her as though spectators at a dramatic performance or who read her as though her autobiographical journal were a novel. The disinterestedness of aesthetic judgment is crucial to its authority, and it facilitates the complex adequation of aesthetic pleasure to social authorization. The scene in Mrs. Jervis's chamber is analogous to those other scenes, but there are important differences. Here the player is unaware that she is performing; moreover, the several spectators have been reduced to one, and he responds not with aesthetic pleasure but with an anticipation of sexual pleasure, a singularly sensible and interested affect that resists the sort of socio-ethical generalization enabled by aesthetic response. In the familiar interior design of Mrs. Jervis's chamber, where the privacy of a bedroom opens into a yet more private closet, Richardson recognizes an apt setting for the aesthetic performance of Pamela's ethical interiority, and he repeats the scenario within the space of ten pages.

Pamela has asked Mrs. Jervis to help her decide how to dispose of her clothing now that she will be returning to her parents: "Now, it seems, she had prepar'd my Master for this Scene, unknown to me; and in this green Room was a Closet, with a Sash-door and a Curtain before it; for there she puts her Sweet-meats and such Things; and she did it, it seems, to turn his Heart . . . ." Pamela's ingenuous particularization of her clothing parcels turns Mrs. Jervis's heart so powerfully (Pamela innocently remarks that "you cry and laugh in a Breath") that when it comes time for her advice, "Alas! my dear Maiden, said she, you make me unable to speak to you at all . . . ." As for Mr. B., Pamela learns later that "he thought two or three times to have burst out upon me . . . ," and "own'd I had made him wipe his Eyes two or three times . . ." (78, 80, 81). Torn between sexual and aesthetic responses, Mr. B. here maintains the aesthetic forms by forbearing (unlike Don Quixote) from forcing the actuality of his spectatorship onto the virtuality of Pamela's socio-ethical performance; but the ambiguity of the scene is challenging.[61] (Later on, when he substitutes reading Pamela's journal for watching her body, Mr. B.'s heart is so moved that "he turn'd away his Face from me" [208], and the sublimation of sexual desire into aesthetic pleasure is complete.) Highmore's illustration of this closet scene (plate 10) is quite faithful to it. Pamela stands in the middle foreground dressed in the principal articles of her country dress, clutching like an infant the bundle of clothing she feels justified in bringing home, while at her feet lie the two bundles she will leave behind because they contain the richer garments given to her by Mr. B. and his mother (note the ribbons and embroidered hem). To Pamela's right sits her primary audience, Mrs. Jervis, leaning forward with hands raised in demonstrative spectatorship. In the background on Pamela's left is the sash door to the closet, behind which we see her secret audience, Mr. B., pushing aside the concealing curtain just enough to reveal Pamela's performance. The three figures exhibit different degrees of presence. Pamela artlessly displays her several "disguises," thereby disabling their capacity for disguise. Mrs. Jervis openly performs the part of accredited audience. And Mr. B., caught in the secretive posture of voyeur rather than spectator, oddly seems to echo Pamela's gesture of self-display while ostentatiously lacking her candor.

In the climactic scene of this series the stage manager is not Mrs. Jervis but Mrs. Jewkes; but once again Richardson maintains dramatic irony—indeed, what we know that Pamela does not know is precisely that she is performing dramatically—while at the same time using first-person retrospection to realign our knowledge with hers. Pamela's previous performance has understandably made her skeptical about what she archly calls her master's "Closet-work" (78), and this time she makes sure that no closet is involved:

> About two Hours after, which was near Eleven o'Clock, Mrs. *Jewkes* and I went up to go to-bed; I pleasing myself with what a charming Night I should have. We lock'd both Doors, and saw poor *Nan,* as I thought, (for Oh! it was my abominable Master, as you shall hear by-and-by) sitting fast asleep, in an Elbow-chair, in a dark Corner of the Room, with her Apron thrown over her Head and Neck. . . . [B]eing not sleepy, and in a prattling Vein, I began to give a little History of myself, as I did once before to Mrs. *Jervis* . . . . [Mrs. Jewkes] heard me run on all this time, while I was undressing, without any Interruption; and I said, Well, I must go to the two Closets, ever since an Affair of the Closet at the other House, tho' he is so far off. So I looked into the Closets, and kneeled down in my own, as I used to do, to say my Prayers; and this with my under Cloaths in my Hand, all undrest, and passed by the poor sleeping Wench, as I thought, in my Return. But Oh! little did I think, it was my wicked wicked Master in a Gown and Petticoat of hers, and her Apron over her Face and Shoulders. . . . [T]he pretended She came to the Bed-side; and sitting down in a Chair, where the Curtain hid her, began to undress [and] . . . came into Bed . . . (173, 175, 176)

We saw above that in the ensuing scene Mr. B.'s desire seems as much epistemological as sexual. Another sign of the scene's semantic thickness is that despite its absence from the scenario, the overdetermined aura of the closet—its simultaneously devotional, epistolary, and sexual privacy—permeates what follows with ethical, aesthetic, and pornographic significance.

Pamela's closet has been the principal site of her letter and journal writing.

However, she tells Mrs. Jewkes that she does not intend to write anymore tonight, and instead she "began to give a little History of myself" that starts with her impoverished childhood, moves to her lady's treatment of her "as if I was a Gentlewoman," and ends with her present anticipation of being "undone" (173–74). The pornographic aspect of Richardson's action depends greatly on the stationary and secreted placement of Mr. B., who by virtue of this placement is, even more than when he spies on Pamela from the greenroom closet, not a spectator but a voyeur—if also an *écouteur* of her history of thwarted upward mobility. In a seeming extension of her sartorial humility in the earlier scene, Pamela is now not simply dressed down to her former station but "all undrest," whereas the partial coverture of Mr. B.'s closet curtain has been enhanced by Nan's gown, petticoat, and apron. Most important, Mr. B. is no longer concealed; he is in plain sight but disguised as a female servant. The image is deeply ambiguous. In Highmore's depiction of the scene (plate 11) light issues once more from the top of the bed but now off canvas on the right. Brilliantly illuminated, Pamela sits on the bed near the center foreground, as she talks undressing herself in graphic illustration of her little history, her humble virtue performed by her willing divestment. In this innocence of disclosure Pamela is contrastively framed by the duplicitous figures of Mr. B. and Mrs. Jewkes, both of whom cover their bodies as she uncovers hers: the "mannish" servant woman pulls up her bedclothes while the master pulls up the servant woman's apron. Does Mr. B.'s disguise "effeminate" him—and if so, in what sense of that labile term?

In *Love-Letters,* cross-dressing is a common method of disguise that Behn employs with an easy and playful insouciance. In *Pamela,* cross-dressing is a much rarer occurrence. When Behn's libertine Philander puts on a maid's "night gown and head dress," he and his father-in-law have an inconsequential but amusingly suggestive encounter. When Richardson's "pretended she" puts on a maid's "gown and petticoat," the disguise is soberly instrumental toward his goal of entrapping Pamela and having his way with her; and its suggestiveness is more disturbing. Although no hint of the sodomitical can be detected in Pamela's master, he is truly besotted by her; yet he expresses his "effeminacy" in ways very different from Sidney's Duke Basilius, Charles I, Behn's Cesario, and the rest. Mr. B.'s abjection is an effect not of the sexual but of the social. His disgrace is not that he is like a woman but that he is like a servant, and his virtual downward mobility is as negatively moralized as Pamela's own humble descent is seen in a positive light. As Pamela puts it early on in the novel: "You have taught me to forget myself, and what belongs to me, and have lessen'd the Distance that Fortune has made between us, by demeaning yourself, to be so free to a poor Servant" (35).

In the half-century that separates Richardson from Behn sexual disguise has become a less common vehicle for experimenting with the boundaries between the realms of the public and the private. And it cannot be a coincidence that in a novel that shares with *Love-Letters* so many boundary concerns of this sort the crucial vehicle of experimentation is not sexual disguise but social mobility. In *Pamela* Richardson is exceptionally interested in the emergent conflict between status and class attitudes toward social relations, as well as in the challenge of representing social change through upward mobility as though it were the on-goingness of social stasis. The challenge was both difficult and unavoidable. The biologization of gender difference that English (and European) culture was experiencing at this time diminished the utility of sexual disguise as a register of fluidity. The sexes were becoming too different to be plausibly used to this end; cross-dressing was coming to mean not a seeming difference but a difference in being. This is to say not that sexual experience now ceases to preoccupy English culture (as the plot of *Pamela* makes clear) but something like the opposite: that the idea of gender difference (hence heterosexual love, marriage, adultery, and separate-spheres ideology) is sufficiently stabilized and objectified that it can sustain much of the weight of the way modern culture tends to approach matters of identity, conflict, and resolution. But as sexuality takes on the capacity to represent identity, it loses the capacity to represent change. In time, protoclass social mobility came to exercise that capacity as, reciprocally, the language of social categorization passed on to sexuality the authority of biological fixity. But for Richardson these themes were dangerously experimental and required some indirection. The strongest argument against understanding *Pamela* as pornography may lie in the recognition that Richardson's fundamental interest there is not in sexual experience "as such" but in the sexualized representation of social experience.

Domesticity and the Closet

Sexuality comes of age in the realm of private experience, which like sexuality takes on, in modern thinking, a more stable and a more normative character. Richardson's depiction of the closet provides a good gauge of this development as it is still in process. In *Pamela* the closet retains its function as the enclave of the male aristocrat and head of household.[62] While still in Bedfordshire Pamela writes that Mr. B. "went into his Closet, which is his Library, and full of rich Pictures besides, a noble Apartment, tho' called a Closet, and next the Private Garden, into which it has a Door that opens" (82). But the closet of Mrs. Jervis, the head domestic servant, though much smaller, is also an interior space of private possession and self-expression "where she has a few Books, and Chest of Drawers, and such-like" (in the closet off the green room Mrs. Jervis also "puts her Sweet-meats and such Things" [64, 78]). Pamela's closet is a multipurpose and ambivalent site, a place of subjection but also subjectivity. In the space of one paragraph Richardson shows her using it both for prayer and for writing: "I went to my Closet; and the first thing I did, on my Knees, again thanked God for the Blessing of the Day . . . . After this, . . . the Pen and my Paper being before me, I amused myself with writing . . ." (295; see also 235). If a closet is (as we have seen) Mr. B.'s hiding place in one of his sexual assaults on Pamela, her closet and its writing implements also provide her refuge from the dread of licit sex when Mrs. Jewkes puts her bedchamber "in Order for a Guest" on her wedding day: "So I refuged myself in my Closet, and had recourse to Pen and Ink, for my Amusement, and to divert my Anxiety of Mind" (291).[63]

Pamela's closet is a privative "Prison" but also a place of negative liberty: "I went up to my Closet, lock'd myself in, and open[ed] my Letter" (155, 118). She conveys this doubleness when she describes her escape plan to her parents: "My Stratagem is this; I will endeavour to get Mrs. *Jewkes* to-bed without me, as she often does, while I sit lock'd up in my Closet; and as she sleeps very sound in her first Sleep, . . . if I can then but get out between the two Bars of the Window, . . . I can drop upon the Leads underneath . . ." (149). And when she finds that her plan must fail because the lock on the back door of the garden has been changed, Pamela's prison becomes, if not her palace, then at least preferable to the alternative of certain discovery: "Then I began to wish myself most heartily again in my Closet, and to repent of my Attempt . . ." (151). Mr. Williams had obtained for Pamela a copy of the garden's back-door key in preparation for this attempt, and we hear much about literal keys in the course of this episode (see 113, 115, 119, 128, 149, 151). Read in the context of the *roman à clef* tradition, these passages may seem momentarily to intimate the revelation of actual particularity. But in *Pamela* the figure of the key has definitively shifted its implication. When Mrs. Jewkes spies her parcel of writings through the "Closet" "Keyhole," Pamela fears that her "private Thoughts" and "Secrets" will become known (197). The key to actual names has modulated to the keyhole that opens into the concrete inner recesses of the mind.

If we back up for a moment, we may gain some perspective on the sort of labor in categorial separation-out that *Pamela* seeks to perform. Richardson had announced such an aim in the preface to the collection of exemplary letters from which his first novel is said to have evolved. Echoing Locke and Defoe, Richardson writes there that "he has endeavoured to point out the duty of a servant, not a slave; the duty of a master, not a tyrant . . . ."[64] *Pamela* carries this labor further by moving from the separation of the private and the public to the separation, within the realm of the private, of two sorts of marriage and domesticity. In Behn's *roman à clef* the genuinely challenging conflict in the private realm is that between the freedom of adulterous love and the constraining coverture of marriage and domesticity. But although the terms of this conflict persist in Mr. B.'s early libertinage, the decisive conflict in Richardson's novel is rather that between the freedom of marriage for love and the constraints of marriages of alliance, convenience, and interest; and the real challenge comes not in deciding which of these is preferable but in reconciling the mobility of class dynamism with the tradition of status hierarchy. By her own terms if not by those of *The Whores Rhetorick,* Pamela vindicates the superiority of the "Mistress"-as-wife to the "Mistress"-as-prostitute by rejecting Mr. B.'s handsome offer that she "be Mistress of my Person and Fortune, as much as if the foolish Ceremony had passed" (166). Richardson's insistence on this difference also flies in the face of the contemporary apprehension that female domestic service and prostitution were largely overlapping professions.[65]

But the vaunted liberation entailed in marriage for love, suffused as it is with the norm of negative liberty that now begins to exert its powerful sway in all domains of modern life, tends to obscure the old pattern of servitude that conjugal coverture itself enforces (this is one reason for the general disdain for marriage in *Love-Letters*). Like the coverage provided by the closet, domestic coverture is double-edged, a palace that is also a prison and a privacy that encloses its own version of publicity. Although fictional precedents already existed—for example, in Mary Hearne's Amaryllis (see above)—Richardson is far from offering Pamela the possibility of a normative domesticity in the absence of marriage. Instead he uses the confrontation between Lady Davers and Mr. B. to affirm that marriage, the hierarchical exception that proves the meritocratic rule of modern existence, is prior to and a precondition for all other social arrangements, including domesticity.[66] But the refusal to separate domesticity from marriage then requires that the domesticity of the housewife be separated out from that of the domestic servant.[67] *Pamela* shows the priority of marriage to all else by featuring a protagonist who is doubly subjected—as a common servant and as a woman—and by separating out these two identities by showing the persistence of her subjection after upward mobility through marriage has erased her commonness. But Richardson's novel also labors to show, first through Pamela's highly productive segregation from the other servants at Lincolnshire and then through her management of the household after marriage, that if a wife continues to be in some sense a servant, her work may also be clearly distinguished from domestic service by the fact of its comparatively "public" status as both an actual and a virtual mode of "government." In this way the arbitrary basis of domesticity in the inequality of marriage is mitigated—or reflected—by the hierarchical division of its labor.

With the possible exception of Richardson's second and crowning success, *Pamela* is by far the most influential domestic novel of the eighteenth century. But to say that it set the pattern is not to say that all its solutions to these problems in separation were embraced by subsequent authors. In the final chapter of this study I will briefly survey four novels that work significant variations on *Pamela*'s precedent and that bring us to the period of the domestic novel's greatest flowering, the nineteenth century.

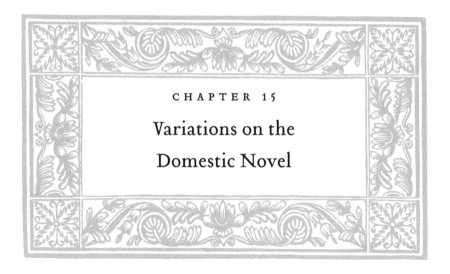

CHAPTER 15

Variations on the
Domestic Novel

Two years after the publication of *Pamela* there appeared a tract that claimed that when the ancients purported to plumb the depths of esoteric, and especially religious, mysteries, they were secretly alluding to the mysteries of female sexuality—"the *characteristical parts* of a woman."[1] Aptly titled *The Secret History of Pandora's Box,* the tract attributes a degree of bad faith to these ancients, who may have secreted their true concern even from themselves because they thought it evil: "Whatever had the air of mystery, engaged their attention and emotion; but by an unparallel'd sort of caprice, all that was most truly profound and secret passed in neglect, and could never obtain an image with religious honours. . . . But perhaps the *Pagans* might say, what I have often heard advanced by people without taste, that these parts were the true *Pandora's* box, and that this box was neither more nor less than an allegory of the characteristical nature of women" (9, 51). Needless to say, the author of this panegyric to the female genitals admits such an allegorical reading only in a positive vein, and the implication is that what once was thought necessary to veil may be embraced, in this enlightened age, for what it is.

FANNY HILL

The Secret History of Pandora's Box might be read as a facetious gloss on the emergence of pornography in the eighteenth century. I have suggested that whereas libertine writing in the early modern period tended to emphasize religious, political, and intellectual modes of antinomianism, pornography as such became recognizable when the sexual element of libertinism evolved from being a means to these other ends to being an end in itself.[2] By this way of thinking, the reputation of John Cleland's *Fanny Hill,* officially titled *Memoirs of a Woman of Pleasure* (1749), as the first native English work of pornography owes to the fact that its libertinism is to an unusual degree specific to the domain of sexuality. Some passages in *Pamela,* we have seen, have a pornographic effect despite themselves because their socio-ethical pedagogy is disabled by the too-sensible energy of their sartorial tropes. By revealing both *Pamela* and Pamela to be a sham, Fielding's *Shamela* makes their pornography intentional, a willful pretence to virtue. In Cleland's *Memoirs* this sense of duplicity is absent because for long stretches the motive to arouse sexual desire and generate sexual pleasure, although nowhere stated, seems to have become paramount.

Not that the pedagogic aim is also absent. Fanny Hill begins the first of her two long letters with a conventionally sartorial claim to historicity: "Truth! stark naked truth, is the word, and I will not so much as take the pains to bestow the strip of a gauze-wrapper on it, but paint situations such as they actually rose to me in nature . . . . The greatest men . . . will not scruple adorning their private closets with nudities . . ."; with this publication Fanny will improve on them by making the naked truth public.[3] To what end? Several times Fanny remarks that her migration to London, like her upbringing, took place in all the vulnerability of pure innocence: "[M]y native purity . . . had taken no root in education . . ." (60; see also 40, 90). The publication of her memoirs is an act of "confession"; perhaps it will provide the reader with the sort of education in vice that she herself found only in the firsthand experience of it (129). At the happy end of her memoirs Fanny associates them with the cause of virtue. "You laugh perhaps at this tail-piece of morality, . . . you may look on it as the paltry finesse of one who seeks to mask a devotee to vice under a rag of a veil, impudently smuggled from the shrine of virtue; . . . or as if a writer should think to shield a treasonable libel by concluding it with a formal prayer for the king" (223). As false panegyric may conceal libel, as outward dress may conceal inner corruption—in short, as "public" disguise may conceal "private" reality—so the claim to good precept may vainly excuse bad example. Nonetheless the justification holds: "[I]f I have painted vice in all its gayest colours, if I have decked it with flowers, it has been solely in order to make the worthier, the solemner, sacrifice of it to virtue. . . . The experiment, you will cry, is dangerous. True—on a fool; but are fools worth the least attention to?" (224).

Since the *Memoirs* make no serious pretence of invading the privacy of any actual particularity, the sort of libel charge to which they were vulnerable came under the law of obscene libel, the corruption of the public.[4] Cleland knew this well, and after a warrant was issued to seize the author, printer, and publisher of his work he defended himself by a range of appeals and, echoing the honorable Rivella, sought mercy for his collaborators: "I am perfectly resigned up to the worst of my fate, but it gives me great pain to see others torn from their families, and business, upon an occasion in which they are entirely innocent."[5] In the event, no legal action was taken against either Cleland or his collaborators in the publication of what by the law should have remained private.

So Cleland apprehended his own legal, but not necessarily his own moral, guilt, and Fanny Hill's memoirs are like Shamela's memoirs without the self-conscious deceit. Where Shamela tells the story of how a whore's pretense to be something else is rewarded by her becoming a wife, Fanny's story tells of how an innocent girl becomes a whore and then, against all odds, gains that same reward. And where Shamela's celebrated maxim highlights her calculating hypocrisy—"I thought once of making a little Fortune by my Person. I now intend to make a great one by my Vartue"—Fanny's opening account of what she has been told of London life has, despite the tell-tale allusion to Fielding's critique, all the earnest naïveté of a Defoevian fable of upward mobility—"[A]s how several maids out of the country had made themselves and all their kin forever, that by preserving their VARTUE, some had taken so with their masters that they had married them, and kept them coaches, and lived vastly grand, and happy, and some, mayhap, came to be duchesses . . ." (41).[6] But if Fanny's vices do not include duplicity, her story is told through ostentatious recourse to the doubling method of metaphor, a method that both recalls the allegorical secret history and complicates Fanny's own pornographic explicitness.

Virtuality through Metaphor

Fanny's metaphors are for the most part familiar ones. Some we have found it instructive to treat as vestigial remnants (e.g., in *Pamela*) of the secret history's full-blown political allegories: thus Charles is Fanny's "master," her "sovereign," her "absolute disposer" (74, 76, 79). Later on Fanny comes under the authority of the kindly bawd Mrs. Cole, who despite her benevolence has her "reasons of state" and preaches "the doctrine of passive obedience and nonresistance to all those arbitrary tastes of pleasure" a prostitute like Fanny is likely to encounter (125, 134). Other metaphors recall the governmental euphemisms of Restoration poems on affairs of state: thus penises are the "first instrument and minister" and the "white staff" (83, 157). Another strain of Fanny's figuration, a vestige of the libertine erotics that aimed at clerical satire, exploits the jargon of religious worship (e.g., 132–33). Yet another draws attention to the status of prostitution as a "trade." With Mrs. Brown Fanny gains "a tolerable insight into the nature and mysteries of their profession," especially through Phoebe, her "tuteress elect" and "manager of her house" (61, 47). But Fanny's apprenticeship in the trade comes to fruition with Mrs. Cole, who "was consummately at the top of her profession . . . ." "[N]ever woman . . . better understood all the mysteries and refinements of it than she did"—for example, "that it was an established rule, and mystery of trade, for me to pass for a maid [i.e., a virgin] . . ." (124–25, 130). The trope of prostitution as an esoteric trade or craft, in particular, is familiar to us from tracts like *The Whores Rhetorick* (1683)—but of course this is less a trope than a literal description, as we have already seen.[7] Moreover, the secrecy of Mrs. Cole's "secret institution" derives not only from its craft status but also from its need to forge an "alliance . . . of a necessary outward decency with unbounded secret liberty . . . ," that is, the need to disguise the illicit nature of its trade behind the illusory facade of a licit one (132, 131). And so, just as it is a "mystery of the trade" that Fanny pass for a virgin, so "[i]n the outer parlour, or rather shop, sat three young women, very demurely employed on millinary work, which was the cover of a traffic in more precious commodities . . . ." In the inner recesses of the house are the several "apartments" of these women, as well as "a spacious drawing room . . . ." And "[a]s soon then as the evening began, and the shew of a shop was shut, the academy opened, [and] the mask of mock-modesty was completely taken off . . ." (132).

The outer/inner, public/private arrangement of the rooms in Mrs. Cole's house parallels the social conventionality with which prostitution had to be practiced in eighteenth-century London, a private secret no less effective for being a public and open secret. Other bawds maintained their professional secrecy by a less elaborate masquerade, made explicit when Charles enables Fanny's escape from Mrs. Brown's authority by confronting her with the charge that she "decoyed" Fanny "under pretence of hiring as a servant . . ." (86). Millinery shops were notoriously one step away from prostitution; so was domestic service.[8] Shortly after hiring her, Mrs. Brown had reassured Fanny that "she had not taken me to be a common servant, to do domestic drudgery, but to be a kind of companion to her . . . ," a remark that reminds us that the most pervasive disguise metaphor, both in Fanny's *Memoirs* and in the profession at large, is probably that of domesticity (46). Brothels are "houses" throughout this richly sedimented discourse, and in the *Memoirs* their business is described as a mode of domesticity in which the conflict between absolute monarch and free subject has been loosely concentrated, as in so many eighteenth-century novels, in familial and generational terms. Mrs. Brown is "Mother Brown," a self-interested parental figure who tries to dispose of Fanny through an "unrighteous contract" with an "elderly gentleman" in something like a mercenary marriage of convenience; Fanny sincerely protests, "but I cannot love you, indeed I cannot!" (53, 54, 56). By contrast, Mrs. Cole is "my good temporal mother," Fanny's coworkers are "the sisterhood" and Mrs. Cole's "daughters," and the entire entourage is "a little family of love" (54, 181, 125, 124, 131). Indeed, Cleland is at some pains to persuade us that the process by which the innocent Fanny is corrupted and becomes a whore is a subtle one, a socializing domestication in prostitution achieved through the signifying figure of domesticity. At Mrs. Brown's she is "allowed to range all over the house, but cautiously kept from seeing any company," and in time "so thoroughly, as they call it, brought over, so tame to their whistle, that, had my cage door been set open, I had no idea that I ought to fly anywhere sooner than stay where I was . . . . [N]othing, in short, was wanting to domesticate me entirely and to prevent my going out anywhere . . ." (60–61). By the time she gets established at Mrs. Cole's Fanny has learned to suspend her disbelief in the fiction of domesticity (and the millinery trade) because she knows her current existence depends on it.

Like Robinson Crusoe, Fanny uses domesticity to familiarize and accommodate a different yet oddly similar way of life. More precisely, like the nobleman in the anonymous *Love-Letters,* Fanny uses domesticity to conceal and reveal an illicit sexuality; and as in that precedent text domesticity abruptly, and terribly, emerges at the end of the story in its own right. Before his disappearance Charles had seemed "born for domestic happiness," and after once "passing me for his wife that he had secretly married and kept private" he leaves Fanny "three months gone with child" and with a "husband . . . gone to sea" (85, 88, 91, 209). But Fanny endures until her inheritance from the mysterious "rational pleasurist" replaces her mock coverture by an opulent mock widowhood (211–12). After Charles's return they are several times taken for husband and wife even before their actual wedding—manifestly a marriage for love—bestows a "legal parentage" on their "fine children" (85, 91, 214, 217, 223). The brutal "domestic" closure of the anonymous *Love-Letters,* I have suggested, domesticates and degrades the ultimate intimacy of same-sex love as its utter antithesis, different-sex murder and infanticide.[9] Seeming almost as tacked-on and unrationalized as that other ending does, the domestic closure of Fanny's *Memoirs* returns the honor of ultimate intimacy to different-sex love and domesticity—even if on the model, disreputable in its own right, by which the private wife is the apotheosis of the public whore.

We may be excused, however, if under the influence of the secret-history tradition we are tempted to read this ending as a concentration of "greater" things. Charles had been betrayed by his "improvident father," who, tricking him into "leaving England," then had him "more strictly watched than a state criminal." Years later, "having heard of his father's death," Charles "had now the world to begin again," and he returns to England in his "ruined fortune" only to be rewarded by Fanny's (84, 92, 93, 216, 217). Consummating his return "after so long a deprival," Fanny is transported by his "scepter-member which commands us all," his "instrument of pleasure and the great-seal of love." Although no stranger to libertinage and the attention of other lovers, she now delights in "a subjection of soul incomparably dearer to me than the liberty of heart which I had been long, too long! the mistress of, in the course of those grosser gallantries, the consciousness of which now made me sigh with a virtuous confusion and regret" (219, 218). Although the analogy she makes is a different one than I am suggesting, Fanny's impulse here "to compare great with less" teasingly invokes the Virgilian tradition by which public are domesticated through private concerns. The reader may muse, for example, that Fanny's financial windfall has placed her in a position comparable to that of Samuel Butler's Widowed England, autonomous and courted by Puritan suitors, and that she now exchanges the liberties of the subject for subjection to the king. This is, of course, no transparent allegory of Charles II's restoration to the seat of England (elsewhere Fanny calls women's "controlling part" the "queen-seat in us, that governs itself by its own maxims of state")—Charles's father sounds as much like Oliver Cromwell as he does Charles I—but rather a historically inflected semantics aimed at evoking the concrete particularity of Cleland's principal characters (176).

Comparative Interiors

Another way Fanny compares great things with less is in the realm of comparative interiors. One day she returns to the "lodgings" in which Mr. H—— has put her up to find "the street-door open . . . I stepped upstairs into my own bedchamber," thinking "to wait upon him in the dining room, into which my bed-chamber had a door," but hearing sounds she "stole softly to the door" and through a convenient "peep-hole" watches Mr. H—— have sex with her maid, Hannah—that is, find an "entrance" where he is soon "lodged" (104–5). Retiring "softly into my closet," Fanny decides to exact revenge on Mr. H—— by seducing "a very handsome young lad" he has just taken into his service. This soon occurs, and on the same dining-room couch. But because the lad, named Will, is both innocent and extraordinarily well hung, penetration is difficult: he finds the "opening" and "gained a lodgment," but once "secure of his entrance" he sticks, finally "withdrawing" from her "quarters" at her cry of pain. After another "entrance," "the soft strait passage" begins to "let him in . . . ." Soon "the soft oiled wards can no longer stand so effectual a picklock, but yield and open him an entrance," Will "gets entirely in," and he ejaculates "into the innermost recesses of my body . . . ." Later his fingers probe "the secrets of that dark and delicious deep . . ." (110–13). On another occasion Will, "settled well in the passage, . . . makes his way up the straights of it . . ."; Fanny gives him "an accommodation, . . . and having drawn him home to me, I kept him fast there . . . ." But one morning a month later "I was in my closet" with Will "when, having neglected to secure the chamber door, and that of the closet standing ajar, Mr

H—— stole in upon us," then, "without saying a word, spun upon his heel and went out. As confused as I was, I heard him very distinctly turn the key and lock the chamber door upon us, so that there was no escape but through the dining room," where Mr H—— is waiting to confront them (118–19, 121).

Fanny's minute account of domestic interiors—rooms both private and, because *en enfilade,* insecure in their privacy[10]—gives us a way of reading her intimate experience in two analogous dimensions of inner space. Her sensitivity to domestic layout is most acute when her own spectatorial secrecy depends on it. On the memorable day that she first masturbates Fanny finds stimulation in a "love-scene" to which she is "spectatress" by the lucky chance of having been in Mrs. Brown's closet when "I heard a rustling in the bed-chamber, separated from the closet only by two sash-doors, before the glasses of which were drawn two yellow damask curtains, but not so close as to exclude the full view of the room from any person in the closet" (64, 61). The next day Phoebe and Fanny enjoy another spectacle by going "down the backstairs very softly, and opening the door of a dark closet, . . . and fastening the door upon us, [where] we had no light but what came through a long crevice in the partition between ours and the light closet, where the scene of action lay . . . ." What they see conforms to how they see it: Polly's "red-centred cleft of flesh"; her client guiding his penis "with his hand to the inviting slit"; and a climax so inflaming that Phoebe draws "me away softly from the peep-hole" to masturbate her before "she brought me again to the crevice so favourable to our curiosity" (66, 67, 68).

Although we might expect the site and language of the back stairs to figure prominently in the scenes of sodomy Fanny describes,[11] Cleland seems to signal his sense of a basic difference between this and vaginal penetration by shifting from imagery of domestic exploration to that of excursion in the out-of-doors. When her coworker Emily is mistaken at a masquerade ball for the boy her shepherd's costume suggests her to be, her companion, having made the crucial discovery ("By heavens, a woman!"), situates her "so that the double-way between the double rising behind presented the choice fair to him, and he was . . . fiercely set on a misdirection" until Emily's gentle resistance checks him and, "turning his steed's head, he drove him at length in the right road . . ." (192). In the very next scene Fanny finds herself in a room in a "public-house" next door to that of "two young sparks." In a "spirit of curiosity" she searches for a prospect onto their privacy until at length she spots a patch on the wall separating her room from theirs. Fanny stands on a chair to reach it, "and with the point of a bodkin soon pierced it and opened myself espial-room sufficent . . . ."[12] From "the very small opening I was posted at" Fanny takes the younger spark "to be a girl in disguise" until "he showed to the open air those globular, fleshy eminences that compose the mount-pleasants of Rome, and which now, with all the narrow vale that intersects them, stood displayed and exposed . . . ." Shocked at "the disproportion of parts," Fanny watches silently as "the first straights of entrance [are] pretty well got through, [and] everything seemed to move and go pretty currently on, as in a carpet-road" (i.e., a smooth road) (193–95).

Fanny shares Cleland's sense of difference. Emily's misdirected companion eventually makes the best of having mistaken her sex, but his first response to it is marked by "an alteration from extreme warmth into a chill and forced civility," and before it is revealed his approach to Emily seems to her alien and culturally unreadable—"a style of courtship dashed with a certain oddity that, not comprehending the mystery of, poor Emily attributed to his falling in with the humour of her disguise . . ." (191). Sodomy is clearly the wrong road to take, and when she sees it enacted between two men Fanny is so incensed at "so criminal a scene" that she intends "to raise the house against them" and ensure they suffer "the very worst of consequences" at the law, far more ultimate than those Cleland himself risks for conviction on a charge of obscene libel. Her righteous aims are foiled, but Mrs. Cole later confirms that what Fanny has witnessed is a matter not just of behavior but of identity: for of all the sodomites she could name there was "hardly . . . one of them whose character was not in all other respects the most worthless and despicable that could be, stripped of all the manly virtues of their own sex and filled up with only the very worst vices and follies of ours . . ." (194–96). Effeminacy is becoming a problem not of excessive liking for women but of being excessively like them, and the increasingly definitive separation between the genders is being reinforced and reciprocated by that between "sexualities."

One of my aims in these pages has been to document Cleland's self-conscious commitment to the metaphorical figuration of sexual activity as something other than itself. And this is perhaps a surprising claim to make about a narrative celebrated for being the first English work of pornography, one therefore dedicated to the depiction of sex and its pleasures as such. Cleland's *Memoirs* make clear how comfortable he felt with the burgeoning and largely French literature of philosophical libertinism and materialism. How is this consistent with his penchant for figuration? Although certain of Cleland's (of Fanny's) figures have a special importance within the argument this study makes—political metaphors, for example, or those of domestic and somatic interiority—his-her penchant for figuration is eclectic and ecumenical, and it is the recourse to metaphors in general that now demands our attention.

Forecasting Charles's first appearance early on in her memoirs, Fanny writes that "love itself took charge of the disposal of me, in spite of interest or gross lust," and after he takes her maidenhead she "returned his strenuous embraces and kisses with a fervour and gust only known to true love, and which mere lust could never rise to" (71, 79). Musing on this difference after having sex with Mr. H——, Fanny conceives it in terms of that between activity and passivity, conscious action and mere passion: "Yet oh! what an immense difference did I feel between this impression of a pleasure merely animal, and struck out of the collision of the sexes by a passive bodily effect, from that sweet fury, that rage of active delight which crowns the enjoyments of a mutual love-passion . . . ." And when Charles returns toward the end of the narrative, their sexual union once again "brought my conscious heart deliciously into play . . ." (101, 218–19). The phrase may allude to the doctrine of "rational pleasure" Fanny has just learned from her benefactor, who "taught me to be sensible that the pleasures of the mind were superior to those of the body . . . . [T]he one served to exalt and perfect the taste of the other to a degree that the sense alone can never arrive at" (211). Fanny's sexual materialism goes beyond and sophisticates a total investment in gross sense experience. Rather, it involves a mediation of opposed categories similar to that Joseph Addison describes in terms of "the Pleasures of the Imagination, [which,] taken in their full Extent, are not so gross as those of Sense, nor so refined as those of the Understanding."[13] Evidently (and with some apparent paradox), the pornographic "woman of pleasure" partakes of the pleasures of the imagination.

Pleasure Itself

Fanny aims at "the nature of pleasure itself, whose capital favourite object is enjoyment of beauty, wherever that rare invaluable gift is found, without distinction of person or station" (120). Anticipating Samuel Johnson, for whom the judgment of Shakespeare's value requires an assessment of the abstract pleasure he promises and gives independent of "personal allusions, local customs, or temporary opinions," Fanny posits an entity—"pleasure itself"—that remains after extraneous factors have been winnowed away.[14] Pleasure itself is therefore a product of disinterestedness. The rational pleasurist is not one who intellectualizes pleasure but one who is best able to give and feel pleasure because not wholly embedded in and habituated to the realm of the personal, local, and temporary senses. As some advocates of scientific disinterestedness argued that the commoner might best command the sort of ethico-epistemological detachment required for generalizable knowledge, so Fanny believes that "the sole pleasures of enjoyment" "in low life are oftener met with, purer and more unsophisticated, than amongst the false ridiculous refinements" of "the great!" One such "low" person is her "new humble sweetheart" Will: "[D]id not his capacity of giving such exquisite pleasure sufficiently raise and ennoble him . . . ?" (120, 116, 117). The abstraction of "pleasure itself" from all its cultivated and corrupting admixtures is demonstrated most radically when Louisa and Fanny seduce Good-natured Dick, the idiot boy who, "poor indeed of habit, poor of understanding," and scarcely articulate, is not only entirely "subjected" to "the common-law of enjoyment" but proves himself an eager and skillful adept. Indeed, Good-natured Dick is the perfect aesthetic agent-subject, overwhelmed by his own performance: "He seemed at this juncture greater than himself: his countenance, before so void of meaning or expression, now grew big with the importance of the act he was upon. . . . I myself was awed into a sort of respect for him by the comely terrors his emotions dressed him in, his eyes shooting sparks of fire, his face glowing with ardours that gave all another life to it . . ." (197, 198, 200). Fanny might be speaking of David Garrick.

One of the practices by which Fanny achieves the abstraction of "pleasure itself" through a methodical equilibration of reason and the senses is the pornographic voyeurism and virtuality in which she becomes habituated. In Mrs. Brown's closet Fanny is overcome by the action before her, "the sound and sight of which thrilled to the very soul of me, and made every vein of my body circulate liquid fires: the emotion grew so violent that it almost intercepted my respiration." This is the limit case of Adam Smith's theory of imaginative identification: "As we have no immediate experience of what other men feel, we can form no idea of the manner in which they are affected, but by conceiving what we ourselves should feel in the like situation. . . . [I]t is by imagination only that we can form any conception of what are his sensations." Fanny is Smith's "spectator," theatrically detached from the "persons principally concerned" and moved to the extremity of vicarious sensation.[15] The author of *Onania* thought that the imaginations accompanying masturbation were as "filthy" as the act itself.[16] But Fanny, in an ecstasy of imaginative identification brought on by watching others perform sex, now discovers masturbation as a definitively literalizing means of (in Smith's words) "bringing the case home to" herself: "I stole my hand up my petticoat, and with fingers all on fire, seized and yet more inflamed the center of all my senses" until she comes—"[a]fter which my senses recovered coolness enough to observe the rest of the transaction between this happy pair" (62–63). "Pleasure itself" is the product, not just of "gross lust," but of the balancing act between sound, sight, and rationally motivated touch made possible by Fanny's self-conscious detachment from the scene itself of activity.[17]

Another method of achieving pleasure itself is (as I have already documented) Fanny's frequent and near-indiscriminate recourse to metaphor. In her figurative style Fanny may have been influenced by her early training in prostitution, for as in the cant discourse of other subcultures, a private language based on figures of speech is a staple of this one. At Mrs. Brown's table, for example, "[t]he conversation was chiefly kept up by the two madams and carried on in double-meaning expressions" that Fanny can only vaguely follow (47).[18] Successful prostitution requires double meaning, as we have seen not just in Fanny's stylistic penchant for metaphor but also as a mode of social practice— thus Mrs. Cole's "shew of a shop," in the daytime and the public front rooms a millinery trade but in the evening and private back rooms a brothel. Fanny describes this institutional masquerade in terms that bring it suggestively close to the ethico-epistemological balance—between the decent and the libertine, the refined and the gross—required to achieve "pleasure itself":

> In short, this was the safest, politest, and, at the same time, the most thorough house of accommodation in town, everything being conducted so that decency made no intrenchment upon the most libertine pleasures, in the practice of which, too, the choice familiars of the house had found the secret so rare and difficult of reconciling even all the refinements of taste and delicacy with the most gross and determinate gratifications of sensuality. (132)

Even more striking are the similar terms in which Fanny, a few pages earlier, thanks her nominal correspondent for sympathizing with the "extreme difficulty" of writing a book so unrelievedly about the *"practice of pleasure"*—"of continuing so long in one strain, in a mean tempered with taste, between the revoltingness of gross, rank, and vulgar expressions, and the ridicule of mincing metaphors and affected circumlocutions . . . ." True, for Fanny metaphor here sounds as much like a part of the problem as it does like the tempering mean by which the problem is solved through the reconciliation of the "gross" and the "refined." But her central purpose is, I think, to compensate for her unavoidable "repetition of near the same images, the same figures, the same expressions" by enlisting her readers in an imaginative identification that will bring home to them what mere words cannot convey by themselves. The problem of the repetitiveness of Fanny's language is related to the problem of the grossness of her subject: both derive from a "uniformity of adventures and expressions, inseparable from a subject of this sort, whose bottom or groundwork [is], in the nature of things, eternally one and the same . . . ." If her language is a "disadvantage," Fanny "trust[s] . . . to your imagination and sensibility the pleasing task of repairing it by their supplements, where my descriptions flag or fail: the one will readily place the pictures I present before your eyes; the other give life to the colours where they are dull, or worn with too frequent handling" (129).

Often Fanny is confident in the power of her metaphors to mediate between the essential sameness of what she describes and what her readers imaginatively feel, and sometimes she reflects self-consciously on that power. Having "spare[d] you the description" of a scene of sexual intercourse by substituting an extended nautical metaphor for it, Fanny cannot resist offering "an excuse I am conscious of owing you for having perhaps too much affected the figurative style; though, surely, it can pass nowhere more allowably than in a subject which is so properly the province of poetry, nay! is poetry itself, pregnant with every flower of imagination and loving metaphors . . ." (207). And sometimes Fanny makes explicit the analogy between the imaginative virtuality of her pleasure as an author and of ours as her readers. Describing the experience of being penetrated by Charles, she lapses: "—oh!—my pen drops from me here in the ecstasy now present to my faithful memory! Description, too, deserts me and delivers over a task, above its strength of wing, to the imagination; but it must be an imagination exalted by such a flame as mine . . ." (220). Fanny now "watches" her memory of the event as she has watched similar events through assorted peepholes, and as we are now asked to "watch" that event through the distantiating peephole of our identificatory imaginations. By this account, the structure of pornographic experience models the aesthetic experience of "pleasure itself."[19]

In fact, Cleland seems to have believed that his singular style might save him from prosecution for (not "pornography" but) obscene libel. In an appeal to the law clerk of the secretary of state he confessed that his printer and publisher "certainly were deceived by my avoiding those rank words in the work, which are all that they Judge of obscenity by, and made them think the Line was drawn between them, and all danger of Law whatever."[20] The misconception that prior self-censorship of this sort would obviate postpublication state censorship (or worse) was presumably Cleland's as well. However, Fanny's defense of the *Memoirs* against not legal but moral vulnerability—her "tail-piece of morality"—may be buttressed by what we have learned about her approach to pornography. By the end of her *Memoirs* Fanny has fulfilled the joint promise of the prostitute as promulgated by *The Whores Rhetorick:* she has become a wife and an author. Properly understood, the author of pornography does not simply justify all manner of vice by insisting on its pedagogic necessity for recognizing virtue. Instead of this too-easy, cynical dialectic Fanny promotes the more strenuous and exacting dialectic of mediation through virtual experience. The character as voyeur, Fanny provides an example of imaginative identification on which to model our own experience in reading the writings of Fanny the author. The filter of pornographic virtuality refines and winnows away the gross sensuality of unmediated, firsthand sexual activity, leaving the residue of "pleasure itself," an aesthetic affect because empirical yet disembedded and detached from its empirical ground. Concluding with a characteristic metaphor, Fanny writes: "Thus, at length, I got snug into port, where . . . I could not help pitying, even in point of taste, those who, immersed in a gross sensuality, are insensible to the so delicate charms of VIRTUE, than which even PLEASURE has not a greater friend, nor than VICE a greater enemy. Thus temperance makes men lords over those pleasures that intemperance enslaves them to . . ." (223). If pornographic voyeurism and fulsome metaphor are two practices by which Fanny abstracts pleasure itself for our consumption, the indispensable third sort of practice is that of publication itself, which ensures that her experiences will also be ours so long as our imaginations meet hers halfway. Cleland's pornography is public not because its intimate privacy refers to political actuality but because it refers to imaginative virtuality.

Tristram Shandy

In *Fanny Hill* our encounter with sexual activity is virtualized and aestheticized by (among other things) Fanny's metaphorical descriptions of it. In Laurence Sterne's *Tristram Shandy* (1759–67) sexual activity as such disappears entirely because it is entirely metaphorical. That is, sex is a sublimated suggestiveness that separates out the concrete capacity for sexual feeling from its actual fulfillment. In Sterne's novel, sexuality saturates men of feeling with the sensible vibrations of a thoroughly sublimated lubricity. Sterne takes Cleland's pornography to the next level and turns it into something else. When Walter says to his brother, "[Y]ou might, at least, know so much as the right end of a woman from the wrong," "Right end,——quoth my uncle Toby, muttering the two words low to himself, and fixing his two eyes insensibly as he muttered them upon a small crevice, form'd by a bad joint in the chimney-piece.——Right end of a woman! ——I declare, quoth my uncle, I know no more which it is, than the man in the moon . . . ."[21] The exchange reminds us of *Fanny Hill* in several ways—the sodomite's mistaking the wrong for the "right road," the "crevice" in the dark closet that reveals Polly's "inviting slit"—but in *Tristram Shandy* the crevices, although omnipresent, only remind us and Sterne's characters of slits, which we never really "see" as Fanny and we see Polly's. By the same token, Sterne's novel is as absolutely domestic as Richardson's is: the only actual space in which events occur is the several rooms, stairs, and floors of the Shandy household. And yet from all this interior space women are for the most part absent; and although Tristram is necessarily the product of sexual intercourse between his father and his mother, the mysteriously caused defect of his reproductive organs gives to "the fortunes of his whole house" a melancholy cast because in all likelihood Tristram represents the end of the family line (vol. 1, chap. 1, p. 3; see also vol. 1, chap. 12, p. 23, and vol. 3, chap. 8, p. 125).[22] The actuality of the Shandy line is on the verge of disappearing from diachronic time, and Tristram's fastidiously full report from the front documents a family life that already seems to exist only in the synchronic, suspended animation of concrete virtuality.

The domestic intimacy of the Shandy household is based not in heterosexual but in homosocial relationships. Men have replaced women, a good deal more thoroughly than Dr. Slop is successful in supplanting the female midwife. Although the marriage settlement of Tristram's mother, Elizabeth, reminds us that men's work is "business" and women's work is "bearing," the unproductivity of labor in both senses of the term seems to be a male failing here (Elizabeth's fortune actually supports the household) (vol. 1, chap. 15, p. 29).[23] So far from being the despised profligacy of the sodomite (or the prostitute or the adulterer), however, unproductivity is revalued here in a positive direction. True, the Shandy men are "effeminate" in the modern rather than the residual sense of the term. But the way they are "like" women is very different from that of the molly, and the innuendo of metaphorical sex in this novel alludes almost exclusively to different-sex rather than to same-sex activity. To appreciate the degree to which "same-sex activity" nonetheless dominates the plot of *Tristram Shandy* we need to pursue metaphorical sex back to what it seems to stand for in this novel, sensibility. Men are like women here because their access to their emotional interiority resembles that with which women in the eighteenth century are increasingly being associated. Uncle Toby is our exemplary man of feeling, and when he forbears from injuring the fly that interrupts him at dinner one evening, Tristram writes that "the action itself . . . instantly set my whole frame into one vibration of most pleasurable sensation . . ." (vol. 2, chap. 12, p. 86).

Sense and Sensibility

Why did the eighteenth-century cult of sensibility celebrate the man rather than the woman of feeling? Like the category of the aesthetic imagination, the idea of sensibility sought to capture that quality of sensation that was rooted in the physical senses but that represented a detached abstraction from sense experience, the virtuality of emotional experience rather than the actuality of sensible experience. Precisely because it is physically responsible for reproduction, "the sex" is too deeply rooted in the senses to mediate the subtilized obliquity of sensibility. Not that sensibility has no linkage to sensible experience. The aristocratic belief that birth makes worth had held the appeal that what could be seen on the outside and in public—rank, regalia, personal display, even refined complexion—was a dependable sign of internal and "private" value. In its preoccupation with the blush, the tear, and the involuntary somatic signs of deep feeling, the cult of sensibility reinvented this notion of the body as a system of socio-ethical signification in terms of a bodily materialism that would evade the ideology of aristocratic privilege. The conception of feminine virtue as internalized honor was crucial to this effort. In *Pamela* and *Clarissa* Richardson would have us see that the honor of corrupt aristocrats is really possessed by those who supposedly exist only to facilitate its lineal passage from male to male. Feminine virtue is expressed both through an active and highly articulate resistance to the encroachments of male aristocracy and, when most under siege, through the mute and involuntary authenticity of bodily sensation.

Sterne borrows from Richardson this counterdiscursive "body language," which provides, in the face of patrilineal ambition, an alternative access to authentic human relations. But he leaves behind the possibility of a militantly active virtue capable of resisting the authority of the line, and he leaves behind the location of either sort of virtue in women. The man of feeling's affectivity is a withdrawal from the publicness of both aggressively male productivity and excessively female reproductivity. Tristram's genital defect and Uncle Toby's wound make them anatomically "like" women, but also unlike women in being liberated from their embeddedness in bodily necessity. Women are compromised by the biological naturalness of their sexual function; men, comparatively free of this imprisonment in the physical senses, are associated not with sex and nature but with gender and nurture. The cultural type of the man of feeling reclaims a recognizably feminine virtue as a distinctively male possession. A feminized hero, the man of feeling reincorporates the normative gender traits within what a patriarchal culture persists in seeing as the normative sex. The hilariousness of Thomas Rowlandson's rendition of the man of feeling (fig. 15.1) turns on the way he desublimates sensibility from the level of the virtual to that of the actual. Rowlandson's country parson has been reading *An Essay on Woman* (1762–63), which protrudes from his pocket and was a parody of Pope's *Essay on Man* that was also, in more or less equal parts, notoriously obscene, misogynist, antisodomitical, and blasphemous in its conflation of libertine sex and Christian ritual.[24] So far from being a man who feels like a woman, Rowlandson's man of feeling likes to feel women; interiority is sartorial, not emotional.

In its broadest significance, the idea of sensibility aims to articulate the relationship between the outside and the inside, the body and the mind, reason and the passions, for a culture that is increasingly invested in categorial separation but also in the conflation of categories made newly possible by the fact of their full separation. In *Tristram Shandy* sensibility comes closest to the status of doctrine through the theory of the hobbyhorse, which in turn derives from the increasingly archaic postulate of the old, Galenic medicine that character is determined by the bodily balance of the four humors. And although I have just suggested its conflationary modernity, in this respect sensibility can also be seen

THE MAN OF FEELING.

Pub.ᵈ Feb.ʸ 29 1788. by Wm. Holland, N.ᵒ 50, Oxford Street.

FIG. 15.1. Thomas Rowlandson, *The Man of Feeling,* 1788, etching. Courtesy of the Lewis Walpole Library, Yale University.

as the last and unlikely gasp of the hierarchical, one-sex model of human sexuality, the traditional dominance of gender over sex still evident in the availability to men of a manifestly feminine norm.[25] This understanding is borne out by the currency of related archaisms in Sterne's novel. For example, Walter's insistence that his wife's marriage settlement limit the number of trips Elizabeth might take to London in anticipation of childbirth is motivated by his belief in the correspondence between the private body and the public state: "[I]t was identically the same in the body national as in the body natural," and "the current of men and money towards the metropolis, upon one frivolous errand or another,——set in so strong,—as to become dangerous to our civil rights . . . ." Indeed, such a policy might "in the end, prove fatal to the monarchical system of domestick government . . . . In this point [Walter] was entirely of Sir *Robert Filmer's* opinion . . ." (vol. 1, chap. 18, pp. 35–36).

Walter's patriarchalism builds on, and agrees with, the humoralism that suffuses *Tristram Shandy* and that sensibility seems in some fashion to modernize. The humoral theory of the hobbyhorse posits a relationship between the soul and the body in which the latter's habitual influence on the former comes in time to seem natural, "beginning in jest,——but ending in downright earnest": "By long journies and much friction, it so happens that the body of the rider is at length fill'd as full of HOBBY-HORSICAL matter as it can hold . . ." (vol. 1, chap. 19, p. 41, and chap. 24, p. 58). This bespeaks the influence of the body on the mind but also of the mind on the body and the passions on reason. Tristram takes so seriously Locke's distinction between reason and the imagination, judgment and wit, that he cannot think of the one without wittily conjoining it with the other, conflating the two in the very process of explicitly separating them out. Like David Hume, Tristram values the Lockean notion of clear and distinct ideas principally for the way it fuels the equally Lockean engine of the association of ideas. This has an important bearing, of course, on the nature of the very work we are reading. Locke's *Essay concerning Human Understanding*, Tristram maintains, is "a history-book . . . of what passes in a man's own mind . . ." (vol. 2, chap. 2, p. 66). Being an autobiographer in the modern mode, he warns us early on that in this "history of myself" "nothing which has touched me will be thought trifling in its nature, or tedious in its telling" (vol. 1, chap. 4, p. 6, and chap. 6, p. 8). Tristram reminds us of both Mr. Spectator— "Is it not much better to be let into the Knowledge of ones-self, than to hear what passes in *Muscovy* or *Poland* . . . ?"—and Dr. Johnson—"[T]he business of the biographer is often . . . to lead the thoughts into domestick privacies . . . ."[26] In Tristram's autobiographical practice, of course, to focus on domestic privacies is rather less voluntary than in those models; and this makes sense, since because the writing of *Tristram Shandy* is Tristram's hobbyhorse, it registers what "has touched me" both as palpable effect and as impalpable affect.

This sort of conflation of the physical and the emotional, of sense and sensibility, of the public and the private, is Sterne's modus operandi. We experience it in the dialectical principle of narration that controls his plot and that Tristram describes in the following terms: "By this contrivance the machinery of my work is a species by itself; two contrary motions are introduced into it, and reconciled, which were thought to be at variance with each other. In a word, my work is digressive, and it is progressive too,——and at the same time" (vol. 1, chap. 22, p. 54). And because *Tristram Shandy* goes both forward and backward at the same time, it stands still—or even produces the net result of negative temporality. This is Sterne's version of preserving "the unity, or rather probability, of time . . ." (vol. 2, chap. 8, p. 79). As playwrights and critics were learning, by reference to the pleasures and powers of the imagination, to justify the divergence of the time represented on stage from the time taken to represent it, Sterne reduces the dramatic conundrum to terminal absurdity by translating it to the medium of narration, where the subjective experience of fabricating a story, and reading it, inevitably outstrips and internalizes the objective story itself just as, in Hume's philosophy, Locke's "reflection" outstrips and internalizes his "sensation."

The demand for dramatic unity of place might seem untranslatable to narration given basic differences between the two media; and in any case, what could be more rigidly localized than a novel whose principal action is relegated to the space of domesticity? Nevertheless Sterne's ingenuity overcomes both problems by suggesting that place, like time, is ultimately an effect of mental interiority. Uncle Toby's hobbyhorse, we know, is the siege of Namur, where he received his groin wound. But his efforts to physically re-create that battle on the table in his room at Shandy Hall are frustrated at every turn by lack of sufficient space, and so he complains to his beloved servant: "I must have some better contrivance, *Trim.*——Can'st not thou take my rule and measure the length and breadth of this table, and then go and bespeak me one as big again?" But Trim has a better idea. Pointing to a map pinned to the wall, he exclaims that little can be done "here upon paper, compared to what your Honour and I could make of it, were we in the country by ourselves, and had but a rood, or a rood and a half of ground to do what we pleased with . . . ." The prospect of accommodating the siege through a closely literal simulacrum of it fills Uncle Toby with joy: "Corporal *Trim*'s description had fired his imagination . . . ." Tristram gives us a precise sense of the actual space Toby contemplates he will use to re-create the siege even as his account acknowledges, in scrupulously bodily terms, the virtuality of that space as it becomes an object of Toby's mental contemplation: Toby has "a little neat country-house of his own," behind which is "a kitchen-garden of about half an acre," at the bottom of which is "a bowling-green" that "instantly presented itself, and became curiously painted, all at once, upon the retina of my uncle *Toby*'s fancy . . ." (vol. 2, chap. 5, pp. 72–75). Maintaining the unity of place turns out to be a simple matter, since actual, exterior space is always a function of virtual, interior space. What is difficult is coordinating the virtual spaces contemplated by different subjects. Later, when the amorous widow Wadman asks Toby, "And whereabouts, dear Sir, . . . did you receive this sad blow?" she "gave a slight glance toward the waistband of my uncle *Toby*'s red plush breeches, expecting naturally . . . that my uncle *Toby* would lay his fore-finger upon the place . . . ." But Toby, "having got his wound before the gate of *St. Nicolas,*" instead gravely lays her finger on that exact spot on the map of the siege (vol. 9, chap. 26, p. 489). Recalling Aphra Behn, Trim says to Toby: "——— for Love, an' please your honour, is exactly like war" (vol. 8, chap. 21, p. 441). In this way Sterne, by a different, first-person route than Fielding but under his in-spiring direction, transforms the actual reference of "chorography" and "topog-raphy" into the virtual, aesthetic reference of "biography."[27]

The Double Failure of the Line

In the practice of Behn and then of Fielding, Sterne could find precedent for the internalization of the virtual reader within the actual text. In all three cases the practice is justified not just by the pleasures of reflexivity but also by the way it facilitates narrative pedagogy, the instruction of the reader by the author-narrator. In *Tristram Shandy* the posited relationship between author and reader can seem as self-consciously and manipulatively virtuosic as the tutorials con-ducted by Fielding, especially the Fielding of *Joseph Andrews* (I am thinking in particular of Tristram's early bouts with Madam [vol. 1, chap. 18, pp. 37–38, and chap. 20, pp. 43–44]). These effects follow the broad logic that is familiar to us from other innovations in the public-private dynamic, especially Shaftesbury's remarks on the implications of print: the separation out of author and reader, although explicit enough in the practice of the rhetorical tradition, becomes so insistent as to solicit the insight of conflation.[28] At least in part because Sterne's first-person narration necessarily brings the narrator more into the thick of things, however, *Tristram Shandy* more often levels the pedagogic relation to one of "conversation" and participatory composition: "Writing, when properly managed, (as you may be sure I think mine is) is but a different name for con-versation: As no one, who knows what he is about in good company, would venture to talk all;———so no author, who understands the just boundaries of decorum and good breeding, would presume to think all: The truest respect which you can pay to the reader's understanding, is to halve this matter amicably, and leave him something to imagine, in his turn, as well as yourself" (vol. 2, chap. 11, p. 83). Tristram's gesture of good will operates as a kind of externalization of the intimate reciprocity that inevitably subsists, as he has told us, within his own and our minds: Tristram the "proper manager" plays judgment to our creative and unpredictable wit. True, he is careful to set a limit on our unpredictability ("Let the reader imagine then, that . . ." [vol. 2, chap. 11, p. 83]). Even so, the conceit of text as conversation effectively affirms a dimension of reflexivity that evades the public-private figuration bequeathed by print circulation by evoking a fiction of face-to-face oral (and, with characteristic suggestiveness, sexual) exchange.

A jest that becomes very earnest, Sterne's indulgence of the pleasures of the imagination turns his novel into an endlessly reflexive exercise in aesthetic disinterestedness in which sensibility is seen somehow to ground the experience of sensation in which it is putatively grounded. Perhaps the most arresting instance of its reflexivity is the way the form and content of *Tristram Shandy* reflect each other in their dual concern with the failure of the line, a formal principle thematized from the outset in Tristram's inability to progress with his life story because he cannot determine ultimate responsibility for "the fortunes of my house." Tristram's failure to impose a progressive order on his narrative line is the irrepressible symptom of his squashed nose and defective penis, his presumed failure to extend his patriline. But *Tristram Shandy* is not only a satire of the male pride in patrilineal inheritance; it also propounds an alternative way for people—indeed, for family members—to interact.

The misunderstanding between Toby and the widow Wadman about the location of his wound exemplifies the futility of linearity, here represented by rational judgment and frustrated by associative wit and the divergent meanings of "place." From the perspective of judgment and patrilineage, the dominant force of witty association threatens to isolate us all in the solitude and solipsism of our individual hobbyhorses, as well as to divert sexual reproduction into the dead-end, virtual vibrations of sensibility. From the perspective of sensibility, however, family ties may consist in the ostensible absence of family ties. As with Toby and the widow, communication and closure between Toby and Walter cannot occur on the level of linear rationality, as a willed meeting of minds on a shared topic of discourse. And yet they do occur when least expected: when, for example, the metaphorical language Walter uses while riding his own hobbyhorse—the word "train," or "siege," or "radical moisture," or "auxiliaries"—happens to intercept Toby's hobbyhorse (vol. 3, chap. 18, p. 141, and chap. 41, p. 178; vol. 5, chaps. 36–37, pp. 300–301, and chaps. 42–43, pp. 306–7). These momentary, involuntary, and fortuitous intersections of divergent bodily humors provide the basis for the sympathetic identification between Sterne's characters and constitute a gentle and silent reproach to laboriously rational and discursive efforts at communication. In a mode that may remind us of Adam Smith's invisible hand, the way to public and social relations lies through individual self-involvement.[29] The distinctive family trait that connects the Shandy males is precisely their difference from one another, the singular and humorous "originality" of their characters. As Tristram remarks, "[T]he hand of the supreme Maker and first Designer of all things, never made or put a family together, . . . where the characters of it were cast or contrasted with so dramatic a felicity as ours was, . . . as in the SHANDY-FAMILY" (vol. 3, chap. 39, p. 176). Sterne's new model of family cohesion substitutes for the organizing principle of diachronic patrilineal inheritance the synchronic community of individuals, isolated monads incapable of rational interaction but conjoined by the involuntary, accidental, and all-powerful forces of sympathetic association. If we set aside as singular to Sterne's imagination the insuperable problem of nonreproductivity, *Tristram Shandy* can be seen to offer not only a radical experiment in private writing but also the paradigmatic depth model of the modern domestic family, which values itself most definitively not as an ongoing public institution but in the affective ties that bind it together in the synchronic space of a single generation or two.

Humphry Clinker

In *Tristram Shandy,* domesticity coalesces as the unexpected residue of failed efforts at a more purposive sort of productivity. In Tobias Smollett's *Humphry Clinker* (1771), domesticity is thrown into high relief against the backdrop of the specious traditionality promulgated by its dominant character, Matthew Bramble. Smollett's full title—*The Expedition of Humphry Clinker*—gives the game away at the outset: despite the splenetic Bramble's garrulousness, this novel is finally not about him at all but about his bastard son, whose "expedition" is only the most eloquent sign of the Bramble family's real nature.[30] *Humphry Clinker* qualifies as a great domestic novel not, like *Tristram Shandy* and *Pamela,* by confining its action to the home but, like *The Pilgrim's Progress* and *Robinson Crusoe,* by leaving home, undertaking adventures that generate images of the household and the family that challenge an older ideal that has been left behind but that still proffers pleasing models for what has replaced it.[31]

When we first encounter Matt Bramble, we are obliged to take his account of Brambleton Hall more or less at face value. His letters home express a familial and "feudal" care for his tenants that evokes an organic community hierarchically stratified by relations of personal dependence. Status and gender distinctions are clearly marked, but they are represented as interdependent and in-separable components of a greater domestic economy. Matt has a gruff but benevolent regard for Higgins the poacher, who no doubt "thought he had some right (especially in my absence) to partake of what nature seems to have intended for common use," and the letters home by Matt's sister Tabitha are even more preoccupied than his with the details of administering the estate, which notably include her authority over the outside work of dairy production (17 Apr., pp. 14–15; see also 26 Apr., p. 44, and 6 May, p. 61).[32] Indeed, Bramble-ton Hall presents the image of a Horatian "country retreat," a sort of pastoral *locus amoenus* where food is "the produce of the natural soil, prepared by mod-erate cultivation" and produced for immediate and local consumption (8 June, pp. 118, 119). Later on in his travels Matt discovers something like a "perfect paradise" in the highlands of Scotland, whose hierarchy of interdependent rela-tions cannot fail to remind us of that other paradise from which this paterfa-milias has strayed: "The connection between the clans and their chiefs is, with-out all doubt, *patriarchal*. It is founded on hereditary regard and affection, cherished through a long succession of ages. The clan consider the chief as their father . . ." (6 Sept., pp. 254–55).

A Family of Originals

However, the Bramble family's traveling entourage is anything but patriarchal. They are in fact (as Matt's nephew Jery calls them) "a family of originals" very recently and haphazardly conjoined by the death of Matt's sister (2 Apr., p. 8). Matt and Tabby are not husband and wife but unmarried brother and sister; Jery and Liddy are their orphaned nephew and niece, who, having been edu-cated apart, have scarcely met each other as the novel opens; in his first letter home Jery speaks of his sister as though of a stranger: "I found her a fine, tall girl of seventeen, with an agreeable person . . ." (2 Apr., p. 8). This is indeed a "traveling" household, one very recently reembedded in family soil, and there is something artificial, even theatrical, about their relations. Liddy addresses one of her correspondents in the following manner: "Having no mother of my own, I hope you will give me leave to disburthen my poor heart to you, who have al-ways acted the part of a kind parent to me . . ." (6 Apr., p. 9). Other parts are taken by other players: the traveling party is completed by Winifred Jenkins, Tabitha's maid, and by Tabitha's dog Chowder, whose health problems preoc-cupy her letters almost as much as Matt's do his. Matt himself is candid about the contingency of the Bramble family: "I an't married to Tabby, thank Heaven! nor did I beget the other two; let them choose another guardian: for my part, I an't in a condition to take care of myself; much less to superintend the conduct of giddy-headed boys and girls" (17 Apr., p. 12).

And yet despite this candor, throughout the novel there is a strong sense in which these highly extended family members variously act out a scenario of strict familial ties and iron-clad obligations as though to mask the tenuous instability of their family commitments. This is evident, for example, in the running subplot of the mysterious Mr. Wilson and his amatory pursuit of Liddy, which punctuates the entire narrative from beginning to end and evokes from her brother an archaic, chivalric outrage against Wilson, whose attentions persuade Jery that he "harbours some infamous design upon the honour of his family": "[M]y blood boils with indignation when I think of that fellow's presumption . . . ." By contrast, the paterfamilias is unperturbed by Wilson's behavior and satirical about Jery's "family-pride": "The rash boy, without saying a word of the matter to me, went immediately in search of Wilson; and, I suppose, treated him with insolence enough. The theatrical hero was too far gone in romance to brook such usage; he replied in blank verse, and a formal challenge ensued" (12 June 12, pp. 144, 145; 8 Aug., p. 224; 17 Apr., pp. 12–13). At a certain point in our reading Smollett's theatricalization of the Bramble family—our sense that it is a performative experiment in achieving what does not come "naturally"—may even begin to infiltrate our experience of Brambleton Hall as a well-nigh poetic ideal that may just be too good to be true.

Interestingly, the artifice of this ideal is most pronounced when evoked by Matt's jeremiads against its pastoral antithesis, the contemporary (and especially urban) Britain he sees in his travels. By Matt's account, social emulation and the allure of upward mobility have engendered a crisis of conspicuous consumption in which everyone apes their betters. Simplicity gives way to complexity, ordered stability to fluidity and mixture, the natural rule of sufficiency and need to the artificial and limitless indulgence of appetite and want. The body politic (to adopt one of Matt's favorite figures of speech) has become "diseased," "infected," "consumed" by a "contagion" for which only the fast-disappearing domestic economy of the countryside, apparently, affords a cure. Or, to adopt another favorite figure, that of tumultuous liquidity, the stable and settled British way of life has been overwhelmed by a "flood," a "tide," a "torrent" of luxury that has "swept away" the balance and tradition of the past—even the relatively recent past of Matt's own youth. Much of this is to be blamed on that "incongruous monster, called the *public*" (29 May, p. 88). Against this monster Matt opposes an antique pastoral idyll in which public sociability and private retreat are coextensive: "From this wild uproar of knavery, folly, and impertinence, I shall fly with double relish to the serenity of retirement, the cordial effusions of unreserved friendship, the hospitality and protection of the rural gods; in a word, the *jucunda oblivia vitae,* which Horace himself had not taste enough to enjoy" (8 June, p. 123).[33]

In its sheer artifice, Matt's pastoral idyll can seem less the ontological antithesis to the social mobility that plagues him in the world at large than its fantastic reaction formation; and this is partly because Matt's judgment is manifestly undependable, even defective. Like the Shandy men, Matt Bramble is a
man of feeling whose hobbyhorse is capable of cutting him off from the outside
world. And like Tristram, Matt finds useful, in accounting for his condition,
the archaic language of the four humors and their circulation throughout the
body (see, e.g., 23 Apr., p. 33). What complicates the character type in Smollett's
rendition, however, is the dizzying reflexivity of Matt's hobbyhorse, however we
choose to define it. On the one hand, we might identify Matt's hobbyhorse as
precisely his obsession with the outside world and how it seems to alter with the
passage of time and his own change of place. On the other hand, it is his obsession with his own inner condition of hypochondria, an external bodily malady
that cannot be separated from his internal mental state. As Matt tells Dr. Lewis,
he has "had an hospital these fourteen years within myself, and studied my own
case with the most painful attention . . ." (20 Apr., p. 23). The problem is that
this program in self-study presumes that separation of mind and body, of subject and object, which Matt's illness precludes: "I find my spirits and my health
affect each other reciprocally . . ." (14 June, p. 154). In fact, Matt's person provides the perfect internalized analogue for what he rails against in the diseased
body politic, the disease of social circulation. This can be seen in Jery's several
diagnoses of his uncle's condition, in which he prefers the emergent language of
sensibility to the residual language of humoral circulation. "I think his peevish-
ness arises partly from bodily pain, and partly from a natural excess of mental
sensibility; for, I suppose, the mind as well as the body, is in some cases endued
with a morbid excess of sensation. . . . He affects misanthropy, in order to conceal the sensibility of a heart, which is tender, even to a degree of weakness. . . .
Indeed, I never knew a hypochondriac so apt to be infected with good-humour.
He is the most risible misanthrope I ever met with" (18 Apr., p. 17; 24 Apr., p.
28; 30 Apr., p. 49).

Jery's figure of "infection" ensures that we see the analogy between the condition of mixture in Matt's person and the condition of the greater body politic,
and this correspondence between the micro- and the macroworld seems appropriate enough to a self-styled patriarchalist like Matt. But it is a paradoxically self-canceling phenomenon, since it consists of a correspondence between
greater and lesser instances of noncorrespondence. What are we to make of this
oddity? In his ideal self-depictions Matt has appeared to us as a traditionalist for
whom the several categories of experience—nature and art, master and servant,
outside and inside work, object and subject, body and mind, public and private—possess a distinction that is not susceptible of separation. And yet his tra-

ditionalism has all along seemed artificially worked up, a response to rather than a precursor of the epochal separations that mark the coming of modernity and that are epitomized for Matt by the current crisis of social mobility and circulation. As Jery's accounts of his uncle's sensibility make clear, contradiction is a central feature of Matt's personality. In schematic terms, it results from his tendency to parody the traditionalist language of distinction to approximate the modern experience of conflation. In Matt's parody the fleeting world of distinction, in which difference is accommodated and contained by the overarching continuum of hierarchy, is both imitated and criticized so as to fabricate a self-consciously sophisticated simulacrum of a world before separation—the modern divisions of labor and knowledge—has taken effect. The emergent culture of conflation, thus likened to the residual culture of distinction, is enabled through similarity to sustain its difference.[34] We can pursue this line of thought by asking how Humphry Clinker's addition to the traveling entourage alters the composition of the Bramble family, a question that also will adumbrate an analogy between Bramble's approximation of the new through parody of the old and Smollett's singular contribution to the domestic novel. Smollett's title concentrates on the expedition of Humphry, not Matt, because his novel is about the setting forth on a journey that is not only physical but also social, the upward mobility of one literally expedited, or "caught by the feet," in the lowest reaches of privative and abject indigence and freed by forces that Smollett invites us to understand in terms both old and new.

Humphry is introduced to the Brambles as the meanest of commoners, "a shabby country fellow" who is "such a beggarly rascal, that he had ne'er a shirt to his back," "a love-begotten babe, brought up in the work-house, and put out apprentice by the parish to a country black-smith" but now so "sick and destitute" that he surely would have perished had Matt's charity not engaged Humphry to replace the postilion responsible for overturning the Bramble carriage. So Matt apparently contributes to the upward mobility he despises; but Winifred's remark that Humphry "had a skin as white as alabaster" warns us that we may be in the territory of that most antiquated of narrative conventions, family romance (24 May, pp. 80–81, 82). Certainly Humphry is as virtuous as they come, and Smollett allows his relationship with Matt to develop in ways that both frustrate and encourage our expectations that Humphry's stock is better than it would appear to be. When, in sincere and utter innocence, he begins to preach the gospel in public places, Matt denounces him as a "wrongheaded enthusiast . . . . [I]f you are really seduced by the reveries of a disturbed imagination, . . . some charitable person might provide you with a dark room and clean straw in Bedlam, where it would not be in your power to infect others with your fanaticism . . ." (10 June, p. 138). Matt's language of "infection" and "enthusiastic" "imagination" invites us to see Humphry through his eyes, as a germ of that social disease which Matt despairs of in the body politic. But we cannot help being reminded, as well, of Matt's own diseased body and the mobile spirits set loose by his uncontrolled sensibility.

Certainly Humphry's spirituality, whatever the ground from which it has been sublimated, is not an isolated case. "[A]ll the females of our family" have been sensibly affected by Humphry's gospel, and Winifred piously points a moral—"[t]he pleasures of London are no better than sower whey and stale cyder, when compared to the joys of the new Gerusalem"—that should give Matt pause, since it associates Humphry's egalitarian Methodist utopianism with Matt's paternalistic pastoral utopianism (10 June, p. 137; 3 June, p. 109). And speaking of sublimates, what about Jery's boiling blood and family pride? As the plot unrolls, we learn to recognize the characteristic enthusiasm of Smollett's women as not religious but amatory. Speaking of his family in the notably quaint terms of "domestic œconomy," Matt writes that it "continues on the old footing.—My sister Tabby still adheres to methodism . . . but I believe the passion of love has in some measure abated the fervour of devotion both in her and her woman, Mrs. Jenkins . . . ." And Jery remarks (reminding us of his sister's infatuation with the mysterious player Mr. Wilson): "Love, it seems, is resolved to assert his dominion over all the females of our family . . ." (15 July, p. 207; 18 July, p. 208). Yet Liddy's love reminds us of nothing so much as Matt's hypochondria. According to him, "[H]er colour fades, her appetite fails, and her spirits flag.—She is become moping and melancholy, and is often found in tears" (8 Aug., p. 235). In Jery's view, we recall, Matt "affects misanthropy, in order to conceal the sensibility of a heart, which is tender, even to a degree of weakness" (24 Apr., p. 28). And in Matt's view, Liddy is "deficient in spirit, and so susceptible—and so tender forsooth!—truly, she has got a languishing eye, and reads romances—" (17 Apr., p. 12).

When Locke warns us about the irrationality of "enthusiasm," his target is manifestly a species of religious excess. When Swift derides the mechanical operation of the spirit, his model of sublimation requires us to see a family resemblance between religious enthusiasm and other sorts of passionate extremity. Smollett would have us generalize more broadly still. Reading *Humphry Clinker* for the passions, we gradually come to see that the one family trait that truly conjoins this family of originals is the symptom of affective access, of sensibility. The Shandy men of feeling experience their kinship at moments when reason and language are most frustrated; in *Humphry Clinker* it is less the characters themselves than we readers who recognize their family ties in the common capacity for sympathetic identification that underlies their voluble disagreements. Smollett's novel is strewn with what its characters refer to generically as "affecting scenes," moving tableaux of familial distress and transfiguration that provide the Brambles a chance to display, with the paradoxical engagement of aesthetic detachment, their sympathetic and charitable responses. Set pieces of sensibility, these scenes theatricalize the pathos of familial instability by including within them the empathy of the Brambles themselves, familial subjects who for a moment become also an objective audience to their own spectacle. The resulting emotion, in luxurious excess of what is strictly proper to the scenes themselves, becomes appropriate by the aesthetic standard of not need but want. The volatility of excessive affect—the self-consciously aesthetic response to life as though it were art and to art as though it were life—is thus paradoxically the stable foundation on which family likeness is grounded, the answer to the question of Bramble family identity.

Family Romance

How do we confirm that Humphry himself is a member of this family? Smollett offers us two different modes of confirmation. On the one hand, we witness Humphry feeling and acting like a Bramble. Smollett's plot features a series of affecting scenes between Humphry and Matt that extends, and positively revalues, the image of noxious liquidity most memorably evoked early on in Matt's mounting hysteria at the infectious corruption lurking in the filthy waters at Bath. This series culminates with Humphry saving Matt's life when the family carriage is overturned in attempting to ford a river swollen by rainwater. Humphry carries Matt ashore "as if he had been an infant of six months" and, putting his commoner training to good purpose, "let him blood in the farrier style. . . . [I]n a little time the blood began to flow in a continued stream . . . ." Unwilling to be "saved" by Humphry's presumptuous piety, Matt is now truly saved by his honest sensibility and his plebeian expertise. The several family members express their fear and relief at this outcome according to their own peculiar sensibilities. In Liddy's case, sensibility takes precedence over genealogy: "'Are you—Are you indeed my uncle—My dear uncle!—My best friend! My father!—Are you really living? or is it an illusion of my poor brain?' . . . As for Clinker, his brain seemed to be affected.—he laughed, and wept, and danced about in . . . a distracted manner . . ." (6 Oct., pp. 313–15). In an exemplary dislocation, the child becomes father of the man. Matt, saved and reborn by his own son, is chastened and purged by exhibiting, in little, the liquidity that almost takes his life. And as if to recapitulate this contradictory drama on the macrolevel of family and nation, Matt quickly rewards Humphry by settling on him an annuity that renders him financially independent. By his own archaic standards Matt thus provides Humphry the social circulation and upward mobility needed to fulfill his status as a dangerous germ of social disease.

But on the other hand, Smollett immediately offers us an alternative way of confirming that Clinker is really a Bramble, one that relieves the danger of Humphry's social elevation by fully indulging the outdated artifice that has been Matt's default mode. With all the self-conscious trappings of romance discovery (including maternal tokens of identity), Smollett reveals that Humphry is really Matt's natural son, born while Matt was still "in the days of hot blood and unrestrained libertinism" and temporarily using his mother's name to raise himself through the inheritance of her estate. And Tabby now affects to see in Humphry's face the signs that "he hath got our blood in his veins" (6 Oct., p. 31). In the romance tradition, family romance—the formal convention of discovered parentage—customarily reconciles outer birth with inner worth, confirming the nobility of character we have already recognized in the foundling or the bastard by disclosing an elevated patriline. Family romance is therefore an apt ally of Matt's "feudal" utopianism because it asserts the hidden continuity and perdurability of a tradition thought to have been lost. The early novel often parodies the family romance, imitating its form but undermining the aristocratic ideology of its content. In *Pamela* (1740) Richardson evokes the expectations of family romance but frustrates them decisively by rewarding Pamela's virtue not through the past but through the future—not with elevated parentage but with an upwardly mobile marriage. Fielding takes the imitation a good deal further in *Joseph Andrews* (1742), ostentatiously orchestrating a series of family-romance discoveries so improbable that we are obliged to believe not the ostensible lesson that birth actually correlates with worth but the skeptical truth that such things only apply in the concrete and virtual particularity of fictional experience.[35]

Here as elsewhere in *Humphry Clinker,* Fielding is Smollett's master; but his treatment of the family romance is indebted to the Richardsonian model as well. Smollett quickly reinforces the aesthetic rather than the strictly empirical credibility of his novel by disclosing that Mr. Wilson is not a lowly strolling player but a gentleman, coincidentally the son of Matt's old college friend. And the double discovery and wedding with which the novel ends, uniting Liddy with "Mr. Wilson" and Humphry with Winifred, is steeped in the language of marvelous metamorphosis and dramatic denouement (14 Oct., pp. 336, 337; 26 Oct., p. 345; 8 Nov., p. 346). But despite Tabby's affectation, we know that it is not the genealogical blood of patrilineage but the "hot blood" of sensibility that marks Humphry a Bramble family member. And although Humphry does turn out to be the son of a gentleman, the revelation feels less like the relatively seamless dovetailing characteristic of the traditional family romance than like the ragged mixture of authentic upward mobility. Indeed, the divergence of Humphry's from Pamela's case is as important as their similarity. Pamela, although a common servant, has been socialized for gentility to such a degree that from the outset she seems wellborn even though she is not. But Humphry, a foundling trained as a country blacksmith and hostler, is ineradicably marked by his commoner upbringing. He will labor as he was bred, as a husbandman on his father's farm, and his demeanor will remain the one to which he was acculturated by his early life. Not ascribed status but lived experience is what determines who we are.

Indeed, under modern conditions of social fluidity and exchange, romance discovery looks "realistic." That is, it is not improbable that Matt should discover his footman to be his son and his family to be a microversion of the burgeoning British nation that has been Matt's spectacle for the past seven months, a heterogeneous assemblage of individuals. So Smollett parodies the antiquated tropes of "romance," preserving while superseding them, an experiment whose results are suggested by the way Jery and Matt use the emergent tropes of the "romantic" (see letters of 3 Sept., pp. 236–44, and 28 Aug., pp. 244–49). Romance becomes romantic through the secularization of spirit, when romance claims to supernatural description can be sublimated into affective response. The sublimity of the Scottish landscape is not a condition of its being but an enthusiastic feeling of its viewer, oxymoronically imagined as that which is ineffably "beyond" imagination. And when both letter writers note that a "Mr. Smollett" has his house at Loch Lomond, they remind us that the liminal experience of romantic sublimity—of being poised between subject and object, imagination and the senses—is also what we feel in the presence of Smollett's reflexive play with romance endings, suspended between the story and its telling, between what is half perceived and half created.

How does Smollett's aestheticizing of romance discovery shed light on the pastoral idyll of domestic economy at Brambleton Hall? Matt's ferocious critique of the modern body politic is never explicitly contradicted any more than is his dejection at his own bodily disorder. Instead Smollett suggests that in both cases the supposedly normative condition of order and stasis may be less the cure than the symptom of disease. At the level of the microbody, Matt reports midway through his travels that "I now begin to feel the good effects of exercise . . . and enjoy a constant tide of spirits, equally distant from inanition and excess . . . ." And toward the end he is convinced that "[w]e should sometimes increase the motion of the machine, . . . and now and then take a plunge amidst the waves of excess, in order to . . . promote a vigorous circulation of the spirits, which is the very essence and criterion of good health" (18 July, p. 219; 26 Oct., p. 339). By the same token, Matt's travels transpire in such a way as to suggest that the pastoralism that urges us to see Brambleton Hall as a *hortus conclusus* in sanctuary from the world is a pleasing fiction, a late allusion to the country house poem. In contemporary Britain, country and city, innocence and corruption, nature and art, are inextricably conflated.

Pastoral as Dialectic

By Smollett's time, centuries-long patterns of cultivation in the British Isles had long since made standard the coding of "south" and "north" as, respectively, "developed" and "underdeveloped." But because the Brambles' leisurely and incremental travel northward is experienced and rationalized as a continuous chain of pastoral movements from "south" to "north," each link in the chain—for example, crossing the Tweed from England to Scotland—is plausible in itself yet radically relativized by its placement in a more comprehensive series. Thus the lowlands are to the highlands as England is to Scotland; and as the irascible Obadiah Lismahago insists, if England is to Scotland as city is to country, then pastoral relation properly understood is one not of separation but of colonial exploitation (see 20 Sept., pp. 275–79). What Matt's professed ideals urge us at each moment to see as mutually exclusive values and behavior are repeatedly seen to overlap, mix, or lapse into indistinguishability. But this is at least in part because the modern circulation of commodities renders city and country, metropolitan and colony, systematically inseparable, two sides of the same coin. Indeed, Matt's ongoing critique of luxury coexists with the accumulation of evidence that he himself is comfortably dependent on its tidal ebb and flow. In Bath he excoriates the "mob of impudent plebeians" whose circulation will increase "till the streams that swell this irresistible torrent of folly and extravagance, shall either be exhausted, or turned into other channels . . . ." But in the very next paragraph Matt remarks to Dr. Lewis, "By your advice, I sent to London a few days ago for half a pound of Genzeng; though I doubt much, whether that which comes from America is equally efficacious with what is brought from the East Indies" (23 Apr., pp. 37–38). Like his bastard son Humphry Clinker, Matt's ginseng is the sign of his secret role in the modern circulation of things. Already in the habit of capitalizing on the international market, Matt is slowly revealed to be fully, and knowingly, submerged in the cultural liquidity from which he stridently attempts to distance himself.

This revelation culminates in the highlands of Scotland. In the bountiful "Scottish paradise" north of Glasgow Matt comes upon a piscatory *locus amoenus,* where all kinds of fish can be found "at the door, for the taking." We might be reminded of Brambleton Hall, whose fish "I can eat in four hours after they are taken" (8 June, p. 119)—except that Matt's improving thoughts take us in a very different direction. What if the clans were given "a taste of property and independence"? "It cannot be expected, that the gentlemen of this country should execute commercial schemes to render their vassals independent; . . .

but a company of merchants might, with proper management, turn to good account a fishery established in this part of Scotland—Our people have a strange itch to colonize America, when the uncultivated parts of our own island might be settled to greater advantage" (6 Sept., pp. 255–56).

Matt's ideology of improvement is yet more evident when he later advises his friend Baynard to improve his decaying estate by the most modern methods of agrarian reform. Indeed, the brief episode provides a clear and instructive model of Smollett's parodic technique—for these are the terms in which Matt describes the modernization he calls for: "With Baynard's good leave, I ordered the gardener to turn the rivulet into its old channel, to refresh the fainting Naiads, who had so long languished among mouldering roots, withered leaves, and dry pebbles.—The shrubbery is condemned to extirpation; and the pleasure-ground will be restored to its original use of corn-field and pasture" (26 Oct., p. 343). Matt's account self-consciously drapes the modernizing improvements to Baynard's estate in the backward-looking language of antique pastoral return, which so diverts us from the material innovations in land use for which the language of improvement itself provided a moralizing euphemism that we are forced to realize that Matt parodies pastoral idyll in order to familiarize a very different agrarian reality. And on the eve of his return home Matt's denial that he has any "cause to complain" of the "œconomy of my farm" suggests either that he is indeed in denial or that Brambleton Hall and its paterfamilias have all along been an exercise in performative archaism. Borrowing a term from E. P. Thompson, the social norm is really social "theater," a performance of pastoral convention that is no less pleasingly virtual than the romance convention of discovered parentage.

Thompson has applied the idea of social theater to the cultural politics of a transitional period, Smollett's own, when the patriarchal control of the rulers and its corollary, the customary rights of their subjects, are in the process of erosion but has not yet been replaced by the modern system of class relations. Under such conditions, the tacit rules of "subordination" need to be reinforced by a more explicit process of "negotiation," and the space opened up between power and authority is a theatrical stage reserved for the self-conscious performance of social roles between which can be sensed the "structural reciprocity" of characters who take part in a searching and unscripted drama.[36] Much of *Humphry Clinker* is illuminated by this hypothesis; but it leaves uncertain whether Smollett would have us see Britain's disease as the fluid mobility of the modern age or the ordered stasis of tradition. When we read Edmund Burke on the "pleasing illusions" of the *ancien régime* we are in no doubt about his preferences.[37] If there is a lesson to be learned from Smollett, it may be less about how to evaluate experience than about how to understand it. In the end, reading *Humphry Clinker* is a lesson in learning to descry, beneath the broad facade of traditionality, the innovative modernizations that that facade helps facilitate and humanize.

Disinterested Narration

To a certain degree this is, of course, Burke's lesson as well. But in Smollett's eponymous hero we have a figure of commoner, and common, understanding that is far from the standard of which Burke approves in 1790. In what sense does Smollett "approve of" his hero? Readers often wonder why Humphry, of all the members of the Bramble family entourage, is the only one who writes no letters. The obvious answers—because he joins the family midstream and has no one to write home to—only rephrases the question. Humphry's normative status for Smollett is signaled by his seemingly contingent, even accidental, appearance in the title and in the plot of the novel. It is not that he is an object who is never permitted to be a subject, a nonliterate "subaltern" denied his "voice," but that as the most abject and unmoored of commoners he functions as Smollett's lowest common denominator and "speaks" for everyone. *Humphry Clinker* is something of an innovation in epistolary form in that it assigns significant narrative roles to five letter writers, who are sharply distinguished from one another in sex, age, social status, cultural attitudes, even epistolary style. Read against Richardson's already canonical precedent, where the letters of the protagonist overshadow all others in both number and authority, Smollett's epistolary novel is manifestly an experiment in the multiplicity and relativity of perspective. Matt's letters to Dr. Lewis are intermixed with the letters of other family members, whose responses to common experiences reflect so broad a range of values as to suggest that in *Humphry Clinker* the truth of things may lie in a composite and mixed view of reality. Smollett's epistolary innovation is clearly coordinated with his insistence on the truth of mixture and fluidity in other respects. The rhetorical dominance of the paterfamilias is theatrically real but a pleasing illusion, since readers learn to factor his views into the more general assessment of things rather than take them as the articulation of that assessment.

Experimentation with modes of novelistic narration recalls contemporary experiments in establishing a standard of scientific, political, and aesthetic disinterestedness once tacit agreement on the coextension of the national and the monarchal interest had begun to fall apart.[38] In *Joseph Andrews,* Fielding countered the putative tyranny of Pamela's epistolary dominance by practicing an omniscient narration at an elevation above and beyond the partiality that is unavoidable in a single character, especially one so ethically defective as Fielding took Pamela to be. In *Humphry Clinker,* Smollett shows that the effect of an impartial—a disinterested—narration can also be achieved without abandoning the epistolary mode, not through overarching detachment but through a protosociological sampling method that appears to derive a general truth from the multifarious data of particularity and disagreement. But Humphry evades the sampling—not only because he does not write letters but also because his leveled status as the most common of commoners qualifies him to represent the common view of things. Amid the sharply differentiated interests of his fellow Brambles (not to mention Smollett's vast, extrafamilial cast of characters) Humphry has no particular interests at all—or interests that particularize him only to the status of the human—and this authorizes him to represent all interests at large. The letters of the other characters participate in the circulation and exchange of things that Matt Bramble is right to see is now the way of the world. But Humphry is himself such a commodity: not an object to be bought and sold, but the abstract measure of common humanity into which all others may be translated and by which all others may be judged. Smollett signals this capacity by making Humphry the blank and receptive register at the heart of social existence, a sensorium of human emotion and fellow feeling whose expedition fulfills what has been only potential in the Bramble family before his arrival. In Smollett as much as in Sterne, disinterestedness goes by the name of sensibility, and the coherence of the domestic household is constituted not by its perdurability over time but by the depth of its punctual moment and by the density and authenticity of its emotional fabric.

PRIDE AND PREJUDICE

The plot of Jane Austen's second published novel echoes with the interplay of privacy and publicity as we have come to understand it in the emergent domestic novel. Taking the long view encouraged by this long study, in *Pride and Prejudice* the vexed relationship between the family and the state that structures much early modern thought on this subject has been decisively internalized and privatized within the realm of the family. This means that the terms of conflict are arguably the same "at foundation" as they were before, but it also means that the separation out of the family from the state inevitably alters the terms of conflict because their foundation has been altered. The light cast by a schematic overview of some of the texts we have read thus far is perhaps worth the risk of making historical relationship look like preordained development. In Behn's *Love-Letters,* the politics of the Exclusion Crisis provide a framework—absolutist tyranny versus the liberties of the subject, paternalist authority versus libertine license—within which struggles between parents and children and husbands and wives become suggestively intelligible as both analogous to and distinct from the public framework. In Richardson's *Pamela,* the political language of absolute tyrant and rebel subject is metaphorical, a skeletal vestige of its former self, not the allegorical signified toward which domestication labors but one of several signifiers of an emergent domesticity of ethical subjects. Even so, Richardson notably relies on the familiar idiom of family politics: Lady Davers had hoped to arrange an aristocratic marriage of alliance for her brother Mr. B., whose ability to resist it is bound up with his ability to make explicit and null the tacit force of his upbringing by recognizing that he was "educated wrong."39

More even than in *Pamela*, family matters in *Pride and Prejudice* rest on a sedimentation of less privatized forms: the constitution of subjective interiority by familial upbringing, the separation of political from ethical subjecthood, the subjection of the subject to state power, the dynastic bedrock of the English polity. The Napoleonic Wars cast the most fleeting of shadows on the national domesticity of village life in Austen's rural England, and that only at the very end of the novel, and only to stress the failure of demobilization to acquaint the Wickhams with the virtues of conjugal domesticity ("Their manner of living, even when the restoration of the peace dismissed them to a home, was unsettled in the extreme").40 The militia regiment stationed at Meryton maintains a subtle background presence throughout *Pride and Prejudice,* of passionate interest to Lydia and Kitty but more subliminal for the other characters and for us, the red coats discreetly scattered among civilian dress at local assemblies, balls, and drawing-room gatherings. As Wordsworth schooled Napoleon at the knee of mother and housewife, so Austen internalizes his wars within the bounds of family life.41 Themes of tyranny and the liberties of the subject have been decisively, and all but invisibly, woven into the fabric of the private realm.

After the restoration of their own peace but before the settlement of their estate, Darcy confides to Elizabeth that he too was educated wrong. "Unfortunately an only son, . . . I was spoilt by my parents, who though good themselves . . . allowed, encouraged, almost taught me to be selfish and overbearing, to care for none beyond my own family circle, to think meanly of all the rest of the world, to *wish* at least to think meanly of their sense and worth compared with my own" (282). Like Mr. B.'s, the lesson was reinforced by a tacit presumption of family integrity ensured by an arranged marriage that would be both patrilineal and endogamous. Darcy's "tacit engagement" to his cousin was long ago projected by their two mothers. "While in their cradles," Lady Catherine de Bourgh protests, "we planned the union: and now, at the moment when the wishes of both sisters would be accomplished, in their marriage, to be prevented by a young woman of inferior birth, of no importance in the world, and wholly unallied to the family!" But the family, once conceived strictly as a project in patrilineage, is now understood to enclose multiple and competing inter-

ests or (in the more personalized language of affective desire) "wishes." As Elizabeth replies, "You both did as much as you could, in planning the marriage. Its
completion depended on others. If Mr. Darcy is neither by honour nor inclination confined to his cousin, why is not he to make another choice? And if I am
that choice, why may not I accept him?" (271). But the sanction of individual
choice is not absolute. Lydia's feared flight with Wickham to Gretna Green and
its promise of clandestine marriage defines its limit in culturally familiar terms
(see fig. 3.4). The ethical norm commonly figured by the privacy and secrecy of
"marriage for love" is damaged considerably by Elizabeth's suspicions of Wickham's ulterior motives ("But why all this secrecy? . . . Why must their marriage
be private?"). "[T]he humiliation, the misery, [Lydia] was bringing on them all,
soon swallowed up every private care . . . ." Their father's "indolence" means
another father will have to be found to protect the family from Lydia's libertinism. And with some irony this turns out to be Darcy, who normatively shrugs
off arranged marriage for himself but just as normatively—and in strict "secrecy"—enforces it for his future sister-in-law (214, 210, 243; cf. 207).[42]

As things develop, the real danger was not clandestine marriage but no marriage at all. According to Elizabeth's aunt Mrs. Gardiner, careless Lydia "was
sure they should be married some time or other, and it did not much signify
when" (245). Lydia is Behn's Silvia without the remorse, and without the sense
to see that to be a dashing man of the sword may only be the outward face of licentious self-service. For Lydia, indeed, intimations of the public world of warfare are a most powerful stimulant to private desire: "Since the ——shire were
first quartered in Meryton," says Elizabeth, "nothing but love, flirtation, and
officers, have been in her head. She has been doing every thing in her power by
thinking and talking on the subject, to give greater—what shall I call it? susceptibility to her feelings . . . ." Surprisingly, it turns out to be not Elizabeth but
Lydia who, irresponsibly enacting his "love of independence," is most truly her
father's daughter (214–15, 234). And in the words of the indolent Mr. Bennet,
"Darcy did every thing; made up the match, gave the money, paid the fellow's
debts, and got him his commission!" (289).

So Darcy is both the independent subject of marriage and the paternalistic
arranger of it. In fact, the latter achievement completes the sequence in which
Austen also turns the aristocratic convention of family romance to her own
ends. The sequence begins at Pemberley, where Darcy's civility and complai-
sance toward Elizabeth's family "connexion," her aunt and uncle the Gardiners,
consoles her "that he should know she had some relations for whom"—unlike
her parents—"there was no need to blush" (193). Later on it is Mr. Gardiner
who first assumes responsibility for arranging the marriage between Lydia and
Wickham, writing to Mr. Bennet of "the engagements which I have ventured to

make on your side" and seeking "full powers to act in your name, throughout the whole of this business," including Lydia's being "married from this house" (i.e., the Gardiners') (229–30). Austen's delicate play here may justly be called an internalization of family romance since although the discovery of "true" parentage is in ethical terms truly ennobling—Mr. Gardiner is "greatly superior to his sister [Mrs. Bennet] as well by nature as education," and his wife is "an amiable, intelligent, elegant woman"—in status terms it is not, nor does it stray beyond the boundaries of the immediate family (108). But paternal surrogacy is taken a step further when Darcy takes over from Mr. Gardiner the role of acting in Mr. Bennet's name and thereby affectively becomes a Bennet "family connexion" before he does so in fact by marrying Elizabeth. Darcy will be present at the arranged wedding, and as Lydia puts it with characteristically lucid crudity, "[M]y uncle was to give me away; . . . But . . . Mr. Darcy might have done as well" (242). In the event, Darcy does indeed do as well.

If we accord Austen's parody of family romance the attention it deserves, the implication is that although inner worth is not a simple function of patrilineal birth, it may be a complex function of primary socialization at the level of family upbringing and susceptible to the force of what Mary Wollstonecraft calls in her more hopeful moods a "revolution" in "individual education."[43] By the same token, the aristocratic institution of the "forced marriage" lives on in Austen's novel—and in its modern posterity—as the deep insight that the negative liberty of the individual subject's freedom to choose is constrained by the invisible shackles of early-childhood formation. Although it entails, like *Pamela,* its protagonist's upwardly mobile marriage, *Pride and Prejudice* achieves "social justice" against not the vertical scale of social hierarchy but the horizontal scale of familial equilibration. The fact that Pamela seems to us relatively unchanging in her character is related to the fact that her arena of action is in this social sense "public," whereas Elizabeth's development is most importantly a "private" accomplishment, a discovery neither of her true parents nor of a husband who improves on her father but of how to re-introject parental exemplarity. As Austen is at pains to make clear without ever questioning her ethical agency, Elizabeth too was brought up wrong. And yet the intersection of the social and the ethical for Austen—and for her modern posterity—is clear from the fact that the precepts taught by parental example center upon the practice of the social institution of marriage. For Behn's Silvia and her world, "marriage for love" means a match willed by the principals, and it can only be a contradiction in terms. Only in the class-based culture of the modern period, when the putatively contractual nature of marriage as a voluntary choice by two individuals begins its slow process of fulfillment in the actuality of cultural custom and marriage law, does the idea of "the marriage choice" itself become fully vulnerable, in turn, to skeptical analysis. How do we adjudicate the comparative authenticity of a volition grounded in more "public," as opposed to more "private," considerations? For the sake of brevity I will tease out one thread of this effort at adjudication from the dense weave of Austen's plot.

Internalizing the Marriage Choice

Beginning with its famous first sentence, *Pride and Prejudice* provides us with an antithetical vocabulary for meditating on the terms of the marriage choice that, although increasingly available to us from other sources, is from the outset deeply embedded in the antithetical attitudes of Elizabeth's parents. And although the theme of "forced marriage" is most effectively internalized by Austen in the general sense of tacit parental influence, early on it is figured more particularly as the sort of influence that elevates "public" necessity over "private" inclination, external and financial over internal and emotional motives, in making the marriage choice. In her own voice Mrs. Bennet echoes the first sentence's necessitarian dictum: "A single man of large fortune . . . . What a fine thing for our girls!" That is, Bingley's "design" (in her husband's arch formulation) must be to marry (1). This is very close to the summary confirmation the narrator provides at the end of the first chapter: "The business of [Mrs. Bennet's] life was to get her daughters married . . ." (3). Mr. Bennet's diffident skepticism expresses on the contrary the belief that any inference of design requires that we first know (in the words of the narrator) "the feelings or views of such a man" (1). His droll rejoinder to his wife is also a serious endorsement of the freedom of the subject: "I will send a few lines by you to assure him of my hearty consent to his marrying which ever he chuses of the girls . . ." (2). When Charlotte Lucas remarks that Jane Bennet would do well to make more "public" her regard for Bingley, Elizabeth makes clear the extent to which she is her father's daughter. "'Your plan is a good one,' replied Elizabeth, 'where nothing is in question but the desire of being well married; . . . But these are not Jane's feelings; she is not acting by design'" (15).

Once the cultural conflict between public and private grounds for marriage—parental forced matches versus children's chosen matches—has been won by the latter, the conflict between public and private sorts of motives is fought out once more within the winner's territory. And at this microlevel of division the tacit distinction between two criteria of choice must become an explicit separation. The most authentically private choice cannot also be the most consciously intended choice: feelings are ranged against design, passion against interest. When the vile Mr. Collins soon forces his attentions on Elizabeth, he seems to confirm both Mr. Bennet on the boorishness of marrying by design rather than according to feelings and Mrs. Bennet on the currency of such motives: "Almost as soon as I entered the house I singled you out as the companion of my future life. But before I am run away with by my feelings on this subject, perhaps it will be advisable for me to state my reasons for marrying—and moreover for coming into Hertfordshire with the design of selecting a wife, as I certainly did" (80). Soon Charlotte assumes the mantle of the exemplary designer by encouraging the addresses of the castoff Mr. Collins. As for Elizabeth, "[s]he had always felt that Charlotte's opinion of matrimony was not exactly like her own, but she could not have supposed it possible that when called into action, she would have sacrificed every better feeling to worldly advantage. . . . [I]t was impossible for that friend to be tolerably happy in the lot she had chosen" (96–97). And she challenges her sister Jane that "you must feel, as well as I do, that the woman who marries [Mr. Collins], cannot have a proper way of thinking. . . . You shall not . . . endeavour to persuade yourself or me, that selfishness is prudence . . ." (105).

Elizabeth's convictions are soon discomfited by the news that Wickham, with whom she has been infatuated, has shifted his attentions to an heiress. Prodded by Mrs. Gardiner's suggestion that this may argue a mercenary motive on Wickham's part, Elizabeth retorts: "Pray, my dear aunt, what is the difference in matrimonial affairs, between the mercenary and the prudent motive?" (118). Now the separation between design and feelings—between public and private, financial and emotional, motives for marriage—is less easily maintained. Much later, however, Mrs. Gardiner describes Darcy's crucial intervention with Wickham in terms that, so far from challenging that separation, turn its established valuation inside out. Since Lydia refused to leave Wickham, "it only remained, he [Darcy] thought, to secure and expedite a marriage, which, in his very first conversation with Wickham, he easily learnt, had never been *his* design. . . . Wickham still cherished the hope of more effectually making his fortune by marriage, in some other country" (245). Lydia's truth to her "feelings" in the marriage choice is not only selfish but deluded, whereas Darcy's fabrication for Wickham of an acceptable "design," patently mercenary, is also patently noble.

The revaluation of outwardly as inwardly motivated choices can be seen in the way a single term shifts its significance over the course of the narrative. Almost from the beginning, not only Elizabeth but we too have been sensitive to Darcy's disdain for her family's "connections." "Darcy had never been so bewitched by any woman as he was by [Elizabeth]," our narrator confides. "He really believed, that were it not for the inferiority of her connections, he should be in some danger" (38). And when Colonel Fitzwilliam tells her that Darcy had "lately saved a friend from the inconveniences of a most imprudent marriage," Elizabeth, rightly suspecting that friend to be Bingley, is convinced that

Darcy's pride "would receive a deeper wound from the want of importance in his friend's connections, than from their want of sense . . ." (143–44). The defining statement of connection in this traditionally public and dynastic sense of the term is made by Lady Catherine de Bourgh, Austen's Lady Davers, who sees in Elizabeth "[t]he upstart pretensions of a young woman without family, connections, or fortune. Is this to be endured! . . . True. You are a gentleman's daughter. But who was your mother?" (272).

But after Elizabeth spurns his awkward expression of his "feelings" for her, Darcy's epistolary reply distinguishes between the merely "objectionable" "situation of your mother's family" and "that total want of propriety so frequently, so almost uniformly betrayed by herself . . . ." By the "most unhappy connection" with Jane from which he sought to preserve his friend, moreover, Darcy means not her outward status but her inner feelings, her apparent "indifference" to Bingley, of which Charlotte had warned and which Elizabeth had explained away as the affect of one admirably devoid of "design" (152). Experiencing his love for Elizabeth as a felt connection to those "beyond my own family circle," Darcy materializes that feeling by his literal presence at Lydia's wedding—"exactly a scene," Elizabeth muses, "and exactly among people, where he had apparently least to do, and least temptation to go." And in a note to her aunt she wonders "how a person unconnected with any of us, and (comparatively speaking) a stranger to our family, should have been amongst you at such a time" (242). Like Sterne's and Smollett's men of feeling, Darcy finds that sensible connection may be most available when the rationality of aristocratic patrilineage is overlooked or ignored. Reduced at this extreme to the irrationality of Lady Catherine's phobic Brambleisms—"Are the shades of Pemberley to be thus polluted?"—family connections are positively revalued in *Pride and Prejudice* as, not the outer-directed deference we show toward a jealous principle that excludes us but an inner-directed embrace of those who sympathetically seek our happiness. The plot-driving problem of the fact that Mr. Bennet's estate is entailed to Mr. Collins is not the diachronic one that the patriline will come to an end but the synchronic one that the present generation—the Bennet girls—will be deprived of financial security. "Unfeeling, selfish girl!" says Lady Catherine to Elizabeth. "Do you not consider that a connection with you, must disgrace him in the eyes of everybody?" To this Elizabeth replies: "I am only resolved to act in that manner, which will, in my own opinion, constitute my happiness, without reference to *you*, or to any person so wholly unconnected with me" (273).

Lady Catherine's selfish recourse to the criterion of "feeling" joins Lydia's at the opposite end of a spectrum that has become a circle whose normative center is the domain of domesticity that, we are given to understand, will prevail at

Pemberley. At the end of the novel Elizabeth leaves behind the parodically defective "domestic felicity" of her parental household at Longbourn, divided, as it was at the outset, between the enduringly "silly" social aspirations of her mother and a father whose libertine independence of spirit we have learned to see harbors a dangerously solipsistic irresponsibility (295). By contrast, Elizabeth and Darcy have already exhibited their capacity to cultivate what at Longbourn was the excluded middle of domestic intimacy, where public and private regard come together in the interior space of minds and houses. If both of them have been brought up wrong, both are reeducated so as to avoid the sort of "forced marriage" that unconsciously perpetuates the pride and prejudice of the parents. Mrs. Gardiner predicts a conjugal reformation for Darcy: "[H]e wants nothing but a little more liveliness, and that, if he marry *prudently*, his wife may teach him" (247). But in his own eyes Darcy has already been reformed: "What do I not owe you!," he exclaims to Elizabeth. "You taught me a lesson, hard indeed at first, but most advantageous," and he explains his surprising "civility" at Pemberley as part of a conscious effort to let "you see that your reproofs had been attended to" (282, 283). So from her future husband's perspective, Elizabeth is already the ethical subject of the domestic realm, the public manager of morals internalized within the private space of the household.

The Third-Person Effect

Elizabeth's reformation is the work of the entire novel, and it too entails a pedagogic relationship. Up to this point, much of my discussion might well have derived from a reading not of Austen's *Pride and Prejudice* but of Frances Burney's *Evelina* (1778), so crucial is Burney to the formulation of the domestic paradigm on which nineteenth-century novel-writing is founded. But *Evelina* is an epistolary novel, and for all its fascination with the letter form, *Pride and Prejudice* makes a crucially different choice of narrative technique. Austen's novel is filled with letters—it is thought to have begun in epistolary form—and recalls earlier experiments of Behn, Richardson, and many others in figuring both interior privacy and its limits. Behn's passage from epistolary to third-person narration within the space of a single narrative is singularly suggestive about the relationship between developments in the apparatus of narration and developments in attitudes toward the dialectic of privacy and publicity.[44] But epistolary and third-person narration also have much in common in this regard. Interesting experiments in narrative hybridization occur in both narrative modes through what might be called a third-person effect—the private made public—that is achieved when characters are explicitly depicted in the process of construing the meaning of letters. For example, the Bennet family's broadly negative attitude toward the fact that their cousin will inherit the family house becomes far more precisely particularized when Mr. Bennet suggests that "if you will listen to his letter, you may perhaps be a little softened by his manner of expressing himself" (46). The remark is directed at Mrs. Bennet, but the result is that we hear not only Mr. Collins's voice in the text of the letter but also those of four family members in varied response to his. The third-person effect produced by the depiction of letter readers in the process of reading is one of both detachment and interiority, and it may remind us of the disinterestedness effect Smollett achieves in *Humphry Clinker* by tacitly juxtaposing the several disparate reactions of the Bramble family to, not a shared letter, but the hermeneutic experience of shared travel.

The effect can be achieved not only by attending to a multiplicity of readers but also by pursuing the developing response of a single one. Later on Elizabeth reads Darcy's long letter over and over, each time correcting errors of construal not only in her previous readings but also in the way she had too hastily and confidently "read" him in actuality. "She grew completely ashamed of herself.—Of neither Darcy nor Wickham could she think, without feeling that she had been blind, partial, prejudiced, absurd" (159). This scene of painfully close reading recalls many similar scenes in earlier narratives, involving forged and pseudonymous letters, in which the truth of the letter writer's actual identity, deeply embedded within the text, is laboriously excavated by a process of increasingly acute rereading. In the third-person sections of *Love-Letters,* for example, the third-person, private-made-public effect is often achieved within an epistolary setting, when characters discover the secret of epistolary identity by multiple readings that reveal a disjunction between style and purported writer, between style and supposed addressee, even between the styles of two letters that claim to be from the same person.

Of course, there are also differences between the ways Behn and Austen achieve third-person detachment through scenes of epistolary reading, especially in the nature of what is revealed. For one thing, the crucial discovery in Behn—this letter is by Brilljard, not Octavio, that letter is intended for Philander, not Octavio—is one of actual identity. In *Pride and Prejudice* letters conceal—and through industrious reading are made to reveal—not the outward identity of their writers but the ethical quality of their motives and sensibilities. This is not to say that Behn lacks interest in any species of personal revelation more interiorized than that of outward identity, but that she and her characters do not conceive the "outer" and the "inner" to be so separable from one another. Rather, external and internal identity are bound together in a relation of distinction that does not admit of that degree of separation out—of inward feeling or motive from outward condition or status—that is required for the further anatomy of interiority into its component parts.

In this respect letters are like clothing. Throughout the development of the secret-history form, forged or concealed letters (or stories) often are linked with sartorial disguises as similarly external and mutually reinforcing methods of characterization. In Sidney's *Arcadia,* Pyrocles and Musidorus use both clothing and tales to conceal their identities from, and to reveal them to, Philoclea and Pamela. In Behn's *Love-Letters,* Brilljard both forges a letter from Octavio and dresses like him. In the anonymous *Love-Letters,* Beau Wilson first misreads the letter and therefore the sex of his noble correspondent, then cross-dresses in order to disguise his own sex. In Richardson's *Pamela,* Mr. B.'s duplicity takes in both deceitful letters and deceitful disguises. The tangibility of identity as an outwardly accessible condition in these examples of personal discovery seems related to the tangibility—the objectivity or objecthood—of the means by which identity is both concealed and revealed, namely, letters and clothing. And we might posit a common root for them in the way traditional tropes like that of family romance tacitly enroll all aspects of identity under the aegis of lineage, all aspects of worth under the tangibility and confident determinacy of birth. Thus in Barclay's *Argenis* the discovery of hitherto concealed letters confirms Queen Hyanisbe's son to be also King Meleander's. But as we have seen, the history of the secret history is one not only of the imitation but also of the criticism of family romance. And the parody of family romance that we see in novels like *Pamela* and *Humphry Clinker* broadly corresponds to the ambition of their authors to separate out and to publicize a private realm of interiority that has a relatively tangential or notional relation to the tangibility of birth and lineage.

There is another difference in the nature of what is revealed by the third-person effect in Behn's and Austen's scenes of reading. In *Love-Letters* the knowledge gained by watching one character read the letter of another character for the most part refines our knowledge of the character of the writer, not that of the reader. Things are rather different in *Pride and Prejudice.* By reading Darcy's letter with a third-person detachment Elizabeth does learn the truth of his interior motives, but this scene of reading is as importantly a reeducation of herself in which she comes to know her own secrets by rereading how she formerly has read other people: "Till this moment I never knew myself" (159). In Austen, what is most private is what is both most deeply felt and most unacknowledged. Elizabeth's development involves the discovery of what has always been there, a secret from herself. Reading letters provides a powerful figure for reading people, both others and oneself, one that privatizes the public activity of social knowledge and publicizes the private activity of self-knowledge. And once tutored by the experience of rereading Darcy through his letter, Elizabeth labors, with a hypercautious attention to the semantic shading of her accumulating verbiage ("respect," "esteem," gratitude"), to read her reading, that is, "to determine her feelings towards" Darcy (200, 201).

Burney's first novel, comparatively contemporary with *Pride and Prejudice,* differs from Behn's *Love-Letters* in similar ways. An epistolary novel, *Evelina* is a remarkable exercise in the overdetermined discovery of outward and inward identity that juxtaposes external (documentary and literal) with internal (emotional and metaphorical) means of revelation while at the same time suggesting, by the careful temporal sequencing of those revelations, which of them has ultimate priority. Belmont first sees the image of Evelina's mother in her face and is overwhelmed by the authenticity of his affective response to this vision. Only afterward does he read the letter from the deceased Caroline that, along with other tangible romance tokens, confirms Evelina's lineage. "Oh, Sir," exclaims Evelina with pointed intensity, "that you could but read my heart!" The effect of Burney's careful sequencing is to admit, rather more than Austen will do, the continuing force of external markers in the knowledge of interiority, while leaving no doubt as to their residual and conventional nature. Most crucially, this entire episode of outward recognition—Burney's version of family-romance discovery, from whose example Austen's profited—is well preceded by Orville's declaration of love for and his proposal to Evelina, internal acts that therefore cannot be influenced by his knowledge of her external lineage. Elsewhere in *Evelina* Burney juxtaposes, with similar results, the actual reading of letters with the virtual reading of people. When Sir Clement writes her in the name of Lord Orville, Evelina's acute and multiple readings of the letter's stylistic solecisms remind us of both Behn's Silvia and Austen's Elizabeth. Like Elizabeth, Evelina pierces to the author's deepest sensibilities, to his internal identity; like Silvia, Evelina is confronted with a forgery of outward identity—and yet despite her insight into the sensibility of the author, her reading fails to infer that the letter therefore must have been written by someone other than Orville.[45]

This discovery is reserved for the more intimate encounter entailed in reading not letters but persons. Shortly before she will see Orville for the first time since receiving the forged letter, Evelina is galvanized by the prospect of a face-to-face encounter and the opportunities for reading character that it will hold: "[S]hould the same impertinent freedom be expressed by his looks, which dictated his cruel letter, I shall not know how to endure either him or myself. . . . [H]e can only gather [my sentiments] from my behaviour, and I tremble lest he should mistake my indignation for confusion!—lest he should misconstrue my reserve into embarrassment! . . . Surely he, as well as I, must think of the letter at the moment of our meeting, and he will, probably, mean to gather my thoughts of it from my looks; . . . If I find that the *eyes* of Lord Orville agree with his *pen* . . . !" (277–78). As Evelina becomes a more practiced virtual reader she becomes more confident in her ability to know Orville's inner feelings. And through this sort of reading (he "not only read my sentiments, but, by his countenance, communicated to me his own") she is enabled to realize, almost as an afterthought, both that the offensive letter was not written by Orville and that it was written by Sir Clement (288; see also 358). As with Austen's Elizabeth, moreover, Evelina's labor in reading the character of the letter writer is continuous with her labor toward self-knowledge. Early on Evelina wistfully complains to her guardian that "there ought to be a book, of the laws and customs à-la-mode, presented to all young people, upon their first introduction into public company." Well before the novel is half-read the reader understands that the book Evelina seeks is the one she is writing about her own discovery, and privatizing internalization, of those public laws and customs (277–78, 288, 84). Yet the very success of Burney's procedure suggests that there is something paradoxical about it. *Evelina* demonstrates that the later-eighteenth-century domestic novel sustains the process of internalization and privatization of which it is itself a product through scenes of reading that are accomplished with equal ease through both epistolary and third-person narration.

Free Indirect Discourse

But the epistolary form of Burney's first novel then seems to be at odds with its substantive implication, its decided valorization of the internal, the metaphorical, and the affective over the external, the literal, and the documentary. This oddity is of course implicit in my description of what is made available through the self-conscious depiction of scenes of reading as a "third-person" effect. And as it happens, after publishing *Evelina* Burney abandoned the epistolary mode to embrace third-person narration, which she learned to practice in an innovative manner that Austen also uses to powerful effect. Free indirect discourse is a method of disclosing characters in the process of gaining self-knowledge that, by refining the virtual institution of the narrator, enhances the structural relation of detachment and interiority whose effect is less subtly available through the actualized fiction of a literal epistolary document—or indeed through the customary practice of third-person narration itself. In the present context, free indirect discourse may be understood as a method not only of reading other characters (as Burney's Evelina and Austen's Elizabeth do) without benefit of reading letters but also of being read without benefit of another character who does the reading. Dispensing with these relatively external mediators of interiority, free indirect discourse replaces them with, not another such mediator, but a sliding movement between character and narrator that figures the micro-oscillation between the "private" and the "public" with remarkable responsiveness and precision.[46]

The following example from *Pride and Prejudice* is the early encounter between Darcy and Wickham, in which Elizabeth reads the two men while we read Elizabeth:

> Mr. Darcy corroborated it with a bow, and was beginning to determine not to fix his eyes on Elizabeth, when they were suddenly arrested by the sight of the stranger, and Elizabeth happening to see the countenance of both as they looked at each other, was all astonishment at the effect of the meeting. Both changed colour, one looked white, the other red. Mr. Wickham, after a few moments, touched his hat—a salutation which Mr. Darcy just deigned to return. What could be the meaning of it?—It was impossible to imagine; it was impossible not to long to know. (55)

Free indirect discourse is notable for the relationship it establishes between what might be called the overarching, "public" detachment of narrative voice and the "private," relative interiority of the character's point of view to which it provides access. Crucial to the effect is that such discourse purports to conflate two separate, public and private, levels of narration. The narrative voice neither offers a neutral description of Elizabeth looking at the two men looking at each other nor frankly informs us of her thoughts at this moment ("she thought to herself"); it subtly modulates from a minutely observed but external plane of description to an interior plane within Elizabeth's consciousness. The effect is achieved by a shift in idiom, from language that is characteristic of the narrator's voice as we have become accustomed to it—dispassionately descriptive, privy to the entire range of experience of which the narration is understood to consist—to language limited by the singularity of viewpoint we have become accustomed to in a particular character, or in any case by the partiality of viewpoint that defines the condition of being a character rather than a narrator.

In this passage we feel the shift at the point where Elizabeth's "astonishment," already conveyed to us from beyond her consciousness, becomes the internal engine of discourse, as though it were spoken by her: "What could be the meaning of it?—It was impossible to imagine; it was impossible not to long to know." This is a particularly eloquent example of free indirect discourse because what is expressed from within Elizabeth's mind—the content of her thoughts—is precisely the fact of epistemological insufficiency that makes her a "private" character rather than a "public" narrator. But even when the contents of the character's discourse do not explicitly reflect its formal partiality, the latter condition is signified by the palpable shift in idiom. Whether free indirect discourse can be said to derive from epistolary form is a problem in the history of narrative style that needs to be addressed from within that history, an ambition that lies beyond this study. What can be said is that free indirect discourse sustains the strategy of the third-person effect to establish a difference between two voices and two viewpoints—the strategy whereby characters subject letters and people to self-conscious interpretation—while smoothing the abrupt shift of difference into a differential continuum that significantly enhances the effect of an incremental process of interiorization and privatization.[47]

The epistemological force of free indirect discourse is fed by many contextual sources, some of which may be highlighted in passing. With the antithetical motives of promotion and prohibition, Protestant casuistry and English libel law conspired to advance a depth model of relative access figured as a journey into the interior that is marked by a sequence of outposts: first action, then speech, finally thought. The perplexity of salvation came to a head in the institution of the private "calling," figured as the external Word, which, accessible as inward thought, also must be fulfilled outwardly as a public "discipline." Official responsibility for the regulation of public print and performance fluctuated between "external" methods of licensing and censoring works before and after the fact and the imposition of an "internalized" self-censorship through a prudent self-discipline. The offensive speech of "public" characters was argued to be ethically coextensive with the offensive thoughts of their "private" authors and thereby subject to state prosecution.[48] These several scenarios bespeak a historical moment when the collectivity of positive freedom, devolving to the "absolute" authority of the state apparatus, comes uncertainly into conflict with the individualism of negative freedom, an evolving principle of "absolute" subjective authenticity. And however else they may differ, these scenarios have in common the premise that the salient point of inquiry is to be found neither in the authority of public exteriority nor in the authenticity of private interiority but in a negotiated passage between them. Dispensing with the comparatively actualized procedure of reading letters for their hidden meaning or of disclosing the secrets of the undressed body, third-person narration that employs free indirect discourse opens up the virtual interiority of character by constituting a "point of view" whose coherence is codependent with that of the narrative voice it momentarily adopts or extrudes. A virtual means of micro-"publication," free indirect discourse, like the actual process of typographical publication on which its existence depends, establishes private personality and the impersonality of public circulation in a single gesture.[49]

Free indirect discourse became fairly common toward the end of the eighteenth century and a familiar, even dominant, narrative technique during the nineteenth, and its historiography therefore broadly corresponds to that of Adam Ferguson's "age of separations." Only when character has been sufficiently separated out from narrator do they acquire the autonomy required for their differential conflation. Crucial to the technique is therefore the experience of difference: not the "content" of public authority or private authenticity but the ongoing formal structure of differential oscillation that defines them in dialectical relationship and creates the sense of a deep interiority by virtue of its excavation from a detached—a "higher" or a more "shallow"—vantage point. There is substantial disagreement among literary critics and historians on this issue.[50] Some critics have argued that the technique enacts the ironizing authority of disciplinary regulation, by which the private individual is constrained through the detached overview of public norms. Others have argued that free indirect discourse subserves the authenticity of the subject, enacting a sympathetic identification of narrator with character by which private individuality is nurtured and sustained through intimate acts of emotional absorption and exchange.

It is not hard to find passages in *Pride and Prejudice* that appear to support both models. The following excerpt seems well described by the latter account of the technique:

> The tumult of her mind was now painfully great. She knew not how to support herself, and from actual weakness sat down and cried for half an hour. Her astonishment, as she reflected on what had passed, was increased by every review of it. That she should receive an offer of marriage from Mr. Darcy! that he should have been in love with her for so many months! (148)

In this sequence of sentences the difference we experience between the external viewpoint with which we begin and the affective interiority that concludes the passage has the effect of accommodating the one to the other with a sense of sympathetic accord that depends entirely on our awareness of the distance we travel in order to get there. Here, on the other hand, is the meeting between Lydia and her future husband:

> All were struck with the stranger's air, all wondered who he could be, and Kitty and Lydia, determined if possible to find out, led the way across the street . . . . Mr. Denny addressed them directly, and entreated permission to introduce his friend, Mr. Wickham, who had returned with him the day before from town, and he was happy to say had accepted a commission in their corps. This was exactly as it should be; for the young man wanted only regimentals to make him completely charming. (54)

Here too the effect of the narration depends entirely on our experience of shifting from an external to an internal point of view, from the open-endedness of wondering who the stranger could be to the too-easy confidence that he is exactly as he should be. Clearly colored by the feelings of the two young women rather than by the more externally descriptive neutrality of the voice that leads us to it, the viewpoint of the concluding sentence is implicitly and ironically undercut by norms that, although (as we have seen) seriously under negotiation throughout this novel, nonetheless already establish Lydia's character as the negative extreme both of her mother's public designs and of her father's private license.

In other words, the juxtaposition of these two passages suggests that the antithetical formulation of the bias that is putatively built into the technique of free indirect discourse is itself vulnerable to questioning. The mechanisms at work in both are the same: the disparity in voices is palpable enough to be felt, in the process of reading, *as* a process; the locus of interiorization is determined by the proximity of the character in question; and the balance of "disciplinary regulation" and "sympathetic identification" depends entirely on the character into whose interiority we are led and on the stage in the development of narrative action at which this happens.[51] A third view of free indirect discourse, however, would dispense altogether with this antithetical formulation of its potential effects. In this view, free indirect discourse is indeed a method of disciplinary regulation, but its rhetorical persuasiveness owes precisely to the fact that it appears to be without rhetoric. The argument here is that the perspectival oscillation entailed in free indirect discourse is no more consciously registered in the experience of the reader than it is in that of the character. Hence free indirect discourse achieves an effect of transparent immediacy whereby representation is transformed into the illusion of the real. Like the character, the reader internalizes the lesson of narration unselfconsciously, as a condition of existence, rather than reflexively, as a movement from the outside inward.

It seems to me that this view of free indirect discourse is also vulnerable, and on a number of grounds. In attributing to its formal work an overarching ideological function it replaces a close attention to the internal nuances of characterization by an external and largely untested theory about the sociology of reader response. It attributes to eighteenth- and nineteenth-century novel readers an inattention to narrative process that is not borne out by their recorded commentary and that may be more pertinent to later readers, who, dulled to the subtlety of the technique by familiarity and overuse, require for their arousal the more ostentatious and extravagant cues of modernist and postmodernist narration. Free indirect discourse is less an ideology than a method of achieving a broad and subtle range of ideological possibilities. A better analogue for it may perhaps be found in the model of the maternal narrator that emerges from the discourse of Eliza Haywood in the *Female Spectator*. "I was willing to treat [my readers]," writes Haywood, "with the Tenderness of a Mother, but not, like some Mothers, to continue my Indulgence to their Ruin."[52] Free indirect discourse is like the rough but tender justice of Charles Gildon's club, which steals and publishes a private letter that describes the victimization of a young girl at the hands of a guardian who believes she lacks "the will to discover it to a Third Person, that might assist her."[53] Reflecting the reciprocity of precept and example Haywood employs to sophisticate formal domestication, free indirect discourse makes available a sliding scale by which minutely calibrated degrees of difference between the public and the private may be achieved and adjusted in the very process of narration.

The example of Haywood reminds us that the differential process of education in which "maternal narration" consists has application not only to the way characters like Elizabeth learn a lesson in figurative reading but also to the way Austen's literal readers are taught to negotiate her novel. Elizabeth's gradual coming to knowledge about herself and others, a microexperience in which free indirect discourse allows us to participate, is broadly analogous to the macroexperience we readers have in coming to know Austen's world at large, a process that includes but is not limited to that of free indirect discourse itself. Adjusted to the conditions of novelistic form, Haywood's differential pedagogy, her oscillation between the exemplary concretion of character and the abstraction of preceptual narration, provides a way of describing this macroexperience—the principal adjustment being the reconception of discursive "precept" as the normative voice of third-person narration. According to this broad analogy, the speech and especially the thoughts of the character stand in relation to the voice of the narrator as actual individuals stand in relation to the virtual collectivity of the public. Our cumulative understanding of Mr. Bennet's character is a case in point. Austen manages our intake of disparate information about him as though she were in charge of our alimentary upbringing. Notably, the similarity between the way in which the first and last chapters of *Pride and Prejudice* begin with the distinctively ironizing authority of third-person point of view suggests that whatever else may develop in the intervening pages, the characters of Elizabeth's parents do not. And yet our understanding of them undergoes a substantial reassessment over the course of the novel, and this is largely owing to both what we learn about Mr. Bennet and how we learn it.

As we have already observed, the remainder of chapter 1 goes far toward establishing our dominant association of Mr. Bennet with the authenticity of "private feeling" over against the superficial venality of his wife's preoccupation with "public design" (1–3). But the rebalancing of that unequal opposition quickly gets going on a number of fronts. For one thing, the narrator soon tells us that Longbourn is "unfortunately" entailed away from the Bennet daughters, a neutral "precept" (this is what can happen in the world of estate settlement) that not only obviates ethical agency by invoking a cause no lower than "fortune" but also suggests a plausibly ethical motive for what otherwise has been conveyed simply as Mrs. Bennet's irrational anxiety about her daughters' marriageability (20). Through the exemplary evidence of dialogue and Elizabeth's reflections, Austen makes us privy both to Mr. Bennet's icy detachment from his wife's flighty efforts at "communication" and to his ironic distance from his duty to provide emotional guidance for his daughters (85, 163). When preceptual generalization recurs, it mixes several points of view so as to diminish the ethical superiority of the father to the mother. The narrator informs us directly of Mr. Bennet's "imprudence" in choosing a wife by the external criterion of "appearance"; we hear—as we have not before—that Elizabeth "had never been blind to the impropriety of her father's behaviour as a husband"; and a hint of his irresponsible self-dramatization is momentarily conveyed to us through the delicate focalization of free indirect discourse: "Respect, esteem, and confidence, had vanished for ever; and all his views of domestic happiness were overthrown" (180). The absolute finality with which Mr. Bennet's feelings of affectionate connection "vanish" is in striking contrast to the way Elizabeth shortly will labor to construe and nurture emergent feelings of "respect," "esteem," and "gratitude" for her future husband in the affective space where "hatred had vanished long ago . . ." (201). Ironically, Mr. Bennet becomes a defective reader of his favorite daughter's feelings. The "forced marriage" plot of which he is guilty consists in imposing his own marital telos on Elizabeth: "My child, let me not have the grief of seeing you unable to respect your partner in life. You know not what you are about" (289).

Before he is supplanted in that important role by Mr. Gardiner and then by Darcy, we are told by the narrator that Mr. Bennet, "a most negligent and dilatory correspondent," has failed to sustain family connections during the crisis of Lydia's elopement, when no more than a punctual letter would have "communicated" much-needed information and relieved the collective "anxiety" at Longbourn (223, 224). We may begin to feel that Mr. Bennet is, like Lady Catherine, one of those heads of household whose lineal family "connections" preclude emotional family connection—were it not that Austen has obscurely provided grounds for doubting the former competence as well, for suspecting, in other words, that Mr. Bennet's affective "imprudence" may be paralleled by financial imprudence, that his conjugal "impropriety" may bespeak personal liability for his lack of absolute property. The narrator soon confirms this suspicion in terms so forthrightly expository that we may well wonder why we were not vouchsafed this information at the outset:

> Mr. Bennet had very often wished, before this period of his life, that, instead of spending his whole income, he had laid by an annual sum, for the better provision of his children, and of his wife, if she survived him. He now wished it more than ever. Had he done his duty in that respect, Lydia need not have been indebted to her uncle, for whatever of honour or credit could now be purchased for her. The satisfac-

tion of prevailing on one of the most worthless young men in Britain to be her husband, might then have rested in the proper place. (233–34)

Our access to Mr. Bennet's mind through free indirect discourse (Wickham is "one of the most worthless young men in Britain") softens the severity of his irresponsibility by ventriloquizing a judgment with which neither we nor the narrator is likely to disagree. It is almost as though Wickham's worthlessness mitigates Mr. Bennet's inveterate disdain for what we now see to be ethically crucial: possessing a "design" for the family's welfare. But has Austen treated us as ethical subjects? Has the information required for an acute reading of Mr. Bennet been imported too suddenly by the narrator "from the outside"? Has our access to Austen's greater "design" been too limited for us to generalize and apply the exemplary lessons of her characters?

Interiority: Characters and Houses

In the domestic novel the deep interiority of characters often is disclosed in complex association with that of houses. In historical terms, developments in the way architectural inside spaces get hived and subdivided bear a loose but fruitful analogy to developments in narrative form. The language itself of early modern domestic architecture—"presence chamber," "(with)drawing room," "privy chamber," "common room," "common passage"—is suggestive for our understanding of how early modern narration discovers new possibilities by explicitating different "points of view" and "voices" that earlier narrative practice had treated as distinct but inseparable functions of a more or less singular discourse.[54] At the height of her frustration over the tendency of "design" and "feeling," Charlotte and Wickham, to bleed into each other, Elizabeth leaps at the prospect of a trip with the Gardiners to the Lake District. A barbed allusion to the lake poets, travel journals, and theories of the picturesque, her words intimate (with an authorial irony) a belief in the possibility that inanimate landscape can be read as though devoid of the ethically problematic: "What are men to rocks and mountains? . . . And when we do return, it shall not be like other travellers . . . . Lakes, mountains, and rivers, shall not be jumbled together in our imaginations; nor, when we attempt to describe any particular scene, will we begin quarreling about its relative situation" (119). The tour of the parsonage at Rosings that immediately follows this passage is an object lesson in the futility of seeking a viewpoint that would escape relativity. It is guided by the tyrannical objectivity of Mr. Collins, by whom "every view was pointed out with a minuteness which left beauty entirely behind." And in contrast to this experience of closely policed reading, the narrative voice modulates along the third-person continuum and momentarily comes to rest, before quickly moving on, in the sycophantic mental space of Mr. Collins: "He could number the fields in every direction, and could tell how many trees there were in the most distant clump. But of all the views which his garden, or which the country, or the kingdom could boast, none were to be compared with the prospect of Rosings . . . . It was a handsome modern building, well situated on rising ground" (121).

When the Gardiners are later obliged to "give up the Lakes, and substitute a more contracted tour," the destination of "a small part of Derbyshire" dear to Mrs. Gardiner naturally raises the idea of a trip to Pemberley as well, which "was not in their direct road, nor more than a mile or two out of it." "The possibility of meeting Mr. Darcy, while viewing the place" disconcerts Elizabeth, but once she is satisfied that the family is not currently in residence "she was at leisure to feel a great deal of curiosity to see the house herself . . ." (182, 183–84). As it happens, meeting the man while viewing the place precisely describes the inexorable progress into the interior that awaits her. Like a cabinet of curiosities, Pemberley will divulge its secrets only to one who brings to its examination the requisite sensibility. If such a cabinet may be seen as the diminutive and private antecedent of the public museum, it is also true that the protoscientific appeal of the cabinet—a little world that wondrously contains the wonders of the world at large—had always involved just this reciprocity between the small and the great, the private and the public. In their leisurely, quasi-touristical approach to Pemberley, Austen's visitors evoke something of the curiosity of the museumgoer—or better, the attitude of those who had begun, in the early part of the previous century, to frequent the great homes of England. Here too the motivation was curiosity: broadly about how those who could not yet be conceived as "the other half" lived, but more specifically about the universe of natural and cultural objects with which the absent owners surrounded, and in that process reflected, themselves.⁵⁵ The stately private home open to public viewing was the same sort of edifice that was celebrated in country house poems of an earlier but largely overlapping period. As we have seen, that poetic subgenre reworked the Virgilian tag *Sic parvis componere magna solebam* in concert with an early modern interest in the series of reflections, from large to small, entailed in the sequence of state, estate, house, and owner. It is, of course, the near side of this sequence, the correspondence between outward house and inward man, that most preoccupies Elizabeth at Pemberley.

Austen narrates the entire experience consummately self-conscious of the interpenetrative relationship between vision and thought, object and subject, sensation and reflection, outside and inside—so much so that Elizabeth's anxious discrimination between the man and the house may quickly come to seem ingenuous. "Elizabeth's mind was too full for conversation, but she saw and admired every remarkable spot and point of view. . . . and, while examining the nearer aspect of the house, all her apprehensions of meeting its owner returned" (185). A personalized touchstone for all that she admires in what she sees, Darcy constantly returns to her thoughts ("She longed to enquire of the housekeeper, whether her master were really absent . . ."). For Elizabeth, inside and outside views are actively interchangeable. Having entered the domestic interior, she "surveys" the dining-parlor as though it were a landscape, then seeks from her interior vantage a succession of viewpoints out onto the landscape, a perspective that emphasizes the dependence of the beauty of its "objects" on the way the subjective relativity of their perception seems to give them an inner life of their own: "Elizabeth, after slightly surveying it, went to a window to enjoy its prospect. The hill . . . was a beautiful object. Every disposition of the ground was good; and she looked on the whole scene, the river, the trees scattered on its banks, and the winding of the valley, as far as she could trace it, with delight. As they passed into other rooms, these objects were taking different positions; but from every window there were beauties to be seen" (185–86). Elizabeth's surrogate eyes, the windows disclose each beauty "in its relative situation": in Pemberley House she experiences a simulacrum of the passage through the Lake District of which she had been disappointed, the natural beauties of the outside not "jumbled together in her imagination" but disengaged, by that framing faculty of inner attention, from their merely sensible grounding.[56]

Against her prejudices Elizabeth gradually learns to trust the housekeeper at Pemberley as truly a keeper of the house in its owner's absence, a guide who, unlike Mr. Collins, knows when, and when not, to frame a view. "'And that,' said Mrs. Reynolds, pointing to another of the miniatures, 'is my master—and very like him'" (186). The miniature—conceived by an Elizabethan practitioner as a "secret" and "a kind of gentle painting"—is, of course, like the capacious landscapes framed by the dining-parlor windows, only one in a succession of viewpoints that have been secreted around the great house.[57] Another is Elizabeth's own picture of Darcy ("And do you not think him a very handsome gentleman, Ma'am?"); yet another is that of Mrs. Reynolds, to whose unrelieved praise of the master of the house Elizabeth listens "with increasing astonishment . . . ." "In what an amiable light does this place him!" she thinks, and the painterly terms of her reflection sustain us in our continuing tour of the domestic interior through lobby and sitting room to the picture gallery, where Elizabeth has the uncanny experience of encountering another image "very like him," "a striking resemblance of Mr. Darcy, with such a smile over the face, as she remembered to have sometimes seen, when he looked at her. . . . [A]nd as she stood before the canvas, on which he was represented, and fixed his eyes upon herself, she thought of his regard with a deeper sentiment of gratitude than it had ever raised before . . ." (188, 189). Like that earlier moment in the tour of Pemberley when room and landscape seemed to exchange places and the object seemed "fixed," in its plastic objecthood, by subjective viewpoint, this moment captures the interpenetrative dialectic of outside and inside, but now at a deeper level of sympathy and "sentiment" and with a deeper penetration into the interior of both house and mind.

Parting from the portrait and the house immediately thereafter, Elizabeth has the apparitional experience of seeing the man—the objectification of the portrait and the subjectification of the house—not once but twice. As inside, standing before the portrait a moment ago, now outside "[t]heir eyes instantly met . . . ." But now it is only once they part again—when Darcy, transfixed, "suddenly recollected himself, and took leave"—that Elizabeth again tries to take his point of view into her own, and now through the agency of not specular presence but free indirect discourse: "[W]holly engrossed by her own feelings, . . . [s]he was overpowered by shame and vexation. Her coming there was the most unfortunate, the most ill-judged thing in the world! How strange must it appear to him! In what a disgraceful light might it not strike so vain a man!" And yet "his behaviour, so strikingly altered,—what could it mean? That he should even speak to her was amazing!—but to speak with such civility, to enquire after her family! . . . She knew not what to think, nor how to account for it" (190, 191). The language of extreme perplexity here may recall that much earlier moment when Elizabeth witnesses the meeting of Darcy and Wickham ("What could be the meaning of it?" [55]). But the similarity is belied by the progress she has made in learning how to read the vast spectrum of experience that is bounded by extremes of public exteriority and private interiority and that encloses a differential each point on which is—once she possesses this key to unlock the secrets of the modern cabinet of curiosities—accessible to all others.

In the terms of the present study, the key to the cabinet of modernity may be epitomized in the understanding that separation is the precondition both for conflation and for reseparation at a deeper level. After Darcy departs abruptly, the three visitors continue their walk through the grounds of the estate, "but it was some time before Elizabeth was sensible of any of it; and, though she answered mechanically to the repeated appeals of her uncle and aunt, and seemed to direct her eyes to such objects as they pointed out, she distinguished no part of the scene. Her thoughts were all fixed on that one spot of Pemberley House, whichever it might be, where Mr. Darcy then was. She longed to know what at that moment was passing in his mind . . ." (191). During her visit Elizabeth has been wistfully aware of the sensible possession her indignant response to Darcy's love has forfeited. "[T]o be mistress of Pemberley might be something!" "Instead of viewing [these rooms] as a stranger, I might have rejoiced in them as my own . . ." (185, 186). And yet her own mind passing beyond sense into the virtual space fixed by her mind's eye, Elizabeth, like Addison's man of a polite imagination, possesses Darcy now more thoroughly than if she owned either him or Pemberley.[58] Soon, when he appears once more, this time to remain with her and her family connections, the conflation of sensibility and sense will have begun in earnest.

The Ideology of the Domestic Novel

It is not uncommon for readers of *Pride and Prejudice* to construe Austen's ending as the culmination of an artful exercise in "conservative" ideology that employs the drama of individual and affective experience to accommodate, justify, and "naturalize" a political scenario of class domination crowned by the marriage of Elizabeth and Darcy. But how might we name the hegemony that Austen would conserve? The figure of Lady Catherine de Bourgh alone reminds us that the novel holds no brief for aristocratic ideology and its dogma that birth is worth. Is *Pride and Prejudice* a naturalization of progressive or "bourgeois" ideology? This reading seems only slightly less implausible, since one of the prejudices Elizabeth learns to shed over the course of the novel is her contrary individualism: the easy progressive inversion of aristocratic ideology, the conviction that *low* birth is worth, a crude parody we see her attraction to just at the moment when she angrily denounces, to Caroline Bingley, its aristocratic antithesis: Wickham's "guilt and his descent appear by your account to be the same" (72). (As her aunt soon after declares with hopeful assurance, "You are too sensible a girl, Lizzy, to fall in love merely because you are warned against it . . ." [111].) Indeed, to imagine that Austen is defending a social status quo based on a marriage plot requires dismissing, as so much cynical window dressing, her efforts to educate Elizabeth and her readers on the folly of either positive or negative standards of freedom unmixed with one another. It is undeniable that the marriage of Elizabeth and Darcy has sociopolitical implications. But the more we read that marriage in the context of the entire novel rather than as a detachable marker of a static ideological dictum, the more we are likely to see *Pride and Prejudice* as a searching inquiry into the grounds for attributing worth given the undependability of both aristocratic and progressive criteria: to understand the novel less as a past- and present-oriented act of conservation than as a future-oriented exploration. This is not to deny the ideological nature of *Pride and Prejudice* but to suggest that in works like it we see best exemplified the ruminative adjudication of public and private values we refer to when we use the term "ideology" with a seriousness that goes beyond dismissive demystification and critique. Austen's novel might better be seen as an actively contradictory process of ideological inquiry rather than as the defense of an already existent ideology.

Reflecting on the broad argument of this study, however, we also need to recognize what was at stake for Austen and her contemporaries in the effort to imagine a realm of private experience that might be separated out from a former embeddedness within a dominantly constitutive "public" realm. From the perspective of ideology theory, the valorization of individual, common life as the key to what is universal because common to us all rightly needs to be understood to signify, at however complex a level of mediation, a sociopolitical practice that has come to dominate much of Western culture even though it is responsive neither to the common nor to the universal.59 Indeed, ideology theory is born of the same historical moment as the domestic novel, and its project is to reshape the old norm of positive liberty for a modern world that would sustain the priority of the collective to the individual without sacrificing the mandatory contribution made to any adequate conception of social justice by the innovative idea of negative liberty. Like ideology theory, the domestic novel labors to conflate the categories of the individual and the social, whose separation out has been the work of the preceding two centuries. But where the classic critique of ideology approaches this shared task from the direction of a renovated public realm conceived, at its most concrete, in terms of a communist or socialist collectivity, the domestic novel is committed to the idea that collective norms can only be a function of individual experience within the realm of the private. The problem with interpreting the domestic novel too quickly according to the model of ideology formation is that it risks obscuring what is most vitally ideological about its project. The domestic novel, and more broadly domesticity as such, is not a discourse that stealthily denies a tacit sociopolitical significance that lies beyond its own will to signify. Rather, it explicitly insists on its own signification of the sociopolitical within the realm of private experience.

As we have seen, the rich lode of domesticity that is deposited by the slow withdrawal of domestication over the course of the early modern period has at its core a conviction of the adequacy of the private to sustain and entail those ultimate human ends to which it had seemed until then no more than a hermeneutic and pedagogic means. Read with an awareness of its sedimented historicity, the domestic novel is striated with the signs of its vigorous effort to, not separate itself from the world, but absorb and incorporate the world within its virtual domain, where the foundational terms of division are continuously rediscovered in successive subdivisions of the interior realm. In the absence of this awareness domesticity becomes only partly legible, occluded by a modern myopia that bears some relation to the tendency to misread the technology of realism in general and of free indirect discourse in particular as an ideology of transparent immediacy rather than a method of mediation more subtle than those it challenges and replaces—indeed, than those by which it is in turn challenged and replaced.⁶⁰ To this extent we have lost the key to the cabinet that holds the secrets of domestic and novelistic practice—which is to say the cabinet of their prehistory. From Walter Scott to Edward Said, Austen's novels have been called to account either for failing to engage the world beyond the domestic confines of private feeling, the middle-class household, and the English nation or for inadequately acknowledging the dependence of these private benefits on public—on class and colonial—exploitation. Without denying the importance of such readings, which understand the domestic novel from a perspective outside its own, it seems equally important to acknowledge that from its own viewpoint this is not a furtive failure—the product of ideological mystification—but an open ideological success. The realm of privacy in modern life is not (only) an alternative to the public but (also) its internalization, a truth that has become best known through the feminist maxim "The personal is political." Nor can we begin to assess the ideological liabilities of domesticity—what it includes, what it excludes—without having recourse to its prehistory of self-conscious inclusion and exclusion, which remains a secret history only with our connivance.

The critique of the domestic novel as at best oblivious to and at worst a palliating naturalization of public injustice conceives it as the domesticating sort of "secret history" that narrative experiments of the past two centuries had been strenuously trying to supersede. By this way of thinking, the project of the domestic novel, more or less like that of the *roman à clef,* is in variable ratios both to reveal and to conceal its public referent. Whatever the utility of this viewpoint, it extends an earlier habit of reading and judging private discourse by the exclusive standard of how well it performs its formal purpose, which is to signify public discourse. And like Eliza Haywood's hostile correspondent in the *Female Spectator,* this viewpoint implies that private discourse in which no such reference, whether explicit or implicit, can be found has the inconsequential triviality of the merely private.⁶¹

But patently public allusion, in Austen and others, is not a stealthy intimation of what is centrally important; it is a remnant of a former system of signification, or a contextual figure for the political conflict that is decisively centered within the private realm. In these terms, Darcy's acutely drawn character is not a means to figure and to understand the status of aristocratic nobility in the early nineteenth century but the end toward whose understanding his social rank makes one crucial contribution. To displace the politics of *Pride and Prejudice* onto what it may, with relative "secrecy," suggest about class conflict ignores how hard, and how successfully, Austen labors to display the politics that inhere within the domestic realm of the family in politically resonant conflicts —between individuals and families, "connections" and "connections," children and parents, upbringing and maturity, feelings and design, subjectivity and subjection, the first person and the third person. As she reads Darcy's letter Elizabeth exclaims: "Till this moment, I never knew myself" (159). Later, when she suddenly encounters Darcy on the grounds of the Pemberley estate, direct and free indirect discourse allows us to witness Elizabeth's new-found self-knowledge in play: "How strange must it appear to him! . . . She longed to know what at that moment was passing in his mind . . ." (191). Like Adam Smith, Austen would have us understand that both self-knowledge and ethical sociability require the sympathetic internalization of the other's point of view as if it were one's own. If we approach the domestic novel as a secret history, we are in danger of missing the singular modernity not only of its focus on the problematic separation out of self from society but also of its conviction that the conflationary project must proceed from, even within, the interior.

Notes

Within the following notes, cross-references to other sections of this book cite numbers of chapters and notes rather than of pages. Sometimes it is the content of the notes that is referred to; more often the citation of two or more notes (e.g., "nn. 14–21") defines a span that refers the reader to a section of the text itself.

For publications before 1800, London is the place of publication unless otherwise stated.

I have refrained from the use of [*sic*] throughout the text and notes.

Introduction

1. Karl Marx, *Grundrisse: Foundations of the Critique of Political Economy* (wr. 1857–58; pub. 1939), trans. Martin Nicolaus (Harmondsworth, UK: Penguin, 1973), 103–5.

2. See ibid., 100.

3. For an expansion of this argument that generalizes beyond the issue of the public and the private, see Michael McKeon, "Tacit Knowledge: Tradition and Its Aftermath," in *Questions of Tradition,* ed. Mark Salber Phillips and Gordon Schochet (Toronto: University of Toronto Press, 2004), 171–202.

4. Philippe Ariès and Georges Duby, gen. eds., *Histoire de la vie privée* (Paris: Editions de Seuil, 1986), trans. Arthur Goldhammer as *A History of Private Life* (Cambridge, MA: Harvard University Press, 1989). *Histoire de la vie privée* documents primarily French history and culture. Volume 3, *De la Renaissance aux Lumières,* ed. Roger Chartier (ill-translated as *Passions of the Renaissance*), approximates the period covered by the present study.

5. Jeff Weintraub, "The Theory and Politics of the Public/Private Distinction," in *Public and Private in Thought and Practice: Perspectives on a Grand Dichotomy,* ed. Jeff Weintraub and Krishan Kumar (Chicago: University of Chicago Press, 1997), 1–42. Weintraub's introduction is the best conceptual analysis I know of, and the collection of essays it introduces is an invaluable resource for both classic and recent writings on the public and the private from a broadly social-scientific perspective.

6. See the discussion of these and other heuristic categories in Raymond Williams, *Marxism and Literature* (Oxford: Oxford University Press, 1977), chap. 8 and passim.

Chapter One | The Devolution of Absolutism

1. Adam Ferguson, *An Essay on the History of Civil Society* (1767), ed. Louis Schneider (New Brunswick, NJ: Transaction, 1980), 183.

2. See ibid., 79–80, 155, 158, 228.

3. See Bernard Mandeville, *The Fable of the Bees* (1705, 1714), ed. F. B. Kaye (Oxford: Clarendon, 1924; Indianapolis: Liberty Classics, 1988), 1:42, 347. Adam Ferguson sometimes seems content to use "society" and "civil society" interchangeably; see, e.g., Ferguson, *Essay,* 57–58. For a comparative overview, see Marvin B. Becker, *The Emergence of Civil Society in the Eighteenth Century: A Privileged Moment in the History of England, Scotland, and France* (Bloomington: Indiana University Press, 1994).

4. See my parallel discussion of the category "class" in Michael McKeon, *The Origins of the English Novel, 1600–1740* (Baltimore: Johns Hopkins University Press, 1987), 163–64.

5. For three distinct and celebrated approaches to the subject, see Norbert Elias, *Power and Civility,* vol. 2 of *The Civilizing Process* (1939), trans. Edmund Jephcott (New York: Pantheon, 1982); Ernst H. Kantorowicz, *The King's Two Bodies: A Study in Mediaeval Political Theology* (Princeton, NJ: Princeton University Press, 1957); and Perry Anderson, *Lineages of the Absolutist State* (London: New Left Books, 1974).

6. See Ernst Cassirer, *The Myth of the State* (Garden City, NY: Doubleday, 1946), chap. 12; Maurizio Viroli, *From Politics to Reason of State: The Acquisition and Transformation of the Language of Politics, 1251–1600* (Cambridge: Cambridge University Press, 1992), passim.

7. *Political Works of James I,* ed. C. H. McIlwain (London, 1918), 333, quoted in J. R. Tanner, *English Constitutional Conflicts of the Seventeenth Century, 1603–1689* (1928; reprint Cambridge: Cambridge University Press, 1961), 20.

8. See McKeon, *Origins,* 177–78.

9. Robert C. Johnson et al., eds., *Commons Debates, 1628,* vol. 3, *21 Apr.–27 May 1628* (New Haven, CT: Yale University Press, 1977), 578–79; John Rushworth, *Historical Collections,* vol. 4 (1692), 425, 428 (font reversed). I have quoted from both recorded versions of Marten's speech.

10. Charles I, "Answer to the Nineteen Propositions," 18 June 1642, in *The Stuart Constitution, 1603–1688: Documents and Commentary,* ed. J. P. Kenyon (Cambridge: Cambridge University Press, 1966), 22–23; Anthony Ascham, *Of the Confusions and Revolutions of Goverments . . .* (1649), 4. Cf. Christopher Hill's thesis of a "revolt within the [English] Revolution" in the introduction to *The World Turned Upside Down: Radical Ideas during the English Revolution* (New York: Viking, 1972).

11. This is one central argument of McKeon, *Origins,* chap. 5.

12. Declaration of 19 May 1642, in Rushworth, *Historical Collections,* 4:702, quoted in Conrad Russell, *The Causes of the English Civil War* (Oxford: Clarendon, 1990), 23–24; Algernon Sidney, *Discourses concerning Government* (wr. 1680–83, pub. 1696), chap. 3, sec. 39, ed. Thomas G. West (Indianapolis: Liberty Fund, 1996), 535, 536. On "the dominant metaphor of legal incorporation" and its decline in the later seventeenth century, see Conal Condren, *The Language of Politics in Seventeenth-Century England* (New York: St. Martin's, 1994), 61–72.

13. See Hannah Arendt, *The Human Condition,* 2nd ed. (Chicago: University of Chicago Press, 1998), pt. 2.

14. See Cynthia B. Patterson, *The Family in Greek History* (Cambridge, MA: Harvard University Press, 1998), chaps. 1, 6.

15. See Josiah Ober, *The Athenian Revolution: Essays on Ancient Greek Democracy and Political Theory* (Princeton, NJ: Princeton University Press, 1996), chap. 11.

16. Aristotle, *Politics*, 1253a, in *The Basic Works of Aristotle*, ed. Richard McKeon (New York: Random House, 1941), 1129, 1130 (hereafter references are to this edition and appear parenthetically in the text). See also Ober, *Athenian Revolution*, chap. 11.

17. On the juridical sense of theory, see Cheryl Anne Cox, *Household Interests: Property, Marriage Strategies, and Family Dynamics in Ancient Athens* (Princeton, NJ: Princeton University Press, 1998), esp. chap. 5.

18. On the *Politics*, see Josiah Ober, "Aristotle's Political Sociology: Class, Status, and Order in the *Politics*," in *Essays on the Foundations of Aristotelian Political Science*, ed. Carnes Lord and David K. O'Connor (Berkeley and Los Angeles: University of California Press, 1991), 133–34; on the *Poetics*, see Michael McKeon, "The Origins of Aesthetic Value," *Telos*, no. 57 (Fall 1983): 63–82. The language of "prescience" and "anticipation" alludes to historical change and not normative progress.

19. See Donald R. Kelley, *Human Measure: Social Thought in the Western Legal Tradition* (Cambridge, MA: Harvard University Press, 1990), 40 and chaps. 2 and 3 passim. On the disparity between juridical "theory" and family inheritance practices in Ancient Rome, see Richard P. Saller, *Patriarchy, Property, and Death in the Roman Family* (Cambridge: Cambridge University Press, 1994).

20. See Jeff Weintraub, "The Theory and Politics of the Public/Private Distinction," in *Public and Private in Thought and Practice: Perspectives on a Grand Dichotomy*, ed. Jeff Weintraub and Krishan Kumar (Chicago: University of Chicago Press, 1997), 11–13.

21. *OED*, 1st ed., s.v. "private," "public."

22. See *Oxford Latin Dictionary*, ed. P. G. W. Glare (Oxford: Oxford University Press, 1982), s.v. "publicus," "privatus."

23. But see Brian Tierney, *Religion, Law, and the Growth of Constitutional Thought, 1150–1650* (Cambridge: Cambridge University Press, 1982), which observes that the Florentine, and hence the modern, separation of the political from the religious is profoundly prefigured in later medieval ecclesiology and political theory. That is, the basic difference we customarily posit between medieval and Renaissance theories of the state becomes complicated as we enter more concrete levels of analysis, a development that nonetheless does not challenge the fruitfulness of the opposition at the more abstract level.

24. See Jürgen Habermas, *The Structural Transformation of the Public Sphere: An Inquiry into a Category of Bourgeois Society* (1962), trans. Thomas Burger and Frederick Lawrence (Cambridge, MA: MIT Press, 1989), pt. 1. See also, on "political economy," William Letwin, *The Origins of Scientific Economics: English Economic Thought, 1660–1776* (London: Methuen, 1963), 217; on the Puritan household, Christopher Hill, *Society and Puritanism in Pre-Revolutionary England* (London: Panther, 1969), chap. 13; and on the gentle household, Lena Cowen Orlin, *Private Matters and Public Culture in Post-Reformation England* (Ithaca, NY: Cornell University Press, 1994). On the domestic economy and the sexual division of labor, see below, chap. 4, nn. 15–43.

25. Francis Bacon, *The Proficiencie and Advancement of Learning Divine and Human* (1605), vol. 2, in *The Philosophical Works of Francis Bacon*, ed. Robert L. Ellis and James Spedding, rev. ed. John M. Robertson (London: Routledge, 1905), p. 81. As we have seen, Aristotle was more careful to discriminate *between* these "simple conjugations" than were many of Bacon's contemporaries. On these matters, see Constance Jordan, "The Household and the State: Transformations in the Representation of an Analogy from Aristotle to James I," *Mod-*

ern Language Quarterly 54, no. 3 (1993): 307–26. I will return to the patriarchalist analogy below, in chap. 3. Plato's *Republic,* in which the nature of the (lesser) soul is sought in its analogous relation to the (greater) state, is to some degree an exception to the rule.

26. For Filmer, "the family *was* a polity, and the polity *was* a household, and the patriarchal, biblical family was not a prototype but was the very wellspring of politics." Gordon J. Schochet, "The Significant Sounds of Silence: The Absence of Women from the Political Thought of Sir Robert Filmer and John Locke (or, 'Why can't a woman be more like a man?')," in *Women Writers and the Early Modern British Political Tradition,* ed. Hilda L. Smith (Cambridge: Cambridge University Press, 1998), 235.

27. [John Milton], *Eikonoklastes: in Answer to a Book Entitled Eikon Basilike . . .* (1649), in *The Complete Prose Works of John Milton,* vol. 3, *1648–1649,* ed. Merritt Y. Hughes (New Haven, CT: Yale University Press, 1962), 486–87; [idem], *A Defence of the People of England* (1651), ed. William J. Grace, trans. Donald Mackenzie, in ibid., vol. 4, *1650–1655,* ed. Don M. Wolfe (New Haven, CT: Yale University Press, 1966), 326–27. My thanks to Erin Murphy for bringing these passages to my attention.

28. John Locke, *An Essay Concerning the True Original, Extent, and End of Civil Government (The Second Treatise of Government)* (1690), bk. 2, chap. 1, sec. 2, in *Two Treatises of Government,* ed. Peter Laslett, 2nd ed. (Cambridge: Cambridge University Press, 1967), 286 (hereafter book 2 is cited as *Second Treatise*).

29. See McKeon, *Origins,* 187.

30. Locke, *Second Treatise,* chap. 2, sec. 14, p. 294; see also chap. 9, secs. 123–31, pp. 368–71. On the compact see generally chap. 8, secs. 95–122, pp. 348–67. See *OED,* s.v. "conflict," v., 3, where the first cited usage is dated 1647.

31. See Locke's critique of enthusiasts in *An Essay concerning Human Understanding* (1690), ed. Peter H. Nidditch (Oxford: Clarendon, 1979), bk. 4, chap. 19, secs. 11, 14, pp. 702, 704: "If they say they know it to be true, because it is a *Revelation* from GOD, the reason is good: but then it will be demanded, how they know it to be a Revelation from GOD. . . . Every Conceit that thoroughly warms our Fancies must pass for an Inspiration, if there be nothing but the Strength of our Perswasions, whereby to judge of our Perswasions: if *Reason* must not examine their Truth by something extrinsical to the Perswasions themselves; Inspirations and Delusions, Truth and Falshood will have the same Measure, and will not be possible to be distinguished."

32. See Gordon J. Schochet, *Patriarchalism in Political Thought: The Authoritarian Family and Political Speculation and Attitudes Especially in Seventeenth-Century England* (New York: Basic Books, 1975), 54–57.

33. In part because the *Two Treatises of Government* announces itself as a refutation of Filmer's patriarchalism, Locke gave to his countertheory a similarly temporal form. But he also believed that "an Argument from what has been, to what should of right be, has no great force . . ." (Locke, *Second Treatise,* chap. 8, sec. 103, p. 354). The distinction between arguments from precedent and arguments from right captures some features of the difference between tacit and explicit knowledge. But the journey from the first to the second tended to involve along the way the effort to explicitate precedent through a theory of origins, and Locke was mindful of the difficulties involved in the notion of a consensual "original" compact that could bind later generations. Indeed, it was partly in order to authorize the binding force of the compact on a posterity that could not have articulated that original choice that Locke

(and Hobbes) invokes "a common distinction of an express and a tacit consent" (ibid., sec. 119, p. 365); Hobbes distinguishes between "Signes of Contract" that "are either *Expresse,* or by *Inference*" (*Leviathan, or The Matter, Forme, & Power of a Common-Wealth Ecclesiastical and Civill* [1651], chap. 14, pp. 66–67). This is one register of the contradiction between the principle of an explicit contract on which the modern theory of the state is based and the virtuality of that contract, which therefore had to be refined for the theory to succeed in tacitly perpetuating the life of the state beyond a single generation. Cf. Jeremy Bentham's observation that "[a]ccording to Locke's scheme, men knew nothing at all of governments till they met together to make one. Locke had speculated so deeply, and reasoned so ingeniously, as to have forgot that he was not of age when he came into the world." "Locke, Rousseau, and Filmer's Scheme," University College, London, MS Bentham 100, in Elie Halevy, *La formation du radicalisme philosophique* (Paris, 1901–3), vol. 1, appendix, 418, quoted in Schochet, *Patriarchalism,* 280.

34. Sir Robert Filmer, *Patriarcha* (wr. c. 1640, pub. 1680), in *Patriarcha and Other Political Works,* ed. Peter Laslett (Oxford: Blackwell, 1949), 54; Sidney, *Discourses,* chap. 1, sec. 3, pp. 12, 13, 16.

35. [Mary Astell], *Reflections Upon Marriage* (1700), 3rd ed. (1706), in *The First English Feminist: Reflections Upon Marriage and Other Writings by Mary Astell,* ed. Bridget Hill (Aldershot, Hants.: Gower, 1986), 102, 76. In fact Astell's royalism consistently takes away with one hand the principle of rational and free agency that it gives with the other: "Far be it from [the author] to stir up Sedition of any sort, none can abhor it more; and she heartily wishes that our Masters wou'd pay their Civil and Ecclesiastical Governors the same Submission, which they themselves extract from their Domestic Subjects" (70).

36. Daniel Defoe, *Conjugal Lewdness; or, Matrimonial Whoredom* (1727), 29, 33, 37, 38, 166.

37. This and the following paragraph rely on a range of studies, including Richard Schlatter, *Private Property: The History of an Idea* (New Brunswick, NJ: Rutgers University Press, 1951); C. B. Macpherson, "The Meaning of Property," in *Property: Mainstream and Critical Positions,* ed. C. B. Macpherson (Toronto: University of Toronto Press, 1978), 1–13; idem, "Capitalism and the Changing Concept of Property," in *Feudalism, Capitalism, and Beyond,* ed. Eugene Kamenka and R. S. Neale (London: Arnold, 1975), 104–24; James Tully, "The Framework of Natural Rights in Locke's Analysis of Property: A Contextual Reconstruction," in *Theories of Property: Aristotle to the Present,* ed. Anthony Parel and Thomas Flanagan (Waterloo, ON: Wilfrid Laurier University Press, 1979); G. E. Aylmer, "The Meaning and Definition of 'Property' in Seventeenth-Century England," *Past and Present,* no. 86 (1980): 87–97; Neal Wood, *John Locke and Agrarian Capitalism* (Berkeley and Los Angeles: University of California Press, 1984); Richard Ashcraft, *Revolutionary Politics and Locke's Two Treatises of Government* (Princeton, NJ: Princeton University Press, 1986); Margaret Sampson, "Laxity and Liberty in Seventeenth-Century English Political Thought," in *Conscience and Casuistry in Early Modern Europe,* ed. Edmund Leites (Cambridge: Cambridge University Press, 1988), 115–16; Thomas A. Horne, *Property Rights and Poverty: Political Argument in Britain, 1605–1834* (Chapel Hill: University of North Carolina Press, 1990); Stephen Buckle, *Natural Law and the Theory of Property: Grotius to Hume* (Oxford: Clarendon, 1991); and J. M. Neeson, *Commoners: Common Right, Enclosure, and Social Change in England, 1700–1820* (Cambridge: Cambridge University Press, 1993), chaps. 1–2.

38. See Alan Macfarlane, *The Origins of English Individualism: The Family, Property, and Social Transition* (Cambridge: Cambridge University Press, 1979); and idem, *The Culture of Capitalism* (Oxford: Blackwell, 1987). In *Human Measure* Donald Kelley argues that the common law prevailed "on the basis of the law of private property, which was a material yet sanctified extension of personal liberty. . . . Eventually, divested of feudal trappings and expressed in the . . . naturalistic terms of Lockean political theory, what might be called the property fetish of common law helped to prepare the way for modern liberal ideology" (171).

39. Daniela Gobetti, "Humankind as a System: Private and Public Agency at the Origins of Modern Liberalism," in Weintraub and Kumar, *Public and Private,* 110.

40. C. B. Macpherson, *The Political Theory of Possessive Individualism* (Oxford: Clarendon, 1962).

41. See Christopher Hill, *Reformation to Industrial Revolution,* Pelican Economic History of Britain 2 (Harmondsworth, UK: Penguin, 1969), 146–48.

42. Daniel Defoe, *The Compleat English Gentleman* (wr. 1728–29), ed. Karl D. Bülbring (London: Nutt, 1890), 62–63; John Lilly, *The Practical Register* (1719), quoted in Aylmer, "Meaning and Definition of 'Property,'" 95. "The abolition of feudal tenures was the basis for the agricultural revolution of the later seventeenth and eighteenth centuries." Christopher Hill, *Intellectual Origins of the English Revolution Revisited* (Oxford: Clarendon, 1997), 319.

43. On the "rebelliousness" of customary culture in this period, see E. P. Thompson, *Customs in Common: Studies in Traditional Popular Culture* (New York: New Press, 1991), 9 and passim.

44. Alan Ryan, *Property and Political Theory* (Oxford: Blackwell, 1984), 46–47. The separation out of the economic from the political domain was achieved, of course, through a number of developments, for example, seventeenth-century debates over the place of merchants and mercantile trade in the greater nation-state. See Mary Poovey, *A History of the Modern Fact: Problems of Knowledge in the Sciences of Wealth and Society* (Chicago: University of Chicago Press, 1998), chap. 2.

45. See Francis Bacon, "Of the True Greatness of Kingdoms and Estates," *Essays* (1612), in Bacon, *Philosophical Works,* 770–74.

46. See the illuminating discussions in Ellen Meiksens Wood, *The Pristine Culture of Capitalism: A Historical Essay on Old Regimes and Modern States* (London: Verso, 1991), 18–19, 24, 27, 78; and Condren, *Language,* 68–69.

47. Joseph Addison, *Spectator,* no. 69 (19 May 1711), in *The Spectator,* ed. Donald F. Bond, 5 vols. (Oxford: Clarendon, 1965) (hereafter references are to this edition and appear parenthetically in the text).

48. For a well-known passage from this formulation, see below, chap. 7, n. 116. On the emergence of the language of interest in the seventeenth century, and on the reversal in attitudes toward how the public interest was to be derived, see J. A. W. Gunn, *Politics and the Public Interest in the Seventeenth Century* (London: Routledge, 1969), xi, 227, 307, and passim.

49. Richard Cumberland, *A Philosophical Enquiry into the Laws of Nature* ([Lat., 1672] trans. 1750), 171, 307, quoted in Gunn, *Politics,* 279, 285. For related arguments, see Gunn, *Politics,* 211–12, 232, 245, 246.

50. Anthony Ashley Cooper, third Earl of Shaftesbury, *Characteristicks of Men, Manners, Opinions, Times . . .* ([1711] rev. 1732), 1:107, ed. Douglas Den Uyl (Indianapolis: Liberty Fund, 2001), 1:67.

51. Adam Smith, *An Inquiry into the Nature and Causes of the Wealth of Nations* (1776), bk. 4, chap. 5, sec. 39, ed. R. H. Campbell, A. S. Skinner, and W. B. Todd, Glasgow Edition of the Works and Correspondence of Adam Smith (Indianapolis: Liberty Classics, 1981), 1:539.

52. Tollemache MSS, Buckminster Park, nr. Grantham, nos. 4109, 4110, quoted in Russell, *Causes,* 24.

53. "A Letter of General George Moncks . . . directed unto Mr. Rolle . . . [and] the rest of the Gentry of Devon," 23 Jan. 1660, in *A Collection of Several Letters and Declarations, sent by General Monck . . .* (1660), 19.

54. "Between 1689 and 1715 twelve general elections were fought, only one less than for the rest of the eighteenth century; indeed, more general elections took place in that short time than in any other period of Parliamentary history, before or since . . . ." J. H. Plumb, *The Growth of Political Stability in England, 1675–1725* (Harmondsworth, UK: Penguin, 1967), 80.

55. For an analysis of this process that aims to assess also the contribution of poetic representation to the interest debate, see Michael McKeon, *Politics and Poetry in Restoration England: The Case of Dryden's "Annus Mirabilis"* (Cambridge, MA: Harvard University Press, 1975), pt. 1.

56. Sidney, *Discourses,* chap. 3, sec. 21, p. 444.

57. Robert Ferguson, *A Representation of the Threatening Dangers* (1689), 6, quoted in David Zaret, "Religion, Science, and Printing in the Public Spheres in Seventeenth-Century England," in *Habermas and the Public Sphere,* ed. Craig Calhoun (Cambridge, MA: MIT Press, 1992), 226.

58. Bernard Mandeville, "An Enquiry into the Origin of Moral Virtue," in Mandeville, *Fable of the Bees,* 1:41–42, 48–49. The deist John Toland sees a comparable impulse to deceive the people in similar terms, as a sort of *arcanum imperii* disseminated at large throughout "the country." Toland's text is the maxim *"that many things were true, which it was not onely useful the People shou'd not know; but that, tho absolutely false, it was expedient the People shou'd believe otherwise.* This is at present the favorite maxim, not of two or three persons only in a country, who juggle with the public, and imagine that deceiving the people is the highest *Reason of State;* but tis likewise the common cant of many others . . . ." [John Toland], *Clidophorus, or, Of the Exoteric and Esoteric Philosophy; that is, Of the External and Internal Doctrine of the Ancients: The one open and public, accommodated to popular prejudices and the Religions establish'd by Law; the other private and secret, wherin, to the few capable and discrete, was taught the real Truth stript of all disguises,* in his *Tetradymus . . .* (1720), 92.

59. Bernard Mandeville, *Origin of Honour* (1732), 40–41, quoted by F. B. Kaye in Mandeville, *Fable of the Bees,* 1:46n1.

60. Positive liberty entails the freedom found in relations with others. On the distinction between positive and negative liberty, of which I make use in this study, see G. W. F. Hegel, *Reason in History* (1837), chap. 3, sec. 3, ed. Robert S. Hartman (New York: Liberal Arts, 1953), 49–50, 54–55, 61–62. Hegel also calls these the objective and subjective aspects of freedom (56). For discussion, see Isaiah Berlin, "Two Concepts of Liberty," in *Four Essays on Liberty* (Oxford: Oxford University Press, 1969), 118–72; Charles Taylor, "What's Wrong with Negative Liberty," in *The Idea of Freedom: Essays in Honour of Isaiah Berlin,* ed. Alan Ryan (Oxford: Oxford University Press, 1979), 175–93; Lawrence Crocker, *Positive Liberty: An Essay in Normative Political Philosophy* (The Hague: Nijhoff, 1980); and Quentin Skinner, "The Idea of

Negative Liberty: Philosophical and Historical Perspectives," in *Philosophy in History: Essays on the Historiography of Philosophy,* ed. Richard Rorty, J. B. Schneewind, and Quentin Skinner (Cambridge: Cambridge University Press, 1984), 193–219. The literature on the distinction between positive and negative liberty is extensive, as is disagreement on the fundamental meaning of the two terms. My own construal of the distinction is heuristic rather than analytic. By my understanding, we can observe in the history of the West a long-term chronology over which the normative status of positive liberty gives way to that of negative liberty, a chronology that is more or less coextensive with the movement from "tradition" to "modernity" and that is paralleled by, for example, the early modern shift in the meaning of the word "individual" from "indivisible" to "singular, independent." See the analysis of *OED* citations in Peter Stallybrass, "Shakespeare, the Individual, and the Text," in *Cultural Studies,* ed. Lawrence Grossberg et al. (London: Routledge, 1992), 593–95. This chronology is complicated, in theory if not in achieved political practice, by my understanding of socialism as an effort to establish a modern regime of positive liberty on terms that diverge from those of tradition.

61. *Memoirs of Thomas, Earl of Ailesbury, Written by Himself,* ed. W. E. Buckley (London: Roxburghe Club, 1890), 1:5. On the cavaliers, see McKeon, *Politics and Poetry,* 81–83.

62. The mounted figure is Sir William Dick, lord mayor of Edinburgh and a well-known merchant who was knighted by Charles I in 1642 but destituted in 1650 by a parliamentary fine levied for lending money to Charles II (*DNB*). The tract in which the image appears was published in 1657, three years after the end of the first of the Anglo-Dutch Wars. On the growth of discontent over the rationale for mercantilist trade wars during the second Anglo-Dutch war, of 1665–67, see McKeon, *Politics and Poetry,* chap. 3. In figure 1 Dick mediates between the late-feudal lord who mobilizes his band of retainers in fealty to his king and the merchant prince whose fealty is as much to his own "profit."

63. *A Remonstrance, Proving that the Confinement of Trade, to particular Companies, is of general Losse to His Majesty, and His People* (1661), broadside; *The Reasons Humbly offered to Consideration, . . . how a Frank and Free Trade to all English Merchants, will be far more advantagious to the whole Land* (1662?), 2.

64. Thomas Johnson, *A Plea for Free-Mens Liberties* (1646), prologue, quoted in Joyce O. Appleby, *Economic Thought and Ideology in Seventeenth-Century England* (Princeton, NJ: Princeton University Press, 1978), 107.

65. On the classical models to which civic humanism was indebted, see above, nn. 13–23.

66. See J. G. A. Pocock, *The Machiavellian Moment: Florentine Political Thought and the Atlantic Republican Tradition* (Princeton, NJ: Princeton University Press, 1975), pt. 3.

67. See Ellen Meiksens Wood, *Pristine Culture,* 70.

68. See Pocock, *Machiavellian Moment,* 462–67.

69. I will return to this question below, in chap. 7.

70. For a fuller version of this argument regarding the dominant scholarship of civic humanism in the past several decades, see Michael McKeon, "Civic Humanism and the Logic of Historical Interpretation," in *The Political Imagination in History: Essays on the Work of J. G. A. Pocock,* ed. DeAnn DeLuna (forthcoming), where I make two basic points: first, that the claims advanced for the influence of civic humanism are inflated and implausible; and second, that the terms in which civic humanism has been expounded most influentially are highly problematic.

71. See, e.g., Pocock, *Machiavellian Moment,* 336–37, 423, 445–46, 464; and idem, *Virtue,*

Commerce, and History: Essays on Political Thought and History, Chiefly in the Eighteenth Century (Cambridge: Cambridge University Press, 1985), chaps. 2, 3, 6. For a study that extends the sway of civic humanism yet further by finding its challenge only in the latter decades of the eighteenth century, see John Barrell, *The Birth of Pandora and the Division of Knowledge* (Philadelphia: University of Pennsylvania Press, 1992).

72. See Ellen Meiksens Wood, *Pristine Culture*, 97–100. The mistaken subordination of the capitalist to the commercial revolution in England (or their erroneous conflation) is a feature of economic historiography that is roughly paralleled in political historiography. The modern proponents of a civic humanist dominance have contributed to a widespread effort in recent years to shift the fulcrum of importance from 1641 to 1688 in locating the long-term origins of modern English political culture. Although I welcome this positive revaluation of the Glorious Revolution and its aftermath, the present study registers at several points my skepticism regarding the (unnecessarily reciprocal) devaluation of the English civil wars and interregnum of 1641 to 1660.

73. See Jean-Christophe Agnew, *Worlds Apart: The Market and the Theater in Anglo-American Thought, 1550–1750* (Cambridge: Cambridge University Press, 1986), chap. 1, esp. sec. 3.

74. Thomas Scott, *The Belgick Pismire* . . . (1622), 32, 34; John Bunyan, *The Pilgrim's Progress from This World, to That which is to come* . . . (1678), ed. N. H. Keeble (Oxford: Oxford University Press, 1984), 73.

75. Ascham, *Of the Confusions*, 27; Locke, *Second Treatise*, chap. 5, secs. 27, 29, pp. 305–6, 307; Hobbes, *Leviathan* (1651), chap. 24, p. 127; William Petty, *Political Anatomy of Ireland* (1691), 63–64, quoted in Appleby, *Economic Thought*, 84; [Richard Allestree], *The Ladies Calling In Two Parts* . . . (Oxford, 1673), b2v (font reversed); [Mary Astell], *A Serious Proposal to the Ladies for the Advancement of their True and Greatest Interest, Part I*, 3rd ed. (1696), in Astell, *First English Feminist*, 155.

76. Henry Robinson, *The Office of Addresses and Encounters* . . . (1650), 2, 4.

77. [Henry Fielding], *A Plan of the Universal Register Office* . . . , 2nd ed. (1752), 5, 7–8, 9, 17–18 (hereafter cited parenthetically in the text). For a discussion of this project, see Miles Ogborn, *Spaces of Modernity: London Geographies, 1680–1780* (New York: Guilford, 1998), chap. 6.

78. See below, chaps. 2, 7. Fielding's idea of a Universal Register Office therefore may be seen as the institutional equivalent of novelistic realism.

79. Ascham, *Of the Confusions*, 30; Edward Misselden, *The Circle of Commerce* (1623), 17, quoted in Julie Robin Solomon, *Objectivity in the Making: Francis Bacon and the Politics of Inquiry* (Baltimore: Johns Hopkins University Press, 1998), 81.

80. Hobbes, *Leviathan*, chaps. 14, 15, pp. 68, 71–72.

81. For this argument see Appleby, *Economic Thought*, 188–91. Cf. Christopher Hill, "From Oaths to Interest," in *Society and Puritanism*, 405: "The supernatural sanction backing the oath of loyalty and the judicial oath—God the supreme overlord—was succeeded in capitalist society by the discovery that it paid a man to make his word his bond because of the rise in social importance of credit, reputation, respectability."

82. Daniel Defoe, *An Essay Upon Public Credit* . . . (1710), 22–23. On Defoe's personalization of public credit see below, chap. 9, nn. 12–18.

83. [Nicholas Barbon], *A Discourse of Trade* (1690), 15, 73; [Dudley North], *Discourse upon Trade* (1691), 14, quoted in Appleby, *Economic Thought*, 169–70, 171.

84. Locke, *Second Treatise,* chap. 5, sec. 31, p. 308; [Fielding], *Plan, 6–7.*

85. See Appleby, *Economic Thought,* 47, 97, 184, 193, and chap. 9 passim.

86. See above, n. 10.

87. James Pitt, *Daily Gazeteer,* nos. 120, 222 (15 Nov. 1735, 13 Mar. 1736), quoted in Shelley Burtt, *Virtue Transformed: Political Arguments in England, 1688–1740* (Cambridge: Cambridge University Press, 1992), 124.

88. Richard Allestree, *The Causes of the Decay of Christian Piety . . .* (1667), 351–52.

89. On these matters, see the thoughtful discussion in C. John Sommerville, *The Secularization of Early Modern England: From Religious Culture to Religious Faith* (Oxford: Oxford University Press, 1992), chap. 1 and passim. See also Michael McKeon, "Tacit Knowledge: Tradition and Its Aftermath," in *Questions of Tradition,* ed. Mark Salber Phillips and Gordon Schochet (Toronto: University of Toronto Press, 2004).

90. See Condren, *Language,* 46, 47. On the Ciceronian etymology of *religio,* see Hannah Arendt, "What Is Authority?" in *Between Past and Future: Six Exercises in Political Thought* (New York: Meridian, 1963), 121.

91. See Christopher Hill's seminal essay "The Spiritualization of the Household," in *Society and Puritanism,* 429–66. On this transfer of authority from the church to the family, see also Elizabeth L. Eisenstein, *The Printing Press as an Agent of Change: Communications and Cultural Transformations in Early-Modern Europe* (Cambridge: Cambridge University Press, 1979), 424–28.

92. This and the following three paragraphs draw on my discussion in McKeon, *Origins,* 189–200.

93. John Foxe, *The Acts and Monuments of John Foxe* (1563, enl. 1570), ed. Stephen R. Cattley (London: Seeley and Burnside, 1839), 8:475.

94. William Perkins, *Workes* (1612), 1:760; John Ward, *God Judging Among the Gods* (1645), 16, quoted in Michael Walzer, *The Revolution of the Saints: A Study in the Origins of Radical Politics* (London: Weidenfeld and Nicolson, 1965), 214, 235. On Puritan industriousness, see also Walzer, *Revolution,* 210–12.

95. See generally Christopher Hill, "Covenant Theology and the Concept of 'A Public Person,'" in *The Collected Essays of Christopher Hill* (Amherst: University of Massachusetts Press, 1986), 3:300–24. On the vacillation in political contexts between an inclusive and an exclusive reading of the contract and the franchise, see also William Haller, *The Rise of Puritanism* (New York: Harper, 1938), 85–91, 168–70; and Christopher Hill, "The Poor and the People," in *Collected Essays,* 3:247–73.

96. See Jonathan Goldberg, *James I and the Politics of Literature: Jonson, Shakespeare, Donne, and Their Contemporaries* (Baltimore: Johns Hopkins University Press, 1983), 115.

97. See Max Weber, *The Protestant Ethic and the Spirit of Capitalism* (1905), trans. Talcott Parsons (New York: Scribner's, 1958). For Adam Smith's analogous, socioeconomic formulation, see below, chap. 7, n. 116.

98. On the relationship between individual and collective tendencies in both Catholic and Protestant teachings, see François Lebrun, "The Two Reformations: Communal Devotion and Personal Piety," in *Passions of the Renaissance,* ed. Roger Chartier, vol. 3 of *A History of Private Life,* gen. eds. Philippe Ariès and Georges Duby, trans. Arthur Goldhammer (Cambridge, MA: Harvard University Press, 1989), 69–109. See also Cecile M. Jagodzinski, *Privacy and Print: Reading and Writing in Seventeenth-Century England* (Charlottesville: Uni-

versity of Virginia Press, 1999), chap. 1, on the proximity of Puritan, Anglican, and recusant Roman Catholic attitudes toward private devotion. The following discussion of casuistry is based upon several essays, in particular Sampson, "Laxity and Liberty," and Edmund Leites, "Casuistry and Character," in Leites, *Conscience and Casuistry,* 72–118 and 119–33, respectively; and Keith Thomas, "Cases of Conscience in Seventeenth-Century England," in *Public Duty and Private Conscience in Seventeenth-Century England: Essays Presented to G. E. Aylmer,* ed. John Morrill, Paul Slack, and Daniel Woolf (Oxford: Clarendon, 1993), 29–56.

99. [David Clarkson], *The Practical Divinity of the Papists Discovered to be Destructive of Christianity and Men's Souls* (1676), 376–77, quoted in Sampson, "Laxity and Liberty," 84. As Sampson and others demonstrate, "probability" is an important term of art in casuistical doctrine.

100. Hobbes, *Leviathan,* chaps. 29, 35, pp. 168–69, 220; John Sharp, *A Discourse of Conscience* (1684), 225, 226, quoted in Roger D. Lund, "Swift's Sermons, 'Public Conscience,' and the Privatization of Religion," in *The Intersections of the Public and Private Spheres in Early Modern England,* ed. Paula R. Backscheider and Timothy Dykstal (London: Cass, 1996), 168; Charles I, *Eikon Basilike,* 11, quoted in Patricia Crawford, "Public Duty, Conscience, and Women in Early Modern England," in Morrill, Slack, and Woolf, *Public Duty,* 61.

101. These statutes were the Corporation Act (1661), the Act of Uniformity (1662), the Conventicle Act (1664), the Five Mile Act (1665), and the Test Act (1673, reinforced and extended 1678).

102. John Locke, "Essay Concerning Toleration" (wr. c. 1667), in H. R. Fox-Bourne, *The Life of John Locke* (New York: Harper, 1876), 1:189, 192. This "divide and rule" argument was already familiar to participants in the toleration debates. In ignoring such advice, Sir Roger L'Estrange, surveyor of the press during the Restoration period, publicized wide-ranging conspiracy theories that rendered explicit the shared interests of Stuart opponents who might otherwise have remained divided. See McKeon, *Politics and Poetry,* 97 and chap. 2 passim.

103. *Et a Dracone: Or, some Reflections Upon a Discourse Called Omnia a Belo comesta . . .* (1668), 9, 40.

104. Herbert Thorndike, *A Discourse of the Forbearance or the Penalties Which a Due Reformation Requires* (1670), 165–66.

105. Benjamin Ibbot, *The Nature and Extent of the Office of the Civil Magistrate. . . . Consider'd in a Sermon . . .* (1720), 6–7, 8, 12. Cf. John Disney, *A View of Antient Laws against Immorality and Profaneness* (Cambridge, 1729), i: "If Impiety or Vice were to be considered only with regard to their consequences in another World, it might be tolerable to leave it to Mens private Reflexion, and to the care of Divines . . . but since they affect the *public* and *present,* as well as *personal* and *future* Interests of Mankind, 'tis fit the Civil Authority should exert itself, in a way of Coercion to suppress such practices." Quoted in Burtt, *Virtue Transformed,* 51.

106. Thomas Sprat, *The History of the Royal Society of London, for the Improving of Natural Knowledge* (1667), 63; [John Dryden], "To the Reader," prefixed to *The Hind and the Panther* (1687), in *The Works of John Dryden,* vol. 3, *Poems, 1685–1692,* ed. Earl Miner and Vinton A. Dearing (Berkeley and Los Angeles: University of California Press, 1969), 120; John Milton, *Christian Doctrine* (translation of *De Doctrina Christiana,* first published in Latin and English in 1825), bk. 1, chap. 27, in *Complete Prose Works,* vol. 6, *ca. 1658–ca. 1660,*

trans. John Carey, ed. Maurice Kelley (New Haven, CT: Yale University Press, 1973), 531–32. That Dryden's statement came after his conversion from Protestantism to Roman Catholicism is, in the terms of this argument, only momentarily surprising.

107. Edward Wettenhall, *Enter into thy Closet: or, a Method for private Devotion. . . ,* "2nd ed." (1668), 9, 5–6, 7; Oliver Heywood, *Closet-Prayer a Christian Duty . . . Tending to prove that the Worship of God in Secret, is the indispensible duty of all Christians . . .* (1687), 4, 82. My remarks on the devotional closet are indebted to the scholarship of Richard Rambuss, *Closet Devotions* (Durham, NC: Duke University Press, 1998).

108. Elnathan Parr, *Abba Father: or A Plaine And short Direction concerning the framing of private Prayer. . . ,* "5th ed." (1636), 2–3; [Francis Osbourne], *The Private Christians Non Vltra, or, a Plea For the Lay-Man's Interpreting the Scriptures. Written by Philolaoclerus* (Oxford, 1656), 3–4; Samuel Clarke on Mary Gunter in Clarke, *The Lives Of sundry Eminent Persons in this Later Age . . .* (1683), 137 (2nd pagination); Thomas Lye, "Sermon XI," in *A Collection of Farewel-Sermons . . .* (1662), 36, quoted in Wendy Wall, *Staging Domesticity: Household Work and English Identity in Early Modern Drama* (Cambridge: Cambridge University Press, 2002), 186; Heywood, *Closet-Prayer,* A3v.

109. Heywood, *Closet-Prayer,* p. 2; Daniel Featley, *Ancilla Pietatis: Or, the Hand-Maid to Private Devotion . . .* (1633), 6; Parr, *Abba Father,* 4.

110. George Herbert, "Confession," lines 9, 1–6, 17–18, in *George Herbert: The Complete English Poems,* ed. John Tobin (Harmondsworth, UK: Penguin, 1991), 117, 118. On the figurative use of architectural terms to express interiority in Renaissance English poetry see Anne Ferry, *The 'Inward' Language: Sonnets of Wyatt, Sidney, Shakespeare, Donne* (Chicago: University of Chicago Press, 1983), 46–47.

111. See generally Christopher Hill, "The Bawdy Courts," chap. 8 in *Society and Puritanism,* 288–332. Hill (304) paraphrases Perkins, *Workes* (1612), 1:530.

112. Leonard W. Levy, *Treason against God: A History of the Offense of Blasphemy* (New York: Schocken, 1981), 302.

113. *Rex v. Taylor* (1676), Keble 607, 621, quoted in ibid., 313–14.

114. *Arguments Relating to a Restraint upon the Press, Fully and Fairly handled in a Letter to a Bencher, from a Young Gentleman of the Temple* (1712), 35, in *Freedom of the Press: Six Tracts, 1712–1730,* ed. Stephen Parks (New York: Garland, 1974).

115. See Hill, *Society and Puritanism,* 331–32.

116. John Disney, *A Second Essay upon the Execution of the Laws against Immorality and Prophaneness* (1710), 48, quoted in T. C. Curtis and W. A. Speck, "The Societies for the Reformation of Manners: A Case Study in the Theory and Practice of Moral Reform," *Literature and History,* no. 3 (1976): 56.

117. *An Account of the Progress of the Reformation of Manners,* 12th ed. (1704), 7, and Edward Stephens, *The Beginning and Progress of a Needful and Hopeful Reformation in England . . .* (1691), 4, quoted in Dudley W. R. Bahlman, *The Moral Revolution of 1688* (New Haven, CT: Yale University Press, 1957), 31 and 33, respectively; see generally chap. 2.

118. Isaac Sharpe, *Plain English Made Plainer* (1704), 10; Henry Sacheverell, *The Communication of Sin* (1709), 14–15; William Nicholson (archdeacon and bishop of Carlisle), in *Letters on Various Subjects . . . to and from William Nicholson,* ed. John Nichols (1809), 1:153–54; and [Philalethes], *Plain Dealing in Answer to Plain English* (1704), 17, all in Bahlman, *Moral Revolution,* 55, 47, 95, 90, 84. Daniel Defoe, *Reformation of Manners* (1702), lines 87–88, in

Poems on Affairs of State: Augustan Satirical Verse, 1660–1714, vol. 6, *1697–1704*, ed. Frank H. Ellis (New Haven, CT: Yale University Press, 1970), 404. On the semantic complexity of contemporary discriminations between "public" and "private" whoring see below, chap. 4, nn. 78–97.

119. Habermas, *Structural Transformation*, 27.

120. See above, n. 54.

121. Pamela O. Long, "Invention, Authorship, 'Intellectual Property,' and the Origin of Patents: Notes toward a Conceptual History," *Technology and Culture* 32, no. 4 (1991): 870.

122. Margaret C. Jacob, *Living the Enlightenment: Freemasonry and Politics in Eighteenth-Century Europe* (New York: Oxford University Press, 1991), 34, 47. The lodges also self-consciously imitated the domestic institutions of the family, among other things using the categories of familial status and place (21 and passim). Jacob quotes an "early" masonic tract that imagines the rude state of nature ameliorated not by contractual agreement but by the building of houses "for convenience, defence and comfort" (58). The notion of domesticity as an alternative to, but modeled upon, polity is central to one major line of argument of the present study.

123. Anthony J. La Vopa, "Conceiving a Public: Ideas and Society in Eighteenth-Century Europe," *Journal of Modern History* 64 (Mar. 1992): 92.

124. Jacob, *Living*, 53, 42.

125. See Habermas, *Structural Transformation*, 30.

Chapter Two | Publishing the Private

1. [Matthew Tindal], *A Letter to a Member of Parliament, Shewing, that a Restraint [of the] Press Is inconsistent with the Protestant Religion, and dangerous to the Liberties of the Nation* (1698), 27.

2. [John Milton], *Eikonoklastes: in Answer to a Book Entitled Eikon Basilike . . .* (1649), in *The Complete Prose Works of John Milton*, vol. 3, *1648–1649*, ed. Merritt Y. Hughes (New Haven, CT: Yale University Press, 1962), 456 (Milton alludes to Matt. 6:6; see above, chap. 1, n. 107); John Dryden, dedication to *The Spanish Friar* (1681), in *Of Dramatic Poesy and Other Critical Essays*, ed. George Watson (London: Dent, 1962), 1:275; Colley Cibber, *An Apology for the Life of Colley Cibber, Comedian* (1740), 86, quoted in J. Paul Hunter, "The World as Stage and Closet," in *British Theater and Other Arts, 1660–1800*, ed. Shirley Strum Kenney (Washington, DC: Folger Shakespeare Library, 1984), 278–79; Lady Sanspareille in Margaret Cavendish, *Youths Glory, and Deaths Banquet, in Playes . . .* (1662), act 2, sc. 5, pp. 131–32; John Aubrey, *Remaines of Gentilisme and Judaisme*, in *Three Prose Works*, ed. John Buchanan-Brown (Fontwell, Sussex: Centaur, 1972), 445, 289–90 (I owe this last reference to Jason Gieger). On the development of this historiography of nostalgia in the later eighteenth and early nineteenth centuries, especially as it centered on the nurse, see Katie Trumpener, *Bardic Nationalism: The Romantic Novel and the British Empire* (Princeton, NJ: Princeton University Press, 1997), chap. 5. James Mulholland argues that it was the consolidation of print culture that brought the category of oral culture into existence. See "The Sound of Print: Voice in Eighteenth-Century British Poetry" (PhD diss., Rutgers University, 2005).

3. Elinor James, *Mrs. James's Reasons that Printing may not be a Free-Trade . . .* (c. 1695–1702), broadside; Sir Roger L'Estrange, *Considerations and Proposals In Order to the Regula-*

tion of the Press . . . (1663), 1; Daniel Defoe, *Applebee's Journal*, 31 July 1725, quoted in Ian Watt, *The Rise of the Novel: Studies in Defoe, Richardson, and Fielding* (Berkeley and Los Angeles: University of California Press, 1957), 53. My thanks to Paula McDowell for acquainting me with James's work. For a depiction of the labor of printing, see below, fig. 6.7.

4. See esp. Mark Rose, *Authors and Owners: The Invention of Copyright* (Cambridge, MA: Harvard University Press, 1993).

5. Joseph Moxon, *Mechanick Exercises on the Whole Art of Printing* (1684), 192–219, quoted in Adrian Johns, *The Nature of the Book: Print and Knowledge in the Making* (Chicago: University of Chicago Press, 1998), 88.

6. [Andrew Marvell], *The Rehearsal Transpros'd: Or, Animadversions Upon a late Book, Intituled, A Preface Shewing What Grounds there are of Fears and Jealousies of Popery*, 2 pts. (1672–73), ed. D. I. B. Smith (Oxford: Clarendon, 1971), 4–5 (hereafter references are to this edition and appear parenthetically in the text); [Tindal], *Letter*, 10, 11, 12. Marvell's spatial association of unauthorized printing with secret "corners" was already standard in state publications. Cf. a parliamentary ordinance of 1649 complaining of "Presses erected in by-places and corners, out of the Eye of Government" and the Printing Act of 1662 (14 Car. 2, c. 33) on the "secret printing in corners," quoted in Harold Weber, *Paper Bullets: Print and Kingship under Charles II* (Lexington: University of Kentucky Press, 1996), 143 and 152, respectively. As we will see, the spatial secrecy of which printing is capable points in the same direction as the recognition of its radical nonspatiality, the virtuality that Marvell adumbrates in his contrast between the literal meetings of "people" in "grounds" and "fields" and the figurative "meetings of letters."

7. John Dryden, *Religio Laici or A Laymans Faith. A Poem* (1682), line 373, in *The Works of John Dryden*, vol. 2, *Poems, 1681–1684*, ed. H. T. Swedenberg Jr. and Vinton A. Dearing (Berkeley and Los Angeles: University of California Press, 1972) (hereafter cited parenthetically in the text).

8. See above, chap. 1, n. 1.

9. *Arguments Relating to a Restraint upon the Press, Fully and Fairly handled in a Letter to a Bencher, from a Young Gentleman of the Temple* (1712), 36–37, and *An Attempt towards a Coalition of English Protestants . . .* (1715), 21, both reprinted in *Freedom of the Press: Six Tracts, 1712–1730*, ed. Stephen Parks (New York: Garland, 1974).

10. [Anne Dutton], *A Letter to such of the Servants of Christ, who May have any Scruple about the Lawfulness of printing any Thing written by a Woman (1743)*, in *Women in the Eighteenth Century: Constructions of Femininity*, ed. Vivien Jones (London: Routledge, 1990), 158, 159.

11. [Daniel Defoe], preface to *The Storm: Or, a Collection Of the most Remarkable Casualties and Disasters Which happen'd in the Late Dreadful Tempest, both by Sea and Land* (1704), A2r–v (font reversed).

12. Martin Billingsley, *The Pens Excellencie or The Secretaries Delight* (1618), C2v–3r, and William Fulwood, *The Enemy of Idlenesse* ([1568] repr. 1621), 1–2, quoted in Jonathan Goldberg, *Writing Matter: From the Hands of the English Renaissance* (Stanford, CA: Stanford University Press, 1990), 130 and 249, respectively; Henry Coventry, in BL, Add. MSS 25125, fols. 31–33, and Philip de Comminges, both quoted in Alan Marshall, *Intelligence and Espionage in the Reign of Charles II, 1660–1685* (Cambridge: Cambridge University Press, 1994), 81–82; "Mr L'Estraings Proposition concerning Libells, &c.," House of Lords Record Office,

quoted in Harold Love, *The Culture and Commerce of Texts: Scribal Publication in Seventeenth-Century England* (1993; reprint, Amherst: University of Massachusetts Press, 1998), 74. On the lack of privacy ensured by the early postal system, see Janet Todd, "Fatal Fluency: Behn's Fiction and the Restoration Letter," in "Reconsidering the Rise of the Novel," special issue, *Eighteenth-Century Fiction* 12, nos. 2–3 (2000): 426–27.

13. Anthony Ashley Cooper, third Earl of Shaftesbury, *Characteristicks of Men, Manners, Opinions, Times* . . . ([1711] rev. 1732), 1:305–6, ed. Douglas Den Uyl (Indianapolis: Liberty Fund, 2001), 1:188–89 (hereafter references are to this edition, which also records the original pagination marginally; citations refer first to the 1732, and then to the 2001, edition).

14. Thomas Sprat, "An Account of the Life and Writings of Mr. Abraham Cowley: Written to Mr. M. Clifford," prefixed to *The Life and Writings of Abraham Cowley* (1668), in *Critical Essays of the Seventeenth Century*, ed. Joel E. Spingarn, vol. 2, *1650–1685* (1908–9; reprint, Bloomington: Indiana University Press, 1957), 137; Dudley, third Baron North, *A Forest Promiscuous of Several Seasons Productions* (1659), A2r, quoted in Love, *Culture*, 41.

15. See Love, *Culture*, chaps. 2 and 3. Love's persuasive corrective to scholarly exaggeration of print's cultural innovation may nonetheless exaggerate scribal publication's importance in teaching print how to be critical of authority (see ibid., chap. 7).

16. David Zaret, *Origins of Democratic Culture: Printing, Petitions, and the Public Sphere in Early Modern England* (Princeton, NJ: Princeton University Press, 2000), 136; Jonathan Swift, *Thoughts on Various Subjects* (1711), in *The Prose Works of Jonathan Swift*, ed. Herbert Davis, vol. 4, *A Proposal for Correcting the English Tongue[,] Polite Conversation, Etc.* (Oxford: Blackwell, 1957), 489 (I owe this reference to Carl Nelson).

17. Margaret J. M. Ezell, *The Patriarch's Wife: Literary Evidence and the History of the Family* (Chapel Hill: University of North Carolina Press, 1987), 68.

18. The argument is made most fully by David Zaret in his "Religion, Science, and Printing in the Public Spheres in Seventeenth-Century England," in *Habermas and the Public Sphere*, ed. Craig Calhoun (Cambridge, MA: MIT Press, 1992), 216–17; and in Zaret, *Origins*, passim. However historical research influenced by Habermas's thesis continues to provide evidence that might push further back the chronology of the public sphere's emergence. For a good account of "news culture" in pre-civil-war England, see Alastair Bellany, *The Politics of Court Scandal in Early Modern England: News Culture and the Overbury Affair, 1603–1660* (Cambridge: Cambridge University Press, 2002), chap. 2.

19. *Some Short Considerations* (1697), 10, quoted in Joyce O. Appleby, *Economic Thought and Ideology in Seventeenth-Century England* (Princeton, NJ: Princeton University Press, 1978), 269n61.

20. See Lois Potter, *Secret Rites and Secret Writing: Royalist Literature, 1641–1660* (Cambridge: Cambridge University Press, 1989), 4; and Weber, *Paper Bullets*, 5–6. Domestic news was first printed four months after Star Chamber, the state licenser, was abolished in 1641; a year later it was being published by at least sixty-four newsbooks (Potter, *Secret Rites*, 5). Cf. Zaret, *Origins*, 175: "More publications appeared between 1640 and 1660 than in the prior history of printing in England, from about 1485 to 1640"; and J. A. W. Gunn, *Politics and the Public Interest in the Seventeenth Century* (London: Routledge, 1969), 1: "Significant discussion about the public interest begins with the civil war."

21. Richard Atkyns, dedication to *Original and Growth of Printing: Collected Out of History, and the Records of this Kingdome* . . . (1664), B2r (font reversed).

22. Cf. [Gabriel Plattes], *A Description of the Famous Kingdom of Macaria* (1641), quoted in Fredrick S. Siebert, *Freedom of the Press in England, 1476–1776: The Rise and Decline of Government Control* (Urbana: University of Illinois Press, 1952), 192.

23. Long Parliament order of 1643, quoted in Zaret, *Origins*, 143.

24. See Siebert, *Freedom*, 204–7, 279–88, 346–63; and Laurence Hanson, *Government and the Press, 1695–1796* (Oxford: Clarendon, 1936), 2, 73–83. Of Parliament's abrupt adjournment in mid–1677 Marvell wrote: "[T]hat which more amazed them afterwards was, that while none of their own transactions or addresses for the public good are suffered to be printed, but even all written copies of them with the same care as libels suppressed; yet they found [the king's] severe speech published in the next day's news book, to mark them out to their own, and all other nations, as refractory disobedient persons . . . gazetted among runaway servants, lost dogs, strayed horses, and highway robbers." [Andrew Marvell], *An Account of the Growth of Popery, and Arbitrary Government in England . . .* (Amsterdam, 1677), in *The Complete Works of Andrew Marvell*, ed. Alexander B. Grosart (1875; reprint, New York: AMS, 1966), 4:406.

25. Atkyns, *Original*, dedication, C2r, B1v (font reversed), E3v, p. 19. Atkyns claims that printing was introduced into England by one of Gutenberg's workmen, whose first production was directly authorized by Henry VI (see C3r).

26. Atkyns, *Original*, C3v, E1r.

27. Quoted in Johns, *Nature*, 311; see also Rose, *Authors*, 23–24. Johns, *Nature*, chap. 4, places Atkyns's advocacy in the context of ongoing controversy about the sociolegal status of printing.

28. John How, *Some Thoughts on the Present State of Printing and Bookselling* (1709), 4, 6, 11–12.

29. Daniel Defoe, *Essay on the Regulation of the Press* (1704), 6–7, and Sir William Blackstone, in *English Reports*, ed. A. Wood Renton, 178 vols. (London: Stevens, 1900–1932), 96:188, quoted in Rose, *Authors*, 34 and 90–91, respectively.

30. See Siebert, *Freedom*, 74–82, 130.

31. James, *Mrs. James's Reasons*; see also idem, *To the Honourable House of Commons . . .* (c. 1696–98), broadside. On this sequence of events from 1662 to 1710, see Donald Thomas, *A Long Time Burning: The History of Literary Censorship in England* (New York: Praeger, 1969), 33; Siebert, *Freedom*, 249; and Hanson, *Government*, 7–11. For books already in print the period was twenty-one years; for those in manuscript, fourteen years from the date of first publication.

32. See David Saunders and Ian Hunter, "Lessons from the 'Literatory': How to Historicize Authorship," *Critical Inquiry* 17 (Spring 1991): 493, 497; and David Saunders, *Authorship and Copyright* (London: Routledge, 1992), 61–69, 170, 185. Nor should the history of copyright be confused with the history of the idea of intellectual property, which pre-exists both patents and copyrights in medieval attitudes toward craft technique—"the belief that knowledge of craft processes and techniques and the development of technological innovations are forms of property with commercial value that are separate from products or devices." See Pamela O. Long, "Invention, Authorship, 'Intellectual Property,' and the Origin of Patents: Notes toward a Conceptual History," *Technology and Culture* 32, no. 4 (1991): 846.

33. L'Estrange, *Considerations*, 2; *Cobbett's Complete Collection of State Trials . . .*, ed. Thomas B. Howell (London: Hansard, 1809–26), vol. 7, col. 1118, quoted in Weber, *Paper Bullets*,

174. On Twyn see Weber, *Paper Bullets*, 156 and generally chaps. 4–5; see also Johns, *Nature*, 135–36.

34. John Dennis, *The Characters and Conduct of Sir John Edgar, Call'd by Himself Sole Monarch of the Stage in Drury-Lane . . .* (1720), letter 1, in *The Critical Works of John Dennis*, ed. Edward N. Hooker (Baltimore: Johns Hopkins University Press, 1943), 2:191.

35. *Cobbett's Complete Collection of State Trials*, vol. 7, cols. 704–5. Cf. Charles I's apocalyptic vision, above, chap. 1, n. 10.

36. See Dustin Griffin, *Literary Patronage in England, 1650–1800* (Cambridge: Cambridge University Press, 1996), 39–43.

37. Norbert Elias, *Power and Civility*, vol. 2 of *The Civilizing Process* (1939), trans. Edmund Jephcott (New York: Pantheon, 1982), 8; Oliver Goldsmith, *The Citizen of the World* (1760–61), letter 84, in *Collected Works of Oliver Goldsmith*, ed. Arthur Friedman (Oxford: Clarendon, 1966), 2:344; *A Vindication of the Exclusive Right of Authors to their own works . . .* (1762), 38–40.

38. See Griffin, *Literary Patronage*, chap. 10 and passim.

39. On the rule of number or quantity, see "The Epistle Dedicatory, to His Royal Highness Prince Posterity," in [Jonathan Swift], *A Tale of a Tub, To which is added The Battle of the Books and the Mechanical Operation of the Spirit* (1704, 1710), ed. A. C. Guthkelch and D. Nichol Smith, 2nd ed. (Oxford: Clarendon, 1958), 30–38.

40. Anthony Ashley Cooper, third Earl of Shaftesbury, "Advice to an Author," in *Characteristicks*, 1:164; 1:264.

41. See Alexander Pope, *Peri Bathous: or, Martinus Scriblerus his Treatise of the Art of Sinking in Poetry* (1727), ed. Edna L. Steeves (New York: King's Crown, 1952), 85 and chaps. 2, 13, 16.

42. For a good assessment of Pope's relationship to patronage, see Griffin, *Literary Patronage*, chap. 6.

43. James Boswell, *Life of Johnson* (1791), entry dated 1754. ed. R. W. Chapman (Oxford: Oxford University Press, 1980), 185.

44. Ibid., entry dated 8 May 1773, 546.

45. Preface to *The Cases of the Appellants and Respondents in the Cause of Literary Property . . .* (1774), sig. av, in *The Literary Property Debate: Six Tracts, 1764–1774*, ed. Stephen Parks (New York: Garland, 1975), and Justice Joseph Yates, in *Millar v. Taylor*, 20 Apr. 1769, in Renton, *English Reports*, 98:234, quoted in Trevor Ross, "Copyright and the Invention of Tradition," *Eighteenth-Century Studies* 26, no. 1 (1992): 3 and 7, respectively. Ross maintains that "the figure of the common reader first appears in tracts calling for the defeat of perpetual copyright . . ." (16). The previous sentences in this paragraph are indebted to Ross's essay.

46. See Ross, "Copyright."

47. See above, chap. 1, nn. 37–39.

48. Michael McKeon, *The Origins of the English Novel, 1600–1740* (Baltimore: Johns Hopkins University Press, 1987), 123–24.

49. Quoted in Potter, *Secret Rites*, 1–2.

50. On the role of print in disclosing the arcana of tradition, see Elizabeth L. Eisenstein, *The Printing Press as an Agent of Change: Communications and Cultural Transformations in Early-Modern Europe* (Cambridge: Cambridge University Press, 1979), 272–302.

51. See Charles Webster, *From Paracelsus to Newton: Magic and the Making of Modern Science* (Cambridge: Cambridge University Press, 1982), 59–60.

52. William Eamon, *Science and the Secrets of Nature: Books of Secrets in Medieval and Early Modern Culture* (Princeton, NJ: Princeton University Press, 1994), 353, 132. Mary Poovey describes early accounting books in terms that evoke the book of secrets: see *A History of the Modern Fact: Problems of Knowledge in the Sciences of Wealth and Society* (Chicago: University of Chicago Press, 1998), 34. However, this sense of the secret as the technical is also inherent in the idea of the craft secret as a knowledge that is, not intentionally concealed, but knowable only by practicing the craft with one's own hands. See Long, "Invention," 860 and n. 37.

53. The point is made by Eamon, *Science*, 195.

54. Alessio Piemontese, *Secretes*, trans. William Warde (1558), fol. *.ii, quoted in ibid., 142.

55. See Eamon, *Science*, 145.

56. Royal Society Misc. MS 4.72, quoted in ibid., 347. As we will see, the welcoming embrace of the "mean" and the "trivial" has a central relevance to the emergence of domestication and domesticity.

57. Thomas Sprat, *The History of the Royal Society of London, For the Improving of Natural Knowledge* (1667), 71, 74, 75. Sprat's aim in the *History*, which soon became central to the Royal Society at large, was to win for the emergent discipline of "science" a positive visibility and stature in the eyes of the British public. See Larry Stewart, *The Rise of Public Science: Rhetoric, Technology, and Natural Philosophy in Newtonian Britain, 1660–1750* (Cambridge: Cambridge University Press, 1992).

58. See Eamon, *Science*, 330–32. The oath is reproduced from Royal Society of London, Boyle Papers, Commonplace Book 189, fol. 13r, in Steven Shapin, *A Social History of Truth: Civility and Science in Seventeenth-Century England* (Chicago: University of Chicago Press, 1994), 403, 404.

59. John Aubrey, *Aubrey's Brief Lives*, ed. Oliver L. Dick (1949; reprint, Harmondsworth, UK: Penguin, 1972), 305, quoted in Eamon, *Science*, 344.

60. Sprat, *History*, 98–99.

61. Steven Shapin and Simon Schaffer, *Leviathan and the Air-Pump: Hobbes, Boyle, and the Experimental Life* (Princeton, NJ: Princeton University Press, 1985), 60.

62. See McKeon, *Origins*, pt. 1, esp. on the strategy of the "claim to historicity." The idea of virtual witnessing has been thoughtfully applied to painting and narrative by John Bender in "Matters of Fact, Virtual Witnessing, and the Public in Hogarth's Narratives," in *Hogarth: Representing Nature's Machines*, ed. David Bindman, Frédéric Ogée, and Peter Wagner (Manchester: Manchester University Press, 2001), 49–70.

63. Jürgen Habermas, *The Structural Transformation of the Public Sphere: An Inquiry into a Category of Bourgeois Society* (1962), trans. Thomas Burger and Frederick Lawrence (Cambridge, MA: MIT Press, 1989), 36–37, 80, 94 (hereafter cited parenthetically in the text). On explicitness, see also 53, 54, 91, 101, 106–7, 117. On 117–40, Habermas discusses the way in which the new realm of the tacit—the natural law of the market and the universal accessibility of its cultural productions—was in turn made problematic by Hegel, Marx, Mill, and Tocqueville.

64. Dario Castiglione, "Opinion's Metamorphosis: Hume and the Perception of Public Authority," in *Shifting the Boundaries: Transformations of the Languages of Public and Private*

in the Eighteenth Century, ed. Dario Castiglione and Lesley Sharpe (Exeter, UK: University of Exeter Press, 1995), 156.

65. Edmund Burke to Bristol Bell Club, 13 Oct. 1777, in *Burke's Politics: Selected Writings and Speeches of Edmund Burke on Reform, Revolution, and War,* ed. Ross J. S. Hoffman and Paul Levack (New York: Knopf, 1949), 119. Burke writes three years after his election from Bristol.

66. Sir William Coventry (1677) in Anchitel Grey, *Debates of the House of Commons (1667–1694),* 10 vols. (London, 1763), 4:385, quoted in David Ogg, *England in the Reign of Charles II,* 2nd ed. (Oxford: Oxford University Press, 1956), 195. The Privy Council required an oath of secrecy.

67. See Zaret, *Origins,* chap. 3. Zaret applies the idea of "the paradox of innovation"—the development of the new through efforts to continue practicing the old—to the public-sphere activity of the revolutionary years (see p. 21).

68. Zaret, *Origins,* 178; see 177–80. But the rise of public opinion cannot be attributed to print alone: see Tim Harris, "Understanding Popular Politics in Restoration Britain," in *A Nation Transformed: England after the Restoration,* ed. Alan Houston and Steve Pincus (Cambridge: Cambridge University Press, 2001), 125–53.

69. PRO, *Calendar of State Papers, Domestic Series* (1641–43), 170, quoted in Zaret, *Origins,* 211. Cf. Sir Edward Dering, in Robert C. Johnson et al., eds., *Commons Debates, 1628,* vol. 3, *21 Apr.–27 May 1628* (New Haven, CT: Yale University Press, 1977), 578–79. To address the king through publication seemed to royalists a violation of propriety comparable to that criticized by Milton in Charles I—that is, publishing one's prayers: see above, n. 2. (I owe this point to Paula McDowell.)

70. John Rushworth, *Historical Collections,* vol. 4 (1692), 170–72; *The Journal of Sir Simonds D'Ewes,* ed. Wallace Notestein, vol. 1 (New Haven, CT: Yale University Press, 1923), 334–40, quoted in Zaret, *Origins,* 237.

71. *Declaration of Some Proceedings* (1648), 25, quoted in Zaret, *Origins,* 240–41; cf. 254.

72. Rushworth, *Historical Collections,* 4:597, quoted in Zaret, *Origins,* 255. Cf., on the problematic notion of tacit consent, above, chap. 1, n. 33.

73. It is through the petitioning, abhorring, and addressing procedures of this period that the party categories of Whig and Tory are often thought to have coalesced. See Mark Knights, *Politics and Opinion in Crisis, 1678–1681* (Cambridge: Cambridge University Press, 1994), esp. chap. 9 on developments of the year from February 1680 to February 1681. Knights is cautious on the question whether full party organization can be attributed to this period of political activity.

74. See Miles Taylor, "John Bull and the Iconography of Public Opinion in England c. 1712–1929," *Past and Present,* no. 134 (1992): 93–128.

75. On the modern nation as an imagined community, see Benedict Anderson, *Imagined Communities: Reflections on the Origin and Spread of Nationalism* (London: Verso, 1983). On the origins of the figure, see below, chap. 9, n. 2. For the lock-and-key symbolism, see also Andrew Marvell, above, nn. 5–6.

76. See Nancy Fraser, "Rethinking the Public Sphere: A Contribution to the Critique of Actually Existing Democracy," in Calhoun, *Habermas and the Public Sphere,* 109–42.

77. The problem in Habermas studies I am trying to confront is related to the scholarly inflation of civic humanism (see above, chap. 1, n. 71). Surprisingly, Fraser identifies the pub-

lic sphere with "the civic-republican model" (113, 129); cf. Michael Warner, *The Letters of the Republic: Publication and the Public Sphere in Eighteenth-Century America* (Cambridge, MA: Harvard University Press, 1990), chap. 2. For a corrective, see Keith Michael Baker, "Defining the Public Sphere in Eighteenth-Century France: Variations on a Theme by Habermas," in Calhoun, *Habermas and the Public Sphere,* 187. Differences in interpretation may owe in part to differences between the broadly European version of civic humanism and the virtualizing and democratizing turn it takes in the revolutionary American context. In a more recent publication, Warner has treated the category of the oppositional counterpublic with a dialectical acuity that acknowledges its status as a situational extension of, rather than (as in Fraser's essay) a structural alternative to, the way a dominant public itself is formed: see his "Publics and Counterpublics," in *Publics and Counterpublics* (New York: Zone Books, 2002), 118–20.

78. In his famous essay *What Is Enlightenment?* (1784) Immanuel Kant went so far as to define the "public use of reason" as "the use that one makes of reason as a *scholar* before the *reading* public. I call private the use that one is entitled to make of one's reason in a *civil post* or office." Quoted by Roger Chartier in his editorial introduction to *Passions of the Renaissance,* vol. 3 of *A History of Private Life,* ed. Philippe Ariès and Georges Duby, trans. Arthur Goldhammer (Cambridge, MA: Harvard University Press, 1989), 17.

79. Critics have pointed out what might be seen as a version of this fiction within the literary public sphere itself. First, the development of eighteenth-century print culture entailed the unprecedented *participation* of women writers and readers. But second, print culture's *representation* of women's activity—even within print, let alone in politics or business—was far more circumscribed than its own example would suggest. See esp. Kathryn Shevelow, *Women and Print Culture: The Constitution of Femininity in the Early Periodical* (New York: Routledge, 1989), 1–2, 14.

80. See Leonore Davidoff and Catherine Hall, *Family Fortunes: Men and Women of the English Middle Class, 1780–1850* (Chicago: University of Chicago Press, 1987); Susan Staves, *Married Women's Separate Property in England, 1660–1833* (Cambridge, MA: Harvard University Press, 1990); Amy Louise Erickson, *Women and Property in Early Modern England* (London: Routledge, 1993); Patricia Crawford, "Public Duty, Conscience, and Women in Early Modern England," in *Public Duty and Private Conscience in Seventeenth-Century England: Essays Presented to G. E. Aylmer,* ed. John Morrill, Paul Slack, and Daniel Woolf (Oxford: Clarendon, 1993), 57–76; Amanda Vickery, *The Gentleman's Daughter: Women's Lives in Georgian England* (New Haven, CT: Yale University Press, 1998); and Paula McDowell, *The Women of Grub Street: Press, Politics, and Gender in the Literary Marketplace, 1678–1730* (Oxford: Clarendon, 1998).

81. Habermas's study has been most controversial in postulating not the emergence but the dissolution of the public sphere toward the end of the nineteenth century under the force of advanced commodity consumption: "The public sphere in the world of letters was replaced by the pseudo-public or sham-private world of culture consumption" (*Structural Transformation,* 160). The transformation brings to a head tendencies toward both the conflation and the polarization of the public and the private, and it marks the historical moment at which quantitative increment—the elaborating extension of the dialectic between dichotomy and continuity—becomes qualitative change. But this dialectic of tendencies is also central to the emergence of the public sphere, and it is unclear why the particular form it

takes at this later stage of development should be conceived as a qualitative and decisive rather than as a quantitative and ongoing transformation.

82. See the thoughtful discussion of Gordon Schochet, who ultimately takes these issues in a direction different from my own, in "Vices, Benefits, and Civil Society: Mandeville, Habermas, and the Distinction between Public and Private," in *The Intersections of the Public and Private Spheres in Early Modern England*, ed. Paula R. Backscheider and Timothy Dykstal (London: Cass, 1996), 261–62.

83. See McKeon, *Origins*, chap. 4, esp. 159–69.

84. Fraser, "Rethinking the Public Sphere," 113, 116.

85. John Earle, *The Autograph Manuscript of Microcosmographie* (Leeds, UK: Scolar Press, 1966), 143, quoted in Love, *Culture*, 193; Love, *Culture*, 194. Love may exaggerate the singularity of Paul's walking as the London center of information exchange before the Restoration. See Bellany, *Politics*, 80–83, on the importance of other places as well, notably the Old and New Exchanges and the law courts. According to Habermas, *Structural Transformation*, 32–36, differences between national cultures made the clientele of both the coffeehouse and the *salon* variable as to both sex and social status. With Earle on oral news compare one of Ben Jonson's characters on the punctual indeterminacy of manuscript newsletters: "I would have no newes printed; for when they are printed they leave to bee newes; while they are written, though they be false, they remaine newes still." *Newes from the New World Discover'd in the Moone* (1620), in *Ben Jonson*, ed. C. H. Herford, Percy Simpson, and Evelyn Simpson, 11 vols. (Oxford: Oxford University Press, 1925–52), 6:514–15, quoted in Love, *Culture*, 10.

86. *A Proclamation to Restrain the Spreading of False News, and Licentious Talking of Matters of State and Government* (12 June 1672); *A Proclamation for the Suppression of Coffee-Houses* (20 Dec. 1675); and *An Additional Proclamation Concerning Coffee-Houses* (8 Jan. 1676), nos. 3570, 3622, and 3625 in *A Bibliography of Royal Proclamations of the Tudor and Stuart Sovereigns and of Others Published under Authority, 1485–1714*, ed. Robert Steele, vol. 1, *England and Wales* (Oxford: Clarendon, 1910), 431, 439. In private Charles referred to coffee-house keepers as "sordid mechanick wretches who, to gain a little money had the impudence and folly to prostitute affairs of state indifferently to the views of those that frequent such houses." H. Thynne to T. Thynne, 19 Sept. 1677, in BL, Add. MS 32095, fol. 38, quoted in Ogg, *England*, 102.

87. Henry Ball to Joseph Williamson, 29 Aug. 1673, in *Letters Addressed from London to Sir Joseph Williamson*, ed. W. D. Christie (London, 1874), 1:194, quoted in Steve Pincus, "'Coffee Politicians Does Create': Coffeehouses and Restoration Political Culture," *Journal of Modern History* 67 (Dec. 1995): 828; [Richard Leigh], *The Transposer Rehears'd: or the Fifth Act of Mr. Bayes's Play . . .* (Oxford, 1673), 36.

88. See Pincus, "Coffee Politicians," 815–16; and Knights, *Politics and Opinion*, 173.

89. *Snotty Nose Gazette*, no. 1 (24 Nov. 1679), quoted in Knights, *Politics and Opinion*, 172.

90. The following paragraph is taken from Michael McKeon "What Were Poems on Affairs of State?" *1650–1850: Ideas, Aesthetics, and Inquiries in the Early Modern Era* 4 (1997): 372–74.

91. [Nahum Tate], "Old England" (1682), lines 23–24, in *Poems on Affairs of State: Augustan Satirical Verse, 1660–1714*, vol. 3, *1682–1685*, ed. Howard H. Schless (New Haven, CT: Yale University Press, 1968), 186; [Henry Mildmay], *The Progress* (1688), lines 1–10, in ibid., vol. 4,

1685–1688, ed. Galbraith M. Crump (New Haven, CT: Yale University Press, 1968), 330–31; *The Mischiefs and Unreasonableness* (1681), 40, quoted in Knights, *Politics and Opinion*, 154. Mildmay alludes to the opening lines of Dryden's *Absalom and Achitophel* (1681).

92. Henry Fielding, *The Life of Mr. Jonathan Wild the Great* (1743), bk. 2, chap. 5, ed. David Nokes (Harmondsworth, UK: Penguin, 1986), 102.

93. *Tatler*, no. 1 (12 Apr. 1709), in *The Tatler*, ed. Donald F. Bond, 3 vols. (Oxford: Clarendon, 1987) (hereafter references are to this edition and appear parenthetically in the text).

94. Joseph Addison, *Spectator*, no. 1 (1 Mar. 1711), in *The Spectator*, ed. Donald F. Bond, 5 vols. (Oxford: Clarendon, 1965) (hereafter references are to this edition and appear parenthetically in the text).

95. See above, n. 20.

96. The dialectical richness of the idea of the domestic is especially evident in this passage, which evokes notions of the private citizen (as opposed to the academic professional), the ethical subject (as opposed to the political subject), and the national (as opposed to the international) newsmonger.

97. Samuel Johnson, *Rambler*, no. 23 (5 June 1750), in *The Yale Edition of the Works of Samuel Johnson*, vol. 3, *The Rambler*, ed. W. J. Bate and Albrecht B. Strauss (New Haven, CT: Yale University Press, 1969), 125–30. For Johnson on the quantitative criteria by which the public passes the last sentence on literary claims see below, chap. 7, nn. 105–7.

98. Shaftesbury, "Miscellaneous Reflections," in *Characteristicks*, 3:14. On Steele and Addison's epistolary policies, see Bond, *Spectator*, 1:xxxvi–xliii; Richmond P. Bond, *The Tatler: The Making of a Literary Journal* (Cambridge, MA: Harvard University Press, 1971), 134–42. See also the thoughtful discussions in Shevelow, *Women and Print Culture*; and Michael G. Ketcham, *Transparent Designs: Reading, Performance, and Form in the Spectator Papers* (Athens: University of Georgia Press, 1985).

99. *Spectator*, no. 457 (14 Aug. 1712). On the hybrid newsletters, see Stanley Morison, *Ichabod Dawks and his News-Letter, with an Account of ther Dawks Family of Booksellers and Stationers, 1653–1731* (Cambridge: Cambridge University Press, 1931). Love, *Culture*, 11, explains that Dawks cast his script typeface in 1696, when the increased circulation of his manuscript newsletter made moving to print unavoidable. The case of *Pope v. Curll* (1741) undertook to decide whether familiar letters were legally "private" or "public," that is, whether they were protected under the 1710 Copyright Act as the private property of the author. Lord Chancellor Hardwicke ruled that Pope owned the letters he had written but not those he had received. See Rose, *Authors*, 59–66.

100. Francis Kirkman, *The Unlucky Citizen Experimentally Described in the Various Misfortunes Of an Unlucky Londoner . . .* (1673), 181–82. In part 2 of *Don Quixote* (1616) the public existence of part 1 leads Sancho Panza to appreciate the attributive powers of print. The duchess wonders whether his master is the same man about whom there is a history in print. . . ." "The very same," says Sancho, telling her that he was the squire she had read about, "if I was not chang'd in my Cradle; I mean, chang'd in the Press." Miguel de Cervantes Saavedra, *Don Quixote*, pt. 2, chap. 30, trans. Peter Motteux (1712), rev. John Ozell (New York: Modern Library, 1930), 639. In alluding to the family romance plot of the changeling Cervantes puns on "cradle," also an instrument of engraving (*OED*).

101. See above, chap. 1, nn. 124–25.

102. In *Tatler*, no. 144 (11 Mar. 1710), Bickerstaff observes that a general extravagance in

equipage "must necessarily get Footing where we have no Sumptuary Laws, and where every Man may be dressed, attended, and carried in what Manner he pleases . . . ." Others knew, however, that even sumptuary laws were an explicitly legalistic intrusion of the state into a formerly tacit politico-social practice. See McKeon, *Origins*, 151.

103. Daniel Defoe, *Conjugal Lewdness; or, Matrimonial Whoredom* (1727), 362; Jonathan Swift, *Examiner*, no. 38 (26 Apr. 1711), in Swift, *Prose Works*, vol. 3, *The Examiner and Other Pieces Written in 1710–11* (Oxford: Blackwell, 1940), 141; Alexander Pope, "A Letter to the Publisher, Occasioned by the present Edition of the Dunciad," in *The Dunciad Variorum* (1728–29), in *The Dunciad*, ed. James Sutherland, vol. 5 of the Twickenham Edition of the Poems of Alexander Pope (New York: Oxford University Press, 1943), 14; Henry Fielding, *Champion* (1741), 1:112 (22 Dec. 1739). In The *Poetaster* (1602) Ben Jonson had depicted satire in a comparably complicated relation to the state and its legal system. See M. Lindsay Kaplan, *The Culture of Slander in Early Modern England* (Cambridge: Cambridge University Press, 1997), chap. 3. The *locus classicus* for this sort of argument is Horace.

104. Warner, *Letters of the Republic*, is particularly attentive to the process of depersonalization entailed in printedness.

105. L'Estrange, *Considerations*, 8.

106. John Milton, *Areopagitica* (1644), ed. Ernest Sirluck, in *The Complete Prose Works of John Milton*, vol. 2, *1643–1648*, ed. Ernest Sirluck (New Haven, CT: Yale University Press, 1959), 720; Jonathan Swift, "The Bookseller to the Reader," prefixed to *A Full and True Account of the Battel Fought last Friday, Between the Antient and the Modern Books in St. James's Library* (1704), in *A Tale of a Tub*, 214; [Jonathan Swift], *Gulliver's Travels* (1726), vol. 11 of Swift, *Prose Works* (Oxford: Blackwell, 1941), xxxiii (on the addition of the letter in 1735, see Harold Williams's introduction, xxiv–xxviii).

107. *The First Satire of the Second Book of Horace* (1733), lines 51–59, in *Imitations of Horace*, ed. John Butt, vol. 4 of the Twickenham Edition of the Poems of Alexander Pope, 2nd ed. (London: Methuen, 1953), 9–11.

108. John Robinson, *New Essays or Observations Divine and Morall* (1628), 135, 137 (I owe this reference to Kimberly Latta); Lord Auchinleck to James Boswell, 30 May 1763, in *Boswell's London Journal, 1762–1763*, ed. Frederick A. Pottle (New York: McGraw-Hill, 1950), app. 2, p. 338; *Diary and Letters of Madame D'Arblay (1778–1840)*, ed. Charlotte Barrett, notes by Austin Dobson (London: Macmillan, 1904), 2:320–21.

109. Using Marvell's figure, Colley Cibber argues that the toxicity of libelous "poisons" that are diffused among an actual, stage "public" is nonetheless greater than that of libels that are circulated through the virtual public sphere of print, where the greater size of the audience is counterbalanced by the separation of its members from each other: "[T]he *quiet* Reader of the same ingenious Matter, can only like for *himself*; and the Poison has a much slower Operation, upon the Body of a People, when it is so retail'd out, than when sold to a full Audience by wholesale." *Apology*, 160, quoted in Hunter, "World as Stage," 278.

110. Both activities evoke the danger of sea travel; and it may be significant that Grotian natural-law theory was an outgrowth of efforts to adjudicate the freedom of the seas, an ostensibly public realm only obscurely and ineffectively subordinated to the positive law of princes. Cf. Hugo Grotius, *Mare Liberum* (1609); Marvell refers to this Grotian doctrine in *The Character of Holland* (1665), line 26. Cf. the capacity of the international book trade to evade national restraints on printing. Of course, "piracy" was the figure contemporaries ap-

plied to unauthorized publication, perhaps because print, like sea travel, was difficult to police; Marvell here extends the term to the "theft" of reputation entailed in printed invective. On the importance of piracy in early modern print culture, see Johns, *Nature,* index, s.v. "piracy."

111. On the perdurability of this maxim in English literature preceding and including that of the Restoration, see J. Douglas Canfield, *Word as Bond in English Literature from the Middle Ages to the Restoration* (Philadelphia: University of Pennsylvania Press, 1989).

112. Samuel Johnson observed the juridical confirmation of this experiential process in the institution of the public domain: see above, n. 44.

113. [Marvell], *Account of the Growth of Popery.*

114. See Hanson, *Government,* 17; and C. R. Kropf, "Libel and Satire in the Eighteenth Century," *Eighteenth-Century Studies* 8, no. 2 (1974–75): 155. "Libel" had to be "published" but not necessarily printed. "The Question of Libells," wrote L'Estrange, "extends it selfe (I conceive) to manuscripts, as well as Prints; as beeing the more mischievous of the Two" because circulated with impunity. "Mr L'Estraings Proposition," quoted in Love, *Culture,* 74. Much of this libelous manuscript circulation owed to the labors of Robert Julian, "Secretary to the Muses"; on Julian as a scribal publisher, see Love, *Culture,* 253–59. Kaplan, *Culture,* 12, says that the common-law courts began to distinguish consistently between written and spoken defamation as "libel" and "slander" in 1660.

115. *Rehearsal* 1, no. 191 (15 Mar. 1707), quoted in Hanson, *Government,* 2.

116. [Thomas Gordon], *Cato's Letters,* no. 32 (10 June 1721), in John Trenchard and Thomas Gordon, *Cato's Letters: or, Essays on Liberty, Civil and Religious, and Other Important Subjects* (originally published in the *London Journal,* 1720–23), ed. Ronald Hamowy (Indianapolis: Liberty Fund, 1995), 1:231, 229. On the uncertainty, see Hanson, *Government,* 17–18. Cf. [William Arnall], *The Case of Opposition Stated, Between the Craftsman and the People* (1731), 39; and Saunders and Hunter, "Lessons," 490. On the idea of libel against the people, see below, chap. 6, nn. 93–98, on Curll's case and the development of the law of obscene libel.

117. See Kropf, "Libel," 162–63. The opinion was that of Justice Matthew Hale in *R. v. Lake* (1670).

118. The appendix to the 2nd edition became a preface to the 3rd: [Mary Astell], *Reflections Upon Marriage* (1700), 3rd ed. (1706), in *The First English Feminist: Reflections Upon Marriage and Other Writings by Mary Astell,* ed. Bridget Hill (Aldershot, Hants.: Gower, 1986), 70; on her discovery of male *Arcana Imperii,* see also p. 131. Astell compares the familial subjection of women to men not only to that of political subjects to their absolute sovereign but also (by virtue of their enforced ignorance of texts, especially scripture) to that of ecclesiastical subjects to the absolute church (see 74).

119. Anne Finch, Countess of Winchilsea, "To Mr. F[inch] Now Earl of W[inchilsea] *Who going abroad, had desired Ardelia to write some Verses upon whatever Subject she thought fit, against his Return in the Evening; Written in the year 1689,*" in *Selected Poems of Anne Finch Countess of Winchilsea,* ed. Katharine M. Rogers (New York: Ungar, 1979), 28–31 (hereafter references are to this edition and appear parenthetically in the text).

120. Finch kept most of her poetry "secret"—that is, unprinted—until 1713. In "The Petition for an Absolute Retreat" (ibid., 59–68) she alludes to James II's deposal: "Back reflecting let me say, / So the sad *Ardelia* lay; / Blasted by a Storm of Fate, / Felt thro' all the *British*

State; / Fall'n, neglected, lost, forgot, / Dark Oblivion all her Lot . . ." (lines 158–63). "Companionate marriage" is a phrase made familiar by Lawrence Stone in *The Family, Sex, and Marriage in England, 1500–1800* (London: Harper, 1977).

121. Jonathan Swift, *Journal to Stella,* ed. Harold Williams (Oxford: Clarendon, 1948), letters 6 (10 Oct. 1710) and 17 (24 Feb. 1711), 1:53, 56, 59–60, 203, 208–9. Swift knew beforehand of the publication of his *Miscellanies* and was the author of most of the *Examiner* papers. Secret codes and ciphers were in widespread use not only by potential state libelers but also by those who kept secret diaries for devotional or other purposes. See Marshall, *Intelligence and Espionage,* 92; and Anthony Fletcher, *Gender, Sex, and Subordination in England, 1500–1800* (New Haven, CT: Yale University Press, 1995), 354. In the domestic sphere such practices might appear to put the husband in the role of the state. Of his wife's spiritual diary S. Bury wrote: "[H]er accounts . . . cannot be recovered by me, nor I believe, by any other, because of many peculiar characters and Abbreviations of her own." *An Account of the Life and Death of Mrs. Elizabeth Bury* (Bristol, 1720), 9–10, quoted in Sara H. Mendelson, "Stuart Women's Diaries and Occasional Memoirs," in *Women in English Society, 1500–1800,* ed. Mary Prior (London: Methuen, 1985), 183.

122. See Swift, *Journal to Stella,* 1:203, 209, 52–53. By the same token, Swift's sense of his difference from the great men he courts can give his accounts of them an ambience of homosociality whose erotic volatility is very different from that of the often infantilized sexuality of his intimate addresses to the women (see 1:5, 59, 208). Swift's sexuality represents one partial adaptation to the emergent modern view that sexual desire is normatively based on the perception of difference. See below, chap. 6, nn. 4–16. In the present context his ambivalence regarding state ministers evokes the parodic doubleness (part imitation, part critique) I have associated with the public sphere.

123. Jonathan Swift, *Examiner,* no. 26 (1 Feb. 1711), in Swift, *Prose Works,* vol. 3, *The Examiner and Other Pieces Written in 1710–11* (Oxford: Blackwell, 1940), 75. Cf. Elinor James on those who "go into holes and corners to Print Treason": *Mrs. James's Application To the Honourable the Commons Assembled in Parliament, On the behalf of the Printers* (c. 1695), broadside.

124. On the Stamp Act of 1712, see Siebert, *Freedom,* 306–18. The strategy of the Stamp Act was almost as old as printing itself: cf. Henry VIII's 1546 proclamation "Prohibiting Heretical Books; Requiring Printer to Identify Himself, Author of Book, and Date of Publication" (38 Hen. 8), proclamation 272, in *Tudor Royal Proclamations,* ed. Paul L. Hughes and James F. Larkin (New Haven: Yale University Press, 1964), 1:373–76.

125. *The Printers Proposal for a regulation of the press* (1712), quoted in Siebert, *Freedom,* 308n11; *The Thoughts of a Tory Author, Concerning the Press . . .* (1712), 2, 22, in Parks, *Freedom of the Press.*

126. *Arguments Relating,* 13, 26, and *Essay for the Press* (1712), 7, both in Parks, *Freedom of the Press.*

127. Dennis, *Characters and Conduct,* letter 3, in *Critical Works,* 2:201; Pope, "Martinus Scriblerus, of the Poem," in *Dunciad Variorum,* in *The Dunciad,* 49. Among the "Libels which have pass'd for Satires" Dennis includes Dryden's *Mac Flecknoe, Absalom and Achitophel, The Medall,* and Garth's *The Dispensary.*

128. See *Tatler,* no. 92 (10 Nov. 1709); Jonathan Swift, *The Importance of the Guardian Considered . . .* (1713), in *Prose Works,* vol. 8, *Political Tracts, 1713–1719,* ed. Herbert Davis and

Irwin Ehrenpreis (Oxford: Blackwell, 1953), 14–15; Hanson, *Government*, 25; *The Doctrine of Innuendo's Discuss'd: or the Liberty of the Press maintain'd . . .* (1731), 6; and *State Law: or, The Doctrine of Libels, Discussed and Examined* (c. 1730), 13, and *Arguments Relating*, 27, both in Parks, *Freedom of the Press*. See generally Hanson, *Government*, 23–28.

129. Addison promised "that in order to outshine all this Modern Race of *Syncopists,* and thoroughly content my *English* Readers, I intend shortly to publish a SPECTATOR that shall not have a single Vowel in it." In the following number (16 July 1714) Mr. Spectator imagines himself at a coffeehouse where "an angry Politician" fulminates against the scandalousness of the previous number.

130. *Doctrine of Innuendo's Discuss'd*, 6, 11; [Philip, Duke of Wharton], *True Briton*, no. 65 (13 Jan. 1725), 552.

131. Hanson, *Government*, 24, citing opinions of 1729 and 1722, respectively. See generally Francis L. Holt, *The Law of Libel* (New York: Gould, 1818), bk. 2, chap. 13, "On the Construction and Certainty of Libel."

132. Recent criticism has variously argued the role of the law in determining the early modern emergence of "literature." See Lennard J. Davis, *Factual Fictions: The Origins of the English Novel* (New York: Columbia University Press, 1983); Annabel Patterson, *Censorship and Interpretation: The Conditions of Writing and Reading in Early Modern England* (Madison: University of Wisconsin Press, 1984); and Catherine Gallagher, *Nobody's Story: The Vanishing Acts of Women Writers in the Marketplace, 1670–1820* (Berkeley and Los Angeles: University of California Press, 1994).

133. [Thomas Shadwell], *The Medal of John Bayes* (1682), lines 7–11, in *Poems on Affairs of State*, 3:81; John Dryden, *A Discourse concerning the Original and Progress of Satire* (1693), in *Of Dramatic Poesy*, 2:126; dedication "To all the Lovers of Wit and Poetry," in *Poems on Affairs of State: from Oliver Cromwell, To this present time* (1698), A8r; [Steele], *Tatler*, no. 92 (10 Nov. 1709); [Addison], *Spectator*, no. 451 (7 Aug. 1712); [Daniel Defoe], *The Family Instructor* (1715), 191; Swift to Pope, 29 Sept. 1725, in *The Correspondence of Jonathan Swift*, ed. Harold Williams (Oxford: Clarendon, 1963), 3:102, 103. Swift suspected that the force of satire was inversely proportional to its generality, which allowed particular readers to see it as having reference to other people. See the prefaces to *A Tale of a Tub* and *The Battel of the Books* in [Swift], *A Tale of a Tub*, 51, 215. But Congreve thought generality might be the key to pedagogy; see his epilogue to *The Way of the World* (1700), lines 16–24. For these passages in Swift, *Battle of the Books*, and Congreve, see below, chap. 14, n. 5, and chap. 13, n. 4.

134. Alexander Pope, advertisement to *Dunciad Variorum*, in *The Dunciad*, 8 (font reversed); see also "Appendix I, The Publisher to the Reader," 201–6 (cf. Pope to Burlington, Jan. 1732, and Pope to Arbuthnot, 2 Aug. 1734, in *The Correspondence of Alexander Pope*, ed. George Sherburn [Oxford: Clarendon, 1956], 3:266, 423); Alexander Pope, advertisement to *The Satires and Epistles of Horace Imitated* (1733) and advertisement to *Epistle to Dr. Arbuthnot* (1735) (font reversed), in Butt, *Imitations of Horace*, 3 and 95 (font reversed), respectively. For Defoe's phrase, see above, n. 11.

135. [Henry Fielding], *Joseph Andrews* (1742), bk. 3, chap. 1, ed. Martin C. Battestin (Middletown, CT: Wesleyan University Press, 1967), 189.

136. "The Trial of Algernon Sidney, at the King's-Bench, for High Treason," in *Cobbett's Complete Collection of State Trials*, vol. 9, cols. 839, 868, 889, quoted in Weber, *Paper Bullets*, 211–13; *A New Song for the Times, 1683,* in *Poems on Affairs of State: Augustan Satirical Verse,*

1660–1714, vol. 1, *1660–1678*, ed. George deF. Lord (New Haven, CT: Yale University Press, 1963), xxxvii. On the separation of thought, speech, and action, see above, chap. 1, n. 106.

137. Jeremy Collier, *A Second Defence of the Short View of the Prophaneness and Immorality of the English Stage* (1700), 104; idem, *A Defence of the Short View of the Prophaneness and Immorality of the English Stage* (1699), 10, quoted in Aubrey Williams, *An Approach to Congreve* (New Haven, CT: Yale University Press, 1979), 61. Collier's view that the publication of vicious examples that were concrete but not actual amounted to something like "public libel" was vindicated by passage of the law of obscene libel in 1728. See below, chap. 6, nn. 93–98.

138. See Michael McKeon, "Prose Fiction: Great Britain," in *The Cambridge History of Literary Criticism,* ed. H. B. Nisbet and Claude Rawson, vol. 4, *The Eighteenth Century* (Cambridge: Cambridge University Press, 1997), 238–63.

139. This opportunity was memorably seized not only by Fielding in *Joseph Andrews* but also a century earlier by the authors of the Grand Remonstrance of 1641, which "talk[ed] of the King as of a third Person." See above, chap. 1, n. 9.

140. [Swift], *Tale of a Tub,* in *A Tale of a Tub,* 7, 8.

141. Collier, *Defence,* 108, 10–11; William Congreve, *Amendments of Mr. Collier's False and Imperfect Citations, &c.* (1698), 9; and James Drake, *The Antient and Modern Stages Survey'd* (1700), 222, 327–28, all quoted in Williams, *Approach,* 78.

142. John Dryden, *Discourse concerning Satire,* in *Of Dramatic Poesy,* 2:131–32.

143. See above, n. 13.

144. See *Characteristicks,* 3:254–57; 3:156–58, where Shaftesbury may be alluding to Collier when he speaks of a writer with whose views on "our *English* STAGE," although those of a "rigid Moralist," he substantially agrees.

145. See the introduction, above. For a relevant effort to assess the similarities and differences between the Greek and the European Enlightenment, see McKeon, *Origins,* 28–32, 134–40.

146. John Locke, *An Essay concerning Human Understanding* (1690), bk. 2, chap. 1, secs. 4, 8 ed. Peter H. Nidditch (Oxford: Clarendon, 1979), pp. 105, 107.

147. Shaftesbury's raillery—his "seeming to be very different from what he really is"—can of course be found everywhere; for example, in the way he toys with the dialectical conundrum that authorial privacy contains a public (i.e., a reflexively readerly) component. Thus his domestic figuration of mental interiority as "home" invites a customary, patriarchalist reading of the mental faculties: "Every Man . . . must of necessity hold his Fancys under some kind of Discipline and Management. . . . The Question therefore is the same here, as in *a Family,* or *Houshold,* when 'tis ask'd, '*Who rules?* or *Who is Master?*'" (*Characteristicks,* 1:323; 1:199). But in Shaftesbury's post-Lockean hands the stern application of patriarchalist analogy is amusingly unsettling, since the internalization of focus, by analogizing the mind ("here") to the state, leaves the family to represent, not the private domain of the small—which customarily confirms the chain of command in the great—but the public domain of the great itself.

148. On these matters see above, chap. 1, nn. 28–30, 73–75.

149. See Charles Taylor, "Modern Social Imaginaries," *Public Culture* 14, no. 1 (2002): 91–124; Benjamin Lee and Edward LiPuma, "Cultures of Circulation: The Imaginations of Modernity," ibid., 191–213; Charles Taylor, *Modern Social Imaginaries* (Durham, NC: Duke University Press, 2004); and Warner, "Publics and Counterpublics," 65–124.

150. See Anderson, *Imagined Communities.*

151. See esp. Lee and LiPuma, "Cultures of Circulation."

152. See Allan Silver, "'Two Different Sorts of Commerce'—Friendship and Strangership in Civil Society," in *Public and Private in Thought and Practice: Perspectives on a Grand Dichotomy,* ed. Jeff Weintraub and Krishan Kumar (Chicago: University of Chicago Press, 1997), 48–49, 52–54; Georg Simmel, *The Philosophy of Money* (1907), ed. David Frisby, trans. Tom Bottomore and David Frisby, 2nd rev. ed. (London: Routledge, 1990), 292–303; and Warner, "Publics and Counterpublics," 74–76.

153. See Charles Taylor's suggestive discussion in *Modern Social Imaginaries,* 93–99.

154. Warner has made this application to the (modern) public in "Publics and Counterpublics."

155. See Charles Taylor, *Modern Social Imaginaries,* chap. 2.

156. Benjamin Lee and Edward LiPuma observe that in this respect the existence of the market has a distinct predication in that its impersonality tends to entail an understanding of its existence as, however willed by its constituent members, nonetheless standing over against their individual agency as the nation-state and the public sphere do not. "Cultures of Circulation," 196.

157. Anderson, *Imagined Communities,* 23, 40, 27.

158. This is a topic that will arise intermittently in the following chapters but concertedly in chap. 7.

159. Cf. McKeon, *Origins,* 118–28; and Michael McKeon, ed., *Theory of the Novel: A Historical Approach* (Baltimore: Johns Hopkins University Press, 2000), pt. 9. Contrast Gallagher, *Nobody's Story,* xv–xviii and passim. Although Gallagher claims here that before the mid-eighteenth century the category of the fictional had no existence in European culture, her argument suggests that what she means is rather that the category had not been explicitly theorized. (I think it had been explicitly theorized by Aristotle, but with no lasting effect; and I cannot see any basis for Gallagher's view of Aristotle and his Renaissance followers as "linking the fictional to the heroic" and thereby failing to theorize fiction as such—that is, as a formal mode independent of particular contents.) In Gallagher's understanding, the evidence that the category of fiction emerged at this time lies in the newfound willingness of authors to proclaim their characters to be "nobody," that is, to have no actual existence. In my view, this understanding is traditional, one of the assumptions that is customary in the tacit practice of story telling and hearing and made explicit only when challenged. What was new in the later seventeenth and eighteenth centuries was a sensitivity to the truth claims of empirical epistemology so intense that it fostered the growth of powerful naive literalisms (in narrative and poetry, what I call the claim to historicity; in drama, the doctrine of the unities of time and place) in reaction to which critics like Dryden, Addison, Fielding, and Johnson began to elaborate the modern view of fiction, which differs from the traditional one not in kind but in the explicitness and precision with which it seeks to describe the psychological state of "believing" a fiction, that is, "believing in" a plausible character without believing his or her actual existence. The strenuousness with which the modern view of fiction came to be articulated against the naive literalisms generated by empirical epistemology is responsible for the optical illusion that this was the first time that the nonexistence of fictional characters was credited. What is new in our period is not fiction as such but the realist and aesthetic formulation of fiction. I will return to these matters below, in chap. 7.

My present inquiry into the modern relation of the public and the private, understood as an inquiry into the relationship between the general and the particular, overlaps in significant ways with Mary Poovey's *History of the Modern Fact.* One major difference between her study and mine is that she approaches the general-particular relationship through a relatively focused history of mathematical quantification, whereas I treat that relationship in broader terms, as a function of more varied epistemological developments.

Chapter Three | From State as Family to Family as State

1. Jürgen Habermas, *The Structural Transformation of the Public Sphere: An Inquiry into a Category of Bourgeois Society* (1962), trans. Thomas Burger and Frederick Lawrence (Cambridge, MA: MIT Press, 1989), 28–31 (hereafter references are to this edition and appear parenthetically in the text).

2. Richard Greenham, *Workes* (1612), 12, quoted in Christopher Hill, *Society and Puritanism in Pre-Revolutionary England* (London: Panther, 1969), 447; John Hayward, *An Answer to the First Part of a Certaine Conference, Concerning Succession* (1603), B4 (I owe this reference to Sue Starke); John Dod and Robert Cleaver, *A Godly Forme of Household Government: for the ordering of private families, according to the direction of God's Word* (1612), A8v, quoted in Susan Dwyer Amussen, *An Ordered Society: Gender and Class in Early Modern England* (Oxford: Blackwell, 1988), 37–38; Richard Hooker, *Of the Laws of Ecclesiastical Polity* (1593–1661), ed. George Edelen et al. (Cambridge, MA: Harvard University Press, Belknap Press, 1977–82), 1:99, quoted in Constance Jordan, "The Household and the State: Transformations in the Representation of an Analogy from Aristotle to James I," *Modern Language Quarterly* 54, no. 3 (1993): 323–24. For Hooker's basic insight, see Aristotle, *Politics,* 1253a–b. In 1658 Edward Gee wrote that since the "publique state or Common–wealth" was established "as a distinct society from that of a household, . . . the paternal power hath been (and that duly, and necessarily) taken to be another, or a distinct authority from that of the Civil Magistrate, and inferior, or subordinate to it." *The Divine Right and Original of the Civill Magistrate from God,* 144–45, quoted in Gordon J. Schochet, *Patriarchalism in Political Thought: The Authoritarian Family and Political Speculation and Attitudes Especially in Seventeenth-Century England* (New York: Basic Books, 1975), 171–72. For an important corrective to modern assumptions that articulations of the patriarchalist analogy can be taken to confirm widespread domestic absolutism at the level of practice, see Margaret J. M. Ezell, *The Patriarch's Wife: Literary Evidence and the History of the Family* (Chapel Hill: University of North Carolina Press, 1987).

3. See Ezell, *Patriarch's Wife,* chaps. 5–6, on Filmer's "In Praise of the Virtuous Wife"; Rachel J. Weil, "The Family in the Exclusion Crisis: Locke versus Filmer Revisited," in *A Nation Transformed: England after the Restoration,* ed. Alan Houston and Steve Pincus (Cambridge: Cambridge University Press, 2001), 101–11.

4. *The Political Works of James I,* ed. Charles H. McIlwain (London, 1918), 272, quoted in Jonathan Goldberg, *James I and the Politics of Literature: Jonson, Shakespeare, Donne, and Their Contemporaries* (Baltimore: Johns Hopkins University Press, 1983), 84; Henry Ferne, *Conscience Satisfied: That there is no warrant for the Armes now taken up by Subjects . . .* (Oxford, 1643), 12, quoted in Mary Lyndon Shanley, "Marriage Contract and Social Contract in Seventeenth-Century English Political Thought," *Western Political Quarterly* 32, no. 1 (1979):

81; *Kingdoms Weekly Intelligencer*, 4–11 July 1646, quoted in Lois Potter, *Secret Rites and Secret Writing: Royalist Literature, 1641–1660* (Cambridge: Cambridge University Press, 1989), 102.

5. The four tracts have been edited by Lois Potter as "The *Mistris Parliament* Political Dialogues," *Analytical and Enumerative Bibliography*, n.s. 1, no. 3 (1987): 101–70. Mrs. London serves as midwife. The lying-in chamber, with its all-female personnel, was traditionally seen as a special place of women's privacy and collectivity. See below, chap. 5, n. 43, and figs. 4.12 and 5.12. The trope of the Mistress Parliament tracts recurs on the eve of the Restoration in *The Famous Tragedie Of the Life and Death of Mris. Rump. Shewing How She was brought to Bed of a Monster . . . her ugly, deformed, ill-shapen, base-begotten Brat or Imp of Reformation . . .* (1660). Customary belief attributed monstrous births to the desirous imaginations of the mothers during pregnancy. See Marie-Hélène Huet, *Monstrous Imagination* (Cambridge, MA: Harvard University Press, 1993).

6. *A New Marriage, Between Mr. King, and Mrs. Parliament. The Banes forbidden by Captaine army, with the Grounds and Reasons he gives for the same* (1648), 4.

7. See Richard Braverman, *Plots and Counterplots: Sexual Politics and the Body Politic in English Literature, 1660–1730* (Cambridge: Cambridge University Press, 1993), 55–56.

8. Sir Robert Hyde in the case of *Manby v. Scott* (1663), 1 Mod. 129, quoted in Susan Staves, *Players' Scepters: Fictions of Authority in the Restoration* (Lincoln: University of Nebraska Press, 1979), 111. As the household was understood to be a "petit commonwealth," so the murder of its head was defined as a crime of "petit treason." On the Treason Act, see Frances Dolan, *Dangerous Familiars: Representations of Domestic Crime in England, 1550–1700* (Ithaca, NY: Cornell University Press, 1994), 21, and on petit treason generally, chaps. 1–3 passim. By the end of the eighteenth century the private charge of murder was being preferred regularly to the public charge of petit treason (ibid., 238), which was not formally abolished until 1828. See William S. Holdsworth, *A History of English Law*, 3rd ed. (London: Methuen, 1922–66), 3:288.

9. John Dryden, "To the Metropolis of Great Britain, The most Renowned and late Flourishing City of London. . . ," prefixed to *Annus Mirabilis* (1667), in *The Works of John Dryden*, vol. 1, *Poems, 1649–1680*, ed. Edward Niles Hooker and H. T. Swedenberg Jr. (Berkeley and Los Angeles: University of California Press, 1956), 48; John Ayloffe, *Britannia and Raleigh* (1674–75), lines 33–34, 98–101, in *Poems on Affairs of State: Augustan Satirical Verse, 1660–1714*, vol. 1, *1660–1678*, ed. George deF. Lord (New Haven, CT: Yale University Press, 1963), 232 (the three virgins are England, Scotland, and Ireland); Elinor James, *To the Right Hon. Convention, Gentlemen, though you have a new name* (c. 1688), quoted in Paula McDowell, *The Women of Grub Street: Press, Politics, and Gender in the London Literary Marketplace, 1678–1730* (Oxford: Clarendon, 1998), 210.

10. [Henry Parker], *Observations upon some of his Majesties late Answers and Expresses* (1642), 18–19, reprinted in *Tracts on Liberty in the Puritan Revolution, 1638–1647*, ed. William Haller (New York: Columbia University Press, 1933), 2:184–85; N.T., *The Resolver Continued: Or, A Satisfaction to some Scruples about the Putting of the Late King to Death* (1649), quoted in Victoria Kahn, "Margaret Cavendish and the Romance of Contract," *Renaissance Quarterly* 50, no. 2 (1997): 533. With this opportunistic regendering of the patriarchalist analogy compare the fate of the fiction of the king's two bodies; see the discussion in Michael McKeon, *The Origins of the English Novel, 1600–1740* (Baltimore: Johns Hopkins University Press, 1987), 179.

11. [John Milton], *Doctrine and Discipline of Divorce* (1644), ed. Lowell W. Coolidge, in *The Complete Prose Works of John Milton*, vol. 2, *1643–1648*, ed. Ernest Sirluck (New Haven, CT: Yale University Press, 1959), 228–29; idem, *A Second Defense of the English People* (1654), ed. Donald A. Roberts, trans. Helen North, in ibid., vol. 4, *1650–1655*, ed. Don M. Wolfe (New Haven, CT: Yale University Press, 1966), 680; [idem], *Eikonoklastes: in Answer to a Book Entitled Eikon Basilike . . .* (1649), in ibid., vol. 3, *1648–1649*, ed. Merritt Y. Hughes (New Haven, CT: Yale University Press, 1962), 421; Henry Neville, *Newes from the New Exchange, or The Common-Wealth of Ladies* (1650), 1–2. On radical sectarian experiments in marriage and sexuality, see Christopher Hill, *The World Turned Upside Down: Radical Ideas during the English Revolution* (New York: Viking, 1972), chap. 15.

12. *A Remonstrance of the Shee-Citizens of London. And Of many thousands of other the free-borne Women of England. Humbly shewing their desires for the attaining of a free trade, for the Kings speedie coming to London, for the maning of their works, and for the redresse of their many other grievances, and burdens they now lie under* (1647), 3.

13. On such petitions, see Sharon Achinstein, "Women on Top in the Pamphlet Literature of the English Revolution," *Women's Studies* 24, nos. 1–2 (1994): 137–40; James Grantham Turner, *Libertines and Radicals in Early Modern London: Sexuality, Politics, and Literary Culture, 1630–1685* (Cambridge: Cambridge University Press, 2002), 88–96.

14. For examples and discussion, see Turner, *Libertines and Radicals*, 96–103.

15. Figure 3.1 reproduces the image as it appears in a tract that revived the trope of the 1640s in the wake of the Exclusion Crisis forty years later.

16. Robert South, "The Virtuous Education of Youth, the Surest, if not Sole way to a happy old Age" (1685), in *Sermons Preached upon Several Occasions* (Philadelphia, 1844), 2:282, and *Marriage Promoted. In a Discourse Of its Ancient and Modern Practice . . .* (1690), 46–47, quoted in Staves, *Players' Scepters*, 115 and 111, respectively; "Epitaph on ABC or elegy on M.P.O.," Bodleian Library, Rawlinson poetry MS 181, fol. 16, quoted in Rachel J. Weil, *Political Passions: Gender, the Family, and Political Argument in England, 1680–1714* (Manchester: Manchester University Press, 1999), 116.

17. The following paragraph is based on Naomi Tadmore, *Family and Friends in Eighteenth-Century England: Household, Kinship, and Patronage* (Cambridge: Cambridge University Press, 2001), an illuminating effort to rethink the history of the family in the early modern period by attending more closely to contemporaries' language use.

18. See McKeon, *Origins*, chap. 4.

19. See Tadmore, *Family*, 39.

20. Ibid., 35.

21. See Lawrence Stone, *The Family, Sex, and Marriage in England, 1500–1800* (London: Harper, 1977), 27–29; Randolph Trumbach, *The Rise of the Egalitarian Family: Aristocratic Kinship and Domestic Relations in Eighteenth-Century England* (New York: Academic, 1978), 129; and Bridget Hill, *Women, Work, and Sexual Politics in Eighteenth-Century England* (Oxford: Blackwell, 1989), 132–33.

22. [Richard Allestree], *The Ladies Calling In Two Parts . . .* (Oxford, 1673), 225.

23. Ellen Meiksins Wood, *The Pristine Culture of Capitalism: A Historical Essay on Old Regimes and Modern States* (London: Verso, 1991), 139.

24. See J. Jean Hecht, *The Domestic Servant Class in Eighteenth-Century England* (London: Routledge, 1956), chap. 3; and Lawrence Stone, *Road to Divorce: England, 1530–1987*

(Oxford: Oxford University Press, 1995), 211–30. On judicial separation, see below, n. 67.

25. See Jack Goody, *The Development of the Family and Marriage in Europe* (Cambridge: Cambridge University Press, 1983), 168–82; and Stone, *Road,* 7, 11, 19, 53, 56.

26. See Goody, *Development,* 148–49; Stone, *Road,* 54–55, 68, 69–70; and Christopher Hill, *Society and Puritanism,* chap. 8.

27. See Stone, *Road,* 66, 71, 79–80, 97, 123, 149, 308; and Staves, *Players' Scepters,* 115.

28. Keith Thomas, "The Puritans and Adultery: The Act of 1650 Reconsidered," in *Puritans and Revolutionaries: Essays in Seventeenth-Century History Presented to Christopher Hill,* ed. Donald Pennington and Keith Thomas (Oxford: Oxford University Press, 1978), 259.

29. Lewis Morris, quoted in John R. Gillis, *For Better, For Worse: British Marriages, 1600 to the Present* (New York: Oxford University Press, 1985), 190, 200–201. On the eve of the 1753 act, Henry Gally remarked that any attempt to reform marriage "would be criticized as an attack on English freedom, for 'liberty, even mistaken liberty, is the darling of the people.'" *Some Considerations upon Clandestine Marriages* (1750), quoted in Stone, *Road,* 121.

30. Henri Misson, *Memoirs and Observations in His Travels over England* ([1698] trans. 1719), 183, 351, quoted in Peter Earle, *The Making of the English Middle Class: Business, Society, and Family Life in London, 1660–1730* (Berkeley and Los Angeles: University of California Press, 1989), 179; Bridget Hill, *Women,* 208.

31. Of course, a marriage contract might also be kept secret from family. See Stone, *Road,* 57.

32. See Gillis, *For Better, For Worse,* 96; and Stone, *Road,* 96–102, 127.

33. See Margaret R. Sommerville, *Sex and Subjection: Attitudes to Women in Early-Modern Society* (London: Arnold, 1995), 174–75 and chap. 7 passim. Cf. Mary Astell's sardonic observation that "the Domestic Sovereign is without Dispute Elected, and the Stipulations and Contract are mutual" in [Mary Astell], *Reflections Upon Marriage* (1700), 3rd ed. (1706), in *The First English Feminist: Reflections Upon Marriage and Other Writings by Mary Astell,* ed. Bridget Hill (Aldershot, Hants.: Gower, 1986), 76.

34. Henry Parker, *Jus populi* (1644), quoted in Shanley, "Marriage Contract," 84; [William Lawrence], *Marriage by the Morall Law of God Vindicated Against all Ceremonial Laws . . .* (1680), 101–2. The subtext of Lawrence's advocacy was the campaign to affirm the marriage of Charles II and Lucy Walter, and hence the legitimacy of their son, the Duke of Monmouth, to succeed the king. See below, chap. 10, nn. 77–86.

35. Locke, *An Essay Concerning the True Original, Extent, and End of Civil Government (The Second Treatise of Government)* (1690), bk. 2, chap. 7, secs. 78, 82, in *Two Treatises of Government,* ed. Peter Laslett, 2nd ed. (Cambridge: Cambridge University Press, 1967), 337, 339 (hereafter book 2 is cited as *Second Treatise*).

36. See Shanley, "Marriage Contract," for examples. Milton's *Doctrine and Discipline of Divorce* (1644) makes full use of this method of inquiry; see his dedicatory epistle: "[A]s a whole people is in proportion to an ill Government, so is one man to an ill mariage. If they against any authority, Covnant, or Statute, may by the soveraign edict of charity, save not only their lives, but honest liberties from unworthy bondage, as well may he against any private Covnant . . . ." *Complete Prose Works,* 2:229.

37. See below, part 3.

38. Thomas Shadwell, *The Lancashire Witches,* act 1, in *The Complete Works of Thomas*

Shadwell, ed. Montague Summers (1927; reprint, New York: Blom, 1968), 4:109, 111; Thomas Otway, *The Atheist,* act 2, p. 379, quoted in Staves, *Players' Scepters,* 113; Richard Leigh, "The Union of Friendship," in *Poems upon several occasions, and, to several persons* (1675), ed. Hugh Macdonald (Oxford: Blackwell, 1947), 50; [Lady Chudleigh], *The Ladies Defence* (1701), lines 139–42, 165–70, in *The Poems and Prose of Mary, Lady Chudleigh,* ed. Margaret J. M. Ezell (New York: Oxford University Press, 1993), 19, 20. The conflict between marriages of convenience and marriage for love is already a staple of Jacobean comedy; what distinguishes Restoration usage is the degree to which it is colored by the discourse of absolutist politics that flourished in the civil-war period.

39. A yet more subtle allusiveness can be seen in Defoe's comparison of children to "slaves" and the victims of "rape" when sacrificed to forced marriages. See Daniel Defoe, *Conjugal Lewdness; or, Matrimonial Whoredom* (1727), 37, 166. Cf. Richard Steele in *Tatler,* no. 91 (8 Nov. 1709), in *The Tatler,* ed. Donald F. Bond, 3 vols. (Oxford: Clarendon, 1987): "Wedlock is but a more solemn Prostitution, where there is not an Union of Minds"; and Joseph Addison in *Spectator,* no. 311 (26 Feb. 1712), in *The Spectator,* ed. Donald F. Bond, 5 vols. (Oxford: Clarendon, 1965), where it is said that successful "fortune hunting" should be punishable as rape. See also *Spectator,* no. 325 (14 Mar. 1712) (hereafter references to these periodicals are to these editions and appear parenthetically in the text).

40. Dorothy Osborne to Sir William Temple, 17 or 18 Dec. 1653, in *Dorothy Osborne: Letters to Sir William Temple, 1652–54: Observations on Love, Literature, Politics, and Religion,* ed. Kenneth Parker (Aldershot, Hants.: Ashgate, 2002), 160. A year after this letter Dorothy and William were married. On the Osborne family, see ibid., 6–7. My thanks to Kevin Pask for this reference.

41. See above, chap. 2, nn. 145–46.

42. At this moment (20 Aug. 1710) Henry Sacheverell, passionate proponent of the absolutist doctrines of passive obedience and nonresistance, was at the height of his celebrity.

43. *Complete Letters of Lady Mary Wortley Montagu,* ed. Robert Halsband (Oxford: Clarendon, 1965), 1:54, 64, 123, 133, 140–41, 151, 157, 159, 162 (20 Aug. 1710–16 Aug. 1712).

44. Lady Mary to Lady Bute, 22 Sept. 1755, in Robert Halsband, *The Life of Lady Mary Wortley Montagu* (Oxford: Clarendon, 1956), 28.

45. See Stone, *Family;* Gillis, *For Better, For Worse,* 21–22, 37, 86; Bridget Hill, *Women,* 185–86; Earle, *Making,* 185–88; and Stone, *Road,* 62, 68. A major contribution to this debate was made also by Trumbach, *Rise.*

46. Ronald Paulson, *Hogarth,* vol. 2, *High Art and Low, 1732–1750* (New Brunswick, NJ: Rutgers University Press, 1992), 219; my remarks have been informed by Paulson's reading of this plate, 214–22.

47. See McKeon, *Origins,* 260–63; and David Toise, "Culpable Passions: The Transformation of Desire and the Development of the British Novel, 1720–1850" (PhD diss., Rutgers University, 1996). This example of the countervailing relationship between passions and interests that Albert O. Hirschman has made familiar differs from his paradigm in attributing to love rather than to economic interest the moderating role. See Hirschman, *The Passions and the Interests: Political Arguments for Capitalism before Its Triumph* (Princeton, NJ: Princeton University Press, 1977).

48. On the conflict between the two kinship systems in eighteenth-century England, see

Ruth Perry, "Women in Families: The Great Disinheritance," in *Women and Literature in Britain, 1700–1800,* ed. Vivien Jones (Cambridge: Cambridge University Press, 2000), 111–31. This conflict corresponds to that between *genos* and *oikos* in Greek antiquity. See above, chap. 1, n. 14.

49. Thomas Shadwell, *The Woman-Captain* (1679), in *Complete Works,* act 4, sc. 1, lines 21, 27, 28; sc. 2, lines 37, 38; sc. 5, line 77. Portion was the share of the parental estate to which a child was entitled under the parental marriage settlement. Jointure was a substitute for dower. See Susan Staves, *Married Women's Separate Property in England, 1660–1833* (Cambridge, MA: Harvard University Press, 1990), chap. 4.

50. Hester Chapone, *Letters on the Improvement of the Mind Addressed to a Lady* (1773), 93, quoted in Amanda Vickery, *The Gentleman's Daughter: Women's Lives in Georgian England* (New Haven, CT: Yale University Press, 1998), 158.

51. [Lawrence], *Marriage,* 71; [Allestree], *Ladies Calling,* 177; [Mary Astell], *Reflections Upon Marriage* (1700), 3rd ed. (1706), in *The First English Feminist: Reflections Upon Marriage and Other Writings by Mary Astell,* ed. Bridget Hill (Aldershot, Hants.: Gower, 1986), 101–2. The absurdity of marriage law is even clearer when its terms are explicitated through comparison to the public model of contractualism rather than absolutism: the protections the "civil society" of marriage provides women from the state-of-nature aggression of others toward themselves and their property are paid for by the loss of both their freedom and their property.

52. Thomas Shadwell, *Bury Fair* (1689), "Epistle Dedicatory" and act 5, sc. 1, ed. John C. Ross (New York: Garland, 1995), 48, 134 (font reversed); Leigh, "Union of Friendship," 49; [Ned Ward], *The Insinuating Bawd: and the Repenting Hart . . .* (1700), 6 (font reversed); [Chudleigh], *Ladies Defence,* lines 64–67, 95–98, in *Poems and Prose,* 17, 18; Sarah Fyge Egerton, "The Emulation," lines 4, 7–10, 15–18, in *Eighteenth-Century Women Poets: An Oxford Anthology,* ed. Roger Lonsdale (Oxford: Oxford University Press, 1989), 31; John Crowne, *City Politiques* (1683), act 5, sc. 3, lines 173–74, 179–84, ed. John Harold Wilson (Lincoln: University of Nebraska Press, 1967), 134.

53. John Wemyss, *The workes of Mr. J. Weemes* (1633), 2:17, quoted in Sommerville, *Sex,* 82; see generally 79–84.

54. On the abolition of feudal tenures, see above, chap. 1, n. 41. The language of "settlement" applied in this period both to the microestate of the propertied family and to the macroestate of England; Acts of Settlement (1662, 1701) marked the new regime on the Restoration of Charles II and the accession of Anne.

55. See McKeon, *Origins,* 153–54; cf. the remarks of Susan Staves in her *Married Women's Separate Property,* 202–3.

56. *The true characters . . .* (1708), 9, quoted in [John Arbuthnot], *The History of John Bull* (1712), ed. Alan W. Bower and Robert A. Erickson (Oxford: Clarendon, 1976), lxxxvii. On pin money, see Staves, *Married Women's Separate Property,* chap. 5.

57. These are the numbers to which Edward Wortley contributed. In letters dated 6, 11, and 12 August 1712, Mary made certain that Edward knew both that the marriage settlement her father had arranged involved considerable pin money and jointure and that she expected neither of him. Montagu, *Complete Letters,* 1:142, 151, 153. On the plebeian practice of wife sale, see below, nn. 65–66.

58. The Grand Alliance had been concluded in 1701 between England, Holland, and Em-

peror Joseph I against France. "Treaty" (as well as "alliance") was commonly used to refer also to a marriage settlement, but Addison plays upon the public, international sense of the term as well. Cf. Oliver Goldsmith, *The Citizen of the World* (1760–61), letter 114, in *Collected Works of Oliver Goldsmith,* ed. Arthur Friedman (Oxford: Clarendon, 1966), 2:440: "The Formalities, delays and disappointments that precede a treaty of marriage here, are usually as numerous as those previous to a treaty of peace." Goldsmith writes in opposition to the 1753 Marriage Act.

59. Locke, *Second Treatise,* chap. 3, sec. 17, p. 297.

60. On international relations as constituting a state of nature, see ibid., chap. 2, sec. 14, pp. 294–95.

61. Ibid., sec. 6, p. 289.

62. Cf. *Spectator,* no. 308 (22 Feb. 1712). *Spectator,* no. 522 (29 Oct. 1712) provides a more positive instance of the carte blanche prenuptial agreement.

63. For a study of this belief and its transformation in the early modern period, see Huet, *Monstrous Imagination.*

64. Daniel Defoe, *Review* 7 (9 May 1710), quoted in McDowell, *Women of Grub Street,* 281.

65. See Stone, *Road,* 141–48.

66. See *Tatler,* no. 223 (12 Sept. 1710); Bridget Hill, *Women,* 219; and E. P. Thompson, *Customs in Common: Studies in Traditional Popular Culture* (New York: New Press, 1991), 427–41.

67. Stone, *Road,* 231–33.

68. Ibid., 303–4, 309–17, quotations on 321, 311. Historical Manuscripts Commission Reports, Rutland MS 22, chap. 2, p. 14.

69. I.e., William and Mary.

70. "The Divorce," in *Poems on Affairs of State: Augustan Satirical Verse, 1660–1714,* vol 5, *1688–1697,* ed. William J. Cameron (New Haven, CT: Yale University Press, 1971), lines 29–32, 37–44, pp. 319–20.

71. See Stone, *Road,* 317–22.

72. *A letter to a gentlewoman concerning government* (1697), 13, quoted in Weil, *Political Passions,* 126. See Weil, *Political Passions,* chap. 5 passim, for other evidence to this effect.

73. Thomas Southerne, *The Wives Excuse: Or, Cuckolds make themselves* (1691), act 1, p. 292, quoted in Staves, *Players' Scepters,* 179; John Vanbrugh, *The Provok'd Wife* (1697), ed. Anthony Colman (Manchester: Manchester University Press, 1982), act 1, sc. 1, lines 69–75, pp. 59–60. Paula R. Backscheider has documented close similarities in theme and language between the notorious parliamentary divorce cases of the 1690s and the drama of that decade in "'Endless Aversion Rooted in the Soul': Divorce in the 1690–1730 Theater," *Eighteenth Century: Theory and Interpretation* 37, no. 2 (1996): 99–135.

74. See Stone, *Road,* 149, 153; and Staves, *Married Women's Separate Property,* chap. 6.

75. Lord Eldon in *Lord St. John v. Lady St. John* (1805), 11 Ves. Jun. 525, 530, 532, quoted in Staves, *Married Women's Separate Property,* 185.

76. Randolph Trumbach, *Sex and the Gender Revolution,* vol. 1, *Heterosexuality and the Third Gender in Enlightenment London* (Chicago: University of Chicago Press, 1998), 392; Justice Buller in *Fletcher v. Fletcher* (1788), 2 Cox 99, 102, quoted in Staves, *Married Women's Separate Property,* 228.

77. See above, chap. 1, n. 9.

78. See Earle, *Making,* 166–67, 171, 173–74; and Bridget Hill, *Women,* chap. 13. In London, even married women could trade independently of their husbands, so long as the trade itself was in a different commodity, by acquiring the status of *feme sole merchant.* See Earle, *Making,* 159–60.

79. See above, nn. 7, 9.

80. William Cavendish, *The Triumphant Widow, or the Medley of Humours* (1677), 97, 98.

81. For the argument that the divine right of kings was not a theory of royal absolutism, see Glenn Burgess, "The Divine Right of Kings Reconsidered," *English Historical Review,* no. 425 (Oct. 1992): 837–61.

82. J. H. Hexter, "The Myth of the Middle Class in Tudor England," in *Reappraisals in History: New Views on Society and History in Early Modern Europe,* 2nd ed. (Chicago: University of Chicago Press, 1979), 114; for Ascham, see Anthony Ascham, *Of the Confusions and Revolutions of Goverments . . .* (1649), 4.

83. "Prerogative" and "privilege" are political terms of art that refer respectively to the authority of monarch and of Parliament and hence constitute the sovereignty of the state in a mixed monarchy.

84. [Mary Astell], *A Serious Proposal to the Ladies, Part II . . .* (1697), 290, in Astell, *First English Feminist,* 179; Chudleigh, *Ladies Defence,* lines 655–62, in *Poems and Prose,* 34.

85. John Dryden, *The Conquest of Granada, Part I* (1672), act 1, sc. 1, lines 205–6, in *The Works of John Dryden,* vol. 11, *Plays,* ed. George R. Guffey and Alan Roper (Berkeley and Los Angeles: University of California Press, 1978), 30.

86. On Dryden, see above, chap. 1, n. 106; on Osborne, above, n. 40; on Shaftesbury, above, chap. 2, nn. 143–47; and on Dennis, John Dennis, *The Characters and Conduct of Sir John Edgar, Call'd by Himself Sole Monarch of the Stage in Drury-Lane . . .* (1720), letter 1, in *The Critical Works of John Dennis,* ed. Edward N. Hooker (Baltimore: Johns Hopkins University Press, 1943), 2:191. For evidence of Dryden's sensitivity, see Michael McKeon, "Historicizing *Absalom and Achitophel,*" in *The New Eighteenth Century: Theory, Politics, English Literature,* ed. Felicity Nussbaum and Laura Brown (New York: Methuen, 1987), 23–40. A century before Dryden, the virtual privacy of the Roman Catholic might be physically actualized as the deprivation entailed in the secret priest hole, as in the following account of the capture of the fugitive Jesuit Edmund Campion: The searchers "being entred with no smal company, sawe walking in the house divers of these that they brought to the Tower: entring farther, up into a Chamber neere the top of the house, which was but very simple, having in it, a large great shelfe, with divers tooles and instrumentes . . . . The simplenesse of the place caused them to use small suspition in it, and were departing againe. But one in the company, by good hap, espied a chinke in the wall of boordes, whereto this shelf was fastened, and through the same he perceived some light, drawing his Dagger he smit a great hole in it, and sawe there was a roome behind it, whereat the rest staied, searching for some entrance into it, which by pulling downe a shelfe they found, being a little hole to one to creep in at: There they entred and found Edmund Campion, the Jesuit and John Peters and Thomas Saltwell, preestes, standing up very closely." Anthony Munday, *A Discoverie of Edmund Campian and his Confederates . . .* (1582), A6–7, in Julian Yates, "Parasitic Geographies: Manifesting Catholic Identity in Early Modern England," in *Catholicism and Anti-Catholicism in Early Modern English Texts,* ed. Arthur F. Marotti (New York: St. Martin's, 1999), 77.

87. Margaret Cavendish, *The Worlds Olio* (1655), "The Epistle" to "The third part of the

first Book," 48 (mispaginated 46); idem, *The Lady Marchioness of Newcastle, CCXI Sociable Letters . . .* (1664), letter 16, p. 27.

88. William Gouge, *Of Domesticall Dvties . . .* (1622), 357.

89. [Astell], *Reflections,* in Astell, *First English Feminist,* 112.

90. Catherine Gallagher's helpful account profits from this sort of contextualization. See "Embracing the Absolute: The Politics of the Female Subject in Seventeenth-Century England," *Genders,* no. 1 (Spring 1988): 24–39. Nancy Armstrong's belief that the modern individual subject first emerges gendered female, and that it does so in explicit disjunction from the political discourse of public subjecthood, is not supported by the evidence. See *Desire and Domestic Fiction: A Political History of the Novel* (New York: Oxford University Press, 1987).

91. For a synthetic study, see Sarah Ellenzweig, "The Tory Roots of Feminism and Radicalism: English Literature and Politics, 1660–1740" (PhD diss., Rutgers University, 2000).

92. [James Tyrrell], *Bibliotheca Politica: Or a Discourse By way of Dialogue, whether Monarchy be Jure Divino . . .* (1692), 10, 11; Samuel Pufendorf, *Of the Law of Nature and Nations* ([Lat., 1672] trans. 1717), bk. 3, chap. 2, ix, p. 186, quoted in Daniela Gobetti, "Humankind as a System: Private and Public Agency at the Origins of Modern Liberalism," in *Public and Private in Thought and Practice: Perspectives on a Grand Dichotomy,* ed. Jeff Weintraub and Krishan Kumar (Chicago: University of Chicago Press, 1997), 114. On the priority of the marriage over the civil contract, see in general Carole Pateman, *The Sexual Contract* (Stanford, CA: Stanford University Press, 1988).

93. George Hickes, *A Discourse of the soveraign Power. In a Sermon . . .* (1682), 21, quoted in Staves, *Players' Scepters,* 117; [Arbuthnot], *History of John Bull,* 26, 25. The Salic law excluded women from dynastic succession in France and Spain.

94. [John Trenchard], *Cato's Letters,* no. 58 (23 Dec. 1721), in John Trenchard and Thomas Gordon, *Cato's Letters: or, Essays on Liberty, Civil and Religious, and Other Important Subjects* (originally published in the *London Journal,* 1720–23), ed. Ronald Hamowy (Indianapolis: Liberty Fund, 1995), 1:399–400. The preceding paragraph is indebted to the illuminating discussion of Sommerville, *Sex,* 225–35 and chap. 8 passim.

95. I substitute Behn and Manley for Chudleigh because of their more demonstrable and outspoken royalism.

96. On the early modern emergence of a system of sexual difference, see Michael McKeon, *The Origins of the English Novel, 1600–1740,* Fifteenth Anniversary Edition (Baltimore: Johns Hopkins University Press, 2002), xxiv–xxix; and below, chap. 6, nn. 4–16.

97. Even though Horace's concluding turn—the moneylender's decision to postpone his rustication—thoroughly ironizes that process. Eighteenth-century imitators of the *beatus ille* often silently omit this part of the poem.

98. Anne Finch, Countess of Winchilsea, "The Petition for an Absolute Retreat *Inscribed to the Right Honble Catharine Countess of Thanet, mention'd in the Poem under the Name of Arminda*" (1713), lines 1–7, 106, 163, in *Selected Poems of Anne Finch Countess of Winchilsea,* ed. Katharine M. Rogers (New York: Ungar, 1979), 59–68. On Finch's politics, see above, chap. 2, n. 120.

99. Lady Mary to Lady Bute, 10 July 1748, 28 Jan., 6 Mar. 1753, in Montagu, *Complete Letters,* 2:403–5, 3:25–28. See Habermas, *Structural Transformation,* 46.

100. Aphra Behn, "The Golden Age. A Paraphrase on a Translation out of French," in

The Works of Aphra Behn, ed. Janet Todd, vol. 1, *Poetry* (Columbus: Ohio State University Press, 1992), lines 83, 97, 111–21, 195–96, pp. 32–35. Behn expands the first-act chorus of Tasso's *Aminta* (1573); the apostrophe to honor and the closing seduction frame are her additions.

101. Mary Leapor, "Man the Monarch" (1751), in *Eighteenth-Century Women Poets,* ed. Lonsdale, lines 1–8, 23, 50–52, 57–65, pp. 202–3.

102. On macropastoralism, see Michael McKeon, "The Pastoral Revolution," in *Refiguring Revolutions: Aesthetics and Politics from the English Revolution to the Romantic Revolution,* ed. Kevin Sharpe and Steven N. Zwicker (Berkeley and Los Angeles: University of California Press, 1998), 284–89.

103. Adam Smith, *An Inquiry into the Nature and Causes of the Wealth of Nations* (1776), bk. 4, chap. 2, ed. R. H. Campbell, A. S. Skinner, and W. B. Todd, Glasgow Edition of the Works and Correspondence of Adam Smith (Indianapolis: Liberty Classics, 1981), 1:454–55.

Chapter Four | Outside and Inside Work

1. For the hypothesis, see above, chap. 2, nn. 148–60.

2. Notably by George Rudé and E. P. Thompson.

3. For some recent scholarship, see Peter Borsay, *The English Urban Renaissance: Culture and Society in the Provincial Town, 1660–1770* (Oxford: Clarendon, 1989), esp. chaps. 6, 11; Penelope Corfield, "Walking the City Streets in the Eighteenth Century," *Journal of Urban History* 16, no. 2 (1990): 132–74; Robert Shoemaker, *Gender in English Society, 1650–1850: The Emergence of Separate Spheres?* (London: Longman, 1998), 269–82; Amanda Vickery, *The Gentleman's Daughter: Women's Lives in Georgian England* (New Haven, CT: Yale University Press, 1998), chap. 6; and Cynthia Wall, *The Literary and Cultural Spaces of Restoration London* (Cambridge: Cambridge University Press, 1998), chap. 5. Wall's account suggests that the need to rebuild London after the Great Fire of 1666 obliged contemporaries to conceive it with an unprecedented self-consciousness about what public space should look like and facilitate.

4. *Boswell's London Journal, 1762–1763,* ed. Frederick A. Pottle (New York: McGraw-Hill, 1950), 68–69, 96, 71.

5. Earlier in the century Richard Steele lodged a similar complaint against the fact that "we the greater Number of the Queen's loyal Subjects, for no Reason in the World but because we want Money, do not share alike in the Division of Her Majesty's High Road. . . . We hang a poor Fellow for taking any Trifle from us on the Road, and bear with the Rich for robbing us of the Road it self." *Tatler,* no. 144 (11 Mar. 1710), in *The Tatler,* ed. Donald F. Bond, 3 vols. (Oxford: Clarendon, 1987) (hereafter references are to this edition and appear parenthetically in the text).

6. [Henry Peacham], *Coach and Sedan, Pleasantly Disputing for Place and Precedence. The Brewers-Cart being Moderator* (1636), C1v, E1r.

7. See John Brewer, *The Common People and Politics, 1750–1790s: The English Satirical Print, 1600–1832* (Cambridge: Chadwyck-Healey, 1986), 26. Brewer's collection and commentary first brought many of these prints to my attention.

8. Margaret Cavendish, *Philosophical and Physical Opinions* (1655), B2v.

9. See Leonore Davidoff and Catherine Hall, *Family Fortunes: Men and Women of the English Middle Class, 1780–1850* (Chicago: University of Chicago Press, 1987), 273.

10. See the balanced perspective of Shoemaker, *Gender,* 10, 318.

11. See Maxine Berg's lucid discussion in "Women's Work, Mechanization, and the Early Phases of Industrialization in England," in *The Historical Meaning of Work,* ed. Patrick Joyce (Cambridge: Cambridge University Press, 1987), 64–65, 96, and passim.

12. Cf. Davidoff and Hall, *Family Fortunes,* 149.

13. Joseph Addison, *Spectator,* no. 81 (2 June 1711), in *The Spectator,* ed. Donald F. Bond, 5 vols. (Oxford: Clarendon, 1965) (hereafter references are to this edition and appear parenthetically in the text).

14. According to Richard Allestree, "[L]adies need not be much at a loss how to entertain themselves, nor run abroad in a *Romantic* quest after foreign divertisements, when they have such variety of engagements at home." [Allestree], *The Ladies Calling In Two Parts* . . . (Oxford, 1673), 230.

15. The following several pages draw on the discussion in Michael McKeon, "Historicizing Patriarchy: The Emergence of Gender Difference in England, 1660–1760," *Eighteenth-Century Studies* 28, no. 3 (1995): 298–300, as well as on sources that complicate that analysis. It should be noted here that although my discussion of the household broadly associates it with the locus of the reproductive family, "[s]chools, colleges, and the inns of court were households in both the literal and figurative senses of the word . . . ." The Renaissance boy "came to maturity in an all-male household that had a sharp sense of its own identity, its own traditions, even its own language." Bruce Smith, *Homosexual Desire in Shakespeare's England* (Chicago: University of Chicago Press, 1991), 84, quoted in Wendy Wall, *Staging Domesticity: Household Work and English Identity in Early Modern Drama* (Cambridge: Cambridge University Press, 2002), 238n48. In this respect, homosocial experience made an important contribution to domestic culture. Explicitly sodomitical experience did too, although in a more mediated fashion. For a reading of a text that highlights the complex parodic relationship between same-sex and different-sex intimacy and domesticity, see below, chap. 12, nn. 61–74.

16. See Susan Cahn, *Industry of Devotion: The Transformation of Women's Work in England, 1500–1660* (New York: Columbia University Press, 1987), 33, 80–81, 89–90; Susan Dwyer Amussen, *An Ordered Society: Gender and Class in Early Modern England* (Oxford: Blackwell, 1988), 43, 68–69; and Bridget Hill, *Women, Work, and Sexual Politics in Eighteenth-Century England* (Oxford: Blackwell, 1989), 35.

17. See Hill, *Women,* 36–37, 50–51; Cahn, *Industry,* 38–39; K. D. M. Snell, *Annals of the Laboring Poor: Social Change and Agrarian England, 1660–1900* (Cambridge: Cambridge University Press, 1985), 22, 62; Deborah Valenze, *The First Industrial Woman* (Oxford: Oxford University Press, 1995), chap. 3 on the dairy industry and p. 47 summarizing other changes in women's agricultural labor; and Shoemaker, *Gender,* 150–59.

18. E. P. Thompson presents evidence that the *charivari,* or "rough music," of the skimmington ride punished a multitude of conjugal sins, not only the inversion of gender authority. See chap. 8 in *Customs in Common: Studies in Traditional Popular Culture* (New York: New Press, 1991), 493ff., 504–5.

19. Samuel Butler, *Characters,* ed. Charles W. Daves (Cleveland, OH: Case Western Reserve University Press, 1970), 81–82.

20. For Hogarth's small illustration, see *Hogarth: The Complete Engravings,* ed. Joseph Burke and Colin Caldwell (New York: Abrams, 1968), plate 88. For another illustration of the passage in Butler that depicts the same tools of labor, see Brewer, *Common People,* 59.

21. Gervase Markham, *The English House-wife* ([1615] 1631), 4, quoted in Wendy Wall, *Staging Domesticity,* 40. For the historian's suggestion, see David E. Underdown, "The Taming of the Scold: The Enforcement of Patriarchal Authority in Early Modern England," in *Order and Disorder in Early Modern England,* ed. A. J. Fletcher and John Stevenson (Cambridge: Cambridge University Press, 1985), 135–36.

22. See Snell, *Annals,* 21–22, 37, 45, 51, 58–62, 157–58. Snell's data comes entirely from the south of England; see Shoemaker, *Gender,* 153–54, on this and other limitations on the generalizability of Snell's work.

23. See Hans Medick, "The Proto-Industrial Family Economy," in *Industrialization before Industrialization: Rural Industry in the Genesis of Capitalism,* ed. Peter Kriedtke et al., trans. Beate Schempp (Cambridge: Cambridge University Press, 1981), 38–73; and David Levine, "Production, Reproduction, and the Proletarian Family in England, 1500–1851," in *Proletarianization and Family History,* ed. David Levine (New York: Academic, 1984), 87–127. On the effect of protoindustrialization on kinship relations, see John R. Gillis, *For Better, For Worse: British Marriages, 1600 to the Present* (New York: Oxford University Press, 1985), 116–21. For a critique, see Rab Houston and K. D. M. Snell, "Historiographical Review: Proto-industrialization? Cottage Industry, Social Change, and Industrial Revolution," *Historical Journal* 27, no. 2 (1984): 473–92. For an overview, see Maxine Berg, *The Age of Manufactures, 1700–1820: Industry, Innovation, and Work in Britain,* 2nd ed. (London: Routledge, 1994), chaps. 3–5.

24. E. J. Hobsbawm, *The Age of Revolution* (New York: New American Library, 1962), 55, quoted in Berg, *Age,* 151.

25. See Berg, *Age,* 140–41, 149, 150, 159–60 (quotation on 160); Valenze, *First Industrial Woman,* 11, 80, 87, and chap. 6 passim; and Shoemaker, *Gender,* 160–71, esp. 168–69.

26. See Berg, *Age,* 160; and Valenze, *First Industrial Woman,* 114. On the technical requirements for the movement from cottage to factory, see Edward Baines, *History of the Cotton Manufacture in Great Britain* (1835; reprint, intro. W. H. Chaloner, London: Cass, 1966), 184–85.

27. See Shoemaker, *Gender,* 160, 161, 175, 194–95, 196–97; Davidoff and Hall, *Family Fortunes,* 274–75; and Anthony Fletcher, *Gender, Sex, and Subordination in England, 1500–1800* (New Haven, CT: Yale University Press, 1995), 240–50.

28. See Berg, *Age,* 157 and chap. 7 passim; Hill, *Women,* chaps. 6, 9 (apprenticeship and occupations); Snell, *Annals,* chaps. 5 and 6 passim (apprenticeship); Peter Earle, *The Making of the English Middle Class: Business, Society, and Family Life in London, 1660–1730* (Berkeley and Los Angeles: University of California Press, 1989), chap. 6 (businesswomen); and Paula McDowell, *The Women of Grub Street: Press, Politics, and Gender in the London Literary Marketplace, 1678–1730* (Oxford: Clarendon, 1998), chap. 1 (women in the book trade).

29. See Snell, *Annals,* 53n36, 215–18, 311–12, 348–49 (quotation on 348).

30. William Perkins, *Workes* (1612), 1:906, quoted in Michael Roberts, "'Words they are Women, and Deeds they are Men': Images of Work and Gender in Early Modern England," in *Women and Work in Pre-Industrial England,* ed. Lindsay Charles and Lorna Duffin (London, 1985), 137. For Dennis, see above, chap 2, n. 34. Roberts points out that the poor's lack of property made them more mobile: "A traveller in Suffolk in the early 1680s saw women 'go spinning up and down the way as I went with a rack and distaff in their hands'" (135). Historical Manuscripts Commission Reports, 13th Report, app., pt. 2 (Portland MSS), 266.

31. Davidoff and Hall, *Family Fortunes,* 272.

32. See Michael McKeon, *The Origins of the English Novel, 1600–1740* (Baltimore: Johns Hopkins University Press, 1987), 165.

33. See Fletcher, *Gender,* 225; Shoemaker, *Gender,* 148–49; and Roberts, "Words," 138.

34. Thomas Powell and unattributed sources, quoted in Roberts, "Words," 141, 142.

35. Andrew Marvell alludes to Primrose's prohibition of female physic when, after extended praise of "Celia," he writes (with ironic alacrity?): "But stay, I slide / Down into error with the vulgar tide; / Women must not teach here: the Doctor doth / Stint them to caudles, almond-milk, and broth [i.e., to customary midwifery]." "To his Worthy Friend Doctor Witty upon His Translation of the 'Popular Errors'" (wr. 1650), lines 27–30, in *Andrew Marvell: The Complete Poems,* ed. Elizabeth Story Donno (Harmondsworth, UK: Penguin, 1978), 62. For a brief consideration of the rise of the professions in a gendered context, see Shoemaker, *Gender,* 179–87.

36. See Davidoff and Hall, *Family Fortunes,* 286; and Shoemaker, *Gender,* 201–3.

37. See Hill, *Women,* 47–50; and Cahn, *Industry,* 47, 99, 120, 158.

38. See Davidoff and Hall, *Family Fortunes,* 32 and chap. 6 passim.

39. See Adam Smith, *An Inquiry into the Nature and Causes of the Wealth of Nations* (1776), bk. 2, chap. 3, ed. R. H. Campbell, A. S. Skinner, and W. B. Todd, Glasgow Edition of the Works and Correspondence of Adam Smith (Indianapolis: Liberty Classics, 1981), 1:330–31. In 1690 Sir Dalby Thomas thought that the category of "Laborious and Industrious People" did not include "Gentry, Clergy, Lawyers, Servingmen, and Beggars," who "are wholly unemploy'd . . . ." *An Historical Account of the Rise and Growth of the West-India Colonies* (1690), 2, quoted in Joyce O. Appleby, *Economic Thought and Ideology in Seventeenth-Century England* (Princeton, NJ: Princeton University Press, 1978), 133.

40. See Nancy Folbre, "The Unproductive Housewife: Her Evolution in Nineteenth-Century Thought," *Signs* 16 (1991): 470–73.

41. See the thoughtful remarks in Cahn, *Industry,* 158; Hill, *Women,* 104; Berg, *Age,* 162–63; and Shoemaker, *Gender,* 145.

42. R. Campbell, *The London Tradesman . . .* (1747), 228. For the assumption that the "apparent Business of a Milliner" is "a mere cloak . . . for lewd females and common prostitutes," see the 1815 public record quoted in Tony Henderson, *Disorderly Women in Eighteenth-Century London: Prostitution and Control in the Metropolis, 1730–1830* (London: Longman, 1999), 159.

43. With reference to the United States in the 1970s it was calculated that "the modern household economy—which encompasses everything from the provision of food and shelter to child care and community services—amounted to nearly one-third of the gross national product. This productive effort, much of it the result of women's work, was needless to say invisible in the national accounts. . . . 'It is difficult to explain how an automobile owned by a cab company is capital equipment whereas it is a consumer bauble when owned by a household.'" Krishan Kumar, "Home: The Promise and Predicament of Private Life at the End of the Twentieth Century," in *Public and Private in Thought and Practice: Perspectives on a Grand Dichotomy,* ed. Jeff Weintraub and Krishan Kumar (Chicago: University of Chicago Press, 1997), 215, quoting Scott Burns, *The Household Economy: Its Shape, Origins, and Future* (Boston: Beacon, 1977), 53.

44. See Hill, *Women,* 125–26, 128, and chap. 8 passim; Davidoff and Hall, *Family Fortunes,* 299, 390; and Berg, *Age,* 137, 160–61.

45. Earle, *Making,* 218.

46. For the comparison of service in households of the lower and higher social orders, see Valenze, *First Industrial Woman,* chap. 9; and Vickery, *Gentleman's Daughter,* chap. 4.

47. Davidoff and Hall, *Family Fortunes,* 394.

48. *Common Sense,* 10 Sept. 1737, quoted in Harriet Guest, *Small Change: Women, Learning, Patriotism, 1750–1810* (Chicago: University of Chicago Press, 2000), 37.

49. *The Art of Governing a Wife; with Rules for Batchelors . . .* (1747), 29.

50. See, e.g., John Dod and Robert Cleaver, *A Godly Forme of Household Government: for the ordering of private families, according to the direction of God's Word* (1612), L6v–7r: "[T]he husband giveth over his right unto his wife: as to rule and governe her maidens: to see to those things that belong unto the kitchin, and to huswiferie . . . ."

51. See above, chap. 3, n. 87.

52. Christopher Hill, *Society and Puritanism in Pre-Revolutionary England* (London: Panther, 1969), chap. 13; [John Milton], *Doctrine and Discipline of Divorce* (1644), ed. Lowell W. Coolidge, in *The Complete Prose Works of John Milton,* vol. 2, *1643–1648,* ed. Ernest Sirluck (New Haven, CT: Yale University Press, 1959), 247; [Allestree], *Ladies Calling,* b2r–v (font reversed); William Gouge, *Of Domesticall Dvties . . .* (1622), 18–19.

53. [John Locke], *Some Thoughts concerning Education* (1693), secs. 39, 40, pp. 41–42; Samuel Johnson, *Rambler,* no. 191 (14 Jan. 1752), in *The Yale Edition of the Works of Samuel Johnson,* vol. 5, *The Rambler,* ed. W. J. Bate and Albrecht B. Strauss (New Haven, CT: Yale University Press, 1969), 234–35.

54. For Chapone, see Hester Chapone, *Letters on the Improvement of the Mind Addressed to a Lady* (1773), 93, quoted in Amanda Vickery, *The Gentleman's Daughter: Women's Lives in Georgian England* (New Haven, CT: Yale University Press, 1998), 158; and Chapone, *Considerations upon the Institution of Marriage* (1739), 6, quoted in Patricia Crawford, "The Construction and Experience of Maternity in Seventeenth-Century England," in *Women as Mothers in Pre-Industrial England: Essays in Memory of Dorothy McLaren,* ed. Valerie Fildes (London: Routledge, 1990), 11.

55. *Satan's Harvest Home . . .* (1749), 45, 47, 48; John Aubrey, *Aubrey on Education,* ed. J. E. Stephens (London: Routledge, 1972), 60, quoted in Fletcher, *Gender,* 307.

56. [Allestree], *Ladies Calling,* b2r–v (font reversed); [George Savile, Marquis of Halifax], *The Lady's New-Year's Gift: or, Advice to a Daughter . . . ,* 2nd ed. (1688), 77–78, 80–81, 26, 27–28; [Mary Astell], *A Serious Proposal to the Ladies for the Advancement of their True and Greatest Interest, Part I,* 3rd ed. (1696), in *First English Feminists: Reflections Upon Marriage and Other Writings by Mary Astell,* ed. Bridget Hill (Aldershot, Hants.: Gower, 1986), 167–68. Margaret Cavendish had written that women "govern as it were by an insensible power" (see above, chap. 3, n. 87).

57. *Marriage Promoted. In a Discourse Of its Ancient and Modern Practice . . .* (1690), 46–47. On the omnicompetent courtier, see McKeon, *Origins,* 184. Wives also were expected to regulate the morals and behavior of their household "domestics," or domestic servants. And although the servant problem was increasingly seen to be an intractable one of social labor, Allestree thought it might be responsive to a pious domestic surveillance: "Now to the well guiding of the *House* by the Mistress of it, I know no better or more comprehensive *Rule,* than for her to endeavour to make all that are hers to be God's *Servants* also. . . . [T]heir own Consciences being the best spy she can set upon them as to their truth and fidelity, and

the best spur also to diligence and industry . . ." (*Ladies Calling*, 224). One of the servants over whom the housewife exercised her governance was the "governess," who extended this "public" function one level down in the private household. In this modern usage the term was an innovation of the period: the *OED* cites as its first instance Steele's language in *Spectator*, no. 314 (29 Feb. 1712), but see Hannah Woolley, *The Gentlewoman's Companion; or, a Guide to the Female Sex . . .* (1675), 4–9.

58. See below, chap. 6, nn. 4–16.

59. Mary Wollstonecraft, *Vindication of the Rights of Women: with Strictures on Political and Moral Subjects* (1792), ed. Miriam Kramnick (Harmondsworth, UK: Penguin, 1975), 129 (hereafter references are to this edition and appear parenthetically in the text).

60. William Godwin, *Enquiry Concerning Political Justice* ([1793] rev. 1798), bk. 1, chap. 3, p. 14. In these years Wollstonecraft and Godwin were acquaintances but not yet lovers.

61. [Allestree], *Ladies Calling*, b3r (font reversed), 3–4.

62. Woolley, *Gentlewoman's Companion*, 108; *The Accomplish'd Housewife; or, the Gentlewoman's Companion . . .* (1745), A1v; *The Lady's Companion: or, Accomplish'd Director in the whole Art of Cookery . . .* (Dublin, 1767), A11r–v; Lady Sarah Pennington, *The Unfortunate Mother's Advice* (1761), 27, quoted in Vickery, *Gentleman's Daughter*, 127; [Halifax], *Lady's New-Year's Gift*, 70; [Eliza Haywood], *Selections from the Female Spectator* (1744–46), ed. Patricia Meyer Spacks (New York: Oxford University Press, 1999), 125–26. With the wife as repository of secrets compare the figure of the secretary, below, chap. 5, nn. 33–41.

63. William Wordsworth, "1801" (1802), in *The Poetical Works of William Wordsworth*, ed. E. de Selincourt, 2nd ed., vol. 3 (Oxford: Clarendon, 1954), 111.

64. See above, n. 58.

65. [John Trenchard], *Cato's Letters*, no. 58 (23 Dec. 1721), in John Trenchard and Thomas Gordon, *Cato's Letters: or, Essays on Liberty, Civil and Religious, and Other Important Subjects* (originally published in the *London Journal*, 1720–23), ed. Ronald Hamowy (Indianapolis: Liberty Fund, 1995), 399–400; Jürgen Habermas, *The Structural Transformation of the Public Sphere: An Inquiry into a Category of Bourgeois Society* (1962), trans. Thomas Burger and Frederick Lawrence (Cambridge, MA: MIT Press, 1989), 46.

66. James Fordyce, *The Character and Conduct of the Female Sex, and Advantages to be derived by Young Men from the Society of Virtuous Women . . .* (1776), pt. 1, p. 6, and William Alexander, *History of Women from the Earliest Antiquity to the Present Time* (1779), 3rd ed. (1782), 1:151, both quoted in Guest, *Small Change*, 156. On the patriotic importance of female learning and of the home, see generally Guest, *Small Change*, chaps. 2, 8.

67. Alexander, *History of Women* (1779), 2:315, quoted in Mark Salber Phillips, *Society and Sentiment: Genres of Historical Writing in Britain, 1740–1820* (Princeton, NJ: Princeton University Press, 2000), 164.

68. See Randolph Trumbach, *The Rise of the Egalitarian Family: Aristocratic Kinship and Domestic Relations in Eighteenth-Century England* (New York: Academic, 1978), 197–224; Valerie A. Fildes, *Breasts, Bottles, and Babies: A History of Infant Feeding* (Edinburgh: University of Edinburgh Press, 1986), 153–55; and Ruth Perry, "Colonizing the Breast: Sexuality and Maternity in Eighteenth-Century England," *Eighteenth-Century Life* 16 (Feb. 1992): 195–96. It was in the later eighteenth and early nineteenth centuries that the unprecedented category "motherhood"—and the assumption that those who give birth to children are naturally and normatively also those who give them nurture—began to become standard. See John R.

Gillis, *A World of Their Own Making: Myth, Ritual, and the Quest for Family Values* (New York: Basic Books, 1996), 152–53.

69. See Katie Trumpener, *Bardic Nationalism: The Romantic Novel and the British Empire* (Princeton, NJ: Princeton University Press, 1997), chap. 5; and Wendy Wall, *Staging Domesticity,* 70–76.

70. Jonas Hanway, memo to Archbishop Secker, Apr. 1762, and idem, *Serious Considerations . . .* (1762), 26, both quoted in James S. Taylor, "Philanthropy and Empire: Jonas Hanway and the Infant Poor of London," *Eighteenth-Century Studies* 12, no. 3 (1979): 294–95. See the discussion in Perry, "Colonizing," 186–87. In her complication of the Victorian image of the housewife as "Angel in the House," Elizabeth Langland is particularly interested in the way the wife's governance of the household entailed, in the office of directing and handling domestic servants, the duties of "class management." See Langland, *Nobody's Angels: Middle-Class Women and Domestic Ideology in Victorian Culture* (Ithaca, NY: Cornell University Press, 1995), 45–49.

71. Hannah More, *Coelebs In Search of a Wife,* 9th ed. (1809), 2:20, quoted in Davidoff and Hall, *Family Fortunes,* 429; see p. 171 for a good account of More's notion of the highly mediated but highly serious efficacy of domestic women in political and public life.

72. Felicity Heal, *Hospitality in Early Modern England* (Oxford: Clarendon, 1990), 393.

73. See Vickery, *Gentleman's Daughter,* 254–57.

74. Smith, *Wealth of Nations,* bk. 4, chap 8, ed. Campell and Skinner, 2:660; Karl Marx, *Grundrisse: Introduction to the Critique of Political Economy* (wr. 1857–58; pub. 1939), trans. Martin Nicolaus (Harmondsworth, UK: Penguin, 1973), 91, 93.

75. Elizabeth Hamilton, *Letters on the Elementary Principles of Education,* 4th ed. (1808), 2:369–70, quoted in Guest, *Small Change,* 325. In chap. 3 Guest discusses ambivalent attitudes toward women's consumption.

76. *Satan's Harvest Home . . .* (1749), 3–5, reprinted with *Hell upon Earth . . .* (1729) in *Hell upon Earth . . . and, Satan's Harvest Home . . .* (New York: Garland, 1985); the author borrows liberally from "Andrew Moreton"'s [i.e., Daniel Defoe's] *Every-Body's Business, is No-Body's Business . . .* (1725), 9, where Defoe also speaks of servants as leading an "Amphibious Life." On the Chelsea parish, see Randolph Trumbach, *Sex and the Gender Revolution,* vol. 1, *Heterosexuality and the Third Gender in Enlightenment London* (Chicago: University of Chicago Press, 1998), 234–47.

77. Campbell, *London Tradesman,* 209. [Bernard Mandeville], *A Modest Defence of Publick Stews: or, an Essay upon Whoring, As it is now practis'd in these Kingdoms* (1724), 20. Women's frequent recourse to marriage after a career of prostitution is hard to document but "probable." Henderson, *Disorderly Women,* 49, 50. On the association of prostitution with the millinery trade see also ibid., 14–15. Trumbach, *Sex,* 120, describes the evolution of "the great streetwalking thoroughfare," bounded at either end by concentrations of bawdy houses. This thoroughfare happens to coincide with the great action of Pope's *Dunciad* (1729–42), "the Removal of the Imperial seat of Dulness from the City to the polite world; as that of the Aeneid is the Removal of the empire *Troy* to *Latium.*" "Martinus Scriblerus of the Poem," in *The Dunciad Variorum* (1728–29), in *The Dunciad,* ed. James Sutherland, vol. 5 of the Twickenham Edition of the Poems of Alexander Pope (New York: Oxford University Press, 1943), 51. From 1750 to 1829, in fact, there was a "precipitate decline in the relative number of commercial sexual transactions being initiated within the boundaries of the old

City of London," although the removal was by no means all westward. See Henderson, *Disorderly Women*, 53.

78. Jeremy Taylor, *The Rule and Exercise of Holy Living* (1650), bk. 4, chap. 8, p. 304; Saunders Welch, *A Proposal . . . To remove the Nuisance of Common Prostitutes from the Streets of this Metropolis . . .* (1758), 7, 19.

79. Henderson, *Disorderly Women*, 180; see also 181–85. According to Henderson, the later-eighteenth-century remoralizing of prostitutes included the idea that most of them had their origins in "threadbare gentility" (188). On the separation of the passions from the interests, see Albert O. Hirschman, *The Passions and the Interests: Political Arguments for Capitalism before Its Triumph* (Princeton, NJ: Princeton University Press, 1977). On the traditional view of women as sexually voracious, see below, chap. 6, n. 15.

80. John Fielding, *A Plan for a Preservatory and Reformatory, for the Benefit of Deserted Girls, and Penitent Prostitutes* (1758), 10, quoted in Miles Ogborn, *Spaces of Modernity: London Geographies, 1680–1780* (New York: Guilford, 1998), 47–48. Fielding aimed to transform prostitutes into housewives and domestic servants (see 15). For an image of a Magdalen penitent, see fig. 4.17.

81. See Steele, *Tatler*, no. 91 (8 Nov. 1709); and Daniel Defoe, *Conjugal Lewdness; or, Matrimonial Whoredom* (1727).

82. A royalist tract of 1647 parodied Leveller-inspired women who sought the public status of citizens as sex-hungry and eager "to be licensed a free trade"—i.e., public whores. See *A Remonstrance of the Shee-Citizens of London. And Of many thousands of other the free-borne Women of England. Humbly shewing their desires for the attaining of a free trade, for the Kings speedie coming to London, for the maning of their works, and for the redresse of their many other grievances, and burdens they now lie under* (1647), 4.

83. *The Wandring Whore* (1663), pt. 6, quoted in Roger Thompson, *Unfit for Modest Ears: A Study of Pornographic, Obscene, and Bawdy Works Written or Published in England in the Second Half of the Seventeenth Century* (Totowa, NJ: Rowman and Littlefield, 1979), 60. On the wandering whore pamphlets of the early 1660s and on precedents for published lists of whores' names and addresses, see James Grantham Turner, *Libertines and Radicals in Early Modern London: Sexuality, Politics, and Literary Culture, 1630–1685* (Cambridge: Cambridge University Press, 2002), 127–39, 140–41.

84. The *Times* report may have been influenced by the famous episode in Frances Burney's *Evelina* (1778) in which the heroine, alone "in the midst of a crowd" at one of London's public pleasure gardens, seeks "protection from insult" from "two ladies" who turn out to be prostitutes (vol. 2, letter 21).

85. [Mandeville], *Modest Defence*, 2, 12, 18.

86. M. Ludovicus, *A Particular but Melancholy Account of the Great Hardships . . . That . . . The Common Women of the Town, Are plung'd into at this Juncture* (1752), unpaginated, quoted in Vivien Jones, "Scandalous Femininity: Prostitution and Eighteenth-Century Narratives," in *Shifting the Boundaries: Transformation of the Languages of Public and Private in the Eighteenth Century*, ed. Dario Castiglione and Lesley Sharpe (Exeter, UK: University of Exeter Press, 1995), 64–65; Welch, *Proposal*, 19.

87. See Henderson, *Disorderly Women*, 28, 31, 50–51; and Tim Hitchcock, *English Sexualities, 1700–1800* (London: St. Martin's, 1997), 95. Streetwalkers sometimes used temporary accommodations—bagnios or hammams (Turkish baths and steam rooms with temporary pri-

vate accommodations) and public houses—that were seen as little different from brothels. Henderson, *Disorderly Women*, 32, 33.

88. See, e.g., *Grub-Street Journal*, no. 12 (26 Mar. 1730), where a recent edition of the Earl of Rochester's poems is treated as though it were a sort of domestic conduct book to be "used by the venerable *Mothers* of Drury-lane in their families."

89. Henry Fielding, *A Charge Delivered to the Grand Jury* (1749), 49–50, quoted in Henderson, *Disorderly Women*, 169–70. Cf. the (albeit simpler) household belongings of another female "cottage industry," that of the flax spinners (fig. 4.8). On the Strand bawdyhouse riot, see Peter Linebaugh, "The Tyburn Riot against the Surgeons," in *Albion's Fatal Tree: Crime and Society in Eighteenth-Century England*, ed. Douglas Hay et al. (New York: Pantheon, 1975), 89–102. On *Onania*, see below, chap. 6, nn. 30–42.

90. Fielding, *Charge Delivered to the Grand Jury*, 46–50, citing R. Burn, *The Justice of the Peace and Parish Officer*, 2nd ed. (1756), 1:132, quoted in Henderson, *Disorderly Women*, 169–70.

91. William Newman (city solicitor), *Parliamentary Papers* (1817), VII, Police Comm., 2nd report, p. 456, quoted in Henderson, *Disorderly Women*, 156. On the techniques of libelers, see above, chap. 2, nn. 128–30.

92. On the "domestically organized brothel" and the "sentimentalization" of prostitution, see Trumbach, *Sex*, 175–76 and chap. 6 passim.

93. J. Massie, *A Plan for the Establishment of Charity-Houses for Exposed or Deserted Women and Girls, and for Penitent Prostitutes* (1758), 23; John Fielding, *Plan for a Preservatory and Reformatory*, 23; and *An Account of the Rise, Progress and Present State of the Magdalen Hospital*, 4th ed. (1770), 20, all quoted in Ogborn, *Spaces of Modernity*, 72. On the Magdalen Hospital, see above, nn. 79–80.

94. On the meaning and context of this category, see Turner, *Libertines and Radicals*, 4–17.

95. *The Poor-Whores Petition. To . . . the Countess of Castlemayne* (1668), and Bodleian Library, MS Don b.8, pp. 190–93, quoted in Tim Harris, *London Crowds in the Reign of Charles II: Propaganda and Politics from the Restoration until the Exclusion Crisis* (Cambridge: Cambridge University Press, 1987), 84 and 85, respectively (see generally 82–91); Samuel Pepys, 25 Mar. 1668, in *The Diary of Samuel Pepys*, ed. Robert Latham and William Matthews, vol. 9, *1668–1669* (London: HarperCollins, 1995), 132. On the cause of the riots and the antiquity of bawdyhouse abuse, see also Turner, *Libertines and Radicals*, 200, 27–29. The apprentices were anticipated weeks before the Restoration by a mock petition to the Parliamentary Convention from the new mistress of the Earl of Pembroke that the new house of Parliament be officially renamed "a *Bawdy-house*." *Phanatick Intelligencer* (1660), 7–8, quoted in Turner, *Libertines and Radicals*, 189.

96. Cf. Thomas Cranley's language in *The Converted Courtezan* (1639), below, chap. 6, n. 42.

97. Jonathan Swift, "A Beautiful Young Nymph Going to Bed . . ." (wr. 1731), in *The Poems of Jonathan Swift*, ed. Harold Williams, 2nd ed. (Oxford: Clarendon, 1958), 2:580–83. This perspective on Swift's satiric target enables us to see his careful itemization of the streetwalker's refuse and prostheses as a mock *blazon*.

98. For a comparison of the Italian and English texts, see James Grantham Turner, "*The Whores Rhetorick*: Narrative, Pornography, and the Origins of the Novel," in *Studies in Eight-

eenth-Century Culture, vol. 24, ed. Carla H. Hay and Syndy M. Conger (Baltimore: Johns Hopkins University Press, 1995), 297–306. See also Bridget Orr, "Whores' Rhetoric and the Maps of Love: Constructing the Feminine in Restoration Erotica," in *Women, Texts, and Histories, 1575–1760*, ed. Clare Brant and Diane Purkiss (London: Routledge, 1992), 195–216. John Wickins was fined forty shillings for printing *The Whores Rhetorick*. See David Foxon, *Libertine Literature in England, 1660–1745* (New Hyde Park, NY: University Books, 1965), 9.

99. *The Whores Rhetorick, Calculated to the Meridian of London and Conformed to the Rules of Art* (1683; reprint, New York: Obolensky, 1961), 20, 24, 28, 105, 36 (hereafter cited parenthetically in the text). On the books of secrets, see above, chap. 2, nn. 52–55.

100. On the tradition of the prostitute's rhetorical and oratorical expertise, see Turner, *Libertines and Radicals*, 22, 37–41. This is more broadly a gendered expertise; cf. the figure of the gossip (see the index).

101. The analogy between religious and amatory intimacy, apart from anticipating the "domestication" of the brothel, has an obvious parodic edge (to which I will return) that is less evident in the parallel with state affairs.

102. See Catherine Gallagher, *Nobody's Story: The Vanishing Acts of Women Writers in the Marketplace, 1670–1820* (Berkeley and Los Angeles: University of California Press, 1994), esp. chap. 1.

103. Turner, "*Whores Rhetorick*," 303; and idem, *Libertines and Radicals*, 324n1, suggest that a whore having sex with both father and son alludes to Charles II and his son, the Duke of Monmouth, and makes the connection to Behn's *Love-Letters* (for a reading of which see below, chap. 11).

104. On the financial situation of widows, particularly those who took over their husbands' trades, see above, chap. 3, n. 78.

105. A counterfeit jewel ground to have many faces.

106. [Samuel Butler], *Hudibras*, ed. John Wilders (Oxford: Clarendon, 1967), pt. 2 (1664), canto 1, lines 304, 441–46, 585–606, pp. 109, 113, 117.

107. Cf. [Mary Astell], *Reflections Upon Marriage* (1700), 3rd ed. (1706), in Astell, *First English Feminist*, 100: "[A] Man, Proud and Vain as he is, . . . may call himself her Slave a few days, but it is only in order to make her his all the rest of her Life." The "plain English" of "the Flatterer's Language" is that "[i]f for nothing else, you'll serve at least as an exercise of my Wit, and how much soever you swell with my Breath, 'tis I deserve the Praise for talking so well on so poor a Subject. We who make the Idols, are the greater Deities; . . . you are therefore only on your good behaviour, and are like to be no more than what we please to make you."

108. At common law, "courtesy" is the husband's right or interest in the wife's real estate, which becomes his at her death. See Susan Staves, *Married Women's Separate Property in England, 1660–1833* (Cambridge, MA: Harvard University Press, 1990), 235. Here dower is conceived analogously as the wife's property by the courtesy of the husband's.

Chapter Five | Subdividing Inside Spaces

1. Max Weber, *The Protestant Ethic and the Spirit of Capitalism* (1905), trans. Talcott Parsons (New York: Scribner's, 1958), 21–22.

2. See John Shanahan, *Elaborate Works: Untangling Drama and Science in Early Modern England* (forthcoming).

3. See the useful caveats of C. R. Hill, "The Iconography of the Laboratory," *Ambix* 22, pt. 2 (1975): 102–10.

4. See Steven Shapin, "The House of Experiment in Seventeenth-Century England," *Isis* 79 (1988): 373–404; and Deborah E. Harkness, "Managing an Experimental Household: The Dees of Mortlake and the Practice of Natural Philosophy," ibid. 88 (1997): 247–62.

5. On this tendency, see Lawrence M. Principe and Lloyd DeWitt, *Transmutations: Alchemy in Art* (Philadelphia: Chemical Heritage Foundation, 2002), on whose commentary I have also relied in my discussion of these paintings.

6. See Marjorie Swann, *Curiosities and Texts: The Culture of Collecting in Early Modern England* (Philadelphia: University of Pennsylvania Press, 2001), 2.

7. See Paula Findlen, "Masculine Prerogatives: Gender, Space, and Knowledge in the Early Modern Museum," in *The Architecture of Science*, ed. Emily Thompson and Peter Gallison (Cambridge, MA: MIT Press, 1999), 35, 36. For images of later cabinet-museums featuring the suspended-specimen motif, see Oliver Impey and Arthur MacGregor, eds., *The Origins of Museums: The Cabinet of Curiosities in Sixteenth- and Seventeenth-Century Europe* (Oxford: Clarendon, 1985), plates 10, 51; Neil Rhodes and Jonathan Sawday, eds., *The Renaissance Computer* (London: Routledge, 2000), figs. 45, 46, 49; *Hogarth: The Complete Engravings,* ed. Joseph Burke and Colin Caldwell (New York: Abrams, 1968), fig. 195; and Barbara M. Stafford, *Artful Science: Enlightenment Entertainment and the Eclipse of Visual Education* (Cambridge, MA: MIT Press, 1994), fig. 172. The motif also received literary treatment. Cf. William Shakespeare, *Romeo and Juliet* (1594–95), act 5, sc. 1, lines 35–49: "Well, Juliet, I will lie with thee tonight. / Let's see for means. O mischief, thou art swift / To enter in the thoughts of desperate men. / I do remember an apothecary, / And hereabouts a dwells, which late I noted, / In tattered weeds, with overwhelming brows, / Culling of simples. Meagre were his looks, / Sharp misery had worn him to the bones; / And in his needy shop a tortoise hung, / An alligator stuffed, and other skins / Of ill-shaped fishes; and above his shelves / A beggarly account of empty boxes, / Green earthen pots, bladders, and musty seeds, / Remnants of packthread, and old cakes of roses / Were thinly scattered to make up a show"; and Mark Akenside, "The Virtuoso; in Imitation of Spencer's Style and Stanza" (1737), st. 6, in *The Poetical Works of Mark Akenside,* ed. Robin Dix (Madison, NJ: Fairleigh Dickinson University Press, 1996), 390: "Here in a corner stood a rich scrutoire, / With many a curiosity replete; / In seemly order furnish'd ev'ry draw'r, / Products of art or nature as was meet; / Airpumps and prisms were plac'd beneath his feet, / A *Memphian* mummy-king hung o'er his head; / Here phials with live insects small and great, / There stood a tripod of the *Pythian* maid; / Above, a crocodile diffus'd a grateful shade."

8. *Philosophical Transactions of the Royal Society* 1 (1666): 321, quoted in Michael Hunter, "The Cabinet Institutionalized: The Royal Society's 'Repository' and Its Background," in Impey and MacGregor, *Origins of Museums,* 159. The cabinet of curiosities took public form not only through the museum but also as popular entertainment. See Richard D. Altick, *The Shows of London* (Cambridge, MA: Harvard University Press, 1978), chaps. 1–2. On the relationship between private cabinets of curiosities and the typographical publication of "cabinets" and "collections" of discursive materials, see Danielle Bobker, "Augustan Interiors: Intimate Spaces and British Writing, 1660–1770" (PhD diss., Rutgers University, forthcoming).

9. John Locke, *An Essay concerning Human Understanding* (1690), ed. Peter H. Nidditch (Oxford: Clarendon, 1979), bk. 1, chap. 2, sec. 15, p. 55.

10. Joseph Moxon, *Mechanick Exercises on the Whole Art of Printing* (1684), and C. H. Firth and R. S. Rait, eds., *Acts and Ordinances of the Interregnum, 1642–1660* (London: HMSO, 1911), quoted in Adrian Johns, *The Nature of the Book: Print and Knowledge in the Making* (Chicago: University of Chicago Press, 1998), 82–83 and 129, respectively.

11. See Leonore Davidoff and Catherine Hall, *Family Fortunes: Men and Women of the English Middle Class, 1780–1850* (Chicago: University of Chicago Press, 1987), 242.

12. John Selden, *Table Talk* (1689), ed. Arthur Warwick (London, 1890), 62, quoted in Alastair Fowler, *The Country House Poem: A Cabinet of Seventeenth-Century Estate Poems and Related Items* (Edinburgh: Edinburgh University Press, 1994), 8; *The Yale Edition of Horace Walpole's Correspondence with Sir Horace Mann,* ed. Wilmarth S. Lewis, Warren Hunting Smith, and George L. Lau, Walpole to Mann, 3 Oct. 1743, in *Horace Walpole's Correspondence,* ed. Wilmarth S. Lewis (New Haven: Yale University Press, 1937–1983), 18:316; Francis Bacon, "Of Building," in *Essays* (1625), in *The Philosophical Works of Francis Bacon,* ed. Robert L. Ellis and James Spedding, rev. ed. John M. Robertson (London: Routledge, 1905), 789–90. See Felicity Heal, *Hospitality in Early Modern England* (Oxford: Clarendon, 1990), 33, 36, 37, 391; and generally Norbert Elias, *The Court Society* (1953), trans. Edmund Jephcott (New York: Pantheon, 1969), chap. 3.

13. Heal, *Hospitality,* 30, 154; see also 29–30.

14. Mark Girouard, *Life in the English Country House: A Social and Architectural History* (New Haven, CT: Yale University Press, 1978), 110. See also David Starkey, introduction to *The English Court: From the Wars of the Roses to the Civil War,* ed. David Starkey et al. (London: Longman, 1987), 4, 5; and Heal, *Hospitality,* 40, 44. On the transformation of eating hall into entrance hall, see also Lawrence Stone, "The Public and the Private in the Stately Homes of England, 1500–1990," *Social Research* 58, no. 1 (1991): 235.

15. [John Pordage], *Theologia mystica* (1683), 149, quoted in J. Andrew Mendelsohn, "Alchemy and Politics in England, 1649–1655," *Past and Present,* no. 135 (1992): 58.

16. Locke, *Essay,* bk. 2, chap. 3, sec. 1, p. 121.

17. See above, chap. 1, nn. 107–9.

18. See Girouard, *Life,* 129; Peter Thornton, *Seventeenth-Century Interior Decoration in England, France, and Holland* (New Haven, CT: Yale University Press, 1979), 296 (on closets, see generally 296–303). Cf. Eliza Haywood's usage in *The Invisible Spy. By Exploralibus* (1755), in *Selected Fiction and Drama of Eliza Haywood,* ed. Paula R. Backscheider (New York: Oxford University Press, 1999), 247: "'Take this,'" says the speaker's mysterious mentor, "giving me a key, 'it will admit you into a closet which no one but myself has ever enter'd;—I call it my Cabinet of Curiosities' . . . . He said no more, but rung his bell for a servant, who, by his orders, conducted me by a narrow winding staircase to the top of the house, and left me at a little door, which I open'd with the key that had been given me, and found myself in a small square room, built after the manner of a turret:—all the furniture was an old wicker chair . . . . [N]ear it was placed a table, not less antiquated, with two globes;—a standish with some paper, and several books in manuscript . . . ."

19. John Donne, "The Canonization" (1633), lines 29–32, in *The Complete Poetry of John Donne,* ed. John T. Shawcross (New York: Anchor, 1967), 98. Nicholas Hilliard, *A Treatise Concerning the Arte of Limning,* ed. R. K. R. Thornton and T. G. S. Cain (Ashington,

Northumberland: Carcanet New Press, 1981), 65, 63, quoted in Patricia Fumerton, *Cultural Aesthetics: Renaissance Literature and the Practice of Social Ornament* (Chicago: University of Chicago Press, 1991), 78; on Elizabethan sonnets and miniatures, see generally chap. 5.

20. Samuel Pepys, *The Diary of Samuel Pepys,* ed. Robert Latham and William Matthews, vol. 9, *1668–1669* (London: HarperCollins, 1995), 415–16.

21. Sir Roger Pratt, *The Architecture of Sir Roger Pratt,* ed. R. T. Gunther (Oxford, 1928), quoted in Thornton, *Seventeenth-Century Interior,* 297.

22. See Girouard, *Life,* 166, 169, 174; and Thornton, *Seventeenth-Century Interior,* 303–15.

23. Leon Battista Alberti, *The Family in Renaissance Florence (I Libri Della Famiglia)* (wr. c. 1434-37, pub. 1734), trans. Renée Neu Watkins (Columbia: University of South Carolina Press, 1969), 209; idem, *On the Art of Building in Ten Books,* trans. Joseph Rykwert, Neil Leach, and Robert Tavernor (Cambridge, MA: MIT Press, 1988), 149, quoted in Findlen, "Masculine Prerogatives," 36.

24. [Samuel Butler], *Hudibras,* ed. John Wilders (Oxford: Clarendon, 1967), pt. 1 (1663), canto 1, lines 175–76, p. 6.

25. William Congreve, *The Way of the World* (1700), act 4, sc. 1, lines 219–23, in *The Complete Plays of William Congreve,* ed. Herbert Davis (Chicago: University of Chicago Press, 1967), 450; Samuel Johnson, preface to *The Plays of William Shakespeare* (1765), in *The Yale Edition of the Works of Samuel Johnson,* vol. 7, *Johnson on Shakespeare,* ed. Arthur Sherbo (New Haven, CT: Yale University Press, 1968), 88, 86; idem, "Milton," in *Lives of the English Poets* (1779, 1781), ed. Arthur Waugh (1952; reprint, London: Oxford University Press, 1968), 1:100. Cf. Mr. Spectator's ambition, above, chap. 2, nn. 94–95. According to Mark Wigley, Alberti's library/study functions as a private "closet": see "Untitled: The Housing of Gender," in *Sexuality and Spaces,* ed. Beatriz Colomina (New York: Princeton Architectural Press, 1992), 347–50. On the patriarchal privacy of records regarding the patrilineal succession in early-Renaissance Florence, see also Stephanie Jed, *Chaste Thinking: The Rape of Lucretia and the Birth of Humanism* (Bloomington: Indiana University Press, 1989), 83–84.

26. See Starkey's discussion in his introduction to Starkey et al., *English Court,* 8–10.

27. See Chris Cook and John Wroughton, *English Historical Facts, 1603–1688* (Totowa, NJ: Rowman and Littlefield, 1980), 21, 25.

28. [Andrew Marvell], *An Account of the Growth of Popery, and Arbitrary Government in England* . . . (Amsterdam, 1677), in *The Complete Works of Andrew Marvell,* ed. Alexander B. Grosart (1875; reprint, New York: AMS, 1966), 4:327. On Louis XIV's administrative structure, see Thornton, *Seventeenth-Century Interior,* 298–99.

29. For more on this type of discourse see below, part 3.

30. [Sir Walter Raleigh], *The Cabinet-Council: Containing the Cheif Arts of Empire, and Mysteries of State; Discabineted In Political and Polemical Aphorisms . . . Published by John Milton, Esq.* (1658), 15, 33.

31. Thomas Randolph, "On the Inestimable Content He Enjoys in the Muses: To Those of His Friends that Dehort Him from Poetry" (1638), lines 47–48, in Fowler, *Country House Poem,* 138–42.

32. See Girouard, *Life,* 130, 135, 149.

33. Angel Day, *The English Secretorie* (1586), 2nd ed. (1599), 2nd pagination (not in 1st ed.), 102–3.

34. John Bunyan, *The Pilgrim's Progress, Part Two* (1684), ed. N. H. Keeble (Oxford: Oxford University Press, 1984), 150, 147.

35. Robert Beale, "Instructions for a Principall Secretarie" (1592), transcribed from Yelverton MSS Cat., BL, Add. MS 48149, in Conyers Read, *Mr. Secretary Walsingham and the Policy of Queen Elizabeth* (Oxford: Clarendon, 1925), 1:428 (app.).

36. Ibid., 431.

37. Day, *English Secretorie,* 2nd pagination, 103, 104.

38. Nicholas Faunt, "Nicholas Faunt's Discourse touching the office of Principal Secretary of Estate, &c.," ed. Charles Hughes, *English Historical Review,* 1905, 500; and Robert Cecil, "The State and Dignity of a Secretary of State's Place, with the Care and Peril thereof," *Harleian Miscellany* 5 (1810): 167, quoted in Richard Rambuss, *Spenser's Secret Career* (Cambridge: Cambridge University Press, 1993), 47 and 37, respectively. On "inward men," see Florence M. Grier Evans, *The Principal Secretary of State: A Survey of the Office from 1558–1689* (Manchester: Manchester University Press, 1923), 2, cited in Rambuss, *Spenser's Secret Career,* 48.

39. See above, chap. 2, nn. 146–47.

40. See above, chaps. 4, n. 62, and 3, n. 89. See Tobias Smollett, *The Adventures of Peregrine Pickle* (1751), chap. 77, ed. James L. Clifford and Paul-Gabriel Boucé (Oxford: Oxford University Press, 1983), 387.

41. See the suggestive argument of Lisa Jardine in "Companionate Marriage versus Male Friendship: Anxiety for the Lineal Family in Jacobean Drama," in *Political Culture and Cultural Politics in Early Modern England: Essays Presented to David Underdown,* ed. Susan Dwyer Amussen and Mark A. Kishlansky (Manchester: Manchester University Press, 1995), 234–54. Jardine discusses this competition in Thomas Middleton and William Rowley's *The Changeling* (1622). See below, chap. 11, for a similar dynamic in Aphra Behn's *Love-Letters Between a Nobleman and his Sister* (1684, 1685, 1687). On the homoerotic element in the master-secretary relationship, see Alan Stewart, "The Early Modern Closet Discovered," *Representations* 50 (Spring 1995): 76–100, revised for his *Close Readers: Humanism and Sodomy in Early Modern England* (Princeton, NJ: Princeton University Press, 1997), chap. 5. There is, of course, a powerful element of the heteroerotic in the modern imagination of the relationship between boss and secretary.

42. *Mundus Foppensis: or, the Fop Display'd. Being the Ladies Vindication, In Answer to a late Pamphlet, Entituled, Mundus Muliebris: Or, The Ladies Dressing-Room Unlock'd, &c. . . .* (1691), A2r–v; Jonathan Swift, "The Lady's Dressing Room," lines 70, 76-77, in *Jonathan Swift: The Complete Poems,* ed. Pat Rogers (New Haven, CT: Yale University Press, 1983), 450. See also Girouard, *Life,* 138, 149–50, 206; John S. Fowler and John Cornforth, *English Decoration in the Eighteenth Century* (London: Barrie and Jenkins, 1974), 80–81; Peter Thornton, *Authentic Decor: The Domestic Interior, 1620–1920* (New York: Viking, 1984), 36; and Thornton, *Seventeenth-Century Interior,* 301, 300, 299, 325, 316, 321, 324–25. Richard Steele's Will Honeycomb takes revenge on his disdainful beloved by corrupting her attendant to place him "early in the Morning behind the Hangings in her Mistress's Dressing-Room," revealing himself just when her face-painting is half completed. *Spectator,* no. 41 (17 Apr. 1711), in *The Spectator,* ed. Donald F. Bond, 5 vols. (Oxford: Clarendon, 1965).

I am not the first reader to think that "misogyny" is far too crude an instrument with which to grasp Swift's subtle ambivalence about women. Disparate themes of revelatory dis-closure—the inside brought to outside view—saturate and complicate his "woman poems," whose reflexivity obliges us to see them also as "poetry poems" that parody the hypocrisy of Petrarchan idealism, especially the *blazon* and its inventory of body parts. For other parodies of the *blazon,* see those by Samuel Butler and the author of *The Whores Rhetorick,* above, chap. 4, nn. 104–7, and by Aphra Behn and Delarivier Manley, below, chap. 11, nn. 33–34, and chap. 13, nn. 30–31.

43. *The Woman's Advocate* (1683), unpaginated, quoted in Anthony Fletcher, *Gender, Sex, and Subordination in England, 1500–1800* (New Haven, CT: Yale University Press, 1995), 187. Adrian Wilson, "The Ceremony of Childbirth and Its Interpretation," in *Women as Mothers in Pre-Industrial England: Essays in Memory of Dorothy McLaren,* ed. Valerie Fildes (London: Routledge, 1990), 82; see also 71, 72–73, 73, 75, 81, 87–88. On petty treason and the parliament-of-women trope, see above, chap. 3, nn. 9, 15.

44. William Hunter, "On the uncertainty of the signs of murder, in the case of bastard children. By the late William Hunter . . . Read July 14, 1783," in *Medical Observations and Inquiries* 6 (1784): 269 (Hunter had died the previous year), quoted in Adrian Wilson, *The Making of Man-Midwifery: Childbirth in England, 1660–1770* (London: University College of London Press, 1995), 181; see generally chaps. 13, 14 and esp. 175–76. Hunter was the author of *Anatomy of the Gravid Uterus* (Birmingham, UK, 1774). On free indirect discourse in novelistic narration, see below, chap. 15, nn. 48–56.

45. Stone, "Public and the Private," 233; following are Stone's suggested categories, 233– 34.

46. Roger North, *Of Building: Roger North's Writings on Architecture,* ed. H. M. Colvin and J. Newman (Oxford: Clarendon, 1981), 32; and Thomas Fuller, *The Holy State,* 2nd ed. (1648), 156, quoted in John Bold, "Privacy and the Plan," in *English Architecture Public and Private: Essays for Kerry Downes,* ed. John Bold and Edward Chaney (London: Hambledon, 1993), 113 and 109, respectively. See also Heal, *Hospitality,* 158; Girouard, *Life,* 120; and Bold, "Privacy," 112, 113–14. In his description of how the devotional closet should be situated, however, Edward Wettenhall thought that the experience of moving from room to room was itself conducive to privacy. See above, chap. 1, n. 107. For the English usage, see Stone, "Public and the Private," 231.

47. Bold, "Privacy," 116.

48. For details, see Girouard, *Life,* 122–23. For a plan of the basement, see Colin Platt, *The Great Rebuildings of Tudor and Stuart England: Revolutions in Architectural Taste* (London: University College of London Press, 1994), fig. 12, p. 38. The use of the back stairs to separate servants from family and guests, a familiar feature of domestic living arrangements in the next two centuries, ensures a different sort of privacy from that enabled by the king's back stairs in the royal household (see above, n. 32).

49. Sir Roger Pratt, "Certain Short Notes Concerning Architecture," in Pratt, *Architecture,* 64, quoted in Girouard, *Life,* 138, and in Bold, "Privacy," 116; North, *Of Building,* 122–23, quoted in Platt, *Great Rebuildings,* 157–58, and in Bold, "Privacy," 115.

50. North, *Of Building,* 25–26, quoted in Platt, *Great Rebuildings,* 136.

51. Bold, "Privacy," 115. On the segregation of servants, see also Heal, *Hospitality,* 155; and Girouard, *Life,* 136, 143.

52. For an early example of the dissociation of the hall from eating, see the plan of Robert Smythson's Hardwick Hall, in Derbyshire, built in 1590–96, in Heal, *Hospitality,* 161. For the

tendency to remove the kitchen, see Girouard, *Life*, 151, 211; and Davidoff and Hall, *Family Fortunes*, 383. However, the open fire and hearth persisted into the nineteenth century, long after technology had made possible and efficient the separation of the stove (for cooking) from the fireplace (for heating), at least in part because the traditional arrangement evoked an image of a pristine and unfragmented domesticity. See Davidoff and Hall, *Family Fortunes*, 380–81.

53. The boundary between inside and outside work within the category of domestic service was permeable. During the seventeenth century, footmen, cheaper because of lower status, began to come into the house to wait at tables, and by the end of the century they had supplanted both gentlemen and yeomen waiters. See Girouard, *Life*, 141–42.

54. See Karl Marx, *Grundrisse: Foundations of the Critique of Political Economy* (wr. 1857–58; pub. 1939), trans. Martin Nicolaus (Harmondsworth, UK: Penguin, 1973), 100, 103–5.

55. See Girouard, *Life*, 204. Cynthia Wall remarks that "in exchange for increasing exclusion from formerly shared space, women were given (or assumed) a separate (but equal?) space of their own." "Gendering Rooms: Domestic Architecture and Literary Acts," *Eighteenth-Century Fiction* 5, no. 4 (1993): 350. However, the medieval custom of seating men and women apart from each other at the dinner itself was still alive, if sporadically so, in the early eighteenth century. See Girouard, *Life*, 148.

56. For Butler, see above, chap. 4, n. 19.

57. Addison speaks of "lying under the Discipline of a Curtain-Lecture" in *Tatler*, no. 243 (28 Oct. 1710), in *The Tatler*, ed. Donald F. Bond, 3 vols. (Oxford: Clarendon, 1987). The image found its best-known modernization in the byplay of Doris Day and Rock Hudson in the 1959 film *Pillow Talk* (dir. Michael Gordon).

58. The full title is *A Curtain-Conference, Being a Discourse betwixt (the late Lord Lambert, now) Iohn Lambert Esq; and his Lady, As they lay a Bed together one night at their House at Wimbleton. Related by the Lady Lambert to Tom Trim, her Gentleman Usher, (one well acquainted with all her Secrets) and now by him Printed for publick satisfaction*.

59. Contrast Lucasta's lover in Richard Lovelace's famous Cavalier poems, who can be both by turns: see below, chap. 8, n. 31.

60. The song was reprinted without the music in *Wit and Mirth or Pills to Purge Melancholy*, vol. 2 (1700), ed. Henry Playford, and in the rev. ed. by Thomas Durfey (1719–20).

61. *Pembroke Papers (1780–1794): Letters and Diaries of Henry, 10th Earl of Pembroke and His Circle*, ed. Herbert, Earl of Pembroke (London: Cape, 1950), 299, 304, quoted in Girouard, *Life*, 206.

62. See Heal, *Hospitality*, 163; and Girouard, *Life*, 145–46.

63. See Bold, "Privacy," 113; Girouard, *Life*, 151–52; and Thornton, *Seventeenth-Century Interior*, fig. 59, p. 60.

64. Philip Yorke in Joyce Goodber, "The Marchioness Grey of Wrest Park," *Bedfordshire Historical Society* 47 (1968): 162, quoted in Fowler and Cornforth, *English Decoration*, 60.

65. Desmond Fitz-gerald, *The Norfolk House Music Room* (London: Victoria and Albert Museum, 1973), 49, quoted in Girouard, *Life*, 197; see also 194–96. On the use of assembly rooms, see also Fowler and Cornforth, *English Decoration*, 76–78.

66. In the following comparison I draw on Stone, "Public and the Private," 237–38.

67. Robert Kerr, *The Gentleman's House: or how to plan English residences from the parsonage to the palace* (1871), quoted in Derek Linstrum, *Sir Jeffry Wyatville, Architect to the King*, Oxford Studies in the History of Art and Architecture (Oxford: Clarendon, 1972), 58. On

tourism, see Stone, "Public and the Private," 248–49; Carole Fabricant, "The Literature of Domestic Tourism and the Public Consumption of Private Property," in *The New Eighteenth Century: Theory, Politics, English Literature,* ed. Felicity Nussbaum and Laura Brown (New York: Methuen, 1987), 254–75; and Ian Ousby, *The Englishman's England: Taste, Travel, and the Rise of Tourism* (Cambridge: Cambridge University Press, 1990), chap. 2.

68. Philippe Ariès, *Centuries of Childhood: A Social History of Family Life,* trans. Robert Baldick (New York: Vintage, 1962), 398.

69. See Platt, *Great Rebuildings,* 150–53, 157.

70. Cf. the composition of George Morland's *The Fruits of Early Industry and Economy* (plate 1).

71. The clerks sleep in chambers on the second floor (not shown).

72. "Explanation of the Draughts of a House Proposed for a Merchant," bound at the end of *Sir John Vanbrugh's Designs for Kings Weston,* Bristol Record Office 33746, printed in John Bold, "The Design of a House for a Merchant, 1724," *Architectural History* 33 (1990): 78–81.

73. Reproductions of the original plans may be found in Kerry Downes, "The Kings Weston Book of Drawings," *Architectural History* 10 (1967): 77–78, figs. 76 and 77.

74. Only the ground floors of these three plans are reproduced, and there is no accompanying explanation.

75. The near side of the back court is occupied by "necessaries," but these are presumably for the clerks rather than for the family, whose close-stools are located more privately in the largest townhouse, within the dark closets of the best chambers on the first floor.

76. See Platt, *Great Rebuildings,* 155–57.

77. Daniel Defoe, *A Tour Thro' the whole Island of Great Britain . . .* (1724–26), ed. G. D. H. Cole (Cambridge: Cambridge University Press, 1927), 2:602 (Everyman's Library ed. [London: Dent, 1928], 2:195).

78. John Wood, *A Series of Plans, for Cottages or Habitations, of the Labourer, Either in Husbandry, or the Mechanic Arts . . .* (1792), 1–6, 35. The relativizing comparison of the palace and the cottage was a common trope. See Samuel Johnson, *Rambler,* no. 168 (26 Oct. 1751), in *The Yale Edition of the Works of Samuel Johnson,* vol. 4, *The Rambler,* ed. W. J. Bate and Albrecht B. Strauss (New Haven, CT: Yale University Press, 1969), 126; Adam Smith, *The Theory of Moral Sentiments* (1759), ed. D. D. Raphael and A. L. Macfie (Indianapolis: Liberty Classics, 1982), 50; and [Hannah More], "The Ploughman's Ditty," line 37, in *Cheap Repository Tracts* (1795). Regarding Wood's ambition to place "himself in the situation of the person for whom he designs," see Adam Smith's remarks below, chap. 7, nn. 110–11. Explicit designs of cottages only began to appear in the mid-eighteenth century, along with the innovative criterion of "comfort" as a standard to be met in architectural plans that mediated between the more traditional, antithetical poles of "necessity" and "luxury." See John Crowley, "From Luxury to Comfort and Back Again: Landscape Architecture and the Cottage in Britain and America," in *Luxury in the Eighteenth Century: Debates, Desires, and Delectable Goods,* ed. Maxine Berg and Elizabeth Eger (Basingstoke, UK: Palgrave Macmillan, 2003), 135–50; see also idem, *The Invention of Comfort: Sensibilities and Design in Early Modern Britain and Early America* (Baltimore: Johns Hopkins University Press, 2001).

79. Thomas Davis, n.d., quoted in Roy Porter, *English Society in the Eighteenth Century* (Harmondsworth, UK: Penguin, 1982), 233. The Marquis of Bath was the owner of Longleat (see figs. 5.18 and 5.19).

80. Dr. Wilan, *Diseases in London* (1801), 255; T. A. Murray, *Remarks on the Situation of the Poor in the Metropolis* (1801), 5; *Middlesex Records, Orders of Court,* Cal., 153; and Francis Place, BL, Add. MSS 35147, fol. 230, quoted in M. Dorothy George, *London Life in the Eighteenth Century* (New York: Capricorn Books, 1965), 86, 87, 88, and 106, respectively.

81. See George, *London Life,* chap. 2. On "privy," see *OED.*

82. Wood, *Series,* 24.

83. Ibid., 27–28.

84. Ibid., 31.

85. Davidoff and Hall, *Family Fortunes,* 367.

86. Thomas Stone, *An Essay on Agriculture, with a view to inform Gentlemen of Landed Property, Whether their Estates are managed to the Greatest Advantage* (1785), 243.

87. William Halfpenny, *Useful Architecture in Twenty-one New Designs for erecting Parsonage-Houses, Farm-Houses, and Inns . . .* (1752), 63, 65.

88. William Halfpenny, *Twelve Beautiful Designs for Farm-Houses . . .* (1750), 25.

89. William Austin, *Haec Homo: Wherein the excellency of the Creation of Woman is described . . .* (1639), 92–93.

Chapter Six | Sex and Book Sex

1. See above, chap. 2, nn. 142–48.

2. Bernard Mandeville, *Free Thoughts on Religion, the Church, and National Happiness* (1720, 2nd ed., enl., 1729), 282–83.

3. PRO, 30/24/27/10, p. 97 (fol. 50r), quoted in Lawrence E. Klein, *Shaftesbury and the Culture of Politeness: Moral Discourse and Cultural Politics in Early Eighteenth-Century England* (Cambridge: Cambridge University Press, 1994), 88.

4. See John R. Gillis, *For Better, For Worse: British Marriages, 1600 to the Present* (New York: Oxford University Press, 1985), chap. 1; Lawrence Stone, *The Family, Sex, and Marriage in England, 1500–1800* (London: Harper, 1977), chaps. 11 and 12; idem, *Road to Divorce: England, 1530–1987* (Oxford: Oxford University Press, 1995), 2, 3; Tim Hitchcock, "Redefining Sex in Eighteenth-Century England," *History Workshop Journal* 41 (1996): 79–80; and idem, *English Sexualities, 1700–1800* (New York: St. Martin's, 1997), 11.

5. See Anthony Fletcher, *Gender, Sex, and Subordination in England, 1500–1800* (New Haven, CT: Yale University Press, 1995), chaps. 2, 19; and Hitchcock, *English Sexualities,* chap. 4. For the extremely influential thesis of a shift from a "one-sex" to a "two-sex" model, see Thomas W. Laqueur, *Making Sex: Body and Gender from the Greeks to Freud* (Cambridge, MA: Harvard University Press, 1990).

6. For a helpful discussion, see Michael C. Schoenfeldt, *Bodies and Selves in Early Modern England: Physiology and Inwardness in Spenser, Shakespeare, Herbert, and Milton* (Cambridge: Cambridge University Press, 1999), 11, 15.

7. See *OED,* s.v. "sex": cf. 1.a (first use citation 1382) and 3 (first use citation 1631). Scholars often acknowledge this abstraction by speaking of modern "sexuality."

8. John Banister, *The Historie of Man* (1578), B1v, quoted in Janet Adelman, "Making Defect Perfection: Shakespeare and the One-Sex Model," in *Enacting Gender on the English Renaissance Stage,* ed. Viviana Comensoli and Anne Russell (Carbondale: University of Illinois Press), 28; R[obert] B[asset], *Curiosities: or The Cabinet of Nature Contayning Phylosophical,*

Naturall, and Morall questions fully answered and Resolved (1637), A5r–6r. The intimate relationship between knowledge and sexual identification is also, of course, as old as Genesis.

9. On this point, see Susan Dwyer Amussen, "'The Part of a Christian Man': The Cultural Politics of Manhood in Early Modern England," in *Political Culture and Cultural Politics in Early Modern England: Essays Presented to David Underdown,* ed. Susan Dwyer Amussen and Mark A. Kishlansky (Manchester: Manchester University Press, 1995), 213–33.

10. Michael McKeon, "Historicizing Patriarchy: The Emergence of Gender Difference in England, 1660–1760," *Eighteenth-Century Studies* 28, no. 3 (1995): 308, 312 (emphasis deleted). Shortly I will suggest a different although broadly complementary way of explaining the emergence of gender difference and sexuality in this period, one that has to do not with the molly subculture but with the sociopolitical status of pederasty. The most important research on the development of a sodomitical subculture in late-seventeenth- and early-eighteenth-century England has been done by Alan Bray, *Homosexuality in Renaissance England,* 2nd ed. (London: Gay Men's Press, 1988); and Randolph Trumbach, in a series of essays that includes "London's Sodomites: Homosexual Behavior and Western Culture in the Eighteenth Century," *Journal of Social History* 11 (Fall 1977): 1–33; "Sodomitical Subcultures, Sodomitical Roles, and the Gender Revolution of the Eighteenth Century: The Recent Historiography," in *'Tis Nature's Fault: Unauthorized Sexuality during the Enlightenment,* ed. Robert Purks Macubbin (Cambridge: Cambridge University Press, 1987), 109–21; "The Birth of the Queen: Sodomy and the Emergence of Gender Equality in Modern Culture, 1660–1750," in *Hidden from History: Reclaiming the Gay and Lesbian Past,* ed. Martin B. Duberman, Martha Vicinus, and George Chauncey Jr. (New York: New American Library, 1989), 129–40; "Sodomitical Assaults, Gender Role, and Sexual Development in Eighteenth-Century London," in *The Pursuit of Sodomy: Male Homosexuality in Renaissance and Enlightenment Europe,* ed. Kent Gerard and Gert Hekma (New York: Harrington Park, 1989), 407–29; and "Sex, Gender, and Sexual Identity in Modern Culture: Male Sodomy and Female Prostitution in Enlightenment London," *Journal of the History of Sexuality* 2, no. 2 (1991): 186–203. This research will be consolidated in the forthcoming second volume of Trumbach's *Sex and the Gender Revolution,* although some of it has already been incorporated in volume 1, *Heterosexuality and the Third Gender in Enlightenment London* (Chicago: University of Chicago Press, 1998). Observing that the specification of the proto-"homosexual" identity roughly coincided with changes in the incidence of and attitudes toward prostitution (including the specification of the meaning of "prostitute," above, chap. 4, nn. 78–79), Trumbach has argued that this should be seen not as a coincidence but as a functional relationship according to which "the sodomite's role was for men what the prostitute's was for women . . . . The majority of eighteenth-century men . . . constructed their masculinity around their avoidance of the sodomite's role and, instead, fervently pursued women and, of course, prostitutes." "Modern Prostitution and Gender in *Fanny Hill:* Libertine and Domesticated Fantasy," in *Sexual Underworlds of the Enlightenment,* ed. G. S. Rousseau and Roy Porter (Chapel Hill: University of North Carolina Press, 1988), 74. On the oppositional social reciprocity between female prostitution and exclusive male sodomy, see, more fully, Trumbach, "Sex, Gender" and *Sex and the Gender Revolution,* 1:9, 69–70, 184–85, and passim. The most controversial aspect of Trumbach's interpretation of this reciprocity is the thesis that an emergent "heterosexual" male anxiety about being identified as an emergent "ho-

mosexual" or exclusive male sodomite led men to an increased engagement in extramarital different-sex activity (including but not limited to sex with prostitutes). This thesis is detachable from, and should not be confused with, what seems to me the less controversial and more important argument that the modern separation out of the two genders as fundamentally different identities and the modern disembedding of male sodomy as not only a despised behavior but also a despised identity have an oppositional social reciprocity.

11. [Delarivier Manley], *The Secret History of Queen Zarah, and the Zarazians* . . . (1705), bk. 2, p. 126.

12. François Poullain de la Barre, *The Woman As Good as the Man: Or, the Equality of Both Sexes* (1673), trans. A.L. (1677), ed. Gerald M. MacLean (Detroit: Wayne State University Press, 1988), 132. Cf. Bernard Mandeville, *The Fable of the Bees* (1705, 1714), ed. F. B. Kaye (Oxford: Clarendon, 1924), Remark (C.), 1:69–72, quoted in McKeon, "Historicizing Patriarchy," 302–3.

13. See Laqueur, *Making Sex*, 8. For a fuller discussion of the relationship between the system of social status and the sex/gender system in early modern England, see Michael McKeon, *The Origins of the English Novel, 1600–1740*, Fifteenth Anniversary Edition (Baltimore: Johns Hopkins University Press, 2002), xxiv–xxix.

14. George Lillo, *The London Merchant: or, The History of George Barnwell* (1731), ed. Lincoln Faller, act. 4, sc. 2, in *The Broadview Anthology of Restoration and Early Eighteenth-Century Drama*, ed. J. Douglas Canfield (Peterborough, ON: Broadview, 2001), 318.

15. This paragraph is based on, and extrapolates from, the suggestive ideas of Thomas A. King in "Gender and Modernity: Male Looks and the Performance of Public Pleasures," in *Monstrous Dreams of Reason: Body, Self, and Other in the Enlightenment*, ed. Laura J. Rosenthal and Mita Choudhury (Lewisburg, PA: Bucknell University Press, 2002), 27–28.

16. See Robert B. Shoemaker, *Gender in English Society, 1650–1850: The Emergence of Separate Spheres?* (London: Longman, 1998), 62–63; on the mother's imagination, see Marie-Hélène Huet, *Monstrous Imagination* (Cambridge, MA: Harvard University Press, 1993). On the cult of motherhood, see above, chap. 4, nn. 67–70. The antithetical sense of the relationship between women and the passions may be reflected in the doublet of the disciplined "housewife" and the lax "hussy." See Wendy Wall, *Staging Domesticity: Household Work and English Identity in Early Modern Drama* (Cambridge: Cambridge University Press, 2002), 17.

17. Hannah Woolley, *The Gentlewoman's Companion; or, a Guide to the Female Sex* . . . (1675), epistle dedicatory, A3v.

18. Elizabeth L. Eisenstein, *The Printing Press as an Agent of Change: Communications and Cultural Transformations in Early-Modern Europe* (Cambridge: Cambridge University Press, 1979), 168.

19. For an argument to this effect regarding the role print played in transforming romance into a coherent canon, see McKeon, *Origins*, 45.

20. See Roy Porter and Lesley Hall, *The Facts of Life: The Creation of Sexual Knowledge in Britain, 1650–1950* (New Haven, CT: Yale University Press, 1995), 33–35, for a summary of the traditional genres of advice, conduct, and information instantiated by *Aristotle's Master-piece*.

21. See Angus McLaren, *Reproductive Rituals: The Perception of Fertility in England from the Sixteenth to the Nineteenth Century* (London: Methuen, 1984), 62–63, who quotes a passage from the 1772 edition making explicit its contraceptive uses.

22. *Aristotle's Compleat and Experienc'd Midwife . . . A Work far more perfect than any yet Extant; and highly Necessary for all Surgeons, Midwives, Nurses, and Child-bearing Women. Made English by W[illiam] S[almon], M.D. The Sixth Edition* (1733).

23. *Aristoteles Master-piece, Or The Secrets of Generation displayed in all the parts thereof . . .* (1684), the first recorded edition.

24. *Aristotle's Compleat Master Piece. . . . The Twenty-Ninth Edition* (1772).

25. *The Works of Aristotle, the Famous Philosopher* (c. 1810).

26. The near nudity of the woman in figure 6.3, however, is only one variation among many; in an otherwise nearly identical frontispiece the woman is clothed. See *The Works of Aristotle. A new edition* (1800?), BL, shelf mark 1578/3732; *Eighteenth Century Short Title Catalogue 1990* (London: British Library, 1990), microfilm reel 3874, no. 3. For Alberti, see above, chap. 5, n. 23.

27. *Aristotle's Master-piece Compleated . . .* (1702) (font reversed); the verses are attributed to William Salmun, whose name appears on a number of these tracts.

28. Cf. the verses with which John Bunyan concludes the first part of *The Pilgrim's Progress from This World, to That which is to come . . .* (1678), ed. N. H. Keeble (Oxford: Oxford University Press, 1984), 134 (font reversed), which strike a similar tone of public-sphere and Protestant self-help: "Now Reader, I have told my Dream to thee; / See if thou canst Interpret it to me; / Or to thy self, or Neighbour . . . ."

29. For one hypothesis of such a tendency and for my reservations about it, see Henry Abelove, "Some Speculations on the History of 'Sexual Intercourse' during the 'Long Eighteenth Century' in England," in *Nationalisms and Sexualities,* ed. Andrew Parker, Mary Russo, Doris Sommer, and Patricia Yaeger (New York: Routledge, 1992), 335–42; and McKeon, "Historicizing Patriarchy," 318n45.

30. On the transfer of slang terms ("he-whore," "molly," "queen," etc.) from female prostitutes to sodomites, see Trumbach, "Birth of the Queen," 137. On the association between sodomy and prostitution and on the sodomite's defiance of procreation and patrilineage, see also Paula Findlen, "Humanism, Politics, and Pornography in Renaissance Italy," in *The Invention of Pornography: Obscenity and the Origins of Modernity, 1500–1800,* ed. Lynn Hunt (New York: Zone Books, 1993), 59, 93, 107; and McKeon, "Historicizing Patriarchy," 309–12.

31. *A Supplement to the Onania . . . to be bound up with either the 7th, 8th, 9th, or 10th Editions of that Book . . .* (n.d.), 19, bound with *Onania; or, the Heinous Sin of Self=Pollution, and All its Frightful Consequences, in both sexes, Consider'd . . . The Eighth Edition* (1723), facsimile ed. (New York: Garland, 1986), separately paginated (hereafter references are to this edition and appear parenthetically in the text). Two recent studies agree that the view of masturbation as an evil and pathological practice is a modern phenomenon that begins with the publication and dissemination of *Onania.* See Jean Stengers and Anne Van Neck, *Masturbation: The History of a Great Terror,* trans. Kathryn Hoffmann (New York: Palgrave, 2001); and Thomas W. Laqueur, *Solitary Sex: A Cultural History of Masturbation* (New York: Zone Books, 2003). Laqueur urges the revival of a former attribution of *Onania* to John Marten (32, 425n15).

32. For Bernard Mandeville, masturbation and prostitution are alternative practices. "Manufriction" is "[t]he first lewd Trick that Boys learn, . . . and when they have once got the Knack of it, they seldom quit it till they come to have actual Commerce with Women: The Safety, Privacy, Convenience, and Cheapness of the Gratification are very strong Mo-

tives . . . ." However, public brothels will help turn such "private Practitioners" from "these clandestine Practices" by providing women with whom to proceed "with the same Convenience, Safety, and Privacy in the one, as well as the other." *A Modest Defence of Publick Stews; or, an Essay upon Whoring, As it is now practis'd in these Kingdoms* (1724), 30, 31, 32, facsimile reprint in Augustan Reprint Society, no. 162, ed. Richard I. Cook (Los Angeles: William Andrews Clark Memorial Library, UCLA, 1973).

33. Unlike libel, masturbation discourse lay under no specific legal prohibition, at least c. 1710, when *Onania* first began to be published. On the formulation of the law of obscene libel in 1728, see below, nn. 93–100. On the book of secrets, see above, chap. 2, nn. 51–55.

34. See above, chap. 2, nn. 158–59.

35. This guilt is customarily mitigated in the case of nocturnal emission or if masturbation and its imagination occur during a dream. Rochester, far less scrupulous about masturbation than the author of *Onania,* draws a fine and ambiguous line in his mock-pastoral story of Cloris: "Frighted shee wakes, and wakeing friggs:/Nature thus kindly eas'd/In dreames raisd by her grunting Piggs/And her owne thumb betwixt her Leggs,/Shees Innocent and pleas'd." "A Song" ("*Faire Cloris* in a Pigsty lay"), lines 36–40, in *The Works of John Wilmot Earl of Rochester,* ed. Harold Love (Oxford: Oxford University Press, 1999), 40.

36. On Protestant conscience—the vocation, the more private authenticity of thoughts over speech and action, and the status of conscience as both "law" and "opinion"—see above, chap. 1, nn. 93–106.

37. Cf. Shaftesbury's desire to overcome the depersonalization of the author that results from publication by making the "obscure implicity Language" of our thoughts "speak out." See above, chap. 2, nn. 144–45.

38. On the 1712 Stamp Act and the 1662 Printing Act, see above, chap. 2, nn. 30–31, 117–18, 123–24.

39. Michel Foucault, *The History of Sexuality,* vol. 1, *An Introduction,* trans. Robert Hurley (New York: Vintage, 1990), 66; Ian Hunter, David Saunders, and Dugald Williamson, *On Pornography: Literature, Sexuality, and Obscenity Law* (London: Macmillan, 1993), 29–30.

40. The remainder of this paragraph is indebted to Edmund Leites, *The Puritan Conscience and Modern Sexuality* (New Haven, CT: Yale University Press, 1986); see esp. his conclusion. However, Hunter, Saunders, and Williamson, in *On Pornography,* do recognize the importance of the role played by Protestant thought in this historical process; see 35, 43.

41. Leites, *Puritan Conscience,* 143–44. On the repressive hypothesis, see Foucault, *History,* vol. 1, pt. 2. The constancy of sex may be a condition of all desire in modern culture. See above, chap. 1, nn. 83–85.

42. Thomas Cranley, *The Converted Courtezan, or, The Reformed Whore. Being a true Relation of a penitent Sinner, shadowed under the name of Amanda* (1639), 22, 76 (font reversed). For a discussion of this tract, see Cecile M. Jagodzinski, *Privacy and Print: Reading and Writing in Seventeenth-Century England* (Charlottesville: University of Virginia Press, 1999), 138–47.

43. However, not all contemporaries found it necessary to subscribe to the logic of this distinction between the virtuality of other products of the imagination and the materiality of masturbation. See below, chap. 15, on Fanny Hill's (i.e., John Cleland's) abstraction of "pleasure itself." On the way eighteenth-century writers came to understand the imagination as a faculty that was grounded in "private" and sensible actuality but conducive to the "public" realm of virtuality, see below, chap. 7. Laqueur's inquiry into the causes of the modern atti-

tude toward masturbation in *Solitary Sex* also leads him to focus on the imaginative powers of masturbation—its autonomy, secrecy, and solitude—as the qualities that make it newly dangerous in a world increasingly dedicated to the freedom of the individual but alarmed by the prospect of an activity that seemed entirely invulnerable to outside control. Stengers and Van Neck, less inclined in *Masturbation* to ask the big question of causation directly, tend to emphasize the marketing brilliance of masturbation's first entrepreneurs, the author of *Onania* and Samuel Auguste David Tissot.

44. John Locke, *An Essay concerning Human Understanding* (1690), bk. 2, chap. 1, sec. 24, ed. Peter H. Nidditch (Oxford: Clarendon, 1979), 118.

45. [Jonathan Swift], *A Tale of a Tub, To which is added The Battle of the Books and the Mechanical Operation of the Spirit* (1704, 1710), ed. A. C. Guthkelch and D. Nichol Smith, 2nd ed. (Oxford: Clarendon, 1958), 266, 287, 163, 157, 165, 164, 167 (hereafter references are to this edition and appear parenthetically in the text).

46. Aristotle, *Poetics,* 1449b.

47. Mandeville, *Modest Defence,* 30, 31.

48. Samuel Pepys, 29 June 1663, *The Diary of Samuel Pepys,* ed. Robert Latham and Williams Matthews, vol. 4, *1663* (London: HarperCollins, 1995), 204 (hereafter references are to this edition and appear parenthetically in the text).

49. See above, chap. 2, nn. 148–58.

50. The plausibility of the analogy between solitary masturbation and the political contract, market exchange, and public opinion depends on the notion that masturbation is, like these other modern practices and unlike the traditional, "face-to-face," and interpersonal practice of copulation, an impersonal and virtual relation—but for the unique reason that its virtual sociability is intrapersonal. Laqueur remarks that "[t]he speculator and the masturbator were playing on the same pitch, but so was everyone who dreamed of contentment through buying just one more thing. . . . Masturbation presented the ultimate challenge to all such views of how selfish desire might be socialized, the limit case, the exemplary case for the challenge it posed" (*Solitary Sex,* 280, 291). Elsewhere Laqueur has compared early modern attitudes toward masturbation and prostitution as two complementary modes of "unsocialized sex" that take it away—respectively, inward and outward—from the social unit of the family. See "The Social Evil, The Solitary Vice, and Pouring Tea," in *Solitary Pleasures: The Historical, Literary, and Artistic Discourses of Autoeroticism,* ed. Paule Bennett and Vernon A. Rosario II (New York: Routledge, 1995), 155–61. My ongoing concern with how the modern realm of the private internalizes the relationship between the public and the private may suggest that one way contemporaries met the challenge epitomized by masturbation was by learning to conceive the realm of individual interiority as not antisocial but a microsocial environment (social psychology, psychoanalysis) in which some of the most pressing problems of sociability might be engaged.

51. Jeremy Taylor, *The Rvle and Exercises of Holy Living . . .* (1650), 80 (font reversed); the author of *Onania* cites this passage (2).

52. For a summary of apprehensions of the moral and social effects of novel reading, see Michael McKeon, "Prose Fiction: Great Britain," in *The Cambridge History of Literary Criticism,* ed. H. B. Nisbet and Claude Rawson, vol. 4, *The Eighteenth Century* (Cambridge: Cambridge University Press, 1997), 248–49.

53. See Ian F. Moulton, *Before Pornography: Erotic Writings in Early Modern England* (Oxford: Oxford University Press, 2000), 5, 8. The genre of the lives of prostitutes was thought to have its origin in Lucian's *Dialogues of the Courtesans.* See Findlen, "Humanism, Politics," 53. Nevertheless I will follow Findlen and an increasing number of scholars in distinguishing the "pornographic," as a specifically early modern emergence, from the universality of the "erotic."

54. For a fuller discussion of the way the rule of female chastity was reconceived in this period, see McKeon, *Origins,* 156–58.

55. Leites, *Puritan Conscience,* 146–47.

56. See *OED,* s.v. "sex," 1.e. But see Mary Wortley Montagu's usage, which applies the phrase to men: Montagu to Anne Wortley, 21 Aug. 1709, in *The Complete Letters of Mary Wortley Montagu,* ed. Robert Halsband (Oxford: Clarendon, 1965), 1:10.

57. See McKeon, "Prose Fiction," 257–58.

58. Hunter, Saunders, and Williamson, *On Pornography,* xi.

59. *Pamela Censured* (1741), 24, ed. Charles Batten Jr., Augustan Reprint Society, no. 175 (Los Angeles: William Andrews Clark Memorial Library, UCLA, 1976).

60. On Pepys's lodgings in the Navy Office, see Pepys, *Diary,* vol. 10, *Companion,* 29.

61. Baudouin also painted a version of this scene in which the lady's dress is hiked up to her waist and the act of masturbation is fully exposed (for the image see Laqueur, *Solitary Sex,* 349). More frankly pornographic for the viewer, it is also perhaps less effective in evoking the liminal virtuality of pornographic reading as experienced by the lady we view.

62. See Hitchcock, *English Sexualities,* 14, 17.

63. See Roy Porter, "Mixed Feelings: The Enlightenment and Sexuality in Eighteenth-Century Britain," in *Sexuality in Eighteenth-Century Britain,* ed. Paul-Gabriel Boucé (Manchester: Manchester University Press, 1982), 8–9.

64. This is documented by James Grantham Turner's study of "pornographic satire," *Libertines and Radicals in Early Modern London: Sexuality, Politics, and Literary Culture, 1630–1685* (Cambridge: Cambridge University Press, 2002).

65. See Peter Wagner, *Eros Revived: Erotica of the Enlightenment in England and America* (London: Secker and Warburg, 1988), 6; Lynn Hunt, "Introduction: Obscenity and the Origins of Modernity, 1500–1800," 10, 18, 36, summarizing the findings of comparatist contributors to *Invention of Pornography* (the exception is Wijnand W. Mijnhardt, "Politics and Pornography in the Seventeenth- and Eighteenth-Century Dutch Republic," 292: "Beginning in the later seventeenth century, pornography was perceived, not only by its producers and consumers but also by official authority, as a separate category"); and Moulton, *Before Pornography,* introduction and pp. 38–39.

66. See the discussion of Christopher Hill, *The World Turned Upside Down: Radical Ideas during the English Revolution* (New York: Viking, 1972), chaps. 9, 10; and idem, *The Collected Essays of Christopher Hill,* vol. 2, *Religion and Politics in Seventeenth-Century England* (Amherst: University of Massachusetts Press, 1968), chap. 10.

67. Cf. David Foxon, *Libertine Literature in England, 1660–1745* (New Hyde Park, NY: University Books, 1965), 50: "It seems that the revolt against authority first took the form of heresy, then politics, and finally sexual license; clearly pornography is closely related to this revolt." On the other hand, Foxon locates the appearance of pornography "as such" in the

great Continental works of the mid-seventeenth century (48). For interesting and rather different discussions of libertinism, see James Grantham Turner, "The Properties of Libertinism," in Macubbin, *'Tis Nature's Fault,* 75–87; and Trumbach, *Sex,* chap. 3.

68. See Richard Rambuss, *Closet Devotions* (Durham, NC: Duke University Press, 1998), passim.

69. On the influence of Aretino in England, see esp. David O. Frantz, *Festum Voluptatis: A Study of Renaissance Erotica* (Columbus: Ohio State University Press, 1989), chaps. 5–8; and Moulton, *Before Pornography,* pt. 2 ("If Castiglione wrote *The Book of the Courtier,* in the *Ragionamenti* Aretino wrote the Book of the Courtesan," 130). Turner, *Libertines and Radicals,* 75, 124, and passim, is attentive to the English mixture of Italian inheritance and native sources.

70. On the Dilettanti Society, see Shearer West, "Libertinism and the Ideology of Male Friendship in the Portraits of the Society of Dilettanti," *Eighteenth-Century Life* 16 (May 1992): 76–104; and Randolph Trumbach, "Erotic Fantasy and Male Libertinism in Enlightenment England," in Hunt, *Invention of Pornography,* 271–82. With the latter effort compare the sodomitical imitation-parody of the marriage sacrament in idem, "Birth of the Queen," 137–38.

71. See Roger Thompson, *Unfit for Modest Ears: A Study of Pornographic, Obscene, and Bawdy Works Written or Published in England in the Second Half of the Seventeenth Century* (Totowa, NJ: Rowman and Littlefield, 1979), chaps. 4, 8; Peter Wagner, *Eros Revived,* chap. 2; and idem, "Anticatholic Erotica in Eighteenth-Century England," in *Erotica and the Enlightenment,* ed. Peter Wagner (Frankfurt-am-Main: Peter Lang, 1991), 166–209.

72. [Andrew Marvell], *The Rehearsal Transpros'd: Or, Animadversions Upon a late Book, Intituled, A Preface Shewing What Grounds there are of Fears and Jealousies of Popery,* 2 pts. (1672–73), ed. D. I. B. Smith (Oxford: Clarendon, 1971), 30–31.

73. Jonathan Swift, *A Discourse Concerning the Mechanical Operation of the Spirit. In a Letter To a Friend. A Fragment* (1704), in *A Tale of a Tub,* 280–81; on Marvell's precedence, see 10.

74. *The Whores Rhetorick, Calculated to the Meridian of London and Conformed to the Rules of Art* (1683; reprint, New York: Obolensky, 1961), 15.

75. Ibid., 129.

76. See below, chaps. 11–13, on the writings of Aphra Behn, Delarivier Manley, and others. See also Paul Hammond, "The King's Two Bodies: Representations of Charles II," in *Culture, Politics, and Society in Britain, 1660–1800,* ed. Jeremy Black and Jeremy Gregory (Manchester: Manchester University Press, 1991), 13–48; Rachel J. Weil, "Sometimes a Scepter Is Only a Scepter: Pornography and Politics in Restoration England," in Hunt, *Invention of Pornography,* 124–53; Harold Weber, *Paper Bullets: Print and Kingship under Charles II* (Lexington: University of Kentucky Press, 1996), chap. 3; and Turner, *Libertines and Radicals,* chaps. 4–6.

77. [John Wilmot, Earl of Rochester], "A Satyr" (wr. 1673), lines 1–22, in Rochester, *Works,* 85–86. I print here what Love calls the "Group-A text."

78. The first listing for the term "private part" in the *OED,* 3.b, is dated 1634 (however, the number of citations is minimal). The more standard term was "privities."

79. "On the Duchess of Portsmouth," quoted in Weil, "Sometimes a Scepter," 143.

80. [John Lacy], "Satire" (1677), lines 7–8, and "Nell Gwynne" (1669), in *Poems on Affairs*

of State: Augustan Satirical Verse, 1660–1714, vol. 1, *1660–1678,* ed. George deF. Lord (New Haven, CT: Yale University Press, 1963), 426 and 420, respectively.

81. On "effeminacy," see McKeon, "Historicizing Patriarchy," 308.

82. See Weil, "Sometimes a Scepter," 142–51, for an interesting discussion of these issues, to which I am indebted.

83. [John Wilmot, Earl of Rochester?], *Sodom and Gomorah* (wr. c. 1673–78), in Rochester, *Works,* 302–33. Harold Love prefers Christopher Fishbourne as its likely author but cannot rule out Rochester. See Rochester, *Works,* 497–98. Hereafter page references are to this edition and appear parenthetically in the text.

84. On the 1670 Secret Treaty of Dover between Charles II and Louis XIV, see below, chap. 10, nn. 70–75.

85. The similarity between the language given to pederasts here to elevate same-sex over different-sex activity and that used by Rochester in his poem of similar theme, "Love to a Woman" (Rochester, *Works,* 38), may support the attribution of *Sodom and Gomorah* to Rochester even as it points the unlikelihood that so different attitudes toward pederasty might have been expressed by the same man.

86. For a brief reading of *The Rape of the Lock* along these lines, see below, chap. 8, nn. 70–74.

87. See above, chap. 1, n. 6.

88. Rochester to Henry Savile, spring 1676, in *The Letters of John Wilmot, Earl of Rochester,* ed. Jeremy Treglown (Chicago: University of Chicago Press, 1980), 117, 119; Sir George Etherege to William Jephson, 8 Mar. 1688, quoted in Harold Weber, *The Restoration Rake-Hero: Transformations in Sexual Understanding in Seventeenth-Century England* (Madison: University of Wisconsin Press, 1986), 49.

89. [John Sheffield, Earl of Mulgrave, Duke of Buckinghamshire], *An Essay upon Poetry* (1682), lines 22–31, in *Critical Essays of the Seventeenth Century,* ed. J. E. Spingarn, vol. 2, *1650–1685* (1908–9; reprint, Bloomington: Indiana University Press, 1957), 288.

90. Charles Wolseley, preface to *Valentinian, a Tragedy, as 'Tis Alter'd by the Late Earl of Rochester* (1685), in Spingarn, *Critical Essays,* vol. 3, *1685–1700,* 15, 17 (hereafter references are to this edition and appear parenthetically in the text).

91. See above, chap. 2, nn. 137–42.

92. See Hunt, "Introduction"; Margaret C. Jacob, "The Materialist World of Pornography"; Kathryn Norberg, "The Libertine Whore: Prostitution in French Pornography from Margot to Juliette"; and Lynn Hunt, "Pornography and the French Revolution," all in Hunt, *Invention of Pornography,* 44, 45; 182; 250–51; and 326, 329, 330–32, 335–38, respectively. These scholars also stress that the effacement of gender difference in pornography of this period was a relative phenomenon. See also Iain McCalman, *Radical Underworld: Prophets, Revolutionaries, and Pornographers in London, 1795–1840* (Cambridge: Cambridge University Press, 1988), chap. 10.

93. For helpful discussions of Curll's case, see Donald Thomas, *A Long Time Burning: The History of Literary Censorship in England* (New York: Praeger, 1969), 78–84; and Hunter, Saunders, and Williamson, *On Pornography,* 50–56.

94. On libel law as aimed at punishing the exposure of real persons, see above, chap. 2, nn. 114–16; on personal reputation as private property, cf. Marvell's language, above, chap. 2, n. 109.

95. *R. v. Taylor* (1676), 1 Vent. 293, quoted in Thomas, *Long Time Burning,* 66; on the Blasphemy Act, see 67. On the relationship between the spiritual and the secular courts in these matters, see also above, chap. 1, nn. 111–14.

96. *R. v. Curll* (1728), in *Cobbett's Complete Collection of State Trials . . . ,* ed. Thomas B. Howell (London: Hansard, 1809–26), vol. 17, cols. 153–60 (hereafter cited parenthetically in the text). Howell includes arguments from the several stages of the attempt to convict Curll over this three-year period; in the following account of Curll's case, for convenience I often do not distinguish these chronologically (or as to individual speaker). Howell also includes material from opinions concerning other cases cited at the time in relation to Curll's.

97. On the norm of "the generality of readers" in libel law, see above, chap. 2, n. 131.

98. According to the account in *Cobbett's Complete Collection of State Trials,* Curll avoided punishment at the hands of the public for his obscene libel by using print to reembed its sexual knowledge within a political context: "This Edmund Curll stood in the pillory at Charing-Cross, but was not pelted, or used ill; for being an artful, cunning (though wicked) fellow, he had contrived to have printed papers dispersed all about Charing-Cross, telling the people, he stood there for vindicating the memory of Queen Anne; which had such an effect on the mob, that it would have been dangerous even to have spoken against him: and when he was taken down out of the pillory, the mob carried him off, as it were in triumph, to a neighbouring tavern" (col. 160).

99. The triptych was first printed in the *Grub-Street Journal,* no. 147 (26 Oct. 1732); the explication appeared in ibid., no. 148 (30 Oct. 1732), which also reprinted the picture (hereafter cited parenthetically in the text).

100. *Grub-Street Journal,* no. 148 (30 Oct. 1732). Where Henley is discussed, the explicator refers us to the note to bk. 3, line 195, of Pope's *Dunciad Variorum* (1728–29).

Chapter Seven | Motives for Domestication

1. Adam Smith, *An Inquiry into the Nature and Causes of the Wealth of Nations* (1776), bk. 1, chap. 1, ed. R. H. Campbell, A. S. Skinner, and W. B. Todd, Glasgow Edition of the Works and Correspondence of Adam Smith (Indianapolis: Liberty Classics, 1981), 1:13–15 (hereafter references are to this edition and appear parenthetically in the text, preceded by the original book and chapter numbers).

2. For one effort in this direction, see Adam Ferguson, *An Essay on the History of Civil Society* (1767), ed. Louis Schneider (New Brunswick, NJ: Transaction, 1980), 25–31.

3. I am thinking here especially of the early modern quarrel of the ancients and moderns, one effect of which was to differentiate "scientific" from "artistic" or "humanistic" modes of knowledge according to the difference between standards of achievement that entail a generalizing norm of incremental and cumulative progress and those that do not. See Douglas Lane Patey, "Ancients and Moderns," in *The Cambridge History of Literary Criticism,* ed. H. B. Nisbet and Claude Rawson, vol. 4, *The Eighteenth Century* (Cambridge: Cambridge University Press, 1997), 34–46. Raymond Williams has remarked how the emergent irreconcilability of material quantity and cultural quality is registered in the resonant ambivalence of the terms "improve" and "interest" in eighteenth-century usage. See *Keywords: A Vocabulary of Culture and Society* (New York: Oxford University Press, 1976), 132–33, 143–44. I will return below to this particular epistemological consequence of the quarrel of the ancients and moderns.

4. John Noorthouck, review of Mrs. Thomson's *The Labyrinths of Life* (1791), in *Monthly Review*, 2nd ser., 5 (July 1791), quoted in *Novel and Romance, 1700–1800: A Documentary Record*, ed. Ioan Williams (New York: Barnes and Noble, 1970), 373. For other instances of this vision, see Michael McKeon, "Prose Fiction: Great Britain," in *Cambridge History of Literary Criticism*, 4:244–46. The *locus classicus* of this vision, applied to the production of not novels but poetry and drama, is Alexander Pope's *Peri Bathous* (1727). See below, nn. 119–26.

5. See above, chap. 1, n. 25.

6. Especially at that historical moment when distinction is poised on the brink of separation, however, the relation between small and great also may serve an ideological more than an epistemological end by self-consciously employing the authority of the great to legitimate the small rather than the familiarity of the small to render greatness intelligible.

7. John Cheke, *Hurt of Sedition* (1549), K3r, and Thomas Gataker, *A Good Wife, God's Gift* (1620), A3v–4r, quoted in Lena Cowen Orlin, *Private Matters and Public Culture in Post-Reformation England* (Ithaca, NY: Cornell University Press, 1994), 88 and 77, respectively.

8. John Milton, *Of Education. To Master Samuel Hartlib* (1644), ed. Donald C. Dorian, in *The Complete Prose Works of John Milton*, vol. 2, *1643–1648*, ed. Ernest Sirluck (New Haven, CT: Yale University Press, 1959), 368–69.

9. Henry Vaughan, *The Mount of Olives*, chap. 24, verse 12, in *The Works of Henry Vaughan*, ed. L. C. Martin, 2nd ed. (Oxford: Oxford University Press, 1957), 177. My thanks to Kristin Girten for this reference.

10. On the instability of Protestant hermeneutics, see Michael McKeon, *The Origins of the English Novel, 1600–1740* (Baltimore: Johns Hopkins University Press, 1987), 74–76, 194–95, and chap. 2 passim.

11. John Bunyan, *The Pilgrim's Progress from This World, to That which is to come . . .* (1678), ed. N. H. Keeble (Oxford: Oxford University Press, 1984), "The Author's Way of Sending Forth his Second Part of the Pilgrim," 139 (font reversed); on parables, see "The Author's Apology for his Book," 4–6 (hereafter cited parenthetically in the text).

12. See Erich Auerbach, *Mimesis: The Representation of Reality in Western Literature*, trans. Willard Trask (1953; reprint, Garden City, NY: Anchor, 1957), 63; and idem, *Literary Language and Its Public in Late Latin Antiquity and in the Middle Ages*, trans. Ralph Manheim, Bollingen Series, 74 (New York: Pantheon, 1965), chaps. 1 and 2.

13. John Dod and Robert Cleaver, *Ten Sermons . . . of the Lords Supper* (1609), 82; William Perkins, *Workes* (1612), 1:758; and Joseph Hall, *The Works* (1628–62), 1:137, all quoted in Charles H. George and Katherine George, *The Protestant Mind of the English Reformation, 1570–1640* (Princeton, NJ: Princeton University Press, 1961), 130, 138, and 139n68, respectively.

14. John Foxe, *The Acts and Monuments of John Foxe* (1563, enl. 1570), ed. Stephen R. Cattley (London: Seeley and Burnside, 1839), 8:493–95 (hereafter cited parenthetically in the text). Cf. Oliver Heywood's advice that when we read Matthew's direction to "enter into thy Closet," although his meaning no doubt is spiritual, nonetheless "we need not interpret the plain word in such a borrowed sense" (see above, chap. 1, n. 107).

15. See McKeon, *Origins*, chap. 8, for an extended argument that Bunyan's literal narrative records the early modern coalescence of the nation-state.

16. On the curtain lecture, see above, chap. 5, nn. 56–60.

17. Matt. 12:50, 19:29.

18. The penultimate paragraph of part 2 tells us that "[a]s for *Christian's* Children, the four Boys that *Christiana* brought with her, with their Wives and Children, I did not stay where I was, till they were gone over. Also since I came away, I heard one say, that they were yet alive, and so would be for the Increase of the Church in that Place where they were for a time" (261).

19. See Barbara J. Lewalski, *Protestant Poetics and the Seventeenth-Century Religious Lyric* (Princeton, NJ: Princeton University Press, 1979), 129–40.

20. George Herbert, "The Bunch of Grapes" (1633), lines 6–11, in *George Herbert: The Complete English Poems,* ed. John Tobin (Harmondsworth, UK: Penguin, 1991), 119–20.

21. If patriarchalist analogies provide the grounds for "political allegory"—the private family signifying the public state—then Dryden's poem invites description as a "mock-political allegory," in which the signifying relationship between private and public balances on the edge of an ironic reversal. For a full discussion, see Michael McKeon, "Historicizing *Absalom and Achitophel*," in *The New Eighteenth Century: Theory, Politics, English Literature,* ed. Felicity Nussbaum and Laura Brown (New York: Methuen, 1987), 25–29; on Protestant poetics and the critics, see 26nn12, 13.

22. George Herbert, "Redemption," in *Complete English Poems,* 35–36.

23. [Jonathan Swift], *A Tale of a Tub, To which is added The Battle of the Books and the Mechanical Operation of the Spirit* (1704, 1710), ed. A. C. Gutchkelch and D. Nichol Smith, 2nd ed. (Oxford: Clarendon, 1958), 73, 74–75 (hereafter cited parenthetically in the text); William Wotton, *Reflections upon Ancient and Modern Learning . . .* (1705), 529; Edward Hyde, Earl of Clarendon, *A Brief View and Survey of the Dangerous and pernicious Errors to Church and State, in Mr. Hobbes's Book, Entitled Leviathan* (Oxford, 1676), 2.

24. John Milton, *Paradise Lost,* bk. 5, lines 304, 306, 377, 396, 328–30, in *John Milton: Complete Poems and Major Prose,* ed. Merritt Y. Hughes (New York: Odyssey, 1957) (hereafter cited parenthetically in the text).

25. Richard Steele, *Tatler,* no. 217 (29 Aug. 1710), in *The Tatler,* ed. Donald F. Bond, 3 vols. (Oxford: Clarendon, 1987) (hereafter references are to this edition and appear parenthetically in the text). Steele's domestication of the scene from *Paradise Lost* has the aim of illustrating the types of the male "bully" and the female "scold." On the skimmington ride, see above, chap. 4, nn. 18–21.

Steele's modernization of Milton is delicately balanced on the edge of the ludicrous. Two centuries later Samuel Butler's modernization of Bunyan confidently plunges over it: Butler's narrator "had also dramatised 'The Pilgrim's Progress' for a Christmas Pantomime, and made an important scene of Vanity Fair, with Mr. Greatheart, Appolyon, Christiana, Mercy, and Hopeful as the principal characters. . . . Mr. Greatheart was very stout and he had a red nose; he wore a capacious waistcoat, and a shirt with a huge frill down the middle of the front. Hopeful was up to as much mischief as I could give him; he wore the costume of a young swell of the period, and had a cigar in his mouth, which was continually going out. Christiana did not wear much of anything . . . ." Butler, *The Way of All Flesh* (wr. 1873–84, pub. 1903) (New York: Modern Library, 1998), 122. My thanks to Carolyn Williams for bringing this passage to my attention.

26. Martinus Scriblerus [Alexander Pope], *Peri Bathous: Of the Art of Sinking in Poetry* (1727), chap. 12, in *Literary Criticism of Alexander Pope,* ed. Bertrand A. Goldgar (Lincoln: University of Nebraska Press, 1965), 76 (hereafter references are to this edition and appear parenthetically in the text).

27. Charles Sorel, *The Extravagant Shepherd; or, The History Of the Shepherd Lysis. An Anti-Romance* . . . (1627–28, 1633–34), trans. John Davies (1654), bk. 13, p. 60 (the speaker is Clarimond). In Bacon's *The Wisdom of the Ancients* ([Lat., 1609] trans. 1619) "naturalization" takes on the literal sense of disclosing a reference to nature. Thus he accommodates Cupid as "*the natural motion of the atom:* which is indeed the original and unique force that constitutes and fashions all things out of matter." *The Philosophical Works of Francis Bacon,* ed. Robert L. Ellis and James Spedding, rev. ed. John M. Robertson (London: Routledge, 1905), 840 (hereafter cited parenthetically in the text). For this reason, Bacon's method is less a hermeneutic accommodation than a euhemerist demystification.

28. [John Dryden], *Absalom and Achitophel* (1681), lines 130–33, in *The Works of John Dryden,* vol. 2, *Poems, 1681–1684,* ed. H. T. Swedenberg Jr. and Vinton A. Dearing (Berkeley and Los Angeles: University of California Press, 1972), 9; idem, *A Discourse concerning the Original and Progress of Satire* (1693), and Dryden to John Dennis, 1694, both in *Of Dramatic Poesy and Other Critical Essays,* ed. George Watson (London: Dent, 1962), 2:88–89, 178.

29. *Spectator,* no. 523 (30 Oct. 1712), in *The Spectator,* ed. Donald F. Bond, 5 vols. (Oxford: Clarendon, 1965) (hereafter references are to this edition and appear parenthetically in the text).

30. William Perkins, *Christian Œconomie* . . . (1609), 3r–v, quoted in Wendy Wall, *Staging Domesticity: Household Work and English Identity in Early Modern Drama* (Cambridge: Cambridge University Press, 2002), 1; William Gouge, *Of Domesticall Dvties* . . . (1622), 18; John Downame, *A Guide to Godliness Or a Treatise of a Christian Life* . . . (1629), 329–30, quoted in John Morgan, *Godly Learning: Puritan Attitudes toward Reason, Learning, and Education, 1560–1640* (Cambridge: Cambridge University Press, 1986), 142–43.

31. Thomas Babington Macaulay, "History" (1828), in *Critical, Historical, and Miscellaneous Essays* (New York: Sheldon, 1860), 1:431–32. My thanks to Jason Gieger for bringing this passage to my attention.

32. Samuel Johnson, *Rambler,* nos. 60 and 4 (13 Oct. and 31 Mar. 1750), in *The Yale Edition of the Works of Samuel Johnson,* vol. 3, *The Rambler,* ed. W. J. Bate and Albrecht B. Strauss (New Haven, CT: Yale University Press, 1969), 321, 21–22; Johnson to Joseph Baretti, 21 Dec. 1762, in James Boswell, *Life of Johnson* (1791), ed. R. W. Chapman (Oxford: Oxford University Press, 1980), 269. Cf. Plutarch, "Alexander," in *The Age of Alexander: Nine Greek Lives by Plutarch,* ed. and trans. Ian Scott-Kilvert (Harmondsworth, UK: Penguin, 1973), 252: ". . . I am writing biography, not history, and the truth is that the most brilliant exploits often tell us nothing of the virtues or vices of the men who performed them, while on the other hand a chance remark or a joke may reveal far more of a man's character than the mere fact of winning battles in which thousands fall, or of marshalling great armies, or laying siege to cities."

33. Tobias Smollett, *Roderick Random,* ed. David Blewett (Harmondsworth, UK: Penguin, 1995), 5.

34. John Dod and Robert Cleaver, *A Godly Forme of Household Government: for the ordering of private families, according to the direction of God's Word* (1612), L7r.

35. Oliver Goldsmith, *Life of Richard Nash* (1762), 2–3; John Bennett, *Letters to a Young Lady* (1789), 184; and *Memoirs of the Life and Times of Sir Thomas Deveil* . . . (1748), 1, quoted in Mark Salber Phillips, *Society and Sentiment: Genres of Historical Writing in Britain, 1740–1820* (Princeton, NJ: Princeton University Press, 2000), 135, 133, and 136, respectively; on these matters, see generally chap. 5 passim.

36. Johnson, *Rambler*, no. 60 (31 Mar. 1750). Cf. Samuel Johnson, *The History of Rasselas, Prince of Abyssinia* (1759), chap. 29, in *The Yale Edition of the Works of Samuel Johnson*, vol. 16, *Rasselas and Other Tales*, ed. Gwin J. Kolb (New Haven, CT: Yale University Press, 1990), 109, where Nekayah speaks of "all the minute detail of a domestick day." For the passage on the public domain, see above, chap. 2, n. 45. On the word "common," cf. the primary sense of the agrarian "common" as land to which all have a use-right and the secondary sense that it is commoners rather than gentle landowners to whom that right is relevant (on use-right, see above, chap. 1, n. 38). As we will see in the cases of Shaftesbury and Addison as well, Johnson's use of the word "vulgar" here is not sociopolitical in its major implication.

37. Johnson, *Rambler*, nos. 60, 4 (13 Oct., 31 Mar. 1750). Johnson alludes here to Pliny's *Natural History* 35.36.85. In derogating the type of the "pretty gentleman" Nathaniel Lancaster economically extends the interplay between social status and generality to include the field of gender difference and sexuality: "*The Pretty Gentleman* is certainly formed in a different Mould from that of Common Men, and tempered with a purer Flame. The whole System is of a finer Turn, and superior Accuracy of Fabric, insomuch that it looks as if Nature had been in doubt, to which Sex she should assign Him." [Nathaniel Lawrence], *The Pretty Gentleman . . .* (1747), ed. Edmund Goldsmid (Edinburgh: Bibliotheca Curiosa, 1885), 25–26.

38. Edmund Burke to Bristol Bell Club, 13 Oct. 1777, in *Burke's Politics: Selected Writings and Speeches of Edmund Burke on Reform, Revolution, and War*, ed. Ross J. S. Hoffman and Paul Levack (New York: Knopf, 1949), 2:119.

39. [William Davenant], *A Proposition for Advancement of Moralitie, By a new way of Entertainment of the People* (1654), 17–18, 9–10, reprinted in James R. Jacob and Timothy Raylor, "Opera and Obedience: Thomas Hobbes and *A Proposition for Advancement of Moralitie* by Sir William Davenant," *Seventeenth Century* 6, no. 1 (1991): 245, 244. Putting a distinct but related meaning on these terms, Edmund Spenser thought his allegory or "historicall fiction" compatible with "the use of these dayes, seeing all things accounted by their showes, and nothing esteemed of, that is not delightful and pleasing to commune sence." "A Letter of the Authors," appended to *The Faerie Queene* (1590), in *Edmund Spenser's Poetry*, ed. Hugh Maclean (New York: Norton, 1968), 1–2.

40. Francis Bacon, "Author's Preface," *The Wisdom of the Ancients*, 823–24.

41. See above, chap. 1, n. 66. The independence of the landed gentleman was said to be guaranteed first of all by his absolute freehold ownership of his property—that is, by his independence both of the sovereign and of the market. For a summary of the civic humanist argument for gentle disinterestedness in sociopolitical matters, see John Barrell, *English Literature in History, 1730–80: An Equal, Wide Survey* (London: Hutchinson, 1983), 31–40. It will be evident from what follows that in my view, Barrell's Pocockian reading attributes to the civic humanist standard of disinterestedness a far more normative and definitive role than is plausible. For Barrell, "the tradition of republican thought" (32) effectively determines the understanding of disinterestedness as a condition of gentility until this view is challenged, first, by early-eighteenth-century efforts to modernize the ideal of the gentleman and, second, by the late-eighteenth-century realization that the proliferating division of labor had rendered untenable the idea that an impartial view of the whole was available to any single perspective. In my reading, the norm of disinterestedness first emerges with the manifest default of sovereign neutrality during the middle decades of the seventeenth century. The

recognition of a multiplicity of interests and occupations that accompanies this default engenders a public debate about the grounds for disinterested judgment in which civic humanism is only one player among several. This is clear already in the last decade of the seventeenth century, when contemporaries tellingly conceived landowners who subscribed to civic humanist ideology as "the landed interest." Cf. W. A. Speck, "Social Status in Late Stuart England," *Past and Present,* no. 34 (1966): 127–29; and idem, "Conflict in Society," in *Britain after the Glorious Revolution,* ed. Geoffrey Holmes (London: Macmillan, 1969), 145. By the early eighteenth century the radical reconception of gentility had been under way in England for well over a century. See McKeon, *Origins,* 156–67 and chap. 5 passim.

For a subtle discussion of disinterestedness and related issues in this period that by a very different route arrives at findings broadly compatible with my own, see Mary Poovey, *A History of the Modern Fact: Problems of Knowledge in the Sciences of Wealth and Society* (Chicago: University of Chicago Press, 1998), chap. 4.

42. See above, chap. 1, nn. 50–65. According to the *OED,* "disinterestedness" was a seventeenth-century coinage. The concept of disinterestedness is as old as stoicism; my limited ambition here is to suggest the degree to which its rethinking in our period depended not only on the influence of ancient texts but significantly on modern intellectual, political, and social change.

43. As we might expect, however, for some time after the Restoration, custom continued to purvey the notion of the sovereign's disinterestedness through the increasingly formulaic bromide that "the king can do no wrong."

44. The language of "refinement" here may seem at first counterintuitive. Especially in social contexts, we tend to think of refinement as valorizing the comparatively elevated status toward which it aims. But if we attend to the full process of refinement—not only where it aims but also where it begins—we see that it also legitimates the lower status as possessing a basis substantial enough to support a transformative rise in status. In social contexts, refinement is an instrument of upward mobility for an assimilative "middle class"; to aristocracy it is beneath contempt. Domestication proceeds from the opposite direction. It is an instrument not of transformation but of accommodation: the value of the lower status lies in the fact of its having been bestowed from above. Refinement is the behavior of the tradesman who internalizes the manners of gentility. Domestication is the story of our "lord" becoming our friend and teacher for a time before returning to the splendor of his father's court. With the construability of "refinement" compare the antithetical implications of the absorption and retention models of social mobility. McKeon, *Origins,* 159–62.

45. I pass over the most radical response—e.g., Bernard Mandeville's—to the question who took on the disinterestedness forfeited by the monarchy: namely, no one at all. For some, that is, the momentum generated by the demystification of monarchal "disinterestedness" quickly overcame the plausibility of disinterestedness as such. Cf. also Thomas Gordon, *Cato's Letters,* no. 40 (5 Aug. 1721), in John Trenchard and Thomas Gordon, *Cato's Letters: or, Essays on Liberty, Civil and Religious, and Other Important Subjects* (originally published in the *London Journal,* 1720–23), ed. Ronald Hamowy (Indianapolis: Liberty Fund, 1995), 1:279: "Every passion, every view that men have, is selfish in some degree; but when it does good to the publick in its operation and consequence, it may be justly called disinterested in the usual meaning of that word. So that when we call any man disinterested, we should intend no more by it, than that the turn of his mind is towards the publick, and

that he has placed his own personal glory and pleasure in serving it. To serve his country is his private pleasure, mankind is his mistress; and he does good to them by gratifying himself. Disinterestedness, in any other sense than this, there is none."

46. Deane Bartlett, *Guardian,* no. 130 (10 Aug. 1713), in *The Guardian,* ed. John C. Stephens (Lexington: University Press of Kentucky, 1982), 433. Bartlett proceeds to base the distinction on the difference between he "whose Occupation lies in the Exertion of his rational Faculties" and he "who is employed in the Use of . . . the organic Parts of his Body," a definition that allows him to exclude all those who spend their time ogling, flirting, cringing, posing, and dressing from the rank of gentry, who rather "imploy the Talents of the Mind in the Pursuit of Knowledge and Practice of Virtue, and are content to take their Places as they are distinguished by moral and intellectual Accomplishments" (433–35).

47. See above, chap. 2, n. 100.

48. The use of the traditional standards of gentility and aristocracy to accommodate emergent social categories is a familiar phenomenon in early modern English culture. A particularly lucid example is the way experimental efforts to construct population tables based on the quantitative criterion of class are infiltrated at certain points by the more familiar and qualitative measure of status group. See McKeon, *Origins,* 165. Cf., on the notional coincidence of aristocracy and sodomy, Michael McKeon, "Historicizing Patriarchy: The Emergence of Gender Difference in England, 1660–1760," *Eighteenth-Century Studies* 28, no. 3 (1995): 309–12.

49. *Spectator,* no. 1 (1 Mar. 1711), in Bond, *Spectator;* see this number also on Mr. Spectator's "small Hereditary Estate" (hereafter references are to this edition and appear parenthetically in the text). On the significance of that estate, see, e.g., Barrell, *English Literature,* 35.

50. See Ros Ballaster's thoughtful remarks on this score in "Man(ley) Forms: Sex and the Female Satirist," in *Women, Texts, and Histories, 1575–1760,* ed. Clare Brant and Diane Purkiss (London: Routledge, 1992), 236–37.

51. Cf. Margaret Cavendish's transvaluation of (not only married) women's lack of the positive freedom of political subjecthood into their possession of the negative freedom of something like ethical subjectivity: "We are not tied to state or crown; we are free" (see above, chap. 3, nn. 87–88).

52. Johnson, *History of Rasselas,* chap. 3, in *Works of Samuel Johnson,* 16:14; *Rambler,* no. 128 (8 June 1751). I think Barrell misreads some related discussions in *Rambler,* nos. 99 and 173 (26 Feb. and 12 Nov. 1751) to conclude that Johnson affirms the capacity of gentlemen alone "to comprehend and describe" "the whole of society . . . ." See *English Literature,* 34. Like *Rambler,* no. 128, these papers in fact offer the gentleman no exemption from the common condition.

53. William Arnall, *British Journal,* no. 74 (31 May 1729), quoted in Shelley Burtt, *Virtue Transformed: Political Arguments in England, 1688–1740* (Cambridge: Cambridge University Press, 1992), 117–18; John Locke, *An Essay concerning Human Understanding* (1690), ed. Peter H. Nidditch (Oxford: Oxford University Press, 1979), bk. 4, chap. 20, sec. 6, p. 711.

54. Robert Boyle, letter c. 1689, in *The Works of the Honourable Robert Boyle,* ed. Thomas Birch, 2nd ed. (London: J. and F. Rivington, 1772), 1:cxxx–cxxxi, quoted in Steven Shapin, *A Social History of Truth: Civility and Science in Seventeenth-Century England* (Chicago: University of Chicago Press, 1994), 176. See Shapin, 83–86 and chap. 3 generally on gentle disinterestedness in natural philosophy. Forty years earlier, when the Royal Society was still only a

dream, Boyle had praised the members of "the *philosophical college*" in rather different terms: as "men of so capacious and searching spirits, that . . . though ambitious to lead the way to any generous design, [are] of so humble and teachable a genius, as they disdain not to be directed to the meanest, so he can but plead reason for his opinion . . . ." Boyle to Francis Tallents, Feb. 1647, in *Works*, 1:xxiv. And see Poovey, *History of the Modern Fact*, 115–16, on Boyle's positive attitude toward the testimony of merchants.

55. Paolo Rossi, *Philosophy, Technology, and the Arts in the Early Modern Era*, trans Salvator Attanasio, ed. Benjamin Nelson (New York: Harper, 1970), ix–x; see generally chap. 1.

56. Robert Hooke, "A General Scheme, or Idea of the Present State of Natural Philosophy . . ." (c. 1668), in *The Posthumous Works of Robert Hooke*, ed. Richard Waller (1705), 63, 62, facs. reprint ed. Theodore M. Brown (London: Cass, 1971); on luciferous (Hooke accidentally writes "luciferous") experiments, see 21. Hooke anticipates the scrupulously defamiliarizing account of the contents of Gulliver's pockets by his Lilliputian hosts. See [Jonathan Swift], *Gulliver's Travels* (1726), pt. 1, chap. 2, *The Prose Works of Jonathan Swift*, ed. Herbert Davis, vol. 11 (Oxford: Blackwell, 1941), 18–20. With Hooke's defense of the "trivial, base, and mean" compare the comments of a contemporary quoted above, chap. 2, n. 56.

57. Robert Hooke, preface to *Micrographia . . .* (1665), a2v, b1r.

58. Thomas Sprat, *The History of the Royal Society of London, for the Improving of Natural Knowledge* (1667), 72. Cf. Oliver Cromwell on the staffing of the republican army: "I had rather have a plain russet-coated captain that knows what he fights for, and loves what he knows, than that which you call a gentleman and is nothing else . . . . It had been well that men of honour and birth had entered into these employments, but why do they not appear? Who would have hindered them? But seeing it was necessary the work must go on, better plain men than none, but best to have men patient of wants, faithful and conscientious in the employment." Crowell to Suffolk County committee, 29 Aug. and 28 Sept. 1643, in *The Writings and Speeches of Oliver Cromwell*, ed. Wilbur C. Abbott (Cambridge, MA: Harvard University Press, 1937), 1:256, 262.

59. Sprat, *History*, 67, 68, 409–10.

60. Francis Bacon, *Novum Organum* (1620), in *Philosophical Works*, 264, 263, 270, 274. In 1667 Richard Allestree identified interest itself as "the great *Idol* to which the world bows . . . ." See above, chap. 1, n. 88. For Smollett see above, n. 33.

61. [John Toland], preface to *Christianity not Mysterious . . .* (1696), xxi, xxii, xx.

62. Sprat, *History*, 73, 66–67, 71–72.

63. Ibid., 97. The year before the publication of Sprat's *History* the Royal Society had established its "repository" of curiosities, which was notable among such collections in providing a nonhierarchical listing of its benefactors and donors. See Marjorie Swann, *Curiosities and Texts: The Culture of Collecting in Early Modern England* (Philadelphia: University of Pennsylvania Press, 2001), 83–90.

64. Hooke, "General Scheme," 61–62.

65. David Hume, *An Enquiry concerning Human Understanding* (1748), sec. 10, pt. 1, 3rd ed., ed. L. A. Selby-Bigge and P. H. Nidditch (Oxford: Clarendon, 1975), 111. Hume also applies these principles to the problem of how to establish disinterestedness in aesthetic judgment. See "Of The Standard of Taste" (1758), in *Essays Moral, Political, and Literary*, ed. Eugene F. Miller, rev. ed. (Indianapolis: Liberty Classics, 1987), 226–49. Cf., e.g., Hume on quantification through perdurability (233) with Johnson, below, n. 105.

66. On experimental repeatability and publication, see above, chap. 2, nn. 61–62.

67. See David Zaret, *Origins of Democratic Culture: Printing, Petitions, and the Public Sphere in Early Modern England* (Princeton, NJ: Princeton University Press, 2000), 257–59; see above, chap. 2, nn. 68–72.

68. [James Madison], *Federalist*, no. 10, in Alexander Hamilton, John Jay, and James Madison, *The Federalist* (1787–88), ed. George W. Carey and James McClellan (Indianapolis: Liberty Fund, 2001), 42–49.

69. Edmund Burke, *Reflections on the Revolution in France*, ed. Thomas H. D. Mahoney (Indianapolis: Bobbs-Merrill, 1955), 86 (hereafter references are to this edition and appear parenthetically in the text). The following discussion of Burke relies in part on Michael McKeon, "Tacit Knowledge: Tradition and Its Aftermath," in *Questions of Tradition*, ed. Mark Salber Phillips and Gordon Schochet (Toronto: University of Toronto Press, 2004), 171–202.

70. See above, n. 38.

71. Boswell, *Life of Johnson*, 316, 317.

72. William Godwin, *Enquiry concerning Political Justice* ([1793] rev. 1798), bk. 5, chap. 15, pp. 140, 132–33, 137.

73. For that argument, see John Barrell, *The Political Theory of Painting from Reynolds to Hazlitt* (New Haven, CT: Yale University Press, 1986). For a counterargument that features Hogarth, see Ronald Paulson, *The Beautiful, Novel, and Strange: Aesthetics and Heterodoxy* (Baltimore: Johns Hopkins University Press, 1996); on the civic humanist interpretation, see xv–xviii. See William Hogarth, introduction to *The Analysis of Beauty* (1753), ed. Ronald Paulson (New Haven, CT: Yale University Press, 1997), 17–20.

74. Samuel Johnson, "Gray," in *Lives of the English Poets* (1779, 1781), ed. Arthur Waugh (1952; reprint, London: Oxford University Press, 1968), 2:464. Gray's celebrated poem is itself, of course, concerned to coordinate the fate of poor commoners with the common fate of all.

75. Thomas Gray, *Elegy Written in a Country Church-Yard*, lines 57–58, in *The Poems of Gray, Collins, and Goldsmith*, ed. Roger Lonsdale (London: Longman, 1969), 127–28.

76. Edmund Burke, *A Philosophical Enquiry into the Origin of our Ideas of the Sublime and Beautiful* (1757), pt. 1, sec. 19, ed. J. T. Boulton (New York: Columbia University Press, 1958), 54 (hereafter references are to this edition, include part and section as well as page numbers, and appear parenthetically in the text).

77. Anthony Ashley Cooper, third Earl of Shaftesbury, *Characteristicks of Men, Manners, Opinions, Times . . .* ([1711] rev. 1732), 1:98, ed. Douglas Den Uyl (Indianapolis: Liberty Fund, 2001), 1:62 (hereafter references appear parenthetically in the text and are to this edition, which also records the original pagination marginally; references refer first to the 1732 and then to the 2001 edition).

Shaftesbury's characterization of Judaism as a faith doctrinally conducive to disinterestedness does not preserve the ordinary Jews of the Old Testament from his withering scorn: "[T]he best Doctrine could not go down without a *Treat*, and the best Disciples had their Heads so running upon their *Loaves*, that they were apt to construe every divine Saying in a *Belly*-Sense . . . . So that it must necessarily be confess'd, in honour of their divine Legislators, Patriots, and Instructors; that they exceeded all others in Goodness and Generosity; since they cou'd so truly love their Nation and Brethren, such as they were; and cou'd have so generous and disinterested Regards for those, who were in themselves so sordidly interested and undeserving" (1:282–83; 1:175–76).

78. Toward the end of the eighteenth century the difference between good birth and good breeding will be axiomatic. Struck by the differences between Orville and Merton, Burney's Evelina muses: "In all ranks and all stations of life, how strangely do characters and manners differ! Lord Orville, with a politeness which knows no intermission, and makes no distinction, is as unassuming and modest, as if he had never mixed with the great, and was totally ignorant of every qualification he possesses; this other Lord, though lavish of compliments and fine speeches, seems to me an entire stranger to real good-breeding . . . ." [Frances Burney], *Evelina, or, the History of a Young Lady's Entrance into the World* (1778), vol. 1, letter 23, ed. Edward A. Bloom and Vivien Jones (Oxford: Oxford University Press, 2002), 114–15.

79. Post-Kantian thought has come to distinguish aesthetic from rational judgment according to its lack of instrumental purpose. But Addison attributes instrumentality—the production of pleasure—to all three of the faculties he considers. What distinguishes the imagination is that the pleasures in whose production it is instrumental are not sensible.

80. Cf. Sprat, *History,* 344, on the "sensible *Pleasure*" to be found in scientific experiment, which is "innocent" and can be enjoyed "without Guilt or Remorse." Joseph Glanvill, like Hooke and Sprat an early expositor of scientific method, describes the pleasure to be had in scientific experiment in moralizing terms that like Sprat's prefigure Addison's, although Glanvill adds an element of the theatrical and the innocently erotic. Given his subject matter, however, Glanvill's discourse has the effect not (as in Addison) of distinguishing aesthetic from scientific disinterestedness but of subsuming the first under the second. The followers of the Royal Society, Glanvill writes, will "find all the innocent *satisfactions* which use to follow *victory, variety,* and *surprise,* the usual sources of our best tasted *pleasures.* And perhaps *human nature* meets few more *sweetly relishing* and *cleanly joyes,* then those, that derive from the *happy issues* of *successful Tryals:* Yea, whether they succeed to the answering the particular *aim* of the *Naturalist* or not; 'tis however a *pleasant* spectacle to behold the *shifts,* windings and *unexpected Caprichios* of distressed *Nature,* when pursued by a *close* and *well managed Experiment.* And the *delights* which result from these *nobler entertainments* are such, as our *cool* and *reflecting thoughts* need not be *ashamed* of. And which are dogged by no such sad sequels as are the products of those *titillations* that reach no higher then *Phancy* and the *Senses.*" *Scepsis Scientifica . . .* (1665), "To the Royal Society," b2v–3r. Cf. Hooke's chaster account of how nature is not pursued but "traced" above, nn. 62–64. Contrast the innocence of eroto-experimental imaginations in Glanvill's analysis with the hyperdepravity of the imaginations that accompany masturbation. See above, chap. 6, nn. 30–34.

81. See the argument of Michael G. Ketcham, *Transparent Designs: Reading, Performance, and Form in the Spectator Papers* (Athens: University of Georgia Press, 1985), 74–81.

82. Addison's other oxymoronic figures are "titular Physitians, Fellows of the Royal Society, Templars that are not given to be contentious, and Statesmen that are out of Business. In short, every one that considers the World as a Theatre, and desires to form a right Judgment of those who are the Actors on it."

83. "Apparent" because the earliest use cited by the *OED* of the financial sense of the term "speculation" postdates this passage by sixty years.

84. See above, n. 68.

85. Cf. Joseph Addison, *Spectator,* no. 409 (19 June 1712), in Bond, *Spectator;* and Hume, "Of the Standard of Taste," 226–49.

86. See *OED,* s.v. "propriety," for a sense of the entanglement of these notions before the eighteenth century. James Boswell later construed the passage as follows: "In reality, a person of small fortune who has only the common views of life and would just be as well as anybody else, cannot like London. But a person of imagination and feeling, such as the Spectator finely describes, can have the most lively enjoyment from the sight of external objects without regard to property at all. London is undoubtedly a place where men and manners may be seen to the greatest advantage." Later in his journal Boswell describes his friend George Dempster's Addisonian view of how happiness is to be attained: "He considered the mind of man like a room, which is either made agreeable or the reverse by the pictures with which it is adorned. External circumstances are nothing to the purpose. Our great point is to have pleasing pictures in the inside." *Boswell's London Journal, 1762–1763,* ed. Frederick A. Pottle (New York: McGraw-Hill, 1950), 68, 203.

87. With Addison's aesthetic virtualization of the land compare George Berkeley's Addisonian *Guardian,* no. 49 (2 May 1713).

88. Thomas Randolph, "On the Inestimable Content He Enjoys in the Muses: To Those of His Friends that Dehort Him from Poetry" (1638), in *The Country House Poem: A Cabinet of Seventeenth-Century Estate Poems and Related Items,* ed. Alastair Fowler (Edinburgh: Edinburgh University Press, 1994), 138–42. On the *beatus ille* trope, see above, chap. 3, n. 97. On the country house poem, see below, chap. 8, nn. 88–93.

89. Andrew Marvell, "The Garden" (wr. c. 1668), lines 41–42, 47–48, in *Andrew Marvell: The Complete Poems,* ed. Elizabeth Story Donno (Harmondsworth, UK: Penguin, 1978), 101.

90. John Dryden, *An Essay of Dramatic Poesy* (1667), in *Of Dramatic Poesy,* 1:51. Lisideius is the speaker. For the *locus classicus* of this dramatic advice, see Aristotle, *Poetics,* 1454b, 1460a.

91. [Charles Cotton], ΕΡΟΤΟΠΟΛΙΣ. *The Present State of Betty-Land* (1684), 14–15. Cotton's elaborately reflexive conceit involves a formal recourse to figuration (agricultural husbandry for sexual husbandry) whose subject matter is the inadequacy of figurative substitutes for the real (pictures for reality). On Aretinian postures and the masturbatory imagination, see above, chap. 6, nn. 30–42, 69, 75. Darby Lewes has coined the term "somatopia" to name the sort of allegorical representation exemplified by Cotton. See *Nudes from Nowhere: Utopian Sexual Landscapes* (Totowa, NJ: Rowman and Littlefield, 2000).

92. John Dyer, "Grongar Hill" (1726), lines 129–30, in *The New Oxford Book of Eighteenth-Century Verse,* ed. Roger Lonsdale (Oxford: Oxford University Press, 1984), 170.

93. Edward Young, *Conjectures on Original Composition. In a Letter to the Author of Sir Charles Grandison* (1759) (Leeds, UK: Scolar Press, 1966), 54. In *Spectator,* no. 606 (13 Oct. 1714), Thomas Tickell extolled "the laudable Mystery of Embroidery" in remarking "[w]hat a delightful Entertainment must it be to the Fair Sex, . . . exempt . . . from publick Business, to pass their Hours . . . transplanting all the Beauties of Nature into their own Dress, or raising a new Creation in their Closets and Apartments."

94. See above, chap. 2, nn. 142–47.

95. Philip Sidney, *A Defence of Poetry* (1595), ed. J. A. Van Dorsten (Oxford: Oxford University Press, 1966), 52, 53.

96. On the scientific debates see generally Steven Shapin and Simon Schaffer, *Leviathan and the Air-Pump: Hobbes, Boyle, and the Experimental Life* (Princeton, NJ: Princeton University Press, 1985).

97. Dryden, *Essay of Dramatic Poesy,* 1:47, 51, 62.

98. Samuel Johnson, preface to *The Plays of William Shakespeare* (1765), in *The Yale Edition of the Works of Samuel Johnson,* vol. 7, *Johnson on Shakespeare,* ed. Arthur Sherbo (New Haven, CT: Yale University Press, 1968), 76–78.

99. Ibid., 79. Cf. Aristotle, *Poetics,* 1453b. Johnson thus applies Addison's point that verbal description distances us more than visual presentation does, yet not so much as to be aesthetically ineffective.

100. See above, chap. 2, nn. 135, 159–60.

101. [Henry Fielding], *Joseph Andrews* (1742), bk. 3, chap. 1, ed. Martin C. Battestin (Middletown, CT: Wesleyan University Press, 1967), 185–88. For the sake of clarity I take the liberty of diluting Fielding's irony by simplifying his use of the term "romance" in this chapter because I am confident that this does not distort his meaning.

102. See above, n. 3.

103. Dryden, *Essay of Dramatic Poesy,* 26.

104. Johnson, preface, 59–60.

105. Ibid., 61.

106. See above, nn. 63–64, 67–68.

107. See above, n. 37. On Burke and duration, see above, nn. 69–70. The logic of the argument against the unities of time and place suggests that Johnson's test of time is one of two available methods of generalizing particular response. Perhaps because the context for this argument was the quarrel of the ancients and moderns and its concern with the scale of diachronic difference, however, the alternative, synchronic method of generalization—the cross-cultural demonstration that at the present moment Shakespeare pleases over and above particular regional, national, and social variations—received less attention from contemporaries; but see below, nn. 121–22.

108. William Wordsworth, preface to *Lyrical Ballads* (1800), 2nd ed. (1802), in *The Prose Works of William Wordsworth,* ed. W. J. B. Owen and Jane Worthington Smyser (Oxford: Clarendon, 1974), 1:119, 157, 141–42, 131, 133, 123, 124, 125. References are to the 1850 ed., which modifies the 2nd ed. of 1802.

109. Ibid., 123, 138, 138–39, 137, 149, 145, 147.

110. See above, chap. 2, nn. 148–58.

111. Adam Smith, *The Theory of Moral Sentiments* (1759), ed. D. D. Raphael and A. L. Macfie (Indianapolis: Liberty Classics, 1982), 9 (hereafter references are to this edition and appear parenthetically in the text).

112. Here as elsewhere, Smith invites fruitful comparison to Edmund Burke's *Philosophical Enquiry into the Origin of our Ideas of the Sublime and Beautiful* (1757), which also is highly relevant to our concern with imaginative disinterestedness.

113. That is, over and above the manifestly dramatic provenance of spectatorship itself. On the one hand, we may recall the way the campaign for the reformation of manners precipitated an insistence on the difference between the ethics of authors and characters, a separation out of what were taken by Jeremy Collier collectively as the "character of the author." Even more directly we are reminded of Shaftesbury's division of the authorial self into "au-

thor" and "reader" (see above, chap. 2, nn. 137–47). On the other hand, Smith's language of the third person evokes the experiments in third-person narration that played an important part in the development of domestic narrative (see below, pt. 3).

114. Not to be confused with the moral sense, which does have some importance here.

115. Like "social psychology," the term "political economy" bears within it the complex history of a former distinction that has been subjected to separation and then to conflation. One difference between them is that in the *Theory* Smith practices a conflative method for which there is as yet no name.

116. Smith also uses the figure of the invisible hand in *The Theory of Moral Sentiments*, 184–85.

117. Richard Steele, *The Trades-man's Calling . . .* (1684), 107.

118. My concern here has been with the correspondence or metaphorical relationship between the systems of sympathy and commodity exchange in Smith's work. *The Theory of Moral Sentiments* also makes what might be called a metonymic argument concerning that relationship. That is, wealth is not only analogous to sympathy in its mode of generation; its possession also constitutes one important impetus for sympathetic response. See 50–61. Here we can see a connection between, on the one hand, Smith's attribution of the persistence and strength of the distinction of ranks to the fact that "the bulk of the people" (53) feel a detached and pleasing identification with the rich and, on the other hand, what I above call the "aesthetic" conservatism of Burke and Johnson.

119. In the following reading I take seriously the conceptual implications of Pope's satire at the risk of seeming to miss the easy lightness of its humor; the two are, I think, compatible.

120. See above, chap. 6, nn. 42–43.

121. On Pope's ambivalence, see above, chap. 2, nn. 41–42, 134.

122. The book of secrets, although related to the political *arcana imperii,* has a more immediate relevance to the scientific *arcana naturae.* See above, chap. 2, nn. 51–57. On the evolution of the cookbook, see below, chap. 10, nn. 38–41.

123. Pope's source for this example may be Bernard Mandeville, *The Fable of the Bees* (1705, 1714), ed. F. B. Kaye (Oxford: Clarendon, 1924), 6th dialogue, 2:284.

124. In his *Letters of Literature* (1785), 483, John Pinkerton fashioned a facetious guide to the Johnsonian test of time, a "table of periods that must pass over different works, before the stamp of lasting worth is put upon them," whose humor also turns upon the problematic correspondence between literary and material productivity (and consumability). The table classifies literature by genres, and whereas the requisite period for "Epic poetry" is "100 years," that for "Panegyrics" is "1 hour" and that for "Pastoral poetry" is "5 minutes." "The reason for the short space allowed for the two last," Pinkerton writes, "is their putrescent quality; which makes it not safe to keep them long before they are eaten." Quoted in J. E. Congleton, *Theories of Pastoral Poetry in England, 1684–1798* (Gainesville: University of Florida Press, 1952), 150.

125. For a recent illumination of this moment, see Jonathan Brody Kramnick, *Making the English Canon: Print-Capitalism and the Cultural Past, 1700–1770* (Cambridge: Cambridge University Press, 1998), esp. 33–39.

126. I have argued that the category of the aesthetic and its peculiar sort of value first coalesces in cultural consciousness as it is separated out not from economic exchange value but

from the literality and locality of a strictly empirical response to sense impressions. John Guillory has made a powerful case for the former narrative as part of a larger argument against the notion that the question of aesthetic value is perennial. See *Cultural Capital: The Problem of Literary Canon Formation* (Chicago: University of Chicago Press, 1993), 303–40. Guillory trains his attention on the period of the formation of political economy, taking the crucial question to be the production of the work of art. In my analysis, the idea of the aesthetic emerges as a question about not objects but responses, not production but the epistemology of consumption, and the crucial context for this emergence is not the later eighteenth century and the rise of the discourse of political economy but the later seventeenth and early eighteenth centuries and their debates over the theory of dramatic response—and, more extensively, the early modern quarrel of the ancients and the moderns. I agree with Guillory that the question of aesthetic value has not always been with us, but see Michael McKeon, "The Origins of Aesthetic Value," *Telos,* no. 57 (Fall 1983): 63–82.

Chapter Eight | Mixed Genres

1. See Michael McKeon, ed., *Theory of the Novel: A Historical Approach* (Baltimore: Johns Hopkins University Press, 2000), 179–83, 265–69, 317–20.

2. See above, chap. 7, n. 25.

3. *Tatler,* no. 172 (16 May 1710), in *The Tatler,* ed. Donald F. Bond, 3 vols. (Oxford: Clarendon, 1987); for Bond's remark, see 2:445n3. Hereafter references are to this edition and appear parenthetically in the text.

4. See Marvin T. Herrick, *Tragicomedy: Its Origins and Development in Italy, France, and England* (Urbana: University of Illinois Press, 1962), chap. 1.

5. See Erich Auerbach, *Mimesis: The Representation of Reality in Western Literature,* trans. Willard Trask (1953; reprint, Garden City, NY: Anchor, 1957).

6. On "domestic tragedy," see Lena Cowen Orlin, *Private Matters and Public Culture in Post-Reformation England* (Ithaca, NY: Cornell University Press, 1994), 8–9.

7. The double-plotted, public-private tragicomedy of the Renaissance was susceptible to narrativization. See the reading of Thomas Deloney's *Thomas of Reading* (1600) in Michael McKeon, *The Origins of the English Novel, 1600–1740* (Baltimore: Johns Hopkins University Press, 1987), 234–37.

8. Cf. Herrick, *Tragicomedy;* Eugene M. Waith, *The Pattern of Tragicomedy in Beaumont and Fletcher* (New Haven, CT: Yale University Press, 1952); Lois Potter, *Secret Rites and Secret Writing: Royalist Literature, 1641–1660* (Cambridge: Cambridge University Press, 1989), chap. 3; and Nancy Klein Maguire, *Regicide and Restoration: English Tragicomedy, 1660–1671* (Cambridge: Cambridge University Press, 1992), who proposes that we treat the dramatic productions of the first decade of the Restoration as comprising two "subgenres" of "tragicomedy," the "divided tragicomedy" and the rhymed heroic play (see p. 3 and passim).

9. See Michael Dobson, *The Making of the National Poet: Shakespeare, Adaptation, and Authorship, 1660–1769* (Oxford: Oxford University Press, 1992), 185: "[T]he very nature of the period's adaptations, with their emphasis on identifying Shakespeare with a strictly domestic and therefore private propriety, helped to render the public performance of his works increasingly irrelevant to his status in British culture." By "domestic" Dobson means both the national and the familial.

10. Frank H. Ristine, *English Tragicomedy, Its Origin and History* (1910; reprint, London: Russell and Russell, 1963), 216.

11. *Spectator,* no. 40 (16 Apr. 1711), in *The Spectator,* ed. Donald F. Bond, 5 vols. (Oxford: Clarendon, 1965) (hereafter references are to this edition and appear parenthetically in the text).

12. George Lillo, *The London Merchant: or, The History of George Barnwell* (1731), dedication and prologue, lines 19–21, in *The Dramatic Works of George Lillo,* ed. James L. Steffensen (Oxford: Clarendon, 1993), 151, 154 (font reversed). Steffensen points out that Lillo's innovation extends to his exclusive use of prose for tragedy as well as to his application of Protestant doctrine to the conflict between "fatality and personal responsibility as the effective force of the tragic action" (113, 119). In this respect, Lillo's George Barnwell and John Foxe's Roger Holland offer the apprentice diametrically opposed models of Protestant tragicomedy; for Foxe see above, chap. 7, n. 14.

13. John Dryden, *Of Dramatic Poesy: An Essay* (1668) and preface to *The Spanish Friar* (1681), in Dryden, *Of Dramatic Poesy and Other Critical Essays,* ed. George Watson (London: Dent, 1962), 1:74 and 274, respectively.

14. The following brief observations are opened out in Michael McKeon, "Marxist Criticism and *Marriage à la Mode,*" *Eighteenth Century: Theory and Interpretation* 24, no. 2 (1983): 141–62.

15. See John Dryden, *Marriage à la Mode,* ed. Mark S. Auburn (Lincoln: University of Nebraska Press, 1981) (hereafter cited parenthetically in the text), act 5, sc. 1, lines 80–125, where the princess Palmyra disdains the socially ambitious Melantha as "impertinent," and lines 438–52, where Rhodophil and Palamede show their deferential "loyalty" to their "long lost King" Leonidas by rushing to his defense.

16. Maguire, *Regicide,* argues that the Stuart court masque lived on, in the first decade of the Restoration, as the Stuart rhymed heroic play, which she also calls the "rhymed heroic masque" (3).

17. See Rosemond Tuve, "Image, Form, and Theme in *A Mask,*" in *A Maske at Ludlow: Essays on Milton's Comus,* ed. John S. Diekhoff (Cleveland, OH: Case Western Reserve Press, 1968), 131; Stephen Orgel, *The Illusion of Power: Political Theater in the English Renaissance* (Berkeley and Los Angeles: University of California Press, 1975), 39; and Erica Veevers, *Images of Love and Religion: Queen Henrietta Maria and Court Entertainments* (Cambridge: Cambridge University Press, 1989), 9–10. See also Ben Jonson, preface to *Hymenaei* (1606): "It is a noble and iust aduantage, that the things subiected to *vnderstanding* haue of those which are obiected to *sense,* that the one sort are but momentarie, and meerely taking; the other impressing, and lasting: . . . This it is hath made the most royall *Princes,* and greatest *persons* (who are commonly the *personaters* of these *actions*) not onely studious of riches, and magnificence in the outward celebration, or shew; . . . but curious after the most high, and heartie *inuentions,* to furnish the inward parts: . . . which, though their *voyce* be taught to sound to present occasions, their *sense,* or doth, or should alwayes lay hold on more remou'd *mysteries.*" In *Ben Jonson,* ed. C. H. Herford, Percy Simpson, and Evelyn Simpson (Oxford: Clarendon, 1941), 7:209. Jonathan Goldberg, *James I and the Politics of Literature: Jonson, Shakespeare, Donne, and Their Contemporaries* (Baltimore: Johns Hopkins University Press, 1983), 56–65, 69–72, suggests that the Jonsonian masque is a formal recapitulation of absolutist *arcana imperii.*

18. Veevers, *Images,* ix.

19. See David Bevington and Peter Holbrook, eds., *The Politics of the Stuart Court Masque* (Cambridge: Cambridge University Press, 1998), introduction.

20. See above, chap. 2, nn. 137–42.

21. John Milton, "Of that sort of Dramatic Poem which is Call'd Tragedy," prefixed to *Samson Agonistes* (1671), in *John Milton: Complete Poems and Major Prose,* ed. Merritt Y. Hughes (New York: Odyssey, 1957), 550 (hereafter cited parenthetically in the text). Milton's preface also remarks that his drama "never was intended" for the public stage. On the distinct modes of "publication" entailed in the oral performance and the literate reading of drama, see Dryden and Cibber, above, chap. 2, nn. 2, 109.

22. For Locke, see above, chap. 1, n. 28. John Guillory sees *Samson Agonistes* as "a prototype of the bourgeois career drama, which conventionally sets the vocation of the husband against the demands of the housewife." "Dalila's House: *Samson Agonistes* and the Sexual Division of Labor," in *Rewriting the Renaissance: The Discourses of Sexual Difference in Early Modern Europe,* ed. Margaret W. Ferguson, Maureen Quilligan, and Nancy J. Vickers (Chicago: University of Chicago Press, 2000), 110. Cf. Steele's reading of *Paradise Lost,* above, chap. 7, n. 25.

23. On the Protestant concept of the "public person," see above, chap. 1, n. 95.

24. With this account of the subjection of the husband compare Milton's language on the subjection of Charles I, above, chap. 3, n. 12.

25. Cf. Mary Astell's admission that she has "Publish'd" and "betray'd the *Arcana Imperii*" of the male sex. See above, chap. 2, n. 118.

26. For Defoe, see above, chap. 1, n. 36. Having been raised by Milton to the status of wife, Dalila is momentarily degraded by the penitent Samson to the status of a "deceitful Concubine" (line 537).

27. The term is Paul Salzman's. See *English Prose Fiction, 1558–1700: A Critical History* (Oxford: Clarendon, 1985), chap. 11.

28. McKeon, *Origins,* 45.

29. See Joel E. Spingarn, *Literary Criticism in the Renaissance,* 2nd ed. (New York: Columbia University Press, 1912), 112–24; Bernard Weinberg, *A History of Literary Criticism in the Italian Renaissance* (Chicago: University of Chicago Press, 1961), vol. 2, chaps. 19, 20; and Alban K. Forcione, *Cervantes, Aristotle, and the Persiles* (Princeton, NJ: Princeton University Press, 1970), chaps. 1, 2 (p. 23 on "heroic poetry").

30. Shakespeare, *Troilus and Cressida* (1603), 1.3.100, 110–11, 118; 3.1.116–23; 2.3.74–76.

31. Richard Lovelace, "To Lucasta, Going to the Wars" (1649), in *English Seventeenth-Century Verse,* vol. 2, ed. Richard S. Sylvester (New York: Norton, 1974), 552–53.

32. When Milton does reflect on what we would recognize as "chivalric romance," he associates it no more with love than with war—"hitherto the only Argument / Heroic deem'd"—under the general category of "Heroic Song," which he is at pains to argue should also encompass the Christian matter of man's first disobedience. See *Paradise Lost,* bk. 9, lines 25–41 (quoted, lines 25, 28–29), in *John Milton,* 379.

33. [Samuel Butler], *Hudibras,* pt. 1 (1663), canto 2, lines 4–8; pt. 2, canto 1, lines 1–6, ed. John Wilders (Oxford: Clarendon Press, 1967), 29, 100 (hereafter cited parenthetically in the text).

34. Quoted above, chap. 4, n. 106.

35. See above, chap. 3, n. 8.

36. In leveling this critique of religious discourse as a mask for political ambition Butler joined a chorus of early-Restoration voices. For some other examples, see Michael McKeon, *Politics and Poetry in Restoration England: The Case of Dryden's "Annus Mirabilis"* (Cambridge, MA: Harvard University Press, 1975), 192–94.

37. On the self-conscious poetics of the doggerel tradition, see David J. Rothman, "*Hudibras* in the Doggerel Tradition," *Restoration* 17, no. 1 (1993): 15–29.

38. John Wilmot, Earl of Rochester, "A Ramble in St. James's Park," lines 89–90, 107–8, 133–34, 165–66, in *The Works of John Wilmot Earl of Rochester*, ed. Harold Love (Oxford: Oxford University Press, 1999), 76–80 (hereafter cited parenthetically in the text). Rochester's most immediate heirs in the desublimation of love poetry are Swift's Strephon and Cassinus. Cf. "The Lady's Dressing Room," "Strephon and Chloe," and "Cassinus and Peter."

39. See above, chap. 6, n. 77.

40. "*Quae sequuntur, in limine thalami regii, a nescio quo nebulone scripta, reperibantur:* 'Bella fugis, bellas sequeris, belloque repugnas, / et bellatori sunt tibi bella tori; / imbelles imbellis amas, audaxque videris / Mars ad opus Veneris, Martis ad arma Venus.'" *Poems on Affairs of State: Augustan Satirical Verse, 1660–1714*, vol. 1, *1660–1678*, ed. George deF. Lord (New Haven, CT: Yale University Press, 1963), 152.

41. On the curtain lecture, see above, chap. 5, nn. 55–60.

42. Pierre Daniel Huet, bishop of Avranches, *The History of Romances* . . . (1670), trans. Stephen Lewis (1715), in *Novel and Romance, 1700–1800: A Documentary Record*, ed. Ioan Williams (New York: Barnes and Noble, 1970), 47.

43. In the preface to *The Hind and the Panther* (1687) Dryden says that although he has given to part 1 of the poem "the Majestick Turn of Heroick Poesie," part 3 "has more of the Nature of Domestick Conversation." Tinged with mock-heroic implication, James II is correspondingly allegorized as a farmer, and the Roman Catholics as "Domestick Poultry." See *The Works of John Dryden*, vol. 3, *Poems, 1685–1692*, ed. Earl Miner and Vinton A. Dearing (Berkeley and Los Angeles: University of California Press, 1969), p. 122; line 995, p. 190.

44. Thomas Sprat, *The History of the Royal Society, For the Improving of Natural Knowledge* (1667), 418; Samuel Butler, *Prose Observations*, ed. Hugh de Quehen (Oxford: Oxford University Press, 1979), 278. For Swift see above, chap. 2, n. 140.

45. [Jonathan Swift], *A Tale of a Tub*, in *A Tale of a Tub, To which is added The Battle of the Books and the Mechanical Operation of the Spirit* (1704, 1710), ed. A. C. Guthkelch and D. Nichol Smith, 2nd ed. (Oxford: Clarendon, 1958), 51 (hereafter references are to this edition and appear parenthetically in the text); Anthony Ashley Cooper, third Earl of Shaftesbury, *Characteristicks of Men, Manners, Opinions, Times* . . . ([1711] rev. 1732), 1:226, 266–67, ed. Douglas Den Uyl (Indianapolis: Liberty Fund, 2001), 1:140, 165; Alexander Pope, *The First Epistle of the Second Book of Horace, Imitated (Epistle to Augustus)*, lines 404–5, 408–10, in *Imitations of Horace*, ed. John Butt, vol. 4 of the Twickenham Edition of the Poems of Alexander Pope, 2nd ed.(London: Methuen, 1953), 229.

46. For a discussion of this phenomenon, see McKeon, *Origins*, 171–73 and chap. 4 passim.

47. [Thomas Gordon], *Cato's Letters*, no. 33 (17 June 1721), in John Trenchard and Thomas Gordon, *Cato's Letters: or, Essays on Liberty, Civil and Religious, and Other Important Subjects* (originally published in the *London Journal*, 1720–23), ed. Ronald Hamowy (Indi-

anapolis: Liberty Fund, 1995), 1:238. For the sexualization of high/low social mixture in popular Restoration verse, see James Grantham Turner, *Libertines and Radicals in Early Modern London: Sexuality, Politics, and Literary Culture, 1630–1685* (Cambridge: Cambridge University Press, 2002), 150–63, 242–51.

48. Henry Fielding, *The Life of Mr. Jonathan Wild the Great* (1743), bk. 1, chap. 4; "Preface"; bk. 2, chap. 1, ed. David Nokes (Harmondsworth, UK: Penguin, 1986), 52, 30, 31, 84–85. Cf. Fielding's domesticating treatment of the mock-heroic simile: "Now *Thetis* the good Housewife began to put on the Pot in order to regale the good Man *Phoebus,* after his daily Labours were over. In vulgar Language, it was in the Evening when *Joseph* attended his Lady's Orders." *Joseph Andrews* (1742), bk. 1, chap. 8, ed. Martin C. Battestin (Middletown, CT: Wesleyan University Press, 1967), 38. With Fielding's satiric conflation of the palace of the great and Newgate prison compare John Wood's humanitarian maxim that "a palace is nothing more than a cottage IMPROVED." See above, chap. 5, nn. 77–78.

49. See McKeon, *Origins,* 383–85.

50. For Swift, see above, chap. 6, nn. 42–43; and for Pope, chap. 7, nn. 119–21.

51. [Jonathan Swift], *Gulliver's Travels* (1726), pt. 3, chap. 6, *The Prose Works of Jonathan Swift,* ed. Herbert Davis, vol. 11 (Oxford: Blackwell, 1941), 175.

52. Francis Bacon, *Novum Organum* (1620), aphorism 120, in *The Philosophical Works of Francis Bacon,* ed. Robert L. Ellis and James Spedding, rev. ed. John M. Robertson (London: Routledge, 1905), 296; Abraham Cowley, "To the Royal Society," st. 7, prefixed to Sprat, *History,* B3r.

53. John Flavell, *Husbandry Spiritualiz'd: or, the Heavenly Use of Earthly Things. . . . Directing Husbandmen to the most Excellent Improvements of their common Imployments. . . . 7th edition* (1705), "The Epistle to the Intelligent Countrey Reader," B2r–v, and "Epistle Dedicatory," A2r, A6r. As these addresses suggest, Flavell shared with others we have read the preoccupation with engaging common people on issues of common interest. See above, chap. 7.

54. John Turberville Needham, *An Account of Some New Microscopical Discoveries . . . Dedicated to the Royal Society* (1745), 1–3, quoted in Marjorie Nicolson, *Science and Imagination* (Ithaca, NY: Cornell University Press, 1956), 221. On Boyle and the practice of "occasional meditation," see J. Paul Hunter, *Before Novels: The Cultural Contexts of Eighteenth-Century English Fiction* (New York: Norton, 1990), 200–208.

55. William Paley, *Natural Theology: or, Evidences of the Existence and Attributes of the Deity, Collected from the Appearances of Nature* (1802; reprint, Boston, 1837), chap. 6, p. 45. On Paley, see Colin Jager, *Romanticism and Design* (forthcoming), chap. 4.

56. Oliver Goldsmith, *The Citizen of the World* (1760–61), letter 89, in *Collected Works of Oliver Goldsmith,* ed. Arthur Friedman (Oxford: Clarendon, 1966), 2:360.

57. Cf. the nineteenth-century maxim that "ontogeny recapitulates phylogeny." See Stephen Jay Gould, *Ontogeny and Phylogeny* (Cambridge, MA: Harvard University Press, 1977).

58. See [Andrew Marvell], *The Last Instructions to a Painter* (1667? 1689), lines 15–18: "Or if to score out our compendious fame, / With Hooke, then, through the microscope take aim, / Where, like the new *Comptroller* [Sir Thomas Clifford], all men laugh / To see a tall louse brandish the white staff." *Andrew Marvell: The Complete Poems,* ed. Elizabeth Story Donno (Harmondsworth, UK: Penguin, 1978), 157. Cf. John Willis and Thomas Brown, "A

Comical Panegyrick on that familiar Animal, by the Vulgar call'd a Louse" (1707), which Richmond P. Bond classifies as a mock heroic in "Register of Burlesque Poems," no. 16, in *English Burlesque Poetry, 1700–1750* (Cambridge, MA: Harvard University Press, 1932), 254. Joseph Roach writes that Hooke's plate "could compete for laurels in the literary genre of the mock-heroic." Roach's aim in this essay is "to interpret the Augustan theater as an instrument, closely analogous to contemporary optical instruments, especially suited to the magnification of behavior." "The Artificial Eye: Augustan Theater and the Empire of the Visible," in *The Performance of Power: Theatrical Discourse and Politics,* ed. Sue-Ellen Case and Janelle Reinelt (Iowa City: University of Iowa Press, 1991), 131, 143.

59. Robert Hooke, *Micrographia . . .* (1665), 78, a2v. For contemporary commentary on the microscope and other optical instruments, see Nicolson, *Science and Imagination;* and Barbara M. Stafford, *Body Criticism: Imagining the Unseen in Enlightenment Art and Medicine* (Cambridge, MA: MIT Press, 1993), chaps. 1, 5.

60. Hooke, *Micrographia,* 175–76.

61. For Chatsworth, see above, chap. 5, n. 63, and fig. 5.19. More immediately Hooke's "discover[y]" and description of the "large Tree" and "the Window" juxtaposed with "my hand and fingers" recalls Gulliver in Lilliput. See, e.g., [Swift], *Gulliver's Travels,* pt. 1, chap. 2, pp. 13, 31.

62. Edmund Burke, *A Philosophical Enquiry into the Origin of our Ideas of the Sublime and Beautiful* (1757), ed. J. T. Boulton (New York: Columbia University Press, 1958), 72. Burke added this passage in the second edition, of 1759. On the sublime of the small, see Kristin Girten, "Meditation, Reflection, and the Sublime of the Small" (PhD diss., Rutgers University, forthcoming).

63. [Eliza Haywood], *The Female Spectator* (1744–46), bk. 15, pp. 155, 147, 148, 153–54, 142, 154, 155.

64. John Dryden, *Mac Flecknoe* (1682), in *The Works of John Dryden,* vol. 2, *Poems, 1681–1684,* ed. H. T. Swedenberg Jr. and Vinton A. Dearing (Berkeley and Los Angeles: University of California Press, 1972) (hereafter cited parenthetically in the text).

65. On the role played by poems on affairs of state in the separation out of poetry from politics, see Michael McKeon, "What Were Poems on Affairs of State?" *1650–1850: Ideas, Aesthetics, and Inquiries in the Early Modern Era* 4 (1997): 363–82.

66. See above, chap. 2, n. 127.

67. For a thoughtful investigation of this possibility, see Patrick J. Daly Jr., "'Rome's Other Hope': Charles, Monmouth, and James in the Summer of 1676," *ELH* 66, no. 3 (1999): 655–76.

68. On the passion for Monmouth, see line 175, p. 59, where Flecknoe-Charles says to Shadwell-Monmouth: "Thou art my blood, where Johnson[-York] has no part . . . ." On the passion for court whores, see lines 70–73, p. 56, on the Barbican: "From its old Ruins Brothel-houses rise, / Scenes of lewd loves, and of polluted joys; / Where their vast Courts the Mother-Strumpets keep, / And, undisturb'd by Watch, in silence sleep." See also lines 122–23, p. 57, Flecknoe's coronation of Shadwell: "*Love's Kingdom* to his right he did convey, / At once his Sceptre and his rule of Sway" (perhaps echoing Rochester's "Satyr on Charles II," line 11: "His scepter and his prick are of a length . . . ." For the context, see above, chap. 6, n. 77. Rochester's poem was already circulating in manuscript when Dryden composed his).

69. "Martinus Scriblerus, of the Poem," in *The Dunciad Variorum* (1728–29), in *The Dunciad*, ed. James Sutherland, vol. 5 of the Twickenham Edition of the Poems of Alexander Pope (New York: Oxford University Press, 1943), 51 (hereafter references are to this edition and appear parenthetically in the text).

70. *The Rape of the Lock*, canto 1, lines 1–3, in *The Rape of the Lock and Other Poems*, ed. Geoffrey Tillotson, vol. 2 of the Twickenham Edition of the Poems of Alexander Pope (London: Methuen, 1940), 144 (hereafter references are to this edition and appear parenthetically in the text).

71. Cf. Samuel Johnson's appreciation of *The Rape of the Lock:* "The subject of the poem is an event below the common incidents of common life; nothing real is introduced that is not seen so often as to be no longer regarded, yet the whole detail of a female-day is here brought before us invested with so much art of decoration, that, though nothing is disguised, every thing is striking, and we feel all the appetite of curiosity for that from which we have a thousand times turned fastidiously away." "Pope," in *Lives of the English Poets* (1779, 1781), ed. Arthur Waugh (1952; reprint, London: Oxford University Press, 1968), 2:316–17. Pope's experiment is older than the eighteenth century. Cf. Wendy Wall's reading of *Gammer Gurton's Needle* (c. 1550–60) in *Staging Domesticity: Household Work and English Identity in Early Modern Drama* (Cambridge: Cambridge University Press, 2000), chap. 2: the play tells the story of "how a missing needle can become the occasion for a complete breakdown in social relations. . . . English comedy is not simply born out of a sense of the inappropriateness of lodging homey truths in grand forms, for the play's 'trifle' turns out to be central to the maintenance of bodies, sexualities, communities, and genders" (63, 86).

72. For other efforts to domesticate ancient poetic machinery, see above, chap. 7, nn. 26–29.

73. For the claim and the interfiliations, see Pope, *Rape of the Lock*, 83, 349. A match between "Belinda" and "the Baron" cannot literally have been Pope's ambition because the latter, Lord Petre, had died in 1713 (see 196n20).

74. On the housewife's unpaid productivity, see above, chap. 4, nn. 37–41.

75. For an overview, see Michael McKeon, "The Pastoral Revolution," in *Refiguring Revolutions: Aesthetics and Politics from the English Revolution to the Romantic Revolution*, ed. Kevin Sharpe and Steven N. Zwicker (Berkeley and Los Angeles: University of California Press, 1998), 267–89. See pp. 268–72 for a defense of viewing pastoral and georgic as continuous rather than oppositional forms, a view I take here as well.

76. George Puttenham, *The Arte of English Poesie . . .* (1589) (Menston, UK: Scolar Press Facsimiles, 1968), bk. 1, chap. 18, pp. 30–31.

77. *Guardian*, no. 30 (15 Apr. 1713), in *The Guardian*, ed. John C. Stephens (Lexington: University Press of Kentucky, 1982) (hereafter references are to this edition and appear parenthetically in the text). Tickell's droll allusion to the regulations of the landed interest should be read in the context of Steele's earlier information that from the *Guardian*'s perspective, the landed and the trading interests are quite complementary. See *Guardian*, no. 6 (18 Mar. 1713).

78. But see Annabel Patterson, *Pastoral and Ideology: Virgil to Valery* (Berkeley and Los Angeles: University of California Press, 1987), 206–14, for the argument that the pastoral contest between Pope and Philips was at least in part a coded quarrel between Tory and Whig politics.

79. Quoted in Richard Wendorf, *William Collins and Eighteenth-Century English Poetry* (Minneapolis: University of Minnesota Press, 1981), 32. My thanks to James Mulholland for bringing this quotation to my attention.

80. The figure of the wolf provides something of an index to what occurs in the transition from Renaissance to Enlightenment pastoral. Spenser's Diggon had used the wolf allegorically, only to be corrected by the literalistic Hobbinol for situating wolves in England: *The Shepheardes Calendar* (1579), "September," lines 147–55; Milton had famously continued the religious allegory in *Lycidas* (1638, 1645), lines 128–31.

81. Alexander Pope, *A Discourse on Pastoral* (1709); idem, "Winter: The Fourth Pastoral, or Daphne," line 14, in *Pastoral Poetry and the Essay on Criticism,* ed. E. Audra, vol. 1 of the Twickenham Edition of the Poems of Alexander Pope (London: Methuen, 1961), 25, 32

82. See John Gay, *Poetry and Prose,* ed. Vinton A. Dearing and Charles E. Beckwith (Oxford: Clarendon, 1974), 1:90–126 (hereafter references are to this edition and appear parenthetically in the text).

83. For helpful annotation of Gay's allusiveness throughout the poem and its introductory material, see ibid., 2:515–40.

84. On the flexible distinction between female "inside" and male "outside" work in the domestic economy, see above, chap. 4, nn. 16–21.

85. See McKeon, "Pastoral Revolution," 272–75.

86. From this perspective, William Collins's "Ode on the Popular Superstitions of the Highlands of Scotland, Considered as the Subject of Poetry" (wr. 1750) may be seen to extend Gay's project in *The Shepherd's Week* to the retrieval of "popular superstitions." For a brief discussion, see Michael McKeon, "Surveying the Frontier of Culture: Pastoralism in Eighteenth-Century England," in *Studies in Eighteenth-Century Culture,* vol. 26, ed. Syndy M. Conger and Julie C. Hayes (Baltimore: Johns Hopkins University Press, 1998), 12.

87. Gay's editors observe (*Poetry and Prose,* 2:535) that he in fact begins "Saturday" with a burlesque of Virgil's Eclogue 4 only to move to an imitation of Eclogue 6, whose substance, an account of the creation and transformation of the world from the Epicurean perspective, Virgil introduces with the humble story of his own first attempts at poetry: "But when I tried her tender voice, too young, / And fighting kings and bloody battles sung, / Apollo checked my pride, and bade me feed / My fattening flocks, nor dare beyond the reed." Eclogue 6, lines 3–6, in *The Works of Virgil,* trans. John Dryden, ed. James Kinsley [Oxford: Oxford University Press, 1961], 24, hereafter cited parenthetically in the text). So Gay's counter-Virgilian diffidence is itself Virgilian, but with the crucial difference that Gay does not reflect the conviction, implicit in Virgil's words here and explicit in the Virgilian *curriculum vitae* from pastoral to georgic to epic, that martial politics are superior to rural privacy.

88. Alastair Fowler, ed., *The Country House Poem: A Cabinet of Seventeenth-Century Estate Poems and Related Items* (Edinburgh: Edinburgh University Press, 1994) (hereafter cited parenthetically in the text). The expansion of the form was already under way at a more modest rate before Fowler's important intervention, ranging from the rediscovery of Emilia Lanier's "Description of Cooke-ham" (1611) to the rereading of Jonathan Swift's poems on his Irish dwelling places by Carole Fabricant in her *Swift's Landscape* (Baltimore: Johns Hopkins University Press, 1982).

89. I pass over here the socioeconomic context that provides this dialectic some explanatory coherence. See Fowler's introduction to *The Country House Poem* for an awareness of

these factors, whose classic presentation with respect to the country house poem was made by Raymond Williams in *The Country and the City* (New York: Oxford University Press, 1973), chaps. 3–6. Aspects of this context have been dealt with at some length in the preceding chapters of the present study.

90. If we include in the country-house genre bawdy verse like "Love's Tenement" (1661), both periodization and typology are complicated by an Interregnum poem that further interiorizes the analogy between outside and inside so that it becomes one between the house and the woman's body, country house and "*Cony-Hall*" (line 8). See *Bawdy Verse: A Pleasant Collection*, ed. E. J. Burford (Harmondsworth, UK: Penguin, 1982), 136–37.

91. See John S. Coolidge, "Great Things and Small: The Virgilian Progression," *Comparative Literature* 7, no. 1 (1965): 8–9. Coolidge argues more broadly that the Virgilian *curriculum vitae* is a temporalization of *Sic parvis componere magna solebam* that figures pastoral, georgic, and epic as a dialectical relation of supersession and fulfillment and that Milton adequated to the typological view of Christian history and of his own performance as a Christian poet whose humble epic both domesticates and exceeds the greatness of its pagan models. For Milton's use of the Latin tag, see *Paradise Lost* (1667), bk. 2, lines 921–22; bk. 6, lines 310–11; bk. 10, line 306. Cf. *Paradise Regained* (1671), bk. 4, lines 567–68.

The schematic nature of the development outlined above can be seen in the example of Pope's *Windsor-Forest* (1713), a relatively late instance of the country house poem in which the house itself plays no part and the distinction between the lesser and the great is rendered all but unavailable. Pope's epic simile, which compares his subject matter—the partridge hunt—with the figure of Britain's militarism, is knit together by the Virgilian line "Thus (if small Things we may with great compare) . . . ." That is, here the great is used to explicate the small, a surprising inversion of formal domestication until we recall that in the complex and self-conscious overlays of which *Windsor-Forest* consists, hunting has already served as the metaphorical signifier of warfare. Such reversals, which are common not only in the "mature" country house poem but (as we have seen) in much of the discourse with which they are contemporary, are characteristic of that stage in the division of knowledge at which the separation and the conflation of categories are working together as antithetical parts of a functioning conceptual unit. But the patent continuity of these poems with their Virgilian model reminds us that the formal problems of domestication, which domesticity both resolves and reformulates, are as old as the distinction between the public and the private itself.

92. On seventeenth-century domestic architecture, see above, chap. 5. The following reflections on "Upon Appleton House" are indebted to Donald M. Friedman, "Rude Heaps and Decent Order," in *Marvell and Liberty*, ed. Warren Chernaik and Martin Dzelzainis (New York: St. Martin's, 1999), 131–35.

93. Luke 10:38–42; see also John 12:1–8.

94. Giles Constable, *Three Studies in Medieval Religious and Social Thought* (Cambridge: Cambridge University Press, 1995), 44, 22; see generally 3–115. A. Pigler cites ninety-five pictorial treatments of this gospel scene in seventeenth- and eighteenth-century Europe. A. Pigler, *Barockthemen: Eine auswahl von verzeichnissen zur ikonographie des 17. und 18. jahrhunderts* (Budapest: Akadémiai Kiadó, 1974), 324–27.

95. Although this painting recently has been attributed to Bueckelaer's circle, I follow the generally accepted ascription. See Franco Pagliaga, ed., *Vincenzo Campi: Scene del Quotidiano* (Milan: Skira, 2000), 198–99.

96. This is one of Vermeer's earliest paintings, and questions have been raised about its attribution.

97. See Keith P. F. Moxey, "Pieter Aertsen, Joachim Bueckelaer, and the Rise of Secular Painting in the Context of the Reformation" (PhD diss., University of Chicago, 1974), 41.

98. For example, the force and complexity of this expressiveness are enhanced by the way the several groupings allude to conventional triangulated compositions in the treatment of other sacred subjects like the Nativity, the Madonna and Child, and the Crucifixion.

99. See, e.g., Kenneth M. Craig, "*Pars Ergo Marthae Transit:* Pieter Aertsen's 'Inverted' Paintings of *Christ in the House of Martha and Mary,*" *Oud Holland* 97, no. 1 (1983): 32–35.

100. See Marta Cacho Casal, "The Old Woman in Velázquez's *Kitchen Scene with Christ's Visit to Martha and Mary,*" *Journal of the Warburg and Courtauld Institutes* 63 (2000): 296–97 and n. 13.

101. A very similar use of space may be found in the representation of other biblical subjects that turn upon the relationship between eating and salvation. The Parable of the Great Supper (Luke 14:12–24) concerns the charitable feeding of the poor and the lame, "for thou shalt be recompensed at the resurrection of the just." Cf. Wtewael's *Kitchen Scene with the Parable of the Great Supper,* Berlin, Staatliche Museen, Bodemuseum. At Emmaus the resurrected Christ reveals himself to two of his apostles by blessing and breaking bread (Luke 24:13–32); cf. Jacob Matham, engraved after Aertsen, *Kitchen Piece with the Supper at Emmaus.* At the wedding of Cana Jesus turns water into wine (John 1:2); cf. Ludger Tom Ring the Younger, *Marriage Feast at Cana,* Kaiser-Friedrich Museum, Berlin.

102. See above, chap. 7, n. 23.

103. See above, chap. 7, n. 24.

104. John Bunyan, *The Pilgrim's Progress from This World, to That which is to come . . .* (1678), "The Conclusion," lines 7–12, ed. N. H. Keeble (Oxford: Oxford University Press, 1984), 134.

105. See Craig, "*Pars Ergo Marthae Transit,*" title; and Constable, *Three Studies,* 133–34 (citing Breughel's *Icarus*).

106. Thus George Ferguson's treatment of Martha and Mary in *Signs and Symbols in Christian Art* (New York: Oxford University Press, 1966), 132–33, passes over the tradition of interpreting their behavior allegorically but focuses on the attributes by which Martha is symbolized.

107. Gotthold Ephraim Lessing, *Laokoon, oder, über die Grenzen der Malerie und Poesie* (1766).

108. See McKeon, *Origins,* chap. 2.

109. See Günther Irmscher, "*Ministrae Voluptatum:* Stoicizing Ethics in the Market and Kitchen Scenes of Pieter Aertsen and Joachim Beuckelaer," *Simiolus* 16, no. 4 (1986): 226. As Irmscher makes clear by studying the kitchen along with the market scenes by these artists, what is central to such paintings is an iconography of alimentary and sexual excess that is available equally in the work of the cook and in the work of the butcher, hence not specifiable to the scene of the domestic as such.

110. See above, chap. 5.

111. See Anne W. Lowenthal, *Joachim Wtewael and Dutch Mannerism* (Doornspijk, The Netherlands: Davaco, 1986), 148.

112. Lowenthal, ibid., 113, writes that in northern European folklore fish are a common symbol of the phallus.

113. The resurrection of Lazarus, we recall, immediately precedes the supper with his sisters Martha and Mary (John 11:1–12:1).

114. Cf. the lady and the dog in Pierre-Antoine Baudouin's, *La Lecture,* plate 2.

115. See Moxey, "Pieter Aertsen," 40; and Craig, "*Pars Ergo Marthae Transit,*" 29–30.

116. Irmscher, "*Ministrae Voluptatum,*" 227, suggests that they are cooks.

117. For some of these details, see the readings of Craig, "*Pars Ergo Marthae Transit,*" 31; Keith P. F. Moxey, "Erasmus and the Iconography of Pieter Aertsen's *Christ in the House of Martha and Mary* in the Boymans–van Benningen Museum," *Journal of the Warburg and Courtauld Institutes* 34 (1971): 335–6; and idem, *Pieter Aertsen,* 46.

118. The word "anachronism" itself enters English usage in the middle of the seventeenth century. See Herman J. Ebeling, "The Word Anachronism," *Modern Language Notes* 52 (1937): 120–21.

119. The term "internalized" is warranted only by our process of reading and not by evidence of historical change.

Chapter Nine | Figures of Domestication

1. For a general treatment, see Michael McKeon, *The Origins of the English Novel, 1600–1740* (Baltimore: Johns Hopkins University Press, 1987), 212–37.

2. [John Arbuthnot], *The History of John Bull* (1712), ed. Alan W. Bower and Robert A. Erickson (Oxford: Clarendon, 1976), 5. For a late-eighteenth-century political cartoon representing Great Britain as John Bull, see fig. 2.2.

The proximity of concentration narrative to the emblem and beast fable traditions can be seen in Richard Lovelace's "A Fly caught in a Cobweb," lines 1–2: "Small type of great ones, that do hum, / Within this whole World's narrow Room . . . ." *The Poems of Richard Lovelace,* ed. C. H. Wilkinson (1930; reprint, Oxford: Clarendon, 1968), 136. See also John Dryden's *Hind and the Panther* (1687), above, chap. 8, n. 43.

3. [Jonathan Swift], *The Conduct of the Allies, and of the Late Ministry, in the Beginning and Carrying on the Present War* (1711), in *The Prose Works of Jonathan Swift,* ed. Herbert Davis, vol. 6, *Political Tracts, 1711–1713* (Oxford: Blackwell, 1951), 56; idem, *A Proposal that all the Ladies and Women of Ireland should appear constantly in Irish Manufactures* (1729), in Swift, *Prose Works,* vol. 12, *Irish Tracts, 1728–1733* (Oxford: Blackwell, 1955), 123–24.

4. [Jonathan Swift], *Examiner,* no. 17 (30 Nov. 1710), in Swift, *Prose Works,* vol. 3, *The Examiner and Other Pieces Written in 1710–11* (Oxford: Blackwell, 1940), 24–25. With the distinction between the name and the thing compare that between libel and satire and actual and concrete particularity as discussed above, in chap. 2.

5. [Jonathan Swift], "The Story of the Injured Lady. Being a true Picture of Scotch Perfidy, Irish Poverty, and English Partiality . . ." (1746), in Swift, *Prose Works,* vol. 9, *Irish Tracts, 1720–1723 and Sermons* (Oxford: Blackwell, 1948), 3 (hereafter cited parenthetically in the text).

6. See above, chap. 3.

7. This reading of Swift's "Story" also may shed light on the venerable and vexing question of his attitude toward women. What is the relationship between Swift's empathetic and

deeply ambivalent identification with Ireland and his impersonation of "her" representative, women?

8. Needless to say, both stories are particularized to a degree that militates against taking them as representative of a single basic difference in narrative form; hence conclusions drawn from this comparison are highly speculative.

9. [Delarivier Manley], dedication to *The Power of Love* (1720), in *The Meridian Anthology of Early Women Writers: British Literary Women from Aphra Behn to Maria Edgworth, 1660–1800*, ed. Katharine M. Rogers and William McCarthy (New York: NAL Penguin, 1987), 143n1. "The Wife's Resentment" derives from Matteo Bandello by way of William Painter's *The Palace of Pleasure* (1566). Hereafter references are to this edition and appear parenthetically in the text.

10. With significant implications for its plot, Manley limits her Anglicization of the novella to language, retaining the Spanish setting: "In Spain they have other maxims than in England; here a person ennobles his wife, there 'tis a reproach for a man of quality and to his descendants, if he chance to mingle with the people" (147–48).

11. *A Review of the State of the English Nation* (1704–13) (hereafter cited parenthetically in the text). For Swift's comparable allegory of Miss Faction, which includes a "Metaphorical Genealogy," see *Examiner*, no. 31 (8 Mar. 1710).

12. With Lady Credit's inconstancy compare that of Mistress Parliament, above, chap. 3, n. 7.

13. Her suitors are therefore in thrall to Lady Credit, "effeminate" in the residual but still active sense of being besotted by her. J. G. A. Pocock has argued on the contrary that this effeminacy is not a residual but an emergent attribution, peculiar to the way civic humanists characterized a new phenomenon, the "hysteria . . . of economic man," who in the eighteenth century (if not later for, e.g., Marx) "was seen as . . . still wrestling with his own passions and hysterias and with interior and exterior forces let loose by his fantasies and appetities, and symbolised by such archetypically female goddesses of disorder as Fortune, Luxury, and most recently Credit herself . . . . [T]he new speculative image of economic man was opposed to the essentially paternal and Roman figure of the citizen patriot." J. G. A. Pocock, *Virtue, Commerce, and History: Essays on Political Thought and History, Chiefly in the Eighteenth Century* (Cambridge: Cambridge University Press, 1985), 113–14. I think Pocock exaggerates the degree to which economic man the *subject*, as distinguished from the *object* of his desires, was associated by contemporaries with "feminine" hysteria, passions, and the like. But even if we take his argument on its own terms, Defoe's eighteenth-century figure of effeminated economic man in fact only extends a seventeenth-century tradition of effeminated political man that includes Philip Sidney's Pyrocles and Duke Basilius, John Milton's and Lucy Hutchinson's Charles I, anonymous's Major General John Lambert, the Earl of Rochester's Charles II, and Aphra Behn's Cesario and Octavio—a series bounded at either end by Shakespeare's and Dryden's Antony (see below, pt. 3; for Lambert and Rochester, see above, chap. 5, n. 59, and chap. 6, n. 77). Pocock mistakes a broad continuity for a radical civic humanist innovation. Defoe's Lady Credit is (in the line of Fortuna) an allegorization of what these earlier texts literalize as wife or beloved to whom the public hero becomes enthralled. Behind this tradition lies the customary apprehension of the disordered household: woman on top, the skimmington ride, the curtain lecture—ultimately Procopius, himself. See *Anecdota*, e.g., i. 12–14, 19–20; ii. 20–23; iii. 1–2.

14. For a comparable moment in another of Defoe's concentration narratives, see *Seldom Comes a Better: or, a Tale of a Lady and her Servants* (1710), 11. Defoe's authorship of this tract has been questioned by, among others, the editors of [Arbuthnot], *History of John Bull,* xx n1.

15. Cf. the experimental effort to accommodate the epistemological category of "disinterestedness" through the social category of gentility, above, chap. 7, nn. 41–53.

16. On the relationship between female chastity and honor, see McKeon, *Origins,* 156–58.

17. On the economic unproductivity of housewives and on the comparison of wives and whores, see above, chap. 4. On whores and sodomites, see above, chap. 6, nn. 28–29. Defoe worked hard to decide the different degrees to which the imagination was an acceptable component (respectively, honor, credit, and fiction) of social, economic, and "aesthetic" experience. See McKeon, *Origins,* 205–6.

18. My thinking about Defoe's Lady Credit has profited from reading and talking with Kimberly Latta. See her essay "The Mistress of the Marriage Market: Gender and Economic Ideology in Defoe's *Review,*" ELH 69, no. 2 (2002): 359–83.

19. Defoe's main rival here may be John Dunton, from whom he learned a great deal in this regard. See George A. Starr, *Defoe and Casuistry* (Princeton, NJ: Princeton University Press, 1971), chap. 1. My claim here is for the brilliance of Defoe's temerity, not necessarily for his originality.

20. Starr, *Defoe.*

21. Defoe, *The Compleat English Gentleman* (wr. 1728–29), ed. Karl D. Bülbring (London: Nutt, 1890) (hereafter cited parenthetically in the text).

22. See above, chap. 1, n. 36 (hereafter *Conjugal Lewdness; or, Matrimonial Whoredom* (1727) will be cited parenthetically in the text).

23. See above, chap. 2, nn. 133–36, 141–42; chap. 6, nn. 93–97; and chap. 7, nn. 73–94.

24. On these matters (and Defoe's involvement in them), see McKeon, *Origins,* chap. 3, sec. 6.

25. [Daniel Defoe], *The Family Instructor* (1715), 8–9 (hereafter cited parenthetically in the text).

26. On the importance of probability in casuistry, see above, chap. 1, n. 99; see also n. 78.

27. On experimental method, see above, chap. 8, nn. 63–65.

28. See above, chap. 8, n. 105.

29. Hereafter cited parenthetically in the text by volume, book, and page number.

30. A likely allusion to Delarivier Manley's Lady Intelligence (*The New Atalantis,* 1709) and to her *Memoirs of Europe* (1710). See below, chap. 13.

31. On the secret history, see below, part 3.

32. See above, chap. 7, nn. 17–19.

33. See above, chap. 2, nn. 94–95.

34. See below, chap. 14, nn. 24–26.

35. With Haywood's maternal figure compare Fielding's parental figure for the role of the narrator, above, chap. 2, n. 135.

36. For Defoe's warnings against unequal matches, see *Conjugal Lewdness,* 213–71.

37. For a broad discussion of the use and significance of such language in the later seventeenth and early eighteenth centuries, see above, chap. 3.

38. See above, chap. 8, n. 63.

39. Haywood's emphasis on the importance of female education, like that of many other

midcentury writers, will be transformed by Mary Wollstonecraft into a powerful, but therefore chastening, sociological principle. See above, chap. 4, nn. 58–61.

40. On the complex and controversial status of the hoop petticoat in eighteenth-century culture, see Erin Mackie, *Market à la Mode: Fashion, Commodity, and Gender in "The Tatler" and "The Spectator"* (Baltimore: Johns Hopkins University Press, 1997), chap. 3.

41. On these matters, see above, chap. 4, nn. 16–47. Cf. Haywood's solicitude in describing how the hoop petticoats of leisured ladies can upset "the numerous Stalls with which this populace City abounds, . . . to the great Damage of the Fruiterer, Fishmonger, Comb and Buckle-Sellers, and others of those small Chapmen" (3.15.185). Contemporaries made the connection between commoners and women as disenfranchised majorities (thus the tendency to see both groups as at risk in reading potentially subversive upward-mobility narratives), and it is not surprising that Haywood should identify with common laborers.

42. Cf. Haywood: "One of the distinguishing Marks of a *bad Taste* in either Sex, is the Affectation of any Virtue without the Attempt to practise it; for it shews that we regard only what we are *thought to be,* not what we *really are* . . ." (3.15.184).

43. On this distinction, see above, chap. 2, n. 78.

Chapter Ten | The Narration of Public Crisis

1. Sissela Bok, *Secrecy: On the Ethics of Concealment and Revelation* (New York: Pantheon, 1982), 5–14.

2. Thomas Sprat, *The History of the Royal Society of London, For the Improving of Natural Knowledge* (1667), 64 (for "cabinets," "closets," and "corners," see pp. 71, 74, 75, 80); [Sir Walter Raleigh], *The Cabinet-Council: Containing the Cheif Arts of Empire, and Mysteries of State; Discabineted In Political and Polemical Aphorisms . . . Published by John Milton, Esq.* (1658), title page; *The Wandring-Whores Complaint for Want of Trading . . .* (1663), title page.

3. Richard Overton, *The Arraignement of Mr. Persecution* (1645), in *Tracts on Liberty in the Puritan Revolution, 1638–1647,* ed. William Haller (New York: Columbia University Press, 1933), 3:230.

4. Procopius, *The Secret History of the Court of the Emperor Justinian . . .* (1674). For recent discussions of the form, see Annabel Patterson, *Early Modern Liberalism* (Cambridge: Cambridge University Press, 1997), chaps. 5–6; and Lionel Gossman, "Anecdote and History," *History and Theory* 42, no. 2 (2003): 143–68.

5. [Antoine Varillas], *Medicis. Written Originally by that Fam'd Historian, the Sieur de Varilles. Made English by Ferrand Spence* (1686; French 1685), "Epistle Dedicatory," A4v–5r, A6r, and "Author's Preface," a4v–a5r, a8r.

6. *Poems on Affairs of State: From the Time of Oliver Cromwell, to the Abdication of K. James the Second . . . Part Two: State-Poems; continued* (1697), "Preface," A2v.

7. On this double sense of secrecy, see Michael McKeon, "What Were Poems on Affairs of State?" *1650–1850: Ideas, Aesthetics, and Inquiries in the Early Modern Era* 4 (1997): 363–82.

8. Francis Bacon, "Author's Preface," in *The Wisdom of the Ancients* ([Lat., 1609] trans. 1619), in *The Philosophical Works of Francis Bacon,* ed. Robert L. Ellis and James Spedding, rev. ed. John M. Robertson (London: Routledge, 1905), 823.

9. [John Toland], *Clidophorus, or, Of the Exoteric and Esoteric Philosophy; that is, Of the*

External and Internal Doctrine of the Ancients: The one open and public, accommodated to popular prejudices and the Religions establish'd by Law; the other private and secret, wherin, to the few capable and discrete, was taught the real Truth stript of all disguises, 85, printed in Toland's *Tetradymus . . .* (1720).

10. On the influence of the *Arcadia,* see Paul Salzman, *English Prose Fiction, 1558–1700: A Critical History* (Oxford: Clarendon, 1985), chap. 10 (hereafter cited parenthetically in the text). Salzman surveys Sidney's influence as a writer of prose fiction and not, more specifically, as a secret historian. For our purposes his most important successor is Mary Wroth's *roman à clef, The Countesse of Montgomeries Urania* (1621) (see Salzman, *English Prose Fiction,* 138–44), whose critical celebrity in recent years may excuse my saying no more about it in this context. In the following discussion of the *Old Arcadia* I have been aided by Annabel Patterson, *Censorship and Interpretation: The Conditions of Writing and Reading in Early Modern England* (Madison: University of Wisconsin Press, 1984); and Blair Worden, *The Sound of Virtue: Philip Sidney's Arcadia and Elizabethan Politics* (New Haven, CT: Yale University Press, 1996).

11. Philip Sidney, *A Defence of Poetry* (1595), ed. J. A. Van Dorsten (Oxford: Oxford University Press, 1966), 43.

12. Philip Sidney, *The Countess of Pembroke's Arcadia (The Old Arcadia),* ed. Jean Robertson (Oxford: Oxford University Press, 1973), 56, 3 (hereafter references are to the *Old Arcadia* in this edition and appear parenthetically in the text).

13. See Patterson, *Censorship,* 33–34.

14. For Shaftesbury, see above, chap. 2, nn. 144–45.

15. For an example of such an articulation, see *Old Arcadia,* 383.

16. See Worden, *Sound of Virtue,* chap. 18 and passim.

17. See ibid., 84–89 and chap. 6 passim.

18. See ibid., pt. 3.

19. On Barclay's *Argenis,* see the useful discussions, on which I have relied, in Patterson, *Censorship,* 188–93; and Salzman, *English Prose Fiction,* 149–55.

20. John Barclay, *Barclay his Argenis. or, The Loves of Polyarchus and Argenis. Faithfully Translated out of Latin into English by Kingsmill Long Esquire. The Second Edition . . . Together with a Key Praefixed to unlock the whole Story* ([1625] 1637) (hereafter cited parenthetically in the text as "Long"), "Epistle Dedicatorie," A3r–v, and "The Key to unlock Argenis," A5v–6r. The key is a translation of one that appeared in the second Latin edition, of 1627.

21. John Barclay, *John Barclay his Argenis. Translated Ovt of Latine into English, The Prose Vpon his Maiesties Command: By Sir Robert Le Grys, Knight . . . With a Clauis annexed to it for the satisfaction of the Reader, and helping him to vnderstand, what persons were by the Author intended vnder the faigned Names imposed by him vpon them . . .* (1629), (hereafter cited parenthetically in the text as "Le Grys"), "The Clavis," 487, 485. The "clavis" is by Le Grys.

22. See above, chap. 7, nn. 78, 85–93.

23. Long attributes the poem to "Ow. Fell." Patterson, *Censorship,* 191–92, suggests how English readers as eminent as Charles I might have seen in *Argenis* a reflection of their own national drama in the late 1620s. With this personification of *Argenis* as a naturalized English princess compare Bunyan's personification of part 2 of *The Pilgrim's Progress* as a pilgrim; Christiana's "key" facilitates a more radical concretization of precept (see above, chap. 7, nn. 17–19).

24. For Haywood, see above, chap. 9, nn. 29–43.

25. Cf. "To the vnderstanding reader," where Le Grys trusts his readers will find in *Argenis* "matter worth their obseruation in seuerall kinds of learning, and not such trash, as to the losse of time and corruption of manners, these Romances are for the most part stuffed withall" (Le Grys, A4v).

26. The Virgin Queen's motherhood confirms the claim by Barclay's spokesman Nicopompus that "there shall be no mans picture to be plainely found there. To disguize them, I will haue many inuentions, which cannot possibly agree to those that I entend to point at" (Le Grys, 131).

27. See below, chap. 14, nn. 23–33, for a discussion of several narratives that Haywood entitles "secret histories."

28. See above, chap. 1, n. 10.

29. Hereafter *The Kings Cabinet Opened* is cited parenthetically in the text. Sixteen forty-five was also the year of composition of a suggestively related alchemical treatise by George Starkey entitled *Secrets Reveal'd: or An Open Entrance to the Shut-Palace of the King: Containing the Greatest Treasure in Chymistry, Never yet so plainly Discovered* (1669). See J. Andrew Mendelsohn, "Alchemy and Politics in England, 1649–1655," *Past and Present*, no. 135 (1992): 54 (and passim on the customary alchemical use of monarchal imagery).

30. [John Gauden], Εικον Βασιλικε. *The Povrtraictvre of His Sacred Maiestie in his Solitvdes and Svfferings* (1649), 189, 192. Gauden is generally accepted as the author of *Eikon Basilike*.

31. James Howell, *Epistolae Ho-Elianae: The Familiar Letters of James Howell,* ed. Joseph Jacobs (London, 1892), 2:658, 1:360, quoted in Patterson, *Censorship,* 217 and 226, respectively. The opening of private letters became standard state practice under Charles II. See above, chap. 2, n. 12.

32. "A Satyr, Occasioned by the Author's Survey of a Scandalous Pamphlet, intituled The Kings Cabinet opened," in *Rump: or an Exact Collection of the Choycest Poems and Songs relating to the Late Times* (1662), 169–70 (hereafter cited parenthetically in the text).

33. Lois Potter, *Secret Rites and Secret Writings: Royalist Literature, 1641–1660* (Cambridge: Cambridge University Press, 1989), 175.

34. Lucy Hutchinson, *Memoirs of the Life of Colonel Hutchinson,* ed. N. H. Keeble (London: Dent, 1995), quoted in James Grantham Turner, *Libertines and Radicals in Early Modern London: Sexuality, Politics, and Literary Culture, 1630–1685* (Cambridge: Cambridge University Press, 2002), 74; [John Milton], *Eikonoklastes: in Answer to a Book Entitled Eikon Basilike . . .* (1649), in *The Complete Prose Works of John Milton,* vol. 3, *1648–1649,* ed. Merritt Y. Hughes (New Haven, CT: Yale University Press, 1962), 419, 421. The critique of male government usurped by the masculine wife, rooted in the disordered household and the skimmington ride, was often transferred to the state political context. See, e.g., below, chap. 11, nn. 15–20. Cf. the preface to *Coll. Henry Marten's Familiar Letters to His Lady of Delight. Also Her kinde Returnes . . .* (1662), A3r: "Sir, These Letters of Yours to Yours, had not seene the world, if you your self had not given just occasion for the incivilitie. There was a time (I would it had never been) when you voted and principally caused the Sacred Letters of your Soveraign, and his Queen (the Cabinet as it was stiled) to be made publick." For deciphering some of these letters, John Wallis, code-breaker extraordinaire, was held partially responsible for the regicide. See Alan Marshall, *Intelligence and Espionage in the Reign of Charles II, 1660–1685* (Cambridge: Cambridge University Press, 1994), 93.

35. On the critique of Charles II, see above, chap. 6, nn. 77–87.

36. By W.M., 4th ed., corrected (1658) (hereafter cited parenthetically in the text). The volume's inner title is *The Queens Cabinet Opened . . .* (C1r).

37. With H.M.'s appreciative preservation of the queen's domestic lore compare John Gay's act of retrieval in *The Shepherd's Week*, above, chap. 8, nn. 82–91.

38. See Wendy Wall, *Staging Domesticity: Household Work and English Identity in Early Modern Drama* (Cambridge: Cambridge University Press, 2002), 28, 53.

39. The term "experiments" reminds us that cookbooks also descend from the late-medieval tradition of the "receipt-book" or book of secrets dedicated to the theory and practice of natural magic. See above, chap. 2, nn. 52–57.

40. See Hannah Woolley, *The Gentlewoman's Companion; or, a Guide to the Female Sex . . .* (1675), A4v. *The Queens Closet Opened* had frequent Restoration reprintings.

41. Indeed, the usurpation of rule republicans saw in the exchange of distaff for scepter seems relevant to the perennial threat of the omnicompetent secretary: for both, hierarchical subjecthood balances on the edge of subjectivity and self-rule.

By the time of Alexander Pope's intervention, the recipe book had evolved from the esotericism of the book of secrets to the domesticity of the housewife's cookbook. See chap. 15, "*A Receipt to Make an* Epic Poem," in Martinus Scriblerus [Alexander Pope], *Peri Bathous: Of the Art of Sinking in Poetry* (1727), in *Literary Criticism of Alexander Pope*, ed. Bertrand A. Goldgar (Lincoln: University of Nebraska Press, 1965), 84–87. Thus in the original version of chap. 15 Pope speaks of the contribution he makes "to the Structure of different sorts of Poetry, as the Receits of good Houswives do to the making Puddings . . . ." So by 1713 the language of the recipe has become a useful technique of formal domestication because it accommodates higher matters through the diction of domesticity: "It would, methinks, make these my Instructions more easily intelligible to ordinary Readers, if I discoursed of these Matters in the Stile in which Ladies Learned in Œconomicks dictate to their Pupils for the Improvement of the Kitchin and Larder." *Guardian*, no. 78 (10 June 1713), 287. In the present context, of course, Pope's use of domestic language aims not to domesticate but to trivialize his subject, modern poetry.

42. See above, chap. 8.

43. E.g., by Thomas P. Haviland, *The Roman de Longue Haleine on English Soil* (Philadelphia: University of Pennsylvania Press, 1931), who usefully includes and discusses *Argenis* among "English Romances in the [French] Heroic Manner" (181).

44. "To the Reader" (1691 reprint), in *Novel and Romance, 1700–1800: A Documentary Record*, ed. Ioan Williams (New York: Barnes and Noble, 1970), 25. See also Nicole Aronson, *Mademoiselle de Scudéry*, trans. Stuart R. Aronson (Boston: Twayne, 1978), 25, 37, 79; and Haviland, *Roman de Longue Haleine*, 70–75.

45. Salzman, *English Prose Fiction*, 189.

46. See Aronson, *Mademoiselle*, 86.

47. John Davies, "To the Ladies," prefixed to *Clelia*, vol. 1 (1655), A2r.

48. [Madeleine de Scudéry], *Clelia*, 1:68–69, 71; the map is printed at A5v–6r. On the map, see Aranson, *Mademoiselle*, 93–94; and Dorothy McDougall, *Madeleine de Scudéry* (New York: Blom, 1972), chap. 4, who reproduces the original French version facing p. 166.

49. [Madeleine de Scudéry], *Ibrahim, or the Illustrious Bassa*, trans. Henry Cogan ([Fr., 1641, 1652], trans. 1674), A3v.

50. [Madeleine de Scudéry], *Clelia,* vol. 4 (1660), trans. G[eorge] H[avers], ii, p. 203.

51. Ibid., 204. Cf. Mr. Spectator's ambition to replace foreign news by "knowledge of one-self," above, chap. 2, nn. 94–95. Amilcar agrees with Herminius, but fears that most readers of such a work "would speak of it but as of a meer trifle, and an unprofitable amusement . . ." (203).

52. For an unusually thoughtful assessment of the problem and responses to many of these questions, see Helen Hackett, "'Yet Tell Me Some Such Fiction': Lady Mary Wroth's *Urania* and the 'Femininity' of Romance," in *Women, Texts, and Histories 1575–1760,* ed. Clare Brant and Diane Purkiss (London: Routledge, 1992), 39–68; and idem, *Women and Romance Fiction in the English Renaissance* (Cambridge: Cambridge University Press, 2000). With respect to Scudéry I think Ros Ballaster is insufficiently attentive to this range of interpretive issues. See *Seductive Forms: Women's Amatory Fiction from 1684 to 1740* (Oxford: Clarendon, 1992), 42–49. Annabel Patterson's argument that there exists "a decidedly feminist impulse" in Scudéry's theory of romance form (*Censorship,* 195–97) is damaged by her misconception that it is a woman, Clelia, and not a man, Herminius, who stresses the importance of representing the "wars of the closet" in the passage quoted above and that what is being defended there is "the new romance" and not "history."

53. The psychoanalytic interpretation of family romance has encouraged a gendering of romance as male and of realism, or a different sort of romance, as female. See Sigmund Freud, "Family Romances" (1909), and Marthe Robert, *Origins of the Novel* (1980), in *Theory of the Novel: A Historical Approach,* ed. Michael McKeon (Baltimore: Johns Hopkins University Press, 2000), 156–77. See also Lisa Honaker, "Reviving Romance: Gender, Genre, and the Late-Victorian Anti-Realists" (PhD diss., Rutgers University, 1993), a study whose central figure is Robert Louis Stevenson.

54. See in general Patterson, *Censorship,* chap. 4; and Potter, *Secret Rites.* But see Nigel Smith, *Literature and Revolution in England, 1640–1660* (New Haven, CT: Yale University Press, 1994), 246–49, on what he calls "Republican Romance."

55. "An Act for subscribing to the Engagement," 2 Jan. 1650, in *The Stuart Constitution, 1603–1688: Documents and Commentary,* ed. J. P. Kenyon (Cambridge: Cambridge University Press, 1966), 341. On the analogy between the marriage contract and the political contract, see above, chap. 3.

56. See Victorian Kahn, "Margaret Cavendish and the Romance of Contract," *Renaissance Quarterly* 50, no. 2 (1997): 526–66. Kahn reads Cavendish's 1656 narrative as exemplary of this sort of accommodation.

57. *Cloria and Narcissus. A Delightful and New Romance, Imbellished with divers Politicall Notions, and singular Remarks of Moderne Transactions . . .* (1653), "To the Reader," A3r–v. Salzman, *English Prose Fiction,* 157n19, attributes this work and its expansion to Sir Percy Herbert.

58. *The Princess Cloria; or, the Royal Romance. In Five Parts. Imbellished with divers Political Notions, and singular Remarks of Modern Transactions. Containing The Story of most part of Europe, for may Years last past . . .* (1661), "To the Reader," A1r (hereafter cited parenthetically in the text). At least one other part of *Cloria and Narcissus* had been published since the first printing of 1653 and incorporated into *The Princess Cloria.*

59. "Antic" expresses a grotesque or bizarre quality associated with the fantastic designs found in ancient Roman remains (*OED*); hence the implication here, perhaps, of a mixture

between literal and allegorical, history and romance, new and old in which the old itself embodies an "antic" formal mixture.

60. Quoted in Salzman, *English Prose Fiction*, 162. A handwritten key appears on the flyleaf of the British Museum copy of the 1665 edition of *The Princess Cloria*, transcribed in Haviland, *Roman de Longue Haleine*, 107.

61. "Advertisement to the judicious Reader," prefixed to [Richard Brathwaite], *Panthalia; or, The Royal Romance* (1659), A2v, quoted in Derek Hirst, "The Politics of Literature in the English Republic," *Seventeenth Century* 5 (1990): 141.

62. For a selection, see *Poems on Affairs of State: Augustan Satirical Verse, 1660–1714*, vol. 1, *1660–1678*, ed. George deF. Lord (New Haven, CT: Yale University Press, 1963). On print culture during this period, see generally above, chap. 2.

63. John Dryden, *Annus Mirabilis* (1667), prefatory "Account," lines 31–32, and line 552, in *The Works of John Dryden*, vol. 1, *Poems, 1649–1680*, ed. Edward Niles Hooker and H. T. Swedenberg Jr. (Berkeley and Los Angeles: University of California Press, 1956), 50, 80. For supporting readings of the poem, see Michael McKeon, *Politics and Poetry in Restoration England: The Case of Dryden's "Annus Mirabilis"* (Cambridge, MA: Harvard University Press, 1975), chaps. 1, 5.

64. [Andrew Marvell], *The Last Instructions to a Painter* (1667? 1689), in *Andrew Marvell: The Complete Poems*, ed. Elizabeth Story Donno (Harmondsworth, UK: Penguin, 1978) (hereafter references are to this edition and appear parenthetically in the text).

65. Cf. the judicial function claimed by the public sphere, above, chap. 2, nn. 91–92, 99–103. On the street as the place of the people and the site of commoner justice, see above, chap. 4, nn. 2–6, and figs. 4.2, 4.4, and 4.5.

66. [John Lacy], "Satire" (1677), lines 13–16, in *Poems on Affairs of State*, 1:426. For the tortoise conceit, see "Upon Appleton House," st. 97.

67. Roger North, *Life of Francis North, Lord Guilford* (1742), 210, quoted in David Ogg, *England in the Reign of Charles II*, 2nd ed. (Oxford: Oxford University Press, 1956), 331; *The Letters of John Wilmot, Earl of Rochester*, ed. Jeremy Treglown (Chicago: University of Chicago Press, 1980), 187. On Chiffinch's office and appointment, see David Allen, "The Political Function of Charles II's Chiffinch," *Huntington Library Quarterly* 39, no. 3 (1976): 277, 281.

68. On the larger context of these matters that is provided by patriarchalist thinking, see above, chap. 3.

69. Treaty reprinted in Ogg, *England*, 344; see pp. 342–48 on both versions of the treaty.

70. Clause 2 of the secret treaty of Dover, in ibid., 345.

71. [Andrew Marvell], *An Account of the Growth of Popery, and Arbitrary Government in England. . . .* (Amsterdam, 1677), in *The Complete Works of Andrew Marvell*, ed. Alexander B. Grosart (1875; reprint, New York: AMS, 1966), 4:281, 248 (text of posthumous 1678 ed., in which Marvell's authorship is identified).

72. See Ogg, *England*, 571–73. On testimony of James's active complicity in the Popish Plot (if not of his readiness to assassinate his brother), see J. P. Kenyon, *The Popish Plot* (Harmondsworth, UK: Penguin, 1974), 160, 176–77.

73. [Marvell], *Account*, 249: "[H]is person is most sacred and inviolable; and whatsoever excesses are committed against so high a trust, nothing of them is imputed to him, as being free from the necessity or temptation; but his ministers only are accountable for all, and must answer it at their perils."

74. Sir Roger L'Estrange, *L'Estrange's Narrative of the Plot. . .* , 2d ed. (1680), 1. Between Marvell's and L'Estrange's narratives was sandwiched the publication of Titus Oates's *True Narrative of the Horrid Plot and Conspiracy of the Popish Party against the Life of His Sacred Majesty* (1679). For a discussion of Marvell's tract as a "secret history," see Annabel Patterson, "Marvell and Secret History," in *Marvell and Liberty,* ed. Warren Chernaik and Martin Dzelzainis (New York: St. Martin's, 1999), 23–49.

75. See Ogg, *England,* 345, 378 and n. 5.

76. See above, chap. 3, n. 68.

77. *His Majesties Declaration to all his Loving Subjects, June the Second, 1680* (1680), 3, 4. On Lucy Walter, see *DNB.*

78. [Robert Ferguson], *A Letter to a Person of Honour, concerning the King's disavowing the having been Married to the D. of M's. Mother,* dated 10 June (1680), 5, 2, 1, 7.

79. [Robert Ferguson], *A Letter to a Person of Honour, concerning the Black Box,* dated 15 May (1680), 1, 3 (font reversed).

80. [William Lawrence], preface to *The Right of Primogeniture, In Succession to the Kingdoms of England, Scotland, and Ireland . . . With all Objections answered, and clear Probation made, That to Compass or Imagine the Death, Exile, or Disinheriting of the King's Eldest Son, is High Treason. To which is added, An Answer to all Objections against declaring him a Protestant Successor, with Reasons shewing the Fatal Dangers of Neglecting the same* (1981), A3r; [John Dryden], *Absalom and Achitophel* (1681), lines 1–2, 5–6, in *Works,* vol. 2, *Poems, 1681–1684,* ed. H. T. Swedenberg Jr. and Vinton A. Dearing (Berkeley and Los Angeles: University of California Press, 1972), 5. For the connection between Lawrence and Dryden's poem, see Mark Goldie, "Contextualizing Dryden's Absalom: William Lawrence, the Law of Marriage, and the Case for King Monmouth," in *Religion, Literature, and Politics in Post-Reformation England, 1540–1688,* ed. D. B. Hamilton and Richard Streier (Cambridge: Cambridge University Press, 1996), 208–30. On the difference between licensed and contract marriage, see above, chap. 3, n. 30.

81. See Michael McKeon, *The Origins of the English Novel, 1600–1740* (Baltimore: Johns Hopkins University Press, 1987), chap. 1.

82. In practice, libel prosecution assigned responsibility for determining whether reference to real people had been made to the jury's judgment of how "the generality of readers" might construe words used "in their true and proper sense." See above, chap. 2, nn. 131–32. Cf. Delarivier Manley's attempt to defend against the charge of libel by denying any intent to make "particular reflections," below, chap. 13, nn. 35–36.

83. The fortunes of Prince Charles after the defeat of royalty provided raw material for other political romances as well, like the narratives of his wanderings after the battle of Worcester, described in McKeon, *Origins,* 213–14.

84. [T.S.], *The Perplex'd Prince* (1682), A4r, A5r, pp. 18, 21, 38, 52, 56, 123.

85. See Michael McKeon, "Historicizing *Absalom and Achitophel*," in *The New Eighteenth Century: Theory, Politics, English Literature,* ed. Felicity Nussbaum and Laura Brown (New York: Methuen, 1987), 23–40. Although I do not use these terms to describe it, something analogous to the public-private dialectic is engaged through Dryden's remarkable tendency to correlate the interplay between type and antitype, anticipation and fulfillment, with that between past and present, sacred and secular.

86. *The Fugitive Statesman, in Requital for the Perplex'd Prince* (1683), 50–51, 26.

87. On the challenge to customary techniques of petitioning in the absolutist state, see above, chap. 2, nn. 69–73.

88. See Judg. 14:18.

89. John Bunyan, *The Holy War, made by Shaddai upon Diabolus, For the Regaining of the Metropolis of the World. or, the Losing and Taking Again of the Town of Mansoul* (1682), ed. Roger Sharrock and James F. Forrest (Oxford: Clarendon, 1980), 29, 28, 139, 116; "To the Reader," 1, 5.

90. Bunyan, *Holy War,* 17. See pp. xxii–xxv and 256 for the reading.

Chapter Eleven | Behn's *Love-Letters*

1. Part 2 of *Absalom and Achitophel* is coauthored by Nahum Tate. For Behn's poetic treatment of the Exclusion Crisis, in which Monmouth is figured, in pastoral, not typological, terms, as the Scotch swain Silvio, see "Silvio's Complaint: A Song, To a Fine Scotch Tune" (1684), in *The Works of Aphra Behn,* ed. Janet Todd, vol. 1, *Poetry* (Columbus: Ohio State University Press, 1992), 82–84.

2. [Aphra Behn], *Love-Letters Between a Nobleman and his Sister,* ed. Janet Todd (Harmondsworth, UK: Penguin, 1996), dedicatory epistle and argument, 3–5, 9 (hereafter cited parenthetically in the text). Cf. Dryden's complication of concealment by revelation, which, given the antiquity of his signifying narrative, involves the ostentatious collapse of historical distance: "Were I the Inventour, who am only the Historian, I should certainly conclude the Piece with the Reconcilement of *Absalom* to *David.* And, who knows but this may come to pass? Things were not brought to an Extremity where I left the Story . . . ." [John Dryden], "To the Reader," prefixed to *Absalom and Achitophel,* in *The Works of John Dryden,* vol. 2, *Poems, 1681–1684,* ed. H. T. Swedenberg Jr. and Vinton A. Dearing (Berkeley and Los Angeles: University of California Press, 1972), 4 (font reversed). For a discussion of *Love-Letters* that undertakes to read its three parts as relatively autonomous narratives, see William B. Warner, *Licensing Entertainment: The Elevation of Novel Reading in Britain, 1684–1750* (Berkeley and Los Angeles: University of California Press, 1998), chap. 2.

3. "The Lord Gray . . . saith that hee marryed [Lady Henrietta's] eldest sister, and expected a maidens-heade, but not findeing it, hee resolved to have one in the family, if any bee left; but lest this should tend towards *scandelum magnatum,* pray keep it to yourself." Historical Manuscripts Commission, *The Manuscripts of Lord Kenyon* (London: Eyre and Spottiswoode for Her Majesty's Stationery Office, 1894), 143, quoted in Alan Roper, "Drawing Parallels and Making Applications in Restoration Literature," in *Politics as Reflected in Literature: Papers presented at a Clark Library Seminar 24 January 1987* (Los Angeles: William Andrews Clark Memorial Library, UCLA, 1987), 33–34.

4. In the same year Grey wrote *The Secret History of the Rye House Plot,* which was not printed until 1754.

5. See above, chap. 10, nn. 77–86.

6. On romance as a mixture of "love" and "war," see above, chap. 8, nn. 28–43.

7. On "The Golden Age" see above, chap. 3, n. 100. For a reading of *Love-Letters* that is especially sensitive to Behn's skepticism regarding the putative improvement of libertinism on paternalism, of republicanism on royalism, see Ellen Pollak, "Beyond Incest: Gender and

the Politics of Transgression in Aphra Behn's *Love-Letters between a Nobleman and His Sister,*" in *Rereading Aphra Behn: History, Theory, and Criticism,* ed. Heidi Hutner (Charlottesville: University Press of Virginia, 1993), 151–86.

8. Cf. Richard Lovelace, "To Lucasta, Going to the Wars" (1649), above, chap. 8, n. 31.

9. Cf. the duel between Philander and Foscario, who "were fainting with loss of blood in each others arms . . ." (105).

10. See Janet Todd's editorial note, 122. Octavio does possess a more general political identity within Behn's fiction as an influential member of the United Provinces' central council (see 131, 134), and Silvia later (192) implies that he is the bastard son of William of Orange. Behn produced no *clef* for her *roman.*

11. Octavian "replaced" Caesar in the Roman republican history to which Behn's names allude, and Philander, for one, associates the Dutch with the Roman republic (130). Moreover, as Cesario is the illegitimate son of the current king, Octavio seems to be the bastard son of the future king, William of Orange (see previous note).

In broadly formal usage, "friendship" tends to designate homosocial ties between male gentility at this time. However, Behn often enough uses the term in a more locally and incidentally gender-neutral fashion. And the formal conception of male friendship was capable of extension to female relations as well, as the innovative example of Katherine Philips in particular demonstrates. See *The Collected Works of Katherine Philips, The Matchless Orinda,* ed. Patrick Thomas, vol. 1, *The Poems* (Cambridge: Stump Cross Books, 1990).

12. On Tory feminism, see above, chap. 3, nn. 81–96.

13. This reading of Silvia is perhaps supported by allegorizations of her predecessors—Argenis, Cloria—as representative of, among other things, a concentrated nationality: cf. *John Barclay his Argenis. Translated . . . By Sir Robert Le Grys . . .* (1629), 487; and *The Princess Cloria: or, The Royal Romance. In Five Parts. Imbellished with divers Political Notions, and singular Remarks of Modern Transactions. Containing The Story of most part of Europe, for may Years last past . . .* (1661), A2v. Cf. also Marvell's Lady State in *The Last Instructions to a Painter* (1667? 1689), in *Andrew Marvell: The Complete Poems,* ed. Elizabeth Story Donno (Harmondsworth, UK: Penguin, 1978).

14. Cf. Shakespeare's Thersites, above, chap. 8, n. 30.

15. In this respect the patriarchal Sebastian treats Octavio as the patriarchal Octavio has treated his sister Calista.

16. On the comparable cases, see above, chap. 10, nn. 14, 33–34. On the skimmington ride, see above, chap. 4, nn. 18–21.

17. Behn also makes Cesario reflect the perfidy Ferguson had attributed to the Duke of York in having, like Charles, sought to disavow his first marriage. On these matters, see above, chap. 10, nn. 77–79. In the background of Behn's characterization of Cesario here is contemporary debate over the competing authority of relatively public and private modes of marriage, a debate that is distinct from, but impinges upon, the Exclusion Crisis. See, e.g., above, chap. 10, nn. 83–84, on *The Perplex'd Prince* (1682).

18. In the case of Monmouth's Rebellion, of course, the illegitimacy involved in contractually replacing the old "husband" (James II) by the new one (Monmouth) was compounded by the rebels' aim to kill James first—that is, to commit "petit treason" against the husband.

19. See above, chap. 10, nn. 16–18.

20. On the double plot as a domesticating device in tragicomedy see above, chap. 8, nn. 7–15.

21. In opening and tampering with Octavio's letter the private "secretary" Brilljard imitates the behavior of the public secretary of state with respect to the newly founded Post Office: see above, chap. 2, n. 12.

22. See above, chap. 6, nn. 3–17.

23. Behn's editor observes (59n) the indebtedness of the scene to Behn's poem "The Disappointment." The self-parody of Philander's tragic heroism suggests also Rochester's "Imperfect Enjoyment," to which Behn's poem alludes. Rochester and his several libertine personae provide a general model for the hero of *Love-Letters*.

24. Our wish to read this encounter as an allusion to the *Old Arcadia*—cf. Basilius's infatuation with the cross-dressed Pyrocles—may be tempered by the recognition that Sidney's influence must have been mediated by that of comparable scenes in Restoration comedy, including Behn's own.

25. And even in the novellas Behn began to write soon after *Love-Letters*. See Michael McKeon, *The Origins of the English Novel, 1600–1740* (Baltimore: Johns Hopkins University Press, 1987), 258–60.

26. See above, chap. 1.

27. See above, chap. 9, nn. 38–43.

28. Although the addition of third-person narration to an epistolary narrative may sometimes be required if a change of scene removes the rationale for correspondence, this is not the case here. In any event, Behn's aristocratic principals, able to rely on servants for the delivery of their letters, correspond with each other in circumstances that normally would obviate epistolary communication.

29. See above, chap. 9.

30. On the other hand, and despite the absence of a diacritical discrimination between epistolary and narrative discourse in the latter parts of Behn's work, the fact of narrative mixture nonetheless does obtrude itself on the reader's consciousness in the latter two parts because the difference between roman and italicized print is internalized within narrative discourse as a discriminant between the narrator's voice and those of her characters. The use of italics to set off dialogue (rather than the less obtrusive quotation marks of modern usage), not uncommon in Restoration typesetting practices, is followed throughout parts 2 and 3 in the first edition (1685, 1687) of *Love-Letters*. The current reprint helpfully restores this usage, which the previous, Penguin edition of 1987 had modernized.

31. See above, chap. 7, n. 113. Of course the impartiality of Smith's internalized spectator bears some relation to the invisibility of the overarching "hand" that reconciles private economic interests in a political economy (above, chap. 7, n. 116). With these compare Addison's "imagination," which names in other terms the synthetic function of a "third person" that oversees the reciprocal refinement of the senses and the domestication of the understanding: above, chap. 7, n. 79.

32. See above, chap. 1, n. 9; cf. chap. 2, n. 72. By Smith's time this will have become a standard way of conceiving the governmental relationship between king and Parliament. See also Hermione's oversight of petitions made to Cesario, above, n. 19.

33. It is worth noting, moreover, that Behn's modulation from epistolary form to third-

person narration is broadly accompanied by a shift from the privative anonymity of part 1's dedicatory epistle, which entails the unmarked implication of male authorship, to a willingness in the latter two dedications to provide a key to authorship in the signature "A.B." (cf. 7 with 120, 255). A spectral personalization of actual authorship, these initials are also a publication (if not a gendering) of privacy. Like Silvia's, Behn's progress through *Love-Letters* is one of increasing publicity.

The subtlety with which Behn learned to balance the public and the private in narrative may owe something to her early experience in the secret service. In 1666 Behn was engaged by Charles II's office of the secretary of state to serve as a spy against the Dutch, with whom England was locked in naval war at the time. From Antwerp she dutifully forwarded intelligence of secret plans to sail the Dutch fleet up the Medway toward London, only to see "her Letter shew'd by way of Contempt, to some who ought not to have been let into the Secret, and so bandy'd about" that her lover William Scot advised her not to expect payment for her work, "and desir'd her therefore to lay aside her politick Negotiation, and divert her Friends with some pleasant Adventures of Antwerp, either as to her Lovers, or those of any other Lady of her Acquaintance: that in this she wou'd be more successful then in her Pretences of State, since here she wou'd not fail of pleasing those she writ to." Behn replied: "Your Remarks upon my Politick Capacity, tho' they are sharp, touch me not, but recoil on those that have not made use of the Advantages they might have drawn from thence, and are doubly to blame. First, in sending a Person, in whose Ability, Sense, and Veracity, they cou'd not confide; and next, not to understand when a Person indifferent tells 'em a probable Story, and which if it come to pass, wou'd sufficiently punish their Incredulity . . . ." "The History of the Life and Memoirs of Mrs. Behn. Written by one of the Fair Sex," in *All the Histories and Novels Written by the Late Ingenious Mrs. Behn, Entire in One Volume. . .* , 5th ed. (1705), 7, 8. Frederick M. Link, *Aphra Behn* (New York: Twayne, 1968), 17, suggests that the author is Charles Gildon. The humiliating event Behn foretold in 1666 did come to pass (see above, chap. 10, nn. 64–65, where Andrew Marvell narrates the prelude to this episode). The epistolary exchange suggests that Behn's decision to write a *roman à clef* about the Exclusion Crisis whose formal method of self-censorship concealed as much as it revealed expressed a sense not only of political but also of sexual constraints on her writing. For similar commentary from Philander to Silvia, see [Behn], *Love-Letters,* 43–44; and for similar advice ventriloquized by Delarivier Manley and Eliza Haywood, see below, chap. 13, nn. 39–40; and above, chap. 9, nn. 29–31.

34. As examples of discursive "art," the *Gazette*'s advertisement and the narrator's account of the investiture ceremony are suggestively comparable to the "black Art" by which Fergusano publishes his *Declaration* (*Declaration of James, Duke of Monmouth, &c.* [1685]) of Cesario's legitimacy, "a pernicious and treasonable Libel," and engineers the "Ceremony" of Cesario and Hermione's mock wedding (402–11).

35. Philander describes Calista's disgust with her husband the Count: "[S]ince she had seen the Charming *Philander* (for so we must let her call him too) his Company and Conversation was wholly insupportable to her . . ." (237). This highly suggestive conflation of character and narrator may also, of course, be the result not of conscious art but of oversight on Behn's part. Elsewhere she achieves a comparable effect by using what might qualify as an early, if momentary, example of free indirect discourse. The narrator describes a meeting between Brilljard and Octavio: "[A]ll their Discourse was of the faithless *Silvia* . . . . [Octavio]

made the amorous *Brilljard* weep a hundred times a-day; and . . . Brilljard no longer doubted but he would indeed no more trust her fickle Sex" (367). Is this the narrator's epithet (cf. her frequent allusions to female artifice), ensuring her distance from Silvia and even her own coverture by an apparently male voice? But we have already heard both Octavio and Philander speak of Silvia's "fickle sex" (see, e.g., 275, 311). Is this the "public" voice of the narrator or the "private" voice of her male characters "published" through third-person narration? On the contemporary explicitation of the difference between character and author as one between public and private voices, see above, chap. 2, nn. 137–42. On free indirect discourse, see below, chap. 15, nn. 46–53.

36. On the coimplication of interest and disinterestedness and on the aesthetic pleasures of the imagination as a privatized experience, see above, chap. 7.

37. On the distinction between "external" and "internal" probability in the developing theory of the novel, see Michael McKeon, "Prose Fiction: Great Britain," in *The Cambridge History of Literary Criticism,* ed. H. B. Nisbet and Claude Rawson, vol. 4, *The Eighteenth Century* (Cambridge: Cambridge University Press, 1997), 255–56, drawing on Douglas Lane Patey, *Probability and Literary Form: Philosophic Theory and Literary Practice in the Augustan Age* (Cambridge: Cambridge University Press, 1984), chap. 5. Silvia's expertise as a "reader" of experience is signaled by her skeptical response to Brilljard's optimistic account of the preparations for Monmouth's Rebellion. Echoing Behn herself in 1666, Silvia "prophesied another End of this high Design then they imagined . . ." and "*would be glad to know what real Probability there is in advancing and succeeding in this Design . . .*" (402).

But the significance of Behn's formal innovations—indeed, the fact of their innovation—needs to be treated with circumspection. The influence of Philip Sidney's *Old Arcadia* is plausible on a number of levels. There is the broad parallel between pairings: Philoclea and Pamela, Silvia and Mertilla; Pyrocles and Musidorus, Philander and Octavio. I have already noted a common interest in, and use of, tropes of sex and status disguise and exchange. The susceptibility of letters by women to being suppressed by men is also a theme in *Love-Letters* that appears first, although sparingly, in Sidney's nonepistolary *roman à clef* (see *The Countess of Pembroke's Arcadia [The Old Arcadia],* ed. Jean Robertson [Oxford: Oxford University Press, 1973], 395–98). So, too, this implication that lovers and readers do not need to be told every detail (see, e.g., *Old Arcadia,* 57, 88, 211). The question of influence is a real one. My central interest, however, lies rather in speculating on the ways in which the two political allegories diverge at the very point of their similarity. Both Sidney and Behn practice versions of the *roman à clef* whose commitment to the disclosure of actual particularity seems partial (on Sidney, see above, chap. 10, nn. 17–19). The *Old Arcadia* appears to proceed on the tacit assumption, still viable in the 1580s, that the categories crucial to its concern—politics and ethics, actual and concrete particularity, the public and the private—are distinguishable but not fully separable from each other, so that what might seem to be opposed values are also parts of a greater whole. With respect to the same categories, *Love-Letters* achieves an effect that is superficially similar to this. But it is generated by an emergent cultural intuition that the public and the private may really be separate domains and by Behn's wish to test this intuition by writing a narrative in which apparently separate categories are experimentally conflated with each other on the level of both form and content. By this understanding, the difference between *Love-Letters* and the *Old Arcadia* therefore marks, in a schematic way, the historical watershed that is the main focus of this study.

38. With these observations compare Ballaster's argument that the narratives of Behn and other women writers of this period are "seductive forms" in the sense that "[t]he telling of a story of seduction is also a mode of seduction." *Seductive Forms,* 24 and passim; on *Love-Letters,* see pp. 100–13.

39. Cf. plate 2.

40. *Spectator,* no. 411 (21 June 1712). See above, chap. 7, nn. 85–86.

41. On the role of the imagination in masturbation, see above, chap. 6, nn. 31–44.

42. This holds not only at the upper but also at the lower levels of the social hierarchy, for reasons having to do not with the need, in gentle families, for heirs to perpetuate estate ownership but with the need, in a domestic economy, to promote production by promoting reproduction. See Alan Macfarlane, *The Culture of Capitalism* (Oxford: Blackwell, 1987), chap. 2.

43. On Bunyan, see McKeon, *Origins,* 297; on Behn, see Ballaster, *Seductive Forms,* 205.

44. See, e.g., above, chap. 6, nn. 68–75.

45. Contrast the case of Miranda, Behn's "Gallopping Nun," in *The Fair Jilt: or, the History of Prince Tarquin and Miranda* (1688), in *The Works of Aphra Behn,* ed. Janet Todd, vol. 3, *The Fair Jilt and Other Short Stories* (Columbus: Ohio State University Press, 1995), 4–48.

46. See, e.g., 58: "Thus with a Thousand Cautions more, which did but raise what you design'd to calm, you made me but the madder to possess: not all the Vows you bad me call to mind, could now restrain my wild and head-strong passion; my raving raging (but my soft) desire . . . ."

47. Cf. Marvell's vision of the disordered "Lady State" in *The Last Instructions to a Painter,* above, chap. 10, nn. 65–66.

48. Thus a signature trope of pornography, the clothing that innocently conceals only to reveal and then conceal again: the "wanton loose negligence" of Silvia's garments, whose "Gown loose . . . was still open and discover'd a World of unguarded Beauty, which she knew not was in view . . ."; the striptease vision of Calista, "wrapt in her Night-Gown only . . . ," letting "go her Gown, which falling open left nothing but her Shift, between me and all her Charming Body . . ." (58, 149, 239). The religious veil is a potent instance of this trope. Ballaster notes, with reference to Behn's work, the currency of "the topos of the desiring nun." *Seductive Forms,* 100; see also Robert Adams Day, *Told in Letters: Epistolary Fiction before Richardson* (Ann Arbor: University of Michigan Press, 1966), 32–40.

49. See above, chap. 6, nn. 38–39.

50. Richard Steele, *Tatler,* no. 185 (15 June 1710), in *The Tatler,* ed. Donald F. Bond, 3 vols. (Oxford: Clarendon, 1987). In *Tatler,* no. 188 (22 June 1710), a reader in whom Mr. Bickerstaff finds an "intellectual Rusticity" writes in to complain that his daughter "has been so undutiful as to fall in Love of her own Head, and tells me a foolish Heathen Story that she has read in your Paper to perswade me to give my Consent. . . . I must therefore desire you to . . . let *Silvia* know, that she ought to act like a dutiful Daughter, and marry the Man that she does not care for" as "Our Great Grandmothers" did.

Chapter Twelve | Toward the Narration of Private Life

1. See [Charles Sackville, Earl of Dorset], "A Faithful Catalogue of Our Most Eminent Ninnies" (1688), in *Poems on Affairs of State: Augustan Satirical Verse, 1660–1714,* vol. 4, *1685–1688,* ed. Galbraith M. Crump (New Haven, CT: Yale University Press, 1968), 191–214;

Aphra Behn, *A Congratulatory Poem to Her Most Sacred Majesty, On the Universal Hopes of All Loyal Persons for a Prince of Wales* (1688) and *A Congratulatory Poem to the King's Most Sacred Majesty, On the Happy Birth of the Prince of Wales* (1688), in *The Works of Aphra Behn*, vol. 1, *Poetry*, ed. Janet Todd (Columbus: Ohio State University Press, 1992), 294–99; and John Dryden, *Britannia Rediviva: A Poem on the Prince, Born on the 10th. of June, 1688*, in *The Works of John Dryden*, vol. 3, *Poems, 1685–1692*, ed. Earl Miner and Vinton A. Dearing (Berkeley and Los Angeles: University of California Press, 1969), 210–21.

2. See J. S. Clarke, *The Life of James the Second* (London: Longman, Hurst, Rees, Orme, and Brown, 1816), 2:192; Historical Manuscripts Commission Reports, Portland MSS, III, 420; [Henry Mildmay], "The Progress" (1689), lines 62, 23–26, 54–57; and "Tom Tiler, or the Nurse" (1688), lines 14–16, all in *Poems on Affairs of State*, 4:xxxviii, xxxix, 331–32, 258. The latter poem imagines (lines 7–8) an upwardly mobile transformation of the bricklayer's trowel to a royal scepter; with this scandalous social mixture compare the scandalous sexual conflation of scepter and prick imagined by Rochester, above, chap. 6, n. 77.

3. William Fuller, *A Brief Discovery of the True Mother Of the Pretended Prince of Wales Known by the Name of Mary Grey . . .* (1696), 13, 6. An accomplice in the plot, Fuller claimed to have carried secret letters from France that "were made up as the Mould of a Button, and so work'd over with Silk, or Silver, and worn on my Cloaths: Others I brought over in the Pipes of Keys . . ." (26–27).

4. On the privatizing function of the gallery or passageway, see above, chap. 5, nn. 16–17.

5. See *The Several Declarations, Together with the Several Depositions made in Council on Monday, the 22nd of October, 1688. Concerning the Birth of the Prince of Wales* (1688). On virtual witnessing, see above, chap. 2, n. 61.

6. [George Hickes], *The Pretences of the Prince of Wales Examin'd, and Rejected. In a Letter to a Friend in the Country* (1701), 7–8. Hickes's tract is an ironic defense of the notion of a plot whose effect is to eloquently refute it. Bays is the incompetent dramatist in *The Rehearsal* (1671), by George Villiers, Duke of Buckingham, and others.

7. *A Full Answer to the Depositions; And to all other the Pretences and Arguments whatsoever, Concerning the Birth of the Prince of Wales. The Intreague thereof detected, The whole design being set forth, with the way and manner of doing it. Whereunto is annexed, A Map or Survey Engraven of St. James's Palace, and the Convent there: Describing the Place wherein it is supposed the true Mother was delivered: With the particular Doors and Passages through which the Child was convey'd to the Queens Bed-Chamber* (1689), 7, 9, 1.

8. Ibid., 9. An analogy between child and book, "suppositious" birth and publication, is implied in the "Author's Apology," which explains the tract's "many gross and unpardonable faults" as an effect of premature and clandestine publication: "[N]ot knowing of its being in the Press till Four Sheets were Printed off, . . . [I] was strangely surpriz'd, when I saw it in an Ayre and Face so Foreign to what I designed it" (A2r–v).

9. *An Account of the Reasons of the Nobility and Gentry's Invitation of His Highness the Prince of Orange into England. Being a Memorial from the English Protestants Concerning their Grievances. With a Large Account of the Birth of the Prince of Wales . . .* (1689), 11, 12. The lying-in chamber was considered a female space: see above, chap. 5, nn. 42–43, and figs. 4.12 and 5.12. On female disinterestedness, see above, chap. 7, nn. 49–52. Although gender is the main criterion of disinterestedness here, it is modified by social status: "[T]he Capacity and Probability of knowing the Facts and the Indifferency of Witnesses of High and Low degree

being equal" in the eyes of the law, the author nonetheless calls for ideal witnesses to be of elevated rank and not "bound to depend upon the Favour of others for their support, like *Nurses* and *Midwives,* and other *Servants*" (13). For a consideration of the significance of this and other aspects of gender difference in discourse on the Warming-Pan Scandal, see Rachel J. Weil, "The Politics of Legitimacy: Women and the Warming-Pan Scandal," in *The Revolution of 1688–1689: Changing Perspectives,* ed. Lois G. Schwoerer (Cambridge: Cambridge University Press, 1992), 65–82. Weil challenges the accuracy of the legal argument made in *Full Answer* (also made in *Account of the Reasons*), 77–78.

10. *Account of the Reasons,* 17, 20.

11. [Jonathan Swift], *A Tale of a Tub,* in *A Tale of a Tub, To which is added The Battle of the Books and the Mechanical Operation of the Spirit* (1704, 1710), ed. A. C. Guthkelch and D. Nichol Smith, 2nd ed. (Oxford: Clarendon, 1958), 173.

12. See *Account of the Reasons,* 18–19; and *Full Answer,* 10ff.

13. *Full Answer,* 10.

14. BL, Add. MS 33286, fol. 20, quoted in Weil, "Politics," 65. Cf. Charles's 1642 prognostication, above, chap. 1, n. 10; and Andrew Marvell's theatricalization of the scene of regicide: "That thence the royal actor born / The tragic scaffold might adorn: / While round the armèd bands / Did clap their bloody hands." "An Horatian Ode upon Cromwell's Return from Ireland" (1650), lines 53–56, in *Andrew Marvell: The Complete Poems,* ed. Elizabeth Story Donno (Harmondsworth, UK: Penguin, 1978), 56.

15. Letters of 22 Sept. and 7 Oct. 1701, in BL, Add. MS. 33286, fols. 11–12, and Bodleian Library, MS Engl. Hist. b.2, fols. 188–89, respectively; and Thomas Wagstaffe, "Innocence Protected" (1692?), in Bodleian Library, MS Engl. Hist. d.1, pp. 3–4, all quoted in Weil, "Politics," 75, 80–81.

16. BL, Sloane MS 2717, fol. 98r, quoted in *Poems on Affairs of State: Augustan Satirical Verse, 1660–1714,* vol. 5, *1688–1697,* ed. William J. Cameron (New Haven, CT: Yale University Press, 1971), 153n23; see 612.

17. For this formulation, see Lois G. Schwoerer, "Images of Queen Mary II, 1689–1695," *Renaissance Quarterly* 42, no. 4 (1989): 729–30.

18. Rachel J. Weil, *Political Passions: Gender, the Family, and Political Argument in England, 1680–1714* (Manchester: Manchester University Press, 1999), 116.

19. Satirists treated her infamy as both public and familial. See Arthur Mainwaring, "Tarquin and Tullia" (1689), a key poem modeled on Dryden's *Absalom and Achitophel* that begins: "In times when Princes cancelled nature's law / . . . / When children used their parents to dethrone / And gnawed their way like vipers to a crown . . ."; Ralph Gray, "The Coronation Ballad, 11th April 1689" (1689), lines 81–83: "O' th' father's side she had honor we grant, / But duty to parents she sadly doth want, / Which makes her a fiend instead of a saint . . ."; and "The Female Parricide" (1690), lines 3, 2, which compares Mary with Lear's Goneril as "unnatural daughters" who "Rebelled for crowns their royal parents wore . . . ," all in *Poems on Affairs of State,* 5:47, 45, 157.

20. *Poems on Affairs of State,* 5:56.

21. See Gen. 2:23–24; and the Anglican marriage service, for which see David Cressy and Lori Anne Ferrell, ed., *Religion and Society in Early Modern England: A Sourcebook* (London: Routledge, 1996), 51–54.

22. Cf. "Hey, diddle diddle." For a brief discussion of this common ballad meter—two

lines of two beats per line alternating with one line of three beats—see Harold Love, *The Culture and Commerce of Texts: Scribal Publication in Seventeenth-Century England* (1993; reprint, Amherst: University of Massachusetts Press, 1998), 232–33.

23. Several poems on Mary's death in 1694 develop the trope of transvestism into a conceit of William and Mary as reciprocal cross-dressers—exchanging "petticoats" for "breeches"—with the implication that "[w]e were mistaken in the choice of our commanders." See *Poems on Affairs of State*, 5:445, 446. Cf. the trope of the effeminated hero and his masculinized beloved, above, chap. 9, n. 13, and chap. 10, n. 34.

24. Already in 1610 James Whitelocke was able to say that "[t]he soveraigne power is agreed to be in the king: but in the king is a two-fold power, the one in parliament, as he is assisted with the consent of the whole state; the other out of parliament, as he is sole, and singular, guided merely by his own will. . . . [T]he power of the king in parliament is greater than his power out of parliament . . . ." *Cobbett's Complete Collection of State Trials . . .* , ed. Thomas B. Howell (London: Hansard, 1809–26), vol. 2, cols. 482–83, quoted in Margaret A. Judson, *The Crisis of the Constitution: An Essay in Constitutional and Political Thought in England, 1603–1645* (1949; reprint, New Brunswick, NJ: Rutgers University Press, 1988), 86–87. On the tradition of "the King in Parliament," see generally Charles H. McIlwain, *The High Court of Parliament and Its Supremacy* (New Haven, CT: Yale University Press, 1910). Is a public-private parallel to be felt between what becomes of the tacit distinction between the king's politic and his natural bodies and what becomes of the distinction between the king's authority in Parliament and out of Parliament?

25. The *OED* notes an obsolete meaning for "jack-in-the-box" or "jack-in-a-box," still current in this period: "A name for a sharper or a cheat; spec. 'a thief who deceived tradesmen by substituting empty boxes for others full of money.'"

A few months after the period this poem depicts and directly after William's decisive defeat of James II at the Battle of the Boyne, Mary, serving as Regent during her husband's absence, divided her time between Hampton Court and Kensington Palace. Both were under repair at the time, and Mary kept William up to date on the progress of work in letters that echo, in architectural terms, the questions of corporate status that Sheppard addresses in his poem. Speaking of one aspect of the repairs at Kensington, Mary writes that "as sone as yt is done your own apartment may be furnisht and tho mine can not possible be ready yet awhile, I have found out a way if you please, wch is yt I may make use [of] Lord Portland's & hee ly in some of ye other roomes, we may ly in your chamber & I go throw ye councel roome down or els dresse there . . . ." A week later she wrote that she had "made use of Lord Portland's closet as I told you in my last I woud . . . ." Mary to William, 26 July, 2 Aug. 1690, quoted in *The Wren Society* (Oxford: Oxford University Press, 1930), 7:136. Mary's disordered syntax underscores the rich ambiguity of what it might mean for her to "make use of" Portland's closet. She seems to float in a liminal space between the poles of several alternatives: bedchamber and council chamber; wife and sovereign; woman and man; private and public; "lying" and not lying with her husband; (cross-?) dressing in the intimate space of the First Gentleman of the Bedchamber, her husband's likely male lover. For another reading of Mary's letter, see Tita Chico, "The Dressing Room Unlock'd: Eroticism, Performance, and Privacy from Pepys to the *Spectator*," in *Monstrous Dreams of Reason: Body, Self, and Other in the Enlightenment,* ed. Laura J. Rosenthal and Mita Choudhury (Lewisburg: Bucknell University Press, 2002), 55–56.

26. See Weil, *Political Passions,* 167.

27. Cf. Toni Bowers, "Queen Anne Makes Provision," in *Refiguring Revolutions: Aesthetics and Politics from the English Revolution to the Romantic Revolution,* ed. Kevin Sharpe and Steven N. Zwicker (Berkeley and Los Angeles: University of California Press, 1998), 66: Anne "chose not to replace maternal imagery but to *redefine* it as a symbolic rather than a literal undertaking. She cast herself not as the physical mother of a particular heir (now an untenable image) but as the symbolic mother of the entire nation."

28. Toni Bowers, *The Politics of Motherhood: British Writing and Culture, 1680–1760* (Cambridge: Cambridge University Press, 1996), 41.

29. See Robert O. Bucholz, *The Augustan Court: Queen Anne and the Decline of Court Culture* (Stanford, CA: Stanford University Press, 1993), 77–83 and passim.

30. *Arguments Relating to a Restraint upon the Press, Fully and Fairly handled in a Letter to a Bencher, from a Young Gentleman of the Temple* (1712), 29–30, 31–32.

31. On these themes in *Queen Zarah,* see Michael McKeon, *The Origins of the English Novel, 1600–1740* (Baltimore: Johns Hopkins University Press, 1987), 233. I will return to *Queen Zarah* in the following chapter.

32. See Weil, *Political Passions,* 164–66.

33. [Arthur Mainwaring?], "*A New Ballad: To the Tune of Fair Rosamund,*" in *Poems on Affairs of State: Augustan Satirical Verse, 1660–1714,* vol. 7, *1704–1714,* ed. Frank H. Ellis (New Haven, CT: Yale University Press, 1975), 309–10. See also idem, "Masham Display'd: To the Tune of *The Dame of Honour,*" in ibid., 319–21; on Churchill's convictions, see 309n16.

34. [Henry St. John], *A Letter to the Examiner* (1710), 12, 13–14.

35. See Weil, *Political Passions,* chap. 8.

36. [John Dunton], *King Abigail: or, The Secret Reign of the She-Favourite, Detected, and Applied; In a Sermon . . .* (1715), pp. 1, 16, sig. A2r, pp. 18, 3.

37. *The Amours of Massalina, Late Queen of Albion, In which are briefly couch'd, Secrets of the Imposture of the Cambrian Prince, the Gothick League, And Other Court Intrigues of the Four last Years Reign, not yet made Publick* (1689), "The Translator to the Reader," A3r. Cf. [Peter Bellon], *The Court Secret* (1689), "Dedication," A3v, which also calls itself a "Historical Novel."

38. *The Secret History of the Reigns of K. Charles II, and K. James II* (1690), 27, 28, 24. For the influence of sexual enthrallment on public policy see, e.g., pp. 49–50, 84–85, 86–87. Embroidering the secret treaty of Dover (see above, chap. 10, nn. 69–72), the author reproduces a 1662 letter from Charles to the pope, pp. 12–18. On Suetonius see "Preface," A2r.

39. *ΕΙΚΟΝ ΒΑΣΙΛΙΚΕ ΔΕΥΤΕΠΑ. The Pourtraicture of his Sacred Majesty King Charles II. With his Reasons for turning Roman Catholick; published by K. James. Found in the Strong Box.* (1694). On pp. 139–41 Charles directs a blasphemous prayer to the god Priapus.

40. [David Jones], *The Secret History of Whitehall . . . Writ at the Request of a Noble Lord, and conveyed to him in Letters, by —— late Secretary-Interpreter to the Marquess of Louvois . . .* (1697), "Preface," A5v, A6r (font reversed).

41. *A Secret History of the Amours and Marriage of an English Nobleman With a Famous Italian Lady* (1712), 8. On Cicero, see p. 4.

42. [Eustache Le Noble], *The Cabinet Open'd, or the Secret History of the Amours of Madam de Maintenon, With the French King. Translated from the French Copy* (1690), sig. A6r, pp. 1–2.

43. See above, n. 2.

44. Pierre Bayle, *The Dictionary Historical and Critical of Mr. Peter Bayle* (1697), 2nd ed., 5 vols. (1734–38), vol. 4, s.v. "Nidhard," n. C, 365–66.

45. See above, chap. 7, n. 86.

46. Richard Steele, *Tatler*, no. 84 (22 Oct. 1709), in *The Tatler*, ed. Donald F. Bond, 3 vols. (Oxford: Clarendon, 1987).

47. See above, chap. 10, nn. 29–35.

48. [Charles Gildon], *The Post=Boy Robb'd of his Mail: or, The Pacquet Broke Open, Consisting of Letters of Love and Gallantry, and all Miscellaneous Subjects . . .* (1692), 2nd ed. (1706). In fact Gildon translated at least part of this work from Ferrante Pallavicino's *Il corriere Svaligiato* (1643) by way of Jean de Préchac's *La valize ouverte* (1680); see "Epistle Dedicatory," iv. Gildon's printer, John Dunton, made some indeterminable contribution to the composition of *Post=Boy*. Years later Gildon published a sequel: *The Post-Man Robb'd of his Mail: or, the Packet broke open . . .* (1719).

49. Gildon, *Post=Boy*, 377–78, 5. The illogic of undertaking "foreign" before "domestic" travels is resisted in David Hume's otherwise similar reflections on his own enterprise: "And as the science of man is the only solid foundation for the other sciences, so the only solid foundation we can give to this science itself must be laid on experience and observation. 'Tis no astonishing reflection to consider, that the application of experimental philosophy to moral subjects should come after that to natural at the distance of above a whole century; since we find in fact, that there was about the same interval betwixt the origins of these sciences . . . . [T]he essence of the mind being equally unknown to us with that of external bodies, it must be equally impossible to form any notion of its powers and qualities otherwise than from careful and exact experiments . . . ." Introduction to *A Treatise of Human Nature: being An Attempt to introduce the experimental Method of Reasoning into Moral Subjects* (1739), ed. L. A. Selby-Bigge (1888), 2nd ed., ed. P. N. Nidditch (Oxford: Clarendon, 1978), xvi–xvii.

50. Gildon, *Post=Boy*, 8, 226, 6.

51. Ibid., 5. On Steele, see above, chap. 2, n. 102.

52. Gildon, *Post=Boy*, 11. As we have come to expect, traditional figures (in this case, chivalric tropes of quasi-legal, extragovernmental intervention in civil matters) are also experimentally and self-consciously applied to render the public-sphere scenario intelligible: one member of the Club proposes that they "relieve the distressed Damsel, that nothing cou'd better deserve the Thoughts of *True Knights of Honour, and Members of Chivalry.* Whether he was serious or no, I won't determine . . ." (6).

53. See above, chap. 11, n. 31.

54. Law, a Scotsman, later gained notoriety as a daring and innovative financier, founder of the first French bank and of the Mississippi Company, whose collapse in the year of the South Sea Bubble forced his flight from France.

55. *The Diary of John Evelyn*, ed. E. S. de Beer (Oxford: Clarendon, 1955), 5:175–76, bracketed words added by de Beer. In an entry for 10 April 1694 Narcissus Luttrell reports that a "duel was yesterday fought between Mr. Lawes and Mr. Wilson in Bloomsbury square; the latter was killed upon the spott, and the other is sent to Newgate . . . ." Like Evelyn, Luttrell is mainly interested in the unsolved mystery of Wilson's rise in status. *A Brief Historical Relation of State Affairs from September 1678 to April 1714* (Oxford: Oxford University Press, 1857), 3:291.

56. Marie Catherine d'Aulnoy, *Memoirs of the Court of England: in the Reign of King Charles II,* 2nd ed. (1708), Aaa1r (hereafter cited parenthetically in the text).

57. With this proliferation of narrator figures compare the similar formal usage in the near-contemporary tract by Daniel Defoe, *A True Relation of the Apparition of One Mrs. Veal . . .* (1706).

58. See above, chap. 9, nn. 11–18.

59. Elizabeth Villiers came to England with Mary in 1689, already a mistress of William of Orange; he cast her off in 1694 (*DNB*). In a copy of the first (1707) edition of d'Aulnoy's *Memoirs* in the British Library (call number 598.d.34), a marginal annotation identifies the great lady as "Castlemaine" (522). Barbara Villiers, Countess of Castlemaine, the celebrated courtesan of Charles II, was by 1694 long out of power. The proposal of Castlemaine, the very type of the she-favorite, as the key to the figure of the great lady suggests a reader response attuned to questions more of concrete than of actual particularity.

60. For a more challenging instance, cf. Aphra Behn's Miranda in *The Fair Jilt: or, the History of Prince Tarquin and Miranda* (1688), in *The Works of Aphra Behn,* ed. Janet Todd, vol. 3, *The Fair Jilt and Other Short Stories* (Columbus: Ohio State University Press, 1995), 1–48.

61. The close similarity in titles clearly distinguishes these two publications from all other entries in Donald Wing, *Short-Title Catalogue of Books Printed in England, Scotland, Ireland, Wales, and British America and of English Books Printed in Other Countries, 1641–1700,* 3 vols. (New York: Columbia University Press for the Index Society, 1945–51). An obscure mixture of parody and plagiarism based on Behn's *Love-Letters* had appeared in 1692: *The Secret Letters of Amour Between the Dutchess and Mynheer.*

62. This may be too cautious, since Rictor Norton has made a strong case for identifying its author as Thomas Gordon and the late nobleman as Charles Spencer, third Earl of Sunderland. See *Mother Clap's Molly House: The Gay Subculture in England, 1700–1830* (London: GMP, 1992), 35–43. Although I find Norton's case persuasive, in the following discussion I have refrained from adopting his identifications pending confirmation by other scholars.

63. The 1745 printing of the tract has been edited by Michael S. Kimmel and reprinted in a special issue of the *Journal of Homosexuality* 19, no. 2 (1990): 11–44, quotations on 13–14, 18 (hereafter cited parenthetically in the text). The reprint of the 1745 version, which does not differ significantly from the 1723 version, reproduces original punctuation and capitalization but not italics.

64. To describe the allegorization that the editor proposes as a "domestication" of same-sex sodomy to the terms of different-sex fornication is particularly apt given the editor's sanctimonious (and self-evidently inaccurate) view of sodomy as "a Sin which is not familiar to our Northern Climate" (14).

65. In his cryptic letter to Law, Wilson seems unaware of the severity of Law's aggression, perhaps even reversing his misconstrual of the nobleman's missing first letter by taking figuratively Law's literal challenge to give "Satisfaction." Wilson also seems to suggest that the supposed family dishonor (cf. Evelyn's account of the dispute about Wilson's sister and Law's mistress) is a cover for "the real Offence" taken by "one we are unable to contend with," perhaps Elizabeth Villiers?

66. On William's court, see Dennis Rubini, "Sexuality and Augustan England: Sodomy, Politics, Elite Circles, and Society," in *The Pursuit of Sodomy: Male Homosexuality in Renais-*

sance and Enlightenment Europe, ed. Kent Gerard and Gert Hekma (New York: Harrington Park, 1989), 349–81.

67. See Michael McKeon, "Historicizing Patriarchy: The Emergence of Gender Difference in England, 1660–1760," *Eighteenth-Century Studies* 28, no. 3 (1995): 309.

68. See ibid., 308. Edward ("Ned") Ward provides an interesting transitional text in *The Secret History of Clubs . . .* (1709): the "Beaus Club" consists of excessively foppish men who are "Effeminate" and have sex with women; members of the "Mollies Club" "mimick all Manner of Effeminacy" but are "*Sodomitical* Wretches" (140, 284).

69. See McKeon, "Historicizing Patriarchy," 311–12.

70. See above, chap. 7, nn. 46–48. Like disinterestedness and the public cachet of printedness, the emergent view of sodomy as an exclusive identity was rendered culturally intelligible at first by association with a familiar category—aristocracy—to which it had no inherent connection.

71. See McKeon, *Origins,* chap. 4.

72. A correspondent of the *Tatler* complained of a certain sort of "*Pretty* Fellows" that "have their Signs and Tokens like Free-Masons . . . ." *Tatler,* no. 26 (9 June 1709), font reversed.

73. *Mundus Foppensis: or, the Fop Display'd. Being the Ladies Vindication, In Answer to a late Pamphlet, Entituled, Mundus Muliebris: Or, The Ladies Dressing-Room Unlock'd, &c. . . .* (1691), 13, in Michael S. Kimmel, ed., *Mundus Foppensis (1691) and The Levellers (1703, 1745),* Augustan Reprint Society, no. 245 (Los Angeles: William Andrews Clark Memorial Library, UCLA, 1988). "Alsatia" refers to the precinct of Whitefriars in the City of London, known at this time as a debtor and criminal sanctuary (*OED*). In replying here to tracts like *Mundus Muliebris: Or, the Ladies Dressing-Room Unlock'd . . .* (1691), the author compares the unlocking of the lady's dressing room to the disclosure of same-sex sociability, which ranges from the luxurious excesses of fop and beau culture to those of the molly underground.

74. The generic pastoral name may have been suggested by Rochester's use of it in several poems. Most pertinently, Chloris is the companionable libertine memorably addressed by the speaker of "The Disabled Debauchee" when he recalls engaging her in a kissing contest to decide "Whether the boy fucked you, or I the boy"; see also the two early songs "As Chloris full of harmless thought" and "Fair Chloris in a pigsty lay."

75. See above, chap. 6, nn. 15, 85–87.

76. For a variation on the motif of the patriarch so tyrannical that he murders the daughter's infant, see below, chap. 14, nn. 32–33.

Chapter Thirteen | Secret History as Autobiography

1. See Michael McKeon, *The Origins of the English Novel, 1600–1740* (Baltimore: Johns Hopkins University Press, 1987), 52–64 and pt. 1 passim.

2. William Congreve, *Incognita; or, Love and Duty Reconcil'd. A Novel* (1692), in *Shorter Novels: Seventeenth Century,* ed. Philip Henderson (London: Dent, 1962), 261, 264. See my reading of *Incognita* in McKeon, *Origins,* 61–63, 263–65.

3. Charles Wilson, *Memoirs of the Life, Writings, and Amours of William Congreve Esq. . . .* (1730), pt. 2, p. 125.

4. William Congreve, epilogue to *The Way of the World*, lines 16–24, in *The Complete Plays of William Congreve*, ed. Herbert Davis (Chicago: University of Chicago Press, 1967), 479.

5. Of course the claim to translation from another tongue was in the case of the English *Argenis* true. Manley's titles also need to be read in the context of the contemporary efflorescence and ambiguity of the "imaginary voyage." See McKeon, *Origins*, 105–6. J. A. Downie recently has assembled evidence that *Queen Zarah* is the work not of Manley but of Joseph Browne. See "What if Delarivier Manley Did *Not* Write *The Secret History of Queen Zarah?*" *Library*, 7th ser., 5 (2004): 247–64. Although Downie's evidence is persuasive, since it has no implications for the minimal use to which I put *Queen Zarah* here I will simply note the reattribution.

6. Preface to part 2 of *Queen Zarah* (1705), A2r–v, in the facsimile edition of *The Novels of Mary Delariviere Manley*, ed. Patricia Köster, 2 vols. (Gainesville, FL: Scholars' Facsimiles and Reprints, 1971), 123–24 (hereafter references to *Queen Zarah* are to this edition and appear parenthetically in the text); dedication to Delarivier Manley, *New Atalantis*, ed. Ros Ballaster (Harmondsworth, UK: Penguin, 1992), 3 (hereafter references to the *New Atalantis* are to this modernized edition and appear parenthetically in the text).

7. On pastoral experiments, see above, chap. 8, nn. 75–92.

8. See Patricia Köster, in Manley, *Novels of Mary Delariviere Manley*, 1:xxiii.

9. See the discussion in Catherine Gallagher, *Nobody's Story: The Vanishing Acts of Women Writers in the Marketplace, 1670–1820* (Berkeley and Los Angeles: University of California Press, 1994), 124–26. On the key to Manley's *Rivella*, see below, nn. 31–32.

10. In the preface to part 2 of *Queen Zarah* (1705), A4r, Manley had called her secret history "a *romantick* Tale of a Tub." See Manley, *Novels of Mary Delariviere Manley*, 1:127. Edmund Curll's key to Swift's *Tale* was published in 1710, a year after the *New Atalantis*. See *A Complete Key to the Tale of a Tub*, reprinted in [Jonathan Swift], *A Tale of a Tub, To which is added The Battle of the Books and the Mechanical Operation of the Spirit* (1704, 1710), ed. A. C. Guthkelch and D. Nichol Smith, 2nd ed. (Oxford: Clarendon, 1958), 329–48.

11. The following two paragraphs are indebted to Paula McDowell, *The Women of Grub Street: Press, Politics, and Gender in the London Literary Marketplace, 1678–1730* (Oxford: Clarendon, 1998), 220–22, 231–65.

12. Cf. Defoe's contemporaneous figure Lady Credit. In the *Female Spectator* Haywood dispenses with the allegory but develops the lesson, latent in Manley's secret histories, that private example is more instructive than public precept (for Defoe and Haywood see above, chap. 9). After the Restoration, the office of the secretary of state was the public apparatus under which news-gathering was officially organized. It involved a vast network of correspondence and manuscript newsletters with exclusive circulation lists. See Alan Marshall, *Intelligence and Espionage in the Reign of Charles II, 1660–1685* (Cambridge: Cambridge University Press, 1994), chap. 1.

13. Intelligence here voices the increasingly patent fiction that the monarch cannot err.

14. On "cabal," see the *OED*. On the Cabal, see David Ogg, *England in the Reign of Charles II*, 2nd ed. (Oxford: Oxford University Press, 1956), 326–30, 344.

15. Other precedents for Manley's female Cabal include Madeleine de Scudéry's *cabala*, Katherine Philips's poetic circle, and Mary Astell's "Protestant monastery." Manley's in turn provided a precedent for Haywood's "Cabal" in the *Female Spectator*.

16. On Silvia, see above, chap. 11, nn. 10–11, 35.

17. On the gossip in the *New Atalantis,* see McDowell, *Women of Grub Street,* 247–59. At its deepest roots this female alternative mode of publicity may be associated not with the public sphere of print but with the orality of the old wives' tale, now officially discredited but for that very reason representative of a "secret" sort of counterhistory (see above, chap. 2, n. 2, and chap. 3, n. 101).

18. On these matters, see above, chap. 7.

19. On the political significance of the cavaliers, see Michael McKeon, *Politics and Poetry in Restoration England: The Case of Dryden's "Annus Mirabilis"* (Cambridge, MA: Harvard University Press, 1975), 81–83. Cf. the similar status of Dorothea in *The Whores Rhetorick* (1683), above, chap. 4, nn. 98–99.

20. Ellen Pollak argues that although first-cousin marriage was not a prohibited degree by civil or canon law at this time, recent changes in the law of guardianship had tarnished marriage between guardian and ward with the obloquy of incest. Pollak is also sensitive to the implications of the analogical relationship between family and state in Manley's work. See "Guarding the Succession of the (E)state: Guardian-Ward Incest and the Dangers of Representation in Delarivier Manley's *The New Atalantis,*" *Eighteenth Century: Theory and Interpretation* 39, no. 3 (1998): 220–37.

21. In fact there are inaccuracies in Manley's account of how and when she learned that her cousin was already married. See Ros Ballaster's introduction to this edition of the *New Atalantis,* viii–ix.

22. Cf. Behn's, above, chap. 11, nn. 26–27.

23. [Delarivier Manley], *The Adventures of Rivella; or, the History Of the Author of the Atalantis. With Secret Memoirs and Characters of several considerable Persons her Cotemporaries. Deliver'd in a Conversation to the Young Chevalier D'Aumont in Somerset-House Garden, by Sir Charles Lovemore. Done into English from the French* (1714). Parenthetical references in the text are to the modernized edition by Katherine Zelinsky (Peterborough, ON: Broadview, 1999).

24. For the history of *Rivella's* commissioning, see Zelinsky's introduction to *Rivella,* 9–11. For the suggestion, see Balaster's introduction to *The New Atalantis,* xviii. In 1725 Curll published a key to *Rivella* that assigns the principal speaker in this conversation a different identity.

25. In her correspondence with Curll Manley implored him, "[F]or God's sake let us try if this affair can be kept a secret. . . . [I]t concerns us all to keep the secret." Curll believed that the reason Manley insisted "that it should be kept a secret during her life-time" was that, as she told him in a letter, "though the world may like what I write of others, they despise whatever an author is thought to say of themselves." See *Rivella,* app. A, pp. 116–17.

26. Cf. these narrative strategies with Behn's shift from an epistolary first person to a narrative third person, and with her preference for surrogate narrators who are male, in *Love-Letters.*

27. Cf. other psychological privatizations of the public-private division: Shaftesbury's "author" and "reader," chap. 2, nn. 146–48; Smith's "myself" and "I," chap. 7, n. 113.

28. [Delarivier Manley], *The Adventures of Rivella . . . The Second Edition. To which is added, A Compleat Key* (1715), A2r–v. The format of the key evolved over time. The keys to Barclay's *Argenis,* almost a century earlier than Manley's, are not parallel tables of this sort but prefaces that identify figures in a more discursive fashion.

29. On this issue in Dryden's essay, see above, chap. 7, nn. 96–97.

30. On the reading of Ovid, see Manley, *New Atalantis,* 35; Zelinsky helpfully includes the three scenes in Manley, *Rivella,* app. B, pp. 121–24.

31. See Zelinsky in Manley, *Rivella,* 20–21.

32. With Manley's foil triad of Lovemore, Rivella, and Hilaria compare Behn's triad of the Princess, Silvia, and Hermione, above, chap. 11, nn. 18–19, 24–25.

33. See Ogg, *England,* 577–78. Cleveland's animus against Montagu may have stemmed not only from his rejection of her but also from the fact of his affair with Cleveland's natural daughter, who may have been fathered by the king. Manley converts this from a potential cause of Cleveland's action against Montagu into the alliance that enables Montagu to act against Cleveland.

34. "I used several arguments to satisfy her conscience that she was under no farther obligation . . . ," Earlier Lovemore had accused Rivella of crediting "[t]he casuists" (69).

35. See above, chap. 2, n. 109.

36. That is, the Copyright Act (1710) and the Stamp Act (1712); see above, chap. 2, nn. 123–25.

37. See above, chap. 2, nn. 133–42.

38. See above, chap. 2, nn. 131–32.

39. See McKeon, *Origins,* 120–22.

40. For this reason it may make sense to read Lovemore's "now" as referring not to the apparent present of the narrative (1710) but to the present of its publication date, 1714. A significant portion of these final pages of *Rivella,* in which Lovemore debates Rivella on the wisdom and meaning of her actions, is preoccupied with controversy about the respective vices of the Whigs and the Tories in which the two parties come to appear mirror reflections of each other and vice comes to reside in party as such (107–9, 111–12, 113). In the coming decades "politics" will have been sufficiently separated out from humanist categories like "ethics" and "literature" to be conceivable, and repudiable, as such. For further discussion, see Michael McKeon, "Cultural Crisis and Dialectical Method: Destabilizing Augustan Literature," in *The Profession of Eighteenth-Century Literature: Reflections on an Institution,* ed. Leo Damrosch (Madison: University of Wisconsin Press, 1992), 52–57.

41. Alexander Pope, *An Epistle from Mr. Pope, to Dr. Arbuthnot* (1735), in *Imitations of Horace,* ed. John Butt, vol. 4 of the Twickenham Edition of the Poems of Alexander Pope, 2nd ed. (London: Methuen, 1953), 95, font reversed (hereafter cited parenthetically in the text).

42. Matt. 6:6; see above, chap. 1, n. 107.

43. Alexander Pope, *The Rape of the Lock and Other Poems,* ed. Geoffrey Tillotson, vol. 2 of the Twickenham Edition of the Poems of Alexander Pope (London: Methuen, 1940), 83; for Tillotson's key, see 349–56.

44. "Esdras Barnivelt," *A Key to the Lock. or, A Treatise proving, beyond all Contradiction, the dangerous Tendency of a late Poem, entituled, The Rape of the Lock, to Government and Religion* (1715), 26, 9, 29, 26, 16.

45. See the copy of the *Key,* bound as a companion volume to the *Rape,* in Princeton University's Rare Book Room (call number Ex 3897.374.13c.2). On Pope's authorship of the *Key,* see Pope, *Rape of the Lock and Other Poems,* 104.

46. See Howard Erskine-Hill, "Literature and the Jacobite Cause: Was There a Rhetoric of Jacobitism?" in *Ideology and Conspiracy: Aspects of Jacobitism, 1689–1759,* ed. Eveline

Cruickshanks (Edinburgh: Donald, 1982), 54 and n. 75. Philip, Duke of Wharton, claimed that on the basis of "Barnivelt's" *Key,* a local JP charged a "Country-Bookseller" with treason for selling *The Rape of the Lock.* See *True Briton,* no. 65 (13 Jan. 1725): 553–55.

Chapter Fourteen | Secret History as Novel

1. See, e.g., Barclay's *Argenis,* above, chap. 10, nn. 21–22.

2. John Locke, *An Essay concerning Human Understanding* (1690), ed. Peter H. Nidditch (Oxford: Clarendon, 1979), bk. 2, chap. 1, secs. 4, 8, pp. 105, 107.

3. See above, chap. 2, nn. 144–45.

4. See above, chap. 7, nn. 112–13.

5. Jonathan Swift, "The Preface of the Author," prefixed to *The Battel of the Books,* in *A Tale of a Tub, To which is added The Battle of the Books and the Mechanical Operation of the Spirit* (1704, 1710), ed. A. C. Guthkelch and D. Nichol Smith, 2nd ed. (Oxford: Clarendon, 1958), 215 (font reversed).

6. See above, chap. 2, n. 135.

7. See, e.g., Nancy Armstrong, *Desire and Domestic Fiction: A Political History of the Novel* (New York: Oxford University Press, 1987), 29.

8. The following paragraphs draw upon my reading of *Robinson Crusoe* in Michael McKeon, *The Origins of the English Novel, 1600–1740* (Baltimore: Johns Hopkins University Press, 1987), chap. 9.

9. [Daniel Defoe], preface to *Robinson Crusoe,* ed. J. Donald Crowley (Oxford: Oxford University Press, 1981), 1 (hereafter references are to this edition and appear parenthetically in the text).

10. [Daniel Defoe], *Serious Reflections During the Life And Surprising Adventures of Robinson Crusoe: with His Vision of the Angelick World* (1720), in *The Works of Daniel Defoe,* ed. G. H. Maynadier, vol. 3 (New York: Sproul, 1903), ix (hereafter references are to this edition and appear parenthetically in the text).

11. See, e.g., [Charles Gildon], *The Life and Strange Surprizing Adventures of Mr. D——— De F——— . . .* (1719), x.

12. For a suggestive argument that in the pre-island portion of the novel Defoe sought to insinuate that *Robinson Crusoe* was a secret history of Robert Harley, Earl of Oxford, see DeAnn DeLuna, "Defoe and the Business of Politics" (in progress), chap. 6, "*Robinson Crusoe,* the Secret History."

13. For Defoe on absolute private property, see above, chap. 1, n. 42. The chronology is subject, of course, to varying interpretation, and some of its details demand more searching construction. Robinson's conversion, for example, occurs in 1660 (103), the year of Charles's Restoration and also of Defoe's birth. For a thoughtful discussion of the significance of this chronology, to which I am indebted, see Michael Seidel, "Crusoe in Exile," *PMLA* 96 (1981): 363–74, revised in *Exile and the Narrative Imagination* (New Haven, CT: Yale University Press, 1986), chap. 1.

14. On these matters, see above, chap. 4, nn. 36–75.

15. The following sentences draw on my reading of *Gulliver's Travels* in McKeon, *Origins,* chap. 10.

16. [Jonathan Swift], *Gulliver's Travels* (1726), pt. 2, chap. 7, *The Prose Works of Jonathan*

Swift, ed. Herbert Davis, vol. 11 (Oxford: Blackwell, 1941), 119 (hereafter references are to this edition and appear parenthetically in the text).

17. Kathryn R. King, *Jane Barker, Exile: A Literary Career, 1675–1725* (Oxford: Clarendon, 2000), 149; see generally chap. 4.

18. Cf. the allusive language of Jacobite regret in Anne Finch's "The Petition for an Absolute Retreat" (1713), discussed above, chap. 3, n. 98.

19. By contrast, a *roman à clef* provoked by the second Jacobite Rising of 1745 is so candid about its political reference as to challenge its status as an allegory. See *The Amours of Don Carlos. A True History, Translated from a Manuscript privately handed about at the french Court* (1745?). Granted, a few central figures bear romance names (Don Carlos is the Young Pretender), but other personages, and most places, retain their actual names. Moreover, the war/love structure of the narrative is so decisively overbalanced toward the latter term that the battle of Culloden is barely mentioned, and Don Carlos's beloved, a woman of "masculine" political sagacity in the line of Queen Henrietta Maria, Behn's Hermione, and Manley's Hilaria, nonetheless writes him that she is so joyous at news of his survival "that she felt no Uneasness about the Loss of the Battle . . ." (127).

20. M[ary] H[earne], *The Lover's Week: or, the Six Days Adventures of Philander and Amaryllis. . .* (1718), A2r–3r, p. 17, and idem, *The Female Deserters. A Novel. By the Author of The Lover's Week* (1719), 108–9, both in facsimile in Mary Hearne, *The Lover's Week and The Female Deserters*, intro. Josephine Grieder (New York: Garland, 1973) (hereafter references are to this edition and appear parenthetically in the text). An immediately identifiable character in the latter work is syncopated as "Sir S. G———th," i.e., Sir Samuel Garth, physician and author of the mock epic *The Dispensary* (1699).

21. Kathryn R. King, "The Novel before Novels (with a Glance at Mary Hearne's Fables of Desertion)," in *Eighteenth-Century Genre and Culture: Serious Reflections on Occasional Forms; Essays in Honor of J. Paul Hunter*, ed. Dennis Todd and Cynthia Wall (Newark: University of Delaware Press, 2001), 47.

22. See above, chap. 13, n. 19.

23. On romance naming, see McKeon, *Origins*, 38–39.

24. See above, chap. 9, nn. 29–43.

25. [Eliza Haywood], *Memoirs Of a Certain Island Adjacent to the Kingdom of Utopia. Written by a Celebrated Author of that Country. Now translated into English* (1725), 1, new pagination following 290. In 1752 there appeared an autobiographical *roman à clef* about a character, Martha Sansom, who figures in Haywood's *Memoirs: Clio: or, a Secret History of the Life and Amours Of the Late celebrated Mrs. S———N———M. Written by Herself, in a Letter to Hillarius* (see the signified of p. 43 in the key to the *Memoirs*, fig. 14.1).

26. The copy belongs to the Princeton University Rare Book Room, call number Ex 3777.2.384.

27. Reprinted in Eliza Haywood, *Selected Fiction and Drama of Eliza Haywood*, ed. Paula R. Backscheider (New York: Oxford University Press, 1999), 83–119.

28. Eliza Haywood, *The British Recluse: or, the Secret History of Cleomira, Suppos'd Dead. A Novel* (1727), reprinted in *Popular Fiction by Women, 1660–1730*, ed. Paula R. Backscheider and John J. Richetti (Oxford: Oxford University Press, 1996), 155 (hereafter references are to this edition and appear parenthetically in the text). On the relationship between the secret history and the true history, see above, chap. 13, n. 1.

29. [Eliza Haywood], *The Mercenary Lover: or, the Unfortunate Heiresses. Being a True, Secret History of a City Amour, In a certain Island adjacent to the Kingdom of Utopia. Written by the Author of Memoirs of the said Island* (1726), in Haywood, *Selected Fiction*, 123, 145, 155, 160, 157.

30. See above, chap. 11, nn. 24–25.

31. Eliza Haywood, *Fantomina: or, Love in a Maze, being a Secret History of an Amour Between Two Persons of Condition* (1725), in Backscheider and Richetti, *Popular Fiction by Women*, 230, 227, 231, 236, 234, 235, 239, 242 (hereafter references are to this edition and appear parenthetically in the text).

32. [Eliza Haywood], *The Fair Hebrew: or, a True, but Secret History of Two Jewish Ladies, Who lately resided in London* (1729), A1–v (hereafter references are to this edition and appear parenthetically in the text). Haywood gives a yet fuller version of this approach in the preface to a narrative that was published fifteen years later, in the first year of the *Female Spectator*'s publication (and signed, significantly, "The Editors"): "The many Fictions which have been lately imposed upon the World, under the specious Titles of *Secret Histories, Memoirs,* &c. &c. have given but too much room to question the Veracity of every Thing that has the least Tendency that way: We therefore think it highly necessary to assure the Reader, that he will find nothing in the following Sheets, but what has been collected from *Original Letters, Private Memorandums,* and the *Accounts* we have been favoured with from the Mouths of Persons too deeply concerned in many of the *chief Transactions* not to be perfectly acquainted with the Truth, and of too much Honour and Integrity to put any false Colours upon it. . . . And if it be true (as certainly it is) that *Example* has more Efficacy than *Precept,* we may be bold to say there are few fairer, or more worthy Imitation." *The Fortunate Foundlings: being the Genuine History of Colonel M——rs, and his Sister, Madam du P——y, the Issue of the Hon. Ch——es M——rs, Son of the late Duke of R——l——d . . .* (1744), A1r, font reversed.

33. The following pages draw upon my reading of *Pamela* in McKeon, *Origins,* chap. 11.

34. Anna Laetitia Barbauld, "Life of Samuel Richardson," in *The Correspondence of Samuel Richardson* (1804; reprint, New York: AMS, 1966), 1:xxi.

35. [Samuel Richardson], *Pamela: or, Virtue Rewarded. In a Series of Familiar Letters from a Beautiful Young Damsel, To her Parents. Now first Published In order to cultivate the Principles of Virtue and Religion in the Minds of the Youth of Both Sexes . . .* (1740), ed. T. C. Duncan Eaves and Ben D. Kimpel (Boston: Houghton Mifflin, 1971), 73 (hereafter references are to this edition and appear parenthetically in the text).

36. On the *Old Arcadia*, see above, chap. 10, nn. 12–18.

37. Letter by Aaron Hill printed in the introduction to the second edition.

38. In the history of the novel the syncopated name persists, long after it has ceased to signify actual particularity, in order to suggest the historylike quality of novelistic characterization.

39. With Mr. B.'s rule about husbands compare the absolutist doctrine that the king can do no wrong.

40. See Ros Ballaster, *Seductive Forms: Women's Amatory Fiction from 1684 to 1740* (Oxford: Clarendon, 1992), e.g., the introduction and conclusion; and William B. Warner, *Licensing Entertainment: The Elevation of Novel Reading in Britain, 1684–1750* (Berkeley and Los Angeles: University of California Press, 1998), 13–14, 41–42, 185–86. Ballaster's term for the first-wave writings is "amatory fiction," while Warner's is "novels of amorous intrigue."

41. Samuel Richardson to Sarah Chapone, 6 Dec. 1750, in *Selected Letters of Samuel Richardson,* ed. John Carroll (Oxford: Clarendon, 1964), 173n68; preface to *A Collection of Entertaining Histories and Novels . . .* (1739), ii, reprinted in Wolfgang Zach, "Mrs. Aubin and Richardson's Earliest Literary Manifesto," *English Studies* 62, no. 3 (1981): 282.

42. [Henry Fielding], *Joseph Andrews* (1742), bk. 3, chap. 1, ed. Martin C. Battestin (Middletown, CT: Wesleyan University Press, 1967), 187.

43. Georg Lukács (by way of Marx) helpfully provides a historical grounding for this development in techniques of characterization in the emergence of the generalizing category of class. See *The Historical Novel* (1938), excerpted in *Theory of the Novel: A Historical Approach,* ed. Michael McKeon (Baltimore: Johns Hopkins University Press, 2000), 237–39; see also 182.

44. See McKeon, *Origins,* chap. 4.

45. When Pamela happily anticipates that she soon will be "out of the House," Mr. B. taunts her with the advice that rather than "return again to hard Work, as you must, if you go to your Father's," she "take a House in London, and let Lodgings to us Members of Parliament, when we come to Town, and such a pretty Daughter as you may pass for, will always fill her House, and she'll get a great deal of money" (71).

46. For *The Whores Rhetorick,* see above, chap. 4, nn. 98–108. For the application to mock-marriage arrangements of the aestheticizing language of "as if," see also Lovemore's offer to Rivella that she "retire to my seat in the country, where she might be sure to command with the same power as if it were her own . . ." (see above, chap. 13, nn. 33–34). Similarly, Mary Hearne's protagonists are brought, respectively, to a *bagnio* and a strange house where they will be "as safe as if you were in the Royal Palace of *St. James's*" (see above).

47. On the several senses of the distinction between "public" and "private" marriages, see above, chap. 3, nn. 28–30.

48. Indeed, one of the examples by which Mr. B. refutes Lady Davers's charge that marrying down has the same consequences for himself as it would for her casts a patriarchalist shadow on his principles: "When the noble Family of *Stuart* ally'd itself into the low Family of *Hyde,* (comparatively low, I mean) did any body scruple to call the Lady Royal Highness, and Duchess of *York*? And did any body think her Daughters, the late Queen *Mary* and Queen *Anne,* less Royal for that?" (349).

49. Andrew Marvell, "An Horatian Ode upon Cromwell's Return from Ireland" (1650), lines 119–20, in *Andrew Marvell: The Complete Poems,* ed. Elizabeth Story Donno (Harmondsworth, UK: Penguin, 1978), 58.

50. In Richardson's continuation of *Pamela* (1741) motherhood becomes central. On the housewife as governor, see above, chap. 4, nn. 48–75.

51. Cf. the recommended furnishings of the model devotional closet, above, chap. 1, n. 107 and fig. 1.2.

52. On aesthetic disinterestedness, see above, chap. 7, nn. 73–109.

53. On the historical significance of housework's unproductivity, see above, chap. 4, nn. 36–43.

54. "Hussy" is derived from "housewife" (*OED*).

55. In the summer of 1691, "[t]alk of Jacobite plots, and of the scheme's of Anne's party and of 'the Commonwealth men' had 'heartily troubled and frighted' [Queen] Mary who burned most of her private papers and kept the journals in a bag tied to her person so that she could burn these too at a moment's notice." Nesca A. Robb, *William of Orange: A Per-*

sonal Portrait (London: Heinemann, 1962), vol. 2, app. A, p. 559. Cf also William Fuller's claim to have secreted letters on his clothing, above, chap. 12, n. 3.

56. The indirection of Manley's autobiography—her self-division into Rivella and Love-more—may be paralleled by Richardson's experiments in a gendered mode of interwriting in which a male voice is parodied—imitated and criticized—by a female voice. The prototype in *Pamela* is Pamela's use of subversive italics to darken the news Mr. B. requires her to send to Mrs. Jervis (93–94, 109). The technique is used subsequently in Pamela's commentary on Mr. B.'s "Articles" (164–67), Lady Davers's oral response to her brother's letter to Pamela (326–27), and Pamela's annotation of Mr. B.'s "lecture" (369–71). Other contemporary uses of the technique can be cited, e.g., Lady Mary Wortley Montagu, "The Reasons that Induced Dr. S[wift] to Write a Poem Called 'The Lady's Dressing-Room'" (wr. c. 1732), and Mary Collier, "The Woman's Labour: to Mr. Stephen Duck" (1739).

57. See above, chap. 6, n. 59.

58. [Henry Fielding], *An Apology for the Life of Mrs. Shamela Andrews. . . .* (1741), in *Joseph Andrews and Shamela,* ed. Douglas Brooks-Davies and Thomas Keymer (Oxford: Oxford University Press, 1999), 310–11. Fielding's Parson Oliver thought the graphic depictions of *Pamela* might be pornographic even in intent: "And notwithstanding our Author's Professions of Modesty, . . . I cannot agree that my Daughter should entertain herself with some of his Pictures; which I do not expect to be contemplated without Emotion, unless by one of my Age and Temper, who can see the Girl lie on her Back, with one Arm round Mrs. *Jewkes* and the other round the Squire, naked in Bed, with his Hand on her Breasts, &c. with as much Indifference as I read any other Page in the whole Novel" (313). *Shamela,* which satirizes *Pamela* not by exposing it as fiction but by insisting more scrupulously on its factuality, is aptly seen as a secret history that supplies actual names ("Booby," not "B——"; "Shamela," not "Pamela"; "the Jacobite Henrietta Maria Honora Andrews," not plain "Mrs. Andrews") and publishes the authentic letters in order to refute the official ones and to "set in a true and just Light" the character of "that young Politician" (title page and 305). Indeed, *Shamela* parodies *Pamela* much as the anonymous *Love-Letters* parodies Behn's *Love-Letters.*

59. See above, chap. 6, nn. 40–41.

60. Cf. Pamela's response to Mr. B.'s offer of diamond jewelry: "What should I think, . . . but that they were the Price of my Honesty; and that I wore those Jewels outwardly, because I had none inwardly?" (166).

61. For Don Quixote, see fig. 7.1.

62. See above, chap. 5, nn. 20–24.

63. The author of *Pamela Censured* (1741) associates the closet's privacy with both reading and sex ("the *Closet Commerce* between the Sexes," 45); see also 25, 54–55.

64. [Samuel Richardson], *Letters Written to and for Particular Friends, On the most Important Occasions . . .* (1741), reprinted as *Familiar Letters on Important Occasions,* ed. Brian W. Downs (London: Routledge, 1928), xxviii. For Locke and Defoe, see above, chap. 1, nn. 28, 36.

65. For *The Whores Rhetorick* on whores and wives, see above, chap. 4, nn. 103–8; for the overlap of domestic servants and whores, see above, chap. 4, nn. 75–77.

66. For a fuller argument of this point, see McKeon, *Origins,* 378–81. On the priority of the marriage contract to the civil contract, see above, chap. 3, nn. 91–94.

67. On the problem of their proximity, see above, chap. 4, nn. 45–47.

Chapter Fifteen | Variations on the Domestic Novel

1. *The Secret History of Pandora's Box . . .* (1742), 25 (hereafter cited parenthetically in the text). The anonymous author may have been inspired by Francis Bacon's *Wisdom of the Ancients* ([Lat., 1609] trans. 1619).

2. See above, chap. 6.

3. [John Cleland], *Memoirs of a Woman of Pleasure* (1749), ed. Peter Wagner (Harmondsworth, UK: Penguin, 1985), 39 (hereafter references are to this edition and appear parenthetically in the text).

4. On the law of obscene libel, see above, chap. 6.

5. John Cleland to Andrew Stone (secretary to the secretary of state), 10 Nov. 1749, quoted in William H. Epstein, *John Cleland: Images of a Life* (New York: Columbia University Press, 1974), 75. On Manley's appeal, see above, chap. 13.

6. Henry Fielding, *Shamela* (1741), in *Joseph Andrews and Shamela*, ed. Douglas Brooks-Davies and Thomas Keymer (Oxford: Oxford University Press, 1999), 329–30. For examples of Defoe's fables, see Michael McKeon, *The Origins of the English Novel, 1600–1740* (Baltimore: Johns Hopkins University Press, 1987), 221–23.

7. See above, chap. 4.

8. Ibid.

9. See above, chap. 12.

10. See above, chap. 5, n. 46.

11. Cf. the anonymous *Love-Letters,* above, chap. 12, nn. 64–65.

12. Cleland's scenes of domestic holes that the heated ingenuity of sexual voyeurism discovers and violates recall the priest holes of an earlier era, also domestic but disclosed through the fervid enthusiasm of religious zeal. See above, chap. 3, n. 86.

13. See above, chap. 7, n. 79.

14. For Johnson, see above, chap. 7, nn. 106–7; but see also nn. 121–22 on Pope.

15. See above, chap. 7, n. 111.

16. See above, chap. 6, nn. 33–34.

17. The same conditions may be had through not voyeurism but book sex. See plate 2.

18. Cf. the language of the molly subculture, one of whose objects of oblique parody was in fact the language of heterosexual prostitution. See above, chap. 12, nn. 72–73. Perhaps the only sort of figuration or "doubling" that Fanny refuses to regard ecumenically is the "double-way" of sodomy (192).

19. Does the dropping of her pen also suggest a momentary turn toward masturbation? Cf. Silvia's "guilty pen" in Behn's *Love-Letters,* above, chap. 11, nn. 38–39. With Fanny-Cleland's lesson in how to be an active and imaginative reader compare also Behn's lessons on how to identify with her characters, above, chap. 11, nn. 36–37.

20. Cleland to Lovel Stanhope, 13 Nov. 1749, quoted in Epstein, *Images,* 77.

21. [Laurence Sterne], *The Life and Opinions of Tristram Shandy, Gentleman,* vol. 2, chap. 7, ed. Ian Watt (Boston: Houghton Mifflin, 1965), 78 (hereafter references are to this edition and appear parenthetically in the text).

22. The cause of Tristram's defect is mysterious because there are too many possible ways of explaining it: his mechanistic conception, his unfortunate naming, the loophole in his mother's marriage settlement, Dr. Slop's new-invented forceps, Obadiah's fateful knotting of

the medical bag, and the accidental circumcision occasioned by the conjunctive carelessness of Susannah, Toby, and Corporal Trim. Like a dream element, Tristram's defect is overdetermined, to be understood by reference not to actual, e.g., causal, relations but to the virtual meaning these relations both conceal and reveal. By a related implication, anatomical difference both is and is not indicative of gender difference.

23. This overstates the case, since Walter does go to the Royal Exchange on occasion, presumably on "business" (see, e.g., vol. 2, chap. 5, p. 71).

24. *An Essay on Woman,* ascribed on its title page to "Pego Borewell," has been attributed to John Wilkes, who was prosecuted for its printing. See Randolph Trumbach, "Erotic Fantasy and Male Libertinism in Enlightenment England," in *The Invention of Pornography: Obscenity and the Origins of Modernity, 1500–1800,* ed. Lynn Hunt (New York: Zone Books, 1993), 277 and the sources cited in n. 22.

25. On the one-sex model, see above, chap. 6, n. 5.

26. See above, chap. 2, nn. 94–95, chap. 7, nn. 31–32.

27. For Behn, see above, chap. 11; on Fielding, see above, chap. 7, nn. 100–101. Despite this, the temptation to read *Tristram Shandy* as an elaborate concentration narrative concerning William and Mary and the failure of the Stuart line may be generated by the similarity between Sterne's reproductively defective hero and the charge leveled at William by Jacobite libels early in his reign. Cf. Ralph Gray, "The Coronation Ballad, 11th April 1689" (1689), lines 37–38, 57–58, in *Poems on Affairs of State: Augustan Satirical Verse, 1660–1714,* vol. 5, *1688–1697,* ed. William J. Cameron (New Haven, CT: Yale University Press, 1971), 41–42, 43: "He is not qualified for his wife,/Because of the cruel midwife's knife,/Yet buggering of Benting doth please to the life./.../An unnatural beast to his father and uncle;/A churl to his wife without e'er a pintle . . . ." The siege of Namur, which occupies so important if privatized a place in *Tristram Shandy,* ended with its fall to William's forces in 1695. On "Benting"—Hans Willem Bentinck—see above, chap. 12, n. 16.

28. For Shaftesbury on the relationship between author and reader, see above, chap. 2, nn. 142–46.

29. For Smith, see above, chap. 1, n. 51.

30. Smollett feeds our uncertainty when, early on, he has Bramble offer his correspondent Dr. Lewis, in a letter dated 23 April, what is in effect an alternative title: "If I did not know that the exercise of your profession has habituated you to the hearing of complaints, I should make a conscience of troubling you with my correspondence, which may be truly called the *lamentations of Matthew Bramble.*" *The Expedition of Humphry Clinker,* ed. Lewis M. Knapp and Paul-Gabriel Boucé (Oxford: Oxford University Press, 1984), 33 (hereafter references are to this edition, consist of letter date and page number, and appear parenthetically in the text). The following discussion draws on Michael McKeon, "Aestheticising the Critique of Luxury: Smollett's *Humphry Clinker,*" in *Luxury in the Eighteenth Century: Debates, Desires, and Delectable Goods,* ed. Maxine Berg and Elizabeth Eger (Basingstoke, UK: Palgrave Macmillan, 2003), 57–67.

31. On *Robinson Crusoe* and *Pamela,* see above, chap. 14; on *The Pilgrim's Progress,* see above, chap. 8.

32. On property as a common use-right, see above, chap. 1; on the domestic economy and the fluid distinction between inside and outside work, see above, chap. 4.

33. Matt quotes from Horace's bk. 2, satire 6; cf. Horace's ironization of the *beatus ille* trope in his second epode, above, chap. 3, n. 97.

34. For a fuller discussion of the relationship between the traditional culture of distinction and the modern culture of conflation, see Michael McKeon, ed., *Theory of the Novel: A Historical Approach* (Baltimore: Johns Hopkins University Press, 2000), 803–8, 851–58.

35. Smollett's contemporary Adam Smith demystified the essentialism of family romance by other means, grounding "the force of blood" not in nature but in nurture, i.e., the empirical experience of the domicile: "In some tragedies and romances, we meet with many beautiful and interesting scenes, founded upon, what is called, the force of blood, or upon the wonderful affection which near relations are supposed to conceive for one another, even before they know that they have any such connection. This force of blood, however, I am afraid, exists no-where but in tragedies and romances. Even in tragedies and romances, it is never supposed to take place between any relations, but those who are naturally bred up in the same house; between parents and children, between brothers and sisters. To imagine any such mysterious affection between cousins, or even between aunts or uncles, and nephews or nieces, would be too ridiculous." *The Theory of Moral Sentiments* (1759), ed. D. D. Raphael and A. L. Macfie (Indianapolis: Liberty Classics, 1982), 222. On family romance, see McKeon, *Theory of the Novel*, pt. 3.

36. E. P. Thompson, "The Patricians and the Plebs," in *Customs in Common: Studies in Traditional Popular Culture* (New York: New Press, 1991), chap. 2. The quoted terms are Thompson's.

37. On Burke, see above, chap. 7, nn. 69–70.

38. On these matters, see above, chap. 7.

39. Pamela too was "brought up wrong." See above, chap. 14, n. 49.

40. Jane Austen, *Pride and Prejudice*, ed. James Kinsley, Isobel Armstrong, and Frank W. Bradbrook (Oxford: Oxford University Press, 1990), 296 (hereafter references are to this edition and appear parenthetically in the text).

41. William Wordsworth, see above, chap. 4, n. 63.

42. Indeed, for both sisters-in-law, since Darcy's assessment of Jane—first negative, then positive—seems to Elizabeth a precondition for Bingley's capacity to act upon his feelings for her (see 143, 283–84).

43. See above, chap. 4, nn. 59–60.

44. See above, chap. 11, nn. 27–35; cf. Delarivier Manley's experiments with a nonepistolary mode of first-person narration, autobiography, above, chap. 13.

45. [Frances Burney], *Evelina, or, the History of a Young Lady's Entrance into the World* (1778), vol. 3, letters, 19, 1, 3, ed. Edward A. Bloom and Vivien Jones (Oxford: Oxford University Press, 2002), 384; see also pp. 351–52, 367, 257–59 (hereafter references are to this edition and appear parenthetically in the text).

46. For a more general discussion of free indirect discourse, see McKeon, *Theory of the Novel*, 485–87, and the readings from Dorrit Cohn and Ann Banfield, 493–536.

47. For a possible instance of free indirect discourse in the third-person narration of Behn's *Love-Letters*, see above, chap. 11, n. 35.

48. On these matters, see above, chaps. 1 and 2.

49. Free indirect discourse therefore may be seen as an articulation, on the level of the sentence, of the abstract and paradigmatically modern relationship between the general and

the particular, the collective and the individual, the public and the private. See above, chap. 2, nn. 148–59.

50. For a range of views, see Margaret A. Doody, "George Eliot and the Eighteenth-Century Novel," *Nineteenth-Century Fiction* 35, no. 2 (1980): 260–91; John Bender, *Imagining the Penitentiary: Fiction and the Architecture of Mind in Eighteenth-Century England* (Chicago: University of Chicago Press, 1987); and William H. Galperin, *The Historical Austen* (Philadelphia: University of Pennsylvania Press, 2003).

51. In practice, moreover, critics disagree not only on what free indirect discourse does but even on what it is. Recognizing it in operation is far from being an exact science, and the difficulties and uncertainties involved in identifying its consistency and scope of variation would seem to support skepticism about its having a determinate ideological implication. For a cogent and helpful discussion of "indefinite" free indirect discourse in Austen's novels that instances the reflections of Charlotte Lucas on her engagement to Mr. Collins (94), see Susan Sniader Lanser, *Fictions of Authority: Women Writers and Narrative Voice* (Ithaca, NY: Cornell University Press, 1992), 73–77.

52. See above, chap. 9, nn. 35–38; see also chap. 10, n. 27. Haywood's innovation may be understood, in turn, in relation to the idea that the emergent figure of domestic wife and mother internalizes, in the private realm of the household, the public authority of the manager or governor. See above, chap. 4, nn. 48–75.

53. See above, chap. 12, n. 52.

54. This is evidently a development in the use of grammatical and syntactical forms (person, voice, tone, embedding, retrospection, etc.) but also in diacritical textual practice (quotations marks, italics, paragraphing and other spacing techniques, etc.). For the architectural language, see above, chap. 5.

55. Ian Ousby suggests that in setting Pemberley in Derbyshire Austen invites the reader to identify it with Chatsworth. See *The Englishman's England: Taste, Travel, and the Rise of Tourism* (Cambridge: Cambridge University Press, 1990), 72–73. A visitor to Chatsworth in 1763 thought its state apartment "of little use but to be walked through." See above, chap. 5, n. 64.

56. For another figure of the relationship between inner eyes and outer windows, see fig. 8.1.

57. On the miniature, see above, chap. 5, n. 19.

58. For Addison, see above, chap. 7, nn. 85–86. In this passage Austen felicitously calls Darcy the property owner the "proprietor" of Pemberley (186).

59. On these two sense of the common, see above, chap. 7, nn. 35–36.

60. On these matters, see McKeon, *Theory of the Novel,* pt. 10.

61. On Haywood's correspondent, see above, chap. 9.

Index

Gouge, William, 151, 183–84, 338
governess: use of term, 760–61n57
government: royal household distinguished from, 228, 229. *See also* state
governors: housewives as, 181–94, 243, 626, 646, 760n50, 839n52
Grand Alliance, 139, 752–53n58
Grand Remonstrance (1641), 5, 69, 532–33
Gray, Ralph, 822n19
Gray, Thomas, 357
great/small relationship: authority and legitimation in, 783n6; in Behn's *Love-Letters*, 511–12; biographer's tasks and, 338–39, 785n32; Christian and scientific ideas about, 404–5, 431; comparisons of, 665; country house poems and, 420–21; critique of, 401; domestication of, 334–36, 410–11; great to explicate small in, 803n91; as hermeneutic and pedagogic method, 326; narrative concretization of, 449; reversals in, 517–18; sublime of, 406, 408; surface/depth in relation to, 403–4; tragicomedy on, 392, 393–94
Greenham, Richard, 112–13
Greenwich Hill, 166, *167*
Grey of Werk, Forde, third baron ("Philander" in Behn's *Love-Letters*): in Behn's *Love-Letters*, 507–19, 520, 524–29, 530, 533–35, 536, 538–43, 545, 818–19n35; political activity of, 507–8
Grotius, Hugo, 139–40, 153, 741–42n110
Grub-Street Journal, 316–18, 764n88
Guardian (periodical), 414–15. *See also* Tickell, Thomas
guild system, 21, 23, 59, 176–77, 207. *See also* freemasonry
Guillory, John, 794–95n126, 797n22
Gunter, Mary, 42
Gwynne, Nell, 305

Habermas, Jürgen: on coffeehouses, 739n85; on consumption, 738–39n81; critique of, 73–74; as influence, 733n18; on literary public sphere, 48, 112, 466; on print, 55; on private autonomy, 157, 191; on private realm, 110–12, 182; on public sphere, 44–48,

56, 70–73, 75, 112, 182; on realm of tacit, 67–68, 736n63; resources of, 79
Hale, Matthew, 43, 313
Halfpenny, William, *265*, *266*, 267
Halifax, George Savile, marquis of, 185–86, 189
Hall, Joseph, 329
halls: access to other rooms via, 252–53, *255*, 256, *257*; fire and hearth in, 770–71n52; shift from great to entry, 220–21, 240, 250
Ham House, 233, 246, *250*
Hampton Court, 559–60, 562, 823n25
Hanway, Jonas, 193, *204*
Harley, Robert, earl of Oxford, 564
Haviland, Thomas P., 811n43
Hayman, Francis, *369*
Hayward, John, 113
Haywood, Eliza: on bad taste, 808n42; Barclay compared with, 479–82; as commoner, 808n41; critique of, 641–42; on female education, 408, 460–66, 530, 807–8n39; on housewife as governor, 189–90, 839n52; influences on, 489; on key to cabinet of curiosities, 767n18; narrative concretization of, 454–58; as narrator/mother, 458–60; secret histories of, 457–58, 631–39; on secrets, 232, 454–55; truth claims of, 833n32. *See also Female Spectator* (periodical)
health: private wealth vs., 21, *22*, 23
Hearne, Mary, 627–31, 658
Hegel, G. W. F., 725–26n60
Help to a National Reformation, A (tract), 44
Henderson, Tony, 763n79
Henley, John ("Orator"), 317
Henrietta Marie, queen of England, 116, 485–87, 520
Henry III, king of France, 480–81
Henry IV, king of France, 293, 480–81
Henry VII, king of England, 221, 223
Henry VIII, king of England, 34–35, 60, 223, *224*, 329, 743n124
Herbert, George, 42–43, 333–34
Herbert, Percy, 812n57
hermeneutics: domestication as, 327–37, 386–87; of king in exile/in state, 493–94; in Martha and Mary's relationship, 428, 432; small/great relationship and, 326